SEEKING THE CITY

Wealth, Poverty, and Political Economy
in Christian Perspective

SEEKING THE CITY

Wealth, Poverty, and Political Economy in Christian Perspective

Chad Brand & Tom Pratt

Kregel
Academic

Library of Congress Cataloging-in-Publication Data

Brand, Chad.
   Seeking the city : Christian faith & political economy : a biblical, theological, historical study / by Chad Brand & Tom Pratt.
      pages cm
   Includes index.
   ISBN 978-0-8254-4304-6
   1. Wealth--Religious aspects—Christianity. 2. Economics—Religious aspects—Christianity. 3. United States—Economic conditions. 4. United States—Economic policy. 5. United States—Politics and government. 6. United States—Social conditions. 7. United States—Church history. I. Pratt, Tom. II. Title.
   BR115.W4B73 2013
   261.8'50973--dc23

2012039490

ISBN 978-0-8254-4304-6

Printed in the United States of America
13 14 15 16 17 / 5 4 3 2 1

To Dr. T. E. Pratt, "Daddy" to me,
who taught me to work, to think,
to love God's Word,
and most of all
to know Jesus Christ
in the forgiveness of my sins.

ᘓ

To Eddie Brand, "Dad," or when I
really felt close to him, "Pops,"
who helped me to be
a better teacher,
and who taught me to love the Lord
and my family.

Contents

Preface

THE STORY OF THIS BOOK begins (for Tom, the oldest of your two writers), in conscious involvement in its many facets, in the academic year of 1964/65 in the deep "valley" of the Texas Rio Grande near Brownsville. One Sunday evening four "preacher-boys" (my mother's favorite name for young men "called to preach" but not yet mature) were returning to the campus of the (then) University of Corpus Christi (now Texas A&M at Corpus Christi) after a day of preaching and testifying in several churches representing the university and the BSU (Baptist Student Union). We had not eaten since noon that day, and by nine o'clock or so we were "starving" as they say and stopped in at the only café we found open that evening along the road in Edinburgh. We sat down at a table in the middle of the almost deserted room and waited for the waitress to come to the table. She was somewhat delayed, but we did not take much notice of it. When she arrived, she was visibly agitated and in an apologetic voice she pointed to three of us and said she could serve us but the fourth would have to go to the back door for service. The fourth happened to be Sidney Smith, a dear friend of my family with whom my sister had served two summers running doing Vacation Bible Schools in East Texas among primarily black congregations and communities. Sid was a student with the rest of us at UCC and among other things was the best ping-pong player I ever knew! He was also "black," or "Negro," as we used the terminology back then.

The strongest irony of the moment was that the woman who made this announcement, with real trepidation I feel, was Hispanic, "Mexican" to us back then, a simple designation of the derivation of the ethnic grouping from which she came. She was employed and under instructions from her manager to carry out the company policy on feeding racial minorities. She herself would only in the most recent years of the time have achieved the right to eat in a place like that and/or work there. My two "white" friends and I were duly shocked and dismayed and put quickly on the spot. I am not ashamed at all to say that as one man we simply rose to leave and one of us (I think I did) said if they would not feed Sid with us, none of us would eat there. We left the establishment quickly and went back to campus hungry, more concerned about what we had experienced together and what it might mean to our friend Sid than we were about our appetites.

Some one of us was the first to apologize to Sid for both what had happened in the café and our own insensitivity to a situation with which he was only too familiar. What is sometimes, or at least has been, referred to as the "black experience" in America had taken us over and made us (the "white dudes") keenly aware of our inadequacies as friends, and at least for me, as Christians. In some sense I would never be the same in my thinking, but it was not as if it was the first time "race" had come up in my life. My dad and mother grew up in east Texas as the youngest born of mothers who gave birth to them in their mid-fourties. They would each have been candidates for abortions of convenience in our time (had the mothers not been the kind of women they were). As the "babies" of the family they were separated from their siblings by time and distance and were thought of in the family, as I grew up around my relatives, as somewhat "odd" in their ideas about culture and race and Christianity. When my dad was "called to preach" and went about it as if he thought it was truly God's plan for his life and his family, it was not well received among the siblings. His and my mother's pursuit of education led them to places no one in the family had ever been or contemplated going and confirmed ideas they had begun to imbibe on their own about the condition of, particularly, Southern Baptist churches and of Texas Baptists in general as well as the larger culture of Texas, the South, and the United States as a whole.

That culture was blatantly and hatefully "racist" at worst and condescending and patronizing mostly at best, with only a few who had any idea what true racial harmony and/or colorblindness might mean. The years that led up to my experience in Edinburgh that night long ago would have at least two of my dad's churches refuse to accept his leadership in announcing to communities that all persons of whatever race, color, or ethnic background were welcome inside their memberships. The ramifications of these acts can be readily imagined. Daddy and Mother were both schoolteachers on the side and had repeated "run-ins" with administrators and other teachers over "integration." Daddy eventually entered the administrative part of the equation and found himself embroiled with school boards over both the moral implications of racial segregation and the actual intent and application of the law in school districts where he served. His final "battle" was in a district on the north side of Waco, Texas, where gerrymandered district lines were used to exclude black students from the high school. His challenge to this policy led to his firing, but only after he had said to them what he said to churches and others: "I was unemployed when I came to this job, and I suppose I can be unemployed when I leave it." He landed in a junior high school in inner-city Waco serving as an assistant principal to a black principal, a man who became a fast and long-time friend to our family.

Sid Smith went on to become a servant to the Lord and Southern Baptists as liaison to black Baptists who wished to be affiliated with the Southern Baptist Convention and/or its work. He had a long and wonderful career and is with the Lord now. I went to Colorado and have spent the last forty-four years (except for two years in the North Charleston area of South Carolina) in the Denver metropolitan area serving mostly lower income churches and neighborhoods, where the economic and educational background of the people as well as the ethnic mixes involved serve to make them mostly what I call "working-class," a mix very similar to areas where I grew up in Texas, except that the churches were almost completely all "white" in Texas. The Colorado churches had no obvious barriers to racial and economic integration nor class-consciousness, but cultural lines were set up as usual in all communities along neighborhood lines, and we always served in the lower-end neighborhoods. And, those churches were predominantly poor and lower middle-class white, with a small percentage of ethnic mix. I might add that my experiences in other parts of the metropolitan area showed no bias one way or the other toward the gospel from poor to rich or any in between. The gospel is truly offensive to all economic, ethnic, and cultural groups, and the poor have no preference for it over anyone else and vice versa.

Economic exigencies and the confrontations of the ministry (not the least over such things as racism) put our family on the edge financially almost all the time, so my wife, Karen, has used her nursing degree off and on all our married life, and I have found myself involved in various business enterprises and moments of desperate need for employment. Consequently, I am deeply familiar with the ins and outs of capitalistic markets from every angle. I have begged (literally) a fast-food outlet manager to hire me in spite of the fact I was obviously "over-qualified" to sweep the floors, clean the toilets, pick up garbage on the lot, and (ick!) scrub the grill. I was a thirty-year-old college graduate and veteran, but unemployed, pastor, and evangelist at the time. I have learned from scratch as a painter's helper the auto body business and operated a body-shop business with up to thirteen employees. I have catered to businesses and churches and the US military and "meals on wheels" and anybody else who would eat my and my sons' BBQ, pizza, and hot-truck offerings.

I have hired some of the worst and some of the best and sought to make business a place of integrity and honesty and customer satisfaction, while on occasion attempting to help the generally unemployable (ex-correctional inmates) and the marginally employable (ethnic and minority youth). I have suffered their conspiracies and thefts and rejoiced in their achievements. I have made money and lost money. I have encountered the EPA, OSHA, IRS, HHS, fire inspectors, health departments, state and county governments, unemployment offices, social services, and every sort of wielder of personal authority within the regulatory atmosphere of modern America. Meanwhile, Karen has served three decades in mostly ICU and Emergency Room settings working evenings and nights so we could hand off our children to one another for care, rather than trusting them to others. As a two-decade veteran of emergency medical services in the Denver area, she has a very clear idea of how care for the indigent and merely uninsured, for the drug-seeking and the drug and alcohol dependent, and for the irresponsible sexual adventurers and the merely young or old and ignorant works in major metropolitan hospital settings.

Frankly, we are deeply grateful to have had the privilege of taking care of ourselves and others by means of capitalistic enterprises. We have also met some wonderful people in the process, among them my colleague and friend Chad Brand, whose family was a member of one of those churches I spoke of above. Neither our family nor Chad's would have come to where we are outside of a free and market-driven society that rewards hard work, education, savings and investment, entrepreneurial enterprise, postponement of gratifi-cation, marital fidelity, and a host of other virtues. As students and teachers of God's Word we have come to believe fervently that there is no "answer" to the world's suffering and poverty in the present age other than the gospel of Jesus Christ that sets a person free to worship God with all he or she is in an atmosphere where nothing is god but God.

All of which brings us again to this book. Sid Smith, a black man from slave heritage in the South, and Chad Brand, a white man from poverty sur-roundings in Adams City, Colorado, and Tom Pratt, child of the culture of truck farmers and dry goods storekeepers in Great Depression–era east Texas, all stand with each other equal at the cross. So far as I ever knew, it never occurred to Sid to call me or someone like Chad a "racist" (as is commonly done in today's American politics) for believing in democratic capitalistic in-stitutions and seeking to get everyone equally involved in its hope for inde-pendence and even prosperity without relying on governmental dependencies. But the years since Sid and I were turned away from that café that night have proved fertile ground for a kind of hatefulness and guilt mongering that make it a constant struggle to know how to approach even men and women like Sid for fear I will inadvertently "offend" the "victim" or cause some unintended discomfort and "prove" to someone that I am a racist. This is what "political economy" as practiced now in the United States has done and is doing to many (I think most) of us. Attorney general Eric Holder recently called us American citizens "racial cowards." Chad and I claim no great courage that others do not have, but it is a mark of my own advancing age and the hope I once held with many in the '60s for a truly colorblind and prosperous society and world that we have written. To whatever degree we can restore the courage that comes from truth telling and believing, we offer the discussion that follows.

Let me (Chad) just add that we believe that this book is needed in our America today. There is so much misinformation in our churches about the way the market works and about the nature of "just generosity" (to use a phrase being bantered around a lot these days) that we believe there is a need-ed corrective. I hear all the time people apologizing for being successful in business and life as if that were something that a Christian ought not to be. We hope to show here that this is simply not a biblical perspective. And the

Seeking the City

situation is probably more problematic today than it has been since the time of the "Robber Barons" (more on them later). Even in the time we have been working on this book, the situation has become more complicated, volatile, and confused. We are hoping to bring some perspective to this.

My background, as Tom has briefly indicated, was growing up in a Denver suburb, the poorest part of town. My high school was half Hispanic, half white. I experienced a call to the ministry when I was eighteen years old, while Tom was my pastor. My ministry has led me to serve churches in five states, and I currently teach theology at The Southern Baptist Theological Seminary and am serving a small congregation, Salyersville First Baptist Church in Salyersville, Kentucky, a church located in one of the poorest counties in the state, with unemployment at 20 percent. I say those things because I probably ought to be sounding the clarion call for redistribution, government assistance at the highest level, and higher taxes on the "rich." But that is not the drum I am beating, for a variety of reasons, not least of which is that if you live in a poor community, you become aware very quickly just how much damage those efforts at redistribution and government assistance have done. A nineteen-year-old student of mine, Jordan Conley, who is from the part of eastern Kentucky where I am now serving my church, related to me how years ago before he was born during the "Great Society" buildup of Lyndon Johnson, the president came to his county and gave a famous speech about his new program, photos were taken and are famously displayed in that county, but the county has never recovered financially from Johnson's program. It is worse off today than it ever was in 1963, the year Johnson took the presidency.

What we are engaging in here is a dialogue that has in recent years taken on the name of "theo-politics" and "theo-economics." We are entering the field of dialogue known as the "political economy," and we are dealing with it from the standpoint of the Christian Bible, the Christian theological heritage, and biblical Christian ethics. But we are playing on the field of *political economy*. So, if there are times in reading this volume that you are not sure whether you are wrestling with political science, with economics, or with theology, then you are right with us! Neither Tom nor I pretend to be political science experts or experts in economics. Tom is a pastor and a businessman, and I am a pastor and a theologian by training. But someone has to speak to the interface be-

Seeking the City

tween these issues, and if the people who have more credentials are not doing it, then we will take our shot and at least open a side of the conversation that has not yet really been broached.

Tom and I believe that for our nation's well-being, and for the church's spiritual vitality, there needs to be a new look at the issues of work, wealth, and stewardship, and it is in hope and expectation that we might do some good, that we offer this book. We realize that the volume you hold in your hand (or are looking at on your screen) is weighty. We make no apology for that in terms of the ground to be covered. We became convinced in the midst of the construction of this book that there was a body of information that needed to be presented, and that without all of it, the story could not be told. Here is our story. It is ours in the sense that we have lived it, and it is ours in the sense that we have assembled it. May the Lord bless you in your reading of the volume, and may he bless our churches with a passion to be Seeking the City.

We both wish to acknowledge the very capable and professional way that the publisher, Kregel, has carried this volume forward to press. Thanks go to Dennis and Paul Hillman for being willing to take on such a project. Thanks to Laura Bartlett for her attention to detail in marketing and other matters. Shawn Vander Lugt has been a pleasure to work with in the editing process. And Paul Brinkerhoff's attention to detail kept us from many mistakes and slip-ups in copy editing. The remaining mistakes are our own.

We have dedicated this book to our fathers, both of whom have gone on to be with the Lord in recent times, but we both know that this book could never have been written without the patience, encouragement, love, and dedication of our partners in life, work, ministry, and stewardship, Karen Pratt and Tina Brand.

Part 1

THE WAY TO THE CITY

A Biblical Journey

Introduction

THE LAST HALF OF THE TWENTIETH CENTURY witnessed an astonishing and more or less peaceful revolution in the political and economic realities of the entire world. "The West won the Cold War. The free nations defeated the totalitarian ones. The capitalists outperformed the statists. The believers outlasted the atheists. The United States of America, flawed and divided as we were, persevered to see the Union of Soviet Socialist Republics and nearly all of its satellites implode."[1] This process is all the more remarkable, coming as it did on the heels of two cataclysmic wars and a worldwide depression.

We are not suggesting that an era in which two major "police actions" (Korea and Vietnam) were fought, the ongoing Cold War threatened the annihilation of the planet during the period from 1945 to the early 1990s, or the fact that literally millions of civilians (besides military personnel) died at the hands of their own governments can be called truly peaceful. But it is wholly remarkable in the history of the world that such astonishing change has taken place without the outbreak of world war on a scale unimaginable. The age of totalitarian Socialist/Marxist governments has (hopefully) passed or is passing (even in China and Cuba), with the hope for millions that they shall never gain ascendancy again. And with them, it was hoped, also passed a way of economics and politics that had threatened all free societies. This was an extraordinary half-century for those who lived through the entire period. The time of fallout shelters, nuclear blast drills in the schools, mushroom clouds in commercials on TV, and the incessant reminder that our system of economics and

---

1   Mona Charen, *Useful Idiots* (New York: Regnery, 2003), 1.

government was in deadly competition with a power that was feared capable of burying us has receded. A new century with no present potential for such a cataclysm has dawned with a burgeoning global community of trade and cooperation (as well as competition) bidding to set the agenda for the foreseeable future.[2] It is the premise of this book that these developments, culminating in events at the beginning of the new century, have recast the terms in which Christians need to think and act ethically as marketplace participants.[3]

When I (Tom), a quintessential baby boomer, was born in 1945, most evangelical Christians were aware of very few ethical dilemmas outside certain personal morality decisions.[4] If there were "business world" decisions to be made, they had primarily to do with the implications of taking home office supplies for personal use and whether it was right to go to work for a beer distributorship—nothing like the current, often bewildering, array of issues faced Christians concerned with conforming their lives to biblical norms.

The problem that, above all others, reared its head to forever dismiss such a simplistic view of Christian morality was racial segregation and its root cause, racism. In a sense, American Christianity has never been the same since 1954 and the Supreme Court decision in *Brown v. Board of Education*. The politics and ethics of race-consciousness now became thoroughly local when it was thrust into school systems across America by the Supreme Court and followed by federal enforcement measures. What had been a simmering back-burner issue for decades was now thrust to the national stage and turned into front-burner news and was made a political call to arms.

For decades since that time, Christian and non-Christian alike have been denied the possibility of quietly ignoring the elephant sitting in the living

---

2   The key word here is "cataclysm." While the threat of isolated terror and nuclear attack is very real, the possibility of an all-out planet-destroying nuclear exchange has passed. The West and the United States won that battle.

3   David Frum suggests that these times look very similar to the conditions at the beginning of the twentieth century. In fact, he calls the current period of adjustment a time of "remoralization." See David Frum, *How We Got Here: The 70s, The Decade That Brought You Modern Life—for Better or Worse* (New York: Basic Books, 2000), 356. For a further in-depth look at this conception, see Gertrude Himmelfarb, *The De-Moralization of Society: From Victorian Virtues to Modern Values* (New York: Vintage Books, 1996).

4   I remember well the high school Sunday seminar discussions guided by ethicist T. B. Maston's *Right or Wrong* (Nashville: Broadman, 1955). This book is still available from used book dealers.

Way to the City

room. It was not that it had never been there before; it was just worked around quietly in polite society. But it was inevitable as the World War II generation came home, having mingled racially even in US-segregated armed services, that things would never be the same.[5] The generations who have come along since that time will have a hard time understanding what a paradigm shift this was for Christians, many of whom had never discussed the problem of racism in moral terms, though, as we shall see, the entire discussion politically in this country was fought out over interpretations of the Bible.

But for others of us, especially those of us who grew to young adulthood during this era, our memories are filled with vivid TV images of high school integration enforced by federal agents in Little Rock, Arkansas, the admission of the first black student at the University of Alabama,[6] the rise of Martin Luther King Jr. and his nonviolent marches (culminating in his eventual assassination),[7] the network news reports of lynchings and successful and attempted assassinations and bombings, the incredible scenes of "race riots" in major cities all across America,[8] and much more. Christians were forced to face a much greater sense of moral responsibility. To a new generation of Christian leadership in the making, Martin Luther King's "dream" that all men and women, boys and girls might one day be judged "not by the color of their skin, but by the content of their character" was not just another sermon; it was a biblical moral mandate. Without question, however, the gathering sense of moral direction was violently changed by the events of April 4, 1968, in Memphis, Tennessee, when rifle fire took the life of Dr. King.

There is a sense in which the bullet fired by James Earl Ray into the body of Martin Luther King Jr., was a "shot heard around the world" just as surely as the legendary first shot at Lexington during the American Revolution. For

---

5   It was not until 1946 that President Harry Truman integrated the armed services of the United States.

6   Even though Governor George Wallace vowed, "Segregation today, segregation tomorrow, segregation forever."

7   Nonviolence was Martin Luther King Jr.'s declared methodology, built on the example of Mahatma Gandhi. Nevertheless, many of King's demonstrations and marches turned violent because of governmental and civilian opposition when these antagonistic entities resorted to violence to stop his work. Taylor Branch, *Parting the Waters: America in the King Years, 1954–63* (New York: Simon & Schuster, 1988), 888–921.

8   More than one hundred cities had riots the day after the burial of King.

Way to the City

many in the generation who became adults during that period (and countless others who came before and since), Dr. King's preaching and actions set a "moral" tone that could invigorate Christian social ethics. What once reverberated as a call to all men and women to rise in righteous indignation and right a long-standing moral wrong was to become in time the mere politics of class envy and warfare. With King's violent departure, a unifying moral theme was lost, drowned by the voices of competing political constituencies demanding a piece of the action. A call to straightforward moral actions was highjacked eventually by forces with another agenda besides mere morality. That object was and is political power.[9]

The American struggle over race became in the last third of the twentieth century a kind of "me-too" political game. It goes like this: If the race question is a moral/political battlefield, what about gender discrimination? What about sexual orientation? What about disability? What about the homeless? And what about any number of other apparent injustices done to any other possible constituency?

To be sure, especially among Christians, but regularly among the general populace as well, the morality card is played to justify political action. But it is with a whole new meaning. For, in the previous eight years of the twenty-first century, events came to bear that produced a new sense of what was moral and what was not. In fact, it was the complete reversal of what existed at the close of World War II where this discussion began. Nowadays *moral* is not a term used to evaluate one's sexual proclivities or one's personal trustworthiness to tell the truth. No. Now *moral* is a litmus test for whether one stands on the correct side of certain political disputes. Morality was not involved in the sexual exploits of the president of the United States in the '90s, in the minds of some, for that was about private behavior, a matter of personal taste but

---

9   There is no way to predict in hindsight what the future work of King and his close associates in the movement would have been had he lived. He, too, might have taken another path as the work continued. We are also aware that history records facets of Dr. King's private and political life that we do not condone. But, it is also true that many men have preached better than they lived and had a salutary influence upon human events. For many who lived through the time, Dr. King's preaching was the spark that lit a flame of genuine Christian social concern. For what still ranks as probably the definitive work on King and this era, see David J. Garrow, *Bearing the Cross: Martin Luther King and the Southern Christian Leadership Conference* (New York: Random House, 1986).

Way to the City

not of morality. Yet according to a very vocal lineup of political pundits and office holders, morality was most certainly involved in such political issues as welfare reform, minimum wage legislation, tax cuts "for the rich," health-care "reform," environmental damage, Medicare benefits, and Social Security (to name but a few). It would seem that *morality* is not what it used to be.[10]

The moral distance that has grown between that earlier time and the present is illustrated in the evolution of the use of terminology associated with the charge of racism. It is now common usage to charge with racism anyone who disagrees with a certain political philosophy. This philosophy is characterized by a conviction that all people of color are the victims of bias and discrimination, whether realized or subconscious, in the mind of the supposed victimizer. Thus, not only is racism the province of the KKK and other obviously race-conscious practitioners of discrimination, but anyone who opposes the politics of a person of color is by default a racist. Strangest of all to many who have lived through the entire sequence of events, the very idea that "color-blindness" should inform our relations among the racial groups is no longer a *moral* way of settling disputes. Rather, it is the very reverse that is now championed. One must discriminate on the basis of race in order to avoid the charge of racism—that is, in certain political situations. In other situations, that may not be the case. But the rules are based on the determinations made by one or more groups that is allowed to call the shots morally—the prior victims.[11] And, the "victim" list has grown longer and broader decade by decade. Most bewildering of all, these prior victims cannot be charged with racism or sexism or hate crime, etc., even if they make such distinctions, because one must have "power" to be called a racist, and a victim by definition has no power. Dr. King's dream has become a nightmare.[12]

---

10 See the discussion of this phenomenon in Shelby Steele, *White Guilt: How Blacks and Whites Together Destroyed the Promise of the Civil Rights Era* (New York: HarperCollins, 2006), 1–6. This is reminiscent of Francis Schaeffer's comment in 1968 that you used to be able to tell a young lady to be a "good girl," and, even if she decided not to take your advice, she at least knew what you meant. Now such advice would be met with a blank stare.

11 And, most importantly, it is the "victims" who determine the fact, extent, and origin of their self-denominated "victimization."

12 Frum opines, and we agree, that additional concomitant forces produced by the Vietnam experience hastened this process of "remoralization." These included government sponsored hyperinflation and the technology explosion. See Frum, *How We Got Here*, 353–54.

Way to the City

Finally, in those last three decades of the twentieth century, voices came to the fore that had long been speaking, though they had not been as respected among the intelligentsia and the political and media elite as they are today. These voices attempted to establish legitimacy in respected circles for the clamor of constant criticism of the American way of life.[13] Their battle cry was that America and the West (but especially the United States) should be ashamed and repent for having gained its wealth at the expense of the poor and weak of the world—both at home and abroad. Born of an almost paranoid guilt about the American success story, it began about the time that the United States and many other Western nations managed to produce a way of life that lifted the masses of people in the West, and especially the United States, above the level of mere subsistence and could produce what had only before been thought of as luxuries. When indoor plumbing, electricity, phones, automobiles, radios, homeownership, and numerous other amenities that went well beyond food and clothing and a place to sleep at night became the norm for millions of working-class Americans and Westerners, the guilt began to pour forth from many directions, but mostly from centers of perceived elite intellectual attainment. The denizens of these locales, mostly institutions of higher learning, but also more bohemian locations such as Greenwich Village and the "open road,"[14] (and of late, the "occupy Wall Street" crowd) were enabled to have the time to contemplate such things because the overflow of American and Western financial success made it possible to have the leisure time to move beyond the mere pursuit of survival.

These self-styled prophets[15] persisted over time until they became entrenched wherever there was political muscle and financial sustenance to protect them. Evangelical Christianity was one of the last places these voices began to be heard. It is clear that in the Christian church there must always be a vital edge of moral authority that challenges the conventions of the age lest we become irrelevant to and, worse, supportive of, an ethics in the public square

---

13 In popular parlance on the talk shows of the '90s, it was the "blame America first crowd." Once the province only of the radical Left, composed of avowed Socialists and Marxists, now apparently mainstream voices were heard.
14 See Jack Kerouac's *On the Road* (New York: Viking, 1957), et al.
15 These are "prophets" in the sense of naysayers against the perceived evil of American society, and also, at times, predictors of doom and gloom.

Way to the City

that condones or ignores real evil.[16] It is apparent in the writing and work of many, who would charge Christians with having exploited "the poor" and other sins against humanity, that they are concerned to maintain this edge. The question before us is whether these charges stick, and if so, what shall we do?

Ron Sider was foremost among many, in his book *Rich Christians in an Age of Hunger*,[17] who forcefully challenged the evangelical community to repent for living a profligate lifestyle at the expense of the weak, poor, and alienated. Professor Sider made it clear in his writings and his public appearances that he meant not just to indict huge multinational corporations and northern hemisphere governments (especially those on the North American continent), but his brush painted as immoral, and in danger of being eternally damned, working-class evangelicals who failed to sign on to such ideas as a "simpler lifestyle,"[18] "graduated tithes," "communal living," and "supporting public transportation with your feet and your vote."[19] Later works have added much to this agenda and the spillover into political advocacy from the evangelical Left and others is evident from local to national and international politics.

---

16 The position of the authors is that evil is both personal, and, because persons inhabit places of power throughout society, institutional. We are convinced, however, that the institutional evil in the world goes far beyond American prosperity.

17 Ronald J. Sider, *Rich Christians in an Age of Hunger: Moving from Affluence to Generosity* (Nashville: Thomas Nelson: 2005). Originally published with subtitle *A Biblical Study*, Downers Grove, IL: InterVarsity Press, 1977. Revised editions published, 1984; Dallas: Word, 1990; 1997 (new subtitle). Citations are to the Thomas Nelson edition. The publication of this book coincided with the founding of Evangelicals for Social Action (ESA) in 1973 and *Sojourners* in 1971, as well as other attempts to implement aspects of Sider's agenda.

18 Suggesting one might eat vegetable protein instead of animal protein, join a food co-op, share appliances, tools, cars, etc.

19 See Sider, *Rich Christians*, 150–66. Professor Sider typically attempts to "have it both ways." He clearly implies the possibility of "going to hell" for ordinary working people who eat bananas and drink coffee because they are participants in "evil structures." (See his use of the story of Lazarus and Dives [Latin, "rich man"], 109.) While stating the obvious that "the affluent North simply is not responsible for all the poverty in the world" (134), nevertheless we are complicit in the same way as Dives and might join him below. See also his use of Paul's teaching on the Lord's Supper, 78–84. This "exegesis" (we will defend our emphasis on this word later in context) is echoed and intensified by Craig L. Blomberg, *Neither Poverty nor Riches: A Biblical Theology of Possessions* (Downers Grove, IL: InterVarsity Press, 1999), 187–89. Sider, besides repeatedly revising his original work, has added to his writings (among others) *I Am Not a Social Activist: Making Jesus the Agenda* (Scottsdale, PA: Herald, 2008) and *Just Generosity: A New Vision for Overcoming Poverty in America*, 2nd ed. (Grand Rapids, MI: Baker, 2007).

Way to the City

Thus was a debate[20] joined that produced point and counterpoint all along the spectrum of Christian advocacy of social responsibility for the weak, poor, disfranchised, alienated, and exploited.[21] The latest wave of evangelical and mainline social activism has taken on the environmental concerns of the political Left and bids to turn it into a biblical mandate for action against "global warming" (now "climate change") based on what we are convinced is a faulty apprehension of the facts about human activity and climate variability and a questionable reading of the Bible and corresponding "Christian" theology.[22] This book seeks to provide a biblical, theological, historical, and economic way forward through these issues. No one aspect of the subject matter seems to satisfy the need for clarity of thought in the current near-maze of literature and political posturing.

In the places where fire and smoke have given way to careful exegesis of Scripture and thoughtful contemplation of ends and means, some consensus among those called variously evangelical and conservative (pejoratively, "fun-

---

20 A battle for some—see, David Chilton, *Productive Christians in an Age of Guilt-Manipulators: A Biblical Response to Ronald J. Sider* (Tyler, TX: Institute for Christian Economics, 1985), repeatedly revised to counter specific editions of Sider's work. These responses to Sider have never been directly answered, and many of Chilton's challenges remain pertinent to this day. Ronald H. Nash, *Why the Left Is Not Right* (Grand Rapids: Zondervan, 1996), details the long history of left-leaning evangelical advocacy to the mid-1990s. For the latest on this "battle," see Joel McDurmon, *God versus Socialism: A Biblical Critique of the New Social Gospel* (Powder Springs, GA: American Vision, 2009). This book challenges the positions of Ron Sider, Jim Wallis, and Tony Campolo.

21 We will be documenting this in the notes as we go along. For a thorough treatment of the debate from all positions, Right, Left, and Center, see Craig M. Gay, *With Liberty and Justice for Whom?* (Grand Rapids, MI: Eerdmans, 1991).

22 Current groups include Evangelical Environmental Network (EEN), whose slogan is "What would Jesus drive?"; the Regeneration Project, with its campaign to halt global warming, Interfaith Power and Light (IPL); Presbyterians for Restoring Creation; the Interfaith Center for Corporate Responsibility; and the National Religious Partnership for the Environment. HarperOne has also recently published *The Green Bible* (San Francisco: HarperCollins, 2008) in the NRSV, which offers selections from the Bible printed in green ink on recycled paper, which that Bible's editors interpret as supporting the leftist environmental political agenda. Selections from *Sojourners'* board chairman Brian McLaren are included as well as numerous other environmental activists. Its perspective is clearly of a piece with prior assumptions that the prosperity of the West is at the expense of the undeveloped world and demands a "Christian" response of repentance and lifestyle change. The American Bible Society has recently published also *The Poverty and Justice Bible* (New York: American Bible Society, 2009) in the CEV with much the same purpose as the above version for environmentalists.

Way to the City

damentalist") has taken place.[23] This continuing attempt to foster a meeting of the minds on the issues that affect Christian moral decision making on economic issues has led to some clarification about the areas of contention. We would hope that there could at least be agreement in these areas and that this book will succeed in advancing the discussion.

WHERE THERE IS AGREEMENT

We propose the following five more or less self-evident conclusions from the current literature.[24]

First, a biblically informed economic outlook is essential for evangelical faith and social interaction. This is a conclusion peculiar to the evangelical wing of Christianity because of the term "biblical." While it is not at times crystal clear what is meant in all camps by "biblical," some attempt to justify one's position from the Scriptures is essential to a call for evangelical consensus.[25] The differences among the disputants concern interpretive details and situational applications and now more and more a decidedly "postmodern" approach to reading the text that seems to assume no indisputable referent as a standard for the textual material other than the reader's own concerns and assumptions. This last is the most deplorable and readers of this work will see we have no sympathy for this approach.

Second and corollary to the first proposition is the growing consensus that the Bible does not explicitly lay out a theory of economics and social

---

23 The current positions of disputants to the general remarks we make here will appear in the text and notes as we go along. We will not attempt any analysis of the current debate over what constitutes an "evangelical" these days. Defining this term is important, to be sure, but is simply not within the mission we have assigned ourselves.

24 For a compendium of "evangelical" thought on the engagement of politics on this and other subjects, see Ronald J. Sider and Diane Knippers, eds., *Toward an Evangelical Public Policy: Political Strategies for the Health of the Nation* (Grand Rapids, MI: Baker, 2005).

25 The latest turn on this discussion uses the term *biblicism* pejoratively to describe a generic attempt to use the Bible as a virtual handbook on any and every topic the Bible might be thought to address profitably from the standpoint of a Christian "worldview" perspective. See especially Christian Smith, *The Bible Made Impossible* (Grand Rapids, MI: Brazos, 2011). We cannot hope to address this subject here, except to state that we think our approach does not treat the Scriptures of the Old and New Testaments as in any sense a "handbook" to anything, and we regard the failure to treat the cross of Christ as the "just"-ifying event of history as the source of many broken attempts to understand the topic we have chosen in this study.

Way to the City

justice, though conclusions are evident in the writings of some.[26] Further, it does not state economic principles as Socialist, Marxist, or capitalist. On the other hand, the Bible does contain enough clear instruction to allow us to deduce its "teaching." The differences concern what it does, in fact, "teach" that should inform those who want to think and act Christianly in the economic marketplace.[27]

Third, Christians should be concerned about the poor, the helpless, and the oppressed. This was never really in dispute, but it was probably on the back burner for many for a number of reasons.[28] The questions being debated today are, what causes the conditions that so concern us, who should be the objects of our concern, how might we go about articulating a truly Christian solution (if one is possible) or at least amelioration, and most troubling, what are the politics (or avoidance thereof) involved?

---

26 With the notable exception of theonomists Gary North, David Chilton, Gary DeMar, et al. However, more recently Sider, *Just Generosity*, and Tony Campolo, *Red-Letter Christians: A Citizen's Guide to Faith and Politics* (Ventura CA: Regal, 2008), are very clear in their political advice to those who would be both moral and truly Christian (as they see it), as is also Jim Wallis in his various writing and speaking efforts. To us these books and speeches look and sound like a primer on the platform of the Democratic National Committee, with very few exceptions. Let the reader read and decide. We concede, without question, that the same can be said of much writing and opining on the other side of the spectrum.

27 The long history of the use of the Bible in American political discourse is far beyond the limits of this book to discuss. Our methodology will be apparent as we seek to explicate Scripture. For salient discussion of the issues in American history, see at least the following: Mark A. Noll and Luke E. Harlow, eds., *Religion and American Politics: From the Colonial Period to the Present*, 2nd ed. (New York: Oxford University Press, 2007); Nathan O. Hatch, *The Democratization of American Christianity* (New Haven, CT: Yale University Press, 1989), esp. chaps. 5 and 6; Mark A. Noll, *The Civil War as a Theological Crisis*, Steven and Janice Brose Lectures in the Civil War Era (Chapel Hill, NC: University of North Carolina Press, 2006); Harry S. Stout, *Upon the Altar of the Nation: A Moral History of the Civil War* (2006; New York: Penguin Books, 2007); Mark A. Noll, *The Scandal of the Evangelical Mind* (Grand Rapids, MI: Eerdmans, 1994); and Mark A. Noll, *America's God: From Jonathan Edwards to Abraham Lincoln* (New York: Oxford University Press, 2002). These works have abundant primary source material in the text and notes for those wanting to document the common use of the Bible in the building and sustaining of the American political and economic structures.

28 One of the most telling analyses of the reason these issues, which were once the clear province of Protestant Christians, became less than compelling to American evangelicals (later called pejoratively and sympathetically "fundamentalists") is to be found in Marvin Olasky, *The Tragedy of American Compassion* (Wheaton, IL: Crossway, 1992). But see also George M. Marsden, *Fundamentalism and American Culture*, 2nd ed. (New York: Oxford University Press, 2006).

Way to the City

Fourth, a marketplace of commerce is necessary to the production of adequate wealth for access to it on a wide enough basis to reach all people. This conclusion has been forced on all but the most dedicated Socialists and Marxists because of the collapse of economic systems all over the world that depend on centralized, coercive government controls for their maintenance.[29] These systems have simply failed, and capitalist institutions have become the order of the new global economy. It is being acknowledged, sometimes grudgingly, that somehow wealth must be produced to reduce the effects of poverty, and a more or less capitalist market-style economy is the best engine for that purpose. The questions concern how much (not whether) government intervention is necessary. We are aware of no one except strict libertarians who advocate what is pejoratively termed "laissez-faire" capitalism, though many are labeled as having such opinions and regularly what is condemned as actually causing economic displacements is falsely so labeled. One question is whether production or distribution are to have the heaviest emphasis, and what the Bible does or doesn't teach about methods of "distribution."

Fifth, American and Western materialistic/secularistic societies are a frightening and challenging menace to biblical Christianity that must be confronted. There are some voices from Left to Right that would attempt to tar others exclusively with a failure to recognize this reality. Sometimes the charge may be correct. But the fact is that no faction has exclusive possession of the blinders of philosophical and theological accommodation to the spirit of the age. The issues we will address relate to the how, the where, and on what grounds this confrontation should take place.

Mankind in the Marketplace

Economists have often referred to man in his interactions in the marketplace of buying and selling as *homo economicus*. Analyses of how *homo economicus* acts and reacts and how outside forces affect him are the rightful province of the general subject of economics and trained economists. Economic theory is

---

29 We are aware that many are now heralding the demise of capitalist, market-oriented economics because of the 2008 global recession. We will be addressing this phenomenon as we go along.

built upon these observations, and some understanding of that discipline is invaluable to anyone wanting to better understand how markets work and what produces wealth and poverty.[30] The authors claim no special expertise in this field, but we will refer from time to time to principles that are both accepted and debated among the experts. We will attempt to simplify without making banal our references to these principles. You will find annotations where appropriate that will assist in further understanding.

However, this is not a book on economics as such. It is a book about Christians and their material and economic life. Since work, earning a living, and dispensing what is earned occupies such a massive proportion of human time, energy, and mentality, economics is arguably man's dominant endeavor. It is, in fact, this pervasive element that drives the modern Christian discussion of the subject.[31] For some, such an all-encompassing monopoly of humankind's best efforts is nothing short of slavery to materialism. In fact, some refer to economics as the "dismal science,"[32] and others critique it as reducing man to nothing but an economic apparatus (see the designation of him above). For others, this enslaving reality is evidence that the Bible's "curse" that man "by the sweat of your brow will eat your food" (Gen. 3:19 NIV) is as powerful as it has ever has been. Whether this dominance of work in order to live is the "curse" or materialistic preoccupation or both and much more is the concern of this book. Christian and non-Christian alike find the economic facts of life intruding upon all segments of existence. Discovering the Christian response to this unavoidable situation is the theme of our book.

---

30 See lucid and readable discussions in Thomas Sowell, *Basic Economics*, 3rd ed. (New York: Basic Books, 2007) and Thomas Sowell, *Applied Economics: Thinking Beyond Stage One* (New York: Basic Books, 2004). Also see Thomas Sowell, *Economic Facts and Fallacies* (New York: Basic Books, 2008), which discusses some of the major misunderstandings in the media and public discussion. For a specifically Christian take on the subject, see Victor V. Claar and Robin J. Klay, *Economics in Christian Perspective: Theory, Policy and Life Choices* (Downers Grove, IL: InterVarsity Press, 2007).

31 See also Gay's characterization of capitalism as "the pre-eminent social issue" (*With Liberty and Justice for Whom?* 1) of our times since the demise of the systems designed to address its problems (Socialism and Marxism) have collapsed late in the previous century.

32 Thomas Carlyle is widely quoted as coining this phrase along with "pig philosophy" to describe the work of Thomas Malthus, Adam Smith, and David Ricardo in economics. See Samuel Gregg, *Economic Thinking for the Theologically Minded* (Lanham, MD: University Press of America, 2001), 9.

Way to the City

Finally, a word about the length and complexity of the material we have come to include here. None of the material we have researched is adequate (and neither is ours) to the task of setting forth and critiquing man's economic life in the light of Scripture and its concomitant theological reflection, history, anthropology, and God at work in his creation with his ultimate glory as the outcome. Further, the explosion of information (and dis- and mis-information) on every possible aspect of this "economy" of life leaves anyone breathless in the contemplation of it. Most frustrating of all to us is the ongoing development of worldwide political exploitation of every facet of existence in its economic implications. The search for "social justice" (really, economic justice) is as long as history, as broad as the human race, as profound as the biblical revelation, as high as the heaven of God, and as complicated as the image of God in man who would be the earth's once and future vice-regent. What we have written here is an attempt to get beyond segmented and oversimplified treatments and give some sense of the immensity of the task of even attempting to plan and engineer mankind's economic present and future. If we can succeed in bringing a healthy humility to would-be prophets, teachers, political manipulators, social engineers, and various other intellectual and moral elites who think themselves capable of running other lives beyond their own, we will have found some sense of contentment in an impossible project. "Establish thou the work of our hands" is our prayer for this project (Ps. 90:17 KJV).

Our plan has been to search out first the biblical basis for an ethical economic life (part 1). This is followed by a historical-theological examination of the attempts in the world of Western civilization, Christendom in its broadest sense, to work out the conclusions of biblical study in their political and economic applications through the various eras of the history of the West (part 2). The third section of the book is designed to engage the present state of affairs from the standpoint of what has been developed in the first two sections (part 3). In the process we have assayed to come to some conclusions that will guide a new generation of biblically informed and theologically engaged Christians in being on mission in the global community. This is obviously an ambitious project, as the length of the book you hold in your hand attests.

We do not apologize for this apparent failure to recognize the short attention span of the generation now enamored of "flash-gatherings" generated by

Way to the City

short "tweets" on the Internet. This work is more a long and continuing blast of the shofar calling an age given to sound-bite crisis-mongering to a contemplative consideration of difficult and at times complicated and unpleasant fact-finding for the purpose of rational action as opposed to emotionally satisfying but soul-destroying and mind-stultifying "do-something-for-the-sake-of-doing-it" activism. We believe this last to be the manner of those who find themselves guilt-ridden by images they do not understand placed before them by "ministers" and politicians whose daily (hourly?) need is for more and more financing of "ministries" and government programs that do not do what they claim to do and many times actually achieve the opposite of their alleged goals.

We believe most Americans who call themselves "Christian," whether the cultural variety or the supposed "born-again" species (so labeled these days increasingly without appropriate examination of the claim) or the "fundamentalist" breed or the "liberal/progressive" community, have in common a general compassion for the "poor" and "less fortunate" and "downtrodden" and "disadvantaged," etc., whether they reside in the United States of America or somewhere else in the global community. No one wishes to harm the "poor" or push grandma over the cliff of unconcern for her Social Security benefits in her old age. In our opinion the constant litany of guilt-mongering and race-baiting and dishonest use of images and "studies" and "crisis" declarations amount to the instigation of class warfare and envy and are the products of political and economic motivations unworthy of Christians. When these same tactics appear in the literature and publicity and appeals of Christian (as they choose to name themselves) organizations, books, sermons, ministries, theologies, etc., it all seems particularly egregious to us.

Consequently, we have felt it necessary to write at length and in some detail from three vantage points. Biblically we believe the theme of seeking out the city that pleases God and is in the best interests of humankind is the nature of the pilgrimage of people of faith (Heb. 11:10, 16). No study that fails to address this overarching theme can hope to begin to establish a biblical mandate for economic life in a fallen world. This theme begins in Eden and concludes with the "download" of the New Jerusalem at the close of the revelation of Jesus Christ. In between we will see a remarkable confluence of

Way to the City

narrative, law-giving, wisdom, and prophetic pronouncements, followed by the inauguration of the kingdom of God in the person and work of the Son of God and his church, that testify to the nature of this pilgrimage of faith across the whole earth to the end of the age. Guided by a single ethic revealed first and comprehensively at Sinai and finally incarnate in the one-and-only Son of God (the *monogenēs*, as opposed to those adopted as sons), the Scriptures of both Testaments expound the theme of the city of the great King to come and the people who will inhabit it.

In the biblical survey of the first section ahead (part 1) we attempt to show that no economic model can claim the loyalty, or at least acquiescence, of Christians that does not take into account this vast panoramic view of humankind in the place and with the destiny that God created them to enjoy and rule. Sin is, of course, the intruder and Satan the purveyor of rebellion against the will of God that constantly spoils the best plans of human beings, for what has now entered into the heart of man must be eradicated for "good" to prevail. Consequently, justice can only be found in the pivotal event of the cross, where "just"-ification is accomplished—a conception that will not allow for mere "fairness"-ification to be substituted in its place. We believe the content of this "justice" is the source of most disagreement among "biblicist"-style (see our note above) Christians when it comes to the discussion of economic systems. Our biblical survey seeks to address this conflict as comprehensively as we can in such a "short" work as this is.

Our second section (part 2) seeks to understand the process and the direction of Christian theological development since the close of the first century. It is perforce historical in its orientation and partakes of political and economic as well as theological concerns. This reflects our own presupposition that theology is by its very nature a reaction to the environment in which it is done, generally interacting for the purpose of both understanding and influencing the prevailing culture and politics. Underlying this presupposition is also the premise that genuine theological reflection seeks to "please God" in some way as a justification for its value. Thus, we seek to find insight into how the church has sought through the centuries to honor and be acceptable to the God of the biblical revelation while evangelizing and influencing the culture around it, particularly, for our purposes, as it relates to economic issues.

Way to the City

This task is also huge and only marginally doable in a "short" work such as this. We have confined ourselves to the general development of Western civilization and its ultimate culmination in the present dominance globally of democratic capitalistic institutions and practices largely traceable to the North American continent, specifically the United States and its English-speaking partners. We do not apologize for narrowing the scope of this investigation in such a manner for three reasons. First, there is little disagreement in the present worldwide economic community that the United States and the former British Empire have had the predominant role of shaping the current global political economy. Second, it is also beyond dispute that the misgivings and criticisms of the evils that may be associated with the ongoing developmental process around the world are directed almost exclusively toward the American version of democratic capitalism as it has been practiced for the last 250 years or so. Third, the theme of the city toward which Christian civilization has been thought to be headed is a dominant theme in the West and still characterizes theological reflection on our economic theme, as it has for two millennia.

Augustine sought to defend the Constantinian model early on. His reflections, while lamenting the Roman excesses and godlessness, nevertheless posit the hand of the God of the Bible as prime mover in the "victory" of Christianity at the very seat of military, political, and economic power. This theme is at the heart of a thousand-year civilization that led to manorial feudalism and the divine right of kings to rule alongside the sanctioning (sanctifying?) authority of the church. It explains much that was deemed acceptable about mercantilism (defined later in this work) as an economic model, and it led to great wealth pouring into the coffers of the church. It also led to great corruption at the heart of the church and its mission and a stultifying of civilizational progress economically and politically. We seek to trace the history of these developments and link them to what follows.[33]

The Reformation sought to address this corruption at first from within and ultimately from the vantage point of outsiders of many stripes. Without

---

33 For the provenance of the Constantinian model for societal and political development, see H. Jefferson Powell, *The Moral Tradition of American Constitutionalism: A Theological Interpretation* (Raleigh, NC: Duke University Press, 1993), esp. 263–85.

Way to the City

dismissing as immaterial the contributions of others, we believe that the foremost among the cultural and political commentators were Luther and Calvin, men with differing visions of the city (or cities), but the so-called "Radical" Reformation of Anabaptist derivation has its part to play as well. Calvin's Geneva, with eventual contributions from the Dutch version of Calvinism, would become the dominant vision that animated several generations of followers who would eventually spawn on the eastern coast of the "New" World a group (really groups) of people animated by the thought of a "mission into the wilderness" that would establish a "city on a hill" for all the world to see (Matt. 5:14). This vision was full-orbed—political, spiritual, ecclesial, economic, missiological—and is generically seen as the Puritan vision and is dominated by a postmillennial version of eschatology, ever optimistic about the American experiment in its Christianized formulation.

Several versions of "Calvinism," influenced by strains of radical separatism (think Anabaptist, Quaker, and others) and Wesleyan Methodism would come to dominate the politics and economics of the North American continent. These would eventually diverge into several streams of theological and political reflection on the culture that lead first, and cataclysmically, to the Civil War and eventually a parting of the ways over the proper way to establish the City on a Hill. One way continued upon a long historic journey of revivalistic upheavals and strong evangelistic appeal with the flavor of social reform centering upon the individual and the church and its local and global mission. The other would take the way of political involvement for the reform of societal inequities that were thought to be at the root of personal sin and corruption. Both had long labored side by side before the war of 1861–65, being biblicist in their preaching and activism, but the war over slavery left them each with a dilemma—how to explain their divergent views of the teaching of Scripture that had led to the nation's greatest human catastrophe.

The sides would eventually part with animosity built up from years of theological and political battle within their respective denominations. One side would be dominated by a political vision of the improvement of mankind and his economic and moral state without the necessity of Christian conversion. The other would maintain the primacy of spiritual renewal through individual salvation and the possibility of societal reform through revivalism,

Way to the City

punctuated now by Wesleyan, holiness, and Keswickian ideals of the supernatural reform of the entire human character.[34] This mission would find expression powerfully in the work of Dwight Moody, Billy Sunday, and eventually Billy Graham of an evangelistic stripe modeled first by Charles Finney.[35]

We are impressed with the conviction from the history and theological considerations of both groups that the vision of the American "dream" of a "city on a hill," that would lead the world to a glorious future, has not been discarded; it has only been modified in opposing directions. Influenced by political progressivism (and Socialistic and Marxist presuppositions), one group seeks the ideal (the utopian vision) through the political system—an ideal of economic "fairness," treated as equivalent to biblical "justice," in what Thomas Sowell has called the "unconstrained vision."[36] This "seeking the city" is best illustrated in our discussions of the development of Wilsonian progressivism and its influence during the time frame of the "Great War," the responses to "the Great Depression," the developments attendant to World War II, and the coming of "the Great Society" legislation. The other side seeks no "ideal" other than the coming premillennial or amillennial kingdom of the great King (the postmillennial dream of the nineteenth century having died on the battlefields of France in the Great War). Meanwhile advocates of this "constrained vision" seek to ameliorate the human condition through personal and ecclesial activism that first seeks the conversion of the individual and goes about "doing good" when it can, while seeking to "do no harm" as spiritual followers of Hippocrates and seeks to model "good citizenship" in a polity of democratic institutions. Generally speaking, we would posit Augustine, John Calvin, and Carl Henry and those who found their delineation of the issues to be profoundly helpful as the leading proponents of this approach.

Our third section (part 3) takes its cue from the clash of these two foundational commitments and notes the points of intersection and disagreement where major disputes tend to divide into differing political loyalties. The his-

---

34 Marsden's discussion, in *Fundamentalism and American Culture*, of the interaction of these developments is particularly helpful.
35 See most definitively on this phenomenon William G. McLoughlin Jr., *Modern Revivalism: Charles Grandison Finney to Billy Graham* (Eugene, OR: Wipf and Stock, 2004).
36 Thomas Sowell, *A Conflict of Visions: Ideological Origins of Political Struggles*, rev. ed. (New York: Basic Books, 2007). We will entertain a lengthy discussion of this book later in chap. 21.

Way to the City

torical setting is the period commencing roughly in 1970 and proceeding to the present, a period coincident with and overlapping Robert Fogel's "Fourth Great Awakening" (cited later in chap. 17) and its emphasis on investing in the business of building "human capital" in the neediest communities left on the planet. Here we seek to clarify a number of issues for Christians caught in a crossfire of ideas and ideals all claiming to proceed from biblical moral teaching. These are all the more important (aside from their claims to biblical warrant) because of the attendant fomenting of a "crisis" mentality associated with political activism and economic difficulty. The complexity of the claims and justifications is daunting, and the intertwining of fact and fiction in the data used is so frustrating at times that it can appear hopelessly muddled. But we believe it is necessary to think straight about the facts of a situation in order to formulate a Christian "solution," if there is one, one that is rational and compassionate at the same time. No one has a commission from the God of the Bible to falsely accuse other Christians of failing to carry out supposed social "mandates" through their having failed to vote for certain politicians or certain pieces of legislation or for having done business with certain corporations or a host of other supposed wrongs. Such false accusations can come from misplaced emphases on scriptural mandates, misunderstood or misrepresented facts in real-life situations of political concern, the creation of "crisis" mentalities where no such crisis exists, or simple insinuations that produce guilt manipulation.

Consequently we have felt it essential to our purpose to clarify the actual economic conditions in the West and especially the United States of America by (1) making as clear as we can the nature of the system(s) under which we operate economically, politically, and socially; (2) attempting to demonstrate the over-all "justice" of capitalistic markets; (3) documenting the sustainability and environmental wisdom and compassion of those markets when they lead to prosperity; (4) questioning as accurately as we can the use and abuse of governmental "solutions" to social ills that may be associated with the displacements of capitalistic markets; and (5) calling to accountability those who would allege from Christian and/or biblical sources that the prosperity of Western Christians is equivalent to the stolen and fraudulent wealth of the "rich" condemned in the Bible and in the politics of the worldwide leftist community. We conclude by suggesting various ways Christians can be involved in

Way to the City

social concern with a rational basis for their compassionate activism. We also provide clear warning about the direction of this world's system of "justice" as opposed to that which the God of the Bible, the Father of our Lord, Jesus Messiah, is in the process of bringing to this earth.

We believe that though the Bible does not spell out an economic or political philosophy as such, that a free-market system of economics accompanied by a political system that elevates human freedom, classically conceived, is most consistent with the teaching of Scripture. We recognize that, since humans are sinners, a system of checks and balances in such a system will be necessary for its success and that the political structure should be concerned to provide an environment that promotes a maximum of equal opportunity for all. We believe that such convictions are implicit in Scripture and found their highest point of historical development in the founding and refounding of the American experiment.[37] We further believe that this structure is under assault in our day and may not survive into the distant future. That is a main part of our concern.

Along the way of this short-but-long presentation we will, especially in the notes, engage some of those who have made some sharp accusations toward other believers, at times implying their eternal doom or unworthiness for fellowship around the Lord's Table (among other things as well) for failing to carry out certain political and economic "mandates" said to be clear in Scripture. Our comments will at times match up to the vehemence of what we consider to be intemperate applications of personal conclusions mistakenly drawn. These comments, of course, represent only the opinions of the authors here and do not in any way reflect on the publishers of this volume, the institutions where the authors are employed, or on anyone quoted in the notes for support of our positions on any issue.

---

37 By "refounding" we refer to the historical impact of the Civil War of 1861–65, a point we will develop in later chapters.

Way to the City

Chapter 1

Seeking the City:
The Metanarrative of Scripture

THE BIBLE BEGINS ITS NARRATIVE in a garden and closes it in a fabulous city. The city of Revelation is clearly juxtaposed against a parody, a whorish imitation of something first contemplated in Israel in Jerusalem, the ideal representation of Mount Zion "on the sides of the north" (Ps. 48:2 KJV). Babylon, the whorish caricature of beauty and wealth, center of all the enmity of the world culture against God and his chosen "seed," having risen long before Jerusalem was anything but a tribal enclave and home to a local priest named Melchizedek (king of righteousness), at last gets her just deserts and makes way for the city coming down from God. Implicit in the "heavenly" Jerusalem imagery is the failure of the earthly Jerusalem to carry out its original mandate. This vision conflates two images—the bride, a designation for the people of God redeemed "from the earth," who is/are the rightful inhabitants and the habitation itself shining in glorious beauty adorned with the wealth of earth that can be mined and/or refined and fished only from the ground and the seas.

She is a technological and moral marvel prepared by creative genius and sacrificial love. Jerusalem, the city of the great King, is the final dwelling place toward which pilgrim people of faith have been pointing for millennia (Heb. 11:10)—a "homeland" rather than a world of sojourning (11:13–16). And only a people who are "righteous" in the sight of God are fit for the city (Rev. 21:27). Astoundingly, between the garden and the city we learn that what was lost at one time has been recovered and "redeemed" by the work of the "just" (righteous) One (Acts 3:14; 7:52; 22:14) who would not give up on the plan to perfect all creation and rule in the presence of his own people. And contrary to some utopian schemes of human imaginings, it is not the garden that is the place of delight and destiny, but the fabulous city with streets of purest gold. The garden has been subsumed by technology around it, though its river flows giving life to all it touches and its "tree of life" gives fruit for all seasons and into it flow all that is of any lasting value from the nations of this world.

Joni Mitchell with her song entitled "Woodstock" was not the first or the last to invoke the utopian dream of "the garden" as man's best hope.[1] Somehow the romantic illusion of "We are stardust / We are golden" that was Woodstock has literally been caught up in "the devil's bargain," it seems to us. That's what "billion-year-old carbon" is like when it has pretentious delusions of grandeur.[2]

Woodstock Nation has finally assumed its full potential for power in the presidency and Congress of the United States and is bent on a return to some yesterday before systemic evil and societal pressures and technology run amok had corrupted all that was once pure and pristine. At least, that's their story and they're sticking to it—if they can just get there before the planet drowns in melting ice caps and burns up from gases breathed out by every human being on the planet and exuded the other way by every bovine raised to feed a rapacious global, but especially American, society.[3]

Thomas Sowell has rightly referred to this conception of the world and its possibilities apart from the direct intervention of God as the "unlimited vision," and John Kekes has added to this analysis in his delineation of the multiple

---

1   See Benjamin J. Wiker, *10 Books That Screwed Up the World: And 5 Others That Didn't Help* (Washington, DC: Regnery, 2008), for a clever and readable survey of the history of this kind of intellectual hypothesizing and pomposity. A companion volume that is more academic and less popular in style is Benjamin J. Wiker, *Moral Darwinism: How We Became Hedonists* (Downers Grove, IL: InterVarsity Press, 2002).

2   "Woodstock," words and music by Joni Mitchell, is a song about the Woodstock Music and Arts Festival of 1969. Mitchell was unable to attend the festival but watched reports on the television, which prompted her to write he song. She first performed and recorded it in 1969 and later released it on her third album, *Ladies of the Canyon* in 1970.

3   Another election has come and gone and the Congress of the United States is changing. Stay tuned.

Way to the City

myths involved in the egalitarian and primitivist notions of societal develop-ment.[4] The ascendant vision of humanity and their world as tending toward the good, because humanity itself, though not entirely good intrinsically, tends to-ward the good anyhow, demands that all pretensions to inequality of outcomes are by nature unjust and due for elimination through whatever means.

The Bible tells a different story. Once there was nothing and God said "'Let there be light,' and there was light." Christian astrophysicists like Hugh Ross will tell you this happened on the order of 13 billion years ago (give or take a few hundred thousand) as we calculate time.[5] Furthermore, he will tell you that this is the precise timing necessary to have produced the civilization we now have that is capable of observing and appreciating the glories of God's good creation—a high-tech global community that "fills" the earth and is ca-pable of sustaining itself[6] and fulfilling the commands of God to Adam and Eve to rule and subdue not just the earth but the heavens as well. "Rather than seeing ourselves as insignificant specks in the immensity of the cosmos, we can consider that immensity an indicator of our worth. It seems the Creator invested a great deal—a universe of 50 billion trillion stars, plus a hundred times more matter, all fine-tuned to mind-boggling precision—for us. If not for the strength and abundance of that evidence in support of the notion, it would seem the height of arrogance."[7] We have no intention of weighing in on the age-of-the-earth controversy in this analysis, but Ross does have a point!

When we consider that the most widely quoted verse in the Bible (John 3:16) states clearly that God "loved" this *cosmos* enough to send his beloved

---

4 Thomas Sowell, *A Conflict of Visions: Ideological Origins of Political Struggles*, rev. ed. (New York: Basic Books, 2007), and John Kekes, *The Illusions of Egalitarianism* (Ithaca, NY: Cornell University Press, 2003). Also see Thomas Sowell, *The Vision of the Anointed: Self-Congratulation as a Basis for Social Policy* (New York: Basic Books, 1995), which points out clearly the mentality of those who deem themselves adequate to the task of egalitarian reforms, and Thomas Sowell, *The Quest for Cosmic Justice* (New York: Free Press, 1999), which delineates the difference between temporal just-ness and eternal or final justice.

5 We are not making any defense here of the young- or old-earth hypotheses, just noting the vastness of a creation that can only be partially understood through inventions like the Hubble Space Telescope.

6 More on the catchword, "sustainability," in a later chapter.

7 Hugh Ross, *Why the Universe Is the Way It Is* (Grand Rapids, MI: Baker, 2008), 41. See also William Dembski, *The End of Christianity: Finding a Good God in an Evil World* (Nashville: B&H; Milton Keynes: Paternoster, 2009), for a theological treatment of the same ideas.

Way to the City

Son for its full redemption, we find ourselves awed by the possibilities that may yet present themselves to the company of "just men made perfect" in the city prepared for them (Heb. 12:23 KJV). The plan has not been diverted or defeated and is still being actively pursued. Wherever men and women use their creative abilities to subdue yet another portion of the planet and bring it into subjection to the needs of humankind and the glory of God, the plan still plays out. Many still suffer in unimaginable, abject poverty, a state they have been in for millennia, not because someone forced it on them, but because that is the state of all human persons in sin until they produce the wealth inherent in the resources (namely, the "stuff" put to use by people and/or God) that God has placed at their disposal. God promises the sun and the rain and the seasons, but he does not break open the ground or plant and cultivate and harvest, nor does he pull weeds or spread stinky fertilizer, and this is the same for the "just and the unjust," according to Jesus. But "manna" all around is not God's way to blessing or prosperity for all; work and creativity and resourcefulness and courage and self-denial and thrift are. From these come his richest blessings though the ground be cursed and life be shortened in death.

The Bible and Christian theology (as we shall demonstrate) consistently teach that men and women do not all obey the commands of God with the same alacrity, and God holds them accountable with relative "blessing" and "cursing" both temporally and eternally. Furthermore, human choices are not determined, and these play out in a diversity of outcomes that no human being has wisdom to fathom, much less control. Within that context human capital ebbs and flows through millennia of genetic and societal development, either cashing in on or paying the debt of legacies beyond anyone's finite ability to predict or remedy. This is the gist of the command in the garden to seek the "knowledge of good and evil" only from God and not attempt to become "gods" in our own stead, sufficient unto every contingency by our own wisdom.

The purpose of this book is to celebrate and commend to rational and sincere Christians the life of creativity and work that God ordained for our good and that is the only way to widespread prosperity for the largest number of people on the planet. (This presupposes that the prosperity-versus-poverty debate

Way to the City

has concluded with a basic shared consensus that it is better to prosper than to be in poverty.[8]) Furthermore, we wish to demonstrate that fallen and sinful people cannot trust to the sheer benevolence of other fallen and sinful people simply because they come bearing "gifts" from governmental entities. To the contrary, it is governments that are the takers from the producers, not the other way around, and they must be the most carefully watched of all, for their goal is to make it "so that no one can buy or sell unless he has the mark, that is, the name of the beast or the number of its name" (Rev. 13:17). The last hundred years of human history witness dramatically to the ongoing attempt of governments to do this very thing, for it is only when every possible freedom of action is coerced out of the economic system that anything like equal outcomes can be foisted upon a gullible and subservient public as an actual living reality—though, of course, the ruling elites will be "more equal"[9] than others.

Jeremiah is famous for relating the Lord's advice to "seek the welfare of the city where I have sent you into exile" (Jer. 29:7), and Bruce Winter has written eloquently on that subject as a matter of expediency for the time in which we live, the time before the *eschaton*, when all Christians must personally seek to be "benefactors" according to the will of God, rather than depending on either the rich or the government to "benefit" them.[10] This plan of action for the helpless and truly needy and abject poor among us is still the rational plan of compassion as well as the biblical one. For "here we have no continuing city but we seek one to come" (Heb. 13:14). We cannot afford the unlimited humanistic vision of egalitarian outcomes, for that way lies poverty for all and the unspeakable mis-

---

8 A conclusion that some whom we will cite as we go along might not endorse explicitly but must surely agree to tacitly, for the political and personal "solutions" they advocate presume that someone must prosper in order to have something to be given or taxed away for "redistribution," and the "poor" will be relatively better off with this largesse passed to them rather than remaining in "poverty."

9 Only the latest in this scheming comes out in the attempt of the Obama administration to restructure health care without having government workers, unions, teachers, and other select "public servants" subject to its mandates.

10 Bruce W. Winter, *Seek the Welfare of the City* (Grand Rapids. MI: Eerdmans; Carlisle, Cumbria: Paternoster, 1994). As this book was being prepared for publication, a book by James Davison Hunter, *To Change the World: The Irony, Tragedy, and Possibility of Christianity in the Late Modern World* (New York: Oxford University Press, 2010), became available. He is essentially addressing this theme in his references to a "new city commons," but we will be going beyond his conceptions, while finding much with which we agree.

Way to the City

ery of slaves whose every action is overseen and coerced by what Paul Rahe calls "soft despotism,"[11] a condition brought on by the perverse tendency of mankind to see to its comforts at the expense of someone else. By using the supposedly benevolent power of the almighty state, men are seduced into believing that all their petty desires and pleasures can be fulfilled without the insecurities inherent in a fallen world rebelling against its Creator, who subjected it to futility of a sort intended to turn its heart back to him (Rom. 8:19–22).

Quoting Alexis de Tocqueville, Rahe makes his point that people of this type have elevated over them

> an immense, tutelary power, which takes sole charge of assuring their enjoyment and of watching over their fate. It is absolute, attentive to detail, regular, provident, and gentle. It would resemble the paternal power if, like that power, it had as its object to prepare men for manhood, but it seeks, to the contrary, to keep them irrevocably fixed in childhood; it loves the fact that the citizens enjoy themselves provided that they dream solely of their own enjoyment. It works willingly for their happiness, but it wishes to be the only agent and the sole arbiter of that happiness. It provides for their security, foresees and supplies their needs, guides them in the principal affairs, directs their industry, regulates their testaments, divides their inheritances . . . .
>
> After having taken each individual in this fashion by turns into its powerful hands, and after having kneaded him in accord with its desire, the sovereign extends its arms about the society as a whole; it covers its surface with a network of petty regulations—complicated, minute, and uniform—through which even the most original minds and the most vigorous souls know not how to make their way past the crowd and emerge into the light of day. It does not break wills; it softens them, bends them, and directs them; rarely does it force one to act, but it constantly opposes

---

11 Paul Anthony Rahe, *Soft Despotism, Democracy's Drift: Montesquieu, Rousseau, Tocqueville, and the Modern Prospect* (New Haven, CT: Yale University Press, 2010).

Way to the City

itself to one's acting on one's own; it does not destroy, it prevents things from being born; it does not tyrannize, it gets in the way: it curtails, it enervates, it extinguishes, it stupefies, and finally it reduces each nation to nothing more than a herd of timid and industrious animals, of which the government is the shepherd.[12]

The final state of the earth and world cultural system dominated by the beastly Roman and Babylonian caricatures of the kingdom of God and the New Jerusalem is said to mark out its adherents with the mark of "a man" whose proclivities are to take the place of God in his "temple." The Bible is clear that the earth is the place of the biblical God's temple, and he is its rightful King. The vision of the anointed ones who would bring ultimate security to earth through government that is secular and self-justifying is the parody that calls for the overthrow of satanic power in the earth by the arrival of the "coming One." It is to this narrative and its commentary that we now turn in some detail.

---

12 Ibid., vi.

Way to the City

Chapter 2

The Narrative Literature
of the Old Testament

MORAL RESPONSIBILITY BECOMES MORE COMPLEX with each passing era in man's supposed development on planet earth. We acknowledge the realities that seem to complicate moral decision making. But we do not mean in so doing to advance the idea that this is actually a "new thing" on earth. In fact, the Old Testament begins the story of man in his moral responsibility by showing how the simple command "you shall not eat" became a matter of apparent ambiguity when the serpent began to question Eve about its simplicity. When she allowed this conversation to sway her from a simple obedience to God's command, life for her and all her descendants became immensely more complicated.

Fortunately, we have not been left with mere complexity. We have been given "a more sure word" (2 Peter 1:19 KJV) to guide us. This "word" preserved through the centuries as the Bible is, in our opinion and that of Leland Ryken,[1] a book that, in all its apparently disparate parts, forms such a unified narrative and message that "the paradoxes of human life are held in tension in what can be called the most balanced book ever written." The Bible is the true metanarrative and foundational document for human understanding of the world, the way it "works," its past rightly interpreted, its present rightly comprehended, and its future fully antici-

---

1   Quoted in David M. Howard Jr., *An Introduction to the Old Testament Historical Books* (Chicago: Moody, 1993), 46.

pated. The reader will be quick to see in this statement our convictions about the Scriptures of the Old and New Testaments and also a foretaste of our methodology in this study of its teachings. We read the Scriptures of the two Testaments of our Bible as "canonical," normative for this inquiry and as Torah, providing a standard from which to make evaluations and judgments.[2] We will leave the defense of the reliability of this methodology to those who have previously fought the battle and rely on the reader to consult the relevant literature.

Our division of the survey of biblical teaching on our subject reflects a fundamental understanding of the differences that exist among the genres of Scripture. However, it is equally integral to our understanding of its teachings that the various parts form an overwhelming unity that is a profound witness to its one supervising Author. The uses of the various genres by the human writers only serve to enhance the profundity of the overall message. There is certainly no competitive tension among the various parts.

This leads us to another underlying assumption. We take as given that the Scriptures we know now as the Old Testament (OT) constantly inform the writers of those we know as the New Testament (NT). They may not be ignored, revised, or taken lightly without great peril to our Christian faith. Moreover, it is not possible properly to teach the NT Scriptures without first having an understanding of how the OT Scriptures prepare us to understand the NT.[3] All too often, Christians think and practice the reverse. Our approach will be to let the OT have its say and seek to follow the NT writers' and Jesus' methodology in allowing the NT to "fulfill" the Old. We take seriously Jesus' teaching on the Mount that "not the smallest letter, not the least stroke of a pen, will by any means disappear from the Law until everything is accomplished" (Matt. 5:18

---

2   See especially on this Gordon J. Wenham, *Story as Torah: Reading Old Testament Narrative Ethically* (Grand Rapids, MI: Baker, 2000). See also Daniel C. Browning Jr., "Torah" in *Holman Illustrated Bible Dictionary*, ed. Chad Brand, Charles Draper, and Archie England (Nashville: Holman Bible Publishers, 2003).
3   See the work of Emil G. Kraeling; A. H. J. Gunneweg, *Understanding the Old Testament*, OTL (Philadelphia: Westminster, 1978); Bernhard W. Andersen; and especially the body of work done by Walter C. Kaiser Jr. See most notably Kaiser's essay, "A Single Biblical Ethic in Business," in *Biblical Principles of Business: The Foundations*, Christians in the Marketplace 1, ed. Richard C. Chewning (Colorado Springs: NavPress, 1989), 76–88. We are also indebted to Dr. T. E. Pratt Sr. (PhD, OT, Baylor University; OT professor at several universities) for his counsel and advice on this subject of OT relevancy.

Way to the City

NIV). Therefore, it is with specific design that we devote as much of our limited space to the OT materials as we do, beginning with the narrative portions.

We see the Bible as *the* metanarrative preserved in and by the commentary of teachers, preachers, and wise men and aided by the choruses of the singers and poets.[4] This cohesiveness and faithfulness to a central theme, the acts of God in the history of the creation, serves to set the Bible apart as a sacred book among the texts of world religions. This feature alone urges us to see history as linear, not cyclical; to see life as ordered by God, not merely fatalistic; to see the material realm as the true locus of God's plan for the ages, not a sort of drive-thru on the way to absorption into "the Force"; to see ourselves as active participants for good or ill in the course of events, not victims of forces outside our ability to affect; and to see the future as an end to be achieved, not a destiny to be accepted.

The narrative sections of both Testaments in our Bible carry us along this winding road from the lessons of the study of the past, to the challenge of the present and the promise of the future. Their content is urged upon us, as it was upon ancient Israel, by way of warning that we not forget the past lest we miss the opportunity of the present and dash the hope of the future (Ps. 106:44–48). Like Henry Ford ("History is . . . bunk!") in the last century, "they soon forgot" (Ps. 106:13). So that we may not become like them, we move now to the biblical history.

The narratives of the Hebrew Scriptures are more voluminous than any other single genre in the OT.[5] Strangely, the literature devoted to understanding these materials as they may bear upon our subject is not proportionately weighted. In fact, there seems to be an almost dismissive attitude displayed at times to the importance of these narrative writings of the OT outside the prophets and portions of the legal sections in dealing with issues ethical. We hope to remedy this oversight.[6]

---

4   For a definitive treatment of this subject, see Walter C. Kaiser Jr., *The Promise-Plan of God: A Biblical Theology of the Old and New Testaments* (Grand Rapids, MI: Zondervan, 2008). This is the culmination of a career of study and contemplation on this theme for Dr. Kaiser.
5   The narratives, of course, are not solely one literary style. They partake to some extent of all the common styles of the OT.
6   This failure to give the OT its due is not just in this subject area but has its roots in a failure to understand the overall position of the OT in the Christian Scriptures. On our current

Way to the City

The book of Genesis, though not the oldest attempt in the ancient world to explain "beginnings,"[7] is arguably on almost any grounds the greatest. Certainly, to a Christian audience it has no parallel. It sweeps us literally from the "big bang" to the dynasties of Egypt in fifty or so pages of any modern English translation. Along the way we are introduced to themes that will not receive their final updates in the corpus of Scripture until we read the closing chapters of the book of Revelation in the NT.[8] We are treated to a vast literary panorama of human drama and divine activity that is breathtaking in its implications for humankind in all our relations to the material world, our fellow creatures, and our God. Nothing like it exists anywhere else in all of human literary history. Further, as Derek Kidner has remarked, Genesis "is in various ways almost nearer the New Testament than the Old."[9] As such, it "begins" to tell the story that will end only in the *eschaton*. To understand where we are today and where we are going, we must know where we came from. Genesis reveals this and much more to us.

However, as in all the biblical narratives we must guard against the blunder of thinking that we have received in writing all there is to know about the events

---

subject, it is evident in the writings of a number of the authors cited in our notes that what really matters in their thinking is what Jesus and Paul had to say. We will address the cited authors' manner of using the OT when we get to their own contributions. We believe Professor Craig L. Blomberg's latest contribution on this subject is characteristic. He devotes only 52 pages (of more than 250) to his discussion of the OT materials and, most tellingly, states that the first major period of the historical books in the Pentateuch (Eden to Sinai) "discloses the least amount of detail about the role of material possessions in the life of God's people" (Blomberg, *Neither Poverty nor Riches*, 33). More on his commentary as we approach the other genres of the OT. The latest from Ben Witherington III, *Jesus and Money: A Guide for Times of Financial Crisis* (Grand Rapids: Brazos, 2010), is even more remiss in this area. He appears simply to dismiss the majority of OT teaching (with the exception of some takes on the Wisdom Literature) as under the "old covenant" and largely irrelevant to NT Christians. *Jesus and Money*, Kindle loc. 486, 2183.

7 Genesis, of course, gets its name from the Hebrew for "beginnings." The book is surely about that before it is about anything else, for nothing is settled here, only begun.

8 See on this theme especially William J. Dumbrell, *The End of the Beginning: Revelation 21–22 and the Old Testament* (Eugene, OR: Wipf and Stock, 2001).

9 Derek Kidner, *Genesis: An Introduction and Commentary*, TOTC (Downers Grove, IL: InterVarsity Press, 1967), 14. The work of N. T. Wright is also quite helpful in understanding the thrust of the work of God as culminating in a complete redemption of the creation as the only fitting conclusion to the long metanarrative of Scripture. See especially N. T. Wright, *Surprised by Hope: Rethinking Heaven, the Resurrection, and the Mission of the Church* (New York: HarperCollins, 2008), and N. T. Wright, *The Resurrection of the Son of God* (Minneapolis: Fortress, 2003).

Way to the City

portrayed. Such is never the case in historical narratives of any culture or religion. What we have is what we were intended to know and, more importantly, what we need to know. Genesis lets us in on the "beginnings" of all the great themes that the biblical literature will return to again and again throughout both Testaments. All the knowledge of God's revelation that eventually joins rivulets and streams of truth into a mighty flowing river of NT fulfillment "begins" in the headwaters of Genesis. For this reason, we will use Genesis as our jumping-off point to explore the OT narratives.

THE SOVEREIGNTY OF GOD

The most obvious beginning in Genesis is God himself and his sovereignty. He is the prime mover from which all has come and apart from which no notion about the material world can be explained or understood. He is not of or from the material world, for he stands apart from it. He has no need for the material world to justify his own being or worth. We may speculate on why he would want to create the universe of material existence, but we cannot posit that he was less than fully God and fully self-sufficient without it. James Weldon Johnson[10] has poetically supposed that God was "lonely" when he said, "I'll build me a world." Johnson further suggested that when all was done except for the creation of man, he said, "I'm lonely still," thus presenting the case for the final creative act. But even Johnson's anthropomorphic poetry is not intended to suggest some lack in God that must be made up by the creation of material things and beings. On the contrary, the all-sufficient God is pictured as operating from the beginning out of an overflow of creative energy that found pleasure and joy ("That's good!") in the accomplishment of his "work."[11]

He existed from eternity in a completely satisfying triune relationship. He needed no one to commend him, for he "saw all that he had made, and it was very good" (Gen. 1:31). This could indeed be the overarching theme of Genesis

---

10 For text and comment on this unique style of sermonizing, see *James Weldon Johnson, Complete Poems*, ed. Sondra Kathryn Wilson (New York: Penguin Books, 2000). Citations here are from *God's Trombones*, "The Creation."

11 But see also the take by Meredith G. Kline in *God, Heaven and Har Magedon: A Covenantal Tale of Cosmos and Telos* (Eugene, OR: Oregon, Wipf and Stock, 2006), that these pronouncements are actually judgmental.

Way to the City

in that the simple command to know what is "good" and what is "evil" from God himself alone and not the forbidden tree is climaxed in the final episode of Genesis with Joseph's declaration, "you meant evil against me, but God meant it for good" (50:20).[12] And so, fittingly, when he had "finished the work he had been doing . . . he rested from all his work" (2:2) This is not stated to suggest that somehow God had become tired of, or even in, his work as we often are. Rather, having "accomplished" and "finished" what he set out to do, he ceased from that activity and, in effect, allowed himself and the creation a time of enjoyment of what had been accomplished. Like a king he has created a realm of rule, planted a garden for his pleasure, "placed" (or, "rested") his image-bearer in it to signify his rule and to take charge for him (to "rule" and to "subdue") and in his "rest" signifies the true goal of the creation itself, thus foreshadowing the role of Sabbath-keeping in man's subsequent pilgrimage (see Exod. 20:8–11, esp. v. 11; cf. Deut. 5:12–15, esp. v. 15). This is the perfect world that for the time being exhibits true submission to the will of its Creator. Yet it does not signify that God has ceased altogether from working.

The theme of God's ongoing work has perhaps its fullest commentary when Jesus corrects the misapprehensions about the Sabbath by the religious teachers of his time. In saying to those zealots for the Sabbath law as they had hedged it about, "My father is always at his work to this very day, and I too am working" (John 5:17 NIV), Jesus illuminates God's "rest." And, for all who will hear, he is urging upon us what is actually taught about God in Genesis. The sovereign God of creation is now at work *in* the material world, though he himself is still not *of* it or *from* it. From the garden which he "planted" to the expulsion of man from it, to the destruction of the earth in the flood, to the confusion of tongues at Babel, to the calling out of a people, to the preservation of that people and the ancient Egyptian civilization and far beyond, God is "working." The poet of Psalm 33 eloquently outlines this multifaceted "working" of the God of the Hebrew Scriptures.

The biblical history bids us to see him working in the lowly families of pilgrim people on the earth, such as the patriarchs and their descendants im-

---

12 This has clear implications for the grand attempts to create "good" for all out of the apparent "evils" of life through governmental means, only to discover we have created more evil rather than less.

Way to the City

mediate and distant. The stories of Hagar and Ishmael, Amram and Jochebel, Elkanah and Hannah, Naomi and Ruth, Jesse and David, and so on tell of his working. The rise and fall of empires such as the Hittite, the Egyptian, the Assyrian, the Babylonian, the Persian, and the Roman show his hand. He works in and watches over the affairs of the nomadic tribes of the Amorites (see, "the iniquity of . . ."), the Moabites, the Jebusites, the Amalekites, the Midianites, the Edomites, and all other manner of "-ites."

He is at work in the exploits of "deliverers" such as Moses, Gideon, Ehud, Deborah, Samson, and Samuel. He is working through men of valor and courage such as Caleb, Joshua, Jonathan, David, Josiah, Asa, and Hezekiah. He is working through the prophets Nathan, Elijah, Elisha, Isaiah, Jeremiah, Ezekiel, and the others. He is working in the twice-widowed Canaanite Tamar, the widowed Moabite alien Ruth, and the exiles Daniel, Shadrach, Meshach, and Abednego. He is at work even when apparently completely hidden in the time of Esther.

His work, of course, will be mirrored in the command to the man and woman to join in the work of the creation, and that command is not superseded in subsequent instructions. He further shows his sovereignty in "blessing" the couple as he commands them to join his work. This blessing is a statement of their supreme position in the creation and an invitation to taste and explore the wonders of the world he has made. It is, sadly, to be matched by a "curse" that follows their sin. But the blessing is to become, even for all that, an ongoing theme in both Testaments of the Bible. Beginning here with the prime directive to rule and to bring into subjection to the will of God the material realm in which they have been placed, his blessing is to follow the human race right to the end of the book of Revelation. The dominion promised with the blessing is, of course, only a derived one and not absolute. But so far as the largesse of God stretches, this blessing assures them they have a mandate upon which to act.

Despite the curse that comes later, this theme of God's blessing will now be played out through the coming ages, passed along from fathers to their offspring, but not without the supervising sovereignty of God.[13] The first blessing

---

13 Fathers bless their offspring (Gen. 9:26–27; 27:27; 48:15; 49:1–28) and God repeatedly renews his blessing (1:28; 5:2; 9:1; 12:3; 24:11). But it is clear the blessing of "good" is now

Way to the City

was universal for the human race. Because of man's move away from his source of authority through rebellion against God, the blessing narrows and expands through the generations of men.[14] After the flood, it is repeated to Noah's family but is later narrowed to Abram personally and his eventual miraculous offspring. From that further "beginning" a promise is made to once again bless mankind universally. That blessing will pass through national Israel and again through a single "house" (David's) and find its ultimate fulfilling in the incarnation. It is no coincidence that Jesus begins his public ministry pronouncing "blessed" again and again from the Mount.

So God in his sovereign work is blessing the creation through the race he began with the formation of Adam and the subsequent creation of his "corresponding" helper. But the blessing came to them in Eden coupled with a command, a moral obligation. Marvelously gifted and wonderfully privileged, the first couple was subjected to God's moral authority, for sovereignty is not mere unrivaled force. It is far more. It is the ability to command respect and reverence through the power of what we sometimes call "character." A "command" such as God first uttered to Adam was not to be enforced by the exertion of physical prowess but was to be a call to follow after one worthy of command. Thus would Adam and Eve become like God and be empowered to achieve the things implicit in ruling and subduing the creation, just as human beings have from time immemorial become like what they follow and worship (see 2 Kings 17:15; Jer. 2:5; Rom. 1:21).[15] But they chose another way.

Now enters the serpent to tempt them with being "as gods," a far less noble goal. What of this interloper? And, what of man's slide into rebellion and the resulting corruption of the creation?[16] Do these not mitigate against the idea of a truly sovereign God who blesses? On the contrary, it is in the arena of the redemption of the creation that he begins to show in another way his

---

filtered through the "bad" that Adam and Eve insisted on tasting for themselves. See Gen. 50:20 for the clear statement of this concept.

14 Erich Sauer, *The Dawn of World Redemption: A Survey of the Historical Revelation in the Old Testament*, trans. G. H. Lang (Grand Rapids, MI: Eerdmans, 1951), 17–95.

15 For a full discussion of what this entails in Scripture, see G. K. Beale, *We Become What We Worship: A Biblical Theology of Idolatry* (Downers Grove, IL: InterVarsity Press, 2008).

16 For a thought-provoking discussion of the implications of "old earth" thinking on the subject of creation's "subjection to decay," see Dembski, *End of Christianity*.

Way to the City

sovereign nature and the power of his blessing by promising to the serpent that a descendant ("seed") of the woman "will crush your head," though the serpent be allowed to "strike his heel" (Gen. 3:15).[17] Even with the "curse" upon the serpent and the ground, God's disciplinary and judgmental work continues as he sees fit. The "enmity" between the "seeds" of the woman and the serpent will continually inform the observant reader of God's continuing supervision of the outworking of this clear promise of redemption for all the creation.

In this way Genesis introduces the story of salvation, and the narratives of the OT again and again return to show prefiguring events in the flood, in Abram's discovery of a sacrificial substitute for Isaac, in Joseph's preceding his family to Egypt, in the exodus, in the ministry and leadership of Joshua and the judges, in the life and times of David the king, and in the lives and ministries of the prophets. All of these culminate in the narratives of the NT toward which they have been pointing to show that God is both sovereign Lord/Judge and Savior.

Most notably these two themes are the impetus for the momentous events surrounding the exodus.[18] Moses, as deliverer and lawgiver, leads a slave people from their bondage to the entrance of the "land of promise." Along the way the gods of Egypt and desert warriors are vanquished as God himself assumes the mantle of holy warrior, for he is a "man of war" (Exod. 15:3). But he will not save his people without subjecting them to the moral obligation of his lordship. It is this juxtaposition of salvation and lordship that explain his dealings with a people he chooses to possess a land he has promised. "The land" assures us that his salvation is indeed to be worked out in a material world that is full of the pilgrim "wandering" of the faithful, but also can find places of "rest" by his grace. Of course, since the fall, there has always been the certainty that "this world" must eventually give way to the "world to come."[19] In that new world, too, there is the promise that man will in fact "subject" its glories through the authority that God delegates to him. What a prospect!

---

17 Derek Kidner is surely correct when he comments, "redemption is about God's rule as much as it is about man's need" (*Genesis*, 70).

18 The most formative moment in the OT record's preparation for the "exodus" of the NT (cf. Luke 9:31).

19 See Heb. 2:5 and Rom. 8:19–22.

Way to the City

The Nature and Calling of Man

We have been giving answers to the implied question, "Who is God?" We turn now to the equally important query, "What is man?" The psalmist, echoed by the writer of Hebrews in the NT, marveled aloud and poetically that God was "mindful" of man at all (Ps. 8:4–6; Heb. 2:6–8). But God's purpose in man is too marvelous to contemplate, for he is/was/will be only a little below God himself. Adam, by design, was created for rule[20] in a universe the complexity of which we are only now in the twenty-first century just beginning to glimpse, though we have suspected it all along. Our science has only touched the hem of the mantle of creation's geometrically multiplied phenomena. It's as if Bill Gates took his toddling son by the hand and walked him into the foyer of Microsoft headquarters and said, "Run this place for me." No, it's far more than that! As the psalmist was attempting to help us see, it is beyond any comprehension for man or angel.

And what of Eve? Without her presence, there is an exclamation—"not good"! But please note, she is presented to Adam as a "helper corresponding to him." There is something profound about God's designation of her as "helper." In fact, the term here is most often used in the Hebrew Scriptures to designate one who assists alongside another in a military manner. She will be "blessed" along with Adam as one who works along with him in the pursuit of God's mandate for their "rule" and "fruitfulness." This can imply nothing less than a full partnership, so God calls "them" Adam.[21] They together in the

---

20 See Peter Gentry and Stan Norman, "Kingdom of God," *Holman Illustrated Bible Dictionary*, 987. Also, see the discussion in Eugene H. Merrill, *Everlasting Dominion: A Theology of the Old Testament* (Nashville: B&H, 2006). Merrill notes, "The technical terms employed are not to be hastily dismissed. The verb, *to rule (rdh)* bears overtones of oppression in some instances and even here suggests dominion of a dictatorial nature. There is to be no question as to who is in charge! This is supported by the companion verb, *subdue (kbš)*, the meaning of which elsewhere is to subjugate (by force) or even to humiliate." *Everlasting Dominion*, 136, 136n10. Note that this is without reference to subsequent sin on the part of Adam and Eve. Man and woman are expected to exert appropriate force to organize and develop the planet and its surrounding environment.

21 There is "mystery" here, as Paul notes (Eph. 5:32), for Gen. 1:27–28 implies that it is in the original union of creation that the "image of God" resides. This cannot be pressed too far, but the juxtaposition of "our image" describing the nature of God begs to be explored in the profundity of man and woman as truly one in Adam. See Anthony A. Hoekema,

stead of all mankind have the dominion over God's creation as his vice-regents. God is Lord! Abraham Kuyper is well known for his assertion, "There is not a single square inch in the whole domain of our human existence over which Christ, who is Sovereign over all, does not cry 'Mine!'"[22] But what is also true is that the "image of God in man" means that we are God's viceroys.[23] This is polemically designed in the Pentateuch to assert that all mankind (and "womankind"!) rule the creation, but not other men.[24] And it is certain that the creation cannot reach its potential in the plan of God without them, for it is less than complete without a man to "till the ground" (Gen. 2:5 KJV).[25]

We cannot speculate fruitfully on what the mental and physical capabilities of the first human beings were. That they were at least potentially capable of fulfilling God's design for them is evident. We have previously noted that the cosmos bears evidence that one day on this earth a high-tech civilization capable of appreciating the entire creation is presupposed. What inherent capacities were present to enable this feat can only be extrapolated from the current fallen state of humankind in general, but the genius necessary for such accomplishment must have been present to exploit.

Within the garden spot of Eden man and woman walk as only kings and gods of ancient Near Eastern cosmologics supposed. Made to enjoy, tend, and create from the land's rich resources, they alone carry the capacity to act from their own will, rather than to *behave* as mere animals. They were given the rich capital of God's image and likeness and all the creative capacity that implies, and the whole earth in its rich resources was theirs to command and exploit (in the best sense of the term).[26] They were not created simply to

---

Created in God's Image (Grand Rapids. MI: Eerdmans; Exeter, UK: Paternoster, 1986), 75–82.

22 Abraham Kuyper, "Sphere Sovereignty" (inaugural address at the founding of the Free University of Amsterdam, October 20, 1880), in *Abraham Kuyper: A Centennial Reader*, ed. James D. Bratt (Grand Rapids, MI: Eerdmans, 1998), 488.

23 Hoekema, *Created in God's Image*, 69–72.

24 We will demonstrate later that politics is necessary or even an option only in a fallen world.

25 It is clear from the beginning that this planet has potential that only mankind can unlock through development in imitation of the creative work of God, contra modern ideas about pristine wilderness as the ideal.

26 Lengthy debate and discussion are evident in the literature on the image of God in man. We find John Walton's take to be the best. John H. Walton, *Ancient Near Eastern Thought and the Old Testament: Introducing the Conceptual World of the Hebrew Bible* (Grand Rapids,

Way to the City

labor and toil and bear offspring, for it is not merely from this that rule and dominance will proceed. This can happen only through the employment of creative genius and, by implications associated with the garden as actually a mirror image of the tabernacle to come, the true worship and fellowship with God that they were intended to enjoy.[27]

Their genius means they will, in the plan of God, not merely dig holes and refill them; they will dig wells in the desert and divert rivers to make gardens. They will not wander aimlessly over the earth and stand fearfully beside the great oceans. They will, instead, observe the stars and learn from their movements and chart their own way, making tracks and roads through uncharted spaces. They will invent sextant and compass and hue trees into shapes that, with sails made from earth's flora and fauna, will send them across vast chaotic waters to new trackless lands. They will not be content to dwell in dank caves in fear of storms and wild animals, choking on the smoke of their campfires and the smell of their own excrement. They will hone wood from the forest, dig metals from the ground, refine alloys with fire, melt sand into glass, and a thousand other creative tasks that will lend themselves to this communal rule upon the earth. They will invent electronic microscopes and computer imaging as they explore the intricacies of plant and animal life in the miracle of the cell. And in sheer celebration of all that is good they will not merely scratch shadowy stick figures into rock but will paint the *Creation of Adam* on the ceiling of the Sistine Chapel and fashion the statue of *David*. Above all, this lowly creature will look to the night skies and see, not gods to be worshipped, but a vast creation to be explored and filled with the glory of the Creator God (if only they had done just this!).

That they were intellectually equipped to have fellowship with God on a personal basis is also clear. This is the purpose of the garden God himself planted. Here is the place where they assume the priestly role of "tending and guarding,"

MI: Baker, 2006), Kindle loc. 2313–24. Man is the image of the king stationed in the king's territory and placed to do the king's work and establish his rule. This contrasts with the ancient Near Eastern idea that the king alone bore the image of a god. See also Beale, *We Become What We Worship* for elaboration on this basic conception.

27   G. K. Beale, *The Temple and the Church's Mission: A Biblical Theology of the Dwelling Place of God*, NSBT 17, ed. D. A. Carson (Downers Grove, IL: InterVarsity Press, 2004).

Way to the City

a harbinger of the later Pentateuchal revelation of the tabernacle.[28] Subduing the outer world (beyond the garden) will take kingly courage and audacity, while the more service-oriented work of the garden is toward God himself and is worship. The man and woman "serve God" in the garden, not the garden itself, and they "guard" like the priests in the tabernacle so that no chaotic elements from the outer world encroach, least of all a "subtle" beast. It also seems obvious that in their innocence they had none of the residual effects that we associate with guilt or shame—inferiority-based pomposity or reticence, self-consciousness, fear of failure, a sense of victimhood, need-based overcompensation, or any number of what we call "dysfunctional" behaviors and mental states. Perhaps, it would be helpful to all of us to try to imagine what would be our true capabilities if we were simply rid of all such baggage and more.

All of this came to the first pair as gifts of God's grace. Since they are given to choose and act and give "names" to other animate life, they exercise from the beginning possession as stewards of God over a vast wealth (capital) that can be developed only in communal arrangements with the offspring to come from their reunion as one. Thus, by implication, the mission of man—denominated by the words "fill . . . subdue . . . dominate"—contains within itself economics and politics.[29] Economics, because no single family, clan, or tribe can fulfill the mission—a situation that will require division of the possession(s) and its stewardship by some means of trade-off, thus creating a market(s). Politics, because it is the rational and morally informed discussion of alternatives that sets value(s) on trade-offs and secures agreement for their allotment in a fallen world. Apart from such arrangements, war is inevitable.

Whatever they were before they disobeyed God, our first parents were

---

28 We concur in the analysis of Calvin Beisner that the two commissions, first to rule and subdue and then to tend and guard, are intended to convey different duties of man in the material world. The fall has complicated both tasks almost beyond calculation. Hence modern confusion over the role of economic and technological subduing and ruling vs. the role of care for the garden, which is no longer accessible. See E. Calvin Beisner, *Where Garden Meets Wilderness: Evangelical Entry into the Environmental Debate* (Grand Rapids, MI: Acton Institute for the Study of Religion and Liberty / Eerdmans, 1997), 9–26.

29 Recent debates about the command to "fill" the earth and the promise of the "blessing" of offspring for this purpose are covered well by Beisner, *Where Garden Meets Wilderness*, 95–112. Nowhere in the narratives of the OT is barrenness of any kind (plant or animal) treated as anything but a problem or even a "curse." The prophets everywhere assume that a return to a primitive and undeveloped state is a punishment and a curse.

Way to the City

never the same afterward. Knowing shame and fear for the first time, they ran from God and tried to cover themselves, first with fig leaves and then with excuses. None of this could restore lost innocence or lead to renewed fellowship with God in Eden or ever after, as the Scriptures of both Testaments confirm. It is notable that the "nakedness" of Genesis 2:25 is one of innocence, while that of 3:7 is from the realization of judgment. This word is one that conveys having been made destitute through the removal of clothing and is best illustrated in the Pentateuch in Deuteronomy 28:48. In that prophetic word Israel is assured that failure to worship God in the prosperity they are about to enjoy will result in being reduced to "nakedness" just like Adam and Eve when they failed the same test. This nakedness is both spiritual and material and is compounded by expulsion from the place of rest and shelter (worship, conveyed in the words "tend/serve" and "guard")[30] into a world of scarcity and wilderness—a theme that continues through Scripture. They can now only know the "good" by passing through the "bad," a course they chose. And their ultimate destiny without eternal life being mediated to them is that they will "return to dust," the undeveloped state of wilderness apart from the creative ("making") activity to which they were originally commissioned.[31]

From this "fall" stem all the evils that will play themselves out in the pages of Scripture, mitigated, of course, by God's saving work and disciplining hand. But first the benevolent and caring God will introduce his image-bearers to the technology that will eventually subdue the planet before them. Seeing the inadequacy of their "clothing" for the task before them, he kills animals and fashions garments more fitting to the arduous ordeal they have brought upon themselves. They are meant to see the Creator subordinating in a terrible way his own creation to their current needs. What a lesson this must have been in the consequences associated with their prime mission, now spoiled by sin, but nevertheless still in force. All technological advance—for that is what making clothing from skins is, when compared to sowing fig leaf loincloths—will have

---

30 Gen. 2:15. This has become a *crux interpretum* for some in the debate on the creation mandate of man before God. We agree with Beisner, noted above. It is clear in the records of the OT that no place of "rest" for the Lord's people and His tabernacle can be secured until the forces of evil and chaos have been subdued. Cf. Exod. 33:14; Deut. 3:20; 12:10 25:19; Josh. 21:44; 22:4; 23:1; 2 Sam. 7:1–17 (esp. vv. 1, 11); 1 Kings 5:4; 1 Kings 8:56; Ps. 95:11; et al.
31 We are indebted to Beisner for a suggestive thought along this line.

Way to the City

its cost in blood and suffering and will require messy and costly cleanup.[32] Humankind will need far more than fig leaves to cover the nakedness they now experience, for eventually chaotic weather patterns, eruptions of earth's planetary tensions, pestilence and disease that will threaten whole civilizations, attacks from wild animals, war, and sheer exhaustion from toil will threaten humanity's very existence on the planet. "Subduing" just got a lot harder!

Soon, the institution of marriage and family is shown to become a caricature of what it was intended to be. The glorious partnership is defiled and perverted by the overbearing tin-god-style man of the house; the subservient, responsibility-averse, mousey little woman;[33] and the rise of a sexuality based on lust rather than love. Families will soon know the intrigue and folly fostered by bigamous marriages that eventually flower into full-blown harems. Adam's hopeful naming of Eve as "mother" becomes her label, not for glory, but for utility (not immediately but clearly an ongoing issue in later stories of barrenness). Her original "fruitfulness" is now to be turned into a kind of mechanistic enterprise to be exploited for economic purposes and social standing. Genesis is only the beginning of a tale for the ages of womanhood exploited in and exploiting her sexuality. It is not without a special irony that "know" becomes "lay" in later narratives, a term used in these stories and in the modern age without even the thought of the long-forgotten "know." Eve's pain in childbirth is matched (and exceeded) by her pain in the loss of one son at the hand of another, as the men assume center stage in the story.

---

32 The obvious lessons from the manner in which Yahweh "clothes" Adam and Eve have far-reaching implications. If Yahweh thinks it inappropriate to send them out into the cursed world without proper clothing and is willing to kill and skin animals to remedy the situation, he is both providing for them and teaching them a lesson. It does not mean that humankind is now empowered merely to exploit the world, but it does show that their ability to go forward with the divine mandate will include things that involve "cracking eggs to make the omelet." The fashioning of skins into clothing explicitly demonstrates technology (no matter how elementary) and its advantages and presages the immediate direction of civilization. It is strange in the light of this obvious lesson to hear advocates for "animal rights" over against those of humans and to note the condemnation of technological advance by many who would have us see Eden as the true destiny of man. We leave the discussion of the typology of atonement in this event to other times and places.

33 For an alternative to this view, see Merrill, *Everlasting Dominion*, 203, noting the work of Susan T. Foh, "What Is the Woman's Desire?" *WTJ* 37 (1974/75): 376–83, who suggests that Eve was actually seeking headship during the temptation experience. Her "desire" toward her husband (Gen. 3:16) is the same as the "desire" of sin toward Cain (Gen. 4:7). In this scenario the attempt of the woman to rule will be put down by the superior violence of the man.

Way to the City

Soon the bully-like Lamech takes two wives and the game is on. Generations of men (literally) pass before us with only the occasional mention of a woman's name among them.[34] In the generation before the flood we see what the woman has become—a "beautiful," "marriageable" object for powerful men to use lustfully.[35] It is probably not saying too much to suggest that the "violence" that eventually grieved God over his creation and that appeared to be man's ongoing pastime was related to this devolution of the woman in the eyes of man.[36] We would hope that the line that produced Noah struggled against this tide in their homes, but the record is silent, except to indicate, inferentially at least, that these men took one wife each. But in God's considered judgment only Noah and his immediate descendants are to be "saved" in the flood. He appears as a lone dissident to the tenor of his times.[37]

The silence about the significance of individual women and the family life of the chosen line is broken with the introduction of Abram and his family. In this pivotal series of events we see how the ravages of sin have corrupted the male-female dynamic even in the families of the "servants of the Lord." The theme of barrenness[38] is introduced as the ultimate disgrace for a person whose only utilitarian function is childbearing. First Sarah, then Rachel finds that life without the ability to pump out babies can be trying, indeed. Both seek to correct this providential oversight by what can only be

---

34 So much for the partnership—the corporation of "Adam & Eve, LLC" will become "Adam & what's her name." Such mentions as named women get are all the more significant, and worthy of consideration, especially for their scarcity.
35 Thorstein Veblen has given witness in our time to the practice of powerful and rich men ("alpha males") in all societies of taking to themselves "trophy women." That old story began with the "men of renown" of Genesis and is seen regularly on the society and political gossip pages of our day. See Thorstein Veblen, *The Theory of the Leisure Class* (1899; repr., London: Penguin Books, 1994), 23.
36 An alternative contributing factor could also be the recognition that no matter how long-lived this early version of men were, they inevitably "died" naturally, as Gen. 5 records again and again. Perhaps then the thought was, it would be better to die in mortal battle?
37 Note also that God is not averse to destroying his own handiwork to preserve man's mission on the earth. So the man is given charge over the preserving of creatures other than humans for the future world, though all others were destroyed, and the "clean" are more in number on the ark—supposedly for food and sacrifice.
38 This "curse" upon the woman in all the narratives regularly is treated as an opportunity for God to work and women to play their part in the salvation story. Strangely, a failure of the man's ability to produce offspring is never considered, even though it is surely as much a part of the human story as the other.

Way to the City

called "sophisticated" means, even for our time. Sarah, to her eventual over-whelming regret, promotes Abram's sexual union with a slave girl. The plot of that story reads, in its inception, its gradual development, and its ultimate denouement, like a script for daytime soap operas. Rachel's story unfolds even more salaciously. Caught up in the competative machinations of two testosterone-hyped businessmen, she joins her sister Leah in a baby-making contest that eventually involves four women and a story that could only be told fully on the big screens of Hollywood.

All of this is not to say that the biblical narrative considers the woman innocent in these events and their original antecedent. She is surely implicated from the beginning in Adam's fall as the one directly inviting him to join her in sin.[39] Her disciplinary sentence implies that in her "submission" to the man there is something less than respect and honor involved. The note in Genesis 6 that her "beauty" was involved in the ongoing lust of powerful men has more than a little suggestion of her exploiting this situation to her advantage.[40] The parts played by Leah and Rachel in the entire story of Jacob call to mind the power of coyness and what we call "passive-aggressive" behavior in modern psycho-speak. This role as exploiter comes to its full expression for her first in the tale of Potiphar's wife and her blatant attempt to corrupt the heroic Joseph. Later, we see a complete role reversal in the pathetic Ahab and the murderous Jezebel.[41] The utter corruption of God's intent for the first institution in society, flowing directly from the first acts of moral irresponsibility, is everywhere evident in the pages of all the literary genres of the Bible.

---

39 It is not necessary to posit some kind of titillating tale of sexual seduction and lust (as some would do) to explain Adam's reluctance to "go it alone" without Eve. She is simply the catalyst for his decision to disobey the command of God. Clearly, though, the NT lays the blame at his feet, not the woman's.

40 See also the stories of Abram's despicable behavior in the face of powerful men in failing his duty to protect Sarai from being absorbed into harems.

41 These lurid stories are not all there is—see also Samson and Delilah, David and Bathsheba, and the unholy alliance of Herodias, Salome, and Herod in the murder of John the Baptizer. All is not lost in the association of men and women, however. See also, Deborah and Barak, Ruth and Boaz, Elijah and Elisha with their two "helpers," Mordecai and Esther, and most importantly Jesus and the women who facilitated his earthly ministry and his own beloved mother, Mary.

Way to the City

THE CORRUPTION OF GOVERNMENTS

But the corruption of home and marriage is just the beginning of what Paul calls the "bondage to decay" (Rom. 8:21). Man's direct accountability to the government of God, at first mediated only through the man to the woman, will in very short order (in the narrative) come to be utterly corrupted in the development of the tyranny of men over their fellows. This will to rule over another, to hold the power of life and death in one's own hand, first manifests itself in the spirit of Cain. In rebellion against the displeasure of God, he responds to the challenge to "rule" over the sin that "crouches" ready to spring upon him by "rising up" against the righteous Abel and taking his innocent life. Implicit in this tale is the competitive desire of men to corner the market on God's "blessing" on their work(s). This makes religious enterprise a "business" from the beginning! God's further challenge to Cain to give an accounting for the welfare of his brother elicits the kind of response that foreshadows the boast of his descendant, Lamech. Cain's denial of the responsibility to guard the welfare of an innocent person (to be his "keeper") is the root issue in all political discourse. Lamech displays the development of this denial in human nature's basic relationships within the entire human family—the tendency to bully and accumulate personal power over others.

It is a matter of some debate what the "mark of Cain" is intended to signify.[42] It is significant to the ongoing narrative, however, that the notable thing about Cain's brief entry is that his son founded a "city" around which clusters the beginnings of culture and commerce, for artisans and artists require community to sell their wares, or at least find patronage for their endeavors. The remark of Lamech regarding his lesser crime, what we might today call manslaughter (killing without prior intent, in contrast to Cain's act), tends in its context to conjure up what will become the *lex talionis*. This city thus becomes a precursor to the "cities of refuge" later in the Pentateuch. This may all be intended to disclose a primeval governance by God himself among men, for it is his provision of a "mark" on Cain that saves him from

---

42 See John H. Sailhamer, "Genesis," in *Genesis, Exodus, Leviticus, Numbers*, vol. 2, *EBC*, ed. Frank E. Gaebelein (Grand Rapids, MI: Zondervan, 1990), ad loc., for full discussion of the alternatives and implications.

Way to the City

the "blood avenger." At the very least we are meant surely to see that the ruler in view is God.

Soon, "men of renown" (lit., men with a name/reputation) walked the earth doing as they pleased,[43] causing God to assert his direct governance once again in the flood. In "pain" and "grief" he "contends" with these "heroes" in their "wickedness," finally meting out judgment and beginning again with one family. But this wiping of the slate has not changed human nature. Far from it! Growing ever more resourceful, human beings launch the first experiment with empire at Babel. Born of an evident sense of insecurity (lest they be "scattered") at the thought of truly obeying the divine command to bring "the whole earth" under God's authority, they set about to "make a name" for themselves and "reach to heaven," with all the overtones of establishing a link to the divine, politically and socially.[44] The proximate methodology was to build a city with a skyscraper at its center that would show off their pretentious self-exaltation and invite the god(s) to descend the tower's stairway and visit the garden prepared for him.[45] God's response to their rebellious ascendancy was to come "down" to "see" their pitiful attempt at utopia and simply "confuse" their language. Thus did "*bab-ili*" (the "gate of God") become "*babel*" ("confusion"), and only the sin for which the future Babylonish state stood ever "reached to heaven" (Rev. 18:5). It should not be missed that all the great cities to come will be modeled on this one as the parody of the heavenly one to come.[46] In the narrative of Scripture Babylon is the whorish mother of all the cities that rise to give mankind security and significance apart from the worship of the one true God. Once again human nature is only constrained, not changed.

Now the narrative proceeds to develop the theme that will dominate Scripture's story till its hopeful conclusion in the final book. Human attempts at

---

43 Perhaps here a reference even to the list that closes out the previous chapter. The narrative of the list of these who lived at length, but just as surely died, is not closed out until Noah's longevity and death are noted later.

44 Note the soon contrast with Jacob's ladder that did find heaven and provide symbolically for communion with the promised "seed." But here, the ladder comes down. It is not raised up.

45 See Walton, *Ancient Near Eastern Thought*, Kindle loc. 1204–15, for this explanation and comment that "with Dostoevsky we can affirm that the tower was not to mount from heaven to earth, but to set up heaven on earth." This will be critical in our final analysis of the significance of Babylon in the Bible.

46 See Jacques Ellul, *The Meaning of the City*, trans. Dennis Pardee (Grand Rapids, MI: Eerdmans, 1970), 1–43, and throughout for an excellent treatment of "city" in Scripture.

Way to the City

government will become more and more corrupt and overwhelmingly tyrannous (a thing foreseen by God's statement in Gen. 11:6, "nothing they plan to do will be impossible for them"), and God will manifest through salvation history his own way. The "heroes" of old in the pre-patriarchal history are soon replaced in the narratives by God's "servant" leaders.[47] These will be the truly heroic figures that walk the pages of the Bible, culminating in the ultimate heroic figure, who alone is "worthy to receive power and riches and wisdom and strength and honor and glory and blessing" (Rev. 5:12 HCSB). All the while these "prophets" and "servants" of "Yahweh" are swaying the world by their faith, the empires of man rise and fall. Though occasionally shown to be less a terror to the innocent than others (for instance, Egypt in the time of Joseph and Persia in the time of Ezra and Nehemiah), the overwhelming picture of governments is that they consolidate their power and wield it in the interests of those who exercise that power to the detriment of those ruled over, many times with great cruelty. To be sure, they are "ordained" by God for his purposes, but they are not for that reason exonerated of the evils they do.[48]

It is surely this factor that weighs heavily in the warnings of Samuel on the eve of the establishment of a kingship in Israel. The descendants of Jacob, weary of pilgrimage and the burden of the tribal duty to subject their "land" to God's authority, long for the security of a king to be their hero and do their dirty work. God's discerning eye and plea for their enlistment in his way of faith is seen in Samuel's farewell speech (1 Sam. 12). Rehearsing the history of God's dealing with them, he charges them with rebellion against God for asking for a king to oppose the Ammonites. In so doing, he shows that this latest action is but one in a series of failures of faith and courage. In contrast to the examples set for them by the patriarchs, by Joseph, Moses, Joshua, Caleb, and the judges, the people have insisted that such individualized and tribalized

---

47 The highest appellation given to leadership in Scripture is to be called the "servant of Yahweh." See, Gen. 26:24; Num. 12:7; 14:24; 1 Sam. 27:12, et al. See also "my servants the prophets," Jer. 7:25 and parallels at 1 Chron. 16:22 and Acts 16:17. Later, we will develop the theme found in the term "shepherd" used repeatedly after the days of David.

48 Paul's comments in Rom. 13 do not establish governments of whatever nature as ultimate in their authority. They derive their legitimacy first from God himself to be sure, but they cannot maintain that legitimacy if they do not serve his purpose in being a punisher of "wrongdoing." N. T. Wright's comments in his commentary on Romans are particularly apropos.

Way to the City

heroics are not for them. As their fathers before them had in the wilderness of Horeb, so they ignored exhortations to faith and courage and resourcefulness[49] and warnings of dire consequences, to their eventual ruin.

Saul's life and rule is a harbinger of what is to come. Shy and insecure at the beginning, but overcome with the need to compensate for his inner failure of courage in the end, he becomes almost a caricature of all that is shown to be wrong with man's rule in the Bible. In asserting his false bravado, he rebels against God. Unable to face up to himself or God, in the person of Samuel, he becomes a tormented, demented figure. Overcome by fits of jealous rage and frustration, he becomes murderous. All this and more are the stuff of human attempts to rule others while being unable to rule oneself. Rome and the whorish Babylon of the last days are inevitable, and their religious pretensions are foreshadowed here.

David's story stands as God's human answer to the call for a king, but even here we see clearly that the failure to rule the sin "crouching at the door" cries out for one to ascend the throne who is truly "worthy" of the ruling authority. As David first flourishes, then wanes, then rises from his shameful failures, our imagination is first charged with admiration and hope, then shocked and saddened, and again made to marvel at the power of grace received (cf. Pss. 32 and 51). David's repentance was immediate and genuine upon Nathan's accusation, and "there is no hint in the narrative that this is anything less than an authentic, rightly intentioned confession. It is presented without irony or suspicion."[50] It is this confounding and exhilarating history that gloriously informs so many of the psalms. But, it is only an earthly glory, as the ensuing developments show.

Solomon's immense wealth and worldwide fame (centered on the city Yahweh has chosen and David acquired), combined with an apparently divine wisdom, is shown later to have been purchased at the price of a growing discontent among the people over heavy taxation and oppressive policies.

---

49 We will have more to say on this major characteristic of humankind in the image of God. Suffice to say here, this is what turns the earth and its raw materials into usefulness for human betterment and advantage, that is, his dominion over the creation as God's steward.
50 Walter Brueggemann, "On Trust and Freedom: A Study of Faith in the Succession Narrative (II Samuel 9–20; I Kings 1–2)," *Interpretation* 26, no. 1 (1972): 8.

Way to the City

Such a scenario should not come as a surprise, given the record of overwhelming opulence combined with decadent sexuality. Finally, the corruption of the institutions of marriage and government are highlighted together in the sad tale of God's own people gone astray. With Rehoboam's promise to dole out more of the same, and then some, a split of the kingdom becomes inevitable. Destruction and captivity cannot ultimately be averted even by the likes of Elijah and Elisha and the whole body of work done by the prophets. Neither can the kingly activities of men like Josiah and Hezekiah and others do more than delay the march of judgment, which Ezekiel eventually sees as the departure of Yahweh from the temple and the city (Ezek. 8–11). We will address this subject more thoroughly in a later chapter.

Were this all there is to the story, this chapter could now be concluded. But, there is more.

The True Heroes

It is now in the OT narrative that a final theme, to which we have made passing references so far, comes to its fruition and prepares for the NT narrative. The earthly kingdom of Israel is no more, but God's people have not disappeared from history. To the contrary, they now shine forth as never before in their heroic character opposing the excesses and evils of the cultures around them. Daniel and his companions are representative of many others like them, how many we aren't told, who refuse to be subsumed in the dominant culture and political situation. Alongside these stand men like Jeremiah and Ezekiel, descendants in kind and spirit of the earlier prophets like Elijah who found out he wasn't really the "only one left." Add to these Esther and Mordecai whose singular stand literally saved the nation from the murderous envy of Haman. And we cannot exit the OT without examining Ezra and Nehemiah and the preachers and others who assisted them. Just who are these people and what is their lineage?

The writer of Hebrews assures us of our perception of them as being the true descendants of Abel. Hebrews 11 bids us see them as among the "great cloud of witnesses," the vast majority of which are unnamed, who urge on the current generation to faith in Christ. They are the ones who stood out in their

Way to the City

time[51] as walking with God (beginning with Enoch) against the tide and spirit of the age. They are the products of a peculiar (for their time) relationship to God and his creation. They are "in it but not of it."

They are the objects of grace. Like Abel, they must bring an "acceptable" sacrifice. They do not lack the normal weaknesses and willfulness of human nature, but they have found a way to overcome in a way that Cain did not. Sometimes, they seem to be types of Christ in their pristine resistance to sin, like Joseph—even though his earlier persona had not engendered hope for what he became in maturity. They achieve what others do not and/or cannot, like Caleb in "possessing" more than his fellows, either in his own tribe or among the tribes of Israel, several of which never "possessed" what was given to them in territory.[52] Other times we marvel at how God could possibly use them, as with David. Mostly, though, they make us admire them for their simple courageous faith that worked, like Ruth, and their indignation at the unbelief of the crowds, like Caleb.

Faith, courage, hope, resourcefulness—these are the hallmarks of people who pass through the "fiery furnace" without being singed and/or who "suffer with the people of God." Human history is, of course, replete with epic tales of such heroes. For this reason, many have undertaken to read the biblical stories as nothing more than the competitive myths of the same ancient characters spun from a different cultural perspective. From this stance, they would assure us there is nothing new here. But we believe there is.

To be sure, these characteristics are not in themselves saving graces. Faith can be placed in a false god. Courage can be misguided or cruel. Hope can be false. Resourcefulness can lead to an undeserved success. In the hands of wicked people, these are the manifestations of the "foolishness" of men. The Bible is clear on this. The human race has from the beginning been possessed of these traits just as they are manifest in God himself. The incarnation fills in

---

51 See Paul's comment on this character trait (Acts 13:36) that commends them not as self-justified before God, but as standing against the backdrop of their generation, which is what all are responsible for. This is the true individualism of Scripture.

52 Judg. 1:27–35 et al. One wonders if this is not ultimately the cause of resort to kingship in the ensuing narrative. The need for a super-achieving hero is part of the ongoing story of Israel and the nations. Nowhere is the accomplishment of such a one diminished intrinsically. On the contrary, it is celebrated and rewarded.

Way to the City

completely what is not said, though implied, previously. In Jesus we have the quintessential man of faith, hope, courage, resourcefulness, and preeminently love. It is this final characteristic that sets him so completely apart, but the other characteristics are seen in abundance throughout the human race with either more or less of all the rest.

The narratives we have surveyed show, not the destruction of these traits in the fall, but their counteraction, in fear and shame and real guilt, and their corruption, in bravado and bullying and murder of innocents, and their abuse in rebellion against God. Paradoxically, it is clear in the disciplinary and judgmental sentence of God in Eden and again after the flood that large doses of all these most salutary features of human nature will be needed even to begin the arduous task God has given to us.

Consider, for instance, what it must have been like to experience the first great nighttime thunderstorm without benefit of modern shelter. The struggle against nature is the first, and perhaps most daunting, of the consequences of the fall. But it is only the beginning, and man's ascent (or descent, depending on perspective) from cave to the moon is no tale of fears followed and shame indulged. Even the Philistines found that "quitting like men" had its advantages.

The truth about man in all his relationships is that he is no "beast of the field" subject to instinct as his guide, the modern religion of Darwinism notwithstanding. The narratives testify clearly that by the superintending grace of God the most astounding reversals of fortune can overtake anyone and that one can succeed in even the most unlikely circumstance. God's heroes count on that possibility.

Without God man may be a barbarian or a philosopher, a serial killer or a preacher, a ruthless dictator or a beloved schoolteacher, a purveyor of child pornography or a Rembrandt. He is seldom as bad as he can be or as good as he can be. It all depends on what he sets his mind and will and effort to. In the Bible these distinctions are seen as the natural state of mankind as corrupted by sin. But all require grace to set them upon the path to become the genuine people of God. The biblical heroes of faith diverge from the "men of renown" because in their walk of hope and courage and resourcefulness they are being made like the God they worship. They are not told to forsake their heroic tendencies but to come to God for forgiveness and a moral and spiritual makeover. They are not expected to restrict their efforts so as not to gain material and sociocultural

Way to the City

success and rewards above their fellows. It is nowhere contemplated that what is needed is egalitarian and communitarian leveling. They must, however, acknowledge that the God of the Bible is the "blessor" (Jer. 17:5–8) in all things.

The apostle Paul will draw this distinction in the NT when he charges humankind apart from God with having become "futile" and "darkened" through "suppressing the truth" in wickedness (Rom. 1:18–23). By way of contrast, he assures the Christian that he or she has not received a "spirit of timidity" but rather one of "power, of love and of self-discipline" (2 Tim. 1:7). And, finally, God himself makes it clear that "the cowardly" and "the unbelieving" will be first into the fire (Rev. 21:8). The "overcomers" of Revelation 2 and 3 are clearly singular personages in the churches and do not gain their "reward" without heroic struggles.

It is as if God in his wisdom set mankind upon the course of self-effort and dared them, male and female, to "boldly go" where none but he had been before. Bill Cosby was famous for suggesting that when God saw Adam and Eve partaking of the forbidden fruit, he caught their attention with a loud whistle and shouted, "All right! Everybody, out of the pool!" This is true insofar as they were barred from Eden and the path to the tree of life. But with reference to how he continued his working toward an eventual new heavens and earth, his mandate to the now fallen race was not to lie down in depression, fear, and shame, but rather to bend their backs with all their might to the task they were given.

Let the woman find a kind of redemption in the pain of childbearing.[53] Let the man find his way through toil and sweat. Let their descendants, generation after generation, learn that the way of sin is indeed "hard." But there is no hint of a justification for the failure to attempt to achieve the original command to "be fruitful," "fill the earth and subdue it," and "rule over" every other creature of God (Gen. 1:28). This command, substantially repeated at the flood with the promise of a regular progression of seasons for sowing and reaping, remains God's first obligation for all men and women.

The narrative shows clearly the economic consequences of man's efforts in a world governed ultimately by the God of the Bible. Scarcity and its companion, poverty, are the direct result of man's spiritual problems. God made

---

53 See Paul's commentary on this (1 Tim. 2:15).

Way to the City

the man and woman and put them in a position to manage and order great abundance. By rebelling against God's authority they reaped the consequences of scarcity. Told to continue with the prime directive, the pair proceeded to wrest a living "from the ground." Soon, various professions and crafts and artistic endeavors are mentioned as being the natural course their work follows. Varying degrees of success and economic reward accompany these efforts. In the ongoing story, those who do as God has directed in his most basic command tend to prosper. The patriarchal narratives show the line of Abram to be at least moderately wealthy for their time—enough to afford generosity and the ability to ignore usurpers and to refuse inappropriate enrichment and to wield political and military power.[54]

The great famine that drove them to Egypt was one example of a force that can impoverish multitudes, but the resourcefulness of Joseph, honed in his trials, is shown to be economic salvation for all, not just the chosen. Of course, the oppression through enslavement that comes upon them at the hands of a corrupt government is another great source of impoverishment. But it is evident throughout that these events, though recurring, are not the way of God's creation but of man's sin. The promise of a "land" to be "possessed" is a promise of prosperity, and it is shown to be real in its fulfillment except when the people "forsake the Lord and serve other gods." The immense wealth of the kingdom is the natural consequence of a productive society that is at least partially in tune with God's express purpose. It is only lost through abuse and as a disciplinary experience.

The success attendant on the worldly pilgrimage of all those who set about to explore the meaning of the command to fruitfulness and dominion is only interrupted by the ravages of sin evident in sickness/disease/deformity, nature's untamed state, and man's interference with his fellow human beings. This is true for all people—not just Abram's descendants, though they are singularly blessed with prosperity in this life and toward God as they prove faithful and are charged with the responsibility of being a conduit for the blessing to pass to all nations. The promise of sowing and harvesting given after the flood is to

---

54 See the stories of Abram and Lot dividing land, Abram refusing spoils of war and the "battle of the wells" in Isaac's time.

Way to the City

the entire race. It says, in effect, go forth and sow, and in the normal course of events you will find a harvest to be gathered.[55]

Unless all peoples courageously accept this mandate for life, there can be no redemption in living. To the degree that God himself has established this as his way of working, it is essential to true eternal salvation and earthly and heavenly prosperity for all. And, finally, to the degree that grace is allowed to work God's own faith, courage, hope, resourcefulness and, ultimately, love into each man, woman, boy, and girl, true heroes will indeed stride the earth.

CONCLUSION

In our century it is fashionable to make men and women the victims of all kinds of systemic, "structural" (current usage: "beyond our control") evil and injustice. Everything from obesity to substance abuse to marital failure to children born out of wedlock to poverty to plain ignorance and illiteracy, not to mention out-right criminality, is seen as really a problem to be addressed "through the system" (current usage: "with a political, governmental answer") and its attempt to get at the so-called "root causes" of such activities (seen as "structural evil"). The narratives of the OT deny this by showing that these evils proceed from human beings themselves and their failure to rule themselves.

The narratives are not complete in themselves alone. They require the giving of the Law and its explication, the observations of the wise, the praises of the poets and singers, and the exhortations of the prophets to finish the story. But no understanding of the other genres is secure without first being grounded in the firm soil of reliably recorded history. Without the narratives, the rest would be speculative musings. We are exercising wisdom, therefore, when we become thoroughly familiar with the actual events as they unfold before our eyes in the Bible. These are not mythic, and therefore unreal, tales of wished-for accomplishments.[56] These are stories of a real and rational

---

55 This "harvest" is not just a promise to an agrarian society but uses the metaphor to include all walks of life. Please note also that the temporary provision of manna in the wilderness was just that, a temporary provision for the time. It is not to be confused with a supposedly normal state or even a more "socially equitable" state where there is not abundance.

56 Modern myths and epic tales of galactic proportions most notably fawned upon in our time are those told in the chronicle of a "galaxy far, far away" ruled mysteriously by "the

Way to the City

God interacting personally with real people in a material world for a definite eternal purpose. He holds these people accountable to his sovereign lordship and seeks them out to save and bless. Though his curse is real, his blessing mitigates and overcomes the curse.

These are real stories of sinful creatures who degenerate into vile actions and habits of life, but who also act in the most unlikely kinds of heroic responses to God's grace and man's depravity. Their world and problems are not all that different from the twenty-first century in the forms their temptations to moral degradation take. Beset by inner perversity and external forces and overcome at times by fear and shame, they must summon the courage that comes from faith in God to "do the right thing." Just so is the dreaded evil of moral relativism and ambiguity defeated.

Force," in the tales of the heroes of "Middle Earth," in the Harry Potter adventures, and in the seldom read yet in their mythical presentations also "romantic" Arthurian legend among others. While literary romanticism has always been a teaching tool in the hands of both fraudulent and well-meaning teachers, those stories have value only insofar as they relate directly to the truth revealed in biblical teachings.

Way to the City

Chapter 3

Words to Live By

A RECENT BOOK[1] BY ANNE HENDERSHOTT, former professor of sociology at the University of San Diego, currently distinguished visiting professor of urban studies at The King's College, New York City, highlights a distressing ongoing trend in the West of the twenty-first century—the surrender of moral categories, by which we once defined deviant behaviors, to complete moral relativism. Besides exalting the bizarre to the more or less ordinary, this practice has the tragic effect of denying the possibility of remedies to debilitating problems. In the resulting chaos it has become commonplace for Americans, Christian and non-Christian alike, to dismiss reprehensible behavior, both public and private, as "not my business" or an occasion for the exercise of "tolerance" or for learning "not to judge." Daniel Patrick Moynihan's phrase for this, "defining deviancy down,"[2] is an apt summary.

It should be obvious to all but the most culturally and sociologically myopic that only rampant disorder and the collapse of civilized societies can follow from such an unchecked deterioration of standards. But as Professor Hendershott notes, the discipline of sociology itself has discarded a previously accepted belief that human beings have unlimited desires, which need to be disciplined or legally conformed to accepted norms, in favor of a culture

---

1 Anne Hendershott, *The Politics of Deviance* (New York: Encounter Books, 2002).
2 Daniel Patrick Moynihan, "Defining Deviancy Down: How We've Become Accustomed to Alarming Levels of Crime and Destructive Behavior," *American Educator* 17, no. 4 (1993–94): 10–18.

where all discussion of deviance is obsolete. Indeed the attempt to label any behavior as wrong or improper or "deviant" from norms of any kind is, it is now supposed, to reject a person's equality or humanity, and to suggest that one's current economic, social, or political situation is a result of such behavior(s) is regarded as "blaming the victim."

Hendershott's writing is notable for being the work of a sociologist, not a theologian. She wants us to appeal to reason or nature or common sense to restore some measure of societal morality that will head off an approaching disintegration of our culture. She surely represents an important minority in the modern West. This minority is troubled by the rapid descent of the dominant culture into evermore offensive and shocking behaviors, but having been stripped of any basis for moral suasion in absolute standards, they are simply struck speechless or stuck with unpersuasive naturalistic appeals. It is just such a dilemma to which the Torah of Scripture speaks.

In his *Critique of Practical Reason* (1788), Immanuel Kant is famous for observing that "[t]wo things fill the mind with ever-increasing awe . . . the starry heavens above and the moral law within me." For several millennia the God of the Bible relied on these factors and his regular workings with individuals and families to convey the meaning of Torah.[3] In this manner the Old Testament (OT) Scriptures convey God's commitment to the essential sacredness of the cycle of life and death—with its round of labor, birthing, family building, social development, nation formation, etc.—and its eternal implications. Religion, with its cultic and philosophical/theological orientation, is not the locus of primary interaction between God and his creation/creatures. Life is.

That the lawgiving at Sinai should have been so delayed speaks volumes. It speaks further volumes that this event(s) assumes such a center-stage position from that point forward. It is clear that what has transpired in the patriarchal history (all of Genesis) is the context for the events in the wilderness of Horeb. It is equally evident that the sudden insertion of the Law is intended as an assertion and revelation of God's complete lordship over all that has been and all that will occur in the history of the created universe. The "coming of

---

3   See previous discussion of "Torah" in chap. 2.

Way to the City

the Law,"[4] as Paul would later speak of it, was not the sudden invention of "true religion" (neither man-made nor God-ordained). It was a manifesto for life (Lev. 18:5) and how it should and could be fruitfully lived out in God's real world. It is what Kaiser has called the "path" that shows the way through the promise-plan of God.[5] And, by the way, it explicitly offers all mankind a "blessing," nay, many "blessings."[6]

To further contextualize this great event, also note that the formalizing of the Law, heretofore allowed to work within the human race as only the dictates of conscience, comes against the backdrop of the great liberation. A "freed" and now free people will for the first time be constituted as a nation "under law." It is telling that this is the only governance God himself has ever specifically instituted among men, that is, the Law in the hands of his chosen and anointed leaders who "judge" the people. God is the only king legitimately reigning in the earth.[7] In a later chapter we will address the prophetic critique of government under Saul and the Davidic dynasty.

Regrettably, far too much has been written and spoken on the subject of work and wealth by evangelical Christians without a serious treatment of the Decalogue and its explication in the Pentateuch. With the exception of Calvin Beisner's study, *Prosperity and Poverty*,[8] no extensive attempt to relate the Sinaitic lawgiving to socioeconomic issues has been done in the current decades-long debate (to our knowledge).[9] What discussion there has been that

---

4 See Rom. 5:20; Gal. 3:17, 19, where it is evident that Paul is arguing that the Law "came" with special purpose and for a specified time. Though perfect in itself, its weakness is found in human nature, not its own lack of holiness or spirituality (Rom. 7:7–14).

5 Walter C. Kaiser Jr., *Preaching and Teaching from the Old Testament: A Guide for the Church* (Grand Rapids, MI: Baker, 2008), 140.

6 This is explicit in the call of Abraham not only to receive but also to give a blessing and is implicit in Deut. 4:5–8.

7 We are cognizant of the fact that the NT sanctions governments as authorized by God (Rom. 13), but it is clear that God's authorization is to be recognized as legitimizing such governance (illustrated in the original reluctance of Saul to serve and of David's humble waiting for God's time to elevate him to the throne) rather than the seizure and bloody defense of thrones that so often occurs in world history. Just as individuals hold "possessions" and "lands" as stewards before God, governments are only his stewards as well.

8 E. Calvin Beisner, *Prosperity and Poverty: The Compassionate Use of Resources in a World of Scarcity* (Eugene, OR: Wipf and Stock, 2001).

9 Walter Kaiser Jr. is the exception to this general rule in his literary corpus and his various speaking appearances. As we were nearing publication of the present work, David L. Baker published a study of the general implications of OT law to our concerns, entitled *Tight Fists*

Way to the City

centers on that portion of the Bible primarily concerns the meaning and relevance of the Jubilee. It is our contention in this chapter that this failure to let the Torah speak in its full context leads to all kinds of exegetical mischief—both misguided interpretation and flat-out omission of pertinent material.

THE TEN WORDS

"Torah" (Heb., "teaching")[10] has little relevancy to any situation past or present unless it is understood in its original historical and literary setting. Further, the Law, as received at Sinai, is not a series of isolated ideas or prescriptions to be understood without a full appreciation of the whole. Nor can any single provision be construed as nullifying another in any context. One cannot simply isolate on a single concept or idea and begin to extrapolate doctrines and applications that will get anywhere near the actual truth revealed.

The "teaching" is a unified body of, first, simple prescriptions and, then, specific developments along lines that suggest further applications. All of this material is set pointedly in a historical context of deliverance from slavery and ongoing nation building. In addition it is presented unambiguously as an entering into of a covenant-related obligation. Finally, it is "given" over a period of years encompassing the events between its first promulgation through the "words" spoken by Yahweh at Mount Sinai and the reiteration of it on the plains of Moab some forty years later by Moses as Israel prepared to enter the land of patriarchal promise under Joshua.[11] Only with such a contextual understanding can we hope to "plow" the "straight line" in Scripture that Paul urged upon Timothy.

The giving of the Law is the central theme of the Pentateuch. "Israel stays at Sinai for eleven months in real time (Exod. 19:1–Num. 10:11) and

---

or *Open Hands: Wealth and Poverty in Old Testament Law* (Grand Rapids. MI: Eerdmans, 2009). However, he does not deal with the Decalogue itself as a single entity.

10 Kaiser notes that this word means to "point [out a direction that one should go in]." *Preaching and Teaching*, 140.

11 Here is a clear instance of our "canonical" reading. We are aware of the traditions about the "deuteronomists."

fifty-seven chapters in narrative time."[12] Sixty-eight chapters precede Sinai and fifty-nine follow it. The giving of the Law is both central to Moses' writings, and Sinai itself is "Israel's largest roadblock to Canaan," in that the nation must pass muster under God's Law before it can enter into his rest.[13]

It is instructive that the Jewish tradition held the entire Pentateuch to be "the Law" (Torah). We have shown in the previous chapter that the narratives of Genesis do indeed "teach" us many things. What we have not previously called to the reader's attention are the many adumbrations of a coming time when assumptions about what is right or moral or correct in humanity's public, private, and religious behavior would be plainly stated. Walter Kaiser is surely not the first or only student of the OT to note that the Decalogue is everywhere anticipated in its various decrees by the actions (as implied to be "right") of characters throughout Genesis.[14] It remained only to reach a fullness of time when Yahweh deemed it appropriate to make the unspoken spoken.

The ten "words,"[15] as they come to us in Hebrew, form the living heart of a broader full body of covenantal stipulations enjoined upon a free and delivered people. As was common in the time of their literary construction, these covenantal stipulations are couched in the form of an ancient Hittite-style vassal treaty.[16] Treaties of this type were common in the Mediterranean region and all had the familiar elements of the names of the parties involved, historical survey of past relations, statement of mutual obligations, listing of witnesses to the process, and warnings of sanctions against any who broke the agreement. In short, the covenant of Sinai was the formalizing of a governmental arrangement between Israel and its God. By this agreement "the

---

12 Stephen G. Dempster, *Dominion and Dynasty: A Theology of the Hebrew Bible*, NSBT 15, ed. D. A. Carson (Downers Grove, IL: InterVarsity Press, 2003), 100.

13 Ibid., 101.

14 For a listing of passages, see Walter C. Kaiser Jr., *Toward Old Testament Ethics* (Grand Rapids, MI: Zondervan, 1983), 82.

15 The Hebrew word so often translated "commandment" (*dabar*) in our English versions is literally "word." See, e.g., Exod. 34:28; Deut. 4:13; 10:4.

16 See OT introductory materials that document these ancient treaties and compare them to similar ancient law codes, such as that of Hammurabi. John H. Walton, *Ancient Near Eastern Thought and the Old Testament* (Grand Rapids, MI: Baker, 2006), has the best current differentiation between the Mesopotamian concept of law and that of the Hebrew Scriptures.

Way to the City

people," or "congregation" become the subjects of the heavenly king.[17] They have a king, but they are not strictly slaves to a capricious will. They have now been given and consent to an arrangement by which they will experience the rule and justice of their ruler/God. This constitutional arrangement serves as the focal point of their formation as the people of the one God.

Our methodology in unpacking the textual material before us in this chapter is everywhere informed by the framework proposed by Walter Kaiser in his book *Toward Old Testament Ethics*,[18] and largely mirrored in the *Expositor's Bible Commentary* on Exodus and Deuteronomy.[19] We note, however, that there is nothing artificial in this approach to the teaching embodied in the Mosaic Law. Rather, the materials themselves give rise to a way of understanding them that is natural and uncontrived.

The Ten Commandments (lit., "ten words") come down to us in the biblical record of Exodus 20:1–17 and Deuteronomy 5:6–21.[20] The record clearly attests to their having been literally "spoken" by Yahweh and then chiseled in stone to be preserved in an "ark" prepared for just that use. Their primary overall form is in succinct negative instructions that get quickly to the core of behavioral issues with Yahweh's decrees. Each of these negatives could have been turned into a positive, as they are elsewhere, but in the initial spoken "word" they are clearly more powerful as they stand.[21]

Note, as well, that though they could have been spelled out as a universal declaration of human rights, they are couched in the second person singular to

---

17 The fact that this lawgiving at that time takes the specific form of a covenant with Israel should not be allowed to obscure its universal applications (cf. Jer. 12 and 18).

18 Kaiser, *Toward Old Testament Ethics*. See citation in n. 14.

19 Walter C. Kaiser Jr., "Exodus," in Genesis, *Exodus, Leviticus, Numbers*, vol. 2, *EBC*, ed. Frank E. Gaebelein (Grand Rapids. MI: Zondervan, 1990), ad loc.; Earl S. Kalland, "Deuteronomy," in *Deuteronomy, Joshua, Judges, Ruth, 1 and 2 Samuel*, vol. 3, *EBC*, ed. Frank E. Gaebelein (Grand Rapids. MI: Zondervan, 1992), ad loc.

20 The careful reader will note the differences of emphasis that attend the second formal rendering of these ten "words" by Moses on the plains of Moab. However, this fact should not lead to an unwarranted pursuit of hypothetical documentary criticism. The two passages are substantially the same, with allowances made for the manner in which Moses wished to reiterate.

21 For an excellent expositional treatment, see R. Albert Mohler Jr., *Words from the Fire: Hearing the Voice of God in the Ten Commandments* (Chicago: Moody, 2009). See also Jochem Douma, *The Ten Commandments: Manual for the Christian Life*, trans. Nelson D. Kloosterman (Phillipsburg, NJ: P&R, 1996), esp. for Douma's discussion of the implied positive form of the negative commands and vice versa.

Way to the City

emphasize the obligation of each person to his neighbor, rather than the modern assertion of personal *freedoms*. The notion of "rights" as commonly used in contemporary discussions—both political and theological—is a "legacy of the European Enlightenment," and is "helpful in forming liberal societies, that is, societies formed without reference to God. No one need feel grateful or to say 'thank you' in a society of rights."[22]

There are three exceptions to the series of negatives: (1) "I being the Lord your God" (2) "Remembering the Sabbath day . . ." (3) "Honoring your father and your mother." A number of commentators have suggested that these positives are a framework from which to view and explicate the Ten Commandments.[23] Our exposition reflects this thinking.

Without question, the position of both the OT and New Testament (NT) is that no law or authority among men is legitimate that does not find its sanction in the One who revealed his own character at Sinai and repeatedly before and after and in many places and ways (cf. Heb. 1). His peculiar relationship to Israel is that he personally intervened in their affairs to bring them "out of the land of slavery." They are consequently "free" with reference to men, but they are obligated to the Sovereign who made them free. It is this massive freedom, which God himself has instigated and sets himself to define, that necessitates the curbing of the fallen race's tendency to run amok.[24] As such, these "words" form the community as it is to be and become going forward. That is, God's language here is *performative* in the most ultimate sense, even more than human efforts at using language in more than an *informative* way.[25] As God's speech created the universe in Genesis 1, so it creates a people here. This is contrary to what we would call the "community-arian" interpretation, common to those who would

---

22   William H. Willimon, "The Effusiveness of Christian Charity," *Theology Today* 49, no. 1 (April 1992): 79–80.

23   See Kaiser, *Toward Old Testament Ethics;* and Kaiser, "Exodus," in *EBC*, ad loc.; and R. Alan Cole, *Exodus: An Introduction and Commentary*, TOTC 2 (Downers Grove, IL: InterVarsity Press, 1973), 149–62.

24   Walter Kaiser comments that this freedom is "so vast" that it is easier to "express a believer's restrictions in a few words." Walter C. Kaiser Jr., *Toward an Old Testament Theology*, (Grand Rapids, MI: Zondervan, 1978), 114.

25   On performative language in the Bible, see especially throughout the volume by Kevin J. Vanhoozer, *Remythologizing Theology: Divine Action, Passion, and Authorship*, Cambridge Studies in Christian Doctrine (Cambridge: Cambridge University Press, 2010).

Way to the City

make the supposed needs and rights of those who make up the community the guiding principle for interpreting the "words" themselves.[26]

The first three commands flow from the impossibility of "a-theism" as a viable construct from which to build a way of life in a world that everywhere bears the marks of intelligent design.[27] These initial three "words" command monotheism (first command), confirm that God is most like man himself (who is his "image," as opposed to any other "form" in the known universe; second command), and does not tolerate the trivial use of his "name" (as revelation of his essential character) for any purpose—conversational, judicial, religious, etc.[28] (third command). The assurance that evil consequences run in the families of those who do not honor God, in a merciful reverse proportion[29] to the blessings that accrue to the families that do honor him properly, punctuates this proviso on the "use" of God's name.[30]

The second group of commands, that is, the fourth command, is linked specifically to the Sabbath and its origin in the creation events. This com-

---

26 This is particularly evident in the work of Sider, Wallis, Campolo, and others we cite in the notes along the way. Sider is especially given to this style of negating the clear mandate of the "words" with a supposed fuller or spiritual understanding of "community." See Sider, *Just Generosity,* and the position taken in his essay by Stephen Charles Mott, "The Partiality of Biblical Justice: A Response to Calvin Beisner," in *Christianity and Economics in the Post–Cold War Era: The Oxford Declaration and Beyond,* ed. Herbert Schlossberg, Vinay Samuel, Ronald J. Sider (Grand Rapids. MI: Eerdmans, 1994), 81–99.

27 Kaiser, *Toward Old Testament Ethics,* 85.

28 The name of God is inappropriate as a casual epithet or as an assurance of veracity when the intent is to deceive or as a name to be taken upon oneself lightly, such as the term "Christian" is frequently used.

29 Daniel Fuller has clearly defended the position that this "mercy" imbedded in the Ten Words constitutes an invitation to faith and trust, not unlike the gospel invitation of the NT. See Daniel P. Fuller, *The Unity of the Bible: Unfolding God's Plan for Humanity* (Grand Rapids. MI: Zondervan, 1992). Within this third "word" can be found the provision of the sacrificial system for sin. Luther also found in these first words the command to "faith" as the first requirement in justification. See on this Mark Seifrid, "Luther, Melanchthon and Paul on the Question of Imputation: Recommendations on a Current Debate," in *Justification: What's at Stake in the Current Debates,* ed. Mark Husbands and Daniel J. Treier (Downers Grove, IL: InterVarsity Press, 2004), 144n29.

30 There is no intent to imply here that God arbitrarily punishes children and grandchildren for the sins of their forebears, but rather an indication of the tendency of evil to become solidified in human character from generation to generation ("third and fourth generation *of those that hate me,*" Exod. 20:5 NIV). By way of contrast, grace can reverse such formations and accrue benefits in greater proportions than the punishments attendant on rebellion. In the background is also the fact that up to four generations could live in the same proximity or compound and be caught in the judgment specifically intended for one.

Way to the City

mand deals with one's right relations with work.[31] In the same way that God "rested" from creative activity, so human persons, having "labored" and "done all their work" are to rest from that activity in full confidence that, just as God can cease from such activity without fear that his kingdom will suffer, so even fallen human beings can rest with confidence that God will continue his providential care of his creatures. Further, no person or beast may be made to labor on the Sabbath so that another may be at ease. All for which each of us is responsible shall be afforded the same "blessing."[32] We will address the implications of this command economically and socially later.

The third grouping of "words" is focused on social obligations—that is, the individual and his neighbor(s).[33] First in both responsibility and fundamental relationship to societal stability is the obligation to family. Without the foundation of the sanctity of familial relations there can be no lasting basis for a stable society. The first command with a specific promise of blessing (and implied curse), the fifth command goes far beyond the mere enjoining of "obedience to parents." It encompasses the full-blown "torah" of the relationships between husbands and wives and their offspring.[34] It implies what is explicit in the injunction against adultery, and it further invites us to contemplate that the values in the "words" that follow are rightly learned first at home and form the foundation of ongoing material blessing.[35] Most important, this is

---

31   Kaiser, *Toward Old Testament Ethics*, 89.
32   The Sabbath law is clearly intended to have wide social and economic implications. Note also how the failure to obey all its provisions resulted in Israel's exile (Lev. 26:34–35; 2 Chron. 36:21). Sabbath observance in the OT includes numerous implications related to both creation (Exod. 20:11) and redemption from Egypt (Deut. 5:15). It is clearly a brake on unlimited economic activity and what we moderns call "workaholism." As such its carryover into the NT era goes far beyond a discussion of what legal day should be observed (cf. Isa. 58:13–14). The Sabbath is a constant reminder of what was lost through sin in the garden. See Harold Dressler, "The Sabbath in the Old Testament," in *From Sabbath to Lord's Day: A Biblical, Historical, and Theological Investigation*, ed. D. A. Carson, Contemporary Evangelical Perspectives (Grand Rapids. MI: Zondervan, 1982).
33   Kaiser, *Toward Old Testament Ethics*, 89–90.
34   See the profound take Malachi has on this subject at Mal. 4:6.
35   As Christopher Wright observes, the harsh punishments enjoined for the failure to observe parented leadership and discipline (Deut. 27:18–21 et al.), indicates that the extended family contemplated (third and fourth generations taught) is the unit explicitly given the land promise by which the blessing continues in Israel. See Christopher J. H. Wright, *God's People in God's Land: Family, Land, and Property in the Old Testament* (Grand Rapids. MI: Eerdmans, 1990), 77–78.

Way to the City

the mandate for cultural stability and building up of what we in our time call *human capital.* Parents inculcate character into their offspring and give them a heritage of blessing that is both material and spiritual, and as they do so societies are built that reflect these values. This is critical to our study, for the promise to be enabled to remain on the land implies a prosperity that cannot be gained in any other way.

The sixth command, "You shall not kill" (strictly, "murder"), gathers up all the possible evil that can be done to the innocent, up to and including the taking of physical life, in a simple negative statement.[36] "So sacred was life, that all violent forms of snatching it away caused guilt to fall upon the land."[37] It does not preclude a "just" or "right" vengeance on those deserving of death. One might take life as a matter of self-defense, in the defense of another innocently attacked, or as a matter of judicial retribution.[38] It is clearly this "word" that is behind case law in the Pentateuch concerning proper societal punishment of crimes against persons and property. The innocent must be acquitted at the tribunal and the guilty must be proportionately punished. This is what defines "justice" in the court—the proper protection of the innocent and proportionate consequences for the guilty.[39] To this standard every individual, society, and government are held by God's law.

The seventh command, "You shall not commit adultery," succinctly sums up all that the greater body of Torah will say about human sexuality. We noted in our previous comment on the fifth command that this one is implied. It is made explicit here to make the issues of sexuality more than just a matter of obligation between husbands and wives. The full commentary of Pentateuchal teaching on sexuality argues not just for fealty in marriage but for true respect for the sexuality first introduced as a gift from God in Eden. As with all the other words of the Decalogue, consequences, both negative and positive, ac-

36 The logic and certainty of our position here can be seen by supposing that the commandment means only that one might merely beat someone almost to death and escape condemnation.
37 Kaiser, *Toward Old Testament Ethics*, 91.
38 Exod. 21:12–14, 28–32; Lev. 17:10–14; Num. 35:9–29; etc. From this proviso also proceeds the doctrine of "just war" and precludes condemnation of those required to participate as agents of legitimate governments engaged in defense of themselves and other innocents.
39 We will take up the discussion of the broader meaning of "justice" again in this chapter and at other times in this book.

Way to the City

crue from either disregard or respect for its teaching. Any society that does not adhere to the proper place and expression of sexuality will find that all sexual promiscuity—that is, sexuality practiced outside the proper union of one man and one woman—is (at the very least) a sin against and an attack upon marriage and the home and has other far-reaching effects on life, health and prosperity (see Heb. 13:4).[40] Thus the use of the word "adultery" guides us to the full understanding of Torah's emphases on appropriate and inappropriate sexual expression, rather than placing a limit on what it is.[41]

The eighth command, "You shall not steal," establishes the principle of personal (or in society, "private" as opposed to "public") property and its protection from the acquisitiveness of fallen human beings. Strictly speaking, theft is any "taking" of that which rightly "belongs" to another by any means other than voluntary surrender or the giving of a gift.[42] The process of illicit acquisition can be blatantly violent and coercive or sly and furtive. One can steal at the point of a sword or gun, or cheat and outwit others in business or government.[43] The word used in the text here is variously used to label among other things, burglary, failure to pay to another what is owed (as in debts or wages), using false weights and measures in business, kidnapping (that is, stealing persons), and subverting the affections of one person for another (that is, stealing the heart, cf. Gen. 31:2; 2 Sam. 15:6).[44] As with the other "words" of the Decalogue, abundant commentary will follow in the Torah and other biblical materials to flesh out the full meaning of this simple negative.

The ninth command, "You shall not give false testimony against your neighbor," undergirds human society's need for integrity in the variegated use of verbal expression and encompasses this need for truth in the prohi-

---

40 The first missionaries to attempt translations of this command in Hawaiian apparently had difficulty fully conveying the intent of this "word." See James A. Michener's fictional account, in humorous overtones, in his novel *Hawaii* (New York: Random House, 1959). The decision was finally made to translate the sixth command as "you shall not sleep mischievously." This secular passage comes very close to the truth we see here.

41 It is tragic that so many men (and women) in public life (political and religious especially) have attempted to hide their shameful sexual practices under the guise of a less than full understanding of what "adultery" truly is.

42 Kaiser, *Toward Old Testament Ethics*, 94.

43 See among others, Exod. 21:16; 22:1–15; Lev. 19:13, 35–36. See also that governmental representatives are indicted for being like those who "move landmarks" in Hos. 5:10.

44 See also Jer. 23:30 for a unique usage of the term in connection with plagiarism.

Way to the City

bition against doing damage to the "neighbor"[45] through a "false" (empty or groundless with reference to concrete realities) "testimony."[46] This "word" is specifically forbidding a harmful "response" in a situation where my neighbor would rightfully expect me to do him no verbal harm. This could certainly be, quintessentially, the circumstance of a court of law, where one might "answer/respond" to questions with a "repeat/return" to a single affirmation of fact. But this is not the only forum in which my neighbor might expect my words to comport with actual verifiable conditions or situations in the physical world so as to cause him no harm. What is enjoined in this ninth "word" is to see that verbal activity (spoken or written) is a force for good or ill that has implications far beyond the casual manner in which it is so constantly used (see also James 3:5–8; cf. Prov. 18:21). It has, ultimately, to do with one's relationship to God himself. "To despise the truth was to despise God whose very being and nature was truth."[47] The use of the Hebrew word for "answer" (which may be used for all manner of "response," verbal and otherwise) implies there are multifaceted ways in which we "speak" to the detriment of others or against their (and God's) just expectations of us.[48]

The final and tenth "word" from Sinai, "You shall not covet," internalizes all that has gone before it by forbidding even the contemplation of disobeying the "words" that have previously protected my neighbor from anything I might do to his hurt. The "word" used here is "covet," but it can be translated just as well "desire" or "delight." How it is to be understood is a matter of contextualizing its usage. It is entirely fitting that the Decalogue moves to this climactic demand. We can now see in graphic relief what the origin of all lawbreaking is—it is within man himself and that simple thing

---

45 It is clear that in the full context of the Decalogue that anytime a conflict arises between the innocent and the guilty, the innocent are to be protected. There should be no angst over the idea that the Hebrew midwives protected innocent babies from the onslaught of Pharaoh, just as many Europeans did the same for the millions of Jews threatened by the Nazis in our time.
46 The literal meaning of this word is "return or response." It is used in a variety of situations in the Hebrew Scriptures.
47 Kaiser, *Toward Old Testament Ethics*, 95.
48 The contextualization of this "word" in Lev. 19:15–16 is instructive, as it enjoins complete impartiality in the courtroom with reference to rich and poor, in contrast to the current US court system, which tends year by year to advance various "causes" at the expense of less favored classes of people.

Way to the City

called "desire." In the prohibition this "desire" is illicit when it involves what is my "neighbor's."[49]

From the literal beginning of our biblical journey in this book we have seen both the simple goodness and the fatal attraction of "desire." The man and the woman were created with desires of every kind and the ability to delight in all manner of pleasurable and good things. God's command to obey him and live, or disobey and die, is founded in the fundamental rightness of desire and delight. In God's creation the question will always be not, "What do you want?" but "What do you want more?" To want, desire, or take pleasure in all the vast possibilities in God's world is good in the context of God's law. To indulge those same motivations in ways that might lead us to harm others or allow such motives to displace God is sin.

"Desire" is not sin.[50] "Desire" for what is another's (from his ox to his wife and every possible thing "else," which is what his "house" is implying) is birthed in "greed" (the lack of an abiding contentment with God and what he has given) and fed by "envy" (the idea that what my neighbor has is really undeserved) until it grows into a rationalization that it is really "only right" that I should have some or all of whatever it is I am fixated upon. This fixation in turn leads to conspiracy in the heart and sometimes with others to commit particular sin. In the courts this is called "conspiracy" and is punishable in proportion to the nature of the crime contemplated. It is a small step from here to committing acts of slander, thievery, murder, and adultery, and of organizing political constituencies around the idea of taking something from others to distribute to oneself and favored others. It was just such a seduction by illicit desire contemplated that plunged the human race into misery in the garden. That tale is made all the more telling for our current discussion by its eloquent emphasis on the mere contemplation of a piece of fruit and the possibility of acquiring a desirable characteristic of God himself ("wisdom"). Such is the legacy of covetousness.

---

49 The Hebrew does not have "belongs" (NIV). It uses a simple possessive that conveys eloquently the sense of personal property and/or ownership and responsibility. For instance, a wife is not a "belonging," but she is in the most intimate sense "mine," or more importantly, "his."

50 Ironically, it is the passing of desire (for food, beauty, sex, life itself, etc.) that so often accompanies the ravages of old age. When desire is gone, the joy of life has passed and death comes on.

Way to the City

But this is not an argument for an ascetic or even an unambitious life. It is a warning about boundaries. It is a directing of desire toward admirable and worthwhile ends. As we shall see later, it is the very heart of biblical ethics to inspire a healthy self-interest—do this and live, even live well; do the other and die, even in great pain and sorrow (Deut. 30:15–20).

COMMENTARIES ON THE TEN WORDS

The Pentateuchal text now moves swiftly into the elaboration of the multifaceted implications of the ten "words" as "spoken" from Sinai. Through the use of formulations intended to be used in case-by-case decision making (casuistic, or "case law" format, designated by the "if/when this . . . then" literary structure) with the occasional insertion of additional injunctions in the same style as the "ten words" ("You shall / shall not . . ." called "apodictic," for that which is universally and always commanded), the Torah becomes a true teacher. It is this extensive commentary that occupies the written record from Exodus 20:22–23:33, resumes in Leviticus 18–20 and other passages, and is once again joined in the book of Deuteronomy 12:1–25:16. In between and mingled with these passages is the ongoing instruction on Israel's obligation to engage in cultic, or ritual, worship in a manner that mirrors God's character. In these sample case studies we learn that the Decalogue is not a minimal statement of terms but a comprehensive overview of the life lived with integrity before God. That is, each simple requirement contains in its full intention all the possible contingencies for each area of life addressed. We urge the reader to consult modern evangelical commentary materials for a thorough discussion of the historical and literary settings in which these various texts are placed. Such a task is beyond the scope of this work. What we can do here is sketch the broad outlines of the biblical materials as they relate to our specific subject.

As we previously argued in the discussion of narrative biblical literature, it is a mistake to attempt to draw out isolated conclusions from individual texts (or even sections) without relating them to their full context (section, book, literature type, OT, NT). No interpretation of casuistic formulations in the Torah can be considered sound that does not follow its roots to the apodictic pronouncements in the "ten words." Further, it is explicit throughout these commentary

Way to the City

text passages that the all-encompassing context is God's covenant with a freed and free people who now are obligated to their suzerain. Explicit also is the assumption that this people will require an atoning provision (acted out ritually in their worship) for their failure to meet their obligations perfectly. It is only in the light of these premises that we offer the following observations.

The Decalogue begins with a statement of obligation to God before anything else. In the commentary texts we also find this direct correlation between who God is and how he "sees" things and how Israel is expected to live.[51] In the same vein is the idea, "You shall not do as the Egyptians (where you came from) nor as the Canaanites (where you are going)," so clearly summarized in the injunction, "You shall not follow a crowd to do evil" (Exod. 23:2).[52] It is this theme that also animates the large body of instruction in the Pentateuch on Israel's worship of God. What is "right in the sight of God" (see further discussion and references below) is not merely a matter of religion or economics but an all-inclusive way to view the entirety of life's decision-making experiences. We would suggest this as the unifying principle that produces some of the seemingly odd juxtapositions of apparently disparate commands (see Exod. 22:16–19). Israel is required to be, like God, "holy."

Strictly speaking, it is not possible to separate one group of obligations from another. To worship God is not merely to engage in cultic or worship observances; it is to live in a certain way. In fact, it is clear in the entirety of the OT witness that the presentation of sacrifice or offering is meaningless apart from obedience to God's explicit commands (1 Sam. 15:22–23). However, no one in the OT record is ever presented as having completely obeyed God in every particular. Hence the system of sacrificial atonement and thankful offerings is instituted in a carefully prescribed ritual process. It is this entire body of obligation to which Israel is joined as a means of being "rightly" related to God. It is a false dichotomy as old as humanity to think it is possible to separate the two things (see Cain and Abel). Therefore, no discussion of the ethical demands of the Law can be fully understood apart

---

51 The use of the phrase "right in the sight of God" will become shorthand for everything that is "just."

52 Part and parcel of Israel's obligations to holiness is that they might be an example to all nations (Deut. 4:6–8; 28:1–14; et al.), presumably so they might follow Israel into blessing.

Way to the City

from the assumptions inherent in Israel's cultic worship. This goes a long way in explaining the form in which these materials have come down to us.

The apparent hodgepodge of commands and "for instances" is the way we encounter life's exigencies (Lev. 19). The Torah teaches us the way that life does. It bids us make note of the way things and experiences in life are intertwined in seemingly unrelated bunches. Only later, it so often happens, do we come to see their relatedness. But we are informed at the outset through the awesome "words" of Sinai that it all comes down to some very basic things. Wherever we may encounter the tough cases and whatever seemingly convoluted form they take, they cannot escape the glare of Horeb's shining cloud. Fundamental to understanding the whole is seeing that all that follows the Decalogue is not an addition to it but an unpacking of its full implications. Therefore, nothing that follows in the "holiness code" or the Deuteronomic restatements or in the setup of the cultic system can rightly be construed to contradict the first "words." They can only be complementary and explicative.

We believe it is the failure to fully account for these factors that leads to interpretive difficulties in so much of the literature on the subject we have chosen here. However, rather than allow others to set the agenda, we will set forth our interpretive schema, which we believe most nearly follows the materials we have in this part of the OT. For a guide to how our interpretation differs from some of our predecessors and contemporaries, please consult the notes associated with this chapter.

ACCOUNTABILITY

Nothing is clearer to the reader of the OT than the concept of accountability—that process by which the world of humanity is brought to experience the consequences, both good and bad, of its actions. What we want to address here is, what is the form and hierarchy of accountability as revealed in the Torah? By "form" we mean, how are consequences mediated to those held accountable? And by "hierarchy" we mean, is the consequence individual or corporate or both?

It is evident from the outset of God's dealings with humankind that there is a fundamental commitment on God's part to hold individuals directly accountable for their actions.[53] However, in his long workings with the family of Abram up to this point, it is also evident that he wills to have "a people" of his own to give light to the nations. Which of these commitments holds sway in the Torah? It is not equivocating, really, to say "both." But by what path does the process work to its inevitable conclusion? It seems clear that it moves from individual to corporate, and not vice versa. It is not a corporate responsibility that leads to an individual one, but the opposite. This is clearly the implication of Deuteronomy 29:18–20, which enjoins corporate responsibility for rooting out individual actions that will taint and mar the national character so as to bring on national disaster.

Beginning with the words from Sinai, couched in second person singular grammar, and following throughout the commentary sections, the overwhelming preponderance of textual material emphasizes individual accountability. Only then, as these individuals assume roles as leaders of families and tribes and/or judges and rulers or teachers do the corporate consequences begin to kick in. Even though God is committed to having "a people," the way to have that is to press upon individuals personal accountability, so they may as groupings become that people he envisions. It is by the accumulation of multiplied individual good and bad, the repeated settling of individual cases by judges, and the repeated teaching of the law by the priests in every town and community that a society "doing right in the sight of Yahweh" is built. It cannot be any other way.

Returning to our two-part question above, what form does this accountability take? To that question we now turn our attention.

MOTIVATION

It is quite often advanced as a biblical ideal that humankind most resembles what God expects when they do what is right and good without reference to personal consequences or rewards. This motivation is called altruism. Is this taught in the Torah? From our discussion of the tenth commandment above, it should be evident that altruism is not something taught there. Desire is not

---

53 The summary statement at Deut. 10:17 (cf. 2 Chron. 19:7) shows that Yahweh fundamentally abhors the tendency to judge by mere outward appearance—and this includes seeing either rich or poor in the light of those appearances!

only a building block of life itself placed in the man and woman at creation, but it is also foundational to the Decalogue and its commentary—both implicit and explicit. It is implicit in the run-up to the sound of God's voice emanating from the mount that it would be exceedingly desirable for the people to come out of that experience alive and not dead. Hence the boundaries set up to keep the irreverently curious from "breaking through" to see God.

It is made explicit in the "first commandment with promise" to honor father and mother, "that your days may be long . . . in the land" that God was giving them (Eph. 6:2; Exod. 20:12). This promise then becomes the seed for a burgeoning harvest of blessings and curses culminating in the long reiterations in Deuteronomy 27 and 28 (cf. Lev. 26). One reads these pages alternately rejoicing and shuddering at the prospects envisioned. All the possibilities from temporal to eternal and material to intangible are foreshadowed in these warnings and promises. We might have lively discussions about just how much of each of these possibilities is implied in each part of the multiplied texts. What cannot be denied is that Torah teaches both/and, not either/or or neither/nor. That is, we should be motivated to do what is in God's Law by both temporal and eternal and material and intangible rewards and punishments. To believe and/or teach otherwise is to miss what both the creation and Torah contend for.

Finally, note that though it is implied that God himself will surely see to the application of consequences, it is the job of duly commissioned judges/rulers to see that proper accountability measures are applied where appropriate.[54] They are to do it with impartiality, honesty, impeccable fairness, and a view to the special cause of any who might be taken advantage of in a given judicial setting (Exod. 23:1–9). Punishments must fit crimes (Exod. 21:12–22:24). The innocent must be acquitted and the guilty punished (Exod. 23:6). In short, judges and rulers are held to the same standard of "right in the sight of God" as individuals are. It is this certainty about reward and punishment that will provide Israel with a stable and ultimately prosperous society. But please note that in the preponderance of the teaching of Torah it is individual attention to these matters, not criminal enforcement, that is the backbone of a "blessed" people.

---

54 The theme of blessing and cursing has been both explicit and implicit prior to this revelation in Israel, but now there is no ambiguity.

Way to the City

WHAT IS JUSTICE?

This question can easily be construed as Pilate's inquiry after "truth"—a cynical commentary on life's impossible quests. Or, it can be construed as begging for the simple answer Jesus gave to a man one day inquiring about the "greatest command" in the Law. Jesus' twofold response, (1) love the Lord your God and (2) love your neighbor as yourself, is quite often laden by readers and commentators with mere sentimentality and used as a means of discarding the explicit teaching of the Bible, particularly the Law as we have been discussing it. Advocates of "justice"—sometimes, "simple justice"—tend to be a part of that latter group and their opponents sometimes sound like Pilate in world-weary response. We think the Bible advocates neither of these.

We have been using the word "right" to describe in summary what God's law requires. It is time to address what this concept involves in principle. Properly understood, "right" and "justice" are synonymous. Merrill states it this way: "Justice is the application of righteousness, especially in situations of legal disposition. Where law is interpreted in a righteous manner, justice will prevail."[55] The Hebrew uses three words to convey the fully nuanced meaning of what is right or just.[56] *Yashar* is the word most often used in the phrase "right in the sight of God," and means essentially "straight" or "correct."[57] It can be used of all kinds of behavior—public, private, religious, or judicial. *Mishpat* properly refers to "that which is correctly decided," and most often refers to judicial situations and is frequently translated in modern versions as "judgments." *Tsedeq* is used to describe that which is objectively "righteous" in the light of God's standards and character.[58] Together, these three terms teach us what "justice" is in the eyes of God and what he wishes to be practiced among people, both individually and judicially.[59]

---

55 Merrill, *Everlasting Dominion*, 60.
56 See standard Hebrew lexicons.
57 See Exod. 15:26; Deut. 6:18; 12:25, 28; 21:9; 2 Kings. 12:2; 14:3; 15:3, 34; etc.
58 Walton notes in *Ancient Near Eastern Thought*, Kindle loc. 3264–74, that the purpose of the Law in Israel is sanctification, meaning that the Law is given to make the people like God before it is strictly about justice.
59 A clear example of apparent misunderstanding here is Ronald J. Sider, "Justice, Human Rights, and Government," in *Toward an Evangelical Public Policy*, ed. Ronald J. Sider and Diane Knippers (Grand Rapids, MI: Baker, 2005), 168–70. Sider's discussion of procedural

Rooted in what God is and what God says, justice is not mere sentimentality or wishful thinking.[60] Such justice is the objective and normative standard
by which God rules and holds humankind accountable. It is propositionally
revealed in the Decalogue and the rest of the Torah. No understanding of "justice" that does not account for this fundamental fact can claim to be fully biblical.[61] It is our contention here and through the remainder of our OT and NT
exposition that there can be no contradiction between the Decalogue and its
Pentateuchal commentary and any other portion of Scripture on the subject
of justice, or any other subject for that matter. What God wants us to know
about justice is revealed in the "words" of Sinai and fleshed out elsewhere.

As we have seen in the narratives, the God of the Bible is fully committed
to the working out of his purposes in the material realm.[62] This is not to deny
his clear eternal intentions, but rather to highlight the profound concern of
the One "who inhabits eternity" (Isa. 57:15) with temporal things. In heaven
and on earth God's will as revealed and developed in the Torah is the delimi-
tation of the boundaries of biblical justice.[63] It cannot possibly be more than
this, but it must not be less. The inadequacy of so much of the Christian

---

and distributive justice mistakes "distributive" as relating to the results of the decisions
made in court procedurally and/or the failure to take procedural action when it is clearly
called for because of fraudulent or violent behavior. This is the clear force of the examples
he calls forth from Scripture as having to do with distributive justice as he denominates
it. This is not the standard meaning of "distributive justice" that causes the tension in our
modern setting. The modern debates have to do with the distribution of economic and
other goods when no procedural justice is thought necessary—i.e., no fraud or theft has
occurred, just unequal "distribution." Most often the so-called standard assumed is one
denominated "fairness," either implicit or explicit. We will have more to say on this later.

60 See Abraham's prayer for Sodom as a profound appeal to the known character of God
before the revelation at Sinai.

61 We will demonstrate throughout our biblical commentary the essential character of justice
as stemming from the Sinai disclosure.

62 These narratives in the Pentateuch in which we can trace the outworking of God's purposes
in the world all have the status of Torah in the Hebrew Bible. Elsewhere, the narratives
"teach," though they reside in the Prophets.

63 This statement reveals a great deal about our understanding of the nature of biblical revelation. While we are cognizant of the process of what some call "progressive" revelation, we
will show in our commentary on the rest of Scripture that, at least in the area of ethics, revelation moves more in the vein of clarification and explanation than it does in a process of
addition. Certainly the incarnation is the very real embodiment of ethical perfection, but
it is not an embodiment of anything not given before in the Torah. See also Walter Kaiser's
helpful discussion of this issue in *Toward Old Testament Ethics*, 60–64. We will comment
further on this issue as our study progresses.

Way to the City

discussion of justice resolves itself into a failure to take into account this ines-capable biblical mandate.[64]

JUSTICE AND JUBILEE

As an illustration of how following the rule we are espousing works itself out, we offer an interpretive framework for understanding the strange-to-our-ears provisions for the various "Sabbaths" enjoined in Torah. From that sentence alone can be discerned a major presupposition of our methodology. The key to understanding the meaning of the Jubilee is to understand the meaning of "Sabbath" in the Decalogue and its commentary.

Modern Christians are accustomed to substituting "Sunday" for "Sabbath" and assuming that "going to church on Sunday" is what "observing my Sab-baths" is all about. This is no more the case than was the practice of the most pious Judaism of Jesus' day. Just as the Pharisees had failed to see that "the Sabbath was made for man," not the other way around (Mark 2:27), too many have seen little more than religious observance in the fourth command.[65] The facts of the case are otherwise.

The profound truth, previously noted, is that this command is an in-vitation to join God in a "rest" mirroring the seventh day of creation. We know that this is its true implication from the explicit extensions of it in the commentaries of Exodus 23:10–13 and Leviticus 25.[66] It is here that we find the conceptual meaning of Sabbath as a deep-seated confidence in God's

---

64 This is a common flaw most notable in the work of Ronald J. Sider, *Cry Justice! The Bible on Hunger and Poverty* (Downers Grove, IL: InterVarsity Press, 1980), which is little more than a compendium of Scripture notations without explication as to the contextual and literary meaning associated with the citations, or how the specific situation in the text relates directly to those of the twenty-first century, who find themselves comparatively wealthy relative to others. Professor Sider appears to assume no explanation is needed for the subject of "justice." We contend this is precisely what is needed, because the implied meaning of Sider's approach is that the "rich" of the West (and especially the United States) are guilty by word-association with the "rich" condemned in the Bible.

65 This is an example we will find repeated in the ministry of Jesus, as he bids us see not some new revelatory teaching but what was all along imbedded in the original "word" from Sinai.

66 See also the similar instructions given in Deut. 15, where the emphasis on "lending" to a "poor brother," without an eye to the approaching time of debt cancellation required by the Law, urges a generosity (lit., "openhandedness") that denies "tightfistedness."

Way to the City

providential care and lordship over all made explicit. To understand its true import, we must, however, stay mindful of the obvious and not-so-obvious contextual situation.

Rooted in the story (Torah) of creation is the inescapable fact that the land (all the lands) is God's. It is his to distribute and allot by nation and by tribal grouping. That he is already and has been doing so is both implicit and explicit in the biblical text. His current work of authorizing and aiding Israel in displacing "the Jebusites" is according to his previous promise and his on-going proof of his faithful and just governance of all creation and whatever it contains. Israel is at once called on to see a promised homeland providentially given, with the prospect of being able to harvest from it great abundance, for it is "a land flowing with milk and honey" (Exod. 3:8, etc.) Among other things, this means they will inhabit "cities you did not build" and take over "vineyards and olive groves that you did not plant" (Deut. 6:11; Josh. 24:13).

Nevertheless, all is not mere distribution of wealth, like so much money lying on the ground.[67] The blessing is in the form of land, which cannot of itself make one wealthy—hence the expression on the American frontier, "land-poor," mean-ing having too much land with not enough other resources to make anything (that is, money or wealth) from it.[68] According to God's command, this land must first be won by supplanting its current holders through courage, resourcefulness, ini-tiative, and, above all, battle. Further, the negative of this course is clearly explicit in that, when some failed to do as commanded in the acquisition ("possession") of land, they would benefit not at all from being "in" the land. On the other hand, if

---

67 Some (notably Blomberg, *Neither Poverty nor Riches*, 195) have attempted to put an inter-pretation of wealth on the use of "manna" in the wilderness, implying that the harvesting of this mysterious (Heb., "What is it?") sustenance was equivalent to the equal distribution of wealth in NT times and our own day. It is clear in the Pentateuchal record that manna was only a temporary provision, very unsatisfying (see Num. 11:4–6) by design to remind the people that they were still on the way to the Land of Promise and not arrived, and ceased the moment the land was entered. Sider makes the similar assumption when he states that the eighth-century B.C. prophets had in mind that the wealth in Israel at that time "was by no means evenly distributed" (*Cry Justice!* 52). He also shares Blomberg's perspective on the "equally distributed" manna (*Neither Poverty nor Riches,* 102).

68 The land is the only commodity in creation that cannot be enlarged and is therefore allotted by tribe, clan, and family and is treated as something that cannot be permanently sold, only rented for its produce. Land cannot be "produced," but it can be creatively "worked" to in-crease wealth. Land is not wealth; wealth is produced when human creativity is applied to it.

Way to the City

a Caleb was capable of acquiring ("possessing") more than he was originally given, it was heartily approved.[69] And it is clear from the context (Josh. 17:14–18) that the envy of other tribes for more land can sometimes involve an apparent unwillingness to deal with the actual allotment they have received at the hand of Yahweh. There is no warrant for a Christian egalitarianism of distribution of anything in either the original dividing of the land among the tribes or the laws concerning Jubilee; Yahweh's distribution is based on divine fiat.

But even when a family and/or tribal grouping succeeded in possessing its allotment, they were not thereby automatically wealthy, in the sense of being able to take a check from *Who Wants to Be a Millionaire?* to the bank. They must now rely once again on the same character traits, by which they had become truly "landed," to produce fruitfulness from their land according to God's promise to Noah that "as long as the earth endures, seedtime and harvest, . . . summer and winter will never cease" (Gen. 8:22) for those who worked the land. It has always been and continues to be so, especially in agrarian societies. The land is the fundamental resource from which wealth is drawn by man's activities according to God's governance of creation.[70]

Against this backdrop the implicit law of the Sabbath is made explicit at Sinai. "Six days you shall labor" is full of the activities that will "possess" and "bring forth fruit" from the land. But "the seventh . . . you shall not do any work" recognizes that the actual "fruitfulness" is God's to give, though it appears to be merely a naturally occurring phenomenon. Israel, and all mankind, acknowledges this fact when deliberately ceasing from labor in the full confidence that the "fruit" will still be forthcoming, even though fully one-seventh of a nation's potential output of productive capacity is apparently foregone.

The passages in Exodus and Leviticus, previously cited, then give further substantiation to this theme. Not only is Israel to observe a weekly Sabbath,

---

69 The careful reader will observe that the ability of Caleb to attain to a greater inheritance is credited to his strong character, a factor that contributes to one's natural abilities, but is not synonymous with them (Josh. 14:6–15). See also Beisner, *Where Garden Meets Wilderness*, 51–52, for delineation of the unequal original distribution of land among the tribes and clans of Israel. Apparently egalitarian distribution was not God's original plan for even Israel.

70 It is surely a mistake for Professor Sider to suggest that "factories" (as we document elsewhere) are somehow equivalent to land in our modern age, for a factory is the product of human ingenuity applied to land/resources. In fact land is only a "resource" in the hand of creative humans or God himself.

Way to the City

but she is also to practice a sabbatical year, letting the land "rest," in the same spirit as the weekly observance. And, as if to shout with the literal voice of the trumpet (*shofar*), every fiftieth year (after seven sevens) a jubilee (lit., "release") allowed for the return to their original land of those who had given up their land as collateral for loans made during the previous forty-nine years. This "release," amounting to a cancellation of debt, prevented an accumulation of the land (the one indispensable resource) into a few hands in a society with an agrarian economy and limited acreage.[71] It is extremely significant that no redistribution of wealth accumulation is commanded or contemplated here. The land is the one commodity that does not grow. It is *returned*, not redistributed, to those who had lost it through whatever circumstances.[72]

Coupled with laws for tithing, charitable giving and allowances (gleaning laws), forgiveness of debts to fellow Israelites, interest-free loans,[73] and compas-

---

71 The narratives have previously shown this sense of indebtedness to God for the land in the life of Abraham, as he can afford to be generous even with his opponents and less morally fit companions (see Lot). Isaac shows this same characteristic in his dealings, but it is mostly missing in the more pragmatic Jacob.

72 Derek Kidner notes that this is where Israel deviated from its neighbors in its Law, as it provided for a "redemption" (Lev. 25:25–28). "It is axiomatic in the ancient world that one paid one's way so long as one had anything to part with—including, in the last resort, one's liberty," commenting on Gen. 47:13–27, especially v. 19. *Genesis*, 211.

73 What is forbidden is putting the "bite" on the neighbor who needs a loan to take care of daily necessities. This is a provision to protect those who need subsistence loans from being driven into debt slavery. See especially on this the comments at Deut. 23:19–20 and Ps. 15:5 by Peter C. Craigie, with 2004 suppl. by Marvin E. Tate, *Psalms 1–50*, rev. ed., *WBC 19*, CD-ROM 59 vols., ed. Bruce M. Metzger, David A. Hubbard and Glenn W. Barker (Nashville: Thomas Nelson, 2007), ad loc. "When the nation was first established, the Israelite economy was by no means mercantile; and loans were made to help persons who had become too poor to support themselves. Assistance to such persons was to be given without interest—not interest of silver (equals "money"), food, or anything that might earn interest (v. 19). But since merchants from other nations might come for business reasons to Israel, or make loans on interest to Israelites, foreigners could be charged interest (v. 20). This rule alleviates the plight of the poor and made it more possible for them to work themselves out of their low estate. Interest is also regulated in Exod. 22:25 and Lev. 25:36–37. The Lord's blessing on their labors in the land they were about to enter was contingent on their following this directive." Craigie's comments continue: "The implied condemnation of usury reflects a quite specific concern in ancient Israel. It is not the case that lending on interest was wrong in principle, but that it normally involved exploitation and abuse. Thus the Hebrew law prevented loans on interest to fellow Hebrews, but permitted them in business transactions with foreigners. . . . The reason was that a fellow Hebrew who was in need of a loan was almost certainly in distress; to make a loan to such a person and charge exorbitant interest would culminate in the aggravation of distress rather than its removal,

Way to the City

sionate indentured servant laws (named "slavery" in our texts), Torah at once recognizes the nature of the human predicament and the principles of personal responsibility.[74] Where charity is truly necessary, it is to be done heartily, with the expectation that God will generously bless the giver (Deut. 15:10).[75] All of these prescriptions may be said to proceed from the concept that fruitful labor and its rewards, provided as they are from a merciful God, are not the same thing as obsessive acquisitiveness—manifest in the proscribed behaviors of commandments six through ten or evident in the inability to rest or sleep "while there is work to be done." Even the idea of "rest from labor" conjures the vision of "thankfulness" in cessation from the arduous part of life captured in the modern shorthand, TGIF.

What Is Not Taught

Finally, we should note what is not taught in the Sabbath laws. First, nothing in these "words" or commentaries proscribes the full development of human potential and initiative, nor do they forbid or denigrate the production and enjoyment of wealth and prosperity. To the contrary, they encourage and literally promise "blessing" on the bold and courageous and obedient, and "cursing" on the timid and cowardly and disobedient.[76] And these blessings and curses are overwhelmingly, if not exclusively, temporal, material, and economic. No prior limits are placed on the amounts of "blessing" that might accrue in individual or societal cases. Thus, there is an overwhelming predisposition toward pushing human potential within the boundaries of God's revealed will.[77]

---

so that if a loan were to be made at all to a fellow Hebrew, it could only be secured by a pledge (cf. Deut. 24:6), without interest."

74 It is this commingling of human responsibility and divine providence that leads to the promise that "There shall not be any poor among you" (Deut. 15:4). The emphasis here is on "not any," as opposed to Deut. 15:11, "there will always be poor." The genuinely helpless or disadvantaged (widows, orphans, disabled, aliens, etc.) will be dealt with by charitable means, but the rest are expected to exercise proper industriousness and depend on God's blessing. This implies what we call "development" in modern parlance. "Societal wealth," a modern terminology we will take up at a later time, is not the product of charity or governmental action but of hard work and human creativity and holy character.

75 For the most recent biblical study in this area, see Baker, *Tight Fists or Open Hands*.

76 See Deut. 28 and parallels, especially Lev. 26.

77 Later biblical materials, which we shall discuss, will highlight some of these limits. Note, further, that the Jubilee redemption has nothing to say about redistributing wealth attained through the use of the land or anything gained through any other business activity, nor is

Way to the City

Nothing in these texts teaches a weakening of the human part of material ownership. In fact, the human ownership of land is strengthened by the Jubilee law in returning it, not willy-nilly to whomever the judge deems "worthy," but to its original "possessor." The only provision in Torah for taking what is in the possession of one and giving it to another is if the receptor of it was the original rightful possessor of it. The explicit concern in such a case is that the original "owner" was somehow deprived of his property by stealth or violence on the part of the one now possessing it. The only "just" thing to do is now to reverse the process judicially. "Sojourning with God on/in the land" does not weaken Israel's hold on it vis-à-vis other human claims—it strengthens that claim. "Sojourning" implies, rather, the temporal and "passing through" aspect of life and begs for an eternal vision.[78]

Nothing in these texts implies or makes explicit that justice is only achieved when the distribution of material "blessings" (for that is what material "fruits" are shown to be) is roughly even across the spectrum of society's variegated landscape. To the contrary, it is explicit that blessings and curses will accrue in more or less direct proportion to the variations in human endeavor to follow in the way of God's commands—both in "possessing the land" and in obeying Sinai's "words." The exception to this is the plain recognition that the truly "innocent" in Israel must be cared for and protected—namely, the widowed, the orphaned, the disabled, the alien (foreigners were not necessarily innocent but disadvantaged by not having full citizenship and privileges in the land), and the like. No one of earthly lineage, however, is empowered to devise a plan of "distribution" that will even out economic and material results. That is God's to give and withhold.

Finally, and perhaps most importantly, nothing in these texts can be construed to imply a utopian outcome for human evolution and achievement.[79]

---

anything in the towns and cities redistributed in any way. It is *all* about the land, which is the *Lord's* and is the commodity that is in limited supply.

78 The land is given to Israel in a provisional promise depending on their own careful observance of all they were commanded to do at Sinai. The previous tenants on the land with God, the Jebusites, had lost the land because of their reprehensible behavior. For the same reason Israel would lose its position on the land in years to come. In this manner God shows his ways are just.

79 This is the abiding dream of many still in our world today. Richard Stearns of World Vision is just the latest to opine exuberantly about "changing the world" through application of a

Way to the City

Rather, these materials affirm a state of human fallenness leading to an absolute necessity that Israel's every step be informed by the law of God—waking and sleeping and rising and going out and coming in, day and night and all seasons, thus establishing a theocracy.[80] Such a condition implies without ambiguity that any attempt to place some kind of czar (Caesar)[81] or other all-powerful person or group in charge of making ordinary human interchange into an idealistic, superaltruistic "just society" is fraught with unforeseen (by earthlings) evils. Even a possible king in Israel must "meditate in God's law day and night" (see Ps. 1:1; cf. Deut. 17:18–20). Judges must not deviate to the right or the left from God's law (Deut. 16:18–20). The reason is clear—all judges and kings are filled with the same tendencies and vices as their appellants and subjects. The human condition knows no exceptions, save the One "who is, and who was, and who is to come" (Rev. 1:4).

In conclusion, Sinai shines with the light of revelation that confirms what has gone before in the narratives. It remains for the embellishment of the preachers and teachers that follow to further uncover the jewels hidden to the eyes of human frailty in its blinding cloud. And we shall find, as Kaiser has taught us, that "the wisdom and the prophetic books of the Bible rely on Torah as being foundational for all they teach and affirm. . . . [T]he heart of the divinely directed life has been laid out in the Mosaic revelation."[82] Having examined the foundation, we now turn to look at the larger structure of OT revelation.

Christianized version of Jubilee. See Richard Stearns, *The Hole in Our Gospel: What Does God Expect of Us? The Answer That Changed My Life and Might Just Change the World* (Nashville: Thomas Nelson, 2009). Stearns take on Jubilee is that it was "God's way of protecting against the rich getting too rich and the poor getting too poor" (22).

80 It is critical to the proper understanding of the covenant that Israel (and by future implication, all mankind) assume the obligation to carefully teach from generation to generation the moral mandates of Sinai (see esp., Deut. 11:16–21) lest God "shut the heavens so that it will not rain and the ground will yield no produce, and you will soon perish" (v. 17).

81 Strange that such positions and nomenclature have been revived under the current US government administration of President Barack Obama.

82 Kaiser, *Preaching and Teaching*, 140.

Way to the City

Chapter 4

Wise Men and Singers

RON SIDER HAS COMPILED as helpful a collection of the biblical material on the subject we are here addressing as can be found anywhere (*Cry Justice!*). However, without clear specification and nuancing, such a collection almost begs to be misinterpreted in the manner that Job's sufferings were misinterpreted by his "friends." Sider's book handles Job in the same way his friends did, implying that his loss of riches was the result of unjust action on his part.[1] Job, of course, is suffering mysteriously (to him and his friends) at the hands of God (through the instrumentality of Satan), and the friends know nothing but the conventional "wisdom" of the day (God punishes/curses the bad and blesses/prospers the

---

1   Ronald J. Sider, *Cry Justice! The Bible on Hunger and Poverty* (Downers Grove, IL: InterVarsity Press, 1980), 48–50. He simply titles the friends' comments as a "charge" and Job's reply as a "defense" without indicating which is the correct and objective view of Job's actual situation (Job 22:5–9; 23:1–2, 12; 24:1–12, 19–22; 29:11–17). This is in effect what the entire book by its style and approach does to the prosperous portion of the globe—condemn those who prosper, by verbal association with the "rich" of the Bible, when it is clear in the Bible that it is not the wealthy per se who are condemned but their actual sins in (1) becoming wealthy at the expense of others, especially the weak and helpless who cannot successfully resist the corruption of governments in collusion with the rich and powerful, or (2) exploiting that advantage with governmental help in the courts or regulatory or tax policy. Witness how Sider's text is interspersed periodically with charts and graphs (without explanation) of the differences in prosperity and poverty between different parts of the modern world. Furthermore, the study questions (199) deliberately bypass the most important interpretive considerations: addressees, historical setting, precise application to time and place, etc., in favor of getting to the "weighty" matters even as they ask leading-the-witness questions to elicit the sought-after answers. This is the essence of guilt by association. The passages from Job we cite here do not even come up for discussion.

good), against which Job mightily defends his integrity until God "answered out of the whirlwind" (Job 38:1). The word translated "answered" in the text is the same "word" uttered on Sinai in the ninth commandment, which forbids a false reply, one not comporting with reality, in a court of law or any other situation that might harm the "neighbor."[2] Furthermore, the friends are roundly condemned for failure to "speak" the "right" thing as Job had done (Job 42:7–9).[3] The implication of this entire scenario, taking into account the book of Job from beginning to end, is to exonerate Job in the implicit court from the charges against him (by "the Satan" and then by his erstwhile "friends") by those unable or unwilling to discern the actual state of affairs.[4] The mission of the wise in Israel is thus commended, for it has reached a conclusion that comports with the realities of the entire cosmic situation in the present age. Job has suffered despite his righteousness and has received a due exoneration from the One who matters most, and Job later resumes being "blessed" in material and intangible ways. As if to underline our conclusion, Job is given double what he had before (42:10), denying anything inherently wrong in having wealth, even massive wealth!

Unlike the wisdom materials of the ancient Near East outside of Israel, the emphasis upon the "fear of Yahweh" controls Israelite point and counterpoint musings upon the nature of life and the world—the milieu of the wise men in all nations. It is the old, old story of "surely God is good to Israel… but as for me" (Ps. 73:1–2); for good or ill, things don't always turn out as expected nor are they always as they seem. This is the place where wisdom is needed. Nowhere is that more true than in the worldly discussion of economics.

---

2   See our previous discussion in chap. 3.
3   The key term "speak" is the same one that designates Sinai's ten "words." "Right" implies that which comports with reality as the embodiment of the truth. Clearly both Satan and the would-be friends have brought a "false witness" against Job. This is not unlike the blanket indictments implied by the attempt to leap from the prophetic and other texts to the modern situation without resort to contextual factors, which Sider implies is not strictly necessary to understand the texts he uses so freely. Such "eisegesis" is not unlike the manner in which "prosperity" and "faith" teachers wrest the text to theirs and their hearers' hurt.
4   This tendency to bring accusation based on false understanding of reality and the text of Scripture can be seen from right and left of the theological political spectrum. One side condemns American lifestyle choices from the standpoint of perverted sexual practice and concludes that the attack on September 11, 2001, was clearly deserved for that reason. The other states just as emphatically that it is American economic life that brought about a justly deserved punishment. See on this the respective pronunciations of Jerry Falwell and Rev. Jeremiah Wright at the time.

Way to the City

Proverbs, Ecclesiastes, Job, and the Song of Solomon contain the stated wisdom of Israel's (and others') sages, but the Psalms also contain a wide variety of Wisdom material in the form of prayers, praises, and exhortations directed at both the congregation in general and the personal self-consciousness of the writers. We will take Proverbs as the underlying base from which one might expect to encounter the exigencies and deviations one finds in the other places of the canon.

Pitfalls to Wisdom

Derek Kidner in the introduction to his commentary[5] on Proverbs says, "it is a book full of wisdom requiring all our wisdom to understand." Presented in Hebrew poetic form and in aphoristic style, it is a book misunderstood almost as widely as it is read and memorized. Since its methodology is topical and not apparently contextually cohesive (except for the occasional lengthened expatiation on a single theme), the temptation is to isolate single verses in our English texts and treat them as assertions of unvarying relationships between actions and outcomes, attitudes and practices, journeys and arrivals, and multiplied variations of the theme of choices and consequences. This kind of interpretive method is at once superficially text-driven and substantially shallow—in other words, unwise.[6]

Four hermeneutical presuppositions prevent our descent into such blunders. The first is to recognize that no single aphorism can in itself exhaust all there is to know about its apparent subject—in part because each proverb has a tendency to have within its seemingly uncomplicated message nuances of other themes explored elsewhere. These texts are part of an "over-all message according to the inspired author's intentions"[7] that requires the interpreter

---

5   Derek Kidner, *Proverbs: An Introduction and Commentary*, TOTC (London: Inter-Varsity Press, 1973).

6   We would also place in this category the conjectures of Ben Witherington III, *Jesus and Money: A Guide for Times of Financial Crisis* (Grand Rapids, MI: Brazos, 2010), to the effect that Proverbs is actually the product of the wealthy and powerful elites and that Ecclesiastes represents a time when disaster has struck.

7   Gordon D. Fee and Douglas Stuart, *How to Read the Bible for All Its Worth: A Guide to Understanding the Bible* (Grand Rapids, MI: Zondervan, 1982), 188. This citation does not

Way to the City

not to atomize them. It is these very subtleties that provoke the "simple" to become either "fools" or "wise"—by heeding or shunning their counsel. Consequently, the wise teacher and student will, insofar as possible, weigh all the teaching of Proverbs on any given topic with careful attention to related shades of insight. This will require, at times, a summary of all that may bear topically on a given subject or idea found anywhere in the book.

The second interpretive rule that must be followed is that each proverbial nugget is placed literarily in an immediate context that bears upon its meaning by association.[8] This is quite often the source of what appears to be mere repetition from another context. The compiler of these materials in effect bids us consider the implications of wise counsel in multiple settings and juxtapositions. This, of course, mirrors life. Attempts at compartmentalization of life's vagaries are futile and foolish, for life happens. It does not organize itself to our will and ways. It simply comes at us like snowflakes driven before the wind. He who would navigate through it wisely and righteously must be prepared to face issues as and where he encounters them. One cannot tell when, where, or how the temptations to sin and foolishness will come or which apparently innocuous moment will be life changing, so one must stay alert to the strange juxtapositions of the trivial and the momentous.

Our third canon of wise interpretation is perhaps more critical to modern evangelical understanding of this portion of the Bible than the other two. It involves the nature of promise and the assertion of eternal, and thus unwavering and unalterable verities, in Scripture. We can illustrate this in many ways, but it can be easily seen in the body of Proverbs itself. Chapter 1:7 says, "The fear of the LORD is the beginning of knowledge; fools despise wisdom and instruction" (NASB). This clearly qualifies as an eternal verity without need for nuanced interpretation. It is in truth a simple variation on the first commandment of Exodus 20. By contrast, Proverbs 3:9–10 says, "Honor the LORD with your wealth and from the first of all your produce; so your barns will be filled with plenty and your vats will overflow with new wine" (NASB). Just as the

---

indicate a blanket endorsement of all that these authors say about the Wisdom Literature of the Bible.

8   Walter C. Kaiser Jr., *Toward Rediscovering the Old Testament*, ed. Lyman Rand Tucker Jr. (Grand Rapids, MI: Zondervan, 1987), 178–82.

Way to the City

statement above requires no qualifications to ascertain its truth content (i.e., its comportment with reality), this statement demands a complete contextualization within the book of Proverbs and the balance of Scripture. If wealth accumulation were merely a matter of "tithing" in the OT sense, then millions of *nouveau riche* would bloom daily on the planet, for who wouldn't pay tithes for such a reward?[9] The fact that no such rendering of this "promise" is valid requires no additional "proof," for the many centuries of recorded time since this was first verbalized have given such a simplistic interpretation to the lie.[10] Nevertheless, many to this very day continue to "claim" the "promise" and urge others to do likewise (usually positing themselves as the recipients of such tithing). This is one of many fallacies (as D. A. Carson has called them) of interpretation that are made by students of the Wisdom material reflecting the lack of Kidner's caution above. We trust we will not be among them.[11]

A fourth and final caveat concerns an all-too-prevalent tendency of New Testament–informed evangelical interpreters. It is the practice of moving quickly away from an interpretive struggle with an apparently difficult passage or statement (like the one with which we have just dealt) to a simplistic and facile "spiritual" or "eternal" explanation. In this case, embarrassed by the idea of getting rich by tithing, or having concluded that no such tit for tat is possible in this world, the student and/or teacher decides this promise must be all about heaven and "pie-in-the-sky bye-and-bye." This, too, we will not do. While the OT affirms the existence of a life beyond the grave, without developing the

---

9 This is the very style of biblical interpretation that informs "prosperity gospel" teaching. For a critique, see Robert M. Bowman Jr., *The Word-Faith Controversy: Understanding the Health and Wealth Gospel* (Grand Rapids, MI: Baker, 2001).

10 We do not deny that God's blessing will come to those who tithe, nor would we assert that those who do not tithe won't become just as rich.

11 Craig Blomberg appears to ignore this caveat, as the title reference of his book reflects not an actual exaltation of the middle position between wealth and poverty but an observation about human frailty. See Craig L. Blomberg, *Neither Poverty nor Riches: A Biblical Theology of Possessions* (Downers Grove, IL: InterVarsity Press, 1999). So also the companion observation about being "overly righteous" or "overly wicked" (Eccl. 7:16–17) is not exalting a middle position between those two alternatives. See on this point D. A. Carson, *Exegetical Fallacies*, 2nd ed. (Grand Rapids, MI: Baker, 1996), Kindle loc. 1354. We believe this is what he calls a fallacy of literary genre. The more appropriate summary advice from the Wisdom material might be "In the day of prosperity be joyful, but in the day of adversity, consider: God has made the one as well as the other, so that man cannot discover anything that will come after him" (Eccl. 7:14 HCSB).

Way to the City

actual dimensions of a world beyond this one—dimensions that would spell out in some way what future and eternal "rewards" one might count on—the OT clearly teaches that material and temporal rewards follow from faithfulness to God. Proverbs reflects this consensus. What it adds is the *how* and *why* of these rewards in practical terms. We will find a much more fruitful avenue for discerning the meaning of the "tithe promise" by studying in Scripture what the wise men see in the character of those faithful enough to God to go on obeying his will (including tithing) long enough to reap benefits—temporal and eternal.

THE BLESSING OF GOD IN PROVERBS

The unique contribution of the book of Proverbs is a well-ordered discussion of how God's goodness, his "blessing," is distributed. Its greatest emphasis is on the temporal, without excluding or de-emphasizing the eternal. A summary statement of its overall teaching (without meaning to oversimplify) would sound something like this: "Blessing" (just like "cursing") is built into the material world God created, and it is obtained through character building. The reverse (cursing) is equally true. It all depends on the kind of character one builds.[12] With this as our launching pad we will suggest what we believe are four unassailable pillars of the life lived wisely.

First, work, or "diligence," precedes virtually all blessings.[13] In fact, we are not aware that Proverbs or any other book in the Bible teaches otherwise. Anything we might call a genuine "good thing" is always preceded by someone's hard work.[14] Thus, it comes before knowledge, wisdom, lasting wealth (as opposed to "fleeting riches"), good relationships, good government, and a host of other "goods" we might name. How could it be otherwise? The prime directive from Eden is to work; the fall only made it harder. The Noahic prom-

---

12 The use of "curse" is not that of the general "curse" resulting from the fall. This can only be reversed with "a new heavens and a new earth." The "curse" we find among the wisdom and moral teachings we have been examining is the direct negative consequence of specific immoral and/or unwise behavior.

13 Prov. 6:6–11; 12:11; 20:13; 23:20; 27:23–27; 28:19; and many others.

14 Even the supposed "luck" of an inheritance or unexpected windfall is to be seen in the first instance as the fruit of prior labors and in the second as an opportunity (as is an inheritance that can be frittered away by lack of due diligence).

ise mitigated that. And everything we have seen in our study so far shows the fruit born by courageous and difficult endeavors. The wisdom of Proverbs is to show its variegated and nuanced influences.

Second, the blessings/fruits of diligence/work piggyback upon one another in beneficial ways. That is, working diligently at something tends to produce the knowledge that leads to "working smarter," as we would say in our time.[15] It will also tend to produce a body of information collected over time, i.e., "wisdom," that leads to the avoidance of wasted time, energy, and resources. This, in turn, produces additional resources to be invested in further productive enterprises. Applying the same principle to relationships, family building, government, or any other life process has the same effect. The outcome is greater than the sum of its parts.

Third, experiencing these things firsthand reinforces the salutary influence of character traits such as delaying gratification till the proper timing in everything, planning for the future, practicing frugality and limiting self-indulgence, and practicing generosity with others (especially the innocent downtrodden).[16] As the cycle of work, fruit bearing, rewards (of all kinds), and character building go around and come around, say the wise men, God's goodness multiplies in the lives of individuals, families, and nations. It is not the result of miraculous intervention or of some esoteric repetition of hidden "steps to victory and prosperity." It is the fruit of good character practiced in life's multiplied opportunities to choose between good and bad, wise and unwise.[17]

Finally, wisdom thus acquired will lead wise people in dealing with other persons properly.[18] The pages of Proverbs are fleshed out with a variety of folk who need the wisdom of the wise. You will meet the "simple" wandering about without purpose, the "fool" blundering on in persistent defiance of the obvious. The "wicked" proceed from mere foolishness to outright mockery and perversity, the "victimized" are seen being deprived of a just enjoyment

---

15   Prov. 4:10–12; 9:7–9; 13:18, 20; 26:16; 24:5–6; and many others.
16   Prov. 5:1–14; 16:3; 20:13; 21:17; 25:16, 28; 27:7; 29:3.
17   Please recognize also as you study these materials that there is no special pleading about the Abrahamic or Davidic covenants here. These teachings are universal for those who "fear the Lord." It is the way of God's creation. To the extent that cultures encourage or discourage this process, they will experience varying degrees of blessing and cursing.
18   Prov. 5:15–20; 6:16–19; 14:18; 15:25; 17:17; 22:22–25; 25:17; 26:7; 29:13; and many others.

Way to the City

of the fruits of their labor (whether material or less transient), and the "poor," who may be so due to a variety of factors, including some or all of the above or the various aspects of the curse brought on by the fall—pestilence, handicaps, disease, widowhood, etc. These folk are never treated as if they are one and the same person, though the simple person might start out poor through lack of experience, remain so because of increasingly foolish behavior, fall in with a wicked crowd and become both like them as well as their apparent victim, living a poor and dissolute life and being taken advantage of by those smarter and more diligent at evil than he. Rather, we are counseled to have a knowing insight into the way that character (and, by implication, cultural mores) must be shaped and taught by all kinds of "teachers"—personal and experiential—to produce beneficial results in life for all kinds of personal situations.[19] Thus do the aphoristic teachings of Proverbs jolt our thinking and our lives first this way, then that. But the conclusion is undeniable: If a person, a family, or a nation wants all the best of what may be made of life material and immaterial, they must listen to the wisdom of the wise.

Job and the Unseen Variable

Craig Blomberg makes Job out to be a "massive counterpoint to the Deuteronomistic cycles of blessing and privation based on obedience and disobedience."[20] Blomberg, though he is a fine scholar who has blessed the church in many ways, has in our opinion misunderstood both Deuteronomy and the Wisdom material, especially Job in his *Neither Poverty nor Riches*. He generalizes that "unseen forces, whether divine or demonic may well be at work in human affairs in ways people will never understand this side of eternity," and so states the obvious (even banal) without adding to the understanding of either the Decalogue (in its context as we have explicated it) and its promises or the Wisdom teachings and their observations about the connectedness of behaviors and results.[21]

---

19 To wit, such apparently contradictory advice as "answer a fool according to his folly" and "do not answer a fool according to his folly" (Prov. 26:4–5).
20 Blomberg, *Neither Poverty nor Riches*, 58. See also Witherington, *Jesus and Money*.
21 For Blomberg's discussion of the Decalogue, see pp. 39–55 of *Neither Poverty nor Riches*.

Job's suffering is clearly *not* of his own making and mystifies him and his so-called friends. The drama that unfolds turns this mystery into what amounts to a courtroom sequence of accusation and witness interrogation (with the friends as prosecution witnesses) and a kind of reversal that bids to put the judge himself on trial (for Job will not go quietly without a personal interview with the judge).[22] But the mystery does not extend to any problems with Deuteronomy's assurances about blessings and curses nor the Wisdom Literature's statements about life's many variables. The very fact that Job has his material and familial prosperity returned in the end serves to reinforce what those other portions of Scripture teach—there are norms of behavior and consequence that are the rule.

Job's case is, in fact, a reiteration of this truth. It required demonic (satanic) activity (with a divine permission) to disrupt the cycle of blessing on a righteous man engaged freely in daily enterprise.[23] Job's character as righteous in God's sight is everywhere and finally vindicated in the story. The temporary condition that makes for the story line is ultimately remedied, and both Torah and Wisdom are upheld. The conflict is over the advice of "friends," in the ancient Near Eastern wisdom tradition, to confess anything willy-nilly that will get the deity to relent and restore Job's fortunes.[24] Job, however, maintains his integrity against all assaults until God "answers," insisting he has nothing

---

22 Thus the "answer" from the whirlwind we noted above.

23 This is why even wicked men prosper materially, unless they are restrained by some higher authority or run afoul of even more wicked men. In the New Testament, the tax farmer Zacchaeus is an example of such a man ultimately restrained by the Savior.

24 See esp. Job 22–23 for the accusation of secret sin from the friends and Job's insistence on his integrity. Related to this, John H. Walton explores the retribution principle and how it factors into the dialogue between Job and his friends: "The Retribution Principle (RP) is the conviction that the righteous will prosper and the wicked will suffer, both in proportion to their respective righteousness and wickedness. In Israelite theology the principle was integral to the belief in God's justice. Since God is just, the Israelites believed it was incumbent on him to uphold the RP. Having a worldview in which God was absolutely just and compelled to maintain the RP, they developed the inevitable converse corollary, which affirmed that those who prospered must be righteous (i.e., favored by God) and those who suffered must be wicked (i.e., experiencing the judgment of God).... In contrast to this Israelite theology [basic acceptance of the RP], the biblical theology of the wisdom literature is more cautious and nuanced. The text never affirms the converse corollary, so it cannot be framed as a biblical teaching. Furthermore, Proverbs couches the RP in proverbial language, Ecclesiastes casts suspicion on it, and the book of Job details its limitations. Thus wisdom literature rejects the RP as providing a theodicy, yet embraces it in its theology." John H. Walton, with Kelly Lemon Vizcaino, *Job*, NIVAC (Grand Rapids, MI: Zondervan, 2012), 39, 44–45.

Way to the City

he knows to confess with specificity.[25] Nowhere is Job's prosperity made out to be an evil of itself—only a pretense for satanic slander. Nor is Job a "counterpoint" to the idea of some Deuteronomic theology that promises unparalleled blessing to the faithful.[26] As we have indicated, this is a *misinterpretation* of both Deuteronomy and Job. Deuteronomy 27–28, the main passage that promises blessing for faithfulness and cursing for unfaithfulness, is a text extended not to *individual* Israelites, but to the covenant *community as a whole*.[27] Individual Israelites will have their fortunes go up and down, but the nation as a whole will be blessed by God if they as a whole remain *faithful*. Job is in no way a "massive counterpoint" to that! Note also that Yahweh does not correct the "Satan" on the issue of whether Job's wealth is a blessing from heaven or not. The tacit assumption is that it is.

So, while Job's wealth is truly a blessing from God, it is not shown to be a digression from Scripture's teaching about the earthly process of its accumulation or the use to which it is put.[28] God's instigation of the dramatic "test" of Job's loyalty to himself is consonant with other biblical warnings about the delusional power of wealth. Job's "patience" (see James in the NT) with the process serves to show clearly that in the end there is nothing *inherently* irresistible in the temptations of prosperity, just as there is not in any other seductive influence.

Chasing the Wind: Ecclesiastes and the Worldly-Wise

Qoheleth[29] bids all who are in earshot to hear his sermon(s) on the "vanity" (lit. "emptiness," or more literally, "vaporous"-ness)[30] of life "under the sun,"

---

25 See John H. Walton, *Ancient Near Eastern* (Grand Rapids, MI: Baker, 2006), Kindle loc. 3499, for the contrast between ancient Near Eastern thought and Job's defense, Job 27:1–9.
26 This is Blomberg's argument. See *Neither Poverty nor Riches*, 58.
27 See, for instance, Paul R. House, *Old Testament Theology* (Downers Grove, IL: InterVarsity Press, 1998), 191–94.
28 No more eloquent defense exists in literature of the unjust accusations against the wealthy than Job's ongoing protest. See esp. 29:11–17 and 31:5–40.
29 Heb., "one who addresses an assembly," or more popularly, "the Preacher." But the term can also entail "one who assembles."
30 The meaning of the Hebrew, *hebel*, is a *crux intepretum* for many as they approach the canonical Ecclesiastes. We agree substantially with the work of Douglas B. Miller, "Qhohelet's Symbolic Uses of *hbl*," *JBL* 117 (1998): 437–54. The word is used in conjunction with

clearly reflecting on and exploring the inadequate perspective of "this world only" thinking.[31] Though it is obvious he has his own faith in the biblical God of the Torah (12:13–14) and a hope for another world and/or existence to come (3:21) as well as an assurance that earthly life itself is a gift from God (2:24), his "preaching" focuses on the apparent futility inherent in the process we have seen elsewhere as the cycle of blessing and cursing, a world where sin and grace coexist.[32] A canonical context for the book in the covenant community of the return from exile is a compelling interpretive pointer,[33] for it is more than simple conjecture to surmise that Qoheleth sees the "bent"-ness of the world as truly God's doing (1:15; 7:13; cf. Job 12:14; Isa. 14:27). Thus the vaporous nature of any human attempt to set things right bids the community to make its way in dependence on the providence of their covenant-keeping God who will ultimately resolve the conflict of blessing and curse in which they have been caught. This in spite of the fact that his ways are at the present time "past finding out."

The Preacher's[34] unique contribution is that of one who has had the opportunity to actually experience all that life "under the sun" can give. He knows firsthand the life of fabulous wealth (2:1–11)—a life without the normal limits imposed on "working people." He had enough to indulge every whim, including time for the contemplation of all life's vagaries. From the sheer possession of vast quantities of those commodities that can be readily converted to other desirable material things, to the expenditure of unlimited

---

numerous observations about the good and evil in life, and begs to be interpreted without forcing a static meaning upon it.

31   For a thorough discussion of the perspective(s) enshrined and canonized in Ecclesiastes, see *The Southern Baptist Journal of Theology* 15, no. 3 (Fall 2011). Particularly helpful are Jason S. DeRouchie, "Shepherding Wind and One Wise Shepherd: Grasping for Breath in Ecclesiastes," 4–25, and A. B. Caneday, "'Everything Is Vapor': Grasping for Meaning Under the Sun," 26–40.

32   We note that the first use of the Hebrew word *hebel* is the sighing (?) breath of Eve as she announces the name of her second child, "Abel" (Gen. 4:2), a possible confession of her own frustrations and a harbinger of her son's fleeting life.

33   See DeRouchie, "Shepherding Wind," 14–15. DeRouchie holds to Solomonic origins for the material canonically placed among the Writings of the Hebrew Scriptures.

34   Solomon is surely the most attractive option as the likely source of such insights as we have here, but consult the standard commentaries and introductions for detailed documentation on origins for this material with this caveat: many have allowed the perplexing nature of the material to color their view of its orthodoxy and intent.

Way to the City

sums on anything that is pleasurable to man, to the ability to engage in any idle avocation or self-satisfying pursuit, such as the study of wisdom, Solomon had it all—at least "all" that one might have or pursue "under the sun." To any and everyone in a potential audience the Preacher is able to say, "Been there and done that." That audience includes the envious who might ask themselves, "What would I do if I were rich?"; the unseeing, who think that all there is is "under the sun"; the wise, who think, as did Job's friends, that everything comes in a neat package; the elite, those in every society who believe they have the ability to lead the way if they possessed the power to be a leisure class. To all these, wealth and power and leisure prove to be vain, empty, devoid of meaning, vaporous—without the benefit of the blessing of God in heavenly perspective (i.e., the one that is not "under the sun").

The key issue for modern students of Qoheleth is whether or not he affirms the fundamental assumptions of the other biblical materials: those who faithfully serve God can expect his blessing and those who do not will receive a curse. The answer to this question is unambiguous.[35] Solomon's sermonizing is neither cynical nor iconoclastic. Rather, through most of the book he speaks of the futility of life on its own merits, but concludes on a note of hopefulness, as long as life is lived with the recognition that God is the source of all that is good: "Fear God, and keep his commandments" (12:13 KJV) for these and other "words of the wise . . . are given from one shepherd" (12:11 KJV), a reference to the Creator who alone deciphers the inscrutable and knows it exhaustively, unlike his creatures.[36] In his bare-knuckle way Qoheleth affirms our ongoing theme that the sovereignty of God, in spite of the sinfulness and depravity of man (7:29) and the brokenness of the cosmos, guides the whole and commands and blesses obedience through the revelation of his "words" and the interpretive work of his Spirit throughout the genres of Scripture. Ecclesiastes in its unrelenting as-

---

35 Contra Blomberg's caricature of the material as a "protest." See *Neither Poverty nor Riches*. Dr. Blomberg is not alone as a skeptic about the nature of this material. We recognize Qoheleth's complexity and edginess, what Brian Borgman refers to as "the shock jock" of Wisdom in "Redeeming the 'Problem Child': Qoheleth's Message and Place in the Family of Scripture," *SBJT* 15, no. 3 (Fall 2011): 62. However, we are more in agreement with the position of Walter C. Kaiser Jr., *Ecclesiastes: Total Life* (Chicago: Moody, 1979), 11, that no book of the Bible has been "so maligned and yet so misunderstood."
36 See Derouchie, "Shepherding Wind," 12–14.

Way to the City

sessment of life's apparently chaotic relationships warns us of "the barrenness of life without a practical faith in God."[37] But it is not a *counterpoint* to "Deuteronomic" theology nor to Proverbs. The conclusion, that there is "nothing better" than enjoying the things that make life tolerable and enjoyable (good food, good times, a good wife, enough money, etc.),[38] is clearly tempered with warnings to "remember your Creator" early and often (11:7–12:14, et al.) because even those blessed by God in this life will inevitably face death ("the curse") and judgment. This is the underlying truth behind the cycle of blessing and cursing (what A. B. Caneday calls the interplay of "insubstantiality, transitoriness, and foulness")[39]—no temporal blessing can overcome the curse of death and all its attendant ministers (i.e., toil, weariness, disease, pestilence, natural disasters, banality, youth and aging, etc.), and no temporal curse need pursue any person into eternity. Such wisdom begs to be juxtaposed with that of the one who said, "Lay not up for yourselves treasures on earth."

Therefore, it is best within the context of honoring God as Creator and giver to *enjoy* what one is given; pay no undue attention to life's inequities, anomalies, and mysteries; take a positive approach to life and work, while ignoring (or at least not giving improper power to) what one cannot control; and diversify your investments enough prudently to anticipate fruit to come from something—even the totally forgotten and unexpected (11:1–6). All else is like "shepherding the wind," or in the modern vernacular, "herding cats."

SONG OF SONGS AND THE JOYS OF LIFE

The juxtaposition of Ecclesiastes and Song of Solomon in our Bibles is surely more than fortuitous—it is profoundly appropriate. Can anything be more striking than the answer of a human love song, informed by a biblical view

---

37 Michael A. Eaton, *Ecclesiastes: An Introduction and Commentary*, TOTC (Downers Grove, IL: InterVarsity Press, 1983), 45. Derek Kidner mirrors this with his view that Ecclesiastes is a "searching criticism of human self-sufficiency." *The Wisdom of Proverbs, Job and Ecclesiastes* (Downers Grove, IL: InterVarsity Press, 1985), 93.

38 See 8:15 and 9:7–10 et al. The summary of 5:18–20 is a clear indicator of the direction one should take when blessed by God with more than adequate material possessions. Enjoy them while you can. There may come a day when you will not be able to do so (6:1–4).

39 Caneday, "Everything Is Vapor," 34. He is following Douglas Miller at this point, n. 33.

of the sexes, to a world-weary sampler (Solomon) of the pleasures inherent in human existence? Solomon (in our thinking) is the focal character in each of these Wisdom books and appears to be drawing us to see how sinful indulgence in multiplied pleasures pales when compared to the overwhelming power and joy of marital love.[40] Canticles celebrates and validates with unbridled exuberance the ancient human practice of lavish expenditure upon our most cherished values.[41] As a kind of exclamation point, this little book bids us see that God takes no pleasure in joys missed, lost, or tossed away in fruitless meandering through life's bazaar. Rather, as in Eden, he bids us plumb the depths and heights of his best gifts within the confines of his revealed will. Let the cup be full and overflow. Bring the best of everything to the celebration!

WISDOM IN THE PSALMS

The book of Psalms begins with what might be called a wisdom poem with eternal moral implications. The exclamation of "blessedness" for "the righteous," contrasted with the pronouncement of doom for "the ungodly," is a paean to material and eternal consequences for earthly actions and worship. As such, it introduces a book[42] that wrestles everywhere with the contrast between God's promise of "blessing" to those who obey him and the apparent ability of the "wicked" to prosper and get away with it, many times at the expense of those more righteous than they. In passages of soaring praise, agonizing despair, profound theological reflection, and soul-searching prayer, the poetry of Israel's experience with life and God leads us to reflect exhaustively on the joys, successes, defeats, and incongruities of time and eternity. The wisdom espoused in many of these poems/songs is reflective of what we see

---

40 This would appear to be true whether one views the male lover as Solomon or an unknown shepherd boy.

41 One is reminded of the assumptions of the two Marys in their dealings with Jesus—one expecting his miracle of winemaking at a lavish feast and the other anticipating his burial with an expenditure of costly ointment, this last over the protest of the bagman, "who cared not for the poor," though he protested loudly (see John 2:1–11; 12:1–8, respectively).

42 See esp. Robert Alter's treatment of the final assembly of the Psalter and the first two poems as introductory, *The Book of Psalms: A Translation with Commentary* (New York: W. W. Norton, 2007). The First Psalm states the basic rule and the Second notes the role of the coming king whose rule we see again as the hope for the future.

Way to the City

elsewhere in the OT Wisdom Literature. Robert Alter is careful to point out also that the language of the Hebrew psalmists is overwhelmingly concrete in its expressions of the expected "blessings," a feature that shows God as the "rescuer" in the situations of life, "where the spiritual was realized through the physical, and divine purposes were implemented in social, political and even military realms."[43] This makes the wisdom of Psalms even more telling for our subject.

The uniqueness of Psalms is that its content is the unabashed interaction with and worship of Israel's God, seen as a universal sovereign and covenant-keeper.[44] This universalism (which we shall see expanded in the prophets) is pertinent to our study, for it moves the concept of "blessing" away from a narrow focus on Israel's singular relationship with Yahweh.[45] We see here a clear emphasis on the rule of God for all undiminished by its mediation through the Abrahamic and Davidic covenants. The blessing of God, with its attendant accountability, is a part of God's evident plan to extend his rule to all peoples in all times and into eternity.[46] Therefore, what we learn about success and failure in life here is applicable at all times and in all cultures.[47] Those who would have us relegate economic and material blessing to Israel only as a part of their peculiar covenantal relationship do not deal with the clear promise to Abraham (which Paul treats as superseding the covenant of law at Sinai) of blessing to all nations on account of him (Abraham).

---

43 Alter, *Psalms*, Kindle loc. 296–317, where he sets forth the case for his translation.

44 Psalm 15 is particularly pertinent with its emphasis on public and economic life as qualifying one to worship. This requires no covenantal signs or externals nor even sacrifice and is in keeping with Solomon's prayer that all peoples might find answers to prayer at the temple (2 Chron. 6:32–33). Most relevant to our study is that the prayers offered here and expected to be heard are for blessings of all kinds including the economic. The person(s) welcomed are also universally designated in Pss. 24:1 and 84:5[6], 12[13]. Note the repeated use of '*adam* in the Hebrew text of Ps. 84.

45 For a thorough and thought-provoking treatment of the universalism of the Psalms, see Walter C. Kaiser Jr., *Mission in the Old Testament: Israel as Light to the Nations* (Grand Rapids, MI: Baker, 2000), chap. 2, Kindle loc. 288–385. Psalm 67 is particularly pertinent to the current discussion.

46 This is a key emphasis in Psalm 33, where the special blessing of Israel (v. 12) is accompanied with an invitation to all nations to join in the blessing of Israel, and Psalm 65 where the invitation is even more specific and individual.

47 Kaiser lays a firm foundation for this assertion in his previously cited works, *Promise-Plan of God* and *Mission in the Old Testament*.

Way to the City

We will mention six of these briefly in the space we have here. First, praise to God is appropriate for all kinds of personal and corporate or cultural good things. These can range from personal prosperity to success in war and cover the full range of human experiences. Nothing is excluded because nothing escapes God's sovereign purview. The theological center for this praise and thanksgiving is that either the God of Israel is the true blessor, or "other gods" are (perish the thought!), or some superstitious process is, or we are just beneficiaries of blind luck. It is clear that the first option is the only one for the psalmists.

Second, prayer is always appropriate in times of gain or loss. And the prayers run the full range of human emotions from complaint to appeals for relief and success to cries for insight and understanding to invocations of revenge and punishment. Nowhere is there the slightest implication of inappropriateness in this praying, as if something were too trivial for God or, obviously, too great.[48] To the contrary, it is in the process of prayer that insight into self and circumstances bursts upon the mind and heart.

Third, this process leads people to other things that may or must be "done" besides the praying and praising. This can range from meditation upon God's law to personal confessions of guilt to testimony to others to a complete reform of one's actions. Neither praise nor prayer is seen as a magic talisman with which to manipulate circumstances for personal advantage. But they are seen as means to corrective actions that will be beneficial to ourselves and others around us, and in the case of a ruler like David, to a nation. This is neither a "name-it-and-claim-it" prosperity gospel nor a "praise-the-Lord-praise-the-Lord" strategy for dismissing pain and loss. It is a biblical way to proceed in life.

Fourth, a lifelong sense of perspective comes from managing life in this way. It is the source of the theology of Psalm 1 and others. A wisdom poem such as Psalm 37 is a puzzle to some, but it is an example of a perspective

---

48 On vengeance, we are aware of the difficulties surrounding the "imprecatory" prayers in the thinking of many. The space of this work does not allow for a full discussion of this issue. We will state our position in two observations. First, no other place in Scripture condemns these prayers (but see our discussion of Jesus' teaching in the Sermon on the Mount). Second, a prayer to God for vengeance is entirely consistent with other places in Scripture that teach us not to take personal vengeance and let God handle it. Imprecatory psalms "guide or channel our anger *to* and *through* God, verbally, rather to or at anyone else, verbally or physically" (Fee and Stuart, *How to Read the Bible*, 182). Where else shall we go but to him for justice to be done?

Way to the City

gained through lifelong reflection, meditation, and prayer, guided by God's law. Thus, its writer can state unequivocally, "I have been young and now I am old but I have not seen the righteous forsaken or his seed begging bread" (v. 25).[49] His faith is based on the long-term observation of life, not the short-term look at current circumstances.[50] He sees at least dimly the outlines of an eternal answer also (vv. 37–38). Even more clear on this is the author of Psalm 73, who can state clearly, "You will guide me with your counsel, and afterward receive me to glory" (v. 24). Throughout the Psalms the promise of blessing is found to be true despite contrary appearances by those with a long view.

Fifth, the psalmists regularly acknowledge the need to avoid sinful attitudes and actions when they are being victimized or are observing the "flourishing" of the wicked. They note how destructive envy can be to one's personal stability (Ps. 73:3). They seek to avoid being like them or imitating their activities (Pss. 1:1–3; 84:10; etc.). They seek not personal vengeance, but God's righteous interventions (Pss. 59, 62, 137, et al.). They wrestle against blaming God and confess their own foolishness and sinfulness (Pss. 32 and 51). They are aware that expressing improperly their profoundest misunderstandings and soul-searchings could be damaging to the immature, so they refrain from speaking out too quickly (Ps. 73:15–16). In these ways the psalmists of Israel highlight the need for self-examination and personal maturity when dealing with life's multiplied vicissitudes. They thus avoid a victim mentality and are better for it in more ways than the spiritual.

---

49 Blomberg, *Neither Poverty nor Riches*, finds this verse as one to "raise serious questions," 61. Does this mean he doubts that it is true (as his statement could be construed) or that it is idealistic (as it appears in his interpretation)? The key words are "forsaken" and "begging bread," terms that denote absolute destitution among those capable of obeying the command to work and using God's wisdom to prosper. It is assumed throughout the OT that the classes of folk (widows, orphans, aliens, disabled) unable to take advantage of God's bounty in the normal way will be taken care of by the believing community.

50 See also Craigie, *Psalms 1–50*, WBC, ad loc., for the same take on this passage as we are defending. Psalm 37:24 in context also sounds like Paul at 2 Cor. 4:7–12 and other places where he suffers want and abounds but is never ever "forsaken." This is ever Israel's hope (Isa. 42:16) and confession (Ezra 9:9). The most profound use of this wording is, of course, Jesus' use of it from the cross in quoting Ps. 22:1. This was coupled with Ps. 16:10 by the church in his case. Finally, Psalm 37 points us to the true ultimate "forsaking" in v. 28, that of the wicked.

Way to the City

Finally, Psalms assures us that sufferings, losses, and defeats come to all without compromising the promise of God to bless the righteous. This is still the case even though the nation be caught up in exile for its sin, and the ideal Zion (the city of Yahweh) seems to have become nothing but a lost dream (Ps. 137). Life, since the fall, encompasses levels of pain that go beyond mere hard work or struggle to achieve goals. Some of it cannot or will not be mitigated and must be endured. However, when endured in the ways the Psalms teach, sufferings become beneficial to us and to others who may be willing to benefit from the experiences of those around them. This last is, of course, the wonderful theme of sacrificial and vicarious sufferings, which culminates in the glory of the cross of Christ and in the lives of those who truly follow him (Pss. 22 and 69 especially). Those who live in this manner in any age or culture will find it a far more rewarding and successful way than that of going through life acting as if the world and life owed them for "all they've been through."

CONCLUSION

In the midst of his defense of his situation, Job recounts at length the assumptions of the wise with reference to their obligations and duties to others: to God, to the afflicted and oppressed, to those who depend upon them, to the young and the old (Job 24, 29 and 31 are particularly striking). All of the Wisdom materials assume these obligations as personal matters of conscience to be attended with great care. We have not enumerated them, because all seem to be in agreement about the teaching of Scripture on these matters and we have previously marked their importance. The burden of this chapter has been that the "blessing" for which all seek, both material and spiritual, is not an unworthy quest and is to be sought and found in the wisdom that only God can give. It is what Satan offered in the garden and could not deliver. Because of this disastrous event, humankind seeks without finding, not because God is not generous and willing to give, but because man from the beginning has sought it apart from the Giver.

Way to the City

Chapter 5

The Prophets and Justice

It has become almost a cliché to associate the preaching and writing of the prophets of Israel with calls for "social justice." This is a valid emphasis in its right context. From the first words of the prophet/judge Samuel inveighing against the greedy and perverse practices of Eli's sons, to Nathan's "Thou art the man," to Elijah's confrontation with Ahab in Naboth's vineyard, to Elisha's denunciation of his acquisitive servant's misuse of Naaman's wealth and position, to the rise of the writing and preaching prophets of the eighth to the fifth century B.C., the work of prophesying in Israel was political and social as well as what we would call "religious." The prophets counsel and condemn kings for their politics and social policies. They warn about the dangers of trusting in wealth and armaments and armies and especially the beastly governments around them that posed as allies.[1] They pronounce judgment on wealthy exploiters of the poor and disadvantaged and upon common (and poor) people who acquiesce in the sins of their leadership. And in countless instances they show what astute observers of contemporary mores they are by the Spirit of the Lord.[2]

---

1 This is surely the most telling observation to be made from the juxtaposition of oracles against the nations among the prophecies to Israel and Judah. Both nations sought alliances with pagan nations rather than turning in repentance their own God, Yahweh. The prophets warned that these nations were in even greater danger than Israel and Judah, for they would never rise again from the ashes of coming judgment.
2 See esp. E. J. Young, *My Servant the Prophets* (Grand Rapids, MI: Eerdmans, 1952); W. J. Beecher, *The Prophets and the Promise* (New York: Cornell University Library, 1905); H. E.

In so doing, these forth-tellers and foretellers from Samuel to Malachi demonstrate God's concern about far more than religion and religious observances and Israel's adherence to cultic form. They are earthy, though not earthbound. They are mostly fearless and pull no punches and court no favors with the mighty; that was the bailiwick of the professional "prophets and sons of the prophets." These men and the occasional woman stand mostly as lonely sentinels, "watchmen," in their times, occasionally seconded by an overlapping ministry of an equally lonely man. What was their "burden," and how did they present it?

A Call to True Worship

Overwhelmingly, these true prophets were concerned with the first three commandments of the Decalogue as their chief indictment against Israel, for the people had persistently failed to worship only Yahweh, had filled the land of promise with idols, and had thus taken Yahweh's name upon themselves in an empty display ("in vain"). No examination of the work and writings of the OT prophets can possibly begin without recognizing this fact. Their primary mission, their pervasive and unending task, was to call God's covenant people first, and through them all peoples, to worship the one true God exclusively and completely. They were not first social and political reformers—they were revivalists and awakeners to genuine faith in God. To the extent that they were on the side of those who had remained faithful to Yahweh in spite of the times, they were comforters of true believers, the "poor" (Isa. 61:1, who are here the "meek" and Isa. 59:20, "those who turn from transgression in Jacob"). But they were decidedly discomforters to the comfortable who were "at ease in Zion."[3]

Freeman, *An Introduction to the Old Testament Prophets* (Grand Rapids, MI: Baker, 1968); and Abraham Joshua Heschel, *The Prophets: Two Volumes in One* (1962; repr., Peabody, MA: Hendrickson, 2007).

3   Compare our thesis with that of Craig L. Blomberg, *Neither Poverty nor Riches* (Downers Grove, IL: InterVarsity Press, 1999), 70: "One has only to read in its entirety virtually any book of prophecy at random to see that at least as serious as the Israelites' ethical sins was their idolatry." We contend that this is upside down. The condemnation of specific sin is a consequence of the overwhelming condemnation of idolatry. They are defenders of the theocracy first, social commentators second; moreover, idolatry is the overwhelming

In the context of this singular mission to call for the true worship of Yahweh as commanded at Sinai, it is surely proper to emphasize the aspects of their message that are what we might call "social." What is not proper is to allow this one facet of their overall message to become a rallying cry for "reforms" in a twenty-first-century setting divorced from a call for the worship of the one true God revealed at Sinai and in the Scriptures. The idolatry charge takes precedence over the social concerns because no true benefaction can happen without the clarity of Yahweh worship. He is the dispenser of "good and evil"[4] and is the source of all wisdom. Only the theocracy can produce the outcomes associated with the wishes of modern "social justice" experimenters. This primary call is grounds for every other application of the further demands emanating from the fire on the mountain in the wilderness. They cannot be made to say something more or less than was revealed there. The Torah of God is the text and context for the preaching of the true prophets. Only "false" prophets would do otherwise—whether "adding to" or "taking away."[5] Zephaniah will call this being "fickle" (3:4 ESV), a word that means reckless or unreliable.

What then is the meaning and content of the call for behavioral change in the prophets? It is the Decalogue in its full contextual development. The logic of it all is inescapable. Just as we have seen in our prior discussion of Torah, each demand of the Law is first dependent on the worship of God and is a reflection of his character. The expansions in case law reflect the same thing—as we saw it, "what is right in the sight of God." The prophets are preachers of God's law to their contemporaries with up-to-date specifics.[6] If there is to be

---

theme of the preaching, which is summarized at 2 Kings 17:6–23; 21:1–26; 23:26–27. This theme is documented in full scholarly detail by G. K. Beale, *We Become What We Worship* (Downers Grove, IL: InterVarsity Press, 2008), Kindle ed. See esp. Kindle loc. 499–506 on these passages. See also Daniel I. Block, "Other Religions in Old Testament Theology," in *Biblical Faith and Other Religions: An Evangelical Assessment,* ed. David W. Baker (Grand Rapids, MI: Baker, 2003), 43–78.

4   See, e.g., Isa. 41:23; 45:7; Amos 3:6.
5   See esp. Jer. 14:13–16; Deut. 18:20; Ezek. 13:6; among many other passages that warn of the danger and doom of the false prophets.
6   See the clear example at Jer. 7:1–11 where the full gamut of sins is specified—with the specifics of disobedience to the Decalogue unpacking the generic reference to social ills—as disqualification of their worship. See also on this Dan. 9 (esp. v. 13), Ezra 9 and 10 and Neh. 9 and 10 and the reform under Hezekiah (2 Chron. 31:20–21), all according to Torah, and

Way to the City

hope in repentance, then that which calls us to repentance must be specified. This is the essence of Yahwistic religion—God's will has been clearly revealed from Sinai onward and the misfortunes of the nation can be traced to the failure of Israel's covenantal obligations. In fact, all the nations will ultimately be held to the same standard in the final assize (Isa. 2:2–5), for "torah" and "word" are the essence of justice (v. 3),[7] just as all nations have the right to come to the temple in Jerusalem and pray to Israel's God for mercy and prosperity (2 Chron. 6:32–33; Isa. 56:7).

The sin(s) of Israel and Judah show up as personal and social and cultural and cultic. But the denunciation is couched, as God's "word" always is, in specific demands aimed at specific sins committed by specific people.[8] Most readers, teachers, and commentators can see this clearly when Amos (2:7) speaks of a man and his son "going in to" the same woman or when Ezekiel (22:11) condemns adultery and incest. But it is not uncommon to see, as an interpretation of prophetic utterances on economic sin, the simple dictum, "God is on the side of the poor,"[9] as if this meant all people not in this category are being condemned as exploiters of the poor and helpless and therefore are responsible for their plight wherever they may be in the world.[10] Others

Josiah (2 Chron. 34:19), that was the result of discovery of the book of the Torah in the temple. Also, see Hos. 4:1–6 and the following context; Isa. 47:9–10; 48:5; Mic. 5:12–6:8; Nah. 1:4; 3:4; and many others. The context of any social commentary is clearly Torah, and the Decalogue in particular. See John Andrew Dearman, *Property Rights in the Eighth-Century Prophets: The Conflict and Its Background* (Atlanta: Scholars, 1988), 58–59, for a listing and chart of the usage by the prophets of the specifics of Pentateuchal citations.

7 Cf. Bruce Waltke's comment on Micah 3:1–4 in *New Bible Commentary: 21st Century Edition*, 4th ed. (Leicester: Inter-Varsity Press, 1994), and his more expanded treatment in Bruce K. Waltke, *A Commentary on Micah* (Grand Rapids: Eerdmans, 2007), 143–57.

8 This is in clear distinction from nations around the ancient Near East who, when experiencing theodicy, did not know what to confess or how to certainly placate their gods. See on this John H. Walton, *Ancient Near Eastern Thought* (Grand Rapids, MI: Baker, 2006), at numerous points.

9 See our discussion of this terminology in chap. 25.

10 An example of this type of extrapolation occurs in Blomberg, *Neither Poverty nor Riches*, 68, where to establish his neither/nor theme he quotes approvingly Kenneth Aitken's commentary on Prov. 30:8: "If individuals and nations were thus contented, two-thirds of the world's population would not be living in poverty." See Kenneth T. Aitken, *Proverbs*, DSB (Edinburgh: Saint Andrews University Press / Philadelphia: Westminster, 1986), 190. We would challenge Dr. Aitken to prove such a bald assertion. After quoting from the prophets several passages of general condemnation of fraudulent and oppressive behavior, Blomberg further opines that "the texts in Amos should give well-to-do Westerners

Way to the City

condemn this interpretive oversimplification as being inconsistent with the clear teaching of Torah (which it is), while muddling the message of Israel's eighth-to fifth-century prophets with "popular social sins in our cultures."[11] Sider is even more strident as he threatens with hellfire "many evangelical leaders," whom he characterizes as "idolatrous heretics" for failing to "teach their people what God tells them to say" about the poor. Rhetorically he asks, "does not the widespread neglect of the poor in the American church mean we are in danger of eternal damnation?"[12] One would question whether there is such a widespread "neglect of the poor," given the "widespread" commitment of evangelical churches to ministering to physical needs.[13]

The prophets never generalize in this way. They have a clear agenda. Lest their message be misunderstood or ignored, they draw their auditors (and readers) in to see in graphic detail what it is God so detests. Namely, it is

---

considerable pause, especially those who seem largely indifferent to the needs of the poor worldwide." *Neither Poverty nor Riches*, 75. He also cites (apparently with approval) Carol and Eric Meyers in their commentary on Zechariah as they "wonder 'whether there is some subconscious critique of a market economy at work here. If buying and selling goods is a merismic construction representing the totality of economic dealings, then on a literal level the message is that such activity cannot have a positive outcome; whatever happens, the flock comes to ruin.'" Carol L. Meyers and Eric M. Meyers, *Zechariah 9–14: A New Translation with Introduction and Commentary*, Anchor Bible 25C (New York and London: Doubleday, 1993), 255, quoted in Blomberg, *Neither Poverty nor Riches*, 75n27. T. Desmond Alexander uses the same guilt by association to condemn "greed" by the use of generalized wealth distribution statistics in *From Eden to the New Jerusalem: Exploring God's Plan for Life on Earth* (Nottingham: Inter-Varsity Press, 2008), 184–85.

11 Blomberg, *Neither Poverty nor Riches*, 70. Just exactly what "popular social sins" he means is unclear, except in his ongoing rhetoric of "neither wealth nor poverty" as a "mandate" (68). While it is surely correct to point out the specific sins of those who exploit the weak in disobedience to the law of God, there is no mandate in any part of Scripture to condemn affluence or richness as a "popular social sin." In fairness, Blomberg does list specifically the sins of Israel delineated by the prophets, but he furnishes no link to the twenty-first century except generalities. He characterizes a "'middle-class' ideal" as inadequate to his own neither/nor theme (because "80% of Westerners consider themselves middle-class") and commends "'give me only my daily bread'" as the apparent "mandate" he seeks, though neither he nor any other advocate for the poor we have researched ever names this "daily-bread-only" theme as a goal for the poor, only for the rich. It is hard to resist the conclusion that this is exactly what Blomberg is driving toward in his book. See particularly p. 245 in his conclusions.

12 Ronald J. Sider, "Are Evangelical Leaders on Their Way to Hell?" pt. 5 in *I Am Not a Social Activist: Making Jesus the Agenda* (Scottsdale, PA: Herald, 2008), Kindle loc. 749–59.

13 One of us (Chad Brand) serves a church in poverty-stricken eastern Kentucky, and my church is a center-point for a very active ministry to the poor that is supported by many churches from Kentucky, Tennessee, Georgia, Ohio, Indiana, and other states.

Way to the City

taking precious goods from the blessing of God and fashioning idols for the worship of that which is vain, vile, and abominable.[14] It is exploiting, oppressing, and defrauding the weak and helpless through dishonest and malevolent business practices sanctioned by rulers.[15] It is accumulating wealth in contravention of the Sabbath mandates, which we discussed in the previous materials on Torah.[16] It is letting God's blessing in material wealth become one's focus of security and a blinder to moral degradation rampant around oneself.[17] It is spending the blessed wealth God has provided on alcohol abuse and partying.[18] It is allowing the allure of wealth and political power to pervert government, so that it becomes no place for "redress of grievances."[19] It is phony repentance (Jer. 34:8–22), trust in political and military power contrary to God's revealed will (see Jeremiah's preaching in the last days of the monarchy),[20] and failure to trust God's ability to restore blessing in contradiction to all apparent realities (Jer. 32–33).[21] And always and everywhere it is adultery and stealing and lying witness in court and murder and Baal worship during

14 Isa. 2:7ff; Jer. 10:3–5; Hab. 1:16ff.; and many others. See esp. Ezekiel's use of "dung pellets" thirty-eight times to designate idols. Block, "Other Religions in Old Testament Theology," 62–64. This is "the evil" in Israel: Deut. 4:25; 13:5[6]; and seven times in the book of Judges.

15 Isa. 3:14–15; Ezek. 22:7, 9, 12–13; 45:9–12; Amos 2:6; 8:5–8; Mal. 3:5; et al. It has been noted in several sources that archaeological discoveries in the northern kingdom at Tirzah show marked differentiation between the tenth and eighth centuries B.C. in the disparity between housing districts of the extremely wealthy and the poorest. The thing that changed was the arrival of a king and kingdom, where there had been none but in Jerusalem before.

16 Isa. 5:8; Ezek. 22:8; Amos 8:5; Mic. 2:2; et al.

17 Amos 4:1–6; Isa. 2:7; Hos. 2:8; Ezek. 16:49; et al.

18 Isa. 5:11–12, 22; 22:13; 28:1, 7; 56:12; Mic. 2:11; Joel 1:5; and many others.

19 Isa. 1:23; 10:1ff.; 56:9–12; Hos. 5:10; Mic. 3:11; Ezek. 22:6; 45:8ff.; et al. See esp. Amos 5:10–15, where the rebuke is despised "in the gate," meaning where the court case is heard. More on this subject below.

20 Note also that the intrigues of the period of Isaiah's ministry (and others) concern the constant temptation to kings in Judah and Israel to engage in foreign alliances with kingdoms such that these kings ultimately will come into judgment against conquerors who in turn will also come into judgment.

21 For just as Israel (and her neighbors) is condemned in no uncertain terms for her lawlessness, she is just as clearly invited to receive mercy in the form of a current reprieve or a future "return" from punishing circumstances or both. In the same vein is Ezekiel's vision(s) of the time of restoration and the "prince" who reverses the habit of the kings foretold by Samuel and illustrated by Jezebel and others, who made it possible in the words of Isaiah to join "house to house" and "field to field" (5:8) through government corruption and individual collusion for dishonest gain, and the failure to enforce the Jubilee law, which would restore to previous owners the family inheritance, not redistribute land to whoever.

Way to the City

the week and then attendance at temple on Sabbath as though all is well (Jer. 7:9–11).[22] Disappointingly, it appears to be quintessentially focused ultimately in Judah's capital city, Jerusalem, as it is characterized a "bloody city" with more the look of Sodom than the "city of the great king."[23]

Finally, as we have seen in all the other OT genres, we see the note of universalism in the prophets. The prophets inveigh against the sins of Israel's neighbors[24] thus showing that the sins that called forth God's word through the prophets is not merely a breach of the special covenantal burden Israel bears, but a failure of all nations to obey God's rule in his creation. Israel's culpability is made worse by her special privilege,[25] but this serves as a reason to make her a spectacle before the nations in her punishment.[26] Just as surely as her pain has been a lesson to the nations, her rejoicing in restoration and return will be an even greater boon to all peoples, both temporal and eternal (Mic. 4:2–5; Isa. 40–66; et al.). And, lest we forget, ultimately the judgment (curse) sent by example upon the nation of Israel shall by the same universal standard be meted out to the nations.[27] Consequently, for Israel or any other entity to seek "justice" through alliances with these governmental powers is to court the final disaster awaiting all the beastly powers on earth—a final and irrevocable end.

Zechariah 14:9 states it succinctly: "And the LORD shall be king over all the earth." This is, of course, an eschatological promise. How one views its applications depends ultimately on the interpretation of eschatology as a theological construct. Most evangelicals of our time hold to either an amillennial or premillennial schema. A few interpreters still hold to a postmillennial system of some sort.[28] The first two systems lead generally to a pessimistic view

---

22 See also Ezek. 18 for the longest litany in the prophets.
23 See Isa. 1 throughout for this indictment of the seat of government and worship as the ultimate problem. Our discussion below will unpack this issue.
24 See, famously, Amos' opening salvos as well as passages in Isaiah, Jeremiah, Daniel, et al.
25 See esp. Ezek. 22 and his repeated emphasis on "in her," that is Jerusalem, as the locale of the great sins.
26 Jer. 22:8; 26:6; Ezek. 5:5–12.; et al.
27 Isa. 40–66; Jer. 46 and on; Joel 3:3; Hag. 2:7; Zech. 14:3–5; et al.
28 Most notably, Reconstructionist (or Theonomic) theologies, though it is not limited to them. On that approach to theology and ethics, see William S. Barker and W. Robert Godfrey, eds., *Theonomy: A Reformed Critique* (Grand Rapids, MI: Zondervan, 1990).

Way to the City

of the possibility of reforming human nature and controlling it to the extent that a utopian vision of social and political interaction can be achieved, that is, without a radical intervention of the rule of God imposed from the heavenly realm. The postmillennial vision has a more optimistic position on the subject.[29] We are of the persuasion that the first two views (especially the second) more nearly represent the proper understanding of the prophets and the rest of the biblical material.[30] This leads us to conclude that the rule of law (especially that revealed in Torah) will continue to be necessary to curb and train human nature in social interaction short of the establishment of God's universal rule "on earth as it is in heaven." To this, the prophets continue to testify.

No study of the prophetic word(s), however, would be complete without coming to grips with the underlying theme, which guides the critique of Israel's governance and sociocultural development. That theme is the failure of the Davidic monarchy to bring in the justice envisioned in Torah. To that we now turn.

THE FAILURE OF HUMAN RULE

It is appropriate at this point to summarize the narrative(s) that inform the prophets as they critique Israelite governmental and social life. What follows is our overview of that critique.

Man was created free under God's rule and as his vice-regent for rule over creation. Redeemed humanity is destined to return to this state in the new heavens and new earth, as we shall see. The original Adamic "rule" is marred, essentially destroyed in its true intent, by our first parents' failure to govern themselves appropriately and to fulfill their original "dominion" in the garden. Between the two termini of history mankind's fallen state intrudes, and thus governments have their function and purpose as sanctioned by the Creator.

---

29 Postmillennialism has had a storied past. Earlier (Puritan and Reformed) versions of postmillennialism held to a Calvinistic view of depravity but contended that a massive revival of evangelical Christianity would convert the world to Christ. Later, liberal versions held that Christian moral principles and the rise of technology and modernity would remake the world into a sort of Christianized utopia. (See, e.g., James Leo Garrett Jr., *Systematic Theology: Biblical, Historical, and Evangelical* [Grand Rapids, MI: Eerdmans, 1995], 2:760–69). More on this later.

30 Sun Wook Chung and Craig L. Blomberg, *A Case for Historic Premillennialism: An Alternative to "Left Behind" Eschatology* (Grand Rapids, MI: Baker, 2009).

Way to the City

The pre-flood world appears to have been "ruled" by "heroic" strong men whose only standard of conduct was their own whims and forcefulness.[31] No external standard called them to "just" governance, so the world became "filled with violence." This violence has its origins not in structural evils but in the "thoughts and imaginations" of mankind's inner nature, and it is a continual and pervasive problem (Gen. 6:5–8).[32] The biblical conclusion is that judgment, in this case the flood, was the only answer to man in his raw and ungoverned state.[33] The effect is that chaos, now evident in sociological terms, returns in the natural world to wreak judgment.

In this environment only Noah "found grace" as a "righteous" man (Gen. 6:9; 7:1) who could be called "blameless" in his time (6:9). The post-flood law is established among men to curb and avenge the violence they do to one another (9:5–6). This rule appears to establish the extreme limit at which vengeance may occur and includes those retributive actions that might accrue to lesser crimes. Further, as the statement of respect for humanity made in God's image, it appears to limit the use of the death penalty.

The patriarchal narratives show plausible examples of the interaction of wealthy nomadic (*habiru*) clans in the ancient Near East with local "kings" in both confrontational and contractual relations (cf. Gen 14, 20–21). This localized and clannish rule is clearly in contrast to early contact with the Egyptian empire and fledgling Babylonian civilization of Nimrod. The intraclan dealings between Jacob and Esau and Jacob and Laban are carried on with no apparent interference or oversight by any other local authorities.[34]

The special case of Sodom and Gomorrah, both of which have "kings" (Gen. 14:2), calls down the direct judgment of God. It is possible that the

---

31 Walter C. Kaiser Jr., *Toward an Old Testament Theology* (Grand Rapids, MI: Zondervan, 1978), 80.

32 Gordon Wenham, *Genesis 1–15*, WBC (Waco, TX: Word Books, 1987), ad loc., comments: "Few texts in the OT are so explicit and all-embracing as this in specifying the extent of human sinfulness and depravity (cf. Ps 14:1–3; 51:3–12 [1–10]; Jer 17:9–10). But that sin has its root in man's thought world is certainly a commonplace of biblical ethics (cf. "You shall not covet," Exod. 20:17)."

33 Erich Sauer, *The Dawn of World Redemption*, trans. G. H. Lang (Grand Rapids, MI: Eerdmans, 1951), 63–80.

34 It is unique to the biblical message that its "heroes" do not come off as ideal characters but as sinners in need of correction by such pagans as Pharaoh, Abimelech, Laban, etc.

Way to the City

"cry" that "went up" to God (18:20–21) is a call for "righteousness and justice" (and is a cry against oppressive governance), standards to which God expects Abraham and his people to adhere (18:19). This seems to explain the extended prayer/conversation/negotiation between Abraham and God on the subject: "Shall not the Judge of all the earth do what is just?" (18:25). Ultimately, judgment again prevails.[35]

Egypt looms large in the last chapters of Genesis as both savior and potential tyrant. Joseph's wisdom and character combined with unlimited power (41:40) "save" Egypt's people but also enslave them as unlanded tenants (47:21, 25). While Joseph is seen as thoroughly virtuous (Gen. 39) and trustworthy, a man "in whom is the Spirit of God," one who was incomparable in discernment and wisdom (41:38–39), a character formed in the crucible of sufferings in the sovereign plan of God, he is nevertheless the one who made slaves of an entire people with the odd exception of the pagan priests (47:26).[36] It is a small step from this to the oppression of Exodus 1 and the "cry" of Israel to God for deliverance.

Pharaoh's tyrannical and godlike claims to ownership over the people of Israel, their children, their labor, their livestock, to the exclusion of all other claims, even the worship of Yahweh (Exod. 5:1–4; 8:25–28; 10:8–11, 24), leads to an ever-widening "judgment" on Pharaoh and his gods (6:6; 7:4; 12:12). This is exactly as it had been promised to Abraham (Gen. 15:14). There is even a hint that the providence that brought Joseph to power and issued in Pharaoh's unparalleled suzerainty (50:19–20) led to this very judgmental confrontation with Pharaoh (Exod. 9:15–17). Judgment again prevails.

Israel's redemption and freedom prepare them for service to Yahweh, as Moses repeatedly tells Pharaoh (Exod. 4:23; 7:16; 8:1, 13, 20, etc.), and thus for his exclusive reign over them, as is celebrated in the hymn of Moses at the sea (15:13–18). Their freedom is not absolute and autonomous, for they have been "redeemed" (15:13) that they might be Yahweh's "slaves," his "pos-

---

35 The recurring theme we cite here has recently been treated more or less exhaustively by James M. Hamilton Jr., *God's Glory in Salvation through Judgment: A Biblical Theology* (Wheaton, IL: Crossway, 2010).

36 This is a harbinger of the mighty wisdom of Solomon, which gained him fame and wealth but which also led to the sense of enslavement among the people that split his kingdom after his death.

Way to the City

session," his "kingdom" as "priests" (19:4–6). Thus, their mission in earthly terms is to exemplify for the nations how a people ruled by God through the instrumentality of his revealed standards should "live" (Deut. 5:5–8), a path hinted at in the exchange over the judgment of Sodom (Gen. 18:17–19).

Though this arrangement is clearly theocratic, it is eventually to be mediated by "wise," "discerning," truth-loving, bribe-hating, God-fearing, and even Spirit-filled men.[37] This is the governance anticipated in advance of the occupation of Canaan.[38] The unit of Torah (Deut. 16:18–18:22) that integrates the institutions of Israel's national life—political and religious, with the religious divided between priest and prophet and the political involving judges and priests (17:8–13)—allows for the possibility of a king "whom Yahweh your God shall choose" (17:15).

All institutions are, of course, subject to Yahweh's direct and indirect supervision by Torah and prophetic word (Deut. 17:18–19; 18:15–22). Significantly, judges are to be chosen by the people themselves, based on their possession of wisdom and reputation among the people (1:15), but a king is to be chosen by Yahweh, "from among your brothers" (17:15). The prohibitions against accumulation of horses, wives, and wealth (17:16–17) are unique in the ancient Near East. Further, the requirement that the future king be a student of Torah (17:18–20) set the spiritual parameters. Thus, contrary to standard practice in the ancient Near East, the king of Israel, should one be needed, is subject to brotherhood, Torah, and Yahweh—making him more a shepherd than a monarch.[39]

---

37 See Exod. 18:13–26; Num. 11:16–30; Deut. 1:9–18.

38 Exod. 21:6; 22:8–9; Num. 25:5; Deut. 16:18; 19:17–18; 21:2.

39 See Timothy S. Laniak, *Shepherds after My Own Heart: Pastoral Traditions and Leadership in the Bible*, NSBT 20, ed. D. A. Carson (Downers Grove, IL: InterVarsity Press, 2006), 94ff., for further documentation. In his commentary J. G. McConville points out three principles arising from this passage: (1) the supremacy of Torah over all and its embodiment of justice/righteousness; (2) the people as the "appointers" of administrators ("judges") among them with God's appointed priests as supreme court; and (3) the prophet as the one who calls all to faithfulness. *Deuteronomy*, Apollos Old Testament Commentaries 5, ed. David W. Baker and Gordon J. Wenham (Downers Grove, IL: InterVarsity Press, 2002) 304–6. Theoretically, this order does not require a king, but it is permitted and he is expected to have his own copy of authorized Torah to "read," "learn," "do," "keep"—(1) that "his heart not be lifted up above his brothers," (2) "that he might not turn aside…to right or left," and (3) "so that he may continue long in his kingdom, he and his children" (Deut. 17:18–20). This system, in following upon the "descent into chaos boh natural and political (in Gen.

Way to the City

It is this governance that prevails until the time of Samuel, the beginning of the period of the prophets we are studying, when the people rebel against Yahweh's kingship and demand a human "king" (1 Sam. 8:4–8). However, the proper relationship of priesthood and judge appears not to have been established until Eli united the offices and Samuel succeeded him (4:18). Moreover, these "judges" are said to be "raised up" (Judg. 2:16) by Yahweh. He was "with them," but it was Yahweh who "saved" them (2:18). He also made it clear that these judges were "commanded" (or, "appointed") by him (2 Sam. 7:11). Even when the Davidic kingship is ratified by the promise of God, the system of local judges carries out the rule of God and his "prince" (7:8), David, and later Solomon (1 Chron. 23:4; 26:29; 2 Chron. 1:2). Significantly, a renewal of this system forms a part of the spiritual reform carried out under Jehoshaphat (2 Chron. 19:5–6) and also appears in the time of Ezra (Ezra 10:14) during the reform over intermarriage.[40]

The Demand for a King

The entire history of the attempt to centralize government in Israel is fraught with ambiguities and outright negativity. It is evident from the beginning that Israel's desire for a "king" to "go out before us and fight our battles" (1 Sam. 8:19–20), the one thing not authorized in Deuteronomy 17, in addition to "judge us," is a call for a kind of security and showiness that Yahweh has not given and that Samuel (at Yahweh's command) warns against.[41] This attitude appears to be characterized in terms of covetousness by Samuel, when he refers to Saul as the one to whom "all the desire of Israel [is] turned" (1 Sam. 9:20 NIV).[42] The prior experiment with the ill-fated requests to Gideon and the per-

---

and Exod.),…with its checks and balances, stand[s] in direct opposition to the monar-chical power politics of Egypt and of its smaller clones in Canaan" (305–6).

40 It is significant that during the conquest of Canaan in the days of Joshua the leadership of Israel is taught about in terms of its own ability under the kingship of Yahweh to fight its own battles and demonstrate its own kingship over the "kings" of Canaan (Josh. 10:22–27). This is done in the ongoing series of battles and is punctuated by a call to courage and trust in Yahweh to do the same thing to all the enemies of Israel.

41 See also 2 Sam. 12:12 where the motivation of fear at the sight of one more threat (Ammonites) seems to be primary.

42 Even more telling is the paraphrase of NLT at this point: "you and your family are the focus of all Israel's hopes." The word for "desire" or "desirable" here as rendered in most

fidy of Abimelech (Judg. 8–9) foreshadowed things to come, even though it is evident that the anarchy of the five citations of Judges is undesirable.[43]

Samuel's warnings about the king go unheeded: his "ways" (lit., "judging" or "manner") will be to "take" (used six times in ESV) what he desires for his own use and that of his "slaves," meaning his own servants (1 Sam. 8:14–15) and subordinates and will do as his title ("king") implies.[44] Samuel warns that the people will one day "cry" (see their "cry" in Egypt against Pharaoh) to Yahweh for relief from this oppression and he will not hear (8:18), for it will be "your king, whom you have chosen for yourselves."[45] Yahweh clearly foreshadows this style of leadership from Saul as oppressive in 1 Samuel 9:17. The translation "restrain" (ESV only) is surely correct, for it is the only place in the OT this word is used to refer to ruling in any sense, and it is always used to convey some sense of negativity.[46]

This certainly sets the tone for what follows. Samuel steadfastly seeks to communicate the true position of Saul as the new leader—he is a "prince,"[47] but the people choose him as "king" and Samuel anoints him as such to "save" Yahweh's people. From here on the situation is tenuous at best, for the people have "rejected" their God who "saves" (1 Sam. 10:19). Saul's career is marked by capricious and rebellious moments and ends in the clutches of witchcraft and suicidal depression, a man rejected of God in favor of another. The idea of dynastic succession (cf. Deut. 17:20) ancient Near Eastern-style is in the background, having been part of the original proposal to Gideon (Judg. 8:22), but it is specifically denied to Saul's line because of his usurpation of priestly duties, as Yahweh seeks "a man after his own heart" to be "prince" over Israel.[48]

---

translations is associated regularly with covetousness (and lust) and is the same root word that characterized Eve's attitude toward the forbidden fruit (Gen. 3:6).

43 See Judg. 17:6; 18:1; 19:1; 21:25.

44 By contrast, it is notable that Yahweh's view of the service of David begins with his being "taken" from the "sheepcote" (2 Sam. 7:8) to be "prince" or commander.

45 This is the earliest warning about how the politics of Israel will play out in the coming exile, first alluded to on the plains of Moab by Moses.

46 For full discussion of this word group, see Ronald B. Allen, "'atsar," TWOT, ad loc.

47 Heb., nagiyd, cf. 1 Sam. 9:16; 10:1; 13:14, as is David, 2 Sam. 6:21; 7:8.

48 1 Sam. 13:13–14—This act of public piety without corresponding private devotion is Saul's practice, as can be seen later in the situation with Amalek. By contrast, we see David's personal devotion and reverence at 1 Sam. 30:6–10 and in the departure from Jerusalem during Absalom's rebellion.

Way to the City

This terminology for designating the future choice has some ambiguities about it. The traditional understanding sees "man after...heart" referring to God's knowledge of David's sincere devotion in contrast to Saul's rebellion. This coincides well with Samuel's references to David as Saul's "neighbor... who is better than you" (1 Sam. 15:28).[49] The other possibility is that this phrase refers to Yahweh's own elective choice as opposed to the action of the people in their earlier demand to Samuel.[50] In either case it is Yahweh's choice to make, though we are left to wonder, given the prior generalized warning about the *mishpat* ("manner") of kings, whether this is an accommodating choice or that now is the correct timing for a choice.

Despite this turn of events, Saul appears to have solidified public approval through waging war against surrounding peoples and collected a standing army (1 Sam. 14:47–52). His campaigns, though defensive rather than expansionist, had the effect of both "deliverance" and the centralizing of his own power.[51] This power is now tested to see if it is at the disposal of Yahweh in holy war or is merely Saul's personal fiefdom (15:1–3). The well-known outcome is that he is charged with "divination" (the "rebellion" that presumes to know the mind of God apart from and subsuming the prophetic word), "idolatry" (the "presumption" that sacrifice could manipulate God's will), and outright "rejection" of the word of Yahweh (15:22–23). This condemnation not only seals the fate of Saul's kingship (the previous confrontation having foreclosed on his dynastic pretentions), it also is couched in the poetic statement of a universal principle that will echo to the last prophetic words of the

---

49 In her commentary Joyce G. Baldwin notes, "What Samuel is at pains to establish once and for all is the essential difference between Israel's monarchy and that of the nations. In Israel the Lord is King, and obedience to him must be paramount. It follows that any sign of a desire for independence of action becomes a disqualification: it is the equivalent of rebellion against the Lord. Already the Lord has selected Saul's successor, who will be *a man after his own heart*, prepared to let the Lord's will, as spoken by his prophet, be the guide of his life." *1 and 2 Samuel: An Introduction and Commentary*, TOTC 8 (Downers Grove, IL: InterVarsity Press, 1988), 105.

50 For this opinion, see John H. Walton, Victor H. Matthews, and Mark W. Chavalas, *The IVP Bible Background Commentary: Old Testament* (Downers Grove, IL: InterVarsity Press, 2000), ad loc.

51 See comments by Carl Friedrich Keil and Franz Delitzsch, *The Books of Samuel*, trans. James Martin, Biblical Commentary on the Old Testament (Grand Rapids, MI: Eerdmans, 1963), 149.

Way to the City

Old Testament (OT; see Mal. 1:10 and its full context). Israel's God is the manipulator, not the manipulated—unlike the gods of the surrounding peoples.

The ambiguity of the whole situation is further emphasized by the interposition within the narrative of Yahweh's conversations with Samuel on the subject of "regret" over the installation of Saul (1 Sam. 15:11, 29, 35). Samuel is clearly "hot" (v. 11) over the change of direction indicated by Yahweh's "regret." After all, had not Samuel himself sought to forestall this entire scenario and been overruled by Yahweh himself? No wonder he "shrieked" all night! That Yahweh is being fair and just in all this is clearly seen as Saul repeatedly refers to Yahweh as "your" (Samuel's) God and carries out a "worship"-ful display only for public consumption (v. 31). This is entirely consistent with all we know of Saul's persona—a man consumed with public perceptions (v. 24), which may very well proceed from some sense of his own inferiority within (cf. 1 Sam. 9:21; 10:22).

Nevertheless, does Yahweh not know this all along and is it not his immutable nature *not* to "regret" or "change his mind" (1 Sam. 15:29; cf. Num 23:19)? How can Samuel maintain his own stature as prophet and anointer of kings in the face of such apparent vacillation? Despite the conundrum, the episode closes with Samuel's "mourning" for Saul and a reaffirmation of Yahweh's "regret" (1 Sam. 15:35).

The narrative continues, without apparent pause, as Samuel once again becomes the messenger of Yahweh (following a rebuke) on a mission for the obvious "king" in the entire sequence. When Samuel is told once again that Saul is "rejected" and that Yahweh "has provided [lit., "seen"] for myself a king" (1 Sam. 16:1), in contrast earlier to "make them a king" (8:22), we cannot be certain if Yahweh had this as a preferred plan all along (thus making the earlier demand by the people premature) or if he is working out his will in spite of the rebellion of his people. The idea of "restrain" in our previous comments would tend to bear out this conclusion. The declarations in 1 Samuel 12:12–25 leave room for either possibility, but the prior deliverance from Philistine oppression by nature miracle (7:10–11) in response to repentance and prayerful sacrifice tend to make a human king superfluous, especially with reference to national security concerns.[52]

---

52 Apparently the previous arrangement of periodic deliverance was popularly judged to be inadequate in light of an immediate Ammonite threat (1 Sam. 12:12) and the ongoing

Way to the City

The repeat of the nature miracle at Gilgal (1 Sam. 12:16–18) would tend to reinforce this conclusion as well. Israel's concern for its security among the nations as well as its desire to be "judged like all the nations" (8:5–6) is declared by Yahweh to be an extension of the rebellion in the nation that has been going on since the deliverance from Egypt (8:8)—the equivalent of idolatry![53]

The resolution of ambiguity and tension over Israel's true kingship is surely seen in the use of the term "prince" (*nagiyd*) to refer to the human personage from the perspective of Yahweh and the prophets[54] and its association with shepherd terminology at David's full accession to leadership at Hebron (2 Sam. 5:2). This terminology defines the ideal human "king" as clearly subservient to Yahweh and his prophets and priests.[55]

Despite his great sin and failures as leader, David personifies this ideal as he is brought up short by the ill-advised first attempt to bring the ark to Jerusalem (2 Sam. 6 vs. 1 Chron. 15:13) and then forbidden to build the central shrine (2 Sam. 7). His respect for the prophetic word and the priestly institution contrasts sharply with that of Saul. Even in his tragic sin and subsequent exposure and humiliation he exemplifies the limitation of monarchy under Yahweh (2 Sam. 12:13; 15:25–26).

The well-known promise(s) of 2 Samuel 7 continues this same theme of David as "shepherd" and "prince" (v. 8), with the addition of "servant," but there is clearly a distant, even eternal horizon involved here as well as a perspective on "house"-building that goes well beyond the temporal (vv. 11–17

Philistine aggression faced by Saul (1 Sam 14:52) and later David. This amounts to a rejection of Yahweh's kingship.

53 Tremper Longman has observed that covenant curses due to general apostasy (idolatry) are described elsewhere in the OT in Lev. 26:19–20 and Deut. 28:22–24, 38–42. Tremper Longman III, "1 Samuel 12:16–19: Divine Omnipotence or Covenant Curse?" *Westminster Theological Journal* 45, no. 1 (1983): 170–71.

54 See 1 Sam. 9:16; 10:1; 13:14; 25:30; 2 Sam. 6:21; 7:8; 1 Kings 1:35; 14:7; 16:2; 2 Kings 20:5; 2 Chron. 11:22. But also note that Ezekiel uses another term (*nasiy'*) to denote the personage envisioned in the era of the ideal temple (e.g., Ezek 34:24; 37:25). For more on this later term, see Walter C. Kaiser, "*nasa, nasiy'* I," *TWOT*, 601.

55 See also that it is Yahweh who is the true "shepherd" of his people and the model for human leadership (Gen. 48:15; 49:24; Pss. 23; 74:1; 77:20; 78:52; 80:1; 95:7; etc.). Tragically, David's great sin is seen as the theft and slaughter of the "ewe lamb" of his "poor" neighbor (2 Sam. 12:2–4).

Way to the City

cf. Ps. 127:1–3), even though Solomon's reign and mission are in the foreground.[56] Solomon is, of course, a prime example of the failure of human delegated authority—marvelously gifted with wisdom, blessed with epiphanic visions, but disobedient to the threefold prohibition against the multiplication of horses, wives, and gold.

Solomon's oppressive policies (1 Kings 12:4) pursuant to his glorification of himself, his kingdom, and even the Lord's house lead to the breakdown of kingdom unity[57] at the time of Rehoboam's assumption of rule (12:16–17). This is the direct result of his failure to assume a role as "servant" and in fulfillment of prophecy and against his father's practices (12:6–15; cf. 11:11). The divided kingdom(s) now assume a direction that can only be called a descent into ultimate judgmental destruction. Once the dominating human monarchy is fully established, the downward spiral is only briefly slowed by the occasional efforts of Davidic descendants[58] in Judah.

This would appear to be the dire end predicted from the outset of the demand for a king—no "cry" would be heard, for consequences are to be carried out against "both you and your king" (1 Sam. 8:25; cf. 8:12; 12:15). This fate, which swallows up people and king, is also what causes such pain and bewilderment to the suffering "remnant"—what Kidner calls "painful tension."[59]

The lure of kingly prerogatives warned about during the initial clamor for a new form of government in the days of Samuel proves too much to overcome. No attempts at establishing treaty relationships with the great powers of the day—Egypt, Syria, Assyria, Phoenicia, Babylon—whether through Solomon's "marriages" or through standard alliances against common enemies, suffice to save the kingdom(s). The Assyrians swallow up the north (722 B.C.) and Babylon carries off the south (607–586 B.C.).

From this point forward there appears to be little interest (at least in the biblical record) in reestablishing the human monarchy. However, there is great interest in what Yahweh may (or may not) do to set someone on the "throne

---

56 See Ps. 89 for a reflection on the need for more than a temporal perspective on this promise.
57 See the "covenant" established at the time of David's accession—2 Sam. 5:3.
58 See Asa, Jehoshaphat, Jehoash (during the lifetime of Jehoiada), Hezekiah, and Josiah.
59 Derek Kidner, *Psalms 73–150: An Introduction and Commentary on Books III–V of the Psalms*, TOTC (London: Inter-Varsity Press, 1975), 319. See also other psalms for this conundrum.

Way to the City

of Yahweh."[60] The history of this concern is undoubtedly the core of the messianic hope and promise. Davidic psalmody repeatedly takes up the theme of Zion as Yahweh's city of rule, the temple as his footstool, and the Davidic king as but a type of the heavenly coming reality.[61]

Isaiah, as premier representative of the early (eighth-century) writing prophets, emphasizes Yahweh as king and the coming one as his ideal ruler in light of the failure of the Davidic monarchy and the capital city with its complement of officials, bureaucrats, and political entrepreneurs.[62] Hosea echoes the theme by harking back to the very beginning of the monarchical regime in Israel.[63] Micah recognizes the need for a remedy and looks to the future (Mic. 5:2). Jeremiah and Ezekiel, during the Babylonian crisis, agree that there is no hope for the Davidic line of their time (Jer. 22:1–23:2; Ezek. 21:25–27). Both agree that a new kind of leader and a new people under a new covenant, and a new Jerusalem are needed.[64]

The psalms of royal idealization[65] do not present prophetic condemnations but offer a call to Israel's kings to measure up to the hope and promise of their Davidic origin. They clearly and repeatedly point to one who will fulfill the promise, of one who will suffer for/with his people (Pss. 22, 69) and will be their shepherd (Pss. 23; 95:6–7; cf., 2:9). The depression, sorrow, and bewilderment seen in the reflection of Psalm 89 on the failure of the ideal king serve to confirm the prophetic word prior and antecedent to the people's relinquishment of their own direct relationship with Yahweh in order to get a king "to fight our battles."[66] Finally, twenty-five years into the exile, Ezekiel is given a vision of an ideal temple and rule to come where the "prince" will no

---

60 1 Chron. 29:23; cf. 17:13–14; 28:5; 2 Chron. 9:8.
61 See Pss. 2, 89, 110, et al.
62 Isa. 1; 6:5; 37:16; 41:21; 43:15; 52:7; cf., 11:1–5; 9:1–7.
63 Hos. 13:9–11; cf., 9:9; 10:9; 11:5.
64 Jer. 31:31–34; 33:14–26; Ezek. 34:1–10; 36:22–38; 37:24–27; 44–46; where the "prince" (*nasiy'*) of a new kind is anticipated. Ezekiel has previously pronounced the doom of David's current line (21:25–27) with anticipation of the fulfillment of Gen. 49:10 as the hope for the future.
65 Pss. 2, 18, 20, 21, 45, 72, 101, 110, 144, etc.
66 See also the story of the Jehoiada/Joash period (2 Chron. 23:1–24:22), which shows clearly the conspiracy of people and king in the treachery of shedding blood. This despite Joash's receiving his copy of the Torah as in Deut. 17 (2 Chron. 23:11) and the "covenant" to "be Yahweh's people" (2 Chron. 23:16).

Way to the City

longer cheat the people in the marketplace or steal their land (Ezek. 45:7–12; 46:16–18), nor shall he be allowed to make a gift of his own land outside his own family except temporarily until the Jubilee.

By way of contrast to all this, Daniel is given visions of the "beast"-ly nature of pagan rule and its ultimate doom at the hands of Yahweh's chosen,[67] an equally stylized negative view compared to the Psalter's view of Davidic rule. Daniel at this point has already interpreted a "word" from Yahweh to Nebuchadnezzar through a dream. This word predicted the descent of the monarch into a beastly state because he would not give glory to the God of Israel for having put him on the throne even of Babylon.[68] Such an assessment of pagan governments is common to the prophets and needs no special citation here.[69] Israel, from Abraham's day forward, has always found itself in juxtaposition to incipient and overpowering empires as well as petty kings. The unique character of the Hebrew Scriptures is that they unrelentingly concentrate on Israel's failure to live up to the call and mission she has been given to exhibit justice/righteousness to the nations.[70] There is no hope for the world in her human rule or rulers. Like the complainers of Malachi's day, the world still cries, "Where is the God of justice?" (Mal. 2:17). "But who can endure the day of his coming?" (3:2). For He will come to purify his own first. And if judgment begins "at the household of God," what will be the fate of "the ungodly and the sinner" (1 Peter 4:17–18; cf. Prov. 11:31)?

---

67 See Dan. 9 and continuing visions and explanations.

68 Dan. 4. Note on this passage the unusual (to us) interpretation of both Hebrew commentators of the intertestamental period and the assessment of Gary Anderson that Daniel actually advises that "almsgiving" (v. 27) will give a reprieve to Nebuchadnezzar from the sentence of Israel's God. Gary A. Anderson, *Sin: A History* (New Haven, CT: Yale University Press, 2009), esp. chap. 9, "Redeem Your Sins with Alms." We will have further comment on the development of this theme of redemptive almsgiving at the close of this section on the OT.

69 It is strange that Blomberg, in *Neither Poverty nor Riches*, simply dismisses the importance of Daniel by stating in a footnote, "In the Hebrew, of course, Daniel is included not with the 'Prophets' but with the 'Writings'; all the more reason why we cannot take his themes as representative of the core of Old Testament prophecy" (70n18).

70 For the most thorough treatment to date of this great theme, see Walter C. Kaiser Jr., *Mission in the Old Testament: Israel as Light to the Nations* (Grand Rapids, MI: Baker, 2000).

Way to the City

The Utopian Vision: Government in the Place of God and Israel's Call for a King

Israel's call for a king in the "days when the judges ruled" (lit., "judged" [Ruth 1:1]) is arguably a call for a utopian answer to the ancient problem of God's "unfair" administration of a sinful world. The theocracy was in disarray for two reasons (apparently) other than the sheer anarchy of the times: (1) the matter of succession—i.e., Eli and Samuel both are failures on this count, even though the level of their own character is decidedly higher than what has gone before (apparently); and (2) (perhaps more importantly) the matter of security—i.e., "someone to fight our battles" appears to call for some sort of mercenary "army" in the place of occasional call-ups of "all Israel." This will require centralization and all its attendant complications. What at first appears to be a "solution" becomes a disaster, as Israel becomes subject to first the exploitation and finally the fate of its kings.[71] This is not undeserved, for it is clear in the prophets that the "servants" of the kings (Dearman designates them as "officials or royal servants")[72] join in the economic oppression of the people as they always do—what Block calls "feudalism"[73]—but it also means that the "remnant" (the primary designees of the term "the poor") will also be carried along in the ensuing disaster. This is the most profound conundrum in the search for justice. It is to this remnant that we owe the record of the story and the hope of a truly "anointed" One, who will fulfill the aspirations of the ages.

The call for justice, for the Christian, comes down to the tension between calling-as-servant and any sense in which some sort of coercion would be justified. "Distributional justice" is coercive by nature. It must take in order to

---

71 See esp. on this exploitation the comments of Daniel I. Block, *The Book of Ezekiel, Chapters 25–48*, NICOT (Grand Rapids, MI: Eerdmans, 1998), 2:724, that the kings are the primary culprits in confiscating the original land possessions and no doubt distributing them by their whims in "feudal" fashion. This he sees being remedied in the land dispersals around the ideal temple. See further Dearman, *Property Rights*, 130–48, for discussion of the likely conditions surrounding Israel and Judah's kingship and aristocracy. None of this situation is analogous to modern market economics and democracies, except that justice must have standards from which to judge.
72 Dearman, *Property Rights*, 133. See esp. the specific designation in Jer. 22:1–5.
73 Block, *Book of Ezekiel*, 2:724.

Way to the City

give. The prophets note that the kings of Israel do this in collusion with their "servants." No governmental coercion may exceed the *lex talionis* according to biblical justice, for that is fundamental to the very definition of justice.[74] The nature of pagan coercion is that it is unjust by definition, for it excludes the worship of Yahweh and has no foundation in Torah upon which to act. The problem with the monarchy in Israel and then Judah and Israel is that what Samuel predicted about the "taking" by kings so they might "give it to their servants" came surely to pass and led to the denunciations of the later prophets.[75] Only theocratic justice is "just" by definition in the mind of the prophets of the OT, for the ideal "Servant" must come to establish this "justice" as a matter of his own commissioning from Yahweh (Isa. 42:1–4).[76] By its very nature this justice begins with the conversion of the human heart and giving of the Spirit in the new covenant before the political kingdom can be established as a working institution upon the earth (Ezek. 36:22–31 and chap. 37; Jer. 31:31–34).

Conclusion

With the foregoing in mind, we can only conclude that the "justice" the prophets envision is exactly what it is in the Torah. The words used are everywhere the same. The emphases on specific failures are the same. The source of the preaching is the same as the Torah—God's speaking, "the word of the LORD." Zephaniah (chap. 3 ESV), during the reign and revival under Josiah, pointed out clearly the fickleness of the enforcement of the law in Jerusalem that led to its downfall. There was a collusion of all in leadership and spiritual direction to subvert the reliable justice of Yahweh:

---

74   See McConville, *Deuteronomy*, on Deut. 17.

75   This and the perversion of the courts so that those who have been defrauded have no recourse is what is repeatedly associated with covetousness and called "unjust gain" (*betsaʿ*; Isa. 57:17 with further examples at Gen. 37:26; Exod. 18:21; Judg. 5:19; 1 Sam. 8:3; Ps. 119.36; Prov. 28:16; Mic. 4:13; Ezek. 22:13, 27.). The attempts of many to associate this idea with the mere acquisition of an amount of wealth judged independently of any given standard of Scripture are ill-conceived and unsustainable.

76   The "prince" of Ezek. 44 and following chapters is another personage who is expected to judge lawfully, but scholarship is divided on whether this one is to be conflated in some way with Messiah.

Way to the City

> Her officials within her
>   are roaring lions;
> her judges are evening wolves
>   that leave nothing till the morning.
> Her prophets are fickle, treacherous men;
> her priests profane what is holy;
>   they do violence to the law.
> The LORD within her is righteous;
>   he does no injustice;
> every morning he shows forth his justice;
>   each dawn he does not fail;
> but the unjust knows no shame.
>
> Zephaniah 3:3–5 ESV

The final verse contrasts the daily reliability of Yahweh with the fickleness (especially) of the prophets whose job it was to keep governmental officials on track. This fickleness in context can only mean inventions of forms of "justice" not consonant with the revealed will of Yahweh in Torah. Therefore, letting "justice roll down" means to practice God's law throughout all of life. To "do justice" is to walk the path of the Torah, no more nor less. To teach otherwise is to "slouch toward Gomorrah" into sentimentality and real injustice. As Dearman states, "The prophets repeatedly accuse various officials as the culprits in the violation of citizens' property rights and not just the anonymous rich as is popularly supposed."[77] This is how to gain money, power, and prestige if government is "on your side."

Jeremiah finalizes the indictment in the last days of the Hebrew monarchy: "From the least of them to the greatest of them, everyone is greedy for unjust gain; and from the prophet to the priest, everyone deals falsely" (Jer. 6:13). This is not merely an indictment of leadership, for he has previously said, "The prophets prophesy falsely, and… my people love to have it so" (5:31).[78]

---

77 Dearman, *Property Rights*, 148.
78 Cf. Mic. 7:1–6, where the problem socially is not "out there" somewhere but in one's very bosom/bed where betrayal sleeps at one's side (v. 5). No stretch of this text and its parallels in the ministry of Jesus (Matt. 10:35–39; Luke 12:53) can account for a theology of class

Way to the City

Jeremiah has sadly come to this conclusion after he has searched high and low for even a single man who "does justice and seeks truth" (5:1 ESV). He goes on to indict them for failing to repent and for hardening their attitudes against Yahweh's law (v. 3). Suddenly, he notes that these he has been searching among are "only the poor,[79] they have no sense;[80] for they do not know the way of the Lord, the justice of their God" (v. 4 ESV). Perhaps he will find more understanding of justice among the "great" (*gadol*, v. 5)? Alas, no! Finally, they must all from poor to great experience God's coming judgment upon Israel (vv. 5–13) for they are all culpable, not just one class or constituency of the people.

In this way do ancient Israel and Judah mirror our own time as constituencies vie to take away the rights and property of other constituencies. Interpretations that make the prophets into class warriors simply fail to grasp their profound insight into human frailty and sinfulness.[81] As Isaiah would and does say, "No one calls for justice; no one pleads his case with integrity" (Isa. 59:4, NIV). This can only mean that without a specific outside standard for what constitutes "justice," all will simply engage in the special pleading that puts themselves in the right. It is called "gaming the system" in our time, and it is a universal practice among rich and poor, young and old, and oppressed and oppressors. Consequently, the need and requirement to practice and teach/preach justice is universal and specific and individual and should be addressed as the prophets do.

---

envy and resentment between the economically differentiated. The problem is far deeper than that and goes to the root issue: all men and women (rich and poor) will game the system to their own advantage and the harm of their neighbors.

79 Using a common word for distinguishing between the rich or powerful and the poor and oppressed (*dal*) as in Exod. 23:3; 30:15; 1 Sam. 2:8; Job 34:28; Ps. 82:3; Prov. 10:15; 19:4; 22:16, 22; and many other passages.

80 A word (*ya'al*) indicating their general foolishness and lack of discretion.

81 See Blomberg's reference in *Neither Poverty nor Riches*, 73, to "urban luxury and extravagance" and "upper class exploitation of the peasants."

Way to the City

Chapter 6

Conclusions from the Old Testament

WHAT THEN IS THE THRUST of Old Testament (OT) ethical and social teachings that will guide us in the search for justice in our time? It is made abundantly clear in the final narratives from the late sixth to the late fifth centuries B.C. in the books of Ezra and Nehemiah and the prophecy of Malachi. Leaders and people returning from the curse of the exile "return" in the spiritual sense to the commands "written in the Law of Moses the man of God" (Ezra 3:2).[1] The final prophetic utterances of Malachi also return to the same theme. The Chronicler, who closes out the Hebrew text, also paints the same picture, as we have previously cited. It is not cultic observance that either pleases God or leads to blessing. In the end it is more profitable in every way to "take to heart" "the commandment" (Mal. 2:1–2), even if the temple doors be shut to prevent sacrifice (1:10), "for the lips of a priest should keep knowledge and people should seek the law from his mouth.... But you have departed from the way; you have caused many to stumble at the law,... because you have not kept my ways but have shown partiality in the law" (2:7–9, our composite translation from several sources). What is assumed in the early narratives and revealed at Horeb is explicated and illustrated and urged upon men and women and boys and girls by every literary and verbal means in the remainder of the OT. Finally, though it awaits its embodiment in the fullness of time, it is the "promise" of the Torah that fosters hope, for, "he will turn the hearts of fathers to

---

1   The final book of the Hebrew Scriptures (2 Chron.) makes it plain that the only way Israel and Judah had ever recovered even a modicum of the long-promised "blessing" was by a return to the Torah of Moses in both faith and practice.

their children and the hearts of children to their fathers, lest I come and strike the land with a decree of utter destruction" (4:6 ESV).

So, the OT closes with only the rebuilding of the temple as a realistic enterprise for Israel as it was constituted in that period, though the city maintains an existence without true freedom to institute a monarchy. With foreign domination as the overriding reality,[2] no return to the society visualized in Torah and attempted from the time of Joshua to the end of the monarchy seems realistic without further interventions by Yahweh in the person of a "coming one."[3] Ezekiel's idealized picture becomes just that—an ideal in need of further revelation on its meaning and intention. We are left with hope, but the hope is in many ways "sick," for "justice" has not been done according to the people, who "weary" the Yahweh by saying "Everyone who does evil is good in the sight of the LORD, and he delights in them" and by asking, "Where is the God of justice?" (Mal. 2:17 ESV).

It is also very clear that the burden of "social justice" is pursued in the specifics of how Israelites treat one another in their regular business dealings. This is evident in the conflicts over loans at interest to those struggling in hard times and the problems associated with intermarriage in Ezra and Nehemiah.

Summarizing then the OT message for our present considerations:

1. Mankind, created in the image of God, was placed in a world made for the sustenance and enjoyment of the race, a prospect only achievable through what we must call "development" and technological advance.

2. Human beings are by creation made directly accountable to the God of the Bible for all their activities. In their original and even "fallen" state they are "free to choose" without coercive interference. The world God created and continues to rule dishes out rewards and consequences at every level of endeavor and interaction. Governments are held accountable to the same standards and find that "history" rewards and punishes them.

---

2 See esp. Ezra 8 and 9 and Neh. 8 and 9 with Daniel's prayer in chap. 9.
3 Cf. Ezek. 21:25–27.

Way to the City

3. The fundamental context of all else for men and women is the obedient pursuit of ruling the creation through work and creative endeavor—seen as adding human ingenuity to natural resources, which are truly only "raw materials" until put into use, to produce a "developed" world from a planet full of potential.

4. Primary to the accomplishment of such a task is faith in its possibilities and hope for the "blessing" of the One who gave the command and set in motion its daily realities. The search for a more "secure" future and prospect leads only to "confusion" and falsification of reality—worse yet, the imposition of overbearing and coercive "rule."

5. The fall of humanity into sin and death did not change the command, but it did change the nature of the realities. The category of "curse" now pervades life, with death being its temporal fruit and damnation its eternal possibility. The "nakedness" of innocence is turned to the "nakedness" of judgment, requiring toil against the curse.

6. The Law given at Sinai at once begins a national experiment in the pursuit of "blessing" and the avoidance of "curse," even as it unfolds man's full obligation to his creator God.

7. Israel's failure to arrive at its full potential for "blessing" and its descent into "curse" foreshadows all of mankind's need for a complete (utopian?) "salvation." The problems arising from the fall are not confined to one nation but are universal. Israel repeats the "fall" of the first couple and becomes "naked" (Deut. 28:48) because she would not worship Yahweh purely in her prosperity and finally serves other masters as "slaves" in her own land according to Nehemiah and Ezra.

8. The utopian hope is not to be achieved by the imposition of temporal empires or systems, but rather by the elevation of a

Way to the City

certain kind of character in (a) man.[4] Heroic characters change systems. Systems and governments cannot produce heroic character. Moreover, they tend to institutionalize and magnify evil in subjugating and exploiting human beings. This is clearly a call for a completely theocratic regime, a new and different kind of Zion, "city of the great king." No "beastly" empire or kingdom can possibly bring "social justice" in the biblical way. This dream awaits the One who comes, upon whose "shoulder" shall be "government."

9.   As the Scripture passages we have cited throughout our study show, the sin of Israel in its social relations is not mere divergence in wealth from one another but specific crimes against the social order and neighbors. For Israel's failure to intercede and its outright instigation and collusion in the profits from immoral behavior, even the Davidic government and capital city have come under judgment.

10.   The weakness brought on by sin, which is evident in even the most heroic of OT "servants of God," demands that someone be "sent" to bring about the realization of the potential waiting in "the whole creation."

11.   This arrival of the One to come will be a day of judgment, as the days of change and transition have always been in the Hebrew Scriptures, and will ensue on the basis of the Torah: "Then I will draw near to you for judgment. I will be a swift witness against the sorcerers, against the adulterers, against those who swear falsely, against those who oppress the hired worker in his

---

4   See on this universal character Ps. 15, where "adam" is the whoever-type character that can find a dwelling in Yahweh's house. See this character's origin from the heart in Deut. 10:12–21. See Micah calling out "O man" (Mic. 6:6–8) with Yahweh's requirements. And, finally, hear Isaiah specify this character in its outward practice (Isa. 33:14–22). Thus do the Law and the Prophets and the Wisdom writers all agree in disparate eras on the character of those who will prosper before Yahweh and in the world.

Way to the City

wages, the widow and the fatherless, against those who thrust aside the sojourner, and do not fear me, says the LORD of hosts" (Mal. 3:5 ESV).

To this explosive possibility we will quickly turn our attention. One issue does concern us at this point, however, for it bears upon a number of discussions between Jesus and the religious leaders of Israel in the New Testament (NT). We have previously mentioned Gary Anderson's work, *Sin: A History*, as both chronicling and advocating a view of almsgiving (charity to the poor) that promises a building up of heavenly merit(s) to be added to the account of those practicing it. These merits serve as balancing weight(s) on the scale of final judgment that will literally free the debtor/sinner (and consequently Israel insofar as they in the aggregate practice almsgiving) "from death" in the eschatological sense. He builds the case from the previously cited dream of Nebuchadnezzar and ancient Hebrew commentary as well as his own considered exegesis.[5] Particularly telling is his apparent acquiescence in an extreme (as we see it) view of the value of almsgiving that will come to the fore in some of our study that follows from the ministry of Jesus. We think it is worth quoting him at length here:

> The point is clear: what one does toward the poor registers directly with God. It is as though the poor person was some sort of ancient automatic teller machine through which one could make a deposit directly to one's heavenly account. Just as an altar was a direct conduit of sacrifices to the heavenly realm, so was the hand of the impoverished soul seeking charity.[6]

This viewpoint is pertinent for two reasons: first, because it shows a strain of Second Temple intertestamental development of Hebrew biblical interpretation that Jesus and the early church would encounter frequent-

---

5   Passages include Dan. 4:27; Pss. 37:21; 112:4–5; Prov. 14:21, 31; 19:17, 28:8; plus mentions of others. Gary A. Anderson, *Sin: A History* (New Haven, CT: Yale University Press, 2009), 138–50.
6   Ibid., 140.

Way to the City

ly. Anderson follows it closely through the ancient book of Tobit.[7] Second, and perhaps more importantly, Anderson is clearly advocating a strain of theological reflection in the church that he traces all the way to Anselm's theory of the atonement and beyond, confuting (as he sees it) the premises and developments that would stem from the Reformation. In the pages that follow here we will maintain the viewpoint that concern for the poor is praiseworthy for all believers, but such concern is hardly the kind of refuge for the sinner advocated here and in some of the other literature we will cite.

---

7   Anderson, *Sin*, 144–46. Clearly Anderson's work requires more detailed refutation than
     we are permitted space in a work of this sort here. His "exegesis" and defense of Roman
     Catholic teaching is at the heart of Reformation debates about the all-sufficient imputation
     of the righteousness of Christ to the believer. As Jesus will say to Simon on a day to come
     in this work, "With man it is impossible, but with God all things are possible."

Way to the City

Chapter 7

The Life, Ministry, and Teachings of Jesus

FUNDAMENTAL TO ANY COHERENT CHRISTIAN THEORY of social ethics is proper coordination of the materials in our modern "Testaments." Land mines of dispute and fallacy challenge all those engaged in such a task. We approach it with due caution, but we also are full of confidence that an integration of the crucial teachings in both Testaments is necessary and possible.

The origin of the designations "old" and "new" in our modern copies of the Bible is, of course, not derived from the written materials themselves. These designations were first imposed on translations from Hebrew and Greek texts in the second century AD Tertullian (around AD 197–200) first used the term "*novum testamentum*" to designate the collection of writings we know as the New Testament (NT). It is only by comparative usage in common parlance that the Hebrew Scriptures can be called "old"—that is, to distinguish them from the "new"-er Scriptures. The concept of "old," as outdated or obsolete or even irrelevant has been imposed on the Hebrew Scriptures by Christian interpreters from the early second century (see Marcion) to the present day. The obvious deficiencies of these interpretations tend to isolate their authors at the fringes of Christian theology and preaching.

Of greater concern for our study is the tendency among modern commentators to relegate our Old Testament (OT) to secondary status for theological and ethical reflection. We have been determined from the genesis of this project not to fall into such a trap. The previous chapters demonstrate our commitment to let the OT have its own say and make its claims on modern people and cultures. For many, the use of the word "testament" after "old" and "new" in our English Bibles amounts to an elevation of the one over the other—as if somehow the writings of the apostles in the first century AD are more reliable or even more "Christian" than those of Moses or Samuel or David. By contrast the apostles and Jesus always honored the OT as Scripture and treated it in their time as the true way to knowledge of God the Father.[1]

This misconception may be mistakenly assumed or earnestly believed because of an improper emphasis on the usage of the word "testament" to head the two collections of texts. The word "testament" is the English equivalent of the Greek word for "covenant." Both groups of texts may rightly be said to contain records of God's covenantal actions with and toward men, but neither is literally a covenant or testament. We affirm that there is a "new covenant" and that this makes some specific things "old."[2] The issue before us will be to determine just exactly what is "old," as in obsolete or abolished, and just exactly what is "new," as in "never before seen/heard," or as in "anticipated and now arrived." The disputations over precisely how to interpret these categories of teaching are the stuff of theological controversy. We trust that what follows will not be merely controversial but will bring further enlightenment to our subject.

Since Jesus himself is the *sine qua non* of God's revelation on all issues, understanding his life, teachings, and ministry with reference to all the other biblical materials is critical. If, in fact, Jesus either in his manner of living and ministering or by his teaching sets aside, abolishes, or unambiguously and unexpectedly modifies prior revelation, we must acknowledge his lordship over all and follow him. If, on the other hand, he confirms, buttresses, and/or extends what has been revealed before his incarnation, we are equally obligated to follow his lead. This goes without saying, but it bears repeating as fundamental to all Christian ethical concerns.

In the interests of telling readers where we sit before delineating where we stand, we here confess our presuppositional bias. Simply stated, if the OT Scriptures are an accurate record of the very words and activities of the triune God, it would be highly problematic (to say the least) if the incarnate manifes-

---

1   See Matt. 22:29; Acts 8:35; 17:11; 2 Tim. 3:16; and 2 Peter 3:16; to name but a few.
2   See most famously the long dissertation by the writer of Hebrews on this very subject.

Way to the City

tation of God through his Son Jesus Christ were to be in any way contradictory to prior revelation. This in no way diminishes the evident sovereignty of a God who "does whatsoever he wills." As Paul says, "Let God be true, though every one were a liar" (Rom. 3:4). But we see nothing in the OT that makes God out to be capricious or arbitrary in his dealings with the created universe or humankind. To the contrary, it is everywhere evident that what is being "revealed" is the utter consistency and reliability of God's character. Israel at the time of Christ was the custodian and steward of the "oracles of God" (Rom. 3:2). Paul here is referring clearly to the experience of a liberated people at Sinai. We would add to this that one does not need Paul's added authority to tell us what is plain in reading the Mosaic account of these experiences.

We are very much aware that various interpretive frameworks have been constructed to account for the "old" and the "new" elements in covenantal dealings that became evident through the work of Christ.[3] In a limited project such as ours there is scant space to interact more than minimally with such constructs. Where necessary we will be noting such interpretive differences that have merit. However, the presupposition we here acknowledge will guide such interactions. We are convinced that the lordship of Christ cannot be seen as different from the lordship of Yahweh. They are one and the same and indivisible. As the writer of Hebrews (1:1–2) put it, he who "spoke" in the past "has spoken" now "in Son" (lit.).[4]

---

3   For a survey of the search for a unifying theme within the diversity of the texts, see esp. Walter C. Kaiser Jr., *Recovering the Unity of the Bible: One Continuous Story, Plan, and Purpose* (Grand Rapids, MI: Zondervan, 2009), and Kaiser's previously cited *The Promise-Plan of God: A Biblical Theology of the Old and New Testaments* (Grand Rapids, MI: Zondervan, 2008). Additionally, see Daniel P. Fuller, *Unity of the Bible: Unfolding God's Plan for Humanity* (Grand Rapids, MI: Zondervan, 1992). As we went to press the latest contributions on this theme are from G. K. Beale, *A New Testament Biblical Theology: The Unfolding of the Old Testament in the New* (Grand Rapids, MI: Baker, 2011), and Peter J. Gentry and Stephen J. Wellum, *Kingdom Through Covenant: A Biblical-Theological Understanding of the Covenants* (Wheaton, IL: Crossway, 2012).

4   For current discussion of the issues surrounding our interpretation of Jesus' teaching and that which has gone before, see Irving M. Zeitlin, *Jesus and the Judaism of His Time* (Cambridge, UK: Polity, 1991); A. E. Harvey, *Jesus and the Constraints of History* (Philadelphia: Westminster, 1982); Roger Mohrlang, *Matthew and Paul: A Comparison of Ethical Perspectives* (New York: Cambridge University Press, 1982). The consensus expressed by Zeitlin is that "the brunt of Jesus' criticism in the Gospel as a whole is directed not against the law itself, but against the prevailing interpretation and practice of it." *Jesus and the Judaism of His Time*, 109.

Way to the City

The Life and Ministry of Jesus

No limited writing such as this can hope to do justice to the infinite splendor that is the life, work, and teaching of the only Son of God. What we will attempt is to relate in a summary fashion this unique life and ministry to the subject we have chosen. This is a daunting task at best and impossible at worst. Attempting to isolate portions of the Gospel record to gain insight for modern readers, as with all biblical studies, is fraught with pitfalls—even more so, since the object of our inquiry is incomparable in person, word, and work. The fact that Jesus came to accomplish and proclaim salvation for all peoples suffuses all else that we might learn from him. His own declaration that "my kingdom is not of this world" would seem to foreclose attempts to make this-worldly conclusions about his teachings. His eschatological pronouncements and his present hidden working and promise of imminent return also warn us to take a cautionary approach to theories of worldly success or failure, poverty or wealth, sickness and health, and weakness and power. Recognizing these underlying themes will remind us of the temporal and limited nature of our current earthly concern, but we obviously do not conclude that this concern is inconsequential or trivial. In fact, it is clear that Jesus is adamant in his insistence that temporal concerns like the use and abuse of money have very real eternal implications (Luke 16:1–15).

A word is in order here on our following division of the Gospel accounts of Jesus' life and work. We have chosen to divide it simply into life, ministry, and teaching. This is a convenience for our purpose, but we trust it is not arbitrary. Clearly, anyone seeking to gain a thoroughgoing familiarity with and mastery of the record of the Gospels needs to delve much more exhaustively into them. We suggest our division as a simplifying way to frame the discussion we have had to this point, as it relates directly to Jesus.

The Life and Character of Jesus

The incarnation constitutes a most amazing affirmation of the physical world and life, fallen though it is. Contrary to other religious convictions worldwide, the Gospels record that the God who created and maintains all that we see, hear, smell, taste, and touch as well as all that we can only imagine has become in-fleshed and humble, to the point of humiliation, though he might easily have sat in magnificent isolation atop Mount Olympus oblivious to all below him. This fact alone is cause for wonder and deep contemplation. After thousands of years of human mismanagement, rebellion, perversion and all the attendant misery, drudgery, exploitation, and sheer lunacy, God chose to "come down" rather than end it all in one final cataclysm—at least for now!

Moreover, the manner of his arrival affirms not only this-worldly life itself but also its processes. Not as a full-grown "deliverer" from the desert but as a babe from his mother's womb does he come—not shrouded in mystery, but announced, attended, and witnessed. With the same needs and weaknesses and the usual provisions of a human baby, he joins the human race—not himself "fallen," but subject to the fallen. As if, also, to emphasize continuity with all that transpires in the OT records,[5] he arrives during a time when the greatest empire up to that time is flexing its muscle in small-town Israel with an oppressive and life-altering tax policy.[6] A harassed family, lacking power and clout, though apparently not destitute, is the human cradle for the nurturing of the Son of God. That family, like so many then and now and from time immemorial, had every reason to play out a victim's role under the circumstances (which became even worse at Herod's behest) but did no such thing. With Joseph and Mary for parents the boy Jesus was in competent and devout human hands, fallen though they were.

Like a previous teacher-prophet in Israel, Samuel, Jesus "grew" in the normal sense and attained "favor" humanly and spiritually (see Luke 2:52; cf. 1 Sam. 2:26). His home was that of what we would recognize as a small business owner, based on personal skills Joseph had learned undoubtedly from hands-on training and experience.[7] Most commentators would also at least suggest that lack

---

5   Surely the meaning of "the time is fulfilled" in Mark's Gospel (1:15) and Paul's "at the right time" (Rom. 5:6) and "when the fullness of time had come, God sent forth his Son, born of woman," etc. (Gal. 4:4).

6   For a helpful summary of the economic life of the land of Israel at this time, see D. E. Oakman, "Economics of Palestine," in *Dictionary of New Testament Background*, ed. Craig A. Evans and Stanley E. Porter (Downers Grove, IL: InterVarsity Press, 2000), 303–8.

7   For pertinent descriptions of Judean life and society of the time, see Anthony J. Saldarini, *Pharisees, Scribes and Sadducees in Palestinian Society: A Sociological Approach*, Biblical Resource Series (Grand Rapids, MI: Eerdmans, 2001) 35–76. For the suggestion that Jesus' family may have been relatively well-to-do for the times, see also Rodney Stark, *The*

Way to the City

of mention of Joseph's actual presence during Jesus' ministry indicates his early death, leading to the reasonable conjecture that Jesus worked at his craft with family sustenance at stake.[8] This would also be consistent with the Jewish tradition expecting teachers to practice a profession for personal and family support.

Jesus begins his public ministry at an age generally conceded to be about thirty, leaving a gap of silence between his bar mitzvah (near the time of the famous visit to the temple with his parents) and the commencement of the bulk of the information we have about his earthly life. Speculation about those years should be circumspect, but we can make some assumptions that are justified by the materials we do have. He must have worked at his trade for the common compensation. He was disparaged for being without rabbinical credentials (though he demonstrates his literacy in reading Scripture in the synagogue) and being commonly known along with his family in the environs of Nazareth. This would tend to indicate he lived the daily life of a craftsman[9] with its attendant burdens and rewards. He would likely have traveled about with his tools to find work wherever it was available, especially in a place like Sepphoris, which was just up the road a few miles and was being rebuilt by the Romans.[10] We also conclude that he must have been a very healthy physical specimen to have assumed a life "on the road" afoot and to have endured as he did such abuse prior to his death.

The beginning of his ministry confirms both his physical stamina and spiritual character. The record of his "temptation" experience is explicit in its inclusion of both. Physical deprivation called forth mental and spiritual testing that reveal his character as a man of faith and integrity with a high sense of divine purpose in his life. Refusing to abuse his power for personal survival or aggrandizement, he chooses the same simple faith in God's providence that he will urge upon others in his short public ministry. In this respect he is the full embodiment of the servant leaders we have seen in the OT Scriptures.

Triumph of Christianity: How the Jesus Movement Became the World's Largest Religion (New York: HarperCollins, 2011), 88.

8　See among others Craig L. Blomberg, *Matthew*, NAC 22 (Nashville: Broadman, 1992), 228.

9　The word commonly translated "carpenter," *tektōn*, can also mean "stone mason" and is used generically for any skilled worker with his hands.

10　This is the famous site where Josephus indicates thousands of Jews had been crucified as an example to all not to cross Rome politically. Could this have been the beginning of Jesus' consciousness of the cross that loomed in his own life?

Way to the City

From a purely human perspective, Jesus' public persona is that of a man completely at ease with himself and anyone he encounters. He is genuinely at home at a festive wedding, in the company of working-class people like his inner circle of disciples, and apparently with more wealthy supporters such as the house of Martha and Mary and others who appear to have contributed to sustaining his ministry. He was unafraid of the powerful and unfazed by contact with the obviously degraded lifestyles of the sexually promiscuous or the hated tax farmers. The poor and the wealthy, the powerful and the weak, the devout and the pagan all found him approachable. In this sense we would say in modern terms that Jesus was a magnificent specimen of human maturity and well-rounded adaptation to the realities around him. He was not an eccentric, except as he saw his mission to disrupt the comfortable. In fact, he was apparently so "worldly" that his critics contrasted him with John the Baptizer—John being characterized as "having a demon" for his ascetic style and Jesus as a "winebibber and glutton" for his manner of life (Matt. 11:19; Luke 7:34).

Finally we note his complete refusal to see his life as being that of a victim. Confrontational throughout his ministry toward all religious and political pretension, he makes the ultimate statement of self- and God-directed intention when he tells his disciples (in passages in John 10, 15, 18–19) and later Pontius Pilate "no man takes my life from me, I lay it down." Apart from the implications for salvation history inherent in this declaration, there is a clear example of what it means to recognize the power and necessity of personal choice in life's defining moments. Had he not lived as he chose to live he would not have faced such a moment. His life moved inevitably toward a certain end, not by the force of Rome or the Jewish religious leaders (who both had/have their moral culpability before God), but by force of his inner sense of direction. This is not merely a divine characteristic but a character trait of all "heroic" human beings great and small, renowned and unheralded. In Jesus we see its quintessential manifestation as both an example to follow and a provision for personal salvation. Jesus was not "other-directed" or "other-motivated" in the sense of letting "others" determine his decisions. Rather, the "other" in his life was his Father—he did what he did for one Other—and thus what he did was, in fact, best for *others*. "I came not to do the will of man, but the will of him

Way to the City

who sent me" was his life force and source.[11] His own characterization of the moral duty of man is embodied in his enumeration of the order of the "great" commandment and the "second" (Matt. 22:34–40)—indicating, as we have shown in the previous chapters, that "on these two commandments depend all the Law and the Prophets." If we are to emulate anyone in our social, political, and cultural life, surely this is the example. It is not man but God who demands first allegiance and will direct us to how we might best give a blessing to our fellows human beings.[12]

Historical Setting

We further note, as a preliminary to examining the specifics of Jesus' teachings, salient features of the socio-politico-theological atmosphere of the first century in Palestine (the Roman name for Judea).[13] As we have seen in the discussion of Jesus' earthly life and that of his family, the nation of Israel was totally dominated and exploited by the political and economic colossus of Rome. Rome was no benevolent patron,[14] except as its local policies required patronage to carry out the will of the emperor. It was a ruthless and militaristic empire, which forced its will on local populations at sword-point. Mass crucifixions were staged to impress unruly provinces and routine confiscation of goods and lands and unspeakable torture were used to enforce the *Pax Romana*.

---

11 See John 4:34; 5:30; 6:39; and other similar passages.
12 In this sense Jesus was not an altruist. He was a man sent on a mission from above. He "served" only one "Master."
13 See among others for background on this section Saldarini, *Pharisees, Scribes and Sadducees in Palestinian Society*; Jacob Neusner, *Judaism When Christianity Began* (Louisville: Westminster John Knox, 2002); Ernst Bammel and C. F. D. Moule, eds., *Jesus and the Politics of His Day* (New York: Cambridge University Press, 1984); Richard A. Horsley, *Bandits, Prophets, and Messiahs: Popular Movements in the Time of Jesus* (Harrisburg, PA: Trinity, 1999); Christopher Bryan, *Render to Caesar: Jesus, the Early Church, and the Roman Superpower* (New York: Oxford University Press, 2005); Geza Vermes, *Jesus and the World of Judaism* (Philadelphia: Fortress, 1984); K. C. Hanson and Douglas E. Oakman, *Palestine in the Time of Jesus: Social Structures and Social Conflicts* (Minneapolis: Fortress, 1998).
14 The latest attempt to set the patronal system of the Roman world in its early Christian context is Alan B. Wheatley, *Patronage in Early Christianity: Its Use and Transformation from Jesus to Paul of Samosata* (Eugene, OR: Wipf and Stock, 2011). The first two chapters of our next section (part 2) also have further data on pertinent issues we discuss in this section.

Way to the City

For all this, however, Rome had its hands full ruling its vast holdings. Wise political policy required that clients be recruited who could assist in pacifying local societies with methods short of raw force. In Rome, as in other empires past and present, the willingness to use and display such force encouraged profit seekers, power brokers, elitists, fearful hoarders of caches of wealth, various wielders of economic power, and outright sycophants to seek this role in the patron-client dance.[15] All of the players sought the one-upmanship of honors conferred, favors owed and received, the status of the "great man," and the strict reciprocity of relationship and arrangements that this system entailed.[16] These recruits in rare cases, such as Herod (Josephus?), were actually installed as local political leaders. Overwhelmingly, however, these clients served as liaisons peddling influence and privilege for their own profit—financial, political, and social.[17]

Among the holders of such privilege and status in Roman-occupied Judea were groups such as scribes, Pharisees, Sadducees (with the subgroups chief priests and elders) and possibly John's generic "the Jews." These groups had economic, political, and social stakes in ingratiating themselves with Rome and its other clients and also in seeing to it that nothing upset this cozy relationship, especially mass movements that tended to destabilize the accepted social networks and political connections.[18] Groups such as the Herodians and the Sicarii (from which Judas probably came) were *personae non gratae*

---

15   Among the hoarders of wealth was the temple, i.e., the priests who were responsible for its upkeep and environs. On more than one occasion the Romans confiscated large amounts from the temple treasuries as general tribute from the Jews. See also note 53 below on *mamona* as the hoarded coinage of this system. Mark Adam Elliott, *The Survivors of Israel: A Reconsideration of the Theology of Pre-Christian Judaism* (Grand Rapids, MI: Eerdmans, 2000), 187–244, has a superb chapter on the historical development of this situation from the Maccabees to A.D. 70.

16   See esp. Wheatley, *Patronage in Early Christianity*, on this prevailing paradigm and the changes Jesus insisted on and the apostles after him sought to bring into the churches.

17   This system of management of conquered territory was simply an extension of Roman cultural, social, and political control. We will refer to it frequently as "patronage" or "patronal."

18   These would be the elites who would contrast with "the poor." On the role of Rome in solidifying these strata in society in the eastern Empire, Peter Oakes says, "Rome reinforced the importance of status and made the hierarchy of status more rigid." *Philippians: From People to Letter* (New York: Cambridge University Press, 2007), 74–75. Oakes notes that Paul's teaching to the Philippian church set the stage for eventual cultural revolution. See Elliott, *Survivors of Israel*, for a full reconstruction of the prevailing structures of dissent and accommodation, politically, socially, and theologically during this period.

Way to the City

to the client groups. The Essenes, in contrast, chose the path of disengagement. Indeed, any mass movement not directly connected to the prevailing patron-client arrangements was bound to attract the opposition of all clients and the attention of the patron, Rome.[19] Thus, the salient comment of leaders prior to Jesus' crucifixion that, unless Jesus is stopped, "The Romans will come and take away our place (the temple)[20] and nation," and its rejoinder that it is better that "one man should die for the people and not the whole nation should perish" (John 11:48–50). The "our place" reference is coincident with Peter's reference to leaving "*idios*" in Luke 18:28.[21] This, the elites were clearly not prepared to do.

The prize for all involved in this charade was a pearl of great price (to use a common phrase of the day) formed by the nexus of power-position-money, not unlike all other societies since the dawn of human group dynamics—power over others, a position in society commanding respect and envy and all the attendant monetary rewards associated with the other two. In first-century Roman Palestine this elite formed by Roman-Jewish collaboration was made up of approximately ten percent[22] of the population—including powerful individuals not necessarily associated with specific groups. The remaining ninety percent were fodder for exploitation. There was no buffering middle class as we know it, though we would probably recognize as middle class the businessmen, artisans, shopkeepers, fishermen, etc., that plied their wares in the towns and countryside. The difference in the modern situation is that the middle class is now much more prosperous, as are the technically "poor," and there is mostly free movement in and out of whatever level of economic and social

---

19 Jesus is pointing to this same relationship (Luke 22:25) when he refers to those who have "lordship" in the human sense as naming themselves and commonly being called "benefactors."
20 For the priesthood this had heavy economic and social overtones.
21 It appears likely that men such as Levi (Matthew), Joseph of Arimathea, Nicodemus, Zacchaeus, and others either were only related on the fringe of these groups or came apart from them when they professed faith in Jesus. This would be what it meant to "forsake all," (Greek, *idios),* meaning "one's own" of whatever value denominated (Luke 18:28 cf. par.) in order to follow Jesus.
22 Estimates of this percentage range from 1 to 13 percent in the current literature on the subject. However, Paul Johnson, *Jesus: A Biography from a Believer* (New York: Viking, 2010), suggests more recently that a relative prosperity had come to ordinary people in Galilee during the reign of Herod. Elliott, *Survivors of Israel,* also suggests this possibility.

Way to the City

class one may find oneself. In Israel in the time of Jesus no such movement was expected, unless it was downward.

The huge majority consisted mostly of farmers and supporting workers, even in towns. Small numbers of artisans, merchants, traders, and assorted small businessmen were a part of the mix—such as, Peter, Andrew, James, John, Levi (the tax farmer), etc. From this mass of the people the elitists extracted what they needed to maintain position, power, and monetary benefits to pass along the upward ladder, which ended on the Tiber. "Tax farmers," such as Zacchaeus and many others along the way, extracted from thirty to seventy percent of the meager production of the mostly agrarian peasantry. Bitter rivalries over limited goods were common among the masses, and constant assaults on their freedom kept them only marginally/nominally above the level of slaves.[23] As in our own day it would be expected that the masses secretly and openly envied and vilified the "rich."[24] Jesus spoke to this, as we shall see.

The most important patron-client relationship for our current study is Rome's exploitation of the Jewish religious educator and priestly classes in Israel and symbiotic effects that obtained from this collaboration. Roman-occupied Israel was founded societally and sought its meaning in Jewish religion derived from its Holy Scriptures and the oral tradition that surrounded, or more literally "hedged it in," and of course the temple itself, the supposed lasting (and last) symbol of God's presence and blessing on Israel. Of course, Jerusalem as the home of the temple and supposed destination of Messiah was the city to which the king would come, as well as the focal point of pilgrimage and/ or burial. Rome sought to maintain order among the mostly religious masses by giving place and position to scribes, Pharisees (insofar as this group sought it politically), and the priestly families (mostly Sadducees), and these in turn

---

23 It was not until the late Middle Ages with the development of commerce and eventual industrialization that this hierarchical situation changed. Any discussion of current conditions in relation to biblical teachings and historical context must take these facts into account. The "poor" of ancient Israel are not analogous to people designated "poor" by American politicians. We will have more to say on this later.

24 See Thomas E. Schmidt, *Hostility to Wealth in the Synoptic Gospels*, JSNTSup 15 (Sheffield: JSOT Press, 1987), for a thorough study of attitudes relative to the contrasts between rich and poor as well as wealth and poverty in the OT period and leading up to the time of Christ.

Way to the City

reinforced their intermediary status by teaching, practice, and attitude—all the while being keenly aware that Israel's hope for a coming kingdom of God and messianic ruler languished under the Roman heel.

In addition, as Stark documents, "the Temple became the dominant financial institution, housing money-changers as well as acting as the state treasury and even as an investment bank—'a depository for capital sums, such as money belonging to widows and orphans or to the rich, who feared for their capital under the often insecure conditions that prevailed.'"[25] Concomitant with this assessment is the certainty that Jerusalem was the economic engine of Roman-occupied Israel. Stark summarizes the prevailing situation thusly: "It was this combination of a rich, relatively worldly priesthood controlling a subsidized state Temple, on the one hand, and 'outsider' political rulers reluctant to coerce religious conformity, on the other, that gave rise to the full range of Jewish religious groups (the Talmud notes twenty-four sects)."[26]

The Pharisee/scribal tradition (which was eventually to emerge as the rabbinic tradition) in general terms maximized its influence over the "people of the land" by feeding the hope for a soon appearance of Messiah with a guilt-mongering adherence to legal and traditional minutiae. Not unlike other health-wealth-prosperity teachers in other ages, they controlled those who listened to them or merely envied them by advocating strict legal-traditional observances, based on the priestly requirements of the Pentateuch, as the way to bring on the messianic age.[27] From their position in the patron-client-people chain, they could offer apparent proof of their doctrine in the visible benefits they gained as abettors of the Roman imperial political scheme. Their portrayal in the Gospels (by and large) as haughty, scheming, lovers of money, who made more of appearances than of inner character, "despising others" while expecting an earthly kingdom to confirm their "righteousness," is entirely consistent with the first-century social dynamics in the literature we cite in the notes.[28]

---

25 Stark, *Triumph of Christianity*, 39.
26 Ibid., 40.
27 See Elliott, *Survivors of Israel*, for the most comprehensive and nuanced treatment of the theological ferment in both sects and among the general populace.
28 We are aware that a school of thought centering on the work of E. P. Sanders has attempted to show that the NT portrayal of the Jewish leadership is essentially unfair. We are not in

Further, the Gospel accounts reflect prevailing opinion among the masses that appears to have been deeply affected by this traditional understanding of Israel's past, present (first century), and future hope.[29] Jesus plays into this dynamic as he addresses his first beatitude to "the poor" (Luke's account in 6:20) without concern for misunderstanding (even as Matthew records the same saying as "poor in spirit," 5:3). Even the most pious of "people of the land," subjected as they were to the situation and interpretation we have been describing, would likely have felt completely disfranchised and hopeless (even in the external sense echoed in the disciples' saying about the difficulty of salvation for the rich, "Who then can be saved?") and extremely vulnerable to religious manipulation. Their teachers were clearly "a cut above" and disdained them, "passing by" the plight of even the most innocent victim, and had no "good news" for them. Jesus, by contrast, labeled his teaching as "preaching the gospel" to the poor. And by "the poor" he meant all those of his time who were not a part of the outrageous political mockery of God's true rule that was first-century Israelite society—social outcasts, brazen sinners, political misfits, the innocents we have encountered elsewhere in the Scriptures, men and women like Jesus gathered around him as intimate followers, and the peasant masses, all without normal access to the social and cultural world of the elite, whether they were rich or poor. Each must face the possibility of becoming outcast from whatever milieu was normal to them. Here is the messianic king, and his retinue is not rulers and the elite but the mass of the people of the time.[30] And they will be subjected to the call to a discipleship of the cross, the focal point of true "good news" for any economic or social or political grouping.

The Sadducee/priestly group differed little from the Pharisee/scribal party in overall attitude and action. Where they did, in our judgment, they would have tended to make matters worse rather than better. In their attempt to

---

agreement with this assessment. See D. A. Carson, Peter T. O'Brien, and Mark A. Seifrid, eds., *Justification and Variegated Nomism, Vol. 1: The Complexities of Second Temple Judaism*, WUNT II 181, *Vol. 2: The Paradoxes of Paul*, WUNT II 140 (Tübingen: Mohr Siebeck / Grand Rapids, MI: Baker, 2001–2004).

29 See esp. the disciples' question, "Who then can be saved?" in the story of the rich ruler (Luke 18:26 cf. par.).

30 This is tantamount to saying that if he came originally to American soil, he would appeal to mass audiences of common people, not just some minority of economically poor or elite. And, there is only one gospel, not one for the poor and one for the rich.

Way to the City

refute the verbal-tradition side of Pharisee teaching, they also rejected the existence of angels as supernatural attendants to God's purpose, and most telling, the possibility of resurrection. This tended to make them even more intent on finding earthly blessing and reward as a confirmation of their righteous condition in the eyes of God. Such doctrinal conviction could not but have enhanced their human tendency to exploit the advantages they had as priestly clients of Rome. Surely this explains the sheer audacity of what Jesus termed turning God's "house of prayer" into a "den of robbers." It is not surprising then that, contrary to the Torah's vision of the Levitical priesthood as a tribe without a "possession," who would teach Israel to seek God aright, they were among the richest and most powerful of the Jews of Jesus' day.

Into this mix of politics, religion, and economics, Jesus came teaching.

Jesus, the Teacher

Jesus used and accepted five titles of distinction to refer to himself—Son of God (used as a confession of faith humanly or a cry of fear demonically, except in John's Gospel, where Jesus himself uses it sparingly to refer to himself), Son of Man (the phrase he most often used when referring to himself), Lord/Master, and Teacher.[31] These last two he uses in the key moment before his death (John 13:13) as a kind of dual designation of his personal relationship with his followers. Together they illuminate both Jesus' persona and his style as one verbalizing the will and Word of God, for the impression of him on the great masses of the people was that he "taught as one who had authority and not as their scribes."[32] Indeed, the overwhelming descriptive phrase for his speaking ministry is "he taught them, saying,..." with the preface, "and he opened his mouth," a way of emphasizing the solemnity along with impling command in his "sayings."

We emphasize this feature of the Gospel records for a specific reason— it shows clearly that Jesus' public and private utterances are to be taken as united in character and source with the "torah" of the OT records. If "torah"

---

31   "The Christ," lit. Messiah, "anointed one," is sparingly used and fraught with difficulties in the charged political atmosphere of the day.

32   Generically he was known as "one of the prophets" to the confessing Simon Peter as he heard it among the crowds.

Way to the City

(teaching) is what describes accurately "the Law" (as distinguished commonly from "the Prophets" by Jesus and his contemporaries), then it can be no mere coincidence that Jesus' speaking work is designated with the same term in such an overwhelming way. Furthermore, Jesus makes it plain that his "words" (like the "ten words" of Sinai) are themselves the source of "life" (John 6:63 and others); just as Moses characterized those other "words" as setting before Israel a choice between life and death (Deut. 30:11–20). It is unfortunate that many throughout Christian history have either neglected this salient fact or have actively sought to drive a wedge between the two "exoduses" (see Luke 9:31), in an apparent attempt to bring greater glory to Christ.[33] Far from succeeding in this endeavor, they have, we believe, tended to obscure the singleness of purpose and intent in the full revelation of God to humankind. Much confusion in the process of interpreting theological and ethical issues results from this hermeneutical propensity. Our purpose here is to avoid a false dichotomy in the ethics of our two "Testaments."[34]

Jesus "taught" and still teaches us with the fully nuanced methodology of a master at his task. Not surprisingly he encompasses all the methods through which Israel (and seekers from all nations) had been taught in the OT Scriptures.[35] Jesus speaks as a new lawgiver making solemn declarations of the will of God for all people just as Moses did. He schools his disciples as a new Samuel, preparing them to carry on the work he has begun. He thunders as one of the eighth century and later prophets with threats of "woe" and promises of "blessing."[36] He speaks words of unparalleled "wisdom" to those who would seek a "better" way. He is a master storyteller who uses narrative structures to provoke searching self-examination by even the most sophisticated listener, overtaking as he does and making new the parable genre. Truly "no man ever spoke as this man" did, and still does.

---

33 For a recent superb treatment that fills this gap, see Rikki E. Watts, *Isaiah's New Exodus in Mark* (Grand Rapids, MI: Baker, 2000). The word "departure" in this verse in Greek is "exodus."

34 Obviously this is a subject for another volume(s), but we simply advance this as our presupposition and trust what follows will justify this assertion.

35 For full treatment of Jesus as sage, see Ben Witherington III, *Jesus the Sage: The Pilgrimage of Wisdom* (Minneapolis: Fortress, 1994). On Jesus as teacher, see Craig S. Keener, *The Historical Jesus of the Gospels* (Grand Rapids, MI: Eerdmans, 2009), 186–237.

36 See Keener, *Historical Jesus of the Gospels*, 238–55.

Way to the City

In such a limited work as ours we can only hope to highlight and illustrate our theme in such a way as to provoke further thought and study. However, we will make every attempt to be faithful to the entire Gospel record, not merely picking and choosing what suits our purpose and paying particular attention to anything in the record that might tend to contradict our analysis. Having stated this proviso, we proceed using the general categories we have mentioned above—Jesus as lawgiver, discipler and mentor, prophet, wise man, and master storyteller.

The Sermon on the Mount

Jesus appears as the new Moses most clearly in Matthew's famous rendering of what we commonly call "The Sermon on the Mount" and Luke's partial parallel to it "on the plain."[37] It is highly significant that Matthew, whom many consider the "most Jewish" of the evangelists, should portray Jesus opening public preaching as a renewal of the ancient theme of "blessing" and its relationships(s) to the ethical/moral demands of God's law. It cannot be coincidental that there is an apparent recalling of the ancient covenantal "words" from a previous Mount. Couched in the language of "blessing" and "fire of hell," Jesus' words clearly are reminiscent of Moses' final reiteration of the words of God on the plains of Moab. And since his audience is primarily, if not wholly, made up of the descendants of Moses' audience, the parallels between the two situations cannot have been lost upon the most devout in Jesus' day. Add to this the fact that the nation of Israel was clearly (apparently) un-"blessed" in the Deuteronomic sense (making them "poor") and apparently "cursed" due to its failure to fulfill God's demands (see Ezra's lament, 9:8–9),[38] and we have a real window through which to view both Matthew's and Jesus' purpose.[39]

37　Clearly space does not permit the discussion here of Synoptic traditions and their nuanced presentations in our Gospels. We will note the pertinent issues as they may arise from our topic.

38　As we have previously noted, Ezra is paralleled here by Neh. 9–10 and Dan. 9. See also N. T. Wright's monumental works on this era and the sense among so many that the exile had never really ended.

39　This is surely the context in which we need to understand the designation "poor in spirit" here in Matthew and "ye poor" in Luke's account. These are the devout in Israel who wonder if God has completely forsaken them. By modern standards, at least ninety percent of the population of the world at that time were "poor," but Jesus is delineating something else in

It is apparent to us that Jesus is encouraging the masses of first-century Jewry and anyone else willing to hear, that even (or especially) those not normally seen as "blessed" can and do find blessing in the kingdom of God. It is arguable that Jesus' ongoing controversy with Jewish religious leaders is being joined here as he issues a challenge that all must consider who is truly blessed of God and in what that blessing consists. We will have more to say on this subject later. In any case, it is clear that a certain character constitutes the "blessed" and assures their standing before God, the Blessor.[40]

Three questions frame our inquiry into Jesus' teaching here: What is the meaning and intent of "blessed"? Does Jesus contradict the Law given at Sinai? What is the meaning and intention of Jesus' radical discipleship commands?

Virtually all commentators are agreed that the "blesseds" Jesus pronounces here are loaded with both eternal and substantive temporal import. Not only is he promising a life beyond this one, but he also pointing to how certain emphases and attitudes in this life produce profound depths of "blessing" now that contradict apparent external conditions. It is a hermeneutical mistake to insist that it must be an either/or choice. It is clearly both/and. It is also a false dichotomy to suggest that Jesus is here somehow saying something that the "blessing" of the OT records does not teach. We have already demonstrated that it is a misunderstanding to see the OT "blessing" as only or even mostly material and temporal. Jesus is telling all who will follow him that the precise character traits that are inherent in those possessing eschatological salvation will have temporal effects as well.[41] As long as God's creation remains as it

---

this "sermon." These are a particular poor, the ones in Israel not seeking relief through the elitist relationships of the day but in God alone. See D. A. Carson, "Matthew," in *Matthew, Mark, Luke*, vol. 8 of EBC, ed. Frank E. Gaebelein (Grand Rapids, MI: Zondervan, 1984), ad loc., for a full discussion. Also see Peter Beyerhaus, "'Blessed Are the Poor in Spirit': The Theology of the Poor in Biblical Perspective," in *God Who Is Rich in Mercy: Essays Presented to Dr. D. B. Knox, ed.* Peter T. O'Brien and David G. Peterson (Homebush West, NSW, Australia: Lancer Books; Grand Rapids, MI: distributed in North America by Baker, 1986), 153–63. See also Blomberg, *Matthew*, 99: "'Poor in spirit,' as a virtue, must refer not to a poor quality of faith but to the acknowledgment of one's spiritual powerlessness and bankruptcy apart from Christ (cf. Goodspeed, 'Those who feel their spiritual need')."

40 Jesus clearly casts himself in the role of the God of the OT, the true Blessor.

41 That is, those "poor in spirit," "meek," "hungry for righteousness," etc. We would advance and support the thought here also that it is best to accept Jesus' assessment of blessedness in poverty as the best way out of poverty and mourning and hunger, etc. Not all are

Way to the City

has been since Noah was promised a stable process, those who take Jesus at his word and regard themselves as truly "blessed" rather than wallowing in their outward circumstances will find it is truly the best and most personally rewarding way to live, in every sense of the word "reward." And, to the degree that "blessed" in the precise Greek rendering can mean "truly happy," they will find the best of what a balanced life short of eternal bliss can provide—once again, in spite of appearances to the contrary. Finally, in the end, as the truly "meek," they will "inherit the earth" literally—the new earth.

Jesus affirms and fills fuller the concept of "blessing." But how does he deal with the Law—specifically its ethical demands? Does Jesus in his most extensive recorded teaching on the moral demands of God contradict the "words" of Sinai? The implications of the answer to this question are critical. If it can be convincingly argued that the answer is yes, then a precedent is set for a hermeneutical process that must end in pitting a NT ethic or morality against its OT equivalent. This is, in fact, a common practice in Christian circles from pulpit to pew and across the spectrum of theological reflection from right to left. As we have stated above, we are presuppositionally opposed to this answer. It creates far more problems than it can ever hope to solve. Imagine a scene where Jesus actually suggests to his audience that he is the unique and only Son of the living God, and among his duties is the task of correcting some of the things his "old man" has said, because after all, we all know how our dads tend to get heavy-handed in exaggerating things!

Nevertheless, do the NT records support our position or contradict it? In Matthew's recounting of Jesus' preaching he moves swiftly from the exhortation for the "blessed" to live as "salt and light" in the present world to a discussion of how this being a "city on a hill" (a harbinger of new thinking on "the city") works out in real life. Suddenly he appears to break with the flow of his previous speaking by going to an aside about his role as teacher vis-à-vis "the Law" and "the Prophets." But this is no *aside*. It is, instead, as plain a statement as can be made about what is the nature of his teaching that follows. Whatever we may say about Jesus' subsequent discourses anywhere in his ministry, we

---

literally and materially poor, but all must be "poor in spirit" to get true blessing, indeed, even to be *saved*.

Way to the City

may not construe his words to be "abolishing" or causing to "pass away" even "the smallest stroke" of the Law until all of it "is accomplished," in the sense of coming into full existence. Further, anyone who "breaks" (or "relaxes," lit., "loosens") the "smallest" of the OT commands will himself find he is "smallest" in the eternal kingdom.

But lest his hearers should mistake this warning to imply that their example in this should be their current religious leadership, he warns that such "righteousness" as they possess will not even permit them to "enter" that kingdom. Clearly Jesus is pointing to himself as the embodiment of obedience to the Law that is alone worthy of emulation. With that said, he proceeds as the prior law-giving did to offer "case studies" (casuistic law) of his own ethical teaching. Each case probes to the full implications of a previous "word"—on murder, adultery, bearing false witness, and so forth.

Murder is shown to proceed from evil attitudes of the heart related to other persons—often first manifested in verbal assault that can become a settled refusal to recognize one's need for reconciliation with an offended "brother" and/or a resistance to meeting obligations that forces a creditor (as anyone we "owe" in any interaction) to take us to court for justice.[42] Likewise, adultery is shown to begin as an affair of the heart and as a sin that cannot escape God's righteous gaze simply because it flies under the screen of legal or societal niceties. The tendency to cover our lies at the expense of others with ever greater oath-takings cannot substitute for "keeping our word" as a simple understanding of God's law in the ninth "word" of Exodus 20 (Matt. 5:33–37).

Jesus next proceeds with a case of the contemporary misuse of a command embedded in biblical teaching about how judges are to determine appropriate punishment for deeds that require societal action (Matt. 5:38–42). The OT materials as we have seen clearly teach that "the punishment should fit the crime"—"crime" here being terminology that subsumes both our "civil" and "criminal" legal terminology. Further, societal courts must be scrupulously "just" and not subject to varying and arbitrary degrees of suasion through attention to class or monetary influence. Jesus makes plain that this command does not sanction

---

42 This is a clear exposition of Lev. 19:17. In fact, we contend that Jesus' tenor throughout his teaching is founded on the implications of the entire Lev. 19 perspective.

Way to the City

either personal retribution or a tit-for-tat self-preservation ethic. He continues with cases where one might actually suffer real injustice voluntarily when it might seem strictly permissible to do otherwise (vv. 39–42). Here is the place one would expect Jesus to advance a social agenda if he had one. But it is clear he is addressing "the poor in spirit" on how to be blessed, not how to acquire the goods of others through governmental action.[43]

In this first of what are sometimes called "radical" demands of Christian ethics, we have an opportunity to probe Jesus' teaching for its real-life implications. Taken one way, these cases would seem to show the true Christian life as one subject to any bully or street mugger one encounters, every frivolous lawsuit seeking to exploit any vulnerability perceived by the avaricious, slavery to anyone with power to compel it, and impoverishment at the hands of deadbeats and chiselers. This cannot be its meaning for several reasons. First, every person is related by mutual obligations to many others before he is to any individual seeking to perpetrate such "evil" on him. It follows that how one reacts in such a situation is not merely a question of personal preservation but of complex intersections of obligation that cause one person's loss to mean loss for others. A father's loss is also a loss for his children and spouse as well as any to which he may owe financial or other compensation. Further, the overall tenor of Jesus' teaching and lifestyle and that of his earliest followers does not demonstrate such a "radical" lifestyle.[44] Jesus is not commanding a voluntary descent into misery with a concomitant descent in varying degrees by all those linked to us by our natural and God-ordained obligations in order to prove some point about generosity. This would be worse than foolishness.

What then is Jesus teaching? It seems obvious to us that he is commanding something like this: Within the context of what the Scriptures teach with respect to all your given personal moral obligations, seek to overcome evil people by doing good to them insofar as it can be done, rather than acting merely retributively and out of direct reciprocal arrangements. This teaching is in itself, "radical," since our natural impulse is to give tit for tat and to harbor resentment against those who

---

43 For an excellent analysis of these texts in Matt. 5, see esp. Frederick Dale Bruner, *Matthew: A Commentary, Vol. 1: The Christbook, Matthew 1–12*, rev. ed. (Grand Rapids, MI: Eerdmans, 2007), 187–280. For a classic expositional treatment, see D. Martyn Lloyd-Jones, *Studies in the Sermon on the Mount* (Grand Rapids, MI: Eerdmans, 1959), 1:149–320.
44 We will discuss the early Acts church at the appropriate time.

Way to the City

have wronged us.[45] Jesus is calling on us to be countercultural.[46] It is manifest in the text that Jesus is speaking of person-to-person interactions, where those with the most knowledge of a specific situation can rightly make such judgments. He is not here advocating either some universal "rule of thumb" for every individual case or an overhaul of societal law and convention, though it is clear if this begins to be put in practice, revolutionary things will happen.[47] Neither is he here advocating the overhaul of the political system, in the way we normally think about that. Still less is he suggesting that humankind and nations should not seek to "resist evil" in its general manifestations morally, politically, economically, militarily, and other ways.[48] Further, Luke's record of Jesus' speaking in this vein and adding "lend, expecting nothing in return" (Luke 6:35), lends credence to the interpretation that Jesus is speaking against the concept of direct reciprocity in relationships that was part of the patron-client atmosphere of the day.[49] He was not advocating that Christians should not expect to repay their debts to one another.

---

45 Anecdotally, one of us (Chad) was preaching through this section of the Sermon on the Mount not long ago, trying to show the "radical" nature of Jesus' demands here. One prominent church member walked out after one of the services and commented, "No one can live like that." Indeed!

46 John R. W. Stott, *Christian Counter-Culture: The Message of the Sermon on the Mount*, Bible Speaks Today (Downers Grove, IL: InterVarsity Press, 1978).

47 Richard Stearns is particularly overwrought, it seems to us, as he repeatedly asserts that Jesus came to start a "social revolution" (*The Hole in Our Gospel* [Nashville: Thomas Nelson, 2009], 20, 22, 67, et al.) and *that* our task is to carry out Jesus' call and mission "for a redeemed world order populated by a redeemed people—*now*" (emphasis his) as the meaning of his proclamation of "the kingdom of God" (Ibid., 16). Ron Sider also states baldly that Jesus was crucified primarily because he was a "dangerous social radical." *I Am Not a Social Activist* (Scottsdale, PA: Herald, 2008), Kindle loc. 702–13. This is not a new conception, and it has all the dangers inherent in any over-realized eschatology.

48 The OT records make clear that the God of the Bible regularly uses national and other duly constituted entities to bring punishment to bear where needed, even when it becomes excessive (see Habakkuk's complaint among others). The whole direction of Torah and Prophets also advocates heroically protecting innocents in our charge. See the discussion of this in Lloyd-Jones, *Studies in the Sermon on the Mount*, 271–89, where he demonstrates the folly of thinking that Jesus here is advocating the end of criminal or civil justice or is advocating pacifism.

49 Halvor Moxnes says of the Lukan quote: "This is the end of the patronal-client relationship in a traditional sense." *The Economy of the Kingdom: Social Conflict and Economic Relations in Luke's Gospel* (Philadelphia: Fortress, 1988), 133. The patron-client relationship involved sometimes complicated obligations with clear demarcations between those who gained superiority by their "gifts" and those who benefited from them. This relationship will have significance in chapters that follow as we continue to explore its influence on the early church and its mission.

Way to the City

Jesus continues by introducing a common misconception of his day embodied in the teaching of contemporary teachers of the law, i.e., "love your neighbor and hate your enemy" (Matt. 5:43–48). That this is nowhere commanded in the OT goes without saying.[50] This idea was nothing but an outright failure to teach God's Word correctly and is reflected later in the cynical question, "And who is my neighbor?" which prompted from Jesus the famous "Good Samaritan" story. In this second of his "radical" demand case studies, Jesus points those who would follow him to the radical activities of the heavenly Father, who clearly has more in mind in the term "neighbor" than a distinction such as, "whoever cannot be classified as an 'enemy'."[51] God's post-flood promise to Noah can readily be seen to encompass even those who make themselves "enemies" to God's kingdom. Those who would prove themselves to be "sons of the Father" will, therefore, practice his love by "praying" even for their own persecutors—without doubt, that they too might become sons of the Father and cease being enemies of God. The "perfection" of the Father is seen in his redemption even of his enemies. This is radical Christianity, and it has its "reward."

Having introduced the category of "reward" (as opposed to the previous warning of "hellfire") to his teaching, Jesus moves easily to a discussion of the nature of the kinds of reward—temporal, illusory, public vs. eternal, substantial, hidden for now. Of particular interest for our study here is the phrase "good deeds" or "acts of righteousness." Typically in first-century Jewish parlance this term denoted personal charitable acts that at best were an expression of devotion to God and his law and of genuine religious fervor and worship.[52] It is clear in the context (Matt. 6:1–18) that it is the proper attitude in worship that is subjected to case study in the topical areas of charity, prayer, and fasting. All appear as virtuous activities deserving of eternal rewards but also subject to abuse by fallen humanity.

---

50 See Lev. 19 for the exact opposite.
51 Lev. 19:33–34 are the culmination of the context of teaching on loving the neighbor.
52 The entire issue of personal "merit" in the pursuit of salvation among the Jews of Jesus' day has come in for rethinking in recent decades. We cannot join that debate here. However, see Gary A. Anderson, *Sin: A History* (New Haven, CT: Yale University Press, 2009), for a thought-provoking study on how the conception of sin as "debt" (the terminology of the "Our Father" as he denominates it) led to Jewish attempts to repay the debt of sin by almsgiving and other good deeds.

Way to the City

Two obvious features of Jesus' teaching here impact our current discussion. The first is that any activity deemed worthy of reward must be a voluntary matter. It cannot be coerced. Otherwise, it would not be considered virtuous. It might be commanded and bracketed with the possibilities of reward and punishment, but it is not by its very nature something to be forced on anyone with these implications. Force inherently negates the categories of reward and punishment. Both Testaments in our modern copies of the Bible support this presupposition.

The second general principle is that truly virtuous deeds must pass muster with God on all counts regardless of the apparent commendation of earthly powers or social conventions. Whether one has actually done "good" depends on God's judgment (cf. its earliest iteration in the story of Cain and Abel). This is the companion NT conception to what we have already seen in the OT materials—"that which is right in the sight of God." It is manifest in this section of Jesus' "Sermon" that there are many ways that humanity can be led astray in the apparent "doing of good" by less than biblical motives and goals. Jesus gives us samples here of the kinds of situations where this can and does regularly occur. In so doing he supports the prior teaching of "the Law and the Prophets." Indeed, it is telling that the prophet Malachi condemns in no uncertain terms such wrongheaded and morally bankrupt attempts to impress God with externals (Mal. 1:6–14).

What follows is another masterful transition from one focal point to its extension. The failure to focus one's attention on the heavenly reward betrays a more deadly lack of loyalty to the proper Master. Jesus makes his point with a kind of wisdom saying (comparing relative values) that bids his audience to think about how one's "treasure" draws the concentration of one's "heart." In stating the obvious he brings clarity to the mind of any who will think along with him. His final statement, "You cannot serve God and money" (lit., "mammon," a more comprehensive term than mere currency),[53] is particularly

---

53 See Hanson and Oakman, *Palestine in the Time of Jesus*, 121–23, defining "mammon" as "stored wealth upon which one places trust." Further, the Aramaic *mamona* for "wealth" denoted the coinage that only the elite could and did collect to use in their exchanges for favor and security in the patronage system of the day. In this sense, one "slaves" for it. See also Ben Witherington III, *Jesus and Money* (Grand Rapids, MI: Brazos, 2010), who in several places (9, 66, 150, 157) seems to disparage the building up of retirement accounts as contrary to Jesus' teaching here. We would only agree with him if he means that putting

apropos among a congregation daily accustomed to the literal implications of "slave" (the root meaning of "serve") relationships all about them. It is not the acquisition of material things he is condemning. It is the tendency to treat them as treasure and to allow them to be an enslaving influence. Seeking rewards in the eternal sphere is the antidote to this mind-set, and the implication is clearly that some will lose reward in the heavenly arena (that is, they have all they will get) because of favoring the earthly. This lays the groundwork for a nonegalitarian world to come.

With a penetrating connective "therefore" (whenever you see this word, ask yourself, "What's it there for?"), Jesus makes it clear that slavery to material things is not the sole (or even the predominant) province of the rich. Keenly aware of the human condition of the vast majority of his audience, he proceeds to speak of things like food and clothing and the "worry" that can drive those who wonder if they will have enough of these necessities daily. Recalling that even creatures of God who are unable to do the things that humans can do to provide for themselves find God's largesse adequate, he bids them reason with him that they (his audience) are in line to receive "much more" than flowers and birds do from God's hand.[54] While Jesus will warn the rich at other times of the "deceitfulness of riches," his emphasis here is clearly on the danger that the more mundane "worries of life" may be the most widespread enemy of "the kingdom of God and his righteousness." It seems to us to go without saying (almost) that nothing here justifies the idea that radical Christians should abandon the usual human process of "sowing and gathering" (in all its implications) in favor of living like birds[55] and flowers in anticipation of some miraculous supply or the largesse pro-

---

one's trust in these things is wrong. Failure to prepare for the declining years of life by savings and investment is an unbiblical way to deal with life's contingencies. Someone will have to take that responsibility for all or most of us near the end of life.

54 Note that "little faith" here is the failure to make rational inferences from the created order.

55 There is a good deal of misunderstanding about the "birds" in this text. If you watch birds in action, they are extremely hardworking and busy in providing for their physical needs. They do not just sit on telephone wires with their mouths open waiting for God to drop seeds in them. Well, except the ones in our bird cages at home who start to squawk "feed me" as soon as they hear us up and about in the morning!

Way to the City

vided by the taxes and fees paid by others, harvested politically.[56] Worry and its companion "seeking" in a kind of feverish frenzy are to be avoided as the key manifestations of "little faith."

Having moved by stages through his moral teaching, Jesus now begins to draw toward a concluding challenge to hear in such a way as to produce action, recognizable "good fruit," and ultimately a "house" that will stand in the coming "storm" of judgment. This process begins with having a discriminating sense of "judgment" that sees oneself and others through the same lens, enabling one to avoid the twin pitfalls of self-deception and gullibility in the face of false prophets. Jesus acknowledges this as a "narrow gate" to enter and a "hard way" to go. But he also affirms that those who go on "asking, seeking, knocking" will "receive, find, and have opened" the "road" to life—both temporal and eternal. No pious and unsubmissive mouthing of "Lord"-ship will suffice for actually walking out this path. Only actually "doing the will" of the Father will avoid his judgment.

At the heart of this final appeal Jesus utters the famous "Golden Rule" statement that is probably rightly taken as a summary of his ethics: "Do to others"—a positive command, contrasting to the common teaching of his day, "do not do to others… what you would have them do to you"—in the context of urging the entry on a life of doing the will of God. And, most importantly, "for this is the Law and the Prophets"—at once summarizing both his teaching and all that has gone before. At the risk of going where no mere man should go, we offer this summary of the Golden Rule in its context: As a moral and wise person who wishes to arrive at an eternal reward and live a productive and God-pleasing life along the way, I must do everything for my neighbor that

---

56 It is strange to us how Craig Blomberg can contend, as he does, that the NT, and esp. Jesus, does not promise "material wealth" as a "guaranteed reward" for "spiritual obedience or even hard work." *Neither Poverty nor Riches* (Downers Grove, IL: InterVarsity Press, 1999), 145 and 242. If the heavenly Father "knows that we have need of these things," where in the world are we supposed to get them if not through the "blessing" on our living and hard work? He would undoubtedly key on his use of the word "wealth," but he continually charges most of the North American church with possessing this very thing, a product overwhelmingly of hard work and Christian discipline. David Platt followed Blomberg on this subject, in *Radical: Taking Back Your Faith from the American Dream* (Colorado Springs: Multnomah, 2010), Kindle loc. 1613–25. Platt does not follow Blomberg's "moderate socialism," but he does advocate some of Blomberg's same hermeneutic, which we find problematic.

Way to the City

will tend to achieve that same goal in his life. Anything else is "foolish" in the extreme and is an ethic that is as shifty as sand in a raging flood. None of Jesus' teachings on money or the poor should lead us to do things to others that will lead them into lives of irresponsibility or laziness or failure to produce so as to be able to do "good" for others from their own resources. Nor should we teach them to seek sustenance from other than the one true Source, to whom we appeal for "daily bread."[57]

We join those of Jesus' day in saying that no teaching in all the literature of mankind is so "amazing" as this, for it bears the "authority" of the Father and the Son.

The Further Teaching of Jesus

A close reading of the Gospels gives the overwhelming impression that Jesus taught predominantly "along the way" of his itinerant mission. The Sermon(s) on the Mount/Plain is matched for length of discourse in passages of parabolic utterance or conjoined sayings, edited possibly for similarity of content or context[58] by the evangelists. None of these other materials, however, matches the evident overall plan of Matthew's famous sermon. We turn our attention now to these teaching moments.

These were opportunities presented by varieties of situations—interaction with the crowds, spoken of disdainfully as "the people of the land" by class- and status-conscious religious leaders; confrontations with those same leaders over their attitudes, teachings, and religious practices; occasions of extended parabolic teaching and prophetic exhortation; propitious one-on-one encounters with earnest seekers and foolish dabblers; and always in the day-to-day mentoring of his inner circle of disciples. In all of these moments Jesus shows

---

57 It is one of the strangest fallacies of interpretation on this section of the Sermon that advocates for the "poor" of our day never stop at being sure that governmental and other programs provide merely "daily bread" for their constituencies. On the other hand the so-called "rich" are constantly warned in the literature of Christian activists for the "poor" about seeking more than "daily bread." This is clearly politics and not biblical exhortation or teaching.
58 Both that of the original hearers and the communities to whom the Gospel writers addressed their work.

his mastery of every contingency, every pretentious claim or boast, and every press conference–like challenge intended to catch him off guard or in some way unsure of himself and his relationship to his Father.[59]

Two things are striking in all these Gospel accounts. First, Jesus models precisely the challenge uttered by Malachi 2:7: "For the lips of a priest should guard knowledge, and people should seek instruction from his mouth, for he is the messenger of the LORD of hosts." He was truly a teacher of "the people," in contrast to the pretenders to that role of the time who sought more to exploit, dominate, and impress their hearers than to humbly guide them to the truth. For this the people "heard him gladly" (Mark 12:37). Second, Jesus' mastery of the minutiae with which he was often peppered in public debate stems from his command of the whole body of the Law and the Prophets. His answers and expositions flow from a settled moral, theological compass established in what has already been revealed. His condemnation of his generation's "teachers" is not for their concern with the contemporary implications of the Law or the Prophets but for the manner in which their "traditions" set aside and made empty the actual commands of God (Matt. 15:6). Thus he could plow a straight course (as Paul exhorted Timothy to do) and cut to the joints and marrow of issues (as the writer of Hebrews commends the power of God's Word), pressing home his message to the heart of the matter and the hearer (Matt. 15:10–20) as we see in the following instances.

Jesus taught as a universal principle that the ordinary "cares of this world" and "the deceitfulness of riches" can blind anyone to the truth and lead to eternal ruin (Matthew 13:22; Mark 4:18–19; Luke 8:14). The rich have their own peculiar temptations to trust in their material successes rather than God (Mark 10:17–31; Luke 12:16–21; 16:19–31), but "worry" over food and clothing (Luke 12:22–31) and undue concern over life's unfairness (Luke 12:13–15) are also threats to one's spiritual well-being.[60] What is most important about the presence of any amount of this world's goods is that they be used wisely,

---

59 See esp. on these varied situations Keener, *Historical Jesus of the Gospels.*
60 Jesus refuses here to address the issue of primogeniture relative to an inheritance and in using the term "all covetousness" makes plain that the one bringing the request for justice to him is the actual covetous one. If Jesus were a social reformer, he would have addressed this matter that was not really changed in the West until the founders of the American republic hammered out compromises on property succession. See on this Thomas G. West,

Way to the City

even shrewdly, in such a way as to accumulate eternal blessings (Luke 16:1–13). This last parable is also noteworthy for its use of a most surprising application that implies wisdom about life and eternity is to be found in some very peculiar situations.

Jesus also consistently taught that the daily calculations prudent people make about relative values in tradable commodities apply to kingdom issues as well. His repeated use of the question "What does it profit?" (Matt. 16:26; Mark 8:36; Luke 9:25) within the context gets the attention of all those accustomed to making trade-offs on a daily basis. The pearl of great price and hidden treasure (Matt. 13:44–46) are examples of things worth great sacrifice, just as eternal values are—in fact, one must be prepared to give all for such things when they are encountered. Thus, following Jesus may cause one to reverse the values of the world completely (Luke 14:7–24) for the sake of eternal reward. This should be seen as the only prudent and wise thing to do, for God himself is the ultimate investor, and he expects a return on investment (Matt. 25:14–30; Luke 19:11–27) for which there will be unequal eternal rewards based on faithfulness and apparent degrees of eternal punishment based on knowledge (Luke 12:47–48).[61] Moreover, he clearly implies that a contract freely entered cannot be used to charge an employer (or Lord) with injustice simply because outcomes appear to be disparate (Matt. 20:1–13, esp. v. 13). This language challenges all who will hear to inventory their stock of goods and values to get a clear picture of their true wealth.

Jesus further makes it clear that material, social, and spiritual resources should be used to benefit others and the kingdom. Tithes and almsgiving in themselves do not bring eternal rewards when the heart attitude is corrupt (Matt. 23:23–25), for there is more to giving than the material thing in itself.[62] In fact, giving what is "inside the cup" is the greater gift (Luke 11:39–42), for it implies more than concern for the immediate physical, material need,

---

Vindicating the Founders: Race, Sex, Class, and Justice in the Origins of America (1997; repr., New York: Rowman & Littlefield, 2000), 37–71.

61 Note esp. in light of our topic that the life to come will have its inequalities based on faithfulness in this life. All rewards will not be the same, nor will punishments. See also Paul's teaching on this subject in 1 Cor. 3:10–15; 9:16–27.

62 See several standard commentaries for the reading that one must give "what is in the cup" first.

Way to the City

reaching out to underlying causes and eternal destinies. This kind of giving is displayed in contrast to mere religious piety in the famous good-Samaritan parable (Luke 10:30–37). Here an outcast from Jewish religious culture demonstrates true neighborliness, the readiness to bring energy and resources to bear upon any situation of opportunity within one's reach. Negatively, the failure of the rich man to come to the relief of Lazarus, the problem on his doorstep, is seen as demonstrating an uncaring and selfish disposition that untreated leads to hell. Further the life to come will see many great reversals of fortune (Luke 16:19–31). In both these cases the emphasis is upon doing what can realistically be done from the standpoint of both the need and the personal resources at hand.[63]

However, giving without reference to discernment of what is best for both the recipient's actual need and the giver's wise use of resources is not commendable—for God himself gives in just this way (Matt. 7:7–11; Luke 18:1–8). We should follow God's example, for opportunities to expend resources of all kinds abound for those who have eyes to see otherwise hidden opportunities to aid "the least" of Christ's "brethren" (Matt. 25:31–46; cf. 18:6).[64] This scene of the judging of "the nations" carries implications for how nations as a whole respond to the missional messengers ("the least") sent to them.

Such giving along the way might also be supplemented by situational divestitures of larger amounts. Zacchaeus, a rich man according to the text (as were all publicans) and known oppressor, was inspired to make restitution even beyond biblical requirements in his euphoria over the forgiveness Jesus

---

63 This moral obligation to discern opportunities to "do good" implies that we cannot plead ignorance in the face of clear injustice, thus justifying our inaction—see, e.g., the failure of "good people" to take a stand in days gone by on such issues as slavery, Jim Crow, and civil rights. However, the attempts of many to tar with this story any who do not agree to a leftist political agenda, as if the modern political situation were as transparent as Jesus' parable, are wide of the mark and demagogic in the extreme.

64 We take this reference to "the least" to be substantially the same as the saying in Mark 9:42 and Matt. 18:6 about "little ones." Marcus J. Borg, *Conflict, Holiness and Politics in the Teaching of Jesus* (Harrisburg, PA: Trinity, 1998), 216, cites Jeremias for this interpretation of "little ones" with which we agree. These least of Christ's "brethren" are his faithful followers. Michael Goulder, "Matthew's Vision for the Church," in *A Vision for the Church: Studies in Early Christian Ecclesiology in Honour of J. P. M. Sweet, ed.* Markus Bockmuehl and Michael B. Thompson (Edinburgh: T&T Clark, 1997), 24, takes the same position. See also Isa. 60 for the eschatological background of this saying, esp. v. 22.

Way to the City

gave (Luke 19:1–10), but there is no indication Jesus insisted on it.[65] The disciples had in some sense "left all" (Mark 10:28), though we are not told that this was a true divestiture, for they did return to their homes and businesses (more on this later). The rich young ruler failed to sell his goods and give the proceeds to the poor because his riches held him in thrall (Mark 10:17–31), much to his eternal detriment, and we add also, his earthly detriment, for Jesus clearly answers Peter's inquiry about the forsaking action of the Twelve with a present and future promise (Luke 18:28–30).[66] In each of these cases the object lesson is not about benefiting the poor but about eternal consequences related to what might be required in following Jesus. The issue is not redistribution of wealth but eternal salvation.[67] Jesus himself said, "The poor you have always" (Mark 14:7; John 12:8), in the context of a lavish outpouring on his own person. Those who sought to make a false dichotomy between this giving and that which directly benefits the poor heard Jesus' rebuke, "Let her alone" (John 12:7).[68] In sum, Jesus taught that kingdom giving is about the attitude of the heart, the presence of opportunity and resources, the demand of kingdom business, and the overflow of grace-inspired gratitude.[69]

---

65 This is one of several incidents with publicans that Luke records positively, indicating that "the poor" of his Gospel includes rich publicans.

66 For those who would deny a material element here, the text is clear. Others will indicate that this can only be from the sharing implicit in Christian community. The fact is, no one will have anything to share with anyone if there is no material promise implicit. You cannot outgive God in this world, or the one to come.

67 Peter's inquiry about who then can be saved (if not a rich man capable of doing generous good deeds and apparently blessed with largesse from God) elicits a response from Jesus on the impossibility of salvation for anyone in the human sense. (See Anderson, *Sin*, on this situation in the time period.) It all depends upon the willingness to follow Christ explicitly. Otherwise, mere divestiture and giving goods away would lead to impoverishment of the rich man with no apparent place to go and no source of sustenance. The key is "come follow me," for Jesus has a new plan for his life. This the rich man refused.

68 Judas was certainly not the first or the last to have an ulterior motive for supposedly giving to the poor—he was getting his cut from the bag like the welfare establishment does today. If all social welfare spending in the United States were simply paid out to the qualified recipients, it would amount to $83,000 a year per person (see chap. 25, n. 11). Unfortunately this tendency has appeared also in American charitable organizations and among well-known advocates and leaders of Christian organizations ministering in fund-raising for poverty relief around the world. Salaries from nearly $500,000 and approaching $1,000,000 can be found. Of course, the American pastorate has also sadly been affected with this disease.

69 In this sense one cannot "serve" God and anything else at all—not even the "poor" or one's family (Matt. 10:34–39) or the "hungry" (John 6:25–27) or the prisoners (see John

John's unique organization of his Gospel around seven "signs" with pertinent teaching emphasizes that temporal miracles and provisions cannot substitute for eternal values and insights. John's conclusion is that despite all the "signs," unbelief was more common among the observers and recipients than faith (John 12:37–50). Particularly apropos of our current study is the story of Jesus' feeding of the five thousand followed by his walk on the water, this last in an apparent attempt to defuse popular enthusiasm over the signs (John 6). His abrupt challenge to those who sought him out "on the other side" of the Sea of Galilee is singularly illustrative of his clear insight into human motives and incentives: "I assure you: You are looking for Me, not because you saw the signs, but because you ate the loaves and were filled" (John 6:26 HCSB). Jesus zeros in on both their need and unbelief and his mission—"Don't work for the food that perishes"; "I am the bread of life"; "Your fathers ate the manna in the wilderness, and they died"; "The one who eats this bread will live forever"; and so on (John 6:27, 35, 49, 58, all HCSB). Jesus is saying to an extremely poor (materially) people that they must cease pursuing a handout, read the "signs" for his true person, and work and believe that, so their true need could be met. As Udo Middelmann puts it, "They saw Jesus as a grand provider without a budget problem! But he taught them that God wanted to reign in their hearts and minds and instruct them about all of life. That would be the way to create food and all other things for life in a manner that no social program or distribution system could provide."[70] In short, he refuses to set up a food kitchen or to let his mission be diverted from its true purpose.[71]

Even his closest followers found these words (teaching) "hard." Why so? Because even a free meal cannot continue in the face of unbelief and the ongoing demands of the kingdom business of calling men and women to follow Christ

---

the Baptizer) or politics. It is just at this point that Gary Anderson, *Sin*, would insert his take on the "merits" of almsgiving (167–70). The best answer to Anderson and others on the issues surrounding the nature of Second Temple theological thought on eschatological salvation (and/or the return from exile) is Carson, O'Brien, Seifrid, *Justification and Variegated Nomism*, 2 vols.

70 Udo Middelmann, *Christianity versus Fatalistic Religions in the War against Poverty* (Colorado Springs: Paternoster, 2007), 51. Of course, undoubtedly many in the crowd that day were thinking of provision that would feed an army to overthrow Rome.

71 John Howard Yoder notes here that Jesus refused to be a "Welfare King." *The Politics of Jesus*, 2nd ed. (Grand Rapids, MI: Eerdmans, 1994), 34.

Way to the City

as Lord. Jesus himself was the only source of spiritual nourishment.[72] The people who sought Jesus out in this instance are no different from those in the days of Moses who begged for food, got manna, learned to despise it, complained till Yahweh sent quail, and then got sick on that, all the while nostalgically remembering leeks and garlic and meat pots from their slave days. Even the poor and needy need a character change. Jesus insists on telling them so in no uncertain terms. This is truly "hard teaching." "Who can hear it?" (John 6:60).[73]

DOING THE WILL OF GOD: THE MINISTRY AND FOLLOWERS OF JESUS

Jesus is plain in his statements to all who hear his teaching that it is not those who only "hear" his teaching but those who "do" his will that please him and receive eternal blessing (Matt. 7:21–27). Setting aside for the moment all the other compelling reasons to study the details of Jesus' ministerial activities, this reason alone compels us to seek out how Jesus actually practiced what he taught others. Further, we want to examine, at least briefly, "those whom he chose" to be with him in his daily itinerancy, for it is clear he is mentoring them in anticipation of the day when they will continue this work after his physical departure ("exodus").

Luke's Gospel (4:16–21) contains a kind of formalized annunciation of the onset of Jesus' earthly ministry. Regardless of the actual timing of this event (likely later than Luke places it), it stands as Jesus' own interpretation of his already burgeoning ministry.[74] A parallel summary statement recounted by Matthew (11:5)

---

72 Merrill C. Tenney suggests that John 6:32–33 "may be an oblique reference to Deuteronomy 8:3: 'Man does not live on bread alone but on every word that comes from the mouth of the LORD.'" "The Gospel of John," in *John–Acts*, vol. 9 of *EBC*, ed. Frank C. Gaebelein (Grand Rapids, MI: Zondervan, 1981), 75.

73 Anyone who has worked with the indigent poor in soup kitchens, food ministries, clothing distribution, and other relief efforts (as we have) is aware (as we are) of this pattern of behavior, especially when a hearing for the gospel is expected. The sense of entitlement on the part of many of those being served (at least in this country) after a time is just overwhelming, with concomitant resistance to and indifference in the face of a gospel presentation. That does not mean that we should close soup kitchens, but it is important to admit that our experience often mirrors that of the Savior in his day.

74 The early church characterized this ministry as "doing good" (Acts 10:38). This is in contrast to pagan ideas of the good and probably refers to his compassionate healing and feeding works.

and Luke (7:22) arises from the wavering faith of the imprisoned and soon to be executed prophet John. John wondered why, if Jesus was the "coming One," that he (John) should be left to imprisonment and even death. The apparent disconnect in John's thinking concerned the strange juxtaposition of Jesus' Jubilee-inspired[75] ministry and John's own apparent destiny. Jesus, seeing this from afar sends a personal "blessed is he" to John with a clear warning not to be "scandalized" by the apparent inconsistencies in the salvation work of Jesus.

John was neither the first nor the last to wrestle with this paradox. From his closest associates to the vast crowds to the Jewish religious leaders to the Judean and Roman political officers, the mystery confounded all. Jesus clearly wanted all who heard and observed him to connect the arrival of Jubilee, "the acceptable year of the Lord," with his lordship, for Jubilee is the ultimate Sabbath, and he himself proclaimed his lordship over the Sabbath (Mark 2:28). Just as in the garden long before, the Sabbath had proclaimed God's mastery over all creation, so now Jesus' mastery of all things shines forth in a ministry of healing, feeding, comforting, freeing, and preaching to all comers, not just an elite few. And this "gospel" with the full challenge to discipleship is for the "poor," not just the wealthy or the elites. They have the privilege of "forsaking all" (including their poverty) to follow him into the new order of things. This is clearly the intent of both the examples Jesus used in the Lukan context to point out that the Jubilee message and benefits are for the believing, not the unbelieving. The attempt to murder him in his own hometown for including believing Gentiles from the OT stories shows how he was understood in his day and should be in ours.[76] It is pertinent to our study that the folk of Nazareth were the "poor" most often highlighted in the modern discussion and they sought to stone him for blasphemy. Furthermore, it is surely an insult to this Israelite group in Nazareth that Jesus interprets the Elijah story as indicative of a search for faith even in widows, who would normally claim benefits simply as Abrahamic seed in the flesh (Luke 4:24–27). Surely Jesus implies here that only in the widow of Zarephath did

---

75 We do not believe the evidence is complete on this supposition of the meaning of "acceptable year of the Lord," but we do not find it objectionable to use the analogy.

76 Our take is contrary to Stearns, *Hole in Our Gospel*, 20–22, who apparently does not connect the languishing of John in the prison as an outright denial of a realized eschatology of social revolution and kingdom-now thinking. John is bid to hold on a bit longer and not be "offended" in Jesus. Of course, that means John will lose his head for now.

Way to the City

Elijah find a believer, while who knows how many others languished in the drought? We assume, of course, that the remnant of a symbolic seven thousand (1 Kings 19) were being nurtured at the Lord's hand by other means. Unbelief knows no monetary or social or political boundaries!

But what of John and others, many others, like him who were not directly touched by Jesus' hand of power, though they believed his words and sought to follow him, however haltingly? Christian theology has been correct in general as it has seen more than the mere physical, temporal, and material in Jesus' miracle working. The world then and now has many times more spiritually blind, deaf, lame, leprous, and imprisoned folk than it does all the physically sick and oppressed and poor combined. Jesus is clearly pointing the way to spiritual healing, bread, and freedom with every miracle of his power. And, we have already heard his teaching that one can "labor" for the bread that "perishes" even as an earlier generation of Israelites "ate manna in the wilderness" and died. This realization must color all our thinking about the power of God through Christ in the present age. He himself declared, "My kingdom is not of this world" (John 18:36).

It is not surprising then that Jesus never laid out a utopian blueprint for change nor engaged in a political struggle to erect structures that would free John and others like him from oppressive and murderous regimes. Neither did he pronounce a universal healing or elimination of hunger and poverty. What he did do was touch life after life with the "finger of God" while pointing to eternal answers for temporal problems. This is the fundamental meaning of what some in our day would call his "power ministry" or some other equivalent to that terminology. Peter effectively confirms our judgment on this subject with his marvelous understatement that Jesus "went about doing good... for God was with him" (Acts 10:38). Luke has previously used the term "benefactor" (Luke 22:25) to describe how those in the then-current system used such activities to lord it over others and acquire name, reputation, and position, not to mention wealth.[77] In his free giving of benefits from the

---

77 Luke uses the verbal form of the term associated with "benefactor" in the Roman patronal system in Peter's statement. See Bruce W. Winter, *Seek the Welfare of the City* (Grand Rapids, MI: Eerdmans; Carlisle, Cumbria: Paternoster, 1994), for a full discussion of this terminology. This attitude toward leaders of charity organizations leads to the salaried

Way to the City

arrival/nearness of the kingdom, he surely has given a harbinger of things to come in the breakdown of the patron-client stratification of society that future practice will bring.

The one permanent earthly structure Jesus did authorize was his church ("assembly" for making decisions in the Greek cities of the time), which he says is placed strategically and spiritually at "the gates of hell," for whatever else its work is, it is to resist satanic evil (Matt. 16:13–19). How this is to be done is evident in the context in which he made this pronunciation. If any are to be a part of this assembly, each must "deny himself... and follow" even to "the cross," the destination to which he himself was headed. Those who heard him that day could not imagine what this meant until it finally came upon them in Jesus' passion. What they could and did do was to "forsake all," follow, and let him lead. This, of course, is the true meaning of all Jesus' "radical demands." It is about his lordship and not the poor (though they might well be the recipients of any literal financial forsaking, but they too must forsake all to follow him)[78] or some idea that his followers had too much and must give it away to be true disciples.

It is the same call as that given to Noah and Abraham and Moses and all who ever tried to do God's will. There is always something to forsake and to deny when God calls. There has always been a going and following that is part of true pilgrimage with God that began with the ancient directive in Eden to "subdue," and it is assumed in the Great Commission to the church to "disciple the nations" (Matt. 28:19–20).[79] The object of this is God's rule over all things from the gates of hell to the highest heaven. In the process and in God's own time all that is "wrong with the world" will be made "right," but trying

---

positions we previously cited and to perquisites that never show up in the audits, and it is surely the ongoing justification for the lavish system of distributing tax money to the welfare establishment, made possible through political manipulation.

78 Note how Luke, the evangelist most often associated with concern for the poor, shows Jesus challenging the crowds to make this radical decision (9:23–27, 57–62; 12:32–34; 14:25–35; and other challenges to follow him in discipleship).

79 It is salient to our study here to mention that missiological history shows that people groups (nations?) who turn fully to the gospel and become disciples of Christ tend to walk out the teaching of Scripture into a much greater prosperity materially than they had before. We will set this forth in greater detail, with all its ambiguities, in the historical section of this volume (see part 2).

Way to the City

to set it right is not what makes him Lord. Making him Lord in fact "on earth as it is in heaven" is what will make things right. This is the true meaning of Jesus' miraculous intervention—his kingdom has broken into this world and will one day "come,"[80] even as he taught his disciples to pray.

Meanwhile, his followers, men and women of every stripe and character, of every economic and political class, and of every social class are united by the need to deny their own brand of selfishness and band together to follow him in "doing good," though it may mean a literal cross, but more likely a figurative one. To businessmen like Peter and John and James and Andrew, it apparently meant periodic but not permanent forsaking of a trade in order to serve the Lord's purposes in their calling. To Matthew it appears to have meant complete separation from tax farming. To Zacchaeus it meant reforming his practices and making restitution above and beyond the requirements of Torah. To the women who were attached to Jesus' ministry it meant both liberation from stigma (see Mary Magdalene and the woman at the well) and support for him in a material vein (see Mary and Martha and others, Luke 8:1–3). To Joseph of Arimathea it meant risking life and limb to obtain Jesus' crucified body and the donation of a tomb. To the seventy-two it meant making "no provision" for the journey and expecting God to provide along the way. To the eleven in the upper room it was the exact opposite (Luke 22:35–38).

The common thread in all this is that Jesus is Lord, and those who would follow him must be prepared at any given time to do what is necessary and/or beneficial to his lordship.[81] Sometimes this is obvious; other times it requires that one have the wisdom of a "serpent" combined with the guileless innocence of a "dove." This is no invitation to pious and/or emotional interpretations of his commands, nor is it an authorization to ham-handed applications of obscure texts or ahistorical applications to modern politics. Jesus lived, taught, and ministered in a world very unlike ours, and attempts to force guilt upon today's working people to "live more simply" in light of some supposed

---

80 We will address this issue further in chap. 9.
81 This is clearly how Paul interpreted what he heard of Jesus' radical demands. He did not live as he did because it helped the "poor" but because it let him be free to "win the more." See 1 Cor. 9 for the way Paul saw this working out in practice. This is surely also the meaning of Jesus' exhortation to obedience in specificity, as opposed to any number of "works" and "deeds" done in apparent public ministry (Matt. 7:21–23).

Way to the City

wrongs done half a world away by unknown perpetrators is not the stuff of "deny yourself, take up the cross and follow me" in first-century Roman Palestine. We will have some suggestions for action on these lines as we draw to the conclusion of this book.

"Final Words"

As a concluding comment on the era of Jesus' public ministry, it seems appropriate to highlight his eschatological teaching with reference especially to the city of Jerusalem of his day (Matt. 24; Mark 13; Luke 21). With sad resignation he began his final teachings lamenting the fate of the city that would be destroyed in the coming Roman annihilation (Matt. 24:37–39). This city chosen in history as the seat of Yahweh's throne and worship was to suffer the same fate as all human cities not in accord with the will of the Father and his Son Jesus. Why? She had become like Sodom and Egypt (Rev. 11:1–13) in her rejection of the Messiah of her hopes and dreams. As Jesus saw it, of course, it was only fitting that a prophet such as himself should face death in Jerusalem (Luke 9:51; 13:33). How shall the promise of Israel's God be vindicated? How shall the "bloody city" of Isaiah realize her mission (Isa. 1:15; cf. Ezek. 9:9)? The remainder of the NT Scriptures will unveil that prospect.

Way to the City

Chapter 8

The First-Century Church
and Apostolic Teaching

IN THE LAST CHAPTER WE NOTED the strategic placement of the church "at the gates of hell." We turn our attention now to this outpost of the kingdom of God seen through the book of Acts and the teachings of the apostles. It will not be long before Luke reveals the true nature of the warfare to which God's assembly is called. But before the cloud of war arrives, there is the wait for a promised empowerment and the day of Pentecost "being fulfilled."

NEW BEGINNINGS: PENTECOST

Most of our readers are, of course, readily familiar with both this event and its precursor in Israel. Pentecost was the national festival celebrating God's blessing in the harvest. All Israel was to gather in what we might today call a great camp meeting and share communal meals and make thankful sacrifice to God for his bounty and see that everyone participated in the festivities and the produce of the land. It was like an all-day-sing-and-dinner-on-the-ground. It is this celebratory gathering that Luke says "was being fulfilled"[1] when the effusion of the Holy Spirit came upon the little band whose destiny it was to be

---

1   See A. T. Robertson, *Word Pictures in the New Testament*, ed. James A. Swanson (Nashville: Broadman & Holman, 2000), ad loc., for descriptive details on this translation.

"witnesses… to the ends of the earth." In the city of Jerusalem and its environs that day were Jewish celebrants from all over the Roman world. In addition, there were "proselytes" (converts) who were adherents to Jewish religion without the racial ties. This conjunction of events and witnesses clearly points to the providential sovereignty of God in salvation history moments.[2]

The term "harvest" now takes on a new and spiritually dynamic meaning as thousands are "added" to the assembly. Daily converts are baptized and join the ranks. More and more from every spectrum of local society and the visiting masses became a part of what can only be seen as an ongoing "Pentecost-al" celebration. The "breaking of bread," the "house to house," the "all things common," the selling and giving "as anyone had need," and the "gladness" and "prayers" all are a continuation and upgrading of the ancient festival of Firstfruits.

Not only is such a thing to be seen as a natural outgrowth of a time, place, and event in salvation history, it should also be seen as a virtual necessity. For, what else could possibly have been done to facilitate the accommodation of such a huge number of foreign visitors? Ancient Jerusalem had no means of feeding, housing, tending and entertaining such crowds for long. If there were not massive sharing and communal arrangements, everyone would simply have had to go home. It is apparent that this did not take place and that the assembly went to great lengths to make things work. And rightly so, at least for a while.

Doubtless, the primary reason for at least a temporary adjustment in living and eating arrangements was that the young church needed to teach and assimilate its variegated membership before many disbursed to the places from which they had come. This true need was naturally fed by an overwhelming enthusiasm born of spiritual life and of wonder at what God might now be doing to the fortunes of Israel.[3] Who would not have wanted to assist this pro-

---

2   Additionally, there were many who had moved from Hellenist regions of the empire to Jerusalem in anticipation of death, desiring to be buried there. This would account for the Hellenist synagogues and the number of widows who became a bone of contention in the congregation later.

3   Some of us, including the authors, have witnessed this very thing happen during times of "revival" in our own country, especially in the South. I (Tom) have personally been the recipient of gifts and provisions that were the direct result of the sense of freedom that can come at times like this.

Way to the City

cess by whatever means were available?[4] Would it not have seemed spiritually dull and niggardly in the extreme, if one believed God was truly at work again in Israel, not to go to any lengths reasonably possible to aid that work? These were exceptional days and unprecedented events. No wonder exceptional and unprecedented arrangements were required.

It was all a part of being led by the Spirit and following Jesus' lordship. Previously, Peter had referred to how Jesus' followers had left all that "belonged" or was related to them (Greek, *idios*, not *pas*, "all" as KJV, NIV, and other versions may imply) in order to follow Jesus.[5] The new identity, distinguishing this new community from the old one, supplied a new meaning to what was one's "own," first seen by Peter (Luke 18:28) as relating to everybody and everything that was in the past before his forsaking it to follow Christ. This would include property but would be even more encompassing than that. When the proceeds of sales of property were "laid at the apostles' feet" for distribution (Acts 4:35), the old system of patronage was stood on its head, for no personal power and expectation of reciprocity could come from the act.[6] These two features would be of particular interest to Luke's original audience.

As if to punctuate the significance of these events, the story of Ananias and Sapphira is a jolting contrast to the joyous and festive atmosphere of the first four chapters of Acts. The story clearly stands as both a warning and an affirmation. It is a warning to all who would falsify and misrepresent spiritual devotion. It is equally an affirmation of the truly unique period in salvation history that is Pentecost. It is reminiscent of the exodus and the heady days of

---

4 Obviously those in the establishment of religion and politics whose fortunes were threatened by such a spontaneous move among the people would oppose it.
5 The disciples' leaving of "homes" or "all" or "all we had," though the word used in Greek is idios not pas, implies a complete reversal of relationships to everything and everybody. See Aaron J. Kuecker's work on the use of *idios* by Luke in both his Gospel (18:28) and Acts to imply a new identity for the congregation through the Spirit. "The Spirit and the 'Other', Satan and the 'Self': Economic Ethics as a Consequence of Identity Transformation in Luke-Acts," in *Engaging Economics: New Testament Scenarios and Early Christian Reception*, ed. Bruce W. Longenecker and Kelly D. Liebengood (Grand Rapids, MI: Eerdmans, 2009), 81–103.
6 This is surely what Jesus is teaching in Luke 14:12–14, when he urges the "ruler of the Pharisees" (14:1) not to invite as guests to his obviously patronal feast those who were capable of reciprocity. For discussion on this, see Stephen C. Barton, "Money Matters: Economic Relations and the Transformation of Value in Early Christianity," in *Engaging Economics*, 49–52.

Way to the City

Joshua's leadership or of David's first attempt to bring the ark of the covenant home to Jerusalem. Instead of all sweetness and light there are moments when God's glory is defended in ways almost beyond our comprehension—Levites draw swords, leprosy attacks Miriam, Achan is stoned, the careless are struck down. Such terrible expressions of divine and direct wrath upon his own people are reserved for these nonpareil moments in the march of kingdom events. They happen so seldom in the overall record that they must be seen for their ability to sear into the memory of those present (and those who read) the reverence in which the events they interrupt must be held.

This is surely significant in Luke's purpose for writing Acts. The apostolic period of ministry is unprecedented in church history and established the fledgling church in all the major population centers of the Mediterranean Roman world, including the capital city. This could not have happened without the special divine interventions, both salutary and judgmental, that aid and abet the apostles' and their companions' work.[7] We believe this is the best light in which to read the narratives in Acts. To read them as literal models of ministry or church life is to miss their larger purpose in the story of Christ's kingdom advance. Attempts to duplicate or overdraw comparisons to these occurrences for contemporary application have and do lead to mischief.

For our purpose here we are particularly concerned with attempts to duplicate or apply as teaching the economic choices made by many in the Jerusalem church and the obvious "spirit" of voluntary pooling of resources for the good of all. The book of Acts is not contending that the model of everyone selling their property and giving the proceeds to the church is a perennial model for the right way to "do church." Failing to see this in the light we advocate misses several obvious factors beyond those we have already mentioned.

First, Luke's narratives and none of the remainder of the New Testament (NT) materials indicate that such a communal situation obtained in any of the other churches or at the time of the effusions of the Spirit in Samaria or at Caesarea or at the time the errant disciples of John were visited with Holy Spirit ev-

---

7   For a contrarian view on this, see Rodney Stark, *Cities of God: The Real Story of How Christianity Became an Urban Movement and Conquered Rome* (New York: HarperCollins, 2007). His take as a sociologist is striking for those of us accustomed to giving God the credit for the expansion of the church through miraculous conversion.

Way to the City

idences at Ephesus. Great joy and special miraculous manifestations were everywhere at these divine moments, but there is no mention of communal pooling
of goods. This does not mean that there was no concern for those in need. Surely
there was. But how the Lord was served in each situation was a function of that
time and place and his leadership, not an attempt to use Pentecost as a model.

Second, there is no record in Acts or the remainder of the NT of preaching
or epistolary teaching that advocates any attempt to repeat the Jerusalem experience. We will address what is taught and preached later, but this absence of clear
teaching should be paramount in whether we see Jerusalem's early experience
as exemplary and repeatable. We think it is exemplary only in the sense that
communal-type sharing on a spontaneous basis in the presence of God's special
blessings has a long history in Christian circles and is good. It is repeatable in
this limited way and for special times and circumstances, but it cannot be made
into a goal for some form of true spirituality or radical Christianity.[8]

Third, there is every reason to question whether it was wise to allow such
a situation to become an ongoing practice and, further, whether it did in fact
assume such a role. It is very clear from Jesus' commissioning of his "apostles"
that he was not enamored of having his church settle in at Jerusalem and enjoy
"the blessing." "Apostle" is the closest NT word for missionary ("sent one") of
our time. To the degree that communal provisions and overindulgence of celebratory religious experience may have delayed the true mission of the church
to be witnesses "to the end of the earth," these good things could have become
the enemy of the best in God's will for his people, since his goal for them was
to scatter. Certainly if such a situation were allowed to become permanent, it
would have been rebellion against the word and will of the Lord Jesus.

The most obvious way of obedience to Christ's command was for those
who were from around the Roman world to return to their homes, after a period of assimilation to the new "people of God," and preach Christ. This whole
process of moving out, with its implications for Samaritans and especially

---

8   Contra Barton, "Money Matters," 58, where he would recommend "the ascetic way" of
     the desert fathers to us as practicing this "new kind of sociality." See also Brian J. Capper,
     "Jesus, Virtuoso Religion, and the Community of Goods," in *Engaging Economics*, 60–80,
     for his two-tiered (at least) idea of the challenge of Jesus to discipleship. The desert fathers'
     experience was nothing like that in Acts.

Way to the City

Gentiles, is at the forefront of Luke's purpose as he tells the story. It is evident to all who read Luke and Paul's writings that this caused a major controversy in the first-century church and that its epicenter was Jerusalem's lack of vision for and/or obedience to the mandate of Jesus. As we have noted elsewhere, the "go" of the Great Commission is assumed, for life is a "going" experience when lived in the way God gave the creation's supervision to humankind. By its very nature it defies the concept of a permanent pooling of goods and settling in to a kind of utopian Christian communalism.

Finally we offer this extrabiblical observation. Every attempt, Christian and otherwise, to impose such a vision—Christian utopian socialism—on any community by teaching or psychological manipulation or by outright coercion has been a failure.[9] The only movement that remains in our time that could claim some form of success is Roman Catholic monasticism, which is certainly not duplicative of the Jerusalem situation and problematic, to say the least, for Protestant Christians. The realization of this historical nonprecedent made visible worldwide in the late twentieth century by the collapse of international Communism and other socialist experiments, has led most mainstream biblical commentators and theologians to abandon attempts to advocate such communal ideas. However, many others have substituted a barely disguised equivalent to what we have criticized. In an attempt to characterize differences in the fortunes and economics of Christian groups and individuals (both within the confines of our own country and those separated by oceans and continents) that they deem to be too disparate and as contrary to Scripture, and in their calling for somehow closing these "gaps" of material wealth, some of them propose exclusion from communion (Lord's Supper) and warn of possible eternal punishment simply for being intolerably wealthy.[10] We con-

---

9 For a survey on this subject, see Norman Cohn, *The Pursuit of the Millennium: Revolutionary Millenarians and Mystical Anarchists of the Middle Ages* (New York: Oxford University Press, 1970). See also Joshua Muravchik, *Heaven on Earth: The Rise and Fall of Socialism* (San Francisco: Encounter Books, 2002), and Thomas Molnar, *Utopia: The Perennial Heresy* (1967; repr., Lanham, MD: University Press of America, 1990).

10 See esp. Craig L. Blomberg, *Neither Poverty nor Riches* (Downers Grove, IL: InterVarsity Press, 1999), 187–88 and 245, where Blomberg says, "[T]here are certain extremes of wealth and poverty which are in and of themselves intolerable…and if left unchecked proves damning," and Sider, previously cited for this charge elsewhere in this book (see introduction, n. 17, and chap. 5, n. 12). Ben Witherington III, *Jesus and Money* (Grand

tend this is no more than changing the terminology and paradigmatic focus of the debate while continuing to mistake the true emphasis of Scripture on this subject. In the Pentecostal narratives Luke is reporting a glorious and wonder-filled moment in salvation history that points us to Christ's lordship, his willingness to endue his people with power for service, his bequeathing a spirit of joy and generosity that overflows, along with an evangelistic zeal that will, through his sovereign activity, reap a harvest. He is not laying down a paradigmatic model for corporate church economics that must be followed legalistically by all churches of all generations.[11]

Besides these legacies bestowed upon the church at Pentecost, two other traditions rooted in prior biblical teaching receive a new justification and impetus. The Old Testament (OT) practice of festive communal meals is carried forward in the churches' "love feasts," associated with the celebration of the Lord's Table. This preceding meal became a source for abuse at Corinth—a subject we will address at the appropriate time. The other tradition carried forward and reinforced is the insistence that Christians must do what is right and possible for those in true need and especially for those in an ongoing state of innocent helplessness, such as widows and orphans and the sick and disabled. This is further embodied by their practice in Jerusalem in the story of the appointing of seven to minister daily to the material needs of qualifying widows, especially those from the Hellenistic dispersion. This practice was doubtless an

---

Rapids. MI: Brazos, 2010), throughout his work wants to substitute the term "community" for "communal," but we cannot see that there is much difference in outcome. Such teaching followed to its inescapable end would make Christians everywhere, who have more to eat than their brethren somewhere, anywhere else in the world, the objects of the wrath of God. What a guilt trip! Furthermore, the use of the word "surplus" to define whatever someone may have left over after the bills are paid and we have eaten enough and been entertained enough and clothed enough sounds a lot like what Marxists and others call "capital." Capital formation for the purpose of being able to engage in business and innovation and entrepreneurial pursuits, the education of the future generation, and compassionate care for the previous generation is essential to the development of the earth and cosmos that humankind was given to rule. Just how much would these would-be planners of personal acquisition and distribution allow a citizen to keep without threatening one with "unworthy" participation in communion or possible eternal damnation?

11 That such economic examples in Luke are far more descriptive than prescriptive is illustrated by the fact that, while there are places in the NT epistles where churches are asked to give generous offerings to other churches in need, nowhere are they told to liquidate their property in order to do so.

Way to the City

outgrowth of the previous Jewish temple funding for widows, which was likely denied to those in the new Christian community.

Perhaps this action should be seen as a moment of separation from the broader Jewish community, signaling as it does the willingness to take up full responsibility for the needs of the new assembly, those who are now "*idios*" to the new community. In the ensuing events, however, Luke is consistent with his ongoing theme of spiritual power bestowed upon those who minister the Word, and it is this work that leads to a clear break with the Jewish community centered in the temple traditions. It is in this immediate context that the outpost of Christ's kingdom learns firsthand that its existence will not be idyllic and that its very life is threatened by dark forces intent on its destruction. Mysteriously it is this very onslaught that leads most surely to the launching of the true mission to which it has been called—witnessing to the end of the earth with an ever-present peril to life and limb, menacing it at every turn. And in further confirmation of sovereign supervision in such matters, it is the fruit of this missionary zeal that ministers materially to the needs of the Jerusalem church—first during the famine of approximately AD 47–49 and again in the later ministry of Paul through the offering collected from the Asian and Greek churches. Both of these should be seen as "relief" efforts not unlike such efforts, Christian and otherwise, in crisis moments of our own time, though for Christians it is truly a "ministry."[12]

THE EPISTLE OF JAMES

Further insight into the early history and teachings of the Jerusalem church is to be found in the NT book that bears the name of its early leader, first mentioned as such in Acts 12:17 at the time of the death of James, the brother of John.[13] This short letter from the half-brother of Jesus is most likely directed toward those Christian Jews scattered from the Jerusalem church by persecution and voluntary movement—many having returned to homes they had before Pentecost. In keeping with the theme of mission we have discussed

---

12 The true meaning of the word "deacon."
13 Further references are at Acts 15:13; 21:18; 1 Cor. 15:7; et al.

Way to the City

above, James refers to them in his salutation as "scattered," or (lit.) "sowed," like seed—a fitting description for witnesses to the ends of the earth.

We will look at the epistle of James for insight into the life situation of the early church, now outside Judea (with implications for Jerusalem) and the pertinent ethical-theological teachings it contains. James makes it clear that the churches of the *diaspora* (those "scattered" Christians) were very much like the Jerusalem church in economic situation—combining members from the poor to the relatively well-off and even rich.[14] As in all people groups, of course, there are the truly helpless, widows, and orphans (1:27).

James plunges quickly into what will be his theme throughout this combination of Jewish wisdom teaching and Greek diatribe—how faith should respond to tribulation and its attendant temptations. His counsel/command is to "count it all joy" (1:2)—i.e., consider the apparent uncontrollability of circumstances ("when you fall into") that produce "trials," which can become "temptations" (same word as "trials") to evil (1:12), as opportunities for growth into maturity (1:3–4). The indispensable additive the Christian brings to such "tests" is an active faith that produces humility.[15] Thus, whether one comes to Christian faith in a "lowly" (poor, humble) state or is made this way in the eyes of society (the man who is "rich" but "made low" by Christian contrition) or by persecution and subsequent loss, both find themselves on equal footing before God and fellow human beings. By contrast the "rich man" (the same person as above but without Christ) will "fade away" like grass "withers," in his "goings."[16] The context of temptation to sin and the need for wisdom is a challenge to both rich and poor in the church to act in faith lest they charge God with their circumstances as an excuse for lawless behavior—samples of which follow in 1:19–22. With the same emphasis as Jesus in the Sermon on the Mount, James urges *doing* as a contrast to only *speaking* (in an uncon-

---

14 See James 1:9–11; 2:1–3; 4:13–17; 5:1–6. There will be disputes in the literature on James as to who the rich are, whether Christian or not, and it appears there may be some mixture involved.

15 For discussion of the theme of humility as guiding James' teaching, see Mariam Kamell, "The Economics of Humility: The Rich and the Humble in James," in *Engaging Economics*, 157–75.

16 This is almost surely the only way to settle what James is saying about both men rejoicing in their current estate in Christ. The rich man by being humbled before Christ, and most likely in these circumstances before the world as well, has avoided the horrible fate contemplated.

Way to the City

trolled way) and *hearing*. His summary action involves assisting the helpless and maintaining personal moral purity (1:27). This is "pure and undefiled" religious sentiment put into action.[17] It is not, of course, all there is to proper religious practice.

James then proceeds to address the issue we have previously seen in first-century Jewry—separations among the religious community based on social class and appearances and patron-client relationships. Jesus spoke to it in dialogue with the Jews, and James addresses it here with the new Christian community. It is apparent that there was great temptation, in the cosmopolitan atmosphere of the churches to which James is preaching, to seek accommodation with an oppressive economic and political situation by offering exalted status to the well-off and/or rich and powerful. This he plainly condemns as contrary to God's revealed will that all people are to be judged without partiality at his tribunal and according to his previous "words." This standard is characterized as the "law of liberty" (2:12 and previously 1:25), standing as it does first on the deliverance from Egypt and now (as it truly always has) upon the finished work of Christ's atonement. By "showing partiality" in church activities and worship, church leaders are becoming "judges with evil thoughts" (a reference to their own inner corruption of motive) and have missed the judgment to which they will be subjected—one based on the "royal law" of neighborly concern for all and any in our purview.[18] In this way God will make "mercy triumph over judgment," for those who have been shown mercy through faith regardless of their prior condition should now practice an impartial mercy among themselves rather than a judgment based on appearances and prior conditions.[19] The supposed "preferential" treatment of the "poor," whether believers or not, cannot be sustained from this passage unless the entire argument is stood on its head. James is clearly not teaching

---

17 This is also the emphasis of Jesus in Matt. 25.

18 Recognizing that the majority of the world at the time were "poor" literally, and God did not go to the rich and powerful echelons of the society of the day to begin his work (James 2:5). It is an exegetical mistake to take a passage about the evil of "partiality" based on appearances and turn it into a justification for preferential treatment of and ministry to the "poor." The argument here is clearly for equality of treatment. On the patronal privilege implications in this passage, see Alan B. Wheatley, *Patronage in Early Christianity* (Eugene, OR: Wipf and Stock, 2011), 26–28.

19 This teaching compares with Jesus, e.g., see Matt. 12:7 with reference to Hos. 6:6 and Mic. 7:18.

Way to the City

that all the "poor" have been "chosen" to be "rich in faith." Nor is he teaching that the "poor" have a preferential option for such faith in the eyes of God.

Continuing with his theme that faith "works," James uses the rhetorical device of diatribe ("What profit?... What profit?"). His illustration is to speak of how ridiculous it would be for a true Christian to encounter a Christian brother or sister having neither adequate clothing nor "daily food" and, instead of "giving the things needed for the body," mouths a quotation from Jesus ("go in peace," Mark 5:34, Luke 7:50) and suggests "warm yourself" and "fill yourself."[20] This illustration in the larger context of discussing faith and works presumes that its hearers will perceive its obvious lesson and apply it to the issue of merely professed as opposed to practiced faith. All can see the necessity of meeting an immediate need for someone of known Christian character rather than mouthing platitudes. So it is also with the broader subject of faith and its consequences.

This theme of professing what one does not then do is expanded next to encompass all the kinds of mischief talkative religion can encompass (James 3:1–12). The third chapter of this epistle closes with a reminder of what true biblical wisdom is all about. Such wisdom produces a "meekness" that informs good "conduct" and "works" and fights off the devilish tendencies to "envy and self-seeking." James here shows that he is truly mastered by the finest in the traditions of Hebrew wisdom literature.

James' next transition is to take envy and self-seeking to its outgrowth in "wars" (ongoing hostility) and "fights" (periodic flareups). He traces these outbreaks of lust and covetousness to a lack of settled confidence in the sovereignty of God over all our affairs. First, he charges his hearers with failure to appeal to God at all. Then, he singles out those who pray in such fashion as to make God a divine "sugar daddy" there to satisfy whimsical and worldly desires. His cure is "submit to God" in humility and wait upon him to "lift" (cf. 1:9) us up. This attitude is contrasted to blaming others, or "judging" others (as in 2:1–4), and once again not being a sincere doer. James further emphasizes the sovereignty of God by condemning the failure to see how fragile human

---

20 We have previously seen that Jesus "went about doing good" as he was able. This is the kind of situation that demands "relief" ministry.

Way to the City

planning and enterprise can be because of the nature of life—"a vapor." Only God knows tomorrow for sure and faithful Christians are bound to take this into account in all their dealings.[21] This seems to us to be the best explanation for the conclusion of 4:17—do good now while you can, and don't put it off till a "better time," for that day may never come, and this "do good" is most likely a reference to the "doing good" we have seen in the life of Jesus.[22] Do your good for others, James says, when and where the opportunity presents itself, for "time waits for" none of us.

James now brings his epistle to a close with a look to the approaching "last days" (5:3). With a scorching blast of prophetic fire he condemns the oppressive forces that try and tempt his hearers. They are the "rich" who have made unjust gain at the expense of their workers[23] and live a life of "luxury" (lit., "voluptuous and wanton pleasure"), "pleasure" ("softness"), and "fatness" ("being nourished as animals for slaughter"). In so doing they have "murdered the just one" (overtones of Christ's death [Acts 7:52] and of James himself, renowned after his martyrdom as "James the Just"), who has been unable to resist them. What these blind plutocrats cannot see, and what James bids his Christian audience to see, is the approach of an eschatological judgment.[24] The

---

21 This does not negate our attempts to be prudent in our plans, nor does it condemn doing business for a "profit." It does recognize that God disposes with or without our plans.
22 See John 9:1–3.
23 It is surely pertinent here that the largest violator of the rule to pay workers their wages and not withhold them is the federal government, not rich businessmen in our day. This device was deliberately introduced during World War II to hide the impact of tax collection. The prevalence of tax refunds without the payment of interest on those funds, after having been withheld for up to a year or more, is unjust in the extreme and a violation of biblical teaching.
24 We have no problem with charging those who live like this with damnable sins. What we do object to is the implication in much Christian evangelical writing and teaching that Americans who work hard and save and invest and build businesses that pay their workers and do honest business fit this category. See esp. on this Blomberg (but he is not alone), *Neither Poverty nor Riches*, 158, speaking of "would-be Christians" (does that mean we are not Christians nor can become so without following his proposed agenda?) who buy goods from corporations he deems to "fail to pay decent wages," or who support "politicians who promise tax cuts for the upper and middle classes, when programs helping the needy at home and abroad are slashed in the process" (This last charge is a caricature cut out of whole cloth and peculiar to only one political party in the United States. At best politicians of both parties only slow the growth of such programs.). "To what extent do the well-to-do Christians in the West and North live lives little different from those described in 5:1–6… even if we plead innocent of the more blatant forms of oppression described in this text?"

Way to the City

Christian should patiently wait and the unrepentant sinner should fear and take warning and repent and believe. Even Christians who excuse themselves from doing the will of God in hard times should remember the Judge "standing at the door" (James 5:9). How much more the unrepentant and unbelieving? Meanwhile, let the assembly of Christians weep, sing, pray, and confess all together with the hope and faith of Elijah and the attention to "saving souls" that this world and its life demand. In conclusion, we see in James' teaching the same ethical themes we have repeatedly found in the rest of Scripture.

THE LIFE AND TEACHINGS OF PAUL

By far the event that more than any other pushed the early church into its intended worldwide expansion was the conversion of Saul of Tarsus, destined to become "apostle to the Gentiles." Luke introduces Saul, a Hellenistic Jew with traditional Jewish training in the Pharisee tradition, as the lead persecutor of Christians in Jerusalem and the surrounding regions. In this role he was hands-on in the murder of Stephen, one of the seven designated to tend to the material needs of the Hellenistic widows. The clear catalyst for the rise of this persecution was the breathtaking preaching of Stephen clearly stating that the purpose of God was no longer served by Jewish exclusivity centered in temple ritual (Acts 7:47–50) and sacrifice (7:42–43). His defense and message before the council of the Sanhedrin surveys Israel's history, highlighting the national failure to respond in faith and loyalty to the grace of God and culminating in the murder of their rightful Lord and Messiah (7:51–53).

The story in Acts tumbles from Luke's pen as he relates in rapid succession Stephen's martyrdom, Saul's maraudings, Philip's (one of the seven) preaching to the Samaritans and the church's recognition of this expansion of the mission as legitimate, the first recorded Gentile convert in the Ethiopian eunuch, and Saul's conversion on the way to expand his murderous harassment of the church. This shocking and sovereign work of God is the beginning of what will become the dominating theme of the remainder of Luke's history—how the church be-

---

The actual guilt or innocence of the described wrongdoing is precisely the point of the passage, not some supposed standard arbitrarily assigned it by the commentator. See also, Sider, "Are Evangelical Leaders Going to Hell?"

Way to the City

came reconciled to the true vision of its Lord. This vision saw the new Israel as characterized by a sanctification and separation of moral character, spiritual life, and servant mission to "the nations" rather than the vision of first-century Jewish leadership of exclusivity centered in the Sabbath, food taboos, ancestral identity, the land, and ultimately the temple. This clash of paradigms will come to dominate the life and teachings of the apostle Paul as well.[25]

The cultural/religious warfare is quickly joined when Saul testifies boldly in Jerusalem to his new faith and must be spirited out of town ahead of a plot on his life—a harbinger of things to come for him in Israel and all around the Mediterranean world. Peter then assumes the mantle of leadership briefly in the Gentile mission by listening to a heavenly vision and the appeal of Cornelius to hear the gospel. In the ensuing events it is clear the Jerusalem church needed the kind of authentication of a work of God, which only a figure with the stature of Peter could provide. But it is Barnabas, as witness and validator of the work of the Antioch church, who sees the opportunity to bring Saul into the execution of Jesus' prime directive.

Once again we see how a sovereign God at work has prepared a man for a moment, just as the Scriptures have recorded such events before again and again. Saul of Tarsus, "who is also called Paul" (Acts 13:9), was born into a Hellenistic Jewish family. A Roman citizen by virtue of his birth into his father's household, he was almost certainly for a time educated in his youth in a Greek school and later was "bought up" (Acts 22:3) in the Jewish faith by the rabbi Gamaliel.[26] The family was apparently well-to-do by first-century standards, giving him a feel for the more cosmopolitan settings in which he would carry out his adult ministry. Nevertheless, he was a tentmaker, or perhaps more accurately a leatherworker, by trade, who had likely been trained by his father. In this respect he would have been thought of as below the station of many in his social class, since his trade consisted of extremely difficult manual labor. On the other hand his skill, physical capabilities due to his practice of the craft, and his willingness to use it

---

25 For a thoroughgoing analysis of these issues, see James D. G. Dunn, *The Partings of the Ways: Between Christianity and Judaism and Their Significance for the Character of Christianity,* 2nd ed. (London: SCM, 2006).

26 See *Holman Illustrated Bible Dictionary*, ed. Chad Brand, Charles Draper, and Archie England (Nashville: Holman Bible Publishers, 2003), ad loc., for documentation.

Way to the City

for the support of himself and his associates would make it possible to offer the gospel message "without charge" (1 Cor. 9:18), in the tradition of Jewish rabbis, and to avoid any appearance of "dishonest gain" or "peddling the word of God" for profit (2 Cor. 2:17; Titus 1:11). This example he set would also allow him to exhort the idle (2 Thess. 3:6–12) and those puffed up with pride in their financial and social position (1 Cor. 4:6–21).

The much-coveted Roman citizenship, which may have been conferred on his father or grandfather as a reward for some military or other service to the empire or possibly as a gift from a master who freed them from slavery, was to be pivotal in his eventual testimony at the emperor's seat of power. It is also clear that he knew when to play this trump card in tense political situations (Acts 16:37–38; 25:9–12), though he had no qualms about laying down his life for his faith and mission as it might become necessary.[27] In this way he exhibited a kind of Christian worldliness, understood in a positive sense. This same canny ability to size up a situation in light of his convictions and sense of calling showed itself repeatedly in his strategic moves from city to city and region to region.[28] He further distinguished himself as a world-wise spiritual tactician in his Jew-first-and-also-the-Greek approach to evangelism, his dialogue with Greek students of philosophy at Athens, his probably decade-long labor to produce a Gentile offering for the Jerusalem church, his final attempt to convert his own people by any means at Jerusalem, and the ease with which he assumed leadership aboard a Roman ship destined for Rome. In every way he exhibited the kind of cosmopolitan personal character, without compromising his moral or spiritual principles, that also characterized Jesus. It is the mark of ancestry, environment, upbringing, education, and the hand of God in salvation that made Paul the man of the hour at this juncture in church history—another of those servant heroes.

It is this kind of man whom God chose to enable and infuse with his word for the churches. The letter to the Romans is, of course, what amounts to a Pauline manifesto of faith and practice for Christians and churches of all locales and ages. It has been considered the least influenced of all his letters

---

27 See 1 Cor. 15:31, 32; 2 Cor. 11:23–27; 2 Tim. 4:6–8.
28 See Stark, *Cities of God.*

Way to the City

by local conditions or controversies.[29] It appears relatively later in his ministry and should, therefore, be expected to contain a true distillation of his teaching as he had practiced it to that time. From it we hear the clear voice of salvation by faith that leads inevitably to works that validate the genuineness of the inner faith and lead to growth into maturity and issue in eternal glorification.[30] We have reaffirmed God's sovereignty in the affairs of men (Rom. 1:18–32) and the utter depravity and inability of humankind to save itself due to ongoing and intractable bondage to sin (3:9–19). And, most telling for our purposes, while the Law is seen to be inherently incapable of bringing salvation (3:19–20), it is affirmed as the final standard by which man is to be judged, the light that reveals his true condition, the good that surfaces his rebellious heart (7:7–25), and the explanation for the wrath of God being poured out on his own Son rather than a deserving human race—"that he might be just and the justifier of the one who has faith in Jesus" (3:26).[31] Paul is also adamant that this was all previously "witnessed by the Law and the Prophets" (3:21) and clearly illustrated in Abraham's experience (chap. 4).

Our purpose here in stating the more or less obvious to serious Bible students is to include Paul among those whose ethics are guided by what is revealed in the OT and especially at Sinai. Moreover, Paul clearly sees this moral/ethical standard as proceeding from God's own character and ministered to the believer in power by God's Spirit (8:1–17). And his summary statement at 13:8–10 equates the love command with the original Ten Commandments.[32] As we shall see, Paul remains faithful to this body of revelation (his own and previous) in the particular and situational teachings we shall examine.

---

29 However, see N. T. Wright, "Romans," in *The New Interpreter's Bible: Acts–1 Corinthians,* vol. 10 (Nashville: Abingdon, 2002), for the case to be made (throughout the commentary) that the ongoing tension in Paul's mission to the Gentiles was the primary cause for the lengthy letter to Rome.

30 Rom. 5:1–11 appears to be the "text" from which this theme is developed through to the end of chap. 8.

31 This is the crowning biblical statement on God's view of justice. Justice is not about sentiment or the wants of human beings. It is about what is "right in the sight of God."

32 It is surely a mistake to expect a pagan world, whether Roman in the first century or the world of the twenty-first century, to understand what love is without any referent in the law of Yahweh. So it is that love is explained and delineated in action by the original "words" from Sinai. So it is also with justice.

Way to the City

Paul's Missionary Plan and Situational Teaching

We are blessed to have in our NT such a plethora of detail concerning the early Christian mission and the large body of writings directed at the ongoing life of new converts organized into local churches. From it we will seek to construct a narrative that gives true-to-the-facts understanding of the Pauline and Lukan materials for the limited purposes we have here. Obviously we cannot hope to do justice to the full range of the life and teachings of Paul anymore than we have to any of the other materials we have examined. However, we are confident that what follows is faithful to the biblical record.

Launching from Judea with a commission from Antioch, Luke tells us, Paul and Barnabas set foot on the island of Cyprus as a first step in their enterprise to evangelize the Mediterranean world. Going first to the synagogues of the Jews, where they would encounter both ethnic Jews and Hellenistic "God-fearers" and "proselytes,"[33] they are soon invited to speak in a completely Gentile setting to the proconsul, Sergius Paulus, who despite opposition by a Jewish sorcerer, is the first convert mentioned by name in the Lukan record of Paul's missionary travels (Acts 13:6–12). This is surely significant as a harbinger of things to come, as Sergius Paulus is neither Jewish nor poor nor powerless. He is a Roman politician with all the appertaining perquisites. This is revolutionary enough that it may have had a significant part in the departure of John Mark from the mission at a later time.

Swiftly Luke records that the next step was Galatia and its collection of towns ("cities"), each with its local synagogue of Jews and its complement of Hellenists, the first being Antioch of Pisidia (13:14–52). It is tragic and regrettable that the success of such a mission, not only with non-Jewish synagogue worshipers but with the Gentile masses as well, should lead to "envy" (13:45) on the part of ethnic Jews.[34] In fact, it was just such success with the masses on the part of Jesus in Galilee and Judea and Jerusalem that had led to Jesus' crucifixion. In that situation it was envy by Jewish leader-powerbrokers who saw their hold on their position threatened by a mass movement of Jewish common-

---

33 The two designations distinguishing the degree of Jewish separation they were willing to take up.
34 This moment is notable for its broad success and its issuance in a decision to "turn to the Gentiles" (13:46).

ers. Here it is just the opposite: a Jewish minority, undoubtedly regarded as a powerless, poor, and disrespected sect, is having its unique religion and cultural monopoly threatened by a vision of the new Israel that would bring into the fold people from all strata of society, regardless of their social rank or financial means, including many who had previously despised and/or oppressed the Jews (see James above). The persecution that is stirred up, coming officially from Roman-sponsored political leadership, is facilitated by the ability of synagogue leaders to influence "leading women" (probably wives of governing men), who were proselytes to Jewish religion. This pattern of local Jewish rejection and incitement of official opposition is to be repeated again and again in Luke's account in Galatia and later in Macedonia and Achaia as well.

It is noteworthy in these accounts that an ethnic Jewish minority should have such an ability to stir up local political opposition. However, when we consider again that Rome's primary concern in the administration of its empire was the maintenance of the famous *Pax Romana* at all costs, we see the same dynamic at work outside Judea and Galilee as we saw in the ministry of Jesus. These Jews whom Paul repeatedly encountered had a different turf to defend, but the methodology was the same. Usually they could find others not inclined to become converts, who had an ox to be gored by Christian success, who could be relied upon to make common cause with them.[35] Thus could a large enough group of petitioners convince local authorities that Christianity posed a threat to the political order. In this way from the beginning have rich and poor, weak and powerful sold their souls for a "mess of pottage."

The return to Judea after this first excursion is important for our study because of the issuing of the Jerusalem Council's directive to Gentile-dominated churches on the subject of Mosaic law-keeping, particularly circumcision, dietary taboos, and sexual immorality. With our limited space we cannot join in a discussion of the ramifications of that directive. However, it is notable that the wording of the directive (Acts 15:23–29) does not include the one thing Paul takes as mandatory for instructing the Galatian churches—"only that we should remember the poor," which Paul says he was "eager to do" (Gal. 2:10). We do not know whether he actually ever verbalized the food taboos, but we

---

35 See the business of idol-making affected in both Philippi and Ephesus.

Way to the City

know he preached sexual purity and here adds what amounts to a consensus of the Council in Jerusalem about ministry to material needs.[36]

Who exactly "the poor" here are (whether the poor in general wherever the churches minister or the poor attached to those churches as members or the poor church at Jerusalem) has been the subject of much debate.[37] The immediate context of the Council would tend to favor the Jerusalem church, ravaged by famine, as the referent for "the poor." The fact that the Antioch church had previously sent a collection for this need and that Paul spent the better part of the next decade gathering another collection for this church would also favor this interpretation.[38] However, in light of the long tradition in Jewish religious practice of making provision for the helpless through temple offerings and of almsgiving in general (confirmed in our previous look at James' teaching), it is likely that some of all three possible recipients are to be "remembered." There is a need for a relief type mission for Jerusalem and an ongoing need in and around each congregation.[39]

Paul confirms this multiple practice of "remembering" the poor elsewhere. In the second Thessalonian epistle from this time period he gives the simple command, which he says he taught them by both example and instruction, "If anyone won't work, neither shall he eat" (2 Thess. 3:10).[40] This implies not only that some form of sharing food with the hungry was a part of early Christian ministry, but that it was to be done so as not to encourage those who "walk in a disorderly manner" (3:11).[41] A further indicator of Paul's practice and teaching on this sub-

---

36 It is striking in this situation, especially in light of the way some commentators take James' general letter to the dispersion, that nothing in the letter he wrote from Jerusalem to the Gentile church mentioned the poor.

37 The entire discussion seems to revolve around the precise dating of the Jerusalem Council relative to the dating of Galatians and a period of famine encompassing this time.

38 See Rom. 15:26 for an additional reference to "the poor" in Jerusalem.

39 Rodney Stark in several of his studies has noted that it is documented that the Christian church in the first three centuries of its life was an impressive force in the Roman world with its charitable activities during famines and plagues and general economic woes.

40 This is surely reminiscent of Prov. 16:26, "a laborer's appetite works for him."

41 See the bountiful literature at this time on the patron-client relationship that would lead to idleness in the pursuit of security through political pull and influence rather than work with one's hands. Bruce W. Winter, *Seek the Welfare of the City* (Grand Rapids, MI: Eerdmans; Carlisle, Cumbria: Paternoster, 1994), is particularly apropos on this subject. Also, most recently, David J. Downs, "Is God Paul's Patron? The Economy of Patronage in Pauline Theology," in *Engaging Economics*, 129–56, discusses at length the exploitative relationship in Roman patronal society.

Way to the City

ject comes near the end of his life in an instruction to his young protégé Timothy (1 Tim. 5:3–16). Here Paul's concern is that "widows who are widows indeed" (v. 3) should be taken care of to the exclusion of those who might be put "in the number" without due consideration of qualifying criteria. Such qualifications begin with age (over sixty) and include past practice as a wife, mother, and Christian who herself practiced "good works," hospitality and service to others (v. 10).[42] This idea of "doing good" is also likely implied in Paul's instruction in Galatians 6:10 in the context of commanding material compensation for "teachers of the word."[43] In this case any opportunity to "do good" is commendable and to be sought out, especially if it is for the Christian brother.

The Second Journey and Corinthian Correspondence

Paul's second missionary circuit begins with a confirmational and strengthening visit to churches begun in the previous excursion. After concluding that the province of Asia was not to be his next evangelistic field, he and Silas with the young Timothy arrive at the port city of Troas. In obedience to a visionary "call" (specifically designating a field of service as opposed to other possibilities noted in Luke's account),[44] these three and Luke proceed to Macedonia where they will begin to encounter a new challenge spiritually, culturally, and politically. Immediately we are introduced to Lydia the cloth merchant as the first convert in the region's foremost city Philippi. She is notable as one who will be characteristic of many of the converts on the Greek peninsula. A well-off woman of prominence, a non-Jewish proselyte with a home large enough to accommodate a "family"[45] (who were baptized with her) and allow for Paul and his party to "stay" with her, she is the firstfruits of a church that is to play a prominent role in Paul's ongoing ministry (see Phil. 4:10–19), especially as it relates to his material needs.

---

42 Note that Paul is concerned that the younger widows might become "idle" and trade in "gossip" and be "busybodies." All this he clearly deplores and expects Timothy and the churches to resist.

43 See Witherington, *Jesus and Money*, ad loc., for a strong defense of this position.

44 This is contra some who would make the universal "call" of the Great Commission open-ended in terms of actual destination.

45 See Robertson's discussion of the term "family," *Word Pictures in the New Testament*, ad loc., indicating that she would have been supporting family members related to her and various servants.

Philippi itself is notable as the first place where Paul experiences pagan opposition and government persecution without apparent incitement by the Jews. This is neither the first nor the last time that genuine Christianity will threaten a "hope of profit" (Acts 16:19) and lead to authoritarian intervention by political groups and individuals. In this case "profit" is in the currency of the material, but Jewish "envy" (as well as all other kinds) has its own currency both material and cultural. Paul asserts his rights as a Roman citizen for the first time (we presume) in connection with his missionary enterprise. This follows the notable conversion of a government official, the jailer, and his "family" or "household." After a final visit with the "brethren" at Lydia's house, the team proceeded to Thessalonica. This last reference (16:40), to a gathering in someone's home, will become a commonplace practice, according to the NT and early Christian traditions. It marks a development that will be helpful to the overall Christian mission, but it will have its problematic side, as we will show later in the discussion of the Corinthian situation.

Already there is at least a hint that Paul may have seen trouble brewing in this arrangement. It smacks of the patronage/client relationship we have described in the discussion of Jesus' ministry. Rich and/or powerful patrons able to provide necessities for no apparent cost to the one benefited tend, if only subtly, to expect some form of compensation that almost always involves undesirable compromises in relationships, principles, or practices.[46] In the Roman world of the time strict reciprocity of various kinds was expected.[47] While there is no hint of this in Lydia herself, and the Philippian church comes in for no criticism in this area in any of Paul's correspondence, it is clear that Paul had to be "constrained" (Acts 16:15) to accept this arrangement. Furthermore,

---

46 There is a distinction to be drawn between strict patronage and "benefaction," but even well intentioned "doing good" could be misunderstood and abused due to societal conventions. See both Winter, *Seek the Welfare of the City*, and Downs, "Is God Paul's Patron?" on this. We will be further dependent upon Peter Garnsey and Richard Saller, *The Roman Empire: Economy, Society, and Culture* (Berkeley: University of California Press, 1987), and J. Nelson Kraybill, *Apocalypse and Allegiance: Worship, Politics, and Devotion in the Book of Revelation* (Grand Rapids, MI: Brazos, 2010), for our ongoing discussion of patronage as experienced by Paul and the churches.

47 See Wheatley, *Patronage in Early Christianity*, 1–2, for the listing of the kinds of reciprocity expected, and his following discussion on how this tended to work out in the era we deal with here.

Way to the City

it is for the first time clearly stated that Paul "travailed and toiled night and day" (1 Thess. 2:9; 2 Thess. 3:8) that he might not be a "burden" or eat "free of charge" at Thessalonica, his next destination. We think it is justified to consider whether he might have clearly set himself on this course after the experience at Philippi. Surely he had no regrets about it after the Corinthian situation ran its course, as we shall soon see.

In rapid-fire sequence Luke records both success and apparent failure in Thessalonica, Berea, and Athens. Bedeviled by Jewish intransigence in Thessalonica, the group nevertheless finds a fruitful hearing among a "multitude of Greeks" and "not a few" of the same "leading women" we have met before. They were houseguests of one Jason, who ran afoul of the Jews and their pagan allies, when the city and its political leaders had to deal with riotous conditions. Jason is apparently of sufficient social stature and financial independence that he can bond ("give security") Paul and Silas out of custody, provided they move on. Berea would have been different in outcome, with success for the word among Greeks and prominent "women and men" as well as Jews, except for the arrival of a contingent from Thessalonica once again inciting mass hysteria.

With this development Paul is personally dispatched out of the city to Athens, where he awaits the eventual arrival of Silas and Timothy. While he is there, he addresses an august group of idle, would-be philosophers, who hear him as those who while away their time by either "hearing or telling some new thing" (Acts 17:21). Despite Paul's effort to adapt his message to such an urbane audience, his first mention of "the resurrection" (17:31) brings laughter and ridicule and a quick dismissal.[48] "Some men" accepted his message, but we never again hear of any fruit out of Athens. This experience no doubt added to Paul's personal concern that he not be classed with such wandering and idle peddlers of "wisdom,"[49] whose livelihood was furnished by rich patrons and

---

48 The concept of the resurrection of the body was held by no one in the Mediterranean world of that day with the exception of (some) Jews and the new Christian faith. N. T. Wright, *The Resurrection of the Son of God*, Christian Origins and the Son of God 3 (Minneapolis: Fortress, 2003), 32–84.

49 Lit., "seed-pickers," in Greek.

Way to the City

the coin of those would pay to hear them "teach."[50] From here Paul rightly concerned to know if the work in Thessalonica (and likely Philippi and Berea) was thriving or perishing, sent Silas and Timothy to minister to them and bring back a report (1 Thess. 3:1–5) while he headed to Corinth.

Upon his arrival in Corinth he encounters the now famous Aquila and Priscilla, Jewish tentmakers driven out of Rome by Claudius Caesar, and strikes up a working relationship with them whereby he can support himself and his ministry while staying in their home (Acts 18:1–4). Upon the arrival of Silas and Timothy with an encouraging report (1 Thess. 3:6–10), Paul changed from a Sabbath-day-only teaching routine to a full time approach,[51] though it is likely he followed the "working night and day" process he practiced in Thessalonica. This led to Jewish opposition and the familiar rejoinder, "From now on I will go to the Gentiles" (Acts 18:5–6).

Titius Justus, a God-fearer and prominent member of a family of potters, provided a place for teaching next door to the synagogue, and Paul moved there from the home of Aquila and Priscilla (Acts 18:7).[52] In short order there is a reversal of the previously monotonous pattern of Jewish rejection followed by incitement to disturbing the peace and governmental and cultural persecution. Instead, Crispus, "the ruler of the synagogue" (18:8) and his household believe and are baptized. The ensuing attempt by the Jews to appeal for Roman intervention fails when Gallio, then procounsul of Achaia, refuses to hear the case and the enraged Jewish mob beats the new ruler of the synagogue, Sosthenes, in Gallio's presence as he turns a blind eye to the whole proceeding. In a final coup de grâce we learn later (1 Cor. 1:1) that Sosthenes has been converted and become a co-worker with Paul. Such is the auspicious beginning of a work that continued for about two years (Acts 18:11, 18). Corinth marks a turning point in Paul's ministry in the Hellenistic/Roman world, as he now has the precedent of governmental non-interference and the conversion of leading Jews to lend new respectability to the Christian movement.

---

50 The implications of the way he was treated in Athens by the Areopagus group tend to this conclusion. He was seen as someone who went about making his living peddling the Word.

51 Made possible by a gift from the Macedonian churches, most prominent of which was surely Philippi (2 Cor. 11:8–9; Phil. 4:15–16).

52 See Robertson, *Word Pictures in the New Testament*, ad loc. for Acts 18:7, for description and discussion.

Way to the City

Corinth, however, is even more notable in our NT for its inordinate occupation of Paul's writing energies (not to mention spiritual capacities!) and the pages of Scripture. This is both bane and blessing. We are indebted to the Corinthians for calling forth so much of Paul's wisdom and inspired insight, but sometimes one is tempted to say, "Enough, already!"[53] Nevertheless, Paul's Corinthian correspondence, containing all or part of perhaps four letters, gives us great insight into both the inner workings of the church itself and also the mind of Paul, and therefore, the Lord.

As we have seen, Corinth is not the first place where Paul saw the conversion of socially prominent or well-to-do persons and families.[54] The conversion of two synagogue rulers is unique up to this point in Luke's account. But, perhaps more striking is the over-representation of Corinthians named in Paul's letters—a total of sixteen individuals plus "Chloe's people"—and the fact that more than half of these may be considered well-to-do by the standards of the time and/or socially and culturally prominent.[55] They had "houses,"[56] and some appear to have employed slaves, were able to travel about the Mediterranean world, and could assist Paul in his work without doing harm to themselves and their families. The fact that Paul says there were "not many"[57] like this (1 Cor. 1:26) only serves to highlight their prominence

---

53 N. T. Wright has a telling summary of the nature of the Corinthian church and the Corinthian street in *The Climax of the Covenant: Christ and the Law in Pauline Theology* (London: T&T Clark, 1993). See also Gerd Theissen, *The Social Setting of Pauline Christianity: Essays on Corinth* (Philadelphia: Fortress, 1982), 69–95, 99–102, for background on this section. Additional documentation may be found in Wayne A. Meeks, *The First Urban Christians: The Social World of the Apostle Paul* (New Haven, CT: Yale University Press, 1983), and Wayne A. Meeks, *The Book of Acts in Its First Century Setting: Volume 2, Graeco-Roman Setting*, ed. David W. J. Gill and Conrad Gempf (Grand Rapids, MI: Eerdmans, 1994). Finally, see Abraham Malherbe, *Social Aspects of Early Christianity*, 2nd ed. (Eugene, OR: Wipf and Stock, 1983), for additional data on the possibility of social mobility in the Roman world of Paul. Movement was possible, but pressures were great.

54 See Rodney Stark's assessment in *The Triumph of Christianity* (New York: HarperCollins, 2011), 88–89, that Paul's reference to "not many" prominent or rich were "called" (1 Cor.1:26) should be seen against the backdrop of the actual percentage of such persons in the general population, not as a generalized indictment of the failure of the "rich" or noble to find salvation. Cf. Stark, *Cities of God*, 50–51.

55 See esp. Theissen, *Social Setting of Pauline Christianity*, on this.

56 This term "houses" in the setting implies more than mere domiciles, including as it does family and servants and any business that might be a part of the extended arrangements.

57 It is possible to translate this phrase simply "some" and the emphasis changes. This may be the best way to take the term. See Stark, *Triumph of Christianity*, 88, cited in n. 54 above .

Way to the City

in the record, but it stands to reason they were not the only representatives of upper class families in the church. As Rodney Stark so eloquently puts it, "[T]he early Christians were not a bunch of miserable underdogs. This always should have been obvious, not only from reading the Gospels, but from asking why and how a bunch of illiterate ignoramuses came to produce sophisticated written scriptures at a time when only the Jews had produced anything comparable."[58]

The resulting clash of cultural associations and social stratification,[59] and financial disparities appear to be at the root of many of the problems in the Corinthian church. This is good from the standpoint that nowhere else in the Roman world was such mixing of social groupings being attempted outside the fledgling "Jesus movement," as Stark calls it. The bad surfaces as these factors were allowed to fester into sore spots, especially by invading the love feasts (1 Cor. 11:17–22), they led to "divisions" (1:11; 11:18), rivalries (1:12–13), law suits (6:1–10), false triumphalism (4:8), and a disparagement of Paul's willingness to support himself without receiving patronage (1 Cor. 9:1–14; 2 Cor. 11:1–15), along with a host of other practical, spiritual, and theological problems. Paul, by way of understatement, attributes this to their inability to eat meat as Christians (1 Cor. 3:2–4), but might be implying even a worse state (13:3–4).[60] For our purposes we will confine ourselves to the implications of their problems for our subject and will finish with a look at Paul's teaching in raising the offering for Jerusalem (2 Cor. 8–9).

Paul's unprecedented success at Corinth led to an influx of large numbers of new converts—"many of the Corinthians," Luke says, believed (Acts 18:8) and Paul is reassured directly by the Lord that "I have many people in this city" (18:10). It should not be thought unusual that in such a place and time a sorting out of relationships would be required, for the Roman world was at that

---

58 Stark, *Triumph of Christianity*, 96.
59 This term signifies the relative permanence of social and economic relationships throughout a lifetime, rather than conditions allowing movement between classes and economic conditions. See Malherbe, *Social Aspects of Early Christianity*, cited above, for exceptions to the general rule. We also use it here to designate various patronage arrangements common to the time and situation.
60 For the best treatment of this subject, in our opinion, see D. A. Carson, *The Cross and Christian Ministry: Leadership Lessons from 1 Corinthians* (Grand Rapids, MI: Baker, 2004).

Way to the City

very moment experimenting with ways to pacify social unrest through political solutions.[61] Paul's lifestyle among them and his insistence on maintaining its essential rightness, even "necessity" (1 Cor. 9:16–18), in the face of criticism and acrimony testify to his own convictions—he must be "all things to all people" (9:19–23) so he might "win the more" (v. 19).[62] He is no wandering cynic (who begged). He steers clear of patronage—either as a teacher/philosopher or as an ethnic Jew-turned-Christian looking for political or social influence. He is a "worker" (not a term of endearment in the Roman world) who does not need to beg for his sustenance (2 Tim. 2:15). Furthermore, he works hard enough so as to have some left over to give to others and provide for his ministry (2 Thess. 3:8; Eph. 4:28).[63] Sometime during this time frame he wrote his second letter to Thessalonica, admonishing them in no uncertain terms how to handle those in the congregation that did not follow his example of laboring "night and day" so as not to be a financial "burden" (2 Thess. 3:6–15).[64] In this way he sought to teach and model to all a fundamental daily Christian walk—to the upper echelons economically and socially he exemplified Christian leadership that intended never to be in the position of being manipulated by the wealthy and/or powerful; to the lower classes he exuded the kind of self-sufficiency in Christ that would lead to contentment (Phil. 4:11) and the sense of being able to "do all things" (Phil. 4:13) through faith in Christ. Work in this way becomes something done "to the Lord" (Col. 3:23; cf. Eccl. 9:10), not for pleasing men. To all, he preached the Christian vision of "one body" put together by God's Spirit—"whether Jews or Greeks, whether slaves or free" (1 Cor. 12:13).

The local love feasts in Christian churches were intended as affirmations of this truth and as extensions of the OT feasts such as Pentecost. They were

---

61 Theissen, *Social Setting of Pauline Christianity*, 106–10. See also Stark, *Triumph of Christianity*, 22, on this subject. Rome was exceedingly fearful of all associations that were not controlled by governmental politics, and only Christians associated regularly with peole not of their class or craft.

62 This passage (1 Cor. 9) is a microcosm of the variegated way in which the radical demands of discipleship for Christ and the cause of "winning" some from all cultures works out. See how Paul speaks of his "rights" (Greek, "authority") as he lays them down without demanding that others do the same. He did not do this as a strategy for helping the "poor" or demanding equality of sacrifice.

63 A practice he continued through his third mission excursion (Acts 20:33–35).

64 He is clear that the congregation is to administer discipline as to a "brother," not an "enemy" (vv. 14–15).

Way to the City

celebrated in connection with "the Lord's Supper" (1 Cor. 11:20), thus lending a solemnity to them that was to temper festivity with contemplation of "the Lord's death" (11:26) in view of his eschatological return. It is, therefore, entirely inappropriate that they should be marred by anything of "divisions" (lit., "schisms," 11:18), especially anything that smacked of social, cultural, or financial separations. This is what was going on in Corinth, and it is clearly a case of social customs of the time being baptized, so to speak, into the new setting, for Paul's reference to "each one takes his own supper" ahead of and in the presence of another so that "one is hungry and another is drunk" (11:21) could just as well have been said of common public banquets given by the government and wealthy benefactors of that time.[65] Paul condemns this as "unworthily" participating in the Lord's Table, for it shows a failure to "discern the Lord's body" (11:29) as being made up of all classes, social, political, and financial.

Two things in chapter 11 are very striking in Paul's final exhortation on this subject. First, he says one who is "guilty" (v. 27) is drinking "judgment" upon himself (v. 29)—this judgment consisting in being "weak and sick" and, most telling for "many," "being in sleep," as in death (v. 30). He follows this with the explanation that such a thing is a "chastening" (v. 32), not a being "condemned with the world." Clearly this says, without giving a universal free ride from judgment at the bar of Christ, that those who have been culpable in the sinful behavior here addressed are still part of the body of Christ.[66] He has already proposed the way to avoid such a thing—"Let a man examine himself" (v. 28). This is a warning that is personal and specific and steers clear of having others seek to discern the thoughts and intents of others.[67]

---

65 See again on this point Theissen, *Social Setting of Pauline Christianity*, 108–9, and Robertson, *Word Pictures in the New Testament*, on what he calls "club feasts."

66 *Contra* Blomberg et al. See n. 10 above and its cross-references to earlier notes.

67 Not to mention their personal balance sheets or the make of car they drive or the square footage of their houses. Blomberg, *Neither Poverty nor Riches*, 187–88, goes so far as to suggest here that those without a "track record" of giving "from their surplus possessions to the poor" might find themselves excluded from the Lord's Supper. We think (if we were to take his suggestion seriously) it is not too outrageous to suggest here that we begin with the 47 percent or more of the American tax-paying public that pays no income taxes, for which redistribution is among the primary purposes. The rest would be exempt from this charge against them if they could produce an income tax return showing that they paid up!

Way to the City

The second exhortation is striking for its simplicity and its apparent common sense. "Wait for one another," he says (v. 33). How full of common courtesy! How understated! Christians should never treat one another with less respect than even the world can recognize as appropriate. We are bound to let such a truth have its say. There is no guilt manipulation in this passage about excessive spending by Christians on ministries other than for the poor and destitute. There is no condemnation of the wealthy and prominent and socially wellborn for their state in life. There is no call to them to divest themselves of their "excess goods" or their "surplus" to give them to the less fortunate in their midst. It is a simple call for Christian courtesy and respect (not a complete abrogation of prior circumstances in life): If you are so hungry as to be unable to do this, "eat at home" (v. 34).

Appropriate to this discussion is the comment of Alan Johnson in his exegesis and application of Paul's teaching on one's life situation in the first letter to Corinth (7:17–24).[68] In that passage Paul advocates remaining in the situation of life one finds when he or she comes to Christ, with a view to doing mission in that circumstance. Johnson relates his own personal experience of seeking to achieve a kind of higher and more radical commitment to Christ. He relates it this way:

> When I became a Christian at the age of nineteen, I was between my sophomore and junior years at a state university in Southern California. My reaction to all my former life and circumstances led me to leave college and join a Christian group that was seeking to live on a higher spiritual level than other Christians. Had I been aware of Paul's teaching in this passage, I would no doubt have remained at the university, to which I later returned after a loss of some time.

Of course, this kind of behavior, such as went on in the Corinthian church, is considered immature and uncouth in cultures all over the world. It shows a

---

68 Alan F. Johnson, *1 Corinthians*, IVP New Testament Commentary 7, ed. Alan F. Johnson and Grant R. Osborne (Downers Grove, IL: InterVarsity Press, 2004), ad loc.

Way to the City

lack of "class" by those in every class who don't know how to behave themselves in social relationships. This same kind of immaturity and apparent patronal-system worldview leads to the kind of party spirit that also plagued the church at Corinth—for each says "I am of Paul," "I am of Apollos," etc. (1:12)—leading to divisive rivalries. These were doubtless fueled by social and financial stratification that would have been dealt with in the world by straightforward separations. In the church at Corinth, for the first time in history all classes and strata of society are being brought together and taught to love one another in spirit and in truth and word and deed as they worship the one God together.[69]

This revolutionary practice is most eloquently grounded in Paul's moral/theological excursus on the principle and practice of love (agape), which he calls the "more excellent way" (1 Cor. 13). Having dealt practically with both social and charismatic divisiveness, he drives his appeal home by making it clear that Christian unity and courtesy are nothing more nor less than what love demands of all. For him, as it was in Torah and in the teaching of Jesus, love is the embodiment of all the pragmatic and moral teaching of both Testaments. Love God / love your neighbor works itself out in all kinds of practical and material and spiritual ways. As an ethical norm, the one-two punch focuses the vertical and horizontal obligations of man without permitting a descent into sentimental and idealistic substitutions of vague standards for moral certitude. The ideal that is to come, when faith and hope have become sight, is that all will know exactly what love demands even as God knows. Until "the perfect" has come, however, Paul's method is to exhort and cajole and teach by every means possible, while maintaining his own strict separation from entanglement.

This last was, as we have already mentioned, a source of ongoing tension between himself and the Corinthians. Paul was clear on the general principle that "those who preach the gospel should live from the gospel" (1 Cor. 9:14).[70] This he had no problem applying to the other apostles and men like Apollos. He, however, insisted as his "freedom" (9:1) and his "right" (9:4–5) that he allowed to "use none of these things" (9:15) because moral "necessity" was

---

69 See Wheatley, *Patronage in Early Christiaity*, on this point with respect to the churches of the first century and beyond.
70 See also 2 Tim. 2:6; Gal. 6:6; 1 Tim. 5:17.

Way to the City

compelling him to preach the gospel freely to his hearers (9:16–18), so that he might not "abuse" his "authority in the gospel" (v. 18). This is language loaded with spiritual insistence in the face of an opposition that is actually questioning his credentials as an apostle (9:1). He concludes this discussion by likening his actions to competitive athletes who run for "the prize" (9:24)—in this case the "crown" to be given as reward in eternity (9:25).

This insistence on a certain ministry style became an even greater bone of contention as communications went back and forth and it seems to have culminated in some parties at Corinth accusing Paul of the "sin" of "abasing" himself, or "being crafty" and snaring them with "guile" so he might "take advantage" of them (2 Cor. 12:16–17)[71] by working with his hands. He, further, added insult to injury (strong irony here) by "taking wages" from the Macedonian churches (2 Cor. 11:9) while he was at Corinth.[72] To make matters worse, there was also a group of "super apostles" (11:5 and 12:11) egging on the parties at Corinth in their disparagement of Paul's lifestyle and ministry. Why didn't Paul just recognize a difficult situation and accept their money and hospitality? After all, if it was all right for Peter and John and Apollos, why not Paul?

We have already noted at length that this was a matter of deep personal conviction for Paul, but why so? Its roots must be deep in the social and political soil of the Roman world we have described. With a huge lower class and peasant population, not to mention a multitude of slaves, the first-century world was dominated by an elite class of well-to-do and socially upper-class types allied with a political/military power without parallel up to that time in history. Those who knew what was best for themselves on a temporal basis worked this system for all it was worth. One went along to get along, to use our modern parlance. We have seen it at work in Jerusalem. It is clearly at work at Corinth and other places Paul journeyed. He is a partial product of its workings. It is unavoidable in many ways. But Paul is uniquely suited of all the churches' leadership of the

---

71   There may even have been some suggesting that Paul was really taking from the offering for Jerusalem and thus gaining advantage over what the Corinthians might otherwise have given him.

72   See Robertson, *Word Pictures in the New Testament*, ad loc., for explanation of the strong sarcasm in the Greek.

Way to the City

time to head Christianity in another direction. He evidently came to the conviction that he must do what he was doing for the sake of the body, otherwise his "boasting" (2 Cor. 11:16–33 and 1 Cor. 9:16) is petty and self-serving.

Paul's abilities as a craftsman in that place and time set him apart from the original eleven apostles, none of whom had such portable skills. Paul could go about the Roman world and find employment with another or set up shop on his own. Peter, Andrew, and John could hardly do so with their fishing business. It was entirely appropriate that those who had no practical means of making a real living while preaching the gospel should receive sustenance from those whom they taught. And, such was the will of the Lord Jesus (Matt. 10:9–15) from their first commissioning. But this would carry its own weight of problems, as we have seen. And it is evident that Paul is right about this concern, since the Corinthians are twisting his own independence financially as an occasion for immature and scurrilous accusations against him. It is this situation Paul is addressing, we believe, as he envisions a day when churches will not be beholden to wealthy patrons with undue influence in their midst, whether of the social, political, or financial variety.[73] Paul is struggling with a group who are not quite willing to "implement a redirection of the honor game."[74]

A second reason Paul would continue to insist on such an arrangement is to be an example of humble servanthood and hard work in the presence of false triumphalism—exhibited in those who were "puffed up" (1 Cor. 4:6), who already were "full… rich… reigned as kings," who were "wise in Christ," who were "distinguished," who were "strong" (4:8–10). This same triumphalism is probably also a characteristic of the "super apostles" we have previously mentioned. In answer to this, Paul says simply, "I urge you, imitate me" (4:16). And this is surely the implication of his ironic "boastings" (11:16–12:10). They boast "one over against another" (4:6) in strength and power while he boasts of weakness and sufferings and humiliations. He is not masochistic in this, for he wishes "you did reign, that we also might reign with you" (4:8).

---

73 Wheatley notes on this subject with reference to the Corinthian situation, "the strongest resistance to the new paradigm [that is, the break down of reciprocity arrangements of patronage] that can be traced in the New Testament is the conflict in the church at Corinth." *Patronage in Early Christianity*, 36.
74 Ibid., 37.

Way to the City

But Paul knows that while the creation "groans and labors" to bring forth the kingdom, even the church is no utopia, and if its members and structure should happen at any time to have abundance, they should act as if they had "received it" and "not glory as if you had not received it" (4:7).

The Offering for "The Poor" at Jerusalem

It follows that those who have received should freely give. From the beginning of our biblical journey in Genesis the idea that all good things come ultimately from God has been a recurring refrain. All people are stewards of God's gifts through the creation and its order indirectly and through spiritual grace directly. In addition all experience serendipitous moments of divine providence. This is the basis of stewardship in the Bible. It does not weaken what is called in our time "property rights" on the horizontal plane, but it adds personal and corporate responsibility as a divine imperative in the vertical plane that must affect the horizontal. The fact is that if God did not give a property right with his gifts, there would be no one to hold accountable for what is done with it, "For who makes you differ?" (1 Cor. 4:7). Consequently, learning how to give generously and wisely is a biblical mandate.

The longest excursus on this practical outworking of biblical morality is 2 Corinthians 8–9. It is highly instructive for our purposes here, so we will work through it as Paul wrote it to the Corinthian church. First, Paul notes that giving in the biblical way is a work of "grace,"[75] which he urges upon Corinth (and us) by way of the example of the Macedonian churches. For, despite "affliction" and "poverty" they "abounded" in "joy," "riches" and "liberality." And this they did by first giving "themselves to the Lord" and then to Paul and his party "by the will of God." This is surely the principle that is at the root of Paul's famous dictum, "Though I bestow all my goods to feed [the poor]... and have not love, it profits me nothing." Giving oneself to the Lord and his will guards against self-serving displays such as Jesus saw at the temple and in his own inner circle (John 12:4–6) as well as giving that does not mirror the manner in which Jesus "became poor" that we might "become rich."

---

75 For the uses of this word group in the context of patronage, and esp. at Corinth, see ibid., 13, 29–35.

Paul makes it clear he is not giving a "commandment" (2 Cor. 8:8) but is testing their sincerity in saying they wanted to participate in the project for Jerusalem in the first place (8:8–11 and 9:1–5). This is certainly the guiding principle for understanding the entire passage, since Paul is never hesitant to give commands and state theological imperatives. In fact, it is the rare exception when he does otherwise. We believe there are two reasons Paul treats this matter so. First, giving is by its nature a voluntary matter—"generosity and not as a grudging obligation… or a necessity… for God loves a cheerful giver" (9:5, 7). Second, giving is situational from both sides. From the giver's side it is based on what one has available for the purpose (8:12). From the recipient's side it is based on the need of the time and place—in this case Jerusalem's impoverishment[76] due to many factors, none of which involved sinful and foolish behavior, for this is "ministering to the saints" (8:4 and 9:1).[77]

Paul also uses the device of positive reinforcement rather than negative guilt manipulation. He does this in two ways. First, he never suggests that they might, in fact, not follow through—"Achaia was ready a year ago; and your zeal has stirred up the majority" (2 Cor. 9:2). The group sent to Corinth (8:16–24) was there in advance of Paul's arrival to make sure they were "ready" (9:3) and that neither he nor they would be embarrassed by his "confident boasting" about them (9:3–5). The second reinforcement is an exhortation based on the nature of God—his ability and willingness to "make all grace abound" (9:8—thus making God the ultimate "benefactor") to the givers as well as the receivers so that they will not only meet the needs in Jerusalem but God will be glorified "through many thanksgivings to God" (9:12). Paul, of course, had previously instructed them on a plan that would assure this positive outcome—"let each of you" on a weekly basis "lay something aside" according to how each may "prosper" so there would be no need for "collections" when Paul arrived (1 Cor. 16:2). In this manner each person and household could make decisions about giving in the calm of private reflection and not in haste or under public pressure.

---

76 Though Paul does not bring in the subject of poverty in Jerusalem as a motivating factor in this case.

77 Many sources now support the idea that this offering was for the relief of famine conditions that were all over the Mediterranean world of the time and hit the Jerusalem congregation hard. It is noteworthy that Paul organized this relief for Jerusalem and not for local situations at this time. The Macedonians are commended for giving in the midst of their own needs.

Way to the City

Consistent with his style in this whole discussion, Paul answers two questions that would naturally arise in the minds of givers. The first concerns the very legitimacy of the collection. In any situation where extraordinary generosity, such as that being practiced in the Macedonian churches, is being urged also upon others, there is bound to be consideration of its justification. After all, nothing we have seen so far in Scripture suggests that God's people should give foolishly or without accountability, for that is the essence of stewardship. To remove all doubt about this situation, Paul assures the Corinthians that he does not expect them to be "burdened" while others are "eased" (2 Cor. 8:13). Rather, he is calling for "equality" (8:14). That is, at this time Corinth has "abundance" and Jerusalem "lacks." In the future this situation might be reversed. Each would be concerned in either situation to meet the other's need.

Furthermore, as Paul writes to the Romans, the Gentiles are "debtors" to the Jerusalem church, for they (Gentiles) have been "partakers of their (Jerusalem's) spiritual things, their (Gentiles') duty is also to minister to them (Jerusalem) in material things" (Rom 15:27). This is very similar to Paul's thinking on compensation for Christian ministers, that those who are taught should share "all good things" with their teachers (Gal. 6:6). In this way there is equality. Paul, then, reinforces this idea from just such a temporary situation in the OT, when Israel was supplied temporarily with sustenance until their arrival in the land that "flowed with milk and honey." That provision ceased when they crossed the Jordan, for it was not intended to be a continuous provision and the more ordinary process of development of one's own "possession" became the norm.

The second concern in all situations like this is the issue of administration in the transfer of the collection to its rightful recipients (2 Cor. 8:16–24). Paul is careful to credential the committee (to use modern terminology) that is assigned this task—Titus and at least two others chosen by the churches and of course Paul himself. This group will insure that all things will be done in an "honorable" manner in the eyes of men and of God—the offering will get to the place and purpose for which it was gathered without fear of pilferage or any questions about the integrity of its custodians.

A final observation is necessary before we leave Paul's hortatory message on giving. Two extremes of interpretation need to be avoided. The first concerns a misplaced understanding of "equality" in 2 Corinthians 8:14, urging

Way to the City

upon Western and especially American Christians, who have more than their brothers and sisters around them or anywhere else in the world, that they are obliged to divest themselves of goods until there is equality throughout the universal church.[78] Of course, it would have been absurd for Paul to have given such advice at Corinth or anywhere else the church grew to any size, for there would no longer have been places to meet, houses of the size needed being available only to the upper class and elites. Further, there would be no surpluses from which to sustain ministries outside the local sphere, such as the Philippian church did repeatedly for Paul. Finally, it is certainly more likely, given Paul's ongoing controversies with this church over the patronage system, that he is substituting the concept of "equality" as a way of assuring the Corinthian Christians that they do not acquire patronal privilege over Jerusalem because of their giving.[79] If anything, the Jerusalem church would have gained the advantage through having been the first "witnesses" to minister spiritually to the Gentiles. But, Paul wants "equality," and thus, all praise in the situation goes to God, not to earthly patrons or benefactors, just as it did in the early Jerusalem church.[80] As Alan Wheatley states relative to all kinds of truly benevolent patronage in this context (first-century Roman world), many favors might be passed back and forth between those seeking mutual "friendship" (what James in his letter appears to be condemning, James 4:4–5) arrange-

---

78 We have elsewhere delineated some of this thinking in the text and notes above.

79 See on this esp. Sze-kar Wan, "Collection for the Saints as Anticolonial Act: Implications of Paul's Ethnic Resconstruction," in *Paul and Politics: Ekklesia, Israel, Imperium, Interpretation; Essays in Honor of Krister Stendahl*, ed. Richard A. Horsley (Harrisburg, PA: Trinity Press International, 2000), 210–15. Additionally, Gordon Fee has opined in this same vein on the equality brought by the eschatological arrival of Christ. See Gordon D. Fee, *Listening to the Spirit in the Text* (Grand Rapids, MI: Eerdmans, 2000), 59–61. See also Garnsey and Saller, *Roman Empire*, 33, and Kraybill, *Apocalypse and Allegiance*, 145, for discussion of the "liturgical system" that designated the patronage relationships of the wealthy in their generosity to the poor and the community. The Greek term *leitourgia* is from this word-group and is commonly used by Paul to describe his service and that of others. This is the word used to describe what both the Corinthians and the Judean church are doing.

80 Most likely also is the background for Paul's burden about the offering from Gentiles to the Jerusalem church in the eschatological promise of Isa. 60:5–17. For the view that Jerusalem might have understood this offering as a kind of "tax" or homage paid by Gentiles to the Jewish nation, fulfilling prophecy, see Dunn, *Partings of the Ways*, 112–13. Paul would surely wish to avoid such an interpretation by Jerusalem. Conversely, he wished the offering to be received and not rejected as tainted by Gentile "impurity" (Rom. 15:27–31), thus solidifying the unity of the Jewish/Gentile churches.

Way to the City

ments, "but the point was never to balance the equation, but to continue the bond and maintain honor."[81] And, since the supreme "benefactors" were the Father and the Son, the new paradigm had all Christian wealth available to all others in need as a matter of stewardship from the heavenly benefactors. Thus, "honor" would flow, not from the few to the many, but from the many to the many and benefaction became a practice from the many to the many not merely from a conspicuous few to the many.[82]

Our second concern as we leave this passage is the attempt by many to read into 2 Corinthians 9:6–15 an emphasis on financial prosperity and this-worldly success for Christians who give generously, especially to the ministers and ministries that teach this doctrine. Just as equality is not about leveling financially among believers, abounding in God's grace is not a promise of financial reward as a *quid pro quo* for giving and/or tithing. Generosity at the right time(s) and place(s) is a grace worked in the lives of believers, who know their Lord's purposeful self-emptying for them has had its desired effect in their lives. Just as he did, they will give and experience both the joy of knowing they have done a helpful and good and righteous thing and the assurance that it is impossible to outgive a gracious God, who sees their needs from eternity and can be trusted to meet them. This is of the same stripe as Jesus' promise to Peter[83] and the promise in Malachi to the tither (3:10–12) and the promises of blessing all through the Scripture. There is material reward, and Paul is as clear as Jesus that the world to come is no egalitarian place of leveling, for there is reward to be gained and lost (1 Cor. 3:9–15; 9:16–27)[84] in the service of the Lord both now and eternally, but the "name it and claim it" (we prefer "blab and grab") gospel is no gospel at all. "Thanks be to God for his indescribable gift!" (2 Cor. 9:15).[85]

---

81 Wheatley, *Patronage in Early Christianity*, 3–4.
82 Ibid., 178.
83 See Luke 18:29–30 where Jesus promises "many times more in this age" to those who have left "*idios*."
84 We will draw some conclusions on this matter in our final chapter. For discussion of the concept of eternal reward in the age to come see Howard Z. Cleveland, "Reward," *Evangelical Dictionary of Theology*, 2nd ed., ed. Walter A. Elwell (Grand Rapids, MI: Baker, 2001), 1031–32.
85 For the latest comprehensive treatment of the ongoing global headway that these "teachings" are making and the appropriate biblical responses, see David W. Jones and Russell S.

Way to the City

Additional Teaching of Paul and Other New Testament Epistles

Nearing the end of his missionary career and of his life, Paul pens the letter to the church at Philippi, which has been faithful to minister to his material needs repeatedly through the years. This missive tells us a great deal about the character of Christian lifestyle as hard-working servant leader/hero develops. Most notable is the manner in which Paul can contemplate both his death and his life. "For me to live is Christ and to die is gain" (Phil. 1:21) is as noble a sentiment and statement of life purpose as can come to the mind of man. It signals a trust in God's sovereign will that issues in "contentment" in whatever condition comes, whether "abounding" or "suffering need" (4:11–12)[86] and the sense of God-reliance that "can do all things" (4:13). This is closely paralleled with the instruction to follow Paul in working and to "aspire to live quietly, and to mind your own affairs, and to work with your hands… so that you may walk properly before outsiders and be dependent on no one" (1 Thess. 4:11–12 ESV), and again, "do [your] work quietly and to earn [your] own living" (2 Thess. 3:12 ESV).[87] This mirrors the mind of Jesus who said no one took his life from him, but he had the ability to lay it down of his own accord. This is clearly the ultimate goal of character in this life for the Christian—a settled reliance on the goodness and gracious empowerment of God, producing a godly self-reliance.

This condition, however, has its enemies. Covetousness, which Paul equates with lust in Romans 7, appears frequently in Paul's lists of what we might call more heinous sins[88] and desiring what belongs to others (envy, Rom. 1:29; Gal. 5:21; 1 Tim. 6:4), both conditions of the heart that can lead to swindling (1 Cor. 5:10), theft (Eph. 4:28), and pursuit of "dishonest gain" (Titus 1:11) in any form. Paul's reason for including this sinful heart attitude on an equal

---

Woodbridge, *Health, Wealth, and Happiness: Has the Prosperity Gospel Overshadowed the Gospel of Christ?* (Grand Rapids, MI: Kregel, 2011).

86   And that knows this state is "great gain" (1 Tim. 6:3–10).

87   This last is in contrast to the activities involved in being "busybodies" (2 Thess. 3:11) in other people's affairs, a reference to the patronal activities of many as clients of powerful "benefactors." This appears also to be the intent of Paul's instruction in Rom. 13:8. See Wheatley, *Patronage in Early Christianity*, 39.

88   See 1 Cor. 5:10–11; 6:10; Titus 1:7.

footing with murder and adultery is that it is equivalent to idolatry (Eph. 5:5; Col. 3:5; cf. Heb. 13:5). Such a turning from God in the heart not only leads to outright crime at times, it can also make one "greedy for gain" (1 Tim. 1:7; 3:8; cf. 1 Peter 5:2), while supposedly serving the church (see also 2 Peter 2:3, 14), "haughty" (1 Tim. 6:17), or simply a "lover of money" (1 Tim. 3:3; 6:10; 2 Tim 3:2). All of these character descriptions refer to those who cannot be relied on to "forsake all" at the Lord's command, for their money and possessions have a stranglehold on their spiritual lives.

Given the dangers attached to earthly wealth and the hold it can gain on anyone (1 Tim. 6:9–10), Paul encourages "the rich" to guard their attitudes and practice benevolence as a way to be freed from wealth's dangers, especially the possibility they might never truly trust God alone for salvation (1 Tim. 6:17–19). Those who have this special "gift" of being able to "give" should do it "with liberality" (Rom. 12:8).[89] Paul and Peter agree that ostentatious display of wealth in the form of clothing and adornment are entirely inappropriate among Christians (1 Tim. 2:9; 1 Peter 3:3–4) since it partakes of both an appeal to worldly values and bespeaks an inner need to be noticed and/or approved for superficial reasons (see esp. Peter on this). Finally, in a word to all (rich or not) who would be truly Christian in both word and deed, as Jesus and James have already emphasized, John warns that anyone who "has this world's goods" and refuses to help a "needy" brother at the time of his need cannot claim to have a heart of Christian love (1 John 3:17–18). More likely he is possessed of love of "the world," which has crowded out the "love of the Father" (1 John 2:15).

THE BLESSING

The theme we have seen since Eden continues in the teaching of the early church. Now it is the followers of Christ who are blessed and pronounce blessings. Early on Peter and John preach to the crowds in Jerusalem that the ancient blessing pronounced to Abraham consists in the sending of Jesus "to bless you, in turning away everyone of you from your iniquities" (Acts 3:26).

---

89 Note once again there is no counsel to divest oneself of all surplus or to "live simply." It is to become a giver. This is the biblical mediating position until one is called on to literally "forsake *idios*."

Way to the City

This theme of forgiveness for sin and justifying grace as the true meaning of the blessing in the present hour, and the harbinger of a universal blessing in the new heavens and the new earth to come, is consistently taught by Paul (Rom. 4:6–9; Gal. 3:8–9, 14) and at least implied by the writer of Hebrews (12:17 and chaps. 6–7). Paul will call it the "fullness of the blessing of Christ" (Rom. 15:29). The cup at the Lord's Table is the "cup of blessing" (1 Cor. 10:16). The full blessing is in "the heavenlies" (Eph. 1:3) and the appearing of the Lord is "the blessed hope" (Titus 2:13). There is no mention of some material element when this term is used in these contexts, as if the promises to the covenant people of the OT had simply been transferred to the Christian church. Nevertheless, we can see no reason to exclude material blessings from the "already/not yet" formulation of eschatological salvation. This blessing is spiritualized and eschatological, but it retains also the universal aspects we have seen before and that Jesus and Paul have stated above. In the end, of course, it must include "inheriting the earth," as Jesus taught (Matt. 5:5), and "inheriting the cosmos," as Paul called it in Romans 4:13. But more on that later.

In addition Christians are pronounced "blessed" when they are enduring temptation (James 1:12), when they are doers and not just hearers of the word (1:25), and when they are reviled and reproached (1 Peter 3:14; 4:14). Christians informed by OT biblical characters count as blessed "those who endured" (James 5:11). And, the man with a clear conscience is blessed (Rom. 14:22). NT believers do and ought to pronounce the blessing. Paul repeatedly pronounces the blessing upon God at the beginning of his letters. He and Peter both commend and practice "blessing those who curse"[90] and James decries the idea that blessing and cursing should come out of the same mouth (James 3:9–10). Finally, Paul in the context of his farewell at Ephesus supplies a saying of Jesus not found in the Gospels, "It is more blessed to give than to receive," implying that hard work that produces enough to assist the mission of Christ has its own rewards (Acts 20:35). Thus does the blessing of Abraham pass upon all the nations. It is notable for what it adds, not for any specific attempt to deduct something from its original intent both material and spiritual.

---

90   See Rom. 12:14; 1 Cor. 4:12; 1 Peter 3:9.

Way to the City

CONCLUSION

The writer of Hebrews is famous for his heroes of the faith hall of fame (Heb. 11). The thing that is most powerful about the passage is his build up to verse 39, where he states flatly that though these all had "obtained a good testimony"—that is, heaven's record of their faith and faithfulness—nevertheless they "did not receive the promise." He goes on in the next verse to state that God's way is to include NT believers in this litany of heroes "that they should not be made perfect apart from us" (v. 40). We should therefore, be prepared for all kinds of glorious victories and painful losses. We may "quench the violence of fire" or "escape the edge of the sword" (v. 34). But we may also have "mockings" and "scourgings," be stoned, "be slain with the sword" and may wander in "deserts and mountains in dens and caves of the earth" (vv. 36–38), for we cannot expect to find the city of peace and security we seek in this present age and place (13:14). The point is that Christians must prepare themselves and must teach as gospel that a faith that follows Jesus will stand ready at any time or place to do whatever must be done to advance the kingdom and glorify God. We have seen this in the OT heroes. We have seen it in Jesus. And again we have seen it in the men and women who followed him in the early church. What remains before his appearing is that we should "lay aside every weight and sin" and "run with endurance the race that is set before us" while "looking unto Jesus" as the one who "endured the cross, despising the shame" (12:1–3) and has now "sat down" at the position of power in God's throne room. If it was so for the blessed Son of God, how can it be otherwise for those who follow him?

Way to the City

Chapter 9

A Better World and the Promise of the Future

Historians record that Abraham Lincoln, whose life was an almost unremitting series of failures until his election to the US presidency, was despondent to the point of suicidal contemplations in the 1840s. His reason ultimately to resist such self-destructive action was that he felt he had not yet done anything (as we would say) to make the world a better place. The world is indeed "a better place" in some sense because of his decision to press on, but it only became so because of the greatest wartime bloodletting in American history.[1] The irony that good men and women (not necessarily eternally justified men and women), on both sides of such a conflict, can have such a vision of the possibilities of life in this world that they would die so that others might experience it is not an exclusively Judeo-Christian legacy. As we document, huge numbers of people paid in blood for a view they had of biblical truth. However, the picture of heroes that emerges from the Bible is unique in world literature, especially since it culminates in the death of Christ, who "while we were yet sinners... died for us" (Rom. 5:8). It is a legacy that issues in the idea that there are some things in life that are worse to contemplate than the possibility of dying while standing or literally fighting for the sake of great principles. It is tragically true

---

1 Many historians today question whether the savagery of that time released on this continent was ultimately necessary. We offer brief comment on this in chap. 24.

in a world such as this, which requires such dying, that there are always those who are willing to kill and risk death to themselves and others whom they coerce for far less principled reasons—self-advancement and power, money, territory, benighted religious zeal, or sheer malice toward other people. The Bible begins this tale of woe just outside the garden with Cain and Abel and traces it through the "men of renown," the Tower of Babel, ancient empires from Egypt to Rome, and then anticipates a grand cataclysm at the end of the current epoch involving the clash of satanic earthly powers and the kingdom of God. "Making the world a better place" can become a hollow slogan when not properly nuanced by this biblical take on humanity, governments, death, judgment, and the end of the age. The tension that exists in the Bible between faith, hope, and love on the one hand and "it is appointed unto man once to die and after this the judgment" (Heb. 9:27) on the other is unavoidable. The question of what is or can be made "better" here and now as opposed to what awaits the consummation of the new heavens and earth is a critical biblical issue for Christians.

No discussion of the biblical view of a better present and a future promise can proceed apart from an examination of the Bible's emphasis on the kingdom of God. We have already seen his kingship (sovereignty) again and again in the Old Testament (OT) from creation on. In the New Testament (NT), John the Baptizer and Jesus preach repentance based on the kingdom's being "at hand" (Matt. 3:2; 4:17). Jesus' public ministry is regularly characterized as the bursting through upon earth and among people of the kingdom of God or heaven. Jesus taught often about the kingdom and answered questions about its nature—sometimes with enigmatic references (parables and others). His final discourse at Olivet is an excursus on how the kingdom will arrive in fullness at the end of the age, and on how one should prepare for and anticipate its arrival (Matt. 24–25 ,and par.). The "gospel of the kingdom" is what is to be preached "as a witness to all the nations" (Matt 24:14). The kingship of Jesus is both asserted and mocked at his crucifixion by the Romans and the Jews (Matt. 27:37, 47).

Prior to Pentecost Luke characterizes the time the resurrected Jesus spent with the apostles as a period of "speaking of the things pertaining to the kingdom of God" (Acts 1:3). Peter characterizes the outpouring of the Holy Spirit as a kingly gift (Acts 2:29–39), which signifies that Christ has assumed David's throne in the heavenly realm. Philip introduces the Samaritans to the gospel

Way to the City

by preaching "the things concerning the kingdom of God" (Acts 8:12). Paul's first missionary journey concludes with a summary statement of his teaching that much tribulation accompanies those who "enter the kingdom of God" (Acts 14:22). The great Ephesian ministry began with a bold proclamation of "the things of the kingdom of God" (Acts 19:8). Finally, Paul takes this same message to the seat of government at Rome (Acts 28:23). James, Peter, and the writer of Hebrews also characterize Christians as having entered into and received the kingdom of God (James 2:5; 2 Peter 1:11; Heb. 12:28).

Just what are these "things concerning the kingdom" that were preached and taught in the early church? What was presented as current and what was promised for the future? And how do these "things" bear upon our subject? To this we now turn our attention.

The "Kingdom" before Christ

John and Jesus opened the era of NT revelation by announcing the nearness of the kingdom of God without fear of introducing an unknown concept to first-century Judaism. Their teaching assumed the audience had some knowledge of the terminology, though it is clear Jesus is at great pains to educate the people in the kingdom's true meaning and dimensions. It is also obvious that this process was designed to dispel any false conceptions of the kingdom that had accrued in the layers of human tradition popularly taught in his time. Both sides of this equation confirm that "kingdom of God" ideas were commonalities in the thinking of both the religious leaders and masses.

Strangely enough, however, the phrase "kingdom of God"[2] appears nowhere in the OT. Nevertheless, the idea of God as a king with subjects and a realm is everywhere.[3] We have already seen the emphasis on his sovereignty throughout the OT literature. His realm is as infinite as his person, encom-

---

2   Or "kingdom of heaven"—a phrase conveying the same content in our opinion, for "heaven" was a euphemism for "God."

3   See our expositions in previous chapters, especially on the prophets and their take on the kingdom. For texts that proclaim God's (Yahweh's) kingship, see Exod. 15:18; Num. 23:21; Deut. 33:5; 2 Kings 19:15; Isa. 6:5; 43:15; Jer. 46:18; Pss. 29:10; 47:2; 93; 96:10; 97; 99:1–4; 145:11–13. See, among many other works, John Bright, *The Kingdom of God: The Biblical Concept and Its Meaning for the Church*, rev. ed. (Minneapolis: Abingdon, 1980).

passing heaven and the created universe, and his rule extends to all nations, not just Israel. That he has allowed an initial and ongoing rebellion to corrupt and pervert both human nature and the natural world in no way detracts from his kingship. To the contrary, he is ever at work in the midst of the chaotic abuse of freedom and liberty that human sin has wrought. His hand is at the helm of history and guides his creation toward its just end. To secure this purpose he has intervened directly in the affairs of people and nations repeatedly in the past and will do so in the future. To this the Law and the Prophets testify.

The language and terminology used to describe this characteristic activity of God is abstract rather than concrete, or what George Eldon Ladd has called "dynamic."[4] That is, it emphasizes not a realm but a reign or rule (Pss. 145:11, 13; 103:19). This rule is to be vindicated in history and will be consummated at the end of history. The OT concept that advances this doctrine is "the God who comes" to bless and judge.[5] This emphasis is unique in the ancient world and continues to challenge the modern world. But it is also a theme subject to misinterpretation and abuse.

As the fortunes of Israel and her kings deteriorated after the days of Solomon, and it began to be evident that even David's line in Judah would fail to maintain its integrity before God, the word of God began to come directly to the prophets warning of judgments to come. The people of both nations, seeing the rise of the threat from Assyria to the east and presuming upon the longsuffering of Yahweh, began to console themselves with visions of "the day of the LORD" as a hoped-for deliverance. Amos sought to disabuse them of this misconception by warning that this much-anticipated day would not bring the light and vindication and blessing they expected but rather darkness and judgment and wrath (Amos 5:18–20). With the Assyrian crisis in the immediate foreground, he visualizes an even greater cataclysm when all of nature will be disrupted in the face of Yahweh's approach (7:4; 8:7–10; 9:5–6). This is not merely poetic hyperbole; it is the stock-in-trade of the Hebrew prophets. They see an immediate need for repentance in the face of a fast-approaching temporal judgment, while making it clear that this hour of wrath is a harbinger of eschatological events to come.

---

4   George Eldon Ladd, *The Presence of the Future: The Eschatology of Biblical Realism* (Grand Rapids, MI: Eerdmans, 1974), 46.
5   Pss. 96:10–13; 98:8–9; 18:7–15; Deut. 33:25; etc.

Way to the City

Micah[6] spoke in the same manner at the same hour but adds the possibility of a great and final salvation. Isaiah preached the same message as well (chaps. 65–66, et al.). Zephaniah's prophecy is from a later time and saw another crisis approaching, but he uses the same methodology. Joel (2:28–32), Jeremiah (chap. 25), Zechariah (entire book), Malachi (chaps. 3–4) and the unique ministries of Daniel and Ezekiel all partake of this verbal/literary style. Their interest in the future is colored by present crises and the need to urge their listeners to repent in the face of both immediate and future judgments and blessings. God's rule in history means that he intervenes temporally to point to a time when he will intervene cataclysmically and eternally to judge and bless.[7] The fact that both events may be conflated in the prophetic message is itself instructive. Each invasion of God's rule in earthly affairs deals with a historical moment and situation and promises a day when the process will be finalized. This is the true burden of biblical prophecy.

Jesus and the Kingdom

The preaching of John, Jesus, and the apostles follows in this train. The people of their day, however, had been hearing another voice. It was the voice of Jewish apocalyptic thought, a vision not of history and its meaning but of a longing for the cataclysmic end of history. Ladd has rightly characterized their writings as dualistic (in the sense of seeing the evil of the present age as mostly the work of Satan and evil spirits), nonprophetic (in the sense of losing the prophets' emphasis on the current judging/blessing acts of God and their relationship to human sin), pessimistic (having no hope except an eschatalogical one), deterministic (nothing new or good can come until certain time periods have elapsed), and ethically passive (almost devoid of any challenge to repentance and faithfulness).[8]

---

6   Micah 4:1–5; 1:2–4; 7:7–20.
7   For a new and dynamic presentation of this theme as the primary motif of salvation history, see James M. Hamilton Jr., *God's Glory in Salvation through Judgment: A Biblical Theology* (Wheaton, IL: Crossway, 2010).
8   Ladd, *Presence of the Future*, 87–101. But see also Mark Adam Elliott, *Survivors of Israel: A Reconsideration of the Theology of Pre-Christian Judaism* (Grand Rapids, MI: Eerdmans, 2000), for a more nuanced understanding of the actual literature of the period. He had the benefit of much greater access to the archaeological discoveries of the last century than did Ladd.

Way to the City

It is this misapprehension of both the kingdom and the prophetic mission of the earlier messengers that animates Jesus' (and John's) preaching/teaching about the kingdom in the NT.

The prior manifestations of God's rule, played out against the backdrop of human aspiration and folly (personal, national, and imperial), serve to usher in for the "fullness of times,"[9] when the person of his perfect rule is manifest among men and as a man. The NT consistently and constantly witnesses that there is no discontinuity among what went before and what is now being manifest and what will be consummated in the future. Any apparent inconsistency is simply a mark of the mystery surrounding God's plans and workings and of the insufficiency of the understanding of these things in the mind of man—a mind seemingly infinitely capable of sloth, folly, and perversity (Mark 4:11–13). Into this mix of personal, national, and imperial misappropriation of God's rule John and Jesus come to preach and in Jesus' case to exercise authority.

This is not the place to engage in a thoroughgoing theological discussion of Jesus' kingdom teaching. We can only note the high points and refer the reader to the broad body of material on the subject. Here we will summarize briefly what Jesus taught: The kingdom is present in his work and that of his disciples,[10] but the power to exorcise demons and/or heal earthly illnesses is no substitute for present and eternal salvation (Matt. 12:43–45; Luke 11:24–26) or the complete elimination of evil powers (Matt. 25:41)[11] and people who follow them. The kingdom is present in the preaching of the gospel (Matt. 4:23; Luke 4:43; Mark 2:2), but "the word" may still be rejected with eternal consequences (Mark 4:14–20). The kingdom is present in the ongoing activity of God as he seeks out "the lost" (Luke 15), invites them to his table (Matt. 22:1–14; Luke 14:16–24), and urges them to fellowship with him as Father,[12] but the rejection of his overtures by men can only lead

---

9   Gal. 4:4; Eph. 1:9–11; cf. Rom 5:6.
10 See Matt. 12:29; Luke 10:17; 11:22; Mark. 6:7.
11 Notice that the "oppression" word-group is most often associated with these demonic powers and suggests to the people that Satan, not Rome or rich people, is the primary oppressor of God's people.
12 Matt. 6:9–10; 13:43; 26:29.

Way to the City

to judgment,[13] and this judgment can descend on cities (Matt. 11:20–24; Luke 10:13–15) and nations (Matt. 21:43). Note that this judgment to come is seen in the background of all kinds of sinful activity: failure to teach the entire Law (Matt. 5:19), hatred and disdain for others (Matt. 5:21–26), careless words (Matt. 12:36–37), judgmentalism (Matt. 7:1–2), failure to forgive (Matt. 18:21–35; cf. 6:12, 14–15), hindering "little ones" in the kingdom (Mark 9:42; Matt. 18:6)[14], hypocrisy (Matt. 23:33), failure to relieve the needy at one's door (Luke 16:19–31), failure to receive and assist the teachers of the gospel (Matt. 25:31–46; Matt. 10:40–42 and its context),[15] and many other sins of omission and commission. We believe it is a complete misapprehension of these last two passages that causes some interpreters (both evangelical and liberal) to place undue exaggerated emphasis in the judgment upon political and personal treatment of the physically and socially "poor."

Finally, and most telling for our present purpose, Jesus taught that the kingdom is supernatural in its origin, its progress and its consummation (Mark 4:26–32), for this is indeed what happens in the material world when seed is planted and a harvest comes through the dynamics of God's creation and Noahic promise. Man may follow the rules for a harvest and cultivate to his advantage, "but God gives the increase." Thus, Jesus teaches that the kingdom can come near (Matt. 3:2 and par.), arrive (Matt. 12:28), appear (Luke 19:11), and be active (Matt. 11:12).[16] Men can enter it, receive it, possess it or inherit it,[17] or they can reject it (Luke 10:11; Matt. 23:13). They can seek it, pray for it to come, and look for it.[18] People can sacrifice for the kingdom (Matt. 19:12; Luke 18:29), preach the kingdom (Matt. 10:7; Luke 10:9), or they can prevent others from entering it (Luke 18:16; cf. 11:52). In none of

---

13 Mark 8:38; Matt. 10:32–33; 25:34.
14 See Morna D. Hooker, *The Signs of a Prophet: The Prophetic Actions of Jesus* (Eugene, OR: Wipf and Stock, 1997), 41–42, for comment on this incident as a definitive moment in Jesus' demonstration of the nature of citizenship in the kingdom. One must be "converted" according to Jesus to be a "little one," i.e., become "poor" (this last is our conclusion on the story). Further, it is the key to "greatness" in the kingdom, a mark of biblical heroism.
15 This is also the emphasis of Paul (1 Tim 5:9–10) on "washing the saints' feet" and John (2 John 10–11) on "receiving" and "bidding Godspeed" to genuine brethren.
16 Verbs listed with "kingdom" as the subject, plus related ideas associated and various Scripture references here and following are mostly from Ladd, *Presence of the Future*, 193.
17 See Matt. 5:20; Mark 10:15; Matt. 5:3, 10; 25:34.
18 Matt. 6:10, 33; Luke 23:51.

Way to the City

these teachings is there a hint that people might establish, build, or bring in the kingdom, nor can they give it to another.[19] Conversely, neither can they destroy it, take it from others, or prevent its triumph. Rather, the kingdom is a gift from the Father (Luke 12:32). Consequently Jesus could confidently go to his crucifixion with the words, "my kingdom is not from this world" (John 18:36), otherwise, his servants would "fight" to prevent his death.

THE KINGDOM IN THE NEW TESTAMENT EPISTLES

We have already noted that the apostles early on and consistently couched their preaching in kingdom terminology. The epistolary materials of the NT help to flesh out for us what they taught. Paul's body of work is, of course, the most instructive. He consistently emphasizes the rule of Christ (as Jesus exalted) over the churches[20] in particular, the present world[21] in a permissive and providential way, and the world to come in an all-encompassing and compelling mandate of righteous wrath and promised blessing.[22] While never equating the church with the kingdom nor participation in the church with belonging to the kingdom, he regularly urges upon the churches such behavior that bespeaks submission to Christ's rule.[23] This is, in fact, Paul's characteristic way of teaching ethics: Jesus Christ is Lord and Head of the church (as a grouping of confessed individual believers). Therefore his subjects should reflect his rule in their behavior. To the extent that the church does this in her corporate life, she is an exhibit for all to see, even to the "principalities and powers in the heavenlies" (Eph. 3:10), of the power and grace of her Lord.

But the church is only *a* (not *the*) manifestation of Christ's rule. The church is more rightly denominated "the people of the kingdom," as Ladd puts it.[24] These people, insofar as they are truly "kingdom people," band together in association for the purpose of preaching the kingdom as Paul did, showing forth kingdom behavior as Paul urges them to do through their ethics and fel-

---

19 Richard Stearns, *The Hole in Our Gospel* (Nashville: Thomas Nelson, 2009).
20 See Eph. 1:22–23; 5:23; Col. 1:18.
21 See Rom. 8:18–25; Eph 1:19–21.
22 See 1 Cor. 15:20–28; 2 Thess. 1:5–10.
23 Eph. 3:15–21; Phil. 2:9–15; Col. 1:13; 3:1–17; et al.
24 Ladd, *Presence of the Future*, 264.

lowship around the table (1 Cor. 11:23–26),[25] and anticipating and awaiting with eagerness the "blessed hope," which is the arrival of the messianic King in his glorious power.

Meanwhile, in the world at large and in the whole created universe a "subjection to futility" (Rom. 8:20) is continuing, implying by the language that there is a ruler who subjects. This is only a temporary situation, however, for the whole creation will be "delivered from corruption" (8:21a), and this deliverance will be coincident with and is dependent upon the arrival of the "glorious liberty of the children of God" (8:21b). Paralleling this condition is the activity of the "rulers of this age" (1 Cor. 2:8) who missed God's revelation by following their own "wisdom" to the dark deed of crucifying (ironically) "the Lord of glory" (v. 8b). Nevertheless, it is the wisdom of God that "ordained" these events, once again asserting the kingdom's rule despite appearances. Even more compelling is Paul's teaching that evil itself is being "restrained" (2 Thess. 2:7) until a time when it will be personified in "the man of sin," or "lawless one" (2:8), whose manipulator is Satan and whose powers will extend to "lying signs and wonders" (2:9). This is the manner of the providential and permissive rule of the heavenly king for the present age—subjection, ordination, and restraint.

Such a situation, where the king can be murdered and his followers are subjected regularly to persecution (1 Thess. 2:14–15), tribulations (2 Thess. 1:4), and death (2 Tim. 4:6; 1 Cor. 15:32), and where men steadily proceed from bad to worse in rejecting the message of the kingdom,[26] cannot be allowed to prevail or go on indefinitely. First, by sending a "strong delusion" (2 Thess. 2:11) to surface in the world the desire to "believe the lie" (v. 11b)—this because they "received not the love of the truth" (2:10)—together with the "pleasure" men take in unrighteous behavior (2:12), and second, by sending the Lord Jesus "from heaven with his mighty angels" (2 Thess. 1:7), God will institute a compulsory rule that cannot be ultimately resisted or denied (1 Cor. 15:25). Finally, the "Son himself…will also be subject to him who put all things under him, that God may be all in all" (1 Cor. 15:28; cf. Phil. 3:21).

---

25 See 1 Cor. 1:7–8; 16:22; Gal. 3:20; 1 Thess. 1:10; Titus 2:13.
26 See 2 Tim. 3:1–9; 4:3–4; Titus 1:10–16.

Way to the City

Other NT epistles confirm and support Paul's theology. James is apparently the earliest to urge faithful and patient behavior on his Christian auditors based on the era in which they live, "the last days" (James 5:3), which will see their tormentors punished, for their cries have reached "the ears of the Lord of hosts" (5:4), whose *parousia* (coming) is "at hand" (5:8), even "standing at the door" (5:9). Peter urges faithfulness and obedience to Christ in the face of "various trials" (1 Peter 1:6), because Christians have a "living hope" (1:3), which is "reserved in heaven" (1:4) and will be manifest "at the revelation of Jesus Christ" (1:7). His explanation of "this salvation" (1:10–12) visualizes prophets of the OT era and the "angels in heaven" eagerly seeking to understand the mysterious working of God's "foreknowledge" (1:2) and "foreordination" (1:20) in the present era. Peter's readers are urged to act out their role as God's "special people" (2:9), even though they live ethically in the world as "sojourners and pilgrims" (2:11). Though they do not rule in this age, because they are obedient to the heavenly ruler, they "may put to silence the ignorance of foolish men" (2:15). They can afford to walk in this fashion because, since his resurrection, Jesus Christ has "gone into heaven and is at the right hand of God, angels and authorities and powers having been made subject to him" (3:22). Their sufferings along the way not only serve to unite them in Christ's sufferings and give them cause to "glorify God" (4:12–16), but they also show that judgment is presently at work in "the house of God" (4:17), a way of speaking of the church. In this way he confirms that the church cannot be synonymous with the kingdom.

Peter's second epistle joins in Paul's warning to Timothy that people who do not hear and obey the truth will corrupt and seduce the church (2 Peter 2:13). In a stinging diatribe he makes clear that judgment will come swiftly and surely (2:4–22). Chapter 3 then parallels Paul's teaching in his Thessalonian correspondence, emphasizing that before "the day of the Lord" arrives "scoffers" will arise to deny that such an event is any longer conceivable (3:3–4), since the length of this era tends to deny the true lordship of the heavenly King—that is, his "promise" has failed. Peter's conclusion is that delay is within the purpose of God (3:9), and the suddenness of the final cataclysm will swallow up the scoffers (3:10). In light of this approaching reality Christians should conduct themselves in a godly manner and anticipate with eagerness the coming of a "new heavens

Way to the City

and a new earth" (3:13), even "hastening" its approach (3:12).[27] Peter does not elaborate on this last idea, but we can only conclude from our current study that Jesus' command to pray for the coming of the kingdom (Matt. 6:10) and his statement that the "gospel of the kingdom" must be preached worldwide "as a witness" (Matt. 24:14) are the catalysts for this exhortation.

The writer of Hebrews has as his primary focus the utter superiority of Christ to all things and persons that came before him. As Son of God he is above the angels (1:4–14), and he is the One to whom all things are being subjected (v. 13). His role as king-priest is mirrored in the mysterious appearance of Melchizedek, "king of peace" and "king of righteousness," in the days of Abraham (7:1–3). Jesus' sacrifice for sin happened "at the end of the ages" (9:26) and he will "appear a second time… for salvation" (9:28). In light of this utter superiority of Christ and his program over all other preceding administrations, Christians are urged to "hold fast the confession of our hope" (10:23), for "yet a little while and he who is coming will come and will not tarry" (10:37). Meanwhile, believers can expect their lives to resemble those of the faithful in prior ages (chap. 11)—a pilgrimage full of uncertainties, challenges, deliverances, temptations, rejection, persecution, torture, and death. This they must endure in faith as an arena for child training (12:5–11), for they/we are "receiving a kingdom which cannot be shaken" (12:28). It follows that ordinary duties and a contentment devoid of covetousness should characterize those expecting to receive such a blessing (13:1–6).

John's ethical concerns in his epistles revolve around the contrast between the love of the Father and the love of "the world" and its "things" (1 John 2:15), seen as a system in rebellion against God. The world is in its "last hour" (2:18), and the spirit of the coming Antichrist is already abroad in it in the form of defectors from among Christian congregations. The world is a place where the Devil and his works, first seen biblically in the story of Cain and Abel, are encountered as hatred for righteous people (3:12–13). It is no wonder that the only thing to be done about this is that the Son of God must "destroy the works of the devil" (3:8). The world loves the message of antichrist-like false prophets

---

27 Note A. T. Robertson, *Word Pictures in the New Testament*, ed. James A. Swanson (Nashville: Broadman & Holman, 2000), ad loc., on this translation of the word used here.

Way to the City

(4:3–5). But Christians can "overcome the world" (5:4–5) by maintaining their faith even though "the whole world lies in the wicked one" (5:19) who manipulates the system behind the scenes by the will of God for the time. Consequently, "keep yourself from idols" (5:21) is a terse but fitting summary exhortation for those who would be *in* but not *of* the world.

Jude's short polemic has the stated purpose of exhorting its readers to "contend earnestly for the faith once for all delivered to the saints" (v. 3). This he does against the same backdrop we have seen in Paul, Peter, John, and Hebrews. Deceptions and defections within the ranks of believers threaten to carry away even those who would be faithful. But since "the Lord comes with ten thousands of his saints" (v. 14), Christians should concentrate on strengthening their faith, prayer, guarding their own spiritual condition (vv. 20–21), and rescuing from the encroaching flames of judgment those whom they can (v. 23).

In conclusion, the correspondence with the churches of the first century that we find in the NT epistles is consistent with the teaching of Jesus and the methodology of the prophets who went before. The kingdom of God has its present manifestation and a future consummation. In light of this the believing community is expected to behave personally and socially as those who expect a future blessing and know they are not exempt from God's judgments present and future. The church is a place for Christ's kingship to be displayed insofar as his will is obeyed. It is also his instrument for good in the private and public lives of the community around it. Paradoxically, it draws upon itself hatred, persecution, and martyrdom the more faithful it is to its true mission. But as it and/or defectors from it depart from Christ's commands and teachings, it becomes an antichrist influence. This tension characterizes the present age and mitigates against utopian visions of change for a truly "better world,"[28] for as John shows, "the world" is the problem.

The Apocalypse of Jesus Christ

John's account of "the revelation of Jesus Christ" rightfully brings to its conclusion the teaching of the Bible about the "things about the kingdom."

---

28 Or Stearns's "social revolution" discussed in his *Hole in Our Gospel*.

Way to the City

Commonly spoken of as "apocalyptic" because of the Greek word translated "revelation," it is often treated as a close kin to the Jewish apocalyptic (so-called) literature produced during the intertestamental period. However, this is a case of *ex post facto* descriptive comment, for it is the Johannine material that is the true apocalypse from which attempts have been made to make applications to the prior Jewish materials and to certain portions of the OT material in the prophets.[29] The adjectival usage of the word "apocalyptic" has, in fact, become a generic denotation for any communication that moves from current conditions and events to visions of impending doom and destruction with overtones of the end of things as we have known them.

We have previously noted that biblical prophecy, with its firm rooting in a God at work in history and an ethical and sociopolitical challenge for the present, stands in marked contrast to intertestamental "apocalyptic." John's "prophecy,"[30] for so it is called, is the last in the line of biblical prophetic works. It is apocalyptic in the strict sense of the term, as it purports to unveil what is mysterious, and it defines the genre that speaks of the end of all things as we know them in the present age. Consequently, it is John's work and all the biblical materials of similar bent that are the plumbline against which all other imitators are to be measured.

The mysteries unveiled in this final vision and those left still shrouded in the mists of symbolic and allegorical language (with conflations of first-century and eschatological events) have spawned a massive literature, not all of which is truly helpful. It is not our purpose to attempt to sort all of this out. We do, however, wish to draw from this prophetic work certain ideas we think are very clear, which bear upon our subject. In so doing, we will clearly betray our presuppositional bias toward the premillennial interpretation, mirroring the work of Ladd, whose work emphasizing the "already-not-yet"-ness of the kingdom seems on target to us, and the work of Craig Blaising and Darrell Bock, whose emphasis on the progressive manifestation of the kingdom dovetails well with Ladd's prior emphases.[31]

---

29 For this description, see George Eldon Ladd, *A Commentary on the Revelation of John* (Grand Rapids, MI: Eerdmans, 1972), 20.

30 See Rev. 1:3; 22:7, 10, 18–19; and the writer himself designated as "prophet," 22:9.

31 See Ladd, *Presence of the Future*; Ladd, *Commentary on the Revelation of John*; George Eldon Ladd, *The Gospel of the Kingdom: Scriptural Studies in the Kingdom of God* (Grand Rapids, MI: Eerdmans, 1959); and Craig A. Blaising and Darrell L. Bock, *Progressive*

John's clearest message is that heaven's hero, the Lamb "bearing death marks" (5:6), is the only one "worthy" (5:2–14) to bring to a close with righteous judgments and rewards the age in which we live and inaugurate the age to come. His worthiness is based in his self-sacrifice and the weight of his character that such love and obedience to the will of the Father imply. Only such a one as he can be trusted to receive and exercise the unlimited "power and riches and wisdom and strength and honor and glory and blessing" (v. 12) that are required to right all wrongs and bring in a new age of true peace and blessing. All others who have exercised power and authority over the lives and fortunes of others are not only pikers in terms of the degree and extent of their powers, but they also lacked the character required to be trusted with anything like life-altering and world-changing force to bring in their flawed and often perverse vision of things as they ought to be. Only the slain Lamb, now risen and ruling, is worthy for such hegemony, no matter what Cain or the mighty men of old or Pharaoh or Goliath or Nebuchadnezzar or Caesar or any other would-be tyrant may think.

Furthermore, not even a Noah or Moses or David or Josiah or Hezekiah or a prophet or an apostle or a pastor of one of the seven churches of Asia, though all may be justified by the blood of the slain Lamb, is worthy. No prior figure, no matter how heroic, is worthy as the Lamb. This is heaven's and John's centerpiece in the apocalypse. Without this One and this truth there is no hope. In him reside all the hopes of mankind for "dominion" and the kingly reign that was envisioned in the beginning. They will reign when he reigns. He secures the promise of the Father.

This figure first appears to John, the exile of Patmos, as "one like the Son of Man" (1:13), whose glory dwarfs the light of the seven golden lamp-stands symbolizing the churches of Asia. He walks among them as their Lord and in prophetic fashion exhorts, challenges, and warns them. Only Smyrna and

---

Dispensationalism (1993; repr., Grand Rapids, MI: Baker, 2002). We would note, as well, that our interpretation has much in common with the amillennial interpretation given by Anthony Hoekema, *The Bible and the Future*, rev. ed. (Grand Rapids, MI: Eerdmans, 1994), who does not overly spiritualize the OT prophecies as some amillennial interpreters do. N. T. Wright has once again added his scholarship to this subject in *Simply Jesus: A New Vision of Who He Is, What He Did, and Why He Matters* (New York: HarperCollins, 2011), a volume with much to commend it and at the same time raising debatable questions.

Way to the City

Philadelphia receive no call to repentance. All are called to endure and "overcome."[32] This last command/promise especially, "He that overcomes," implies that conditions are such that individuals must be prepared to stand alone if need be to reap the reward promised—repeated descriptions of eternal salvation. This repeated call to individual heroic action in the hope of salvation, coupled with the repeated call to the "angel" (messenger or pastor, in all likelihood[33]) of five of the churches to call for a general repentance in the congregation away from deeds and attitudes specified, indicate that the churches are not the hope for a better world. Their own internal flaws and their consequent failure to mirror Christ's glory to the world, especially if they do not adequately repent, make the case that they can only be poor and hazy reflections of the glory that must come and that is to come. Meanwhile, "he that has ears to hear" must "keep the words of the prophecy of this book" (22:7), for the Lamb is Lord of the churches and will judge them as he does all the world.

John's next vision of the Christ is the one we began with here and is given for the purpose of revealing his lordship over the current age in the unrolling of the scroll. We believe this is symbolic of his rule in history, for the first four seals picture the march of empires, war, famine, and death. The fifth seal sees martyrs slain "for the word of God and the testimony which they held," (6:9) crying out for justice and the vengeance of God in the terminology of those wearied by delay ("How long, O Lord"). The sixth seal ushers in an eschatological moment signifying the end of what now is systemically and in all creation. This parallels the manner in which previous prophets saw the end of all things. This is the answer to the prayer of the martyrs and, by implication, that of all world-weary Christian pilgrims, for all the heroes are not dead yet.[34]

After the interlude of chapter 7, the culminating events of the end of the age are announced by successive trumpets heralding massive natural and cosmic di-

---

32 Rev. 2:7, 11, 17, 26; 3:5, 12, 21. Note that all the calls to "repent" and to "overcome" or "conquer" are addressed to a singular "you," implying either the "messenger" of each church or each member individually or both. "Overcomers" are individuals, not the collective.

33 Of the "angel's" identity in these greetings, Augustus H. Strong said, "So, too, in Rev. 2:1, 8, 12, 18, and 3:1, 7, 14, 'the angel of the church' is best interpreted as meaning the pastor of the church." *Systematic Theology: A Compendium Designed for the Use of Theological Students*, 3 vols. in 1 (Old Tappan, NJ: Revell, 1907), 916.

34 This is basically Ladd's approach to the interpretation of the first six seals. *Commentary on the Revelation of John*, 79–120.

Way to the City

sasters, the release from restraint of demonic power, and the resulting torments of "those who dwell on the earth,"[35] a reference to those whose mind-set makes them at home and at rest in the present age and on the present terrestrial creation. These can be contrasted with the martyrs and the pilgrims and "those who are coming out of great tribulation" (7:14), who are looking for new heavens and a new earth (2 Peter 3:13). Dwellers on the earth do not repent of all kinds of immoral behavior no matter the pressures brought to bear on them (Rev. 9:20–21).

The "little book" (Rev. 10:2) appears to symbolize a shorter period (in contrast to the seven-sealed scroll) in which the Christ will exercise his lordship. Its contents are both "bitter" and "sweet" to John. The sweet is undoubtedly the arrival at last of deliverance and justice for the faithful, but the bitterness is just as certainly the terrible vengeance that shall fall upon the earthbound we have previously described. These are portrayed as rejoicing and celebrating over the martyrdom of the two prophets who "tormented" them (11:10) and as giving their "worship" to "the beast" who wields full political, economic, and religious power (13:11–18). Here in chapter 11 of John's book it is revealed that Jerusalem in the earthly realm is perhaps the worst sinner of all in that she became the perpetrator of murder against the very Son of God and his followers. This is certainly a monstrous evil, that all earthly types of power and authority should at last become concentrated in a single coercive governing force, perverting the whole plan of God, wielded by a single personality and acceded to by all those who are caught up in deception and/or cowardly enough to prefer life as slaves rather than death in faithful resistance. They will be deceived because "they received not the love of the truth" (2 Thess. 2:10), and they will choose temporary life over eternal glory because they lack the courage of the heroes of the faith (Rev. 21:8; cf. Heb. 12:1–4).[36]

The vision presented in the interlude of Revelation chapter 18 fills out the picture of the last great monstrosity that bids all peoples everywhere on earth to give allegiance or die. It is personified in the first empire of the biblical record. We have seen how God viewed the first human attempt to circumvent the prime directive to go out into the earth and subdue it and bring it into the service of God and man

---

35   See Rev. 3:10; 6:10; 8:13; 11:10; 13:8–14.
36   This is surely the intent of the "cowardly" and "faithless" (ESV) being first into the fire in 21:8.

Way to the City

and create a "heaven on earth" in the words of Dostoyevsky.[37] At Babel the choice to seek security above courageous obedience led first to a sovereign scattering and eventually to a wicked empire.[38] John sees this same evil in the final convulsions of a corrupt world system. The collusion of the "kings of the earth" with "the merchants of the earth" (vv. 3, 9, 11) and the "shipmasters" and "sailors" (vv. 17–19) in concert with the Babylonish idea of seeking security in ungodly alliances is rightly called whorishness and fornication. For this is a kind of ultimate evil—using government's coercive powers to acquire and manipulate wealth for imperial control of the lives and livelihoods of others—is a complete perversion of God's original command to subdue and have dominion over the earth and all creation. It is surely the collusion of the "fascism" we will address in future chapters. The prophetic charge is that "all the nations" (v. 3) have drunk the intoxicating nectar of governmental power being manipulated for the aggrandizement of the elitist few at the expense of those loyal to Christ, who are unable or unwilling to play Babylon's game.[39] It was peculiarly the game of Rome, the certain object behind the imagery of Babylon in John's vision, as we document extensively in the early chapters of the next section of the book. This is hellish work, for it acquires wealth through intrigue, reputation (the "name" of Gen. 11:4), coercion, and the politics of preferential legalities, rather than God-honoring labor, toil, thrift, and deferred rewards. Such wealth and power is destined to be "made desolate in one hour" (Rev. 18:19).

Babylon is symbolic of all the great imperial visions that have been swept away in the march of God's sovereignty throughout history. Some have been

---

37 Fyodor Dostoyevsky, *Brothers Karamazov*, trans. Constance Garnett (New York: Random House, 1950), 25–26.
38 This search for security through government is among the principles first articulated in the West by John Locke, and Thomas Jefferson followed in his train during the time of the American founding. See Peter Augustine Lawler, "Religion, Philosophy, and the American Founding," in *Protestantism and the American Founding*, ed. Thomas S. Engerman and Michael P. Zuckert, Loyola Topics in Political Philosophy (Notre Dame, IN: Notre Dame University Press, 2004), 166–67.
39 For compelling views of the state of the Roman central geographical region on the Italian peninsula, see Peter Garnsey and Richard Saller, The *Roman Empire: Economy, Society, and Culture* (Berkeley: University of California Press, 1987), and J. Nelson Kraybill, *Apocalypse and Allegiance* (Grand Rapids, MI: Brazos, 2010). The Italian peninsula and Rome itself were largely unproductive of the necessities to sustain the population. Consequently, the rest of the empire fed the elite of government and their various patronage-generated relationships. It was not unlike the concept of the administrative state we will explore later in the next section and will find growing in its influence in the West.

Way to the City

directly destroyed by God's revealed actions (Israel and ancient Babylon), others have been shown to be unable to resist his mighty works even as they continued to stand (Egypt), but all have passed from the scene just as surely as Rome did after its long run. All of them partook of Babel's failed promise to deliver security and wealth through unholy and unbiblical departures from God's rule fueled by covetousness, envy, and power-mongering. Just as in the past, whatever final form the utopian vision takes, it will be judged by the one who rules "with a rod of iron" (Rev. 19:15). The warning to all is not to become worshippers of such a vision—particularly when it involves one's own security and livelihood (13:16–18), for this is "the mark of the beast" (v. 16; 20:4)—a vision, namely, that mankind is able to build the perfect world without God.

To those who, through the faith they hold in "the testimony of Jesus" (19:10) and the courage they show in doing God's will (20:4; 22:14), overcome by endurance and patience (14:12–13), the heavenly king will at last come to rule first on the old earth and finally over a new heaven and a new earth (21:1). This is the better world, which utopian visions of the present age can only imagine. Such a world must have the right king, the right subjects, and be a place without a curse from sin's presence (22:3). Naturally (rather, supernaturally) it must be given from above and come down from the "Father of lights," as James would say. Only in such a world can scarcity be eliminated, for this is what gates of pearl, streets and walls of gold, foundations of "precious" stones, unpolluted water, and unlimited access to the tree of life is all about. To those whose values have been purified, the unlimited enjoyment of wealth is both uncorrupting and inconsequential beside the greater good of being in full partnership with the rule of God (22:5). Here and here alone can the commission and the promise of human dominion be realized. Finally, the blessing first pronounced in Eden, renewed to Noah, narrowed, with a universal focus, to Abraham, continued in the same particular sense at Sinai and the house of David, becomes truly universal and eternal for all who are "in Christ" (Eph. 3:1–6).

CONCLUSION

John's account of the unveiling of Christ in his kingdom power closes out the Bible's ongoing polemic against the tendency of government, religion, and the masses of the people to confuse the roles they have been assigned to create a false god.

Way to the City

God's world was created for men and women to rule and subdue by adding their labor and God-given ingenuity to natural resources for the production of goods and wealth as God's stewards. Sin's ravages first dethroned God in the hearts of men and women individually and then proceeded—first by one-on-one coercion born of religious envy (Cain and Abel), then by the false heroism of small-time despots (Lamech and the so-called men of renown), then by joining forces to seek security apart from God (Babel)—to create political, religious, and cultural structures that would make God irrelevant. In time great empircs that slaughtered and enslaved whole civilizations took the place of God. Tragically, millions upon millions whom God created freely and voluntarily to exercise their stewardship under his leadership and that of his own special kind of servant hero/leaders were martyred or shackled or, worse, cooperated with evil despots for their own advantage.

The Law said that government's job was to stand as an impartial arbiter (Lev. 19:15, et al.), dispensing punishment to the evil and justice to the righteous. The Davidic ruler was enjoined to "crush the oppressor" (Ps. 72:4, et al.) of the needy and afflicted. But the prophets found that even in Israel there was rampant the coercive oppression of those in league with government to seize and defraud the property of others and otherwise rob them and do violence to them by "legal" mcans.[40] This is perversion of the mandate to both individuals and governments. Free men and women under God who trust him to reward their efforts are promised his faithfulness in all kinds of ways so long as they work diligently, plan prudently, live thriftily, strive courageously, give generously, and worship the One who gives good gifts. Government is best when it confines its business to arbitration between those aggrieved and their clear oppressors and is at its worst when it makes its own increase a goal and uses the moral perversity of its subjects to practice favoritism through legalized immoralities and presumes to have the wisdom of God to "make a better world" or some such monstrosity.

Freedom to make voluntary exchanges with others on economic, social, and cultural matters is inherent in God's creation and mandates to humankind. Going about the earth and through life is the essence of fulfilling the stewardship given to free people under the command of God. Such free movement and free exchange tend to challenge people to look to God for help and sustenance and to

---

40   See Isa. 10:1–2; Mic. 2:2; 6:12; and many others.

Way to the City

show courage and ingenuity under his leadership, rather than receive a "mark" that makes them a part of an earthly fraternity. Those who mistake moral and physical freedom for autonomy and libertinism will pay the price eternally and should be made to pay the price temporally by governing authorities. When, instead, the cowardly and covetous and greedy look to governments to sanction and aid their efforts, they make government a God. To whatever extent large masses of people can be persuaded to make the choice for government over God, the kingdoms of this world will grow at the expense of those who are making a different choice.

Government elites have consistently justified their activities by asserting some form of divine or moral right to do what they do. It is, therefore, no surprise to see in the Bible's final prophetic words a picture of a great whore aided by religious perversity and deception convincing a world full of peoples and nations that God is not the great blessor, government is. To those whose stock-in-trade is not loving, seeking, and doing the truth, the pull of this great lie is irresistible. In this way a world gone astray from its true king can be convinced to surrender its liberty to one who sits in the place of God.

Finally we note the obvious throughout the biblical survey we have traversed and especially "what the Spirit says to the churches." The Bible as a whole and John's final record are written to the *believing community* as such, not to the world. The churches, like Israel, are custodians of the "oracles of God" to the world for sure, but they are first to hear and obey the Word. This final book and the entire biblical record are overwhelmingly a call for the faithful to get their own house in order, not seek to get the world's twisted caricatures and dreamy, vaporous hopes in line with God's revelation. Thus, the King's promise to "make all things new" assures us of his sovereign intention and our subordinate role. Just how people of faith should relate to this promise is the stuff of aspirations for the "city which hath foundations." The next two sections of this volume will wind their way through the contortions and machinations of would-be world-changers against the backdrop of the biblical journey. Qoheleth is not the only one who has found this ongoing attempt to be a "shepherding of the wind."

Way to the City

Part 2

THE STRUGGLE
FOR THE CITY

Rome, Geneva, and the City on a Hill

Chapter 10

Self-Denial and World-Denial in a Giant Empire of Extravagance

THE PREVIOUS CHAPTERS HAVE DEMONSTRATED that Scripture has a very full and somewhat complex set of teachings on work and the acquisition of and stewardship of wealth. We have shown that Jesus, the prophets, and the apostles taught that thrift and generosity are important principles. But we have also made it clear that Scripture does not prohibit one from benefiting materially from the fruit of one's labor—in fact, the Bible teaches that material prosperity is often, though not always, a blessing from God. Scripture also teaches that labor, even manual labor, is honorable and good. The question now before us is, just how has the church over the centuries understood and applied Scripture on these important matters? What has been the church's theology of money? What has been its theology of work and labor? A corollary question concerns how the churches, or at least how individual theologians whose work has contributed to these matters, understand the nature of the human condition.

Questions of politics and economics are always bound up with one's doctrine of man, or of "humanity," as it is currently being discussed. We have to recognize with John Caputo, that "theology goes all the way down," that is, down into things like *politics* and *economics*, and the church has known that *intuitively* since the earliest days. Even its attempts to deny it were tacit recogni-

251

tions that it could not avoid the questions.[1] This chapter will address the church's attitude from the end of the first century into the period known as the Patristic Age (roughly AD 100–600). The next chapter will conclude that material and continue on to the high Middle Ages (the thirteenth century and somewhat beyond). In order to do that, the early church's historical and cultural context will be established in order to understand the similarities and contrasts of the Christian view over against *prevailing* cultural norms.

A Word about History

"All attempts to understand the past are indirect attempts to understand the present and its future."[2] H. Richard Niebuhr knew how to write an *opening line* for a book! We fully concur with his sentiment and are happy to make the point at the outset that this rather extensive survey you are about to peruse is not *just* about the past, but about where we are right *now*, and where we anticipate (fear?) that we are *headed*. We are aware of the dangers of interpreting the past with the future and the present in mind. We have frequently been reminded of the danger of *anachronism* (reading later events back into the past narratives of people who had no way of anticipating those developments), and of the "Whig" interpretation of history (telling the story only from the standpoint of those who eventually won in the various conflicts). You, the readers, will be the judge as to whether we have been sufficiently *careful* not to fall into these traps.

Several things must be kept in mind in reading this history. *First*, theology is always done in a specific *context*, a context that includes prevailing political, religious, and socioeconomic factors. No one simply does an exegesis of a text and then produces a "pure theology," one that is not affected by the intellectual and social conditions in which the church carries out its calling. Even the biblical writings themselves were produced in specific historical situations. So, the Old Testament book of Daniel gives us a statement about *how* one should relate to the *political* context. Daniel and his friends make it clear that they are going

---

1   John Caputo, *Radical Hermeneutics: Repetition, Deconstruction, and the Hermeneutic Project* (Bloomington: Indiana University Press, 1987), 224.
2   H. Richard Niebuhr, *The Kingdom of God in America* (New York: Harper & Brothers, 1937), 1.

Struggle for the City

to obey God *rather* than the king of Babylon, if they have to choose, and that they are willing to pay for their obedience with their very lives. Had Daniel been born during the reign of King David in Israel, his reaction to the state would have been very *different*—he would likely have been a "friend" of the state.

In light of that, it is not surprising that Christian thinkers through the ages have been, alternatingly, friendly toward the state or hostile toward the ruling powers. Is the state governed by King David or by King Nebuchadnezzar? It makes a difference! Similarly, Christian thinkers have sometimes *affirmed* the economic structures of their world and sometimes found them *wanting* in some specific area. If the dominant economic structures are *oppressive* toward the poor while giving great favoritism to the wealthy, one would expect that the primary economic response would be against the greatest oppression. In other words, one might not expect to find a well worked-out theory of Christian economics when the common people of the day are starving to death and the wealthy are sitting on top of hoards of food and gold, especially if those conditions are what they are *because* of preferences established by the ruling elite.[3] Because of that, it might be the case that some very well known and beloved Christian writers would have a lopsided and *skewed* theology of possessions. It is not hard to see why that would be the case. We will have to keep that in mind as we survey Christian history.

Another thing to keep in mind is that ancient and medieval writers, whether pagan or Christian, did not actually work out in an intellectual way what we would call "systems of economics," with a notable exception or two that we will encounter along the way. That is *not* to say that they did not think philosophically or theologically about economic issues. At least as far back as Plato, we have thinkers who gave a great deal of attention to economic concerns. What they did not do, however, was to think through the entire range of economic issues that we now know affect the whole exchange process. So,

---

3   Truth is, there was really no such thing as an "economic theory" in general that significantly impacted the world of commerce on a large scale until Adam Smith published his *The Wealth of Nations* in 1776 (for full citation, see chap. 15, note 63). For more on Smith and the development of economic theory, see Mark Skousen, *The Making of Modern Economics: The Lives and Ideas of the Great Thinkers*, 2nd ed. (Armonk, NY: M. E. Sharpe, 2009), 13–46. But as we will demonstrate in the chapter following this one, the pieces of the economic puzzle had *already* been laid out in Catholic Scholasticism.

Struggle for the City

Plato constructed a model of the ideal society, the *Republic*, in which he contemplated various professions, and how many workers each would be required in order for the republic to function well. He also discussed such issues as private property and governance. But he had no sense of the issue of supply and demand, of distribution factors, of the total impact of tariffs and duties, of the concept of free markets or the impact that controlled production and distribution would have on the overall economy. Plato gave no attention to such questions, though his student, Aristotle, did.

Aristotle came close to inventing economics. A theory of economics addresses the question of exchanges of goods and services for some kind of payment in return. Any theory has to address four questions: For *whom* is this transaction taking place? *What* is exchanged or consumed? How can one *produce* that which is exchanged? How can one measure *equilibrium* in the exchange, or, to put it in other terms, is the exchange fair?[4] Human beings produce, exchange, distribute, and use human and nonhuman goods. Aristotle "provided a theory of final distribution" and offered opinion on production and equilibrium but did not conceive of personal distribution nor did he address the issue of use or utility.[5] That would come in the fifth century from Augustine, but would not be bundled all together into one big package until Scholasticism[6] accomplished it in the thirteenth century and afterward. More of that later.

Instead, what we will note during our historical survey is that theoretical thinkers (sometimes) and societal architects (more often) simply organized local economies in ways that benefited the *ruling elite* as much as possible, sometimes with no real consideration about what such organizations might mean fifty or a hundred years down the line. Further, those "societal architects," as we have called them, were generally just the ruling elites and their

---

4   John Mueller, *Redeeming Economics: Rediscovering the Missing Element* (Wilmington, DE: ISI Books, 2010), 20.
5   Ibid., 22.
6   *Scholasticism* is a term that "simply stands for the theology and philosophy and subsidiary disciplines of the schools of western Europe in the great period of medieval culture." Eugene R. Fairweather, trans. and ed., *A Scholastic Miscellany: Anselm to Ockham*, Library of Christian Classics (Philadelphia: Westminster, 1956), 18. The "schools" mentioned here were the great monastic schools that arose in Western Europe in the eleventh century, followed by the rise of the medieval universities, such as those in Paris, Oxford, Cambridge, and Bologna, founded just before the year 1200.

Struggle for the City

henchmen, a collection of individuals that would include scholars, bishops, various levels of nobility, and others. Scholars and churchmen were often the *hired guns* of the ruling elites—scholars because they could receive patronage,[7] and influential churchmen (generally, bishops and abbots) because they often wanted a piece of the ruling pie and because of the influence they had over the masses. Marx was at least partly right about that.[8]

The net effect of all of that is that most of the thinkers who commented on economic issues, some of whom did protest the brutality and oppressiveness of the system, had no clear ideas about economic *theory* or systems. So, to look to Tertullian or Marcus Aurelius for a comprehensive economic theory is to look in vain. With some thinkers, and Calvin and Thomas Aquinas would be examples, we find ourselves closer to something like a theory of economics in totality. It has been thought that economics as a theoretical discipline is a product only of the Enlightenment. Certainly it took on a new theoretical cast with thinkers such as David Hume and Adam Smith, but the essential pieces of the economic puzzle were assembled by the Scholastics in the universities, based on the previous work of Aristotle and Augustine.

All of that is to say that any survey of the church and its response to poverty, overwork, political oppression, and all that goes with that, must recognize the limitations of the project. I say that in part because some surveys do not admit this, and so they give the impression that there is a unified Christian intellectual response to political and economic situations and that this response is virtually unanimously in line with later "prophetic" or "liberationist" responses to the state and the economy.[9] Such claims, tacit or explicit, are *deceptive*. We believe they are often *intentionally* deceptive.

---

7   Alan B. Wheatley, *Patronage in Early Christianity* (Eugene, OR: Wipf and Stock, 2011), 52–188.

8   Marx's notion that religion is the opiate of the people is historically true, though we certainly would reject the notion that this is *all* that religion is. Karl Marx and Friedrich Engels, *The Communist Manifesto*, trans. Samuel Moore (1884; repr., New York: Washington Square, 1964), 38.

9   Justo Gonzàlez, for instance, surveys the patristic literature and argues that the early Christian approach to wealth was consistent with what we would today call "prophetic" or "liberationist" trends. What he fails to note is that these people were almost all writing within the context of oppressive systems of wealth that kept the underprivileged in a virtual state of poverty. *Faith and Wealth: A History of Early Christian Ideas on the Origin, Significance, and Use of Money* (Eugene, OR: Wipf and Stock, 1990).

Struggle for the City

We also make this point at this juncture in the argument in order to say that historical analyses are not generally as satisfying as one might hope. The data just *are* what they are. We might *wish* a certain "heroic" figure in the history of the church had sided more with our own conclusions. But if that is not the case, we have to note that and go on. But we do more than note it; we also note that there may have been reasons for his or her myopia. Then again, maybe not. In this part of our analysis, we will simply let history be what it is, as best as we can tell it.

We need simply to say what this analysis is and what it is not. This is not a history of economics, though it includes discussions of economic history. This is not a work on political science, though we will certainly examine political history. This part of our study is both less ambitious and more ambitious than either of those things. This is an examination of the history of political economy as it relates to the history of Christianity.

WHAT THE CHURCH INHERITED: THE ROMAN EMPIRE, POLITICS, AND ECONOMICS

We cannot dwell on these issues in detail, for the sake of time, but it is important to make a few observations on the state of the political and economic world into which the church was thrust in the first century. We have developed some of this material in the chapters on the New Testament, but a further investigation here will be helpful as a prelude to examining the early church's wrestling with the economic and political issues of the time.

The Political Context of Early Christianity

Rome as the political entity of history lasted about 1,250 years, roughly from 750 BC to a little short of AD 500.[10] The first 250 years may be designated the Roman *Monarchy*, the next 480 years or so the Roman *Republic*, and the final

---

10 The traditionally accepted, though often disputed, dates are April 23, 753 BC for the founding of the Roman *Monarchy*, and 510 BC for the founding of the Roman *Republic*. For the dispute over the dates, see John Nobel Wilford, "More Clues in the Legend (or Is It Fact?) of Romulus," *The New York Times*, June 12, 2007.

Struggle for the City

five hundred years the Roman *Empire*.[11] The first period was the period of initiation of Roman domination of its immediate environs, of consolidation of power under a strong monarchical government, and of statist control of the economy through controlled trade. The second period witnessed the growth of local economies due to common law approaches to trade, of a lessening of political control due to the influence of the Roman Senate, and, as a result, of the flourishing of Rome. During this time Rome consolidated its power by conquering the Etruscans, the Sabines, the Samnites, and most of the Greek colonies in Sicily and southern Italy. The Punic Wars of the second and third centuries BC brought the Carthaginian Empire under its sway, and then the consolidation was complete when, after the battle of Corinth in 146 BC, Rome established its control over Greece.[12] By 134 BC the Iberian Peninsula was also under Roman governorship (though there would be pockets of resistance for more than a century), thus making the Mediterranean Sea a Roman lake.[13]

The third period displays, for the rest of history to observe, the development of an *imperial* structure, a structure in place even before there was anyone with the title "emperor." This was the inevitable result of the consistent conquest of lands in all directions. N. T. Wright describes how Rome's imperial structure ripened toward centralized political control: "By the middle of the first century B.C.E., its network of provinces and client regimes had become increasingly difficult to govern by the system of roving magistrates, and it was vulnerable to the ambitions of powerful individuals."[14] The first of these was Julius Caesar, who was assassinated for his ambitions. Out of this political chaos, empire emerged, in spite of the Senate's opposition. Julius Caesar was, more technically, a *dictator* rather than emperor, and was murdered on March 15, 44 BC, as a result. But the notion of one-man rule did not die with him.

---

11 This third number is based on the beginning date of 27 B.C., when Octavian established the Principate, and a concluding date of 476 B.C., when the last traditional Roman emperor was defeated by the Hunnic prince Odoacre, the city then falling under his dominion.

12 Christopher S. Mackay, *Ancient Rome: A Military and Political History* (Cambridge: Cambridge University Press, 2004), 61–88.

13 Ibid., 89–93.

14 N. T. Wright, "Roman Empire," in *Dictionary for Theological Interpretation of the Bible*, ed. Kevin J. Vanhoozer (Grand Rapids, MI: Baker, 2005), 695. Wright uses the nomenclature "B.C.E.," but we are content to use the more traditional, "BC" and "AD"

Struggle for the City

Octavian, or Caesar Augustus, the adopted heir of Julius Caesar, would be the first occupant of the imperial throne, ruling all of Rome for forty-five years. Octavian defeated Marc Antony at the Battle of Actium in 31 b.c., thus eliminating all real opposition to his plan to become the first emperor, after which he four years later established the Principate in 27 b.c., a governing system that allowed an emperor to be ruler of Rome for life.[15] Though he kept the Senate in place, his rule was absolute. He took the name "Augustus" and had himself appointed *Pontifex Maximus*, chief priest, and "from the time of Augustus onward the emperor became the chief focus of all Roman religious ritual."[16] This would later have *ominous* implications for the spreading Christian churches.

Augustus followed this by initiating a series of building projects, social reforms, and economic programs that would make Rome the greatest city in the Western world.[17] It was the greatest city in the Western world in that it was the largest and in that its rulers controlled such a large domain, though not necessarily in other ways.[18] Establishing the so-called *Pax Romana*, Octavian would be only the first in a series of emperors who would maintain authority over a governing structure that dominated a realm that stretched from Germany to North Africa, from the British Isles to the western steppes of Russia.[19] Due to the fact that his accession led to the period of peace, Octavian was hailed as a savior and wonder-worker.[20] This five-hundred-year period would conclude with the eventual dissolution of what had been an enormous geopolitical marvel.

---

15   Mackay, *Ancient Rome*, 182–91.
16   Richard Overy, ed., *The Times Complete History of the World*, 8th ed. (London: Times, 2010), 100.
17   J. A. Crook, "Political History, 30 BC to AD 14," in *The Cambridge Ancient History*, vol. 10: *The Augustan Empire, 43 BC–AD 69*, 2nd ed., ed. Alan K. Bowman, Edward Champlin, and Andrew Lintott (Cambridge: Cambridge University Press, 1996), 73–93.
18   Its massive population meant that parts of the city were immersed in squalor.
19   While "*Pax Romana*" is often portrayed as a positive contribution, it actually points to the reality that Rome had crushed all military and political opposition within the confines of its imperial borders and so was in complete control. This control was often brutal, and included, of course, the enslavement of vast indigenous populations. Fergus Millar, *The Emperor in the Roman World, 31 BC–AD 337* (New York: Cornell University Press, 1977), 368–74.
20   J. A. Crook, "Augustus: Power, Authority, Achievement," in *Cambridge Ancient History*, vol. 10: *The Augustan Empire, 43 BC–AD 69*, 123–46.

Struggle for the City

The older Roman ideology, according to which Rome was naturally free and was the instrument for bringing freedom and hope to the rest of the world through its military power, "was transferred to the claims of Augustus and his family."[21] Rome believed it was *inherently* just ("Iustitia" became a goddess during the reign of Augustus), and because of this, the emperors considered Rome's imperial ambitions to be justified.[22] What could be *better* for the world than Roman domination? As a result of the *Pax Romana*, Rome was the beneficiary of a vast economic boon that was based on an intricate system of taxation, enslavement, and governing bureaucracies in the colonies.[23] The benefit was spread around to some degree in terms of the kind of *federal* employment needed to maintain such a massive organization, but beyond that employment, the financial benefits were primarily directed *inwardly* toward the city of Rome and its intricate web of politicians, patrons, and patricians.[24]

Taxation in the Roman Empire

Taxation was crucial. By the first century B.C., Roman citizens within Italy paid no *direct* taxes to finance its wars, since the government was supported by wealth flowing in from the provinces.[25] Empire, though, brought about the need for a standing army, an army that stood consistently at about 350,000 men, so Augustus levied inheritance taxes, estate taxes, property taxes, and he and his successors monopolized and "nationalized" industries so that the state might have sufficient resources to fund its rapidly expanding interests.[26] Local taxes were levied to prop up local manifestations of the Roman state, and "indirect taxes" (*vectigalia*) such as customs duties were levied to help fill the increasingly voracious need of the Roman Empire for cash. These duties would

---

21 Wright, "Roman Empire," 695.
22 Ibid.
23 See the discussion in D. W. Rathbone, "The Imperial Finances," in *The Cambridge Ancient History*, vol. 10: *The Augustan Empire, 43 BC–AD 69*, 309–23.
24 For a concise survey of this period economically and its ensuing effects, see R. Glenn Hubbard and William Duggan, *The Aid Trap: Hard Truths about Ending Poverty* (New York: Columbia University Press, 2009).
25 C. Webber and A. Wildavsky, *A History of Taxation and Expenditure in the Western World* (New York: Simon & Schuster, 1986), 109.
26 Ibid.

Struggle for the City

be as high as twenty-five percent of the value of the cargo in the provinces, but as low as five percent in Italy itself.[27]

Judean farmers were expected to turn over *one-third* of their grain production to the Roman authority, and that percentage was fairly typical of other provinces. In addition there was the annual Judean temple tax of half a shekel. Taxes continued to be collected even when their original purpose no longer applied. Emperor Vespasian demanded that Jews continue to pay the temple tax even *after* the temple was destroyed in AD 70.[28] In addition, Rome had the authority to seize property, whether land, livestock, or implements, from the provincial populace when needed. It also had the authority of almost unlimited conscription of young men into the military.[29] Rome is a clear example of the fact that a government truly shows its power to dominate in its authority to tax and to tax *at will*.

The way Rome handled its treasury changed from the republic period into the period of empire.[30] In republican Rome, the central state treasury was the *aerarium* and was located in the temple of Saturn. That treasury continued into the imperial period, but was designated *aerarium Saturni* to distinguish it from the *aerarium militare*, established by Augustus in 6 BC, with the exclusive purpose of paying veterans' benefits.[31] The governing bodies in the colonies each had their own *fiscus*[32] (basket) into which various taxes were deposited and out of which expenses were taken. Eventually the revenue collected in those *fisci* would be sent on to Rome. In the empire, in addition to the *aerarium Saturni* and the *aerarum militare* the emperors held their own *fiscus*, known as the *patrimonium*, handled by their own household, out of which expenses and patrimony would be issued.[33] Such patrimony, toward soldiers, toward provincial governors, toward senators, was an important component in maintaining the image of a powerful but benevolent Rome. *Benevolent*, though, was not always how the empire was perceived by its client states.

---

27 Rathbone, "Imperial Finances," 114. Realize that there was no "Italy" in the modern sense until the nineteenth century, but we will use that term to refer to the Italian peninsula and its various city states.
28 Josephus, *Jewish War* 7.6.6.
29 Rathbone, "Imperial Finances," 112–14.
30 Mackay, *Ancient Rome*, 170–76.
31 Rathbone, "Imperial Finances," 320.
32 Hence, our word *fiscal*.
33 Rathbone, "Imperial Finances," 320.

Struggle for the City

Rome: The City

In the late republic period, the governing Senate believed that it was necessary to increase the population of the city of Rome itself, "either because of fear or success,"[34] that is, to engender fear in its enemies and to give a sense of the success of the emperors. In the early third century BC the population was somewhere between 150,000 and 200,000. In the middle of the first century BC, 320,000 persons were registered as recipients of free wheat. The size of the city at its peak, during the reign of Octavian, has been hotly debated with some historians seeing it leveling out at 350,000 and others believing it surged up to 800,000 or even a million residents in the second century AD.[35] Due to the fact that the number of aqueducts was constantly being increased from the first to the fourth centuries (from nine to nineteen), it is likely that the larger numbers are the most accurate. This would make population density somewhere between two hundred and three hundred persons per acre—more than modern Calcutta.[36]

Whichever figure is correct, Rome was a large city. It was not primarily economic forces but *political* ambitions that drove the emperors to labor hard to maintain such a large city: "Political forces, even more than economic factors, drive urban civilization."[37] As one scholar notes, "The size of Rome hence represented an ideological commitment to a particular historical narrative, a particular notion of emperorship, and a particular idea of empire."[38] There are three reasons for this. *First,* a large and thriving Rome allowed emperors to defend the notion that their governance was an extension of the republic, the center of "Old Rome." That was important to keep the Senate loyal

---

34 Raymond Van Dam, *Rome and Constantinople: Rewriting Roman History during Late Antiquity* (Waco, TX: Baylor University Press, 2010), 8.

35 Richard Duncan-Jones, *The Economy of the Roman Empire: Quantitative Studies,* 2nd ed. (Cambridge: Cambridge University Press, 1982), 259–87, opts for the smaller numbers, while Keith Hopkins, *Conquerors and Slaves, Sociological Studies in Roman History 1* (Cambridge: Cambridge University Press, 1978), 96–98, argues for the larger figure.

36 John E. Stambaugh, *The Ancient Roman City* (Baltimore: Johns Hopkins University Press, 1988).

37 Alberto F. Ades and Edward L. Glaeser, "Trades and Circuses: Explaining Urban Giants," *Quarterly Journal of Economics* 110, no. 1 (1995): 195–227. We are indebted to Raymond Van Dam for direction to this resource.

38 Van Dam, *Rome and Constantinople,* 18.

Struggle for the City

to the newer regime. *Second,* the emperors needed a large stage on which to demonstrate their imperial power, and the massive city provided that. *Third,* the magnificence of Rome "sent messages to provincials," messages that they were secure with the might of Rome protecting them, and that if they were compliant, the greatness that was Rome might one day be *shared* with them.[39] Size was crucial for the emperors to send the kind of message to the provinces and to the world that would enable them, generation after generation, to *re-main* Roman emperors.

The city of Rome produced nothing. It "conquered other lands, tried to manage their imperial affairs through currency, and imported stuff from these conquered lands,"[40] but it manufactured nothing, produced nothing, and con-tributed nothing material to the world around it. There was a constant need for grain imports to Rome. In the early years of empire, soldiers were also farmers of fairly small plots of land, about five to ten acres each. The spread of empire brought, of necessity, war. These soldier-farmers had to leave their farms, sometimes for extended periods in order to fight. Returning home, they often found their land overrun or in such a condition that it was simply not worth trying to restore it. Many sold their farms to wealthy citizens who would buy up vast stretches of land, and cultivate it with *slave* labor. This brought them great wealth, but also created a larger demand for slaves, which, in a kind of endless cycle, created the need for new wars so that new slave labor could be created and then imported.[41]

In the late republic and early imperial periods, first the Senate and then the emperors attracted people to Rome by providing a large amount of free food, especially grain, grapes, and oil. Grain came from conquered North Africa, while wine and oil came from conquered Spain and Gaul. The amount of grain that it took to feed the citizens of the city of Rome was somewhere between two hundred and four hundred thousand tons a year, and the oil and wine shipments required some 750 shiploads per year.[42] In the third century

---

39 Three reasons quoted from Van Dam, *Rome and Constantinople*, 22. See his fuller discus-sion, 18–24.
40 Douglas Wilson, *Five Cities that Ruled the World: How Jerusalem, Athens, Rome, London, and New York Shaped Global History* (Nashville: Thomas Nelson, 2009), 98.
41 Pliny, *Natural History* 1.18.21.
42 Van Dam, *Rome and Constantinople*, 10.

Struggle for the City

pork was added to the entitlement, so that eventually the citizens of the city were parodied as "Piglet" and "Sausage" by provincials. "The food supply of Rome had become, literally, pork barrel politics."[43] Indeed! The emperor Trajan, the "most aggressive emperor of the Principate,"[44] expanded the benefice to include spectacular gladiatorial events at Circus Maximus. After he defeated the Dacians, he presented games at Rome that lasted 123 days, featuring combats between 10,000 gladiators and that witnessed the slaughter of 11,000 animals.[45] Bread and circuses, and all provided *nearly free* of charge by the outlying citizens of the empire!

By the middle of the third century this network began to break down under the increasingly expensive weight of its own maintenance. The rhetoric of Roman "freedom" was also becoming obviously more and more difficult to sell. The third century was marked by massive destabilization and decentralization.[46] The empire was put up for sale by the soldiery and often wound up in the hands of the highest bidder. More than sixty emperors governed the empire in that century, but for most of that time the "empire" was divided into smaller units ruled by competitors to the "throne." Military service became hereditary and new taxes were raised to support the army, but senators and others withdrew support from emperors over whom they had no influence.[47]

The Roman Empire and the Church

Christianity struggled under the massive weight of Rome. At the height of the Roman Empire at the end of the *Pax Romana* (roughly AD 193, at the death of Emperor Commodus), the profile of leadership was one in which a centralized executive power held sway over approximately 65 million people, covering territory estimated to be 2.2 million square miles.[48] The third cen-

---

43 Ibid.
44 Mackay, *Ancient Rome*, 225.
45 Van Dam, *Rome and Constantinople*, 21.
46 Mackay, *Ancient Rome*, 266–82.
47 Overy, *Times Complete History of the World*, 102.
48 This is out of an estimated world population of 300 million. "Roman Empire Population," UNRV Roman Empire, http://www.unrv.com/empire/roman-population.php (accessed December 21, 2011).

Struggle for the City

tury, as we have noted, saw this break down. That was a difficult time for the Christian church. Internal difficulties were compounded at the borders, as it became more and more difficult for Rome to hold the barbarians at bay. That led to even further economic and political problems within the empire. Many Romans blamed the difficulties on the growing Christian church, and, as a result, persecutions of Christians became more intentional and more severe. Three empire-wide persecutions were launched, one by Emperor Decius, AD 249–51, one by Emperor Vallerian, AD 258–60, and finally, the Great Persecution of Emperors Diocletian and Galerius, AD 303–11.[49] Later, Augustine in his work *The City of God*, contrary to the typical Roman interpretation of the empire's problems, laid the blame at the feet of the pagan religions of the Romans, with their sordid sexuality and their brutality.[50] The standard Roman rationale for its political problems was misplaced and Augustine's was overly simplistic. An economic assessment of the decline is not hard to arrive at, considering the nature of Roman exploitation and the difficulty of maintaining the administration of such a vast enterprise. One thing would become clear in the declining conditions that marked the third century: harsh economic times for the whole of Rome resulted in even more harsh times for the Christians within the empire.[51]

Late in the third century Rome was reunited under the heavy hand of Diocletian (AD 284), and then later, and more decisively, of Constantine (AD 312), who, in an effort to keep Rome unified, *moved* the capital to the more centrally located Byzantium, and, quite humbly, renamed it for himself— Constantinople. The accession of Diocletian marked a turning point in Roman political life. Historians have observed that the rule that Rome exercised became far more dominating from this point down to the end of the empire, and refer to this period, in contrast to the *Principate* (governance by a prince, 27 BC–AD 284), as the *Dominate* (governance by a lord, AD 284–476) and the emperor's home as the *domus divina* (house of God). As intrusive as Rome had been in the early period of empire, it would be far more oppressive in the

---

49 Diocletian took the unusual move of retiring from the emperorship in AD 305, but his program of persecution was carried on by his successor, Galerius.
50 Augustine. *The City of God* 1.1.
51 Mackay, *Ancient Rome*, 283–90.

Struggle for the City

decades after Diocletian took the throne. Previously senators and equestrians had carried out public works; now these would fall under the authority of the emperor, thus demanding even higher taxation. This would be carried on by the emperors who succeeded Diocletian, including Constantine.[52] One year after the Battle of the Milvian Bridge, in which Constantine defeated his most serious competitor to sole emperorship, the ruler signed the Edict of Milan, which granted *legitimacy* to the Christian church, a legitimacy that would, essentially, never be revoked.

The Edict of Milan also became the first step in the initiation of the emperor-Christians.[53] From that point on, Christians in the empire had to face only the same difficult economic times faced by everyone else. While some early Christian writers associated Rome with Babylon, the new generation, represented by Eusebius, saw Rome and Emperor Constantine in almost eschatological and messianic terms. Eusebius wrote that "on his own, God, the ruler of the entire universe, selected Constantine."[54] In these words, "Eusebius had transformed Constantine from a soldier emperor characteristic of the third century into God's chosen ruler."[55] For that church father, Constantine united once and for all universal church and universal empire, each of which was meant by God for the other.[56] Eusebius compared Constantine's victory at the Milvian Bridge with the glorious victory of the Israelites in the exodus.[57] The interesting wrinkle in all of this was that emperor-Christians also claimed to be divine.[58] Eusebius himself reflects this dilemma in his *Oration in Praise of Constantine* where he nearly equates Constantine with Christ—as Christ leads the heavenly armies so Constantine leads the earthly ones and each is "like a prefect of the great Emperor [God]."[59] Eusebius "developed a providential account of history in which God guided Rome's ascent so that the church would

---

52 "Diocletian," in *The Oxford Dictionary of the Christian Church*, 3rd ed., ed. F. L. Cross and E. A. Livingstone (Oxford: Oxford University Press, 1997), 483.
53 Charles Freeman, *A.D. 381: Heretics, Pagans, and the Dawn of the Monotheistic State* (New York: Overlook, 2009), 13.
54 Eusebius, *Ecclesiastical History* 8.13.14.
55 Van Dam, *Rome and Constantinople*, 26.
56 Eusebius, *Ecclesiastical History* 8.
57 Ibid. 9.9.
58 Freeman, *A.D. 381*, 12–26.
59 Eusebius, *Oration in Praise of Constantine* 1.6.

Struggle for the City

acquire worldly political authority through a Christian emperor."[60] This was the closest Christianity came to developing a political theology comparable to other nations, and even this would collapse a century and a half later.

Fascist Rome

As a political entity, imperial Rome was a *totalizing* state.[61] One of its symbols was the *fasces*, a bundle of sticks lashed together around a single rod, with an axe wrapped into the bundle. This depicted the notion that there was a single ruling entity, bound together with a group of smaller and weaker entities, with the threat of the *axe* should anyone seek to unbind the bundle. The term *fascism* grew out of this image. In our time, of course, fascism is a disreputable term, largely because of the two most obvious Fascist rulers of the twentieth century—Hitler and Mussolini. But the term did not used to have such an unpalatable connotation, and many early twentieth century "Progressives," such as President Woodrow Wilson, could accurately be described as "fascist."[62]

Fascism sought absolute control over its subjects, and it believed that it had the right to fashion whatever laws were expedient that might enable it to maintain that control. As we have noted already, Rome believed that its governance was inherently *just*, and so, what was good for Rome was good for the provinces. To the Romans this was a righteous form of governance; the provinces would not see it that way in large part. Fascism often believes it is wearing a serene face, but others perceive it to be not a grin but a *leer*. Rome was a truly fascist empire.[63]

---

60 Mark Lilla, *The Stillborn God: Religion, Politics, and the Modern West* (New York: Vintage Books, 2007), 43.

61 Not exactly a *totalitarian* state in the modern sense, since that requires a greater communication and travel technology.

62 Jonah Goldberg, *Liberal Fascism: The Secret History of the American Left from Mussolini to the Politics of Meaning* (New York: Doubleday, 2006), 25–120; Volker Losemann, "Fascism," in *The Classical Tradition*, ed. Anthony Grafton, Glenn W. Most, and Salvatore Settis (Cambridge: Harvard University Press, 2010), 352–54.

63 It may be more precise to designate Rome as "statist." A statist style of governance is one in which heavy authority is invested in the federal governing body, which then seeks to control every facet of its subjects' lives. "Fascism" is one version of statism.

Struggle for the City

THE ECONOMIC CONTEXT OF EARLY CHRISTIANITY

Christianity crept its way into this Roman world in the first century under the leadership of a handful of missionaries and evangelists whose enterprising ministries drove them all across the Mediterranean world within the first century of the church's existence. By the centennial celebration of its existence, the church may have numbered around fifty thousand adherents in a Roman world of somewhere near 60 or 65 million people.[64] Christianity first grew up among hellenized Jews (like Paul) who then, partly because their Hellenization made them comfortable in conversing with Gentiles, were able to make the message understandable to the non-Jewish Greco-Roman people. It would also seem that there was enough cross-fertilization between Gentiles and Jews in the Roman cities that Gentiles knew something about Jewish worship and beliefs. So, the growth of the church took place primarily in these Greco-Roman cities that stood at various crossroads of the empire. That positioning enabled the church to grow dramatically over the next two centuries.[65] By the end of the third century the Christians were a thriving, if at times beleaguered, presence in the Roman Empire. So, how did they match up to Greco-Roman mores on matters such as work and the management of wealth?

We have argued from Scripture that the biblical teaching honors hard work, generosity, and thrift as important virtues. These values are found clearly in both Old and New Testaments, and were generally well-practiced by Israelites or Jews. But the wider world of Jesus' day did not always extol those virtues. Plato argued that manual labor was to be done by artisans who were slaves, not by thinkers or "philosophers." This was part of Plato's social philosophy that the *polis* was to be comprised of three ranks of persons—gold, silver, and bronze; the *gold* were the philosophers who governed (Guardians), the *silver* were the administrative class (Auxiliaries), while the *bronze* were the workers (Producers). To ask the gold to do manual labor would be to subvert the very order of the *polis*, something Plato found to be immoral. We

---

64 Robert Wilken, *The Christians as the Romans Saw Them* (New Haven, CT: Yale University Press, 1984), 31.
65 James Davison Hunter, *To Change the World: The Irony, Tragedy, and Possibility of Christianity in the Late Modern World* (Oxford: Oxford University Press, 2010), 49.

Struggle for the City

should all operate according to the station of life that is granted to us by birth, whether rulers, auxiliaries, or producers.[66] Ancient philosopher Archimedes was *ashamed* for having constructed devices that aided him in his geometrical calculations, thus involving himself in manual labor.[67] The Roman philosopher Cicero complained similarly that daily work was *unbecoming* to freeborn men.[68] Lynn White noted, "In the classical tradition there is scarcely a hint of the dignity of labor."[69] Patricians and other freemen were supposed to live lives of languid luxury, leaving *labor* to the unfortunate and to slaves.

Slavery was virtually a universal reality in the ancient world. When one considers the seven wonders of the ancient world, it is sobering to reflect on the fact that they were all built with slave labor. Aristotle and Plato not only assumed that slavery was a way of life, but also *defended* it. Plato's ideal republic would keep slaves in their place, and Aristotle contended that some people are naturally suited to slavery, but that *citizens* of the *demos* (the city state) were not so suited: "From the hour of their birth, some are marked out for subjection, others for rule."[70] Aristotle argued that slavery is natural, expedient, and just.[71] The famous philosopher also believed that, since a slave is only a "living tool… therefore there can be no friendship with a slave as slave."[72] "Without slaves to do the labor, Aristotle argued, enlightened men would lack time and energy to pursue virtue and wisdom."[73] In addition, Plato defended the notion of using *brutality* in dealing with slaves, since they are little more than brutes themselves and are not capable of life in normal society.[74] The ancient world was almost unanimous in its denigration of work and manual labor and its assignment of manual labor to slaves or to the lowest classes of society.

---

66 Plato, *Republic* 1.
67 L. D. White, "The Significance of Medieval Christianity," in *The Vitality of the Christian Tradition*, ed. George F. Thomas (New York: Harper and Brothers, 1945), 91.
68 Cicero, *De officiis* 1.150. See the discussion in Alvin J. Schmidt, *How Christianity Changed the World* (Grand Rapids, MI: Zondervan, 2004), chap. 8.
69 White, "Significance of Medieval Christianity," 91.
70 Aristotle, *Politics* 1:1254.
71 Ibid. 1:1255.
72 Aristotle, *Nichomachean Ethics* 8.11.
73 Rodney Stark, *The Victory of Reason: How Christianity Led to Freedom, Capitalism, and Western Success* (New York: Random House, 2005), 27.
74 David Brion Davis, *The Problem of Slavery in Western Culture* (Ithaca, NY: Cornell University Press, 1966), 66.

Struggle for the City

Generosity was also foreign to the classical mind-set. Whereas early Christians were well known for their generosity, the non-Christian world was not. Roman pagans practiced *liberalitas*, not *caritas*.[75] In other words, Romans gave, expecting to get something in return for their gift, as we discussed earlier in this chapter and in the biblical analysis concerning Roman patronage.[76] When one gives in order to receive something in return, that "gift" is usually given, not to those who are in need, but to those who *already* have plenty, or at least in order to receive something that one wants, and so the recipient can *respond* in kind. Part of the problem in the Roman context was that their religious traditions did *not* emphasize charity. There was no theology of grace, and so no corresponding concept of *caritas* (benevolent love). There was also no notion of community participation in the religious traditions. Priests performed at the temples; everyone else was a mere spectator. "People only went to temples; they did not *belong* to them."[77] Such a religious experience calls for no transformation of life and for no participation in the religious communal life of the people.

The early church differed from its Roman context in *all* of these areas. Regarding labor, early Christians emphasized both that sloth was a sin and that labor was to be *honored*. The *Apostolic Constitutions* (AD 375) condemned sloth in a way reminiscent of Paul in 2 Thessalonians. Monastic communities also emphasized the importance of labor for the spiritual man.[78] Basil of Caesarea in the fourth century argued that, "work preserves us from evil thoughts."[79] Work was not an option, but a *necessity* for early Christianity, and not merely a pragmatic necessity, but a biblical and theological one.

On the issue of slavery, the apostle Paul argued that there is neither "slave nor free" in Christ (Gal. 3:28). In his letter to Philemon he urged the slave owner to treat his returning slave as an *equal* to himself, an attitude that would

---

75 Gerhard Ullhorn, *Christian Charity in the Ancient Church* (New York: Charles Scribner's Sons, 1883), 7–9.

76 Wheatley, *Patronage in Early Christianity*, 1–8. For our discussion of Roman patronage with its expectation of reciprocity, see chap. 8.

77 Stark, *Triumph of Christianity*, 10.

78 We will offer some criticisms of monasticism along the way, but there were certainly some laudable features of monastic life.

79 See Schmidt, *How Christianity Changed the World*, 196.

Struggle for the City

eventually undermine slavery as a practice. The early Christians regularly freed their slaves. St. Melania emancipated 8,000 slaves, St. Ovidius freed 5,000, the Christian Chromatia freed 1,400. Augustine argued that slavery was a sin. The very nature of Christianity itself, if it is followed faithfully, drives a *stake* in the heart of slavery.[80] On the issue of generosity, Christianity was able to bring about a revolution in the way people perceived those in need because of its theology of sin and grace. A second-century Christian writing, *The Shepherd of Hermas*, teaches, "Give simply to all without asking doubtfully to whom you give, but give to all."[81] Grace and generosity virtually *define* the Christian ethic.

Before we proceed to discuss the development of Christian attitudes toward political economy, we must consider one other issue that will be a crucial point in the development of the West and of the church as part of that heritage. That issue is *reason*. The Christian faith, of all the world's religions, is the one faith that has encouraged or, more likely, demanded that a rational process ought to take place whereby our understanding of the world would progress over time, enabling us bit by bit to *understand* and *exercise dominion* over that world. One scholar notes that it remains to be seen why capitalism "developed only in Europe." His answer is, that if one digs deeply enough, one will discover that "the truly fundamental basis not only for capitalism, but for the rest of the West was an extraordinary faith in reason."[82] This is even true in the arena of doctrinal development, as any historian of theology would be able to confirm. Our theological claims do not spring fully formed simply from the words of the Greek New Testament, but are the product of centuries of *logical* and *dialectical* refinement. "While all the other world religions emphasized *mystery* and *intuition*, Christianity alone embraced *reason* and *logic* as the primary guide to religious truth."[83] The other world religions have not produced an academic theology that has experienced growth and development in anything like the manner that Christianity has. So reason, progress, the development of wealth, the development of technology all stem from this fundamental difference. We will see that develop through the course of this historical analysis.

---

80 Ibid., 274.
81 Quoted in ibid., 127.
82 Stark, *Victory of Reason*, x.
83 Ibid.

Struggle for the City

So, just what has been the church's understanding about wealth, politics, work, material possessions, and the poor? These historical chapters will attempt to present a survey of answers to that question.

Ultimate Rejection of Materialism: Gnosticism

Some early Christians sought complete separation from the world. Most of these sought such separation because they recognized that the world was filled with sin and vice, and they were committed to a life of holiness. Others interpreted Jesus' teaching on this differently and sought separation because of their belief that the physical, material world itself was *intrinsically* evil and had been since its creation. These latter individuals formed Christian fellowships based on a new theology that is generally known as *Gnosticism*.[84] Gnosticism was an attempt to blend Christian thought with certain Greek philosophical tendencies and with the ecstatic mystery religions that were popular in the second century, perhaps even with Persian Zoroastrianism.[85] In common with the mystery religions, the Gnostics held that salvation came through initiation into a *mysterious* and occult organization, one that guarded its secrets closely. "This was the secret knowledge that the Gnostics claimed to possess. It was acquired, however, not by perseverance in moral rectitude but by sudden *illumination* that enabled them to understand the ways of God, the universe, and themselves."[86] In common with the Greek philosophical schools (Platonism and Middle Platonism), the Gnostics taught that the world was split into two realities, the physical and the spiritual, and that the physical was intrinsically inferior to the spiritual.

Gnostic teachers took this Greek view one step further than the philosophers, though, contending that the material world was positively evil by virtue of the fact that it *was physical* and material. They perceived that the physical/material world offered pleasure but it also offered pain and suffering.[87] That very fact must mean that the physical is a pale shadow of the spiritual, and that the

---

84 Gnosticism did exist outside Christianity, but its greatest efforts were aimed at gnosticizing the church.

85 Alastair H. B. Logan, *Gnostic Truth and Christian Heresy: A Study in the History of Gnosticism* (Peabody, MA: Hendrickson, 1996), 53.

86 W. H. C. Frend, *The Rise of Christianity* (Philadelphia: Fortress, 1984), 199.

87 Logan, *Gnostic Truth and Christian Heresy*, 167–96.

Struggle for the City

spiritual was the real. Final salvation for the Gnostic "Christians," would come when, having full knowledge of these truths and having been initiated into the cult, one would escape from the bonds of this world and return to the realm of pure spirit.[88] Death alone would not suffice—one had to die a Gnostic believer.[89]

The key to Gnosticism was its denial of the traditional Jewish doctrine of *creation*, which might well suggest that Gnosticism grew up in regions where there was interaction with Judaism.[90] Gnostics held a defective view of Christ. Christ could not have taken "flesh" on him, since the material world is evil, so the Gnostic "Christians" were forced to deny the humanity of Jesus. The Bible, of course, teaches clearly that Jesus was in every way a human being (John 1:14; Heb. 2:14–18).[91] Gnostic teachers were also heretical in their view of salvation, arguing that redemption comes through knowledge (*gnosis*), while Scripture is clear that salvation comes by grace through faith (Rom. 3:21–26; Eph. 2:8–9).[92] Most importantly for our discussion, the Gnostics were sub-biblical in their understanding of creation. Though Gnostic opinions varied on just how the world came to be,[93] they were unified in their conviction that the physical universe was not made by the God and Father of Jesus Christ. This flies in the face of Genesis 1, where God not only creates the world, but also offers his own assessment of the created world, that it is "very *good*" (v. 31). The material world was considered inherently bad by these early cultists.[94]

It naturally followed that the Gnostics considered physical work to be far inferior to "spiritual" values, such as meditation, chanting, spiritual conversation, and prayer. Valentinian Gnosticism divided the world of men into three groups—the carnal, the soulish, and the spiritual.[95] The carnal were those who were merely people of flesh, with no interest in spiritual matters at all. The soulish were Christians

---

88 Edwin M. Yamauchi, *Pre-Christian Gnosticism: A Survey of the Proposed Evidences* 2nd ed. (Eugene, OR: Wipf and Stock, 2003), 13–28.

89 "Gnosticism," *Oxford Dictionary of the Christian Church*, 683–85.

90 Diarmaid MacCulloch, *Christianity: The First Three Thousand Years* (New York: Penguin Books, 2009), 122.

91 Logan, *Gnostic Truth and Christian Heresy*, 223–26.

92 Ibid., 211–40.

93 Irenaeus discusses more than twenty varieties of Gnosticism in his book *Against Heresies*, which was the first major critique of Gnostic thought.

94 This is the central tenet of all Gnostic thought. Kurt Rudolph, *Gnosis: The Nature and History of an Ancient Religion* (Edinburgh: T&T Clark, 1983), 57.

95 Valentinus (d. 165) was one of the more influential Gnostic teachers in the second century,

Struggle for the City

(or religious people), but they were Christians who had not been introduced to the true *gnosis*. Both of these types were still people of this world, people who concerned themselves with the things of this world, including the matters of earning a living, purchasing and selling, or tilling the soil. The Gnostic, however, was *beyond* such concerns, and was willing to leave them all in the hands of God.[96] This constituted for them a rejection of the spirit of greed that drives some to amass hordes of wealth, but in addition it rejects all commitment to material concerns *whatsoever*. Gnosticism is the ultimate rejection of regard for the mundane affairs of life in any real sense. Such an attitude, though it seems to be "spiritual," is far removed from biblical notions of the nature of our living in this world.

Most early Christians correctly perceived that Gnosticism was not a viable Christian alternative, since it denied a number of key doctrines. The encounter with Gnosticism, though, had a salutary effect on the development of early Christianity. The conflict between the competing groups caused the orthodox party to think through issues they had not previously considered. As a result of this interaction, the orthodox gained new insights. "Christianity for the first time became a philosophical religion grappling with deep moral and intellectual problems, as well as being the Way preached by Jesus and Paul."[97] That kind of approach would stand the church in good stead in the rough waters that lay ahead.

Affirming the Spiritual Over the Material: Renouncing the World and Its Possessions

Gnosticism appealed to the desire on the part of some to express a faith of heroic proportions. The major problem was that it was heretical to the core. There were some in the church who wanted to stay close theologically to "the faith once delivered to the saints," while upholding the standard that Jesus demands a *profound* commitment from Christians. The Lord had told his disci-

---

and his views eventually became the standard form for most Gnostics by the end of the century. "Valentinus," *Oxford Dictionary of the Christian Church*, 1675–76.

96 Ignatius noted that the Gnostics had no interest in offering aid to those in physical or financial distress: "For love they have no care, none for the widow, none for the orphan, none for the distressed, none for the prisoner, none for the hungry or thirsty." Ignatius, *To the Smyrnaeans*, 3.

97 Frend, *Rise of Christianity*, 197.

ples that they were *not* to be "of the world" (John 15:19). To be "of the world," in this way of thinking, is to live one's life concerned about the things of this world, things such as families, professions, and money.

Tertullian and "Holiness"

Tertullian (ca. AD 160–225) represents one of the strongest voices for a radical interpretation of the call to discipleship in the early church. Attempting to apply a "Christ against culture"[98] model to every area of life, Tertullian urged Christians to repudiate philosophy, to refuse any participation in worldly government (such as in a position of magistrate or soldier), or worldly entertainment (such as the theater), and to live lives of complete holiness. This was part and parcel of his overall doctrine of humanity, namely, that we have inherited a nature of sin from our parents. Tertullian sometimes claimed that anyone who sinned after baptism would be forever lost.[99] In the area of ethics, not only did he forbid divorced persons from remarrying—he made the same restriction for widows and widowers, since a decision to remarry must come only from a desire to have sex.[100] It is hard to imagine a more dramatic call to depart from "the world" than this, though it has been argued that he only meant to apply this to older widows.[101] At the same time, he did not want Christians to be of no usefulness in the wider world. "We sojourn with you [unbelievers] in the world, abjuring neither forum, nor shambles, nor bath, nor booth, nor inn, nor weekly market, nor any other places of commerce....

---

98 H. Richard Niebuhr placed Tertullian as one of the prime examples of a "Christ against culture model." Though Niebuhr oversimplifies at times, his book is still a good representative study in the various ways Christians engage culture. H. Richard Niebuhr, *Christ and Culture* (New York: Harper Torchbooks, 1951), 52.

99 On other occasions, though he still held this view, he made a distinction between different "kinds" of sins. This appears to be an early form of the later distinction between *mortal* and *venial* sins that would become prominent in some circles.

100 Early in his writings Tertullian preferred that widows remained unmarried while later he insisted on it. Everett Ferguson, "Tertullian," in *Early Christian Thinkers: The Lives and Legacies of Twelve Key Figures*, ed. Paul Forster (Downers Grove, IL: InterVarsity Press, 2010), 93.

101 David E. Wilhite, "Tertullian on Widows: A North African Interpretation," in *Engaging Economics: New Testament Scenarios and Early Christian Reception*, ed. Bruce W. Longenecker and Kelly D. Liebengood (Grand Rapids, MI: Eerdmans, 2009), 235–42.

Struggle for the City

We sail with you and till ground with you."[102] Christians are to be *in* the world to its benefit, but perhaps not *of* the world in the sense of *enjoying* the good things that the world has to offer.

Tertullian applied a similar approach to the question of wealth and stewardship. Christians should separate themselves from any interest in wealth, and should even hold wealth in contempt.[103] Rather, they should commit themselves to a communal purse, if not a communal lifestyle.[104] As this church father puts it, Christians have "all things in common except wives."[105] Tertullian was not advocating that Christians owned all things in common, but that they ought to make available to others, specifically the needy, what each had in his possession.[106] Commenting on Matthew 5:40, "If someone wants to sue you and take your undergarment, give him your cloak as well," Tertullian said that believers should be ready to give away *all* of their possessions to anyone who asks for them.[107] He was also opposed to the charging of interest on loans in any measure at all. Partly because of that conviction, he forbade Christians from dabbling in the financial affair of others in much the same way that he exhorted them not to serve as soldiers or magistrates.[108] Tertullian's conviction was that Christians should be glad to cast away earthly ornaments that they might inherit the heavenly.[109]

Rejecting the Worldly Church: Anchorites and Cenobites

Tertullian's theology of separation from the world brought him one step short of actually leaving society physically. The stance he advocated, though, was consistent in every other way with the rise of *monasticism* in the same century. Monasticism was a new path for Christian living that exemplified self-denial,

---

102 Tertullian, *Apology* 42.
103 Tertullian, *Patience* 7.2.
104 In the mid-second century the *Didache* had strongly promoted charity toward those in need, but not communalism and not to the degree found in Tertullian. See the *Didache*, or *The Teaching of the Twelve Apostles* 12–13.
105 Tertullian, *Apology* 39.
106 David Batson, *The Treasure Chest of the Early Christians: Faith, Care and Community from the Apostolic Age to Constantine the Great* (Leominster: Gracewing; Grand Rapids, MI: Eerdmans, 2001), 65.
107 Tertullian, *Flight in Persecution* 13.
108 Tertullian, *Against Marcion* 4.17.
109 Gonzàlez, *Faith and Wealth*, 122.

Struggle for the City

discipline of the flesh, and solitude or physical separation from the world. In some ways, it is *odd* that monasticism would have developed in Christianity, since the Christian faith affirms the incarnation of Christ and God's act of creating the material world. The other great world religion that has a heavy monastic presence is Buddhism, a religion that has at its center nothingness and the annihilation of the self. None of that is true of Christianity.[110] In addition, Judaism, in many ways the forerunner of Christianity, is inherently anti-monastic with its emphasis on family and children. Monasticism constituted a "silent rebellion" over against excesses in the church, excesses that had grown over time.[111] We will explore that idea further.

One of the earliest known monks[112] was the Egyptian, Anthony (ca. AD 251–356).[113] In AD 276 at the age of twenty he heard a sermon on the rich young ruler. Jesus told that man to sell all he possessed and then to come and follow him.[114] After hearing the sermon, Anthony immediately left his rich and comfortable home and set out to be a hermit monk (an anchorite), living out his long life in the Egyptian desert.[115] He was convinced that living a life of poverty, focused on prayer and spiritual warfare, was the only way for him to be a disciple of the Lord. He would stand through the day for hours, holding his arms out in the sign of the cross, as a warrior for the Lord. Many young Egyptians heard his story, and by the middle of the fourth century the desert was filled with hundreds of young "poor men for the gospel." They engaged what they considered to be the spiritual problems associated with the lure of wealth, and they solved them by a rigorously ascetic lifestyle.[116]

---

110 Udo Middelmann, *Christianity Versus Fatalistic Religions in the War against Poverty* (Colorado Springs: Paternoster, 2007), throughout, but esp. 41–67.

111 A. M. Alchin, *The Silent Rebellion: Anglican Religious Communities, 1845–1900* (London: SCM, 1958). Alchin used this term (also the title of his work) to refer to Anglican "monasticism" in the nineteenth century, but it is a helpful concept to apply back to the early monastic movement.

112 The word *monk* comes from the Greek word *monachos* and means "solitary." The earliest monks were solitary hermits, though the later practice was generally communal. We are using the word generically to refer to both types.

113 We know that he was not the earliest because even in his own biography he talks of other young men he had known of in childhood, but their stories are lost to us.

114 Matt. 19:16–23; Mark 10:17–24; Luke 18:18–24.

115 The best primary source information on Anthony comes from Athanasius' book *The Life of Anthony*.

116 A. H. M. Jones, *The Later Roman Empire, 284–602* (Oxford: Blackwell, 1964), 2:792.

Struggle for the City

What made such a life so attractive to so many? Christianity was an illegal religion in the Roman Empire. Christians were often persecuted and sometimes killed for their faith up through the early part of the fourth century. Because persecution was such a constant reality in the church, a fairly high percentage of church members were actually very committed to their faith. That is not to say that there were no *nominal* Christians in those days, but it was the case that one had to think twice before being baptized, and so make public a profession of faith in Jesus, something that was considered illegal (*religio illicitas*) by the state. In spite of that, there was a significant percentage of the very rich who identified themselves with the church.[117] This was true from the earliest days of Christianity.[118] Persecution, though, made one think twice. That same persecution, especially in the early fourth century, *fueled* the ranks of monks who fled to the desert to escape.[119]

Changes came after AD 313. As we have already noted, in 312 Constantine won the battle at the Milvian Bridge against Maxentius, thus eliminating the last threat against him from within the empire. The night before the battle he had a vision of a cross of light or of the *chi-rho*, a common Christian symbol of the time, and a voice spoke to him, saying, "In this sign conquer."[120] After winning the battle, Constantine took this as an indication that Christianity was the true religion, thus converting to the faith; the next year he issued the Edict of Milan, legitimizing Christianity. (It is at least possible that he had been converted to Christianity earlier, since he already had Christian bishops in his entourage when he marched on Rome.[121]) Over the next few years the once-persecuted faith would become the preferred religion of the Roman Empire.[122]

---

117 Rodney Stark, *The Rise of Christianity: A Sociologist Reconsiders History* (Princeton, NJ: Princeton University Press, 1996), 29–48.

118 Ignatius, writing to the Romans early in the second century about his impending trial there, asked that Christians not interfere with the justice system to help him to be pardoned. Only persons of privilege would have had such clout. Ignatius, *To the Romans*, 4.

119 MacCulloch, *Christianity*, 207.

120 In some accounts it was a "cross of light" or of gold.

121 Michael Grant, *Constantine the Great: The Man and His Times* (New York: Scribner's, 1994), 146.

122 There is a debate as to Constantine's motives for legalizing Christianity. In 1925 historian Shirley Jackson Case made an argument that the persecution of Diocletian was a bad political decision because by AD 300 half the empire had become Christian and that Constantine simply was doing the wise thing. "The Acceptance of Christianity by the Roman Emperors," in *Papers of the American Society of Church History* 8, 2nd ser. (New

Struggle for the City

For the harried Christians it was a wonderful thing now not to have to go to worship services in fear that they might be arrested. And yet, over the decades that followed, the church began to *change*. It was no longer illegal to be a Christian. Quite the contrary, it was now considered *respectable* to be a disciple belonging to Jesus; nearly all good Romans were now in the church. It should come as no surprise that many would join the church for less than appropriate reasons, and so, many unregenerate people were suddenly "Christians." Others were baptized for all the right reasons, but because the call to discipleship was not quite so daunting as it had been in the days of persecution, their faith was often not very deep and their churches became less distinct as "companies of the committed."[123]

By the end of the fourth century, Jerome and other significant figures would argue that the legitimization of the Christian church had led to its moral and spiritual dissolution.[124] For many, the call to the desert was in reality a protest against the spiritual decline of the church. There would be no more martyrdoms, and so, "[i]n default of any more martyrdoms provided by Roman imperial power, [the monks] martyred their bodies themselves, and thus they annexed the esteem which martyrs had already gained among the Christian faithful."[125] That assessment might be a bit too general, but it is clear that the anchorite (hermit) monks were the *new martyrs*.[126]

In the fourth century a new kind of dedicated life became more and more common. Monastic *communities* began to sprout up. The new heroes of Christianity had a choice between living out their lives as spiritual hermits, wrestling the powers of darkness alone, or of joining with like-minded groups of men or women in *common-life* communities,[127] who would submit together to the threefold

---

York: G. P. Putnam's Sons, 1928), 62. Those numbers may not be accurate, but the argument stands even with the smaller number.

123 This line is taken from the title of the book by Elton Trueblood, *The Company of the Committed* (New York: Harper & Row, 1980).

124 J. N. D. Kelly, *Jerome: His Life, Writings, and Controversies* (London: Duckworth, 1975), 129–40. It needs to be noted that Jerome was not known for his graciousness or affability, but his sentiment is probably correct.

125 MacCulloch, *Christianity*, 206.

126 For a fascinating discussion of the Irish monks as "white martyrs," see Thomas Cahill, *How the Irish Saved Civilization: The Untold Story of Ireland's Heroic Role from the Fall of Rome to the Rise of Medieval Europe* (New York: Nan A. Talese, Doubleday, 1995), 151–84.

127 They were known as *cenobites*, in contrast to the hermit *anchorites*, from the Greek, *koinos bios*, or "common life."

Struggle for the City

vow: poverty, chastity, obedience.[128] Over time the community model became the most prominent. Benedict of Nursia (AD 480–547) is one of the best-known exemplars of this model, known to later monastics as the "Father of Monks."

Early monasticism was an Eastern phenomenon, in Egypt or other parts of North Africa, and then in Syria and Asia Minor. This led Eastern Christians to believe that their spirituality was greater than that of Western Christians. Western monasticism was not far behind, though, and Martin, a soldier in Gaul, entered monastic life in AD 361. He was able to "fascinate young aristocrats from important Gallo-Roman families" to join him in the monastic life of contemplation and evangelism.[129] Early on, monasticism, whether Eastern or Western, was primarily a career for the penitent *wealthy*.

The monastic orders, such as the Benedictines early on, and later the Cluniacs, Dominicans, and others, did not generally reject the notion of owning private property. Rather, they held that property ought to be owned *communally*.[130] In the ideal monastic situation the "brethren" were equal in every way, including their possession of the property on which they worked.[131] This was of course only an *apparent* ownership, since the property was not "listed" in the name of all of the resident monks, nor could they pass anything on to family upon their death. The message was clear—none of the monks owned anything privately for *himself* (the vow of personal poverty), but all possessed all things in common. Eventually, many of the orders, especially the Benedictines, became quite well off through their agricultural prowess, often wine-producing along with other lucrative ventures, and in many other ways. It is hard to argue against success.[132]

---

128 This was the standard monastic vow as formulated classically by Benedict around the year AD 500 but which had been used in some form even earlier.

129 MacCulloch, *Christianity*, 313.

130 Eleanor Shipley Duckett, *The Gateway to the Middle Ages: Monasticism*, Ann Arbor Paperbacks (1938; repr., Ann Arbor: University of Michigan Press, 1961), 3:122–73.

131 Not all monks came from wealthy backgrounds. Some came from poor homes, the monastery actually providing a better life than they had ever known before. W. H. C. Frend, *The Early Church* (1965; repr., Philadelphia: Fortress, 1982), 629–33.

132 Duckett, *Gateway to the Middle Ages*, 122–73. It does also seem to be the case that the Benedictines' eventual wealth led to the decline of their order, and the need for new reforming orders, such as the Cluniacs, around the turn of the millennium. Justo L. Gonzàlez, *The Story of Christianity*, vol. 1: *The Early Church to the Dawn of the Reformation* (New York: HarperCollins, 1984), 277–81.

Struggle for the City

According to the prevailing theory of spirituality that developed in both the Eastern and Western churches, the separated and personally impoverished monastic life, therefore, was the most godly kind of life one could live. The highest spiritual goal one could have was to live the *vita apostolica*, the life lived by Jesus and the apostles, who had neither purse, wallet, nor sandals.[133] Such a life could only be lived in its fullest sense by those who had taken monastic vows. Even laymen such as Peter Waldo (or Valdes), who sought ways in the twelfth century to live the *vita apostolica*, did so only by first *ceasing* all secular work and taking a vow of poverty.[134] Thomas Aquinas would later say that taking the cowl was like a second baptism—it purified one's soul—and was the most certain route to heaven that one could take.[135] This of course created a two-tiered conception of spirituality in the Roman Catholic Church. The truly spiritual were the monks and others who had taken the vow. They were the elites—the *heroes* of the church. Everyone else was apparently content to live out a less-committed Christian experience.[136]

Applying this conception of spirituality to private ownership of property and the possession of wealth was quite simple. Godly people renounced private ownership and lived a communitarian or completely isolated existence. Those, on the other hand, who possessed their own property, especially the rich, were living a *substandard* life of Christian discipleship. They had failed, like the rich young ruler, to leave all behind and follow Christ. One could see this division between the two kinds of "Christians" in the world in spectacular ways with the dazzling giants in the monastic movement, such as Simeon the Stylite, who lived for thirty years atop a stone pillar in Asia Minor and was thus considered a paragon of godliness. Located on a major Syrian thoroughfare, Simeon preached every day to those wayfarers who would pause to hear him. He was an example of severe and austere commitment. But the distinction between the two kinds of Christianity was no less real

---

133 Bernard McGinn, *The Flowering of Mysticism: Men and Women in the New Mysticism, 1200–1300* (New York: Crossroad, 1998), 4–6.

134 Ibid., 6.

135 Roland Bainton, *Here I Stand: A Life of Martin Luther* (Nashville: Abingdon, 1950), 33.

136 This assessment is not intended to be a full statement about the values and demerits of monasticism. There is no doubt that many good things were promoted and accomplished by the monastic system—the translation of Scripture, the furthering of theological discourse, missions and evangelism (esp. with people like Martin of Tours), the composition of hymns, etc. Nor are we alleging that there were no genuinely spiritual persons in the history of Catholic and Orthodox monasticism—quite the contrary is true.

Struggle for the City

among the more normal monastic communities—the truly dedicated must *leave* behind everyday existence and be cloistered away from the artifacts of normal life in order to be devoted truly to God. Further, since the monks had proved that communalism, not acquisitiveness, was the key to general economic success, it only remained to convince the *rest* of society that this was so. The *Corpus Christi*, that is, the entire church, simply needed to copy the communalist economic microcosm exemplified so clearly by the Benedictines.

To sum up, the Gnostic denigration of that which is physical and material has a parallel in the monastic movement insofar as the monks promoted a retreat into spiritual enclaves and flight from this world.[137] Monasticism did not, of course, adopt the cosmology or the Christology of Gnosticism.[138] At least, most did not, though the Spanish Priscillian may be the exception.[139] Nor were most monks committed to a total escape into the realm of the spiritual or mystical—many monasteries required manual labor, though it was manual labor in the monastery, not in the town. "The widespread belief in the antinomy between flesh and spirit and salvation as escape from the trammels of the one into the realms of the other engendered rigid asceticism both within and outside the Christian movement."[140] The *spiritual man* "takes no thought," literally, for the mundane concerns of the world.[141] He is beyond all of that.

That, however, is only part of the story. Monasticism was a complex and many-layered phenomenon, and we will visit it again after we have explored what other Christians taught about wealth and work.

---

137 Herbert B. Workman, *The Evolution of the Monastic Ideal from the Earliest Times Down to the Coming of the Friars: A Second Chapter in the History of Christian Renunciation* (1913; repr., Boston: Beacon Press, 1962), 38–66, as noted by Kenneth Scott Latourette, *A History of the Expansion of Christianity*, vol. 1: *The First Five Centuries*, Contemporary Evangelical Perspectives (New York: Harper & Row, 1970), 354.

138 A case can be made that certain individuals in the monastic tradition held positions that were Gnostic or Manichean or pantheistic. This was especially true of some of the monastic mystics.

139 J. Stevenson, *Creeds, Councils and Controversies: Documents Illustrating the History of the Church, AD 337–461*, rev. by W. H. C. Frend (London: SPCK, 1989), 159–63; Henry Chadwick, *Priscillian of Avila: The Occult and the Charismatic in the Early Church* (Oxford: Oxford University Press, 1976), 57–110.

140 Latourette, *History of the Expansion of Christianity*, 1:354. Latourette here is referring to both Christian and non-Christian forms of monasticism.

141 We have argued that Jesus did not mean that we should never think about material issues when he spoke these words, but rather that we should not be filled with anxiety over material/financial difficulties (Matt. 6:25–34). See earlier discussion of Jesus' teaching in chap. 7.

Struggle for the City

Chapter 11

Using Wealth or Enjoying Wealth?
From the Fathers to the Scholastics

Not all early Christian thinkers were as "holiness" in orientation as the monks, as Tertullian, or as the Gnostics. Some early Christian thinkers believed that financial resources, even wealth, could be used for the positive good. These questions would receive renewed importance when the giant Roman Empire was taken out of the picture in the fifth century. In time, even the monastic communities found that such goods and resources were useful for more than just taking men out of the world to protect them from their own "flesh." This chapter will spell this out in detail.

Theologies of "Possessions"

Most early Christian thinkers did not have the same kind of negative attitude toward wealth and possessions as Tertullian and the monastic communities. Several thoughtful churchmen and intellectuals in the patristic church sought a more biblically and rationally integrated approach. We will examine only two of those persons for the sake of space.

Clement of Alexandria: Work as Care for the Soul

If Tertullian represents the "otherworldly" approach to the spiritual life, Clement of Alexandria (ca. AD 150–215) takes us virtually in the oppo-

site direction. As head of the catechetical school in Alexandria, he sought
to develop a fully Christianized philosophy, both for defensive (apologetic)
purposes and as a constructive model to use in teaching Christians wise living.[1] Clement sought for a synthesis between Greek thinking and the New
Testament, even going so far as to claim that philosophy could provide the
answers for some of the questions that theology asks.[2]

   In his philosophical/theological inquiry Clement squarely addressed economic issues. Fundamental to his understanding was a distinction between the
ownership of capital and its *use*.[3] As for ownership, Clement recognized that
each person owns his own possessions. However, though we have ownership,
we are required to relinquish what we have to others in *usage*: "By possession
they are other peoples', and become theirs by possession; by use they are the
property of each one of us."[4] Clement is apparently arguing that Christians
may accumulate capital so long as they are willing to give some of it away to
those in need, and this thinker, living in a city the size of Alexandria, would
likely have seen many needy Christians.[5] Wealth is not *inherently* injurious,
only *potentially* so, and can "contribute to [one's] advantage if he knows the
right use of" it.[6] In a sermon on the rich young ruler ("Who Is the Rich Man
Who Shall Be Saved?"), a sermon that makes clear he is speaking to wealthy
Christians, Clement states that Jesus' command to sell all is not meant to
be taken *literally* by all persons, but is a counsel "to detach the soul from
unworthy thoughts."[7] He insists that Christians ought to be industrious and
hard working in their places of employment. This is partly the case because it

---

1   Judith L. Kovacs, "Clement of Alexandria," in *Early Christian Thinkers: The Lives and
     Legacies of Twelve Key Figures*, ed. Paul Foster (Downers Grove, IL: InterVarsity Press,
     2010), 68.
2   Jaroslav Pelikan, *The Christian Tradition*, vol. 1: *The Emergence of the Catholic Tradition
     (100–600)* (Chicago: University of Chicago Press, 1971), 46–48.
3   Barry Gordon, *The Economic Problem in Biblical and Patristic Thought*, Supplements to
     Vigiliae Christianae 9 (Leiden: E. J. Brill, 1989), 85.
4   Clement, *Miscellanies* 4.13, quoted in Gordon, *Economic Problem in Biblical and Patristic
     Thought*, 85.
5   In Rome, for instance, in the year AD 248, there were 155 clergy ministering to the needs
     of about 1,500 widows and others with no income. David Batson, *The Treasure Chest of the
     Early Christians* (Leominster: Gracewing; Grand Rapids,MI: Eerdmans, 2001), 94.
6   J. Stevenson, ed., *Creeds, Councils and Controversies*, rev. by W. H. C. Frend (London:
     SPCK, 1989), 188–89.
7   Kovacs, "Clement of Alexandria," 73.

Struggle for the City

is important to care for the body, "the care for which is required by the very care of the soul,"[8] and partly because having command of the necessities of life makes us free to serve God more robustly.[9] But the chief end of all of this is that Christians may support those who are destitute so that they too might have the same benefits. Christian entrepreneurs, then, are valuable to the kingdom, but only insofar as they are able to be conduits of wealth to the needy by donation. This is not as austere as Tertullian, who called for a common purse for church members, but it is still exacting in its expectations that those who *have* will share with those who *have not*.

Augustine on Economics and the City

None of the Christians we have examined so far developed anything like a consistent economic philosophy. That would soon change. Aurelius Augustine (AD 354–430) is the most important theologian of the first millennium of the church. His writings cover virtually every area of the theological curriculum, and in addition he addressed many mundane and "secular" matters from a theological perspective. Augustine wrote during a period of economic decline in the empire; indeed, Rome was in decline in every way measurable. The previous century had witnessed the loss of venture capital as well as the steady elimination of arable land due to neglect and poor management.[10] This coupled with a decline in birth rates in the patrician class, and the Roman citizenry in general, caused the Senate to move more and more slaves and mercenaries into the ranks of the army, thus *diluting* the quality of the once-indomitable Roman military machine.[11]

Small wonder that early in the fifth century barbarians surged across the Rhine and began the systematic process of toppling the decaying giant that had been the Roman Empire. Part of Augustine's legacy is that he wrote the epitaph of Rome at the same time that he mapped out some of the uncharted contours of Christian thought. He certainly gave the church a theology of

---

8   Clement, *Miscellanies* 4.5.
9   Gordon, *Economic Problem in Biblical and Patristic Thought*, 86.
10 Ramsey MacMullen, "Social Mobility and the Theodosian Code," *Journal of Roman Studies* 54, pts. 1–2 (1964): 50.
11 Christopher S. Mackay, *Ancient Rome: A Military and Political History* (Cambridge: Cambridge University Press, 2004), 331–32.

Struggle for the City

history, previously unexplored, in his *City of God*, and was the first to pen a theological autobiography, the *Confessions*. In a similar way the African father was the first to develop a comprehensive system of economic ethics. He is an important figure for the development of *political economy* in the church as well as for the doctrines of salvation, the Trinity, and the church.

Aurelius Augustine was born in Thagaste, in the Roman Africa province, which is now modern Algeria. He was the son of an unsophisticated, though devout, Catholic mother and a pagan father. His family was among the Roman citizenry and he early showed signs of brilliance.[12] He studied rhetoric in Carthage and then became teacher of the same subject at the "university" there, eventually moving on to teach in Rome, and then to Milan, the *greatest* of the Western Roman cities of the time. Teaching rhetoric was considered to be one pathway to success and to enter the highest echelons of Roman society, which was what Augustine hoped for, but it was a challenge to a young man from the provinces. Augustine had rejected his mother's Catholic faith at about age fifteen, moving successively to the cult known as Manicheanism, then to paganism, then to Neoplatonism, before being finally converted through the influence of a Christian friend, through the preaching of Bishop Ambrose in Milan, and through reading the Pauline epistles.[13] He was now an exemplar of "a faith which united the imperious nobleman [Ambrose] in the pulpit with the elderly woman from a provincial backwater."[14] He later returned to Africa, where in AD 395 he became bishop of Hippo Regius.

As much as anything, Augustine represents the flowering of *rational theology* in the early centuries of the church, a rational theology that begins with faith, but moves on toward evidence, sensory experience, and then to rational knowledge that elevates the Bible over all, but which integrates that with a chastened philosophical understanding.[15] In regard to his theology of possessions, Augustine was concerned about the extreme asceticism that was to be found among early monks. While he recognized that people can be too

---

12 His early life is covered by himself anecdotally in his book titled *Confessions*.
13 Augustine, *Confessions* 1–8.
14 Diarmaid MacCulloch, *Christianity* (New York: Penguin, 2009), 302.
15 Etienne Gilson, *The Christian Philosophy of Saint Augustine*, trans. L. E. M. Lynch (London: Victor Gollancz, 1961), 27–112.

Struggle for the City

acquisitive and proud of what they have, he also believed that there was a role for commerce and that wickedness was not *inherent* in commercial activity.[16] He was also convinced that *price* was not merely a function of seller's costs but also of the interest on the part of the purchaser to obtain that which was for sale. "In this way, Augustine gave legitimacy not merely to merchants but to the eventual deep involvement of the church in the birth of capitalism."[17] That will be clear not only for later Protestantism, but for Catholicism as well.

Augustine made three major contributions to the Christian theology of possessions.[18] First, he made a distinction between *material things* themselves and the *possession* of those things. Appealing to the Christian doctrine of creation, he argued that the things themselves are intrinsically good, since they were made by a good God.[19] So the wood and stone of a house are good things, but whether it is appropriate for one to own such a house is quite another question, which brings us to his second contribution.

Augustine also made a distinction between *using* a material possession and *enjoying* it. "Some things are to be enjoyed, others are to be used, and there are others which are to be enjoyed and used."[20] Think again of the house we mentioned above. It is one thing to use the house for basic needs—shelter, a place to raise the family, a means of hospitality. It is another thing to take *pride* or joy in the house for its own sake, say, because of its size or beauty. If we enjoy the house in that manner, we are in serious danger of *idolatry* and of violating the command not to love the world. Augustine argues in several of his discussions of ethics that the intent of the *heart* is what is crucial in determining the moral nature of one's action.[21] So, one might have a large and beautiful house, as long as one is not proud of it and does not enjoy it *too much*.

---

16 John W. Baldwin, *The Medieval Theories of the Just Price: Romanists, Canonists, and Theologians in the Twelfth and Thirteenth Centuries*, Transactions of the American Philosophical Society, new ser. (Philadelphia: American Philosophical Society, 1959), 15.
17 Rodney Stark, *The Victory of Reason* (New York: Random House, 2005), 58.
18 A convenient summary of Augustine's economic beliefs is found in John Schneider, *Godly Materialism: Rethinking Money and Possessions* (Downers Grove, IL: InterVarsity Press, 1994), 26–33.
19 Augustine, *City of God* 12.9
20 Augustine, *On Christian Doctrine* 1.3.9.
21 Augustine, *Psalms* 147.12; *Psalms* 95.15, cited in Justo L. Gonzàles, *Faith and Wealth* (Eugene, OR: Wipf and Stock, 1990), 215–16.

Struggle for the City

Thirdly, the African father maintained that the absolute best that one could do with possessions is to *give* them away. When it comes to economic transactions, they are of two kinds: "sale or gift."[22] Augustine was the founder of a monastery, even if he did not remain there throughout his ministry. Though he did not promote extreme asceticism or demand absolute poverty in his order, he still promoted the *ideal* of communalism.[23] One who becomes poor for the sake of the gospel will be rich in heaven, and that is a much *better* state. This is part and parcel with Augustine's overall understanding of *love*, key to understanding his thought as a whole. We all have self-love and love for the other. We will generally have greater love for our own children than we will the children of others. That is understandable, but it ought not to mean that we do not have *any* love at all for those not close to us.

With regard to his discussions of *distribution* (whether by sale or gift) and his discussion of *utility*, Augustine made original contributions to economics, contributions that would be picked up by Thomas Aquinas in the thirteenth century in explicating a fully developed economic theory.[24] We will come back to that later. Augustine left to the world a legacy of a fairly thoroughgoing theology of labor, wealth, and stewardship.

The other issue that concerns us about the great African father is his philosophy of history and his views on governance, spelled out most intricately and authoritatively in *City of God*. He wrote the book to answer the concerns of a man named Marcellinus about the reliability of the Bible and the validity of the Christian faith. Marcellinus was a fellow Christian, but being a Roman civil servant he had heard many criticisms of Christianity from other state employees, especially African proconsul Volusianus, who wished for a *return* to the pagan religions of the past.[25] Emperor Theodosius I had proscribed

---

22 Augustine, *On Free Will,* Anti-Pelagian Writings, Nicene and Post-Nicene Fathers, vol. 5, ed. Philip Schaff (Grand Rapids: Eerdmans, 1956), 2.11..
23 His views on this were very close to those of Basil the Great and John Chrysostom, both of whom were roughly his contemporaries. It must be recalled that he did not live a communal lifestyle as a bishop, but he still considered it to be an important option.
24 John Mueller, *Redeeming Economics* (Wilmington, DE: ISI Books, 2010), 21–25.
25 R. W. Dyson, "Introduction," Augustine, *The City of God against the Pagans*, ed. and trans. R. W. Dyson, Cambridge Texts in the History of Political Thought (Cambridge: Cambridge University Press, 1998), xii. In the penning of this volume, Augustine also had other pagan Roman critics of Christianity in mind such as Nectarius of Calama and "the philosophers

Struggle for the City

the pagan religions in 384, and made Christianity the *official* religion of the empire in 392.[26] In 410 the Visigoths, under the leadership of Alaric, sacked the city of Rome, and, though the sack was relatively mild in comparison with similar events at the time (the Visigoths were Christians, though of an Arian bent), the citizens of Rome were shaken to the core. Rome considered itself to be the eternal city. How can an eternal city be *sacked* in such a fashion? Many Romans of the more traditional mind-set blamed the abandonment of the older religions and the commitment to Christianity as the reason why Rome had fallen.[27] This criticism was the occasion for the book, "the most self-conscious book he ever wrote,"[28] though it is likely Augustine would have written a similar book in any event, since he had previously alluded to the "two cities" in other writings.[29] In setting this forth, Augustine would "set the tone for Christian political theology for many centuries."[30] We still speak of these issues in language set in stone by Augustine, namely, the "Two Cities."

Augustine contended that the two cities first presented themselves in opposition to one another when the satanic rebellion took place.[31] This book does not constitute a "theory of politics" in the way a modern work might do; such a task was really not even feasible at a time when the centuries-old institutions were cracking.[32] It is a ranging work filled with biblical interpretation

---

Augustine knew so well—the Platonici." Peter Brown, *Augustine of Hippo: A Biography* (Berkeley: University of California Press, 1967), 301–3.

26 In spite of the formal outlawing of pagan religion, there was no prosecution toward those who continued the old ways, and Theodosius himself appointed nearly as many open pagans to high government posts as he did Christians. Among the poor urbanites and rural Romans, paganism persisted for decades, or longer. Christianity at this time was largely confined to the more well to do and to slaves. Rodney Stark, *Triumph of Christianity* (New York: HarperOne, 2011), 189–93.

27 Christians in "New Rome" (Constantinople) did not count Alaric's victory to be the fall of Rome, since they saw themselves (the Eastern empire) to be the true successor. Jaroslav Pelikan, *The Excellent Empire: The Fall of Rome and the Triumph of the Church*, Rauschenbusch Lectures 1, new ser. (San Francisco: Harper & Row, 1987), 77.

28 Brown, *Augustine of Hippo*, 303.

29 Dyson, "Introduction," xiii.

30 Mark Lilla, *Stillborn God* (New York: Vintage Books, 2007), 43.

31 Augustine, *On the Literal Interpretation of Genesis* 11, 15, 20.

32 "The conditions of the early fifth century did not stimulate St. Augustine or anyone else to undertake a work of social construction." Edward R. Hardy Jr., "The City of God," in *A Companion to the Study of St. Augustine*, ed. Roy W. Battenhouse (Oxford: Oxford University Press, 1955), 274.

Struggle for the City

and comments on history (like most of Augustine's writings) that, by the time it is done, leaves the reader with some pretty clear notions of what the author believed about these matters. When God made the first couple, their life was one of *complete* love and happiness.[33] They were given only one prohibition. But they had the full capacity to violate the prohibition, since they were made with free will, and violate it they did.[34] Because of their sin, their nature and the nature of their offspring was *changed* for the worse, so that "bondage to sin and the necessity of death were transmitted to their posterity."[35] This is a crucial element to understand in all of Augustine's mature theological writings.[36] Man, created with the gift of free will, still retains the power of choice, but even that has been tainted by sin.[37] Humanity was created to love God supremely, and to love themselves only secondarily, but now, apart from the aid that comes from the grace of God, people love themselves supremely.[38] Such is the nature of sin, that as much as anything else it is constituted of tainted love.

It is no surprise that Adam's son, Cain, after murdering his own brother, founded the first city. Augustine believed that had there been no sin, there would never have been a political state, for, though man is naturally sociable, he is not naturally political.[39] Human beings were intended to be lords over herds and flocks, but not over other people; yet now, governed by the impulses of self-love, people have a lust for mastery, what Augustine calls *libido dominandi*.[40] The state is a manifestation of all of this, and can only be so. Whereas Plato and Aristotle considered the state to be *natural*, Augustine sees it as sinful even at its *best*. Even good judges, because they do not know people's hearts, have to resort to force to discern the truth, and the wisest of them can only pray to be released from their responsibilities.[41]

---

33 Augustine, *City of God* 14.10.
34 Ibid. 14.13.
35 Ibid. 14.1.
36 Paul Rigby, "Original Sin," in *Augustine through the Ages: An Encyclopedia*, ed. Allan D. Fitzgerald (Grand Rapids, MI: Eerdmans, 1999), 107.
37 Augustine, *City of God* 14.11.
38 Ibid. 15.1.
39 Ibid. 19.5.
40 Ibid. 19.15, 14.13; Augustine, *On Christian Doctrine* 1, 23.
41 Augustine, *City of God* 19.6.

Struggle for the City

God in his infinite wisdom and foresight knew all of this would be the case. He determined within himself that he would provide an alternative to the sinful city of self-love. Those who are not members of the elect are citizens of the *civitas terrena*, or even of the *civitas diaboli*, while the elect are members of the *civitas dei*. The members of each city are unified by allegiance to a common object of love, meaning, by "love" (or "loves") "a variety of attitudes toward things we possess, as well as a wide range of human appetites and aversions toward things we do not possess."[42] But in each city it is a different kind of love. The citizens of the City of Man (or "Earthly City") are marked by self-love, while in the City of God the population's love is directed primarily toward God.[43] These are "fundamental orientations of the members of the two cities."[44] The one city glories in itself, while the other city glories in God.[45] Whereas previous philosophers Plato and Aristotle (for instance) thought of man as finding his place in life, his distinctive contribution as occurring in the city (the City of Man in Augustine's scheme), the African father rejects that notion and contends, rather, that man only finds his true home in the City of God.

True community occurs when people gather around something that they all love together. Love of an object spontaneously gives birth to a society of those who have the same object of love. "He who loves God is, by that very fact, brought into a social relationship with all those who love him."[46] The City of God is not to be equated to the church, because not all persons in the visible church are regenerate.[47] "The church is not a perfect society, but a body in which saints and sinners are 'mixed' (*corpus permixtum*)."[48] This City of God on earth is but a prelude to the heavenly city that awaits in the new heavens and new earth. For Augustine, "heaven is not longed for because the apparent goods of earth are bad but because they are not good enough."[49] And for him the final eternal state is physical—the new earth.

---

42 Paul Weithman, "Augustine's Political Philosophy," in *The Cambridge Companion to Augustine*, ed. Eleonore Stump and Norman Kretzman (Cambridge: Cambridge University Press, 2001), 235.
43 Augustine, *City of God* 19.24.
44 Weithman, "Augustine's Political Philosophy," 236.
45 Augustine, *City of God* 6.12.15–19. See Brown, *Augustine of Hippo*, 310.
46 Gilson, *Christian Philosophy of Saint Augustine*, 172.
47 Ernest L. Fortin contends that Augustine "occasionally equates the City of God with the church." "Civitate Dei, De," in *Augustine through the Ages*, 199.
48 Williston Walker, *A History of the Christian Church*, 4th ed. (New York: Scribner's, 1985), 205.
49 Hardy, "City of God," 273.

Struggle for the City

Augustine rejected the assertion of Rome that it is the seat of justice. Cicero had taught that real justice is found in the commonwealth, but Augustine argues that Rome was *never* a commonwealth, that is, a moral community. Rome lacked justice in two ways—it never *acknowledged* the true God as God and it acted in *immoral* ways toward its enemies and its citizens alike.[50] This was, essentially, why Rome eventually fell. "Rome and other empires, as expressions of the earthly city, had to succumb. If they once became great and powerful, this was only because God so willed it."[51] Rome became great, in the providence of God, but it was still an empire built on sin. In the providence of God Rome had a task, "but once that historical mission was accomplished Rome fell as a result of her sin and idolatry," in Augustine's view.[52] At their worst, nations are little more than *robbers* who steal from their people but do it, as it were, *legally*. That is a snapshot of nations at their worst, but even then they have a role to fill. *Bad* government is better than *no* government. "[Augustine] formulated a view of the earthly city that admitted, and worked with, imperfections such as unjust regimes and criminal elements. Even in an imperfect setting, he urged Christians to be good citizens and required officials to be impartial."[53] Augustine was no anarchist nor was he an idealist; he believed that nations can be better, but only if they are led by Christians.

Justice is the goal of government. "True justice exists only in the society of God, and this will be truly fulfilled only after the judgment. Nevertheless, while no society on earth can *fully* express this justice, the one that is more influenced by Christians and by Christian teaching will more perfectly reflect a just society. For this reason, Christians have a duty toward government."[54] This is not exactly the same goal that Eusebius previously expressed with regard to Constantine. The "idea of a Christian empire such as Eusebius of Caesarea had envisaged can never be a perfect reality on earth."[55] *Just* government is the goal, though one *unattain-*

---

50 Augustine, *City of God* 19.21; 2.21.
51 Justo L. Gonzàlez, *A History of Christian Thought*, vol. 2: *From Augustine to the Eve of the Reformation*, rev. ed. (Nashville: Abingdon, 1987), 54.
52 Ibid.
53 Andrew Knowles and Pachomios Penkett, *Augustine and His World*, IVP Histories (Downers Grove, IL: InterVarsity Press, 2004), 147–48.
54 Robert E. Webber, *The Church in the World: Opposition, Tension, or Transformation?* (Grand Rapids, MI: Zondervan, 1986), 71.
55 MacCulloch, *Christianity*, 305–6.

Struggle for the City

able in this age. Even though a Christian state will still be tainted by sin and depravity, Christian rulers can give to subjects examples of godliness and humility.[56]

Though all of this does not represent what we would today call a *theory* of political science, it does represent the longest and most sustained treatment of the role of the state from any Christian writer for a long time to come, and it set forth an *ideal* of government that "Christian Kings and Magistrates" sought to follow for centuries. The manner in which they did so did not always live up to the African father's ideal.

THE FALL OF ROME AND THE AFTERMATH

Augustine's *City of God* was written, as we noted, as an *apologetic* for Christianity after the sack of Rome. The sack by Alaric was only the beginning of the end for the once great republic and then empire. Other "sacks" occurred in the years that followed, and, little by little, the once-considered-inviolable Roman Empire began to disintegrate. The history of that disintegration is not our concern here, but in the city's final days the last Roman emperor, Romulus Augustus (an ironic name), was deposed by an army led by the mercenary Odoacre in AD 476. In reality, the Roman Empire died "not with a bang but with a whimper," as it had been almost totally in the hands of foreign kings and princes long before. What next?

The Fall of Rome

The fall of Rome is one of the most celebrated events (or, more correctly, series of events) in history, and often historians (like Edward Gibbon) have bemoaned the fact that "Great Rome" with all its splendor, might, and glory was taken down by a bunch of petty and uncultured thugs, and then it was succeeded by a cobbled group of political entities with no sense of the technological and intellectual power of that which they tore down. These ridiculous kingdoms came more and more to be dominated by the Roman Catholic Church, until it finally dominated the whole lot by the eleventh and twelfth centuries. That, however, is a misunderstanding of the real events.

---

56 Augustine, *City of God* 5.24.

Struggle for the City

In one real sense the fall of Rome was the collapse of a *city*, not the ending of a civilization. We have pointed out earlier in our historical survey that Rome was a *bully*. It was a fat, lazy bully whose very existence depended on slavery, war, redistribution of wealth, and favorable *privilege* granted by the state to a chosen few. It deserved to go down. It needed to be plowed under. Thank God for the destruction of Rome and its empire! That city's collapse was the only hope for Western Europeans to be able to have a fresh start on building their own civilizations. That is not to say that everything got better in "Europe" after the fall. The Roman Empire was replaced briefly with a much smaller Hunnic Empire (the rule of the Huns) and then with no empire and older systems of trade and travel broke down,[57] but from the standpoint of history, the fall of Rome was a *good thing*.

Not only is the fall of Rome sometimes misunderstood, but what happened afterwards has *certainly* been misstated. Enlightenment figures like Gibbon and Voltaire claimed that the fall of Rome plunged Europe into the "Dark Ages," from which it would take centuries to emerge. Voltaire called this period a time when "barbarism, superstition, [and] ignorance covered the face of the world."[58] Of course, in true hubristic fashion, those same figures (Voltaire and Gibbon) argued that the Dark Ages only finally ended with—them! The fall of the empire in actuality meant that those parts of Europe that had been under its domination, liable to be invaded, and taxed beyond their ability to bear, were now free. But free to do what? Again, common convention is that Europe went into a cultural and scientific decline. That is simply *not* true. Rome itself had actually been in scientific stagnation for a long time. What was the last Roman invention? The Romans were good engineers, as is proven by their ability to bring water many miles from mountains into their cities through aqueducts, but all the labor to accomplish that was done by *slaves*. They employed concrete to make domed roofs, but they were not the inventors of concrete. As one scholar puts it, "[D]espotic states discourage and even prevent progress."[59] With the despot gone, what would happen next?

---

57   Peter Heather, *Empires and Barbarians: The Fall of Rome and the Birth of Europe* (Oxford: Oxford University Press, 2009), 331–85.
58   Voltaire, *Works*, vol. 12, quoted in Stark, *Victory of Reason*, 35.
59   Ibid., 37.

Struggle for the City

Technological Innovations in the Wake of Rome's Fall

Innovations in production, in war, and in transportation came with the passing of the Roman Empire.[60] In *production*, wind and water mills exploded into Europe in the ninth and tenth centuries, a development that the Romans had no use for, since they had slaves who could provide them all the manpower they needed. With the ending of slavery, power for sawing lumber, for turning lathes, grinding knives, and hammering metal was needed, and water and wind power was useful for these tasks. Enterprising people invented the *horse collar*. Oxen collars were not appropriate for horses due to their different physiology, but in Rome no one thought of simply altering the collar. Horses are better suited to plowing and can plow twice as much ground in a day as oxen, so this increased agricultural productivity. Horses could also pull much heavier plows than oxen, and so the larger plows were fashioned, enabling farmers to plow some land previously unavailable to them. Europeans also developed the *three-field system*, leaving behind the two-field system, which enabled them to increase productivity by thirty or thirty-five percent.[61] In Slavic lands, due to increased farming technology, the amount of land under the plow increased by two hundred percent in the eighth century.[62] "This was critical to state formation in a number of ways."[63] Chimneys, clocks, and eyeglasses were all developed during the period that Voltaire and Gibbon designated as the so-called Dark Ages.

Western Europeans also advanced warfare technology in the centuries following the loss of Roman hegemony. Somewhere around AD 700 the Franks invented the *stirrup*. Without the stirrup heavy cavalry was not possible, since a charge with lances is impossible unless the rider can brace himself. At the Battle of Tours in AD 732 and then again four years later at the Battle of Narbonne, Charles Martel likely employed heavy cavalry against the invading Muslims who

---

60 The material in these paragraphs is taken from Stark, *Victory of Reason*, 38–50, and from Heather, *Empires and Barbarians*.
61 For this discussion about increased agricultural productivity, see Stark, *Victory of Reason*, 42.
62 Heather, *Empires and Barbarians*, 545–48.
63 Ibid., 546. Heather elaborates that large crop production was necessary to maintain armies, to establish social distinctions, and to increase populations that in turn allowed for larger construction projects. Increased farm production was necessary for the building of modern society.

Struggle for the City

were intent on turning Western Europe into a Muslim caliphate. Martel and his stirruped heavy cavalry prevailed in both instances, both very important victories.[64] The use of *gunpowder* in fighting first with cannons and then with muskets was also developed toward the end of the Dark Ages. The Chinese had first invented gunpowder but only used it in fireworks. The Europeans used it more effectively in warfare. Europeans also invented the *rudder* placed at the back of a ship for steering. The Greeks and Romans steered with oars, but the rudder made for a better fighting ship, especially when combined with *cannons* and the *compass*, the former invented sometime in the eleventh century and the latter invented much earlier.[65]

There was also new technology in land transportation. Much has been made about the Roman roads, and, while there were many of them, and they could certainly guide one to the destination, they were poorly built and completely unsuitable for large wagons. Their primary purpose was getting soldiers to the battle, but even the soldiers normally walked on the turf *beside* the roads rather than on the roads themselves.[66] Roman wagons did not have a front *pivot*, their wheels were not capable of turning, and they were relatively small since they had to be pulled primarily by oxen in the absence of adequate horse collars. In the Dark Ages, enterprising persons changed all of this, along with figuring out how to harness horses and/or oxen *side by side* and in *front* and *behind* one another, familiar to us from movies featuring stagecoaches and wagon trains. Of course, they had to build roads and bridges to accommodate these better and larger wagons, and they did, roads far *better* than the ones built by Rome.[67] These were all innovations that had to wait till Rome was gone and the "Dark Ages had dawned." "In fact, it was during the 'Dark Ages' that Europe took the great technological and intellectual leap forward that put it ahead of the rest of the world."[68] Thank God for the Dark Ages! The enterprising spirit and *creativity* of human beings will find a way when they

---

64 See under the next heading's section of our treatment.
65 Stark, *Triumph of Christianity*, 239–44.
66 Stark, *Victory of Reason*, 49.
67 Michael Postan, "Chapter IV: The Trade of Medieval Europe: The North," in *The Cambridge Economic History of Europe*, vol. 2: *Trade and Industry in the Middle Ages* (Cambridge: Cambridge University Press, 1952), 147.
68 Stark, *Triumph of Christianity*, 240.

Struggle for the City

are out from under the heavy and dictatorial hand of an oppressive, fascist government that *steals* their resources and *enslaves* their people.

An Augustinian Christian Empire?

A monumentally important event occurred in the year AD 620 when an obscure religious leader named *Muhammad* (AD 570–632) became the ruler and prophet of the Arabian city, Medina. Ten years later he led a successful attack on the city of Mecca, with the result that most of the Arabian peninsula was under his control.[69] Though he died only two years after that, his successors, the caliphs, continued his policy of conversion by conquest, and in eighty years the Middle East, North Africa, and most of the Iberian Peninsula were under their control. They did not force conversions on monotheists, but they did make it difficult for non-Muslims to subsist under their rule.[70]

Muslim ambitions were large, and in AD 732 they attempted an assault on the west-central European mainland. Near the French city of Tours they encountered the *major domus* of the Frankish Merovingian king, a man named Charles Martel. Martel was the chief aristocrat in the service of King Pippin II,[71] and he led probably the only army in Europe at the time that could stop the invading Muslims. He was successful in his battle, for reasons that we have mentioned elsewhere, and he drove the invading army back across the Pyrenees. If not for that win, we might have grown up reading the "King James Version" of the Qur'an! In 752 Charles' son, also named Pippin, not content with being merely *major domus* deposed the last Merovingian king and had himself crowned King of the Franks.[72] Thus began the Carolingian Empire, so well known to us in later times.

Pippin ("the Short") set out to expand his empire, but that great task would be carried out in a spectacular way by his son, Charles (Karolus Magnus, born

---

69 Fazlur Rahman, *Islam*, 2nd ed. (Chicago: University of Chicago Press, 2002), 11–29.

70 In the eighth century, for instance, John of Damascus was a bishop of the Catholic Church under Muslim governance. But Christians and Jews could not vote, own a horse, carry a sword, or propagate their faith. Robert Spencer, *The Truth about Muhammad: Founder of the World's Most Intolerant Religion* (Washington, DC: Regnery, 2006), 153.

71 Chris Wickham, *The Inheritance of Rome: A History of Europe from 400 to 1000* (New York: Viking, 2009), 111–29.

72 Heather, *Empires and Barbarians*, 367.

Struggle for the City

742, ruling from 768–814), known to posterity as Charlemagne. Though the Frankish kings had been at least *nominally* "Christian" since King Clovis in 496 had his army baptized by priests sitting on tree branches while the soldiers marched beneath and were sprinkled with holy water, Charlemagne took his faith *seriously*. "World-changing events depend on the merging of two kinds of power: military might and the force of an ideology."[73] Charlemagne's combination of military might and intense faith in the gospel story would create the greatest example of militant Christianity yet seen.[74] European society in the seventh to the tenth centuries "had developed into three social classes: those who worked (the peasants), those who fought (the rulers and the knights), and those who prayed (the priests and the religious)."[75] A veritable contradiction in terms, Charles was a devout man in his faith, yet fierce and violent in his warfare; he ate large, drank large, was fiercely loyal to his subjects, doted on his children, and treated disloyalty with swift vengeance.[76] At the end of his life he donated two-thirds of his personal wealth to the church. Charlemagne could read (but could not write well), and his favorite book was Augustine's *City of God*, which he read in his palace at Aachen, but also carried with him on his campaigns against, for instance, the Saxons.[77] He believed that he was bringing the City of God to the "European" world of his day, and in one blazing symbolic act, he stated his intentions for all to see.

Charles had been building empire for several decades, but he was merely the king of Francia, and the various foreign nobles who sat under his hegemony were always just a tavern-fight away from mutiny. Pope Leo III was having difficulties with Irene, empress of the Eastern Roman (Byzantine) Empire, traditionally considered to be the protector of the papacy.[78] Each man had something he needed, so on Christmas Day 800, the pope crowned Charlemagne "Emperor of the Romans," thus inaugurating the "Holy Roman Empire."[79] Pope Leo gave

---

73 Derek Wilson, *Charlemagne: A Biography* (New York: Vintage Books, 2007), 6.
74 Ibid., 6–7.
75 James R. Payton Jr., *Getting the Reformation Wrong: Correcting Some Misunderstandings* (Downers Grove, IL: InterVarsity Press, 2010), 101.
76 Wilson, *Charlemagne*, 29–31, 101–2, 123–25, 148–50, 154–55.
77 Ibid., 125–29, 196.
78 This was the Iconoclastic Controversy, but it does not concern us in this discussion.
79 Judith Herrin, *The Formation of Christendom* (Princeton, NJ: Princeton University Press, 1987), 305.

Struggle for the City

Charles his credentials, and Charles pledged himself as the papacy's defender[80] along with confirming his father's granting of the Papal States to the church.[81] This act would bring about a *marriage* between church and state that was more visible even than that cemented by Constantine in the Old Roman world. But it would prove to be a *shaky* marriage through the centuries. Shaky, indeed! This is the moment in time that a symbiotic relationship between church and state was forged that would have untold consequences, not only for Catholicism, but even for the early Protestants. One could argue that religion and "secular" governance were *already* linked at the local level, a linkage that would go on even beyond the Reformation. That is true. But *this* was the event that placed that linkage at the highest echelon of both sides (the temporal and the spiritual) of the governing of human lives in the Middle Ages.

Charlemagne built an empire that would endure beyond his death, though not in the same state of *health* that it was at the time of his death.[82] His combination of Christian faith and morality, combined with the emerging relationship of feudalism, "which bound lords and vassals together with bands of mutual responsibility," created the phenomenon of *chivalry*.[83] He also set a pattern, an ideal for what a Christian monarchy could be, that would become *mythic* in the centuries that followed. Here was the City of God come to overspread the City of Man. We do not think that the Saxons saw it that way, and neither do we, but Charlemagne certainly did.

Catholic "Capitalism" and the Aftermath

We have already discussed monasticism and its call to leave the world and enter the cloister of the faithful few. There is more to the story, however, and at this point we need to examine the way in which the monastic system, building

---

80 Wilson, *Charlemagne*, 79–82.
81 This was done in his father's day by producing a forged document called "The Donation of Constantine," in which the emperor supposedly granted large tracts of land in "Italy" to the pope, to rule in Constantine's stead when he relocated the capital to Constantinople. Herrin, *Formation of Christendom*, 297, 399–400. The document also gave the pope in Rome primacy over all other churches and bishoprics, including Constantinople, Antioch, Jerusalem, and Alexandria.
82 Heather, *Empires and Barbarians*, 368.
83 Wilson, *Charlemagne*, 148.

Struggle for the City

on the innovations we have just detailed, was able to *spike* the markets with new wealth and even more technological innovations. We have already noted that the Greek intellectual world denigrated trade, commerce, and manual labor as being below the dignity of cultured men. But we have also already seen that Christian thinkers like Clement of Alexandria and Augustine had defended such activities as being not only legitimate, but specifically *Christian*. This view of commerce was actualized in some of the monastic communities in the years after the fall of Rome.[84] It may seem odd to those who only saw the monasteries as the locus of the vow of poverty that some of them would also be the place of great commerce, but it is an important part of the story.

There were great monastic estates that engaged in agriculture, at first to sustain their own personnel, but later for commercial purposes. The church was one of the great landowners in the medieval world because of the vast monastic estates and, after the eighth century, because of Frankish King Pippin III's gift of the Papal States to the pope.[85] The monasteries made use of the new inventions, the horse collar, the heavy moldboard plow, the three-field system, and others in their agricultural work. As time went by and they became adept at their work, they went a long way beyond subsistence agriculture. Remember that these were men who had no wives, no family, and lots of time on their hands, as well as a need to expend energy, for *more* than one reason. These large and profitable monastic estates were the result.

One scholar has noted that these monasteries developed more than just a sort of proto-capitalism, but an actual truly commercialized *system*.[86] What the monks achieved was a sort of "religious capitalism," and along the way they established a pattern in which the church would set the economic tone for the Western economy.[87] One of the ways the church had for years generated revenue was by saying masses for the wealthy, who remunerated them for doing so.[88] This money was often plowed back into the monastic estates for further economic development, so that by the High Middle Ages there were huge mo-

---

84 Stark, *Triumph of Christianity*, 244–46.
85 MacCulloch, *Christianity*, 348. See our earlier discussion in this chapter.
86 Randall Collins, *Weberian Sociological Theory* (Cambridge: Cambridge University Press, 1986), 47.
87 Ibid., 55.
88 Stark, *Victory of Reason*, 58.

Struggle for the City

nastic estates, one in Hungary that had more than 250,000 acres under plow.[89] Cistercian houses (a monastic order that was begun in the tenth century as a reforming order) often held estates larger than 100,000 acres, with some of the Cistercian monasteries at work raising fine horses. The earliest capitalists then were not Dutch bankers or Genevan merchants, or even Venetian shipbuilders, but monastic farmers, vintners, and equestrian managers. Out of this trade they were able even to become bankers, lending money to the European nobility. Capitalism was born, nearly a *thousand years* before the Scottish philosopher Adam Smith wrote his famous book.

The Crusades and Market Innovation

Monastic innovation was not the only kind of capitalism that inserted itself into the medieval world. Another version of that sort of innovation was crucial to the propagation of the "Crusades." The Crusades are a much-studied series of events that have inflamed the emotions of historians and apologists for centuries and will likely do so for many years to come. Our purpose here is not to defend or criticize, but to demonstrate the *financial* impact of the Crusades on the development of the West and to examine their overall impact on the church.

Europeans first began to make pilgrimages to the Holy Land[90] in the aftermath of Constantine's conversion to Christianity. His mother, Helena, visited Jerusalem, supposedly finding there the True Cross, an incredibly *lucky* find, especially in light of later archaeologists' difficulties in finding much of anything! The first known pilgrim from the West was a man from Gaul (France) who made the journey in 333.[91] Early Christian thinkers such as Augustine, Jerome, and the Cappadocian Fathers discouraged pilgrimages as having no spiritual benefit in the lives of the pilgrims, but that did not stop people from making the trip. Sometimes the trips involved large groups, such as the journey made at the expense of Robert II, Duke of Normandy, in 1026, a pilgrimage led by Richard,

---

89 Ibid., 59.
90 The land of Israel came to be known as the "Holy Land" late in the period of the Crusades, in the late thirteenth century. Douglas Harper, "Holy Land," *Online Etymology Dictionary*, http://www.etymonline.com/index.php?term=Holy+Land.
91 Teddy Kollek and Moshe Pearlman, *Pilgrims to the Holy Land: The Story of Pilgrimage Through the Ages* (New York: Harper & Row, 1970), 38.

Struggle for the City

Abbot of St. Vannes, a very well known religious man in Europe.[92] On this particular pilgrimage, when the party came to the holy sites, the abbot would explain to them what each location was, and often with great emotion and eyes filled with tears, he would further describe the nature of Jesus' toils and travails.[93] These experiences were very popular among those who could afford them.

In the eleventh century a series of developments led to renewed conflict between Muslims and Christians. The first, in 1009, was when the Muslim caliph tore down the Church of the Holy Sepulcher, a church built by Constantine to commemorate the resurrection of Christ.[94] Pilgrims on their way to the holy places had to walk past the carnage, and even though a makeshift building was reconstructed, the damage was visible. These pilgrims increased in numbers throughout the century as new pilgrim routes were opened up.[95] The second major event was the Battle of Manzikert in 1071, fought between the Byzantine emperor Romanus and the newly emerging Muslim power from the East, the Seljuk Turks. Romanus lost the battle, and the Turks shut down the pilgrimage routes.[96] Christian pilgrims caught in the crossfire were slaughtered, as were Christian people still living under Muslim rule, since the new overlords were even less sympathetic to "infidels" than their predecessors. All of this led to a call for Crusade against the Muslim "murderers."

For the next two centuries Christian crusaders made their way East to what most of them called *Outremer* ("over the sea" in French). The First Crusade (1096–99) was successful in that the Europeans won over the Muslim forces and held the Kingdom of Jerusalem till 1187. In the middle of that time (1145) a Second Crusade was launched to reinforce the Christian kingdom. After the defeat of Christian forces in 1187 by the Kurdish general Saladin, a Third Crusade left in 1189, led by august kings, such as Richard the Lionheart and Frederick Barbarossa. Richard fought Saladin to a draw, but only received minor concessions. None of the remaining five crusades would

---

92 R. W. Southern, *Making of the Middle Ages* (1953; repr., New Haven, CT: Yale University Press, 1992), 51.
93 Ibid., 52–53.
94 Rodney Stark, *God's Battalions: The Case for the Crusades* (New York: HarperOne, 2009), 90.
95 MacCulloch, *Christianity*, 382.
96 Stark, *God's Battalions*, 92–95.

Struggle for the City

win any victories in *Outremer*, though the Fourth Crusade would witness the conquest of the Byzantine Christians by the Catholics.[97]

While the Crusades were not overall successful in terms of their primary goals, the economic impact of the Crusades is almost impossible to overstate. Crusaders had to raise revenues for the vast expenditure involved in taking armies for extended periods. Most barons owed their lieges only forty days per year of fighting, anything over that had to be paid for, and the same arrangement prevailed in the relationship between knights and their own lieges.[98] Huge tracts of land had to be *mortgaged*, causing a shift in landholdings in France, England, and the Italian city-states. Similarly, Louis VII of France in 1146 levied huge taxes on the clergy to pay for the costs of sending armies to reinforce the aging crusaders of the First Crusade. Since the church started this, it ought to shoulder much of the burden.[99] This may well have been the first time in European history that a tax was levied on *income* rather than merely on property or on import/export of goods.[100]

The *second* economic impact had to do with trade. The crusaders were exposed to exotic new commodities in *Outremer*, causing an increased desire on the part or Europeans for coffee, pepper, silks, and other rarities. "In the great trade-boom which followed the Crusades, when the Mongolian peace opened all Asia to their agents, they [the four great Italian city-states] eclipsed all their rivals in the rising economic boom."[101] In each of these cities in the thirteenth century, "the mercantile classes rose to political power" and set the foundations for the rise of the modern world of trade.[102]

A *third* economic impact was even more profound and concerns primarily the city of Venice. The Venetians, who were the greatest Mediterranean shipbuilders of the time, had been involved with the Crusades ever since the First Crusade in a variety of ways. In 1201 as French leaders began to plan the Fourth

---

97 See Steven Runciman, *A History of the Crusades*, 3 vols. (Cambridge: Cambridge University Press, 1951–54).

98 Steven Runciman, *A History of the Crusades*, vol. 1: *The First Crusade and the Foundation of the Kingdom of Jerusalem* (Cambridge: Cambridge University Press, 1951), 231.

99 Stark, *God's Battalions*, 238.

100 Elizabeth Siberry, *Criticism of Crusading: 1095–1274* (Oxford: Clarendon, 1985), 120.

101 H. R. Trevor-Roper, "The Medieval Italian Capitalists," *Historical Essays* (1957; repr., New York: Harper Torchbooks, 1966), 19.

102 Ibid., 19.

Struggle for the City

Crusade, they made arrangements with the *doge* (duke) of Venice to provide ships to carry 4,500 horsemen (and their horses) and 30,000 foot-soldiers.[103] This required tremendous innovation, including devising leather slings in the lower holds of the ships for suspending the horses in air for transport. Since the ships were ordered on credit, it required the assembling of one of the first great joint-stock corporations with hundreds of investors placing capital in expectation that the crusaders, when they took possession in 1202, would have the required funds, 84,000 silver marks, to pay them back. They did not.[104] Furious at the lack of funds from the French, the *doge* demanded to be taken on the crusade and then instructed the French to attack the rebellious city of Zara on the Dalmatian coast. They plundered that city and then went on, not to *Outremer*, but to Constantinople, which they attacked and also plundered so that the *doge* could recoup the shortfall from the French.[105] One scholar notes, "There never was a greater crime against humanity than the Fourth Crusade."[106] All of this is sordid to the extreme, but the development of a joint-stock corporation for the purpose of large economic projects would spell out the future of world innovation. The Crusades helped at least to launch that innovation in finance.

Thomas Aquinas and the Synthesis of the Catholic Heritage

Thomas Aquinas' (1225–74) position was in many ways similar to that of Augustine. Thomas was born to an affluent family. His parents wished for their bright young son to carry on the family heritage, not in the family business, but as a Benedictine monk, and so at age five he was sent to the Benedictine monastery of Monte Cassino, with the family's expectation that he would one day rise to the position of abbot of that great monastery.[107] Thomas was pleased to take holy orders, but he wanted to be, not a respectable Benedictine monk, but a Dominican, a new order of monastics that were considered

---

103 Peter Ackroyd, *Venice: Pure City* (New York: Nan A. Talese, Doubleday, 2009), 162.
104 Ibid., 162–63.
105 Ibid., 163–65.
106 Steven Runciman, *A History of the Crusades*, vol. 3: *The Kingdom of Acre and the Later Crusades* (Cambridge: Cambridge University Press, 1953), 130.
107 "Thomas Aquinas, St.," *The Oxford Dictionary of the Christian Church*, 3rd ed., ed. F. L. Cross and E. A. Livingstone (Oxford: Oxford University Press, 1997), 1614.

Struggle for the City

to be little more than a cult by many.[108] His family tried various ploys, even locking Thomas in the family villa for two years and offering him a prostitute to show him the pleasures of the flesh in order to dissuade him. (Benedictines by then were known to have an occasional "Saturday night out," but the Dominicans were fervent ascetics!)[109] The young man was adamant, though, and soon afterward, escaped from home and joined a Dominican monastery. After an education at Paris under Albert the Great, among others, Thomas would become the *premier* theologian/philosopher of the Roman Catholic Church in the Middle Ages.[110]

A great man is often enabled to *become* great in part by accidents of timing. Thomas was the beneficiary of scholarly work that was being done by others at about the time of his birth. In the second decade of the thirteenth century a group of scholars, Muslim, Jewish, and Christian, gathered together in Toledo and in an amazing demonstration of scholarly *camaraderie*, translated many of the works of Aristotle into Latin that had previously been available only in Greek and Arabic.[111] This joint effort ought to be seen as "an acute source of embarrassment"[112] for many modernists, who believe that in this period of the "Dark Ages" only prejudice, ignorance, and intolerance were the hallmarks of the day. The attempt on the part of modern scholars to ignore the remarkable advances that were taking place in the early thirteenth century amounts to "the rewriting of history that we associate with Stalinism in the Soviet Union—the 'airbrushing' out of figures and events embarrassing to the current regime."[113] Enlightenment figures wanted their readers to think that advances had come only when the hated church was being marginalized, but this was not the way it *really* was.[114] In the end, only the *Catholics* of the three groups would benefit

---

108 New monastic orders often faced an uphill battle in earning the respect of the wider church.
109 We mean this only in terms of comparison. Benedictines were no longer the paragons of purity they once represented.
110 This affirmation did not come immediately, and in the thirteenth century Thomas' theology came under occasional condemnation.
111 Richard E. Rubenstein, *Aristotle's Children: How Christians, Muslims and Jews Discovered Ancient Wisdom and Illuminated the Middle Ages* (New York: Harvest, 2004), 15.
112 Ibid., 9.
113 Ibid., 284.
114 The Enlightenment is variously dated, but the period of roughly 1650–1800 is commonly accepted.

Struggle for the City

long term from this endeavor, so that "farsighted popes and bishops therefore took the fateful step that Islamic leaders had rejected."[115] Though neither pope nor bishop, Thomas Aquinas was one of those who used this rediscovery of Aristotle to *advance* the learning of Christianity in ways that many have forgotten, including in the areas of economics and politics.[116]

He founded his *economic* views on two basic premises. *First,* Thomas affirmed, based on *natural law* theory, that humans have the right to proprietorship over goods—the right to *private property*. This was, in his view, a natural right, and he further contended that God had given men the power, found in human reason, to use those things that were placed at their disposal.[117]

The Dominican monk held that private ownership was necessary due to the human condition of sin. If a thing belongs to *everyone*, no one takes care of it, and so private ownership of property is necessary to the stewardship of God's gifts to us in this world.[118] Further, since what one possesses is one's own, anything that infringes on this right is a *sin*. Larceny and pillaging, then, are sins against God because by stealth or force one takes that which God has given to someone else.[119] Of course, Thomas recognized that this notion of private ownership could lead to abuse on the part of the rich, and that recognition led him to his other claim.

Thomas's *second* premise was that, again according to natural law, the *use* of all things is available to all persons. Private ownership does not negate the truth that all of the goods of this world have been given to all people. Some obviously have more of the world's goods in their own possession than others. God intends for them to use only that which they need to safeguard against want and neglect. The amount of goods that they possess over and above what they really need is given to them in trust, so they might distribute that to oth-

---

115 Rubenstein, *Aristotle's Children*, 9. Even Byzantine Christianity did not advance very far through this resurgence.
116 We need to make clear that the rediscovery of Aristotle was a mixed bag for the church, especially in the area of *theology*, as the Protestant Reformers would later make clear. But in the fields of mundane knowledge, the recovery of the Greek thinker was revolutionary.
117 Thomas Aquinas, *Summa Theologica,* trans. Fathers of the English Dominican Province (London: Burns Oates & Washbourne, 1912), vol. 10, II-II, Q. 66, ad. 1.
118 Etienne Gilson, *The Christian Philosophy of St. Thomas Aquinas,* trans. L. K. Shook (New York: Random House, 1956), 315.
119 Ibid., 315. An exception to this will be noted in the next paragraph.

Struggle for the City

ers who are in need, should such a need arise. Thomas believed that there was nothing intrinsically immoral about being rich, but that the rich, by virtue of their privilege, had certain *responsibilities* to society. If a rich man does not distribute his wealth to those in need, he is in effect a robber, since those goods actually belong to the needy by right.[120] Further, if a poor man is in *urgent* and *manifest* need, he is justified in taking what he needs from the rich (who are obviously not fulfilling their God-ordained role), even if he is forced to use trickery or violence.[121] It is not wrong for the rich to be rich, but it is also not wrong for the poor to take what they need for subsistence, but only for subsistence. This was *not* a proto-Marxist position of virtually even distribution, however, since the goods were still at the discretion of their owners, and governments were not to be the arbiters of distribution.

In commerce and trade Thomas shows himself to be a truly *medieval* man, and a medieval man of the monastery at that. In buying and selling, Thomas thought that the best scenario was that *no one ever profited* from any exchange, but rather, that persons would simply trade with one another for the things they could not produce for themselves. His was essentially a *barter* system with no profit motive.[122] Thomas conceded that this would probably not work in the real world, since men were motivated by a desire for gain. He then proposed a compromise, one in which profits would be as low as possible on any goods sold or traded, and further urged that the state monitor such transactions to ensure that profits were minimal. Fundamental to his position was the idea that "there is something essentially base in commerce as such."[123] That is, the desire to make a profit in trade was essentially a sinful motivation. This *contrasts* with the position of Augustine that we have already surveyed, for the African father argued that profit in trade is *acceptable* as long as there is no fraud or larceny.

There is one more thing about Thomas' economic theory, and it may be the most astounding thing of all to later interpreters. Recall that in the previous chapter we noted that any thorough system of economics must address four

---

120 Thomas Aquinas, *Summa Theologica*, II–II, Q. 66, Art. 2.
121 Ibid., II–II, Q. 66, Art. 7.
122 Ibid., II–II, Q. 77, Art. 4.
123 Gilson, *Christian Philosophy of St. Thomas Aquinas*, 325.

Struggle for the City

questions: For *whom* is this transaction taking place? *What* is exchanged or consumed? How can one *produce* that which is exchanged? How can one measure *equilibrium* in the exchange, or, to put it in other terms, is the exchange fair? The four issues are final distribution, utility, production, and equilibrium.[124] We noted that both Aristotle and Augustine came close to inventing a complete economic system in terms of these four questions, but both fell slightly short. Where they failed, Thomas succeeded.

In 1250 Albert the Great gave lectures to his students on the recently rediscovered (and translated into Latin) *Nichomachean Ethics* of Aristotle. Thomas, his assistant, took notes on the lectures and then prepared Albert's commentary for publication. Three of the four elements of economic theory are found in Thomas' own later commentary on the *Ethics*, and the fourth is found in his commentary on Aristotle's *Politics*. The same material is found in Thomas's *Summa*. We will present it here in brief. He wrote, "Thus it seems that one person is a friend of another if he acts the same way for a friend as he might for himself."[125] If he does so, he will provide goods or services for the "other." That is *distribution*. Second, the Catholic Doctor wrote, "The prices of things saleable does not depend on their degree of nature since at times a horse fetches a higher price than a slave, but it depends on their usefulness to man."[126] That is *utility*. He also addressed "*equilibrium* conditions,"[127] and "*production*."[128] That covers it all. And in the Scholastic tradition that followed him, his discussions are repeated over and over again. So, why did this not result in a revolution in economic activity? In part it did, but on a very limited scale. Again the question, Why? We will answer that in a later discussion (see chap. 15).

Thomas was a man of his times and his religious heritage. He could not see that the rising tide of mercantilism[129] was compatible with Scriptural teach-

---

124 Mueller, *Redeeming Economics*, 22–26. In this discussion we are indebted to Mueller's interpretation of Thomas and have followed closely his citations of the "Angelic Doctor."
125 Thomas Aquinas, *Commentary on Aristotle's Nichomachean Ethics*, rev. ed., Aristotelian Commentary Series, trans. C. I. Litzinger (1271–72; Notre Dame, IN: Dumb Ox Books, 1993), 548.
126 Ibid., 567.
127 Ibid., 294–96.
128 Thomas Aquinas, *Commentary on Aristotle's Politics*, trans. Richard J. Regan (1271–72; Aristotle's Politics Aristotle's Politics Indianapolis, IN: Hackett, 2007), 1271–72. For all these references we are indebted to Mueller, *Redeeming Economics*.
129 We will discuss mercantilism at length in chap. 15.

Struggle for the City

ings on earning and wealth and longed instead for a "simpler day."[130] More importantly, though, Thomas' own abandonment of wealth for the monastic life surely left its imprint on his understanding of the community of goods and of the profit motivation in any sense. Those who wanted to gain from commerce would eventually, like the rich young ruler, go away grieved, for they seek to own much property (Mark 10:17–22).

How should we evaluate this? Our analysis of the biblical text has made it clear that there is no justification for arguing that all things belong to all people, that the rich have a responsibility simply to *empty* their coffers regularly just as a matter of course to care for the poor, or that a desire to make a *profit* is inherently sinful. Further, though the Bible certainly enjoins us to be charitable, it also teaches that material blessings come from God and that they can be passed on to our children, which means that we are not all required to give them all away in order to be spiritual people. It seems, then, that though we can learn *much* from Tertullian, Clement, Augustine, the monastics, and Thomas, on issues related to economics, at the end of the day their overall theories of biblical economy do *not* completely pass the biblical test.[131] We would note, however, that the times in which they lived may have made it difficult for them to get the whole picture.

One more issue related to Thomas—his understanding of Christian *politics*. With the publication of Thomas' *Summa*, the Christian world received its most comprehensive account of Christian doctrine to that time, but also "the most coherent account of Christian political life."[132] Borrowing from Aristotle again, Thomas expressed the idea that humans are political animals, and that "political life can contribute to human perfection."[133] Thomas' approach is based on the idea that the incarnation of Christ makes the possibility of a truly Christian

---

130 There was a period of "capitalistic" surge in the thirteenth and fourteenth centuries, though this was halted by the Black Plague and did not rise again for about two hundred years.
131 Batson is apparently of the opinion that the Patristic Age lends to us in the twenty-first century a full-orbed perspective on the responsibility of the church, the state, and Christians on these matters. The church is in the final analysis a charity-dispensing body and it ought to treat its purse as communally owned. *Treasure Chest of the Early Christians*, 114–19. We do not concur that this is *all* that these early fathers of the church and monks teach us.
132 Lilla, *Stillborn God*, 46.
133 Ibid., 46–47.

Struggle for the City

state, with a truly Christian monarch, an *actual* possibility.[134] His view is somewhat more optimistic than that of Augustine, in spite of the fact that Thomas did *not* deny that Augustine's view of sin was correct. Certainly Charlemagne's rule was an early *attempt* at something like Thomas' position, though he may have inadvertently made it clear that in the end it is not entirely possible in this present age. The intrusion of Aristotle into the picture is likely what makes Thomas' political theology more sanguine about the possibility of a Christian state.[135] Later, both Calvin and the Puritans of Boston would borrow elements of this position to construct their own political theologies.

Finishing Off the Middle Ages

Before the rise of a permanent mercantile culture, the economies of Europe were almost exclusively agricultural in nature. In regions where the land had all been claimed by families or barons, there was little hope of increasing wealth, except by war or discovery of new lands.[136] This meant that the best hope a poor man had was, either by stealth or ingenuity (or murder), to displace someone ahead of him in the food chain. The characteristic Christian responses to money issues are probably predictable in such a context: *criticisms* of those who were excessively acquisitive and *greedy; exhortations* to those who had wealth to *give much of it away* to those who were destitute and had no prospects for wealth; the *departure* from the culture on the part of some persons very serious about their religious commitment and a flight into *communities* (monasteries) where virtues such as prayer, poverty, and godliness were emphasized; and a *distinction* between the *possession* of goods and the *use* of those same goods. From the Gnostics to Augustine and from the monastic communities to Thomas Aquinas, these were the kinds of reactions that came from the church.

The most common theme during this early period is the affirmation of the need for *charity* on the part of the *rich*. The rich have become that way

---

134 Paul E. Sigmund, "Law and Politics," in *The Cambridge Companion to Aquinas*, ed. Norman Kretzman and Eleonore Stump (Cambridge: Cambridge University Press, 1993), 217–31.

135 Lilla, *Stillborn God*, 47–48.

136 For a clear presentation of this situation, see Thomas G. West, *Vindicating the Founders: Race, Sex, Class, and Justice in the Origins of America* (1997; repr., New York: Rowman & Littlefield, 2000), 37–70, for a broader historical analysis than just recent history.

Struggle for the City

either by inheritance or greed, in the opinion of most critics of the wealthy in the ancient and medieval church. Now, if they will but give of their bounty, they will save their own souls and save many poor peoples' bodies along the way. The typical "money sermons," then would have been exhortations against laziness and greed, but little else besides. Beginning in the sixteenth century a new set of issues comes to the forefront. As the world enters a period in which a *mercantile* class will set the pace for the growth of wealth, and in which new vistas of exploration and discovery are on the horizon, will the church discover any *new* insights for how to deal with the blessings and blight of money? As the Roman Catholic hegemony faces its first real threat in nearly a thousand years, will the new religious orders (the various Reformers) carve out a new perspective on economic issues?

Among the developments that are sometimes forgotten during this era, because of the obviously overwhelming significance of Luther's act of defiance at Wittenberg (and the seemingly greater one at Worms, as we will see in the next chapter), is the establishment of what would come to be known as the School of Salamanca in 1526. Established by Francisco de Vitoria, a Jewish convert to Christianity who had studied at the Sorbonne in Paris, it would become the center of economic thought that shook much of the cultural and political world of Emperor Charles V to its roots. Founded when Vitoria became the chair of theology at the University of Salamanca, Spain, and upon his assembling of a group of "natural law" thinkers, the school was at great pains to revive the thought of Thomas Aquinas whose proofs argued that "all law was God's law and that no man—not even a lord—could know it completely."[137] These "Schoolmen" insisted that all men were generally capable of discerning God's law by reason and were consequently capable of ruling themselves. They further reasoned that since the discovery of the "New World" it had become evident that this was clearly the will of God for mankind.

From this seedbed would come the germinal ideas leading to Locke's concept of the social contract, Adam Smith's and the eighteenth-century philosophers' views on property rights and profit-making, and Carl Menger's theories of mar-

---

137 Eric Robert Morse, *Juggernaut: Why the System Crushes the Only People Who Can Save It* (Austin, TX: New Classic Books, 2010), 30.

Struggle for the City

ginal utility in the nineteenth century. The Spanish Scholastics did not, in fact, succeed in producing a finished system of coherent thought on these subjects, but they did anticipate by many years the eventual consolidation that would inform Adam Smith's *Wealth of Nations* and the Austrian school of economics of another generation. (Again, we will cover all of these issues in later chapters.) Among the many contributors from this school and other places during the late Scholastic period are Jean Buridan (1300–58) and his pupil Nicolas Oresme (1325–82) on the theory of money, Martin de Azpilcueta (1493–1596) on the relationship between supply and pricing, and Thomas de Vio, Cardinal Cajetan (1468–1534), defending the morality of *foreign exchange* markets and the understanding of the future value of money.

Perhaps most important for our study were several contributors to the modern theory of value as a function of subjective choice and determination—the idea that any object has more value than merely the sum of its material components and the labor attached to its production. That is, *each person* has a (or more than one) scale of *personal* valuation that determines his or her own conception of the *value* of any object. Augustine had commented on this subjective valuation in *City of God* and men like Pierre de Jean Olivi (1248–98) and 150 years later San Bernardino of Siena (1380–1444), Luis Saravia de la Calle (sixteenth century), Cardinal Juan de Lugo (1583–1660) and Luis de Molina (1535–1600). As Thomas Woods put it, "The just price of goods is not fixed according to the *utility* given to them by man, as if, *caeteris paribus*, the nature and the need of the use given to then determined the quantity of price…. It depends on the relative *appreciation* which each man has for the use of the good."[138]

These ideas and many more become the driving force(s) that fuel the economic, political, and theological revolution that we know as the Reformation. That will be the focus of our next chapter.

---

138 Thomas E. Woods Jr., *How the Catholic Church Built Western Civilization* (Washington, DC: Regnery, 2005), 160 (emphases added). The paragraphs above are indebted to Woods, *How the Catholic Church*; Morse, *Juggernaut*; and Stark, *Victory of Reason*. See also the first volume in Murray N. Rothbard's massive work *The Austrian Perspective on History of Economic Thought*, vol. 1: *Economic Thought before Adam Smith* (Auburn, AL: Ludwig von Mises Institute, 2006).

Struggle for the City

Chapter 12

The Reformation and Political Economy

JOHN FLETCHER HURST HAS WRITTEN a book entitled *Short History of the Reformation*.[1] It is certainly possible to get the main events of the Reformation out in a little over a hundred pages, but the full story is extraordinarily complex and, for some of us, has occupied years of our academic life in an attempt really to understand all of the twists and turns of this revolution in Europe. For our purposes in this book, the Reformation is being presented as a largely religious and theological revolution (or set of revolutions) that also had huge political and economic ramifications. While we are convinced that the initial movement was theological and religious and that theological issues continued to drive the reforms for decades, we also know that there was more to it than simply that. Political, philosophical, and economic concerns were intertwined with the theological, and for good reason. It is the case that "financial... concerns are not separate from but rather an extension of theological (in this case Christian) beliefs" in ways that are profound and complex in the Reformation.[2] The same can be said of political concerns, as we will attempt to demonstrate.

---

1   John F. Hurst, *Short History of the Reformation* (New York: Harper & Bros., 1884).
2   David W. Hall and Matthew D. Burton, *Calvin and Commerce: The Transforming Power of Calvinism in Market Economies* (Philipsburg, NJ: P&R, 2009), xvii. These authors make this case specifically about the work of Calvin, but similar comments could be offered about at least some of the other major Reformers.

BACKGROUND TO THE REFORMATION: A BRIEF
INTRODUCTION TO THE RENAISSANCE

The Scholastic Movement (thirteenth century and after), which we discussed in the previous chapter, was a kind of "Little Renaissance" in that it brought classical learning (Aristotle, and eventually Plato) to the fore, but it was a movement still generally under the governance of churchly direction, even if the universities were not controlled by the papacy. In the fourteenth, fifteenth, and sixteenth centuries a Renaissance appeared that was more expansive in terms of the areas of culture that were involved and in its extension beyond the universities. We need to take brief cognizance of this Renaissance because of its implications for political economy and for its importance to the Reformation that followed.

The Renaissance began as a *humanist* endeavor to recover the classical world and to appropriate its treasures for a modern context. The term "humanism" was not used at the time, and the term does not imply that they rejected God, church, or religion, but it is still the right word.[3] The Renaissance began in the wake of the Black Death of 1347–51, which probably killed somewhere between thirty and sixty percent of the population of Europe. People thought they were experiencing the *end* of the world.[4] As the renewal movement progressed and flowered into the beautiful works of art and literature that we associate with this period, it would seem to many that they had experienced the *rebirth* of that world.

In many ways the Renaissance became a new way of looking at the world, but it incorporated an old way of doing it. It is not insignificant that Italy became the springboard for the renewal since the Italian peninsula had the advantage of "the encyclopedia of antiquity buried beneath it."[5] The emphasis on "humanism" more than anything else was a focus on *freedom*. This focus on freedom included at least two elements—*free will* in a theological sense and *freedom of speech* in a more political sense.[6] The form of freedom in the first sense would come to clash with Reformation ideals, at least with most of the

---

3   Diarmaid MacCulloch, *Christianity* (New York: Penguin Books, 2009), 574.
4   Rudolph W. Heinze, *Reform and Conflict: From the Medieval World to the Wars of Religion*, Baker History of the Church 4 (Grand Rapids, MI: Baker, 2005), 19.
5   MacCulloch, *Christianity*, 575.
6   Bard Thompson, *Humanists and Reformers: A History of the Renaissance and Reformation* (Grand Rapids, MI: Eerdmans, 1996), 343–49, 390, 648–49.

Struggle for the City

major Reformers, but the freedom of speech would echo down the halls of Wittenberg and Geneva even as they would in Florence.

One key figure is Niccolò Machiavelli. A Florentine, Machiavelli came along at the height of the Renaissance and was learned in languages and in philosophy. A man with a broad and extensive résumé, his most important contribution was his political essay, *The Prince*, a book he dedicated to his chief patron, Lorenzo ("the Magnificent") de' Medici. This work represents a shift from *idealism* in politics to *realism*.[7] He primarily describes how political power is acquired, and only secondarily how it should be used. He contends that a prince is not necessarily a man known for strong ethics and that this is entirely appropriate. The one man who exemplified Machiavelli's model prince at the time was Duke Cesare Borgia, a ruthless but very successful son of Pope Alexander VI, Rodrigo Borgia.[8] He held up as laudable Borgia's actions after becoming the Duke of Valeninois, wherein he assassinated his chief opponents.[9] On the other hand, Machiavelli urged princes not to take the land or the women of those they are forced to kill, since that will create a rebel class among their sons.[10] In addition, as to the question whether a ruler ought to desire to be loved by his people, the Renaissance scholar believed it was better for a ruler to be *feared* over being loved.[11] For Machiavelli, all of this was necessary in order to preserve the peace and to enable the duke to govern a *stable* and *secure* land, which should be the *chief* goal of any prince.

Machiavelli went on to question what he considered to be the Renaissance assumption that humans are both *good* and *rational*. The renewal movement in general sought to rectify what was considered to be the darker side of the Augustinian view of man with a more Pelagian ideal of moral goodness. Machiavelli rejected that. Since human evil is a reality, and good princes recognize that, this is

---

7 Mark Lilla, *The Stillborn God* (New York: Vintage Books, 2007), 107.
8 Niccolò Machiavelli, *The Prince,* trans. and ed. Peter Bondanella, Oxford World's Classics (1532; Oxford: Oxford University Press, 2005), 15. He also notes the weaknesses of Borgia's style, namely, that he rose to power on the backs of others.
9 Ibid., 57–62.
10 Ibid., 58.
11 Ibid., 57–58. As Machiavelli says, "Men are less hesitant about injuring someone who makes himself loved than one who makes himself feared;… fear is sustained by a dread of punishment that will never abandon you."

Struggle for the City

the very fact that brings about the *need* for government.[12] This is perhaps the origin of what later scholars will call *Realpolitik*, that governing is about *hard* and *brutal* realities. Monarchs need to be realistic about the state of affairs and recognize that hard realities call for hard actions. Machiavelli exemplified that in a stark manner.

The other aspect of the Renaissance that will come to bear on our examination is its *literary* focus. Figures such as Desiderius Erasmus and Johannes Reuchlin, with their major accomplishments with the Greek and Hebrew text, will impact the coming generation of Reformers, though not at the very beginning. Neither Erasmus nor Reuchlin was amenable to the Reformers (Reuchlin being great uncle to Philipp Melanchthon), though they were both aware of Catholic "difficulties."[13] Erasmus' publication of the Greek New Testament in 1516 will prove to be a *monumental* aid to Luther and Calvin and others in their exegetical endeavors, especially since he also provided a new Latin translation to go along with it, to help show where and why the Latin Vulgate got it wrong.[14] The Greek New Testament, the first to appear in the relatively new age of the printing press, was one of the most important accomplishments of the time. Reuchlin provided similar services for the Hebrew Old Testament. The generation of scholars that would include the major Reformers would now be able to read the Bible in its original languages, an opportunity that actually made the Reformation possible and whose importance virtually cannot be exaggerated. Now, on to Martin Luther.

MARTIN LUTHER AND THE THEOLOGICAL AND POLITICAL EARTHQUAKE

The Saxon reformer Martin Luther actually first came to the wider public eye as a Reformer due to an issue of church *finances*.[15] On October 31, 1517 Luther posted a document that he titled, "Ninety-Five Theses," to the door of the castle

---

12 Thompson, *Humanists and Reformers*, 301–3.
13 "Reuchlin, Johannes," *Oxford Dictionary of the Christian Church*, 3rd ed., ed. F. L. Cross and E. A. Livingstone (Oxford: Oxford University Press, 1997), 1389; Justo L. Gonzàlez, *The Story of Christianity*, vol. 2: *The Reformation to the Present Day* (New York: HarperCollins, 1985), 9–12, 42–43.
14 MacCulloch, *Christianity*, 596.
15 He was already known to some members of his monastic order, the Augustinians, as a feisty doctor of theology who had been agitating for theological and ethical reforms in the church for more than a year previous to the Ninety-Five-Theses posting.

church in the city of Wittenberg, where Luther was professor of Bible at the university of the same name. This was the conventional way of "choosing" someone to a public debate. The person he was challenging was a Dominican friar named John Tetzel, and the occasion was the sale of *indulgences*. An indulgence was a certificate issued by the church hierarchy that granted the recipient or someone of his choosing some leniency regarding *purgatory*. The Roman Catholic Church taught that nearly all Christians would enter purgatory at death in order to be "purged" for the actual sins they committed in life. While Christ had atoned for original sin at the cross, that sacrifice was not sufficient to remit the penalty for *actual* sins, an atonement that would be secured by long years of suffering in the fires of purgatory.[16] However, the church claimed to have the authority to make some exceptions in the case of people who had done some extraordinary duty in service of the church (such as participation in the official Crusades), or in special cases, to those who made financial contributions to the church.

The Crisis

In 1517, Pope Leo X issued an indulgence to be sold in parts of Germany to procure funds in part to finish the construction of St. Peter's Basilica. He was assisted in that endeavor by Albrecht, archbishop of Magdeburg, an extreme example of the European noblemen who regarded the church as an asset to be exploited for their families. Albrecht was also seeking papal dispensation to become archbishop also of Mainz.[17] The proceeds from the sale of indulgences would enable Leo to continue his church construction and enable Albrecht to pay back the bankers from whom he had borrowed money to get the papal dispensation. Any person who made the designated indulgence contribution would be given a receipt *certifying* that a dead relative could be released from purgatory as compensation for purchasing the indulgence. John Tetzel was selling these indulgences in the city of Jüterbock, not far from Wittenberg, and was making extravagant claims: "As soon as the coin in the coffer rings, / The soul from purgatory springs."[18] Some Witten-

---

16 Bernhard Lohse, *Martin Luther: An Introduction to His Life and Work*, trans. Robert C. Schultz (Philadelphia: Fortress, 1986), 8–11, 42–45.
17 Diarmaid MacCulloch, *The Reformation* (New York: Viking, 2003), 117.
18 Roland Bainton, *Here I Stand: A Life of Martin Luther* (Nashville: Abingdon, 1950), 78.

Struggle for the City

bergers had purchased the indulgences and when Luther found out, he challenged Tetzel to a debate.

The German Bible professor believed that the sale of indulgences represented nothing less than *extortion* on the part of the church, an extortion made possible because the common people gullibly believed that such transactions actually could take place. He, however, had become convinced, in his study of the Bible, that indulgences were not real, and concluded that, if the pope actually believed that purgatory *did* exist, and that he *could* exempt people from suffering there, he ought to let *everyone* out, not merely the ones whose families were financially able to make the required contribution.[19] But Luther viewed the doctrine related to indulgences, and many other doctrines of the church, as *distortions* of the gospel, a gospel Luther had come to grips with over the course of several years of teaching Psalms, Galatians, and Romans. By sometime late in 1515 he had come to affirm that justification was granted by God directly to the soul that believed in Christ and Christ alone for salvation.[20] The church, on the other hand, had largely taught that justification was granted by God through the sacraments of the church to those who lived lives of appropriate faith and charity and who were in good standing with the church when they died. This was due in part to the wedding of Greek (Aristotelian) philosophy with Christian doctrine, wherein "reconciliation was understood as effecting a new ontological relationship between the divine and the human."[21] Luther would seek to change that.

The shift in the doctrine of justification caused by Luther's teaching had implications that were far reaching. It made it clear to those who affirmed it that the focus was now on the *individual*. "Every man, individually, is an epitome," in the Lutheran understanding.[22] The locus of authority for Luther was

---

19 Later, around 1530, Luther would reject the doctrine of purgatory altogether.

20 Alister E. McGrath, *Luther's Theology of the Cross: Martin Luther's Theological Breakthrough* (Malden, MA: Blackwell, 1985), 141–47. MacCulloch places it later, in 1517. *Reformation*, 123.

21 Timothy George, *The Theology of the Reformers* (Nashville: Broadman, 1988), 63. In order to substantiate his assessment, George quotes in his study in this place from Catholic scholar Hans Küng, *Justification: The Doctrine of Karl Barth and a Catholic Response*, trans. Thomas Collins, Edmund E. Tolk, and David Granskou (New York: Thomas Nelson, 1964).

22 A. S. P. Woodhouse, *Puritanism and Liberty: Being the Army Debates, 1647–49* (London: J. M. Dent and Sons, 1938), 40, quoted in Sacvan Bercovitch, *The Puritan Origins of the American Self* (New Haven, CT: Yale University Press, 1975), 11.

Struggle for the City

Scripture, but the hinge on which that authority turned in the lives of people was now not the church but the self—the individual choice to believe the gospel. Protestantism's most radical contribution to both the theology and the politics of the time lay here in its doctrine of *justification*. Each man stood alone before God with nothing between save Christ alone. Since man stood alone before God, he might also stand alone before the king. In Luther's view, as in the Protestant view in general, that king (or noble, or prince) did not necessarily have the authority of the church or the Bible supporting his every whim.[23] The individual, in Reformation Europe, had a new role over against that same role in the past.[24] Eventually, Luther's doctrine of justification came to be determinative of his position on his whole understanding of theology, hermeneutics, the canon of Scripture, and his views on human nature.[25]

It is not our purpose in this chapter to follow the career of Martin Luther after these events, but a brief word is necessary to lay the groundwork for what follows. Luther's posting sparked a series of debates between himself and several significant theological heavyweights from the church, especially Johann Maier of Eck. This all culminated in Luther's being summoned to the Imperial Diet in April 1521, the annual gathering of emperor, electors, princes, and leading churchmen to carry out imperial political business. That year, one item of business was a certain Saxon Bible professor who had aroused papal ire and would now be dealt with in what amounted to a court of law. Luther stood before the Diet, defended himself, and claimed that he would stand by his writings since he was convinced by Scripture that he was correct, and he would not allow papal decrees or decisions of church councils to *trump* the Bible.[26] The Diet eventually condemned Luther's writings and called for his formal arrest

---

23 We will explore in the pages ahead the various views on governmental authority held by various wings of the Reformation.
24 These ideas were present in some sense in Renaissance thought, but the differences between the two understandings of human freedom were profound—the Renaissance focus was not on justification by faith, or upon the reality of divine judgment, or on the depravity and bondage of the soul; quite the contrary. Those doctrines in many ways drove the Reformers.
25 James R. Payton Jr., *Getting the Reformation Wrong* (Downers Grove, IL: InterVarsity Press, 2010), 94–95.
26 The literature is immense, but see, for instance, Thompson, *Humanists and Reformers*, 381–412; Heiko A. Oberman, *Luther: Man between God and the Devil*, trans. Eileen Walliser-Schwarzbart (New York: Doubleday, 1992), 175–206; Bainton, *Here I Stand*, 68–190.

Struggle for the City

and trial as a heretic. He was successful in eluding arrest due to the support of the elector (duke) of Saxony, and he would go on to lead a major portion of the Holy Roman Empire to support his reforming efforts.

Impact on the Church

The Reformation began as a debate over the church's *finances*. And as it progressed, the church's finances were affected dramatically. The eventual loss of several provinces of the Holy Roman Empire, parts of the Low Countries, numerous "free" cities, England, and other regions would make a huge impact on Roman Catholic finances and would result in more than a century of cajoling, debate, war, and intrigue. The Reformation begun by the writings and debates of the Saxon professor Luther would *remake* Europe and the new world being explored and colonized at the same time into a completely different image than had prevailed for the previous millennium.

Reformation theology was not simply a new view of one's relation to God, as if that were something isolated from the rest of reality. A new view of one's relation to God affects everything in life, including how one understands politics, economics, and society. "The noted Reformation scholar Roland Bainton once remarked that when Christianity takes itself seriously, it must either renounce the world or master it."[27] The former attitude was characteristic of much of medieval Christianity with its monastic orders, as we have seen, with its notion that holiness entailed retreat from the world and with its exemplification of the value of poverty.

Vocation and the Priesthood of All Believers

The Reformers, on the other hand, attempted to master the world under the *hand of God*. One of Luther's greatest contributions to the church of his time and after was his understanding of the nature of *vocation*. In the Middle Ages the notion had developed that the clergy of various kinds were the truly *holy* ones,

---

27 Quoted in Alister E. McGrath, *Reformation Thought: An Introduction*, 3rd ed. (Malden, MA: Blackwell, 1999), 263.

Struggle for the City

since they were pursuing a vocation that entailed separation from secular life and a dedication to the service of God exclusively. This belief led to a "two-tiered" understanding of the nature of Christian humanity. One segment of humanity sought the life of holiness because they sought a vocation of holy living. The rest of humanity was mired in the things of *this* world and had a much less likelihood of ever attaining salvation. This was the major conviction that had driven Luther to join an Augustinian monastery.[28] When he abandoned monasticism, he also abandoned its understanding of human spirituality.

Luther the Protestant contended that all persons were called to a vocation, and that whether that vocation were "sacred" or "secular," the important thing was to follow the calling of God on one's life.[29] All persons should work, for work was honorable. "God wills that man should work, and without work He will give him nothing. Conversely, God will not give him anything because of his labor, but solely out of His goodness and blessing."[30] Even Adam was called to work, and even that in his pre-fallen condition. Luther noted, "How much more perfect [work] would have been in that garden in the state of innocence. But it is appropriate here also to point out that man was created not for leisure but for work, even in the state of innocence."[31] This conviction was closely tied to Luther's understanding of the priesthood of *all* Christians. The calling to the ministry does not make one closer to God, nor does it give the minister or "priest" a special standing before the Lord. All Christians are priests, and therefore all Christians have equal access to God and have equal responsibility to help others find the Lord in their own lives.[32]

For the Reformers, the real vocation of the Christian "lay in serving God in the world."[33] Real Christianity was to be found in the cities, villages, and rural life of the secular world, not in the cathedrals or in monastic cells. It is important

---

28 Bainton, *Here I Stand*, 37–51.
29 Martin Luther, "The Freedom of the Christian" (1520), in *Three Treatises*, 2nd rev. ed. (Minneapolis: Augsburg, 1998), 23.
30 Martin Luther, *The Christian in Society II*, trans. and ed. Walther I. Brandt, vol. 45 of *Luther's Works*, American Edition, ed. Jaroslav Pelikan and Helmut T. Lehmann (1522–24; Minneapolis: Fortress, 1962), 327.
31 Martin Luther, "Exposition of Gen. 2:14" (1535), quoted in *What Luther Says: An Anthology*, comp. Ewald M. Plass (St. Louis: Concordia, 1959), 3:1494.
32 Martin Luther, "The Babylonian Captivity of the Church" (1520), in *Three Treatises*, 76.
33 McGrath, *Reformation Thought*, 263.

Struggle for the City

to recognize that medieval Christianity was almost totally *monastic* in nature, especially before the rise of the universities around the year 1200. The monastery was all there was to the Christian heritage.[34] The universities changed that, but only partly. The rise of the universities meant that there was now some aspect of Western culture not dominated by the monastic orders, but in effect the culture of the church was still almost thoroughly monastic until the Reformation began to spread across Europe. The monastic mind-set was, however, increasingly alien to the common man, especially after the printing press made information more and more available to more and more people.

A classic example comes from one of the famous devotional writings of the late Middle Ages, Thomas à Kempis' *On the Imitation of Christ*, the first chapter of book 1 being titled "Of the Imitation of Christ, and Contempt for the World and All Its Vanities."[35] Thomas died in 1471 and his book was popular in Germany in Luther's day. Its very title and first chapter title illustrates the point.[36] For monastic spirituality it is the cloister over against the world. This doctrine left little hope for the farmer, the mechanic, and the blacksmith. Luther's doctrine would change that, and his views on *vocation*, as much as his teaching on justification, fired the imagination of the German people. In fact, the two teachings—justification and vocation—are directly related to each other. Justification by faith alone entailed a *new view* of vocation, and the new understanding of vocation contains implications for the political and economic orders that were monumental. Over time, these new understandings would change the worlds of government and economy just as dramatically as Luther's view on justification changed the ecclesiastical world.

How did this new view of vocation work itself out? The secular realm is part of God's territory, but so is the church. For Luther, the church is the *communio sanctorum*, the sacred gathering. Its members are *all* priests. The Saxon Reformer developed these ideas early on in his analysis of monastic vows written in 1521. Though he did not at that time reject monasticism wholesale, he

---

34 Ernst Robert Curtius, *European Literature and the Latin Middle Ages*, trans. Willard R. Trask, Bollingen Series 36 (1953; Princeton, NJ: Princeton University Press, 1990).
35 Thomas a Kempis, *The Imitation of Christ*, intro. John R. Tyson (New York: Barnes & Noble), 2004.
36 McGrath points this out in *Reformation Thought*, 264.

Struggle for the City

denied that only monks and priests were "called." Rather, as we have noted, Luther applied the notion of vocation to every individual, thus sanctifying even "secular" vocations. One might even say that Luther's approach sanctifies *especially* secular vocations, since clerical work was *already* sanctified. Since all believers are priests to one another, and all have the responsibility of serving one another, the clergy no longer had an exclusive right to the concept of a "calling." All are called.

"Calling" understood in this way had huge implications both for church and for the community. "Luther brought down the community of saints out of heaven and down to earth."[37] He did not reject the clergy as a calling or profession, but rather argued that other work is sanctified along with the calling to pastor. In addition, it is only with a non-Catholic ecclesiology (doctrine of the "church") that any concept of the sanctity of work can be articulated. The reason is that Catholicism sacralizes the church in such a way that nothing else *can* be considered sacred. Its sacralization of the communion of the saints in a manner unique to all other societies means that the workplace could *never* be seen as sacred in the manner that Luther articulated.

This constituted a major revision of the church's understanding of the nature of work and of the life of the common man. In terms of community Luther's view made it clear that "[t]he 'Saint's Rest' was in the world to come: in this he was to labour at his calling. Business henceforth became a sacred office in which it was a man's bounden duty to do his utmost *ad majorem Dei gloriam*."[38] The fact that Europe was about to pass from an agricultural/manorial economy to one that entailed greater trade, and a focus on capital certainly would aid the reform movements.[39] "Man was no longer made for a function: a function was made for man."[40] Luther would do his part to help to create the new world.

---

37 Paul Althaus, *The Theology of Martin Luther*, trans. Robert C. Schultz (Philadelphia: Fortress, 1966), 298.
38 R. H. Murray, *The Political Consequences of the Reformation: Studies in Sixteenth-Century Political Thought* (1926; repr., New York: Russell & Russell, 1960), 61.
39 J. A. Sharpe, "Economy and Society," in *The Sixteenth Century*, Short Oxford History of the British Isles, ed. Patrick Collinson (Oxford: Oxford University Press, 2002), 17–45.
40 Murray, *Political Consequences of the Reformation*, 61.

Struggle for the City

Two Kingdoms

In comparison to other contemporary voices calling for reform, Luther was much more conservative than many, but one aspect of his work served to *undermine* the nature of the Catholic view of the relationship between church and state.[41] Pre-Christian pagan conceptions of the state fused religion and state, as we noted in the earlier historical analysis. The emperors were worshiped in ancient Rome. Jewish-Christian understandings of church and state tended to set church and state, if not in opposition, at least as contrasting and separate spheres. That recognition fueled the Augustinian understanding of the Two Cities as well as the medieval distinction between emperor and pope or patriarch, though, as we have also seen, the pre-Christian unity of these spheres sometimes surfaced in the medieval world.

During late antiquity a fusion between state and religious authority was often attempted. Papal supremacy over political rule was claimed by Pope Gelasius in 494. He wrote to the emperor Anastasius, "There are, august emperor, two means by which the world is chiefly ruled, the sacred authority of the priesthood and the royal power. Of these the responsibility of the priests is more weighty."[42] Perhaps the best example of this assertion of authority occurred when Pope Gregory VII excommunicated Emperor Henry IV, declaring his subjects no longer under his rule. Henry made his way to the pope's winter lodgings in the Alps, knelt in the snow for three days and finally had his infraction absolved, reluctantly, by the pope. Henry would have the last word, as he later besieged Gregory in Rome.[43]

This wrestling with one another on the part of popes and kings or emperors over who really had the power was a common conflict in the Middle Ages. Luther called for a kind of return to Augustine on this matter in one respect, though his views are not completely consistent with those of the African father.

---

41 By "conservative" we mean that Luther was willing to conserve more of both Catholic theology and especially liturgy than Reformers such as John Calvin, Ulrich Zwingli, Thomas Müntzer, Menno Simmons, and Martin Bucer. See the discussion in Bainton, *Here I Stand*, 265–85.

42 Quoted in Brian Tierney, *The Crisis of Church and State, 1050–1300* (Englewood Cliffs, NJ: Prentice-Hall, 1964), 13.

43 Justo L. Gonzàlez, *The Story of Christianity,* vol 1: *The Early Church to the Dawn of the Reformation* (New York: HarperCollins, 1984), 286–91.

Struggle for the City

Augustine's approach saw the Two Cities as constituting a duality, but a duality that would hopefully be short-lived as the two parts (or the many parts) would finally work together as a semi-sanctified Christian society. Luther's approach would not be exactly the same, though he does maintain the idea of a duality.

Luther's approach to the relation between church and state has often been referred to as the doctrine of the "Two Kingdoms," though scholars generally recognize that the German Reformer never used that actual phrase himself.[44] Here is what he said:

> For God has established two kinds of government among men. The one is spiritual; it has no sword, but it has the word, by means of which men are to become good and righteous, so that with this righteousness they may attain eternal life. He administers this righteousness through the word, which he has committed to the preachers. The other kind is worldly government, which works through the sword so that those who do not want to be good and righteous to eternal life may be forced to become good and righteous in the eyes of the world. He administers this righteousness through the sword.[45]

Luther's views on this matter have been often misunderstood, even by Luther scholars.[46] Some have argued, for instance, that Luther contended for the autonomy of the secular authority from the sacred.[47] Conversely, a famous religious sociologist, Ernst Troeltsch, contended that Luther had promoted a dual morality for Christians, pitting the Decalogue over against natural law

---

44 Lohse, *Martin Luther*, 188.
45 Martin Luther, *Lectures on Isaiah: Chapters 1–39*, trans. and ed. Herbert J. A. Bouman, vol. 16 of *Luther's Works*, American Edition, ed. Jaroslav Pelikan and Helmut T. Lehmann (1527; Minneapolis: Fortress, 1969), 99.
46 For an assessment of how Luther has been misinterpreted, even in his own house, see William J. Wright, *Martin Luther's Understanding of God's Two Kingdoms: A Response to the Challenge of Skepticism*, Texts and Studies in Reformation and Post-Reformation Thought (Grand Rapids, MI: Baker, 2010), 17–43.
47 Reinhold Seeberg, *Textbook of the History of Doctrines*, vol. 2: *History of Doctrines in the Middle and Early Modern Ages*. trans. Charles E. Hay (Grand Rapids, MI: Baker, 1966), 273.

Struggle for the City

morality.[48] These understandings do not represent Luther's position. Rather, Luther contended that there are two "governments," that is, God rules in two ways, in a secular and a spiritual manner. God rules through the sword of secular authority and through the word of the church's proclamation.[49]

The two-kingdom idea was not primarily a political notion for Luther, but rather represented his overall worldview.[50] It underlay his whole understanding of the relationship between God and Satan, heavenly versus temporal, law and gospel, and so was a permeating or controlling idea in his theology.[51] Further, secular authority comprehends more than merely government and the state but includes all secular functions. In other words, "reason" governs all questions about life in this world.[52] Luther believed in natural law, though he preferred phrases such as "law of creation," and he believed that this natural law came from God and that it was good, though not entirely sufficient in itself.[53] The kingdom of this world was consistent with the law of creation, but the kingdom of Christ with the work of the Holy Spirit. The two were not opposed to one another, but they were also not the same in Luther's understanding.[54]

Beyond that, Luther argued that government can and should exist in such a way that cares for the needs of the people, and if it does not, then the people should stand up for what is right. However, he was opposed to "revolution" unless it could be established that the ruler was insane. He held to this view because he "derives the state, not from below, but exclusively from above, from God's plan of salvation [and] insists on its distinct character as a state whose essence is authority."[55] Since the authority of the state is directly granted by God, rebellion is virtually *unthinkable*. This lay, partly, behind his refusal to

---

48 Ernst Troeltsch, *The Social Teaching of the Christian Churches*, trans. Olive Wyon, Library of Theological Ethics (1931; repr., Louisville: Westminster/John Knox, 1992), 2:507–8; see Wright, *Martin Luther's Understanding*, 26.
49 Lohse, *Martin Luther*, 189.
50 Althaus, *Theology of Martin Luther*, 253.
51 Wright, *Martin Luther's Understanding*, 114.
52 Lohse, *Martin Luther*, 192.
53 Martin Luther, "Commentary on Psalm 101" (1534), in *Selected Psalms II*, trans. and ed. Jaroslav Pelikan, vol. 13 of *Luther's Works*, American Edition, ed. Jaroslav Pelikan and Helmut T. Lehmann (Minneapolis: Fortress, 1956), 160.
54 Wright, *Martin Luther's Understanding*, 127–71.
55 Karl Holl, *The Cultural Significance of the Reformation*, trans. Karl and Barbara Hertz and John H. Lichtblau, Living Age Books (New York: Meridian Books, 1959), 50.

Struggle for the City

support the peasants in their 1525 revolt against the nobility.[56] Luther did, however, advance the notion that civic freedom of conscience was one of the implications of justification by faith, and, since he believed that civil authority was granted by God, but not in an absolute sense, his view "set a rigid limit to the absolute power of the state."[57] John Calvin would later take this matter in a direction that Luther refused to go.[58] The churches should be free to call their own pastors, and to govern their affairs without interference from the state. "The realm of faith needs freedom, but the realm of temporal order needs coercion and rules. True Christians can know clearly where the boundaries lay, but there are very few true Christians, so they ought to submit to worldly powers."[59] This was not an airtight philosophical position, but the broad contours are pretty clear.

Luther rejected the idea that the pope should rule over the secular realm. The problem, Luther contended, lay in a general misunderstanding on the part of the Catholic Church about the nature of ministry, the nature of the church, and the nature of Christ. The Christ we worship is first of all Christ crucified. The ministry of the church ought also to be a ministry of the cross. When popes assumed the governance over kings and emperors, they were attempting to be vicars of Christ glorified, when they ought to be vicars of Christ crucified.[60] The pope's task is not to rule the world but to propagate the gospel.[61]

Christians, of course, are citizens of both kingdoms in Luther's understanding. Because of that, they ought to exercise stewardship in the civic realm.[62] Their first allegiance is to Christ and his church, but the secular realm is established also by God and so demands their allegiance.[63] For Luther, the secular realm ought also to honor Christ and carry on its "ministry" in conscious service of Christ. As George notes, one should not confuse Luther's distinction between two governments as some kind of early version of separation of church and

---

56 Bainton, *Here I Stand*, 270–77.
57 Holl, *Cultural Significance of the Reformation*, 51.
58 See the discussion on Calvin below.
59 MacCulloch, *Reformation*, 152.
60 McGrath, *Luther's Theology of the Cross*, 176–81.
61 George, *Theology of the Reformers*, 99.
62 As we will see, Luther's position on this will differ from the Radical Reformers.
63 William A. Mueller, *Church and State in Luther and Calvin: A Comparative Study* (Nashville: Broadman, 1954), 36–45.

Struggle for the City

state.[64] "The pastor urged his flock to obey the temporal authority, while the prince protected the church from the violence of the mob."[65] The believer is part of both governments, but in each, Christ is supreme.

JOHN CALVIN: REFORMING ALL OF LIFE

John Calvin was the most important leader in the second generation of the reform that swept across northern and parts of Western Europe.[66] If there is any one unifying characteristic of Calvin's reforming ideology, it is that all of life must be shaped by Scripture to bring glory to God.[67] This overriding conviction drove Calvin to articulate and push for reform in every realm of life in the city of Geneva, where he spent most of his ministry years. This conviction caused both Calvin and the leaders of the city great consternation and contains many controversial elements, but the end result is a massive and thorough worldview centered around the glorification of God in this age.

Geneva

Calvin came to Geneva in 1536, having only within the previous three years moved his allegiance to the new religious reforming ideals sweeping Europe. He had just published a medium-sized volume titled *The Institutes of the Christian Religion*, a book that gained immediate recognition and made the twenty-six-year-old author a sensation nearly overnight.[68] On his way to Strasbourg, where he hoped to rent a small house and settle down to the quiet life of being a Christian scholar, he was forced to make his way through Geneva, because the road to Basel and Strasbourg was blocked due to troop movements as war dragged on between Francis I of France and Charles V, Holy Roman Emperor. Calvin was "forced to go

---

64 George, *Theology of the Reformers*, 101.
65 Ibid.
66 Bruce Gordon, *Calvin* (New Haven, CT: Yale University Press, 2009), 121–44. This is probably the best biography of Calvin, simply as the story of his life.
67 George, *Theology of the Reformers*, 163, 172.
68 Herman Selderhuis, *John Calvin: A Pilgrim's Life*, trans. Albert Gootjes (Downers Grove, IL: InterVarsity Press, 2009), 34–58.

the long way around, by way of Geneva, where he stayed overnight."[69] He stayed more than overnight.

William Farel lived in Geneva, having recently been hired by the town leadership to reform the churches of the city and to help make a complete break with Roman Catholicism. Other Swiss cities were doing the same, and only a year before Calvin's arrival, the people of Geneva had thrown the Catholic leadership out of the city, had eliminated the statues and relics, and had demanded religious reforms from the city council. "The Genevan Reformation *preceded* Calvin's arrival."[70] Before that, the bishop of Geneva had ruled the city; now it was under *magistrates*. Farel convinced Calvin to join him in the task of bringing substantial biblical reforms to the churches of Geneva, but only after first threatening him with *condemnation* from God. The reform task took the rest of Calvin's years with the exception of one three-year interruption.

That God Would Be All

Calvin believed that all of life should come under the guiding hand of God and his Word.[71] Representing Calvin's vision, Abraham Kuyper said, "The religion of man upon this earth should consist in one echoing of God's glory, as our Creator and Inspirer."[72] Like Luther, the Geneva Reformer contended that one of the problems with historic Catholicism was that it tended to a two-tiered spirituality, with some persons being expected to bring all of their life under the rule of God (the various clergy), while others (the laity) did not labor under the same strictures. Not so for Calvin. With Luther, he held firmly to the *priesthood* of all believers.[73] This would constitute one of his greatest objections to Augustinian theology, though in many areas he was a fan of the

---

69 Thompson, *Humanists and Reformers*, 486.
70 Bernard Cottret, *Calvin: A Biography*, trans. M. Wallace McDonald (Grand Rapids, MI: Eerdmans, 2000 / Edinburgh, Scotland: T&T Clark), 114.
71 John Calvin, *Institutes of the Christian Religion*, vol. 1, trans. Ford Lewis Battles, ed. John T. McNeill, Library of Christian Classics 20 (Philadelphia: Westminster, 1960), 1.1.1.
72 Abraham Kuyper, *Lectures on Calvinism* (1899; Grand Rapids, MI: Eerdmans, 1931), 46.
73 Brian G. Armstrong, "The Changing Face of French Protestantism: The Influence of Pierre Du Moulin," in *Calviniana: Ideas and Influence of Jean Calvin*, ed. Robert V. Schnucker, Sixteenth Century Essays and Studies 10 (Kirksville, MO: Sixteenth Century Journal, 1988), 139–40.

Struggle for the City

African father. Augustine's ecclesiology was problematic in that he "remained the Bishop" and so stood between the Triune God and the layman.[74] Though Calvin believed in the office and calling of pastors and elders, he did not place them on a different *par* from the layman. The Genevan Reformer believed that all persons in all walks of life should be guided in every area of life by God's Word. Every area of life—not just the "spiritual" life, but politics, relationships, economics—every area of life should be governed by God.[75] Calvin argued that there ought to be order in all of these areas and that this order can only come from obedience to God's Word.[76]

Work and Wealth in Geneva

On the subject of *economics* and its relationship to the community and to the church, Calvin had a more thoroughgoing and comprehensive model than anyone up to his time.[77] His work was an advance on Thomas' in that he sought specific pastoral applications of his views in the community life of Geneva, while Thomas's views remained more abstract and untested. He argued that the Bible gives us clear guidelines on what wealth actually is, how wealth should be accrued, how it should be used, and the dangers and advantages of handling wealth. He also developed a working model for how wealth ought to be handled by a community and *when* and *how* it ought to be *redistributed* to the needy.

Calvin taught that wealth in and of itself was neither moral nor immoral. "He was not opposed to the market per se and even became involved in financial transactions by recommending speculative investments to friends and by securing loans for recently arrived immigrants."[78] Wealth is, in fact, part of the created

---

74 Kuyper, *Lectures on Calvinism*, 48.
75 Nelson Kloosterman, "Calvin on Ethics," in *Calvin for Today*, ed. Joel Beeke (Grand Rapids, MI: Reformation Heritage, 2009), 195–210.
76 Lucien Joseph Richard, *The Spirituality of John Calvin* (Atlanta: John Knox, 1974) argues just this point throughout his work. See esp., Calvin, *Institutes*, 3.2–3.7.
77 Several monographs have been written in the last fifty years that are of great help in understanding Calvin's views on these issues. A small sampling includes André Biéler, *Calvin's Economic and Social Thought*, trans. James Greig, ed. Edward Dommen (Geneva: World Alliance of Reformed Churches, 2005); Jeannine E. Olson, *Calvin and Social Welfare: Deacons and the Bourse Française* (Selinsgrove, PA: Susquehanna University Press, 1989); Hall and Burton, *Calvin and Commerce*.
78 Gordon, *Calvin*, 297.

Struggle for the City

order, since creation contains within it the seeds of prosperity, a prosperity that God intended for his people to use in their *subduing* and exercising dominion over the earth.[79] The earth is a well-furnished house that offers to Adam an abundance of good things. The man had the right to exercise watch-care and dominion over this creation, a right given to him by the Lord himself.[80] Calvin believed that human beings ought to excel in *all* that they undertake, including the arts, theology, and business. If humanity is going to conduct commerce, it ought to do so with integrity, but also with a view to doing it to the very best of their *ability*. Those who do so will likely earn profits in their business undertakings. Calvin taught this with fervor, and partly as a result of this, Geneva during his time became a *bustling* center for economic development.[81]

Geneva underwent demographic and economic turmoil during most of Calvin's tenure there, due to the unsettling effect of the Reformation in France and the Swiss Confederacy and due to various wars, especially those between France and the Emperor and between the Emperor and the Turks. Geneva was a haven for tens of thousands of refugees fleeing persecution mostly from France and the Holy Roman Empire. "Prior to Calvin's immigration in 1536, for example, Geneva had fifty merchants, three printers, and few, if any, nobles. By the late 1550s Geneva was home to 180 merchants, 113 printers and publishers, and at least seventy aristocratic refugees who claimed nobility."[82] Calvin's views on the value of work and creation of wealth gave to these individuals the right and the inspiration to use their gifts to create opportunities for themselves in business and craftsmanship.

Calvin also recognized that the Bible supports the private ownership of property. This is especially clear in the Old Testament (OT), but it is also a New Testament (NT) notion. Only on rare occasions does Jesus instruct a person to abandon all his wealth, and the reasons appear to be specific to that particular individual. In his commentary on the rich young ruler, for instance, Calvin writes,

---

79 John Calvin, *Commentaries on the First Book of Moses Called Genesis*, vol. 1, trans. John King, Calvin's Commentaries, ed. David W. Torrance and Thomas F. Torrance (Eng. trans., 1847; repr., Grand Rapids, MI: Eerdmans, 1963), 82.
80 Ibid., 99.
81 Hall and Burton, *Calvin and Commerce*, 26.
82 Ibid., 27.

Struggle for the City

But if we are not prepared to endure poverty, it is manifest that covetousness reigns in us. And this is what I said at the outset, that the order which Christ gave, to sell all that he had, was not an addition to the law, but the scrutiny of a concealed vice. For the more deeply a man is tainted by this or the other vice, the more strikingly will it be dragged forth to light by being reproved. We are reminded also by this example that, if we would persevere steadily in the school of Christ, we must renounce the flesh. This young man, who had brought both a desire to learn and modesty, withdrew from Christ, because it was hard to part with a darling vice.[83]

The biblical model of economy is that one ought to *earn, save*, and *give* all that he can, and any impediment to this is an *inefficiency*.[84]

The Geneva Reformer believed in the importance of *investment*. In order for investment to be as productive as it possibly could be, it had to be free from the threat of confiscation, which he argued was a form of theft. There are three kinds of theft, in Calvin's view. Some thefts occur by violence, others by fraudulent deceit, and still others by legal means. Theft by legal means occurs when our property is taken from us by the government or by the courts and given to someone else through no fault of ourselves, but simply for the purpose of redistribution at the government's whim.[85] People have a right to the *property* that God has granted to them in his providence and any attempt to remove that from them is *theft*, whether done by violence or by legal obfuscation. It is important to recognize that God has granted to each individual what he has determined, in his providence, that he would give to him. Living by faith means that we are content with what we have, though at the same time it is right and just to seek more, but to seek more by lawful means of *industry*, and not by envy and theft.

Because he had a profound view of human depravity, Calvin also recognized that humans could act sinfully with regard to their possessions and wealth.[86]

---

83 John Calvin, *A Harmony of the Gospels: Matthew, Mark and Luke*, vol. 2, trans. T. H. L. Parker, Calvin's Commentaries, ed. David W. Torrance and Thomas F. Torrance (Eng. trans., 1845; repr., Grand Rapids, MI: Eerdmans, 1972), ad loc.
84 Olson, *Calvin and Social Welfare*, 37.
85 Calvin, *Institutes*, 2.8.45.
86 See T. F. Torrance, *Calvin's Doctrine of Man*, new ed. (Grand Rapids, MI: Eerdmans, 1957).

Struggle for the City

This is true in a variety of ways. For one, since the fall of Adam, humans have been mired in a condition of sin, and as a result they have to battle with the sin of slothfulness. As Hall and Burton observe, "Sloth and selfishness, in the changed universe, have become more normal than industry and stewardship."[87] Because of this, a *work ethic* is required of us. Individuals will seldom work hard for nothing, and so the Calvinist view of depravity entails the notion that we will get paid at the *end* of a job rather than at the beginning.[88] That would not have been the case with Adam before the fall. Before the fall he could live in a garden, could pursue his work with no downward pull of a sinful nature leading him to slothfulness or neglect, and all was well.[89] But the garden is *gone*, and we are now surrounded by thorns and thistles, and work is done and bread is earned by the sweat of the brow. That very sweat sometimes becomes a deterrent to hard work.

Depravity can also cause persons to seek for someone *else* to do their work for them rather than to do it themselves. In Calvin's Geneva, there was a well-developed system of care for the poor, but it was also tempered by a recognition that people can and will take advantage of generosity and that there must be checks and balances on just how generosity is carried out. This was carried out through a system known as the *Bourse française*. "There was an effort in Geneva to maintain the image of the *Bourse française* as a fund to help people who were considered worthy, rather than as an institution that indiscriminately aided everyone."[90] There were times when the *deacons*, who were commissioned to carry out the work of helping the poor and handling the money, declined to help a person who requested assistance due to laziness on that person's part. Social ministry was not a substitute for industry and hard work; it was used to help the *truly* needy. While some have argued that the situation early in the book of Acts entailed some form of Christian socialism, Calvin did not agree. For him, discord in the church was "remedied not by an equalization of wealth, but by a spirit of unity," and that when goods were sold, the proceeds were not equally

---

87 Hall and Burton, *Calvin and Commerce*, 53; Torrance, *Calvin's Doctrine of Man*, 65.
88 Hall and Burton, *Calvin and Commerce*, 54.
89 Harro Höpfl, *The Christian Polity of John Calvin*, Cambridge Studies in the History and Theory of Politics (Cambridge: Cambridge University Press, 1982), 153–60.
90 Olson, *Calvin and Social Welfare*, 139.

Struggle for the City

divided but given to each as he had genuine need.[91] Further, there was no mandate that those with possessions *had* to sell them to help the wealthy, in Calvin's view. Such a choice was purely *voluntary*.

In Geneva there was a genuine need for philanthropy. Due to the persecution of Protestants in many parts of Europe, cities like Zurich and Geneva became havens for refugees. During Calvin's time in Geneva the population of the city more than doubled at its peak. When he arrived in 1536 there were between 8,000 and 10,000 inhabitants; by 1560 that number had swelled to 21,000.[92] Many of them had come there because of Calvin's pamphlets, written to encourage oppressed Catholics sympathetic to the Reformation to come to cities like Geneva.[93] One of the reasons that refugees preferred Geneva to other Reformed cities was that there was little pressure from the *trade guilds* to keep them out. In most Swiss cities the trade guilds were represented on the city councils and used their considerable influence to prevent refugees from admission to the cities, since such persons represented labor *competition*. The guilds were not represented on the city council of Geneva.[94]

Calvin, like the Reformers in the other haven cities, worked hard to provide shelter, food, and work for these refugees. He preached that landlords should not charge them higher rates and that merchants should employ them, even if it was more costly to employ them at first.[95] In addition, he worked hard in teaching them biblical views on *work* and *wealth* so that they could learn to be *prosperous* and *industrious* in their own areas of training and expertise. The *Bourse* (the diaconate) even conducted *job training*.[96] Begging was forbidden, but the *elderly* and the *infirm* were carefully cared for by the deacons in the city. *Orphans* were a constant challenge, but they were seen to by the *Bourse*

---

91 John Calvin, *Commentary on the Acts of the Apostles*, vol. 1, trans. W. J. G. McDonald, Calvin's Commentaries, ed. David W. Torrance and Thomas F. Torrance (Eng. trans., 1844; repr., Grand Rapids, MI: Eerdmans, 1972) 193; Hall and Burton, *Calvin and Social Welfare*, 67.

92 Philip Benedict, "Calvin and the Transformation of Geneva," in *John Calvin's Impact on Church and Society, 1509–2009*, ed. Martin Ernst Hirzel and Martin Sallmann (Grand Rapids, MI: Eerdmans, 2009), 11.

93 Gordon, *Calvin*, 198–200.

94 Benedict, "Calvin and the Transformation of Geneva," 5.

95 Mark Valeri, "Religion, Discipline, and the Economy in Calvin's Geneva," *Sixteenth Century Journal* 28, no. 1 (1997): 123–42.

96 Olson, *Calvin and Social Welfare*, 39–40.

Struggle for the City

as well. What was *not* done in Geneva was a redistribution of wealth through city *taxation*. The people gave to their churches and the churches cared for the poor, and in other cases individuals gave privately to the care for the poor and the infirm. What would be true in Scotland with regard to social welfare was also true in Geneva: "The answer to poverty was still found in individual benevolence exercised either privately or through the Church."[97] For Calvin, *forced* redistribution by the state was nothing short of *legalized theft*.

Calvin's view on *interest* charged on loans differed from the medieval Roman Catholic tradition. In the ancient world, both Plato and Aristotle considered interest on loans to be contrary to nature. In the patristic period there was no uniform tradition, though the *Apostolic Canons* did not allow *clerics* to loan on interest. In the Middle Ages, however, both Thomas Aquinas and John Duns Scotus *condemned* the practice of charging interest, lumping any such charge in with the Bible's condemnation of usury.[98] Even Luther and Melanchthon were opposed to interest, though their views were not as strict as those of Thomas. Calvin, though, taught that interest on loans ought to be *allowed* by the city leaders since he knew that those who borrow were sinners, and as such, some would *renege* on repaying their loans.[99] He argued, though, that no more than a 5-percent rate ought to be allowed, since, in the same way, those who loan money were sinners, and if allowed would extort money from the very needy who might be incentivized to borrow unwisely. Those who charged more than five percent were brought before the church and banned from the Lord's Supper.[100] Calvin's views were progressive for the time, even as compared with those of Luther, who opposed any form of "usury." As one historian has noted, "Calvin was bridging to the seventeenth century, Luther to the fifteenth."[101] The future lay with Calvin.

---

97 Geoffrey Bromiley, "The English Reformers and the Diaconate," in *Service in Christ: Essays Presented to Karl Barth in Honor of His 80th Birthday*, ed. James I. McCord and T. H. L. Parker (London: Epworth, 1966), 113.
98 "Usury," *The Catholic Encyclopedia*, rev. ed., ed. Robert Broderick (New York: Thomas Nelson, 1990).
99 Gordon, *Calvin*, 297.
100 David W. Jones, *Reforming the Morality of Usury: A Study of the Differences That Separated the Protestant Reformers* (Lanham, MD: University Press of America, 2004), 107–33.
101 Jack Cashill, *Popes and Bankers: A Cultural History of Credit and Debt, from Aristotle to AIG* (Nashville: Thomas Nelson, 2010), 65.

Struggle for the City

This set of convictions comes about as close as possible to a full-blown pragmatic economic theory in a time when the word *economics* in the "science of wealth" sense had not yet been coined, and in the work of a thinker who did not have a well-developed epistemological system. Though he was familiar with the philosophers, he vowed "not to follow the philosophers farther than is profitable."[102] Calvin had a *biblically* defined understanding of work, of wealth, of welfare, of property, and of the relation of all of that to the church and the government. His views would be transferred in the next several generations to a group of people whose homeland was England, but many of whom would make their way to the New World, where they would have the freedom to implement them in specific and dramatic ways.

Governing Geneva

On political theory, Calvin's ideas were complex and in many ways new. He opposed the notion of fusing secular government and church government. Calvin "advanced a doctrine of separation of church and state, [but] not separation of religion and state."[103] Calvin's approach to state government is that it should be both *respected* and *limited*. It should be respected because it is appointed by a sovereign God, but it should be *limited* because those who govern are *sinful* men who will be tempted to use government for their own selfish purposes. In his famous lectures on Calvinism given at Princeton, Abraham Kuyper stated that the Calvinistic "political faith" is based on three assumptions: only God is sovereign in the destiny of nations; sin has broken down God's direct governing of people, necessitating human rule; and people never have authority over fellow human beings except that which is given by God.[104] How did the Genevan Reformer work these ideas out?

Civil government is a force for good and is the instrument God uses to keep society from descending into chaos. If not for civil government, depraved

---

102 Calvin, *Institutes*, 2.2.4. See the discussion in François Wendel, *Calvin: Origins and Development of His Religious Thought*, trans. Philip Mairet (Grand Rapids, MI: Baker, 1997), 32–45.
103 G. Joseph Gattis, "The Political Theory of John Calvin," in *Politics and Public Policy: A Christian Response*, ed. Timothy J. Demy and Gary P. Stewart, Christian Response Series (Grand Rapids, MI: Kregel, 2000), 97.
104 Kuyper, *Lectures on Calvinism*, 85.

Struggle for the City

men would act in whatever manner they wished, since they would know they would go "scot-free."[105] God governs through human rule. And since this is the case, it ought to be *godly* men who bear the task of governing, men serving as "vicars of God" (or, God vicariously).[106] This part of the *Institutes* was written in part as a critique of what he perceived to be the Anabaptist anarchists, "who would have men living pell-mell like rats in straw."[107] Government is necessary and the best governors were godly men.

Government had a positive and not merely a negative role in Calvin's thought. It was "to cherish and protect the outward worship of God, to defend sound doctrine of piety and the position of the church, to adjust our life to the society of men, to form our social behavior to civil righteousness, to reconcile us with one another, and to promote general peace and tranquility."[108] So, magistrates ought to be chosen both for their judicious *wisdom* in governing and for their *piety*. Their task was not merely to keep the unruly from having their way, but to promote goodness and righteousness in society.

Calvin was opposed to revolution and rebellion. He did condone *resistance*, but not *rebellion*, contending that if a nation has a wicked ruler, it may be God's way of punishing the people for their sins. He cites in particular the case of Nebuchadnezzar from Daniel as a biblical example.[109] He believed that if a ruler was treating his people unjustly, lesser magistrates should take the matter in hand and deal with it.[110] He went so far as to say that the lesser magistrates *must* take this issue in hand. If they do not do so, "their dissimulation is not free from nefarious perfidy, because they fraudulently betray the liberty of the people, while knowing that, by the ordinance of God, they are

---

105 John Calvin, *Institutes of the Christian Religion*, vol. 2, trans. Ford Lewis Battles, ed. John T. McNeill, Library of Christian Classics 21 (Philadelphia: Westminster, 1960), 4.20.2. Book 4, chap. 20 of *Institutes* is where Calvin devotes attention to the question of civil government.
106 Calvin, *Institutes*, 4.20.6.
107 Ibid., 4.20.7. We are convinced that Calvin's understanding of the Anabaptists was defective, based only on the radical tendencies of some revolutionaries who had caused considerable *angst* in Europe through political unrest and war.
108 Ibid., 4.20.2.
109 Ibid., 4:20.25–29.
110 W. Fred Graham, "Calvin and the Political Order: An Analysis of the Three Explanatory Studies," in *Calviniana*, 51–61.

Struggle for the City

its appointed guardians."[111] Revolution was not permitted, though resistance was. The limitations to resistance are profound but betray Calvin's strict convictions about the sovereignty of God.[112] Some of his followers would later extend the notion of resistance by "lower magistrates" to include the possibility of rebellion, in *limited* and *extreme* instances.

What kind of government would be best suited to these ends? Like both Augustine and Thomas Aquinas before him, Calvin believed it was possible to construct a *political theology*. To position him relative to the two previous thinkers, Calvin was as fully committed to the doctrine of depravity as Augustine had been, though he had *higher* hopes for government than the African father. He was less sanguine about the possibility of a godly monarch than was Thomas, but held out that a Christian state *could* be formed.[113] In a manner reminiscent of Aristotle, Calvin did not believe there was only one kind of appropriate government, but he did believe that some were better than others.[114] Entrusting power to one person alone, or only to a few elites was dangerous, as noted above, due to sin. In his lectures on Amos 7 he excoriated governing authorities in England and Germany, noting particularly that Henry VIII was a "blasphemy." Of the German Lutheran nobles, he likewise asserted that they should not "become chief judges as in doctrine as in all spiritual government," but should use their temporal power to "render free the worship of God."[115] Rulers should be godly men, but they should not enforce doctrinal uniformity, only orthodoxy.

Calvin argued for a "system compounded of aristocracy and democracy."[116] By "aristocracy" he did not mean a hereditary class, but a class elected by their fellows.[117] That was the very kind of government that existed in Geneva when he arrived, and while Calvin often found himself at odds with key leaders of the Little

---

111 Calvin, *Institutes*, 4.20.31.
112 William R. Stevenson, "Calvin and Political Issues," in *The Cambridge Companion to John Calvin*, ed. Donald K. McKim, Cambridge Companions to Religion (Cambridge: Cambridge University Press, 2004), 181–86.
113 Lilla, *Stillborn God*, 70.
114 Gattis, "Political Theory of John Calvin," 99–100.
115 John Calvin, *Commentaries on the Twelve Minor Prophets: Joel, Amos, Obadiah*, vol. 2, trans. John Owen, Calvin's Commentaries 8, ed. David W. Torrance and Thomas F. Torrance (Eng. trans., 1846; repr., Grand Rapids, MI: Eerdmans, 1950), 349–50, quoted in Gattis, "Political Theory of John Calvin," 101.
116 Calvin, *Institutes*, 4.20.7.
117 Gattis, "Political Theory of John Calvin" 100.

Struggle for the City

Council (the highest ruling council in the city), he always defended the type of government found in the city.[118] Citing David in the OT, Calvin contended that rulers had the right to go to war when facing wickedness or in self-defense, but never simply to wreak vengeance or to inflict undue cruelty.[119] Magistrates were to protect their people from robbers and invaders and to use force if necessary; if they did not do so, they were as bad as the robbers or invaders.[120]

Calvin was a *covenantal* theologian, though it would not be till the next generation that covenantal *theology* would be worked out fully. He saw a significant continuity between old and new covenants, especially in terms of the doctrine of the *church*. So, for him, baptism was the extension of circumcision into the new covenant—it was the *sign* of the covenant in the same way.[121] In a similar way, a Reformed community in the modern world was to reflect Jerusalem of the OT. That was what Calvin was trying to accomplish in Geneva—to make Geneva the modern *equivalent* of the Davidic city. That was why all of these reforms were necessary, not merely optional. "Calvin's Genevan church was intended by Calvin to be exemplary."[122] For him the concept of a fully *secularized* state was unthinkable, though, as we have already noted, he did not want the two spheres to be fused or overly cooperative.

One of the great questions that has been raised by historians is whether or not Calvin's views were the basis of later *republicanism*, such as that which prevailed in the American experience in the 1770s and '80s. The best answer seems to be that Jefferson and Madison worked out an approach to government that was consistent with some Calvinist ideals, especially in regards to human depravity and the need for limited government, but clearly not identical.[123] Calvin favored the idea of *decentralization* in governance, an idea consistent with Jeffersonian politics.

---

118 David W. Hall, *Calvin in the Public Square: Liberal Democracies, Rights, and Civil Liberties*, Calvin 500 Series (Philipsburg, NJ: P&R, 2009), 71–77.
119 Calvin, *Institutes*, 4.20.10.
120 Ibid., 4.20.11.
121 Shawn D. Wright, "Baptism and the Logic of Reformed Paedobaptists," in *Believer's Baptism: Sign of the New Covenant in Christ*, ed. Thomas R. Schreiner and Shawn D. Wright, NAC Studies in Bible and Theology (Nashville: B&H, 2006), 228–56.
122 Höpfl, *Christian Polity of John Calvin*, 121.
123 See the helpful discussion in D. G. Hart, "Implausible: Calvinism and American Politics," in *John Calvin's American Legacy*, ed. Thomas J. Davis (New York: Oxford University Press, 2010), 65–88.

Struggle for the City

One scholar has argued that a synthetic reading of Calvin shows that he held to five principles—"fundamental law, natural rights, contract and consent of people, popular sovereignty, resistance to tyranny through responsible representatives"— what this interpreter calls the "five points of political Calvinism" that would later be a description of republicanism in essence.[124] But he would likely not have favored the exact system we now have in the United States. As one historian has put it, "Modern Democracy is the child of the Reformation, not of the Reformers."[125] Modern republicanism is a sort of working out of the basic ideas that come from the Reformation, but it is not found in the Reformers' teachings explicitly.

Taxation in Geneva

Taxation is of course a place where economics and politics come together. Though it is often not the case, one might hope that taxation theories would be based on an overall world-and-life view. Calvin recognized that taxes were allowable, even necessary, but only within prudent limitation. Taxes should "support only public necessity."[126] He feared that sinful components within government would impose inordinate taxation simply for their own purposes: "To impose them upon the common folk without cause is tyrannical extortion."[127] Taxes that were too heavy represented, as we discussed above, governmental theft and extortion, a theft as reprehensible as burglary. As we pointed out above, taxes were not to be used to support the indolent, who were not to be supported at all, nor even those who were justifiably dependent on public support, as *they* were to be cared for by freewill offerings.

Beyond the matter of taxation, how should governments enact legislation? On the *basis* for legislation, Calvin certainly argued that the Bible was to be the foundation for all law. He did not teach, though, that every aspect of Mosaic legislation had a place in a modern state.[128] In that sense, as well as

124 Herbert D. Foster, "International Calvinism through Locke and the Revolution of 1688," *American Historical Review* 32, no. 3 (1927): 487, quoted in Jeffry H. Morrison, *John Witherspoon and the Founding of the American Republic* (Notre Dame, IN: University of Notre Dame Press, 2005), 81.
125 G. P. Gooch, *English Democratic Ideas in the Seventeenth Century*, 2nd ed. (Cambridge: Cambridge University Press, 1927), 7.
126 Hall, *Calvin in the Public Square*, 78.
127 Calvin, *Institutes*, 4.20.13.
128 Hall, *Calvin in the Public Square*, 79.

in other ways, his position differed from later "theocracy" views, such as those represented by the modern "Theonomy" school.[129] The other basis for civil legislation in Calvin's teaching was *natural law*. He clearly taught that the natural man has an "implanting" and an "imprinting" of the law of God on the human heart; Calvin draws this conclusion from Romans 2:14–15: "Since then all nations, of themselves and without a monitor, are disposed to make laws for themselves, it is beyond all question evident that they have some notions of justice and rectitude… and which are implanted by nature in the hearts of men."[130] In this, his position is similar to that of Thomas, previously considered. The main difference between them is that whereas "Thomas spoke of conscience as reason's application of general precepts to particular moral acts, Calvin (more resembling Luther) speaks of conscience as awareness of God's law and judgment."[131] Thomas saw the connection between natural law and the conscience as an *indirect* connection, while Calvin believed it was *direct*. The Reformer in Geneva thought through the wide range of these issues related to the economy, governing, and the human condition in a very thoughtful and advanced way. Even if we do not agree with all of his conclusions, we can be impressed with the thoroughness and consistency of his exposition.

THE RADICAL REFORMERS: REFORM WITHOUT THE MAGISTRACY

On January 21, 1525, a small group of men gathered in the home of Felix Manz (1498–1527) in the Swiss city of Zurich. For some months Manz and his friends, Conrad Grebel (ca. 1498–1526), Georg Blaurock (1492–1529), and

---

129 Two key examples of the theonomic approach (also called Christian Reconstructionism) can be seen in Rousas John Rushdoony, *The Institutes of Biblical Law* (1973; repr., Philipsburg, NJ: P&R, 1980); Gary North, *Political Polytheism: The Myth of Pluralism* (Tyler, TX: Institute for Christian Economics, 1989). Also see Greg L. Bahnsen, Theonomy in Christian Ethics, 3rd ed. (Nacogdoches, TX : Covenant Media Press, 2002).

130 John Calvin, *The Epistles of Paul the Apostle to the Romans and to the Thessalonians,* trans. Ross Mackenzie, Calvin's Commentaries, ed. David W. Torrance and Thomas F. Torrance (Eng. trans., 1849; repr., Grand Rapids, MI: Eerdmans, 1959), ad loc.

131 David VanDrunen, *Natural Law and the Two Kingdoms: A Study in the Development of Reformed Social Thought*, Emory University Studies in Law and Religion (Grand Rapids, MI: Eerdmans, 2010), 101.

Struggle for the City

others, had been convinced that the Catholic Mass and other Catholic teachings were contrary to Scripture. They had followed the lead of their teacher and mentor, Ulrich Zwingli (1484–1531), in calling for *reforms* in the churches of their city. Zwingli wished for these reforms, but was constrained by the slow hand of the city council, which, though it had ousted the Catholic bishop from leadership, was slow to authorize any real changes in the worship in the city's churches.[132] But the students of Zwingli wanted even more. Though they agreed with Reformers like Luther that much needed to be changed, they differed with the other Reformers on the *nature* of the church and the *timing* of baptism. They had concluded that infant baptism was an *abomination* and that only *believers'* baptism was consistent with the NT.[133] To be even more specific, what they were contending for was not merely believers' baptism understood generically, but *disciples' baptism*, since baptism was to be reserved for "committed disciples who had shown by their steadfast faith, self-discipline and whole-hearted following of the ideals of the gathered community that they were genuine disciples."[134] That January evening they acted on their convictions. After prayer, Georg Blaurock stood up in the midst of their meeting and asked Grebel "for God's sake to baptize him with the true Christian baptism upon his faith and knowledge," whereupon Grebel complied, and then Blaurock baptized the *other* adults in the room.[135] They then pledged themselves as true disciples of the Lord "to live lives separated from the world and to teach the gospel and hold the faith."[136] Thus began the movement commonly known as *Anabaptism*, but better known to modern scholarship as the Radical Reformation.[137]

---

132 Harold S. Bender, *Conrad Grebel, c. 1498–1526: The Founder of the Swiss Brethren Sometimes Called Anabaptists*, Studies in Anabaptist and Mennonite History 6 (Goshen, IN: Mennonite Historical Society, 1950), 89–135.

133 The real position of Zwingli on the timing of baptism is difficult to ascertain. One of his students, Balthasar Hubmaier, claimed that in May 1523, Zwingli had declared that infant baptism was unbiblical, but by late fall 1524 he held firmly to infant baptism. C. Arnold Snyder, *The Life and Thought of Michael Sattler*, Studies in Anabaptist and Mennonite History 27 (Scottdale, PA: Herald, 1984), 69.

134 Payton, *Getting the Reformation Wrong*, 161.

135 William R. Estep, *The Anabaptist Story: An Introduction to Sixteenth-Century Anabaptism*, 3rd ed. (Grand Rapids, MI: Eerdmans, 1996), 13–14; MacCulloch, *Reformation*, 145–46.

136 Estep, *Anabaptist Story*, 14.

137 This term was coined by George Huntston Williams, *The Radical Reformation* (Philadelphia: Westminster, 1962).

Struggle for the City

It may seem an *incidental* thing to us, this evening baptismal event with only a dozen or so obscure figures present, but in reality it constituted a very tiny (at the time) but extremely significant *revolution* in theology.[138] The age-old practice of infant baptism with its implications for politics and social relations was immense.

> Social expectations, legal enactments and interpersonal relationships all built on this foundation. So to deny that the paedo-baptism[139] of all was legitimate and to insist on a later baptism of only a few could not be simply a personal decision with the goal of pursuing greater spiritual fidelity. It inevitably also entailed a stinging indictment of the Christian faith of the others and of the legitimacy of the civil state.[140]

As much as anything, the Radical Reformation constituted a new way of understanding the church—"new," that is, insofar as it is difficult to find others who sympathized with them any time in their own recent memory.[141] For them the church was a *believers'* church (with a lowercase c) since they did not hold to a monolithic established church.[142] Menno Simons (1496–1561), one of the important theologians in the movement, argued that he was simply applying Luther's doctrine of justification by faith to the doctrine of the *church*. If people are justified by faith alone, then only such justified people ought to be "members" of the church. The church then is a "believers' church" in the

---

138 This was not the first such "anabaptism," a term that means "rebaptism," but it is the one that involved the baptism of the real architect of the new movement, a movement that, though "obscure" at the time, would be revolutionary, as we will demonstrate.

139 The term *"paedo-baptism"* refers to the practice of "infant baptism."

140 Payton, *Getting the Reformation Wrong*, 164–65.

141 This is a debatable observation, of course. Scholars have argued for many parallels throughout the patristic and medieval periods, and we would recognize that groups like the Waldenses appear to have similarities to the Radical Reformers in their doctrine of the church. The Waldenses seem to have retained infant baptism, though some of them seem to have added a second baptismal rite for initiates into the movement. Cf. "Waldenses," *Oxford Dictionary of the Christian Church*, 1714–15, and Caroline T. Marshall, "Waldenses," *Evangelical Dictionary of Theology*, 2nd ed., ed. Walter A. Elwell (Grand Rapids, MI: Baker, 2001), 1252–53. But the Waldenses were only one small group in the history of the church, and their theology of baptism was not the main focus of their concern.

142 Estep, *Anabaptist Story*, 33.

Struggle for the City

sense that only those are members of the visible church who are, by their own testimony at least, members of the mystical body of Christ.[143] Menno further argued that the NT only depicts and teaches the baptism of those who have made a conscious choice to become disciples of Jesus and that this was consistent with his views on the nature of the church. Luther had done much good in his reforming efforts, as would Calvin, but not enough. While the Magisterial Reformers wished to "*reform* the church on the basis of the Word of God, the Radical Reformers were more concerned to *restore* the primitive church which they believed had 'fallen' or apostatized."[144] Menno viewed his work as a furthering or a *completion* of what Luther had started.

The implications of such a set of convictions are *momentous*. If the church is made up only of a believing community, Menno further contended, then it alone is responsible for its ministry, its leadership, its support, and its own reform efforts. This entailed a staggering impact politically. In all of the other reform efforts in Germany, Geneva, Basel, Strasbourg, Zurich, and other places (including England), those efforts were supported by, and in some cases even initiated by, the political authorities.[145] This in effect "put the state in a position of dominance in the life of the church."[146] Additionally, these reforms were carried out for the most part only under the approving watch-care of town councils, nobles, princes, and other political leaders. Grebel, Manz, and the other key leaders of the new Radicals *rejected* this out of hand. The church needs no assistance in carrying out its reforms. Whenever the government adds its lending hand to reform efforts it also looks for some kind of payback as well as complete cooperation with the political realities that are in place, whether those political realities are just or not. The Anabaptists in effect said, "We do not need the government's help in carrying out our reforms, and we do not want its interference."[147] It was a truly *radical* position; but these men were not, in all likelihood, fully prepared for the storm that was about to be unleashed on them.

---

143 Thompson, *Humanists and Reformers*, 464.
144 George, *Theology of the Reformers*, 286–87.
145 Williams, *Radical Reformation*, 234–41.
146 Bender, *Conrad Grebel*, 99.
147 Williams, *Radical Reformation*, 846–65.

Struggle for the City

The practice of "rebaptism" (the meaning of the term *Anabaptist*) was outlawed in Zurich. Felix Manz was executed early in 1527 for "rebaptizing" persons, who in a twisted sense of irony was then himself executed by drowning.[148] The Radicals were *proscribed* all over Europe, with the exception of Holland. The reason is that their convictions challenged one of the most long-standing and universal beliefs of Western (and indeed Eastern) Christendom, the belief that church and state were in some sense two sides of the same coin.[149] It is not that everyone else saw church and state as the *same* thing. It is not even that kings and popes always got along well. We have seen that this was often not the case. But the common belief—so common that it was part of the fabric of their very lives—was that there was only one *state* (in any given geographic area) and there was also only one *church*, and people just believed that this seamlessness was requisite to a *stable* society. To contend for a different political reality was tantamount to treason or *sedition*; to contend for a different ecclesiastical reality was to commit the very *same crime*. Starting a new church was seen as rebellion and insurrection. This was at least the view that outsiders took of the *Anabaptists*, as they called them, a name that "came to be used in a general pejorative sense to describe those who were believed to oppose the existing social and political order."[150] There is only one way to deal with usurpers. This is why Manz was drowned by the Zurich authorities, in a kind of parody of his own baptismal practice.[151] But the Radicals believed that practicing mandated infant baptism in the context of an *established* church was to confuse the church with the world.[152]

The Anabaptists were attempting to break a millennium-old assumption. Their beliefs were counter to Augustine, contrary to the practice of the medieval

---

148 Ibid., 137–39. The Radicals denied that this was "rebaptism," since they were convinced that this baptism, i.e., the "christening," was not actually baptism.
149 The Eastern Orthodox view differed in some key ways from the Western Catholic view, mostly in that in the East, patriarch and emperor were seen as the two heads of society and generally tended to work hand in glove. In the West there was much greater friction between pope and emperor, but in spite of that, there was a unanimous sense that only one church was legitimate and that church and state were conjoined in some fashion.
150 Christopher Hill, *The World Turned Upside Down: Radical Ideas during the English Revolution* (New York: Viking, 1972), 22.
151 Bender, *Conrad Grebel*, 160–62.
152 MacCulloch, *Christianity*, 164.

Struggle for the City

popes, counter to the convictions that launched the Inquisition, and they were inconsistent with the compromise position of Luther or the rational approach of John Calvin. Their belief was also not consistent with their own *local* situation in Zurich in which Zwingli was willing to allow the city council to set the tone and the pace of reform, in effect, to *govern* the church's affairs. "The decision of Conrad Grebel to refuse to accept the jurisdiction of the Zurich council over the Zurich church is one of the high moments of history, for however obscure it was, it marked the beginning of the modern 'free church' movement."[153]

Furthermore, this action by "Grebel and the Swiss Brethren who gathered around him in the ensuing year(s) planted the seed out of which has come, through the influence of the Anabaptists in Holland and England, the modern Protestant commitment of freedom of *conscience*, freedom of *religion*, *voluntary* church membership, and *separation* of church and state."[154] These are truly *monumental* issues! Grebel would pay for his actions with imprisonment in Zurich in 1525/26, but would be released and then die in August of 1526, probably from the plague, in Maienfeld.[155] Living only to the age of twenty-eight, he had founded a theological *revolution* that would live on for generations.

All of the previous theologies we have discussed here advocated the view that there can be only *one* government and only *one* church in any locale, and that there was some kind of mutually supportive *symbiosis* between them, even though leaders of church and state did not always agree on how to handle any given situation. For the previous "Great Tradition," the two (state and church) had to find a way to work together for moral, economic, political, and ecclesiastical advancement, in effect, to create a *Christian society*. But this was not so for the Radicals, and in many places they paid a great price for their "sedition." They did not see themselves as *rebels*, of course, but were simply calling for a *new model* of church-state relations, a model that actually would be tentatively attempted in the Low Countries by the 1540s.[156] This does *not* mean that the Radicals in Zurich were advocating *separatism*. They rejected

---

153 Bender, *Conrad Grebel*, 99–100.
154 Ibid., 100.
155 Ibid., 162.
156 What happened in Holland cannot be called religious *liberty* in the later sense of that term, but it certainly did represent some level of religious *toleration*. Because of this, many Anabaptists fled to Holland, where "going Dutch" meant going an easier way.

Struggle for the City

the Catholic Church and the idea of a state church, but they did wish for "one united church, not a little church outside the big church, for they believed that the majority of the people would accept their program."[157] They wanted *one church*, but not a church under the bootheel of the city council.

Many of the Radicals advocated economic and political reforms that were consistent with their views on the church. Menno, for instance, urged that genuine Christians cannot serve in the political sphere at any level, since to do so would be to violate one's exclusive vows of allegiance to Christ alone. Even voting in elections was for him a violation of one's dedication to Christ.[158] While not all Mennonites have followed Menno's views consistently on this, it is still the case that the Anabaptist tradition has maintained at best a neutrality and at worst a hostility to political involvement on the part of its adherents.

Jacob Hutter (1500–1536), who was martyred in the same year that Menno was converted to the new movement (and as he said, to Christ), along with his followers believed that the early church in Acts practiced true communalism, and so, in seeking to emulate what they believed to be the ancient practice of the church, they formed communal living arrangements and all the members of any one church lived in the same large building, farmed the same land, took their meals together, worshiped together, and shared all things in common, except wives.[159] No one had any money, which they considered to be evil, and the community traded goods and services for those things that they could not make or grow.[160] Part of the motivation for this practice early on lay in the volatile economic situation in Europe in the 1520s and after. Trade with Asia and new wealth pouring in from America (especially gold from South America) displaced many craftsmen and artisans, causing many of them to have to move to new locations to find work, work that often was not to be found there, either.[161] The Hutterite communities *honored* craftsmen and welcomed these displaced persons and their families into their fold.[162]

---

157 Ibid., 104.

158 George, *Theology of the Reformers*, 289.

159 Williams, *Radical Reformation*, 233–34, 412–17.

160 James Stayer, "The Anabaptist Revolt and Political and Religious Power," in *Power, Authority, and the Anabaptist Tradition*, ed. Benjamin W. Redekop and Calvin W. Redekop, Center Books in Anabaptist Studies (Baltimore: Johns Hopkins University Press, 2001), 61–63.

161 Franklin H. Littell, *The Origins of Sectarian Protestantism: A Study of the Anabaptist View of the Church* (New York: MacMillan, 1964), 124.

162 Stayer, "Anabaptist Revolt," 62.

Struggle for the City

Eventually, many of the Anabaptist groups found their way to the Netherlands.[163] Only there could they practice their faith without fear of arrest or *worse*. The reason for this was that the Dutch were a tolerant people. In the mid-sixteenth century they were at war with Spain, a war in which the pope sided with Spain. It seemed odd to the Dutch (northern Netherlands) that the pope would side with *one* Catholic nation over against another Catholic nation when they were at war. This eventually led the northern Netherlands to break with the papacy and become Reformed, but in the meantime, the Dutch were tolerant of religious diversity.[164] There was even a phrase for it—"Go Dutch!" It meant to go the easy way, the tolerant way. In our day it simply refers to a cheap date, but even the modern usage retains something of the original meaning—the easy way. Radical Reformers and others found northern Netherlands to be a hospitable place.

For the Radical Reformers there was no such thing as the City of God in *this age*, unless it could be construed as a separated community of believers only, such as in the Hutterite communes. The City of God was purely *eschatological* for most of them, especially for Conrad Grebel and Menno Simons—the "heavenly Jerusalem and myriads of angels" (Heb. 12:22). Because of that, they could not affirm any *divinely* sanctioned ruling authority in this age. Governance had to be more humble than that. Menno would not even participate in the governing process but encouraged his followers to "come out from them." Their hope lay in another dimension.

If the year 1600 marks some kind of arbitrary boundary to what was the "Reformation Age," then it certainly presented to the outside observer a very different Europe from the one that people would have seen a century earlier. Those differences were theological, ecclesiastical, political, and economic. In the next chapter we will witness the political, economic, and ecclesiastical impact of these developments.

---

163 Williams, *Radical Reformation*, 8–11, 341–50.
164 MacCulloch, *Christianity*, 639–40.

Struggle for the City

Chapter 13

Mercantilist Economics at Its Best (or Worst) in England and France

THE AFTERMATH OF THE REFORMATION was a transformed Europe. When the sixteenth century dawned, Western Europe was essentially united under the aegis of *one church*, the church in Rome. By century's end there were at least four "branches" of Christianity—Catholic, Lutheran, Reformed, and Anglican, and one more if the Anabaptists are included. But even that characterization is too simplistic. The Reformed churches differed from one another, partly due to national differences between the Dutch, the Swiss, the Scots, and other geographical distinctions. Scandinavian Lutherans held some views different from their German brethren. In the Anglican Church there were two major parties, the high church and the Puritan. If we looked even closer we would find that even this description does not adequately convey the multiplicity within Protestant Christianity. Differences also prevailed in Catholicism.

Europe's transformation, however, was not merely ecclesiastical. Increased nationalization, new trade routes, and the challenges and rewards of colonization made the Continent very different in 1600 than it had been in 1500. This chapter will examine some of these changes and will also demonstrate how the whole subject of the "economy" gave rise eventually to the new discipline of "economics." We will first see how a "mercantilist" approach to government's attempt to dominate a nation's economy was attempted by the Tudor dynasty in England, and how it was then perfected in the next century by the French. We will attempt to sketch the impact all of that had on the Christian faith, especially with the New World of America on the horizon.

England in the Sixteenth Century: The Implementation of Mercantilist Economics

The spirit of Calvin eventually caught on in the English-speaking world even more dramatically and intensely than it did on the Continent. It was not obvious that this would happen in the early years of the English "Reformation." The story of that series of events is well known, but a brief synopsis is in order.

Two Henrys

Henry VII died in 1509, having introduced the Tudor dynasty to the throne in 1485. Henry had come to power in the wake of the Wars of the Roses between the House of Lancaster and the House of York, represented by the red and white roses, respectively, wars which left a power vacuum within the English nobility. Henry VII waltzed confidently into that vacuum, becoming the most powerful monarch in Europe at the time. Henry's oldest son, Arthur, had died seven years earlier than his father, in 1502. Arthur had been married the year before to Catherine of Aragon in a political marriage, he being fifteen years of age and she, sixteen. Catherine was daughter of Ferdinand and Isabella of Spain and the marriage was arranged largely as a strategy against France and the Netherlands on the part of both countries. When Arthur died the next year, King Henry, wishing to keep the king and queen of Spain as allies and to secure the remainder of the very large dowry she brought (the total was two hundred thousand crowns), instructed his next eldest son, Henry, to wed his brother's widow, which the young Henry dutifully did. A papal dispensation was necessary since the marriage was contrary to canon law, which held that a man could not marry his brother's widow.[1] Though Henry dutifully obeyed his father it is also the case that there was apparently deep

---

1 J. H. Merle d'Aubigné, *The Reformation in England*, trans. H. White, ed. S. M. Houghton (London: Banner of Truth, 1962), 1:112.

Struggle for the City

affection between the two of them. Henry wrote Catherine's father after the nuptials, "If I were still free, I would choose her for wife before all others."[2] That sentiment would eventually fade. In 1509, that second son became King Henry VIII (1491–1547) of England.

Catherine bore her husband the king, in order, a stillborn daughter; a son who lived only fifty-two days; a son who died immediately after birth; a stillborn son; a daughter, Mary, who would one day be queen (born in 1516); and a daughter who lived only a few hours. She was unable, unfortunately, to give Henry what he most wanted, a male heir. Being the dashing, virile, and handsome young man that he was[3] as well as being king of England at a time when kings often took other lovers, Henry had various affairs and dalliances, one of which actually produced a son, Henry Fitzroy, later made Duke of Richmond.[4] But that son would not qualify as heir since he was *illegitimate*.

Eventually Henry would seek a divorce from his Spanish queen, but the pope, Clement VII, beholden to Catherine's nephew, Emperor Charles V who had supported Clement's aspirations to the papacy, refused to grant a divorce or an annulment.[5] "The power to issue matrimonial dispensations was one of the most effective and lucrative means of papal control,"[6] and *control* was what Clement exercised in this matter.[7] He in fact suggested that Henry, rather than receiving an annulment of his marriage to Catherine, merely take another wife alongside Catherine, advice Henry had no interest in taking.[8] The king then sought the advice of English and foreign universities in what became known as the "Great Matter," sending a Cambridge doctor of divinity, Thomas Cranmer, who was also chaplain to the Boleyn family, abroad to

---

2   Alison Weir, *Henry VIII: The King and His Court* (New York: Ballantine Books, 2001), 15.
3   Most people are familiar with the portraits of Henry as an old man, corpulent, besotted, and made pudgy from too hedonistic a life, but as a young man he was a champion athlete, hunter, and jouster.
4   Weir, *Henry VIII*, 215. He may have also fathered other, unacknowledged children, even perhaps one or two through his mistress Mary Boleyn, sister to his later wife, Anne, who had been his mistress before Anne. Ibid., 216.
5   D'Aubigné, *Reformation in England*, 2:278–91.
6   G. W. Bromiley, *Thomas Cranmer: Archbishop and Martyr* (1956; repr., Greenwood, SC: Attic, 1977), 12.
7   For an examination of the whole "Great Matter," see Diarmaid MacCulloch, *Thomas Cranmer: A Life* (New Haven, CT: Yale University Press, 1996), 41–78.
8   Bromiley, *Thomas Cranmer*, 14.

Struggle for the City

seek opinion. Cranmer eventually informed the king that the majority opinion of university faculties that he consulted with were convinced that he did
not *need* a divorce, only an annulment, and that most of them agreed that the
king's case was *just* in light of the violation of canon law that brought about
the marriage in the first place.[9]

The long and short of it was that Henry appointed Cranmer as Archbishop of Canterbury, whereupon the new Archbishop granted the King
his annulment, allowing him to marry his quite pregnant mistress, Anne
Boleyn.[10] Anne soon gave birth to a daughter, Elizabeth, and Parliament
passed, in 1534, the Act of Supremacy, which made the English monarch the
head of the churches in England. The Church of England was "reformed,"
and Henry was its head. Not everyone was pleased with this development.
John Fisher, Bishop of Rochester, and Thomas More, Lord Chancellor, both
refused to affirm the Act of Supremacy. Fisher would "give no answer to the
demand that he should recognize the king as head of the Church."[11] Thomas
More likewise refused, replying that all he could meditate on was Christ's
passion. Fisher met the executioner's axe on June 22, 1535, donning his best
clothes with the comment, "This is my wedding day, and I ought to dress
as for a Holiday."[12] A fortnight later More met the same fate with the same
dignity. "So ended the life of Thomas More, one of the few Londoners upon
whom sainthood has been conferred and the first Englishman to be beatified
as a martyr."[13] It was deadly dangerous to resist the king. But the Church of
England was "reformed."

Or was it? It was certainly *disconnected* from the Roman papacy. But
Henry's personal theology was still very, very Catholic: Catholic without the
pope.[14] Cranmer, the new Archbishop, wanted very much to move the Anglican Church in the direction of *substantial* reforms—he was a supporter of

---

9 MacCulloch, *Thomas Cranmer*, 42.
10 Archbishop Warham had died in August 1532, and Henry took that occasion to implement
   the final step in his plan to have his marriage to Catherine annulled and then to marry
   Anne, the appointment of Cranmer. Bromiley, *Thomas Cranmer*, 22–28.
11 J. H. Merle d'Aubigné, *Reformation in England*, trans. H. White, ed. S. M. Houghton
   (London: Banner of Truth, 1962), 2:219.
12 Ibid.
13 Peter Ackroyd, *The Life of Thomas More* (New York: Nan A. Talese, Doubleday, 1998), 406.
14 Susan Doran, *The Tudor Chronicles* (2008; repr., New York: Metro Books, 2009), 161.

Struggle for the City

Luther's general theological ideas—but the king was not interested in that, at least not early on. Eventually Henry would allow for some minor changes to doctrine and polity, such as the publication of an English translation of the Bible, but more substantial reforms would have to wait.[15] When Anne Boleyn proved incapable of producing a male heir, Henry accused her of adultery and had her executed, then married Jane Seymour, who subsequently gave birth to a son, Edward. The King was jubilant, weeping with joy so that Hugh Latimer, later bishop, wrote, "We all hungered for a prince so long there was so much rejoicing as at the birth of John the Baptist."[16] Henry had his boy.[17]

Henry made other contributions to the Protestantization of England, but some of the impact was unintentional or ancillary to Henry's primary goals, which were generally avaricious. After the passage of the Act of Supremacy, Henry began to dismantle the *monasteries*.[18] If there is no papacy in England any more, who needs the institutions that support it, especially the monasteries? There were about eight hundred of these, some very small, some large and influential, whose total value constituted "one-fifth of the kingdom's landed wealth."[19] Henry seized 399 of them initially, expelled their occupants, and sold the land and buildings off for pennies on the dollar to the rising gentry class of the *nouveaux riche* that were emerging at the time.[20] This had the dual effect of ingratiating the new nobility to Henry and of adding to the royal coffers. As the later founder of the True Levellers, Gerrard Winstanley would note, "ecclesiastical questions were also in part economic."[21] But that is not the end of that story. What Henry had no way of knowing was that this class would eventually side mainly with the New Protestants in the decades ahead, even, by the next century, with the Puritans.[22] Eventually all eight hundred monasteries would be liquidated.

---

15 Bromiley, *Thomas Cranmer*, 46–63.
16 Quoted in Weir, *Henry VIII*, 396.
17 Diarmaid MacCulloch, *The Boy-King: Edward VI and the Protestant Reformation* (New York: Palgrave, 1999), 1–39.
18 Weir, *Henry VIII*, 382–89.
19 Ibid., 385.
20 MacCulloch, *Thomas Cranmer*, 151–56.
21 Christopher Hill, *God's Englishman: Oliver Cromwell and the English Reformation*, Crosscurrents in World History (New York: Dial, 1970), 19.
22 Weir, *Henry VIII*, 386.

Struggle for the City

Tudor Economics

In spite of the auctioning off of the monastic houses, though, Henry died in debt; his courtly tastes were simply too expensive.[23] Though Henry's prerogatives to take what he wanted were significantly more limited than the later French kings' would be (due to the differences between English and French law), he took what he wanted when he could. The monastery seizures were a fortunate by-product of the Act of Supremacy, and one that would not be without its own set of *controversies* for the king and his heirs. In all, Henry was a classic example of a monarch dominating his subjects, granting them few liberties, and exploiting the economy for his own purposes. This was the *mercantilist* way.

England, like much of the rest of Western Europe but at a more *accelerated* rate, was emerging from the manorial and feudal approach to the economy, a style that had prevailed since the end of Roman times. New wealth and the rise of a merchant class was providing new opportunities for financial growth, especially in light of the rise of more powerful national governments, England being among the first to gain that power in the early sixteenth century, as a result of the previously mentioned wars among the noble classes. England was still behind the Spanish, who were plundering the Americas for gold, and the Dutch, who were finding more creative ways to become wealthy, but England was slowly rising. Her larger population, in contrast to the smaller Holland, and the shared powers between Crown, nobility, and gentry, in contrast to France's domination of the merchant class by the king, resulted in a faster climb to prosperity. "Decisions taken [during the seventeenth century, especially] enabled England to become the first industrialized imperialist great power."[24] But those developments were yet decades away; in terms of world economy it was too slow for Henry, but he was still master of his fate in his own country. This enabled Henry to assert his authority over the entire national economy and bend it to his will, which he did, to his own personal benefit.

Henry's extravagance stood in stark contrast to the bleak and dreary condition of the vast majority of his subjects. Villages were depopulated

---

23 Ibid., 54.
24 Hill, *God's Englishman*, 14.

Struggle for the City

because there was not sufficient food and because houses, bridges, and other structures were in a deplorable condition, according to a 1542 document known as *Complaynt of Roderyck Mor*.[25] This situation resulted in there being many unemployed vagrants across the countryside during the middle and end of the sixteenth century. The combination of a growing population and economic inflation were the main causes of so much discontent. The population of London rose from 60,000 in 1520 to 200,000 in 1603. One East Anglia family had 3,000 sheep in 1544, but only four years later the size of the flock was 4,200; such rapid increases depleted grass supplies.[26] England was, literally, "pestered with people,"[27] due to factors which are not entirely clear to scholars, though it was likely in part a result of young people marrying earlier than before since they were living displaced lives.[28] Those who marry early tend to have more children. This rise in population generated an inflationary spike in prices, since demand went up without a corresponding increase in supply. After the death of Henry, his son's administration tried to deal with this by appointing study commissions, who then recommended a series of "enclosure" laws, secluding land away from use in free grazing. Predictably, these laws were unpopular.[29] The result of all this was economic displacement on a large scale.

The Tudor monarchs, Henry and his three children, were forced to intervene in the economy more than previous kings. Emerging from a manorial (or feudalist) economic system into a mercantile one had enabled European monarchs to have more influence over their economic situation, since the economy was becoming more manageable (or, perhaps, easier to manipulate), and since *intellectuals* were beginning to have some idea about how to do that. The Tudor monarchs "transformed England from a feudal society to a centralized

---

25 Penry Williams, *The Tudor Regime* (1979; repr., Oxford: Clarendon, 1981), 139.
26 Alan Simpson, *The Wealth of the Gentry, 1540–1660* (Cambridge: Cambridge University Press, 1961), 183–84.
27 J. D. Chambers, *Population, Economy and Society in Pre-Industrial England* (Oxford: Oxford University Press, 1972), 27.
28 Williams, *Tudor Regime*, 142.
29 Jennifer Loach, *Edward VI*, ed. GeorgeBernard and Penry Williams, Yale English Monarchs (New Haven, CT: Yale University Press, 1999), 59–69.

Struggle for the City

state."[30] These rulers were motivated in doing so by various forces. They feared insurrection from a disaffected populace, and there had been more than one coup in England in previous centuries. They knew that foreign threats of invasion were always real, and Spain attempted to do just that in 1588, though the Spanish Armada failed abysmally. The Tudor monarchs were deeply concerned to maintain the value of the British pound in foreign commerce. Perhaps more than anything else, they longed for the *glory* of court and Crown, and money was necessary for that.[31] Commenting on Henry VIII in this regard, one historian has noted that, "He was covetous, prodigal, capricious, suspicious."[32] These traits caused him, and to some degree, at least his two daughters, to attain more control over the nation's economy than any dynasty before them.

The net effect was that they enacted a veritable plethora of regulations, about three hundred of them in all, most of which were "penal" in nature—that is, they prescribed some penalty to be inflicted on offenders. Many of these regulations had to do with textiles and concerned issues such as starching, stretching, the numbers of threads per inch, packaging, and so on, regulations that we have become familiar with in our day but that were new at the time. The interesting thing was that some textile companies, those that had curried favor with the king (or the queen) would be exempted from compliance, while other companies were levied heavy fines for failure to comply.[33] One law issued during the reign of Mary I limited the number of looms that could be owned by rural clothiers and weavers, again, to grant preferred treatment to weavers in London, who in turn could bestow preferential treatment and economic favors to the Crown.[34]

Other regulations had to do with supporting the apprenticeship regulations of the various trade guilds. The guilds pressured the Crown to support their guidelines and rewarded the kings and queens with various amenities to prevent

---

30 Michael Allen Gillespie, *The Theological Origins of Modernity* (Chicago: University of Chicago Press, 2008), 210.
31 Williams, *Tudor Regime*, 144.
32 J. H. Merle d'Aubigné, *The Reformation in England*, trans. H. White, ed. S. M. Houghton (London: Banner of Truth, 1962), 2:493.
33 Williams, *Tudor Regime*, 145–49.
34 Ibid., 155.

Struggle for the City

non-guild workers from competing.[35] In many industries, workers who wished to switch to a different kind of employment had to obtain government *approval* to do so, approval that might only be granted upon the payment of a *fee*. This governmental *tinkering* with the economy was planned, structured, and had as its net effect governmental control over England's financial markets, and the lining of the state's pockets with as much money as it could justify taking. Only the inefficiency of governmental regulators, poor communication, and inferior technology kept it from being even more intrusive.

Even more overbearing than the Tudors' manipulation of the domestic economy was their control over foreign trade, as might be expected.[36] The more that national identity displaced the previous internal feudal allegiances, the more the newly authoritarian kings and queens attempted to manipulate their economies in order to serve their own purposes. The old manorial system was bad in that it left vast majorities of the population in abject poverty; the new mercantile system was *almost* as bad in that it allowed those in power to determine just *who* would receive favored economic status, while those "outside" continued to live, generally, in abject *poverty*. This was as true of imports as it was of that productivity that was purely domestic.

From Henry to Edward

One other issue related to Henry VIII's particular contribution is salient. Beginning in 1538 the king initiated some reforms of the church, such as the destruction of shrines and relics. This was consistent with the dissolution of the monasteries but did not provide any personal financial incentive to the king in doing so. The previous year he had also allowed for the publication of the Bible in English, the Tyndale/Coverdale Bible.[37] By the end of 1538 nearly all of

---

35   Margaret G. Davies, *The Enforcement of English Apprenticeship: A Study in Applied Mercantilism, 1563–1642*, Harvard Economic Studies 97 (Cambridge: Cambridge University Press, 1956), 244–56.
36   Williams, *Tudor Regime*, 165–70.
37   F. F. Bruce, *History of the Bible in English: From the Earliest Versions*, 3rd ed. (Oxford: Oxford University Press, 1978), 57–59; Derek Wilson, *The People's Bible: The Remarkable History of the King James Version* (Oxford: Lion, 2010), 50–54; A. G. Dickens, *The English Reformation*, 2nd ed. (University Park: Pennsylvania State University Press, 1989), 131.

Struggle for the City

the monasteries had been suppressed and emptied of their residents. Henry's contribution to reform was nearly complete, or as complete as he wished for it to be. At the end of the day, Henry was still essentially personally committed to a Roman Catholic faith, though he had labored for a "middle way" in his public commitments.[38] On December 30, 1547, he commended his soul to "the glorious and blessed Virgin," and asked that masses be said for his soul.[39]

It would be Henry's son, Edward (1537–53), who would move the Church of England in the direction of substantial reforms, under the direction of Cranmer, when he became king at the demise of his father in late 1547, though it may be the case that Henry was on the verge of moving in more substantial reform directions shortly before his death.[40] Edward was only nine years old when he came to the throne, but he had been mightily influenced by his mother's family, who were committed to the new Protestant ideals, and by Cranmer.[41] Edward and his advisors, especially the Duke of Somerset, were astute and careful in the manner in which they introduced substantial reforms to the churches. Edward's new Protestant Prayer Book, for instance, was carefully worded so as not to offend any but the most contentious of Catholics.[42]

In spite of the attempts at being careful and deliberate, the new reforms were not met with universal approbation, as one might have expected, since the young "Josiah"[43] was interfering with traditions that dated back centuries. There were *riots* in parts of England in 1549 due to the new way of doing church, especially in the West and the South.[44] Other unrest in England was political and economic during the young king's rule, probably mainly caused by a sudden spike in population between 1541 and 1551, a spike that put great

---

38 G. W. Bernard, *The King's Reformation: Henry VIII and the Remaking of the English Church* (New Haven, CT: Yale University Press, 2005), throughout and then 589–606.
39 Timothy George, *John Robinson and the English Separatist Tradition*, NABPR Dissertation Series 1 (Macon, GA: Mercer University Press, 1982), 9.
40 Diarmaid MacCulloch, *The Boy King: Edward VI and the Protestant Reformation* (New York: Palgrave, 1999), 57–59.
41 His reforms included, but were not limited to, a new Book of Common Prayer, abolishing the requirement for clerical celibacy, offering the liturgy in English, abandoning the sign of the cross, etc.
42 Dickens, *English Reformation*, 219.
43 See MacCulloch, *Boy King*, 63, for the comparison with the young king of Judah.
44 Loach, *Edward VI*, 70–88.

Struggle for the City

strain on food production.[45] Still, he and his cause *survived* the uprisings and it appeared that nearly thoroughgoing reforms of the English Church would soon take hold. But it was not to last. Edward, who had always been sickly,[46] was afflicted with consumption at age sixteen and died, leaving the throne to his Catholic half sister, Mary, who immediately repealed the Act of Supremacy and initiated the process that she hoped would reinstate the papacy.[47]

Rome, Again

Under Mary (1516–58), Protestants were forced to flee, conform, or die. Nearly a thousand pastors fled to the Continent, where many of them took studies with the major Reformers such as John Calvin and Heinrich Bullinger.[48] Lutheran cities were largely closed to them for various political reasons, so the vast majority came under the wing of Calvin, Bullinger, Bucer and a few others, that is, under a type of Protestant theology that was *covenantal* and *Reformed*.[49] Lutheranism made a greater distinction between the church and the world than did "Calvinism," as we have seen, and held to a more rigid distinction between state and church, with the church under the jurisdiction of the state. The Reformed, while still advocating "two kingdoms," saw church and state more closely aligned, with the state governed by godly rulers, the church led by godly pastors, and both entities standing on similar footing, even though the church's reforms were often *tempered* by state *management*.[50]

Mary's rule, though it caused a serious disruption in the lives of the Protestant pastors of the realm, would not be long in duration, lasting only a little over five years. When these banished pastors, often known later as the "Marian Exiles," returned to England half a decade later, they would come

---

45 Ibid., 58.
46 MacCulloch, *Boy King*, 150; Loach, *Edward VI*, 159–69.
47 There is no doubt that the rapidity of Edward's changes in the church actually helped Mary in some ways, since many were still disaffected by the sudden changes mandated by the young king and longed still for "older ways."
48 Christina Hallowell Garrett, *The Marian Exiles: A Study in the Origins of Elizabethan Puritanism* (Cambridge: Cambridge University Press, 1938), 1–29.
49 Bruce Gordon, *Calvin* (New Haven, CT: Yale University Press, 2009), 259–66.
50 Quentin Skinner, *The Foundations of Modern Political Thought*, vol. 2, *The Age of the Reformation* (Cambridge: Harvard University Press, 1978), 3–15, 189–358.

Struggle for the City

back as well-educated Reformed pastors whose time in Europe had bestowed upon them even greater biblical and theological *firepower*. Their training on the Continent would also give to their view of the relationship between church and state a flavor very distinctly "Calvinistic" and covenantal. That would have huge implications in the decades to come, as we will see.

In the meantime, Mary exercised her revenge on Cranmer and the other church leaders who had cooperated with her father's plan to divorce Mary's mother and who had been complicit in driving the papacy out of England. Cranmer was executed in March 1556.[51] He had committed the dual offenses of reforming the English Church and granting Mary's father his requested annulment from her mother. Around three hundred other bishops and churchmen would also lose their lives. But Mary's reign of terror was to be fairly short-lived as she died in November 1558, childless. The reintroduction of Catholicism to the realm was, likewise, not long-lived, as Elizabeth, the last of the Tudors, would return to the policies of her father, Henry VIII, and her brother, Edward VI, or at least to some *version* of their "reformation."

Trade Is War: The Rise of the European Merchant Kings

The seventeenth century witnessed the ending of the old Europe and the birthing of a new one. The birth pangs, however, were severe, indeed! The Peace of Westphalia, which brought an end to the Thirty Years War in 1648, the last of the great religious wars between Protestant and Catholic, resulted in the emergence of the modern nations of Europe. Specifically, "The positive interpretation of Westphalia regards it as the birth of the modern international order based on sovereign states interacting (formally) as equals within a common secularized legal framework, regardless of size, power, or internal configuration."[52] While this was to be a process not quite complete until the nineteenth century, it was

---

51 MacCulloch, *Thomas Cranmer*, 594–605.
52 Peter H. Wilson, *The Thirty Years' War: Europe's Tragedy* (Cambridge: Harvard University Press, 2009), 754. Wilson goes on to qualify that assessment slightly by saying the process was already under way before Westphalia and continued to develop after 1648, but the general consensus still stands.

Struggle for the City

certainly occurring in the seventeenth. The formation of these nations, especially modern France, Holland, and Switzerland, resulted in political forces trying to find a way to make those nations increase in their wealth, since national *wealth* was seen to be tantamount to *political* power.[53]

The Rise of the Individual

Before the rise of the modern world there was the notion that everyone had a *place* to fill, a task that had been given to each person, and that each person ought to be *content* with that and not attempt to change anything about it. In Chaucer's *Canterbury Tales* the Parson says, "God had ordained that some folk should be more high in estate and in degree and some folk more low and everyone should be served in his estate and in his degree." Stick to what is yours. If you are a lord, then be a lord, and if you are a peasant, be content with that. Every political theorist from Plato to Aristotle to Augustine to Thomas Aquinas agreed on this. For Plato, a *just* society was a "society in which the members of every category of citizen perform only the function appropriate to that category."[54] Socrates actually states that it is *immoral* for a working-class man to seek to be something else other than a working-class man, that is, to be in government or to be a nobleman.[55] We all have our place and we should be content with that. Humans are equal to one another only in that they are all humans and share in a common *humanity*. They are not equal in *opportunity*, however, but are virtually locked in to a status in life from which there is little hope for deviation. They should accept that and go on with their lives. From Plato to Chaucer, that was considered to be part of what it meant to be a moral person.

As we have seen, though, the Renaissance and Reformation brought attention to *individuals*, to their own choices, and made it clear that such static roles might not be fixed. Individuals were worth something, and they had the ability to make choices that could change their lives in dramatic ways. That

53 Rondo Cameron and Larry Neal, *A Concise Economic History of the World: From Paleolithic Times to the Present*, 4th ed. (New York: Oxford University Press, 2003), 129; Wilson, *Thirty Years' War*, 371.
54 Quoted in W. R. Runciman, *Great Books, Bad Arguments: Republic, Leviathan, and the Communist Manifesto* (Princeton, NJ: Princeton University Press, 2010), 23.
55 Plato, *Republic* 2; see discussion in Runciman, *Great Books, Bad Arguments*, 25.

Struggle for the City

idea would grow only more and more common with the passing of time in early modern Europe and would spill over beyond Protestant borders into Catholic thought as well. What was happening from the Reformation on to the late eighteenth century was a rising tide of individualism, and with it an attendant political philosophy of *republicanism*, and with those a concomitant notion of a freer *economy* than had prevailed before all of this. These were, however, ideas slow to flower.

The Rise of Wealth

Trade was also growing in Europe in the seventeenth and eighteenth centuries. Wool was being shipped out of England. Fishing industries in Denmark were helping the economy of that nation. Banking was a prominent business in Holland.[56] In Venice the shipping trade had been making that city wealthy since the time of the Crusades, and by the seventeenth century the Venetians had major competition from the Spanish, the English, and the Dutch.[57] There were medieval trade fairs in which goods were exchanged by either barter or for coin or bullion. They had been around for some time, but by the seventeenth century they were growing in prominence and in the variety of goods that they could feature and sell.

There was also an increasing acceptance of *materialism* that was also in part a result of the Reformation. We pointed out in our discussion of the Reformation that both Luther and Calvin had a different philosophy of *money*, of loaning money, of profits in business, and of the value of material things than had been common in Catholicism. *Greed* was one of the seven deadly sins for Catholics, and as we have seen in a previous chapter, the most "holy" people of all renounced *all* worldly things. But the idea had begun to develop that having *some* possessions was not necessarily wrong.[58] We saw in our discussion of

---

56 Cameron and Neal, *Concise Economic History of the World*, 131.
57 Gregory Clark, *A Farewell to Alms: A Brief Economic History of the World*, Princeton Economic History of the Western World (Princeton, NJ: Princeton University Press, 2008), 166–92. They had had competition from the Portuguese in the previous century, but more about that later.
58 Tom Bethell, *The Noblest Triumph: Property and Prosperity through the Ages* (New York: Palgrave Macmillan, 1998), 19–32.

Struggle for the City

the Reformation, and we will see again in our discussion of American Puritanism, that Calvinism teaches that a *chastened* and disciplined sort of selfishness is not necessarily an evil in itself. This idea took root in the early seventeenth century, even in Catholic circles, and there was an increasing tendency for Europeans to want to have some luxuries in life—at least those who can afford them. A defense of the practice of holding private property will be mounted in the seventeenth and eighteenth centuries, and by the 1870s even the Catholic papacy will weigh in, arguing for the right of property.

The Dutch Make Their Mark

One of the most important developments in the early seventeenth century was the ratcheting up of trade between Europe and the "East Indies," a term that designated the lands from Egypt and India to Indonesia and Japan. Several European countries competed for the products that came from there, but the two nations that wound up at the head of the pack in the seventeenth century were England and the Netherlands. The Netherlands was arguably the *wealthiest* and most *technologically* advanced of the European nations in the seventeenth century.[59] Amsterdam was the *center* of international commerce in the early 1600s and the Dutch East India Company was the world's first-ever joint-stock company with a permanent share capital.[60] This giant corporation boasted 150 merchant ships and forty enormous warships, and it employed fifty thousand people at its peak, of whom ten thousand were private military men.

The eventual wealth and dominance of the Dutch East India Company was due in large part to its cornering the market on Indonesian spices, especially nutmeg, cloves, and mace.[61] Originally, nutmeg and mace were to be found only on five islands in the Banda Island group in eastern Indonesia. The two spices come from the same tree, and they were coveted (along with cloves,

---

59 By midcentury the Netherlands controlled half of Europe's foreign trade. Stephen R. Bown, *Merchant Kings: When Companies Ruled the World, 1600–1900* (New York: Saint Martin's, 2009), 52.

60 Earlier we noted that Venice produced joint-stock corporations as early as the time of the Crusades, but these were temporary ventures.

61 For a thorough treatment of this, see Michael Krondl, *The Taste of Conquest: The Rise and Fall of the Three Great Cities of Spice* (New York: Ballantine Books, 2007).

Struggle for the City

also from Indonesia) by Europeans for their flavoring, aromatic, and supposed medicinal uses. The Romans first learned of the spices through traders who brought them to India and Arabia, and sought them out to bring new life to drab foods.[62] For the Europeans, though, they had greater value as personal *fragrances* to be worn in pouches and situated in strategic places on one's body or in clothing. European hygiene at the time left something to be wanted, and long rides in closed carriages at close quarters could be quite an olfactory *ordeal*. So, the aromatic spices were coveted by the *gentry* and *noble* classes. Arab merchants had discovered the islands in the medieval period and began selling the spices to Venetian traders, though they did not divulge the whereabouts of the source. In August 1511 Alfonso de Albuquerque, a Portuguese nobleman and admiral, defeated an Arab force at Malacca in Indonesia, and thus discovered the whereabouts of the Spice Islands. He seized control of the trade for the newly wealthy and powerful nation of Portugal, though in 1519 Magellan sailed to the same islands and injected Spain into the market as well.

The Portuguese knew that they had superior maritime technology in the early sixteenth century, and they exploited that superiority both militarily and in commerce, virtually *uniting* those two spheres. "The Portuguese government was the first to attack the principle—common throughout the region—that the sea belonged to no one, and the first to use force to redirect trade."[63] They built forts at Malacca and Hormuz and claimed *exclusive* rights to the pepper trade and the right to sink any ship that attempted competition in that trade. Theirs was a brief foray into government-sponsored, terrorist-supported, mercantilist economics and trade. The counterattack came from the Turks initially and eventually from the Dutch and the English.[64]

By 1600 Portugal's tiny size was making it difficult for the enterprising little country to continue to compete with the large European nations, nations that now had the same nautical technology as the small Iberian coun-

---

62 J. Innes Miller, *The Spice Trade of the Roman Empire, 29 B.C. to A.D. 641* (Oxford: Clarendon, 1969).

63 Kenneth Pomeranz and Steven Topik, *The World That Trade Created: Society, Culture, and the World Economy, 1400 to the Present*, 3rd ed., Sources and Studies in World History (New York: M. E. Sharpe, 2013), 19.

64 Ibid., 18.

Struggle for the City

try.[65] Beginning in 1603, the Dutch engaged in a decade-long struggle to oust both the Portuguese and the Spanish from their hold on the spice trade, and in result the Dutch now *monopolized* the trade.[66] The Dutch East Indies Company was given sole authority to trade for spice by the States General, the government of the Netherlands. They were also given full permission to maintain that exclusive trade by the States General, *no matter what.* The *no matter what* eventually included war with the British, plus torture and execution of scores of natives as well as of many Japanese. In the words of Jan Pieterszoon Coen, the man who was appointed by the Company to manage the work in Indonesia, writing to the Council that governed the Company, "Your Honours should know by experience that trade in Asia must be driven and maintained under the protection and favor of your Honours' own weapons, and that the weapons must be paid for by the profits from the trade; so that we cannot carry out trade without war, nor war without trade."[67] This is *mercantilist* economics at its very core—big profits, big government that grants favored status and monopolistic authority and the right to use force to select business ventures, and trade *as war.*

Around the world similar events were transpiring in the one Dutch colonial holding in North America, but with very different results. In September 1609 the Dutch mariner Henry Hudson dropped anchor off the coast of what we would later call Coney Island, and then proceeded to sail his "full-rigged ship *Half Moon* 150 miles up the river later named for him, reaching as far as present-day Albany."[68] He, of course, was looking for a northwest passage to the East Indies and was not much interested in anything else this new land might offer. The next year a group of Dutch merchants launched what they hoped would be a lucrative fur-trapping business. These were *practical* men who were not interested in the "pie in the sky" of hidden sea routes to fabulous

---

65 Portugal's population was only two million at the time, and the continuous wars that would be waged over the spice trade and other areas of trading, the continuous shipwrecks, and other misfortunes took a heavy toll on the young male population. A. R. Disney, *A History of Portugal and the Portuguese Empire: From Beginnings to 1807,* vol. 1, *Portugal* (Cambridge: Cambridge University Press, 2009), 280–325.

66 Bown, *Merchant Kings,* 24–38.

67 Ibid., 38.

68 John Steele Gordon, *An Empire of Wealth: The Epic History of American Economic Power* (New York: HarperCollins, 2004), 4.

Struggle for the City

lands; they were more interested in the "soft gold" that was right under their noses up the Hudson, Connecticut, and Delaware rivers.[69] As the epicenter of their trading efforts, they constructed some ramshackle huts at the southern tip of Manhattan Island and proceeded quietly to become rich.[70]

By 1621 the extent of the possibilities to generate a lucrative trade for pelts had become obvious to observers in the Netherlands, and in that year another joint-stock corporation came into existence, the Dutch West India Corporation, and two years later it was granted exclusive monopolistic authority to trade in the colony then known as New Netherlands. It was a joint-stock company whose goal was to earn profits for its stockholders, but once given monopolistic status by the States General it would eventually also be "driven by geopolitics."[71] Whether those two goals were compatible was a question that would be raised in a baptism of fire.

The first two decades of the new Company's charter witnessed a host of challenges to the stability of the enterprise. One had to do with a lack of clear objective for those who worked for the Company. Were they there to trade for furs or to act as agents provocateur against Spanish trading efforts? The directors of the company wanted them to engage in *both*, since profits were obtainable from both. These are very different activities, but we have already noted how the Portuguese and the Dutch in Asia often blurred the lines between commerce and acts of war. Both sets of activities earned very lucrative rewards.

Another challenge involved the desire of the settlers to have opportunities to have farms and raise cattle and crops along with their Company work. The Company viewed that as *conflict of interest*, and over the entire time the Dutch held New Netherlands this would be a source of conflict. They did not even build a church for seventeen years. This was, technically, not a colony, but a work outpost, as far as the Company was concerned.[72] In addition, the first two governors were brutal men who hired "Indian Fighters" to harass and murder

---

69 Bown, *Merchant Kings*, 71.
70 For a fascinating read through the primary sources of the history of this part of colonial development, see Russell Shorto, *The Island at the Center of the Earth: The Epic Story of Dutch Manhattan and the Forgotten Colony That Shaped America* (New York: Vintage Books, 2005).
71 Poweranz and Topik, *World That Trade Created*, 157.
72 Gordon, *Empire of Wealth*, 38.

Struggle for the City

local Native Americans in an attempt to frighten them into submission. Though the Company was not *theoretically* opposed to such tactics (the East India Company employed them regularly), when they backfired the directors removed those governors. Even the brilliant and remarkable Pieter Stuyvesant was unable to resolve the differences between the settlers and the directors.

England Takes Over

The question of who would win out, the settlers or the directors of the Company, would eventually be settled, not by the Company or the States General, but by the English. The outbreak of the First Anglo-Dutch War in 1652 made the earlier conflicts in New Amsterdam seem remote and petty. Stuyvesant constructed a palisade around the settlement to prepare in case armed conflict found its way across the Atlantic. It was to no avail. "After the restoration of the English monarchy in Britain [in 1660], the English moved quickly to reestablish their authority along the Atlantic coast from Newfoundland to Florida."[73] When an English fleet anchored in the harbor in September 1664, the people of New Amsterdam marched out of their walled city and welcomed the new conquerors with open arms. They had more hope to gain freedom from the conquering English than they had been able to secure from their *own* government back home.[74]

The Second Anglo-Dutch War, which ended with the Treaty of Breda in 1667, made it finally clear that the Dutch would not have any hope for the return of New Amsterdam to them. In return the Dutch regained Surinam (Dutch Guiana) and the nutmeg island of Run as part of the settlement. "What was to become the most famous city in the world was bargained away for a tiny and barren nutmeg island in Indonesia and some South American slave-dependent sugar plantations."[75] The one concession Stuyvesant bargained for before surrendering the palisade was that the residents of New

---

73 William J. Bennett, *America: The Last Best Hope*, vol. 1, *From the Age of Discovery to a World at War, 1492–1914* (Nashville: Nelson Current, 2006), 44. The "Restoration" will be explained later.

74 Jenny Uglow, *A Gambling Man: Charles II's Restoration Game* (New York: Farrar, Straus and Giroux, 2009), 315.

75 Bown, *Merchant Kings*, 100–101.

Struggle for the City

Holland would be granted *liberty of conscience* in matters related to religion, so that its inhabitants would not be coerced into following the established faiths of the English colonies, a concession that was granted. That left a little bit of "going Dutch" there after the departure of the Netherlanders as governors.[76]

France and the Origin of "Economics"

Since nation building was the order of the day, the mercantilist economics of the time was really a matter of intellectuals and activists serving their lords or their sovereigns in helping to build national power. One of the most important ways of developing national power was through the accumulation of *gold*. The thought of the day was that *wealth* was a matter of how much gold a country had. This was the mercantilist philosophy of wealth—wealth is constituted in gold and silver bullion or coin, but *especially* in gold. Each nation wanted to have more gold than other nations, since that was in itself what constituted wealth.[77] It is not that previous cultures had not recognized the value of gold for an economy, but it was at this time—the time of new gold discoveries in South and Central America—that intellectuals and kings developed this as a philosophical/economic system of thought. And so, their lust for gold *grew* since they were convinced that this was the way to win the wars that were so frequent between the European powers—both the trade wars and the actual wars. As we have seen, the two were inextricably intertwined and often indistinguishable.

A Mercantilist Nation

European nations were plundering the Americas (South and Central America) for their gold reserves and bringing ship after ship back to Europe, laden with bullion. Lords often had "war chests," which were, literally, large chests filled with gold and silver coins and bullion. This wealth would be used to finance war and other matters of concern. Of course, if one has more gold, one can loan money to businesses in one's country, businesses that might build things like

---

76 Ibid., 102.
77 Mark Skousen, *The Making of Modern Economics*, 2nd ed. (Armonk, NY: M. E. Sharpe, 2009), 17.

ships and cannons. It served a similar role as *credit* does in our modern economies, but of course, there were limitations, since credit is a fluid matter; but if it
is all based on gold, then it is limited to the actual amount of gold that is in the
treasure chest.[78] This mercantilist understanding of the economy worked best
when it was conjoined with a powerful *state*, since the state could, then, cause
the economy to work in the manner dictated by its leaders, or *leader*.

The mercantilist system can, perhaps, best be viewed by taking a snippet
out of the history of France in the 1660s and afterward. Louis XIV was king,
having taken the throne at age four, though his rule was directed and guided
by Cardinal Mazarin until the Cardinal's death, when Louis was eighteen.
Louis was a very devout Catholic, though he was opposed to both to the
extreme French nationalist Catholics (Gallicans) and to the *extreme* papalists
(Ultramontanists).[79] When he assumed full duties as king, Louis retained the
services of Mazarin's financial secretary, Jean-Baptiste Colbert. Colbert possessed the ability to put the resources of France at the disposal of the young
king in a way previously unseen on a national scale. Louis was determined
to hold absolute sway over his people, much as Philip II had held the reins
of power in Spain in the previous century.[80] These men, who ruled their own
countries for seventy-two and seventy-one years, respectively, held to *divine
right* views on the role of the king.[81] Louis was an absolutist monarch and the
implications of that for a national economy were about to be applied for the
first time in history.

A prominent debate of the time in France was between the Ultramontan-
ist party and the Gallican party. The Ultramontanists (a term that means "over
the mountains" in an obvious reference to the papacy in Rome) held that the
pope ought to have final authority in France not only in spiritual matters, but
temporal ones as well. The Gallicans (a term that pointed to the ancient name

78 Mark Skousen, *Economics of a Pure Gold Standard*, 4th ed. (Atlanta: Foundation for
    Economic Education, 2010).
79 Emmanuel Le Roy Ladurie, *The Ancien Régime: A History of France, 1610–1774*, trans.
    Mark Greengrass, History of France (1991; Oxford: Blackwell, 1996), 21–22.
80 Geoffrey Parker, *The Grand Strategy of Philip II* (New Haven, CT: Yale University Press,
    2000), 92–93 and throughout.
81 John Neville Figgis, *The Theory of the Divine Right of Kings* (1896; facsimile repr., London:
    Nabu, 2010).

Struggle for the City

of the region, Gaul) held, to the contrary, that the pope had spiritual authority only and that political, temporal power was in the hands of the French governing authorities, especially the king. With his absolutist views in place, it comes as no surprise to anyone that Louis, and his court with him, sided with the Gallicans, though he was, as noted, "[hostile] toward the extreme Gallicanism of various individuals in his entourage."[82] He was a Gallican, but he considered the extremists to be closer to the Protestant Huguenots than to a historic love of France. So, what of his policies on finance and trade?

Jean-Baptiste Colbert

Finance Minister Colbert observed that much trade between nations was carried out on the seas.[83] Since that was so, if France wished to get the greatest *advantage* in the acquisition of gold and to get the upper hand in trade, it should go to war with the nation that had the greatest *amount* of trade on the high seas, so under Colbert's advice France started a war with the Dutch. He advised the king to burn as many Dutch ships in 1672 as the French navy could possibly burn. This was because he believed that France needed the upper hand in trade no matter what the moral cost might be. France had to be bringing in more gold than any other country, whether by war or trade, and again the two practices were *not* far apart. In fact, in mercantilist economics, as we have seen, there is a sense in which trade *is* war. Those nations that had for centuries fought wars with each other over land and possessions, now fought each other both literally by war for gold and in trade wars also for the same commodity.

Colbert's aim was to make France the *greatest nation* in the world and to do so by meticulous management of *every* aspect of the French economy. The first step in launching such a venture was to control information. Max Weber has noted that state paperwork engendered the need for bureaucracy, which can be defined as "the exercise of control on the basis of knowledge."[84] To centralize a government

---

82 Le Roy Ladurie, *Ancien Régime*, 21.
83 Jacob Soll, *The Information Master: Jean-Baptiste Colbert's Secret State Intelligence System,* Cultures of Knowledge in the Early Modern World (Ann Arbor: University of Michigan Press, 2009), 36.
84 James E. King, *Science and Rationalism in the Government of Louis XIV, 1661–1683* (Baltimore: Johns Hopkins University Press, 1949).

Struggle for the City

one first had to identify its archives and to centralize them.[85] A person in a suffi-cient position of authority might then control the flow of information—all infor-mation, potentially—and thereby control the entire economy. This was Colbert's aim, and he established a strategy for doing this at every possible level.[86]

Colbert employed the assistance of intellectuals, merchants, military men, and a host of others in his scheme to have the Crown dominate *every* area of French cultural and political life.[87] He used intellectuals to develop an intricate system of espionage that enabled him to follow the movements and machina-tions of nobles, of foreign sailing vessels, of merchants in the colonies, and of church officials, in essence forming "a centralized, internal corps of professional state observers whose writings would have concrete results."[88] Only the *Jesuits* had ever worked harder to formulate a system of espionage like that developed by Colbert.[89] Indeed, Colbert had early on trained to be a Jesuit priest.

But there were other issues for Colbert. In mercantilist economics it is expedient for the government to be in control of the economy of the *nation* as well, to the degree that it could. Colbert built France into the one nation of its time that was actually capable of doing so, far more than England, Holland, or the previously strong but now much weakened Spain.[90] Much of this had to do with the previously noted absolutism that underlay Louis's policies. France had nothing similar to the English Magna Carta, a regulative device that lim-ited the authority of the monarch in that country. The French *Parlement* held much less authority than its English counterpart, due both to the constitutions of France and to its recent history at that time. All of this allowed Colbert to run roughshod, with virtually no restraint.

Colbert's power also played into the Crown's interests. Since the court of the king was a significantly large contributor to economic exchange in France,

---

85 Le Roy Ladurie, *Ancien Régime*, 162–63.

86 Soll, *Information Master*, 1–33.

87 Frances A. Yates, *The French Academies of the Sixteenth Centuries*, Studies of the Warburg Institute 15 (London: University of London, Warburg Institute, 1947).

88 Soll, *Information Master*, 71, see also 67–83.

89 See Allan Greer, ed., *The Jesuit Relations: Natives and Missionaries in Seventeenth Century America*, Bedford Series in History and Culture (Boston: St. Martin's Press, 2000); Jonathan Wright, *God's Soldiers: Adventure, Politics, Intrigue, and Power—A History of the Jesuits* (New York: Doubleday, 2005), esp. 228–42.

90 Le Roy Ladurie, *Ancien Régime*, 178.

Struggle for the City

Colbert had a platform from which he issued strict regulations on such things as manufacturing. In the manufacture of cloth, just like in England, there were rigid guidelines on how many threads per square inch there had to be on various kinds of cloth—not simply for the garments of the court, but for all manufacturing. He applied similar regulations and standards to virtually all industry, and even to the production and distribution of food. Government inspectors went around investigating manufacturing plants to be sure they were up to the required standards. He was responsible for helping to organize the tax base of the nation and oversaw the *intendants*, whose responsibility it was to gather taxes from the people.[91] Colbert attempted to "increase the productivity of the French economy in much the same way that a drill sergeant tries to enhance the performance of his soldiers."[92] He built many very good roads in France, but he built them by forced, compulsory labor. He passed laws demanding child labor. Children who did not enter the workforce by age of six were fined. France must be productive, and even productive to the point of forcing children to work.

Colbert's accumulation and control of data was enormous. He kept elaborate "inventories, scrapbooks, journals, and ledgers for each tax farmer, region, different tax and different royal expenditure."[93] He required his assistants to master double-entry bookkeeping and to manage all national, regional, and district accounting data using that method. He built his own library to be second in size only to the Royal Library, and there, along with an extensive book collection, he kept all his notebooks, journals, and folders containing the data his agents had amassed in their efforts to catalogue the economy, the travels of nobles, the state of foreign trade, and information of foreign domestic life—hundreds of thousands of individual documents and collections of material, all of it organized in such a way that he, the Information Master, could put his hands on just the required piece of paper or ledger within moments. The nineteenth-century editor of Colbert's papers offered his opinion that Colbert was truly obsessed with knowing, literally, everything that could be known about every nook and cranny of the large

---

91 Soll, *Information Master*, 68.
92 Cameron and Neal, *Concise Economic History of the World*, 149.
93 Soll, *Information Master*, 64.

Struggle for the City

and expansive French countryside and city life in the twenty-two years that he served Louis XIV.[94]

Such a project had never been possible before on such a grand scale in a nation as expansive as France. What made it possible was the confluence of several streams: Louis's absolutism, the French system's restraint on local power as over against the monarchy, France's economic health (at least compared to her neighbors) in Louis's early rule, and Jean-Baptiste Colbert's unique genius. Without him, and in far advance to any sort of data storage and quick retrieval system, none of this would have worked. A testimony to that fact is seen in the rapid dismantling of much of the system after his death in 1683.[95] The state remained strong, largely due to the continued shadow of Colbert falling across Louis' administration, but the system broke down without the spiderlike man sitting in his library, hunting down papers and issuing orders to hundreds of agents who would go out to fetch new data and issue new mandates that came with all the authority of the Crown.

Fascism in France under Louis

In a very real sense, the administration of Louis XIV was Rome *redivivus*. It was the first great *administrative state* of the modern world. The modern rebirth of Rome had begun with the Renaissance, the very name of that movement being testimony to that fact.[96] Yet the stirrings of old Rome in Northern Italy resulted in the restoration of the spirit of Rome's *cultural* achievements, but not its *administrative state*—that would have to wait for Louis and his "Information Master."[97] In Louis, Paris had *become* Rome, and in some ways in a far more controlling and administrative fashion than old Rome ever could have been. What also contributed to this was the relationship between church and state and the prevailing theological orthodoxy. In some European countries at the time, notably England, Scotland, the Netherlands, parts of Germany and parts

---

94 Ibid., 4.
95 Ibid., 153–68.
96 Bard Thompson, *Humanists and Reformers: A History of the Renaissance and Reformation* (Grand Rapids, MI: Eerdmans, 1996), 32–38.
97 Soll, *Information Master*, 16–17.

Struggle for the City

of the Swiss Confederation, Reformation theology was transforming people, government, church, and the economy. Louis did everything in his power to hold the French Protestants, the Huguenots, at bay, preventing them from exerting any significant influence on government or the nation at large.[98]

Colbert was successful. *Price stability* never wavered during his administration.[99] There was no *monetary devaluation* in the years that he controlled the nation's economy. He led France to develop industrially in a way that it had never done before, in part to try to catch up with the Dutch. In silk manufacturing, in ribbon-making, in printing, in the manufacturing of silk hosiery on a loom, the finance minister took France to new heights, even though those heights were doomed to fade in the later years of Louis XIV's reign.[100] Many nations, then and *since then*, could wish for such success over such a lengthy period of time.

There was, however, also a significant amount of *corruption* that stemmed from Colbert's backroom machinations, and not an inconsiderable amount of it attached to Colbert himself, who amassed a huge fortune and an even larger library, at a time when that was what often made a man respectable in the eyes of others, especially of intellectuals, who otherwise considered Colbert to be their inferior. Payments to spies along with favorable status given to certain industries or to certain manufacturers within industries was common in Louis's France. Freezing out nobles who were not loyal to Louis, bribes paid to others—all of this was common to the French Crown as well. It was also true of other European states at the time, but none of them exhibited the truly *dominant* administrative state in the way France did. None of them was as thoroughly "fascist," in the way we have employed that term in this book, in the way that France was. In Louis's reign, with Colbert as his chief industrial and financial architect, France was fascist in an unprecedented fashion for a nation of its size. France never became as *financially successful* as the Dutch *before* them or the British *after* them, but it did *control* the economy in a far more absolutist fashion than either of the other nations.

---

98 Le Roy Ladurie, *Ancien Régime*, 147–48.
99 Ibid., 169.
100 Ibid., 171–78. The loom itself was a "machine" that was composed of 3,500 metal parts and had been invented at the end of the sixteenth century.

Struggle for the City

The First "Economists"

Colbert did not carry out his work without opposition. His insidious efforts to control France's entire economy actually called forth the first efforts at *intellectual reflection* on the task of economics in the form of a *school* that we have come to know as the *Physiocrats*. They were thoroughly opposed to the kind of fascist tinkering and control that Colbert exhibited. Instead of having the government control everything, which often led to war, poverty, political favoritism, and oppression, the Physiocrats wished to propose a new approach to political economy. They were the first set of thinkers known as "economists," in French, "*Les Economistes*," a term that means the "rule of nature."[101] They were the first to propose the notion of *laissez-faire*, a term that simply meant, "let it be."[102] Apparently the Dauphin of France once commented to François Quesnay, one of the chief Physiocrat philosophers, that governing was very difficult. Quesnay replied that governing was actually not difficult. The Dauphin then asked Quesnay what he would do; the philosopher replied, "Nothing."

Quesnay and his associates, such as Anne-Robert-Jacques Turgot, believed that if the government would simply leave the economy alone, it would all work out. Turgot was actually a successor to Colbert's position during the reign of Louis XVI, though with obviously *different* priorities.[103] He was eventually forced out by a coalition of nobles, tax farmers, and the aristocracy, each seeking only his own interests and each believing that his *own* interests were paramount, a trend that did not begin and would not end with the French economy of the time. This bickering and the inability of the French kings in the eighteenth century to get a handle on the situation would lead to mounting debt and lack of productivity, eventually leading to the French Revolution.[104]

The Physiocrats recognized that the economy included several groups: peasants, landlords, aristocrats, merchants, and the king. But they believed that if the king would simply let everything be, that a "natural" equilibrium

101 Cameron and Neal, *Concise Economic History of the World*, 149.
102 Mark Skousen, *The Big Three in Economics: Adam Smith, Karl Marx and John Maynard Keynes*, Gale Virtual Reference Library (New York: M. E. Sharpe, 2007), 42.
103 Skousen, *Big Three in Economics*, 43.
104 Clark, *Farewell to Alms*, 230.

Struggle for the City

would work itself out over time.[105] This was due to the fact that self-interest was the motivation of every participant in the economy and that each individual was best suited to determine what goods were best for *him*, and what exactly he wanted from life. So, if everyone were simply allowed to pursue their own interests, without governmental *interference or preference*, everything would work out, since the economic system itself depended on a *network* of interrelated individuals each working at the same goal. In the aftermath of Colbert's tinkering, this seemed all the more obvious to the Physiocrat economists. Government interference and micromanagement (to use a term from our time) simply caused that process to become more *sluggish* and also brought corruption and oppression into the mix.

So, the government should just "let it be." In some ways, this was a bit naïve, especially since in France at the time there was little recourse for the peasant class, and the Physiocrats knew this. But their work was prescient of a more sophisticated model that would arise in the late eighteenth century in Great Britain. After a survey of some important developments related to our narrative in England, we will turn to that model.

---

105 Cameron and Neal, *Concise Economic History of the World*, 149.

Struggle for the City

Chapter 14

From England to America

THE BATON OF LEADERSHIP in the world economy would pass from the Dutch to the English by the late 1600s. We will give some reasons why the leadership changed, but the "why" is not our main concern. It is *what* that leadership is going to mean for England, though even moreso what it will mean for *America,* that is our major concern. In this chapter, we will begin to turn our attention to the main concern we have in writing this book—the question, "What is America to do?"

FROM MERCANTILIST KINGS TO ENTREPRENEURIAL PURITANS

Mary I of England died in 1558. Since she had no issue (children) and her husband had no claim to the Crown, when she died the throne was passed to the last living child of Henry VIII, Elizabeth (1533–1603). She was twenty-five years old and unmarried.

Queen Elizabeth I

Elizabeth had learned, so she claimed, from her two sibling monarchs about how *not* to handle the relationship between Crown and church. It is difficult "to be certain about Elizabeth's personal beliefs because she had to hide them for much of her life, and she became very skilled at telling people what she knew they wanted to hear."[1] She certainly had advisors, and they were likely at odds with each other about what should be done. In the end she chose a middle path, one that was neither Calvinist nor Catholic, but somewhere between.[2] We may not know what she thought, but we do know what she did. First, she drove Catholicism back out of England by reenacting the Act of Supremacy and then the Act of Uniformity, both in 1559, thus bringing to a final end efforts at reuniting London (or Canterbury) and Rome.[3] She then restored Cranmer's and Edward's Book of Common Prayer to the churches. She lifted the ban on clerical marriage that had been reinstated by Mary. But having taken those measures, she was not inclined to advance much further in reforming the Church of England. As we noted of her father in the previous chapter, Elizabeth was committed to the "Middle Way."

Elizabeth understood that the mass of people in the churches did not so much mind what theology was being preached from the pulpit—even predestination—but they could grow quite surly when the visible *accoutrements* of worship were altered. So, in 1567, Elizabeth made it clear to the bishops that ministers (or priests) were to continue to wear the same *vestment* (robe) that had been worn for decades when administering their pastoral duties.[4] To many of the pastors, and especially those who had been to Geneva and Zurich during the Mary years and had seen what *real* Reformed worship was like, this was nothing less than theological and ecclesiastical *compromise*, the wearing of the "rags of popery."[5] What Reformed pastor could stand to preach the pure Word of God while wearing a Catholic robe, knowing all that it symbolized? Most of these English divines were convinced that they should

---

1   Rudolph W. Heinze, *Reform and Conflict: From the Medieval World to the Wars of Religion* (Grand Rapids, MI: Baker, 2005), 238.

2   Patrick McGrath, *Papists and Puritans under Elizabeth I*, Blandford History Series, Problems of History (London: Blandford, 1967), 1–26.

3   Diarmaid MacCulloch, *Christianity* (New York: Penguin Books, 2009), 670.

4   This "Vestment Controversy" became the real dividing line between Elizabeth and her more zealous reformers. Patrick Collinson, "The 'Nott Conformytye' of the Young John Whitgift," in *Godly People: Essays on English Protestantism and Puritanism*, History Series 23 (London: Hambledon, 1983), 325–34; Patrick Collinson, "The Reformer and the Archbishop: Martin Bucer and the English Bucerian," in *Godly People*, 39–40.

5   Earle E. Cairns, *Christianity through the Centuries: A History of the Christian Church*, 3rd ed. (Grand Rapids, MI: Zondervan, 1996), 328.

Struggle for the City

follow the Bible in setting their church governmental and worship polity, not *merely* in its teachings about God and salvation.[6]

Elizabeth had other ideas about the matter. For her it was more import-ant to keep ancient traditions, and in her mediating Protestant thinking, the clothing one wore in the pulpit had little or no theological significance; it did, however, have great significance for tradition and order. She promised the protesting bishops that in time the restrictions on clerical dress would be relaxed and asked the ministers to "tarry" with her but insisted that such measures were necessary for maintaining order and peace in the church. She well remembered the riots of 1549 when her half-brother attempted more substantial reforms.

The Reformed pastors had two options. They could yield to the queen and the bishops and wear the hated garments or they could resign their churches. Some were fortunate enough to have wealthy parishioners who could set them up as "lecturers" after they resigned, and so they could offer weekly "lectures" (sermons in some place other than a church) and continue to minister, though not in a fully pastoral manner.[7] They were not in a *church* and there was no administration of sacraments, but as lecturers they could still "preach."

Others made the decision to remain as pastors and wear the hated robe. They decided that their calling was to *pastor* and that they could only *purify* the lives and doctrine of their people by continuing in that capacity. Some of them held personally to Presbyterian views of church government, oth-ers believed churches should be independent from one another with a more "congregational" polity. They were united in their belief that Episcopal polity was wrong and, generally, also in their broadly "Calvinistic" views on salva-tion, but they made the compromise and stayed in. They soon were handed the nickname "Puritan."[8] As time went by, this loose-knit group of Anglican pastors would develop their own views on the relation between church, state,

---

6 Leland Ryken, *Worldly Saints: The Puritans as They Really Were* (Grand Rapids, MI: Zondervan, 1986), 112–15.

7 Paul S. Seaver, *The Puritan Lectureships: The Politics of Religious Dissent 1560–1662* (Stanford, CA: Stanford University Press, 1970).

8 Originally the term "Puritan" referred only to that generation of state-church Reformers who determined to compromise with the queen over the Vestment Controversy, though,

Struggle for the City

and monarchy, views that were not completely uniform with one another but generally at odds with the "high-church" Anglican leadership.

From Henry to Elizabeth, and on into the next century, with the brief exception of the rule of Mary, Rome was rejected as the seat of the English Church. But what took its place? It was not exactly a new Romanism, yet it was also not exactly the kind of Reformed church or church and state relationship represented by the views of Luther or Calvin, though it was closer to Luther than to Calvin. What happened in this odd and unique confluence of Canterbury and London in which the monarch was the head of the church and exercised that headship through the Archbishop? London and Canterbury *together* form a kind of Jerusalem, but only in an *authoritative* sense; not *necessarily* in a pietistic sense.[9] Both the Henrician (Henry VIII) and the Elizabethan reforms were essentially about form and authority, not theology.

The basic idea for this view of state over church, princes over bishops, stemmed from the writings of Renaissance humanist Marsiglio of Padua, who contended that the state is omnipotent, self-sufficient, and entirely responsible for supplying for the needs of the people in this present life.[10] The state also derives its authority from the people, in Marsiglio's view. The church supplies for the needs of the people in the life to come. Because of that, in this age, according to a historian of England's version of church and state relations, "the Church can have no authority, no property, no jurisdiction save those which the state sees fit to lend it."[11] This position came to be known as Erastianism. The church has no temporal authority in this age—it has spiritual authority, but that is all. The church in turn is under the authority of the state, in the English situation, that is, under the monarch of England.

---

later, it will come to be used of a broader group that really had nothing to do with that controversy.

9   Philip E. Hughes, *Theology of the English Reformers* (Grand Rapids, MI: Eerdmans, 1965), 225–62.

10 See Marsiglio of Padua, *Writings on the Empire: Defensor minor and De translatione Imperii*, trans. Cary J. Nederman and Fiona Watson, ed. Cary J. Nederman, Cambridge Texts in the History of Political Thought (1326; Cambridge: Cambridge University Press, 1993).

11 A. G. Dickens, *The English Reformation*, 2nd ed. (University Park: Pennsylvania State University Press, 1989), 84.

Struggle for the City

The Puritans, God, and Vocation

So, what of these Puritans, these "reformers within the reform"? What did they believe about humanity, state, and economy? The Puritans inherited their views on worship, work, and wealth essentially from Calvin and other thinkers in the "Reformed" (non-Lutheran Protestant) tradition, but added their own "English" twist. To get the picture it will be helpful to take a brief snapshot of the overall English economy and social situation at the time.

A lot of people sat around doing nothing in England during this period—whether it was lords and courtiers or peasants—due to the aforementioned economic hardships. London was generally an exception to this malaise, noise filling the city constantly, "noise associated with energy, and specifically with the making of money."[12] But much of the rest of the country was in financial straits. In Thomas More's *Utopia*,[13] written during Henry's reign and constituting the first delineation of the hopes for the New World by an Englishman, More painted what he considered to be the ideal society that might be constructed in "America," which of course, had been "discovered" but not yet *colonized* by the English. Thomas More was critical of the idleness of people under Henry's reign, the idleness of *both* nobles and peasants. So, he wrote of a new world in which *everyone* worked. But even in More's fiction, people do not work much—only a few hours a day. And work is depicted in largely *negative* terms, especially manual labor, which is to be *despised*. More important, for More, is *intellectual* activity and the opportunity for "gentlemen" to sit and engage in pleasant discourse, an engagement anticipated, as we have seen, as far back as Plato's *Republic*. For More, work is not personally satisfying, but merely a means of self-discipline.[14] This is what one might have been expected from an English aristocrat at the time. "Work" was used by More as a rhetorical device to lecture the *lower classes* on idleness and drunkenness.

What about Puritan views on the matter? William Perkins, who taught theology at Cambridge during the reign of Elizabeth, argued in contrast to More

---

12 Peter Ackroyd, *London: The Biography* (New York: Nan A. Talese, Doubleday, 2001), 67.
13 Thomas More, *The Complete Works of St. Thomas More*, vol. 4, *Utopia*, ed. Edward Surtz and J. H. Hexter, Yale Edition of the Complete Works of St. Thomas More (1516; Eng. trans., 1551; New Haven, CT: Yale University Press, 1965).
14 J. H. Hexter, *More's Utopia: The Biography of an Idea*, History of Ideas Series 5 (Princeton, NJ: Princeton University Press, 1952), 84.

Struggle for the City

that as soon as Adam was created, God assigned him work, the cultivation of the garden. Perkins noted that, "Adam in his innocence had all things at his will, yet then God employed him in a calling."[15] Perkins recognized that work is not a consequence of sin, and is a means of fulfillment, rather than of punishment.[16] Perkins went on to make the point that there is no distinction between manual labor and other activities, whether vocational or aesthetic. The covenant is both conditional and unconditional.[17] This view was in direct contrast to most of the consensus of Western thought before him, with the noted exceptions of Calvin and Luther, the Reformation theology restoring a biblical approach to these issues. For Perkins and other Puritan writers, all callings are worthy. Cotton Mather stated, "Oh, let every Christian walk with God when he works at his calling, act in cooperation with an eye to God, act as under the eye of God."[18] God looks at the *heart* of the worker, not at the *kind* of work he does. Work was not merely a matter of the imposition of *society*, but of *divine* vocation.

Puritan Joseph Hall contended that work is a personal demand made on every Christian who follows his own calling in willing obedience to God.[19] The chain of command here runs from God to man to society, not from God through society to man. Perkins noted, "A vocation or calling is a certain kind of life ordained and imposed on man by God for the common good." This is an explicit critique of the idea that *society* can or should energize all men to do the right thing. Doing the right thing begins with an individual *before God* (*coram Deo*). That is why the later New England Puritans would employ the jeremiad, a denunciatory sermon preached on social occasions, to call the people to do their vocational and spiritual duties before God in the New World.[20] They, further, did not make a hard distinction between vocational and spiritual duties, but rather conceived of them as of *one* piece.

---

15 William Perkins, *The Works of William Perkins*. trans. Ian Breward, Courtenay Library of Reformation Classics 3 (Abingdon Berkshire: Sutton Courtenay, 1970), cited in Ryken, *Worldly Saints*, 34. We have cited a similar concept already from Luther.

16 William Perkins, *Treatise of the Vocations, or, Callings of Men* (London: Printed by Iohn Legat, printer to the Vniuersitie of Cambridge, 1603), cited in Ryken, *Worldly Saints*, 27.

17 Diarmaid MacCulloch, *The Reformation* (New York: Viking, 2003), 379.

18 Cotton Mather, *A Christian at His Calling* (Boston: Sewall, 1701), cited in Ryken, *Worldly Saints*, 27.

19 Charles H. George and Katherine George, *The Protestant Mind of the English Reformation, 1570–1640* (Princeton, NJ: Princeton University Press, 1961), 136.

20 Charles E. Hambrick-Stowe, *The Practice of Piety: Puritan Devotional Disciplines in Seventeenth-Century New England* (Chapel Hill: University of North Carolina Press, 1982), 54–90.

Struggle for the City

The classic study of Puritan attitudes toward piety and wealth is Max Weber's book *The Protestant Ethic and the Spirit of Capitalism*.[21] Though the book traces the "Protestant ethic" back to Calvin, Weber devotes the majority of his treatment to the English Calvinists, the Puritans, as well as to Methodism and to the Baptists. Weber believed there to be a *causal* relationship between the value that the Puritans and other Protestants placed on the practice of piety and on the energetic, calculating spirit that he considered to be the genius of capitalism and of Western civilization. He contended that "ascetic Protestantism" was the most influential intellectual contribution to the spread of the capitalistic spirit in England and America, even though that trend is inherently conflicted.[22] That "ascetic Protestantism" carried three central aspects: a methodical-rational organization of life, a psychological certainty of salvation associated with this spirit, and the sense that providence lends dignity even to mundane activities such as work.

Weber's contribution has been subjected to heavy critique. The first aspect of this "spirit" that he notes—the methodical-rational organization of life—has some validity, and certainly Puritans, Methodists, and Baptists sought to live their lives that way. But so did medieval monks, yet they are not usually painted with the colors of "capitalism," though as we have seen, some were *exactly* that.[23] As to Weber's second assertion, that financial and vocational stability were to be identified with a "psychological certainty of salvation," this is even more *dubious*. If such an allegation is made toward New England Puritanism, it has to be stated that there was a *great deal* of doubtfulness about salvation among this group, in spite of the fact that they were financially and vocationally very stable.[24] As to the third point, that providence lends dignity to mundane activities, this is certainly true, but a belief in providence also provides encouragement to those who are not vocationally or financially well off. Weber's arguments are helpful and somewhat insightful, and it is the case that Puritanism contained a strong work ethic, but ultimately Weber's argument does not provide a real explanation for the "spirit of capitalism."[25]

---

21 Max Weber, *The Protestant Ethic and the Spirit of Capitalism*, 3rd ed., trans. Stephen Kalberg (1930; Los Angeles: Roxbury, 2002). Original German text composed in 1904–5.
22 Ibid., 53–102.
23 Weber makes no note of the "capitalism" of the medieval monks.
24 We will explore this in more detail later.
25 Michael Novak is the best at describing this "spirit," and he is Catholic. See our citations of him throughout the book.

Struggle for the City

Alongside the Puritan Independents, Scottish Covenanters, so-called from the Solemn League and Covenant they signed with the British as part of their agreement to aid Cromwell in the English Civil War in the 1640s, developed an entire theological *framework* for church and state relations. The Covenanters had a high view of kingship, but they opposed any concept of the divine right of kings and urged that kings were themselves *under* the law. The best known of the Covenanters, Samuel Rutherford in his famous *Lex Rex*,[26] presented a theory of *limited government and constitutionalism*. His argument was based on Deuteronomy 17, and it articulated the rule of law rather than the rule of men, supported by such notions as the separation of powers and the "covenant," the precursor to the social contract theory of governance. Rutherford also contended that monarchs had limited authority over the church.[27] This laid the foundation for the later work of Hobbes and Locke, whose political philosophies would be laid out in the context of a very strong and virile monarchy in the later third of the seventeenth century. But Rutherford's arguments also brought the ire of the restored King Charles II, who in 1660 publicly burned his *Lex Rex*, deprived him of his position at St. Andrews, and charged him with treason.[28] Rutherford died soon after so that no trial was held.

The Stuarts, Separatism, and America

The situation in Scotland and England came to a sort of merger in 1603. Queen Elizabeth died leaving neither husband nor children, the last of the Tudor dynasty. Parliament, expectedly, offered the crown to the heir presumptive, the King of Scotland, who was also related to the Tudors, James Stuart. In that year, King James VI of Scotland became King James I of England. Puritans in the universities, in the churches, and in Parliament saw this as a hopeful moment; after all, Scotland had been state church Presbyterian since 1574. Perhaps the

---

26 The title of the book implies that "the law is king." It was an explicit refutation of the doctrine of *Rex Lex*, "the king is the law." Samuel Rutherford, *Lex Rex, or, The Law and the Prince* (1843; Farmington Hills, MI: Gale, 2010).

27 Meic Pearse, *The Age of Reason: From the Wars of Religion to the French Revolution, 1570–1789*, Baker History of the Church 5 (Grand Rapids, MI: Baker, 2006), 269.

28 "Rutherford, Samuel," *Oxford Dictionary of the Christian Church*, 3rd ed., ed. F. L. Cross and E. A. Livingstone (Oxford: Oxford University Press, 1997), 1429.

Struggle for the City

king would at least bring in Presbyterianism as an option for English subjects, alongside the Anglican episcopacy (the rule of the church by bishops).

Such thoughts were naïve in the *extreme*. As King of Scotland James had found himself from his early days in conflict with Presbyterian leaders.[29] Though he would get along well with Puritans in England, it was only so by putting them in their *place*.[30] At the Hampton Court Conference in 1604 when some Puritans hoped the king would begin abolishing the episcopacy and moving in the direction of Presbyterianism, he made it clear that he would "harry out of the kingdom" anyone who pursued such notions seriously.[31] He was now *head* of the church and no longer had to suffer the contentious and pesky theologians of his Scottish Presbyterian homeland.

When Elizabeth was queen there had arisen a small but significant movement of Separatist "churches." Consciously violating the Queen's Act of Uniformity (1559), these "churches" met in homes, in barns, and in the open air, believing that the episcopacy that was the Church of England was "no church," since it stood in violation of various biblical mandates for what a church was.[32] The non-separating Puritans, on the one hand, were convinced that there was intended to be a national element in their churches, but the Separatists rejected this, contending that there was no necessary *national* element at all in a "pure" church.[33] Rather than the *parish* being the basic unit of the church, it was the *congregation*, a congregation that "elected its own officers, disciplined its own members, and administered the sacraments only to its committed initiates."[34] Even before separatism this position had been defended by William Tyndale, who had translated the Greek word *ekklēsia* in his New Testament as "congregation," rather than as "church."[35] This was new to England. As one historian has stated it,

29 John Macleod, *Dynasty: The Stuarts 1560–1807* (New York: St. Martin's Press, 1999), 131–33.
30 Ibid., 148.
31 MacCulloch, *Reformation*, 497.
32 B. R. White, *The English Separatist Tradition: From the Marian Martyrs to the Pilgrim Fathers*, Oxford Theological Monographs (Oxford: Oxford University Press, 1971), 20–43.
33 Ibid., 26.
34 Timothy George, *John Robinson and the English Separatist Tradition* (Macon, GA: Mercer University Press, 1982), 43.
35 Brian Moynihan, *God's Bestseller: William Tyndale, Thomas More, and the Writing of the English Bible—A Story of Martyrdom and Betrayal* (New York: St. Martin's Press, 2002), 72.

Struggle for the City

in the Anglican Church, "[t]here had been no voluntary gathering of believers."[36] Now there was, in Separatism, though the potential *price* was high.

What mattered to them was whether a church was organized according to *Scripture* and whether its polity was faithful to God's Word, a view they held in common with many Presbyterians.[37] They thus held firmly to the regulative principle in worship, that is, that everything in corporate worship must conform to the pattern *described* and *prescribed* in the NT. They opposed the normative principle, the notion that anything is allowable in corporate worship as long as it is *not forbidden* in the NT.[38] They also affirmed that only people who were regenerate could be *members* of these churches. As Henry Ainsworth, one of the leading figures in Separatism put it, "[P]eople must be regenerate and born agayn [sic], before they may be admitted into any particular church."[39] The net result of this conviction then led them to form conventicles, separate locations for public worship away from the Anglican churches, conventicles whose membership was comprised of the *regenerate*; to do otherwise would be sin and would be no real worship.

The movement was encouraged by a 1582 book written by Robert Browne,[40] *Reformation without Tarrying for Anie* [sic], a book whose title was a conscious response to the queen's promise of fifteen years earlier, that if pastors would be patient, she would allow piecemeal reforms in worship.[41] In 1587 John Field declared that "seeing we cannot compass" reforms "by suit or dispute," then it is "the multitude and people that must bring the discipline to pass which we desire."[42] Unfortunately for the Separatists, toleration was not to be the order of the day under Elizabeth. In 1586 John Greenwood and Henry Barrow started a Separatist church they called the *Pioneer Church*, a name consciously chosen to send

36 Edmund S. Morgan, *Visible Saints: The History of a Puritan Idea* (Ithaca, NY: Cornell University Press, 1963), 25.
37 Hughes, *Theology of the English Reformers*, 178, 181.
38 George, *John Robinson and the English Separatist Tradition*, 115.
39 Perry Miller, "The Marrow of Puritan Divinity," in *Errand into the Wilderness* (Cambridge, MA: Harvard University Press, 1956), 48–98.
40 For Separatism before Browne, see George, *John Robinson and the English Separatist Tradition*, 10–38.
41 White, *English Separatist Tradition*, 49.
42 Quoted in Patrick Collinson, "John Field and Elizabethan Puritanism," in *Elizabethan Government and Society: Essays Presented to Sir John Neale*, ed. S. T. Bindoff, J. Hurstfield, and C. H. Williams (London: University of London Press, 1961), 159.

Struggle for the City

the signal that they were going back to the book of Acts—the earliest days of the church. The next year they were both arrested and, after spending six years, off and on, in "The Clink" in London, they were hanged for sedition.[43] They were only *hanged*, and not also *burned*, since their crime was only *sedition* and not also *heresy*.[44] Bloody Mary? How about *Bloody Bess*?[45] Separatism was not to be tolerated since, as was much the common belief of the day and as we have already argued, church and state were seen as opposite sides of the *same* coin.[46]

Separatism grew under King James, though he was almost as relentless as Elizabeth in attempting to stamp it out, at least early in his reign. Separatist pastors such as Francis Johnson, John Robinson, John Smyth, and Thomas Helwys were forced to flee with their churches to Holland, to "go Dutch," as the Anabaptists had done nearly a century earlier.[47] Eventually, in James' later years, Separatist churches were given a bit more latitude in England, but under the rule of his son, Charles I (king from 1625 till 1649), persecutions were increased, especially after Charles appointed William Laud Archbishop of Canterbury in 1633.[48]

What about those Separatists in Holland? Did they remain there, eventually to be assimilated into the culture and life of the Netherlands? Some of them did. But not all, since Englishmen do not see themselves as *Europeans* and chafed at their sons growing up and not speaking the "King's English" as their mother tongue.[49] In 1611 a small group, under the leadership of Thomas Helwys, returned to England and established a church in Spitalfield (a name not derived from any uncouth oral practice but from the fact that it was located near a hospital). This group had gone to Holland in 1607, led by Helwys and John Smyth.

---

43 It was nicknamed "The Clink" for obvious reasons.
44 That dual punishment was the fate of, for instance, John Oldcastle in 1417 in England, who was "hanged for his treason, [and] was simultaneously burnt for his heresy." Moynihan, *God's Bestseller*, xxv.
45 She also had sixty Jesuits executed for refusing to leave England in the 1580s. Susan Doran, *The Tudor Chronicles* (2008; repr., New York: Metro Books, 2009), 336. Overall, Elizabeth may have executed as many as Mary had on religious grounds. The majority were Catholics, but some were separatists.
46 Dickens, *English Reformation*, 311–12.
47 White, *English Separatist Tradition*, 91–115.
48 Charles Carlton, *Charles I: The Personal Monarch*, 2nd ed. (New York: Routledge, 1995), 138–40, 158–69.
49 There is a French proverb that states, *L'Angleterre une Isle!* (England is an island!) That is more than just an observation of geography.

Struggle for the City

After two years, in 1609, they rejected infant baptism, took baptism as believers, and reconstituted themselves as a new church based on the principles of believers' (or disciples') baptism and regenerate church membership.[50] The "Baptists" had arrived, but their return to England was fraught with peril. Helwys was arrested in 1612 and apparently died in prison four years later.[51]

One of the other Separatist churches in Holland that included John Robinson, William Bradford, and William Brewster, likewise became disenchanted with Dutch life in 1620. But by then there was a new option—America! In the early seventeenth century, English joint-stock corporations formed to make money from the New World, and enlisted people from various walks of life and with differing motivations—religious, financial, personal—to go there and labor so that both worker and company would benefit. The joint-stock approach was the only possibility since James I was strapped for cash,[52] but it turned out to be the best thing for virtually everyone, since each part of the process—stockholders, workers, towns and villages in America, and the Crown—all benefited and something beautiful, the entrepreneurial system, was shown to be not only workable but the best *possible* structure of finance in a fallen world. So, members of this Separatist church (not all of them), which they had named the Pilgrim Church, boarded the Mayflower and sailed to the new English colonies across the Atlantic. They had made compact with the Virginia Company to land in the north of that colony, but bad winds and inaccurate charts caused them to land instead at Plymouth, on Cape Cod.[53] Their pastor, John Robinson, had intended to join them later from Leyden, but died unexpectedly, leaving them pastorless for a number of years. They all nearly died the first winter, but the colony survived and thrived for a number of years, caught between Anglicans to the south, and, shortly thereafter, Puritan Congregationalists to the north.[54] Meanwhile, what was happening back in the homeland?

---

50 H. Leon McBeth, *The Baptist Heritage: Four Centuries of Baptist Witness* (Nashville: Broadman, 1987), 33–34.

51 Ibid., 38.

52 Thomas A. Askew and Peter W. Spellman, *The Churches and the American Experience: Ideals and Institutions* (Grand Rapids, MI: Baker, 1984), 26.

53 William Warren Sweet, *The Story of Religion in America*, 2nd ed. (1930; New York: Harper & Row, 1950), 44–45.

54 Ibid., 45–48.

Struggle for the City

King Charles early on came to accept the French notion that kings ruled by *divine right*, as French kings had believed even before his time, and needed little if any consent from the governed.[55] His father before him had also affirmed this idea, arguing before Parliament in 1610 that "[t]he state of monarchy is the supremest thing on earth: for Kings are not only God's lieutenants on earth, and sit upon God's throne, but even by God himself are called Gods."[56] But the difference between the two of them was that, "unlike his father, [Charles] was no pragmatist."[57] As we have noted previously, England was also *no France*. The Magna Carta, British Common Law, and centuries of tradition drew out the limitations of English kings. Though James and Charles attempted to solve the nation's (and their own) financial problems by supporting "the monopoly [that] London export companies [had] against interlopers, [by slowing] down industrial development" and controlling it "through guilds and monopolies," and by "suppres[sing] middle men," these British monarchs had not Louis XIV's power or savvy.[58] Instead, they were forced to do so through "professional informers, an unpopular and bribable class, and by unpaid justices of the peace, frequently themselves the employers against whom the regulations were directed."[59] Charles decided he could not brook any more *interference* from his political rivals, and in 1629 he sent Parliament *home* in response to a bill called the Petition of Right, an attempt to draw further limitations on the King's authority; Parliament would not be recalled by the King till 1640, when he needed them to enact a tax in response to a threatened Scottish invasion.[60]

Charles was especially opposed to Puritanism. Again, the difference between him and his father on this matter was apparent, since James had curried the Puritans' *favor*, while at the same time not granting them concessions. The situation had changed somewhat since James had had dealings with these Calvinists.

---

55 Macleod, *Dynasty*, 158.
56 Carlton, *Charles I*, 10. Elizabeth had probably also believed in the divine right of *queens*, but she had been too prudent to "thrust her views down her subjects' throats." Christopher Hill, *God's Englishman: Oliver Cromwell and the English Reformation* (New York: Dial, 1970), 15.
57 Macleod, *Dynasty*, 158.
58 Christopher Hill, *The Century of Revolution: 1603–1714*, Norton Library History of England (New York: W. W. Norton, 1982), 22.
59 Ibid., 23.
60 We will return to these events after narrating the early Puritan migration to "America."

Struggle for the City

Significant change had taken place in the universities that encouraged Charles's position. Arminianism had gained the upper hand among English theology professors, and by 1625 they had the majority at both Cambridge and Oxford. Calvinism was outlawed at Oxford in 1626 and at Cambridge in 1632.[61] Many Puritans feared that this was but a prelude to the return of the papacy. Charles opposed them directly and legally and since the House of Commons was filled with Puritans, they saw the dissolving of Parliament in 1629 as an *ominous* sign. Economic pressures were applied to the Puritan establishment as well, by threatening the rights of *inheritance* of landowners, special *tithes* on towns that allowed Puritan "lectureships," and the attempt to seize back the *estates* of those who had purchased monasteries under Henry VIII.[62] These served the *dual* purpose of stabbing at the Puritan party (who were mainly of the gentry class) and of raising federal revenues without convening Parliament to levy *traditional* forms of taxation; in reality they were little more than economic *bullying* by Crown and church. Many Englishmen responded to the dissolution of Parliament by taking ship. From 1629 to 1641 more than twenty thousand Englishmen left England for Massachusetts, not counting wives and children.

Massachusetts and the Fervency of Vocation

Virginia had been the destination for early immigration, placing the first permanent settlement there in 1607, but Virginia was heavily controlled by agents of the Crown, and the Church of England's presence was *strong* and *intrusive*. The new immigrants did not want to escape from the English frying pan only to find themselves back in the American *fire*. The Puritans who made their exodus to Massachusetts Bay were not attempting to set up a *new* church, at least not in the beginning. They saw themselves as Anglicans, but as Calvinistic, Puritan Anglicans who were being increasingly *pressed* over their preaching and their doctrine in England, and especially so after Archbishop Laud began indicting Puritan pastors for heresy in 1633.[63]

---

61 Nicholas Tyacke, *Anti-Calvinists: The Rise of English Arminianism, c. 1590–1640*, Oxford Historical Monographs (Oxford: Clarendon, 1987), 77.
62 Hill, *God's Englishman*, 19–20.
63 Carlton, *Charles I*, 138–40.

Struggle for the City

Against all odds, the Massachusetts Puritans were successful economically, socially, religiously, and in every other measurable issue. They *should* have failed. They were literally launching an "errand into the wilderness," and it should have been a wilderness that ate them up. They were operating in a land of rock-filled soil, short growing seasons, brutal winters, and no precious metals that might draw fortune hunters. Yet, they thrived. Why? "Massachusetts Bay Colony… succeeded for two overriding reasons: it freed the economy of anachronistic restraints; and it recognized the link between land ownership and productive behavior."[64] These hardy individuals compensated for the harshness of life with an "*overbelief* which impelled them to endure the poverty, despair and peril of life between a savage sea and an ominously unknown continent."[65] A brief explanation is helpful here.

The lure of America was primarily an *economic* lure, the more so if one sailed for Virginia, but also eventually for the Puritans of Massachusetts Bay. In England there was no more easily obtainable land; America would be the land of *opportunity*. The years between 1500 and 1620 had witnessed a *doubling* of the population of England and Wales, extensive enclosures, considerable geographical mobility, and the disruption of traditional economic alignments due to a doubling of prices.[66] English society had been transformed, and made more transitory. According to one study, in 1641 only sixteen percent of farming families had lived for a century in the same village.[67] This was new—social dislocation had always been less of a problem in England than in Europe. But American opportunities beckoned.

For the Puritans there was the added bonus, and in many cases the most compelling factor, of freedom from the onerous hand of Charles, Laud, and the Star Chamber, the court where many Puritans were put on trial for their beliefs. In the year 1600, England's population stood at about five million. In

---

64 Stephen Innes, *Creating the Commonwealth: The Economic Culture of Puritan New England* (New York: W. W. Norton, 1995), 5.
65 H. Richard Niebuhr, *Kingdom of God in America* (New York: Harper & Brothers, 1937), 7 (emphasis added).
66 Peter Laslett, *The World We Have Lost: Further Explored*, 3rd ed. (New York: Routledge, 2004).
67 Philip J. Greven Jr., *Four Generations: Population, Land, and Family in Colonial Andover, Massachusetts* (Ithaca, NY: Cornell University Press, 1970).

Struggle for the City

the rest of Europe the populations stood at anywhere from fourteen persons per square kilometer to twenty-eight or even thirty per square kilometer.[68] In England the number was something over forty people per square kilometer. This constituted a substantial increase from the year 1500.

The growth of population had put a great strain on agricultural output in both England and Europe, partly because there had been no corresponding increase in agricultural technology. This resulted in what has been called the *Price Revolution*—the increase in the cost of food, especially grains, through the century.[69] The seventeenth century witnessed a series of bad harvests, outbreaks of plague, and European wars (especially the Thirty Years War), all of which would cause a population decline in that century. In addition to all of this, governments, whether at the national or local levels, constantly tinkered with the economy. That tinkering, some of which we have already discussed, kept the economics of England and Europe on an unsure setting through the seventeenth century. All of that would change in Massachusetts.

The Puritans of Boston organized a commonwealth that linked "capitalism" to the redemptive community, perhaps based on their knowledge of what Calvin had done in Geneva.[70] After all, some of their fathers had been there during the reign of Queen Mary. *Nowhere* else in English America would the population have access to the same level of prosperity, educational opportunities, family stability, material culture, or life expectancy as in Massachusetts.[71] The children raised in this part of the new world constituted "the most literate society in the world."[72] This colony "established a flourishing, diversified, family-based economy within a generation of its founding."[73] This stands in contrast to the strictly Anglican colony of Virginia, which experienced early and rapid financial failure. Virginia had been advertised as a land of "fair meadows and goodly tall trees with such fresh waters running

---

68 Rondo Cameron and Larry Neal, *A Concise Economic History of the World: From Paleolithic Times to the Present*, 4th ed. (New York: Oxford University Press, 2003), 96.
69 Ibid., 105–6.
70 Innes, *Creating the Commonwealth*, 6. The term *capitalism* and the economic theory that underlies it had not yet been established, though, as we have seen, Catholic Scholastics had formed the basic intellectual elements.
71 Nathan Rosenberg and L. E. Birdzell Jr., *How the West Grew Rich: The Economic Transformation of the Industrial World* (New York: Basic Books, 1986), 193.
72 Francis J. Bremer, *John Winthrop: Biography as History* (New York: Continuum, 2009), 53.
73 Innes, *Creating the Commonwealth*, 6.

Struggle for the City

through the woods" that a visitor "was almost ravished at the first sight thereof."[74] Yet, it quickly became a place of famine, disease, and misery. Though originally a project of the Virginia Company (as Massachusetts was of the Massachusetts Bay Company), a joint-stock corporation, by 1624 it became a "royal Crown colony after the failure of the profit-sharing arrangements between investors and settlers and the use of land grants to attract labor."[75] In England critics complained that the settlers who had taken ship for Virginia were lazy and filled with moral shortcomings.[76] But the real difference may lie in the fact that those who went to Massachusetts were generally on an *errand* that was greater than mere search for gain and the opportunity for leisure, while many in Virginia were allured by just such things, quick profits, and the retirement to the lifestyle of the English gentry.

The early settlers in Virginia were *not* a people specifically passionate about *faith and family*, but those in Massachusetts were. There the family was *crucial* and so strict laws and rules governing family life were important.[77] While *technically* wives were subordinate to their husbands in Puritan homes, "in practice they shared in the management of their households," so that the focus was on "marriage as companionship [and]… partnership."[78] Similarly, in nearby Plymouth Colony, the so-called, "Old Colony" (where the Pilgrim Church had landed in 1620) very strict regulations were developed concerning the relations between husbands and wives and parents and children. Men were often chastised and even fined for treating their wives badly in public.[79] These colonies were *patriarchal*, but it was a patriarchalism tempered with Christian sanctification.

These Englishmen were *not* driven from their homes in England to the shores of New England. Later immigrants, especially in the nineteenth century, might be viewed as those who are "the uprooted." This was not the case with these Puri-

---

74 David Bertelson, *The Lazy South* (New York: Oxford University Press, 1967), 20.

75 Stanley L. Engerman and Robert E. Gallman, "The Emergence of a Market Economy before 1860," in *A Companion to 19th-Century America*, Blackwell Companions to American History, ed. William L. Barney (Oxford: Blackwell, 2001), 121.

76 Bertelson, *Lazy South*, 21–24.

77 Ryken, *Worldly Saints*, 73–90.

78 Bremer, *John Winthrop: Biography as History*, 14. The Massachusetts Puritans also allowed women in the congregation broad scope in involvement in church conference discussions. Ibid., 42.

79 John Demos, *A Little Commonwealth: Family Life in Plymouth Colony* (New York: Oxford, 1970), 82–106.

Struggle for the City

tans. Rather, they came on an *errand*. In his classic essay, Perry Miller notes that the word "errand" had evolved in its connotations over time. "Originally, as the word first took form in English, it meant exclusively a short journey on which an inferior is sent to convey a message or to perform a service for his superior."[80] But the word later came to have a different connotation: "It came to mean the actual business on which the actor goes, the purpose itself, the conscious intention in his mind."[81] It was in this sense that the Puritans' exodus was an *errand*. "These Puritans were not driven out of England (thousands of their fellows stayed and fought the Cavaliers)—they went of their own accord."[82] Though many, perhaps two-thirds, of these settlers came as indentured servants,[83] they went to carve out a better future for their progeny, to build, in Winthrop's words, "a city upon a hill"![84] They went out to seek a city; not indeed the heavenly one, but one that could be as close to that as possible.

The Covenants and "Visible Saints"

Basic to the identity of the Massachusetts community, and somewhat less so the Plymouth one,[85] was a twofold understanding of "covenant."[86] God had made a covenant with Adam based on works, a covenant based on perfect obedience that incorporated all of life, both mundane and spiritual. But Adam broke that covenant by sin and so God made a new covenant of grace with Abraham that promised eternal life to those who had faith. But now, in a fallen world,

---

80 Perry Miller, "Errand into the Wilderness," in *Errand into the Wilderness*, 3.
81 Ibid.
82 Ibid., 4.
83 Engerman and Galliman, "Emergence of a Market Economy," 122. The estimated two-thirds who came as indentured servants was the number for *all* the thirteen colonies in the early decades of immigration, but the number is likely fairly indicative of New England as well.
84 Quoted in Francis J. Bremer, *John Winthrop: America's Forgotten Founding Father* (Oxford: Oxford University Press, 2003), 29, 308. Note that this is not the same book by Bremer on Winthrop that we cited earlier.
85 The Plymouth group was made up of Separatists who had previously fled to the Netherlands and then took ship to America in 1620.
86 This "covenantal theology" was rooted in the writings of Calvin and the other non-Lutheran Reformers, but developed in full form only in the 1550s and afterward. See, for instance, Michael Scott Horton, *God of Promise: Introducing Covenant Theology* (Grand Rapids, MI: Baker, 2006).

both covenants were in effect, with the covenant of works governing mundane life (work, society, government) and the covenant of grace determining spiritual life, since the covenant of works could not now save anyone.[87] Preachers preached from both covenants, issuing "ethical appeals" and urging "moral reforms" from the previous covenant and calls for conversion from the latter.[88] On the one hand, "civil society" was the "sphere of uncoerced association positioned between the patriarchal household and the state."[89] They realized they had the opportunity to erect a *new thing* in the wilderness. "The founding vision was to erect a cultural and social order completely under God's sovereignty as revealed in the Bible."[90] This sphere was to be nurtured in a common commitment both to the laws of the community, which were derived mutually from Scripture and natural law,[91] and to the authority of the church, nestled in God's Word and made apparent in the preaching of the pastors.[92]

That they drew upon natural law as well as Scripture might seem odd to some, since the Puritans are usually seen as *theocrats* who needed nothing but the Bible for exercising jurisprudence.[93] But John Cotton and other New England divines of this time were also *Englishmen*, and as Englishmen they appealed to British common law, especially in their Election Day sermons.[94] John Davenport, for instance, appealed to the "light of nature," "Profane authors," and "the Consent of all Nations" in his discourse on the responsibilities of civil magistrates.[95] Winthrop insisted that the laws in Massachusetts model the pattern after which the English law code had developed, slowly, organical-

---

87 E. Brooks Holifield, *Theology in America: Christian Thought from the Age of the Puritans to the Civil War* (New Haven, CT: Yale University Press, 2003), 40.

88 Ibid., 40.

89 Innes, *Creating the Commonwealth*, 6.

90 Askew and Spellman, *Churches and the American Experience*, 32–33.

91 VanDrunen, *Natural Law and the Two Kingdoms*, 229–34.

92 Harry S. Stout, *The New England Soul: Preaching and Religious Culture in Colonial New England* (Oxford: Oxford University Press, 1986), 13–49.

93 That is the position advocated, apparently wrongly, by Mark A. Noll, *America's God: From Jonathan Edwards to Abraham Lincoln* (New York: Oxford, 2002), 33–36.

94 Keith L. Griffin, *Revolution and Religion: American Revolutionary War and the Reformed Clergy* (New York: Paragon House, 1994), 26.

95 John Davenport, *Discourse about Civil Government in a New Plantation Whose Design Is Religion* (Cambridge, MA: Printed by Samuel Green and Marmaduke Johnson, 1663), 23–24. Note: This work has been wrongly ascribed on title page to John Cotton. Cf. Cotton Mather's *Magnalia Christi Americana* (London: Printed for T. Parkhurst, 1702), bk. 3, p. 56.

Struggle for the City

ly, over time, rather than simply importing the Mosaic code *theocratically* as the basic standard. "These standards angered some who wished the City on a Hill to be a new Jerusalem modeled on biblical patterns."[96] The debate would continue long after Winthrop's death.

Scripture did also play a role in the organization of civil society. Even as Moses had instructed the people of Israel in Deuteronomy 28 that they must collectively honor the covenant that God had established with them in order for them to dwell at peace in the land under the protection of God, so, argued Davenport, Cotton, and others, the people of Massachusetts must *collectively* honor their covenant with God in order to thrive. Here was another version of *Geneva*, a theology of politics helping to formulate a political theology of governance. From such preaching there quickly developed the notion that here was a new covenanted people who were recapitulating, in some sense, the people of Israel in their exodus and entry upon a new land.[97] Massachusetts *was* the new Canaan and the Puritans a new Israel, at least in the view of some.[98]

Central to their views on civil society was the idea, already established in the writings of John Calvin, that *godly* magistrates should exercise authority under God and according to his Word. Magistrates, in this understanding, were nearly as important as pastors, and like pastors, they were to be *men of God*. These were to be men who had gone through the fire of their own conversion experience and who had proven the genuineness of their conversion by the life they lived. "The New England Puritans were the only founders of any commonwealth in the Western world to make political leadership contingent on the authenticity of an inward experience."[99] In Massachusetts the decision was made early by John Winthrop and others that pastors could not serve as magistrates, so that there would be no situation such as had developed in England where all bishops were members of the House of Lords and held temporal as well as spiritual authority.[100] The situation in New England, though, sometimes led to conflicting opinions between magistrates and pastors, as had previously been the case in Geneva,

---

96 Bremer, *John Winthrop: Forgotten Founder*, 308.
97 Stout, *New England Soul*, 166–84.
98 It was not until the 1650s and 1660s that these ideas took firm hold.
99 George McKenna, *The Puritan Origins of American Patriotism* (New Haven, CT: Yale University Press, 2007), 28.
100 Bremer, *John Winthrop*, 33.

Struggle for the City

and it also often led citizens to ask whether or not such men had true conversion experiences. Is it not possible that a moral magistrate is simply that—a moral man? Further, Winthrop was *always* the mediating voice early on. As we will see in a later discussion, questions such as that would contribute to the eventual evaporation of the so-called Puritan canopy.

The other aspect of covenant that was crucial to these people was the *new covenant* experience of saving grace, saving grace manifested in an experience of conversion that was identifiable and palpable. Really, for the first time, we have here a communal theological belief that holds that conversion is an identifiable experience and that maintains that such an experience is necessary for *full* church membership.[101] One might argue that this conviction is *implicit* in Protestant theology's affirmation of justification by faith alone, but the fact is that it was *only* in Massachusetts and Plymouth Colonies where such a practice was first established and where it became an ecclesiological issue. In New England, under the tutelage of pastors such as Thomas Shepherd and Thomas Hooker, the stages under which regeneration would take place were identified. "Preparation" was required, which "meant driving the soul to contrition and humiliation, and most of the New Englanders agreed that it was necessary."[102] This required a ministry that would focus on *sin* in its preaching, so much so that Thomas Shepherd tried, in the words of one of his auditors, "to pound our hearts all to pieces."[103] This was the only way that "visible saints" could become *visible*. It would later have its own backlash.

It has been argued that what the Puritans considered to be the most important aspect of their doctrine of the church, the notion of the *visible saint* as alone sharing in full church membership, was also a *weakness*. "Protestantism liberated men from the treadmill of indulgences and penances, but cast them on the iron couch of introspection."[104] That may be, though it is not necessarily the case that it always happened to be so or that it was necessarily the case. Further, this notion of the new covenant experience of conversion was tied, by Cotton and others, to

---

101 Morgan, *Visible Saints*, 64–112.
102 Holifield, *Theology in America*, 43.
103 Ibid., 43.
104 Perry Miller, *Roger Williams: His Contribution to the American Tradition*, Makers of the American Tradition (New York: Bobbs-Merrill, 1953), 207–8.

Struggle for the City

the "corporate covenant" notion of the Commonwealth, with the *conclusion* that the City Set Upon the Hill could only be what it was intended to be if everyone, or nearly everyone, would undergo a genuine and visible conversion experience.[105] This is predicated, of course, on a Calvinistic view of depravity. Because humans are innately sinful, they need both a conversion experience and systems of authority to keep them disciplined, even *after* they have been converted.

Social Structure of New England

The social structure that prevailed in Massachusetts was shaped by a Calvinist social ethic, an ethic that placed family first, church second, and commonwealth third. The doctrine of *vocation*, borrowed from Calvin, Luther, and their Puritan mentors back at Cambridge, William Perkins and William Ames, shaped the doctrine of work and made labor a *sacred* thing, grounding all "striving behavior in communal obligation."[106] This "capitalist" system, in a manner not significantly different from the way Adam Smith would define capitalist motivation a century later, recognized that individuals would work out of a self-motivation to improve their lot, but also knew that such self-motivation *could* become sinful excess.

Thomas Shepherd reminded the saints that self-interest was a "raging Sea which would overwhelm all if it have not bankes."[107] Here was an attempt to bridge what Émile Durkheim has called the "duality of human existence," that is, the attempt to combine in one person or movement both interest-motivated and altruistic-motivated action.[108] Massachusetts would become successful by fostering a "distinctive civic ecology" based on strong families and town organizations and by creating a "religiously based culture of discipline" that fostered hard work and generosity so the rich and mighty would not eat up the poor. This allowed the New England colony to become the New World's first "capitalist commonwealth."[109]

---

105 Morgan, *Visible Saints*, 35.
106 Innes, *Creating the Commonwealth*, 7.
107 Stout, *New England Soul*, 21–22.
108 Émile Durkheim, "The Dualism of Human Nature and Its Social Condition," in *On Morality and Society: Selected Writings*, ed. Robert N. Bellah, Heritage of Sociology (Chicago: University of Chicago Press, 1973), 149–68.
109 Innes, *Creating the Commonwealth*, 9.

Struggle for the City

Church and State

That is not to say that everything in the "capitalist commonwealth" was laudable. John Cotton's commitment to the "corporate covenant" led him to brook little or no *dissenting* voices. Cotton was a titanic intellectual figure, and upon his coming to Massachusetts, some people "could hardly believe that God would suffer Mr. Cotton to err." Virtually from his arrival in Boston in 1633 he clashed with Roger Williams, a Puritan Calvinist who was a Separatist in his beliefs and who had been there two years previous to Cotton, and with Anne Hutchinson.[110]

Williams disagreed with the degrees to which Cotton wished to extend the "corporate covenant" notion, since for Cotton that meant the ministers in the colony needed to walk lock step on nearly *all* theological matters. Williams walked lock step with *no one*, as subsequent events would make clear. Previous to Cotton's arrival Williams had attempted to serve the church in Salem as teacher, thinking that this church, unlike the Boston church, held to *Separatist* sympathies, but he had departed in disgust when he found that they were not Separatists at all.[111] Williams' rejection of Cotton's (and Shepherd's) notion of the corporate covenant was based on his rejection of their Old Testament hermeneutic, a hermeneutic in which they increasingly transferred Israel's theocratic governmental structure to the governing structure of the *churches* of New England.[112]

Anne Hutchinson, likewise, found herself at odds with the colony's leadership, and eventually with Cotton. Hutchinson contended that the immediate leadership of the *Spirit* in one's life should take the place of both the corporate covenant notion and any real understanding of assurance of salvation, beliefs that led to the accusation of *antinomianism*, that is, that Hutchinson rejected the law of Scripture for her own *immediate* experience of God.[113] In that day, to be called

---

110 Larzer Ziff, *The Career of John Cotton: Puritanism and the American Experience* (Princeton, NJ: Princeton University Press, 1962), 90, 212–16, 134–47.

111 Edwin S. Gaustad, "Roger Williams and the Principle of Separation," *Foundations* 1 (1958): 55–64; John M. Barry, *Roger Williams and the Creation of the American Soul: Church, State, and the Birth of Liberty* (New York: Viking, 2012), 201–2. We do not agree with Gaustad's or Barry's belief that Williams was a social theorist first and a theologian second.

112 James P. Byrd Jr., *The Challenges of Roger Williams: Religious Liberty, Violent Persecution, and the Bible* (Macon, GA: Mercer University Press, 2002), 53–86.

113 Central to her position was the belief that assurance of salvation came from the "witness of the Spirit" and not from an examination of one's works.

Struggle for the City

"antinomian" would be similar to being called a "nihilist" in our day.[114] Clearly not a good thing! At first, Cotton wished to be sympathetic toward Hutchinson, his own views being similar,[115] but Thomas Shepherd, newly arrived from England and being opposed to the "spiritist" view would have none of it.[116]

Williams, having gone to Plymouth Colony in 1631, returned to Salem in 1633, to the *chagrin* of the authorities there. A man who was never sure about the genuineness of *anyone else's* faith (he even refused to pray with his wife since he was not sure that she was a worthy saint[117]), he had found the Plymouth Colony also to be *insufficiently* Separatist to his liking, and left under a *mutual* agreement about his departure.[118] As events transpired, Williams and Hutchinson were forced to leave, both initially to Rhode Island, where Williams founded Providence Plantation. "Given their background of persecution in England, one might imagine that the Puritans of New England would look more favorably on religious freedom, but in Massachusetts the Puritans' idea of religious liberty extended only to the freedom given non-Puritans to leave the colony."[119] A few years later Williams would pen a treatise exposing Cotton's heavy-handed measures, *The Bloudy Tenent of Persecution*.[120] The two would engage in pamphlet warfare for some time afterward over the notions of religious liberty and the role of the state in enforcing theological *uniformity*.[121] Though many religious establishments (state churches) considered themselves to be Christian commonwealths (or nations), as the Puritans of New England certainly did, "Williams argued that the coming of Christ had rendered all nations 'merely civil' in nature, not spiritual."[122] Anne Hutchinson agreed with Williams, following him to

---

114 Edmund S. Morgan, *The Puritan Dilemma: The Story of John Winthrop*, 2nd ed., Library of American Biography (New York: Pearson Longman, 2006), 134.
115 Ziff, *Career of John Cotton*, 201–2.
116 Bremer, *John Winthrop: Biography as History*, 40–41.
117 Ibid., 38. From our standpoint we are convinced that she must have been saved since few wives in *history* would have put up with that!
118 Byrd, *Challenges of Roger Williams*, 190.
119 Thomas S. Kidd, *God of Liberty: A Religious History of the American Revolution* (New York: Basic Books, 2010), 40.
120 Roger Williams, *The Bloudy Tenent of Persecution for Cause of Conscience: Discussed in a Conference between Truth and Peace*, ed. Richard Groves, Classics of Religious Liberty 2, (1644; Macon, GA: Mercer University Press, 2001).
121 James Leo Garrett Jr., *Baptist Theology: A Four-Century Study* (Macon: Mercer University Press, 2009), 109–13.
122 Kidd, *God of Liberty*, 43.

Struggle for the City

Rhode Island. After the death of her husband, though, Hutchinson moved with her children from Rhode Island to Long Island in New Netherlands. There she and five of her children were killed by Native American Indians, who reportedly burned the family alive in their house.[123]

It is hard to imagine any positions to be more polar opposite than the Massachusetts Puritans' and Williams' respective stands on the public role of religion. "To Williams, the church was so sacred that state support would soil it. To the Puritans, religion was so important that it demanded state support."[124] For Williams, state support of religion would inevitably entail state support of only *one form* of religion and that would rob individuals who were persuaded to *another form* of religious expression to sacrifice their "natural right" to worship in the manner they chose.[125] This was, literally, unconscionable for Williams. He fought against this the rest of his life in sermons, speeches, writings, and disputations.[126]

An epilogue to this debate is appropriate. Within a decade of the disputes between Williams and Cotton, "American society embraced the principles of voluntarism and tolerance in faith in a spirit not of secularism, but of piety."[127] In 1656 the former governor of Massachusetts, Henry Vane, "was expounding the principles of civil and religious liberty, arguing that they were inseparable and that the freedom of religious belief was essential to the maintenance of a Christian society."[128] Paul Johnson goes on to comment, "This document [Vane's proposal], and the sentiments it articulated, were more instrumental in determining the spirit of the American Constitution in religious matters than were the writings of the Enlightenment."[129] Cotton's compatriot, in the end, sided with Williams over Cotton himself.

---

123 John Winthrop, *A Short History of the Rise, Reign, and Ruin of the Antinomians* (1644; London: Printed for Tho. Parkhurst, 1692), preface.
124 Kidd, *God of Liberty*, 43.
125 Edmund S. Morgan, *Inventing the People: The Rise of Popular Sovereignty in England and America* (New York: Norton, 1988), 142.
126 Byrd, *Challenges of Roger Williams*, 128–82.
127 Paul Johnson, "The Almost-Chosen People: Why America Is Different," in *Unsecular America*, Encounter Series 2, ed. Richard John Neuhaus (Grand Rapids, MI: Eerdmans, 1986), 4.
128 Ibid.
129 Ibid.

Struggle for the City

England: New and Old

New England would be the *only* culture in which Calvinistic Puritanism would take root and maintain some semblance of its effect for decades. By 1641 Puritanism had reached its peak in England. Just the year before, as we noted in our earlier discussion, King Charles had recalled Parliament to deal with the Scottish threat of invasion. He needed Parliament in order to secure the funds necessary to prosecute a war. The Scots had been provoked by Archbishop Laud's attempt to force them to adopt the Anglican Prayer Book in 1637 and to submit to five bishops sent there from England.[130] They threatened war. Charles had to pay them off, but they marched to the north of England in further threat, thus necessitating Parliament, or what became known as the "Long Parliament."

When the members of Parliament convened they expressed their anger and frustration at being kept out of the governing process for eleven years by *impeaching* Archbishop Laud and others.[131] They passed further legislation that prevented the king from *excluding* them from service in the future. Then a series of events brought on a national crisis. An Irish rebellion in 1641 caused panic; the king attempted to arrest five leaders of the opposition party to him in the House; disaffection toward the king began to spread across the land, and Charles was forced to flee to Nottingham.[132]

In 1642 the king made *war* on the Puritan wing of Parliament, and the populace that supported it, and the English Civil War ensued. Parliament entered into a treaty with the Scots, "The Solemn League and Covenant," which secured Scottish support in the war against Charles, with the pledge that the English Church would become state church Presbyterian when the conflict was over. The king would lose the war (or, wars), and in the end, his head, as well.[133]

---

130 Charles Firth, *Oliver Cromwell and the Rule of Puritans in England*, Heroes of the Nations (London: Oxford University Press, 1900), 40–41.
131 Hill, *Century of Revolution*, 94. Laud would be executed in 1645.
132 Ibid., 95.
133 The cause of the English Civil War is a complex matter. Conrad Russell argues that there may have been little that Charles could have done to avoid it, but certainly his policies exacerbated what would probably otherwise have been a later development or a smaller conflict. Conrad Russell, *The Causes of the English Civil War*, Ford Lectures (Oxford: Clarendon, 1990), 1–25, 212–19.

Struggle for the City

In the war Oliver Cromwell, a member of Parliament, began as a captain in the army opposing the king, but swiftly moved up the ranks once his prowess was proven in battle and when his negotiating skills between various factions in the army became apparent.[134] The tradition in the English military was that "gentlemen" were chosen for officers while men of lower standing were not. Cromwell preferred what he called the "free way" to the "formal way."[135] He believed that if one chose men according to the two criteria of their *ability* and their *love* for God and country, then "honest men will follow them.... A few honest men are better than numbers."[136] This of course flew in the face of *tradition* and was subversive to a heritage that took a *hierarchically* graded society for granted. Cromwell cared not that many found his philosophy to be novel, and in the end, the *success* of his New Model Army proved him correct.

In 1644 Parliament convened the Westminster Assembly, with the ostensible goal of forging the path for a possible English Presbyterianism, in keeping with the Solemn League and Covenant.[137] Some wished for no state church. But, "The idea of a single state Church was so deeply embedded in the thought of the propertied that freedom to choose one's religion seemed in itself subversive."[138] The assembly would meet for three years and would fashion one of the most *influential* bodies of ecclesiastical material in the history of the church—the Westminster Confession and the Westminster Shorter Catechism being the two best-known documents from this assembly.

But by the end of the three years, there was little popular or parliamentary sympathy in the direction of an English Presbyterian Church. Rather, the larger number of Englishmen favored the views of the one man whose military prowess had given such an aid in winning the war—Oliver Cromwell. Cromwell was an "Independent," what would later be known as a *Congregationalist*. His convictions in this direction had been settled when a host of his troops who were fully committed to Independency acquitted them-

---

134 Hill, *God's Englishman*, 55–70.
135 Ibid., 66.
136 Ibid., 67.
137 Parliament did order the rudiments of a Presbyterian system for England in 1646 and 1647. Williston Walker, *A History of the Christian Church*, 4th ed. (New York: Scribner's, 1985), 555.
138 Hill, *Century of Revolution*, 143.

Struggle for the City

selves well at the Battle of Marston Moor in 1644, a significant victory in the war against the king. God *must* have blessed their faithfulness, in Cromwell's opinion.[139] In the end, the Independents also won the day in the Westminster Assembly when, led by such stalwarts as John Owen and Thomas Goodwin, they rejected the Solemn League and Covenant and with it any notion of state church Presbyterianism.[140] The Scots, of course, never forgave them and blamed Owen and Goodwin and the others for their later fate in the Restoration of the monarchy.[141]

From 1649 to 1653 Parliament ran the country, having abolished the Anglican Church and having eliminated the office of bishop. During this period there was great religious liberty, with even groups like Quakers, Levellers, and Diggers seen by many to be seditious, enjoying freedom to convene and to propagate their views.[142] For the first time, really, in English history there was no persecution of dissent, since, in a very real sense, where there is no *established* church, there is no such thing as "dissent."

It became clear though that Parliament could not act as an *executive* body. So, in 1653 Oliver Cromwell was drafted to be Lord Protector. He reorganized the churches in England, trying to provide "faithful preachers" for every pulpit. He protected Quakers and Jews and championed the cause of the persecuted Vaudois (Waldensian) Protestants in France.[143] This period, known as the Commonwealth, came remarkably close to later republican ideals, though, in the absence of the franchise or vote on the part of the common man, true republicanism cold never be a reality—governing decisions

139 Antonia Fraser, *Cromwell: The Lord Protector* (New York: Alfred A. Knopf, 1974), 135.
140 William Haller, *Liberty and Reformation in the Puritan Revolution* (New York: Columbia University Press, 1955), 336–41.
141 Fraser, *Cromwell*, 227. Charles took advantage of the Scots' displeasure in 1648 and induced them to assist him in a reinvasion of England with the promise that he would establish Presbyterianism if Parliament would not, but the attempt was dashed by Cromwell's army.
142 The Quakers, founded by George Fox, were religious enthusiasts who looked primarily to the "inner light," or the voice of the Holy Spirit, rather than basing authority on the teachings of Scripture. The Levellers were an early form of democratic movement, while the Diggers (or "True Levellers") constituted an early form of what we would call a form of socialism, since they called for the digging up of landmarks or property boundaries (abolition of private property). Christopher Hill, *The World Turned Upside Down: Radical Ideas during the English Revolution* (New York: Viking, 1972), 13, 86–120.
143 Hill, *God's Englishman*, 149–54, 165.

Struggle for the City

in England to this day are still being made by people who are not themselves selected by the populace. Key theological leaders, such as John Owen, came close to espousing republicanism explicitly during this time (in his *Brief Declaration and Vindication*), even though it was considered to be a heretical belief by many.[144] John Milton, who served in a high office in Cromwell's administration, *explicitly* espoused republicanism, and paid for it when the interregnum[145] came to an end.[146]

Cromwell's vigorous promotion of the Christian faith in his own country was, however, seen by some as Puritanical meddling, a fact that ensured the decline of Puritanism after Cromwell's death in 1658. History puts many things in perspective. "Cromwell was very far from being the Puritan killjoy of vulgar convention."[147] But the perception was there at the time. Following Cromwell's death, his son Richard was not able to hold the reigns of power in anything resembling the manner of his father, and so, Parliament was presented with a dilemma: how to maintain political and military equilibrium in a world that included France, Spain, and the Netherlands, traditional enemies of England? The answer? The return of the king.

The Restoration of the British monarchy in 1660 brought with it a return of religious persecution, though newly crowned King Charles II had at first promised "a liberty to tender consciences."[148] The monarchs had, since the time of Henry VIII, been the earthly heads of the Church of England. The Civil War and the Commonwealth of Cromwell had ended all of that, but only *temporarily*. Charles insisted on the restoration of the Act of Supremacy once he was on the throne. In 1662 Parliament passed the Act of Uniformity, requiring all English pastors to subscribe to the Anglican rite. That meant the restoration of the Anglican Church as the only legitimate church on England's soil.[149] All ten thousand of England's churches were restored to the episcopacy

---

144 John Owen, *A Brief Declaration and Vindication of the Doctrine of the Trinity*, vol. 2, *The Works of John Owen*, ed. William H. Goold (Edinburgh: Banner of Truth, 1965), 336–440.
145 Literally, "the period between the kings," 1649–60.
146 Christopher Hill, *Milton and the English Revolution* (London: Faber and Faber, 1977), 461–64.
147 Hill, *God's Englishman*, 198.
148 Martin Sutherland, *Peace, Toleration and Decay: The Ecclesiology of Later Stuart Dissent*, Studies in Evangelical History and Thought (Carlisle, UK: Paternoster, 2003), 2.
149 Hill, *Century of Revolution*, 166–71.

Struggle for the City

of the church, and dissent was outlawed. About two thousand pastors were *expelled* in the Great Ejection, including a third of the London clergy.[150]

Such a religious solution only made sense to Charles, whose court soon became the center of corruption and good taste, as nobles and intellectuals curried favor with the king by giving lip service to his glories. That was not all that was wrong with Charles's court. Shortage of finances for his extravagant living led him into secret intrigues with his cousin, the Sun King, Louis XIV of France.[151] At the Secret Treaty of Dover (1670) he promised to make war on the Protestant Dutch and to promote Roman Catholicism in England in exchange for gold. That is, in spite of the formal enforcement of the Act of Uniformity, for money Charles secretly promoted Catholicism.[152] During this same period his armies were killing thousands of Scottish Covenanters, who refused to yield to the episcopacy and were forced to meet in secret conventicles throughout the countryside.[153] Charles was, thus, killing people for opposing the Anglican Church and promoting the opposition to the Anglican Church at one and the same time—all for profit.[154]

On his deathbed Charles made public his earlier conversion to Roman Catholicism, a "secret" which was not really very secret.[155] He left no legitimate son as heir, though he had eight sons and five daughters, so his brother the Duke of York became King James II. James' Catholicism was far more public than had been the case with his brother. Immediately he initiated a pro-French, pro-Catholic policy (his second wife was French). The British nobles were hopeful that nothing would come of this, since James' oldest child, Mary, was wed to the Dutch Protestant Prince William of Orange and she would likely succeed her father as queen. But in early 1688 James' wife's pregnancy became undeniable.

Seven bishops opposed James's religious views publicly, and he had them arrested and tried, though they were acquitted in June of that year, the same month

---

150 Jenny Uglow, *A Gambling Man: Charles II's Restoration Game* (New York: Farrar, Straus, and Giroux, 2009), 193.
151 Hill, *Century of Revolution*, 185–89.
152 Antonia Fraser, *Royal Charles: Charles II and the Restoration* (New York: Alfred A. Knopf, 1979), 275, 347.
153 Pearse, *Age of Reason*, 269; Jock Purves, *Fair Sunshine: Character Studies of the Scottish Covenanters* (London: Banner of Truth, 1968).
154 Uglow, *Gambling Man*, 240.
155 Hill, *Century of Revolution*, 169.

Struggle for the City

that James's wife, Mary, gave birth to a *son*, a son who would now displace Mary as successor to James. At that point a group of political figures known as the Immortal Seven, including the Bishop of London, invited William of Orange to accede to the throne.[156] In November William did just that, and "sent James II and VII [he was also King of Scotland] packing from his Atlantic thrones."[157] William invaded England with an army numbering twenty-one thousand, the largest attempted invasion since the Spanish Armada exactly one hundred years prior.[158] With his large standing army deserting to the other side, James sent his wife and new son to France and then fled the country dressed as a woman. England would not again walk the path again that Mary Tudor had led, and James knew that it would mean his life if he tarried.

The people of England welcomed the invaders. While William had brought with him an impressive army, it would not be necessary to use it. Mobs throughout the country rose against their governors. Townspeople purged their district of military governors. The people of England, by the "desperate thousands" (desperate because if William were unsuccessful they would be guilty of treason) welcomed the Prince of Orange in an almost giddy fashion. "England had new rulers who, it appeared, were placed on the throne by the will of the English people."[159] Indeed, it did!

Co-regents William and Mary were crowned in 1689, and the same year Parliament passed the Act of Toleration, granting religious liberty to dissenters, a liberty *never* to be revoked.[160] The same year Parliament published the "Declaration of Rights," a document that, as much as anything, *resembled* the sentiments of both the Magna Carta of 1215 and the later Declaration of Independence of 1776. The American colonists of almost a century later were beholden to the political philosophy advanced by a Dutch prince in an English context, but one birthed by a host of Baptists, Levellers, Puritans, Quakers,

---

156 Ibid., 171.
157 MacCulloch, *Reformation*, 581.
158 See further discussion in Steve C. A. Pincus, *England's Glorious Revolution 1688–1689: A Brief History with Documents*, Bedford Series in History and Culture (New York: Bedford / St. Martin's Press, 2006), 3.
159 Ibid.
160 Though it nearly was by Queen Anne in 1714, being stopped only by her death the evening before she was to sign the new legislation.

Struggle for the City

and Independents, all of whom made their contribution. The ensuing "Glorious Revolution" (1689) restored the advances that had been made by Cromwell, Rutherford, Milton, and others during the interregnum. William and Mary also brought their country to renewed greatness in Europe by helping to seal the downfall of France in the War of Spanish Succession (1701–14).[161]

No political figures have been without some stain on their character, but William and Mary held to philosophical and theological convictions that kept in *check* the kinds of tendencies that were so common among state figures of their day—they did not utilize office for enforcing their religious views or to curry financial favor and support for favored nobility. A sort of Calvinistic *protorepublicanism* ruled the hour. Full religious *liberty* was still a long way off, but religious *toleration* was, in England, pretty much to stay.

---

161 Hill, *Century of Revolution*, 221–27.

Struggle for the City

Chapter 15

Republicanism and Free Markets

THE EIGHTEENTH CENTURY REALLY WAS the beginning of the *modern world*. Scientific developments, political revolutions, and new ways of understanding how economies of nations actually worked catapulted the West into an entirely new self-understanding and paved the way for the increased wealth that would mark the modern world out as being fundamentally *different* from everything before about the year 1700. Century markers are, of course, arbitrary. No one woke up on January 1, 1701, and said, "At last, the modern world." Looking back, though, it is clear that the eighteenth century witnessed massive *changes* in virtually every area of thought and life, but nothing was more profound than the shifts in politics and in the way people understood the economic and political world. Here we will begin in the mid-seventeenth century and examine a series of thinkers whose writings in many ways created the modern world.

LOCKE, HOBBES, HUME, AND MONTESQUIEU: CONTRARY AND COMPLEMENTARY VIEWS ON POLITICAL, RELIGIOUS, AND ECONOMIC LIBERTY

From Locke to Montesquieu, English and European thinking on politics and economics and their relationship to church and religion in general took on a whole new cast. We need to examine that development before looking at a figure who drew together many of the strands, authoring an important book in the year 1776.

Locke and Religious Liberty

The English Civil War and its aftermath created a whole new *context* for understanding the merits or demerits of republicanism. But those insights had to
await the "Glorious Revolution" of 1689 that came with the reign of William
and Mary for any kind of realization on England's home soil. And it is important to note that even the Glorious Revolution did not result in a republican
government in England. But in the middle of the Restoration period, in 1665,
England sent a diplomatic mission to Cleves—a Prussian city, also a Lutheran
city. One member of the delegation was a young scholar who had written treatises defending the authority of government over all areas of life, and especially
over religion. He had accepted the view promoted by the Tudors of the previous century and the Stuarts (and the French Bourbon kings) of his own time
that any kind of religious dissent was *dangerous* and threatened to *undermine*
society. In Cleves, the young John Locke (1632–1704) found a city in which
several Protestant faiths existed peacefully alongside Roman Catholicism. As
he put it, "They quietly permit one another to choose their way to heaven."[1]
Locke's world was transformed overnight.

This visit to Cleves brought about a paradigm shift in Locke's thinking.
"Over the next few years it gradually dawned on the young scholar that religious dissent is not the cause of political conflict over religion. Rather, the
outlawing of religious dissent is the cause of political conflict over religion."[2]
Locke would make a major contribution in the development of a philosophical commitment to *religious liberty* in England and the Western world as well
as to the nature of government in general.

Toleration of religious opinion was nothing new. The Romans, as we have
shown, tolerated the religious views of the provinces, after a fashion. The
Dutch had been tolerant of religious diversity, all the while having a state
church that was, successively, Roman Catholic and then Reformed. They even

---

1   John Locke, "Introduction," *The Reasonableness of Christianity: As Delivered in the
    Scriptures*, ed. John C. Higgins-Biddle, Clarendon Edition of the Works of John Locke
    (1695; Oxford: Clarendon, 1999), lxxxv.
2   Greg Forster, *The Contested Public Square: The Crisis of Christianity and Politics* (Downers
    Grove, IL: InterVarsity Press, 2008), 143.

Struggle for the City

had a term for it: "Go Dutch." To "go Dutch" meant to "go the easy way," that is, the tolerant way, since the Dutch allowed Jews, Anabaptists, and other movements the freedom to live and practice their faith in the Low Countries.[3]

Still, though the Dutch were tolerant, their system did not allow for full freedom of conscience in the way Locke would articulate. That is clear from, among other facts, the way the Remonstrants were treated after the Synod of Dort in 1619. Representing the Arminian party that was rejected at that Synod, they were forced to abandon their pulpits since they could not affirm the Canons (the decisions) of the Synod.[4] At one level one might just consider that to be a church issue. It was more than just a church matter for them, however, as the Synod was called by the Dutch government, and the resultant expulsions were enforced by the same Dutch government.[5] Toleration is not the same thing as full freedom of conscience, though it is certainly better than *oppression*.[6]

Locke's world was very different from ours. The Reformation had brought many states out from under the hegemony of the Roman Catholic Church, and at first most of those states were under the direction of one specific form of Christianity: Geneva was Reformed, England was Anglican, and Saxony was Lutheran. A number of battles had been fought between Lutheran, Catholic, and Reformed forces, but in 1555 the Peace of Augsburg was affirmed. It stated that the religion of the sovereign, whether king, duke, or prince, would be the religion of the land—*cuius regio, eius religio*.[7] But that turned out to be only a temporary solution, for two reasons.

First, what if a king died and his heir was from a different branch of the church? That is what happened in 1618 when the Lutheran king of Bohemia died childless, and his throne was granted to his brother, the Elector of the Palatinate, who was a Catholic. The ensuing confrontation that took place between the Bohemian nobles and the representatives of the new king in an upper floor of the palace in Prague witnessed an event known as the "Defenestration

---

3   Williams, *The Radical Reformation*, 347–48, inter alia.
4   Williston Walker, *A History of the Christian Church*, 4th ed. (New York: Scribner's, 1985), 542.
5   Dirk Jellema, "Dort, Synod of," *The New International Dictionary of the Christian Church*, rev. ed. ed. J. D. Douglas (Grand Rapids, MI: Zondervan, 1978), 310.
6   Forster, *Contested Public Square*, 145.
7   Walker, *History of the Christian Church*, 465, 529.

Struggle for the City

of Prague." (The German word for "window" is *Fenster*, originally from Latin *fenestra*,[8] so you can probably figure it out.) The delegation was thrown from the window to the rocks below. None of the men died, but the insult was met with a declaration of war.[9] The Thirty Years' War was on.

The second problem with the Peace of Augsburg solution was that the situation in each place did not remain static in the years following the settlements. So, as we have already seen, when traditional Anglicanism came into conflict with Puritan Anglicanism, the resulting debate was not merely ecclesiastical but also *political* and *economic*. In that case, Parliament came mostly to support the *Puritan* wing, and the end of the matter was the English Civil War. Something very similar took place in France, though there the Protestant party was put down by the Catholic one.[10] These were the issues Locke faced in attempting to draw up a defense of freedom of conscience, plus one more beside that we have discussed previously. Even a century after the Reformation there were many who believed that membership in an alternate Christian tradition from the prevailing national one (or civic one, in the case of some of the free cities of Europe) entailed a treasonous attitude toward the government. So, even in the late seventeenth century, British citizens who were Catholic were still eyed with suspicion—and sometimes deservedly so!

In 1689, the year of the Glorious Revolution, Locke wrote "A Letter concerning Toleration."[11] Defending himself by using both the New Testament and moral persuasion, Locke made a firm case for *toleration*. From the NT he noted that meekness and charity ought to be extended toward all, and he cited Paul's appeal that the "weapons of our warfare are not of the flesh" (2 Cor. 10:4).[12] Calvin had argued for religious *uniformity* on the basis of the Old Testament,

---

8 Douglas Harper, "defenestration," *Online Etymology Dictionary*, http://www.etymonline. com/index.php?term=defenestration.

9 Peter H. Wilson, *Europe's Tragedy: A History of the Thirty Years War* (London: Allen Lane, 2009), 3–4. He subtitles the event as "Three Men and a Window."

10 In 1598 King Henry IV passed the Edict of Nantes, which granted Protestants in France toleration, but the edict was revoked in 1685 by Louis XIV "who desired to have one state, one ruler, and one faith." So, two hundred thousand Huguenots were forced to flee. Earle E. Cairns, *Christianity through the Centuries*, 3rd ed. (Grand Rapids, MI: Zondervan, 1996), 310.

11 John Locke, "A Letter concerning Toleration" (1689), in *Locke on Toleration*, ed. Richard Vernon, Cambridge Texts in the History of Philosophy (Cambridge: Cambridge University Press, 2010).

12 Forster, *Contested Public Square*, 155.

Struggle for the City

but Locke observed that there is now no theocratic community under the new covenant, a covenant that comprises a people from every nation and tongue. So, under the new covenant, religious *establishments* ought to be *rejected.*

He did not, however, simply leave it at that. Locke further argued that "the things that count for the survival of the community are the shared rules of social interaction, not religion as such."[13] The differing Christian communities differed on theology, but not on *justice.* People do not have to agree on religion in order to agree on the *moral* rules that govern a society. Furthermore, a person could not really be "saved" by conforming to the religious demands of the state, since salvation is by faith out of personal volition and not merely by *formal* conformity to an *ecclesiastical* tradition.[14]

Locke went on to observe that most civilized societies have similar laws when they treat the moral issues of their society alone, absent the theological or religious issues. The reason for this lies in *natural law,* which has been imparted by God to *all* persons, with the result that they will believe many of the same things in matters of justice and morals, even if they belong to completely different religions, say, Judaism or Islam.[15] People may not *know* that the source of human law is the divine law written on the conscience, but it is there, nonetheless, and that enables people to work out moral and legal systems in whatever part of the world they may live.[16] As Locke put it in his *Essay Concerning Human Understanding,* "[M]orality is the proper science and business of mankind in general; (who are both concerned and fitted to seek out their *Summum Bonum*)."[17] Human beings are predisposed to seek out that which makes them most happy, and it is the job of government to establish that on the broadest base possible, to create the greatest happiness for the people as a *whole.*[18] For Locke, this meant that religious *liberty,* not merely religious toleration, is *necessary* for a just society in the modern world.[19]

---

13 Ibid., 157.
14 John Locke, *An Essay Concerning Human Understanding,* ed. Peter H. Nidditch (1689/1690; Oxford: Oxford University Press, 1979), 4.19.10.
15 Roger Woolhouse, *John Locke: A Biography* (Cambridge: Cambridge University Press, 2007), 285–88.
16 Locke, *Essay Concerning Human Understanding,* 1.3.6.
17 Ibid., 4.12.11.
18 Ibid., 4.12.13.
19 Woolhouse, *John Locke,* 310–12. So Locke's argument here is somewhat of an advance over his previous "Letter concerning Toleration."

Struggle for the City

Religious allegiance to one church, or to church at all, must never be coerced. These ideas were already "in the air" when Locke was writing his books, and even before. When Johann Maier of Eck, Luther's Catholic inquisitor at the Diet of Worms, called upon King Sigismund to suppress the Reformation in Poland, Sigismund replied, "Permit me sir to be the king of both the sheep and the goats." His son, Sigismund II claimed to be "king of the people but not of their consciences."[20] Locke was able to build on the work of those who had gone before, especially those who had drunk deeply at the well of the Reformation and had imbibed its real significance—*individual liberty*—something that even the first and second generation of Reformers did not always do.[21]

Locke also made important contributions to notions of rights and of property. He argued that human beings have been given natural rights by God, rights that include *life*, *liberty*, and the pursuit of *property*. He contended that property existed *before* government, and therefore government has no right to dispose of the property of lawful citizens without *due process*. But at this point, Locke seems to be somewhat confused, at least that is how it seems to those of us who read his work in light of later developments. Locke held that ownership of property is created by the application of labor, and he then tied that notion to what he called, "the labor theory of value." Locke's labor theory of value seems wrongheaded, or at least it does to us. By this idea he meant that all monetary value of a commodity is connected to the amount of labor that it took to create that commodity. (Karl Marx would later adopt a similar notion.) Clearly, though, this is not the case. The same amount of labor may go into the creation of a beautiful work of art that goes into building a well-proportioned pile of garbage in one's backyard, but it is obvious that they are not of equal value.[22]

Hobbes and *Leviathan*

Thomas Hobbes (1588–1679) held views very different from those of Locke on the absolute power of the sovereign in England, but was a co-contributor along

---

20 Diarmaid MacCulloch, *The Reformation* (New York: Viking, 2003), 192.
21 With the exception of Conrad Grebel, Menno Simons, and others of the Radical Reformation.
22 Mark Skousen, *The Making of Modern Economics*, 2nd ed. (Armonk, NY: M. E. Sharpe, 2009), 54.

Struggle for the City

with Locke on the topic of natural rights and on government requiring the consent of the *people*. Entering this world on April 5, 1588, he was born prematurely when his mother heard the report that the Spanish Armada was on its way. He later wrote in his *Verse Life*, that "Mother Dear did bring forth Twins at once, both Me, and Fear."[23] His life seems to have been marked by that *fear*, over and over again.

Hobbes and his political views can only be understood against the backdrop of the political struggle between Parliament and king, the struggle that eventually cost King Charles I his life. Hobbes was engaged in writing several scientific treatises during this time, and his sympathies lay directly with the monarchy and against the rising Puritan party that was so influential in Parliament. He said as much in his book *De corpore politico* in 1642. When, that same year, war broke out between Crown and Parliament and one of the king's ministers was sent to the Tower for defending the very ideas that were spelled out in Hobbes' book, Hobbes fled to France where he spent a year in exile.[24] He spent much of his time from 1646–48 in France as tutor to the prince of Wales (later Charles II).[25] It was during this time that he wrote *Leviathan*, published in 1651.

Hobbes argued that the state of nature, that is, the natural state without government, is a state in which all persons would have the natural right to all things. Such a position, however, is practically untenable, since everyone would seek to take what he or she wants from whomever has it, and so, the state of nature is for Hobbes, a state of *war*.[26] This war would be a "war of all against all."[27] He further stated that if a man would only look within himself, he would know "what are the thoughts and passions of all other men."[28] In keeping with the empirical method that had been founded by Francis Bacon and furthered by John Locke and Isaac Newton, Hobbes noted "that *wisdom* is acquired, not by reading of *books*, but of

---

23 Thomas Hobbes, *Elements of Law Natural and Political* (1640/1650; New York: Penguin Books, 1994), 254.
24 Michael Allen Gillespie, *The Theological Origins of Modernity* (Chicago: University of Chicago Press, 2008), 218.
25 "Hobbes, Thomas," *Oxford Dictionary of the Christian Church*, 3rd ed., ed. F. L. Cross and E. A. Livingstone (Oxford: Oxford University Press, 1997), 776.
26 Thomas Hobbes, *Leviathan*, ed. J. C. A. Gaskin, Oxford World's Classics (1651; Oxford: Oxford University Press, 2008), 13.
27 Ibid., 13.
28 Ibid., 11.2.

Struggle for the City

men.[29] In other words, if we are really honest, we will know what the danger is to live in society without a strong hand of government. Left in the state of nature, Hobbes famously argued that people would live lives that are "solitary, poor, nasty, brutish, and short."[30] The state of nature is a state of war. "That is why the natural social condition of mankind is war—if not explicit, armed hostilities, then a perpetual state of anxious readiness in preparation for conflict."[31] This *pragmatic* and *dark* anthropology, right or wrong, stands behind Hobbes' politics.

To prevent this catastrophe of all against all from actually happening, men in a state of nature concede to a *social contract* and set forth a civil society, a society in which they cede their natural rights in exchange for protection from the others in the state of nature.[32] Though they have a natural right to life and liberty, they must not maintain that right as something inalienable. Hobbes believed that people possessed these natural rights, as Locke also argued, but his position obviously *differed* from Locke's mature views, as Locke would argue that these rights *are* inalienable. Hobbes contended that government, monarchy in this case, had the authority to *override* peoples' natural rights when it had a compelling interest to do so. Such governmental authority, even if it advances to become outright *oppression*, is the price people pay for *security* from one another.

Hobbes believed that what people wanted and needed more than anything else was a sense of security that government would protect them from *other people*.[33] For him, fear was the most natural human passion, and the basic fear among all fears is the fear of violent *death*. Government may not be able to eliminate the possibility of violent death taking place, but it can give itself to the regulation of the kind of violence that people in society inflict on one another.[34] A sovereign can apply himself (or herself) in seeing to it that such collisions are lessened.

In spite of the monarchy's authority to exercise total authority over all spheres of life, including religion, it ought to *seek* to rule by *consent*.[35] Hobbes

---

29 Hobbes, "Author's Introduction," *Leviathan*.
30 Hobbes, *Leviathan*, 13.9.
31 Mark Lilla, *The Stillborn God* (New York: Vintage Books, 2007), 82.
32 A. P. Martinich, *Hobbes: A Biography* (Cambridge: Cambridge University Press, 1999), 230–35.
33 Hobbes, *Leviathan*, 18.
34 Gillespie, *Theological Origins of Modernity*, 208.
35 Hobbes, *Leviathan*, 20.

Struggle for the City

was not in favor of the divine right of kings, even if he did speak out in favor of men (James I and Charles I) who held to that belief. Hobbes believed that *just* monarchs would gain consent when they can. He also made a role for religion in this, a very important role. Hobbes may have been the "first thinker to suggest that religious conflict and political conflict are essentially the same conflict."[36] Because of that, the religious problem and the political problem must "be solved together, or not at all."[37] The way this is solved is by making the sovereign not only lord of the nation, but lord in the church as well, that is, by making the king "an earthly God."[38] This was shocking to many of Hobbes' contemporary readers, still reeling from the specter of the Thirty Years' War, for they expected from him a more *secular* solution. In reality, though, his solution *was* a secular solution, for he did not contend that the church over which the king presided was the "one true Church." Hobbes had now substituted a kind of "earthly religion" for the "One, Holy, Catholic Apostolic Church," with the king of England as its head. His solution to the problem of all against all is one nation, one sovereign, one church, but it was a *pragmatic*, not a *dogmatic*, solution.

There are many inconsistencies in Hobbes' politics. Many of his arguments are based on faulty *anthropology* (nature of man) and a naïve understanding of human *psychology*.[39] He was certainly no Augustinian or Calvinist, but his view of human depravity (humans are *brutes*) was darker than theirs, with little gleam of the possibility for redemption, aside from a political one *external* to the soul. His position also assumes that only a powerful *monarch* could maintain order and he never explores the concept of separation of powers.[40] Though he claims to reject the divine right of kings, the book comes awfully close at least to contending for the *naturally religious* right of kings. But the one thing Hobbes did accomplish was to demystify and demythologize the theological basis for governance.[41] If theologians were to make a case for the theological basis for some political arrangement, they would have to come to grips with

---

36 Lilla, *Stillborn God*, 80.
37 Ibid., 81.
38 Hobbes, *Leviathan*, 15.8.
39 Gillespie, *Theological Origins of Modernity*, 246–54.
40 W. R. Runciman, *Great Books, Bad Arguments: Republic, Leviathan, and the Communist Manifesto* (Princeton, NJ: Princeton University Press, 2010), 67.
41 Lilla, *Stillborn God*, 89.

Struggle for the City

Hobbes's demystification, a project that would be taken up in earnest in the next century by a Scottish philosopher to the north.

David Hume and the Cradle of Economics

David Hume (1711–76) taught philosophy in Scotland and was a man whose writings covered a wide and ranging set of ideas. His religious writings were quite controversial, but our concern here is primarily with his thoughts on *economics* and *politics*. Hume entered the University of Edinburgh at the unusually early age of ten (fourteen was normal) and he published his *A Treatise of Human Nature* at the age of twenty-six, earning him immediate fame. One of Hume's biographers suggested that his essays constitute the "cradle of economics."[42] Hume made several important contributions to the study of the economy, though his work in this area was not as monumentally significant as that of his friend and fellow also in Edinburgh, Adam Smith. Hume treated questions related to political economy as integral to question on ethics and jurisprudence. The science of man is based on observation and experience and our experiments here arise "from a cautious observation of human life."[43] This is Hume's basic approach to all science, so there is no surprise that he would employ this method here. Hume believed that human nature was a *constant* in all parts of the world and in all ages and that an examination of a large enough grouping of people in one place at one time will tell you what they would be like in all times and places.[44] With this, he considers that his observations about history and about what is happening in his world at the time enable him to draw his own conclusions about political economy *everywhere*. At the same time, Hume was skeptical about the "common man," even as he was skeptical about drawing out any conclusions about such things as causation, and he held that commerce was really the great *polisher* of the common man.[45]

---

42 John Hill Burton, *Life and Correspondence of David Hume* (Edinburgh: University of Edinburgh Press, 1846), 1:354.

43 David Hume, "Introduction," *A Treatise of Human Nature*, 2nd ed., ed. L. A. Selby-Bigge and P. H. Nidditch (1739–40; Oxford: Clarendon, 1978), xvi.

44 David Hume, *Enquiries concerning Human Understanding and concerning the Principles of Morals*, 3rd ed., ed. L. A. Selby-Bigge and P. H. Nidditch (1777; Oxford: Clarendon, 1975), 83.

45 David Hume, *David Hume's Political Essays*, ed. Charles W. Hendel, Forum Books 11 (New York: Liberal Arts, 1953), 47.

Struggle for the City

The Scottish philosopher held that the basis for economic transactions is the *self-interest* of man. We have self-interest and we have a desire that others would see us in a positive light. "There are few persons, that are satisfy'd [*sic*] with their own character, or genius, or fortune, who are not desirous of showing themselves to the world, and of acquiring the love and approbation of mankind."[46] So, we are interested in economic transactions because of the *pleasure* they bring us and because they bring the added pleasure of other people being sympathetic with that which brings us pleasure.[47] This, of course, *could* be a *detriment* to society since it would turn all persons into acquisitive and selfish brutes, the economic equivalent of Hobbes' "all against all." Hume observed, though, that people also derive a certain selfish pleasure from being thought of as *generous*. We "receive a pleasure from the view of such actions as tend to the peace of society, and an uneasiness from such as are contrary to it."[48] It is still self-motivation, but it is a self-motivation that extends charity to others, which tends to bring some *redemption* to the apparent self-centeredness of it. Hume did not so much see humans as rational creatures but as *clever animals* that will use means to achieve ends or purposes that were predetermined by their sentiments.[49]

Hume considered the role of history and of historical development as a key component to an understanding of political economy. As people in prehistorical times moved from gathering to sedentary agriculture to manufacturing, each new development brought with it an increased desire for more of such changes. This had happened especially in the previous century to his country as the nation of England witnessed a rapid rate of economic growth in comparison to previous times, albeit an unsteady one.[50] Success breeds a greater desire for more such success. This becomes a sort of engine that drives progress, and progress is a good thing for Hume. For centuries societies and economies were relatively *static* and unmoving from generation to generation, but the previous two centuries to Hume had witnessed extensive *change* and progress.

---

46 Hume, *Treatise of Human Nature*, 331–32.
47 John Mueller, *Redeeming Economics* (Wilmington, DE: ISI Books, 2010), 81.
48 Hume, *Treatise of Human Nature*, 533.
49 Mueller, *Redeeming Economics*, 78.
50 David Hume, *The History of England: From the Invasion of Julius Caesar to the Revolution in 1688* (1778; Indianapolis: Liberty Classics, 1983), 6:148.

Struggle for the City

The Scotsman also called attention to the importance of international *trade*. As we have observed in previous discussions, the nations of Europe were wary of reciprocal international trade. They were happy to *export* their goods to other nations in order to trade for their gold, but they generally *opposed imports*, since importing would drain their gold reserves and send them elsewhere. But that situation is untenable over the long run, since it entails the notion, as we have already pointed out, that trade *is* war. Hume had the insight to see this, and offered his own analysis. In an essay called, "Of the Jealousy of Trade," Hume pointed out that England's "situation" was vastly improved over what it had been two centuries before, when "all the arts both of agriculture and manufactures were then extremely rude and imperfect."[51] This is because trade had slowly improved between those nations, and so, "the encrease [*sic*] of riches and commerce in any one nation, instead of hurting, commonly promotes the riches and commerce of all its neighbors."[52] This is a bit naïvely stated but is generally true, as later economists will spell out in more careful detail.

Hume did not believe, in contrast to Locke, that humans had a *natural* right to private property, but he did believe that, since resources are limited, the possession of private property was *justified*. If all goods were unlimited and freely available, then private property would be an "idle ceremonial," and not worth fussing over. Though not a Calvinist (that's an understatement!), Hume was realistic about the dark side of human nature (though his "man" was not as dark as Hobbes'), and so he resisted any effort to argue for equal *distribution* of property. Any attempt on the part of the government to redistribute property on anything like an equal basis would be destructive of *thrift* and *hard work*, since if humans did not need to be thrifty and industrious in order to be successful, they would not be.[53] In a manner similar to his friend Adam Smith, whose contributions to economics will be taken up shortly, Hume believed that trade was a stimulus for economic growth and that governments should take down barriers to trade. Finally, Hume demonstrated how an increase in a nation's gold supply brings with

---

51 David Hume, "Of the Jealousy of Trade," in *Essays, Moral, Political, and Literary*, ed. Eugene F. Miller (Indianapolis: Liberty Fund, 1987), Library of Economics and Liberty, http://www.econlib.org/library/LFBooks/Hume/hmMPL29.html (accessed March 25, 2011).
52 Ibid.
53 Norman Kemp Smith, *The Philosophy of David Hume: A Critical Study of Its Origins and Central Doctrines* (New York: Palgrave Macmillan, 2005), 243.

Struggle for the City

it an attended rise in *inflation*. The more gold that is in an economic system, the more prices of goods and services will rise until *equilibrium* is reached. This had happened, of course, in both Spain and Portugal in the sixteenth century, but Hume was the one who was able to show *why*. So, along with Adam Smith and John Locke, Hume helped to put the final intellectual nails in the coffin of the mercantile system, though as with all economic evolutions, the rudiments of mercantilism would linger on for a long time.

Montesquieu

We need to examine the work of one more important European intellectual before turning our attention to Adam Smith. Charles de Secondat, Baron de Montsquieu, was born in southwest France in 1689, the year of England's Glorious Revolution. That event in English history, along with the *Acts of Union 1707* that brought England and Scotland together to form *Great Britain*, were quite influential in the thinking of the young scholar/nobleman. Montesquieu minimized the roles of individuals in history, arguing that certain changes are inevitable, not because of the genius of one particular man, but because of the cultures of ideologies that are formed by the movements of history.[54] No doubt Louis XIV, who died before the young scholar published this idea, would have disagreed.

In his massively influential *The Spirit of the Laws*, the baron made a case for a new kind of governmental *organization*. His work divided French society into three classes—the monarchy, the aristocracy, and the commons. He further argued that there are two kinds of governmental powers—the sovereign and the administrative. The sovereign has authority, but not absolute authority. The administrative is divided into executive, legislative, and judiciary branches that are *separate* from and *dependent* on one another so that none of them trumps the others.[55] This latter idea was the most *radical* since, if implemented, it would

---

54 Paul A. Rahe, *Montesquieu and the Logic of Liberty: War, Religion, Commerce, Climate, Terrain, Technology, Uneasiness of Mind, the Spirit of Political Vigilance, and the Foundations of the Modern Republic* (New Haven, CT: Yale University Press, 2009).

55 Charles de Secondat Montesquieu, *The Spirit of Laws*, trans. Thomas Nugent, rev. J. V. Prichard, Bohn's Standard Library (1748; G. Bell & Sons, London, 1914), 233, Liberty

Struggle for the City

have eliminated the notion of the three estates of the French monarchy—the clergy, the aristocracy, and the people at large who were represented by the Estates General. This would have *eradicated* the last element of the older feudalistic (manorial) structure. As we know, and will see later, it was this latter structure that would impact the formation of the American Constitutional government.

ADAM SMITH AND THE MAJOR DEVELOPMENT OF "THE DISMAL SCIENCE"

As we have seen, various thinkers have given serious consideration to the interface between theology, politics, and economic issues. We have also seen that Thomas Aquinas articulated a fully developed theory of economics in the thirteenth century and that this theory was followed by other Scholastics and had an impact on later churchmen like John Calvin. The year 1776 witnessed the publication of a book that would initiate a new *era* in economic history, an era that would both help to close the door on one phase of economic history and open doors to new hopes, though those open doors would not all be the best pathways. In that year, a Scottish "moral philosopher" named Adam Smith published *The Wealth of Nations*, a volume destined to rock the intellectual world almost as powerfully as the revolution of that same year rocked the international world of politics.[56]

Building on the Foundation of Others

Sometimes it seems as though a mystical sort of synchronicity brings apparently disparate forces together at the same moment. The late eighteenth century witnessed revolutions of various sorts—the two most prominent being the French and American revolutions, one of which created a new republic, and the other of which eventually created a new *despotism*. But political revolutions were not the only type of that genre. The Industrial Revolution in England was

---

Library of Constitutional Classics, http://www.constitution.org/cm/sol.htm (accessed March 28, 2011).

56 The full title is *An Inquiry into the Nature and Causes of the Wealth of Nations*. See full citation in note 63.

whipping into fever pitch at about the same time as the American Revolution, with new technologies such as the steam engine, the spinning jenny, and just a few years later, in America, the cotton gin. While America was still largely agrarian, England was becoming an industrial powerhouse.[57] This revolution in technology was preceded, about a century earlier, by a scientific revolution known to us as the Enlightenment. That movement, insofar as it can be called a "movement," itself built on the foundation of the Protestant Reformation, which was ushered in at least partly as a result of the Renaissance, an intellectual and artistic explosion that was also preceded by the Scholastic tradition of the twelfth and thirteenth centuries. What seems clear from this is that there is no *mystical* synchronicity but, rather, movements and individuals building their innovations, in part, on foundations laid by others.

Smith himself appears to have been influenced in part by the prior work of a Dutch-born Englishman, Bernard Mandeville (1670–1733). Mandeville is (or was) famous for his allegorical portrayal of humankind in their economic relationships as a hive of bees, written as a poetic piece in 1705.[58] In the poem the bees are all motivated by "vicious drives" such as avarice, luxury, debauchery, waste, intemperance, gluttony, and the like and are exceedingly prosperous. One day they pray, hypocritically it would seem, for *virtuous* character to replace their vices. When their prayers are answered affirmatively, suddenly they are plunged into poverty. The *moral* is obviously that neither "the designs of the state" nor "the benevolence of individuals" leads to prosperity but only all pursuing "self-interest," here seen as common *vices*. Smith clearly saw it *differently* and sought to cast a new moral understanding around the creation of societal and personal wealth.[59]

It is not mere happenstance that the Industrial Revolution, the Declaration of Independence, and Adam Smith's famous volume all came at about the same

---

57   Peter Mathias, *The First Industrial Nation: An Economic History of Britain, 1700–1914* (London: Methuen, 1969), 481–86.

58   Originally titled "The Grumbling Hive" (1704) the poem later was published as a book. Bernard Mandeville, *The Fable of the Bees: And Other Writings* (1714; Indianapolis: Hackett, 1997), 19–35. See Forrest McDonald, *Novus Ordo Seclorum: The Intellectual Origins of the Constitution* (Lawrence: University Press of Kansas, 1985), 109, for this connection. It appears Smith is bringing the appropriate moral tone to the more crass interpretation of Mandeville.

59   We will note later in this volume that Smith sought to show that for the first time in human history there was a way out of the mass poverty of ages gone by in human history. See chap. 25, "Social Justice and Distribution."

Struggle for the City

time. (It is a bit odd that the Declaration and *Wealth of Nations* happened the same year, though!) These are connected to one another, even as they built on the foundations laid by Renaissance and Scholastic scholars, and on the religious ideologies of the Protestant Reformers and the Evangelical Revivalists (the latter will be discussed later in our presentation). The *individualism* implied in Luther's doctrine of justification by faith, the notion of personal *responsibility* found in Calvin's views on work, and the concept of political *freedom* in a state with a division of powers articulated by both Locke and Montesquieu all came together in Smith's volume and drove him to articulate a view of economics that is implicit in many of those earlier thinkers but which never did quite come together until his efforts to do so in his work. As Skousen puts it, "Prior to this famous date, six thousand years of recorded history had passed without a seminal work being published on the subject that dominated every waking hour of practically every human being: making a living."[60] His assessment might be somewhat of an overstatement in light of the fact that the Scholastics had already anticipated Smith, but their work had made little impact outside of the scholarly world. That history changed in a single day.

"Natural Liberty"

Smith's *basic* ideology can be easily summed up, even though his tome was nearly a thousand pages long. He believed in *free trade*, the *division of labor*, and the development of *industrial technology*. Throughout the book Smith advocated the principle of "natural liberty," which meant, for him, that people ought to have the freedom to do what they want with little interference from the state, so long as they are law-abiding citizens.[61] This is especially the case with reference to economic decisions.[62] Smith believed that economic freedom was a basic human *liberty*, a view that he held, as we have seen, in common with John Locke, who affirmed that we have inalienable rights to life, liberty, and the pursuit of

---

60 Skousen, *Making of Modern Economics,* 13. We have mentioned Thomas Aquinas as developing these ideas, but even in his work they are not all presented in the same writing.

61 Recall Cromwell's "free way" versus "formal way" in the treatment of his men within the military; not an *economic* issue for Cromwell, but similar in *conceptual* substance.

62 Mark Skousen, *The Big Three in Economics: Adam Smith, Karl Marx and John Maynard Keynes* (New York: M. E. Sharpe, 2007), 10.

property. In *Wealth of Nations*, Smith argued, "To prohibit a great people... from making all that they can of every part of their own produce, or from employing their stock and industry in the way that they judge most advantageous to themselves, is a manifest violation of the most sacred rights of mankind."[63] This Scottish philosopher made it his point to stand up for those rights.

What was this "natural freedom"? For our Adam Smith, it included the right to *buy* goods from any source *without* having to pay crippling tariffs if the goods happened to be imported. It included the right to seek any kind of *employment* one might desire. This was heavily restricted in most European countries in Smith's day by both government regulations that required workers to obtain government *permission* to change jobs and by the *stranglehold* that trade guilds had on most skilled labor, trade guilds that held their authority by government sanction.[64] Natural liberty for Smith also entailed the right to *pay* any wage that the market might bear and to *charge* any price for goods that the market might sustain, without the government setting standards for such things, arbitrary or otherwise. It also included the freedom to generate, accumulate, retain, and pass on capital and wealth to the *next generation* (or to anyone else) without government intrusion in the process.[65] Adam Smith encouraged "the virtues of thrift, capital investment, and labor-saving machinery as essential ingredients to promote rising living standards."[66] In short, he promoted the concept of economic freedom in just about *every* sector of a nation's economic life.

The most obvious implication of "natural liberty" was *free trade*. Smith wrote during a time when trade was anything *but* free. Since the prevailing belief of mercantilism was that wealth was defined in terms of the accumulation of silver and gold, any threat to that supply was tantamount to a *military* threat, as we pointed out in the previous chapter. Because of that, most European countries had elaborate *protectionist* policies in matters of trade. High import tariffs were

---

63 Adam Smith, *An Inquiry into the Nature and Causes of the Wealth of Nations*, ed. Edwin Cannan, Modern Library of the World's Best Books (1776; New York: Modern Library, 1965), 549.
64 Skousen, *Big Three in Economics*, 11–12. Smith was not opposed to guilds as such but only to the way in which European governments and the guilds colluded to keep labor expensive to the detriment of the consumer.
65 We have already noted how Crown and church under Charles I attempted to skim or even confiscate inheritance property.
66 Skousen, *Big Three in Economics*, 11.

Struggle for the City

used to make it economically difficult for foreign countries to sell their goods in other countries—the cost passed on to consumers made it difficult for any but the richest of persons to buy those commodities.

Presumably that policy protected domestic production and manufacturing. Of course, what really happened was that other countries enacted similar protective tariffs, thus preventing exports, which in turn *damaged* the economy of the producing nation that wanted to sell its goods in other countries. Smith argued that this circular policy of protection and threat helped no one in the long run, except the *governments* that collected the tariffs. When international trade itself is viewed as a kind of warfare, almost no one is helped and nearly everyone is hurt. Both producers and consumers are pinched. So, Smith argued for massive *reductions* of tariffs as a means to causing the wealth of all nations to increase.[67]

The second implication of "natural liberty" was the *division of labor*. Many trades had been regulated by government, by trade guilds, and by lack of technological advance so there were many barriers to a worker being able to be hired and to have mobility in the work place. But in the area of technological development and innovation that came with industrialization, some of that was already beginning to change in Smith's day. His most famous example of the division of labor is his discussion of the "pin factory."[68] In previous generations a single individual would apprentice and then eventually master the skill of making pins to be used by seamstresses. There were many steps in making pins—cutting the wire, straightening the wire, sharpening the point, making the head, packaging the pins, and so forth. Pin-makers carefully protected their trade so they could keep the price of pins high and so they could earn a good profit, and forces within government and the guilds helped keep them protected.

Smith proposed, however, that an assembly-line process made more sense. Rather than have one man working, and making, perhaps, twenty pins in a day, Smith conjectured that ten workers, each of whom was adept at only one part of the process—cutting wire, sharpening points, etc.—that such persons, because they were not having to stop over and over again in the day to change work stations, to "saunter" as he put it, could be far more productive. He estimated that the

---

67 See the chart in Skousen, *Making of Modern Economics*, 195, for the correlation between reduction of tariffs and economic prosperity in the history of the American economy.
68 Smith, *Wealth of Nations*, chap. 1.

Struggle for the City

twenty pins made by one man per day might actually exceed forty-eight thousand pins made by ten people operating under the principle of the "division of labor." This would create more productivity, would employ more people in the making of pins, and would cause the cost of pins to decrease substantially, which, in turn, would lower household expenses, freeing up capital to be used to purchase other commodities, which, in turn, would create more jobs. Someone is hurt in the division of labor of course—the master pin-maker, who now has to find other employment—but vast numbers of other people are helped in the process.

The third entailment of "natural liberty" would be to encourage *industrial technological development*. If the government and the guilds no longer controlled manufacturing and commerce, entrepreneurs and inventors would have a financial incentive to devote creative energy and time to technological development. When we think of the late eighteenth to the mid-nineteenth centuries, we think of a time of great *technological* advances. The steam engine (used on both land and water), the spinning jenny, the cotton gin, agricultural advances such as the McCormick reaper and the John Deere steel plowshare and new forms of milling grain and many other examples could be adduced to demonstrate how the Scientific Revolution had impacted and produced the Industrial Revolution.[69]

It is not merely coincidence that many of these new inventions were created in Britain, where governmental changes were giving greater freedom to individuals, and in the new United States of America, where the government laid a lighter hand on business and inventive creativity.[70]

Smith believed that a greater degree of liberty granted by governments would *inevitably* result in more new inventions that would make labor easier, faster, and more profitable. He was convinced that there was nothing wrong and everything right with all of this.

How did some of these new inventions make such a difference? There were two types of inventions in England that gave rise to industrialization: macroinventions and microinventions. Thomas Newcomen's steam engine

---

69 Robert C. Allen, *The British Industrial Revolution in Global Perspective*, New Approaches to Economic and Social History (Cambridge: Cambridge University Press, 2009), 188–95.

70 John Steele Gordon, *The Business of America: Tales from the Marketplace—American Enterprise from the Settling of New England to the Breakup of AT&T* (New York: Walker, 2001), 247–51.

Struggle for the City

and James Hargreaves' spinning jenny were macroinventions. "They set in train long trajectories of advance that resulted in great increases in productivity."[71] Microinventions were the various applications that were put to use by these larger changes in manufacturing and transportation technologies.[72] So, a steam engine could be placed on water or on rails. These macroinventions also spun off into new areas of creativity for men who were constantly looking for more efficient ways to do things. Back to Smith.

Competition

"Natural liberty" then was the key to economic development and the rising wealth of nations. It gave to enterprising individuals like Newcomen and Hargreaves the sense that they could develop new ways of doing things and not have to *battle* incessantly with the *government* to be able to implement their new ideas. There were, in addition, two other elements that we will discuss more briefly. The first is *competition*. Smith writes, "Every man, as long as he does not violate the laws of justice, is left perfectly free to pursue his own interest his own way, and to bring both his industry and capital into competition with those of any other man, or order of men."[73] Individuals in Smith's perspective have the right to compete with one another in the production and exchange of goods and services. Competition, in Smith's view, is a sign of a *healthy* economy. There are several *threats* to competition, most of which are represented by the two regular sources of difficulty Smith had already identified: *government* and protectionist trade *guilds* or *unions*. The greatest threat to productivity comes when the two of these *collude* to stifle competition.

Governments can and do give preferential treatment either to certain sectors of the economy or to certain competitors for the market within the economy or to the guilds and unions. This is, in fact, the historic trend of governments all over the world. Some sector of the economy or some union or some wealthy entrepreneur provides needed political support to governmental leaders, and, in turn, they are rewarded with special government protection or

---

71   Allen, *British Industrial Revolution in Global Perspective,* 136.
72   Ibid., 136–37.
73   Smith, *Wealth of Nations,* 651.

endorsement. This undermines competition and, in the long run, eviscerates the freedoms of the people and generally causes an increase in the cost for goods and service for all. To put it practically, government preferential treatment creates *unemployment* and rising *inflation*, along with other economic difficulties. We noted earlier that Locke argued that religious dissent was not the cause of political dissent over religion; instead it was the outlawing of religious dissent by the government that was the cause. This had its parallel in the economic world.[74] Here it is not economic competition that created business and economic *inefficiency*; rather, it was the government's granting special treatment to certain sectors of the economy that created those problems.

Justice in the Capitalist System

Alongside "natural liberty" and "competition," Smith identifies one other important component to the development of wealth, and that is *justice*. "Justice," for Smith, means that the economic actions of individuals must be just and honest. This is an important aspect of Smith's philosophy that is sometimes ignored by his critics. Economic exchanges ought to be done in a just and honest manner. "Capitalism" (not Smith's word, by the way) is not greed endorsed by political entitlement. The following statement by Smith incorporates all three elements: "Every man, as long as he does not violate the laws of justice, is left perfectly free to pursue his own interest his own way, and to bring both his industry and capital into competition with those of any other man or order of men."[75] In other words, the process works as people pursue their own interests, but it only continues to benefit the whole of an economy if they pursue their interests in a just and *honest* manner. Dinesh D'Souza interprets Smith in this way, "Capitalism civilizes greed in much the same way that marriages civilizes lust. Greed, like lust, is part of our human nature; it would be futile to try to root it out. What capitalism does is to channel greed in such a way that it works to meet the wants and needs of society."[76] Without that, there is a breakdown.

When these three components come together in a nation's economy, ar-

---

74 Skousen, *Making of Modern Economics*, 33.
75 Smith, *Wealth of Nations*, 651.
76 Dinesh D'Souza, "How Capitalism Civilizes Greed," *Forbes*, October 9, 2000, http://www.

Struggle for the City

gued Smith, there will develop a "natural harmony" of interests between workers, landlords, entrepreneurs, and investors. In the pin factory, workers and managers have to work together to accomplish their tasks. The division of labor was, for Smith, the key to a productive economy.

The Invisible Hand

Consider the manufacture of a wool coat. There are dozens of steps in the process of growing the wool, shearing the sheep, making the cloth, producing the dye, and bringing other cloths such as cotton into the process. There is the manufacture of buttons, of a fur collar, and many other steps besides. Large numbers of workers, most of whom never meet one another, are involved in making a single woolen coat. Each of their labor contributes to the other, though they never meet. Nor will they likely meet the eventual purchaser of the finished product—the retail consumer. At every step along the way people are simply pursuing their own self-interests—working to earn a paycheck, operating a business for profit, working to put food on the table for the children, participating in a craft for various reasons, and shopping at the consumption end of the chain—and the net result is that everyone gets something out of it, something that they want.

Why does each one do that? Because each one is seeking his or her own *self-interest* of providing for the family, of paying for college education, of purchasing a larger house to accommodate the growth of the family, and so on. "By pursuing his own self-interest, every individual is led by an *invisible hand* to promote the public interest."[77] The larger part of this particular paragraph from Smith is worth quoting:

> It is not from the benevolence of the butcher, the brewer, or the baker, that we expect our dinner, but from their regard to their own interest. We address ourselves, not to their humanity, but to their self-love.... Every individual... who employs capital...

---

forbes.com/global/2000/1009/0320030a.html, quoted in Skousen, *Making of Modern Economics*, 28.
77 Smith, *Wealth of Nations*, 423 (emphasis added).

Struggle for the City

and labours… neither intends to promote the public interest, nor knows how much he is promoting it… he is led by an invisible hand to promote an end which was no part of his intention…. By pursuing his own interest he frequently promotes that of society.[78]

Through the concept of the "invisible hand," Smith contends that if an economy is just left to operate, it will do so in such a way that peoples' needs are met through the *hydraulic* process of working and living, buying and selling, and running businesses and employing personnel.

Though this part of Smith's argument has sometimes been vilified by critics as "Smith's grabbing hand," this is to misunderstand his whole point. He is simply saying that an economic system in this age in which we live is not intended to and *never* could work simply on an *altruistic* basis and no other. Rather, each man or woman, knowing his or her own needs and the needs of the family, will work to supply those needs. Each one has a motivation, a strong motivation, to provide for his or her family, and a much smaller motivation to provide for someone else's family.[79] After all, the other person's family is not his or her *primary* responsibility—it is the responsibility of the father or husband or wife or mother of that family. But each one working to supply the needs of his or her *own* family will contribute to the *whole* enterprise. Would there be abuses to the system that might arise? Certainly, and it would not be long before German critics would identify the difficulties as "*Das Adam Smith Problem.*"[80] We recognize the potential difficulties and will take them on later in this discussion.

Smith's views on free trade spilled over into his understanding of *religious freedom*. He lived, of course, in a country (Scotland) that had a state church, though by his day there was a great deal of religious liberty in his country, the "Glorious Revolution" having spilled over into Scotland from England, especially after the *Union*. Smith believed that "a great multitude of religious sects" would promote toleration and would be a healthy thing for a nation.[81] In other words, what he

---

78 Ibid., 423.
79 We discussed this same notion in our material on Augustine earlier (see chap. 11).
80 See the critique in Mueller, *Redeeming Economics*, 49–77.
81 Smith, *Wealth of Nations*, 744.

Struggle for the City

thought was good for the economy—freedom from government intrusion—he also believed was good for church and religion. Leave it alone and let it be.

Smith's book was not met with universal acclaim, though initially it was hard to find any *substantial* critics. Certainly in the next century the book would have plenty of detractors, as we will note. But the book has received high praise, even from those who, at the end of the day, do not accept his system of economics. English historian Henry Thomas Buckle opined that in terms of its eventual impact, the book "is probably the most important book that has ever been written."[82] Readers on both sides of the Atlantic found this tome to be extremely helpful in understanding just what *economics* is and just why nations had struggled for centuries to generate and sustain wealth over time. The book just "made sense" to many people in its day, not the least of which were intellectuals and industrialists in the new world of America.

One other issue has to be dealt with in understanding Adam Smith's contribution to economics before we offer some criticism of the project as a whole. As we noted earlier, Smith argues that the primary motive for economic activity is "self-interest." Everyone, pursuing the need to take care of the needs of themselves and their family, will engage in work, commerce, and buying and selling. But that is not the only motivation for Smith. The other is "sympathy." Smith developed this idea in an earlier work, *The Theory of Moral Sentiments*.[83] In economic terms, this meant that both buyer and seller engage in a transaction that is mutually beneficial, and that this is what brings satisfaction to the transaction.[84] Smith argued that everyone has a basic desire to be accepted by others. (We saw Hume making a similar argument.) In preindustrial times this manifested itself in village life where everyone knew everyone else and where it was important to build good relations so that one's business and personal life could prosper. Even in the industrialized city, though, this would still be necessary, since over the long run a good reputation would be important for success. But these two motivations might appear to be at odds with one another. German philosophers believed they were, and designated

82 Quoted in Skousen, *Big Three in Economics*, 12.
83 Adam Smith, *The Theory of Moral Sentiments*, ed. Knud Haakonssen, Cambridge Texts in the History of Philosophy (1759; Cambridge: Cambridge University Press, 2002).
84 Lars Tvede, *Business Cycles: From John Law to Chaos Theory* (Amsterdam: Harwood, 1997), 29, quoted in Skousen, *Making of Modern Economics*, 32.

Struggle for the City

this motivation crisis, "*Das Adam Smith Problem*." It was not a problem for Smith himself, however, since it was his belief that economic activity and moral behavior were not contradictory to each other.[85]

A Mild Rebuke

It is probably apparent that we think well of the overall project Smith assembled. But there are some difficulties. As we pointed out in the material on Thomas Aquinas, the world's first thoroughgoing economic theorist, there are four important elements in any full treatment of the topic—production, exchange (or equilibrium), distribution (or final distribution), and use (or utility). Smith knew of all this, as he had been trained by Frances Hutchinson (1694–1746), who was well versed in Scholastic economics.[86] Yet, in *Wealth of Nations*, Smith reduces the outline to only two components, leaving out consideration of final distribution and utility, apparently for the sake of simplicity, but also because his own personal beliefs caused him not to regard a separate treatment of these issues as necessary to an understanding of political economy. In one of the most famous passages in the book, one that we have quoted here with some approbation, Smith stated that "the butcher, the brewer and the baker" do not provide their services out of the interest of humanity, but for their own self-interest. This is true insofar as it goes, but Smith could have fine-tuned this a bit by borrowing from Augustine's notion of *personal distribution*, where he distinguished between *beneficence* and *benevolence*. "The main reason the brewer, the butcher, and the baker doesn't serve his customers from *beneficence* is not exclusively self-love, but rather because each is faced with the fact of scarcity."[87] Smith would have done better had he made that distinction.

Adam Smith was not a genius in a vacuum who created a new system *de novo* that suddenly changed the world. Rather, he was a man of his time who brought together a set of ideas whose time had come. Schooled in Scholastic economics, the heir of Locke's conception of religious liberty, the dialogue

---

85 Athol Fitzgibbons, *Adam Smith's System of Liberty, Wealth, and Virtue: The Moral and Political Foundations of* The Wealth of Nations (New York: Clarendon, 1995), 3–4.

86 Ian Simpson Ross, *The Life of Adam Smith* (Oxford: Clarendon, 1995), 53–54.

87 Mueller, *Redeeming Economics*, 56.

Struggle for the City

partner with Hume in his own creative attempts to reconceive the nature of wealth and exchange, Smith was the *synthesizer* who brought the strands together at a time when the nation of England was on the precipice of industrialization in a way previously unanticipated. He was the *right man* in the *right place* at the *right time*, in spite of the formal shortcomings of his own system. So, what would be the outcome of these Enlightenment reflections on political economy? We will now turn our attention to that question.

Struggle for the City

Chapter 16

Viva la Revolución!

THE EIGHTEENTH CENTURY WOULD BE the century in which two extraordinary revolutions would establish the agenda for the future of the West. The American Revolution would set the course for America's development right on through the twentieth century and beyond, while the French Revolution would set the table for European political struggles throughout the nineteenth century.

THE AMERICAN EXPERIMENT

England was where the Industrial Revolution first took root, but it would be in America, the nation founded the same year as Smith's *Wealth of Nations* was published, where the project would make the greatest long-term impact. In order for Smith's project to be undertaken in full measure, several freedoms were needed.

The Need for Freedom in a Free and Productive Land

First, *political freedom* was a necessity, a political freedom that respected private property and contracts. Entrepreneurs and business owners need to have a share in the governance of their world, the world where they were engaged in economic exchanges. Some kind of republicanism or *democratic republicanism* was important toward achieving this necessary freedom.[1] Through the Middle

---

1   Eric Foner, *The Story of American Freedom* (New York: Norton, 1998), 12–28.

Ages the authorities, whether kings, barons, or other types of unelected political powers, often saw fit to confiscate the property of those under their jurisdiction. Then again, in various sorts of ways the governments at various levels controlled prices, production, and distribution. It was against this "mercantilist" system of political economy that we have discussed extensively in previous chapters that Smith had dedicated his efforts.

Only a political economy that eschewed mercantilism could witness whether or not Smith's theories might be workable. The American form of government as it crystallized in the Constitution offered that very kind of *political* freedom, since most government officials in the federal system would be elected in some form by qualified holders of political franchise, and since, for a variety of reasons, mercantilist public policies previously ascendant among the colonies were rejected, modified, or compromised at the Constitutional Convention in 1787.[2] Similarly, though not to the same degree, England had developed by the nineteenth century into a parliamentarian monarchy that had some republican features in it. But our primary focus will be on the American developments. What emerged in these developments is that political freedom is a necessity, a freedom also exemplified in free elections.

Second, freedom of *press/speech* is crucial to a free-market political economy. This is the case since the press needs to be free to disseminate information about the nature of the exchange of goods and services and about the ethical status of various industries. It must also be free to report on any alleged *government intrusion* into the economy. There must be no coercion from the state

---

2   On this history and its ultimate settlement among the colonies/states at the Constitutional Convention, see Forrest McDonald, *Novus Ordo Seclorum* (Lawrence: University Press of Kansas, 1985), esp. chaps. 3, 4, and 8, and Forrest McDonald, *E Pluribus Unum: The Formation of the American Republic, 1776–1790*, 2nd ed. (Indianapolis: Liberty Fund, 1979). The various original colonies had mercantilist structures to protect their varying economic interests primarily against foreign competition and interference. They would typically make exception for their sister colonies, but not always, and such sectional conflict led to much wheeling and dealing in the making of the Constitution. It was finally settled that only Congress (the one envisioned in the new constitution) would be allowed to establish "navigation acts," which were designed to control exports and imports to the benefit of the new and several United States. On the theological/religious clash and settling of sectional differences, see Mark Valeri, "Calvin and the Social Order in Early America: Moral Ideals and Transatlantic Empire," in *John Calvin's American Legacy*, ed. Thomas J. Davis (New York: Oxford University Press, 2010), 19–42.

Struggle for the City

over the press, and there must be freedom for one member of the press to monitor whether other members of the press are being *manipulated* by business interests or the government for their own purposes.[3]

Third, freedom of *markets* is fundamental to this system. That is almost by definition basic to Smith's (as it was to Thomas Aquinas' before him) approach to economics. The concept of free markets is discussed at length elsewhere in this book,[4] but here what we need to note is that the American government (as established in the Constitution) early on played only a marginal role in manipulating markets, in interfering with production, and, for the most part, in overly taxing products for consumption by the populace.[5] Many factors contributed to the prosperity that this produced. "The widespread distribution of land" had powerful consequences, as here, "one's livelihood was not dependent on the goodwill of another, as was the case presumably with tenants, serfs, indentured servants, wage-workers, or chattel slaves."[6] Others made their living in trade, especially seafaring trade. "New England Yankees made themselves one of the world's great seafaring peoples," showing that they had "a remarkable amount in common with the Dutch—another seagoing, predominantly Calvinist people who combined agriculture with commerce."[7] Still others engaged in fur trading, manufacturing, and animal husbandry. There seemed to be an almost *infinite* number of opportunities for these new Americans.

The free market means small government regulation of trade, low tariffs on goods imported, low taxes on sale of goods, and not preferring one industry

---

3   Robert W. T. Martin, *The Free and Open Press: The Founding of American Democratic Press Liberty, 1640–1800* (New York: New York University Press, 2001).

4   For our discussion of free markets, see the chapters in part 3.

5   John Steele Gordon, *An Empire of Wealth: The Epic History of American Economic Power* (New York: HarperCollins, 2004), esp. 98–112. This is contra the British activities justified through the Navigation Acts of the seventeenth century, which were intentionally intensified in their enforcement during the run up to the revolutionary period. These Acts were designed to force all commerce on the sea through the British Isles before engaging North America, whether export or import, and see that both capital shipbuilding and employment at sea remained under exclusive British control.

6   Daniel Walker Howe, *What Hath God Wrought: The Transformation of America, 1815–1848*, Oxford History of the United States (New York: Oxford University Press, 2007), 37. This does not apply to all Americans, since some were slaves, etc.

7   Ibid., 47.

Struggle for the City

or one company over against others. Though there was considerable disagreement on such matters as the *national bank*, how to handle *national debt*, and
on whether the federal government had any right at all to *tax* goods and services *within* this country, the early American experiment was closely aligned
with Smith's ideology on this particular issue of markets.[8] It is necessary, of
course, for governments to impose some health and safety standards, to regulate weights and measurements, and to insure that certain services are made
available to the public,[9] but beyond some *important* regulations, government
should not manipulate the economy. This was the belief of the founders.[10]

Though it was not a unanimously held view earlier on, by 1791 the fourth
freedom that is necessary to a free economy had been agreed upon: *religious*
freedom. The Constitution as first composed did not provide for guaranteed
freedom of religious expression, only for no religious test for pubic office. The
fires of the *Great Awakening* from earlier in the century had inflamed many
colonials, especially the Baptists, with a passion to see a nation that would
abandon European-style religious establishments and provide for full religious
freedom for *all* persons. Virginia Baptist John Leland met with James Madison in March 1788 and eventually convinced the man who was expected to
be the congressman from that district after the fall elections, that religious
liberty needed to be guaranteed in an amendment to the Constitution.[11] Such
a guarantee was necessary to a free-market economy since the European mer-
cantilists had been *parasitical* on established religions to gain favors with the
government, a government that granted the religious establishment in the first
place.[12] The United States would be the first nation in the modern world to
make this guarantee.

---

8   Paul Johnson, *A History of the American People* (New York: HarperCollins, 1997), 212–17.
9   Wayne Grudem, *Politics according to the Bible: A Comprehensive Resource for Understanding Modern Political Issues in Light of Scripture* (Grand Rapids, MI: Zondervan, 2010), 274.
10 William J. Bennett, *America: The Last Best Hope*, vol. 1, *From the Age of Discovery to a World at War, 1492–1914* (Nashville: Nelson Current, 2006), 143–53.
11 Thomas S. Kidd, *God of Liberty* (New York: Basic Books, 2010), 223.
12 Greg Forster, *The Contested Public Square* (Downers Grove, IL: InterVarsity Press, 2008), 154–58. We have documented many cases of this in our earlier discussion. For instance, recall from chap. 14 how Louis XIV restricted Protestants but gave full support to the Catholic Church's spiritual authority.

Struggle for the City

Returning to the Narrative

As the founding fathers of the new American republic would eventually begin the task of defining themselves, first through the Articles of Confederation and then through the Constitution of 1787, it would become clear that their new system of government was *well suited* to the freedoms articulated above. They believed that nature established laws and rights that were consistent with what they had inherited from the broad British Christian theological tradition, both Anglican and Puritan. They also believed that revolution was a right granted to them by "nature and nature's God." In 1802 Baptist pastor John Leland delivered to then-new president Thomas Jefferson a 1,235 pound block of cheese. The red crust of the cheese was adorned with the words, "Rebellion to tyrants is obedience to God."[13] That would be a *common*, if not unanimous, sentiment in the new nation.

The new Americans affirmed that their rights as individuals in compact with one another guaranteed them the right to be free from oppression, and they recognized that governing would at least in part be an *adversarial* endeavor that would require a division of powers between the various branches of government. They hoped that the country would not divide up into parties, and that the adversarial nature of government would not be too divisive to be workable. Their hopes for a one-party system endured for twelve years and then were dashed in the election of 1800 when a two party system first emerged, never to be done away with again. But even that did not halt the experiment—it merely modified it.[14] But we are getting ahead of ourselves.

Diversity in the Colonies

Though these events are well known and part of our national intellectual heritage, we need to look at several components of this history with specific questions in mind. One question has to do with the rise of *republicanism* in America. Certainly the English Civil War of the 1640s and the brief es-

---

13 Kidd, *God of Liberty*, 4.
14 John E. Ferling, *Adams vs. Jefferson: The Tumultuous Election of 1800*, Pivotal Moments in American History (New York: Oxford University Press, 2005).

Struggle for the City

tablishment of the Commonwealth in England lurked behind their thinking. The writings of Locke, a very influential thinker for early America, were an intellectual touchstone for these "founding fathers." And just as certainly the heritage of John Calvin, funneled through the New England Puritan tradition, was a key component of their new political heritage. But none of these was *specifically* "republican" in the way we usually think of that term. We need to examine that issue so we may better understand the convictions about liberty, revolution, and the "consent of the governed" more fully. We will also need to take a look at *economic* developments and convictions on the part of the early republic, and especially the attitudes about economic issues on the part of the Christian leadership of early America.

There were, of course, four separate identities in terms of religious orientation in early colonial America. *Puritans* had made Massachusetts into a financially lucrative world and practiced their Puritan and Congregational faith with varying levels of consistency through their first hundred years. Then there were the *Pilgrim Separatists* who landed at Plymouth. They became more integrated with the Puritans of New England through the seventeenth century but still maintained an individual religious identity as Plymouth Colony until they were annexed by Massachusetts in 1691. A major part of the colonial population was under the established *Anglican* church, especially Virginia, New York, the Carolinas, and Georgia.[15] Finally, there were the colonies of Pennsylvania and Rhode Island, colonies that were havens for religious dissent and that offered broad religious *liberty*, with no established church.[16] In the early days of this diversity, the early and mid-1600s, it seemed as though these four divergent groups had in common only that they were (mostly) Englishmen. In other ways they were so *different* that it had been incumbent on at least some of them to flee the homeland in order to be away from *other* Englishmen. We will now turn our attention back to those New England Puritans in taking our next step forward in the narrative.

---

15 New York, though technically Anglican, enjoyed broad religious freedom.
16 There were some Roman Catholics in Maryland early on and Dutch Reformed in New York and New Jersey, but these were minority populations.

Struggle for the City

The New England Problem

We left our early New Englanders with them establishing a *covenanted* community of entrepreneurs under the direction of *godly* magistrates and pastors. We noted there that this situation prevailed for a number of decades, but it was not to be a *permanent* situation. In order to ensure that the corporate covenant aspect of their community remained strong, they required, as we have already discussed, that everyone admitted to full church membership must be able convincingly to relate a *conversion* experience and to live in a manner that demonstrated the reality of that conversion. Only those who could do that would be admitted to the Lord's Supper and so to full church membership.[17] In addition, only full church members could have their children baptized and only male full church members could vote in elections.[18]

Around three decades after the Puritans began to arrive in New England a *crisis* began to loom. Fewer and fewer adults were personally claiming ownership to the covenant so as to be "visible saints," that is, fewer were testifying to a conversion experience. "Owning the covenant" and a personal conversion experience were one and the same thing in the early days. This meant that increasing numbers of children were *not baptized*, and so not part of the larger "covenanted community," and that fewer young men were eligible to vote. Both of these matters—unbaptized children and men unable to vote—posed serious threats to both the spiritual and the "secular" mission of the Puritan community.[19]

So, a compromise decision was reached known as "The Half-Way Covenant." This agreement extended *partial* church membership rights, including baptism, to the children of those who would live up to the expectations of the corporate civic covenant and who would submit to church discipline, even though they were, technically speaking, unconverted.[20] This meant in

---

17 Edmund S. Morgan, *Visible Saints* (Ithaca, NY: Cornell University Press, 1963), 131.

18 John Adair, *Founding Fathers: The Puritans in England and America* (London: J. M. Dent, 1982), 209–38. The qualification to this final issue was that excommunicated members *still* had the franchise.

19 Mark A. Noll, *America's God: From Jonathan Edwards to Abraham Lincoln* (New York: Oxford University Press, 2002), 31–50.

20 Robert A. Handy, *A Christian America: Protestant Hopes and Historical Realities* (New York: Oxford University Press, 1971), 13.

Struggle for the City

essence that the two aspects of the covenant, the corporate covenant and the experience of the new covenant gift of salvation, had been *divided* from each other. A person could affirm the corporate covenant (the covenant of works) without having been converted under the covenant of grace. This Half-Way Covenant solved the immediate crisis, allowing the baptism of unconverted church members and maintaining an electorate, but it set the stage for another crisis that would be, arguably, even *more* profound in the next century.[21]

Great Awakening

It is important to recall a point that we established earlier. In the Reformed and Puritan view of *community*, "[a]t each point in the movement's history the same central Puritan vision endured: the magistracy guaranteed the social conditions under which the laity, part volunteers and part conscripts, pursued their individual destinies in a collective context interpreted and mediated by the clergy."[22] This belief had created a situation in New England in which the theological standards earlier articulated by English Puritans took root. This was organized around three themes: "the centrality of the new birth, the assumption of a unified society, and the church as the central link between personal religion and national reform."[23] Early New England, at least, was inherently "Christian," whatever one might say about Virginia or the other colonies.

All of this, as we have already noted, was tied together through the notion of a corporate covenant, and the "reach" of this covenantal language constituted what one historian calls the "Puritan canopy" for the theology of this people.[24] They lived beneath it, it *defined* them, and it *protected* them. It protected them, that is, until the canopy began to be removed. That occurred surprisingly early in the process.

The New England Puritans had organized a commonwealth where all levels of organization were shaped by divine reality, and it was done so by

---

21 Robert G. Pope, *The Half-Way Covenant: Church Membership in Puritan New England* (1969; Eugene, OR: Wipf and Stock, 2002).
22 Stephen Foster, *The Long Argument: English Puritanism and the Shaping of New England Culture, 1570–1700* (1991; repr., Chapel Hill: University of North Carolina Press, 1996), 288.
23 Noll, *America's God*, 38.
24 Ibid., 39.

Struggle for the City

"constituting the male church members and the voting (freemen) as the same group."[25] That required, of course, a rather careful steering around obstacles and a sometimes heavy-handed approach to dissent. It also required at a certain point the redefinition of what a church member really *was*. In all that, the Puritan canopy held together, though as we have seen, only with the modification of the Half-Way Covenant. But the Great Awakening and its aftermath would unravel the threads of the canopy and leave it tattered and ruined.

The Great Awakening was the American version of what was really a transatlantic, multinational series of religious awakenings that were occurring roughly contemporaneous to one another.[26] It may be too much to claim that there was actually a *movement* that can be designated the "Great Awakening." No one used the phrase during the period of the revivals. The first major history of America, George Bancroft's *History of the United States* (completed in 1874) does not use the phrase. Joseph Tracy may have coined the phrase in his 1842 best seller, *The Great Awakening*.[27] Whatever we conclude about the notion of the Great Awakening, here was at least a series of spiritual renewals in various American colonies, renewals that were loosely tied together through the itinerant ministry of George Whitefield over the course of several decades.[28] In one sense, the Awakening (or series of renewals) was a kind of response to the Half-Way Covenant or to what that Covenant had wrought.[29]

Jonathan Edwards (1703–58) came to pastor the Northampton Congregational Church in 1729. By his testimony, what he inherited from his grand-

---

25 Ibid., 40.
26 Earle E. Cairns, *An Endless Line of Splendor: Revivals and Their Leaders from the Great Awakening to the Present* (Wheaton: Tyndale, 1986), 31–36.
27 Joseph Tracy, *The Great Awakening: A History of the Revival of Religion in the Time of Edwards and Whitefield* (1842; Carlisle, PA: Banner of Truth, 1976).
28 There is considerable discussion taking place as to whether there ever was a Great Awakening, or whether it might be historical fiction. We will continue to use the traditional labels, but we are aware that modifications may need to be made to the traditional story line. See Jon Butler, *Awash in a Sea of Faith: Christianizing the American People*, Studies in Cultural History (Cambridge: Harvard University Press, 1990), who rejects the idea that there was any sort of unified awakening across the colonies, and Frank Lambert, *Inventing the "Great Awakening"* (Princeton, NJ: Princeton University Press, 1999), who affirms the traditional view with some modifications.
29 Cairns, *Endless Line of Splendor*, 31.

Struggle for the City

father Solomon Stoddard (who had pastored the church for fifty-nine years) was a church filled with "Mr. and Mrs. Goodman, but not Mr. and Mrs. Gospel."[30] He laid the blame for that largely at the feet of the men who had framed the Half-Way Covenant, since they had allowed unconverted persons to have membership in and in some places, including Northampton, partake of the Lord's Supper in the churches. The *churches*, and by association the *magistracy*, were under the control of mostly *unregenerate* persons. All of this was contrary to the vision of the early New England pastors, who had begun arriving exactly one century before Edwards became pastor of the church. Edwards was not alone in that conviction. Increase Mather, son of Richard Mather and father of Cotton Mather, had argued in his 1702 book, *The Glory Departing from New England*, that the people had lost the passion and love for God that had been characteristic of the first generations of New Englanders.[31] In some churches the Lord's Supper was even given to the unregenerate in hope that it might be a means of grace, another reason why Mather was convinced that the "glory" had departed.[32]

The Great Awakening from the standpoint of Edwards, one of its two most significant purveyors (along with George Whitefield), was specifically about restoring one element of early New England religion—*piety of the heart*, an experience created by justifying grace. What had happened as a result of the Half-Way Covenant is that New Englanders lived lives representing common grace—the grace of God experienced by all persons, even the unregenerate—but not saving grace.[33] Later, Edwards would argue that gracious affections toward God are exercises of the will or the heart made possible by the supernatural influence of the Spirit.[34]

---

30 Ibid., 44.
31 Increase Mather, I*chabod, or, A Discourse, Shewing What Cause There Is to Fear That the Glory of the Lord, Is Departing from New-England* (Boston: Printed by Timothy Green, 1702), cited in Cairns, *Endless Line of Splendor*, 39–40.
32 E. Brooks Holifield, *Theology in America* (New Haven, CT: Yale University Press, 2003), 67.
33 Noll, *America's God*, 45. See Jonathan Edwards, *A Humble Inquiry*, in Jonathan Edwards, *Ecclesiastical Writings*, Works of Jonathan Edwards, vol. 12, ed. David D. Hall (1748; New Haven, CT: Yale University Press, 1994), esp. 260–85, for his response.
34 Jonathan Edwards, *Religious Affections*, Works of Jonathan Edwards, vol. 2, ed. John E. Smith (1746; New Haven, CT: Yale University Press, 1959), 200–239. See the excellent treatment of this in William Breitenbach, "Piety and Moralism: Edwards and the New

Struggle for the City

Yet, while Edwards sought to restore one element of early Puritan piety, he removed another one. The early Puritans, in their focus on people becoming "visible saints," believed that young persons had to go through an intense process of "preparation" to get to that point, something we alluded to earlier. The process was well spelled out, was intense, involved the scrutiny of church elders, and became increasingly intrusive over time. The difficulty presented by this *preparationism* is likely one of the reasons for the decline in testimonies of conversion in the 1650s that led to the Half-Way Covenant. If that is what conversion is, thought many, then who can go through all of that? Better to trust to the *mercy* of God than to the *scrutiny* of the elders and the magistrates![35] Edwards rejected preparationism. In the revival, a four-year old girl, Phoebe Bartlett, in his church was converted, and Edwards affirmed the genuineness of the conversion.[36] One of the reasons he was convinced that such a thing could happen was that his own wife, Sarah Pierpont Edwards, claimed to have been converted at age four or five.[37] Edwards' theology held out the possibility of immediate conversions carried out by the sovereign Spirit on the heart of any person, *no matter what age.*

Most important with reference to the inherited Puritan tradition, Edwards *rejected* the notion that one can be a member of the church without being a *visible saint.*[38] This was a return to the original vision of the Puritan fathers, but a vision that had been modified by the Half-Way Covenant in order to maintain the corporate covenant vision. Edwards explicitly *rejected* the concept of a *corporate covenant* for New Testament saints. There is now no external covenant, only an internal covenant by which one knows Christ as personal Lord and Savior, a covenant that is manifest corporately, not in *society* or in *national identity*, but in the *church* only.[39] It seems that Conrad Grebel has triumphed over Calvin![40]

Divinity," in *Jonathan Edwards and the American Experience*, ed. Nathan O. Hatch and Harry S. Stout (New York: Oxford University Press, 1988), 182.

35 Morgan, *Visible Saints*, 62.

36 George M. Marsden, *Jonathan Edwards: A Life* (New Haven, CT: Yale University Press, 2003), 249.

37 Ibid., 242.

38 Edwards, *Humble Inquiry*, 174.

39 Ibid., 272. See the discussion in Noll, *America's God*, 44–47.

40 Not that Edwards was taking up the Anabaptist cause, as that sect was still being vilified in Edwards' day.

Struggle for the City

In 1750 Edwards took the decisive step of *barring* from the Lord's Table those who had no testimony to a saving conversion.[41] His grandfather, Solomon Stoddard, had extended the Half-way Covenant even beyond its original reach to allow the unconverted to the Lord's Table in hopes that this might *convert* them.[42] Edwards' act ended more than seventy years of tradition in that church; he was summarily dismissed by a vote of 230–23.[43] The Puritan canopy had been rent to shreds. Noll's comment is instructive here: Edwards "highlighted but also dismembered the Puritan concept of covenant," and this had the net effect of "weakening one era's theological canopy without offering anything to take its place and so opened thought to a subtle, yet powerful, move from theology to politics, and intellectual leadership to a shift from the clergy to men of state."[44] That seems to be precisely the case. New England made the shift from *Puritan* to Yankee, and it was the tenacious Jonathan Edwards who forced the matter and brought about the shift, or at least the final stage of the move.[45]

We need to look at another aspect of the "Awakening" before we move on. A great deal of the preaching that brought about the awakenings was itinerant preaching. Edwards traveled up and down the Connecticut River Valley between 1737 and 1741, preaching in other men's churches, and many remarkable conversions occurred during this time.[46] In 1740 George Whitefield (1714–70) preached four sermons in Edwards' church, "which greatly moved Edwards and his congregation, and a new revival broke out which continued for two years."[47] William Tennent and James Davenport took this to still higher levels by preaching in other men's parishes,[48] and then, especially, the Englishman George Whitefield extended such "invasions" in numerous towns

41 Marsden, *Jonathan Edwards*, 359–61.
42 Cairns, *Endless Line of Splendor*, 44.
43 Ibid., 46.
44 Noll, *America's God*, 50.
45 Richard L. Bushman, *From Puritan to Yankee: Character and the Social Order in Connecticut, 1690–1765*, Center for the Study of the History of Liberty in America (Cambridge: Harvard University Press, 1967).
46 The famous sermon "Sinners in the Hands of an Angry God" was preached at Enfield, not Northampton. Marsden, *Jonathan Edwards*, 219–22.
47 Thomas A. Askew and Peter W. Spellman, *The Churches and the American Experience* (Grand Rapids, MI: Baker, 1984), 43.
48 Kidd, *God of Liberty*, 22–23.

Struggle for the City

over several of the colonies.[49] By 1742 out of a population of about 300,000, between 25,000 and 50,000 new converts had been added to the churches since 1734.[50] These revivals constituted "an outpouring of the Holy Spirit," which "consisted of deep conviction, followed by sound conversion, upon many souls about the same time and under the same religious instructors."[51] America was changing, and changing because of the *gospel*.

Slaves were also converted in the revival. Between 1714 and 1760 the number of black slaves in America jumped from 58,850 to 310,000, "largely because of the diminishing number of indentured servants" and the need for labor.[52] Race-based slavery at this time was not mainly a Southern phenomenon, but was found in *all parts* of the country with *New England* merchants heavily involved in the slave trade as a means of acquiring wealth.[53] In Edwards' church six slaves had been converted in 1734–35 and were added to the church, with a total of nine joining during his tenure there.[54] This was a controversial matter, especially in the South, where more and more slaves were being accumulated throughout the eighteenth century. British courts had determined that *baptized* slaves had to be set *free*, so American slaveholders were uneasy about the evangelization of their *property*.[55] But many were saved in the revivals.

Revival also spread south. New Light Congregationalist-turned-Baptist Shubal Stearns (1706–71) arrived in North Carolina in 1755, settling in the Sandy Creek vicinity of Guilford County.[56] He was one who had been converted in the earlier awakening in New England and was now a "Separate Baptist," a split having taken place within the Baptist faith between "Regular Baptists" (who rejected the Awakening) and "Separates" (who affirmed it).[57] From the mother church in Sandy Creek sprang many other churches

49 Harry Stout, *The Divine Dramatist: George Whitefield and the Rise of Modern Evangelicalism*, Library of Religious Biography (Grand Rapids, MI: Eerdmans, 1991), 61–68.
50 Askew and Spellman, *Churches and the American Experience*, 43.
51 Mark A. Noll, *The Rise of Evangelicalism: The Age of Edwards, Whitfield, and the Wesleys*, A History of Evangelicalism 1 (Downers Grove, IL: InterVarsity Press, 2004), 15.
52 Askew and Spellman, *Churches and the American Experience*, 47.
53 Ibid., 48.
54 Marsden, *Jonathan Edwards*, 255–58.
55 Askew and Spellman, *Churches and the American Experience*, 48.
56 H. Leon McBeth, *The Baptist Heritage* (Nashville: Broadman, 1987), 227.
57 John B. Boles, *The Great Revival, 1787–1805: The Origins of the Southern Evangelical Mind* (Lexington: The University Press of Kentucky, 1972), 4.

Struggle for the City

throughout North Carolina, so much so that this part of the country, which had very few Baptists, would eventually become identified as a Baptist *haven*. Others joined Stearns in this work, including former Anglican John Waller, while Stearns founded eighteen churches and baptized more than two thousand people.[58] This was the only significant movement of revival in the South before the Great Revival of 1801.[59]

There is a significant question that lies before the student of early American "politics," now that we have used that term of the American situation. The question is: how does the American historical context move from Puritanism to republicanism so quickly? What was the process that took us from *Puritan* to *Yankee* in the course of a generation? We may recall that England came close to a sort of republicanism after their Civil War of the 1640s and the Commonwealth government that ruled in the wake of the early Stuart kings. It stopped short of republicanism in the Commonwealth, though, and subsequently reinstated the monarchy. What was it that led the Protestant citizens of the American colonies to move away from centuries of tradition and adopt a *new form* of government? And why would they break with their mother country in the very first place? The answer lies in the amazing ministry of George Whitefield.

Until recently, many historians of colonial religion have despised Whitefield. One famous historian called Whitefield, "repulsive, reckless, irresponsible, whining, sanctimonious."[60] We will offer a different opinion. By his own testimony, George Whitefield went to the colonies in the first place because he was convinced that the clergy in the Anglican colonies were *incompetent* and *corrupt*. His first trip in 1738 (to Georgia) was attended by *remarkable* instances of repentance and renewal in the churches. Writing in his own *Journals* later he noted that the Church of England might "flourish" in the colonies if her ministers were "found faithful." Only bad ministers were sent there, and the result was a lukewarm church.[61] Whitefield's approach to *evangelism* actually mirrors

---

58 Askew and Spellman, *Churches and the American Experience*, 44.
59 Boles, *Great Revival*, 4–5.
60 Perry Miller, *Jonathan Edwards* (1949; repr., Amherst: University of Massachusetts Press, 1981), 142. Miller considered Edwards to be the "American Augustine," but apparently thought Whitefield to be the American philistine.
61 George Whitefield, *George Whitefield's Journals, 1737–1741, to Which Is Prefixed His "Short Account" (1746) and "Further Account" (1747)* (1905; Gainesville, FL: Scholars' Facsimiles

the kind of *market economy* that America would soon become, since he used dramatic "marketing" in announcing his meetings ahead of time, and he felt no compunction about entering into "competition" with established ministers in the towns he visited.[62] Whitefield was a preaching *entrepreneur* in a land that would soon become a land filled with the same spirit toward the economy. To a certain degree that was what the Great Awakening was all about.

Whitefield's preaching struck a note even more clear and *arresting* than had Edwards's. Returning for a second and much more expansive preaching tour in late 1739, the Anglican priest scoured the colonies with his call for "regeneration," and the bestowal of the gift of the Spirit to American church members. People in the Church of England rarely (with the exception of the Puritan wing, now become the Congregationalists in the New World) emphasized any sort of "personal connection to God" as part of the Christian experience, but instead believed that "a person inherited their [*sic*] religion via family tradition and intellectually agreed upon church doctrines."[63] Whitefield, having been converted through the ministry of Charles Wesley several years before,[64] came preaching that *genuine* Christianity was *regenerate* Christianity. Such an experience normally does not occur in an *instant* but entails a *period* of time of conviction of sin, seeking the Lord, and finally bursting through with sweet *assurance*.[65] The result of regeneration is the gift of the *Spirit* to the believer, a gift that brings about transformation of character.[66]

Whitefield was confessionally a Calvinist, subscribing to the Calvinistic *Thirty-Nine Articles* of the Church of England, even requiring the students enrolled in his New World college to memorize the confession.[67] Like Edwards,

---

and Reprints, 1969), 386–87. We are indebted to Roger Finke and Rodney Stark for this citation, Roger Finke and Rodney Stark, *The Churching of America, 1776–1990: Winners and Losers in Our Religious Economy*, 2nd ed. (1992; New Brunswick, NJ: Rutgers University Press, 2005), 39–40.

62 Fink and Stark, *Churching of America, 1776–1990*, 49–53.
63 Jerome Dean Mahaffey, *The Accidental Revolutionary: George Whitefield and the Creation of America* (Waco, TX: Baylor University Press, 2011), 4.
64 Stout, *Divine Dramatist*, 19–22. For a fuller account see Timothy L. Smith, ed., *Whitefield and Wesley on the New Birth* (Grand Rapids, MI: Zondervan, 1986), 39–49, most of which is Whitefield's own account of his conversion from his *Journals*.
65 Mahaffey, *Accidental Revolutionary*, 23.
66 Smith, *Whitefield and Wesley on the New Birth*, 92–105.
67 Stout, *Divine Dramatist*, 272. This college was formed in Whitefield's later years, in Georgia.

Struggle for the City

whom we have discussed, Whitefield was a *Calvinist* who *urged* his auditors to seek to be converted. But he went beyond Edwards in this matter. Edwards, who had done a careful reading of Locke and believed that one could discern through "affections" (emotions) the reality of God working in the heart, and so to find a sense of *assurance* with that, found it difficult to take the matter much *further*.[68] Whitefield, though, believed that "the prepared heart had a choice," and that it was the job of the preacher to challenge his hearers to *make* that choice.[69] This constituted a seismic shift in American religion, especially in New England, with the *new birth* eventually being associated with "the pursuit of happiness," a key theme in decades ahead.[70]

In his fifteen-month tour of America that began in November 1739, Whitefield ignored denominational barriers by preaching in outdoor events that brought together Anglicans, Presbyterians, Congregationalists, and others.[71] This brought colonists *together*, making them for the first time since the earliest colonization a *family*, a family knit together by the "new birth" that thousands were experiencing all over the land.[72] The concept of the new birth was even more significant for the people of *that* time than it is for *us*, since the message was a new one (Anglican priests had neglected this biblical theme) and since farmers and midwives, both very common in the day, connected *intuitively* to the imagery.

The newly regenerate saw themselves as *spiritual equals* to many pastors, since they had now shared the same Holy Spirit with them. This of course caused *consternation* to the older institutionalized clergy who rejected Whitefield's message and resulted in the formation of "New Light" congregations in New England to be set alongside the "Old Lights." These New Lights "were those who had begun to see themselves as Americans."[73] Old Lights, like the respectable Boston pastor Charles Chauncy, "preferred a top-down society led by a king and

---

68 Mahaffey, *Accidental Revolutionary*, 34.
69 Ibid., 36. Whitefield would still affirm that the Holy Spirit does the hard work, not the person.
70 Alan Heimert, *Religion and the American Mind, from the Great Awakening to the Revolution* (Cambridge: Harvard University Press, 1966), 43.
71 Stout, *Divine Dramatist*, 49–65.
72 Mahaffey, *Accidental Revolutionary*, 50.
73 Ibid., 53.

Struggle for the City

lords, while the New Lights favored a strong, grass-roots, parliamentary self-rule, with loyalty to the king as symbolic of their devotion to the British Empire."[74] What had begun as a revival of *religion* was morphing into a new conception of *society*. Older European social divisions based on *blood* and *soil* were giving way to a new kind of unity based on a *common* conversion experience.

War between France and England in 1745 drove Whitefield to further reflection on not merely the *social*, but the *political* implications of the new birth. The combined power of France and the papacy attempted a coup to reinstate the Stuart monarchy in the form of James II's grandson, "Bonnie Prince Charlie." England was triumphant in fighting off the Catholic advance, but it all made Whitefield recognize that though he was loyal to King George II, "he could envision the Church of England becoming as oppressive as the Catholics."[75] While the conflict hung in the balance, Whitefield preached a sermon in which "he promoted religious liberty by speculating about life under a Roman Catholic-dominated government."[76] From this point on, his sermons would be peppered with *republican* ideas, many derived from Locke. It needs to be said that republicanism did not flow from politics to religion, but rather in the reverse direction.[77] What began as a revival in the churches, a revival of *spiritual egalitarianism* under the heading of the new birth available to all, moved in the next generation to become a revival of hatred of political oppression and a love of *political egalitarianism*. Whitefield was the man who sparked this revival. The colonies would never be the same.

Among other impacts, the Great Awakening had at least done this to America: It "gave a distinctive American flavor to a wide range of denominations."[78] Not everyone accepted the revivals, of course, and in every denomination there were detractors.[79] The churches were changed in five ways by the Awakening: "evangelical vigor, a tendency to downgrade the clergy, little stress on liturgical

74 Ibid.
75 Ibid., 102.
76 Ibid., 107.
77 Noll, *America's God*, 83.
78 Johnson, *History of the American People*, 116.
79 C. C. Goen, *Revivalism and Separatism in New England, 1740–1800: Strict Congregationalists and Separate Baptists in the Great Awakening* (1962; repr., Middletown, CT: Wesleyan University Press, 1987).

Struggle for the City

correctness, and even less on parish boundaries, and above all an emphasis on individual experience."[80] The same writer identified Revelation 21:5 as the key text to the revivals, and also the key text for the American experience as a whole: "Behold I make all things new."[81] Before the Awakening each of the colonies saw itself as relating to the Crown *individually* as colonies, as the Spanish colonies would continue to do for a hundred years; the Awakening had left the impression with its supporters that they were all part of *one grand cause* that gave them more in common with *one another* than they had with their English relatives. "Historians agree that this national revival prepared Americans for the national revolution that was to follow in just thirty years. Religious cooperation thus prepared the way for political and military cooperation."[82] The Awakening *facilitated* the Revolution. "The Revolution could not have taken place without this religious background."[83] The Great Awakening was "really the beginning of America's identity as a nation—the starting point of the Revolution."[84] The philosophy of Locke and the careful theology of Edwards were channeled through the fiery rhetoric of Whitefield, "providing a vocabulary everyone could understand."[85] One could almost say, "No Whitefield, No Revolution!"[86] The Great Awakening was a defining hour for the colonies, whichever way we attempt to explain it as a historical phenomenon.

From Colony to Republic: A New Kind of Freedom

The American Revolutionary War looms large in the consciousness of all informed Americans. It is not only important, though, as a tale of war and independence; there are aspects of it that are also as crucial to our analysis of *politics*, the *economy*, and their relation to the *church*. "The American Revolu-

---

80 Johnson, *History of the American People*, 116.
81 Ibid.
82 Askew and Spellman, *Churches and the American Experience*, 47.
83 Johnson, *History of the American People*, 117.
84 William G. McLoughlin, "The Role of Religion in the Revolution: Liberty of Conscience and Cultural Cohesion in the New Nation," in *Essays on the American Revolution*, ed. Stephen G. Kurtz and James H. Hutson (Chapel Hill: University of North Carolina Press, 1973), 198.
85 Mahaffey, *Accidental Revolutionary*, 188.
86 From the dust jacket of Mahaffey, *Accidental Revolutionary*.

Struggle for the City

tion is the single most crucial event in American history."[87] But we wish to be clear about this part of the story. We are not attempting here to tell the *story* of the American Revolution. Important as that is, it is not specifically germane to our subject. All we will do in this part of the narrative is to ask the question, "Was the Revolution justifiable economically, politically, and theologically?" It is an important question in our day as even *some* conservatives, politically and theologically, have concluded that it was *unjust*.

Mid-eighteenth-century America was a time and place of expansion as the frontier extended further and further west, an extension hampered by both Native Americans and the French, who were loath to cede the Mississippi Valley to the English and the colonists. Most of the colonial English in the colonies worked very hard. "Work was a duty imposed by God and approved by Him as right and good."[88] Many of them were remarkably successful. Commerce centered in the cities and generated great fortunes. "The great landowners along the Hudson Valley in New York and the big planters in Maryland, Virginia, and South Carolina may have possessed even greater wealth" than those in the cities.[89] The French and Indian War, "the first world war in human history,"[90] caused a brief halt to all of that, but the British (the colonial militias and the British army) won and France was checked. A series of challenges coming from the British Crown, though, would change things forever.

George III became King of England in 1760, right in the middle of the war with the French. He acceded to the throne upon the death of his grandfather, George II, the young man's father, Frederick, having passed away in 1751 when the boy was thirteen years old.[91] The chief influence on the young George growing up were his possessive *mother* and her dominating *friend*, the

---

87 Nathan O. Hatch, "The Democratization of Christianity and the Character of American Politics," in *Religion and American Politics: From the Colonial Period to the Present*, 2nd ed., ed. Mark A. Noll and Luke E. Harlow (New York: Oxford University Press, 2007), 112.

88 Robert Middlekauff, *The Glorious Cause: The American Revolution, 1763–1789*, 2nd ed., Oxford History of the United States (1982; New York: Oxford University Press, 2005), 5.

89 Middlekauff, *Glorious Cause*, 39.

90 Johnson, *History of the American People*, 121. The war lasted from 1754–60 in North America and from 1756–63 in Central and South America, in the Caribbean, in India, and in Europe.

91 Antonia Fraser, ed., *The Lives of the Kings and Queens of England* (New York: Alfred A. Knopf, 1975), 274.

Struggle for the City

Earl of Bute, whom George would spend years of his life trying to please.[92] This influence was to *mark* him for the of his life and may be one of the explanations for his implacable approach to the American colonials. "In Bute's unpracticed hands the prince's insecure, rather rigid personality grew more rigid and no more confident," and he became "proud and intolerant of others whose views did not agree with his or his tutor's."[93] The king would always be a weak and ineffective administrator.

The spark that ignited the events that *led* to the Revolutionary War was a military battle between a young lieutenant colonel from Virginia named George Washington and a detachment of French soldiers at Fort Duquesne, near modern Pittsburgh. He and his detachment of volunteers and Indians came upon the French suddenly, and when the French soldiers went for their muskets, the young officer later testified, "I ordered my company to fire."[94] This brought on a French retaliation, and the French and Indian War in America, and a worldwide conflict that brought the Spanish in on the side of the French and the Prussians on the side of the British.[95] The cost of the war would send England into a financial tailspin, necessitating a major overhaul of its revenue-raising systems.[96] Massive tax increases were levied in England itself, and then, in 1764, the Crown turned its head to the *American colonies* for their assistance.

The first was the Sugar Act, a tax on molasses brought from the British West Indies and used in the distilling of rum, and a tax on other imports such as cloth, coffee and wine.[97] This brought about a reaction, though one a little slow in developing, since parliamentary law, stemming from the Magna Carta in 1215, stated that the people cannot be levied a tax by Parliament unless they have representation in Parliament. The colonies had no representation on that body. The next year witnessed a new decision by Parliament, the Stamp Act, a tax on many printed documents that required such documents to be printed on stamped paper produced in London, carrying an embossed revenue stamp, in

---

92 Ibid., 276.
93 Middlekauff, *Glorious Cause*, 21.
94 Johnson, *History of the American People*, 124.
95 Ibid.
96 The debt in 1763 was more than 122 million British pounds. Middlekauff, *Glorious Cause*, 61.
97 Kidd, *God of Liberty*, 32–33.

Struggle for the City

effect, a tax on *everyone*. This time the response was not slow developing. To the colonists, this was ridiculous, and seemed to be nothing but invasive *intrusion* not for regulatory purpose, but just to *extort* money from the Americans.[98] In 1767 Parliament passed the Townsend Duties, import taxes on tea, glass, paper, and paint. The colonists became even more vocally agitated than before, and the British summarily increased the size of their troop presence in Massachusetts.[99]

It seemed more and more to the Americans that King George III and his Parliament saw them, the colonials, as primarily a *source* for raising *revenue*. In debate, Parliament regularly referred to the colonials, in the words of MP Charles Townsend, as "Children planted by our Care, nourished up by our Indulgence until they are grown to a Degree of Strength and Opulence, and protected by our Arms," but who were unwilling to contribute to their own support.[100] Townsend clearly had no idea of the *travail* that most Americans had gone through to eke out their livings in the harsh wilderness that was America both at their initial arrival and in the drive west to frontier. Donning powdered wigs and living in comfort, most of them were cared for by servants and did little, if any, *manual labor*, in the tradition of "gentlemen" that goes all the way back to Greek and Roman philosophers we have already documented. How could they understand *America*? Both King George and Parliament, for the most part, turned a deaf ear to the remonstrations coming from across the Atlantic. Between 1764 and 1774 the Americans feared that the next shoe to drop would be a *religious* one. When the Quebec Act was passed in 1774, a law allowing Roman Catholicism in Quebec, a British colony, colonists feared that next would be the appointment of an Anglican bishop to oversee all the colonies, and the specter of *religious persecution* for dissent from Anglicanism once again seemed to loom large.[101]

When we look back at all these events, it may seem to us as though their taxation level was not all that high in *comparison* to ours.[102] It may also seem

---

98 Middlekauff, *Glorious Cause*, 74–97.
99 Kidd, *God of Liberty*, 57.
100 Middlekauff, *Glorious Cause*, 78.
101 Kidd, *God of Liberty*, 59, 69–70. Recall that the Stuart kings were *secretly* amenable to Roman Catholicism, even though they were *publicly* Anglican.
102 Or, if they could have looked forward to our time, they might well wonder why we have put up with our present level of taxation.

Struggle for the City

that allowing religious pluralism in Quebec was a *rational* act of modern men. It may seem like much ado about nothing. But we cannot read history backward, a tactic known as the "Whig interpretation of history." We have to put ourselves in their shoes, if we can. To them, a financially strapped federal *bureaucracy* had summarily added several new taxes aimed at retrieving *revenue* from "children" nourished by English "indulgence" and was enforcing the taking of these taxes more *fiercely* than ever. Coupling this with imposition of the previously laxly enforced Navigation Acts[103] produced what the colonies considered to be *intolerable* economic and political burdens. The British government would not listen to embassies from the colonies sent to complain, the ineffective and self-absorbed king refusing to grant them any legitimacy.

The colonials had a major legal point of order—the English had never levied taxes without *representation*. England would not listen. They were allowing a Catholic bishop to take residence in territory contiguous to the colonies and their territories. By 1765, the word "popery" meant not just Catholicism, but any form of *overweening oppression*.[104] They were gesturing at sending an Anglican bishop to guide the religious life of Americans. And the colonials had good memories—they recalled that a century before Charles II had forced a new governor onto Massachusetts, one who had ruled the Puritans with an iron fist.[105] *This* king seemed just as implacable as that one had a hundred years before. Evangelical minister Benjamin Throop spoke for many when he stated, "We could not long expect to enjoy our religious liberties, when once our civil liberties were gone."[106] The increasing conflict with England was becoming, in the words of Patrick Henry, a "holy cause of liberty," a cause fueled by convictions that arose in the Great Awakening, and by the experience of the Americans, by both plowshares and swords, wresting the New World into a land that yielded to their iron wills.

One of the key intellectual architects of the Revolution was the Scots Presbyterian immigrant John Witherspoon. Witherspoon had been trained in

---

103 See note 2 in this chapter for documentation.
104 Ruth H. Bloch, *Visionary Republic: Millennial Themes in American Thought, 1756–1800* (1985; Cambridge: Cambridge University Press, 1988), 54.
105 Kidd, *God of Liberty*, 31.
106 Ibid., 34.

Struggle for the City

the Scottish Common Sense School of Moral philosophy founded by Francis Hutcheson and Thomas Reid. This school of thought was in many ways a response to the kind of skepticism that Reid believed was implicit in Locke, but which found full flourishing in David Hume, who was convinced that it was impossible to make any conclusions about such things as *causation*. Among other conclusions, Hume employed this metaphysical skepticism to question all attempts to draw the conclusion that God must *exist* on the basis of the existence of the world—the popular cosmological argument for the existence of God.[107] Hume argued that we cannot know things *in themselves*, but only *representations* of those things generated in the mind.[108] Thus, the world outside our own intellection is anybody's guess. Reid replied with his notion of "common sense," and complained that only a *philosopher* would articulate the kind of skepticism inherent in Hume's theory. Instead, Reid contended, many things that we know are a result of "axioms, first principles, principles of common sense, self-evident truths" that everyone in the world operates under and that demonstrate their veracity just by the manner in which the world works.[109]

Witherspoon brought this Common Sense philosophy with him to the presidency of Princeton in 1768. Inherent in this methodology was a political *pragmatism* that caused Witherspoon to recognize very quickly that Britain's political and economic machinations in the colonies were counterproductive to its desire to maintain loyalty in the colonies.[110] Though the Presbyterian minister and college president had little in common with the increasingly agnostic Thomas Paine in doctrinal matters, he was an enthusiastic admirer of Paine's aptly named, *Common Sense* tract, calling for American revolution.[111] The two greatest influences on Witherspoon's revolutionary theory were "the

---

107 Robert J. Fogelin, "Hume's Scepticism," in *The Cambridge Companion to Hume*, ed. David Fate Norton, Cambridge Companions to Philosophers (Cambridge: Cambridge University Press, 1993), 90–116.

108 Ibid., 94–98.

109 Jeffry H. Morrison, *John Witherspoon and the Founding of the American Republic* (Notre Dame, IN: University of Notre Dame Press, 2005), 54.

110 Ibid., 59–63. For further treatment of the Scottish Enlightenment's influence on the American Revolution, see Garry Wills, *Inventing America: Jefferson's Declaration of Independence* (Garden City, NY: Doubleday, 1978).

111 Thomas Paine, *Common Sense* (Philadelphia: Printed, and sold, by R. Bell, in Third-Street, 1776).

Struggle for the City

liberal Whig theorists and the Protestant Reformers."[112] The "Whig" side of the equation entailed an acceptance of a republican theory of government and so a rejection of monarchy on principle.[113] On the side of the "Protestant Reformers," those men (especially Calvin) rejected the divine right of kings and extolled popular sovereignty and the sacredness of contracts.[114] Though Calvin had eschewed notions of revolution, he had recognized the legitimacy of *magistrates* coming together to resist the tyranny of a king. "Witherspoon appears to have considered the Continental Congress just such a magistracy, appointed to protect the people's freedom and to restrain a willful British ministry and Parliament."[115] The president of Princeton held these views so strongly and publicly that some in Britain called the Revolutionary War the "Presbyterian Rebellion."[116]

But there is something else here that is often missed by a simply historical *reportage* of the events. If we could think their thoughts with them, we would find that the colonials had already decided—at least the majority of them. They had carved out a land with their bare hands, as we already noted, and they had left every vestige of what it meant to be "European" (and at *some* levels Englishmen still carried some of that sheen) behind them, many of them a generation or two ago.[117] They were already "Americans" by 1776, and the American Revolution was an *inevitable* event. Even so loyal a son of England as George Washington would venture in 1774, "that the Measures which [the] Administration hath for sometime been, and now are, most violently pursuing, are repugnant to every principle of natural justice."[118] The fact that they had grown greater than their fathers who came across the ocean was the key component. "It is the development of this view to the point of overwhelming

---

112 Morrison, *John Witherspoon*, 78.
113 Daniel Walker Howe, *Making of the American Self: Jonathan Edwards to Abraham Lincoln* (1997; Oxford: Oxford University Press, 2009), 54, 132–41. The Whig party of the mid-nineteenth century held to a similar but not identical ideology as the Whigs of the Revolution.
114 See our earlier discussion of Calvin in chap. 12
115 Morrison, *John Witherspoon*, 80.
116 Ibid., 6.
117 Gordon S. Wood, *The Idea of America: Reflection on the Birth of the United States* (New York: Penguin, 2011), 34–35.
118 Ellis, Joseph J., *His Excellency: George Washington* (New York: Alfred A. Knopf, 2004), 63.

Struggle for the City

persuasiveness to the majority of American leaders and the meaning this view gave to the events of the time, and not simply an accumulation of grievances, that explains the origin of the American Revolution."[119] They were *not children* and would not be treated as such. When the time for a declaration for war came, they were up to the task. The Revolution was on.

One other point needs brief attention with regard to politics, economics, and theology in the American Revolution. This war, like other later wars, such as the Civil War and the two World Wars of the twentieth century, would transform both America and its churches. We will offer a brief comment here on how it changed America, and later on how it changed the churches of America. America's society and economy were *transformed* by the war itself. "The inexhaustible needs of the army—for everything from blankets and wagons to meat and rum—brought into being a host of new manufacturing and entrepreneurial interests and made market farmers out of husbandmen who before had scarcely traded out of their neighborhoods."[120] No event in the eighteenth century accelerated the *capitalistic* development of America more than the Revolutionary War.

FRANCE: A REVOLUTION OF A DIFFERENT COLOR

The American Revolution would not be the only national revolution of the late eighteenth century. The French Revolution (1789–99) saw that nation move from a *monarchy* to a *republic* to an *anarchic state* to a *constitutional democracy* to an *empire* in the space of ten years. Several years of famine and severe food shortages, coupled with crippling debt, created a severe economic crisis. The later Bourbon kings made *foolish* decisions relative to the French economy that devastated it.[121] Louis XV spent massive amounts of money fighting the British in the American colonies in what was known in Europe as the Seven Years' War

---

119 Bernard Bailyn, ed., *Pamphlets of the American Revolution, 1750-1776* (Cambridge, MA: Belknap Press of Harvard University Press, 1965-), I, viii. Quoted in Wood, *Idea of America*, 36.
120 Wood, *Idea of America*, 136.
121 William Doyle, *The Oxford History of the French Revolution*, 2nd ed. (Oxford: Oxford University Press, 2002), 66–85.

Struggle for the City

(1756–63) and in America as the French and Indian War (1754–63).[122] Then his grandson Louis XVI (also known as Louis the Last) poured more resources into the American Revolutionary War, a billion *livres* to be exact,[123] resources he did not have, and so had to borrow heavily from European banking houses.[124] Diminished harvests resulted in massive starvation for many of the poor of the nation, all the while the nobility were conspicuous in their lavish *consumption*. Free trade of grain was suppressed by *contrôleur général* Joseph Terray in 1770, resulting in the people accusing King Louis XV and his ministers of consolidating a "famine pact" to drive prices up for their own aggrandizement.[125] The French federal government ran budget deficits every year from 1756 till the outbreak of revolution.[126] Add to this the problem of how to care for large numbers of veterans of the wars against the British, massive unemployment, high bread prices due to the crop failures, and new Enlightenment ideals about the *equality* of all men, and you have a severe crisis.[127]

In 1789 the Estates General was called into session, something that had not happened since 1614.[128] The Estates General was made up of the First Estate, the clergy; the Second Estate, the nobility; and the Third Estate, the commoners of France. The kings had governed absolutely in the meantime, but the crisis of 1789 made it clear to many intellectuals, nobles, church leaders, and activists that the monarchy could not deliver them in the present hour. Together they formed a National Assembly that arrogated to itself the task of governing the nation in the stead of the king. The ideas of Montesquieu, which had been adopted to great benefit in America, were rejected in

---

122 Emmanuel Le Roy Ladurie, *The Ancien Régime: A History of France, 1610–1774*, trans. Mark Greengrass, History of France (1991; Oxford: Blackwell, 1996), 247–50. See our earlier discussion in chap. 13. The French and Indian War (1754–63) was the American theater of a larger war fought between the British and French known as the Seven Years' War (1756–63). The first two years of the war were fought in the American colonies, but in 1756 it escalated to a larger theater in other parts of the world.

123 Johnson, *History of the American People*, 168.

124 Doyle, *Oxford History of the French Revolution*, 79–80.

125 Le Roy Ladurie, *Ancien Régime*, 428.

126 Ibid., 493.

127 For a discussion of the Enlightenment ideals about humanity in modernity, see Michael Allen Gillespie, *The Theological Origins of Modernity* (Chicago: University of Chicago Press, 2008), 44–100.

128 Doyle, *Oxford History of the French Revolution*, 86–111.

Struggle for the City

his home country by the monarchy, and now they would also not be adopted by this newly formed National Assembly.[129]

Louis XVI responded to the Estates General by closing the building in which the Assembly was meeting and restructuring the finance ministry. Many Parisians interpreted this to be an attempted coup on the part of the king against the National Assembly. With much of the French Guard now supporting them, insurgents stormed the Bastille, where there was a large cache of weapons and ammunition, and which many considered to be a *symbol* of the now-tyrannical *Ancien Régime*. The National Assembly thus became the de facto governing body in the stead of the monarchy. The royal family attempted to leave Paris secretly, but was found out, and brought back.[130] In January 1793, Louis XVI was found guilty of various crimes and beheaded. Albert Camus commented that this constituted "an act that secularized the French world and banished God from the subsequent history of the French people." Perhaps.

In the fall of 1793 the Committee of Public Safety, led by Maximilien Robespierre, took control through a coup and unleashed the Reign of Terror in which more than 16,500 people were executed, mostly by the guillotine, though some historians put the number as high as 40,000.[131] Robespierre set price controls on all foodstuffs and many other goods, sent troops into the countryside to seize crops and arrest farmers, prosecuting anyone who resisted or attempted to preserve their own property from being seized by the committee's agents. He also clamped down on the church and set about a *scorched earth* tactic in dealing with bishops. What led him to take such Draconian measures?

Robespierre was a fervent disciple of Jean-Jacques Rousseau, who contended that individuals who live in such a way that they place the general will of the public first are truly "free" and "just," while those who do not live in such a way are criminals or heretics. Government, Rousseau believed, "was originally invented to protect and nurture greed." Primitive people would have had no need for any elaborate scheme of property rights and so no need for government, but "government would have arisen when people decided that they wanted to accumulate ever-greater amounts of property to have the

---

129 Le Roy Ladurie, *Ancien Régime*, 502.
130 Doyle, *Oxford History of the French Revolution*, 112–35.
131 Ibid., 247–71.

Struggle for the City

satisfaction of owning more than their neighbors."[132] Rousseau stated, "The first man who, after enclosing a piece of ground, took it into his head to say, 'This is mine,' and found people simple enough to believe him, was the real founder of civil society."[133] Those who refuse to live for the common good above all else must be forced to bend to the general will by the state. The state, as it were, "forces" them to be "free." In so doing, it may have to suspend all of the usual devices of democracy, such as free elections, representative bodies that reflect the views of the majority of the public, and free speech, since those are "hardly ever necessary where the government is well intentioned. (The specter of Marx looms ever closer.) For the rulers know that the general will is always on the side which is most favorable to the public interest, that is to say the most equitable; so that it is needful only to act justly to be certain of following the general will."[134] Robespierre was simply applying Rousseau to the situation in Paris in 1793. "The people is always worth more than individuals," as he himself put it.[135] Worth so much more, in fact, that the slaughter of tens of thousands of resisters is justifiable—in the name of "justice."

The French Revolution was the first in a line of revolutions that would lead to authoritarian and totalitarian states.[136] It was a *fascist* revolution in that, though it cast out the "demonic" religion represented by Roman Catholicism and the First Estate, it then capitulated to a new religion, the religion of the *state*.[137] It was also the first revolution in modern times that purported to be more *democratic* for having removed the standard devices that had historically attended true efforts at democratic governing, again, such as free speech, representative

---

132 Forster, *Contested Public Square*, 212.

133 Jean-Jacques Rousseau, *Discourse on the Origin of Inequality among Men*, trans. and ed. Helena Rosenblatt, Bedford Series in History and Culture (1754; Eng. trans., 1761; New York: Bedford / St. Martin's Press, 2011) part 2, cited in Forster, *Contested Public Square*, 213.

134 Jean-Jacques Rousseau, *The Social Contract and Discourses*, trans. G. D. H. Cole, Everyman's Library 660 (1762; Eng. trans., 1913; New York: Dutton, 1950), 297.

135 Quoted in Gertrude Himmelfarb, "The Idea of Compassion: The British vs. the French Enlightenment," *Public Interest* 145 (Fall 2001): 20. http://www.nationalaffairs.com/ public_interest/detail/the-idea-of-compassion-the-british-vs-the-french-enlightenment.

136 For a discussion of the difference between authoritarianism and totalitarianism, see Michael G. Roskin, Robert L. Cord, James A. Medieros, and Walter S. Jones, *Political Science: An Introduction*, 9th ed. (Upper Saddle River, NJ: Pearson Prentice Hall, 2006), 71–90.

137 Doyle, *Oxford History of the French Revolution*, 391–425.

Struggle for the City

government, and freedom from governmental invasion of private property without proper warrant.[138] In France, the *real problem* was *not* the *economy*. Certainly there were bumps and difficulties with food production and distribution, but the essential problem was not the economy itself, not before the Revolution and not after the Revolution. The problem was governmental *manipulation* of the economy. And it is also the case that during the revolutionary period, the policies of the revolutionary leaders made matters worse. There was a general assumption "that under the new regime there would be guaranteed supplies of cheap bread." In the eyes of most, "failure to achieve this would mean betrayal of the Revolution."[139] Revolutionary France became something of a *revived Rome*, but in this case a revived Rome in a state of *chaos*, as if Rome had been revived only in its own final decades of corruption and demise.

That kind of manipulation was something the American founding fathers wanted to avoid, at least most of them. The question is, when the government believes that it knows best for the people and ignores their express wishes in adopting and enforcing legislation, how is this, philosophically, any better than the Committee of Public Safety? How is it any different in any country when the government wants to force legislation that the majority of people do not want? The difference between the French Revolution and the American Revolution could not have been more profound.

---

138 Forster, *Contested Public Square*, 212–13.
139 Doyle, *Oxford History of the French Revolution*, 401.

Struggle for the City

Chapter 17

A New Beginning:
The New Nation as an Economic Leviathan

Before looking at the interplay between the church and market issues in nineteenth-century America, we wish to give a brief overview of the expansion of the American economy in the postwar years of the American Revolutionary War (1775–83). This second world war[1] had left the Americans in a *terrible* economic condition in terms of debt, this in spite of the incredible entrepreneurial spirit that had prevailed during the war. Economies boom during war and they struggle in the immediate aftermath. "The war brought to the Thirteen States, now united after a fashion, immense miseries, losses, benefits, and unexpected blessings."[2] Native Americans had probably the worst lot, since they had assisted the British more than assisting the Americans, and were left out at the Peace of Paris (1783). Slaves lost out, since they got nothing and even worse than nothing when the new Constitution essentially legitimized lifelong slavery. Americans were divided from one another between those that had supported the British (Tories) and the Patriots. Women lost out, as many of them lost brothers, fathers, husbands, and sons in the bitter fighting.[3] Still, the Americans had earned their freedom, and

---

1   So designated due to the fact that the American War of Independence, similar to the French and Indian War, or Seven Years' War, included combatants from numerous European countries and Central America, and involved economies as far away as India.

2   Paul Johnson, *A History of the American People* (New York: HarperCollins, 1997), 168.

3   For a survey of all of this, see ibid., 167–77.

they had learned during the heat of the fighting how to make a living in this new world. Now, what would they do with it?

What the new Americans did have was a *nation*, and land to govern. But how would they find a way to capitalize on their winnings? At first they feared having any kind of strong *federal* government, since that was what they had just thrown off. Their first constitution was the Articles of Confederation, produced in 1776–77 as a governing document for the new nation, a nation still at war. They were not really interested in *theory* at this point, since they were at war; they just needed some kind of practical guide.[4] The Articles gave little power to Congress, essentially making each state an independent entity, much like the Swiss Confederacy had been for a long time.[5] The Articles served fairly well enough in the war years, but troubles loomed in 1783 after the signing of the peace treaty with England. Even before that, things were touch and go. Two years elapsed between the English surrender at Yorktown and the signing of the Treaty of Paris. During those two years there was much fear of what lay ahead, and of republicanism, specifically.[6] Many Americans urged the Congress to renegotiate with the Crown and return to the status of colonists. That, of course, did not happen, primarily because of the leadership of George Washington.[7]

Just how was the United States to function as a *national* identity? Even more, how could the Articles of Confederation maintain this nation of producers? "Not the defects of the Articles of Confederation, but this promotion of entrepreneurial interests by ordinary people—their endless buying and selling, their bottomless passion for luxurious consumption—was what really frightened the Federalists."[8] Or did it? Eventually, when Congress convened in the Summer of 1787 the members of that body determined that the Articles could not stand as a foundation that would keep America safe in an unsafe world, and based on the principles of government outlined by Montesquieu that we outlined in our earlier discussion, fashioned the United

---

4   Ibid., 158.
5   Robert Middlekauff, *The Glorious Cause: The American Revolution, 1763–1789*, 2nd ed., (New York: Oxford University Press, 2005), 624.
6   William M. Fowler Jr., *American Crisis: George Washington and the Dangerous Two Years after Yorktown, 1781–1783* (New York: Walker, 2011), 110–11.
7   Ibid., 1–2, 87–89, 100–101, 137–40.
8   Gordon S. Wood, *The Idea of America* (New York: Penguin, 2011), 139.

Struggle for the City

States Constitution.[9] It was ratified two years later and the Bill of Rights added another two years later.[10]

It is important to make a clear distinction at this point. In the eighteenth century, England stumbled into its modern Parliamentarian form of government and used Montesquieu's distinction between legislative, executive, and judicial powers, but its form of government still conflated these powers in certain ways. In the British system the ministers of the Crown are simultaneously members of Parliament, thus blurring the legislative and executive powers together.[11] It was this *linkage*, what Americans called "corruption," and what David Hume called "influence," that the colonials had objected to. Parliament could not resist King George's policies because they were beholden to him. This was why when the Constitution was written, it was written with a clear and distinct and *complete* separation of powers in mind. There would be no crossing over between the powers for "influence" that had so corrupted the British Parliamentarian version of republicanism. At least, that was what the founders *intended*. The point here is that American democracy is based on *mistrust*, and that is a good thing![12] Though most of the founders were not orthodox Calvinists (indeed, some were merely rational theists or even deists) they were savvy and experienced enough to know that political power placed in too few hands has a corrosive tendency. We do not trust our politicians to behave themselves, so we have built as many checks and balances into the system as we can to keep their hands out of the cookie jar, as it were.

After a postwar period of inflation, nation inventing, and wrangling over matters such as the national bank, America's economy (which had been generally healthy in the prewar period and during the war) soared forward once again.[13] Though the country was deeply in debt to the tune of about 54 million dollars, it "was, probably, in per-capita terms, the richest country in the

---

9   Johnson, *History of the American People*, 160. See earlier discussion of Montesquieu in chap. 15.

10 There was significant objection to the new Constitution, with the most vocal attack coming from Patrick Henry. Thomas S. Kidd, *Patrick Henry: First among Patriots* (New York: Basic Books, 2011), 183–212.

11 Wood, *Idea of America*, 180.

12 Ibid., 183.

13 For a thorough discussion of all of this, see Charles Rappleye, *Robert Morris: Financier of the American Revolution* (New York: Simon & Schuster, 2010).

Struggle for the City

world, even though Britain was emerging as the first great industrial power."[14] America was poised to make its impact on the world economy.

Cotton, New Technologies, and Slavery

One of the first impacts is also one that we now approach with deep regrets: cotton. The larger issue was *textiles*. Before the new inventions of the eighteenth-century Industrial Revolution, it took a woman (nearly all spinners were women, hence the original sense of the term, "spinster") nearly twenty days to spin a pound of cotton into thread. This was done at home, and it took four women to supply one loom for turning the thread into cloth. In 1733 a new loom was invented called the *flying shuttle*,[15] but what was needed was not faster looms but faster spinning, or *lots* more women! The solution came in 1764 when James Hargreaves, previously mentioned in our narrative, invented the *spinning jenny*, a machine that could spin eight threads at a time. But that made little difference on any grand scale because preparing cotton for spinning was such a tedious process. A field hand could easily pick fifty pounds of cotton in a day of harvesting, but it then took twenty-five man-days of labor to separate the seed from that same fifty pounds.[16] In 1793, though, Eli Whitney, right after graduating from Yale, invented the *cotton gin*, a simple machine that separated the seed from the fiber. The time it took to separate seed from fifty pounds of cotton dropped from twenty-five man-days to *one*. This was a remarkable advance in efficiency.

Of course, this was both good and bad. It was good insofar as cotton textiles could now be produced very cheaply, especially with the new technology for spinning and weaving in place. But cotton was expensive to produce, costing about seventy percent more to produce per acre than corn.[17] It was impossible to hire enough wage earners to be able to work the fields and still turn a profit for cotton farmers, in part because *freeborn* wage earners were few and far between in an America that promised virtually *free* land just a little to the west of current

---

14 Johnson, *History of the American People*, 213.
15 John Steele Gordon, *An Empire of Wealth* (New York: HarperCollins, 2004), 88.
16 Ibid., 83.
17 Ibid., 86.

Struggle for the City

settlements. The solution was already at hand—the large population of lifelong chattel slaves that had been brought from Africa. In 1793 many of them were serving as slaves in northern states (only one state, Vermont, had abolished slavery as of 1793), and now, with cotton in such demand, some 835,000 of them were "sold south" between 1790 and 1860. The price of slaves went from about $300 to about $2,000, and the South became wealthy in turn, producing about seventy percent of the world's cotton by 1850.[18] Of course, it also created untold *misery* in terms of sexual and physical abuse of slaves, families torn apart, and something we will discuss later, the "theological problem of slavery."[19]

Railroads

One early problem encountered by anyone seeking to move through the United States was its huge size. By 1845 more than half of the population lived west of the Alleghenies, and just getting there from New York or Charleston was daunting and frustrating.[20] A stagecoach ride from Memphis to Philadelphia took three weeks! One of the early stated goals with regard to railroads was to stabilize the Union and promote trade. This, of course, created a conflicted process that would persist for decades, since trade is based on *competition* while Union is predicated on *cooperation*. "The two forces never coexisted peacefully."[21] Before the arrival of railroads in about 1829, virtually all long-distance travel was limited to *waterways*. In those days, regional speech accents were nearly always connected to a river valley, rather than a region, like "Southern" or "Yankee." Early locomotives and passenger cars were primitive and unsafe, causing governments, local, state, and federal, eventually to have to pass hundreds of *regulations*.

People began flocking west, which both enriched the west and depleted the east of available labor. People left their hometowns, causing the breakup of extended family situations that had so defined much of American life before the 1830s and '40s. "Before the construction of railroads in New England,

---

18 Ibid., 85, 87.
19 Mark A. Noll, *The Civil War as a Theological Crisis*, Steven and Janice Brose Lectures in the Civil War Era (Chapel Hill: University of North Carolina Press, 2006).
20 Sarah H. Gordon, *Passage to Union: How the Railroads Transformed American Life, 1829–1929* (Chicago: Ivan R. Dee, 1997), 14.
21 Ibid., 23.

Struggle for the City

travel beyond the boundaries of a hometown or region were uncommon."[22] In 1831, the year that Boston got the railroad, one prominent Bostonian declared in a public meeting "that if people could come from Springfield to Boston in five hours, an average of nine people would come every day."[23] How could Boston manage all of that? Seemingly the prospect of nine strangers in Boston in a single day was a bit overwhelming in 1831.

Real advances would take several decades. In 1857 railroads connected the cities of the East with the Mississippi River for the first time.[24] The disparity between North and South in the sectional conflict of the 1860s would also have a railroad component, in several ways. There were no railway connections between northern states and southern states before the war. In addition, the size of rail gauges in southern states was different, so that southern troops traveling from North Carolina to Tennessee were forced to change trains at the state line.[25] But the biggest disparity lay in the *amount* of railroad track in north and south. The North had four times more miles of track than the South had. This was due to the fact that the North was much more heavily industrialized, but also because "the South saw land in a more traditional light, as *home and heritage*, not just as a *natural resource* to benefit capital and state."[26] However we understand the issue, the railroads were a key component of expanding American wealth.

We could discuss the telegraph, steamships, American ingenuity in mining, northern farming techniques and new inventions such as the John Deere steel plowshare and the McCormick reaper, tools that made it possible for farmers to plow the deep rooted grasses up from the plains of Illinois and Indiana. The point is that Americans, with a spirit unfettered (or *little-fettered*) by government were free either to produce or not produce. That freedom created a financial and industrial *juggernaut* long before two twentieth century world wars would cast America into the world's limelight. Now there is another question that needs to be addressed. How were American Christians and churches *using* their wealth, and how were they doing holding on to "the *faith* once delivered to the saints" (Jude 3)?

---

22 Ibid., 47.
23 Ibid., 49.
24 Ibid., 106.
25 Ibid., 133, 137.
26 Ibid., 136.

Struggle for the City

REVIVALISM AND SOCIAL REFORM

The aftermath of the American Revolution witnessed a new wave of revival, often called the Second Great Awakening. If America was not a Christian nation at the time of the Revolution it *soon became one* when the fires of revival scorched college campuses (like Yale and Hampden-Sidney), churches in the Shenandoah Valley, and camp meetings over the Cumberland into Kentucky and Tennessee.[27] Out of the revival at Hampden-Sydney College in 1787 James McGready, Presbyterian stalwart, emerged and would take reins of leadership for many years in the western states.[28] Jonathan Edwards' grandson, Timothy Dwight, president of Yale, saw *hundreds* of students converted, students that had been heavily influenced in their early educational training by deists and skeptical Enlightenment philosophers such as Voltaire and David Hume.[29] But under Dwight's pastoral presidency these students turned from *skepticism* to the *gospel,* and many of these converts, such as theologian Nathaniel Taylor, pastor Lyman Beecher (the father of Harriet Beecher Stowe), and John C. Calhoun would exercise *intellectual* and *political* leadership of the nation in the early nineteenth century.[30] Because of that, the nineteenth-century legacy of the United States would be remarkably *different* from that of France, Italy,

---

27 The debate over whether America was *founded* as a Christian nation is complex and beyond the scope of this book to articulate. Certainly Massachusetts was colonized by sincere Christians, but that fervor had diluted by 1776. Virginia was a different matter. A sample of the literature would include Mark Noll, Nathan O. Hatch, George Marsden, *The Search for Christian America* (Westchester, IL: Crossway, 1983); John D. Woodbridge, Mark Noll, Nathan O. Hatch, *The Gospel in America: Themes in the Story of America's Evangelicals* (Grand Rapids, MI: Zondervan, 1979); Donald W. Dayton, *Discovering an Evangelical Heritage* (New York: Harper & Row, 1976); Edwin S. Gaustad, *Faith of Our Fathers: Religion and the New Nation* (San Francisco: Harper & Row, 1987); M. E. Bradford, *A Worthy Company: The Dramatic Story of the Men Who Founded Our Country* (1982; repr., Westchester, IL: Crossway, 1988); Michael Novak and Jana Novak, *Washington's God: Religion, Liberty, and the Father of Our Country* (New York: Basic Books, 2006); Peter Lillback, with Jerry Newcombe, *George Washington's Sacred Fire* (Bryn Mawr, PA: Providence Forum, 2006).

28 John Wolffe, *The Expansion of Evangelicalism: The Age of Wilberforce, More, Chalmers and Finney,* History of Evangelicalism 2 (Downers Grove, IL: InterVarsity Press, 2007), 48.

29 Marvin Olasky, *Fighting for Liberty and Virtue: Political and Cultural Wars in Eighteenth-Century America,* American Experience (Wheaton, IL: Crossway, 1995), 207; John R. Fitzmier, *New England's Moral Legislator: Timothy Dwight, 1752–1817,* Religion in North America (Bloomington: Indiana University Press, 1998).

30 Fitzmier, *New England's Moral Legislator,* 15–16, 56–58, 177–78.

Struggle for the City

or Germany. "The Christian religion remained an enduring element of imponderable magnitude in American life and thought, simultaneously progressive and conservative, a source of both social reform and divisive controversy."[31] In America, the church as an evangelistic and social force would have influence far outweighing the same institutions in Europe, or even in England.

The Second Great Awakening's fires eventually cooled down, but its impact was felt throughout the nineteenth century. Though, as we have noted, some historians dispute the degree to which America was a "Christian nation" in 1776, there is little dispute that it was a Christian nation (insofar as we can even use that language) a half-century later. The census of 1860 reported 38,183 church buildings, one for every 608 persons. Between 1832 and 1854 the population had grown by eighty-eight percent, while the number of evangelical clergy had grown by 175 percent.[32] One-fifth of Americans were members of an evangelical church in 1855, but there is indication that more than another one-fifth attended church regularly. Nearly *half* of Americans were weekly or near-weekly church attenders.[33]

Shifting of the Center of Gravity

One shift that had occurred was in the *kinds* of churches Americans were now joining. In the early colonial period the Congregationalists and the Anglicans (Episcopalians) had dominated the ecclesiastical landscape. Baptists were a tiny minority, even in 1700, trailing slightly behind the Presbyterians. Francis Asbury came to America in 1771 to lead the fledgling Methodist work here. Even at the beginnings of the Revolutionary War the situation had changed only little. "In 1776 the Congregationalists, Episcopalians, and Presbyterians seemed to be the colonial denominations."[34] Fifty-five percent of those who belonged to a church belonged to one of these three. By 1850 the Congrega-

---

31 Daniel Walker Howe, *What Hath God Wrought: The Transformation of America, 1815–1848* (New York: Oxford University Press, 2007), 836.
32 Timothy L. Smith, *Revivalism and Social Reform in Mid-19th-Century America* (New York: Abingdon, 1957), 17.
33 Mark A. Noll, *America's God* (New York: Oxford University Press, 2002), 55.
34 Roger Finke and Rodney Stark, *The Churching of America, 1776–1990*, 2nd ed. (New Brunswick, NJ: Rutgers University Press, 2005), 55.

Struggle for the City

tionalists had dropped from 20.4 percent of all church adherents in America to four percent. Episcopalians had moved from 15.7 percent to 3.5 percent, while Presbyterians had shifted from nineteen percent to 11.6 percent.[35]

What caused this shift? Older historians argued that the state of religion declined during the Revolutionary War and in its aftermath. William Warren Sweet referred to this period as "the period of the lowest ebb-tide of vitality in the history of American Christianity."[36] That sentiment could be found in many other "standard" works, but it simply is *not true*. What had happened was a *denominational shift*, away from the three churches listed in the previous paragraph and toward the Methodists and the Baptists. By 1850 the Methodists had captured 34.2 percent of the churchgoing population and the Baptists had garnered 16.9 percent, and by century's end the Baptists would be larger still. Catholics were growing as well. So, the shift did not occur because of a *decline* in religion but because of a *shift* away from the older traditions to the new "upstarts."

Previous scholars like William Warren Sweet and Sidney Ahlstrom may have arrived at the conclusion that religion declined during this time from a statement made by an aging Lyman Beecher, the redoubtable Congregationalist minister who *despised* Baptists and Methodists for their lack of an educated ministry and for their emotional style of worship.[37] The Congregational, Presbyterian, and Episcopal churches were all derived from a *European* style of religious establishment, one in which privilege and bloodlines play a role and one that depends for its support on state *establishment* and *taxation* of the populous.[38] In addition, these older European denominations lauded the importance of an excellent education.[39] That meant Harvard, Yale, William and Mary, and so on. The problem was that these schools, dependent on European intellectual development, had *secularized* early on. Pastors in those

---

35 Ibid., 56.
36 William Warren Sweet, *The Story of Religion in America*, 2nd ed. (New York: Harper & Row, 1950), 223.
37 Finke and Stark, *Churching of America, 1776–1990*, 58–59.
38 Though the Congregational Church was an American institution and not a European one, it was initiated by first generation Englishmen who were used to state support of religion and exclusive establishment.
39 See Beecher's views on this and how it was likely one of the reasons he was disaffected toward the relatively uneducated Baptists and Methodists. Stuart C. Henry, *Unvanquished Puritan: A Portrait of Lyman Beecher* (Grand Rapids, MI: Eerdmans, 1973), 172–77.

Struggle for the City

churches were, first and foremost, *scholars*, and they were all imbibing from the streams that ran from the *lecterns* of Europe. We have already pointed out that the American Revolution is the single most important event in American history, and not just because it was our political "break" with England. It is also important because "[t]he generation overshadowed by it and its counterpart in France stands at the fault line that separates an older world, premised on standards of deference, patronage, and ordered succession, from a newer one to which we are attuned since it continues to shape our values."[40] This is an important perspective.

America was *different* from Europe. We have argued previously that, even before Adam Smith's book, America was already de facto, basically a *free-market* economy. We have shown that George Whitefield appealed to that spirit when he itinerated across the colonies, preaching in other pastor's "parishes," and using market methods to promote his revivals. Whitefield's success was remarkable, in our view both because he had a remarkable *calling* and giftedness from God and because he had the *savvy* to make people aware that he was coming to town. Further, Baptists early on and later Methodists demonstrated that one does not require state tax support and exclusive establishment in order to be able to build churches and call pastors. The point is that Baptists and Methodists were carrying out church growth in the *same way* that early American entrepreneurs built their businesses—not by seeking government monopoly and subsidy, but by offering the best ministry they could offer and by making participation a purely *voluntary* matter.[41]

We can press this matter further. The period from 1776 till 1830 left the same indelible imprint upon the *structures* of American life as it did upon our *politics*. But it is necessary to recognize that, aside from land and the enormous size of the country, *religion* made the biggest impression on the lives of people during this period. One can see this by looking at the extreme difference between British Methodism after the death of Wesley in 1791 with the American version under Asbury. In England it immediately became a centripetal *bureau-*

---

40 Nathan O. Hatch, "The Democratization of Christianity and the Character of American Politics," in *Religion and American Politics: From the Colonial Period to the Present*, 2nd ed., ed. Mark A. Noll and Luke E. Harlow (New York: Oxford University Press, 2007), 94.

41 Finke and Stark, *Churching of America, 1776–1990*, 55–116.

Struggle for the City

cracy under the heavy, centralizing hand of Jabez Bunting. In America, it was centrifugal, creative, entrepreneurial, and there was almost no central *authority*.[42] The American experience was untrammeled and unregulated. Within a few years of Jefferson's election in 1800, "it became anachronistic to speak of dissent in America."[43] If there is no one norm to which all must conform, then *every* speech is a *dissenting* speech, and the very notion of dissent disappears, at least for a while.

Churches and religious movements in the early 1800s operated in a climate "in which ecclesiastical establishments had withered."[44] This attitude had little to do with polity and much to do with the incarnation of popular culture, an incarnation that brought together a *populist* spirit, a *democratic* attitude, and a belief that here, where there were seemingly endless opportunities for advancement in personal success, there was also the possibility for endless *advancement* in the kingdom of God. Campbellites, Baptists (at least those west of the Alleghenies), Methodists, Mormons, and others held to the same spirit, and they carried with them the sense that God would work in their lives every *single* day if they would just be faithful *to* him and faithful *to hear* him.[45] Religion was the most driving force in American culture from 1780 till 1830, especially in the western part of the country, and that impression remains in many ways even today.

From Evangelism to Moral Reform

Both the First and Second Great Awakenings had divided denominations. New and Old Light Congregationalists, New and Old Side Presbyterians, then New and Old School Presbyterians, and Separate and Regular Baptists were names taken by groups that, respectively, either affirmed the revivals or did not.[46] Churches and pastors generally *gravitated* to one side or the other, depending on whether or not they believed the awakenings were from God.[47]

---

42 Hatch, "Democratization of Christianity," 95.
43 Ibid.
44 Ibid., 96.
45 Ibid., 100–115.
46 Earle E. Cairns, *An Endless Line of Splendor* (Wheaton, IL: Tyndale, 1986), 85–116.
47 Ibid., 45.

Struggle for the City

By 1840, though, polarization over the revivals had begun to wane. Though formal divisions remained in the denominations, functionally the walls began to come down. New Lights and Old Lights no longer spent all of their time and polemical energy battling one another. Most (though certainly not all) among America's evangelicals had come to believe that the revivals had at least *some* validity. By 1840, "The argument was no longer over revivals or measures, but only the theological framework within which their success was to be interpreted."[48] Some of these revised opinions were a result of pragmatic considerations. There was evidence, for instance, that Baptists in Kentucky, Tennessee, Arkansas, and Texas had lost as many as three thousand churches to the rising Disciples movement led by Alexander Campbell and Barton Stone, and that a significant portion of these left due to a great deal of Baptist antirevivalism.[49]

One factor that led to the increasing acceptance of revivalism was a change in the *nature* of the revivals. In the early heat of the Second Great Awakening camp meetings and other revival venues had witnessed emotionally charged displays of piety. People got the jerks, they rolled on the ground, "treed the devil," spoke in tongues, danced and laughed in the Spirit, and barked like dogs. One Baptist pastor related how he was caught behind a wagon filled with people returning from a camp meeting and how he had to ride along behind them for hours, listening to them "bay like a bunch of spaniels."[50] By 1840, and in the aftermath of the Finney "crusades," the decline of uncouth practices brought a greater respectability to "revival."[51] "Even at the camp meetings they placed great emphasis upon the 'blessed quietness' of the Spirit's presence and expected leaders to restrain the fervor of the flock."[52] That being the case, the revivalist tradition began to move in a different direction, the direction of *social reform*—Christian education, temperance reform, relief of the poor, and the abolition of slavery. That is, the revival tradition took on reforms that

---

48 Smith, *Revivalism and Social Reform*, 55.
49 Albert Henry Newman, *A History of Baptist Churches in the United States*, rev. ed. (Philadelphia: American Baptist Publication Society, 1898), 440–41.
50 Robert A. Baker, ed., *A Baptist Source Book: With Particular Reference to Southern Baptists* (Nashville: Broadman, 1966), 46.
51 Charles E. Hambrick-Stowe, *Charles G. Finney and the Spirit of American Evangelicalism*, Library of Religious Biography (Grand Rapids, MI: Eerdmans, 1996), 131–64.
52 Smith, *Revivalism and Social Reform*, 60.

Struggle for the City

would bring the church increasingly into a dialogue with governments, mostly state and local at first, but eventually federal. Who, after all, was really responsible for effecting such reforms?

Charles Finney burst on the scene in 1824, preaching a series of impassioned revivals in a manner similar to Whitefield over a period of eight years, which ended in 1832. Finney's theology was very different than that of Whitefield and represented almost a total rejection of the earlier evangelist's Calvinism. Finney defined "free will" as the "power to choose in every instance in accordance with moral obligation, or to refuse so to choose."[53] This led him to postulate that people had the *natural* ability to receive Christ, and based on that he used various "new measures" to excite "decisions" in his meetings.

Finney's shift from mass evangelistic meetings to moral reform and education is a classic example of that trend from this period.[54] Finney, preaching in Oberlin on the national day of fasting in 1841, denied that humanity's root problem was individual sin only, but was also what he called "national sins." God "deals with nations.... Each nation is regarded by God as a unit."[55] Finney decried several "national sins" in general: the "outrageous injustice with which this nation has treated the aborigines [Native Americans] of this country"; the "hypocrisy upon which the Revolution was based" since slavery was still ensconced; national desecration of the Sabbath; the "national love of money" exemplified in American industry and acquisitiveness; the "disgusting licentiousness and intemperance" of congressmen; the legal sanctioning of duels by the government; and the "wickedness of political contests."[56] In 1842, after a five-year hiatus from his evangelistic ministry, he returned to the "sawdust trail," but this time not merely as an evangelist, but as a moral crusader as well.[57]

Most significantly for our study, some of the theological underpinnings of the Second Great Awakening were decidedly un-Calvinistic and have been labeled as "Pelagian" for their dependence on "means" to produce "revival" and reliance on

53   Charles Finney, *Finney's Systematic Theology*, comp. and ed. Dennis Carroll, Bill Nicely, L. G. Parkhurst Jr. (1846–47; Minneapolis: Bethany House, 1994), 32. Note: This is the 1878 edition of Finney's *Lectures on Systematic Theology*.
54   Hambrick-Stowe, *Charles G. Finney*, 198–227.
55   Finney, quoted in Hambrick-Stowe, *Charles G. Finney*, 200.
56   Ibid., 200–201.
57   Ibid., 204.

Struggle for the City

an anthropology that did not take as seriously the depravity of man as had the previous Awakening.[58] Some of this reasoning is specious, as we have already witnessed Whitefield using "means" in his itinerant ministry, but there certainly were substantial *differences* between Whitefield and Finney, differences of both style and content. In New England many Congregationalists and Presbyterians in their theological reflections on the experience of revival moved in the direction of what came to be known as the "New Divinity." Their thinking is peculiar for having wed rationalistic Scottish philosophy, emphasizing human ability to act virtuously, to a broadly Calvinistic understanding of the need for conversion. Baptists and Methodists, for the most part, did not follow that course.[59]

Two strains would come out of this supposed "modified Calvinism"—one eventually issued in the Unitarian schism and the other led to an activism aimed at fighting humanity's inner corruption through movements of "moral reform and social benevolence." What Fogel calls an "army" of "missionaries and humanitarians" set up a *plethora* of new organizations that they hoped would lead to "the benevolent empire." This proclivity could lead someone like Charles Finney to declare, in various times and places, that salvation requires that "the reborn become totally unselfish or totally altruistic." Christians can realize "holiness and virtue" through the exercise of "disinterested benevolence." They must be committed to "the universal reformation of the world," to the "complete and final overthrow" of "war, slavery, licentiousness, and all such evils and abominations" in order to "make the world a fit place for the

---

58 We are indebted to Robert W. Fogel, *The Fourth Great Awakening and the Future of Egalitarianism* (Chicago: University of Chicago, 2000), 93–94, for his analysis here and throughout this paragraph. He draws extensively from the works of Sydney E. Ahlstrom, *A Religious History of the American People*, 2nd ed. (New Haven, CT: Yale University Press, 2004), 430–77; Whitney R. Cross, *The Burned Over District: The Social and Intellectual History of Enthusiastic Religion in Western New York, 1800–1850* (1950; repr., Ithaca, NY: Cornell University Press, 1982); and William G. McLoughlin, *Revivals, Awakenings, and Reform: An Essay on Religion and Social Change in America, 1607–1977*, Chicago History of American Religion (Chicago: University of Chicago Press, 1978).

59 See, for instance, *Princeton versus the New Divinity: the Meaning of Sin, Grace, Salvation, Revival* (Edinburgh: Banner of Truth, 2001), a reprinting of a series of essays, mostly from *The Princeton Review* in the nineteenth century, critical of the New Divinity movement. For a more favorable, but still critical, assessment see Douglas A. Sweeney, *Nathaniel Taylor, New Haven Theology, and the Legacy of Jonathan Edwards*, Religion in America (Oxford: Oxford University Press, 2003), 24–36, 99–107.

Struggle for the City

imminent return of Christ."[60] Finney here wraps *evangelism, social reform,* and an early Holiness version of *sanctification* all into *one* piece.

The passionate Americanism of Finney and his converts became known as "religious ultraism," driven by a belief in the possibility of the "ultimate perfection of society" and the fear that unless this agenda was constantly promoted, the "natural tendency toward degeneracy" would prevail.[61] Thus did a movement among evangelicals that originally concentrated on "issues and methods relatively remote from politics (such as persuading individuals to abstain from intoxicating liquors or persuading prostitutes to reform themselves)" become one that "gradually reasserted their influence in the political arena."[62] This politicization was probably *inevitable,* but it did subtly *transform* the message of salvation by grace through faith to one of salvation by social transformation of *culture.* The old emphasis on regeneration was not removed, but it was in *certain* ways eclipsed.

Holiness and Social Reform

The year 1858 would take the scattered energy of revivalism with its newly renovated reputation and channel that into a mighty force. The "Prayer Revival" of that year transformed evangelical Christianity for the latter half of the nineteenth century.[63] This was a revival with little pastoral leadership, a revival that included female leadership (especially Phoebe Palmer), and a revival that was transdenominational, including even the Unitarians. Though some have contended that there are purely sociological explanations for the "revival," such as the Financial Panic of 1857 and continued agitation over extending slavery into the territories, most religious historians today would accept the revival as a *genuine* religious movement that swept across the entire nation.[64] It is what came *out* of the revival that concerns us. The revival renovated Methodism and its emphasis on sanctification as an identifiable second blessing after salvation. Phoebe

---

60 Fogel, *Fourth Great Awakening,* 94.
61 Ibid.
62 Ibid., 95.
63 Kathryn Teresa Long, *The Revival of 1857–58: Interpreting an American Religious Awakening,* Religion in America (New York: Oxford University Press, 1998).
64 Ibid., 116.

Struggle for the City

Palmer's "double cure" doctrine—in which she interpreted the phrase from the hymn "Rock of Ages," "Be of sin the double cure, / Save from wrath and make me pure," as two separate experiences—became a launching pad for both a new kind of spirituality and a new kind of ethics.[65] Popular Baptist evangelist of the time A. B. Earle put it this way: "The ethical ideals to which Emerson and Henry David Thoreau aspired on a highly sophisticated level, plain men of the time sought at a Methodist mourners' bench or class meeting."[66] The Holiness Movement, with its second blessing view of sanctification wedded to a committed social ministry and linked to a genuinely American consciousness, was on.

In the aftermath of the Revival of 1858 American evangelicals turned increasingly to a focus on social issues. "The rapid growth of concern with purely social issues such as poverty, workingmen's rights, the liquor traffic, slum housing, and racial bitterness is the chief feature distinguishing American religion after 1865 from that of the first half of the nineteenth century."[67] This was true nearly across the board in American Christianity, and is of course especially true of "progressive" or liberal Christianity. "Such matters in some cases supplanted entirely the earlier pre-occupation with salvation from personal sin and the life hereafter."[68] But it was also true of *evangelicals* at a significant level. Smith goes on to say, "The quest for perfection joined with compassion for the poor and needy sinners and a rebirth of millennial expectation to make Protestantism a mighty social force long before the slavery conflict erupted into war."[69] In other words, by around 1860, led especially by Methodism (the most dominant denomination in America at the time), evangelicals launched a social reform program that would consume much of their energy through the rest of the century. But one has to ask the question whether the social reform aspect began to take the place of genuine evangelism defined in biblical terms.

---

65   Charles Edward White, *The Beauty of Holiness: Phoebe Palmer as Theologian, Revivalist, Feminist, and Humanitarian* (Grand Rapids, MI: Francis Asbury, 1986), esp. 105–60. The hymn "Rock of Ages" was penned by Augustus Toplady, a Calvinist who would have been incensed to know that his words were taken in this way.
66   A. B. Earle, *The Rest of Faith* (Boston: James H. Earle, 1871), quoted in Vinson Synan, *The Holiness-Pentecostal Movement in the United States* (Grand Rapids, MI: Eerdmans, 1971), 30.
67   Smith, *Revivalism and Social Reform*, 148.
68   Ibid.
69   Ibid., 149.

Struggle for the City

What was the state of the poor in America? America was the land of opportunity, but entrenched poverty became a reality by 1837 when waves of immigrants began to flood the coastal cities. In the 1820s and '30s more than 667,000 overseas immigrants entered the United States.[70] Before around 1800 poverty was taken care of almost exclusively by families, and in the absence of that, individual churches would do what they could with situations with which they were familiar.[71] Churches learned quickly to distinguish between the deserving poor and the undeserving, between those who were poor because of a case of bad luck and those who were down in the pit because they were drunks.[72] As industrialization worked its way into the same cities, it became a mixed situation, since industrialization provided jobs, but those same jobs attracted more immigrants, and an endless cycle settled in. Great inequalities existed in the cities during early industrialization, and this caused a certain amount of resentment, as is witnessed by the invention of the word millionaire around 1821.[73] On the other hand, the inequalities between rich and poor did not change substantially over the next several decades of early industrialization, and we will return to this theme toward the end of chapter 19, "Rebuilding a New Nation."[74] This situation also created a new missionary opportunity for churches since most of the poor immigrants did *not* attend church.

Chapel of the Good Shepherd in Boston is an example of this wedding of *spirituality* and *social* concern. Pastor Frederick Huntington employed the assistance of a doctor in his congregation, Dr. Charles Cullis, a "homeopathic physician," to help with the medical needs of the people who were helped by the Chapel.[75] Relying entirely on freewill faith gifts (similar to George Müller in England), the Chapel built eleven cottages to house the *needy*. The minis-

---

70 Howe, *What Hath God Wrought*, 526.
71 Marvin Olasky, *The Tragedy of American Compassion* (Wheaton, IL: Crossway, 1992), 13.
72 Ibid., 10–13.
73 Edward Pessen, *Riches, Class and Power before the Civil War* (Lexington, MA: D. C. Heath, 1973), 32, 70. See also Douglas Harper, "millionaire," *Online Etymology Dictionary*, http://www.etymonline.com/index.php?term=millionaire. The word *billionaire* entered American English in 1844. Ibid., http://www.etymonline.com/index.php?term=billionaire.
74 Donald Adams, "Prices and Wages," in *Encyclopedia of American Economic History: Studies of the Principal Movements and Ideas*, ed. Glenn Porter (New York: Charles Scribner's Sons, 1980), 229–46.
75 Smith, *Revivalism and Social Reform*, 173.

Struggle for the City

tries that engaged in such activities saw themselves as doing evangelism and social ministry for the purpose of the improvement of society, in true *postmillennial* fashion.[76]

Both evangelicals and liberals at this time held to a postmillennial eschatology, believing that the millennial reign of Christ had arrived, a reign evidenced by the upsurge of social ministry on the part of the church. The idea, going all the way back to the Puritans (and maybe Augustine), was that once the church came to a position of dominance in the world, virtually all of society would come under its aegis, and *nearly everyone* would be converted to the faith. That situation would then prevail for a lengthy period of time, at the end of which the new kingdom of Christ would dawn. The difference between evangelicals and liberals in the 1850s and down to the end of the century was that evangelicals held to the absolute need for a personal conversion experience for all persons and to the literal truth of what the Bible teaches about the second coming of Christ, while liberals increasingly abandoned belief in the infallibility of the Bible and, for some at least, in the need to believe in Jesus to find "salvation." In addition, by the 1880s the postmillennial understanding would be edged out by a resurgent premillennialism on the part of evangelicals. But at the time of the Civil War that was not even on the horizon.[77]

In the 1860s and '70s there was no federal program for poverty relief, nor were there state programs. Relief societies did organize in the cities, though, to assist the "worthy poor." The Boston Provident Association, established in 1851, gave food, clothes, coal, and other commodities (though not money) to those willing to work, but it refused to help drunkards.[78] The idea was that the "city could reflect the countryside when discipline and love were twins, not opposites."[79] Churches, working with local governments, provided for the relief of the genuinely poor and infirm who could not help themselves.

Charles Brace founded the New York Children's Aid Society in 1853. The streets of New York were filled with orphaned boys who were thieves, pick-

---

76 Premillennialism was growing at this time and by 1875 would begin to take the place of postmillennialism in America.
77 For a discussion of eschatology as a political issue, see Russell D. Moore, *The Kingdom of Christ: The New Evangelical Perspective* (Wheaton, IL: Crossway, 2004), 25–80.
78 Olasky, *Tragedy of American Compassion*, 29.
79 Ibid., 30.

Struggle for the City

pockets, and hoodlums. Brace reached out to them but *required* them to attend church services specifically designed for their age and status. They were usually moved out to live with families in the countryside who needed help on the farm. The program was very structured and little leeway was given for rebellion. By the 1860s the Society was placing two thousand children per year, and by the 1870s it was placing twice that many. By the end of the century the Society's limited records showed that three placed-out children had become governors, 498 were merchants or businessmen, eighty-one were teachers, and so on.[80]

Several observations are important at this point. *First,* these programs were based on belief in a *free-market* understanding of economics. They did not seek aid from federal or state agencies but believed that individuals, societies, and churches should do what they could for poverty, usually in the name of Christ. It was workers and business people who were digging in to their *own* pockets to help. The records in most eastern cities right up to the end of the nineteenth century show that these organizations took care of the needs of the poor and the dispossessed, including orphans, in ways that were very adequate.

Second, since the relief was local, there was a great deal of *accountability*. Wedding "discipline and love" meant that they could weed out the drunks and malcontents who were looking only for a handout, not a hand-up. *Third,* one of the implications of all this was that churches, even evangelical churches, began to see a primary focus of ministry to outsiders as a *social* one, something we have already noted with the shift in the ministry of Charles Finney. In the early years of this trend, evangelicals tended to keep evangelism and social ministry together, but when the evangelism is *not* successful and the social ministry *is*, social ministry can eventually become the primary focus. The question now has to be faced, however, as to just how Christians understood this market-driven economy that was able to do so much to help the poor. Certainly it is a good thing to take one's possessions and use them to help others, but is it not at least possible that the free-market system itself is flawed? And if so, how can it be an instrument in the hand of God in ministry? Christians in the nineteenth century debated that question at length, and it is to that debate that we now turn.

---

80 Ibid., 33–39.

Struggle for the City

CHRISTIAN THEOLOGY AND THE RESPONSE TO AMERICAN "CAPITALISM"

Because America was a place where there was little regulation of the economy, by modern standards, Adam Smith's ideas seemed to bear themselves out, in many cases even before his book appeared. After all, Smith's book was just the distillation of previous wisdom gathered in one place. New England was financed early on by joint-stock corporations, especially the Massachusetts Bay Company and the Plymouth Bay Company. Virginia was also financed in this way in the beginning. The men who founded these companies back in England were known as "*adventurers.*" That seems an odd name for men who never left home, but it was a term etymologically related to our modern term *venture capitalist.* These men went out on a limb and invested their own money in a "venture," which might not meet with success, and yet they did so with the expectation that they would realize a profit. The venture was relatively free from government regulation, and the profit would, hopefully, be relatively free from government *monitoring* since it was obtained outside the normal network of government oversight.[81] The New World of British colonization in the Western Hemisphere would seem to offer a pragmatic testing ground for ideas like those later represented in Smith's philosophy.

Specific intellectual responses to Smith after his book appeared in America were mixed. This was to be true in the general intellectual world and in the world of Christian intellectuals. In America the two "worlds" were not widely separated until late in the nineteenth century. In this way, America was different from Europe and even England, where the Enlightenment had created two intellectual communities, one of them broadly Christian,[82] and the other decidedly non-Christian, and even in some cases anti-Christian.[83] In America, the thinking world of the early nineteenth century was still, generally, a *Christian* intellectual world. Stew-

---

81 John Steele Gordon, *The Business of America: Tales from the Marketplace—American Enterprise from the Settling of New England to the Break-up of AT&T* (New York: Walker, 2001), 4–6.

82 From the broadly Christian intellectual community, thinkers such as Isaac Newton, John Locke, Dugald Stewart, and Thomas Reid come to mind as being significant Enlightenment intellectuals who maintained some kind of commitment to evangelical Christianity.

83 From the decidedly non- or anti-Christian intellectual community, figures such as Voltaire, David Hume, Immanuel Kant, Charles Fourier, and Auguste Comte are key exemplars.

Struggle for the City

art Davenport has identified three early-nineteenth-century responses to the new "political economy" ideology hinted at by the Physiocrats and developed by Smith and his disciples: the *clerical economists*, who were supporters of Smith's approach; the *contrarians*, who opposed it; and the *pastoral moralists*, who adapted it to their own moral ideology.[84] All three groups were represented by avowedly Christian thinkers, each of whom claimed that his theory was completely *consistent* with biblical ethics and the teachings of Jesus. Just how did each group make its case?

The "clerical economists" were supportive of America's rapid rise to commercial success and were further *sanguine* about Smith's overall approach to political economy. They supported free trade, the division of labor, and the rapid evolution of industrialized technology. They held these views in spite of the so-called *Das Adam Smith Problem*. These individuals were well-known Christian leaders, mostly educators, who did not believe that Smith's approach to political economy was anti-Christian or necessarily injurious to the spiritual life of those who were being affected by it in the marketplace.

One of the most outspoken supporters of Smith was Baptist minister and professor of moral philosophy Francis Wayland. At the heart of Wayland's own moral theory lay a commitment to Scottish Common Sense Realism. This was a worldview articulated by, among others, Thomas Reid and Dugald Stewart. Reid and Stewart were convinced that God had established the world according to certain natural moral laws and that humans had been endowed by God with the ability to discover what those laws were.[85] Wayland and the other political economists contended that Smith's approach was *intuitive*, that it was *pragmatically* advantageous, and that its *utility* was being proven in the material success of the American experiment. So, for Wayland, the proof lay in a mix of natural theological intuitions, utilitarianism, and American millenarianism. He articulated this confluence of biblical and Scottish Common Sense Realism related to the economy in 1837 in his book, *Elements of Political*

---

84 Stewart Davenport, *Friends of the Unrighteous Mammon: Northern Christians and Market Capitalism, 1815–1860* (Chicago: University of Chicago Press, 2008).

85 Nicholas Wolterstorff, *Thomas Reid and the Story of Epistemology*, Modern European Philosophy (2001; repr., Cambridge: Cambridge University Press, 2004), 46. Reid and Stewart saw themselves as standing in a long line of classical Christian thought (Augustine, Anselm, Thomas, some Reformed theologians) that affirmed both natural and revealed theology.

Struggle for the City

Economy.[86] For Wayland, "The principles of supply and demand were seen as part of the divinely ordered structure of the world."[87] As a college president and professor, he also wished to extend the scope of these ideas to the point of changing the college curriculum to include more practical disciplines.[88]

Further, Wayland believed that being wealthy was not a sin. "The right of property is founded on the will of God... as made known to us by natural conscience, by general consequences, and by revelation."[89] The primary example he pointed to was Nicholas Brown, patron of Brown University. At Brown's funeral Wayland noted that the man had combined a gift for making money with a commitment to Christian ideals of *benevolence.* Wayland further observed that Brown had done so, not at the end of a life dedicated to making a fortune, like some who after "the love of wealth, eating like a canker into his soul, had paralyzed every generous sentiment," and who then give away a fortune as if to *atone* for their greed.[90] No, he said, Brown had done so all his life. Brown's life and work were clear evidence that God had given good gifts to his people in common grace, and that those gifts could be expanded upon, grow, and then be used for purposes that were *both* humanitarian and spiritual.

Wayland combined this view of the economy with his own Baptist beliefs in democratic process. As we have already noted, *some* Anabaptists eschewed any political involvement because of their view that Christians owe allegiance to Christ and Christ alone, and therefore serving in the *military* or even *voting* in elections was a violation of one's holiness. But the Baptist groups that grew out of English Separatism did not generally follow Anabaptist teaching on politics and the state. They held to more mainstream and Reformed (or Lutheran views) that Christians live in two worlds simultaneously. Because of their *ec-*

---

86 Francis Wayland, *Elements of Political Economy* (1837; London: Cassell, Petter and Galpin, 1856).

87 David W. Bebbington, *Baptists through the Centuries: A History of a Global People* (Waco, TX: Baylor University Press, 2010), 124.

88 Davenport, *Friends of the Unrighteous Mammon*, 35–41.

89 Francis Wayland, *Elements of Moral Science* (1835; New York: Nabu, 2010), 210, 211.

90 Francis Wayland, *A Discourse in Commemoration of the Life and Character of the Hon. Nicholas Brown: Delivered in the Chapel of Brown University, November 3, 1841* (Boston: Gould, Kendall and Lincoln, 1841), quoted in Mark S. Schantz, *Piety in Providence: Class Dimensions of Religious Experience in Antebellum Rhode Island* (Ithaca, NY: Cornell University Press, 2000), 124.

Struggle for the City

clesiology, which held that local churches are autonomous and make their own decisions without reference to church hierarchy, they tended to be, possibly, even more committed to democratic processes than even the Reformed and Lutherans. Wayland the Baptist then held to the necessity of free markets and the value of republican democracy as all being consistent with his interpretation of the Bible in its views on church, society, and government.

It was not Baptists alone who held such views, however. Methodists and Presbyterians weighed in on the matter with similar arguments. "Honest John Hogan" was a Missouri Methodist minister and a grocer, banker, railroad speculator, and manufacturer. By the mid-1800s he was also one of the *wealthiest* men in Missouri but remained a local Methodist pastor into his old age.[91] He defended his wealth by noting that he used his money to help others and that God had blessed him with it. By the 1840s Presbyterians had split into Old School and New School factions, generally over various theological issues including how one articulates the doctrine of original sin. Within both factions, however, one could have found those who saw America's new wealth as a *gift* from God and as something that could be used in his service. While they both issued stern warnings about the *danger* of wealth, especially for young men newly removed from the farm to the city, they agreed on the helpfulness of prosperity.

Philadelphia Old School pastor George Junkin, for instance, argued that the new manufacturing prosperity was not the farmer's "most sure market."[92] Almost identical advice was being given by figures such as fellow Philadelphian Albert Barnes and Henry Ward Beecher, men who were clearly identified with the progressive New School faction.[93] While it might seem, as we discussed earlier in the development of republicanism, that the new views were inimical to traditional Calvinist theology, even among the most orthodox there developed, mainly due to an appeal to natural law, a way to bring

---

91 Richard Carwardine, "Charles Sellers's 'Antinomians' and 'Arminians': Methodists and the Market Revolution" in *God and Mammon: Protestants, Money, and the Market, 1790–1860*, ed. Mark A. Noll (New York: Oxford University Press, 2001), 83–84.

92 Richard W. Pointer, "Philadelphia Presbyterians, Capitalism, and the Morality of Economic Success," in *God and Mammon*, 175.

93 George Marsden, *The Evangelical Mind and New School Presbyterianism: A Case Study of Thought and Theology in Nineteenth-Century America*, Yale Publications in American Studies 20 (New Haven, CT: Yale University Press, 1970), 67–103.

Struggle for the City

together what might be called the *Puritan ethic* and *Benjamin Franklin's* ideas about developing moral society.[94]

On the other side of the debate lay a group known to historians as the "contrarians."[95] Chief among them were Presbyterian layman and industrialist Stephen Colwell and sometime minister and educator Orestes Brownson. Colwell married into wealth and spent most of his adult life managing his father-in-law's iron foundries. But he traveled widely in Europe and there witnessed what he thought to be the *natural result* of political economy—a starving working class made of the many and an opulent ownership class made up of the very few. He believed the same thing was happening in the United States of America in the 1830s and '40s. He laid the blame for all of this on the explicit *self-centeredness* of Smith's approach. Tell people that satisfying their own interests and their own needs is appropriate and right, and they will do just that, and the devil take the *rest*. "It may be worth inquiring whether the principles upon which free trade is urged will not go far in their ultimate conclusions to dissolve the whole fabric of human society," he wrote at one point.[96] He opposed free trade, the division of labor, and the development of industrial technology. All of it, he was convinced, was evil and could not be reformed.

Orestes Brownson concurred with Colwell, at least in the early years of his writing.[97] Brownson loathed economic *inequality* during the period before 1840. He especially was angry at anyone who argued that God approved of such inequality in the name of progress and civilization.[98] He contended that the gospel *itself* was against any sense of inequality. The clerical economists had argued that class distinction is not important and that it may lie even in the providence of God. Brownson replied that social and economic inequality were created by men and that such inequalities must now be reversed in the name of progress, even if that meant an assault on *private property*. He was not opposed to private property *per se*, but he was against any kind of *hereditary* property. He was not, then, a communist, but did call for the state to reform all laws related to wealth

---

94 Pointer, "Philadelphia Presbyterians," 176.

95 Davenport, *Friends of the Unrighteous Mammon*, 107–38.

96 Stephen Colwell, "The Smithsonian Bequest," *Biblical Repertory and Princeton Review* 14, no. 2 (1842): 394–95, quoted in Davenport, *Friends of the Unrighteous Mammon*, 114.

97 Brownson was a man whose ideas seemed always in flux, and up to 1840 he was opposed to Smith's views, though after 1840 he was at least more friendly to them.

98 Fogel, *Fourth Great Awakening*, 320.

Struggle for the City

inheritance.[99] The basis for his views was primarily religious in nature—he believed the Bible was against the call to financial success.

Brownson and Colwell also had the advantage of calling to their aid Smith's own later disciples in economics both from England, Thomas Malthus and David Ricardo. Though they generally agreed with Smith's understanding of markets, these two men presented a *dour* outlook on the possibility of political economy raising a significant hope for higher standards of living for the future. Ricardo argued that in an economic system where there were three groups, landlords, capitalists (entrepreneurs), and workers, in the end *only* the landlords would prosper. This was due to what he called the "law of diminishing returns" (Ricardo coined the phrase), the idea that if wages went up, wealthier workers would have more children, which would mean more mouths to feed, and hence, higher costs. So, "in proportion as wages rose, profits would fall."[100] Malthus, an ordained Anglican minister and son of a well-to-do father, became famous for his views on population. He contended that populations grow *geometrically* but that agricultural output grows only *arithmetically*. Therefore, it was inevitable that population would soon (he believed within fifty years) outgrow food supplies and that there would be a massive food shortage, which in turn would cause war and revolution.[101]

Brownson and Colwell were thus able to bring Smith's own disciples into the debate on their side. All in all, they believed they had shown that if the best-case scenario came to pass, greed and inequality would reign in America, and if Ricardo or Malthus were correct, the situation would be far worse. They were not merely trying to bring a pessimistic, "Calvinistic" view of the darker side of sin to their advantage, but rather were making their case based on *economic* arguments. Their view had the earlier support of Francis Asbury, leading Methodist evangelist who had died in 1816, just as the "market revolution" (commonly dated 1815–46, from the end of the War of 1812 to the

---

99 Davenport, *Friends of the Unrighteous Mammon*, 137.
100 David Ricardo, *On the Principles of Political Economy and Taxation*, vol. 1 of *The Works and Correspondence of David Ricardo*, ed. Piero Sraffa (Cambridge: Cambridge University Press for the Royal Economic Society, 1951), 111.
101 Thomas Malthus, *An Essay on the Principle of Population*, ed. Anthony Flew (1798; New York: Penguin Books, 1985).

Struggle for the City

Mexican-American War) was getting started.[102] Asbury was deeply concerned about two things—ministers developing a love for and need for money, and ministers abandoning their circuit ministries for a more settled approach.

The clerical economists, then, supported America's rapid rise to industrial leadership and wealth and the philosophy that supported and informed that rise. The contrarians were opposed to such industrialization and wanted the US government to intervene. There was also a *third* group, identified by Davenport as the "pastoral moralists," a group less well-identified ideologically, but people who recognized the danger inherent in industrialization, free trade, and the division of labor, yet who were not *philosophically* opposed to it. Among them was William Arnot, who warned, "Among the elements of the nation's greatness lie the seeds of sure decay. The very abundance of our material resources, and the very excess of our mercantile enterprise, seem to be forcing into earlier maturity the vices that will lay our glory in the dust."[103] These pastoral moralists were ministers first, and so found themselves from time to time having to warn their people, pastorally, of the danger that lay in the accumulation of wealth. These men, including Presbyterian pastor Henry Boardman, Unitarian pastor Andrew Peabody, and Congregationalist pastor Joseph Emerson, were not ideologically opposed to capitalism but were concerned about what capitalism might become in the hands of entrepreneurs.

These were three responses to the rise of industrialization and to the philosophy that underlay it. All three responses were from antebellum American Christian leaders, some educators, some captains of industry, some pastors. What none of them suspected was that there was lurking in the shadows a much more strident voice, one that was not buttressed by quotes from the Bible, but one that would sound a clarion call against Smith's "capitalism." In the aftermath of America's great struggle from 1861 to 1865, that voice would gain a hearing. But war would come first, a war that concerned bodies and souls, prices and principles. The outcome is known to us, but it was not known to them that witnessed its coming.

---

102 David Hempton, "A Tale of Preachers and Beggars: Methodism and Money in the Great Age of Transatlantic Expansion, 1780–1830," in *God and Mammon*, 123–46; Carwardine, "Charles Sellers's 'Antinomians' and 'Arminians,'" 83.

103 William Arnot, *Race for Riches, and Some of the Pits into Which the Runners Fall: Six Lectures Applying the Word of God to the Traffic of Men* (Philadelphia: Lippincott, Grambo, 1853), 57–58, quoted in Davenport, *Friends of the Unrighteous Mammon*, 171.

Struggle for the City

Chapter 18

Economics and War

IN OUR NARRATIVE WE FIND ourselves in the early nineteenth century. We have seen America go through its *greatest* and most defining crisis—the American Revolution. We have also witnessed the degree to which Americans, with this vast landscape before them, turned the nation into a marvel of economic success, and at the same time we have observed that religion flourished, and especially flourished on the frontier (west of the Allegheny Mountains) with people approaching their faith in much the same way that they approached life and making a living—with earnestness. Before continuing with the story, we need to look at some developments in economics from Adam Smith to the time of America's *second* great defining crisis.

AFTER ADAM SMITH: CARRYING ON THE CONVERSATION IN THE HEAT OF THE NINETEENTH CENTURY

The science of "economics" was all the rage after Smith, and various thinkers in different parts of the world wanted to add their own touch to the work of Smith. The rapid development of industrialization and its impact on the social structure of, first England, and then America, and eventually other parts of Europe drove this passion for the new science. Not all of the developments were salutary, of course, and that very fact also contributed to the interest.

Smith's "Disciples"

Adam Smith had left a great legacy, but his "disciples" were a mixed lot. J. B. Say (1767–1832) was sometimes called "The French Adam Smith." Say was in many ways the only real disciple of Smith in his day, since his views not only were consistent with the Scottish philosopher but he actually *improved* on and *expanded* Smith's contribution.[1] First, he extolled the role of entrepreneurs in the economic world. The *entrepreneur* creates new products and develops ways of managing labor and resources. He finds efficient ways of doing these things in order to maximize profits, and maximized profits means *employment* for more people and *lower costs* for the consumer. Say also further expanded the understanding of the relation between supply and demand. "Supply creates its own demand" was the way Say put it.[2] This was an advance on the work that Smith had done, but fully consistent with Smith's own contribution.

Not all of Smith's followers would "do him proud," however. Smith had believed that a free-market economy would result in a rising economic status for virtually *all* thrifty and hard-working persons. But two British economists whom we have briefly discussed in a previous chapter were men who claimed his mantle but who took economics in a *different* direction. We will examine their work in more detail here. Thomas Malthus (1766–1834) was convinced that the one obstacle to Smith's belief that prosperity would come only if the markets were free was the problem of *population*. England's "first professor of political economy,"[3] Malthus argued that pressures on limited resources would keep people on the very edge of subsistence.[4] He argued that food production increases *arithmetically*, but that populations grow *geometrically*, and the *disparity* between the two would mean that in the future the prospects were bleak for human survival, let alone human

---

1   John Mueller, *Redeeming Economics* (Wilmington, DE: ISI Books, 2010), 71–72.
2   Mark Skousen, *The Making of Modern Economics*, 2nd ed. (Armonk, NY: M. E. Sharpe, 2009), 52–54. For the definitive study in our time of this subject, see Thomas Sowell, *Say's Law: An Historical Analysis* (Princeton, NJ: Princeton University Press, 1972).
3   Sylvia Nasar, *Grand Pursuit: The Story of Economic Genius* (New York: Simon & Schuster, 2011), 4.
4   Thomas Malthus, *An Essay on the Principle of Population*, ed. Antony Flew (1798; New York: Penguin Books, 1985).

improvement.[5] In his "law of population," Malthus contended that because of the "decreasing proportion of produce which must necessarily be obtained from the continual additions of capital applied to land already in cultivation," the end would be an ever-increasing shortage.[6] In other words, philosophically and ideally, he thought Smith was right, but because of the population problem, Malthus believed that Smith's views would never see *fulfillment*.

Charles Dickens lampooned Malthus' views in his *A Christmas Carol* (1843). Ebenezer Scrooge, upon being told that many poor people would rather die than go to the Poor Houses, replied, "If they would rather die, they had better do it, and decrease the surplus population."[7] Of course, as we know today, Malthus was *spectacularly* wrong. He had no way of anticipating that the technology of food production would advance to such a degree that we would be able, 150 years later, potentially to feed the entire world and even *twice* the population with the advanced technology that we now have. Not even Smith could have foreseen that, of course, but Smith expected that entrepreneurs would find ways to *solve* various problems that would arise to threaten the economy and that smart and incentivized people *would* solve those problems, unless governments interfered with the process. Irrigation techniques, new farming technology, genetic experimentation with farm products, and various other developments have all created a whole new *environment* in food production. Malthus, of course, could not have known what would happen.[8] Further, Malthus "had assumed that pay was strictly a function of the size of the labor force. More workers meant more competition among them, hence lower wages."[9] That is, he assumed that the economy was a *zero-sum* game, something that modern economists reject. His prophecies all went awry. Modern doomsayers need also to be informed that what has happened in the past to doom-and-gloom prophecies may well happen to the similar ones being made today and in the future.

David Ricardo (1772–1823) was a close friend of Thomas Malthus and was a firm believer in *free trade*. He was successful in encouraging the British

---

5   Nathan Rosenberg and L. E. Birdzell Jr., *How the West Grew Rich* (New York: Basic Books, 1986), 7.
6   Malthus, *Essay on the Principles of Population*, 225.
7   Quoted in Mueller, *Redeeming Economics*, 75.
8   Skousen, *Making of Modern Economics*, 82–86.
9   Nasar, *Grand Pursuit*, 38.

Struggle for the City

Parliament to repeal the Corn Laws in 1846, a high tariff on agricultural goods that the British had imposed many years earlier.[10] Yet, his overall impact on economics was in *contrast* to the impact of Adam Smith. He believed in the "labor theory of value," which was earlier introduced by Locke and which would later be a key component in Marxist thought. He argued that the theory of political economy proposed by Smith was partially true, but that it would lead to nothing more than subsistence wages for the vast majority of the population.[11] And, rather than believing that the political theory of economics actually could have practical benefits in the lives of common people, he saw it as little more than an analytical tool that scholars could use in the classroom. If it is possible to be damaged more by one's friends than one's enemies, Adam Smith probably was thus damaged by this tandem of Malthus and Ricardo. Thomas Carlyle, who knew the work of Malthus and Ricardo, was referring to their arguments when he labeled economics, "The Dismal Science."

Karl Marx

Enter Karl Marx. Marx is in many ways the *opposite* of Adam Smith. The Scotsman had argued that when every man pursues his own self-interests, "this would result in an outcome beneficial to all, whereas Marx argued that the pursuit of self-interest would lead to anarchy, crisis, and the dissolution of the property-based system itself."[12] Smith had a generally positive outlook on the human condition if only governments would honor man's "natural liberty." Smith believed that the "invisible hand" would boost everyone along and raise all ships, while Marx believed that the "iron fist of competition" would pulverize workers, even while it enriched those who owned the means of production.[13] Why was Karl Marx's outlook so gloomy, and how did he make the case for his view?

Karl Marx (1818–83) was born to a Jewish family in Trier, in the Kingdom of Prussia. Prior to his birth, his father converted to Lutheranism, in part

---

10 The tariff in 1846 stood at fifty percent. Nasar, *Grand Pursuit*, 33.
11 Mueller, *Redeeming Economics*, 70–71.
12 John E. Roemer, *Free to Lose: An Introduction to Marxist Economic Philosophy* (Cambridge, MA: Harvard University Press, 1988), 2.
13 Ibid., 3.

to advance his *career* as a lawyer. His mother converted later, and Karl himself was baptized at age six. His father wanted him to study law, but Karl was interested in studying philosophy at the University of Berlin. The shadow of Hegel still loomed large at the university there, but not everyone at Berlin was a faithful disciple of the great man's ideas.[14] The left-wing Hegelians consisted of a group of philosophers and writers whose central influences were Ludwig Feuerbach and Bruno Bauer, men who had opposed Hegel's metaphysical assumptions while still accepting his *dialectical method* as a tool for critiquing the prevailing conservative political and religious views of the time.[15] Hegel had substituted the concept of *Geist* (Spirit) for "God," but the Young Hegelians were convinced that this still kept the specter of religion in Hegel's system.[16] They wanted to eliminate that element *completely*, but the historical dialectic, the movement of history from one kind of culture, encountered by an alternative, with a new synthesis emerging from the conflict, was still important to them. They believed, however, that what drove this process was not some mysterious and ineffable *Geist*, but simply *history itself.*[17] Marx had also been heavily influenced by Ludwig Feuerbach, a left-wing Hegelian, who had held that Christianity (and other religions) make "God" in their image, and not the other way around.[18] As Friedrich Engels would comment, "In one blow it… placed materialism back upon the throne…. We were all for the moment Feuerbachians."[19] The combination of Hegel, especially a left-wing reading of him, and Feuerbach would determine the *course* of the movement.

---

14 Hegel died in 1831, several years before Marx arrived there to study. We will discus Hegel's philosophy in some detail later in this chapter and the next (chap. 19).

15 Mark Skousen, *The Big Three in Economics: Adam Smith, Karl Marx and John Maynard Keynes* (New York: M. E. Sharpe, 2007), 64–67.

16 James C. Livingston and Francis Schüssler Fiorenza, *Modern Christian Thought*, vol. 1, *The Enlightenment and the Nineteenth Century*, 2nd ed. (Minneapolis: Fortress, 2006), 229–35.

17 This also showed Marx's rejection of the Hegelian metaphysic, which was represented after Hegel by philosophers such as Friedrich Wilhelm Joseph Schelling, who doubted the real existence of the material, external world. It was against this "idealistic" position that the left-wing Hegelians took their stand. For them, the dialectical process was driven by historical, materialistic factors.

18 Livingston and Fiorenza, *Modern Christian Thought*, 1:222–26.

19 Karl Marx and Friedrich Engels, *Collected Works, 1845–47*, vol. 5: *Theses on Feuerbach, the German Ideology, and Related Works*, trans. Clemens Dutt, W. Lough, and C. P. Magill (New York: International Publishers, 1976), quoted in Saul K. Padover, *Karl Marx: An Intimate Biography* (New York: McGraw-Hill, 1978).

Struggle for the City

Once he finished doctoral studies, Marx went to work editing a political periodical in Prussia, but censorship issues caused him to resign and move to Paris, the central gathering place for revolutionaries from other parts of Europe. There he met Friedrich Engels, and the two collaborated on several books, most famously *The Communist Manifesto* in 1848. From 1845 to 1849 Marx lived, variously in Paris (twice), in Brussels, in Cologne, and finally, in London.[20] The various political revolutions in Europe in 1848 were the cause for much of this itinerancy, since several state and local governments expelled Marx for his radical views. The European powers were all in flux in the post-Napoleonic world due to the twin challenges of the need for a new political identity and the rise of industrialization in much of Europe, the net effect of which was the *displacement* of the inhabitants.[21] Arriving back in London in May 1849, Marx would remain there the rest of his life. In the early 1860s he began researching and writing a multivolume work, the final volume of which would not be published until after his death, a work known as *Capital* (*Das Kapital* in German).[22]

Marx's view of history was that history is driven by movement from the fragmentary to the complete, driven by individuals and movements that seek for such a completed system. It is a progressive unfolding that is mostly gradual, but that occasionally surges forward in a kind of leap that takes the world (or some part of it) to a whole new level of consciousness and experience.[23] He contended that the material world is what is *actually* real, that "God" is only a concoction of man, and that our ideas about the world are *consequences*, rather than causes, of the world around us.

In terms of economics, Marx believed that being *human* involves an effort at the *transformation* of the natural world around us. We do that by *labor*, and

---

20 Skousen, *Making of Modern Economics*, 137–38.
21 Michael Burleigh, *Earthly Powers: The Clash of Religion and Politics in Europe from the French Revolution to the Great War* (New York: HarperCollins, 2005), 112–43. See also the excellent study by Mike Rapport, *1848: Year of Revolution* (2008; repr., New York: Basic Books, 2010), esp. 1–41.
22 Marx in his correspondence called this work, "Outlines of a Critique of Political Economy." Nasar, *Grand Pursuit*, 14. See full citation of Marx's work in note 26.
23 Skousen, *Big Three in Economics*, 67–73.

Struggle for the City

so, one's labor power is crucial to a person's efforts at being truly human.[24] Marx contended that every economic system that had ever prevailed in civilization robbed the majority of people of their ability to do just that. The older *feudal* (manorial) system had granted the right of true humanity to only a handful of people, the *barons*, the *bishops*, and perhaps a few privileged others. (We know that *mercantilism* was an improvement over that since it gave a larger group of people economic power, but still limited it to a small group of elites, just not landed elites. Marx made no mention of mercantilism.) *Capitalism* was even better in that more people have some access to goods and services needed for happiness than was the case with either feudalism or mercantilism.[25] But capitalism, in Marx's view, was only *quantitatively* better than feudalism, not qualitatively. For Marx, capitalism overcame older economic forms when the majority of people began to sell their labor as a commodity because they no longer had land. Those who sell their labor are the *proletarians*; the ones who buy that labor are the *bourgeoisie*.[26] Those who own the means of production (the *bourgeois*) employ the workers to produce goods, goods that are sold in the market, and a *profit* is generated. Marx called that profit "surplus value" and argued that it was really owed to the workers, since it was their "surplus labor" that made it possible.[27] Profits were *inherently* unjust, in Marx's view, since the *owners* of the *means of production* did not generate them themselves. In some ways, this harks back to Thomas Aquinas' argument that profit in business is a *sin*; the difference is that Marx did not believe in sin.

The *new problem* of poverty in London began around 1750 when new inventions brought new jobs to the city. Of course, poverty itself was nothing new. But industrialization had brought a note of change. "In the coun-

---

24 As we have already shown in an earlier part of our study, this "labor theory of value" was first proposed by Locke, though he had a very different political motivation for this view.

25 The term *capitalism* was coined by Thackeray, but Marx used the term to refer to Smith's philosophy, and Marx's historical analysis is flawed in many ways. For one, as this volume has shown, there was a stage between feudalism and capitalism known as mercantilism, which was not acknowledged by Marx, though he did recognize that the feudal system underwent changes with the rise of a middle class in Europe.

26 Karl Marx, *Capital: A Critique of Political Economy*, vol. 1, trans. Ben Fowkes (1867; Eng. trans., 1887; New York: Penguin Books / London: New Left Review, 1976), 742.

27 Mueller, *Redeeming Economics*, 76; Marx, *Capital*, 1:555.

Struggle for the City

try, hunger, cold, disease, and ignorance appeared to be the work of nature. In the great capital of the world, misery seemed to be man-made, almost gratuitous."[28] Here, from about 1750 to about 1840 misery would often be the order of the day, since people were cramped together in squalid tenements with little or no public sanitation, eking out whatever miserable living they could. The power of industrialization had transformed the British economy; in real dollars the gross domestic product of England had *quadrupled* from 1750 to 1850, "growing more in a hundred years than in the previous thousand."[29] But the incomes of workers had risen only about thirty percent in that same period. That would change much for the better over the next several decades, but at the time of Marx's writing and research, conditions were deplorable.[30]

Capitalism, in Marx's view, has the ability to be a very powerful economic system because it is constantly improving the means of production.[31] It can do this because of the advances in technology and because it has so much surplus value to work with. Marx expected, though, that a crisis would come upon capitalism when profits would eventually fall even as the economy was growing. One crisis would eventually become many separate crises, and the resulting trauma would in the end collapse the system when the proletariat, out of frustration, would eventually rise up and wrest the means of production from the hands of the bourgeoisie. "The worse things got, he reasoned, the better the odds of revolution."[32] Marx and Engels argued that this eventuality was "inevitable."[33] "Workers of the world, unite!"

Karl Marx's solution to the problem engendered by capitalism was a *revolutionary socialism*, and in so doing, saw himself as exposing the doctrines of

---

28 Nasar, *Grand Pursuit*, 21.
29 Angus Maddison, *Statistics on World Population, GDP and Per Capita GDP, 1–2008 AD*, Groningen Growth and Development Centre, University of Groningen, Netherlands, http://www.ggdc.net/maddison/oriindex.htm (Original Maddison Homepage).
30 See the details in Nasar, *Grand Pursuit*, 26–40. It was much worse in London and Liverpool than in villages and the countryside because, in this age before the discovery of the germ theory of disease, people were thrown together and shared all things in common, including disease.
31 Skousen, *Making of Modern Economics*, 150–53.
32 Nasar, *Grand Pursuit*, 36.
33 Mueller, *Redeeming Economics*, 76.

Struggle for the City

Smith, Malthus, Ricardo, and other economists, as a "false religion, just as radical German religion scholars had exposed biblical texts as forgeries and fakes."[34] He opened his book *The Communist Manifesto*, coauthored with Friedrich Engels, with this line, "The history of all hitherto existing society is the history of class struggles."[35] Socialism was the new order of the day, and it had been invented by Germans.

Their solution to the ever-present process of class struggles entailed a *ten-point program*, summarized briefly in this way: (1) abolition of property in land, (2) a heavy progressive or graduated income tax, (3) abolition of all rights of inheritance, (4) confiscation of the property of emigrants and rebels, (5) centralization of all credit in the hands of the state, (6) centralization of the means of communication and transportation in the hands of the state, (7) extension of factories and instruments of production owned by the state (along with reclamation of waste lands by the state), (8) equal obligation of all to work, (9) combination of agriculture with manufacturing industries and the gradual abolition of the distinction between town and country, and (10) free education of all children in public schools.[36]

Every part of this program was important to Marx and Engels, but some of the items were more *crucial* than others. They truly believed that private property was the root cause of strife, class struggle, and even slavery. The point of the *Communist Manifesto*, and the Marx and Engels program in general, "was to prove 'with mathematical certainty' that the system of private property and free competition couldn't work and hence that 'the revolution must come.'"[37] They agreed with French anarchist Pierre-Joseph Proudhon, "Property is theft!"[38] They opposed *all* religion, believing that "religion is the opium of the people," since churches had used religion to keep workers from revolution for *generations*. They recognized that the means of accomplishing

34 Nasar, *Grand Pursuit*, 37.
35 Karl Marx and Friedrich Engels, *The Communist Manifesto*, trans. Samuel Morse, ed. Joseph Katz (1848; New York: Washington Square, 1964), 57. The book was first published in 1848, the "year of revolution."
36 Marx and Engels, *Communist Manifesto*, 94. They spell out their ten-step-program on this page.
37 Nasar, *Grand Pursuit*, 37.
38 Marx and Engels, *Communist Manifesto*, 82.

Struggle for the City

these goals would have to done through a *despotic* and *violent* overthrow of existing powers, but that the ends will justify the means.[39]

Marx and Engels were not alone in their advocacy of socialism/communism in the nineteenth century. Other philosophers were calling for similar changes in understanding how politics and economics should be construed and employed by intellectuals and by governments. None of this should come as a surprise to anyone who understands that millions of peasants had moved from farms to the cities, that those cities were initially *incapable* of accommodating the new inhabitants, and that unemployment was epidemic in most of the cities of Europe.[40] This refugee situation was very *different* from the one Calvin managed in the 1550s. For the moment it is important to note that Europe was gladly passing along its problems created by the Industrial Revolution, and American businesses were actively recruiting workers in Europe.[41]

This displacement caused many, at least a half-million persons a year after 1845, to emigrate to America.[42] This of course placed huge strains on the *resources* in the American cities, especially New York early on, then Detroit and Chicago, as they attempted to accommodate these huge numbers of mostly poor and unskilled new workers. Those willing to move west had less trouble since the country had vast resources to accommodate nearly an unlimited number of people.[43] But, as we have seen, that kind of life brought its own difficulties, at least to the first generation or two. So, we ought not to be surprised that a Marx would feel called to urge a new paradigm.[44] His voice was, in fact, similar to that of Charles Dickens, in whose books we find much the same situation as painted by the Prussian philosopher. Marx and Dickens gave similar analyses of the situation; the difference lay in their view of the future. For Marx the future was bleak and dark, with no possibility of societal redemption, while Dickens believed that Scrooge might be converted and share all good things with the Cratchits.

39 Ibid., 92.
40 Rapport, *1848*, 113.
41 Paul Johnson, *A History of the American People* (New York: HarperCollins, 1997), 514.
42 Howe, *What Hath God Wrought*, 822–27.
43 Johnson, *History of the American People*, 513–14.
44 Skousen, *Making of Modern Economics*, 227–46.

Struggle for the City

The American Economy at Midcentury

In 1850, midcentury, had the last president born before the Constitution, President Zachary Taylor, looked around himself, he would have witnessed a very different America from the one he had known as a boy. The fifty-year span of time was not without its bumps (two wars and several financial crises), but overall, it was a time of burgeoning growth.

The Politics of Economic Growth

In early nineteenth century America, the birth rate *exploded*. The 1800 census recorded just over 5.3 million Americans. By 1810 there were a little over 7.2 million citizens. In 1820 the numbers stood at a staggering 9.64 million. No nation in history had ever witnessed that kind of growth, and while some of it was due to immigration, the majority was from the vigorous expansion of large families that went with economic and religious intensity. One congressman from the period put it like this: "I invite you to go to the west, and visit one of our log cabins, and number its inmates. There you will find a strong, stout youth of eighteen, with his Better Half, just commencing the first struggle of independent life. Thirty years from that time, visit them again; and instead of two, you will find in that same family twenty-two. That is what I call the American Multiplication Table."[45] That trend continued at varying levels of pace throughout the nineteenth century, so that the population continued to grow about 35 percent per decade in this entire period.

The country followed what might be called a "Hamiltonian economic policy." That included tariffs, the formation of a central bank (a debated issue that would continue to be controversial for decades), the "use of public debt to provide a form of financial intermediation and to attract foreign capital," patent protection for inventors, encouragement of immigration to attract laborers, restrictions on use of foreign vessels for trade, and "related pro-industry, pro-

---

45 *Congressional Globe*, 29th Congress, 1st Session, January 10, 1846, 211, quoted in D. W. Meinig, *The Shaping of America: A Geographical Perspective on 500 Years of History, vol. 2, Continental America, 1800–67* (New Haven, CT: Yale University Press, 1993), 222, cited in Johnson, *History of the American People*, 283.

Struggle for the City

growth measures."[46] In implementing these policies, the country's first secretary of the treasury urged Congress to adopt policies of debt, high taxation, protectionism, and tax subsidies for business that had the potential for massive abuse in the future.[47]

Immigration was likewise trending upward. In contrast to the early colonial period when passage across the Atlantic was expensive and often purchased at the expense of becoming someone's servant for years, in 1800 passage was cheap. One could board a freight ship in Liverpool for a mere ten pounds. Water was provided, though not food, and when one arrived in New York, that person simply debarked the ship and went where he *wished*.[48] From 1810 to 1820 it has been estimated that one hundred thousand Europeans entered America without having to show a single piece of paper. That easy entrance into the nation ended in 1820, with laws passed after the country's first large-scale economic disaster.

The Panic of 1819 was *inevitable*. In 1791 Congress chartered a national bank (for twenty years) for handling issues related to credit, loaning money, and being an institution for investment. Both the government and individuals could borrow from this bank.[49] There was much debate about the wisdom of this, as we have noted, with the party of Jefferson being *opposed* to such an institution. With Jeffersonians in the majority in 1811 when the charter expired, they voted against renewing the charter.[50] Between 1816 and 1821 six new states were created. All of the states, seeing the need for banks, allowed for the creation of such institutions, "and they duly sprang up, good, bad, and indifferent (mostly the last two)."[51] States issued bank notes with little care to how many they printed. New England banks refused to take bank notes from the South, and Boston notes were constantly declining in value.[52]

---

46 Stanley L. Engerman and Robert E. Gallman, "The Emergence of a Market Economy before 1860," in *A Companion to 19th-Century America*, ed. William L. Barney (Oxford: Blackwell, 2001), 127.
47 Thomas J. DiLorenzo, *Hamilton's Curse: How Jefferson's Archenemy Betrayed the American Revolution—and What It Means for Americans Today* (New York: Crown Forum, 2008), 41.
48 Johnson, *History of the American People*, 284.
49 Jonathan R. T. Hughes and Louis P. Cain, *American Economic History*, 7th ed. (Boston: Pearson Addison Wesley, 2006), 235.
50 Ibid., 236.
51 Johnson, *History of the American People*, 285.
52 Hughes and Cain, *American Economic History*, 236–37.

Struggle for the City

The federal government realized that a crisis was brewing and chartered the Second National Bank in 1816, but it had *little* oversight. The rise in cotton prices caused the price of land to rise, but people only needed to put two percent down on the purchase while the bank financed the rest. Often, the bank even allowed purchasers to pay even the second installment (payments once per year) on credit, based on land value. Payments were often made with dubious paper money from somewhere out of state. These bills of exchange "raced around rapidly from one debtor to another, accumulating interest charges and yielding less and less of their face value…. It was a typical bit of nineteenth-century ruin-finance, beloved of Dickens and Thackeray, who used such devices to get their gullible heroes into trouble."[53] All that was needed was a financial *crisis* to tip the scales. That came in 1819.

Cotton buyers in Liverpool suddenly began purchasing Indian cotton, rather than American. The price of New Orleans cotton was cut in half.[54] This hit land prices, which dropped about 75 percent. The banks' collateral on all of those loans was suddenly worthless and they went out of business by the hundreds. By the year of the Panic, "the price of agricultural exports was less than half what it had been a year before."[55] Manufacturers were unable to secure loans and they went out of business. Of 2,325 cotton mills in Philadelphia in 1816, only 149 still remained in 1819.[56] This caused many in the nation to look askance at immigrants, since they represented competition for any sort of job one might find. But, such concerns were needless, since America recovered quickly from the economic bust, and within a year or two it was barely a blip on peoples' memory. One of the likely reasons the recession did not last was because the federal government was not yet "smart" enough to try to fix it! This Panic would, however, lead to Andrew Jackson's "war on Hamilton's bank, a war that he eventually won."[57]

If we look to one of those log cabins mentioned some paragraphs earlier, albeit a very fine specimen in this case, we can see something of the frontier

---

53 Johnson, *History of the American People*, 286.
54 Ibid., 287.
55 DiLorenzo, *Hamilton's Curse*, 68.
56 Johnson, *History of the American People*, 288.
57 DiLorenzo, *Hamilton's Curse*, 68.

Struggle for the City

American spirit at work. Henry Clay's transplanted hometown of Lexington, Kentucky, was a thriving crossroads, with a diversified economy in the first half of the nineteenth century.[58] Located in the fertile Bluegrass country of central Kentucky, it boasted the first *newspaper*, the first *library*, and the first *college*, Transylvania University, west of the Appalachians.[59] On his plantation, Ashland, just outside of the town, Clay grew hemp, with a labor force of fifty slaves. He also had part ownership of a rope factory in nearby Louisville that used his raw material. His career synthesized agriculture, commerce, and industry, and he sensed an impulse toward public service that would enable him to bring these concerns to fruition on a larger scale.[60] His desire was to create a harmony of various economic interests in Kentucky and in the nation at large, a system that he himself called, "The *American System*."[61]

The American System represented "a full-blown systemization of the Republican nationalism" that had come to expression in Madison's message to Congress after the War of 1812 had ended.[62] His first State of the Union address after that conflagration was sent to Congress on December 5, 1815, and included what later came to be known as the "Madison Platform."[63] He called for a (new) national bank that could offer credit for expanding markets (a change of tune for his political party), some restrictions (though not many) on imports, a plan for establishing roads and canals into western markets and resources, and low, virtually *no*, federal taxes on any domestic progress.[64] Governments would commit to build harbors, hasten industrialization, speed Western expansion, and bind the Union together.[65] It was this vision that had led to the building of the Erie Canal, such a huge boon to America's economic growth in the 1820s and '30s.

---

58 Clay had been born in Virginia, but moved to Kentucky in 1797, at age twenty.
59 Howe, *What Hath God Wrought*, 270.
60 Ibid.
61 Daniel Walker Howe, *The Political Culture of the American Whigs* (Chicago: University of Chicago Press, 1979), 123–49.
62 Howe, *What Hath God Wrought*, 270.
63 Joyce Lee Malcolm, "The Novelty of James Madison's Constitutionalism," in *James Madison and the Future of Limited Government*, ed. John Samples (New York: Cato Institute, 2002), 43–57.
64 Howe, *What Hath God Wrought*, 79–89.
65 Robert V. Remini, *Henry Clay: Statesman for the Union* (New York: W. W. Norton, 1991), 223–27.

Struggle for the City

Clay believed that the American System "constituted the economic basis for social improvement" that would not create "division between haves
and have-nots" but that would enable all to improve themselves.[66] Some assistance would come to farmers and planters from the federal government,
which would provide that assistance through rather high tariffs on imports[67]
and through sale of its vast holdings in land to corporations and others. This
assistance would be parted out to any who could qualify. The approach was
not completely laissez-faire and granted favored trade to other Western Hemisphere nations,[68] but it was "American" in the sense that it was based on the
belief that Americans were *entrepreneurial*, and even poor Americans, if given
a small boost, would find a way to prosper.[69]

American Successes in an Industrial Society

The American economy had experienced unrestrained growth overall, due at
least in part to Clay's "American System," although that growth had both negative and positive implications. The biggest negative implications had to do
with *slaves*, on whose backs much of the progress had been built but who had
experienced little benefit from it, and on Native Americans, who were forced
further and further into managed enclaves as a result of American success.[70]
The generation that fought the Revolution gradually abolished slavery north
of the Mason-Dixon line and the new northern states, such as Ohio, never
knew it. Meanwhile, slavery became even *more* necessary to the economy of
the South in years after the Constitution was ratified.

Both before and after the Panic of 1819, America's economy blazed forward. The Louisiana Purchase of 1803 provided much more territory for
Americans to utilize. Before that, America was about the size of Ireland, while

---

66 Howe, *What Hath God Wrought*, 270–71.
67 Understandably, this was the most controversial aspect of the plan.
68 This philosophy had been promoted by President Monroe and is known as the Monroe
    Doctrine. There was no "textbook" laissez-faire economic model in this period in America.
    Engerman and Gallman, "Emergence of a Market Economy," 132.
69 Maurice G. Baxter, *Henry Clay and the American System* (Lexington: University Press of
    Kentucky, 1995), esp. chaps. 4 and 5.
70 James M. McPherson, *Battle Cry of Freedom: The Civil War Era*, Oxford History of the
    United States 6 (New York: Oxford University Press, 1988), 6.

Struggle for the City

a few years after 1850, with the Mexican Cession to add, America was the most populous nation in the world with the exception of Russia and France.[71] America was being especially noticed for its progress in manufacturing in the years before the Civil War, especially in the making of firearms. The French had experimented with producing interchangeable parts for muskets as early as 1780, but those parts were made individually by skilled craftsmen. In 1851 American companies began making each part by a special-purpose machine that could make each one *exactly* the same every time, thus making truly interchangeable parts.[72] In 1854 Samuel Colt had told a committee of Parliament in England, "There is nothing that cannot be produced by machinery!"[73] That is a truism for us, but it was not so as recently as the mid-nineteenth century.

On the precipice of war, America was as prosperous as she had ever been. There was, of course, a dark underside to the belly of this beast. Its *philosophy*, racism, was rife throughout the nation. But its *economics*, slavery, was a purely sectional issue. If America's first national crisis was the Revolutionary War, it was about to face its second one when the elections of 1860 loomed on the horizon.

Upon the Altar of the Nation: The American Civil War

Many Americans in our time have forgotten the historical context in which the Civil War was fought, so we need to recreate some of that before the war can make any sense to us, if indeed it can even then. America, as we have discussed, was booming. Two large events had ceded to the Americans a land more vast than almost anyone in 1860 could really conceive. Entrepreneurial people were, though, moving quickly across the western and southwestern parts of the country and transforming the land into a settlers' paradise. Mormons had flooded into "Deseret" (Utah) beginning in 1847 and had quickly left the footprint of civilization on that large tract. Forty-niners and others in their wake were spread

---

71 Ibid., 9. The Mexican Cession was the territory ceded to the United States by the Mexican government at the Treaty of Guadalupe Hidalgo, the treaty that brought to an end the Mexican-American War of 1846–48.
72 Ibid., 15.
73 Eugene S. Ferguson, "Technology as Knowledge," in *Technology and Social Change in America*, ed. Edwin T. Layton Jr. (1973; New York: Joanna Cotler Books, 1974), 23–24.

up and down the California coast and many places farther inland from there. Small settlements had cropped up in Oregon, Washington, Wyoming, New Mexico, and the Dakotas. These people settling these new "territories" had every intention of following in the footsteps of Missouri, Kansas, Nebraska, Iowa, and other former territories in eventually becoming states. So, just how did those territories become states with full representation in Congress?

Preparing a Nation for War

In 1819 there were eleven slave states and eleven free states. A kind of balancing act had been taking place that kept parity between the two, since there was a sort of *gentleman's* agreement that would keep the Senate in parity, with equal numbers of senators from slave and free states.[74] The philosophy of slavery had been evolving since the late eighteenth century when many slaveholders voiced the position that, though they *kept* slaves, they did not *like* the institution and thought it likely to fade away. This had been the expressed position of slaveholding presidents such as Jefferson and Madison.[75] Southern slaveholders often felt the need to *apologize* for owning slaves. But by 1816 that was changing, largely because the South had so much money invested in slaves and because the institution of slavery was making so much of a return on its investment.[76] By the time James Monroe became president in 1820, many political leaders and Southern intellectuals were praising slavery, and a kind of "maturation of proslavery thought" came along so as to begin "the prolonged crisis of the Union."[77] Southerners had turned from *apologizing* for their unique institution to being its *apologists!*

By 1819 the territory of Missouri had acquired more than sixty thousand residents, the number required for statehood, and its residents petitioned Congress for that status in February of that year. The border between slave states and free states had been determined to be the southwestern boundary

---

74 Howe, *What Hath God Wrought*, 125–47.
75 Ibid., 261, 442, 587.
76 Johnson, *History of the American People*, 312.
77 Elizabeth Fox-Genovese and Eugene D. Genovese, *The Mind of the Master-Class: History and Faith in the Southern Slaveholders' Worldview* (New York: Cambridge University Press, 2005), 80.

Struggle for the City

of Pennsylvania, a boundary determined by English astronomers and survey-ors Charles Mason and Jeremiah Dixon in settling a dispute between Pennsylvania and Maryland, and so it was known ever after as the Mason-Dixon line.[78] That line existed in the minds of Americans all the way to the Mississippi River, but it had not yet been extended into the lands of the Louisiana Purchase. Missouri's petition would take it there, if granted, since Missouri was home to about ten thousand slaves, though the Mason-Dixon line cut the territory in two.

In response to the request from Missouri a New York congressman introduced an antislavery bill that would have prevented this decision, and it passed in the House, but predictably, not in the Senate. John Quincy Adams and John C. Calhoun famously battled this out, with Adams arguing that the South ought to be allowed to *secede* from the Union and just end the matter right there, and with Calhoun asserting that parity ought to remain and that the South, for now, was *still* in the United States of America.[79] It is small surprise that this debate would be held by senators from Massachusetts and South Carolina, the two most *radical* and *polarized* states in their respective sections of the country.

It was Henry Clay of Kentucky who worked behind the scenes to engineer a proposal that the best solution was a compromise that allowed Missouri to come into the Union as a slave state, but that for every slave state a free state be admitted, and vice versa.[80] In this case, Missouri would come in, and so would a new northern state in which Maine would be carved out of the northern part of Massachusetts. The bill stipulated that no new slave states would be organized in the northern parts of the Louisiana Purchase. This became known of course as the Missouri Compromise (1820), and it settled the waters, sort of, for at least a while. But it also resulted in the "Denmark Vesey" slave rebellion in South Carolina, in the "upsurge in attention to slavery nationally," and in being a *harbinger*, though no one could predict it at the time, of the Civil War.[81]

---

78 Johnson, *History of the American People*, 317.
79 Howe, *What Hath God Wrought*, 154–60.
80 Ibid., 151–56.
81 Mark Noll, *God and Race in American Politics: A Short History* (Princeton, NJ: Princeton University Press, 2008), 30.

Struggle for the City

By the 1830s in the North, abolitionist sentiment was growing under the leadership of editorialist William Lloyd Garrison of Boston and others. Great Britain ended its experiment with slavery in 1833. Driven by William Wilberforce and his "first great object" (we might say, "objective"), that is, of eliminating the slave *trade* in Britain and its colonies, the battle was long and difficult. Wilberforce experienced an evangelical conversion in 1787, and from that point on, as a member of Parliament, he worked year in and year out to abolish slave trading. Year after year he brought motions, made long (as long as four-hour) speeches detailing the horrors and inequities of the trade, was defeated over and over again, until finally on February 23, 1807, he accomplished his goal, a twenty-year-long battle that ended the slave trade.[82] He would also live to see the end of slavery altogether in Britain. William Gladstone, future prime minister of England, visited the aging Wilberforce on July 25, 1833, and informed him that the very next day a bill would be introduced in Parliament to bring slavery to an end in the British Empire. That bill would pass, and *two days later* the man most responsible for ending slavery in Great Britain died near his family.[83] But slavery was not dead in America, though voices calling for *abolition* grew steadily after the British ended slavery.

Abolitionist sentiment spiked dramatically after Congress passed the Fugitive Slave Law in 1850, a component of the Compromise of 1850 in which California was admitted into the Union as a free state, *without* the admission of a corresponding slave state. The Constitution already contained language providing for the return of runaway slaves if they were found in other states, but it made no provision for how that was to happen. A 1793 law allowed slaveholders to pursue their slaves across state lines and to bring the matter before local magistrates to prove their claim.[84] The federal law made no provisions for *habeas corpus* or the rights of slaves to defend themselves in court, though several Northern states passed their own legislation to keep matters from getting out of hand. The Fugitive Slave Act of 1850 stated that US marshals were required to assist slaveholders or professional slave catchers to carry

---

82 Kevin Belmonte, *Hero for Humanity: A Biography of William Wilberforce* (Colorado Springs: NavPress, 2002), 101–49.
83 Ibid., 325–26.
84 McPherson, *Battle Cry of Freedom*, 78.

Struggle for the City

out their task, or risk a fine of $1,000.[85] The stipulations of the statute seemed to most Northerners at the time to be rigged in favor of the slaveholders and not the alleged slaves.[86] Indeed, in the decade of the 1850s, 332 slaves were returned and only eleven declared free.[87]

The Slave Law incited abolitionist sentiment and sent it into *fever* pitch in England, but more importantly in places like Boston and Philadelphia. By this time in England there was real "abhorrence" of Negro slavery, seventeen years after its abolition.[88] Then, when slave catchers came to Boston to retrieve two escaped slaves, abolitionist pastor Theodore Parker hid them in his house and vowed that he would shoot to kill anyone who tried to retrieve them. He stated, "I would rather lie all of my life in jail, and starve there, than refuse to protect one of these parishioners of mine."[89] William Lloyd Garrison wrote one editorial after another calling the law a *scandal*, and he was joined by Frederick Douglass, "a self-taught former slave and militant abolitionist orator without peer."[90] Charles Finney, former evangelist turned college professor and then president, was also a committed abolitionist. These men were joined by Harriet Beecher Stowe, daughter of famed Congregationalist pastor, Lyman Beecher, and sister of the New York pastor, Henry Ward Beecher, probably the most famous preacher in the North, when in 1852 she published *Uncle Tom's Cabin*, a novel about the misery of slavery. It was a publishing *sensation*. When Lincoln met her in 1862 he reportedly offered, "So you're the little woman who wrote the book that made this great war."[91] She at least contributed much to antislavery sentiment.

---

85 Holman Hamilton, *Prologue to Conflict: The Crisis and Compromise of 1850* (Lexington: University Press of Kentucky, 1964), 204–8.

86 McPherson, *Battle Cry of Freedom*, 80.

87 Ibid., 80.

88 David Goldfield, *America Aflame: How the Civil War Created a Nation* (New York: Bloomsbury, 2011), 83. Many Southerners believed the abhorrence for slavery expressed by the English was contrived as a ruse to break up the Union. Ironic!

89 Theodore Parker to Millard Fillmore, November 21, 1850, Boston, quoted in Philip S. Foner, *History of Black Americans*, vol. 1: *From Africa to the Emergence of the Cotton Kingdom*, Contributions in American History 40 (Iowa City, IA: Praeger, 1975), 37, cited in McPherson, *Battle Cry of Freedom*, 82.

90 Harry S. Stout, *Upon the Altar of the Nation: A Moral History of the Civil War* (2006; New York: Penguin Books, 2007), 1.

91 Quoted in Thomas F. Gossett, *Uncle Tom's Cabin and American Culture* (Dallas: Southern Methodist University Press, 1985), 166.

Struggle for the City

War seemed close at hand from 1854–56. Stephen A. Douglas, senator from Illinois, proposed legislation that would establish a large new state out of the Nebraska Territory, but in keeping with the (spirit of the) Missouri Compromise, it would be divided into two states with the southern one, Kansas, being allowed to *determine* its own slave or free soil destiny by "popular sovereignty," that is, a vote of its founding settlers.[92] His rationale was that this process would facilitate the construction of a transcontinental railroad since it would bring people into the new states.[93] The problem was that the Compromise of 1820 stipulated no slave states in the northern parts of the Louisiana Purchase, so that part of the 1820 Compromise would have to be repealed by a new bill, a bill that was presented in and passed Congress, the Kansas-Nebraska Act of 1854. Both slavers and antislavers moved into the new state of Kansas, but at the first election the slavers won by a landslide, though there were many examples of fraudulent voting. They then installed their own governor and legislature and made it a *crime* to harbor fugitive slaves, a crime punishable by death, along with another law making it a felony to question slave-holding in Kansas.[94] The antislavers organized (unlawfully) their own constitutional convention, elected another governor and legislature, and set about to battle with the slavers. Bible-thumping antislavery clergymen from the North proved "expert gun-runners, especially of what were known as 'Beecher's Bibles,' rifles supplied by the bloodthirsty congregation of the Rev. Henry Ward Beecher."[95] Slavers *sacked* Lawrence, the capital city for the antislavers, and burned the governor's house. The antislavers compared that attack to the sack of Rome by the Visigoths.[96] In response an antislaver named John Brown attacked a pro-slave settlement in the state and killed five men in cold blood.[97] "Bleeding Kansas" became in essence a preview of what was to follow half a decade later.

Dred Scott was a slave. His owner was an army surgeon named John Emerson. Billeted in various places, including what later became Minnesota and Illinois, Emerson took Scott with him. After Emerson died, Scott's friends en-

---

92 Goldfield, *America Aflame*, 95–104.
93 Johnson, *History of the American People*, 427.
94 McPherson, *Battle Cry of Freedom*, 146; Goldfield, *America Aflame*, 113.
95 Johnson, *History of the American People*, 429.
96 Goldfield, *America Aflame*, 114.
97 For a careful examination of all of this, see McPherson, *Battle Cry of Freedom*, 145–69.

Struggle for the City

couraged him to sue for freedom from Emerson's widow on the grounds that he had spent two years in a free state and two more years in free territory. He sued in St. Louis and won the first two cases, but had the decision overturned by the Missouri Supreme Court.[98] It then passed to a federal appeals court, which upheld the Missouri ruling. Scott's attorneys then appealed to the highest court in the land, which took the case and gave a ruling in February 1857.[99]

The US Supreme Court, led by Southerner Robert Taney, had a majority of Southerners, along with one "doughface," a term coined in the Missouri debates to refer to Northerners who voted the way Southerners voted. President-elect Buchanan saw this case as an opportunity "to resolve the slavery extension issue that had poisoned congressional debate and plagued administrations from James K. Polk forward," and he, in clear violation of the *separation of powers*, then "corresponded with two associate justices of the Supreme Court and chatted with the chief justice to the effect that it would be really nice if they could put this problem to rest once and for all."[100] The court upheld the appeals court ruling that Scott could not be freed, but went one step further and declared that blacks could not be citizens. Since blacks were not part of the "sovereign people" who made the Constitution, "they were not included in the 'all men' whom the Declaration of Independence proclaimed 'created equal.'"[101] Most of the nation was flabbergasted by this ruling, but it became the law of the land. President Buchanan, who was inaugurated only two days before the court handed down its decision (he knew ahead of time what was coming), could not have been more *pleased*, but the sweeping decision had the effect of rendering the Missouri Compromise theoretically *unconstitutional*, and of mandating that neither Congress nor state legislatures could ban slavery *in any event*.[102] The country was inching closer to the moment of decision.[103]

---

98 The case initially went to court in Missouri in 1847, but the appeals process dragged out nearly ten years. Goldfield, *America Aflame*, 139.
99 The full narrative is found in McPherson, *Battle Cry of Freedom*, 170–81.
100 Goldfield, *America Aflame*, 139.
101 McPherson, *Battle Cry of Freedom*, 174.
102 Goldfield, *America Aflame*, 140. The decision caused an eventual drop in railroad stocks, since Americans were now fearful of migrating to Kansas and Nebraska, for fear that the "blood on the plains" would erupt into full-scale war. A major economic recession hit the nation within months of the ruling.
103 This all makes it clear that "without the problem of the West the sectionalization of American politics would either have proceeded very differently or not at all." John

Struggle for the City

Only one element remains in our "background to the war" discussion: the presidential election of 1860. In 1858 Abraham Lincoln ran for the Senate seat of Stephen A. Douglas, and though he lost the race, the seven public debates between him and Douglas put him in the public eye of all Americans.[104] The most important thing they learned about Lincoln was that he was *adamantly* opposed to extending slavery into the remaining territories.[105] In fact, Lincoln let it be known in the election campaign that he would be willing to give to slaveholders major *concessions*. He was even willing to support a constitutional amendment that would guarantee the right of the South to their slaves into *perpetuity* and he supported colonization in Africa for those who were freed, but he would not support the right of states to secede from the Union, and he would not allow expansion of slavery further into the territories.[106] Kansas was the last of that.

The 1860 election was something of a very messy party with four presidential candidates on the ticket. The Northern Democrats nominated Stephen Douglas, but the Southern Democrats would not have him, so they nominated Kentuckian John C. Breckinridge on a proslavery ticket. The Whigs took another shot (their last) at the presidency and nominated John Bell of Tennessee. The Republicans nominated Lincoln, who won the presidency against the split Democrat ticket, a split that resulted in political suicide for the Democratic party.[107] Since Lincoln's position on slavery in the territories was so well known and so firmly held, the Southern states felt they had no option. On December 20, 1860, South Carolina *seceded* from the Union. The two major issues they listed as *rationale* were that states had the right to determine their own destinies over against an intrusive federal government and that Lincoln's refusal to extend slavery into the territories would eventually weaken the South's position. Ten more states would follow South Carolina in the ensuing months.

Ashworth, "The Sectionalization of Politics, 1845–1860," in *A Companion to 19th-Century America*, 28.

104 Allen C. Guelzo, *Lincoln and Douglas: The Debates That Defined America* (New York: Simon & Schuster, 2008), 89–182.

105 Johnson, *History of the American People*, 444.

106 Stout, *Upon the Altar of the Nation*, 14.

107 Johnson, *History of the American People*, 450.

Struggle for the City

President Lincoln would be forced to decide whether he was willing to let the Southern states go. If he let them go, the United States would be smaller by nearly one-half in territory and one-third in population, but it would not be faced with dealing with slavery on the same scale as it did when the Confederate states were in the Union.[108] To bring them back would mean an *invasion* of the South. The South, for her part, was hopeful that Lincoln would do nothing and just let them go. At first, many voices in the North were content to let the Southerners leave.[109] But not Lincoln. He was deeply committed to preserving the Union, no matter what! Of course, in early 1861, no one had any idea what would be entailed in the "no matter what!" They would soon find out. His first significant offensive would come in July and would take place near a Virginia town named Manassas, the Battle of Bull Run, the first battle of a war that would last nearly four bloody years.

It is not in our purpose to chronicle the Civil War, any more than we told the narrative of the Revolutionary War. But we do wish to give some analysis of the churches and their relationship to the war as well as a few final numbers.

Churches in North and South during the Civil War

For decades preachers in America had debated whether or not the Bible encouraged or even *condoned* slavery. The issue is complicated, and we deal with the hermeneutical and biblical questions on slavery in what follows in this chapter, but the point is that preachers and theologians in the nineteenth century came to differing conclusions, with some noting that the Bible allows slavery and others that it did not.[110] For American Protestants at midcentury, what the Bible articulated as truth *was* truth. The "evangelical community" in America had always emphasized the fact that "the Bible is the Word of God

---

108 Four states that allowed slavery did not secede: Missouri, Kentucky, Maryland, Delaware. Had there been no war, those states likely would have kept the institution of slavery for some years to come and remained in the Union.
109 McPherson, *Battle Cry of Freedom*, 246–50.
110 Some of the key combatants on the proslavery side were Baptist Richard Furman, Presbyterian James Henley Thornwell, and even *Northern* Bible scholar Moses Stuart. Those on the antislavery side included Henry Ward Beecher, Charles Finney, and Tayler Lewis.

Struggle for the City

in a cognitive, propositional, factual sense."[111] "If the Bible was God's revealed word to humanity, then it was the duty of Christians to heed carefully every aspect of that revelation."[112] Even when German scholarship was calling those things into question, and the British began a slow drift of following in their steps, American evangelicals were holding firm. Not all American churchmen, of course. The Puritan Congregationalists had begun the drift into Unitarianism in the latter third of the eighteenth century, and the German scholarship was encouraging some of them to continue that trend. Edward Everett was the first American scholar to earn a PhD in a German university, and in 1820 he brought German biblical criticism to Harvard.[113] By 1852 Congregationalist minister and theologian Horace Bushnell was calling for a new understanding of the Bible that brings it into alliance with *poetry* and that to take it literally or to believe in its infallibility was a mistake.[114] Bushnell called for a rejection of the "old theology" (orthodoxy) and the substitution of a new theology in which the Bible is mined only for its images and in which Trinitarianism and orthodox Christology are replaced with an "instrumental" view.[115] It is *stunning* to imagine that the denomination that claimed John Cotton and Jonathan Edwards would be the *first* in America to slide into liberalism! But Presbyterians, Methodists, and Baptists, the three largest Protestant denominations in 1850, were committed to the inspiration of the Bible, "from Genesis to maps."

The slavery conflict began to *change* all of that. By 1860 some few American elites were abandoning the Bible as a source for knowledge, truth, and morality. Some of the first such Americans included jurist Oliver Wendell Holmes Jr., elite literati like William Dean Howells, and politicians like William Henry Trescot.[116] William Lloyd Garrison, the abolitionist we have cited previously in our study, was not quite so negative toward the Bible as those

---

111 Mark A. Noll, *Between Faith and Criticism: Evangelicals, Scholarship, and the Bible in America*, Confessional Perspectives (San Francisco: Harper & Row, 1986), 6.

112 Mark A. Noll, *America's God* (New York: Oxford University Press, 2002), 386–87.

113 Paul C. Gutjahr, *Charles Hodge: Guardian of American Orthodoxy* (Oxford: Oxford University Press, 2011), 88–89.

114 Livingston and Fiorenza, *Modern Christian Thought*, 1:108.

115 Robert Bruce Mullin, *The Puritan as Yankee: A Life of Horace Bushnell*, Library of Religious Biography (Grand Rapids, MI: Eerdmans, 2002), 63–64, 134–37, 149–50, 157–60.

116 Mark A. Noll, *The Civil War as a Theological Crisis* (Chapel Hill: University of North Carolina Press, 2006), 31.

Struggle for the City

men, but he made it clear that "[t]o say that everything in the Bible is to be believed, simply because it is found in that volume, is... absurd and pernicious."[117] This conviction allowed Garrison to *discard* texts from the Bible that seemed to promote slavery as a benign or at least as a neutral matter.[118] No one would ever accuse Garrison of being either *benign* or *neutral* toward slavery! In 1860 and 1861 American Christian people were forced to decide what they believed the Bible *taught* about slavery. Even though the war early on was not a war for abolition but for restoring *Union*, no Southerners and few Northerners could retain an attitude of neutrality to what many believed to be the cause of the war that was killing its boys and eventually its civilians.[119]

The problem was for them, the question, "How do you know who's right on the question of slavery in the Bible?" Equally scholarly people stood on both sides of that hermeneutical question, North and South, Baptist and Methodist, Presbyterian and Catholic. James Henry Thornwell, Southern Presbyterian, had written, "The Scriptures not only fail to condemn slavery, they as distinctly sanction it as any other condition of man. The Church was formally organized in the family of a slaveholder [Abraham]."[120] *This* was the theological crisis. "The theological crisis of the Civil War was that while voluntary reliance on the Bible had contributed greatly to the creation of American national culture, that same voluntary reliance on Scripture led only to deadlock over what should be done about slavery."[121] The failure to find a solution would lead many of the denominations in America in the next decades to begin to doubt the intrinsic *authority* of Scripture, doubts that were flying over Europe already, but doubts that would have a new *twist* in the American context *because* of the Civil War.[122]

117 William Lloyd Garrison, *Liberator* 15 (1845): 186, quoted in Wendell Phillips Garrison and Francis Jackson Garrison, *William Lloyd Garrison, 1805–1879: The Story of His Life, vol. 3, 1841–1860* (New-York: Century, 1885), 146, cited in Noll, *Civil War as a Theological Crisis*, 31.
118 Noll, *Civil War as a Theological Crisis*, 32.
119 McPherson, *Battle Cry of Freedom*, 234–75.
120 James Henry Thornwell, *The Collected Writings of James Henry Thornwell, vol. 4, Ecclesiastical*, ed. John B. Adger and John L. Girardeau (Richmond, VA: Presbyterian Committee of Publication, 1873), 385; quoted in Thomas A. Askew and Peter W. Spellman, *The Churches and the American Experience* (Grand Rapids, MI: Baker, 1984), 117.
121 Noll, *Civil War as a Theological Crisis*, 159.
122 There were also mediating figures in the controversy, such as Charles Hodge, who believed that Africans were inferior to whites, but who hoped for an improved situation in the

Struggle for the City

A secondary issue on the biblical and ethical question of slavery is that the discussions of it were often not well *nuanced*, on either side. Southerners who defended slavery on the grounds that it was allowed in the Old Testament failed to note that so-called *biblical* slavery was not *race-based*.[123] In the OT also, slavery was generally not lifelong servitude but was only *temporary*. Abolitionists also failed to be nuanced, arguing that New Testament salvation *demands* abolition, yet forgetting Paul's words to Philemon regarding his returned runaway but now Christian slave Onesimus.[124] In the heat of battle, many words were uttered, but there was often a lack of *clear thinking* on the matter on both sides of the debate. That was the *theological crisis* over Scripture that was raised, and as we shall see in a bit, this predicament lingered on *after* the war and created a *crisis of authority* in the major Christian denominations. In fact it may have been the *defining* epistemological issue in the distinctly American denominations in the years after the war.

What kind of day-to-day impact did the war have on Christians and Christian churches? In a much greater way than in the North, Southerners were called upon to see the new Confederate government as a *God-inspired*, God-anointed government. The Constitution of the United States did not even mention God, but the Confederate Constitution explicitly declared its Christian identity, "invoking the favor and guidance of God."[125] The national motto was *Deo Vindice*, "with God as our defender." Northern Christians began to agitate in sermons and editorials for the United States to follow suit, but there was little will to do that in Congress. Southerners contrasted their document with the one that had been written by infidels and *deists*.[126] "This meant that the South was now in a position more analogous to that of ancient Israel with its theocratic constitution or to Puritan New England than to the North."[127] The Confederate army was like Israel, under Gideon, fighting the Midianites. Most of the war was waged in the South, with the significant exceptions of Antietam and Gettysburg. The

---

future. David Torbett, *Theology and Slavery: Charles Hodge and Horace Bushnell* (Macon, GA: Mercer University Press, 2006), 88–90.

123 Noll, *Civil War as a Theological Crisis*, 63.

124 Ibid., 33, 40. We have already considered these texts in our biblical discussion in part 1.

125 Stout, *Upon the Altar of the Nation*, 47.

126 Ibid., 48. That was *their* claim, though we reject it as a general assessment.

127 Ibid., 47.

Struggle for the City

South, like Israel, faced a much larger force, a force that, then as now, attacked Israel from the *north* (Judg.7:1).[128] At least that was its self-perception.

The South also called for far more *fast days* than did the North. Over the course of the war, Jefferson Davis called for *ten* fast days, Lincoln only for *three*.[129] The South pursued its fast days with more fervor, shutting down all commerce, all schools, and the people committing themselves to religious services. Soldiers in the South, along with civilians, were instructed to live more righteous lives to bear out the justice of their cause.[130] Southern preachers revived the jeremiad sermons that had been the stock of Puritans in the early colonial period, as we have already discussed.[131] Again, in the North fasts were also held, and one in the city of Boston, for instance, was taken very seriously with all businesses closing.[132] The Congregationalist Unitarians may have shed their doctrine of the Trinity, but they still remembered their Puritan roots. New York City was another matter; commerce there never ceased, but churches still observed the fast days. One of Lincoln's informants expressed concern that the Confederate soldiers were "praying with a great deal more earnestness" than his own troops."[133] Perhaps, and perhaps, over the course of the war, they needed to.

Many Christian ministers and theology professors from the (now empty) religious colleges came and worked as chaplains. One such Confederate chaplain, Robert Bunting, kept a diary of his daily activities, and virtually every day contains records of prayer meetings, writing letters for soldiers, Bible study, attendance upon the sick, mail delivery, and preaching.[134] He asked for strict adherence to his spiritual regimen from his brigade and reported that his men all attended every service, with the exception of about a dozen who preferred gambling to church services.[135] In the winter of 1863-64 a great revival broke out among the Confederate soldiers at Orange Courthouse, Virginia. Estimates vary from 100,000 thousand to 200,000 conversions occurring in both armies

---

128 Daniel W. Stowell, *Rebuilding Zion: The Religious Reconstruction of the South, 1863–1877* (New York: Oxford University Press, 1998), 37.
129 Stout, *Upon the Altar of the Nation*, 48–50.
130 Goldfield, *America Aflame*, 319.
131 Stout, *Upon the Altar of the Nation*, 49. See our discussion of Puritan preaching in chap. 14.
132 Ibid., 76.
133 Askew and Spellman, *Churches and the American Experience*, 121.
134 Stout, *Upon the Altar of the Nation*, 214–15.
135 Ibid., 215.

Struggle for the City

during the years of the war.[136] Men in such circumstances often find themselves susceptible to the prompting of the Spirit. Others become more and more bitter.

Those killed in battle were often seen as *martyrs*. This came sooner to Southerners since they believed they had been wrongfully invaded by Lincoln's army. Their young men were doing the "Lord's work."[137] The idea came slower to the North, primarily because Lincoln had prosecuted the war as a means of returning the Confederacy to the Union. It was a war waged to maintain the American identity that had been carved out, not in the Constitution, but in the *Declaration of Independence*, that all men are created equal.[138] That was Lincoln's "Bible," his defining text, and that defining text drove him to use whatever means he had to return America to that standard— *all* of America. But somewhere during the first two years of the war the focus turned to the *abolition* of slavery, and when that happened, Northern casualties could *also* be seen as martyrs. "They were willing to transform death into martyrdom if it was grounded ethically in abolition."[139] The war created too many of these martyrs.

The need for charity abounded during and after the war. In 1861 the United States Sanitary Commission was organized, under the leadership of Unitarian minister Henry Bellows.[140] "Commission workers cared for the sick and wounded, provided food for soldiers, and drove ambulance wagons."[141] The American Bible Society provided every Union and every Confederate soldier with Bibles. The United States Christian Commission was formed out of the YMCA to distribute religious and popular literature to word-hungry soldiers. As the Union army pushed farther into the South, there was need to care for blacks who were now destitute. Voluntary societies stepped up and offered help.[142] None of these was operated by any government bureaucracy, and all were managed by churches through donations given by individuals.

One theological issue American Christians faced in the war was how to continue to construe their doctrine of the *providence of God*. The people prayed for the

---

136 Askew and Spellman, *Churches and the American Experience*, 121.
137 Stout, *Upon the Altar of the Nation*, 86–91.
138 Ibid., xix, 29.
139 Ibid., 82.
140 Askew and Spellman, *Churches and the American Experience*, 122.
141 Ibid.
142 Ibid.

Struggle for the City

battles—one group of Americans praying for Confederate victory and another for Union victory on the field of battle. Most of the battles were won by one side or the other, one sign that this first modern war was different from most of the battles from older times. Confederates scored the first victory, then had some setbacks, then regained ground and it was back and forth through 1862, with victories for the South at Seven Days, loss at Stones River, and strategic loss at Antietam.[143] The Confederates did well in 1863 at Chickamauga and Chancellorsville, but also lost major battles at Gettysburg, Vicksburg, and Chattanooga.[144] Then the tide turned against the Confederacy in 1864 with inconclusive larger battles, but with a loss of the *means* to continue the war.[145] Both sides invoked the same God, asking him to help their cause and at the end of the day recognizing, whatever the outcome, that his will was done. Over and over they did this.

Southern Presbyterian John Adger, once the war was over, went to great lengths to insist on "the justice of the Southern cause," but also conceded that "there was one error… into which we acknowledge that some Southern ministers sometimes fell." That error was to believe "that God must surely bless the *right*." What the Southerners had learned through the disposition of the war was that God often lets "the righteous… be overthrown." Godly ministers may pray, but the outcome is left with God. His conclusion was, "Yes! the hand of God, gracious though heavy, is upon the South for her discipline."[146] In some places, Christian fervor waned, and the "carnage turned soldiers and civilians away from theological explanations, if not from their faith."[147] It was not simply faith in the Bible that was at stake for Civil War America, but faith in God himself.

A related issue had to do with military *protocol* in relation to civilians and how the churches would cope with that. The army leaders on both sides had been trained at West Point, believed the same doctrines of war, understood the same tactics and strategies in battle. One of their deepest held convictions was

---

143 McPherson, *Battle Cry of Freedom*, 464–78, 580–83, 538–44.
144 Ibid., 672–76, 639–45, 647–63, 627–38, 678–81.
145 Ibid., 689–830.
146 John Adger, "Northern and Southern Views of the Province of the Church," *Southern Presbyterian Review* 16, no. 4 (March 1866): 398–99, 410, quoted in Noll, *Civil War as a Theological Crisis*, 77–78.
147 Goldfield, *America Aflame*, 320. Revivals in Mobile, Alabama, fell flat in 1864, perhaps out of a foreboding sense that the end was near.

Struggle for the City

that war was for *soldiers*, not for civilians.[148] This conviction held for the first year-and-a-half. In October 1862 William Tecumseh Sherman, attempting to hold on to his victory in Memphis, sustained a series of guerrilla attacks from Confederate fighters. In response he destroyed the town of Randolph, Tennessee. When the next attack came he destroyed all homes, farms, and crops along a fifteen-mile stretch south of Memphis. "When a Memphis woman objected, Sherman replied that God Himself had destroyed entire populations for far lesser crimes."[149] This would be especially the lesson learned late in the war through Sherman's march to the sea, exercising a final "vengeance upon South Carolina" for starting this whole mess.[150]

One more thing needs to be said before we make a few comments about the economic impact of the war and then move on. The Civil War was, as we indicated earlier, the *second* defining moment in America's history, which is why we have given it so much attention in our narrative. A third will come in the next century, and we will also give it a close look later. That sense of a sentiment that a new time was here can be heard in the voice of a Negro slave from North Carolina, who, upon hearing in early 1863 of the Emancipation Proclamation, replied, "These are the times foretold by the Prophets, 'When a Nation shall be born in a day.'"[151] But had that day actually yet arrived?

A newcomer to the United States may have made the most telling comment on the nature of slavery, and the war, and the "new day." His name was Philip Schaff, and he was a native Swiss who had studied in Germany, then accepted a call to teach at the German Reformed seminary in Mercersburg, Pennsylvania. In 1861 he penned a review article in the Mercersburg Review in which he called for the gradual, voluntary end to slavery, but noted also that, "*The negro question lies far deeper than the slavery question.*"[152] Schaff, it turns out, was quite prescient. The Civil War did solve the *slavery* issue, once and for all, but neither the war, nor twelve years of "Reconstruction"—that

---

148 Stout, *Upon the Altar of the Nation*, 61.
149 Ibid., 155.
150 Ibid., 415–18.
151 Quoted in William S. McFeely, *Frederick Douglass* (New York: Simon & Schuster, 1992), 212, cited in Goldfield, *America Aflame*, 267.
152 Philip Schaff, "Slavery and the Bible," *Mercersburg Review* 13 (April 1861): 316–17, quoted in Noll, *Civil War as a Theological Crisis*, 51.

Struggle for the City

is, oversight from the federal government over the governing policies of the eleven rebel states, nor decades of Jim Crow and prejudice—none of these had solved the so-called Negro question. We will have to see whether that does get some kind of solution later in our story.

The Cost of Freedom

Shelby Foote fittingly cites Greek philosopher and astronomer Anaximander at the conclusion of his three-volume analysis of the war. "It is necessary that things should pass away into that from which they are born. For things must pay one another the penalty and compensation for their injustice according to the ordinance of time."[153] The war was effectively over in April 1865, as Lee's surrender brought a kind of ending, and then in May as President Johnson's ratification of the Thirteenth Amendment brought freedom to all of the former slaves, another kind of ending. But at what cost?

The North, out of two million soldiers and sailors, had 640,000 casualties, killed and wounded. The number of dead for the North stood at 365,000, and those deaths came from combat, disease, drowning, sunstroke, and suicide.[154] The South had placed about 750,000 men in uniform and of them 450,000 were casualties, killed or wounded, which makes it more than half of the total number of soldiers. Of that number, about 256,000 were dead, bringing the official total of the dead to 623,026.[155] "The butcher's bill thus came to no less than 1,094,453 for both sides, in and out of more than 10,000 military actions, including seventy-six full-scale battles, 310 engagements, 6,337 skirmishes, and numerous sieges, raids, expeditions, and the like."[156] If this was the *second defining moment* in American history, it had demanded an astounding sacrifice for its redemption.

The financial cost of the war will never be known. It is hopelessly multifaceted. The sheer cost of war *material* was monumental. The loss of *earnings*

---

153 Quoted in Shelby Foote, *The Civil War: A Narrative*, vol. 3, *Red River to Appomattox* (New York: Random House, 1974), 1040.
154 Ibid.
155 Ibid.
156 Ibid.

Struggle for the City

and *trade* during the war made for a huge difficulty even for returning Union soldiers, especially since inflation had doubled the cost of goods in the intervening years. The overwhelming loss of property in the South through four years of having war waged almost exclusively on its territory would take years to recover, far more than the twelve years of "Reconstruction," a term that did *not* refer to the rebuilding of the Southern economy or infrastructure.

America would recover. "From the flame and ashes of the Civil War emerged, not instantaneously as in the Oriental fable, but slowly and gradually, a phoenix-like apparition—a new country, in the main a creation of evolution rather than revolution, its golden wings and feathers mingled with more familiar and time-tested adjuncts of flight and splendor."[157] Was this a necessary war? Perhaps not. Those who engage in "What if?" examinations of history have played out many scenarios. But even as in other relationships of life the conflicts we engage in are conflicts that are now part of the narrative of things past. In human relationships we do not always learn from our conflicts the morning after. So it would be with this national conflict.

---

157 Allan Nevins, *The War for Union, vol. 4, The Organized War to Victory: 1864–1865*, Ordeal of the Union 8 (New York: Scribners, 1971), 392.

Struggle for the City

Chapter 19

Rebuilding a New Nation

In 1865, with the fires of war barely subsided, a president barely buried, and a transcontinental railroad halfway built, America was on the verge of a new era. But not all of it was consistent with the ideals that had brought our foundation, and much of it would be tested in the fires in the sixty or so years that intervened between the previous defining crisis and the one that loomed, albeit unseen, on the horizon.

PROGRESSIVISM IN POLITICS, ECONOMICS, AND THEOLOGY

America was like a new nation after the Civil War. Everywhere there was struggle, though the struggle in the South was far more intense than that in the North. But before long it was clear that new realities were emerging. The world was changing, and changing as much in America as anywhere else.

Progressive Politics and Economics

The American Civil War marked several turning points, but one of them concerned how some American intellectuals viewed the founding fathers. Writing a couple of decades after the war, future president Woodrow Wilson, for example, stated his belief that Jefferson and others (especially Madison and Hamilton) among the founders endorsed a political philosophy that was no longer tenable and that, in fact, they did not in any demonstrable sense hold to a *democratic* understanding of governance.[1] Wilson contended that only now, in the 1880s, had America herself actually developed into a constitutional democracy that had any hope of providing leadership for the watching world. He further argued that the American Constitution itself had to be either *rejected* or completely *reinterpreted* for the new generation. For him, the only possibility for the Constitution still to serve as the basis for American government was if it was seen as some kind of "living" document that could be completely reinterpreted for every new generation.[2]

This new approach would come to be called by the name "Progressivism," and was fast becoming the accepted version of American political philosophy in the major universities. By the time Wilson became president, in 1913, Progressivism would *dominate* the *social science* departments in most major eastern US universities.[3] Where did such a vision come from, and what would be its impact on politics and economics in the decades that lay ahead?

The intellectual basis for Progressivism lay in the confluence of the English Historical School associated with Edmund Burke and the historicist philosophy sparked by the work of Georg Hegel. The Historical School taught that progress in the philosophy of governing was inevitable but that it was also slow and progressive.[4] Burke was opposed to "revolutions" in general, believing that sudden "jerks" were disruptive to the inevitable and gradual flow of historical development. Burke was especially critical of the French Revolution (less so of the American) since in France it radically overturned the institutions of society, including Crown, church, and the nobility. Burke argued that the evolution of governing philosophy ought to find ways to work with the prevailing institutions, institutions that will themselves have to adapt to the changes that occur, and so evolve along with them.

---

1   Paul Johnson, *A History of the American People* (New York: HarperCollins, 1997), 629–30.
2   Paul Carrese, "Montesquieu, the Founders, and Woodrow Wilson: The Evolution of Rights and the Eclipse of Constitutionalism," in *The Progressive Revolution in Politics and Political Science: Transforming the American Regime*, ed. John Marini and Ken Masugi, Studies in Statesmanship and Political Philosophy (Lanham, MD: Rowan & Littlefield, 2005), 133–62.
3   Thomas G. West, "Progressivism and the Transformation of American Government," in *The Progressive Revolution in Politics and Political Science*, 13–34.
4   Greg Forster, *The Contested Public Square* (Downers Grove, IL: InterVarsity Press, 2008), 218–24.

Struggle for the City

Wilson accepted this new Historical School's premises, arguing that the American Revolution itself was *unfortunate*.[5] He contended that if the more moderate voices had been heard, such as that of Washington, the revolution could have been avoided, and America would gradually, over time, have emerged from colonialism to become an independent nation, with a governing structure more like the British system, rather than the one it did eventually develop in 1787. As he put it, "How much happier [America] would be now, if she had England's form of government instead of the miserable delusion of a republic.... I venture to say that this country will never celebrate another centennial as a republic. The English form of government is the only true one."[6] The American republic in its current form was, for Wilson, inherently *unstable* and would probably not last till the end of the twentieth century.

Wilson went on to argue, though, that the Burkean ideal was *insufficient* left to itself. Merely to contend that governments would slowly move forward to better models was not enough. Burke's model was far too conservative for Wilson, but in Georg Hegel's writings the future president found an approach that provided the final pieces of the ideological puzzle Wilson was attempting to arrange.[7] Hegel contended that history was being driven forward by a powerful subterranean force that he called the *Geist*, a force that was causing to emerge a new kind of political reality that would be marked by *justice* and equity in *all ways*.[8] Hegel believed that the state was itself becoming "rational," and such rationality demanded the fusion of government and civil society into an organic whole, thus creating a new kind of nation in which government was no longer to be thought of as a threat to the rights of individuals. That belief was common among the founders and provided the basis for their constitu-

---

5   Johnson, *History of the American People*, 634.
6   Woodrow Wilson, "From Wilson's Shorthand Diary," July 4, 1876, in *The Papers of Woodrow Wilson*, ed. Arthur S. Link (Princeton, NJ: Princeton University Press, 1966), 1:148–49, quoted in Ronald J. Pestritto, *Woodrow Wilson and the Roots of Modern Liberalism*, American Intellectual Culture (Lanham, MD: Rowan & Littlefield, 2005), 49–50.
7   Carrese, "Montesquieu, the Founders, and Woodrow Wilson," 150–51.
8   G. W. F. Hegel, *Elements of the Philosophy of Right*, trans. H. B. Nisbet, ed. Allen W. Wood, Cambridge Texts in the History of Political Thought (1821; Cambridge: Cambridge University Press, 1991). The *Geist* should not be seen as comparable with or as a counterpart to traditional Christian views about God, except perhaps in some kind of purely pantheistic sense, as the *Geist* for Hegel is completely immanent in this world.

Struggle for the City

tional conviction that government should be limited and divided into three inviolable branches.[9] The founders *agreed* that government ought not to be a *threat*, but they would not have agreed with Hegel (or Wilson) that the hope of the nation lay in an *all-encompassing* state that itself had evolved to the point of being inherently just. Quite the *opposite*, and here is where Wilson's views conflicted with theirs.

Hegel's new governmental power would be used on *behalf* of the people and would create genuine freedom, construed in ways not previously imagined. "Government would free men of economic necessity thereby creating the possibility of genuine human freedom."[10] The enlightened class that was sympathetic with these new ideas about the state would provide the "technical rationality" to carry this project out and would do so by making use of the *research university*, which would undercut the older philosophical mind-set that undergirded the liberal arts system in the American university. The new university, working with the new political bureaucracy, "of necessity, becomes the institutional heart of the administrative state."[11] This "administrative state" would provide the leadership needed to take the country in directions that *previous* generations were simply unable to fathom. It would, of course, have to be granted *sweeping powers*. It should come as little surprise that Wilson once kept Congress in continual session for a year and a half.[12] Not even Lincoln had been able to pull that off.

Darwin would propose his theory of natural selection and biological evolution in his publication in 1859 of *On the Origin of Species*. This theory of a purely immanent origin and development of biological life on the planet fit in very well with Hegel's philosophical immanentism. Darwinism did not merely revolutionize biology and the other natural sciences but transformed other areas of investigation in the *social sciences*, as many of them found reasons to incorporate, with often unexpected results, the concept of natural selection and gradual evolution in the realms of psychology, sociology, and political sci-

---

9 John Marini, "Progressivism, Modern Political Science, and the Transformation of American Constitutionalism," *The Progressive Revolution in Politics and Political Science*, 221–22.
10 Ibid.
11 Ibid.
12 Jonah Goldberg, *Liberal Fascism* (New York: Doubleday, 2006), 105.

Struggle for the City

ence.[13] Most important of these applications for our study is what came to be known as "social Darwinism," the belief that poverty and its attendant ills were a matter of genetic development and hereditary transference. This would lead to a direction of thought advocating the elimination of such hereditary strains in the human race by even biological means—that is, genetic engineering. Its opposite was that evolutionary development might even breed this problem out of existence.

Wilson's conception of *democracy* entailed a dramatically different understanding than that of the founders, and he *readily* admitted that. He was very clear about this. The rise of the new social sciences—psychology, sociology, and political science—in the nineteenth century made it inevitable that the founders' approach had to be rejected, based as it was on philosophical and religious convictions that no longer prevailed. "The theoretical foundation of the new disciplines rested upon a rejection of the philosophic authority upon which early American political thought was based."[14] These new social sciences, unlike the natural sciences, were predicated on the assumption that "History, not nature, provided the meaningful knowledge as regards politics and society."[15] Wilson's concept of the nature of man, the nature of society, and the nature of nature differed widely from that of Washington and Jefferson.

How did the focus on the new social sciences result in a divergence with the founders? One issue important to the founders was *separation of powers*. Wilson and the new political science, however, viewed this as an *impediment* to progress.[16] Again, Wilson contended that the first generation of Americans had a flawed view of liberty—for them, liberty meant protecting individuals from the threat that can come from an overweening and powerful federal government.[17] Perhaps, in some sense, they were justified in holding that view due to the times in which they lived (though Wilson believed the founders overreacted), but that is *no longer* the case. Now we live in a time (again—Wilson was writing this in 1889) in which the federal government has been trans-

---

13 Charles E. Merriam, *A History of American Political Theories*, Citizen's Library of Economics, Politics, and Sociology (New York: Macmillan, 1903), 305.
14 Marini, "Progressivism," 223.
15 Ibid., 225.
16 Johnson, *History of the American People*, 629.
17 Carrese, "Montesquieu, the Founders, and Woodrow Wilson," 149–50.

Struggle for the City

formed into an instrument for *good*. The checks and balances of the separation of powers are now an impediment.[18]

The new, post-Civil War American political philosophy into which government will be increasingly transformed will be more *democratic* than anything that has gone before. It will be more democratic because it will be a *living, organic* extension of the peoples' will. To divide this government over against itself is wrong. As Wilson wrote in *The New Freedom*, "No living thing can have its organs offset against each other, as checks, and live."[19] Separation of powers is both *inefficient* and *irresponsible*, in Wilson's view. America needed a new vision to march into the twentieth century. Only in this way can an American *utopia* be achieved.

Wilson called for the instatement of a new political structure that would substitute a *parliamentary* form of legislature for the existing one and that would install a cabinet-level administration that would link the executive and legislative branches so they would no longer be at odds with one another. A parliamentary form of government allows fewer checks on those in leadership. Later, when he was president, Wilson claimed that he was the right hand of God, and that to stand against him was to thwart divine will.[20] Well, if the *administrative state* is the realization of the *Geist*, then what other conclusion could one draw? In fact, the leaders of the legislative branch *should* serve in the cabinet of the executive branch to ensure optimal cooperation, under this new view.[21] *Gridlock* would be done away with. Or so the theory went.

Wilson's theory also separated *politics* and *administration*. On the political side, elections would bring people into power, but those very people needed to recognize that it would not be their own wisdom that ought to guide their administration but the advice of *scientific experts* in the bureaucracy, the *mandarins*, or the "masterminds."[22] Neither politicians nor the common people really knew

---

18 Goldberg, *Liberal Fascism*, 88. Recall our earlier mention of President-elect Buchanan colluding with the Supreme Court on the Dred Scott case as an example of subverting the separation of powers.
19 Quoted in Pestritto, *Woodrow Wilson*, 124.
20 Goldberg, *Liberal Fascism*, 85.
21 From Wilson's essay, "Cabinet Government in the United States," written in 1879, quoted in *Papers of Woodrow Wilson*, vol. 1: *1856–1880*, cited in Pestritto, *Woodrow Wilson*, 125.
22 Mark Levin, *Ameritopia: The Unmaking of America* (New York: Simon & Schuster, 2012), 37.

Struggle for the City

what was best for them, but politicians hopefully have the good wisdom to defer to *intellectuals* on matters related to administration.[23] This was a radically different philosophy than had prevailed with the founders, or even with such later presidents as Lincoln, who believed they were elected because the people (or at least some majority of them) believed in them and believed in their political convictions. Franklin, Washington, Madison, Lincoln and the other previous architects of the American republic believed that the country should be guided by those with some stake in the game, whether planters, yeoman farmers, businessmen, lawyers, or those who had served in the military, but not by mandarins or masterminds of the latest trends in European philosophy.

The *anthropological* and *economic* implications of this are not that hard to imagine. Anthropologically, Wilson took his cues from Hegel. The *Geist* was driving humanity onward to higher stages of corporate perfection. One of the ways this was happening was through the new *social sciences*.[24] These, coupled with the obvious advances in natural science and technology that were attendant on (or precedent to) the Industrial Revolution made it seem, intuitively, as though this corporate improvement in human perfection was *attainable*. Such a set of beliefs was what caused Wilson to believe that the new administrative state that was just right around the corner would be the most *just* that had ever governed—after all, it would express the political and social will of a people who were on the verge of becoming one with the *Geist*. "It was Wilson who first introduced America to big, benevolent government."[25] He introduced us to it, but he was only the first in a *line* that has become increasingly longer.

Hegel's philosophy was based on an ideological construct of *history as process* but was not based on an understanding of the actual *experience* of human beings. Hegel's philosophy was developed in his study and in the classroom, not in the mix of encountering human life in its daily reality. It was *speculative*, not based on experience, something Hegel despised. Critiquing Friedrich Schleiermacher's[26] theology of "experience" (*das Gefühl*), Hegel once commented that if the essence of religion consists in the feeling of absolute depen-

---

23 Pestritto, *Woodrow Wilson*, 133–97.
24 Marini, "Progressivism," 233–37.
25 Johnson, *History of the American People*, 637.
26 More on Schleiermacher in this chapter shortly.

Struggle for the City

dence, "then the dog would be the best Christian."[27] That set his anthropology apart from both the Christian doctrine of man that arose in the Reformation (based on the Bible) and the Lockean understanding of the human condition that was instrumental in assisting the founders in the task of nation forming. It could be argued that the founders brought together Reformation ideology with that of Locke and the tradition he followed. Locke saw himself as representing Christian morality and religion, while at the same time grounding politics and the authority of government in natural law that was accessible to reason.[28] Hegel, and his followers, including Wilson, assumed a more Pelagian understanding of the human condition, at least in terms of the soon-perfectibility of the human condition as the *Geist* brings about the utopian modernity.[29] The "fall of man" in Hegel's thought was a move from "innocence to self-consciousness," and though that presented a challenge, it was the necessary step to perfectability.[30] This is a human condition in which not Nature, but Will, plays the dominant role. That Will, then, once it becomes public in the governmental *administration* in the secular "millennium" that is about to dawn, will bring about a whole *new society* that is rooted in social justice.[31]

What is the nature of that social justice? Democracy! Democracy, that is, according to Wilson's interpretation of *democracy*, an interpretation different from the founders. This is a democracy of *effect*, not a democracy of *opportunity*. This understanding of democracy would tend to redistribute resources, over time, so that all shared everything in a rough sort of *equality*. This democracy differed little from the socialist ideal that was being implemented in parts of Europe at the time that Wilson was serving as US president. Wilson himself said that Socialism was similar to his own proposal and that the only reason he did not affirm Socialism was that he thought it too *artificial*. But he applauded its economic egalitarianism of *effect* as the model that ought to be the goal of all modern nations.[32]

---

27 Quoted in Livingston and Fiorenza, *Modern Christian Thought*, 1:117.
28 Forster, *Contested Public Square*, 187–97, and see our earlier discussion of Locke in chap. 15.
29 Recall that Pelagius did not believe humans were sinners by nature.
30 Georg Wilhelm Friedrich Hegel, *Lectures on the Philosophy of Religion,* vol. 3, *The Consummate Religion,* trans. R. F. Brown, ed. Peter C. Hodgson, Lectures on the Philosophy of Religion (1821–31; Berkeley: University of California Press, 1985), 301. Hegel sided with the *serpent* in the "fall," not with God.
31 Marini, "Progressivism," 234.
32 Pestritto, *Woodrow Wilson*, 80.

Struggle for the City

The government has the responsibility, then, to enact policies that will make wealth inequities far less extreme. That is what a *just* social policy would do in a nation whose government reflects the arrival of a true democratic spirit. And of course it will need to *control the economy* in order to bring about the desired effect. As one Progressive put it, "Laissez-faire is dead. Long live social control."[33] So, we have here the new humanity and an administrative state that has evolved to the point where it can truly rule in *justice*, and all supported by an economy that has been placed at the feet of the *administrative state*. Sounds like heaven! Or some other place, perhaps?

Progressivism in Theology and Religion

Liberal theology had seized the major European religion and theology faculties by 1870. The two most basic components of liberal theology are a commitment to the prevailing scientific spirit and a full acceptance of the results of literary criticism.[34] In the nineteenth century the commitment to science meant an affirmation of the theory of *evolution*. This was the case even before Darwin's *On the Origin of Species* in 1859, since evolutionary Lamarckianism goes back to the early century (i.e., to French botanist and zoologist J. B. P. Lamarck, 1744–1829). Liberalism's commitment to prevailing scientific orthodoxy led its adherents to reconsider the traditional Christian doctrine of *creation*, driving many of them in the direction of discarding the doctrine of God's *transcendence* and resorting to a radical form of *immanence*.[35] There are many problems with this, not the least of which is that the Bible does not present God to us in this way, but also because it is difficult to maintain the *personhood* of God in such a view. Friedrich Schleiermacher left the legacy of an immanent God with no real *personhood* who nonetheless somehow cares about the depth of our *concerns*. The Berlin theologian described religion as "the immediate feeling of the Infinite and

---

33 Quoted in Michael McGerr, *A Fierce Discontent: The Rise and Fall of the Progressive Movement in America, 1870–1920* (New York: Free Press, 2003), 282. McGerr does not give the Progressive "reformer's" name.
34 Gary Dorrien, *The Word as True Myth: Interpreting Modern Theology* (Louisville: Westminster John Knox, 1997), 10–72.
35 Stanley J. Grenz and Roger E. Olson, *20th Century Theology: God and World in a Transitional Age* (Downers Grove, IL: InterVarsity Press, 1992), 24–61.

Struggle for the City

the Eternal."[36] How such an "Infinite" could make a difference in our lives in any way except an *aesthetic* one is not clear at all in Schleiermacher's writings.[37]

In addition, liberalism's commitment to a full acceptance of the results of literary criticism, in the nineteenth century at least, entailed a rejection of the *authenticity* of most of the Old Testament, including a revising of the history of the Jewish people, since if the documents telling their history are not authentic, then the *history* itself is bogus.[38] These documents (the OT) might still have some "religious" or poetic value as *classics*, but their putative claims to being derived from divine *revelation* cannot be accepted. This is in part because Immanuel Kant, Prussian philosopher who died in 1804, argued that humans can only know what they are *constructed* to know and *that* only includes the artifacts of the *empirical* world around us.[39] We can *believe* in other things beyond the empirical world, but we cannot *know* them. Since God is *not* an artifact in this world (though Kant believed in God), he cannot be *known*, nor can God cross over the gap from his existence in the realm of *noumena* to our existence in the realm of *phenomena*. So, the claim of the prophets, "Thus saith the Lord" is *illusory*. The New Testament must also be subjected to this same analysis, and the results, in the mind of liberals by say 1900, was that it fared little better than the OT.[40]

These two basic features of liberal theology, the unquestioned acceptance of evolutionary scientism and the unquestioned affirmation of literary criticism, with its *historicist*[41] understanding of the past, crossed the Atlantic in

---

36 Friedrich Schleiermacher, *On Religion: Speeches to Its Cultured Despisers*, trans. John Oman (1799; Eng. trans., 1893; New York: Harper, 1958), 15–16, and throughout.

37 For the mature development of his ideas regarding religious experience, God, and creation, see Friedrich Schleiermacher, *The Christian Faith*, 2nd ed., ed. H. R. Mackintosh and J. S. Stewart (1830–31; Eng. trans., 1928; repr., Edinburgh: T&T Clark, 1948), 3–93, 149–55, 194–232.

38 Julius Wellhausen, *A Prolegomena to the History of Israel*, Scholars Press Reprints and Translations (1878; Eng. trans., 1885 ed.; repr., Atlanta: Scholars Press, 1994). Originally published in German in 1878, this book gave the fullest treatment to the critical understanding of the OT in its day.

39 Immanuel Kant, *Critique of Pure Reason*, trans. and ed. Marcus Weigelt, based on trans. Max Müller, Penguin Classics (1781; New York: Penguin Books, 2008).

40 These notions of criticism had taken root in German universities as early as the late 1700s, and had slowly wound their way through academia to the churches there by the mid-nineteenth century.

41 *Historicism* is the idea that we can only accept interpretations of the past that are consistent with our own experience of the world and with the assured beliefs of the scientific community.

Struggle for the City

the 1840s in a strong way. Congregationalist pastor and theologian Theodore Parker preached a sermon in 1841 that denied both biblical inspiration and the deity of Christ.[42] He claimed that the Bible must be treated like every other "historical phenomenon… subject to the laws of historical inquiry."[43] Congregationalist theologian Horace Bushnell, whom we have alluded to earlier, in 1849 began to promote the new theology.[44] In 1881, after a five-year-long heresy trial in Scotland in the Presbyterian church concluded with an exoneration of OT professor William Robertson Smith, professors Charles Briggs and A. A. Hodge, editors of the *Presbyterian Review*, published a series of essays in that journal on the issue.[45] In that early American context, Princeton Seminary (especially Charles Hodge) took the more traditional and conservative stance over against the more liberal position taken by Union Seminary (Briggs) in New York City.[46] This would warm up to be an issue that American theologians would be forced to deal with, and Briggs and Hodge would take opposite sides in the debate.[47] Recall also that a major historical precedent for the American debate had been the inability of Northerners and Southerners to sort out just what the Bible did teach on *slavery*. For the new liberals there was a reason—the Bible itself was filled with *contradictions* and could no longer be looked to in order to decide such issues. It would now be the new social sciences in the universities that would help us sort those things out.

It is important to recognize that this is not just some airy theological debate. If the Bible does not come by inspiration from God, then Christianity has lost its base, its foundation. If religious knowledge only comes through natural

---

42 George Marsden, "Theodore Parker," in *The New International Dictionary of the Church*, rev. ed. (Grand Rapids, MI: Zondervan, 1988). The sermon was titled "A Discourse on the Transient and Permanent in Christianity" (Luke 21:33), preached in 1841 as an ordination sermon in Boston and later published as a book (see bibliography).

43 Jerry Wayne Brown, *The Rise of Biblical Criticism in America, 1800–1870: The New England Scholars* (Middleton, CT: Wesleyan University Press, 1969), 166.

44 Sidney E. Ahlstrom, *Theology in America: The Major Protestant Voices from Puritanism to Neo-Orthodoxy*, American Heritage 73 (New York: Bobbs-Merrill, 1967), 317–70.

45 Mark A. Noll, *Between Faith and Criticism* (San Francisco: Harper & Row, 1986), 15–18.

46 See the discussion in the Noll book for the debate between conservatives and liberals on biblical authority between 1880 and 1974. See also Paul C. Gutjahr, *Charles Hodge* (Oxford: Oxford University Press, 2011), 227–34, 240–50, 273–76.

47 An insightful analysis of one participant's journey through these issues can be found in Grant Wacker, *Augustus H. Strong and the Dilemma of Historical Consciousness* (Macon, GA: Mercer University Press, 1985).

Struggle for the City

knowledge or through some vague conception of "the Spirit," or if it is simply one other kind of discipline like sociology, economics, or biology, and if all of these items are in a "web" where they are of equal value to one another, then we have to reconceive the nature of our faith. Charles Hodge contended that Christianity itself was at stake and argued that the very "words employed" in the Bible are inspired.[48] If the Bible was an inspired record of truth, then it had to be correct in all of its details, even to the level of word choice.[49] Hodge argued that there is no such thing as a "wordless thought," and so, in contrast to the new liberalism encroaching on some American pulpits, form and substance had to come together. There could be no "inspiration of the ideals" of the faith without also *plenary verbal* inspiration of the words of the text.[50] Increasingly, pastors who adopted some version of the new liberalism, such as the aging Henry Ward Beecher of New York, Phillips Brooks of Boston, or eventually Harry Emerson Fosdick of New York, proclaimed versions of the faith that were, more or less, dramatically different from "the faith once delivered to the saints" (Jude 3).[51] That this is so will be evidenced in the seventy or so years after the importation of liberalism into America in about 1840, to which we will subsequently return.

CHARITY, ENTREPRENEURS, AND THE CHURCH

The close of the nineteenth century and the opening of the twentieth century are the occasion of a number of developments historically, politically, economically, and theologically that affect our study. In that period industrialization

---

48 Charles Hodge, "The Inspiration of Holy Scripture," *Biblical Repertory and Princeton Review* 29, no. 4 (1857): 675. Excerpts from and a brief commentary on this article can be found in Mark A. Noll, ed., *The Princeton Theology 1812-1821: Scripture, Science, and Theological Method from Archibald Alexander to Benjamin Warfield* (1983; repr., Grand Rapids: Baker, 2001), 135–41.
49 Hodge, "Inspiration of Holy Scripture," 675.
50 Ibid., 677.
51 Beecher, for instance, in reference to evolution, believed that science was "the deciphering of God's thought as revealed in the structure of the world." James C. Livingston and Francis Schüssler Fiorenza, *Modern Christian Thought*, vol. 1, *The Enlightenment and the Nineteenth Century*, 2nd ed. (Minneapolis: Fortress, 2006), 263. On Phillips Brooks, see Charles W. Fuller, *The Trouble with "Truth Through Personality": Phillips Brooks, Incarnation, and the Evangelical Boundaries of Preaching* (Eugene, OR: Wipf and Stock, 2010), 12–43, 78–108. On Fosdick, see our later discussion in chap. 20.

Struggle for the City

accelerated even faster than it had moved previously, and it witnessed the consolidation of several major industries that depended on size for their efficiency. Oil, steel, transportation (railroads and eventually automobiles), electricity, machinery building, chemicals, food production, communications, and finance, among others, geared up to serve a continent and ultimately the world. Bigness in these areas led to demands economically, socially, and politically that washed over into cultural and religious areas in *unprecedented* ways. This was the "Gilded Age."[52] There were a few dozen big companies in the middle of the nineteenth century, but with natural resource discoveries and new technologies, by the 1880s all of American life seemed to loom *larger and larger*. Changes accelerated and led to accentuations in human need and misery that produced cries for "big answers" to match big *problems*.

Social Problems in the Late Nineteenth Century

Immigration, the first big answer to the labor shortage, peaked in the 1880s and again in the decade after 1900.[53] By the mid-1880s America was receiving about five hundred thousand immigrants per year.[54] Between 1865 and 1900 the American population grew from 31 million to 76 million. Prior peak periods, such as the 1840s, had seen mass migrations to the western frontiers—remember Horace Greeley's famous advice, "Go West, young man," a slogan that was an attempt to move the problem of unemployment and slums *out* of the eastern cities onto the *frontier*. During those last decades of the nineteenth century, after the frontier had been virtually fully occupied, at least in terms of free land, concerned social activists, religious and secular, began to believe the problems were just too big for the prior answers rooted in *private action*, no matter how such private relief organizations had *proliferated*.[55]

---

52 Sean Dennis Cashman, *America in the Gilded Age: From the Death of Lincoln to the Rise of Theodore Roosevelt*, 3rd ed. (New York: New York University Press, 1993).
53 Johnson, *History of the American People*, 513–14, 661–62.
54 Mark A. Noll, *The Old Religion in a New World: The History of North American Christianity* (Grand Rapids, MI: Eerdmans, 2002), 124.
55 This is strange in some ways, for in first half of the nineteenth century the total investment by Christian organizations and their affiliates in social action and evangelization exceeded the entire budget of the federal government. See George McKenna, *The Puritan Origins of American Patriotism* (New Haven, CT: Yale University Press, 2007), 3.

Struggle for the City

Christian relief organizations flourished in the last half of the nineteenth century. Charles Spurgeon in London led his church to great efforts at ministering to physical needs, along with spiritual needs. Even before he came to pastor in that city, his predecessor, John Rippon, had erected a building he called the *Almshouses* in which needy widows lived *free* of charge and were granted a small weekly stipend.[56] Spurgeon himself built new dwellings for the women, seventeen small houses, and provided them also with food, clothing, and other necessities.[57] His church also constructed *orphanages* for both boys and girls, a project that began with a £20,000 donation from a Mrs. Hillyard, the widow of a Church of England clergyman.[58] The amount of philanthropy that came through this one evangelical Baptist church in London is almost impossible to exaggerate.

D. L. Moody also was a compassionate supporter of those who were down and out, especially in Chicago where he developed a reputation for "ministering to young men in a city of young men," and particularly those in the "center of the city who had been abandoned by churches that had fled to 'nicer neighborhoods.'"[59] British Baptist minister F. B. Meyer, often known for his Keswick spirituality, published in 1894 *The Bells of Is, or Voices of Human Need and Sorrow*, to publicize the plight and need of *released prisoners* in Leicester.[60] Baptist churches in America regularly placed a collection box out when they took the Lord's Supper, a collection to be used for *relief* of members of their congregation. In those times many Christian people took great pleasure in being the *instruments* of God in making a difference in the plight of the "unfortunate." But in the minds of many, what was really needed was a *government* response.

Books began to come off the presses extolling the virtues of *public response* to social pressures. Among them were publications by ministers, intellectuals,

---

56 Arnold Dallimore, *Spurgeon: A New Biography* (Chicago: Moody, 1984), 125.
57 Ibid., 125–26. For some years Spurgeon paid these expenses out of his own pocket, though eventually the church took responsibility for it.
58 Ibid., 126–28. One computation measuring the "real value" of this gift given in 1866 puts it at $2.1 million USD (or perhaps more) in 2011. Lawrence H. Officer and Samuel H. Williamson, "Computing 'Real Value' over Time with a Conversion between U.K. Pounds and U.S. Dollars, 1830 to Present," MeasuringWorth, http:// www.measuringworth.com/ exchange/ (accessed February 27, 2013).
59 Bruce J. Evensen, *God's Man for the Gilded Age: D. L. Moody and the Rise of Modern Mass Evangelism* (Oxford: Oxford University Press, 2003), 126.
60 David W. Bebbington, *Baptists through the Centuries* (Waco, TX: Baylor University Press, 2010), 126.

Struggle for the City

and literati of various sorts, all urging a kind of "social universalism." The list includes William Dean Howells, Hamlin Garland, Laurence Gronlund, Daniel De Leon, Richard Ely, George Herron, William H. Fremantle, and Mark Matthews among others.[61] Richard Ely founded the American Economic Association with the idea of promoting his universalistic idea that "the exercise of philanthropy" is "the duty of government."[62] Ely appealed to economists and theologians to come together in an all-out call to the "philanthropy of governments, either local, state, or national."[63] He believed that only "coercive philanthropy" held the hope of establishing "among us true cities of God." These ideas found buyers for books including *Social Aspects of Christianity, and Other Essays* (Ely), *The World as the Subject of Redemption* (Fremantle), and *The Christian Society* and *Between Caesar and Jesus* (both by Herron). These and other writings came to be known as the "social gospel." What could be more *suited* to an inherently religious nineteenth-century progressive American context than a "social gospel"?

The Social Gospel

The so-called social gospel went well beyond anything seen up to that point. William H. Fremantle (1831–1916), an early British "Social Universalist," opined that collectives such as governments had the power to break down man's selfishness and make him *better*. He wrote that government "has the power of life and death over our persons. Hence it calls forth a worship more complete than any other."[64] Only government, he continued, "can embrace all the wants of its members and afford them the universal instruction and elevation which they need."[65] He did not

---

61 See, e.g., Dale E. Soden, *The Reverend Mark Matthews: An Activist in the Progressive Era* (Seattle: University of Washington Press, 2000).

62 Richard Ely, *Social Aspects of Christianity, and Other Essays* (New York: T. Y. Crowell, 1889), 92, quoted in Marvin Olasky, *The Tragedy of American Compassion* (Wheaton, IL: Crossway, 1992), 120–21. In this section of our book we are indebted to Olasky's prior work, esp. chap. 7, "And Why Not Do More?" By the way, for those who are critical of Olasky, President Clinton used his work as a base for reforming welfare in the 1990s; not that he followed him fully.

63 Ibid., 121.

64 W. H. Fremantle, *The World as the Subject of Redemption*, 2nd ed., Bampton Lectures, 1883 (1885; New York: Longmans, Green, 1907), 278–80, quoted in Olasky, *Tragedy of American Compassion*, 122.

65 Ibid.

Struggle for the City

blush to assert, "When we think of [the Nation] as becoming, as it must do more and more, the object of mental regard, of admiration, of love, even of *worship* (for in it preeminently God dwells) we shall recognize to the fullest extent its religious character and functions."[66] His call was ultimately for a government with supreme power to impose his vision, led by those with "a clear intellectual perception" of the need for such power and ways to exercise it. He concluded, "The good thus aimed at, both temporal and spiritual, is so great that we cannot despair of attaining it."[67] Fremantle's approach might have some value in a British situation where church and state were still *fused*, but it would have been more *problematic* in the American context. Yet based on its own premises, it makes a certain amount of sense. What could be more Progressive, more Hegelian, and more Christian (in a new *liberal* sense of the term) than a nation that had become the *incarnation of God*?

Less dramatically, in America Washington Gladden (1836–1918) served as pastor of churches in New York and Massachusetts from 1860 to 1882, and then First Congregationalist Church in Columbus, Ohio, from 1882 to 1914. He felt the need to look for "new religious categories to cope with the changing situation" in America, postwar and in light of massive immigration.[68] He was the pioneer of the social gospel in America.

Unlike Bushnell, whose liberal theology did not really have a social focus, Gladden's did. Gladden emphasized personal responsibility, along with a *modest* government regulation, to accomplish his goals of correcting the imbalance between rich and poor.[69] Gladden wrote in his book *Applied Christianity*, "The great inequalities arising from the present defective methods of distribution will only be corrected through a deepening sense of the obligations imposed by the possession of wealth. The economic law, like the moral law, can never be fulfilled without love."[70] The two were linked inextricably for Gladden.

---

66 Fremantle, *World as the Subject of Redemption*, 278–79, quoted in Olasky, *Tragedy of American Compassion*, 122 (emphasis added).

67 Fremantle, *World as the Subject of Redemption*, 309, quoted in Olasky, *Tragedy of American Compassion*, 123.

68 John Woodbridge, Mark A. Noll, and Nathan O. Hatch, *The Gospel in America: Themes in the Story of America's Evangelicals* (Grand Rapids, MI: Zondervan, 1979), 53.

69 Christopher H. Evans, *The Kingdom Is Always but Coming: A Life of Walter Rauschenbusch*, Library of Religious Biography (Grand Rapids, MI: Eerdmans, 2004), 53.

70 Washington Gladden, *Applied Christianity: Moral Aspects of Social Questions* (Boston: Houghton, Mifflin, 1887), 37, quoted in Evans, *Kingdom Is Always but Coming*, 53–54.

Struggle for the City

Pastoring in the increasingly Unitarian Congregationalist church, when the new liberalism began to make itself known in American church life, Gladden gladly embraced it, while still retaining something of an evangelical *spirit* and *terminology*.[71] He saw himself as "reformist and idealist," but not as revolutionary. "Gladden repeatedly assured that the socializing spirit of modern liberal Christianity did not lead to socialist politics."[72] Gladden laid out his views in *The Church and Modern Life*.[73] He argued that the church's gospel now included "Christian nurture," but even more than that; he also argued that the gospel was equally tied in with emphasizing *profit sharing* in businesses, the support of *unions*, and industrial *arbitration*. By "Christian nurture" he meant, borrowing from Bushnell, *"[t]hat the child is to grow up a Christian, and never know himself as being otherwise."*[74] This was a rejection of the *conversionist* tradition that we have discussed, beginning with the Puritans and continuing even more so in the revivalists Edwards, Whitefield, and Finney. This is not *evangelism* in the Whitefieldian sense and fits in perfectly well with a liberalized Unitarianism, though also, oddly enough, with pre-Great Awakening Presbyterianism, so that even so stalwart a theologian as Charles Hodge of Princeton did not substantially disagree with Bushnell and Gladden on the issue of nurture, though he was certainly no social gospeler.[75] Gladden was a warmhearted man who believed that people needed Jesus, but who also believed that the *rich* had the duty to give up massive amounts of their wealth to bring about *equity* between rich and poor, and was under the impression that if they would do so, justice would be accomplished.

The son of German immigrants, Walter Rauschenbusch (1861–1918), would take the social gospel to new heights of theological reflection and recognition. Rauschenbusch's father, Augustus, had grown up in Germany in a Lutheran Pietist environment, but after coming to America in 1846, he converted to

---

71 C. George Fry and Joel R. Kurz, *Washington Gladden as a Preacher of the Social Gospel, 1882–1918*, Texts and Studies in the Social Gospel 5 (Lewiston, NY: Edwin Mellen, 2003).

72 Gary Dorrien, *The Making of American Liberal Theology*, vol. 2, *Idealism, Realism, and Modernity: 1900–1950* (Louisville: Westminster John Knox, 2003), 73.

73 Washington Gladden, *The Church and Modern Life* (Boston: Houghton Mifflin, 1908), 42–53, 94–107.

74 Horace Bushnell, *Christian Nurture*, Twin Brooks (1861; repr., Grand Rapids, MI: Baker, 1979), 10.

75 Noll, *Princeton Theology 1812–1821*, 176–84.

Struggle for the City

the *Baptist* faith, being baptized in the Mississippi River in Missouri, and shortly afterward taking a Baptist pastorate.[76] Augustus's version of the Baptist faith was stern, conservative, and authoritarian. Brooking no defection from that faith on the part of his family, Augustus demanded that his children find a place of *conversion* for their souls, and he further demanded that they not *deviate* from his conservative beliefs.[77] This was difficult for young Walter, since he was increasingly drawn to the liberal voices of Horace Bushnell and Henry Ward Beecher.

As we have already noted, it was advancing *immigration* more than anything else that called forth the social gospel movement, immigration coupled with problems of alcohol abuse and domestic violence and sexual sins.[78] The immigration issue hit Rauschenbusch hard since his father was an immigrant and most of his contacts were in the German immigrant community. The other issue, of which we will have more to say later, was that many of the business moguls whose corporations were becoming truly giants of industry, were also deeply religious men, like the Baptist John Rockefeller.[79] It was to their Christian principles, which linked them to Jesus and his ethic, that the social gospelers appealed.

Along with the liberal emphasis on biblical criticism and evolution, Rauschenbusch had also been heavily influenced by German theologian and ethicist Albrecht Ritschl (1822–89). Ritschl was heir to the long "quest for the historical Jesus" of nineteenth-century fame, and while he was unable to make the same kinds of "metaphysical" (theological) claims for Christ that the early church had, he was convinced that Jesus represented the *apex* of ethics in the ancient world. Ritschl also believed that the "kingdom of God" was social and grounded in the fabric of history.[80] Ritschl wrote, "Jesus himself… saw in the Kingdom of God the moral end of the religious fellowship he had to found."[81] Ritschl argued that Jesus saw his entire ministry as related to the establishment of this kingdom in himself, as he was "the only one qualified

76 Evans, *Kingdom Is Always but Coming*, 8.
77 Ibid., 19.
78 Bebbington, *Baptists through the Centuries*, 127–29.
79 Evans, *Kingdom Is Always but Coming*, 51.
80 Ibid., 92.
81 Albrecht Ritschl, *The Christian Doctrine of Justification and Reconciliation*, vol. 3, *The Positive Development of the Doctrine*, 2nd ed., ed. H. R. Mackintosh and A. B. Macaulay, Library of Religious and Philosophical Thought (1874; Edinburgh: T&T Clark, 1902), 12.

Struggle for the City

for his special calling, the introduction of the Kingdom of God."[82] But Jesus intended that the church that he founded would carry out the twin goals of justification and reconciliation within society and thus realize *to some extent* the kingdom of God in this age, through the transformation of community; not merely the church community, but society itself.[83] "When the social gospel appeared toward the end of the century it came as the heir of this living movement which had proceeded in dialectical fashion from individual to communal hope."[84] True, but the *communal* here was not confined to communities of faith (churches) but extended to *society* at large.

For Rauschenbusch, as well, the social gospel was the *extension* of the kingdom of God on earth. Rauschenbusch, who pastored a German immigrant church near Hell's Kitchen in New York City's Bowery district in his early ministry, noted that in the year 1891, "Christ's conception of the Kingdom of God came to me as a new revelation."[85] This "new revelation" occurred after a year of travel and study in Germany where he was immersed in, among others, the theology of Ritschl.[86] In his first book (undiscovered and unpublished for fifty years), the New York pastor announced that, "Christianity is in its nature revolutionary."[87] In 1907 he published his first really important work, *Christianity and the Social Crisis*, in which he contended that the essential Christian task was "to transform human society into the Kingdom of God by regenerating all human relations and reconstituting them in accordance with the will of God."[88] Later, he would criticize the inherited *tradition* of the doctrine of

---

82 Albrecht Ritschl, *Instruction in the Christian Religion*, trans. Alice Mead Swing, in Albert Temple Swing, *The Theology of Albrecht Ritschl* (1875; Eng. trans., 1901; repr., New York: Kessenger, 2007), 195.

83 Ibid., 179. Ritschl did not believe the kingdom was fully realizable in this age but that it could in some sense be established through the church's ministry in society. David L. Mueller, *An Introduction to the Theology of Albrecht Ritschl* (Philadelphia: Westminster, 1969), 175–79.

84 H. Richard Niebuhr, *Kingdom of God in America* (New York: Harper & Brothers, 1937), 161.

85 Walter Rauschenbusch, *Christianizing the Social Order* (New York: Macmillan, 1912), 93.

86 Evans, *Kingdom Is Always but Coming*, 90–94. He never became a "disciple" of Ritschl's since he found too many problems, mostly political, with the German theologian's position, but the influence is there, nonetheless.

87 Walter Rauschenbusch, *The Righteousness of the Kingdom*, ed. Max Stackhouse (Nashville: Abingdon, 1968), 1.

88 Walter Rauschenbusch, *Christianity and the Social Crisis* (New York: Macmillan, 1907), xi.

Struggle for the City

salvation in the church: "The main aim set before Christians was to save their souls from eternal woe, to have communion with God now and hereafter, and to live God-fearing lives. It was individualistic religion, concentrated on the life to come. Its social effectiveness was largely a by-product. What, now, would have been the result if Christianity had placed an equally strong emphasis on the Kingdom of God, the ideal social order?"[89] That was the task Rauschenbusch set for himself.

Several principles undergirded his efforts. The first was *freedom*, but freedom construed *collectively*. In 1896 he wrote, "Now men are free, but it is the freedom of grains of sand that are whirled up in a cloud and then dropped in a heap, but neither cloud nor sand-heap have any coherence."[90] True freedom is collective, not, as the American founders had believed, individual. The next great principle, he announced, "is *association*."[91] He argued that "individualism means tyranny"[92] and that there was a need for new *forms* of association to rescue those who are gripped by poverty. Redemption must be social for both Rauschenbusch and the other representatives of the social gospel, and part of the new association that was needed was association with *government*. Rauschenbusch would no doubt have argued that Progressivism was, as in the title of one of Washington Gladden's books, "applied Christianity."[93] This is to be carried out by a conjoint plan bringing church together with government agencies. "The problem of Christianizing the social order welds all the tasks of practical Christianity with the highest objects of statesmanship. That the actual results of our present social order are in acute contradiction to the Christian conceptions of justice and brotherhood is realized by every man who thinks at all."[94] It goes without saying, but it was said, that in such a world it is *immaterial* whether one is converted to Christianity or not, for "social wrongs" cause individual problems, which will disappear as soon as the social setting is

---

89 Walter Rauschenbusch, *The Social Principles of Jesus*, ed. Henry H. Meyer (New York: Methodist Book Concern, 1916), 73–74.
90 Walter Rauschenbusch, "The Ideals of Social Reformers," *America Journal of Sociology* 2 (September 1896): 208–10, quoted in McGerr, *Fierce Discontent*, 66.
91 Ibid.
92 Rauschenbusch, "The Ideals of Social Reformers," 211, quoted in McGerr, *Fierce Discontent*, 59.
93 Gladden, *Applied Christianity* (1887); quoted in Goldberg, *Liberal Fascism*, 87. .
94 Rauschenbusch, *Christianizing the Social Order*, viii.

Struggle for the City

changed.[95] Personal piety was important in his own life, and he did believe in a future second coming of Christ,[96] but those things had to take a secondary role. The end goal for Rauschenbusch was "social redemption," the world set right under the kingdom of God through the ethics of Christ.[97]

In a very real sense, this is a *revived Augustinianism.* It is not a revival of Augustine's views on *man* or *salvation,* for Rauschenbusch was gesturing that original sin is more *societal* than individual, and so *redemption* must take place in that realm, as well. But Rauschenbusch's developed theology *did* contain its own version of the City of God.[98] It was not really *Augustine's* City of God, where the individual *conversions* of the mass of humanity would result in a society where *justice* prevails more often than not. It was not a revival of *Charlemagne's* version of the City of God, brought on and maintained by a combination of fierce *militarism* and warm *piety.* It was not *John Calvin's* City of God, nor that of the Massachusetts *Puritans* in which *godly pastors* and *godly magistrates* worked hand in hand to bring Christian *government* and Christian *charity* to a world of otherwise rebellious and obstreperous citizens. It was instead a City of God in which the *enlightened* church with a *liberalized* theology would cooperate with an *enlarged* administrative state that would use its coercive powers to equalize the distribution of goods to all citizens so that *none* would be in want, and thus bring the *kingdom of God* to the modern world. At least in part.

At this point a question has to be raised. If Rauschenbusch's program is indeed an *Augustinian* model, what has become of the Anabaptist/Baptist heritage? Rauschenbusch was, after all, a Baptist. The British social gospel approaches were based on at least a semi-Erastian understanding of the relationship between church and state (see the discussion of Henry VIII in chap. 14), and Gladden's

---

95 That being said, it is important to acknowledge that Rauschenbusch valued his pietistic Christian conversion and that his writings all conveyed that deep pietism, overlaid with his moderate theological liberalism.

96 Dorrien, *Making of American Liberal Theology, 1900–1950,* 2:92.

97 See David W. Bebbington, *The Dominance of Evangelicalism: The Age of Spurgeon and Moody,* A History of Evangelicalism: People, Movements and Ideas in the English Speaking World 3, ed. David W. Bebbington (Downers Grove, IL: InterVarsity Press, 2005), for a broader treatment of the social gospel, including especially elements from the British context.

98 Gary Dorrien calls his position "The Kingdom as Political Theology." Dorrien, *Making of American Liberal Theology, 1900–1950,* 2:87–93.

Struggle for the City

Congregationalist position could hark back to the *collusion* between the church and the governing order in earlier Massachusetts. But Rauschenbusch was a *Baptist*, a Baptist who was critical of Ritschl's attempts at Christianizing the German world with his "kingdom now" emphasis. How then can he justify the efforts to enlist the administrative state in support of his efforts to *bring* the kingdom of God into the world of his day? Was not Conrad Grebel rolling over in his *grave* in Maienfeld when Rauschenbusch was publishing his major writings? And what of similar free-church models today that seek also to *coerce* citizens to support a "social justice" system derived from their interpretations of the Bible, one enforced by the coercive *fiscal* strategies of an overpowering federal government? We will discuss these questions further in later chapters.

Evangelical Approaches to the Social Order

The great irony of these developments is that at this same time conservative (later to be labeled "fundamentalist") evangelical Protestant elements in the churches were actively involved in the ongoing task of social reform through application of the authentic gospel in a holistic understanding of the church's mission. George Marsden documents these activities as *intense* and *extensive*, driven as they were by a deep sense of calling to mission and belief in the power of holiness and spiritual anointing to enable believers in the work of redemption of the whole person. This was a powerful wave of activism led by the likes of A. J. Gordon, J. M. Gray, J. Wilbur Chapman, A. T. Pierson, R. A. Torrey, Stephen H. Tyng Sr., Stephen H. Tyng Jr., A. C. Dixon, Russell Conwell, the redoubtable General William Booth of the Salvation Army, and many others associated with local church ministries and the D. L. Moody evangelistic crusades.[99] The entire list of worthies would read like a who's who of holiness, Keswick, revivalist, Calvinistic, dispensational premillennialist church leaders and pastors of the day.

The first of the publications promoting a "social" application of the gospel, *The Christian Herald* (originally *The Christian Herald and Signs of the Times*), was founded in 1878. It became a rallying point for thousands and published largely

---

99   We have alluded to some of these previously.

Struggle for the City

premillenialist contributors such as Gordon, Pierson, Samuel Kellogg, and England's Charles Spurgeon. This weekly journal, sponsored by theologically conservative Christians, would eventually reach a circulation of a quarter million and become decidedly "progressive" in its politics, but through about 1910 it was instrumental in the distribution of millions of dollars to famine relief, overseas orphanages, its own Bowery mission, and a summer home for tenement children.[100]

What Marsden calls the "Great Reversal" in conservative evangelical attitudes toward social reforms and political involvement was to ensue, beginning about the turn of the twentieth century and become full-fledged by about 1930. Prior to this time the premillennial (now also dispensational) persuasions of the vast majority of conservatives and their concern for personal holiness and the life of "overcoming" through Keswickian ideas had *not* produced a dramatic subordination of social concern to a more *individualistic* interpretation of salvation through the gospel.[101] This was to *change* over time. The reasons are complex, and we will address them shortly, again using Marsden's helpful analysis.[102]

The Third Great Awakening

As the evangelical position was evolving, we see three streams had now joined into a mighty river of social activism as the twentieth century dawns (what Robert Fogel calls the "Third Great Awakening"). First, a high spirit of *optimism* gripped social activists with a resolve to make universal social justice real

---

100 See George M. Marsden, *Fundamentalism and American Culture*, 2nd ed. (New York: Oxford University Press, 2006), 80–85, for documentation on the above two paragraphs. Additionally, we found both Paul A. Carter, *The Spiritual Crisis of the Gilded Age* (DeKalb: Northern Illinois University Press, 1971), and Daniel Walker Howe, ed., *Victorian America* (Philadelphia: University of Pennsylvania Press, 1976), helpful in understanding this period.

101 Cf. Rauschenbusch's comment quoted earlier in the text above from *Social Principles of Jesus*, 73–74 (cited in note 89).

102 We commend Marsden's work *Fundamentalism and American Culture* as the most objective and conclude here that the immense pressures brought on by the Great War and its aftermath and the ongoing slide of the liberal Christian tradition into leftist and Wilsonian politics, coupled with the threat of Darwinism in its multifaceted applications and widespread concern over the rising Bolshevik international threat eventually forced conservative evangelicals to make choices they would rather not have been required to make.

Struggle for the City

through *governmental* solutions. While praising the past efforts of churches, businesses, individuals, and philanthropic organizations, the ongoing campaign was to *diminish* these in order to make way for the new national and *political* reality. In 1899 the *Christian Oracle*, a magazine of progressive mainline Christianity, changed its name to the *Christian Century* in anticipation of triumphs to come. "With their mastery of nature the men of the twentieth century will learn how to master themselves. They will solve the social problem."[103] It is hard to imagine any statement more triumphal than that, and in light of where we *are* more than a century later, it seems to be filled with a bit of *arrogance* and *hubris* that were *unfounded.* At the time, no doubt, it seemed possible. Technology, the new leadership role of America in the world, and a growing sense of moral brotherhood made *everything* seem possible in the new century. They had no way of anticipating the terrible *ordeal* that was about to grip the world. *Christian Century* became a major purveyor of new ideas that had been incubating throughout the *previous* century, mostly in liberal theological circles.

Second, in the new theological and political context man was no longer *individually accountable* for his social situation because of sin. The Bible was not to be taken completely seriously in its diagnosis of man's condition because the Bible had been *discredited* in the highest intellectual circles. Of course, there was no reason to believe anyone would actually go to *hell,* so why should anyone have to suffer in *this life* either? Universalistic *theology* was now wed to universalistic *sociology.* And since *government* was the entity charged with accomplishing this utopian dream, *it* was to be criticized if anyone went unfed or unclothed or unhoused or remained wallowing in drug addiction and inebriation.[104]

Third, a grand *coalition* now stood on the precipice of a new century—Progressivism, Marxism, theological liberalism—ready to bring in the sacred/secular millennium! They would have their opportunities to *renovate* the Western world. First they would put the so-called robber barons to heel with *antitrust* legislation in the new century. Then the Great War would give

---

103 *Christian Century*, November 23, 1899, 4.
104 See Olasky, *Tragedy of American Compassion*, chap. 8, for much of the documentation in this section.

Struggle for the City

Woodrow Wilson a chance to advance his Progressive agenda in the *aftermath* of war throughout the world, even if not so successfully in America. The Great Depression would offer Franklin Delano Roosevelt almost unfettered leave to meddle with his new toy, the American government and its *economy*. Finally, the ugly leftovers of slavery and racism would grant Lyndon Johnson an opportunity to birth the Great Society, an almost complete *remaking* of America, only to be rivaled by events in the twenty-first century that followed. Those developments all lie yet ahead, and they were all supported to one degree or another by the leftist theological coalition that succeeded in dominating the *mainstream* Christian denominations in the twentieth century. But before we survey those developments we must first examine the rise of a powerful form of free-market industrialization that would dwarf anything seen before the Civil War.

THE TURN OF THE CENTURY: ROBBER BARONS, THE GROWTH OF INDUSTRY, AND REGULATION

Beginning in the aftermath of the Civil War in the North, and by the late seventies in the South, the American economy went into high gear, and it remained at a high pace into the late 1920s, with the exception of several recessions and one "depression" in the 1890s. This was a period of new inventions and new applications of relatively recent inventions. This period witnessed the rise of some of the most iconic figures in American business and financial history, names that are even now virtually *household* words. Some of these entrepreneurs are popularly lauded and others are popularly vilified (and some are both), but they are well known to us, though *who* they really were and *what* they really did has been lacquered over by generations of traditional interpretations and misinterpretations motivated by various political, religious, and economic forces. As we will show, some of these men are not near the "sinners" some have made them out to be (though we all are sinners), and while they might not quite make *sainthood*, at least some of them did make important positive contributions to the American economy and to various institutions in our country.

Struggle for the City

Market Entrepreneurs and Political Entrepreneurs

This period is often known as the Age of the Entrepreneurs, but not all entrepreneurs are alike. Economist Thomas DiLorenzo has made a distinction between *market entrepreneurs* and *political entrepreneurs*. "A pure *market entrepreneur*, or capitalist, succeeds financially by selling a newer, better, or less expensive product on the free market without any government subsidies, direct or indirect."[105] This person is *philosophically* and *pragmatically* committed to the basic ideals laid out by Adam Smith that we have discussed at length. Such an entrepreneur attempts to please the consumer, whether through the quality, quantity, or cost (or usually, some combination of those) of that which is produced, whether goods or services. Pleasing the consumer means *sales* and *productivity*, and thus is the pathway to business success. "By contrast, a *political entrepreneur* succeeds primarily by influencing government to subsidize his business or industry, or to enact legislation or regulation that harms his competition."[106] This type of "entrepreneur" accomplishes his or her goal, which is generally the same goal of the market entrepreneur—sales of goods and services—primarily by currying political favor, not by producing something of superior *quality*.

DiLorenzo gives this illustration. If you are in the mousetrap industry, you can become successful by building *better mousetraps* than other manufacturers and so attract a customer base and convince consumers that you have a better and more economically viable product than your competitors. On the other hand, you might instead lobby Congress to prohibit the importation of (or charge a heavy tariff on) all foreign-made mousetraps. The first is *market*

---

105 Thomas J. DiLorenzo, *How Capitalism Saved America: The Untold History of Our Country, from the Pilgrims to the Present* (New York: Crown Forum, 2004), 111. In this section of our book we have benefited very much from the writings of DiLorenzo as well as from Gabriel Kolko, *The Triumph of Conservatism: A Reinterpretation of American History, 1900–1916* (Chicago: Quadrangle Books, 1963). These two volumes featured detailed statistical and analytic studies of business in this period. Also of great help on these matters are Burton W. Folsom Jr., *The Myth of the Robber Barons: A New Look at the Rise of Big Business in America, 1840–1920*, 6th ed. (Herndon, VA: Young America's Foundation, 2010), originally published as *Entrepreneurs vs. the State* (1987); Ron Chernow, *Titan: The Life of John D. Rockefeller, Sr.* (New York: Random House, 1998); John Steele Gordon, *An Empire of Wealth: The Epic History of American Economic Power* (New York: HarperCollins, 2004).
106 DiLorenzo, *How Capitalism Saved America*, 111.

Struggle for the City

entrepreneurship whereas the second is *political*. The American economy has always included a combination of both types, "self-made men and women as well as political connivers and manipulators," and the late nineteenth century witnessed the increase of both types, *in spades*.

The reason it is important to distinguish between the two philosophically and historically in this discussion is that *only* the market entrepreneur is a *real capitalist*; the political entrepreneur is a "neomercantilist."[107] The reason is clear. The mercantilist economies, like those of Charles II of England and Louis XIV of France, were comprised of heavy government intrusion into the economy to satisfy king and/or merchants or both, but only those merchants or industries that, for whatever political reason, curried favor with the *Crown*.

The "Robber Barons"

Enter the "robber barons."[108] We know their names: Rockefeller, Vanderbilt, Stanford, Carnegie, Morgan, Dodge, Ford. To the casual American with a typical education some of these names sound more sinister than others, but they all call to mind some image such as the Disney character Scrooge McDuck, a man (or talking waterfowl, we presume) sitting on a large pile of gold coins in his basement, dolling out mere pennies, if even that, to others who happen to be in need. According to the "canonical" interpretation passed down in the most common version of the story, these men starved their workers practically to death, in Ebenezer Scrooge (before his conversion) fashion. They required workers to labor in *fetid* conditions in *dangerous* workplaces. They squeezed out competitors and left them and their families standing in food lines, so the robber barons could gain a little larger share of the market. After driving out the competition, they drove up prices and became enor-

---

107 Ibid.
108 There really were literal robber barons in northern Europe in the 1100s. They were men who set up tollbooths to extract (extort) "taxes" on shipments up the Rhine River. Originally there were nineteen of these stations, which grew to forty-four in the 1200s and more than sixty in the 1300s. In contrast, the seminal work on the subject of the great industrialists as "robber barons," establishing the ongoing public consciousness of this era, is Matthew Josephson, *The Robber Barons: The Great American Capitalists, 1861–1901* (1934; repr., New York: Harcourt, Brace & World, 1962).

Struggle for the City

mously wealthy because consumers no longer had access to the same products at a lower cost. This is the kind of picture painted by muckraking journalists in the first decade or so of the twentieth century, especially writers like Ida Tarbell and Upton Sinclair.[109] Certainly there are some glimpses of the truth in these kinds of accounts, but it is a far different picture when one looks at the *whole*. Let's take a look at some key aspects of the post-Civil War economy and see which entrepreneur is *which*.

The railroad industry had been growing dramatically since the 1820s, and we have already discussed some aspects of that. The postwar situation was the time when the transcontinental railroad revolutionized American transportation and shipping. The American railroad was arguably the greatest *technological* feat of the nineteenth century, surpassing even the building of the Erie Canal in the 1820s, itself a huge accomplishment, and the construction of the Panama railroad in 1855.[110] Commissioned by Lincoln in 1863 at a dramatic moment in the Civil War when the war could have gone either way, this railroad for the first time *connected* the eastern and western halves of the United States and *decreased* travel time across the country remarkably.[111] At the time when the West was opening up to pioneers and merchants, travel from the Missouri River to the Pacific Ocean by wagon took four to six months and was fraught with dangers. The new railroad, completed in 1869, enabled one to traverse that same distance in *six days*.[112]

The railroad was constructed by the Union Pacific and Central Pacific companies, both of which were formed primarily for this purpose, and the task was accomplished through massive land grants from the federal government, as well as through loans from the US government and from foreign sources, and in various other ways. Leland Stanford, president of the Central Pacific, used his California political connections (he had previously been governor and US senator there) to have laws passed that prevented any competition to his railroad in the state.[113] In the years during and after the construction of the transcontinental

109 Ida M. Tarbell, *The History of the Standard Oil Company*, 2 vols. (New York: Macmillan, 1904); Upton Sinclair, *The Jungle* (New York: Doubleday, 1906).
110 Stephen E. Ambrose, *Nothing Like It in the World: The Men Who Built the Transcontinental Railroad, 1863–1869* (New York: Simon & Schuster, 2000), 86–88.
111 H. W. Brands, *American Colossus: The Triumph of Capitalism, 1865–1900* (New York: Doubleday, 2010), 40–64.
112 *Ibid.*, 372–74.
113 Folsom, *Entrepreneurs vs. the State*, 22. Note: Current edition (6th) is titled *The Myth of the Robber Barons* previously cited in note 105.

Struggle for the City

railroad, the railroad companies were able to sell off massive portions of the un-used land grants and made huge profits for themselves, profits from land *given* to them by the federal government. That seems somewhat inappropriate on the surface, but it is *more* than inappropriate. These two giant enterprises had an unfair advantage over other competitors that had received no such aid from the public treasury.[114] This is a classic case of *political entrepreneurship*.[115]

Evidence is clear that the construction process itself was filled with waste and corruption. Railroad executives stole money from the treasury, a very large treasury, since the government loaned the railroad companies anywhere from $16,000 to $48,000 per mile of track laid (depending on whether it was on flat, hilly, or mountainous terrain). The Union Pacific executives created their own coal company, mining coal for two dollars per ton, then selling it to their railroad for six dollars a ton, pocketing the profits.[116] Other examples of mas-sive fraud, misuse of public funds, and outright theft on the part of many of the principal actors in the building of this railroad could be adduced if space permitted. It was one giant *seizure of wealth* by men well connected politically who figured out how to use those connections to their advantage. They were *thieves*. They were just *really big* thieves who used the state and federal govern-ments to carry out their massive theft.

One might respond to this by saying, in effect, "Well, it takes the federal government and its special favors to enable corporations to build something as massive and expansive as the transcontinental railroad, and any time you have lots of money floating around among entrepreneurial men, you are going to have some corruption." (That sounds strangely like the observation that when alpha males are given political power, well, many of them are simply going to be sexually promiscuous, so we should just overlook it.) The *evidence* just does not bear out the claim, however, that only the federal government can carry off something so massive as construction of a transcontinental railroad.

James J. Hill (1838–1916) was another late nineteenth-century entrepre-neur who owned a railroad company. Hill was a devout Protestant who was

---

114 Albro Martin, *James J. Hill and the Opening of the Northwest* (New York: Oxford University Press, 1976), 411.
115 See the entire account in Ambrose, *Nothing Like It in the World*.
116 DiLorenzo, *How Capitalism Saved America*, 111.

Struggle for the City

heavily influenced by a Quaker teacher, William Wetherald, in high school in Canada. At age twenty-five he married a devout Irish Catholic woman, and throughout his later years he gave generously to both Protestant and Catholic charities and causes.[117] Hill built the *second* transcontinental railroad, the Great Northern, from 1886 to 1893. He did it all without *any* government funds or subsidies.[118] Hill accomplished the entire project by hard work, planning, and judicious purchasing of property along the route of the railroad, with financing from J. P. Morgan. He then sold much of the land he bought to immigrants at very good prices (for them) and transported them for free to their new homesteads in the Northwest if they *promised* to farm near the railroad, knowing that he would earn profits from them by shipping their goods to market. This was *market entrepreneurship* at its best!

One of Hill's watchwords was *efficiency*, since he was using his own money and resources. He was committed to *thrift*, a quality he had learned from his Quaker teacher. He was remarkably capable in planning and strategy, as can be seen from a look at his whole life as a businessman. For instance, once he had finished building the railroad he invested in steamships and so initiated a new period in trade with the Far East. He built his railroad much *cheaper*, with *better materials*, and with fewer instances of need for reconstruction or rerouting, something that plagued the first transcontinental for ten years after its completion. He said he wanted an efficient way for immigrants and others to make their way West, and commented, "We do not care enough for Rocky Mountains scenery to spend a large sum of money developing it."[119] His was "the best constructed and most profitable of all the world's major railroads."[120] Hill was a market entrepreneur, by conviction and by determination. He was not a saint and certainly had flaws, but his kind of "capitalism" was not tainted by governmental cronyism.[121]

The difference between the manner in which the two railroads were constructed was like night and day. That is because one was built under political *intrigue* and the other out of a commitment to sound business and finance

---

117 Brands, *American Colossus*, 467.
118 Michael P. Malone, *James J. Hill: Empire Builder of the Northwest*, Oklahoma Western Biographies 12 (Norman: University of Oklahoma Press, 1996), 102–50.
119 Ibid., 366.
120 Ibid., 102.
121 Ibid., 185–225.

Struggle for the City

principles. There were entrepreneurs, and then there were *entrepreneurs* in the railroad business. Some strong-armed and cozied up to governments at all levels in order to achieve monopolistic status, preferential treatment, subsidies, land grants, and money. Small wonder that their projects were run inefficiently with massive corruption. That was the pattern they themselves set. Then there were rich men like Hill who did it on their own, and provided services for hundreds of thousands of Americans for decades to come.

Another giant industry in the late nineteenth century was *oil.* The depletion of whales in the 1850s caused a sharp rise in the cost of whale oil, a standard product used to light the interior of homes after dark.[122] Only the affluent could afford to light their parlors every evening by that time. Lard oil, tallow, cottonseed oil, and other illuminants were available, but nothing that "burned in a bright, clean, safe manner."[123] The solution to the problem turned out to be oil, crude oil. The first petroleum oil wells were drilled near Titusville, Pennsylvania, in 1859, though at first it was not clear just what use the substance could be put to. The next year a chemist named C. A. Dean distilled the first kerosene from the Pennsylvania oil.[124] It was an illuminant, and a *better* one than was available at the time.

Raised by a mother who had been converted in the fires of the Second Great Awakening, John D. Rockefeller (1839–1937) was raised to fear *God* and his *mother*—his father was something of a flimflam man. Young John himself had a dramatic conversion experience as a teenager, and maintained a commitment to God and church throughout his life. In 1862 at age twenty-three he was already in business with several partners when he was given an opportunity to invest in the new technology, which seemed to hold real promise for wealth. He and his partners put up $4,000, at the time a huge investment, to build a refinery in Cleveland, Ohio.[125]

Rockefeller was a man *consumed* with involvement in the details of his business. He felt the need to know *everything* and to be involved in every single part of his business enterprises, being religious not only about *religion*, but also about

---

122 Chernow, *Titan: The Life of John Rockefeller, Sr.,* 73.
123 Ibid., 73–74.
124 Ibid., 75–79.
125 Ibid., 77–80.

Struggle for the City

business and about *making money*. "Like James J. Hill, Rockefeller paid meticulous attention to every detail of his business, constantly striving to cut his costs, improve his product, and expand his line of products."[126] Rockefeller, as the years wound on, was obsessed with "high-volume, low-cost production in order to maintain market share, even if he temporarily *sacrificed* market share."[127] He pioneered such practices as "vertical integration," in which he made his own barrels and wagons, developed his own coal mines, and controlled almost everything himself, with the exception of transportation. Nothing escaped his attention.

Within a few short years there were hundreds of competitors in the kerosene business, since kerosene was such an increasingly valuable commodity. Many of them had difficulty in maintaining their viability, and Rockefeller bought out hundreds of them. He was a fierce competitor in business, and this competitive spirit incited some of his harshest *critics*. Ida Minerva Tarbell wrote a series of harshly denunciatory articles, published in *McLure's Magazine* in 1902 and 1903, later published as *The History of the Standard Oil Company*.[128] It was hardly objective journalism—Tarbell was sister to the treasurer of Pure Oil Company, Standard Oil's largest competitor, which was unable to keep up with Rockefeller's cost-cutting. This story is like so many of that era: a businessman makes consumers (ordinary working people) who value a dollar and the price of goods his primary object for satisfaction and service. Others do not follow suit in his industry and find the competition hard and exacting. Rather than accept the fact and move on or sell out at a profit or any one of a number of things, they complain to government politicos and to willing media types who are all too glad to carry the water of grievance and envy.

Tarbell herself was of humble family (as was Rockefeller), and she considered that the business giant had robbed America of some of its *innocence*.[129] Her arguments were emotional, ad hominem, and illogical (claiming that Rockefeller was hurting common people, when he was making fuel cheaper and cheaper for the mass population). She was successful, though, in getting a

---

126 DiLorenzo, *How Capitalism Saved America*, 121.
127 Chernow, *Titan: The Life of John Rockefeller, Sr.*, 257.
128 DiLorenzo, *How Capitalism Saved America*, 123. For a full citation of Tarbell's published work, see note 109.
129 Chernow, *Titan: The Life of John Rockefeller, Sr.*, 435–50.

Struggle for the City

segment of America to wonder whether men like Rockefeller were not merely grasping, greedy men who cared only about money and not about *people*. That assessment, popular then and now, remains with us till this day.

What did happen was that Rockefeller's Standard Oil accomplished *two* things simultaneously. It increasingly grew to have a larger and larger share of the market for kerosene, though it never did become a monopoly. It also drove the cost of kerosene in the American market down and down and down. Its market share rose from four percent in 1870 to twenty-five percent in 1874 and eighty-five percent in 1880.[130] At the same time, its large share of the market eventually enabled it to set the price for kerosene, and, contrary to what has often been alleged, it drove the price *down* rather than up. His company was able to cut the cost of refining from three cents a gallon in 1869 to less than *half a cent* by 1885.

Correspondingly, Rockefeller oversaw the drop in retail price from thirty cents a gallon in 1869 to less than eight cents in 1885. This was partly due to drop in crude prices but more to the *efficiency* of the Rockefeller organization and the development of the so-called tank-wagon system for delivering the final product.[131] It was also due to the fact that his large volume of production got him lower prices for transportation. By 1882 Standard refined nine out of every ten barrels of oil produced in the United States.[132] The cheaper price, of course, drove more competitors to either sell or enter other businesses. Since they could not compete at that level, more criticism of the "cutthroat" Rockefeller was fomented by muckrakers. The truth is that competitors were driven out of their previous businesses and into others or went to work for Rockefeller at lucrative salaries and usually with stock in the companies he owned. Rockefeller was a *brilliant* businessman, and competing with him was extremely *difficult*, because he knew how to get costs down and lower the prices. And virtually every family in America had *cheap* fuel for lighting their homes. Rockefeller believed in "doing good by doing well."[133]

---

130 Dominick T. Armentano, *Antitrust and Monopoly: Anatomy of a Policy Failure* (1972; New York: John Wiley & Sons, 1982), 58.
131 Chernow, *Titan: The Life of John Rockefeller, Sr.*, 258.
132 Brands, *American Colossus*, 91.
133 Ibid., 92. Brands uses this phrase in dealing with the contribution of Andrew Carnegie, but it likely fits Rockefeller as well as it does the steel giant.

Struggle for the City

Life is filled with *trade-offs*. That is simply the way it is in the real world where we live. The political covering for government's interference in the business process has always been supposedly to help the "common man," the average American, the consumer, the poor, and the like. Rockefeller was the friend of *all these* in his pricing and his drive for efficiency. And, in the process he saved the whales from extinction.

The word *Realpolitik* refers to the fact that in the political rough and tumble of life, politics faces hard realities. Ideological considerations aside, at some point politics has to deal with the *real situation* one is facing, not some *ideal* situation one might wish for.[134] There is also a kind of "*Realeconomik*." It is valuable and important to think about what economic conditions would be ideal, but then at some point to realize that we have to deal with the world in which we live. We do not live in heaven or some kind of utopian paradise; we dwell in *this* world. It could not be simultaneously the case that every competitor to Standard Oil in business could make the same profits that they made early on and remain in business alongside Rockefeller and *at the same time* offer to American people more and more affordable kerosene. In the world of *Realeconomik*, in this age, it will always be the case that some are *helped* and others are *displaced* in any given situation of economic transition. That is not the last word, of course, but it is a part of the story that has to be considered and understood. In the age to come that will no longer be the case; but we still live in *this age*.

Schumpeter and Commercial Activity: "Creative Destruction"

All of this may sound harsh and unkind, but it ought not to be interpreted that way. It is simply a description of life in this world. An early twentieth-century political economist that we have referred to briefly has described this for us very well. Joseph Schumpeter was an Austrian economist who came to America to teach at Harvard in 1932. Born in 1883, the year that Marx died, Schumpeter did more than any previous economist to extol the importance of *entrepreneurs*. He recognized that entrepreneurs, like Rockefeller and Hill, make life *easier* for many as a result of their innovations and inventions, but noted

---

134 We realize that the term often has a darker and more sinister connotation, but here we are simply employing it in its neutral and generic implications that there is a real-life political situation that has to be faced at some point.

Struggle for the City

also that they bring a *destabilizing* influence into the market. For Schumpeter, capitalism can "never be stationary." The industrial process "incessantly revolutionizes the economic structure from within, incessantly destroying the old one, incessantly creating a new one."[135] The Austrian economist labeled this process "creative destruction" and offered that this process is *inevitable* in a fluid environment in which the state allows for the market to develop on its own terms.[136]

Here is how it works. Someone has an idea for a new mousetrap (to use an example we have already employed), an idea that attracts attention when it is produced and marketed because it is better than anything previously available. It is so good that consumers shift their buying patterns so much that the sale of older mousetraps drops by fifty percent. Demand drops and the manufacturer of older mousetraps is forced to lay off workers. Suppliers to the older company receive fewer orders and they, in turn, lay off workers. The new company is flourishing. It is hiring new workers at a steady rate to keep up with demand. It is also purchasing more and more supplies and raw materials from its vendors, who, in turn, hire new employees and purchase more from their suppliers. Consumers are *elated* and mice are dying by the *truckload*, but some people have to go find new jobs.[137] Creative destruction.

Think about it like this. Walmart[138] builds a store in a medium-sized town in Kentucky that previously had nothing like a Walmart anywhere nearby. What happens? Small mom-and-pop stores are negatively impacted since they have to sell groceries and other items at a higher price. They simply do not have the wholesale buying power of a Walmart. Consumers, who have to watch their budgets and buy things at the lowest possible prices, shift their purchasing to the new superstore. The small stores go out of business, and the

---

135 Joseph A. Schumpeter, *Capitalism, Socialism, and Democracy*, 3rd ed. (1942; New York: Harper & Row, 1950), 82–83.
136 Ibid., 82.
137 No actual mice were hurt in this narrative!
138 When we use an example like this, we are thinking of Walmart as it was conceived by the founder, Sam Walton. This was his vision. We realize that in reality, a company such as Wal-Mart Stores, Inc., is subject to the lure of political entrepreneurship like any other and that in some places and some times it might also be corrupted. We are dealing here with the basic principles upon which the company was built. More discussion of Walmart later in the book.

Struggle for the City

families that own them have to find other means of employment. But young families that had to devote, say, thirty percent of their income to food and clothing now spend only twenty-five percent on that and are now free to use that extra five percent for other items, which means that another segment of the market is receiving revenue that it did not receive before.

Creative destruction. This is what industrialization did to the economy of the West in the nineteenth century. It is what the automobile did to the buggy-whip industry in the 1920s. Is it good or bad? The answer depends in part on what one *means* by "good" and "bad." It is *not* a moral issue at heart; but in terms of outcome, it is good if you benefit from the new resource, and it is bad if you lose your job. It is *both*, depending on who gets helped and who gets hurt. But if not for the process of creative destruction, we would all still be living in caves and heading out every morning in hope of killing something so that the family might have dinner.[139]

That brings us back to Standard Oil. Several antitrust bills had passed through Congress in the 1890s and the first decade of the twentieth century.[140] A "trust" is simply a *conglomerate* of business arrangements made by a single company or individual in an attempt to gain a large advantage over a certain segment of the economy. Some perceived these trusts to be a threat to *democracy* and to *free trade* insofar as they might become a threat to consumers. If a company devised means to drive out competition and then jack up the price of goods and services since it was now the "only game in town," then that would constitute a *threat* to the market, specifically to *consumers*. Tarbell alleged that Standard Oil had done just that. She claimed that Rockefeller had violated the Sherman Act, which declared "unlawful trusts and combinations in restraint of trade and production." One does not have to be a lawyer to recognize that this language is *ambiguous* in the extreme and could be subject to almost any kind of interpretation in a court of law, depending on the disposition of the judge. Still, the claim was made that Standard Oil was in violation.[141]

The evidence, though, indicates exactly the *opposite*. We do not even need Rockefeller's aspiration, noted earlier, *not* to raise prices but rather to give con-

---

139 Mark Skousen, *The Making of Modern Economics*, 2nd ed. (Armonk, NY: M. E. Sharpe, 2009), 430.
140 In particular, the Sherman Antitrust Act of 1890 and the Clayton Act of 1914.
141 See Chernow, *Titan: The Life of John Rockefeller, Sr.*, 537–56, for discussion of these issues.

Struggle for the City

sumers the best product at the cheapest possible price. The statistical data bear that out. As we have already noted, by the middle of the first decade of the twentieth century the price of kerosene had declined three hundred percent from its high in the 1870s. If antitrust legislation has as its goal the protection of consumers, the case against Standard Oil seems "ludicrous."[142] In 1906 the federal government filed suit to dissolve Standard Oil under the dictates of the Sherman Antitrust Act. Five years later the Supreme Court broke the company into a group of smaller companies, having found it guilty of violating the 1890 legislation, ambiguous though it was.[143]

We are not arguing that Rockefeller was a saint or that he always acted appropriately in business dealings. He was a passionate, competitive, aggressive man in his business dealings, and there are plenty of actual situations where someone might consider him to be at fault. What we *are* arguing is that he became the victim of *political entrepreneurship* (as we defined it earlier) as it employed the assistance of the federal government to stifle his industry. He was punished in the courts because he was *big* in a time when *just being big* was considered bad. And he refused to deal with the government in the way the *political entrepreneurs* had done. Rockefeller and other market entrepreneurs of his day, men like J. P. Morgan and Andrew Carnegie, "came of age in an era of unprecedented government corruption and never would be able to conceive of government as a suitable instrument for reforming and regulating the economy."[144] One has to wonder whether history is, in a way, repeating itself in our own day.

If we look at other industries, we would find similar trends in terms of market share and costs. The United States Steel Corporation, more commonly known as U.S. Steel, was a large conglomerate of companies that gained a significant share of the market for steel and iron in the late nineteenth century, but which saw that share diminish steadily in the early twentieth century. In 1907 a large gathering of top steel executives from around the country gathered together to try to come to an agreement about fixing steel prices.[145] If they

---

142 DiLorenzo, *How Capitalism Saved America*, 126.
143 Chernow, *Titan: The Life of John Rockefeller, Sr.*, 554. Chernow's presentation of the case and the issues generally exonerates Rockefeller of wrongdoing, but not everyone in Standard Oil was innocent (see 537–60).
144 Gordon, *Empire of Wealth*, 222.
145 Gabriel Kolko, *Triumph of Conservatism* (New York: Free Press, 1977), 35.

Struggle for the City

could agree on a fixed price, then they would not have to worry about competitive pricing but could set the price as high as possible and know that the price would stay there. This is known as "rationalizing" (a different usage from our common sense of the term as used in this book), and the goal in steel and other industries was to *rationalize* the process in order to prevent annoying fluctuations in the market. But we are not surprised, in light of Schumpeter's conclusions, that they were unable to do this.

So, the market fluctuated, and U.S. Steel's share of the market dropped from 62.9 percent of the market for ingots and castings in 1905 to 52.5 percent in 1911 and 46.2 percent in 1921.[146] Similar trends can be seen in the automobile industry, agricultural machine industry, telephone industry, and other industries across the board. But the second and third decades of the new century witnessed an array of antitrust enactments that in effect enabled the federal government to *regulate* and *control* American business more and more.

The political arena would witness the playing out of the struggle to understand, critique, and/or justify what was happening in big business. William Jennings Bryan, erstwhile Democratic presidential candidate (he would be nominated three times, but never win the presidency), defending yeoman farmers against the interests of industrialists, gave what came to be his most famous speech, when he urged, "You shall not press down upon the brow of labor this crown of thorns, and you shall not crucify mankind upon a cross of gold," referring to the gold standard, which he believed was stultifying the ability of small businesses to flourish.[147]

The first decade of the new century really witnessed the end of big-muscled, hard-hitting, "get out of my way or I will run you over" (terminology we use here as reflecting the attitudes of populist movements) big business in America, but not for the reasons commonly thought. The ingenuity of American business saw to it that the companies would grow and proliferate and the economy would operate at near full throttle for the first three decades of the new century, even though some industry leaders would feel chastened by the example of Standard Oil.

---

146 Ibid., 37.
147 Michael Kazin, *A Godly Hero: The Life of William Jennings Bryan* (New York: Alfred A. Knopf, 2006), 61.

Struggle for the City

Of course, in the new setting, businesses increasingly maneuvered their way to the government and its regulatory power in order to *limit competition* and guarantee *higher prices*. The early twentieth century would witness an increasing contrast between *market* entrepreneurs and *political* entrepreneurs. Historians almost universally refer to this period (1898–1916) as the Progressive Era, so named for the judgment that the progressive ideas about government and social needs that we have previously surveyed now hatched in public demand for accountability by business to government in the name of *social justice*.

Ironically, it was an era driven by the politics of men like Theodore Roosevelt, president and Rough Rider and lifelong "conservationist." In August of 1910 he famously founded his Bull Moose Party to focus attention on what he called a "new nationalism" and a Fair Deal for the "common people." But this was not his first foray into populism, the attempt to move the masses of the people with themes that resonate, regardless of their merit or lack thereof when scrutinized in rational terms and realistic categories. Roosevelt loved being known as the "trust buster," having had his administration file the antitrust case against Standard Oil in 1906 (a decision not handed down till 1911 after he left office). He encouraged Progressives to push for the income tax (on the "rich" only at that time) after it was struck down by the Supreme Court. He inflamed the masses with tough talk about the evil of wealthy people of his time with statements such as "too much cannot be said against the men of great wealth." He vowed to "punish certain malefactors of great wealth," sounding rather like Hillary Clinton and others in the primary campaign run-up to the US presidential election of 2008.

Roosevelt, himself an inheritor of wealth that he did not build on his own, saw big business as inherently monopolistic and dangerous. He assumed that what he saw on the surface of anecdotal situations was in fact the accurate take on the situation.[148] The fact was that though TR saw an America run over with monopolies, his vision was impaired. Monopolies by their very nature are evil in the eyes of the public because of their ability to run others out of their

---

148 Jim Powell, "Obama and Teddy Roosevelt: Both Progressives, Both Clueless about the Economy," *Forbes*, December 8, 2011, http://www.forbes.com/sites/jimpowell/2011/12/08/obama-and-teddy-roosevelt-both-progressives-both-clueless-about-the-economy/. See also Powell's biographical work on Roosevelt, Jim Powell, *Bully Boy: The Truth about Theodore Roosevelt's Legacy* (New York: Crown Forum, 2006).

Struggle for the City

business field, push prices up, and take advantage of their positioning in the market by withholding supplies. All over the America of that day prices were falling and supplies were abundant, with low inflation and some of the lowest business failure rates in the history of the country. Nevertheless, even as Roosevelt called for "big government" to rein in the businessmen, other "business" was afoot, though it was not obvious to all observers.

As Robert Higgs has shown, the facts differed widely from the public perception, for it was in reality the business community that wised up to the possibilities of a real *partnership* with government. It was *they* who began to lead the way to controls and regulations that would solidify their positions in the economy and squeeze out competition.[149] By the time of the American entry into World War I, "[t]he dominant ideology of political and economic elites had become one that not only tolerated a greatly expanded role for government in economic decision making; it positively insisted on such activism."[150] This era would provide the impetus for events that would transpire during the succeeding critical periods of 1916–18, 1930–33, and 1940–45.[151]

The Great War would present the occasion for America to take decisive leadership of the world economy. We have already discussed at length Woodrow Wilson's notion that the *administrative state* could and should control every area of life. Though he ran on a platform of no entry into the European war in 1916, it was only a brief period after his inauguration before he announced plans to send troops to France and Belgium. Americans should not have been surprised, since Wilson had written years before that a war can allow a leader the opportunity to enact changes in governing that might not be possible in other situations. A *crisis* should not be allowed to go to *waste*! It was the opportunity for the American president to assert *unheard of* authority over the economy and its political connections, while monitoring dissent in the body politic.[152] Higgs is worth quoting at length here:

---

149 Robert Higgs, *Crisis and Leviathan: Critical Episodes in the Growth of American Government* (New York: Oxford University Press, 1987), esp. chap. 6.
150 Ibid., 121–22.
151 Ibid., 106. Higgs throughout his study insists that the crises he covers did not *require* big government answers, but they were used to further ideologies already ascendant or in place.
152 See Higgs throughout *Crisis and Leviathan,* chap. 7, emphasizing the manner in which national, state, and local government monitored its citizens' lives and turned neighbors and local business people into enforcers of petty regulations that some called "patriotic meddling."

Struggle for the City

The American economy remained, as late as 1916, predominantly a market system. The next two years, however, witnessed an enormous and wholly unprecedented intervention of the federal government in the nation's economic affairs. By the time of the armistice, the government had taken over the ocean shipping, railroad, telephone, and telegraph industries; commandeered hundreds of manufacturing plants; entered into massive economic enterprises on its own account in such varied departments as shipbuilding, wheat trading, and building construction; undertaken to lend huge sums to businesses directly or indirectly and to regulate the private issuance of securities; established official priorities for the use of transportation facilities, food, fuel, and many raw materials; fixed prices of dozens of important commodities; intervened in hundreds of labor disputes; and conscripted millions of men for service in the armed forces. It had, in short, extensively distorted or wholly displaced markets, creating what some contemporaries called "war socialism."[153]

Among the administrative enforcer types on Wilson's team was a man named Herbert Hoover, head of the United States Food Administration. The "lessons" he would learn here about government manipulation of the economy would lead the nation to the brink of economic collapse.

---

153 Ibid., 123.

Struggle for the City

Chapter 20

From the Great War to the
Great Depression and Its New Deal

THE TWENTIETH CENTURY COULD, arguably, be dated from 1914 till 2000. The momentous events related to the Great War really make those first fourteen years of the century to fit more with the nineteenth century than the twentieth. We will begin to look first at the postwar prosperity and then follow that with an analysis of the Great Depression and will discuss its causes and its effects.

THE GREAT WAR

The Great War, later known as World War I, was one of the momentous events of European history, and in a way signals the end of the nineteenth century and the beginning of a new world order. Because America was more impacted by World War II, we will only give a short treatment of the first war. We think it is likely that histories written by the middle of our current century will just refer to these as the World War, parts 1 and 2, since many of the chief combatants were the same in each case. The Great War turned out to be the "primal tragedy of modern world civilization" and the reason why the twentieth century became such a "disastrous epoch for mankind."[1] The United States was a powerful nation at the outset of the war but was not a

---

1   Paul Johnson, *A History of the American People* (New York: HarperCollins, 1997), 642.

world power; it would emerge as one of the great world powers by 1918. Even with that, the war was a *tragedy*.

The United States did not enter the war until early 1917. By that time the warring nations were harnessing their entire economies to the effort of winning the conflict. When America did join in, American churches supported the war effort enthusiastically. They often adopted resolutions that used language such as "hellish Huns" and "sinister black eagle." The churches bordered on becoming government agencies in helping the war effort.[2] "Fundamentalists" were at first excoriated for not fully supporting the Wilsonian tack, but they eventually came on board after powerful elements in the broader ecclesial community attacked them in the popular press.[3] The large denominations organized war commissions, mobilized chaplains, in a way similar to what they had done in the Civil War, and added a drive to defeat John Barleycorn to their war concerns. In the eyes of many, the two were connected, since Germany was the seat of much of the beer brewing industry, even though many of those brewers had emigrated to America and set up shop here. This two-fisted effort (no pun intended) resulted in Prohibition being adopted only a year after the war was over, with the Eighteenth Amendment achieving ratification in October 1919, and taking effect January 16, 1920.[4]

The big black mark on the church's reputation in the war was the way it treated pacifists and conscientious objectors. Because Americans, including American Christians, saw the war as almost a holy war, almost a modern crusade, pacifists were seen almost as traitors to the cause.[5] Quakers, Mennonites,

---

2   Thomas A. Askew and Peter W. Spellman, *The Churches and the American Experience* (Grand Rapids: Baker, 1984), 180.

3   Shirley Jackson Case, professor of early church history at the Divinity School of the University of Chicago, went so far as to suggest that premillennialism was sinister in its origins and intents and was being supported by "[t]wo-thousand dollars a week" emanating from unknown sources, "but there is a strong suspicion *that it emanates from German sources. In my belief the fund would be a profitable field for governmental investigation.*" Quoted from the *Chicago Daily News*, January 21, 1918, in *The King's Business* 9 (April 1918), 276, cited in George M. Marsden, *Fundamentalism and American Culture*, 2nd ed. New York: Oxford University Press, 2006), 140.

4   Mark A. Noll, *A History of Christianity in the United States and Canada* (1992; repr., Grand Rapids, MI: Eerdmans, 2003), 296–97. See esp. Daniel Okrent, *Last Call: The Rise and Fall of Prohibition* (New York: Scribner, 2010), esp. 7–52, 227–46, 329–54.

5   Sidney Ahlstrom, *A Religious History of the American People*, 2nd ed. (New Haven, CT: Yale University Press, 2004), 883–89.

Struggle for the City

and Jehovah's Witnesses were subject to ridicule, harassment, and even imprisonment for their religiously motivated refusal to support the war. This would be the last war where such a thing as intolerance of pacifism would happen on a large scale.[6] And when the war was over, America was ready to take her place as a favored nation in this world.

THE ROARING TWENTIES AND THE GREAT DEPRESSION

No single issue defined the American economic and political situation in the twentieth century more than the *Great Depression*. Though in the twentieth century the United States fought two world wars and several smaller wars, undertook massive new entitlement legislation, tripled in population, shifted population's center of gravity to the West and the South, attracted massively larger numbers of immigrants from south of the United States and from Asia, the Great Depression (and its aftermath) was the *defining* event in the middle of all of those other developments that altered our self-conception as a nation. If the American Revolution and the documents that surrounded it (Declaration of Independence and Constitution) defined our identity for the first eighty years of our existence, and the Civil War redefined our identity for the next seven or so decades, the Great Depression and its aftermath accomplished much the same thing for the twentieth century. And this is not only true of our *political economy*, it is also true for the nature of the *Christian faith* and the religious identity in the churches of America.

The Twenties as Boom Time

The American economy *boomed* during the war years, and after an economic recession in the early Twenties, it surged again in the middle and later part of the decade. It was not the "Roaring Twenties" of popular lore, but it was a time of prosperity and economic growth. The automobile proved to be a new part of the economy that would transform American economic life in ways beyond calculation. The internal combustion engine was invented in

---

6   Askew and Spellman, *Churches and the American Experience*, 180–81.

Struggle for the City

1876 by a German engineer and the carburetor was invented in 1893.[7] With those two technologies in place, automobiles appeared at a rapid pace in both Europe and America. In 1903, fifty-seven companies built cars in the United States alone. But in classic social Darwinian fashion, that number would decline, until today there are only about two-dozen automobile manufacturers in the entire world. Henry Ford was the son of a Dearborn, Michigan farmer. Not well educated or well read, Ford was fascinated with mechanics from his youth. In 1896 he built his first automobile in a carriage house behind where he was living.[8] By 1923 Henry Ford's auto plant was producing six thousand cars a day. Then, by 1925 that number was up to 8,500 cars a day and in 1929 it stood at nearly twelve thousand, that from a man who in 1903 had started with a handful of employees and $27,000 in his pocket from investors.[9] Just to understand what a difference a decade had made, the American automobile companies had produced 1,658,000 cars in 1919, but in 1929 that tripled to 4,587,000 cars. In 1919 there were 1.12 cars registered for every ten households; ten years later there were 3.15 cars for every four households.[10]

By 1920 Ford was producing half the cars in the world. What made him so productive? Ford introduced the Model T in 1908. It was priced at $850, a much lower price than most other cars at the time, and much cheaper than the European models. But in 1913 the entrepreneur introduced the assembly line approach to manufacturing. He had visited a meat-packing plant and decided that if animals could be disassembled on a line, the reverse process could be employed for manufacturing autos.[11] By 1916 the price had dropped to $360 and Ford sold more than 730,000 Model Ts. By the 1920s, and despite inflation caused by World War I, the price was set at $265. It was largely a result of the assembly line approach, but even more, it was careful attention to every *detail* of labor management that enabled the automaker to be able to

---

7   John Steele Gordon, *An Empire of Wealth: The Epic History of American Economic Power* (New York: HarperCollins, 2004), 296.

8   Ibid., 297.

9   Amity Shlaes, *The Forgotten Man: A New History of the Great Depression* (New York: HarperCollins, 2007), 39.

10 Gene Smiley, *Rethinking the Great Depression: A New View of Its Causes and Consequences*, American Ways (Chicago: Ivan R. Dee, 2002), 4.

11 Gordon, *Empire of Wealth*, 298.

Struggle for the City

build a car so cheap that his own workers could buy one, workers that earned an industry-high five dollars a day.[12]

The automobile turned out to be a *transformative* technology, like electricity at about the same time, and like the computer chip later in the century.[13] In 1900 there were about two hundred miles of paved roads in the United States. By 1920 there were 369,000 and by 1929, 662,000 miles of paved roads.[14] In 1905 the first purpose-built gas station opened in St. Louis. Gasoline at the time was being sold at general stores and blacksmith shops, with many of the latter closing up in the early years of the twentieth century or being converted to gas stations and mechanic garages. Corporate *logos* began to appear on roadside signs, since a traveler in a car did not have time to read a long sentence while traveling at thirty or forty miles an hour. A new demographic region, the suburbs, began to be developed on the periphery of cities since commuting either to the job or to the train station was now possible.

Farm families now had the ability to abate the sense of loneliness many of them experienced before the car, when walking to a neighbor's house was too time-consuming since they lived several miles away.[15] The *rural* economy changed as well. In 1900 one-third of the farmland was devoted to fodder for the nation's large population of horses and mules. As farmers turned more and more to internal combustion-driven vehicles for their work, the nature of farming and what was grown on the farm also changed, causing a considerable amount of difficulty for farmers, especially after the war ended in 1918.[16] America led the way. In 1924 the four leading European car manufacturers turned out only eleven percent as many automobiles as those built in the United States.[17]

Electricity was also making a huge difference in the economy and was becoming, like the automobile, a kind of *background* technology that would affect

12 Stephen Meyer III, *The Five-Dollar Day: Labor Management and Social Control in the Ford Motor Company, 1908–1921*, SUNY Series in American Social History (New York: State University of New York Press, 1981).

13 David A. Hounshell, *From the American System to Mass Production, 1800–1932: The Development of Manufacturing Technology in the United States*, Studies in Industry and Society 4 (Baltimore: Johns Hopkins University Press, 1984), 249.

14 Gordon, *Empire of Wealth*, 299.

15 Meyer, *Five-Dollar Day*, 85.

16 Gordon, *Empire of Wealth*, 300–301.

17 Johnson, *History of the American People*, 723.

Struggle for the City

other technologies. British physicist Michael Faraday had proven the fact of
electricity and magnetism in 1831, and its first practical usage was with the
telegraph. Thomas Edison would be the first great purveyor of electricity, but
only after first inventing the industrial research laboratory in Menlo Park, New
Jersey.[18] It was in that laboratory that he invented the phonograph (1877) and
the electric light (1879).[19] Once he had invented the incandescent light bulb,
Edison knew that there would have to be some kind of system that would enable
the bulbs to be used by people in buildings, so he "set about to build a generating plant and lay electric lines in a one-square-mile area of Manhattan business
district" in 1880.[20] Working at night so as not to disturb traffic during business
hours, he dug trenches, sent out crews to homes and businesses to wire up stores
and houses of those willing to participate in his "experiment," and solved many
problems he encountered on the fly. The solutions for the problems he encountered during this two-year period of preparation for the first electrified city resulted in 102 patents in the year 1882 alone.[21] On September 4, 1882, Edison
threw the switch, and lights came on in buildings all over the district. "By that
evening it was obvious that something important had happened."[22]

More orders were put in immediately to light more of Manhattan. Sam
Insull of Chicago, Edison's former secretary, was using Thomas Edison's inventions to light that city and countryside with electricity.[23] Similar projects began
to sprout up almost immediately in other towns and cities. That electrification
was being made possible by the construction of new *hydroelectric* dams. The first
such dam in the age of electrification had been completed in 1927, the Wilson
Dam near Muscle Shoals, and it was designed to provide electricity for the rural
and small-town communities in Alabama. The future looked bright—literally!

The electrification of America was fast becoming a reality, with fifteen percent of homes electrified by 1910 and sixty-eight percent in 1930. Similarly,
factories were using electricity. By 1909 electric power accounted for twenty-one

---

18 Randall E. Stross, *The Wizard of Menlo Park: How Thomas Alva Edison Invented the Modern
World* (New York: Crown, 2008), 83.
19 Ibid., 102.
20 Gordon, *Empire of Wealth*, 303.
21 Stross, *Wizard of Menlo Park*, 147.
22 Gordon, *Empire of Wealth*, 303.
23 Shlaes, *Forgotten Man*, 21–23.

Struggle for the City

percent of primary horsepower in manufacturing, a figure that would grow to fifty percent in 1919 and seventy-five percent in 1929. That was a *huge* development. It meant that buildings and machines no longer had to be oriented to a power source, like a water wheel. You could build a plant anywhere, and you could organize the machinery in ways that made for more efficiency, not merely as in the past to relate to the location of power sources. In the 1920s mechanical refrigerators were entering the market, and about eight percent of households had one by 1930. Washing machines went from single digit percentages in 1920 to twenty-five percent of households by 1930. Radios went from single digits in 1920 to about forty percent of households in 1930. All of this was facilitated by electricity.[24] America was on a boom. Movies, radio programs, the 1927 Yankees—it is hard to express how different the world seemed even compared to what it had looked like ten or twenty years earlier.

The Twenties was a decade in which youth and youth culture first emerged as having a separate identity. It was in this decade that the word *teenager* was coined.[25] Disposable income, the automobile, and relaxed standards in culture paved the way for such teenagers to become a target for *marketing*. In that decade nineteenth-century private academies gave way to twentieth-century high schools, and such public venues mandated a "social education" to go along with, and to some degree to supplant, the traditional forms of education.[26] Adolescence became less of a time of *preparing* for adulthood and more of a time of *delaying* it. A symbiosis came into existence, for the first time in history, between a "self-standing youth culture and a self-conscious entertainment industry."[27] This would have huge implications for the economy, for the churches, and for families.

One development, though, seems incongruent to the culture of the Roaring Twenties: Prohibition. The Eighteenth Amendment, passed by a Congress that believed this was what the people wanted, ratified by the states in October 1919, was signed into law January 16, 1920. Why did the country so readily

---

24 For these statistics and many others, see Nathan Rosenberg, *Technology and American Economic Growth*, Harper Torchbooks (New York: Harper & Row, 1972).
25 Quentin J. Schultze, *Dancing in the Dark: Youth, Popular Culture, and the Electronic Media* (Grand Rapids, MI: Eerdmans, 1991), 14–45. The terms *adolescent* and *adolescence* came into vogue at this time.
26 Ibid., 36.
27 Ibid., 38.

Struggle for the City

turn to federal legislation in dealing with the issue of alcohol? The churches, especially the Protestant churches, were at the heart of this development.[28] Preachers such as Billy Sunday, R. A. Torrey and J. Wilbur Chapman poured themselves into this crusade right after the turn of the century.[29] Sunday especially saw his task as the salvation of urban America.[30] The cities were places of sin and degradation, and something had to be done about the abuse, the laziness, the sordidness of city life. Women wanted Prohibition as a way of taming their husbands and also as an issue linked to women's suffrage.[31] Prohibition was of course, government intrusion into the lives of individuals, and most Americans, especially Protestants, had avoided sanctioning government intrusion, but this was somehow *different*, or so it seemed. "Though individualistic Protestants were constantly criticizing liberal efforts to remake the world through law, they were eager to do so themselves on this issue," agreeing with Gladstone that "it was the duty of government to make it easy to do right and difficult to do wrong."[32] Prohibition would endure throughout the 1920s and into the early years of the Great Depression. Herbert Hoover, whose entire presidency was encompassed by the Prohibition years, referred to it as the "noble experiment."[33] It was an experiment that would not endure long.

Calvin Coolidge

The Twenties was a boom decade in terms of manufacturing, but the tone in the White House during the middle of that decade was *muted*. Calvin Coolidge had been vice president to Warren Harding, and when Harding collapsed and died on August 2, 1923, Coolidge became president. He would subsequently run for reelection once, in 1924, and win, putting him in office till January 1929. So, he was president during most of the great business years of the decade.

---

28 For a full discussion of Prohibition, see James H. Timberlake, *Prohibition and the Progressive Movement, 1900–1960* (Cambridge, MA: Harvard University Press, 1963).
29 Martin E. Marty, *Righteous Empire: The Protestant Experience in America,* Two Centuries of American Life (New York: Dial Press, 1970), 214.
30 Lyle W. Dorsett, *Billy Sunday and the Redemption of Urban America*, Library of Religious Biography (Grand Rapids, MI: Eerdmans, 1991), 85–123.
31 Okrent, *Last Call*, 62–66.
32 As quoted by Marty, *Righteous Empire*, 213.
33 Askew and Spellman, *Churches and the American Experiment*, 181.

Coolidge was a famously quiet man who was absolutely committed to the rule of law and to a laissez-faire approach to politics and the economy. He oversaw a time of real prosperity and believed that he had no mandate, indeed no right, to *tinker* with the economy. He sought to follow the advice of Lord Salisbury, who had governed England earlier: "The country is carried comfortably down the river by the current, and the function of government is merely to put out an oar when there is any danger of it drifting into the bank."[34] Like Queen Elizabeth I of England, he was "a supreme exponent of masterly inactivity."[35] Coolidge believed that the president ought not to cater to people who wish an audience with him. As he stated it, "Nine-tenths of a president's callers at the White House want something they ought not to have. If you keep still they will run out in three or four minutes." His attitude toward work and welfare was expressed in these words: "Government cannot relieve from toil. The normal must take care of themselves. Self-government means self-support.... Ultimately, property rights and personal rights are the same thing."[36] His governing approach also led him to sneer at Prohibition; the federal government had no business legislating on such issues. Though he could not repeal Prohibition, he did little to strengthen its enforcement.[37] Every tub must sit on its own bottom.

This was not the common governing policy in the world of that time, though from our distance we may think that it was. Most of those who came to power in the early 1920s stand in stark contrast to Coolidge. Mussolini became Italy's fortieth prime minister in 1922, soon calling himself *Il Duce* ("The Leader"). Stalin came to power in the Soviet Union the same year as Coolidge, Chiang Kai-shek in China began ruling in 1925, Reza Shah over Persia also in 1925. All of these "took government into corners of their country it had never before penetrated."[38] The fact is that the Twenties and Thirties were decades in which governing in many places in the world became more

---

34 Quoted in Calvin Coolidge, *Mind of a President: As Revealed by Himself in His Own Words; President Coolidge's Views on Public Questions Selected and Arranged by Subjects,* ed. C. Bascom Slemp (Garden City, NY: Doubleday, 1926), 83.
35 Johnson, *History of the American People,* 715.
36 Ibid., 716.
37 Okrent, *Last Call,* 227–28.
38 Johnson, *History of the American People,* 717.

Struggle for the City

heavy-handed and top-heavy than had previously been the case in most of these countries; just think of Hitler and FDR.[39] Calvin Coolidge may have been the last laissez-faire president until Ronald Reagan.

The Crash of the Market

Herbert Hoover was inaugurated as president in 1929. He had run on the campaign promise of a chicken in every pot and a car in every garage. It looked as though his presidency would witness just that kind of boom. But after only nine months, something bad happened.

One sign of the booming economy of the late 1920s was the advance in the stock market. If one takes July 1926 as the base month for analysis and index at 100, one can then compare that with development over the ensuing years. The same month in 1927 it was 112, and a year after that it was 148.[40] By September 1929 it stood at 216. An investor who bought $1,000 worth of those stocks in 1926 had $2,160 in just over three years, and that does not count dividends. Such an increase was quite remarkable!

There were signs of weakness in the economy, however. Business investment in equipment and technology had declined in 1928 and 1929 over previous years. Auto sales were down a bit in 1929 from the previous year, and other industrial production was down as well. The Federal Reserve had issued a warning in February 1929 that it would not support bank loans for stock speculation. But everyone from the new president to the Harvard Economic Society was touting the soundness of the nation's economy.[41]

That would change quickly. The stock market peaked on September 3 at 381. It declined to 320 on October 20. The last two weeks of October 1929, saw the market fluctuate dramatically. Panic ensued on Tuesday, October 29, when sixteen million shares were dumped. The index fell forty-three points in one day, with some

39 See "The First Despotic Utopias," chap. 2 in Paul Johnson, *Modern Times: The World from the Twenties to the Nineties*, rev. ed. (New York: HarperPerennial, 1991).
40 Charles P. Kindleberger, *The World in Depression, 1929–1939*, History of the World Economy in the Twentieth Century 4 (Berkeley: University of California Press, 1973), 111–13.
41 John Kenneth Galbraith, *The Great Crash, 1929*, Discus Book (1954; New York: Avon Books, 1979), 127–28.

Struggle for the City

stocks being down fifty percent by the end of the trading day. Goldman Sachs, for instance, one of the most glamorous of investment trusts, was down forty-two percent in one day.[42] By December the market had fallen to 147 and a year later it was down to 102. In July 1932 it had cratered to thirty-four points, compared to the 100 index number of July 1926, down more than eighty-five percent from its high in September 1929.[43]

What caused all this? It was nothing new, of course, as there had been at least twelve previous financial crises (crashes) in the American economy through the nineteenth and early twentieth centuries.[44] Yet what caused the 1929 crash? Some have argued that people just got carried away with speculation. But this does not seem to be the case. Economist John Kenneth Galbraith lists five major weaknesses that laid the groundwork for the crash: unequal income distribution, unstable business organization at the corporate level, weak banking structure, international financial troubles, and ignorance of financial realities by the nation's leaders.[45] Not all of these are of equal significance, and one or two of them are actually debatable as to whether they played a role at all.

What made it all worse was the practice of allowing people to purchase stocks on the *margin*, that is, of putting only a small percentage down when purchasing stocks.[46] Lots of people were in the market in 1929 in comparison to earlier times. There was booming growth in the 1920s, with all of the new technology in cars, refrigerators, washing machines, and such commodities. The general public was buying stock for the first time. An article appeared in the *Ladies' Home Journal*, August 1929, entitled "Everybody Ought to Be Rich," which encouraged housewives to get into the stock market. The timing is ironic![47]

The market crashed. That means that people began selling stock at an accelerated speed. Massive selling causes, in supply-and-demand fashion, prices to go

---

42 Lance E. Davis, Jonathan R. T. Hughes and Duncan M. McDougall, *American Economic History: The Development of a National Economy*, rev. ed., Irwin Series in Economics (Homewood, IL: Irwin, 1965), chap. 23.

43 Galbraith, *Great Crash, 1929*, 78–112.

44 R. C. O. Matthews, *The Business Cycle*, Cambridge Economic Handbooks (Chicago: University of Chicago Press, 1959).

45 Galbraith, *Great Crash, 1929*, 157–65.

46 Shlaes, *Forgotten Man*, 41.

47 Samuel Crowther, "Everybody Ought to Be Rich: An Interview with John J. Raskob," *Ladies' Home Journal* (August 1929): 9, 36.

Struggle for the City

down. Brokers were hit with the demand for cash when the selling began. They naturally called for the *margins* (that is, the loans advanced on trading accounts for the purchase of stocks) to be paid in full; people ran to the banks, and a *domino* effect began.[48] But a recession was already on its way long before the crash occurred. "Prosperity began to fade in early 1929, although the public did not begin to realize it until after the sensational stock market crash in October."[49] The recession would follow after.

The Churches of America Respond to the Economic Crisis

The market crash and the depression that followed impacted churches in America in dramatic ways, but the churches that were so impacted had already been enduring a struggle of their own, some for decades and others for at least ten or fifteen years. We have discussed the rise of theological modernism in the American churches in the wake of the Civil War, in part because of the "theological problem" that was sparked by the interpretation of the Bible's teaching on slavery and the "Negro problem." That modernism spread through many Northern denominations, especially the Presbyterians, the Congregationalists, the Episcopal Church, and the Northern Baptists. By the turn of the century the theological institutions of those churches and many of the more prominent pulpits in large cities came increasingly under the influence of liberal thought.[50] Conservatives in those denominations protested, but many did not realize just how dramatically their churches would change in the decades ahead. Many of these churches had endured some diversity in the past, but now it seemed that the unorthodox elements were about to *take over*.[51]

These shifts coincided with transitions in the intellectual culture of America in general. Secularism had begun to settle in even before the Great War, and after the war it made its presence known in spades. "Peacetime normalcy

---

48 Peter Rappoport and Eugene N. White, "Was the Crash of 1929 Expected?" *American Economic Review* 84, no. 1 (March 1994): 33.
49 Paul Studenski and Herman E. Kroos, *Financial History of the United States: Fiscal, Monetary, Banking, and Tariff* (New York: McGraw-Hill, 1952), 353.
50 Marsden, *Fundamentalism and American Culture*, 22–25.
51 Bradley J. Longfield, *The Presbyterian Controversy: Fundamentalists, Modernists, and Moderates*, Religion in America (New York: Oxford University Press, 1991).

accommodated and accelerated the trend toward secularization in American society."[52] H. L. Mencken and others like him had been accusing the churches of America of promoting outmoded ideas and backward lifestyles.[53] Throughout the late nineteenth century, but now even more dramatically, science came to have a determinative role in matters of truth. Freudianism in psychology and pragmatism in philosophy were ruling those realms in the universities of the nation.[54] Whereas religion and the churches were still given a respectable nod in the intellectual culture of America before the war, this was increasingly becoming not the case in the postwar period.

The Twenties would witness a dramatic shift in the Northern Presbyterian and the Northern Baptist denominations.[55] From 1919 to 1923 the conservatives, now labeled "fundamentalists," within those two denominations would attempt to drive the modernists from positions of leadership in their churches.[56] They were unsuccessful in both cases. The result was that, in essence, the educational and denominational *institutions* went over to the modernists, along with many of the larger churches, and the conservatives were left with their pulpits and their frustrations. At this point it will be helpful to give a brief description of the differences between the two groups, since some of the differences have as much to do with *social issues* as they do with theology or attitudes to biblical authority.

There was great diversity among the *fundamentalists*. Some were Southern, rural, Baptist premillennialists; others were Northern, urban, Presbyterian amillennialists. J. Gresham Machen was representative of the latter classification. Professor of New Testament and apologetics at Princeton Seminary, Machen was from a wealthy family and had done doctoral study in Germany with some of the most *prestigious* liberal theologians of the time.[57] That study, in fact, had brought him to the brink of modernism himself.[58] But only to the

---

52 Askew and Spellman, *Churches and the American Experience*, 183.
53 Marsden, *Fundamentalism and American Culture*, 187–88.
54 Askew and Spellman, *Churches and the American Experience*, 183.
55 Louis Gasper, *The Fundamentalist Movement, 1930–1956*, Twin Brooks (Grand Rapids, MI: Baker, 1963), 21–25.
56 Marsden, *Fundamentalism and American Culture*, 153–75.
57 C. Allyn Russell, *Voices of American Fundamentalism: Seven Biographical Studies* (Philadelphia: Westminster, 1976), 146–50.
58 Marsden, *Fundamentalism and American Culture*, 132.

Struggle for the City

brink; Machen became perhaps the *leading* defender of theological orthodoxy. He argued that the Bible is based on *fact*, on the narration of *actual events*, and that any affirmation of the Bible's authority entailed its infallibility and inerrancy. To question that is to impugn the authority of Christ, a first step in moving in the direction of *infidelity*.[59] Machen contended that this was what liberalism was engaged in, and in his seminal work critiquing liberalism, titled *Christianity and Liberalism*, he argued that liberal theology was no longer Christian but was in Martin Marty's words "a sellout, treason."[60] To Machen "[t]heological liberalism was not a new variation of Christian thought... but the basis of an essentially new religion."[61] Machen went further: "A separation between the two parties in the Church is the crying need of the hour."[62]

This Princeton scholar and other leaders of the conservative movement "felt that moderates should leave the denominations and found new ones devoted to their novel theology with its faith in mankind and science."[63] For Machen, Christian preaching must be based on *scholarly* exegesis and clearly articulated *theology*. This brought him into conflict with *some* fundamentalists who believed that pious preaching alone was enough, as long as it was Bible-based. Machen thought such a conclusion to be unbiblical, since the leading evangelist of the New Testament was a classically educated *intellectual*.[64]

On political and social issues Machen may have appeared to be *atypical* of other fundamentalists, who were inclined generally to focus on issues like alcohol, gambling, Darwinism in the schools and elsewhere, Sabbath observance, theater-going, prostitution and other sexual sins, and the threat of international Communism, but not on political matters of social concern like unions, income disparity, or welfare.[65] Machen, though, was *deeply* concerned about *politics*. He frequently wrote letters to *The New York Times* and other

---

59 J. Gresham Machen, *Christianity and Liberalism* (New York: Macmillan, 1923), 20, 70–75.
60 Martin E. Marty, *Modern American Religion*, vol. 2, *The Noise of Conflict, 1919–1941* (Chicago: University of Chicago Press, 1991), 179.
61 George M. Marsden, *Reforming Fundamentalism: Fuller Seminary and the New Evangelicalism* (1987; repr., Grand Rapids, MI: Eerdmans, 1995), 32.
62 Machen, *Christianity and Liberalism*, 160.
63 Askew and Spellman, *Churches and the American Experience*, 185–86.
64 Machen, *Christianity and Liberalism*, 162.
65 Later in this chapter we will detail the rise of populist enthusiasm for economic issues among Southern fundamentalists. This is another story.

Struggle for the City

newspapers that dealt with social and political matters, but he clearly subordinated social issues to theology and the Bible.[66] Engagement with the culture was *crucial*, and pastors were to be educated in *all* of the intellectual currents of the time, though their primary task was *theological and pastoral*.[67]

Still, Machen's ideas about the relationship of Christianity to the culture were *nuanced*, and are important enough to give some further details. For him, "spiritual liberty was markedly different from civil liberty."[68] Both were important, the first to the church and the second to people as citizens of the United States. To fail to make this distinction would result in error in one of two ways—for liberals, the failure to make the distinction results in the social gospel; while for fundamentalists it results in a "program for Christian America."[69] The spiritual nature of the church meant that its goal was to achieve *spiritual ends* (the kingdom of the Lord) through *spiritual means* (such as preaching and the sacraments).[70] Its goal was not to achieve political ends *as the church*, though certainly individual Christians ought to be involved in politics, and ought to bring their Christian convictions to the ballot box.

Machen's position *differed* in some important ways from other Reformed or Calvinistic understandings of the relationship between Christ and culture, especially in the political realm. The intellectual program of Dutch Reformed theologian and Netherlands prime minister (1901–5) Abraham Kuyper flowed from his conviction that "[t]here is not a square inch in the whole domain of our human existence over which Christ, who is sovereign over all, does not cry, 'Mine!'"[71] Kuyper fleshed that out in his Stone Lectures at Princeton University in 1898 in which he boldly exclaimed that the triune God must exercise

---

66 Ned B. Stonehouse, *J. Gresham Machen: A Biographical Memoir*, 2nd ed. (Grand Rapids, MI: Eerdmans, 1955), 82–86.

67 Machen, *Christianity and Liberalism*, 118–19.

68 D. G. Hart, "Introduction: The Forgotten Machen?" in J. Gresham Machen, *Selected Shorter Writings*, ed. D. G. Hart (Phillipsburg, NJ: P&R Publishing, 2004), 13.

69 Ibid.

70 D. G. Hart, "The Spirituality of the Church, the Westminster Standards, and Nineteenth Century American Protestantism," in D. G. Hart, *Recovering Mother Kirk: The Case for Liturgy in the Reformed Church* (Grand Rapids, MI: Baker, 2003), 51–65, esp. 58–65.

71 Abraham Kuyper, "Sphere Sovereignty" (inaugural address at the founding of the Free University of Amsterdam, October 20, 1880) in *Abraham Kuyper: A Centennial Reader*, ed. James D. Bratt (Grand Rapids, MI: Eerdmans, 1998), 488.

Struggle for the City

his sovereignty in "the State,… in Society,… and in the Church."[72] Christ cries "Mine!" over all of this, and those three "spheres" must work together to see that it will be so.

Kuyper's vision for the state is Augustinian to the core, and perhaps more than Augustinian. It is important, however, to note what he was *not* calling for. He was not defending the older European notion of one state church that was all-encompassing. The reason is that "*government lacks the data of judgment* [necessary for it to authorize only one Church], and because every magisterial judgment here *infringes the sovereignty of the Church.*"[73] These spheres do not trump one another. "The sovereignty of the State and the sovereignty of the Church exist side by side, and they mutually limit one another."[74] Still, this is a *grand* and *totalizing* vision for society, based on the notion of a Christianized culture and a mandate for religion that encompasses all of life.

Machen's approach is not so totalizing. The church is to refrain from activity that Scripture does not explicitly sanction for the church, whether *political* declarations or *humanitarian* assistance.[75] God does call *individual* Christians to be involved in these activities, however, and they ought to be involved in them alongside both believers and nonbelievers. Machen was convinced that his treatment of these issues did not negate his integrity as a *Reformed* theologian. He contended that the American situation had allowed Reformed theology in some ways to be purged of European *baggage* that was not necessary to it. He seems clearly to have had both the state church situations of previous centuries and the "Christian society" approach of the current Dutch situation in mind.[76]

Harry Emerson Fosdick, erstwhile Baptist and Presbyterian, pastor and seminary professor, will serve as our representative of modernism on this subject. He believed that the church should be the champion for *economic reform* in the nation, for *redistribution* of wealth, and for *empowering unions* to dis-

---

72 Abraham Kuyper, *Lectures on Calvinism* (1899; Grand Rapids, MI: Eerdmans, 1931), 79.
73 Ibid., 105.
74 Ibid., 107.
75 Hart, "Introduction: The Forgotten Machen?" 14.
76 See his discussion in J. Gresham Machen, "The Responsibility of the Church in Our New Age," in Machen, *Selected Shorter Writings*, 364–76.

Struggle for the City

cipline big business.[77] In the teeth of the Great Depression, Fosdick preached a sermon he titled "The Ghost of a Chance." It was a passionate message denouncing economic *injustice* and pointing out the *flaws* of capitalism. This sermon caused Congressman Hamilton Fish Jr., "chairman of the original House committee investigating 'Reds,' to classify him with the 'pink intellectuals and sobbing socialists.'"[78] Fosdick was no Marxist, and was committed to democratic principles his whole life, but he often threw sympathetic *support* behind Socialists and Communists, defending their right to a "place at the table" in American discourse.

At the beginning of the decade of the Twenties, long before preaching the sermon noted above, Fosdick had pronounced on the nature of social concerns for the church in *Literary Digest* magazine. He was convinced that the church needed to engage in calling for social reforms of business, government, and other institutions of public life.

> Repress the endeavor to apply the principles of Jesus to social order; repress the agencies that seek the amelioration of human relations in industry; try to keep the economic situation static in a dynamic world; and when you have long enough represt [sic] the possibilities of orderly social progress you will get the inevitable consequence, disorderly social revolution.[79]

For Fosdick, the *social* implications of the gospel took precedence over the *personal* implications of salvation for one's soul. Previously the social gospelers and the Progressives alike "held an unreservedly optimistic view of the State, and they were as eager to grant the State control over the economic areas of life as over such moral areas as liquor, prostitution, gambling, and lurid literature."[80] Fosdick considered himself to be a disciple of Rauschenbusch, and

---

77 Marty, *Noise of Conflict*, 2:52–55.
78 Robert Moats Miller, *Harry Emerson Fosdick: Preacher, Pastor, Prophet* (New York: Oxford University Press, 1985), 469.
79 Taken from *Literary Digest*, June 18, 1921, quoted in Robert Moats Miller, *American Protestantism and Social Issues, 1919–1939* (Chapel Hill: University of North Carolina Press, 1958), 33–34.
80 Miller, *Harry Emerson Fosdick*, 478.

Struggle for the City

stated, "We are not here simply to save people out of the world but to save the world."[81] There is a direct line of continuity from the social Christian movements of the late 1800s to the position of this New York pastor, though this newer "social gospel" was "detached from its evangelical roots."[82] Fosdick and his fellows went much further than the older social gospel did in *eviscerating* the heart of Christian theology.

With Machen we noted that while he was concerned with political and social matters, he subordinated all that to the *Bible* and to the concerns of *theology*. The *opposite* was true of Fosdick. Referring to the Bible as a "priceless treasury of spiritual truth," he also made it clear that he rejected the doctrines of verbal *inspiration* and *inerrancy*.[83] While later parts of the Bible, especially the Gospels, might speak today with some kind of authority, the earlier Scriptures "started from primitive and childlike origins and, with however many setbacks and delays, grew in scope and height toward the culmination in Christ's Gospel."[84] Fosdick regarded God as mainly *immanent* in this world, which brought the accusation of pantheism, an accusation that was probably not accurate.[85] The "divinity" of Jesus consisted of his unique spiritual *consciousness*, not in his identity as the God-man, an idea Fosdick had learned from older liberal William Newton Clarke.[86] *Experience* comes before theology for Clarke and Fosdick and others in the Schleiermacher tradition. This whole approach constituted a failure to recognize what Kuyper had observed about this experiential approach, that "the root of every heretical phenomenon lies in the human heart; each one of us carries the germ of it within."[87] The New York pastor had little confidence that theological statements

---

81 Ibid., 480.
82 Robert D. Linder, "The Resurgence of Evangelical Social Concern (1925–1975)," in *The Evangelicals: What They Believe, Who They Are, and Where They Are Changing*, ed. David F. Wells and John D. Woodbridge (Nashville: Abingdon, 1975), 198.
83 Harry Emerson Fosdick, *A Guide to Understanding the Bible: The Development of Ideas within the Old and New Testaments* (1938; repr., Whitefish, MT: Kessenger, 2003); Miller, *Harry Emerson Fosdick*, 403–8.
84 Harry Emerson Fosdick, *The Modern Use of the Bible* (New York: Macmillan, 1924), 8.
85 Miller, *Harry Emerson Fosdick*, 402.
86 Gary Dorrien, *The Making of American Liberal Theology*, vol. 2, *Idealism, Realism, and Modernity: 1900–1950* (Louisville: Westminster John Knox, 2003), 359.
87 Abraham Kuyper, "Modernism: A *Fata Morgana* in the Christian Domain," (Amsterdam: H. de Hoogh, 1871) in *Abraham Kuyper: A Centennial Reader*, 98.

Struggle for the City

could clarify much of *anything* about the doctrines of the Trinity or the second advent of Christ and the future state, among other theological issues.[88] Christians should affirm these things, but even where the Bible made clear statements about such matters, Fosdick considered it *risky business* to make firm pronouncements, at least in part because the Bible was not to be taken literally. Christians should follow their *hearts*, in Fosdick's view, rather than requiring reflective theology to drive them. But in following this methodology, it ought to be clear to the reader of Fosdick's work that he reads Jesus only through the eyes of one who *wishes* to find in the Galilean a social reformer with the *same* ideas as the modern liberal, whereas if one reads carefully, one finds Jesus teaching about future rewards and punishments, who expects God to bring about a cataclysmic end of the world, and who clearly espouses his own second advent, all things Fosdick refused seriously to consider.[89]

Bible scholar and Moody Bible Institute professor Wilbur Smith wrote to Fosdick, stating in criticism, "It was nothing less than heartbreaking" to hear Fosdick plead with his audience "to follow their instinct for beauty, to cultivate a sense of honour, that these things would lead them into a religious life or experience."[90] To Smith this was *empty humanism*.[91] What is obvious from all of this is that Fosdick, in contrast to Machen, subverted *theology* and *evangelism* to the more important tasks for the church of modern times, involvement in *political* action and *social* reform in the name of Jesus. As we have seen, however, his "Jesus" is a very selective one.

The two factions, the fundamentalists and modernists, battled out their differences through the early and middle years of the Twenties in annual meetings of their denominations, in print, through sermons, and in the newspapers. Just before the 1922 Northern Baptist Convention, Fosdick famously preached a sermon he titled "Shall the Fundamentalists Win?" Clarence Macartney, pastor of Arch

---

88 Miller, *Harry Emerson Fosdick, 416.*
89 See the excellent review of Fosdick's book by J. Gresham Machen, "Review of Fosdick's *Modern Use of the Bible*," in Machen, *Selected Shorter Writings*, 455–68, on this particular point, 458.
90 Wilbur Smith to Harry Emerson Fosdick, February 15, 1932, Wilbur Smith Papers, Fuller Theological Seminary Archives, quoted in Marsden, *Reforming Fundamentalism*, 36.
91 See Smith's lament about the later history of Fuller Theological Seminary that in some ways has followed in Fosdick's footsteps. Wilbur M. Smith, *Before I Forget: Memoirs* (Chicago: Moody, 1971), 294.

Struggle for the City

Street Presbyterian Church in Philadelphia and one of the great preachers of the time, responded with a sermon he titled "Shall Unbelief Win?"[92] One might win the *pamphlet* warfare, however, and still lose the *real* war. Fosdick's famous sermon helped to galvanize the modernists and moderates a few weeks later at the Northern Baptist Convention, and they rejected an effort on the part of conservatives and fundamentalists to adopt a confession of faith for the denomination.[93]

Fundamentalists among Northern Presbyterians also had hopes dashed when the 1924 General Assembly affirmed a platform called the Auburn Affirmation, a statement that allowed churches and pastors some latitude in the way they interpreted the Westminster Confession, the confessional standard of Presbyterians.[94] Northern Baptist and Northern Presbyterian fundamentalists lost out in *both* denominations. "Usually the balance of political influence resided with a moderate middle party, generally evangelical in viewpoint but not militant enough to join with the more determined fundamentalists in order to root out liberal clergy."[95] That did not happen in 1922 and 1924. The reluctance of the moderates to vote with the fundamentalists led to the modernists *taking over* the denominational machinery.[96]

The *apparent* culmination of this conflict was the Scopes Trial in 1925.[97] This trial in Dayton, Tennessee, which featured a public school teacher, John Scopes, under *indictment* for teaching evolution, and the outcome caused many people in America to consider these "fundamentalists" to be ignorant *hayseeds*, which was not an accurate assessment of the leadership of the movement at all.[98] The trial featured two titanic attorneys, popular atheist Clarence Darrow for the defense and former presidential candidate and redoubtable Presbyterian layman William Jennings Bryan for the prosecution.[99] Bryan *won* the case, though Scopes was later

92 Longfield, *Presbyterian Controversy*, 9–11.
93 Ahlstrom, *Religious History of the American People*, 910–13.
94 Marsden, *Fundamentalism and American Culture*, 180–81.
95 Askew and Spellman, *Churches and the American Experience*, 186.
96 Ibid., 186–87.
97 We say *apparent* because that was how it seemed to many at the time, partly because of the specific events and partly because of the way the *media* reported on the events.
98 Joel A. Carpenter, "From Fundamentalism to the New Evangelical Coalition," in *Evangelicalism and Modern America*, ed. George Marsden (Grand Rapids, MI: Eerdmans, 1984), 3–16.
99 Michael Kazin, *A Godly Hero: The Life of William Jennings Bryan* (New York: Alfred A. Knopf, 2006), 45–79, 262–95.

Struggle for the City

exonerated. But though Bryan won the case, the fundamentalists *lost* in public perspective.[100] One liberal critic observed, "For the first time in history, organized knowledge has come into open conflict with organized ignorance."[101] Bryan lay *dead* in his sleep a few days after the trial, and fundamentalism become associated with anti-intellectualism. "In short, the term [fundamentalism] that originally had referred to an orthodox ministerial effort, largely urban, to oppose theological liberalism in the Northern denominations came to connote hostility to modern culture and social change."[102] Perception is the cruelest form of reality.[103]

The trial sundered conservatives and liberals even *further*, and by the early 1930s several new denominations and associations had formed in both the Baptist and Presbyterian camps. The fundamentalists (many of them) from these mainline denominations left to form new churches, new schools, and new mission boards.[104] Further, in the aftermath of the separation, fundamentalism, though it remained strong and vibrant, "retreated from any significant and formative influence in the cultural and intellectual centers of society."[105] The fundamentalists focused on *evangelism* and *eschatology*, especially dispensational premillennialism, and with the focus on the returning Christ as the only hope for society, many of the fundamentalists gave little attention to matters of systemic sin or social *justice*.[106] Fundamentalists also tended to focus less on *theology* (except the particular points where they differed from their less-stringent but still-conservative brethren) and concentrated on "fighting their new mortal enemy, modernism and its social gospel."[107] When the *economic* depression began to sink in and to work its impact, many Northern Christians had already

---

100 Linder, "Resurgence of Evangelical Social Concern," 195.

101 Maynard Shipley, *The War on Modern Science: A Short History of the Fundamentalist Attacks on Evolution and Modernism* (New York: Alfred A. Knopf, 1927), 4.

102 Askew and Spellman, *Churches and the American Experience*, 187.

103 The play and later film made about the trial, *Inherit the Wind*, is a total refabrication and caricature of the actual events to the point of being laughable.

104 Gasper, *Fundamentalist Movement*, 21–39.

105 Askew and Spellman, *Churches and the American Experience*, 188.

106 Carl Henry will make this a point of critique with his important book published in 1947, a treatment we will examine later in this discussion in chap. 21.

107 Linder, "Resurgence of Evangelical Social Concern," 197. Baptist pastor W. B. Riley, speaking in 1919 at the World Conference on Christian Fundamentals, had dubbed the social gospel, "social service Christianity." Ibid., 198. See Wm. B. Riley, "The Great Commission," in *God Hath Spoken* (Philadelphia: Bible Conference Committee, 1919).

Struggle for the City

been dealing with an *ecclesiastical* depression for several years, and the economic problems would only drive them farther apart from one another.

Several things happened as a result of the economic privations of the Great Depression. Some denominations, mostly among mainline liberal churches, that had struggled to maintain their own structure, merged. These mergers were done, in part, to economize their expenses at the level of denominational *hierarchy*. Southern and Northern Methodists ended their alienation, and other groups merged to form the Evangelical and Reformed Church in 1934. The liberal denominations were responding in a *centripetal* manner to the Depression, since their numbers had already been dwindling and the bad economy only made matters worse.[108] The problem is that the mergers did not work over the long run, and merged denominations would later merge with other merged denominations in order to find some way to survive. In addition to those denominational mergers, in rural communities several churches would come together and merge into a "community church." But in both cases, the numbers just continued to *dwindle*. The reason for the decline is that in both the *rural* mergers and in the *denominational* mergers, the choices of church goers were ignored in favor of some kind of sociological analysis, and they simply did not want to be a part of what they were left with in the way they loved going to the churches they had before the mergers.[109] People want what they want, not what some denominational *bureaucrat* determines to give them.

Liberal churches also gave strong support to labor and to unions. In 1931 Methodists in Lawrence, Massachusetts, passed a resolution condemning the abridgment of civil liberties of textile workers in that town during a strike.[110] The Federal Council of Churches also gave its approbation to labor and against corporations during most of the period.[111] But it is also clear that many of these mainline, liberal denominations went through hard times of their own, and not exclusively economic ones. These groups experienced an "institutional 'religious depression' to match the nation's economic depression."[112] They were unable to

---

108 Ahlstrom, *Religious History of the American People*, 920–21.
109 Roger Finke and Rodney Stark, *The Churching of America, 1776–1990*, 2nd ed. (New Brunswick, NJ: Rutgers University Press, 2005), 197–234.
110 Miller, *American Protestantism and Social Issues*, 275.
111 Ibid., 279.
112 Noll, *History of Christianity in the United States and Canada*, 432.

Struggle for the City

cope with the financial hardship of the Depression, a new phenomenon since churches both moderate and conservative had generally been able to make a huge dent in the difficulties faced by church members in previous recessions. An editorial in *Christian Century* in 1935 stated it thus: "The Christian church has come into the depression wholly unprepared to take account of it, and to minister to the deepest human need which it discloses."[113] The *Christian Century*, of course, is a liberal publication catering, then and now, to mainly liberal churches. Such churches would never fully recover in either numbers or influence.

Other denominations, on the other hand, underwent something like a *revival*, especially the Holiness, Pentecostal, and fundamentalist churches.[114] Southern Baptists grew in the decade from four million to five million, and Seventh-Day Adventists increased by more than fifty percent.[115] Southern Baptists had been growing since the Civil War, and that growth surged through the 1930s. The likely reasons are as follows: they provided an alternative to secularization; they were more fully democratic than other large denominations; their local congregations were autonomous (hence, entrepreneurial, or potentially so); their seminaries served the churches rather than becoming independent "divinity schools"; many clergy remained bivocational and did not require fully-funded salaries, so churches could invest in other things needed for growth.[116] The Great Depression did not hamper that process appreciably.

This is also the period when the transiency sometimes known as the "great migration(s)" of fundamentalist Christians and their denominational affiliates out of the South (particularly) and into the North and the Southwest caused the beginning formation of the future Religious Right. They went looking for work and survival wherever they could find it and carried their pietistic faith and brand of "folk religion" as some would come to call it.[117]

---

113 "Why No Revival?" *Christian Century* 52 (September 18, 1935): 1168, quoted in Askew and Spellman, *Churches and the American Experience*, 190.
114 Ahlstrom, *Religious History of the American People*, 920.
115 Noll, *History of Christianity in the United States and Canada*, 432. We cite the Adventists as an example of a church that has (or at least had) a heavy eschatological focus, as did Southern Baptists at the time.
116 Finke and Stark, *Churching of America, 1776–1990*, 186–88.
117 See esp. James N. Gregory, *The Southern Diaspora: How the Great Migrations of Black and White Southerners Transformed America* (Chapel Hill: University of North Carolina Press, 2005), and other sources we will cite later.

Struggle for the City

The more conservative churches also formed new organizations in the wake of the challenges presented by the economic privations. They disagreed with the Federal Council of Churches on most theological issues, though not necessarily with its views on labor during the difficult years,[118] but they felt need for some kind of coalition that could provide mutuality of support and encouragement across denominational lines without at the same time creating a kind of lowest common denominator of theological belief that appeared to be happening at the Federal Council.[119] In 1942–43 the National Association of Evangelicals (NAE) was formed. When, a few years later, the World Council of Churches rejected both Communism and laissez-faire capitalism, in expectation that the United Nations would be able to create some kind of economic utopianism, members of the NAE were there to claim that this would only come about when the "World Sovereign Himself" would accomplish this.[120]

The liberal churches of the Great Depression turned back to the social gospel message, with some, such as the National Council of Methodist Youth, endorsing Socialism in 1934 as the way out.[121] In 1932 the Commission of Appraisal of the Laymen's Foreign Missions Inquiry of the Congregationalist Church "issued a report entitled *Rethinking Missions* that called on foreign workers to stress social outreach rather than evangelistic preaching."[122] The Federal Council of Churches in 1932 called upon the federal government to rescue the nation through government action and economic planning.[123] The new Fellowship of Socialist Christians, formed in 1930, issued a manifesto that spoke of "class struggle" and warned that "class war" would result "if the inequities of the social order were not removed."[124] All of this points to the massive impact that the Great Depression had on modernist and liberal Christianity.

Liberal theology did not remain static through this period. The Great War and the economic woes of the world worked their impact on theological minds such

---

118 Some individual conservative churches stood up for labor during the strikes, though they sometimes paid a heavy price. Miller, *American Protestantism and Social Issues*, 286.

119 Marty, *Righteous Empire*, 248–49.

120 Ibid., 249.

121 Ahlstrom, *Religious History of the American People*, 922.

122 Noll, *History of Christianity in the United States and Canada*, 432.

123 Miller, *American Protestantism and Social Issues*, 268. "Economic planning" is a code term for Socialism.

124 Ahlstrom, *Religious History of the American People*, 923.

Struggle for the City

as that of Swiss pastor Karl Barth, a man who had worked as a volunteer chaplain with German soldiers during the war. Trained in the best liberal tradition, Barth had grown disillusioned when his favorite professors signed a pact supporting the Kaiser's war plans.[125] Barth's theology moved back toward classical doctrinal expression and a reappropriation of patristic and Reformation theology. He along with others in Europe developed a "neo-orthodoxy" that, while it still affirmed biblical criticism, was much more affirmative of the teaching of the Bible on human sin, God's transcendence, and Christ's atonement.[126] Karl Barth, Emil Brunner, Friedrich Gogarten, and, to a lesser degree, Rudolf Bultmann initiated a theological revolution in Europe that would also spread to England and the United States.[127]

In the United States the neo-orthodox spirit was imbibed by Reinhold Niebuhr and his younger brother, H. Richard Niebuhr. The two men had started out as committed *liberals*, with Reinhold committed to the history of religions (*Religionsgeschichtliche Schule*) school of theology that was prominent in Germany. Reinhold Niebuhr explained that "the Bible vanishes as any supernatural authority and Christianity is forced to compete with all religions upon a common basis."[128] Reinhold still demonstrated a commitment to classical liberal views in his book *Leaves from the Notebook of a Tamed Cynic*, published in 1929. In his book *The Social Sources of Denominationalism*, Reinhold's brother, H. Richard Niebuhr, had followed liberal theologian Adolf von Harnack in attempting to free Christianity of the "strange interpretation of the faith" that had been subverted to "problems and methods of Greek philosophy," by which he meant the development of orthodoxy in the early church.[129]

Then came the market crash. In 1932 Reinhold published *Moral Man and Immoral Society*, in which he found the prevailing assumptions of lib-

---

125 Stanley J. Grenz and Roger E. Olson, *20th Century Theology* (Downers Grove, IL: InterVarsity Press, 1992), 65–67.

126 See esp., Karl Barth, *Epistle to the Romans*, trans. Edwyn C. Hoskyns (1918; Eng. trans., 1933; repr., New York: Oxford University Press, 1968), and his 14-vol. *Church Dogmatics*, trans. and ed. T. F. Torrance and G. W. Bromiley (Edinburgh: T&T Clark, 1936–68).

127 James C. Livingston and Francis Schüssler Fiorenza, *Modern Christian Thought, vol. 2, The Twentieth Century*, 2nd ed. (Minneapolis: Fortress, 2006), 62–94.

128 Reinhold Niebuhr, "Yale-Eden," *Keryx* (December 1914), 57, quoted in Dorrien, *Making of American Liberal Theology, 1900–1950*, 2:439.

129 H. Richard Niebuhr, *The Social Sources of Denominationalism*, Living Age Books (1929; repr., New York: Meridian, 1957), 11–12.

Struggle for the City

eralism to be "lacking the realism with which to combat the problems of a technological and industrial society."[130] This book was the "most disruptive religio-ethical bombshell of domestic construction to be dropped during the entire interwar period," a work in which Niebuhr made it clear that labor unions, corporations, and sovereign states are "by their nature incapable of altruistic conduct."[131] In the book, Niebuhr "embraced a Christian variant of Marxism, which provided an explanation for the impending collapse of bourgeois civilization and an antidote to the pious moralism [i.e., social gospel] of liberal Christianity."[132] Niebuhr was specific: "Marxian socialism is a true enough interpretation of what the industrial worker feels about society and history, to have become the accepted social and political philosophy of all self-conscious and politically intelligent industrial workers."[133] Here was a stark *realism* about the nature of human sin, almost more Augustinian than the African father himself, but a realism linked to a *Socialist* prescription of the way out. Niebuhr sounds almost like a conservative in his railings against sin, but that was only because he believed that Protestant liberalism "had forsaken its biblical and classical roots."[134] In his Gifford Lectures given in 1939 he is even more blistering, calling for a rejection of Classical and Romantic views of human nature and reasserting a biblical realism that acknowledges both the greatness and the tragedy that is the human condition.[135] This is true of individuals and of nations. Niebuhr himself would confess, "In general my position has developed theologically to the right and politically to the left of modern liberal Protestantism."[136] He "blasted the optimism and sentimentality of social-gospel liberalism, but never doubted that Christians are called to create a just society."[137] He believed that Christian theologians should "attempt the

---

130 Askew and Spellman, *Churches and the American Experience*, 192.

131 Ibid., 941.

132 Dorrien, *Making of American Liberal Theology, 1900–1950*, 2:450.

133 Reinhold Niebuhr, *Moral Man and Immoral Society: A Study in Ethics and Politics* (New York: Scribner's, 1932), 144.

134 Dorrien, *Making of American Liberal Theology, 1900–1950*, 2:451.

135 Reinhold Niebuhr, *The Nature and Destiny of Man: A Christian Interpretation*, vol. 1, *Human Nature*, Gifford Lectures 1939 (New York: Scribner's, 1941), 1–53, and throughout.

136 Reinhold Niebuhr, "Dr. Niebuhr's Position," *Christian Century* 50 (January 18, 1933): 91–92, quoted in Dorrien, *Making of American Liberal Theology, 1900–1950*, 2:451.

137 Gary Dorrien, *The Making of American Liberal Theology*, vol. 3, *Crisis, Irony, and Postmodernity: 1950–2005* (Louisville: Westminster John Knox, 2006), 13

Struggle for the City

impossible," so that "a progressively higher justice and more stable peace can be achieved."[138] Christianity and Marxism, in his view, were both *realistic* and *utopian*, and since they shared that in common, they should join hands in making this "higher justice and more stable peace." The City of God would have to be constructed with Karl Marx as one of its architects. Augustine was back, but with a liberal and a Marxist twist.[139]

H. Richard Niebuhr also pointed out, especially in his book *The Kingdom of God in America*, that the churches were susceptible to being overtaken by the *values* of the larger society in America and that this had in fact happened in liberal Christianity.[140] Liberalism, and its concomitant political/economic program, did not have the answers to the *deepest needs* of Americans. "It [liberalism] became as intent upon its conservation and defense as orthodoxy had ever been."[141] Despite good intentions, it provided no answers when the economic crisis loomed. This Niebuhr was more sanguine toward the social gospel movement than was his older brother Reinhold and believed that Rauschenbusch, at least, still spoke with a *Pauline* voice.[142] But their solution was still, ultimately, no *real* solution. "The Depression unquestionably obtained for Social Christianity a voice in the churches which it had not had before."[143] That is true, but it is also true that a deep criticism of "Social Christianity" was arising within the liberal tradition. That much is clear, but what was the response of conservatives?

With the exception of some Southern populists, conservatives generally did not call on the *government* to solve the economic problems. Many of their leaders were laissez-faire, or nearly so, in their economic philosophy and believed that, as the country had emerged from previous recessions and depres-

---

138 Niebuhr, *Moral Man and Immoral Society*, 256.

139 In the interest of precision, it must be noted that Niebuhr was not blind to the oppressive tendencies of Soviet Marxism and that as time went by, his criticisms of Marxism became more severe. Langdon Gilkey, *On Niebuhr: A Theological Study* (Chicago: University of Chicago Press, 2001), 45–48.

140 H. Richard Niebuhr, *Kingdom of God in America* (New York: Harper & Brothers, 1937), 164–98.

141 Ibid., 196.

142 Ibid., 162, 194. This book was written five years after Reinhold's *Moral Man and Immoral Society*.

143 Ahlstrom, *Religious History of the American People*, 923.

Struggle for the City

sions, so it would from this one.[144] Even within the liberal churches, there were organized countermovements to the actions of, say, the Federal Council.[145] Southern Baptists in 1938 termed the American economic system the "best in the world."[146] There had been some recovery by then from the worst days of the recession, but such optimism probably also grew from Southern Baptists' own growth and their general *faith* in a providential God.

One thing seems clear about the Great Depression and the churches of America. If there was a divide between conservative and liberal (or fundamentalist and modernist) before the recession set in, that divide yawned much, much *wider* after ten years of economic woes. The conservative churches were generally larger and stronger after the Depression was over, while the liberal churches were smaller than they had been, yet they still retained dominance in "national religious life, in both sheer numbers and cultural leadership."[147] If the Great Depression and its aftermath actually was one of the three great defining moments in American *history* (the other two being the Revolutionary War and the Civil War), then it was also one of the great defining moments in the American *churches*. There is no going back. But we still have not been able to discern the causes of the recession throughout this period of American history. It is to that question that we now turn, and the answers will hopefully enable us to discern which "theological solutions" were the more accurate.

Understanding the Great Depression

The "Crash of '29" was deep and painful. It is important, though, to understand what a stock market crash *is*. A crash pulls money out of the bank accounts of investors who are forced to make their margin calls (demands to repay loans made to buy stocks), and this may cause them to go *bankrupt*. It lowers the *value* of cor-

144 Noll, *History of Christianity in the United States and Canada*, 433.
145 Ahlstrom, *Religious History of the American People*, 923.
146 Ibid., 924.
147 Lyman Kellstedt, John Green, Corwin Smidt, and James Guth, "Faith Transformed: Religion and American Politics from FDR to George W. Bush," in *Religion and American Politics: From the Colonial Period to the Present*, 2nd ed., ed. Mark A. Noll and Luke E. Harlow (Oxford: Oxford University Press, 2007), 269.

porations that have public ownership. It can have a deep impact on banks when those who are forced to pay their margins withdraw all of their funds, and so, it may result in bank runs and bank closings. It did all of those things in 1929.[148] It can also damage future investment, both because investors now have less liquidity (that is, cash on hand) and because there may develop a tendency not to *trust* markets on the part of those who have been financially hurt. A crash reduces the value of tangible assets and deteriorates household balance sheets. Consumers are forced to reduce their spending in an effort to rebuild their budgets.

But that is about it. Imagine that the house you live in was suddenly worth half what it had been worth the day before. That is troublesome, especially if you have to try to sell it at the new price. But you *still* have a job and you can still purchase groceries and other commodities. The stock market crash *itself* did not close any factories. Also, the stock market crash in and of itself did not cause the terrible financial chaos that followed it; that was due to other factors, and at this point we will discuss just what those factors were.

By most analyses, the Great Depression lasted nearly four years.[149] It was the longest, deepest recession in American history, though the recession of the mid-1890s was nearly as bad. In any case, what made it happen, and what made it so bad? First, as we have said, the Crash of '29 did not *cause* the Great Depression. Few students of the crash, outside of the Marxist interpreters, see it that way, though popular perception often has been that "We had a crash, and then the Great Depression followed." But this is simply *not* the case. Rather, the crash was a symptom of larger problems in the economy. "Neither the stock market crash nor the antecedent speculation has usually been thought a decisive cause."[150] It is just not as simple as all that. The stock market was not a "superficial phenomenon,"[151] and its fall was significant, but it was not the single *cause*.

Further, the Great Depression was already underway when the US stock market crashed in 1929—it was underway in other countries. Due to circum-

---

148 Galbraith, *Great Crash, 1929*, 175–92.
149 Some interpreters link the several recessions that recurred in the 1930s into one long depression. See, e.g., Pierre Berton, *The Great Depression, 1929–1939* (Toronto: McClelland & Stewart, 1990).
150 John Kenneth Galbraith, *Money: Whence It Came, Where It Went* (Boston: Houghton Mifflin, 1975), 183.
151 Kindleberger, *World in Depression, 1929–1939*, 127.

Struggle for the City

stances far too complex to treat here, European and Asian nations had already entered a deep recession, some of them as early as 1927. These recessions actually helped to trigger the US market crash.[152]

Turning a Stock Market Crash into a Great Depression

If the market crash of 1929 did not cause the Great Depression, what did? Few events have been studied more than this phenomenon, and though some disagreements still persist, there is a general consensus among economic historians (except the persistently Marxist and neo-Marxist interpreters) today about the major causes of the Depression. The consensus is that a combination of business activities and government interference in the economy are what resulted in a lengthening depression.

First, there was a stagnation in aggregate *demand* on the economy during the late 1920s and into the '30s. Declines in business investment beginning in 1926 presented a problem that was not perceived at the time, since normally statistics like this are not clear until a few years later. In 1932 and 1933 business investment was down to about one percent. But the decline in investment after the housing boom was over, following the Great War, eventually impacted the nation's economy. That is due to the fact that the manufacturing of heavy equipment, the kind that factories use, was behind normal pace during all of these years from 1926 onward. There was also a decline in demand from the *government*. The federal government ran budget surpluses all through the 1920s, which means that it was soaking up money that was not available in the market. To put it differently, it was taking from the private sector what would ordinarily have been spent, saved, or invested. A federal budget surplus sounds like a really good thing to those of us who live in the twenty-first century, but it is not *necessarily* or *exclusively* a good thing, and running one year after another eventually damaged the resiliency of the economy.

Second, in face of the crisis, Congress passed, and President Hoover signed into law, the Smoot-Hawley Tariff (1930). This raised tariff costs on many

---

152 For a fuller explanation of these matters, see Smiley, *Rethinking the Great Depression*, 31–70.

imported goods to around fifty percent of their retail price. This tariff was urged on the government by American industry, which was responding in a knee-jerk reaction to imports flooding the market. It was, in industry's mind, a way to protect American jobs and is another example of the kind of result that occurs when government and industry try to *collude* to *manage* the economy. Tariffs, while necessary at a certain level, become counterproductive when they are raised too high, and they have never proved themselves beneficial to the larger economy, since by their very nature they concern only a small segment of it. Foreign countries need American dollars so that they can in turn purchase American products, and, as economists expected at the time, the huge tariff increase would simply cause foreign governments to raise *their own* tariffs, shut out American products, and cause American workers to be laid off. That is exactly what happened. Shock waves were sent to foreign countries, further exacerbating the depression in Europe and Asia; that in turn pulled their gold out of American banks, causing more of them to collapse. Who ever said doing *something* is better than doing *nothing*?

Third, Hoover convened meetings with captains of industry. He convinced them that the biggest mistake they could make was to lower the wages of their employees. He believed that *farm prices*, costs of *goods and services*, and *wages* had to be kept high so that incomes would remain stable and that this would enable the country to pull out of the depression. The heads of major corporations agreed, with Henry Ford actually increasing wages.[153] This was what the labor unions had been asking for—a wage floor, even though it was not sustainable by the market—and Hoover gave it to them.[154] Of course, what this meant was that when the bottom fell out, as it inevitably would in such a top-managed situation, it fell out *dramatically*. It is hard to imagine how anyone could have thought this was a logical thing to do, but the "emergency" thinking seemed to justify doing *anything* just to be doing *something*.[155] The ensuing unemployment drop was staggering!

---

153 Thomas J. DiLorenzo, *How Capitalism Saved America* (New York: Crown Forum, 2004), 166.
154 Murray N. Rothbard, *America's Great Depression*, 5th ed. (1963; Auburn, AL: Mises Institute, 2000), 212.
155 See Higgs, *Crisis and Leviathan*, chap. 8, for full discussion of the implications of this policy and many others.

Struggle for the City

In the midst of this, the Hoover administration did make a move that seemed salutary, and by some modern economic interpretation was the right move, but this is by no means noncontroversial. The president initiated genuine public works programs, and so stimulated the economy by *government* spending. The largest project he initiated was the Boulder Dam, now known as the Hoover Dam in honor of the president. It was a *genuine* works program that had the overall purpose of helping to electrify the nation. It put thousands of men and women to work and was the kind of government spending program that could (and did) benefit the economy for generations to come.[156]

On the other hand, because the federal government managed the project, it helped cause a decline in *private* sector construction, which dropped drastically in 1930, and it had the effect of putting the government into *competition* in the electrical and construction businesses against private interests.[157] In other words, one is left to wonder why Hoover did not instead let that project be carried out by private companies at every level of the operation, companies that were more suited to such a project. Instead, companies went out of business that could have done the work. These were *unintended consequences*, but Hoover should have been able to anticipate it since he had himself been secretary of commerce under Coolidge and had been part of the excesses of the Wilson administration, as we noted previously.

The likely reason Hoover empowered the federal government to build the dam was due to his Progressive political beliefs, the same beliefs that led Wilson to believe in an overarching administrative state. Hoover was a social engineer as well as an actual mechanical engineer who had made a fortune between 1900 and 1915 managing mining projects around the world. He was in fact known by his friends as the "Great Engineer." He had been influenced by one of the greatest architects of the Progressive movement, sociologist Thorstein Veblen. Hoover had read Veblen's two key books, *The Theory of the Leisure Class* (1899) and *The Engineers and the Price System* (1921), and was captivated by them.[158] Veblen presented the *engineer* as the one person who could solve the problems

---

156 That is in contrast to many other government "stimulus" projects that would come in the next decade that did not benefit the overall economy very much at all. They simply put some people to work on the government dole for a temporary period of time.
157 Joan Hoff Wilson, *Herbert Hoover: Forgotten Progressive*, ed. Oscar Handlin (1975; repr., Long Grove, IL: Waveland, 1992), 146.
158 Johnson, *History of the American People*, 736.

Struggle for the City

still confronting humankind. The engineer was a benevolent person who was out to replace business, out to replace competition, and out to run the economy on a purely *benevolent* basis.[159] Hoover was known to say, "When you know me better, you will know when I say a thing is a fact, it *is* a fact."[160] He would know what to do in a crisis situation and the people should let him take charge.

Hoover believed he had been equipped with the *tools* to fix this difficulty; that was in fact part of the problem. Hoover and others believed that the managed economy of the Soviet Union was doing *well* and that they ought to be able to do something *similar* in America. They did not realize that the only reason the Soviet situation looked so good was because the Soviets were lying through their teeth, and with the lack of a free press in that nation, there was little hope of finding out the truth for some time to come. So, Hoover looked for ways to manage the American economy out of the Depression by tinkering with this or that aspect of the economy, always under the pressure of "crisis" thinking that said "do something, anything" *now*. This is what Austrian economist Friedrich Hayek has called the "fatal conceit," the idea that a planner or group of planners can ever process *all* the information necessary actually to be able to manage the economy of a nation, especially one as large and diverse as the United States.[161] The stimulus plan was simply another aspect of that attempt to plan, manage, and control the American economy.

But the stimulus plan had another built-in and unintended consequence for Hoover. A nation that had run ten straight years of surplus suddenly had a budget deficit in 1930 and an even larger one in 1931. Half of government spending in 1932 was deficit spending. Hoover had to run for reelection in 1932, and his opponent, Franklin Delano Roosevelt, ran against Hoover on the platform of a balanced budget. This resonated with many of the people, who understood little of macroeconomics, since, after all, the country was in a deep recession, and Hoover was running up the tab.[162]

---

159 John B. Diggins, *The Bard of Savagery: Thorstein Veblen and Modern Social Theory* (London: Branch Line, 1978).
160 Quoted in Arthur Schlesinger Jr., *The Crisis of the Old Order: 1919–1933*, Age of Roosevelt 1 (1957; repr., New York: Houghton Mifflin, 2003), 8 (emphasis added).
161 F. A. Hayek, *The Fatal Conceit: The Errors of Socialism*, Collected Works of F. A. Hayek 1, ed. W. W. Bartley III (Chicago: University of Chicago Press, 1991), quoted in DiLorenzo, *How Capitalism Saved America*, 162.
162 Johnson, *History of the American People*, 740.

Struggle for the City

Hoover sensed his vulnerability, and, in what historians will later determine was a *fourth* major cause of the Great Depression, Congress passed and Hoover signed into law a massive *tax increase* in 1932. This was the worst thing a president could do in the face of a deep recession since it takes further buying power out of an economy already crippled by other factors. Hoover lost the reelection bid by a landslide, and FDR took the presidency in March 1933, and promptly forgot his campaign promises to balance the budget, driving deficits higher than they had *ever* been under Hoover.[163]

The *fifth* major contributing cause to the deepness of the Depression was the Federal Reserve and its policies in response to the economic crisis. Congress had created the Federal Reserve in 1913 following the recovery from what has been called the Panic of 1907. That year, a deep recession and a series of bank closings that followed made it clear to many American leaders that we were having trouble managing our economy, and the idea was that as *efficiency* was becoming the watchword in the business world, perhaps the federal government needed a mechanism for interacting with the economy that would enable government and business to come together and work to prevent future recessions, or at least to diminish their impact. There are serious questions to be asked about whether the Fed should have ever been given the authority to regulate the money supply, but the fact is that it had that power. Throughout the 1920s it kept rates low enough so that money and credit were readily available, perhaps too ready, but then it suddenly closed off the *spigot*.

In 1929 the Fed had begun to constrict the money supply by raising interest rates, one contributing factor to the crash. It was concerned that the economy was moving too rapidly and that this would cause *inflation*. So, it raised rates. But then the Fed did exactly the wrong thing. After the crash, it should have *lowered* interest rates to make credit available, but instead it raised them further, causing a decrease in the *money supply*. The actual money supply decreased by four percent between the end of 1928 and the end of 1930.[164] It

---

163 By 1936, FDR's first bid for reelection, the deficit was sixty percent higher than the highest it had been under Hoover.
164 Shlaes, *Forgotten Man*, 90.

Struggle for the City

declined by another 12 percent in 1931.[165] It did so under the maintenance of Hoover's tinkering.[166]

Nearly a hundred years earlier, in 1837, while Martin Van Buren was president, there was a similar depression. Van Buren, a man who held strongly to laissez-faire convictions, did nothing about it, even though his own advisors encouraged him to jump in and tinker with the economy. He refused to do so and the depression was short-lived.[167] The constriction by the Fed in 1930 prolonged the problem. Oddly enough, Hoover felt energized by this—"another rescue opportunity in the offing"[168] for a Progressive-era president who believed that an energetic federal government could fix anything, given sufficient resources (that is, total authority and the power to spend). His optimism was short-lived. It was Hoover's incessant interfering in the economy that turned an *average* recession into the Great Depression.[169]

The Marxist interpretation of the Great Depression was that people speculated too much, workers were not allowed to share in the profits of their companies, individuals became greedy and pulled their money out when there was a sign of danger, and thus the *crash caused* the Great Depression. Marxists believe that capitalism creates unbalanced accumulations of wealth that inevitably lead to a crisis. Marxist intellectuals had predicted that as long as capitalism reigns, there will be numerous "crashes" and crises every few years, and they saw the Great Depression as the *vindication* of their view. As we have tried to demonstrate, this interpretation is almost exactly wrong and is opposed to the actual facts of what did take place.

By the end of Hoover's term, unemployment stood at 24.9 percent. Landlords could not collect rents, so property taxes went unpaid. City revenues evaporated, impacting schools, city services, and other programs. Children by the hundreds of thousands were unable to go to school, and many who did go were malnourished. Approximately 1,500 colleges went under, putting intel-

---

165 Milton Friedman and Anna Jacobson Schwartz, *A Monetary History of the United States, 1867–1960*, Studies in Business Cycles 12 (Princeton, NJ: Princeton University Press, 1963), chap. 7.
166 DiLorenzo, *How Capitalism Saved America*, 175–78.
167 Ibid., 158.
168 Shlaes, *Forgotten Man*, 91.
169 DiLorenzo, *How Capitalism Saved America*, 178.

Struggle for the City

lectuals out of work. "Thus impoverished, writers and intellectuals generally veered sharply to the left in these years."[170] This was made more the case since the standard interpretation of the Depression for years was that it was the fault of greedy *rich* people.

These intellectuals, people like Edmund Wilson, would carry on this leftist legacy for decades, even generations. Paul Johnson writes, quoting Wilson in his *Shores of Light* published in 1952, that "[t]he age of influence was now dawning for American writers, especially the younger ones 'who had grown up in the Big Business era and had always resented its barbarism, its crowding out of everything they cared about.' For them 'these years were not depressing but stimulating. One couldn't help being exhilarated at the sudden, unexpected collapse of the stupid gigantic fraud. It gave us a new sense of freedom; and it gave us a new sense of power."[171] In many universities these leftist Marxist intellectuals still wield the power *decades* after their cherished interpretation of the Great Depression has been debunked.[172]

A New Dealer

In 1932 Franklin Delano Roosevelt took the presidency with about sixty percent of the vote. His election was made simple by virtue of the terrible economic situation and Hoover's apparent failure to change that. Hoover had failed to understand one thing about business downturns—that they serve *essential purposes*. "They have to be sharp. But they need not be long because they are

---

170 Johnson, *History of the American People*, 743. Though he did not lose his job, as we have seen, this is exactly what happened to Reinhold Niebuhr, a veer to the *political left*.
171 Edmund Wilson, "The Literary Consequences of the Crash," *Shores of Light: A Literary Chronicle of the Twenties and Thirties* (New York: Farrar, Straus and Young, 1952), 498, quoted in Johnson, *History of the American People*, 743. Wilson was only one of many in the time who held to messianic ideals in politics. See his magnum opus, *To the Finland Station: A Study in the Writing and Acting of History* (1940; New York: Farrar, Straus and Giroux, 1972). This book of often turgid prose details his take on the history of Socialist and Communist ideas. Wilson joined other would-be world changers such as John Dewey and Walt Whitman in Wilson's hope for a world based on his reading of the Old Testament prophets.
172 It is simply a fact that about the only Marxists left in the world are found in China, Cuba, Venezuela, North Korea, and American state universities. See Dinesh D'Souza's documentary film *2016: Obama's America*, directed by Dinesh D'Souza and John Sullivan (2012; Santa Monica, CA: Lionsgate, 2012), DVD, http://2016themovie.com/.

Struggle for the City

self-adjusting. All they require on the part of governments, the business community, and the public is patience."[173] Roosevelt would also fail to understand the same principle, even more so than Hoover. In his first campaign speech he appealed to a person he labeled "the forgotten man." Roosevelt claimed that big business and big businessmen were to blame for the Great Depression. These greedy men, trading stocks in New York, playing with the destiny of the poor man, the old man, the union worker—these greedy men had plunged the country into economic chaos, and now any man in need of government assistance was in fact "the forgotten man."

One member of Roosevelt's "brain trust," Ray Moley, suggested the metaphor of the forgotten man, once he had read at some point. Ironically, Roosevelt and Moley completely *misused* the metaphor. The image actually comes from a lecture by Yale philosopher William Graham Sumner. In Sumner's speech the "forgotten man" was actually not the poor man or the man in need of assistance, but the *average taxpayer*. He said that if person A sees something wrong and that a person X is suffering, and he goes to person B to discuss the problem, the two of them then propose a law to help X. But then it is person C who actually pays the taxes to help X. Sumner argued that C is the "forgotten man," the man nobody notices, but the one who actually gets it done. Roosevelt used this plaintive and heart-wrenching metaphor about the *forgotten man* to point out the need of the man on the soup line, and the plea was effective. The problem was that he and his speechwriters got the point completely wrong.[174] That misunderstanding serves as a veritable parable for how Roosevelt and his New Dealers got the whole thing wrong, and how easy it is for governments to continue to do so.

On March 5, 1933, FDR convened a special session of Congress. He issued a series of presidential proclamations, closing the banks, and keeping them closed for about a week.[175] This was due to the fact that bank runs had devastated many banks during the years of the Depression. Then, he attempted to enact one new policy after another. What should we do? Anything. When you are drowning you will reach out for anything that might save you. But what if

---

173 Johnson, *History of the American People*, 735.
174 Shlaes, *Forgotten Man*, 12–13.
175 Ibid., 157–58.

Struggle for the City

the thing you grab actually ensures that you will remain in the water for a good deal longer? In the first hundred days Congress passed fifteen major bills that dealt with almost every aspect of the economy. Many were contradictory, and most were later ruled unconstitutional.[176] It was billed as the New Deal, but it differed very little from some of Hoover's last-ditch efforts at manipulating the economy. This would later be admitted by Rexford Tugwell, one of Roosevelt's key advisors: "We didn't admit it at the time, but practically the whole New Deal was extrapolated from programs that Hoover started."[177] The New Deal was begun by Hoover[178]; Roosevelt was just a new *dealer*.

The idea was that the new administration could accomplish what Woodrow Wilson had wanted to do, Progressive that he was, but was unable to pull off. Wilson had wanted America to take the lead in forming a whole new world order by using the disruption caused by the Great War. Of course, in order for America to take that lead, it would have to become fundamentally a different country than it had been in the long nineteenth century.[179] The war (the Great War) seemed to provide a needed *catalyst*. "Hence all fascistic movements commit considerable energy to prolonging a heightened state of emergency."[180] Never waste a crisis! But at the end of the war, Americans wanted nothing to do with the new League of Nations, and they were content to continue being the kind of republic they had been following their own remaking at the end of the Civil War; they were not enamored with the new Progressive ideas fostered by Wilson, and the "heightened state of emergency" had passed in America, though not in Europe. Roosevelt had a new opportunity created by the Great Depression. The key was to seize control of the economy by *dominating* every sector of it and utilizing it for the purpose of the *administrative state*. Political columnist Walter Lippmann actually told Roosevelt in a meeting at Warm Springs, Georgia, Roosevelt's retreat location,

176 H. W. Brands, *Traitor to His Class: The Privileged Life and Radical Presidency of Franklin Delano Roosevelt* (New York: Doubleday, 2008), 223–65.
177 Quoted in *The Reader's Companion to American History*, ed. Eric Foner and John A. Garraty (Boston: Houghton-Mifflin, 1991), 514.
178 Johnson, *History of the American People*, 740.
179 The phrase "long nineteenth century" refers to the tendency of some historians to argue that the nineteenth century really lasted from 1789 till 1914.
180 Jonah Goldberg, *Liberal Fascism* (New York: Doubleday, 2006), 43.

Struggle for the City

"The situation is critical, Franklin. You may have no alternative but to assume dictatorial powers."[181] He nearly did.

Something very similar was happening in two depression-ravaged nations in Europe—Italy and Germany. Benito Mussolini had been enacting coercive economic policies in Italy for several years when Roosevelt was inaugurated in 1933. At the same time Adolf Hitler was beginning his sweeping plan of renovating the entire German economy, which was in even worse condition than the Italian and American ones due to war reparations that had been in place since the Treaty of Versailles in 1919.[182] Once Hitler was in power he established "state capitalism" as a way to reward the industrialists, who profited further from the Nazis' attempt to exterminate the Jews, many of whom were financially successful.[183] This state capitalism was really just a reworked form of Socialism, an intellectual project worked out in the nineteenth century by mostly German thinkers, as we have already noted.[184]

Roosevelt was a great *admirer* of both men in 1933, and for a number of years after that. Of course, we think of those two revolutions as Fascist in nature, and from our vantage point, *Fascist* means something dark, evil, and sinister. But the term did not have that connotation at the time, and plenty of American intellectuals were glad in 1933 and even in 1937 for America to follow in those *fascist* footsteps as *quickly* as it possibly could. After all, there were examples of semibenevolent fascist regimes in the past—think of Rome and France. At first, it appeared that Italy and Germany were merely modern versions of that kind of fascism. Of course, in America one needed a serious motivation to follow such a new course. The Great Depression gave the new president that opportunity. His answer was the New Deal legislation, a sweeping remaking of the American political economy.

---

181 Quoted in Jonathan Alter, *The Defining Moment: FDR's Hundred Days and the Triumph of Hope* (New York: Simon & Schuster, 2006), 5.

182 Margaret MacMillan, *Paris 1919: Six Months that Changed the World* (New York: Random House, 2002), 166–205.

183 Goldberg, *Liberal Fascism*, 57.

184 See the trenchant discussion about Germany as the root of Socialism in Friedrich Hayek's famous book/essay, *The Road to Serfdom*, 50th anniversary ed. (Chicago: University of Chicago Press, 1994), 1–12. The book was first published in 1944.

Struggle for the City

What Was Being Dealt

"No series of events in modern history is surrounded by more mythology than the New Deal, inaugurated by the 'Hundred Days.'"[185] The story of young Washington hurling the silver dollar across the Potomac is *nothing* compared to this myth. Let's look at the basic elements.[186] One element of the New Deal was *industrial regulation*. The National Industrial Recovery Acts (1933) set up a National Recovery Administration (NRA).[187] It attempted to set up codes and standards for fair business competition, codes that included fair wages, work hours, amount of goods produced, typical work day, and so on. Once these standards were approved by the NRA they had the force of law. The NRA had a little blue eagle logo that was used to indicate industries and companies that were in *compliance* with NRA regulations. The basic idea here is to set up a government-run monopoly in each area of industrial economy.[188]

Each industry was to agree to keep wages high and not to undercut one another on prices. All businesses would coordinate and agree *not* to compete. The fundamental strategy was to keep *production down*, ensure that wages were high, and that prices were also high. The language used to pass and promote such legislation deliberately avoided what this kind of collusion had once been called: *cartelization*, previously considered abominable behavior by such men as the "robber barons." Within a year *ninety percent* of industrial workers were in companies covered by NRA regulation. The federal government was in control of industrial output, and it passed out favors to those companies that curried its favor. *Political entrepreneurship* had won the day![189] A lot of this would later be found to be *unconstitutional* by the Supreme Court, but that all takes time, and while the legal battles *dragged on*, so did the recession.[190]

---

185 Johnson, *History of the American People*, 753.
186 Most of this narrative is taken from an amalgam of reading Shlaes, *Forgotten Man*, Eric Foner, *The Story of American Freedom* (New York: Norton, 1998), Brands, *Traitor to His Class*, and Anthony J. Badger, *The New Deal: The Depression Years, 1933–1940* (1989; repr., Chicago: Ivan R. Dee, 2002). Specific footnotes will point to specific important points in the narrative.
187 Shlaes, *Forgotten Man*, 150–52, 201–2.
188 Brands, *Traitor to His Class*, 279–89.
189 See our previous discussion in chap. 19.
190 Badger, *New Deal*, 116–17.

Struggle for the City

The New Deal also addressed the *agricultural* industry with the Agricultural Adjustment Administration as a sort of "twin for the NRA."[191] This led to the formation of a series of laws labeled the Agricultural Adjustment Acts. Roosevelt and his supporters wanted to be sure that farmers could earn as much as they had back in the years just before and during the Great War.[192] American farmers *flourished* during the Great War because European countries bought their produce in great amounts and, therefore, at really good prices (supply and demand, again). But farm prices had fallen off after the War because European countries were rebuilding their own economies and could not afford American produce—they were growing their own once again. Most of these Acts were *also* found to be unconstitutional, but Congress and the president just kept passing new ones, hoping that something might *stick*.[193] The whirlwind nature of all of this legislation brought Roosevelt to a fever pitch and those who were with him as well. One of Roosevelt's aides, Irving Fisher of Yale, wrote to his wife, "I feel this work marks the culmination of my life."[194] Heady, indeed!

They set up federal crop insurance to guarantee against disasters. They established the Commodity Credit Corporation to try to keep prices high. They established the food stamp program for the poor and the school lunch program. Both of these had as their *primary* purpose, not helping the poor, but setting up *demand* for agricultural commodities in order to keep the price high. Subsidies like this and many others survive today, even though most American agriculture is carried on by massive corporations, to the detriment of what were once called (and still are) "family farms." Another important point is that these programs were disproportionally focused on poor African Americans and their smaller farms in the South. Over time, this would leave them painted with the stigma of "welfare" more than white farmers.[195]

Some of these programs were successful in keeping farm prices up and farmers then, quite naturally, produced more and *more* output. However, this renewed

---

191 Shlaes, *Forgotten Man*, 152.
192 Badger, *New Deal*, 161–62.
193 Brands, *Traitor to His Class*, 263.
194 Shlaes, *Forgotten Man*, 153.
195 Foner, *Story of American Freedom*, 208.

Struggle for the City

608

commitment to output had the deleterious result of driving prices back down again, a problem that American agriculture has had to deal with throughout the rest of the century. Because of that, the federal government has repeatedly tinkered with farm prices and subsidies, right down to the twenty-first century.[196]

Banking and finance were also on the agenda for the New Deal. The Federal Deposit Insurance Corporation (FDIC) was established to insure *deposits*.[197] The Federal Housing Administration (FHA) was established to help people get access to *home loans*.[198] The Security and Exchange Commission (SEC) regulated stock transactions and various other aspects of the securities industry.[199] One of the most controversial bills, at least from later perspective, was the Glass-Steagall Act of 1933. It separated commercial banks from investment banks and prevented banks from trading in securities such as *stocks*. This was so as to keep banks from being involved in speculation, though it is the case that there is no real evidence that banks had done much of this sort of thing.[200] This controversy remains with us to the present day as we see the rules first rescinded and then reinstated, adding constant *uncertainty* to the marketplace and begging for ongoing political interference or even corruption.

Other new agencies were the Civil Aeronautics Board to regulate plane fares and to keep them high enough so that the airlines would remain *solvent*. The Federal Communications Commission was created to regulate radio and telegraph. A similar agency had been put in place when Hoover was commerce secretary, and he had used it then to control what *kinds* of companies were able to use the airwaves. More of that sort of regulation will now be possible under the New Deal. The Interstate Commerce Commission, which already regulated the railroads, now was enabled to regulate interstate trucking. So, there was a vast network of new regulations all coming in within a couple of years that placed the federal government over virtually *every* area of national business and economy.[201]

---

196 Badger, *New Deal*, 162.
197 Ibid., 72.
198 Foner, *Story of American Freedom*, 210.
199 Shlaes, *Forgotten Man*, 199, 297.
200 Brands, *Traitor to His Class*, 262–64.
201 Badger, *New Deal*, 245–50.

Struggle for the City

What's the Big Deal?

Those of us who have come along after all of that may have simply grown up with the recognition that "Well, of course the government regulates plane fares and charges radio and television stations fees and controls what they can broadcast. Has it not always been that way?" The answer is, "No! It came in with the New Deal." It came in under a president who believed that the administrative state had the right and the ability to govern almost *every* detail of the economic life of the nation. In his second inauguration address Roosevelt said that he was seeking "unimagined power."[202] Like Woodrow Wilson, he believed he had the best and brightest advisors, people who could understand how to command the economy. Unlike Wilson, he was a poor judge of character and intelligence, in spite of the fact that he regularly referred to his "brains trust." "In fact this too is largely myth."[203] There was no intellectual center to Roosevelt's program—there was no *program*, just a variety of attempts to try things to see if they would work. This president admired what was happening in Italy and Germany under Mussolini and Hitler, respectively, places that were trying to carry out the Hegelian ideal that we discussed earlier (see chap. 19), at least in the 1930s, and he wanted to see the same kinds of things happening here. The European fascism seemed to be having good results; why could not the same thing happen here? Ironically, it was Democrats, such as William Green, president of the American Federation of Labor, who said that Roosevelt's program smacked "of fascism, of Hitlerism, and in some respects of sovietism."[204] Harsh criticism of Roosevelt was not limited to the Republican right.

Unions received a new impetus and new empowerment due to the New Deal. There had been trade and labor unions in the United States since very early times, a development from the trade guilds of the older European economic system, though they never had the same hold on the economy here that they did in Europe. After all, American economics owed much to Adam Smith's political economy, and Smith's philosophy had little sympathy with the trade guilds that colluded with governments to get what they wanted, at the expense of consumers. But various industries and trades did develop

---

202 Shlaes, *Forgotten Man*, 10.
203 Johnson, *History of the American People*, 760.
204 Quoted in Brands, *Traitor to His Class*, 333.

Struggle for the City

unions in America, such as hatters, teamsters, and so on. In 1886 several of them formed into the American Federation of Labor.[205]

They had little power, however. When the Hatters Union went on strike in 1908, the courts ruled that the very fact that they went on strike put them in violation of the Sherman Antitrust Act and held each of them personally liable. In 1935, under New Deal sponsorship, the remaining independent unions joined together to form the Congress of Industrial Organizations.[206] This covered autoworkers, steelworkers, and so on, so that they could not be pitted *against* one another. Later the two organizations linked together to form the AFL-CIO. The Wagner Act of 1935 set up a national labor-relations board to *oversee* union elections *nationwide*. In 1930 only about twelve percent of American workers were in unions, but by 1940 that number would be up to thirty percent, a dramatic rise in one decade, basically due to the New Deal legislation and the impact of the Great Depression. In some places unions were forced on companies in brutal ways. The Ford Motor Company had long held out against unionization, but in 1934 Ford security workers beat a striker and violence ensued.[207] Similar events were occurring around the country.

The original Social Security Act was passed in 1935. The tax on employers and the old-age benefit system were two different laws. Roosevelt set it up that way in the first place because he *feared* that an omnibus bill that included both would be struck down by the Supreme Court, which was declaring much of his New Deal legislation unconstitutional. So, the system was never set up to have accounts established for current workers that they could draw upon in the future. It was a *current* tax on *current* employers and then a *separate* arrangement of payments to retirees.[208] This would come to have huge repercussions in later years.

There was much more, but these are the most important provisions for our purposes here. Did the New Deal work? In some ways it "appeared" to do so, in the same way the logic of correspondence between events appears to "prove" some propositions. The economy hit bottom in 1933. The next year witnessed a slight recovery, which is why some historians date the Great Depression as only from 1929

---

205 Philip Dray, *There Is Power in a Union: The Epic Story of Labor in America* (New York: Doubleday, 2010). This is primarily a historical narrative.
206 Foner, *Story of American Freedom*, 200.
207 Shlaes, *Forgotten Man*, 323–24.
208 Badger, *New Deal*, 227–35.

Struggle for the City

through 1933, but the upswing that followed really cannot be considered to be a genuine "recovery." The years 1935 and 1936 see some real improvement, yet then there is another deep crash in 1937, with the market dropping more than fifty percent in seven months, with no real recovery until late 1939. The New Deal enacted a high tax on the rich in 1937, and this removed buying power from the economy. The Federal Reserve also made bad decisions, in ways we have seen before. It is also the case that the full impact of New Deal regulatory agencies was being felt in 1937, causing more expense to manufacturers, thus cutting profits and hindering their ability to hire and to purchase equipment. Does this sound familiar?

Numerous questions with not-so-satisfying answers have been raised in recent scholarship concerning this period. The questions are persistent: Why did New Dealers make it more difficult to hire workers? Why were taxes on individuals and corporations raised in such a fashion as to triple collections during the period and double their percentage vis-à-vis the gross domestic product? Why was so much "recovery" money directed to the nonpoor? Why were policies enacted that pushed up the cost of living? Why were crops and foodstuffs and animals destroyed while people were starving? Why were 150 law suits filed by the Justice Department against businesses? Why were blacks harmed by the new labor laws? The list is endless, it seems.[209]

As the Depression slugged along, various intellectuals were trying to explain it, and many of them were urging various political solutions other than those being tried by FDR. We have already discussed the *Marxist* view that this financial crisis demonstrated the bankrupt moral basis of *capitalism*. Some intellectuals in the Western world agreed with the Marxist view, but it had little hope of being the dominant view in Washington or London. Another interpretation that became a favored one in much of the non-Communist world was that of John Maynard Keynes, who in 1936, right in the middle of the Depression, published *The General Theory of Employment, Interest, and Money*.[210] Keynes opposed both Adam Smith's free-market approach and Marx's completely controlled economy approach.

---

209 For a full discussion of these and many more issues, see Jim Powell, *FDR's Folly: How Roosevelt and His New Deal Prolonged the Great Depression* (New York: Crown Forum, 2003).

210 John Maynard Keynes, *The General Theory of Employment, Interest, and Money* (London: Macmillan, 1936).

Struggle for the City

Keynes believed that capitalism was inherently *unstable*, which is why it kept slipping into recessions and depressions every so often. What it needed was neither a governmental master who could control it all the time nor a drunk capitalistic system (in his view) that went wherever it chose regardless of the effect. Instead, "all that was needed was for government to take control of a wayward capitalist steering wheel and get the car back on the road to prosperity."[211] It did this not by older methods of cutting prices and wages, but by running deficits, spending money on public works, and tinkering with the money supply. Keynes believed that unemployment had one basic reason—*inadequate demand*. "When anyone cuts down expenditure,… next morning someone for sure finds that his income has been cut off…. The fellow who wakes up to find out that his income is reduced or that he is thrown out of work… is compelled in his turn to cut down his expenditure, whether he wants to or not…. Once the rot has started, it is most difficult to stop."[212] If that was the case, then the "fix" is also quite simple—expansionary fiscal policy. Curiously, FDR attempted to do just some of these things in the New Deal. The fact that they did not work did not deter Keynes, who merely thought that FDR was not receiving the right kind of advice.[213] Still, even today, Keynes' approach is dominant in many academic and political circles and has become the *sine qua non* of Paul Krugman (erstwhile Enron advisor and present *New York Times* columnist) and the Barack Obama economic team (see "stimulus" as the operative policy answer to economic displacements).

Shortly after the Depression had ended, and during World War II, an Austrian intellectual named Friedrich Hayek responded to Keynes and to the generally accepted belief on the part of English intellectuals that Fascism (the kind of fascism now out in the open in Germany and Italy) was a capitalist *response* to Socialism. Hayek, in his now-famous *Road to Serfdom*, contended that this was

211 Mark Skousen, *The Making of Modern Economics: The Lives and Ideas of the Great Thinkers*, 2nd ed. (Armonk, NY: M. E. Sharpe, 2009), 325.

212 John Maynard Keynes, *The Collected Writings of John Maynard Keynes*, vol. 21, *Activities 1931–1939: World Crises and Policies in Britain and America*, ed. Donald Moggridge (London: Macmillan, 1982), 134, 144.

213 Todd G. Buchholz, *New Ideas from Dead Economists: An Introduction to Modern Economic Thought*, rev. ed. (New York: Plume, 1999), 229–52.

Struggle for the City

nonsense.[214] This "Austrian economist" (who was forced to flee first to Cambridge and eventually came to America to teach) believed that both Marxist Socialism and Keynesianism were dead wrong. In contrast to those two, he argued, "only capitalism makes democracy possible."[215] Quoting Lord Acton, "Power tends to corrupt, and absolute power corrupts absolutely," he penned a chapter entitled, "Why the Worst Get on Top." Here he sought to explain why people like Hitler, Stalin, Mussolini, and even Roosevelt get elected or in some other way rise to the top during crises. They were charismatic figures who arose during times of crisis and convinced the people that they had a solution, one that could be implemented *only* from the top down with *near-total control*.[216] We have already noted Hayek's point that the problem with planned economies (whether Socialist, statist, or some hybrid) is that no one person or committee has the wisdom to plan a nation's economy.[217] He made a similar observation in *Road to Serfdom*.

And because all the details of the changes constantly affecting the conditions of demand and supply of the different commodities can never be fully known, or quickly enough be collected and disseminated, by any one center, what is required is some apparatus of registration that automatically records all the relevant effects of individual actions and whose indications are at the same time resultant of, and the guide for, all the individual decisions.[218]

But this is not possible even in the age of supercomputers. It is impossible to *plan* an economy. At the heart of the little volume though is a chapter entitled, "Planning and the Rule of Law," in which the Austrian economist makes it clear that planned economies, even those on the level of Keynesian planning, eventually cannot live under the rule of law.[219] Hayek offered Roosevelt very different advice than had Keynes.[220] Back to the New Deal.

214 Hayek, *Road to Serfdom*, 13–27.

215 Ibid., 69–70.

216 Ibid., 148–67.

217 F. A. Hayek, "The Use of Knowledge in Society," *American Economic Review* 35, no. 4 (September 1945): 526–28; also see the excellent treatment in Nicholas Wapshott, *Keynes Hayek: The Clash That Defined Modern Economics* (New York: W. W. Norton, 2011), 29–45, 154–70, 247–65.

218 Hayek, *Road to Serfdom*, 55.

219 Ibid., 80–96.

220 Sylvia Nasar, *Grand Pursuit* (New York: Simon & Schuster, 2011), 401–2. The two men, Hayek and Keynes, did remain friends in spite of their very different perspectives on political economy.

Struggle for the City

The problem with the New Deal was that very little of it was really intended to *increase productivity*. That was never its real *purpose*. Roosevelt's idea was that we as a nation should produce a lot *less* and keep wages and prices *high*. Stop competition, cut production, pay high wages, and keep prices as high as possible. Is that seriously a *solution* to a *recession*? And what happens when unemployment hits twenty-five percent, as it did? The New Deal was a Progressive *philosophical* solution that was being thrown at what was in reality was a *pragmatic* problem.[221] Roosevelt did not understand macroeconomics, he did not understand how to empower business to stimulate the economy, and even more importantly, he did not understand the "forgotten man."

Robert Higgs argues cogently about the extended misery of this period that the greatest contributor to ongoing economic depression was "regime uncertainty." By this he means that business people and ordinary investors had no confidence in the law and their property rights because of the continuing onslaught of New Deal legislation against the business community and the capricious nature of the taking away of those rights so they might be dispensed to *others* on the political inside. Aggregate private investment in the economy did not grow for the decade of the Thirties, as we have noted above. It did not reach what might be called *normalcy* until after the end of World War II in 1947. This lack of confidence in investment during the period 1935–40 was brought on by the second wave of enactments, which Higgs calls the "Second New Deal" (after 1935). It was not until 1940, on the eve of the war, that Roosevelt began to *divest* his inner circle of anti-business advisors and administrators in favor of pro-business consultants and politicians. The war did not cause the recovery that began about 1947 and continued through the 1950s, but it was an *interregnum* in which the Rooseveltian interference was set aside in an effort to win a war that must be won.[222]

It is obvious that we now live in a world of economic and political institutions that are *largely* the result of New Deal interference and experimenta-

---

221 Eventually Roosevelt gave up on using the term "progressive" and replaced it with the word "liberal." Foner, *Story of American Freedom*, 200–201.
222 For the full analysis and documentation on this opinion, see Robert Higgs, *Depression, War, and Cold War: Challenging the Myths of Conflict and Prosperity* (Oakland, CA: Independent Institute, 2006), chap. 1.

Struggle for the City

tion and their aftermath. This is clearly a mixed bag of regulatory and tax-and-spend-and-borrow methods of control that is labyrinthine in the early twenty-first century. It *saps* human initiative and rewards *irresponsible* and sinful behavior at every turn and fails to hold the true culprits of economic difficulty and disaster *accountable*. But here is its most egregious effect: The most important legacy of the New Deal is a certain system of belief, the now-dominant ideology of the mixed economy, which holds that the government is an immensely useful means for achieving one's private aspirations and that one's resort to this reservoir of potentially appropriable benefits is perfectly legitimate. To take—indirectly if not directly—other people's property for one's own benefit is considered morally impeccable, provided the taking is effected through the medium of the government.[223]

The promise of social security (the general value, not the program) and something-for-nothing has taken hold of the body politic and shows little sign of abating almost eighty years later.

The Churches as Players in the Game

Recessions have consequences. "The Great Depression has ended the Republican dominance of national politics that began in 1896."[224] Protestants, even conservative Protestants, turned out in large numbers for FDR in 1932. But at the end of the New Deal period, what would the assessment be in the churches?

Roman Catholicism in America was surging at this time, much as fundamentalism was, and especially so on the economic front. The medieval Catholic thinker Thomas Aquinas had been rediscovered in American Catholic circles, and his emphasis on *rationality*, on the *sacraments* of the church as a unifying force for all Catholics, and on faithfulness to the Catholic *traditions* brought a surge in Catholic churches.[225] The years before the recession had witnessed the rise of a Catholicism that had all the characteristics of revivalistic funda-

---

223 Higgs, *Crisis and Leviathan*, 195.
224 Kellstedt et al., "Faith Transformed," 269. Republican dominance of national politics actually began in 1860, with only a couple of Democrats being elected in the intervening years.
225 Noll, *History of Christianity in the United States and Canada*, 433.

Struggle for the City

mentalism, and it brought renewed personal commitment to many members.[226] Whether Catholic or Protestant, people who have an enthusiasm for their faith and who hold its tenets as cherished ideals to be believed and lived have an easier time getting through life's difficult times than those who do not.

Many of these people originally had high hopes for Roosevelt's New Deal, including a galvanizing figure in the church of that time, a man named Charles Coughlin. Father Coughlin pastored in Detroit, a city hard hit by the Great Depression. For the first several years under Hoover, the economy was a regular feature of his sermons, and in 1932 his message was "Roosevelt or Ruin."[227] By 1934, however, he had changed his tune. His concern was not that Roosevelt was doing too much, but that it was too little. He advocated a virtual takeover of the entire economy by the federal government.[228]

Elsewhere, historian Thomas Sugrue notes the preaching of a black pastor in inner-city Chicago at the time: "Let Jesus lead you and Roosevelt feed you!"[229] This cry from the cities highlights the debate of the time exacerbated by race relations all over the nation, as black Americans were hit harder by the Depression than any others. Famously, Gunnar Myrdal would publish (with acclaim in black and white press alike) his bestseller, *The American Dilemma: The Negro Problem and American Democracy*, in 1944, advocating boldly "social engineering" (with reference to racial implications in its economic effects), but during the mid-1930s Roosevelt was too concerned about defending in the courts the work he was doing elsewhere in the economy to endanger it with outright provocation of the Southern wing of his own party.[230] Myrdal and many (most?) others at the time believed in a "solution" that did not involve structural economic change but "social change," a process of persuasion, education, and cajolery that would lead to a race-blind (or color-blind)

---

226 Finke and Stark, *Churching of America, 1776–1990*, 117–55.

227 Ahlstrom, *Religious History of the American People*, 928.

228 Noll, *History of Christianity in the United States and Canada*, 504.

229 Quoted in Thomas J. Sugrue, *Sweet Land of Liberty: The Forgotten Struggle for Civil Rights in the North* (New York: Random House, 2008), 50.

230 See ibid., 58–63. Myrdal was finishing his two-volume tome for publication in 1942 as the impact of World War II was being felt all over the country in racial relations. Sugrue is at great pains to show in his volume, *Sweet Land of Liberty*, that the race problem in America was not a regional problem, except as the Democrat Party was dominated by the South, which had a veto on race-based legislation. Nevertheless, his book is a study of the problem in the North.

Struggle for the City

society, because after all, "People are all much alike on a fundamental level, and they are all good people. They want to be rational and just." Not everyone, black or white, would have agreed with that assessment.

On the other hand the modern world called for big solutions, and these big solutions were beyond the pale for many denominations. The Congregationalist Church had been almost completely dominated by its capitulation to liberalism and Unitarianism. Episcopalians, Northern Presbyterians, Northern Methodists, and Northern Baptists were headed toward liberalism at least in their institutions, even if many churches were still evangelical. One historian noted, "With its basic theological insights largely emasculated, Protestantism was robbed of any independently grounded vision of life and became more and more the creature of American culture rather than its creator."[231] Such churches basically accepted Roosevelt's New Deal as a political version of the social gospel and as a "paternal substitute for traditional church charity."[232] *Conservative* churches were not so roundly dejected in the wake of the New Deal, *nor* were they as *sanguine* about Roosevelt's policies; and what no one in the church or society in general knew in 1940 was that they were on the verge of war and revival.

So, what we got through the Depression was the "solution"; meanwhile the real "solution," World War II and postwar prosperity, was on its way. What was next for America and her evangelicals?

---

231 Winthrop Hudson, quoted in Askew and Spellman, *Churches and the American Experience*, 190.
232 Ibid.

Struggle for the City

Chapter 21

Pearl Harbor, Woodstock, and the Great Debate

Our story has taken us through some tough economic, political, and theological storms. But as they say, "You ain't seen nothing yet." From the Forties till now has been a turbulent time. Let's take a peek.

War and Its Wake

Fundamental transformations came into American society beginning in the Forties. Some of them had already been working their way into the nation in the previous decade, but the Second World War and its effects on our culture fundamentally transformed American politics and the American economy, even as it affected those same aspects of nations in the rest of the world. The churches were especially impacted, in ways that we will explore in this chapter.

The Second World War

World War II and its aftermath brought the Great Depression, however it is defined, to a final end.[1] America was called upon for the first two years of

---

1   Anthony J. Badger, *The New Deal: The Depression Years, 1933–1940* (1989; repr., Chicago: Ivan R. Dee, 2002), 310–11.

the war in Europe to produce war *material* for the Allied forces, and it did so. It went so far as to transform its great factories into weapons manufacturing plants. Under the banner "arsenal of democracy," a brilliant Rooseveltian wordplay, Americans *sacrificed* and *worked* and *produced* the expanded manufacturing capacity that would turn into prosperity after the war years. Detroit built no cars from late 1942 till 1946. But the auto plants built tanks and trucks and jeeps first for England and the other Allies, and then, after 1941, for its own troops. In January 1941, FDR asked Congress for means to arm England and America as well, just in case we were drawn into the war. The Lend-Lease Act passed in Congress in March, authorizing the administration to provide supplies to "any country whose defense the President deems vital to the defense of the United States."[2] The "Prosperity Wartime" was on.

America entered the war in December 1941. In October 1942 Roosevelt "visited a Chrysler factory in Detroit that built tanks, a Ford facility in Willow Run, Michigan, that produced B-24 bombers, an Allis-Chalmers plant in Milwaukee that made ammunition," along with a "Boeing plant in Seattle that assembled B-17s, and a Kaiser yard in Portland, Oregon, that constructed cargo ships."[3] He also dropped in on an Alcoa smelter in Vancouver, Washington, that turned bauxite into aluminum, and a Higgins yard in New Orleans that churned out landing craft."[4] These visits were timed to coincide with congressional elections that were only a few weeks away, but the tour itself demonstrates the extent to which American industry was supporting the war effort, and this is only a sampling.

All of this manufacturing caused the gross domestic product of the United States to soar from 1940 through 1945. This war, as much as any war in recent memory, seemed to be *just* and seemed to have been *inevitable*. We were attacked, and so we replied in kind. The Japanese had assaulted us, and had done so with war preparations "that were a characteristic combination of breathtaking efficiency and inexplicable muddle."[5] They had no plan for a protracted

---

2   Jonathan R. T. Hughes and Louis P. Cain, *American Economic History*, 7th ed. (Boston: Pearson Addison Wesley, 2006), 526.
3   H. W. Brands, *Traitor to His Class*: The Privileged Life and Radical Presidency of Franklin Delano Roosevelt (New York: Doubleday, 2008), 533.
4   Ibid.
5   Paul Johnson, *A History of the American People* (New York: HarperCollins, 1997), 778.

Struggle for the City

war, and when America did not capitulate immediately, they knew they were in trouble, as they were.[6] We responded and did so with a vengeance. But once again the demand for action on a national scale in an "emergency" brought forth ever-increasing intrusions by government into private business and homes and institutions that carried forward the ideology of big government to the rescue. America's economy became, like it never had before, a "command economy," that is, an economy under the command of the centrally planning federal government.[7] *Big government* in America had happened before, during the Revolutionary War, the Civil War, and the Great War, and was not new, but the wartime economy was a harbinger of just *how big*, big could be.

Postbellum

When the war was over there was the usual economic hangover that comes after war—a recession.[8] We had one and it was bad, but it was partially offset by the fact that returning GIs took their savings from their military service and bought homes and cars, and those who had simply worked through the war and bought bonds with surplus money that could not be spent on goods not being produced for consumer purposes began to spend, and so, by 1947 the economy was booming again.[9] It boomed right through the 1950s with only a small snag or two along the way. The war had sent many migrants from rural America to the cities of the North and West, "permanently altering the nation's social geography,"[10] even as the Great Depression had sent many Southern farmers to California. It was a new America.

The postwar world was a fast-changing world. The major European powers had been *colonial* powers. Since the late fifteenth century Spain and Portugal had been developing major colonial holdings around the world. Within a hundred years they were joined by England, France, and the Netherlands, and after that the Germans and a few other European nations. But World

---

6 Ibid., 779.
7 Hughes and Cain, *American Economic History*, 527.
8 James T. Patterson, *Grand Expectations: The United States, 1945–1974*, Oxford History of the United States 10 (New York: Oxford University Press, 1996), 39–60.
9 Ibid., 61–81.
10 Eric Foner, *The Story of American Freedom* (New York: W. W. Norton, 1998), 219.

Struggle for the City

War II had exhausted those nations financially and politically, and it became clear after the war that such *exhaustion*, coupled with indigenous new *resistance* to colonialism in general by those "third world" nations, was going to spell the end of virtually all colonialism.[11] India, Canada, parts of Southeast Asia, Africa, South and Central America, and on and on, European powers were *decolonizing*.[12] Philosophically it was certainly a good thing; pragmatically in some places it only created a new set of problems—poverty, revolution, the possibility of new kinds of colonialization. "It is impossible to make any truthful generalization about colonialism. The same is true of the decolonizing process."[13] All of these things did happen, and the dust has not settled yet and may not for a long time to come. What emerged from the war was that there were now two great superpowers, in terms of military might, international influence, and economic power. At least, that was how it seemed in the 1950s as we settled into what came to be called the Cold War.

The Churches, the War, and What Came After

In our discussion of the Great War, now designated as World War I, we noted the large number of pacifists and conscientious objectors who had refused to enter the war. The two years of war before the attack at Pearl Harbor witnessed an intense debate in churches over the most Christian *position* on war, with a significant *minority* in the churches, whether students, pastors, or laymen holding to a pacifist position. But the attack on Pearl Harbor ended *most* of that.[14] The number of conscientious objectors in the 1940s dwindled down to about twelve thousand.[15] The churches supported the war. They "took up without reluctance their wartime tasks; but a more tempered and mature view of global war's grim business replaced the unrestrained crusading enthusiasm

---

11 Johnson, *History of the American People*, 806.
12 For a brief overview, see Raymond F. Betts, *Decolonization*, 2nd ed., Making of the Contemporary World (New York: Routledge, 2004), 20–37, and throughout.
13 Paul Johnson, *Modern Times*, rev. ed. (New York: HarperPerennial, 1991), 506.
14 Thomas A. Askew and Peter W. Spellman, *The Churches and the American Experience* (Grand Rapids, MI: Baker, 1984), 194.
15 Sydney E. Ahlstrom, *A Religious History of the American People*, 2nd ed. (1972; New Haven, CT: Yale University Press, 2004), 949.

of 1917–18."[16] The churches for the most part did *not* glorify the war, nor did they have the same kind of crusading spirit that had existed in the earlier wars. For mainline churches this may be partly due to the influence of liberalism and neo-orthodoxy with their altered theology of sin and their rejection of any sort of postmillennialism.[17]

During the Second World War, social changes that resulted from an all-out mobilization for war had an impact on religious as well as cultural matters.[18] The massive recruitment and industrial expansion caused a change in *gender* roles that did not completely revert to prewar status when the hostilities were ended.[19] Education changed as a result of the war, since the GI Bill made it possible for many more people to attend college than before; many of them went to religious schools. The self-identity of many of the nation's blacks was also altered during the war, since many of them had fought alongside whites.[20] Their lives, on the *average*, improved in the late 1940s.[21] Their prospects did not improve as quickly or as thoroughly as white Americans, but it did seem to be a harbinger of better things to come.[22] But painful days were ahead as a direct result of increased expectations and white intransigence. Even more, the increased productivity of the war years caused Christian people in the churches to have a greater sense of security and of hopefulness after the decade of depression, in spite of the fact that they were at war.[23] And of course, the successful prosecution of the war made Americans believe that it was worth all of the sacrifice. "America's sacrificial defense of the 'four freedoms' seemed to enhance the value of each, including the freedom of worship."[24] Indeed!

---

16 Askew and Spellman, *Churches and the American Experience*, 194.
17 Ahlstrom, *Religious History of the American People*, 949.
18 Mark A. Noll, *A History of Christianity in the United States and Canada* (1992; repr., Grand Rapids, MI: Eerdmans, 2003), 437.
19 Patterson, *Grand Expectations*, 10–38.
20 Noll, *History of Christianity in the United States and Canada*, 437.
21 Patterson, *Grand Expectations*, 19.
22 Martin E. Marty, *Modern American Religion*, vol. 3, *Under God, Indivisible, 1941–1960* (Chicago: University of Chicago Press, 1996), 65–75.
23 Ahlstrom, *Religious History of the American People*, 950.
24 Askew and Spellman, *Churches and the American Experience*, 195. The "four freedoms" here are politics (the right to vote), speech/press, markets, and religion, as we detailed in a previous discussion (see chap. 16).

Struggle for the City

The ending of the war witnessed something of a "revival" in American houses of worship, if one looks at the numbers of people joining and attending churches. Some of this was a result of the postwar baby boom, which "created countless new families for whom attachment to church became as normal as increased personal prosperity and a move to the suburbs."[25] One might argue that this was as much *cultural* as it was "spiritual." "Being a church member and speaking favorably became a means of affirming the 'American Way of Life,' especially since the USSR and its Communist allies were formally committed to atheism."[26] In part, then, this "revival" was a response to the Cold War that settled into the American situation as the United States and the USSR competed with one another in the nuclear arms race. But that is only part of the explanation. Culture critic Will Herberg saw this growth, which also included Catholic and Jewish expansion, as a merging of all faiths into the "culture religion" of the "American way of life."[27] From 1940 to 1970 church affiliation rose from forty-nine percent to more than sixty-two percent.[28] Most major denominations grew during this period, but those experiencing the greatest growth were conservative (or even fundamentalist) churches and "third force" churches, churches that were Pentecostal or charismatic in one way or another, with these latter churches increasing their membership from four hundred to seven hundred percent.[29] It is not likely that such a surge is due *only* to civil or cultural factors, even if those do play some part in the explanation.

G. K. Chesterton once called America "a nation with the soul of a church." Post–World War II America actually lived up to that description perhaps more than at any time since the Second Great Awakening. In 1967 Robert N. Bellah of Harvard published an essay entitled "Civil Religion in America." His opening statement is, "There actually exists alongside of and rather clearly differentiated from the churches an elaborate and well-institutionalized civil

---

25 Noll, *History of Christianity in the United States and Canada*, 437.
26 Ahlstrom, *Religious History of the American People*, 951.
27 Will Herberg, *Protestant-Catholic-Jew: An Essay in American Religious Sociology*, rev. ed., Anchor Books (Garden City, NY: Doubleday, 1960), 72–98.
28 Ahlstrom, *Religious History of the American People*, 952.
29 Ibid., 959.

Struggle for the City

religion in America."[30] He went on to argue that this must be understood *sympathetically* because it owns "its own seriousness and integrity and requires the same care in understanding that any other religion does."[31] That can be seen very clearly in this postwar period. On Flag Day in 1954 President Eisenhower signed legislation that added "one nation under God" to the Pledge of Allegiance. He contended that this new pledge would enrich a world in which there were so many people "deadened in mind and soul by a materialistic philosophy of life."[32] In 1956 the phrase "In God we trust" (as used by Lincoln in the Gettysburg Address) was "raised from the semiofficial it has had since 1865 as a device on our coinage to become the country's official motto."[33]

Eisenhower "presided benignly over what was termed, 'Piety on the Potomac,' a generalized form of the Christian religion very much in the American tradition, with no stress on dogma but insistence on moral propriety and good works."[34] It made some people *feel* safe in an increasingly unsafe world to have some religious tradition to participate in. That Eisenhower did not really understand the heart of Christianity very well can be seen in his 1954 announcement, "Our government makes no sense unless it is founded on a deeply felt religious faith—and I don't care what it is!"[35] The extent to which this generally Christianized character of America had colored our political life can be seen in John F. Kennedy's conclusion to his inaugural address: "With a good conscience our only sure reward, with history the final judge of deeds, let us go forth to lead the land we love, asking His blessing and His help, but knowing that here on earth God's work must be truly our own."[36] That was Jack Kennedy, not George Washington!

---

30 Robert N. Bellah, "Civil Religion in America," *Daedelus* 96, no. 1 (1967): 1. See also, Robert N. Bellah and Phillip E. Hammond, *Varieties of Civil Religion* (San Francisco: Harper & Row, 1980), 1–26.
31 Bellah, "Civil Religion in America," 1.
32 Quoted in Stephen J. Whitfield, *The Culture of the Cold War*, American Moment (Baltimore: Johns Hopkins University Press, 1996), 89, cited in Patterson, *Grand Expectations*, 329.
33 Ahlstrom, *Religious History of the American People*, 954.
34 Johnson, *History of the American People*, 840.
35 Quoted in Dwight D. Eisenhower, "The President's Religious Faith," interview by Paul Hutchinson, *Christian Century* 71 (March 25, 1954), 365, quoted in Johnson, *History of the American People, 840*.
36 John F. Kennedy, "Inaugural Address," January 20, 1961, *Public Papers of the Presidents of the United States* (Washington, DC: United States Government Printing Office, 1961), 3, quoted in Perry C. Cotham, *Politics, Americanism, and Christianity* (Grand Rapids, MI: Baker, 1976), 127.

Struggle for the City

Was the attitude of fundamentalism about social issues changed by the late 1940s? Recall that most fundamentalists (Machen and the Presbyterians being the exception) were *not* keen to give great attention to social matters, at least not beyond the kinds of individual sins that they regularly preached against. But in the postwar period, that began to change. A coalition of fundamentalists during the war (in 1942) had formed the National Association of Evangelicals. Preferring the term "Evangelical" to the (now) more pejorative "fundamentalist," they charted new territory theologically, educationally, and also in terms of a new focus on social issues.[37]

The movement was not something completely novel but had been forming in the late 1930s in places like Wheaton College where a youthful Billy Graham enrolled in 1940. Scholars there such as J. Oliver Buswell and Gordon Clark were preparing a new generation of fundamentalists to move away from *separatism*, that is, the need to abandon their denominations when heresy arose. This had "plagued Protestant reformers in America since the first Puritans set foot on Plymouth Rock."[38] The Wheaton faculty were also encouraging their students that a strict dispensational premillennialism, which to some in fundamentalist circles was a "tenet of orthodoxy," was *not* endemic to holding to the fundamentals of the faith.[39] In addition, they were leading them to abandon the focus on less significant issues, such as opposition to card-playing and theater-going and to get serious about *serious matters*. Though still committed to the fundamentals, this younger generation was willing to rethink some of these other social issues.[40] Gaining momentum in the war years, the new evangelicals were poised to make their own impact when the dust of battle finally settled.

The leading intellectual of the group in the late Forties was a young former journalist with two earned doctorates by 1949, one in theology and the other in philosophy. Carl F. H. Henry in 1946 authored the book *Remaking the Modern Mind* (1946). This book put him on the map as a young (thirty-three years old

---

37 George M. Marsden, *Reforming Fundamentalism* (1987; repr., Grand Rapids, MI: Eerdmans, 1995), 32–52.
38 Ibid., 6.
39 George M. Marsden, "From Fundamentalism to Evangelicalism: A Historical Analysis," in *The Evangelicals: What They Believe, Who They Are, Where They Are Changing*, ed. David F. Wells and John D. Woodbridge (Nashville: Abingdon, 1975), 127.
40 Marty, *Under God, Indivisible*, 3:152–54.

Struggle for the City

at the time) fundamentalist theologian with a firm grasp of the intellectual issues of the time. He argued that the previous three decades had demonstrated that modern Western culture had collapsed because the "philosophical premises on which it was based had proved too flimsy to support the weight of civilization."[41] The premises he spoke of were the components of *modern humanism*. The roots of this system lay in the Renaissance and the Enlightenment that followed, with its focus on scientism, the immanence of God seen in evolutionary forces, the development of Scripture out of purely natural insights, and "the continuing revelation of God especially in the growing application of Christian principles to society."[42] The two world wars had shown that the most developed intellectual society in history (Germany) was *not* thereby the most moral society, but instead that it was willing to initiate military conflict and genocide (the Holocaust) that had swept almost the entire world into misery and pain.

The following year Henry wrote what would prove to be his most noted early work, *The Uneasy Conscience of Modern Fundamentalism*. In the introduction to the volume, Harold John Ockenga wrote, "The church needs a progressive Fundamentalism with a social message."[43] Henry offered critiques of both modernism and fundamentalism on the issue of social concern. He blamed modernism for collapsing the Christian faith into *nothing more* than social justice, and he accused fundamentalism of virtually *ignoring* matters of social concern that are actually raised by the Bible itself. Henry argued that early Christianity did not "chart the course for social reform," rather, "it furnished the basic principles and the moral dynamic for such reform, and concentrated on regeneration as the guarantee of bettered conditions."[44] He noted that Augustine's *City of God* insisted that "the temporal and eternal cities exist concurrently in history, as against the view that the kingdom of God is to be identified with super-history alone," a view which was characteristic of much of fundamentalism.[45] He further observed that the reforming work

---

41 Marsden, *Reforming Fundamentalism*, 78.
42 Marsden, "From Fundamentalism to Evangelicalism," 124.
43 Harold J. Ockenga, "Introduction," in Carl F. H. Henry, *The Uneasy Conscience of Modern Fundamentalism*, new ed. (1947; Grand Rapids, MI: Eerdmans, 2003), xx. This citation is from the 2003 edition that contains a new "Foreword" by Richard J. Mouw.
44 Henry, *Uneasy Conscience of Modern Fundamentalism*, 37.
45 Ibid., 38.

Struggle for the City

of John Calvin, in distinction to that of Luther, had involved "an articulate statement not only of dogmatics [theology] but of the social implications of redemption."[46] That was the historic tradition of most of the church.

Modern fundamentalism, though heir apparent to "the Great Tradition" of the past since it has maintained its commitment to the authority of Scripture, in contrast to the mainline denominations of the day, is yet "a stranger, in its predominant spirit, to the vigorous social interest of its ideological forebears."[47] As a result, "it does not challenge the injustices of totalitarianisms, the secularisms of modern education, the evils of racial hatred, the wrongs of current labor-management relations, the inadequate bases of international dealings."[48] Henry urged fundamentalism to reform its ways and to "express the genius of the Christian tradition: (1) That Christianity opposes any and every evil, personal and social, and must never be represented as in any way tolerant of such evil; (2) That Christianity opposes such evil as the only sufficient formula for its resolution, the redemptive work of Jesus Christ and the regenerative work of the Holy Spirit."[49] In other words, the substitutionary atonement of Christ and the new birth brought about by the Holy Spirit are the basis for dealing with evils, whether personal or social. With such a formulation it is small wonder that this book is credited with helping to herald "the dawn of an evangelical awakening."[50]

Henry went on to point out that there was an odd similarity between fundamentalists and modernists when it came to dealing with social evil. Both of them were driven by their *eschatology*. Fundamentalists held to a delayed-kingdom theology, that the kingdom will only come in the future after the second advent of Christ. Modernism, by contrast, believed that the kingdom of God was here in toto right now.[51] There is no future kingdom to be established at the second coming, since modernists did not generally believe in a second coming.[52] Since

---

46 Ibid., 39.
47 Ibid.
48 Ibid.
49 Ibid., 40
50 Rudolph Nelson, *The Making and Unmaking of an Evangelical Mind: The Case of Edward Carnell* (Cambridge: Cambridge University Press, 1987), 64.
51 Henry, *Uneasy Conscience of Modern Fundamentalism*, 42.
52 Recall the earlier discussion of Fosdick, who refused to speculate on future eschatology, esp. on the second coming of Christ (see chap. 20).

Struggle for the City

God is radically *immanent* in liberalism and since there is no clear outline of a future existence, the kingdom here and now is the *only* kingdom there will ever be, and so the churches should mobilize governments and the generosity of individuals to bring the kingdom about. Henry's response against both of these eschatological "extremes" is to see that the kingdom is both already and not-yet, that "the kingdom exists in incomplete realization.[53] To Henry, "[t]he task of the Bible student is to discover (1) in what sense it is here; (2) in what sense it is to be further realized before the advent of Christ; and (3) in what sense it will be fully realized at the advent of Christ."[54] One observer of Henry's theology puts it like this: "Henry self-consciously develops his ecclesiology within the context of his commitments to inaugurated eschatology and holistic soteriology."[55] In this formula lies the basic theological framework for Henry's social ethic.

For Henry, the "supernaturalist framework of historic Christianity" is the "lone solution of modern dilemmas."[56] In other words, only a chastened and reformed fundamentalism (or, evangelicalism) can provide the answers to social evil, since only it "insists upon a personal God, as against impersonal ultimates whether of space-time or *élan vital* variety."[57] Only historic Christianity "insists that man's uniqueness is a divine embodiment rather than a human achievement." Likewise, the biblical religion "insists that man's predicament is not an animal inheritance nor a necessity of his nature but rather a consequence of his voluntary revolt against God." The fundamental faith "insists that salvation can be provided only by God, as against the view that man is competent to save himself." Genuine Christianity "insists that the Scriptures are a revelation lighting the way to the divine incarnation in Jesus Christ as the Redeemer of mankind, as against the view that they stand among many other

---

53 George Eldon Ladd was most responsible for popularizing the "already and not-yet" distinction in American evangelical theology. For a discussion of his views on eschatology, see John A. D'Elia, *A Place at the Table: George Eldon Ladd and the Rehabilitation of Evangelical Scholarship in America* (Oxford: Oxford University Press, 2008), 72–80.

54 Henry, *Uneasy Conscience of Modern Fundamentalism*, 48.

55 Russell D. Moore, *The Kingdom of Christ* (Wheaton, IL: Crossway, 2004), 138–39.

56 Henry, *Uneasy Conscience of Modern Fundamentalism*, 57.

57 Ibid., 58. The term *"élan vital"* was used to refer to some of the neo-liberal theologies that were sometimes designated "personalism" or "personalist" philosophy. See also Gary Dorrien, *The Making of American Liberal Theology*, vol. 2, *Idealism, Realism, and Modernity: 1900–1950* (Louisville: Westminster John Knox, 2003), 286–355.

Struggle for the City

records of religious experience without a difference in kind." Historic Christianity "insists that history is bound up with man's acceptance or rejection of the God-man, rather than that history is primarily what happens among nations." Finally, biblical faith "insists that the future is not an open question, but that world events move toward an ultimate consummation in a future judgment of the race."[58] Only *this* kind of Christianity can make a difference in the world in a way that God intends.

Henry does not call this "social justice" since that designation would imply that the kingdom of God is *here* and that justice can be truly distributed.[59] Henry's "inaugurated eschatology" (*already, but not-yet*) does not allow for such a belief. But the church must engage in social ethics *alongside* its engagement in evangelism, and all of this is based on the redemptive work of Christ and the regenerative power of the Holy Spirit, as we have already seen in his exposition. In many ways, Henry's approach to these matters was similar to that of J. Gresham Machen, whose position we outlined earlier. In the evangelical community Henry's book about modern fundamentalists' uneasy conscience caused "quite a stir."[60] But more than six decades later it is clear that this understanding of theology and ministry brought about a new phase of evangelical engagement in the postwar period.

CIVIL RIGHTS AND THE GREAT SOCIETY

Americans prospered in the years after the Second World War. With seven percent of the world's population in the late 1940s it produced forty-two percent of the world's income.[61] American workers produced fifty-seven percent of the world's steel, forty-three percent of its electricity, sixty-two percent of oil, eighty percent of automobiles. Our caloric intake was about fifty percent higher than that of people in Western Europe.[62] America again demonstrated that if left to its resources, it could engineer huge comebacks.

---

58 Henry, *Uneasy Conscience of Modern Fundamentalism*, 57–58.
59 David O. Moberg, "Fundamentalists and Evangelicals in Society," in *The Evangelicals*, 143–69.
60 Carl F. H. Henry, *Confessions of a Theologian: An Autobiography* (Waco, TX: Word, 1986), 113.
61 Patterson, *Grand Expectations*, 61.
62 Ibid., 61–62.

Struggle for the City

Not everyone participated in that prosperity. We have previously noted that black Americans saw an increase in prosperity, but not to the same degree as whites. The same was true for Hispanics.[63] Government assisted in this expansion. Though federal spending declined after the war was over—not a surprising matter, as federal spending went from $95.2 billion in 1945 to a postwar low of $36.5 billion in 1948—federal spending overall remained much higher than it was *before* the war. State and local spending more than doubled between 1945 and 1948, much of it in building schools and roads.[64]

There was a series of social and political issues that the country began to tackle in about the mid-1950s and for several years following. The three American presidents of the period, Dwight D. Eisenhower, John F. Kennedy, and Lyndon B. Johnson, would be placed in position to lead the nation through one of its most internally turbulent times in its history and to deal with those issues that were being raised by various segments of society. Though Americans were vastly more wealthy than the rest of the world, there were parts of the economy where people did *not* have a significant share in those economic advantages, especially people in the inner cities and others who were on the fringe of the economy, such as single mothers, an increasing statistic in the period.[65] Lyndon Johnson would oversee the largest portion of the realignment of government and social issues, through what became known as the "Great Society." There are three significant aspects of the Great Society, a term coined by John F. Kennedy, though Kennedy was more likely to appeal to what he called the "New Frontier."[66] We will examine those three aspects next.

Civil Rights

The first issue confronted by Johnson's Great Society was *civil rights*. The civil rights issue in Johnson's day was the near end of a long road that goes back to the first lifelong black servitude in America, an indentured servant named Punch who was sentenced to lifelong servitude in 1637 for trying to run away.

---

63   Ibid., 62.
64   Ibid., 64.
65   Ibid., 536–37.
66   Johnson, *History of the American People*, 873.

Struggle for the City

"Color-consciousness has always blighted life in the United States."[67] Black slavery had been a scourge ever since that first lifelong servitude, and especially so when, after the invention of the cotton gin in 1793, cotton production became far less costly, resulting in slavery becoming an almost exclusively Southern phenomenon. White plantation owners offered the gospel, in some measure, to black slaves, though the motivation for doing so was often not the most altruistic.[68] Slavery was abolished in 1863 by the Emancipation Proclamation, the Fifteenth Amendment of 1865 then giving black men the franchise. But in Reconstruction South, Jim Crow laws made the life of black people very different from the life of white people. We have examined these issues in detail earlier in our study.

The roots of the civil rights movement are long and complex. W. E. B. Du Bois wrote *The Souls of Black Folks* in 1903, articulating the ways in which Negroes in post-Reconstructionist America were limited, discriminated against, and treated as inferior to whites.[69] He rejected the *accommodationist* approach represented by Booker T. Washington of the Tuskegee Institute in Atlanta and called for full recognition of equality between the races. But he also rejected the notion, earlier defended by Frederick Douglass, that Negroes should integrate into white society, arguing that Negroes are instead members of a vast historic race and that they should maintain the dignity and antiquity of that heritage.[70] Du Bois was not raised in the South and had not endured Jim Crow until he moved to Atlanta in 1897 at age twenty-nine. His approach to the "black issue" was therefore not indicative of the more prominent experience in the post-slavery South.

One thing is clear of the majority of black civil rights advocates: deeply held religious fervor, and mostly *evangelical* Christian fervor, constitutes the most important ingredient in the movement.[71] Blacks constituted nearly sixteen million Americans in 1950 and about nineteen million in 1960.[72] Blacks

---

67 Patterson, *Grand Expectations*, 375.
68 Albert J. Raboteau, *Slave Religion: The "Invisible Institution" in the Antebellum South*, updated ed. (1978; Oxford: Oxford University Press, 2004), 95–150.
69 W. E. B. Du Bois, *The Souls of Black Folks* (Chicago: A. C. McClurg, 1903).
70 David Levering Lewis, *W. E. B. Du Bois: A Biography*, updated ed., ed. Kendra Taira Field (New York: Henry Holt, 2009), 123.
71 Mark Noll, *God and Race in American Politics* (Princeton, NJ: Princeton University Press, 2008), 102.
72 Patterson, *Grand Expectations*, 380.

Struggle for the City

had originally voted Republican, because that was the party of Lincoln, but with the advent of FDR's New Deal they switched allegiance en masse, not because FDR was pro-black, but simply as a "pragmatic political response."[73]

The year 1954 saw the landmark court case, *Brown v. Board of Education of Topeka*, "perhaps the most important single Supreme Court decision in American history,"[74] decided in the US Supreme Court. It ruled that "Separate but Equal" laws were unconstitutional, and that schools must begin the process of desegregation.[75] The US Congress debated legislation in the late 1950s that would extend civil rights issues further. In 1957 the Senate passed a weak civil rights bill that guaranteed voting rights to blacks, a bill that could have gone further if not for resistance on the part of Southern legislators.[76]

In some parts of the South little happened for the next ten years after the Supreme Court ruling, but civil rights legislation in 1964 did force the hand of cities to begin the process of *integrating* schools. Churches of the Deep South often did not support the new legislation, except Progressive and liberal forces. That was probably understandable given the times, though it is also *unfortunate*. Hearts needed to be changed, and many of them eventually were. After it became clear that the new social reality did not destroy the American system, many of the more hard-bitten opponents of civil rights offered their apologies and did their best to make amends.

Here is an abbreviated narrative of the civil rights movement, a movement that is generally dated 1955–68, though some would push the beginning date back to 1945.[77] After the *Brown* decision by the court, on December 1, 1955, Rosa Parks refused to give up her seat on a public bus for a white passenger in Montgomery,

---

73 Nancy J. Weiss, *Farewell to the Party of Lincoln: Black Politics in the Age of FDR* (Princeton, NJ: Princeton University Press, 1983), 220, quoted in Noll, *God and Race in American Politics*, 105.

74 Patterson, *Grand Expectations*, 953.

75 A. Powell Davies, "The Supreme Court Decision," in *Rhetoric, Religion, and the Civil Rights Movement: 1954-1965*, ed. Davis W. Houck and David E. Dixon, Studies in Rhetoric and Religion 1 (Waco, TX: Baylor University Press, 2006), 36–41.

76 Robert A. Caro, *The Years of Lyndon Johnson*, vol. 3, *Master of the Senate* (New York: Alfred A. Knopf, 2002), 970–75.

77 Johnson, *History of the American People*, 954; Steven F. Lawson and Charles Payne, *Debating the Civil Rights Movement, 1945-1968*, 2nd ed., Debating Twentieth-Century America (New York: Rowan & Littlefield, 2006). More on the sheer economics of this issue later in this chapter.

Struggle for the City

Alabama. She was arrested, tried and convicted for disorderly conduct, whereupon fifty black leaders in the city organized and boycotted the buses for 381 days until the buses were finally desegregated.[78] The leader of the Montgomery Improvement Association was a young Baptist minister named Martin Luther King Jr. King was a well-educated black man with a PhD from Boston University.

The influences on King's theology were broad and diverse. He had drunk deeply at the well of social gospel, taking his seminary degree at Rochester Theological Seminary where the specter of its older theological teacher, Rauschenbusch, still loomed large.[79] He also learned much from his Boston professor, philosopher Edgar S. Brightman, whose *personalist* philosophy "contended for a heightened evaluation of human free will along with a stronger sense of God as bounded by the actions of the humans he had created."[80] But the more important theological influence on King was Reinhold Niebuhr, the neo-orthodox theologian we discussed earlier (see chap. 20), whose views on the deeply entrenched *evil* in the world and in its institutions appealed to King's concerns for justice.[81] Like Niebuhr, King had little faith in voluntaristic cooperation, a conviction that caused both men ultimately to reject the simplistic notions inherent in the social gospel. Niebuhr considered the social gospel to be *idolatrous*, and King agreed.[82] On the subject of human nature, King was closer to orthodoxy than to liberalism, holding an almost Augustinian (but really more Niebuhrian) strong doctrine of human depravity. This made King something of a "Conservative Militant."[83] Nor did the black pastor glorify all of the motives of his own movement. He realized that *coercion*, the kind of coercion that the civil rights movement would have to employ, carried with it its own moral challenges, but "what makes King a world-historical figure is his Niebuhrian pessimism about human institutions and his Niebuhrian insistence that coercion is tragically necessary to achieve justice."[84] His plan would work.

---

78 Marty, *Under God, Indivisible*, 3:387–88.
79 Taylor Branch, *Parting the Water: America in the King Years, 1954–63* (New York: Simon & Schuster, 1989), 74.
80 Noll, *God and Race in American Politics*, 108.
81 Branch, *Parting the Waters*, 91, 99.
82 David L. Chappell, *A Stone of Hope: Prophetic Religion and the Death of Jim Crow* (Chapel Hill: University of North Carolina Press, 2004), 27, 45, 53.
83 August Meier, "The Conservative Militant," in *Martin Luther King, Jr.: A Profile*, ed. C. Eric Lincoln, American Century Series (New York: Hill and Wang, 1970), 144–56.
84 Chappell, *Stone of Hope*, 53.

Struggle for the City

But to leave the story with an emphasis only on "influences" in regard to just his educational résumé is not enough. King was from Baptist pastor stock. His father, the "foundational theological influence on young Martin's life,"[85] was a deeply committed evangelical Christian and had taught his sometimes-skeptical son to look to God and to be a man of faith. That would stand King in good stead in the more difficult days of his struggle. King himself would write, "In the truest sense of the word, God is a living God. In him there is feeling and will, responsive to the deepest yearnings of the human heart; *this* God both evokes and answers prayer."[86] During the dark days of the Montgomery boycott, King experienced a sort of transcendental encounter with God that brought him great peace.[87] A colleague of one of the authors (Chad), who has studied King carefully for years gave this general assessment of the man and his theology: Though he had been trained as a liberal, when his house was attacked one night with his little girl inside, his evangelical fervor and commitment to the message of the Bible marked him for the rest of his life.[88]

The narrative continues in 1957 when nine high school students in Little Rock, Arkansas, challenged the segregation policy of the city and attended an all-white school.[89] They had to be escorted by federal troops. In 1960 a sit-in was launched by young blacks at a Woolworth's store in Greensboro, North Carolina, a sit-in that spread to other cities in the South.[90] The movement gained momentum slowly from 1960 to 1963, the year that the Southern Christian Leadership Conference elected to protest the segregation of downtown businesses in Birmingham, Alabama. The protest was *peaceful*, but the protesters were faced with an injunction prohibiting their march to the coun-

---

85 William H. Brackney, *A Genetic History of Baptist Thought: With Special Reference to Baptists in Britain and North America*, Baptists (Macon, GA: Mercer University Press, 2004), 457.

86 Martin Luther King Jr., *Strength to Love* (1963; repr., Philadelphia: Fortress, 1981), 155, quoted in Brackney, *Genetic History*, 460.

87 Branch, *Parting the Waters*, 162.

88 Thanks to Professor Kevin L. Smith of The Southern Baptist Theological Seminary for this observation. For documentation on King's conversion, see Chappell, *Stone of Hope*, 216.

89 For the telling of this tale from the inside, see Carlotta Walls LaNier, with Liza Frazier Page, *A Mighty Long Way: My Journey to Justice at Little Rock Central High School* (New York: Random House, 2009).

90 Lawson and Payne, *Debating the Civil Rights Movement, 1945–1968*, 18–19; Patterson, *Grand Expectations*, 430–31.

Struggle for the City

ty building. Eugene "Bull" Connor, commissioner of public safety responded with brutal force.[91] King was among those arrested, and it was from the
city jail that he wrote his famous "Letter from Birmingham Jail."[92] That same
year witnessed the march on Washington where King delivered his famous
"I Have a Dream" speech,[93] having now become the recognized leader of the
movement. In that speech/sermon, the black leader proclaimed, "We are not
satisfied, and we will not be satisfied until 'justice rolls down like waters, and
righteousness like a mighty stream,'" citing the prophet Amos (5:24) in the
recognizable cadences of the King James Version of the Bible.[94] King would
during these days appeal to the same kind of populist spirit that we discussed
in the America of the early 1800s. But more than that, he was a prophet, not
merely a black activist; and that prophetic stance riveted the attention of a
nation, even *some* who were, in their hearts, battling with inherited racism.[95]
He wanted to give people what he called "a sense of somebodiness," or in the
language of an earlier Methodist preacher, "an abiding confidence that he was
a subject of that powerful kingdom whose Prince cared for his subjects."[96] St.
Augustine, Florida, witnessed the next major events, including another arrest
of King, to which a large number of Jewish rabbis responded by coming to the
city and organizing a pray-in, resulting in their being arrested as well.

The year 1964 witnessed the passing of the Civil Rights Act in Congress.
President Kennedy had proposed such legislation, but did not live to see it
enacted. It became one of the first major components of Lyndon Johnson's
Great Society proposals.[97] Johnson was a man who, though a Southerner, had
deep sympathies for those who were left behind by the systems of justice, a

---

91 S. Jonathan Bass, *Blessed Are the Peacemakers: Martin Luther King, Jr., Eight White Religious
    Leaders, and the "Letter from Birmingham Jail"* (Baton Rouge: Louisiana State University
    Press, 2001), 88–109.
92 Ibid., 110–30.
93 Patterson, *Grand Expectations*, 482–85.
94 Quoted in Branch, *Parting the Waters*, 882.
95 Chappell, *Stone of Hope*, 44–66.
96 John M'Lean, ed., *Sketch of Rev. Philip Gatch* (Cincinnati: Swormstedt and Poe, 1854), 135,
    quoted in Nathan O. Hatch, "The Democratization of Christianity and the Character of
    American Politics," in *Religion and American Politics*, 2nd ed., ed. Mark A. Noll and Luke
    E. Harlow (New York: Oxford University Press, 2007), 101.
97 Robert Dallek, *Lyndon B. Johnson: Portrait of a President* (New York: Oxford University
    Press, 2004), 135–45.

Struggle for the City

sympathy that stemmed from his own experiences as a young man growing up in a poor white family in Texas. Passing the civil rights legislation was one of his first great passions after inheriting the mantle of leadership from the assassinated Jack Kennedy.[98] Southern senators filibustered the legislation for fifty-four days, but on July 2 President Johnson signed it into law. That legislation was followed the next year by the Voting Rights Act, precipitated by the arrest of King and 250 supporters in a protest against voting restrictions in Selma, Alabama.[99] This act suspended poll taxes, literacy tests, and authorized federal supervision of voter registration in districts where such tests were being utilized. Four years later, King would be dead, killed by an assassin's bullet in Memphis. Clearly, though, the accomplishments of the previous thirteen years were nothing short of *remarkable*.

How did the churches respond to all of this? The answer is complex, but we must deal with it in brief. The liberal denominations generally welcomed the new developments and the new federal laws, as well. Many conservative churches were in the South, for reasons we have discussed elsewhere. At the national level, many southern denominations, including the Southern Baptist Convention, called for an end to segregation, as early as the late Fifties.[100] At the state level, though, Deep South Baptists resented the calls from people like ethicist T. B. Maston to affirm the equality of the races.[101] "During the decade after 1957, white Alabama Baptists basically planted their feet next to George Wallace's and refused compromise or moderation."[102] Wallace himself would be elected governor in 1962 for the first time and on Monday, January 14, 1963, "stood on the steps of the state capital in Montgomery and took the oath of office near the spot where Jefferson Davis, a hundred years before, had taken the oath of office as president of the Confederate States of America."[103] In the inaugural speech that followed Wallace proclaimed "segregation

---

98 Robert A. Caro, *The Years of Lyndon Johnson*, vol. 4, *The Passage of Power* (New York: Alfred A. Knopf, 2012), 484–502.

99 Patterson, *Grand Expectations*, 579–84.

100 Wayne Flynt, *Alabama Baptists: Southern Baptists in the Heart of Dixie*, Religion and American Culture (Tuscaloosa: University of Alabama Press, 1998), 459.

101 T. B. Maston, *The Bible and Race: A Careful Examination of Biblical Teachings on Human Relations* (Nashville: Broadman, 1959), 1–52, 105–17.

102 Flynt, *Alabama Baptists*, 459.

103 Bass, *Blessed Are the Peacemakers*, 18.

Struggle for the City

now… segregation tomorrow… segregation forever." Many white Baptists, Pentecostals, and other conservatives of the Deep South gave a hearty "Amen" to that assessment.

Denominations were one thing; individual pastors were something else. Many Southern fundamentalists had perhaps their darkest hours between 1954 and 1968. Fundamentalist editor and evangelist John R. Rice, as quoted by Wayne Flynt, "denounced the *Brown* decision as a product of 'left-wing thought' and predicted that it would result in the 'mongrelization of the race and the breakdown of all the Southern standards of culture.'"[104] Baptist pastor W. A. Criswell told the South Carolina legislature in 1956 that he favored segregation and that people should "stick with their own kind."[105] By 1968 when he was elected president of the Southern Baptist Convention, though, Criswell had moderated his views and both he and Rice later apologized for their earlier sinful words and deeds.[106] In the wake of the April 1968 murder of Dr. King, Criswell committed the denomination to end segregation in churches and housing and to support full civil rights for all Americans.[107] He went on to urge Baptists and others to repudiate using the Bible in defending segregation.[108] It had taken much to move some Southern evangelicals in the right direction on the race issue, but as they say, "Better late than never." It would take a younger generation of Southern evangelicals to make the final push, and in 1995 the Southern Baptist Convention publicly at its full annual meeting repented of past racism.

Why did the civil rights movement succeed in accomplishing its goals? One might argue that the time was just right, that a new generation did not harbor the same degree of racism that Americans manifested before 1950. But that is simply not enough, left alone. There were certainly racist demagogues in the South, but many segregationists were of milder temperament and sought to maintain segregation by making schools and other institutions

---

104 Quoted in Flynt, *Alabama Baptists*, 458.
105 Ibid.
106 Ibid.
107 Noll, *God and Race in American Politics*, 134.
108 Mark Newman, *Getting Right with God: Southern Baptists and Desegregation, 1945–95*, Religion and American Culture (Tuscaloosa: University of Alabama Press, 2001), 80.

Struggle for the City

both separate and *truly equal.*[109] At the end of the day, "their lack of radicalism, as much as their racism, hindered them."[110] The eventual success of the civil rights movement would, in many ways (though still only partially), finish the job begun by Washington, Jefferson, Witherspoon, and then Lincoln. If all men are endowed by their creator with "unalienable rights," then that must, by definition, extend to black men and women as well. Martin Luther King Jr. and those who labored alongside him deserve to be named among the heroes of democracy in our nation's history.

The Johnson administration had acted well with regard to the race issue. But there were other components of the Great Society legislation.

The War on Poverty

In his State of the Union address in January 1964, Johnson announced, "This administration today, here and now, declares unconditional war on poverty in America."[111] Kennedy had been planning something similar before his assassination, and Johnson now carried on with the plans. In 1962 Michael Harrington had published *The Other America*, in which he claimed that as many as twenty-five percent of Americans were in deep financial need.[112] Johnson believed, as did many people still at the time, that FDR's New Deal legislation had pulled the country out of the Depression and that what was good for America then—giant federal programs of spending and control—would be good for America now in its current crisis of economy.[113] Johnson was committed to FDR-style reforms and had served as the Texas director of FDR's National Youth Administration from 1935–37. For him, FDR was the model to emulate.[114] He needed more than anything else to get Congress to go along

---

109 Chappell, *Stone of Hope*, 153–78.
110 Ibid., 178.
111 Lyndon B. Johnson, "Annual Message to the Congress on the State of the Union," January 8, 1964, *Public Papers of the Presidents of the United States* (Washington, DC: United States Government Printing Office, 1964), quoted in Dallek, *Lyndon B. Johnson*, 153; also see Caro, *Passage of Power*, 4:546–49.
112 Michael Harrington, *The Other America: Poverty in the United States* (New York: Scribner's, 1962), 171–96.
113 Patterson, *Grand Expectations*, 534.
114 William E. Leuchtenburg, *In the Shadow of FDR: From Harry Truman to Ronald Reagan* (Ithaca, NY: Cornell University Press, 1983), chap. 4.

Struggle for the City

with him, and his years as a senator from Texas, and especially as senate majority leader,[115] had prepared him well for that task.

Johnson believed it was time to give all Americans "the benefits of a fully financed welfare state."[116] It was in a speech given at the University of Michigan, May 22, 1964 that he stated, "[I]n your time we have the opportunity to move not only toward the rich society and the powerful society, but upward to the Great Society."[117] By "Great" he meant "magnanimous," he meant a great state, for Johnson was not interested in anything *small*. Like the late Roman emperors, the Bourbon kings of France, and the Stuart monarchs of England, he wanted America and its government to be *larger than life*. In November 1964 he would be elected president, handily defeating Barry Goldwater of Arizona, a man from a small state who believed in limited government. There was very little that was limited about Lyndon Johnson.[118]

Aside from the civil rights legislation we have already discussed the other new laws and bureaucracies would be large and costly. This would be especially the case for the "welfare" legislation. The Omnibus Housing Act, or Fair Housing Act (1968), provided funds to build housing for poor and middle-income families. This was augmented the same year by the Housing and Urban Development Act. The Demonstration Cities and Metropolitan Development Act (1966) provided money to help abolish ghettoes and to build city parks. The Urban Mass Transportation Act (1964) provided funds to cities for the development of bus systems and other forms of public transport. The Head Start Act and the Higher Education Act (1965) introduced better educational opportunities for poor people. The Clean Water Restoration Act (1966) allocated funds into antipollution campaigns. The Wilderness Areas Act (1964) put nine million acres of land out of the reach of developers. Each of these required new levels of bureaucracy, and that meant *money*.

---

115 Or just "Leader," as he was often called. Caro, *Master of the Senate*, chap. 25, "The Leader."
116 Johnson, *History of the American People*, 873.
117 Lyndon B. Johnson, "Remarks at the University of Michigan" (commencement address, University of Michigan, Ann Arbor, Michigan, May 22, 1964), in *Public Papers of the Presidents of the United States: Lyndon B. Johnson, 1963–64*, vol. 1, entry 357 (Washington, DC: Government Printing Office, 1965), 704–7, Lyndon Baines Johnson Presidential Library, Austin, Texas, last updated June 6, 2007, http://www.lbjlibrary.net/collections/selected-speeches/november-1963-1964/05-22-1964.html.
118 Patterson, *Grand Expectations*, 538.

Struggle for the City

During the five-year Johnson administration, federal spending on education rose *fivefold*. On health care, spending more than tripled. By 1971 America was spending more on welfare programs than on defense. From 1949 to 1979 defense costs rose ten times, but welfare costs rose *twenty-five* times.[119]

Critics coined a phrase about all of this spending and restructuring: "throwing money at problems." But that was not how the president saw it. Johnson was attempting to present the war on poverty not as an income re-distribution, "but as an opportunity to extend to all Americans the promise of the American dream. Lyndon Johnson married ideological conviction to the politics of the liberal consensus."[120] This commitment was not new to the president. As far back as 1944 he had been committed to the idea that the philosophy of free enterprise, i.e., capitalism, should be replaced with the notion of equal opportunity for all persons, and that if local communities were unable to provide that equal opportunity, he expected, in his own words, "to vote for whatever legislation is necessary to let the Federal Government do it. If that be enlarging the power of the Federal Government, and if that be centralizing more power in Washington, make the most of it."[121] This was a fundamental philosophical shift away from the economic philosophy that had characterized early American beliefs. It would be too much to call this Socialism, but it is a turn in the *direction* of Socialism and away from the market economy convictions that had made America such a great economic power. The justification was that this constituted *social justice*, but as the philosopher Friedrich Hayek has noted, social justice is "the Trojan Horse through which totalitarianism has entered many societies in the world."[122] Just claiming "social justice" itself is not enough.

---

119 The statistics and details in this paragraph come from Johnson, *History of the American People*, 874–75.

120 Gareth Davies, *From Opportunity to Entitlement: The Transformation and Decline of Great Society Liberalism* (Lawrence: University Press of Kansas, 1996), 31.

121 Quoted in Robert Dallek, *Lone Star Rising: Lyndon Johnson and His Times, 1908–1960* (New York: Oxford University Press, 1991), 288.

122 F. A. Hayek, *Law, Legislation and Liberty*, vol. 2: *The Mirage of Social Justice* (Chicago: University of Chicago Press, 1976), 130. In this work Hayek also asserted that social justice construed as an intentional effort at equal income distribution is "a hollow incantation" (xii), "absurd" (64), "a mirage" (64), "a quasi-religious superstition" (66), and a concept that "does not belong to the category of error but to that of nonsense" (78).

Struggle for the City

Health Care

The third component of the Great Society legislation concerned health care. Medicare and Medicaid both passed in 1965. In that year, half of senior adults over the age of sixty-five had no health insurance.[123] The original plan was to provide health care only for these individuals through Medicare legislation, but at the last minute, Congressman Wilbur Mills of Arkansas, influential chairman of the House Ways and Means Committee, added Medicaid to the legislation, thus offering federally funded health care services to the uninsured, no matter what age. This fundamentally transformed health care in America.[124] Growing quickly, these two programs reached one-fifth of the population by 1976.[125] By 1968 low-income people consulted doctors more regularly than did high-income people, and though death rates of low-income seniors declined over the next few years, there is no proof that it was because of Medicare, since those numbers had been changing even before the advent of Medicare.[126] Nevertheless, with the emplacement of these last major pieces of the long-developing Progressive agenda the stage was set for a longer-growing dependency upon federal largesse and activism to "make the world a better place," or so it seemed. For this is the *Fabian road* to Socialism; increment by increment pieces are put in place that, once tasted by the public, cannot be easily displaced and must continue to be fed.[127]

What would the story look like without the intervention of the elephant that was by then sitting squarely in the Oval Office of the White House, threatening to blow the Great Society and all its claimed and hoped-for glory apart? We have a hard time knowing our own world, much less being able to play with

---

123 Patterson, *Grand Expectations*, 573.
124 Allen Matusow, *The Unraveling of America: A History of Liberalism in the 1960s* (Athens: University of Georgia Press, 2009), 228.
125 Ibid., 228–29.
126 Theodore Marmor and James Morone, "The Health Programs of the Kennedy-Johnson Years: An Overview," in *Toward New Human Rights: The Social Policies of the Kennedy and Johnson Administrations*, ed. David C. Warner (Austin: Lyndon B. Johnson School of Public Affairs, University of Texas, 1977), 173.
127 The term *Fabian road* comes from the socialist Fabian Society in England and denotes the strategy of incremental implementation of Socialism until it becomes plain to the majority of the population that full-blown Socialism is the country's only hope.

any confidence that "what if" game of history with Lyndon Johnson. Johnson would depart from the political wars in 1968, disgraced with the legacy of Vietnam, a war he had inherited from his more heralded predecessor. He rode out of town a beaten "cowboy" of sorts, who wished with all his heart never to preside over an American defeat abroad and to be remembered for a compassionate and magnanimous mustering of huge American resources for the elimination of poverty in his own lifetime and ours. The whole thing depended on a "guns and butter" strategy, as it was then known, and hung by the thread of the printing press cranking out American dollars without end, or so it seemed.

A Conflict of Visions

How should we assess all of this massive invasion of traditionally private sector concerns on the part of the federal government? One way is to look a it philosophically. Economist Thomas Sowell has cogently argued that all consistent political positions arise out of a vision, a vision that entails "a sense of *causation*."[128] "*If* causation proceeds as our vision conceives it to, *then* certain other consequences follow, and theory is the working out of what those consequences are."[129] How does that play out through our historical analysis?

Though there are many different political theories, when you boil them down they can all be represented by two visions about political means and goals: the *constrained* vision and the *unconstrained* vision. The constrained vision recognizes that life in this world will never be perfected in any given society and that everyone will have to be content to live with trade-offs. The unconstrained vision has the goal of the *perfectibility* of society by removing all barriers to political idealism.[130] The constrained vision gives much credence to *pragmatic* solutions to problems, and so holds that even common people with little education can do much to improve society. The unconstrained vision believes that *intellectuals* are better prepared to make the world better, and so "professors in a university turned statesmen" may be the best prescription for

---

128 Thomas Sowell, *A Conflict of Visions: Ideological Origins of Political Struggles*, rev. ed. (New York: Basic Books, 2007), 6.
129 Ibid.
130 Ibid., 14–24.

Struggle for the City

improving our world.[131] We have seen this previously in the administration of Woodrow Wilson, and it is here in spades in the Barack Obama White House.

When it comes to *social processes*, the constrained vision "puts little faith in deliberately designed social processes, since it has little faith that any manageable set of decision makers could effectively cope with the enormous complexities of designing a whole blueprint for an economic system, a legal system, or a system of morality or politics."[132] One is reminded here of Hayek's comment on *command economies* that we have discussed earlier (see chap. 20). No man or group of men could ever know everything necessary to be able to determine supply, demand, production, price, the cost of labor and management, the quality of product, and countless other variables necessary to planning a nation's economy. The unconstrained vision sees it differently. Building in part off of engineering models developed by engineer-turned-economist Thorstein Veblen, the unconstrained vision sees the solution to social problems as merely a matter of "technical coordination" by experts.[133] All such problems are *theoretically* solvable; you just have to put together the right team of smart people. The unconstrained vision believes that *utopia* can be achieved in this world that we live in. But in order to be able to pull it off, the *administrative state* has to be given the kind of power and authority that it takes to make it all happen.

In our *historical survey* we have already encountered both visions a number of times. The Roman Republic represented the constrained vision, but Roman Empire the unconstrained vision. Calvin represents the constrained vision, though a *qualified* version of it.[134] He did not believe that the city council of Geneva should control everything, though he did place high value on the leadership of godly magistrates and pastors. The Puritans of Massachusetts could have hurled headlong in pursuit of the unconstrained vision[135] had it not been

---

131 Ibid., 43.
132 Ibid., 68.
133 Ibid., 72. Also see discussion of Veblen's exaltation of the engineer as problem solver in chap. 20.
134 See Sowell's discussion of nuanced versions of both visions within Calvin in *Conflict of Visions*, 99–126.
135 Best represented in a book by Edward Johnson with the running title *Wonder-Working Providence of Sions Saviour in New England* (Printed for Nath: Brooke at the Angel in Corn-hill, 1654). He averred that the "Lord had assembled his Saints together" in the new World, "the place where the Lord will create a new Heaven, and a new earth in, new

for wise counselors such as John Winthrop and Henry Vane. As it turned out, they evolved into a *nuanced* version of the constrained vision. France under Louis XIV with his minister of finance, Colbert, depicts the unconstrained vision *unleashed*, as the Crown attempted to control every aspect of French economic life even with its limited transportation and information technologies. The Stuart kings of England practiced a nuanced version of the unconstrained vision, limited by the nature of shared governance with Parliament—they could not do everything they wanted, and when they tried, one of them lost his head. Hobbes gestures toward the unconstrained vision, but Locke, Montesquieu, Hume, and Smith *clearly* prefer the constrained. The American Constitution is a classic model of the constrained vision, and Witherspoon's theoretical articulation of its basis in the Protestant Reformation and Scottish Common Sense philosophy underscores that. Hegel and Marx clearly represent the unconstrained vision with some nuance, especially in Hegel's call for a dominating state. J. Gresham Machen is a clear advocate of the constrained vision, but Rauschenbusch and Fosdick sought out mandated governmental authority to solve social problems.[136] Reinhold Niebuhr is somewhat conflicted on this matter as he recognized that both coercers and the coerced were unjust (though not equally so), and Martin Luther King Jr. also inherited the mantle of the (somewhat conflicted) constrained vision. Presidents Woodrow Wilson and Franklin Roosevelt were unconstrained in their attempts to govern all of American life from the top, but Eisenhower was not. Lyndon Johnson takes his place alongside Wilson and FDR.

Paying the Piper

The financial price for all of this would come to roost in the next three presidencies, as "stagflation," the worst of all possible economic worlds, it would seem, sank its fangs into first Richard Nixon (the supposed conservative who introduced wage and price controls, the end of the gold standard, and the Environmental Protection

---

Churches, and a new Common-wealth together." Quoted in Michael Knox Beran, "Obama in the Bunker," *National Review*, February 20, 2012, 36.

136 It could be argued that Kuyper tends toward the unconstrained vision in his totalizing Christian society, though he divided decision making into the three "spheres."

Struggle for the City

Agency (EPA), among other big government panaceas), then Gerald Ford (he of the WIN—Whip Inflation Now—buttons), and later Jimmy Carter (the Southern Baptist and the only president to admit "lusting in his heart" to *Playboy* magazine). In 1980 Americans would turn to Ronald Reagan as the antidote to Carter's "malaise,"[137] and the years of the "misery index"[138] in hope for better things to come.

At the bottom of it all, Johnson's Great Society, though it had salutary results in the area of civil rights, was a giant attempt to seize the government for a specific set of philosophical and economic agendas. "Lyndon Johnson seems like an odd choice for liberalism's deliverer. Then again, he was no one's choice. An assassin's bullet anointed him for the job."[139] Johnson was a New Dealer, so we ought not to be surprised that he would enact the same kind of liberal, attractive kind of fascist policies that were utilized by Wilson and FDR before him. His Great Society, as he stated it, rests on *abundance* and *liberty* for all. But when you look at it in terms of the man himself and his overweening *ambitions*, it sounds like the voice of a Roman emperor trying to encourage people from Naples to relocate to Rome.

Transition: The Rise of the Religious Right and the Evangelical Left

Several developments in the life of the nation and three events characterize our summary of this period. *First*, it is not really possible for anyone who did not live through the Vietnam War era to understand how this seemingly unending struggle radicalized a generation coming to adulthood during its height and waning days. Primarily because of the Selective Service System's draft laws and the politics of their application, all young American males were forced to consider the impact of possible war service on the future of their lives. Recent experiences with protest over Iraq and Afghanistan bear *no resemblance* to those days because

---

137 "Malaise" was the term used by Mr. Carter himself of the end of his administration, in a national address, counseling, with advice from his young daughter Amy, accepting American limitations in all areas of life. See Kevin Mattson, *"What the Heck Are You Up To, Mr. President?" Jimmy Carter, America's "Malaise," and the Speech That Should Have Changed the Country* (New York: Bloomsbury, 2010).
138 A designation by the Reagan camp for the total of unemployment and inflation percentages that had ravaged America in the preceding years.
139 Jonah Goldberg, *Liberal Fascism* (New York: Doubleday, 2006), 229.

Struggle for the City

the United States is now served by fully trained volunteer armed forces. To know that one's politics and convictions on social issues directly affect the future or lack thereof for oneself individually has a definitely clarifying and intensifying effect on one's advocacy and actions related to those concerns. In this case the nation was rent from border to border with violence and struggle unparalleled in a land with no actually warring armies or bands of guerrillas.[140]

The presence of exemptions in the draft "lottery" process made matters even worse, it seemed. It was widely felt that the draft was unfair on its surface by its exemption of certain factions, notably college students, since college attendance was not economically accessible to all. It was charged then and in ongoing commentary over the years that *black youth* were particularly abused by this system, with a higher percentage of them going into the armed forces and suffering disproportionate deaths and wounding in Vietnam itself. The fact that this was untrue (blacks suffered generally the same percentage of service and casualties that their numbers in the population represented) did not then, nor does it seem at times now, affect the perception. It served only to inflame and ratchet up emotions in subsequent debates.

Second, the ongoing process of protest and radicalization exacerbated the usual and timeworn process whereby the young are finally disconnected from dependency on the older generation and set out upon their own. The political left exploited this situation to mobilize cadres of students and hangers-on who made their presence felt in the hallways and administration buildings of colleges and universities and in the streets and at political events with outrageous language, garb, personal hygiene, public drunkenness and drugged posturing, and public sex acts never before seen in American civilized society. All this was intended to convey not just the usual rights of passage of youth to adult responsibility, but more so the outright *rejection* of American moral legitimacy embodied in their parents' generational lifestyles and the institutions that symbolized them. The Occupy Whatever "movement" of 2011–12 is a mere

---

140 The popular music of the time is one gauge. Buffalo Springfield's haunting "For What It's Worth" (1967); Crosby, Stills, Nash, and Young's strident line "Four dead in Ohio" from their protest song "Ohio" (1970); John Lennon's cynical "Imagine" (1971); Joni Mitchell's "Woodstock" (1970) with its call to go "back to the garden"; and Arlo Guthrie's satirical "Alice's Restaurant Massacree" (1967) are just a sampling of the *angst* music of that generation.

Struggle for the City

shadow of the bygone era, though its tawdry style and spread of filth and disease and criminal activity bids comparisons.

Third, the civil rights struggle had become more intense as the implications of the 1964 Civil Rights Act were being played out across the country. Dr. King's and Robert Kennedy's assassinations served to lend moral power to the protests in the streets and everywhere else. Students who wished to make a meaningful contribution beyond posturing in the streets and hallways of academe joined the struggle in the South and some paid for it with their lives as well. On the other hand, conservative students found themselves morally conflicted about how to register legitimate and prophetic protest to American failings without joining the riotous scenes in the streets.[141]

Woodstock, Explo '72, and the Chicago Declaration

It was during this period that two contrasting events were sponsored at the student level and a third at a higher and more sophisticated level that serve to delineate the separations in a generation and tell the story of the next forty years of political and moral public posturing for this generation. *First*, the gathering at *Woodstock* (1969) achieved an almost overnight mythical status as some kind of dawning of a new age of consciousness that surely could not help but bring in the *utopia* envisioned for so long by so many.[142] What it really turned out to be was an orgy in the mud and filth of a farm field, staged for the benefit of rock bands and "artists," that illustrated the *bankruptcy* of a "movement" gone amok. Attended by something like five hundred thousand people, or several million if you believe the testimony today of all those who claim to have been there, its usefulness is largely *symbolic* in the minds of those who honor it. But at the time it had and continues to have its mythical effects upon media and memory.

Second, a group of evangelical leaders in the right wing of that movement staged an event in Dallas, Texas, in 1972, called Explo '72 and dubbed the Great

---

141 This would be the case with one of the authors, Tom. I lived through this period on a college campus and was a college debater researching and debating these issues year by year as well as preaching to small congregations.
142 Nearly all of the books that have been written about Woodstock celebrate its "beauty," "wonder," magic," and its milestone status in expressing a vision for a generation.

Jesus Rally, or *Godstock* by some. It was attended on its last night by 150,000 or so teens who had generally behaved themselves and comported themselves in public for a week like future citizens of the country their pastors and adult leaders loved and revered. They listened to preaching, sang and danced to Christian rock and roll, and at times swooned to the performance of Johnny Cash, the *headliner* of the entertainment. Organized and promoted by the likes of Bill Bright (Campus Crusade for Christ), Billy Graham, and E. V. Hill (black pastor from the riot-torn district of Watts in Los Angeles), it was nevertheless *avoided* by most from the *evangelical left*. This was undoubtedly a *political* gathering, though it was not *billed* as such. Those dimensions have been widely explored, and we would not dispute them. Richard Nixon, running for reelection that year, would have loved to appear at the meeting, but advisors to Bill Bright urged a noninvitation. Nixon did send a telegram of greeting, saying that "the way to change the world for the better is to change ourselves for the better through deep and abiding commitment to spiritual values."[143]

Third, a gathering took place in Chicago during the Thanksgiving weekend of 1973. Titled in a more common language, compared to the previous two, the "Thanksgiving Workshop on Evangelicals and Social Concern" was notable for its inclusion of both "young Turks" and elder statesmen from the evangelical community. Coordinated by Ron Sider, who hoped it would be the catalyst for his Evangelicals for Social Action organization, it was attended by such luminaries as Frank Gaebelein, Carl Henry, Rufus Jones, and Paul Rees, representing generally an older and more conservative point of view, and Jim Wallis, Donald Dayton, Nancy Hardesty, Vernon Grounds, James Dunn, Foy Valentine, John Howard Yoder, and a number of others representing the newer more liberal

---

143 Nixon's telegram quoted in John Geoffrey Turner, "Selling Jesus to Modern America: Campus Crusade for Christ, Evangelical Culture, and Conservative Politics" (PhD diss., University of Notre Dame, 2005), cited in Darren Dochuk, "Evangelicalism Becomes Southern, Politics Becomes Evangelical: From FDR to Ronald Reagan," in *Religion and American Politics: From the Colonial Period to the Present*, 2nd ed., ed. Mark A. Noll and Luke E. Harlow (New York: Oxford University Press, 2007), 298. Sources for information in this section are numerous, but the best summary of Explo '72 and its historical antecedents and effects is Dochuk, "Evangelicalism Becomes Southern, Politics Becomes Evangelical," 297–328. This essay is the precursor of Dochuk's work in *From Bible Belt to Sun Belt: Plain-Folk Religion, Grassroots Politics, and Rise of Evangelical Conservatism* (New York: W. W. Norton, 2011). See also John Egerton, *The Americanization of Dixie: The Southernization of America* (New York: Harper's Magazine Press, 1974).

Struggle for the City

point of view and the *radical left* of the time among evangelicals on social issues. The meeting is remarkable for having come up with a document of less than five hundred words, The Chicago Declaration,[144] that all could sign, though it did not get into *specifics* as to its recommendations for change. That process would work itself out over the next three or four years. Some have suggested over the years that Sider, a supporter and worker for the George McGovern campaign against the incumbent Richard Nixon, organized this, hoping to get a mailing list to use for his own political causes, presidential candidate George McGovern chief among them, but this cannot be known.

"Texas Theology" in the Sun Belt

These two latter meetings have implications for our conclusions in this section of the book and lead to what follows in part 3. Explo '72 can be rightly seen, we think, as the culmination of a decades-long process whereby Southern conservative (pejoratively, fundamentalist) Christians arrived on the political stage with the ability to *affect elections* and policy by their *united presence*. Their journey into political relevance began in the shadows of the Great Depression as the "migration" we referred to in passing earlier. Moving out of the South in droves (some calculate from census figures as many as 15 to 20 million), they settled heavily in the West, especially Southern California and in cities of the Midwest and Northeast. Unlike many portrayals of them in popular media and hagiography, they went overwhelmingly, as *Christians*, with a sense of mission, like the "errand" of the Puritans before them, "as if they were a godly vanguard sent off into the wilderness to save themselves and their people."[145] Rather than seek to return "home" after the national crises of depression and war, they stayed to change the culture into which they had been sent.

Historian Darren Dochuk calls the theology to which they were committed, "Texas theology." He traces this "theology" to the areas from which many of these folk had come, west of the Mississippi, and through which they had passed espe-

---

144 Available at several points on the Internet and memorialized in the book by Ronald J. Sider, ed., *The Chicago Declaration* (Carol Stream, IL: Creation House, 1974).
145 Dochuk, "Evangelicalism Becomes Southern," 300. For full documentation, see Dochuk, *Bible Belt to Sun Belt*.

cially on the way to Southern California, on the famous Route 66. He opines that the term itself originated at The Southern Baptist Theological Seminary as a *pejorative* used by "moderates" in the various theological controversies of the Southern Baptist Convention.[146] Dochuk characterizes it thus: "Certain of the absolute rightness of their doctrine, impassioned with the cause of evangelical democracy, and dedicated to those leaders most willing to flex their muscles on behalf of such sacred causes, evangelicals who were nurtured in this belief system exuded a gritty determination… in comparison to northern evangelicals, who turned 'serious, quiet, intense, humorless, sacrificial, and patient' in the peak religious experience, they were always 'busy, vocal, and promotional' and 'task-oriented.'"[147] He goes on to note that these particular evangelical leaders "and institutions assumed responsibility for protecting society from those who would undermine them. Distinctions between religion and politics ultimately held little meaning in this crusade since a threat to independence in one sphere was considered a threat in both. 'Apolitical' in its emphasis on the altering of social and political systems through acts of individual initiative rather than institutional restructuring, southern evangelicalism was, in other words, never un-political or anti-political; quite the contrary." Though there was a strong tradition of the church as "spiritual," Dochuk avers, "proud southerners always knew 'how to play political hardball when the prayer meeting let out.'"[148] Tennessee Williams and Walker Percy could undoubtedly add an "Amen" to that assessment.

---

146 Dochuk's lone source on this point appears to be Paul Harvey, *Redeeming the South: Religious Cultures and Racial Identities among Southern Baptists 1865-1925*, Fred W. Morrison Series in Southern Studies (Chapel Hill: University of North Carolina Press, 1997), 151. The quotation at this point (293n33) is from the W. O. Carver papers at The Southern Baptist Seminary and refers to a conversation at the meeting of the Baptist General Convention of Texas in 1908 between Carver and Leonard Doolan. The occasion was the era of the establishment of The Southwestern Baptist Theological Seminary in Waco, Texas (later moved to Ft. Worth in 1910). Harvey notes that the mission and intent of the Ft. Worth school was decidedly and pointedly different from the Louisville institution, so that students imbibed instruction in practical church growth and management with "the best Baptist orthodoxy, but that means a militant orthodoxy." Their older brothers among Southeastern Baptists complained of a "Texas theology" in the western institution that was "not the most tolerant kind." When Tom grew up in Texas around this type of conversation in Baptist circles, Southwestern Seminary in Fort Worth was referred to in a kind of elitist jargon as a "preacher factory."
147 Harvey, *Redeeming the South*, 302.
148 Ibid., 302–3.

Struggle for the City

Southern California was not the only place this particular "theology" took root. Over the years the experience of uprootedness and pilgrim journey removed the prior propensity to Southern populist movements such as the "ham-and-eggers" and others led by the likes of Huey Long, Colonel Bilbo, and Pappy Lee "Pass the Biscuits" O'Daniel, all of which made their political living making big promises from the federal government to constituencies.[149] Eventually, the descendants of these pilgrims delivered support and votes to the likes of Richard Nixon, Ronald Reagan, and George W. Bush. These politicians represent a wide diversity in political philosophy[150] despite all wearing the "conservative" label, but they are mostly united in general opposition to the welfare state and attacks on capitalism and American exceptionalism.

So in the 1930s, '40s, and '50s the Southern migration proceeded to dig in and build, it seemed, churches in every little storefront grouping (now strip malls), and eventually, megachurches in places like Orange County, California, Hammond, Indiana, and Detroit, Michigan, and scores of other places wherever they went. They scratched and clawed economically and ended up in war material factories and dozens of supporting businesses. Pastors with little theological training and less financial support became bivocational church builders with the business acumen and political savvy to survive. And out of these groupings inside and out of denominational affiliations they built institutions like Pepperdine University, Harding College, John Brown University, Oral Roberts University, Oklahoma Christian College, Fuller Theological Seminary, LeTourneau Technical College, and others for educating young Christians as evangelical en-

---

149 Dochuk, *Bible Belt to Sun Belt*, 11.

150 See Richard Nixon as described above who, when questioned in national media about his economic policies, stated in 1971 after taking the United States off the gold standard, "I am now a Keynesian in economics." This statement is widely misquoted as something like "We're all Keynesians now," but this quote is actually taken out of context from statements made by Milton Friedman in "We Are All Keynesians Now," *Time* magazine (December 31, 1965, and clarified in a letter in the February 4, 1966 edition, "Letter: Friedman & Keynes"). Friedman was making historical analysis of the Keynesian "solution" to the Great Depression as compared to historical developments in the 1960s. Note also that the "supply side" economics of Reagan bears little resemblance to the "compassionate conservatism" and huge government deficit of the George W. Bush administration on such programs as "No Child Left Behind" and the Medicare drug benefit program. It is also notable, in this vein, that Jack Kennedy and Lyndon Johnson promoted "supply side economics" in order to raise the revenue required for their social programs in 1963 and 1964. Caro, *Passage of Power*, 4:466–83.

Struggle for the City

trepreneurs and professionals and teachers and lawyers and most of all, capital-istic survivors in a world at first inhospitable to them and their aspirations.[151] To them capitalistic institutions and freedom for entrepreneurial experimentation were the answer to the disheartening displacements of depression and war, not the enemy to be expunged from national life.

The Great Debate

Explo '72 was almost a coming-out party announcing a generation ready to claim a world with *entrepreneurial Christianity* at its best. The meeting that produced the Chicago Declaration was of a *different sort* altogether. Producing a document full of the confession of sin against "those suffering social abuses," they referred to an "unjust American society," "the economic rights of the poor and the oppressed," "the historic involvement of the church in America with racism and the conspicuous responsibility of the evangelical community for perpetuating the personal attitudes and institutional structures that have divided the body of Christ along color lines," and failing to "condemn the exploitation of racism at home and abroad by our economic system."[152]

They called on evangelicals to "demonstrate repentance" by confronting "the social and political injustice of our nation" and the "materialism of our culture and the maldistribution of the nation's wealth and services." Stating it in no uncertain terms, they said, "We recognize that as a nation we play a crucial role in the imbalance and injustice of international trade and devel-opment. Before God and a billion hungry neighbors, we must rethink our values regarding our present standard of living and promote more just acqui-sition and distribution of the world's resources." They accused the nation of "a proud trust that promotes a national pathology of war and violence which victimizes our neighbors at home and abroad." They said evangelicals "have encouraged men to prideful domination and women to irresponsible passivi-

---

151 Dochuk, *Bible Belt to Sun Belt*, 167–95, 326–61.
152 The materials we cite here in what follows (may be found published together in the following study guide: Augustus Cerillo Jr. and Murray W. Dempster, *Salt and Light: Evangelical Political Thought in Modern America*, Christian College Coalition Study Guides 3 (Grand Rapids, MI: Baker, 1989).

Struggle for the City

ty." They finished as they had begun with a declaration of loyalty to the lord-ship of Christ over all of life in the endeavor to right these confessed wrongs. Fifty-three signers, including the group of "conservative" spokesmen noted above and others, joined in this declaration. It remained to be seen how the implementation of the words would produce an agenda and how that would play out among the signers.

Prior to this time, as we have noted, Carl Henry had taken the lead in calling forth "fundamentalist" evangelicals to Christian social involvement. His was a well-nuanced and thoughtful call that took into account the history of theological controversy and sociopolitical activism of the previous hundred years or so of American history. We have documented this history and noted that those who came to be pejoratively labeled as "fundamentalists" did not lack for involvement in the neediness of their neighbors. They simply did not agree with the Progressives and social gospelers about motivations or means or ends and opted to go their own way through individual and local church and parachurch organizations—a process that began in the days of the Second Great Awakening and Finney's leadership. The tensions we have outlined were coming to a head in the clashes of the Sixties, and evangelicals were among those caught up in the struggle to define the *nature* of Christian involvement and social and political issues. Nowhere is this struggle more clearly seen than in the series of essays that passed between Carl F. H. Henry and Lewis B. Sme-des between October 1965 and June 1966.[153]

Henry's opening essay is found in *Christianity Today*, October 8, 1965, "Evangelicals in the Social Struggle."[154] He carefully delineates the reasons for past (at the time) political noninvolvement of evangelicals and defends their apparent inactivity from the parameters we named above. Motivationally, evangelicals could not reconcile the attempts of Protestant liberal "modern-ists" to "achieve the kingdom of God on earth through political and economic changes."[155] As Henry put it, "The modernists so excluded supernatural re-

---

153 Ibid., 26–28. Note that Henry was *Christianity Today's* founding editor (until 1968). Smedes and Henry went back and forth as their essays were published in the magazine.
154 Carl F. H. Henry, "Evangelicals in the Social Struggle," *Christianity Today* 10 (October 8, 1965): 3–11, cited in Cerillo and Dempster, *Salt and Light*.
155 Ibid., 28.

Struggle for the City

demptive facets of the Christian faith and so modified the proper content of the Christian ethic that, as evangelicals saw it, they had altered the very nature and missions of the church."[156] Having long since jettisoned a biblical theology of the wrath of God "and dissolved his righteousness into benevolence or love," they go on in some circles to deny even his objective existence, while others disown his transcendence or even his relevance. Consequently, "evangelicals who insist on obedience to divinely revealed precepts, and who hold that redeemed men alone can truly fulfill the will of God and that only men of good will can enlarge the boundaries of God's kingdom, are caricatured as 'rationalists.'"[157] The nonevangelical is thus motivated by and engaged in an "existential involvement on an emergency basis,"[158] while the evangelical is engaged in evangelism and worldwide mission and the practice of a supernatural *agape* (*love*) with a view to a coming kingdom. Nevertheless, the secularist or nonevangelical insists on agitating for laws "to compel others to act in a predictable, principled way."[159]

Evangelicals differ on goals as well. Since the age to come is the only utopian possibility to sinful humankind, no current system offers such hope. Nevertheless, social engineers of the present age have embraced everything from pacifism to Socialism to Soviet Communism and the depredations of those who would turn the kingdom of God into a vision of repudiation of *private property, inequality of wealth*, the *profit motive*, and even a person's *right to work* "apart from compulsory union membership."[160]

The conflict over method, as Henry saw it, is even more contemporary for those of us living in the post-Bush presidential era. Henry stated in 1965, "Just as in his theological view of God the liberal dissolves righteousness into love, so in the political order he dilutes social justice into compassion." It is this viewpoint that produces the *welfare state*. "This confounding of justice and love confuses what God expects of government with what he expects of the church, and makes the state an instrument for legislating partisan and

---

156 Ibid.
157 Ibid.
158 Ibid., 27.
159 Ibid., 28.
160 Ibid., 30.

Struggle for the City

sectarian ideals upon society." Therefore, "[c]urrent proposals to detach the gospel from 'right-wing' social reaction and current pleas for 'political compassion' are rooted in leftist political ideology more often than in an authentic spiritual view of the role of government."[161] Henry has much more to say than we can recount here, but his abiding advice may be best when he notes that biblical Christians who know how painful the pursuit of social justice can be in a fallen and tragic world will "avoid both the *Liberal* error of 'absolutizing relatives,' as if these were identical with the will of God, and also the *Fundamentalist* temptation to consider any gain short of the absolute ideal in history as worthless or unworthy."[162] Somehow, a road must be struck between these two extremes.

The ensuing dialogue[163] by written exchange is exceedingly irenic and mostly repetitive, for Dr. Smedes repeatedly seeks to draw Dr. Henry out on the specifics of legislative remedies to social problems, and Henry insists again and again that there is not a specifically Christian or evangelical answer in most cases. Smedes refers several times to a "God-willed structure for society," while forgoing specifics *despite* Henry's call for them in order to debate them. Henry makes it plain he is on the *side* of civil rights legislation but is *less* supportive of welfare state attempts to give economic heft to these rights. Smedes insists that there cannot be real rights without the latter sorts of legislation, and Henry is wary of the consequences of *economics* being included in *inalienable rights*. Henry insists that government cannot engage in acts of "compassion" or benevolence (seen as categories of ethical "good"), and Smedes cannot see why not. Earlier, in 1968 Henry had already spelled out his views on the church and social justice in a letter to J. Howard Pew, a position that does not include the kind of activism represented by Smedes and Sider. Henry's position was:

> 1. The Bible is critically relevant to the whole of modern life and culture—the sociopolitical arena included. 2. The institutional church has no mandate, jurisdiction or competence to endorse political legislation or military tactics or economic specifics in the name of

---

161 Ibid., 31.
162 Ibid., 33.
163 Ibid., 40–58.

Struggle for the City

Christ. 3. The institutional church is divinely obliged to proclaim God's entire revelation, including the standards or commandments by which men and nations are to be finally judged, and by which they ought now to live and maintain social stability. 4. The political achievement of a better society is the task of all citizens, and individual Christians ought to be politically engaged to the limit of their competence and opportunity. 5. The Bible limits the proper activity of both government and church for divinely stipulated objectives—the former, the preservation of justice and order, and the latter, the moral-spiritual task of evangelizing the earth.[164]

This statement is remarkably similar to the approach we previously detailed in examining Machen and is completely consistent with a *constrained vision* of the roles of church and the state.

Ultimately Smedes indicates his full *support* of the *Great Society* programs of the day including "a massive governmental attack on the intolerable slums of our great cities."[165] He calls for this under the category of "social justice," not "compassion," though he has already argued for "compassion" previously. He offers, with reference to the "massive" nature of the task, that "it has been demonstrated that nothing less than a massive onslaught will do the job. And it is just because social justice requires the doing of these things that their being done badly is regrettable and *intolerable*" (emphasis added).

Smedes admits that it appears he and Henry have a difference of opinion about the value and/or mission of big government, but he does not think they really differ in that regard. He finally suggests that Henry and many other evangelicals do not agree with him "on the subject of justice and rights among men because we have a significant shading of difference in our theology concerning man." He would characterize this difference as a juxtaposition of the individual and government as "two polar existences in society. And this helps explain why many Evangelicals are apprehensive of

---

164 Quoted in Henry, *Confessions of a Theologian*, 270–71. The material quoted here is taken from correspondence between Carl F. H. Henry and J. Howard Pew in January 1968.
165 Quoted in Cerillo and Dempster, *Salt and Light*, 57.

Struggle for the City

governmental action in the sphere of economics and welfare."[166] The conclusion for Smedes was that "Evangelicals have a personal ethic for regenerate individuals. They do not have an ethic that prescribes a way of action and form for human society."[167]

Henry and Smedes both attended the meeting in Chicago and signed the declaration that came from it. They represent a mediating presence from different points of view. The ensuing attempts to hammer out an actual evangelical agenda for "action," as Sider's organizational name advocates, was to founder through 1974 and 1975 and conclude in 1976 with no clear agreements and with the final meeting not attended by any of the "conservative" parties. There were recriminations all around for any and everyone. "Blacks accused whites of racism, women complained about sexist language, activist whites belittled academic theorists, and evangelical political radicals vigorously debated political liberals over strategies of social change. The unraveling of the evangelical coalition for social action mirrored the more general sociopolitical unraveling of the nation."[168] Perhaps more accurately, Smedes and Henry represented positions that might be called "center-left" and "center-right," respectively, but the bigger noise was being made by those on the extremes.

Intensifying the differences among the parties was the publication and reaction to the publication of Richard Quebedeaux's book, *The Young Evangelicals*.[169] Carl Henry reviewed the book and reacted to its implications in *Christianity Today* in April 1974.[170] Among other criticisms, Henry notes that the "new kind of evangelism" advocated by the radical evangelicals (among whom Quebedeaux lists InterVarsity and Christian World Liberation Front) is in fact a "tag line that seems brand-restrictive to the correlation of evangelism with criticism of American policy in domestic and foreign affairs." He notes that the radicals blame fundamentalism and evangelicalism for "the contemporary ecological crisis," because orthodoxy

---

166 Ibid.
167 Ibid., 58. The conclusion is that the Calvinist tradition "provides the most promising base on which to develop one."
168 Ibid., 67.
169 Richard Quebedeaux, *The Young Evangelicals: Revolution in Orthodoxy* (New York: Harper & Row, 1974).
170 Carl F. H. Henry, "Revolt on Evangelical Frontiers," *Christianity Today* 18 (April 16, 1974): 5–8.

Struggle for the City

"does not emphasize God's revelation in nature." Further, they charge evangelicals with "merely treating the symptoms of social injustice rather than *curing* [the disease itself]," a condition no less "heretical" to the radicals than theological *liberalism*.

Henry correctly denominates this as ancient Marxism that has "long derogated Christianity's social concern as merely a dispensing of aspirin whereas the overcoming of alienation (i.e., the class struggle) requires major surgery (socialist revolution) to remove objectionable social structures (capitalism). Such an estimate caricatures the tidal wave of human compassion unleashed upon the world by Christianity, oversimplifies the problem of alienation, confuses capitalism with the devil, divinizes socialism, and suffers from utopian enthusiasm."[171] The twenty-first-century litany of "taxing the rich," wealthy nations giving to poorer nations, "more equitable distribution of wealth," "ecological crisis," among others, has its most recent origins in this early diatribe by Quebedeaux. What the evangelical left was actually doing was advocating a moderate form of liberation theology, a blending of Marxism with the Sermon on the Mount, a theological approach common in Latin America, and later with some American black and feminist theologies.[172]

Primary among the radicals were Jim Wallis, whose original publication, *The Post-American*, speaks volumes (only later did it assume the name *Sojourners*); John Alexander, editor of *The Other Side* (designating the "have-nots" in American society, originally named *Freedom Now*); and Sharon Gallagher, editor of *Right On!* (renamed to *Radix* in 1999). Wallis would answer Henry in the June 21, 1974, issue of *Christianity Today*.[173] Noting that Henry appears to have confidence in the basic positive nature of the American system, Wallis nevertheless insists that "most young evangelicals do not feel it is possible to do that and still be faithful to the biblical mandate to seek justice for the poor and oppressed, who experience the consequences of US wealth and power in

---

171 Quoted in Cerillo and Dempster, *Salt and Light*, 74.
172 See the various essays in Ronald H. Nash, ed., *Liberation Theology* (Milford, MI: Mott Media, 1984); see also Carl E. Armerding, ed., *Evangelicals and Liberation*, Studies in the World Church and Missions 6 (Grand Rapids, MI: Baker, 1977); and for black liberation theology, see Anthony B. Bradley, *Liberating Black Theology: The Bible and the Black Experience in America* (Wheaton, IL: Crossway, 2010).
173 Jim Wallis, "Revolt on Evangelical Frontiers: A Response," *Christianity Today* 21 (June 21, 1974): 20–21, quoted in Cerillo and Dempster, *Salt and Light*, 80.

Struggle for the City

basically negative ways." He further avers that "many evangelicals insist that the call to discipleship demands fundamental breaks with the dominant values and life-style of the majority culture and provides the Christian with a different agenda than that of our political economy."[174] Wallis finally declares that "[a] biblical protest is being mounted against the brutalities of war and global dominance, a materialistic profit culture, institutionally structured racism and injustice, and government by deceit and manipulation."[175]

Henry notes that the radical agenda states that "our faith must be distinctively Post-American," in distinction to Henry's "Supra-American," and is tantamount to venturing a "final judgment upon the nation that God has not yet uttered." He then wisely suggests that "[e]stablishment evangelicals should consider the challenge posed by the young evangelicals as a summons to reinforce what is good, to debate what is controversial, and to give a biblical reason for disowning the remainder."[176]

Ron Sider would eventually convert his organizing attempt in the Chicago meeting under the original Evangelicals for Social Action banner into a full-fledged advocacy organization of the same name. *The Post-American* would become *Sojourners* based on the idea that these folk are "sojourners in a strange and doomed land." By 1986 Wallis was calling the political religious right "wolves in sheep's clothing," whose concerns about the Soviet threat "became more important in evangelical sermons than the words of Jesus," thus imposing on evangelical tradition "an alien and false gospel." He continued by saying, "The biblical gospel is a threat to the wealth, power, and violence of the American establishment, so it was replaced with an American gospel that sanctions the values of the system as it aggressively reasserts its power."[177] So much for irenic dialogue! Wallis is, of course, not less irenic than some of his "opponents" by this time. But the position of Wallis and Sider, philosophically, when it comes to the enlistment of the administrative state in order to enact social reforms in the service of the church, is a blatant example of the *uncon-*

---

174 Ibid.
175 Ibid., 81.
176 Ibid., 77–78.
177 Jim Wallis, "A Wolf in Sheep's Clothing: The Political Right Invades the Evangelical Fold," *Sojourners* 15, no. 5 (May 1986): 20–23.

Struggle for the City

strained vision and constitutes a rejection of the best of Reformed, Anabaptist, revivalistic, and evangelical interpretations of the role of the church and its relation to the surrounding culture.[178]

Whatever hope there might have been for dialogue disappeared in 1973 with the *Roe v. Wade* decision on abortion. Most "religious right" and even many moderate evangelicals and large segments of the general US population perceived this decision as an invasion by a nonelected body into areas better left to local communities and political entities. It was *inflammatory* on its own merits and added fuel to other controversies because the clear implication seemed to be that the federal government intended to have its way with every community in the country regardless of the principles of *representative government*. Add to this its emotional and moral implications and you have a struggle/war that is four decades long and shows no signs of abating. Now we will turn our attention to the actual political and economic issues that form the substance of the abortion debate in our contemporary culture added to the conflict already in place concerning the other issues we have detailed throughout the historical section of our study.

---

178 Though the Anabaptist position has been co-opted by modern defenders of the kind of position represented by Wallis and Sider, our treatment of Conrad Grebel and his distinction between the role of church and the role of government declares otherwise.

Struggle for the City

Part 3

AWAITING THE CITY

How Should We Then Live?

Chapter 22

Western Civilization and the American Dream

FORMER BRITISH PRIME MINISTER Margaret Thatcher, in her book *Statecraft: Strategies for a Changing World*, describes the essential character of American society at the beginning of the twenty-first century in this way: "America is more than a nation or state or a superpower; it is an idea—and one which has transformed and continues to transform us all. America is unique—in its power, its wealth, its outlook on the world. But its uniqueness has roots, and those roots are essentially English.... [I]t was from our Locke and Sidney, our Harrington and Coke, that your Henry and your Jefferson, your Madison and Hamilton took their bearings."[1]

Dinesh D'Souza is advocating much the same analysis of Western and American civilization when he says, "I want to suggest that the reason the West became the dominant civilization in the modern era is because it invented three institutions: science, democracy, and capitalism."[2] D'Souza goes on to credit this "unique expression" of human aspirations to "the influence of Athens and Jerusalem—Athens representing the principle of autonomous reason and Jerusalem

---

1   Margaret Thatcher, *Statecraft: Strategies for a Changing World* (London: HarperCollins, 2003), 20, 22. This is also the outlook of Melanie Phillips in her recent book *The World Turned Upside Down: The Global Battle Over God, Truth, and Power* (New York: Encounter Books, 2010). Contrast this view with that of the Obama administration, which denies the exceptionalism implicit in Thatcher's accolades.
2   Dinesh D'Souza, *What's So Great about America?* (Washington, DC: Regnery, 2002), 61.

representing the revealed truths of Judaism and Christianity."[3] Certainly our study of biblical truth and historical theology has born out this analysis.

David S. Landes has copiously documented the wide diffusion and current domination of these ideas (with, to be sure, varying degrees of benefit and/or damage) in his volume *The Wealth and Poverty of Nations*. Noting the widespread distribution of the products of modern technology, science, manufacturing and the like, he opines, "Until very recently, over the thousand and more years of this process that most people look upon as progress, the key factor—the driving force—has been Western civilization and its dissemination: the knowledge, the techniques, the political and social ideologies, for better or for worse. This dissemination flows partly from Western dominion (for knowledge and know-how are equal to power), partly from Western teaching, and partly from emulation."[4] We concur.

While none of the above-mentioned commentators has a uniquely Christian perspective, they each in their own way confirm the essential truth of our premise that the American and Western conception of the world has produced the most prosperous and dynamic period in the history of human activity on the planet.[5] Prior to September 11, 2001, the unhindered continuation of this

---

3   Ibid., 62. See his full discussion of this phenomenon in 60–67.
4   David S. Landes, *The Wealth and Poverty of Nations: Why Some Are So Rich and Why Some Are So Poor* (New York: W. W. Norton, 1998), 513. Additionally, see Nathan Rosenberg and L. E. Birdzell Jr., *How the West Grew Rich: The Economic Transformation of the Industrial World* (New York: Basic Books, 1986), for corroboration. Extensive studies in the development of cultures and economies have also produced such supporting evidence as Lawrence E. Harrison and Samuel P. Huntington, eds., *Culture Matters: How Values Shape Human Progress* (New York: Basic Books, 2000); Lawrence E. Harrison and Jerome Kagan, eds., *Developing Cultures: Essays on Cultural Change* (New York: Routledge, 2005); and the companion volume, Lawrence E. Harrison and Peter L. Berger, eds., *Developing Cultures: Case Studies* (New York: Routledge, 2006). Sociologist Peter L. Berger, *The Capitalist Revolution: Fifty Propositions about Prosperity, Equality, and Liberty* (New York: Basic Books, 1986), did pioneering work along this same line. Finally, see the very factual and at times whimsical Anthony Esolen, *The Politically Incorrect Guide to Western Civilization* (Washington, DC: Regnery, 2008).
5   See Gregory Clark, *A Farewell to Alms: A Brief Economic History of the World* (Princeton, NJ: Princeton University Press, 2008); Rondo Cameron and Larry Neal, *A Concise Economic History of the World: From Paleolithic Times to the Present*, 4th ed. (New York: Oxford University Press, 2003); and Robert William Fogel, *The Escape from Hunger and Premature Death, 1700–2100: Europe, America and the Third World*, Cambridge Studies in Population, Economy, and Society in Past Time 38 (Cambridge: Cambridge University Press, 2004); and Deidre N. McCloskey, *The Bourgeois Virtues: Ethics for an Age of*

dominance might have seemed to be an unchallenged foregone conclusion. However, the events of that day set in motion a surprising storm of anti-American, anti-Western sentiment, not only in the radical Islamic world of the terrorists but also in the nearly dormant world of the political and religious Far Left.[6] With the rise of European political opposition to American and British hegemony at the United Nations, the violent protests and demonstrations against "globalism" at numerous international forums, and the rise of worldwide demonstrations against American-led policies opposing terrorist organizations and states, a new wave of questioning threatens to break this millennium-long domination of Western and (later) American ideals. Further, with the election of Barack Obama, whose wife claimed during the campaign of 2008 that this period was the first time in her life that she was proud of her country,[7] a new era of apologetic posturing before the world for past "sins" and "blunders" seems to have become the order of the day.[8]

Commerce (Chicago: University of Chicago Press, 2006), for documentation of the massive and sudden move from poverty to prosperity in Western civilization. This book reprises Adam Smith's themes with new insights and updating.

6 This "dormancy" is not that of noninvolvement or lack of life, but rather one of inability to organize and motivate numbers of people to take to the streets in demonstrations or to make strident and unfounded claims that might sound credible to some. An example is the call of tenured professor Nicholas DeGenova of Columbia University for "a million Mogadishus" to decimate the American military, cited in Ron Howell, "Radicals Speak Out At Columbia 'Teach-In,'" *NewsDay*, March 27, 2003, http://www.freerepublic.com/focus/f-news/878685/ posts. For analysis of this phenomenon at home and abroad, see Paul Hollander, ed., *Understanding Anti-Americanism: Its Origins and Impact at Home and Abroad* (Chicago: Ivan R. Dee, 2004); Olaf Gersemann, *Cowboy Capitalism: European Myths, American Reality* (Washington, DC: Cato Institute, 2004); and Daniel J. Flynn, *Why the Left Hates America: Exposing the Lies That Have Obscured Our Nation's Greatness* (Roseville, CA: Crown, 2002); and the more popular style of Michael Medved, *The 10 Big Lies about America: Combating Destructive Distortions about Our Nation* (New York: Crown Forum, 2008). From a more theological perspective, see Meic Pearse, *Why the Rest Hates the West: Understanding the Roots of Global Rage* (Downers Grove, IL: InterVarsity Press, 2004).

7 Michelle Obama further asserted at various times that "Americans are 'cynical' and 'mean' and have 'broken souls' and that the lives 'that most people are living have gotten progressively worse since I was a little girl.'" Quoted in Paul Anthony Rahe, *Soft Despotism, Democracy's Drift* (New Haven, CT: Yale University Press, 2010), Kindle loc. 78.

8 For positively nuanced approaches to the good and bad of American dominance on the world scene, see Niall Ferguson, *Colossus: The Price of America's Empire* (New York: Penguin, 2004), who decries America's lack of "guts" to impose its will on the world for its (the world's) own good (301); Andrew J. Bacevich, *American Empire: The Realities and Consequences of U.S. Diplomacy* (Cambridge, MA: Harvard University Press, 2002); and Michael Mandelbaum, *The Case for Goliath: How America Acts as the World's Government in the 21st Century* (Cambridge: Perseus, 2005).

Awaiting the City

Evangelical Christians, born and raised under the dominance of the previously cited ideals, rightly wonder whether their assumptions and conclusions about the essential "right"-ness of their institutions, based as they are on such ancient conceptions of reality, can still be supported by valid Christian propositions. With Christian missions and missionary families now on the cutting edge of terror warfare, decisions about these issues carry more than mere theological and psychological consequences.[9]

The American Success Story

The two-hundred-plus-year-old American experiment represents the pinnacle of the millennium-plus ascendancy of the West and its politics, ideas, economics, and military prowess. As Margaret Thatcher and Melanie Phillips demonstrate, this ascendancy finds its current impetus from the culmination of English cultural domination and the carving of the democratic republic on the shores of the American continent. Most observers would concede as axiomatic that the United States now *dominates* the world as did ancient Rome, but *not* in the fascist way that Rome thrust itself on its world and then devoured all of its resources with little or no recompense. America is the dominant power in the world not as a military *terrorist*, but as a military *savior* and an economic engine and benevolent rescuer in time of need. We have made foreign policy mistakes and Americans are sinners, like everyone else, so it would be *false* to see America in messianic terms. America is a "hyper-power," as French foreign minister Hubert Vedrine labeled her,[10] a hyper-power with generally altruistic passions.

---

9 Recent events in the news in places like Yemen and the Philippines and the Islamic world, where American missionaries have been deliberately killed or wounded or were bystanders harmed in terrorist acts, serve to emphasize the current cost calculation in human terms for missionary service. Southern Baptist Convention news service Baptist Press regularly uses pseudonyms for the names of those in mission service when reporting their experiences.

10 We will not contend, as some in our time do, that Rome in its vicious rule and military tyranny is anything like the current version of the United States. Rather, the degree of influence and power in comparative terms for the age in which each existed is parallel. See sources on American empire listed above. In stark contrast to Rome as well as more recent fascist world powers, we recall the famous commentary titled "The Americans" by Canadian broadcaster Gordon Sinclair, originally written for a regular broadcast on CFRB radio in Toronto on June 5, 1973. The inspiring tribute to this nation's many deeds of

Consider the dimensions and implications of this hegemony. Economically American production and consumption dominate a new global community.[11] American companies maintain operations in countries around the world from North America to every continent on the planet. American consumers trying to buy exclusively American products can no longer be sure their new Ford sedan wasn't built by Chinese, Mexican, or European workers. American credit card and computer users will never know if the customer service representative they accessed by phone or e-mail works in Chicago or New Delhi. The favorite goods appearing in American malls fuel economic development all over the third, and now, the fourth world.[12] Kids from all over the globe (even those on welfare and food stamps in this country, native and illegal) wear products with American athletic team logos made all over the world.

Further, American markets now extend to all areas of the globe, with American companies like Walmart, Ford, McDonald's, Microsoft, and a host of others calculating market share and advertising budgets in euros, yen, pounds, reals, and whatever will bear the marketing. Leadership elites worldwide fear that such American success in their markets will, in fact, succeed in altering their cultures as well. This fear goes a long way in explaining global anti-American sentiment.[13]

It is not just that the gross domestic product (GDP) of the United States dwarfs the GDP of dozens of countries combined. Numerous state economies do the same. Some state governments collect more in taxes from this economic

---

valor and beneficence throughout its history came during one of America's darkest hours, the Vietnam War, and was revived following the terrorist attacks of September 11, 2001. Original script online at http://www.tysknews.com/Depts/Our_Culture/americans.htm.

11 Michael Novak, *The Spirit of Democratic Capitalism*, 2nd ed. (Lanham, MD: Madison, 1991), 20–22.

12 Consult some of the standard world informational economic texts to find out detail on the various designations for economic classifications by country.

13 Witness the past public relations attempts by the French government to cause French citizens to boycott McDonald's. This has not succeeded, as McDonald's marketing strategies win the day. Introducing the McBaguette, as the French call it, among other attempts to please local clientele, "McDo—as the French call it—is trying to appeal to national culinary tastes elsewhere in Europe too. The company has devised around twenty locally tailored menu items in some fourteen European countries, including Finland, where it offers the Rye McFeast, a burger served on a rye bun, and Spain, where it offers the tomato-based soup Gazpacho." Marion Issard, "To Tailor Burgers for France, McDonald's Enlists Baguette," *Wall Street Journal*, February, 24, 2012, http://online.wsj.com/article/SB 10001424052970204778604577241312286387028.html.

Awaiting the City

engine than the GDP of many of these countries combined.[14] A more dubious indicator of "superiority" is the fact that under the current Obama administration's budget proposals, the *deficit spending* of the United States government tops the GDP of India, Russia, Brazil, Spain, and Canada combined.[15] Walmart alone would be the thirty-first-ranked economy in the world if it were classified as a single country (just behind Saudi Arabia). It is the sixth-ranked single export partner for the Republic of China.[16]

This economic power is not just the projection of a handful of wealthy "robber baron" type individuals or a few giant corporate boardrooms. It is the overwhelming and inexorable, even volcanic, eruption of a society-wide acquisition of immense wealth. Masses of ordinary working people participate with their families in burgeoning purchasing power and accumulated net worth. Average real per capita income in the United States is $43,512, compared to $29,796 in the EU.[17] Furthermore, this prosperity is "distributed"[18] far more equitably than anywhere else in the world at any time in the history of the world.[19] Cries that economic inequality is growing in the United States

---

14 Check out statistics in C. Alan Joyce, Sarah Janssen, and M. L. Liu., eds. *The World Almanac and Book of Facts, 2009* (New York: World Almanac Books, 2009).

15 Cited by American Enterprise Institute scholar Kevin A. Hassett, "World-Class Deficit," *National Review*, March 23, 2009, 6, reposted, http://www.aei.org/article/economics/fiscal-policy/a-world-class-deficit/.

16 Bethany Moreton, *To Serve God and Wal-Mart: The Making of Christian Free Enterprise* (Cambridge: Harvard University Press, 2009), 6.

17 Figures are for 2008 from the Economic Research Service (http://ers.usda.gov/) cited in Philip Klein, "Wrestling with Capitalist Pigs," *American Spectator*, April 2009, http://spectator.org/archives/2009/04/09/wrestling-with-capitalist-pigs.

18 The term "distributed" is widely used with ignoble intent as if wealth were something lying around on the ground like manna to be harvested. We will have more to say on this later. For now we use the term advisedly.

19 See W. Michael Cox and Richard Alm, *Myths of Rich and Poor: Why We're Better Off than We Think* (New York: Basic Books, 1999), and Alan Reynolds, *Income and Wealth*, Greenwood Guides to Business and Economics (Westport, CT: Greenwood Press, 2006), for detailed analysis of this issue complete with extensive data in tables, charts, and graphs. The latest reflections on the nature of inequality of outcomes in American society are documented in Ron Haskins and Isabel Sawhill, *Creating an Opportunity Society* (Washington, DC: Brookings Institution Press, 2009), and Claudia Goldin and Lawrence F. Katz, *The Race between Technology and Education* (Cambridge, MA: Harvard University Press, 2008). The conclusion from statistical studies shows that the most prevalent reason for inequality of income distribution is rising illegitimacy ("nonmarital births"), with the remainder accounted for by the failure to be educated to compete in the current economic and technological atmosphere and the failure to work.

Awaiting the City

are simply not based in fact.[20] They do not take into account the actual individual conditions that apply but simply tally statistical categories.[21] They do not track the change in the composition of households over time.[22] They do not account for large numbers of legal and illegal immigrants coming into the workforce at the lowest levels. They do not account for the social selectivity that takes place when people in the same or near categories marry each other and form new households.[23] Further, with reference to the raw statistical studies, they do not account for the change in accounting that resulted when the IRS approved the use of the S-Corporation in tax reporting.[24] And perhaps most importantly, they do not account for *realistic* measurements of the physical and economic nature of the disparities in practice between real households in differing categories in a society where all are growing more prosperous.[25] As a final, though disconcerting indicator of success, the recent run-up of unemployment in the United States over seven percent was immediately labeled a "crisis" (now about 7.5 percent at this writing and previously higher) at a time when French president Sarkozy was boasting that 7.2 percent was the best figure in France in twenty-five years.[26]

---

20 See Thomas Sowell, *Intellectuals and Society* (New York: Basic Books, 2009), 35–45, for a succinct summary of the nature of the statistical claims, which attempt to show American economic inequities as a growing menace. Sowell documents, as do many others, that naysayers are using statistical figures that do not reflect the actual human conditions involved, that is, size of households, economic mobility, ages of individuals, actual wealth accumulation, and other factors. In addition, the critical statistics do not account for government transfers through cash, food stamps, rent assistance, and a host of other benefits.

21 That is, they do not show people moving up and down the scale of categories rather than staying in one place.

22 That is, they do not show the massive change from two-parent nuclear families where both parents and some children may work to masses of single-parent households with children where no one may work full-time.

23 This results in disproportionate multiplication at the top end of the categorical scale when, for instance, a lawyer marries a banker and both continue to work.

24 This change in procedure moved large amounts of statistically significant "income" from corporate ledgers to individual income tax filings. These filings are the source of the "inequality" statistics cited in polemical reportage of "gaps" that are allegedly growing between "rich and poor."

25 That is, the differences between a family in the lower categories and those in the higher mean that the lower end will be replacing the dishwasher this year and the upper will remodel the kitchen. Why this should constitute a biblical, theological, or historical reason for relief is never explained by the advocates of response to statistical studies of this type.

26 Previous unemployment numbers in France regularly hovering near fourteen percent, and others in Europe around seventeen percent.

Awaiting the City

Furthermore, to be classified "poor" in America is now a dubious statistic based on an annual income of approximately $11,000 for an individual and $22,000 for a family of four that does not include the approximately $8,000 per person spent on average by the states for additional social welfare services to this classification of people and the federal outlays not channeled through the states (needs-based federal/state outlays are more than $1 trillion and rising as we go to publication).[27] Total social transfer spending by government entities now amount to approximately $2.9 trillion annually (approximately twenty percent of GDP), and private charities chip in another approximately $0.5 trillion. This amounts to almost twenty-eight percent of US GDP, and has been so for decades.[28]

Dinesh D'Souza has rightly noted that hundreds of thousands in the United States now live a lifestyle that "would scandalize much of the world and every previous generation that has gone before them," and the world wants to go where the poor people are fat.[29] The so-called "poor" in this country on average have and use the kind of consumer goods (multiple color TVs, air conditioning, microwaves, musical sound systems, computers, etc.), own multiple automobiles, eat the kinds and amounts of food, and live in the kinds and size of housing (much of it personally owned) that have been considered middle class for generations in the rest of the world.[30]

Let the record also show that no nation on earth has attempted to do more with its wealth to *benefit* the downtrodden, alienated, destitute, marginalized,

---

27 See article by Heritage Foundation expert Robert Rector, "The Facts about Poverty in America," *Human Events*, February 7, 2012, 13, http://www.humanevents.com/2012/02/07/the-facts-about-poverty-in-america/, for breakdowns on "means-tested" programs spending (i.e., Medicaid, Food Stamps, rent support, etc., not including Unemployment Insurance, Social Security, or Medicare) through state and federal programs.

28 Information in this paragraph comes from the U.S. Census Bureau, Department of Health and Human Services, the Central Intelligence Agency Web site, and Infoplease.com. The total outlay of goods and services and cash expenditures amounts to approximately $83,000 per person in the "poor" and near-poor category (see chap. 25, n. 11). See also careful and detailed documentation in William Voegeli, *Never Enough: America's Limitless Welfare State* (New York: Encounter Books, 2010).

29 Dinesh D'Souza, *The Virtue of Prosperity: Finding Values in an Age of Techno-Affluence* (New York: Simon & Schuster, 2000), 15. D'Souza details this prosperity in 14–15.

30 Information available from US government services departments (Census Bureau, HUD, Commerce, Energy, etc.) and online. See esp. Robert P. Murphy, "Michigan's Poor: How Much Do Numbers Alone Really Tell Us?" Viewpoint on Public Issues, Mackinac Center for Public Policy, March 1, 2004, http://www.mackinac.org/6312. See also Robert Rector, "Romney Right: Poverty Safety Net Huge," *Human Events* (February 13, 2012): 19.

Awaiting the City

and racially excluded of the earth. Whether it has been in private charity, religious activism, whole country and regional reconstructive efforts, ongoing foreign manpower and monetary assistance, liberal immigration policies, or massive commitments to domestic welfare programs, American attempts to ameliorate the human condition are unprecedented.[31] Once again, none of this would be possible without the vast resources provided by millions of enterprising American citizens and businesses.[32]

The latest calculations available show that the amounts of United States spending on aid and development outside this country are also staggering—belying the image created in the media both domestically and abroad that Americans are stingy. This canard is usually tied to a misunderstanding of the way people, businesses, and government in the United States do benevolence and relief. Governmental assistance for international aid by the United States outstrips anything done anywhere else in the world (about $40 billion annually), though as a percentage of GDP it is not large. However, it is seldom noted that the private sector in the United States is the engine of relief and development that makes the most difference. That amounts to sixty percent of all worldwide charitable contributions (as of 2005), a figure that is now approximately $300 billion (as of 2007),[33] and now eighty-five percent of all expenditures for foreign aid from the United States. Not included in any of these numbers is a typical year when $6.2 billion came from the military budget to fund emergency efforts or $160 billion was sent home by immigrants (legal and illegal) to third- and fourth-world countries, especially Latin America, and $600 billion in free-trade imports came from the same parts of the

---

31 Marvin Olasky, *The Tragedy of American Compassion* (Wheaton: Crossway, 1992), esp. 6–23, 99–115, 134–50. See also, Tommy Newberry, *The War on Success: How the Obama Agenda Is Shattering the American Dream* (Washington, DC: Regnery, 2010), 31–32, for the latest breakdown on American governmental and private generosity to the world.

32 See Voegeli, *Never Enough*, for argumentation that this is precisely the condition necessary to sustain the welfare state and the Left knows it, but they are bent on ever-increasing demands and regulations anyway.

33 For documentation on the latest figures in this paragraph, see Don Eberly, *The Rise of Global Civil Society: Building Communities and Nations from the Bottom Up* (New York: Encounter Books, 2008), Kindle loc. 681ff. See an issue of weekly economic and financial newsletter by Jeff Thredgold, "Happy Talk," *Tea Leaf*, April 15, 2009, at http://www.thredgold.com/tealeaf/090415.pdf, for this latest estimate of charitable giving in the United States. This is twice the percentage of GDP of the next most generous private giving nation, Great Britain.

Awaiting the City

world.[34] Moreover, the government and US businesses and benevolent enterprises invest untold amounts in human capital and resources sent to poverty-stricken areas for direct hands-on assistance and educational efforts that cannot be tracked or calculated. The massive response to the Indian Ocean tsunami of 2004 is typical in our current time frame.[35] At that time fully thirty-six percent of all Americans got involved at some level of giving, so that in the end the American Red Cross stopped accepting money and one group, Doctors without Borders, began offering donors the option of refunds and placement of gifts in other areas of the world.[36]

Science and Technology

But the American success story is not just economic. The United States and the West lead the world in science and technology. Leadership in science and technology is first a product of *inquisitiveness, initiative*, and the willingness to accept *progress and change*.[37] The spirit of the first settlers on American shores is also the spirit of Kitty Hawk, Menlo Park, the space shuttle *Challenger*, and Silicon Valley.[38] No society in human history has done so much to further the mandate to subdue and rule over God's creation for the benefit of all mankind.

This kind of leadership cannot be isolated from economic success—in fact, they go hand in glove. No innovation of a scientific or technological

---

34 This last amount is in contrast to the heavily protected industries in other developed nations that will not allow such imports. This is a continuing major issue in worldwide negotiations over relief for poverty in the world.

35 See Eberly, *Rise of Global Civil Society*, chap. 7, locs. 1666–1803, for full treatment of this event.

36 More recently, the Haitian government appears to have been overwhelmed and embarrassed by American relief efforts directed at earthquake victims and stopped supplies from entering the country unless they administered and took a percentage for themselves.

37 Robert Nisbet, *History of the Idea of Progress* (New York: Basic Books, 1980), 3–9, 237–96. See Udo Middelmann, *Christianity versus Fatalistic Religions in the War against Poverty* (Colorado Springs: Paternoster, 2007), and Darrow L. Miller, *Discipling Nations: The Power of Truth to Transform Cultures* (Seattle: YWAM Publishing, 1998), for discussions of the worldviews that hinder vast regions of the world from actually setting about to change their conditions and world environment.

38 This vast reservoir of inventive production is the exclusive characteristic of Western civilization compared with the remainder of the world and its history. See D'Souza, *What's So Great about America*, 60–61; Middelmann, *Christianity versus Fatalistic Religions*. It is this technology, wherever it appears, that limits the damage, human and material, caused by such events as tsunamis, earthquakes, and hurricanes.

nature can occur without massive investment in research and development—many times over years and decades. This requires the *accumulation of capital* (i.e., profits, that bad word) not earmarked for mere survival. On the consumer side, nothing can be developed for the use and benefit of mass markets unless there are those with sufficient wealth to pay for the first products on the market, which will be disproportionately expensive.

Some products are so expensive at the beginning that only huge entities like governments can be the first buyers. Such projects as highways, super-computers, weapons and security systems, aircraft, and space technology are instances of this kind. On the other hand, thousands of products start out as items that only the very *wealthiest* of individuals could afford to purchase and use, thus proving their utility for mass markets and refining their production process and cost. These consumer goods can be as beneficial and essential as new cures for deadly illnesses or as apparently frivolous as digital media players. The American market system has succeeded in a manner that no other has in bringing to all of humanity the by-products of putting men on the moon (to use one example)—in medicine, miniaturization in all technologies, transportation, communications, and cooking the family dinner. So, too, the same market process puts computers in the homes of the lowest economic classes and makes available life saving and enhancing drugs and procedures at affordable prices to all people.[39] The American dream is a scientific and technological miracle.

As with each of the preceding areas, the American dream leads the nations of the world in virtually every kind of endeavor. Militarily she is unmatched in the ability to secure the benefits of freedom and democratic institutions anywhere such action is needed. And because the American military is subject to civilian control, manned by volunteers with high motivation and trained in up-to-the-minute technologies, and supplied by a market economy producing constant innovation and advancement of technologies, it surpasses all military

---

39 In America and around the world American medical technology is made available no matter the cost to the destitute, alien, homeless, and otherwise completely deprived multitudes. This would not be possible without the experimentation and marketing that the United States consumer provides. Canada now faces the fact that because it has stifled the process for drug manufacturers in its own country, it must rely on American firms to develop its drugs.

Awaiting the City

forces on earth in the ability to achieve its objectives while minimizing collateral damage to nonmilitary personnel and property. This principle has been a cornerstone of just-war ethical discussion for millennia.[40] It is, in fact, the American military umbrella that allows free countries everywhere to minimize and/or eliminate altogether their military budgets and turn their resources to internal social concerns.

Further, no nation or society has actually put in place the technology and mechanisms that the United States has for protecting the planet's environment and resources. The cities of the Communist bloc, when it was still functional, were often filthy and depressing places to live. Much of the third world today is filled with pollution caused by lack of modernization. Once again markets, technology, and economic realities have combined over time to preserve habitats and reclaim lost ones, keep skies blue and clean up those polluted by industrial development, protect endangered species and repopulate nearly extinct ones, leave wilderness pristine and reclaim lost ones, and point the way for the world of nations and cultures to do the same.[41] The American way has been to recognize a need to do something about environmental problems, let American business make a *market* out of it (or encourage and mandate solutions through tax and regulation policies) and, as with so many other things, *general prosperity* will pay for it.[42]

---

40 See Victor Davis Hanson, *Carnage and Culture: Landmark Battles in the Rise of Western Power* (New York: Random House, 2001), for the good and the bad of the way Western cultural ideas and ideals influence the course of history through even war-making.

41 See Bjørn Lomborg, *The Skeptical Environmentalist: Measuring the Real State of the World* (Cambridge: Cambridge University Press, 2001), for the most detailed look at the actual state of the environment now and historically. See Ronald Bailey, ed. *Earth Report 2000: Revisiting the True State of the Planet* (New York: McGraw Hill, 2000), for additional documentation. For more readable and popular treatments, see Christopher C. Horner, *The Politically Incorrect Guide to Global Warming and Environmentalism* (Washington, DC: Regnery, 2007); Ronald Bailey, ed., *Global Warming and Other Eco-Myths: How the Environmental Movement Uses False Science to Scare Us to Death* (New York: Forum, 2002); and Joseph L. Bast, Peter J. Hill, Richard C. Rue, *Eco-Sanity: A Common-Sense Guide to Environmentalism* (Lanham, MD: Madison, 1994). For a Christian perspective without the crisis mentality of the left, see E. Calvin Beisner, *Garden Meets Wilderness: Evangelical Entry into the Environmental Debate* (Grand Rapids, MI: Acton Institute for the Study of Religion and Liberty / Eerdmans, 1997), a corrective to evangelical missteps in this area.

42 For a good discussion of the appropriate roles of government and private enterprise in working out ecological issues, see Richard Pipes, *Property and Freedom* (New York: Alfred A. Knopf, 1999), 248–53.

Awaiting the City

American Success Exported

The success of this process in the United States and the world is apparent everywhere in the world. Perhaps the greatest indicator of the singular success of the American experiment is the millions of people who have and are voting for it with their feet. Undeniably, for all the world's people, the one symbol of hope for a better life is the United States. Just as the original European settlers of the North American continent braved any danger and set aside all fears to plant their hopes and dreams in free soil, millions since then, trusting to God and their own initiative, continue to make the journey from poverty and oppression to opportunity and freedom. And, universally they end up better off in every way by multiplied degrees of any measurement. Paradoxically, even those brought here against their will as slaves would find their descendants far better off than the descendants of those families they left behind in Africa.[43]

These developments are so powerful that the debate about Socialism, Communism, and capitalism as producers of wealth is moot, and Communism is a failed experiment on the ash heap of history. Capitalistic institutions and ideas have won by the sheer force of their obvious success and the absence of any this-world rival from the other ideologies, though critics abound.[44] As even long-dead Communist dictator Deng Xiaoping once said, "It's glorious to be rich." No economic engine of any human past has approached the marvel of the West, the recession of 2008 notwithstanding. The "American

---

43 This is one reason the discussion about "reparations" to descendants of slave families has no ethical currency. See also D'Souza's chapter, "Two Cheers for Colonialism" in *What's So Great about America,* for a take on the residual effect of British and other imperial policies. Also, see Keith B. Richburg, *Out of America: A Black Man Confronts Africa,* (1997; repr., New York: Basic Books, 2009). Thomas Sowell has published decades of studies in a trilogy detailing the nature of culturally based changes that have benefited groups coming in contact with advanced civilization and/or overcoming negative encounters. See *Race and Culture: A World View* (New York: Basic Books, 1994); *Migrations and Cultures: A World View* (New York: Basic Books, 1996); and *Conquests and Cultures: An International History* (New York: Basic Books, 1998).

44 Critiques such as there are do not advocate a return to previous versions of Socialism or Marxism. They do decry the materialistic bent of capitalistic institutions and their perceived selfishness and neglect of more humanitarian, artistic, and altruistic pursuits. For the best recent defense of capitalistic hegemony in the world, see Jay W. Richards, *Money, Greed, and God: Why Capitalism Is the Solution and Not the Problem* (New York: HarperOne, 2009).

Awaiting the City

dream" is an economic *miracle*, unprecedented in human history that is now becoming the possession of the rest of the world as it adopts capitalistic market economics.[45] The world is becoming "flat," as Thomas Friedman has labeled it, due to "the rise of the rest."[46]

We do not mean by this enumeration of external criteria for evaluating success to give short shrift to other values. Nor do we mean to be merely jingoistic in hyping American superiority. Throughout the remainder of this book we will be highlighting underlying philosophical and theological underpinnings of the American story and interacting with deserved criticism. But before moving to the next stage in our argument, we note a final piece in the successful mosaic that is the American idea.

It is now a common political strategy to discount and depreciate the cultural diversity and tolerance of American society. This practice is to ignore the very real truth of history that no society in the prior history, or for that matter current practice, of human governance has committed so many human and material resources to the ideal of building one people out of multiplied ethnic, racial, and religious constituencies.[47] From its beginnings in the break from the British Empire, the attempt to treat all men as created equal—stated clearly in the founding documents—has led the world in the struggle for freedom and equal opportunity for all, regardless of apparent differences of external

---

45 Globally, the adoption of capitalistic economics and market systems has reduced the so-called bottom billion of apparently intractable poverty (those existing on less than $1/ day) to a number more like 350 million. See the latest statistical studies on the movement out of extreme poverty in the world, published by economists Maxim Pinkovsky and Xavier Sala-i-Martin, "Parametric Estimations of the World Distribution of Income" (NBER Working Paper, No. 15433, National Bureau of Economic Research, Cambridge, Massachusetts, issued October 2009), http://www.nber.org/papers/w15433, cited in Kevin A. Hassett, "The Poor Need Capitalism," *National Review*, November 23, 2009, 11, reposted http://www.ncpa.org/sub/dpd/index.php?Article_ID=18694.

46 Thomas L. Friedman, *Hot, Flat, and Crowded: Why We Need a Green Revolution and How It Can Renew America* (New York: Farrar, Straus and Giroux, 2008). Friedman is ironically arguing for a continuance of American dominance through green technologies, not a downsizing of American productivity. He sees this as the way to outdo the Chinese in the future. See also Fareed Zakaria, *The Post-American World* (New York: W. W. Norton, 2008), for his take on "the rise of the rest" as the world embraces economic development.

47 We deplore the current fad of promoting what amounts to tribalism in American society under the guise of a redefining of the meaning of diversity. It can only lead to a new Balkanization of the culture.

Awaiting the City

appearance, philosophy, class, sex, or national or ethnic origin.[48] America's greatest bloodletting in war was ultimately, if not immediately, to rid the continent of slavery. Its educational system was founded with the idea of giving every person, regardless of prior culture or language or economic status, an opportunity to succeed in life. Its political institutions provide the mechanics for peaceful change and redress of grievances. Its free nongovernmental institutions allow any person or group to gain economic power, to publish and propagate dissenting views, to sue for compensation and reparation, and to organize as necessary to secure any of the foregoing results.

The history of the world to the present century is largely a story of oppression and exercise of raw coercive force to achieve domestic and international self-aggrandizement. In that history the United States of America has been singularly committed to *benevolent ends* and *nonimperialist designs*. Whether in the actual production of peaceful and noncoercive change for humanity's knottiest societal conflicts or in exercising force for the greater good of the largest number of people, the American dream enacted is utterly unique and is proving itself an exportable commodity in the world.

The latest testimony to this phenomenon is from Indur Goklany in his massive documentation of the current state of the world. He begins with the assessment of Dickens at the beginning of the Industrial Revolution in England, that the cities of Great Britain were little short of a living hell (*The Old Curiosity Shop*), or so it seemed. But this was only a temporary way-stop on the road to massive changes for the better. Societies around the world (having grown from approximately 750 million in 1750 to 6.5 billion today)[49] now bask in economic and technological conditions that are unprecedented in the history of mankind on the planet. Each society has undergone massive changes that started with worsening environmental, resource, and human conditions, but which inevitably improved as wealth was created to overcome obstacles to

---

48 For an appreciation of the actual attitudes and intentions of the founders on equality for all and other pertinent issues, see Thomas G. West, *Vindicating the Founders: Race, Sex, Class, and Justice in the Origins of America* (1997; repr., New York: Rowman & Littlefield, 2000).

49 This factor alone should give pause to those insisting on the deteriorating conditions on the planet, for it is the very progress we here cite that has allowed human beings to flourish as never before on the planet. The problem is not environmental degradation to the hurt of humankind, but the exact opposite.

Awaiting the City

further progress. Thus, today not only in Great Britain and the United States, but all over the world, as Goklany notes, "the average inhabitant of planet earth is… wealthier, freer from hunger and disease, and likely to be longer lived than ever before. And although epidemics, floods, droughts, and other natural disasters still occur, their consequences, while still severe, are generally not as lethal·as in times past, except where poverty stalks the land because of war—civil or otherwise—and dysfunctional government policies." The process of change has freed individuals from the limits of caste and race and gender prejudices, bestowed property rights to millions, expanded the middle class, and provided the benefits of education and opportunity through democratic institutions to countless who had never dreamed of such possibilities. In addition, the improvement of environmental standards and conditions as societies have grown wealthier has allowed people everywhere to remedy things that Dickens first deplored (and well beyond that), so that we can now afford to measure "one molecule of pollutant among a billion other molecules, [and] we feel beset by trace gases and debris of human origin in the atmosphere and the stratosphere, in the Arctic and the Antarctic, at the bottom of the ocean and at the top of Mt. Everest." Goklany further opines that we can now indulge ourselves in a "romanticized view of nature" that was never possible before, Malthusian fear-mongering notwithstanding.[50]

The Idea of Progress

Explaining all the reasons for the American (and now the world's) success story is a task far too large for this chapter, or even this book. Nor is it within our focus to attempt such a labor. But among the reasons is one that is quite fundamental, and it is a reason that ties the American story both to the best insights of classical antiquity and to the evangelical strand of the Christian heritage—the idea of progress.

---

50 Indur M. Goklany, *The Improving State of the World: Why We're Living Longer, Healthier, More Comfortable Lives on a Cleaner Planet* (Washington, DC: Cato Institute, 2007), Kindle loc. 34–66. McCloskey, *Bourgeois Virtues*, and Goklany's book are the latest overall documentation on the issues of population and economic growth and environmental sustainability that we have seen. Earlier and even more detailed is Julian L. Simon, ed., *The State of Humanity* (1995; repr., Oxford: Blackwell, 1998). All are massively documented.

Awaiting the City

Both Hellenism and the Roman world at their best taught that man has the ability and the obligation to rise above his surroundings and make for a better life. Prometheus takes fire from the gods and, though he pays dearly for it, gives the gift to men, who begin the conquest of their world. Protagoras argued that "man is the measure of all things." By that he was not excluding the Greek gods but was preaching that humans must make their way in this world, if they are to make a way at all. Plato, likewise, though he is often accused of being overly concerned with the otherworldly realm of the "Forms," was equally committed to life in this world. In Plato's *Laws*, he argues that men have developed over time from lives that were simple and filled with hardship to life in the *polis*, which, though at times is complex and hard, is yet far superior to the older days.[51] The Roman Seneca took a page from Plato's book and urged that for primitive people there was no such thing as justice, nor did they understand self-control or bravery. Now it may be that both Plato and Seneca were guilty of cultural chauvinism, but it is also clear that they believed that their cultures were evidence of the progress of man.[52]

Early Christians held similar views, though not for the same reasons as the pagan writers.[53] Though these ideas show up earlier than the fifth century, it is especially in the writings of Augustine that the notion of the progress of God's creation can be clearly seen. In his great book on the philosophy of history, *The City of God*, Augustine compares the growth of humankind with a river, which moves inexorably toward its goal.[54] The African father also criticizes the notion of time that is found in those who believe that time is cyclical. For him the Bible taught that time is linear, moving from creation, through the history of Israel, to redemption in Christ, on to the millennial kingdom, and finally to eternal bliss.[55] Even his settled view on the millennium shows his commitment to progress, for he was essentially a postmillennialist in his later writings

---

51   It is unlikely that Plato had anything more than mere impressionistic and legendary knowledge of these older times.

52   We are indebted to Nisbet, *History of the Idea of Progress*, 10–46, for this information.

53   The classic book by J. B. Bury, *The Idea of Progress: An Inquiry into Its Origin and Growth* (1920; New York: Dover, 1987), argues that progressive insights were not present in Christian theology. There is no doubt that Bury was mistaken in this assessment.

54   Augustine, *City of God* 22.

55   Ibid. 20.

Awaiting the City

(though he might not have recognized that). He argued that the church would see the City of Man overwhelmed by the City of God through the preaching of the gospel and that Christ would return only when the millennium had run its course.[56] It is also the case, of course, that Augustine was at the same time *pessimistic* about man—he affirmed a strong doctrine of depravity. But this depravity would not keep even the City of Man from making progress through history, and since Christ's redemption of his church meant that the church would grow—Paul, Augustine reminded his readers, did compare the church to a human body, which also grows—progress was inevitable for the kingdom, which, like the mustard plant, would one day dominate the garden.[57]

Both the Reformation and the American Puritans recaptured this same spirit, but we have already said enough about them in previous chapters for this to be plain. What ought to be plain to even the casual reader is that the American experiment has been heavily committed to the idea of progress, indeed, that this idea is almost identical with America and Americans at their best.

This has been the case at least sense the Revolutionary War. It might be no real accident that Adam Smith's *Wealth of Nations*, which laid out the blueprint for how a nation could acquire wealth through technological progress, was published in 1776. The book was almost an advertisement for what was already beginning to take place "across the pond" and what was developing even more rapidly in England. What we do see in the history of America is a clear example of "sustained growth."[58] It is *progress* that, though it has had fits and starts, has maintained America's momentum decade to decade. We will argue in the course of the remaining chapters that though there is the potential for such a trend to become demonic, overall—treated correctly—the idea of progress is not only in keeping with the best of the Western heritage but is also rooted in Scripture and the best theological reflection as we have tried to present it in the foregoing chapters.[59]

---

56 Anthony Hoekema, *The Bible and the Future*, rev. ed. (Grand Rapids, MI: Eerdmans, 1994), 132.

57 Nisbet, *History of the Idea of Progress*, 47–76.

58 Max Weber, *The Protestant Ethic and the Spirit of Capitalism*, 3rd ed., trans. Stephen Kalberg (1930; Los Angeles: Roxbury, 2002). Original German text composed in 1904–5.

59 C. S. Lewis argues against this other potentially demonic form of "progress" in "Is Progress Possible? Willing Slaves of the Welfare State," *God in the Dock: Essays on Theology and*

Americans at their best have operated under the assumption that knowledge is cumulative and that its "applications to human betterment are continuous and never-ending."[60] The Chicago World's Fair of 1893 provided a showcase for America's fascination with progress. More than twenty-seven million people visited the six-hundred-acre exhibit, where they seized "the living scroll of progress, inscribed with every successive conquest of man's intellect."[61] George Westinghouse's huge electric generators were on display, and it would seem that the worry that had been raised about the usefulness of alternating current was laid to rest in that fair. Probably few present realized that they were observing the beginning of a revolution. George Ferris debuted his massive "Wheel" there for the first time, and it turned out to be the most popular attraction. Hundreds of exhibits and thousands of artifacts were on display, most with the primary goal of impressing the visitors with the technological prowess of man (especially American man) at the close of the nineteenth century. The history speaks for itself.

As a final word for this section, it needs also to be noted that the idea of progress was *not* invented during the Enlightenment. This is the allegation of Jean-François Lyotard in his *Postmodern Condition*, when he argues that the idea of "performativity," that we ought to get maximum output for minimum input, is a thoroughly modern idea.[62] While the idea may have received a kind of industrialized and scientized application in the years since Isaac Newton and Robert Boyle laid the groundwork for modern industrialization, the fact is that these ideas can be traced back to the pre-Socratic philosophers and to early Christianity. Christians do not have to live in dread of what the latest postmodern thinker has to say about the human heritage, for often as not, they have a terrible sense of history. The idea of progress seems quite clearly to be hardwired into the human psyche. Hardwired by God, in our opinion.

Ethics, ed. Walter Hooper (1970; repr., Grand Rapids, MI: Eerdmans, 2008), 311–16.

60 D'Souza, *What's So Great about America*, 63.

61 Nisbet, *History of the Idea of Progress*, 204.

62 Jean-François Lyotard, *The Postmodern Condition*, trans. Geoff Bennington and Brian Massumi, Theory and History of Literature 10 (Minneapolis: University of Minnesota, 1983), chap. 1.

Awaiting the City

The New Challenges

Prior to the latter half of the previous century, the popular consensus in the United States espoused the values we have outlined above. The spirit of American individualism and capitalistic entrepreneurial enterprise was nurtured by what Paul Johnson has described as a high level of religiosity coupled with an equally high degree of moral and ethical agreement as to the proper functioning of public institutions.[63] This consensus maintained a more or less balanced view of the interaction between rights and duties. John Winthrop's vision of the City on a Hill, later updated in Lincoln's characterization of the American Union as "the almost chosen people," became the more generic and nebulous formulation of President Dwight Eisenhower in 1954: "Our government makes no sense unless it is founded on a deeply felt religious faith—and I don't care what it is."[64]

There is a sense in which Eisenhower's statement, uttered during the national debate over placing the words "under God" in the Pledge of Allegiance to the flag, was a clear indicator of the sea change to come. The adoption of the phrase "In God we trust" as the national motto two years later only served to further the perception of that era as the high water mark of American civil religion—not the beginning of a renaissance of true Christian religious fervor.[65] From the perspective of events that have transpired in the half-century since that time, those days play like the last gasp of a waning civilization.

Eisenhower, and millions more like him in that era and today, did and do care exactly what kind of religious faith sustains our public institutions. The consensus of the past was that the moral and ethical foundation of society was to be found in the Bible and especially its revelation of the Decalogue. Though there is still widespread adherence to this simple standard, the consensus has been stood on its head. Other voices and constituencies now dominate the public forum once ruled by the received wisdom of the entire Judeo-Christian tradi-

---

63   Paul Johnson, "God and the Americans," *Commentary* 99, no. 1 (January 1995): 25–45.
64   Paul Johnson refers to this species of American as *"homo Americanus religiosus."*
65   What had been gradually seeping into Christian dialogue, the nontheological and anti-intellectual, antirational approach to religious practice, now is in full bloom in Ike's statement.

Awaiting the City

tion. It is this challenge, or better, these challenges, that pose the greatest threat to a new generation of would-be American dreamers, both religious and secular.

Such a moral and ethical confrontation has not arisen in a decade or even a half-century. Through gradual attrition, the original theological and biblical presuppositions of the "dream" have been eroded and forgotten in the minds of the general populace over time.[66] What was once embedded in the documents that birthed the nation no longer carries even the force of shibboleth or platitude. The current rage is outright denial and excoriation of any perceived "duties" in the name of "rights" that cannot possibly be given without taking from someone else. Charles Murray has rightly noted in a review of Thomas Sowell's *A Conflict of Visions* that the political climate on the Left makes no attempt to argue, as it once did, that to improve man's physical and economic condition is to engender in him the seeds of his own moral and cultural improvement.[67] Instead, it simply argues that "fairness" or cost-efficiency or saving the planet demands the redistribution of wealth and benefits, regardless of any moral considerations in the persons receiving largesse.

Consider a couple of examples of the dimensions of this great reversal. For instance, an essentially Christian and clearly compassionate policy inviting "millions longing to be free" to join in the American idea and the opportunity for prosperity and success has been turned into cries for the preservation of "diversity" at the

---

66 For varied takes on the "American dream," see Jennifer L. Hochschild, *Facing Up to the American Dream: Race, Class, and the Soul of the Nation*, Princeton Studies in American Politics (Princeton, NJ: Princeton University Press, 1995); Jason DeParle, *American Dream: Three Women, Ten Kids, and a Nation's Drive to End Welfare*, (New York: Viking, 2004); Jim Cullen, *The American Dream: A Short History of an Idea That Shaped a Nation* (New York: Oxford University Press, 2003). The last is a history of the term and its meaning and use. David Platt is one of the latest to opine on the implications of the American dream for Christians. See David Platt, *Radical: Taking Back Your Faith from the American Dream* (Colorado Springs: Multnomah, 2010). Our criticisms of the Platt material are substantially those of Kevin DeYoung, "Getting to the Root of *Radical*: A Review and Response," review of *Radical: Taking Back Your Faith from the American Dream* by David Platt, The Gospel Coalition Blogs, May 25, 2010, http://thegospelcoalition.org/blogs/kevindeyoung/2010/05/25/getting-to-the-root-of-radical/.

67 Charles Murray, "Thomas Sowell—Seeing Clearly," review of *A Conflict of Visions: Ideological Origins of Political Struggles* by Thomas Sowell, *National Review*, December 19, 2005, Book Reviews, reposted, http://www.aei.org/article/politics-and-public-opinion/thomas-sowell--seeing-clearly/.

Awaiting the City

expense of full integration into a "melting pot" society.[68] Prior generations came to this land seeking only freedom and opportunity. Now, even illegal entrants to the country and murderous enemies of its citizens expect their "rights" to be protected and expect as well to be the recipients of our generous welfare and education systems.[69] The very ideas of freedom and opportunity contain within them the duties to be responsible for oneself, to work hard, to get an education, to save and invest, to be faithful to family and neighbors, and a host of other common virtues. Without these philosophical and moral foundations, freedom becomes "free for what?" Opportunity becomes "opportunity to do what?"

Ponder also how an essentially Christian philosophical conception of "unalienable rights" given by the "Creator" has been turned into the idea of "provisions." The rights first conceived by the founders of the United States were not things "provided" to states or individuals. Rather, they were statements about areas of life no government would be allowed to invade, coerce, limit, tax, etc., without the due process of law. "Life, liberty and the pursuit of happiness" is a fundamental statement about the right to be left alone so long as I do not harm the innocent neighbor. The concept of "pursuit" implies my own effort and enterprise, not that of another on my behalf. Today's pursuit of rights is not typically this. It is, rather, an attempt to *get* from government (and necessarily, therefore, from fellow citizens) the provisions that *I* deem necessary to *my* happiness. The truth is that no government can "provide" anything. It must first take from someone in order to provide for another. In Christian thought and that of the philosophical forebears of the American Revolution, God is the true "provider," and governments are to be facilitators of an appropriate atmosphere of law allowing human beings freely to pursue his will. In such an atmosphere they will typically prosper. Rights are, by their very nature, fundamental and limited because they involve the same rights of the neighbor. "Provisions" by government fiat necessarily involve doing harm to one for the benefit of another.

---

68 Numerous studies have shown that the best and fastest way to succeed economically and culturally in America is to join the team, learn the language, go to the schools, and be immersed in the culture.

69 It has become a building block of leftist dogma to understand "rights" in this fashion as well. See also the attorney general of the United States, Eric Holder, proposing to try terrorist attackers of US targets as criminals under US law and subject to its provision of rights to citizens.

Awaiting the City

These are but two examples among many of the ways in which Christian propositions have been co-opted and reversed and then fed to the public in the West and America as truly compassionate and Christian ideals. It is this kind of philosophical reversal that feeds so many current movements from feminism to environmentalism to internationalism to Islamic terrorism. When such a process of mental gymnastics feeds itself on human jealousy, envy, fear, and moral relativism, good becomes evil and heroes become villains, addicts become victims and terrorists become patriots, the innocent can be plundered and the criminal can receive a solicitous hearing. All of this can go on while Christians who have never changed their essential convictions pass from being just plain Christians in the public eye to being vilified as "fundamentalist zealots," at the same time that the real zealots who literally murder thousands of innocents must be "understood" and "given a fair hearing" because their acts are said to stem from "underlying grievances."

A Christian Response

How does one maintain a truly Christian perspective and public stance in the face of such developments? How should we live, and how should we speak?

Obviously it is too late to long nostalgically for the return of the day of "*homo Americanus religiosus*." We have arrived at this place in part because this species held sway for too long. And, besides, we can no more reverse the historical clock fifty years than Islamic fundamentalists can reverse it seven centuries. What we must do is get a firm grip on *biblical* and *theological* foundations for what is so often called a "just society" and contend for and embody it wherever there is opportunity and need. We cannot afford to be silent, to lapse into sentimentality, to allow fear and irrationality to control the conflict, or to permit our true or perceived guilt to set the agenda. Too much of what is accepted as "Christian" dialogue and ideology is in part or the whole a combination of these common ways of dealing with nettlesome issues.

By way of telling the reader where we *sit* before telling you where we *stand*, we offer the following summary observations that should be more or less clear from the foregoing discussions in the previous sections. First, no Christian can rightly defend without reservation any human institution or system. All human things are perforce *flawed*, whether overtly or covertly. Our Christian Revolu-

Awaiting the City

tionary War fathers believed, rightly, that strong political opinions and commitment to country were consistent with following Jesus as Lord, but they also
knew that these were separate issues as we have seen in previous chapters (see
development of Christian political thought in part 2).[70] Therefore, our defense
of anything American or Western must be true to this standard.

Second, our standard for comparison begins and finally ends with whatever we have found the Bible to teach on the subject. We have also sought
to be cognizant of and aided by the theological reflections and philosophical
propositions of those who have gone before us. However, we will not shy away
from asserting the authority of the Scriptures over *any and all* other claims to
knowledge of the truth, nor will we bound simply by theological constructs
that served the past well but do not translate to the present.[71]

Third, our process of critique and defense will be rational—as opposed to
gnostic (i.e., having special powers or access to secret things), sentimental (i.e., just
feeling good about an idea), polemical (i.e., seeking out the opportunity to inflame
emotional responses and controversy), anecdotal (i.e., drawing conclusions with
sweeping effects from isolated cases), or irrational (i.e., using any or all of these
other approaches to avoid dealing with reality). We do not believe in the religion
of rationalism—the idea that all of reality can be known by the power of unaided
human reason. However, we do believe that *God* is rational, the *universe* he created
is clearly observable as rational, and that *Christian faith* is rational.[72]

---

70 Nathan O. Hatch, *The Sacred Cause of Liberty: Republican Thought and the Millennium in Revolutionary New England* (New Haven, CT: Yale University Press, 1977), esp. chaps. 2 and 3; Steven J. Keillor, *This Rebellious House: American History and the Truth of Christianity* (Downers Grove, IL: InterVarsity Press, 1996), 59–102.
71 Noel Weeks, *The Sufficiency of Scripture* (Edinburgh: Banner of Truth, 1998); John MacArthur, "The Sufficiency of the Written Word," in *Sola Scriptura! The Protestant Position on the Bible*, ed. Don Kistler (Morgan, PA: Soli Deo Gloria, 1995), 151–83.
72 In defense of this conviction, see, for instance, Kenneth D. Boa and Robert M. Bowman Jr., *Faith Has Its Reasons: An Integrative Approach to Defending Christianity; An Apologetics Handbook*, 2nd ed. (Colorado Springs: Biblica, 2005); J. P. Moreland, *Scaling the Secular City: A Defense of Christianity* (Grand Rapids, MI: Baker, 1987); Phillip E. Johnson, *Reason in the Balance: The Case against Naturalism in Science, Law, and Education* (Downers Grove, IL: InterVarsity Press, 1995); Ronald H. Nash, *The Word of God and the Mind of Man: The Crisis of Revealed Truth in Contemporary Theology*, Contemporary Evangelical Perspectives / Bibliology (Grand Rapids, MI: Zondervan, 1982); and Rodney Stark, *Victory of Reason: How Christianity Led to Freedom, Capitalism, and Western Success* (New York: Random House, 2005).

Awaiting the City

Fourth, we will attempt to retain a healthy respect for the power of idealism and the radical demands of God's Word, while eschewing the evils of utopian conceptions. It is clear that God's intention for man on this earth is for the highest possible aspirations to motivate and drive his every endeavor. However, it is also clear that sin resides in all activities human, even in the work of those who are regenerate. As Luther said, we are *simul iustus et peccator*—righteous in the sight of God because of Christ, yet still battling the "flesh." Because the kingdom of God is both "already" and "not yet," we can expect no triumphalistic realization of either a worldly or Christian utopia in this age, either in community or individually in our own hearts.[73] God's present providential oversight includes death at every turn and an approaching cataclysm that shall issue in a "new heavens and a new earth," which he alone can produce.

CONCLUSION

Finally, it is clear from the foregoing that our bias is toward Western and American civilization. History, unrevised by modern hagiographers, is the record of a line running from Jerusalem through Athens, Rome, Wittenberg, Geneva, Runnymede, Boston, and Philadelphia and stretching to the present telling the story of how Judeo-Christian documents, institutions, and practices have, in fact, been a city on a hill and a light to the world. It is also evident that the world banks on this and depends on it, even in the midst of demonstrations and hate-filled diatribes against the supposed evil American Satan.

---

73 Both corporate and individualistic "utopias" abound in Christian history. See our citations in chap. 10, "Self-Denial and World-Denial in a Giant Empire of Extravagance." The Oneida Community, monastic orders, and various Anabaptist communalists held out the hope for realizing the kingdom in this age through social reconstruction, but all inevitably fell short. Mystics and radical charismatics of various types have offered the full realization of the kingdom in this age as an inner experience, but they have left flat and frustrated those who took them seriously. See, for instance, Ray Yungen, *A Time of Departing: How a Universal Spirituality Is Changing the Face of Christianity*, 2nd. ed. (Eureka, MT: Lighthouse Trails Publishing, 2006); Donald S. Whitney, "Doctrine and Devotion: A Reunion Devoutly to be Desired," Christ Community Church, February 15, 2003, http://www.glenwoodhills.org/article.asp?ID=740, taken from Donald S. Whitney, "Unity of Doctrine and Devotion," in *The Compromised Church: The Present Evangelical Crisis*, ed. John H. Armstrong (Wheaton, IL: Crossway, 1998); Robert M. Bowman Jr., *The Word-Faith Controversy: Understanding the Health and Wealth Gospel* (Grand Rapids, MI: Baker, 2001).

Awaiting the City

Two scenarios illustrate the point. When the British ruled their far-flung empire long ago, they were both revered and excoriated as the current American-style worldwide dominance is today. But the most telling insight into the true nature of British rule was the one burned into world memory by India's Gandhi. His concept of nonviolent protest was posited on one clear perception of the mores brought to the Orient by the English. He knew that if he lay down in front of a train as an act of protest, the train would stop. The British conscience would not allow otherwise. In this manner he eventually succeeded in exercising effectual power against a vastly superior foe.[74] No such tactic would have had a ghost of a chance in Nazi Germany, Napoleon's France, Stalin's Soviet Union, or in any other empire.

Except for one—the modern American "empire." When American troops entered Iraq in 2003, the same scenario was enacted on the screens of millions of television sets around the globe. Iraqis suffering under the brutal regime of Saddam Hussein were encouraged to welcome American soldiers as liberators, not conquerors, and Iraqi fighters were urged to surrender rather than die in futility. Many did just that. But the desperate and despotic regime then resorted to the tactic of faking surrenders to lure American troops into ambushes. Finally, civilians were forced at gunpoint to drive suicide vehicles loaded with explosives to be blown up at checkpoints manned by troops trained to treat civilians as noncombatants. The vile regime and the chaotic roving quasi-revolutionary-dissident bands that followed it were plainly trusting that coalition soldiers would carry the moral and ethical fundamentals of their civilization onto the battlefield and into the streets of the cities.

Nothing illustrates more clearly the clash of cultures steeped in differing values and religious ideas. We would not excuse or defend Western and American immorality and debasement. But neither will we engage in a guilt trip that will not defend the good and heroic. They who will not rise to defend the good and innocent are doomed to be enslaved and consumed by evil.

---

74 This same presumption about the nature of the American conscience guided the nonviolent thought and practice of Dr. Martin Luther King Jr.

Awaiting the City

Chapter 23

Moral Complexities
in the Twenty-First Century

THE APPARENT COMPLEXITIES OF PERSONAL moral decision making in the face of economic, social, and political realities in daily life have been intensifying for the past hundred fifty years in American society, as we have previously documented, but seem to have been further catalyzed by events early in the twenty-first century. We will take them more or less chronologically.

GEORGE W. BUSH AND THE CHALLENGES OF THE MODERN PRESIDENCY

The *first* was the two-term presidency of George W. Bush, whose early and continuing emphasis was on something called "compassionate conservatism."[1] This theme, though later eclipsed by events so overwhelming as to make it seemingly irrelevant, characterized an attempt to cloak "conservatism" in a label that would combat the ongoing charge of "mean-spiritedness" against those on the right from those on the left of the political spectrum. Its usefulness gradually drained away, and it was ultimately discarded as the Bush presidency became embroiled in an unpopular war and fought through one

---

1   See Marvin Olasky, *Compassionate Conservatism: What It Is, What It Does, and How It Can Transform America* (New York: Free Press, 2000), for a full statement of what is meant by this terminology. The book's foreword is written by George W. Bush.

economic crisis early on and ended with an even greater one. Along the way were battles over tax "reform" and policies said to benefit "the rich" over "the poor," and foreign businesses over Native American ones (read "outsourcing"). Further battles ensued over farm subsidies benefiting huge corporate producers (as opposed to "family farms") and industries like steel that could not compete with foreign rivals. Lately it is "bailouts" and "stimulus," and "Main Street" versus "Wall Street," and government takeovers of auto companies, financial institutions, and the health-care industry.

In each of these developments Christians could find important reasons to wonder where they should stand on the issues. For instance, should "rich" Americans get more in tax-cut revenues than "poor" Americans, many of which paid no income taxes to begin with?[2] Should government revenues be used to fund grassroots efforts at correcting social ills through religious organizations? What is the role of American trade and farm policy on third-world and fourth-world economies, especially the "poor" of those lands? More importantly, what is the true impact of an environmental policy that subsidizes ethanol production[3] from corn in such volume that the price of tortillas sold to the poor in Mexico City skyrockets and food commodity prices all over the world are distorted as more and more land that once stood ready to produce surpluses for the poor are now used to produce gasoline supplements that benefit primarily huge multinational corporations? Or, perhaps even more critically, what will be the impact of global-warming (now "climate-change") induced policies on the poorest of the world? These are but a few of the political decisions that raised questions from the early days of the Bush presidency onward. It was widely perceived, and probably correctly so, that the direction of presidential leadership was informed by the highly confrontational campaign that revolved repeatedly around economic issues. The president saw his credibility at stake in attempting to pursue a promised agenda that was both "compassionate" and "conservative" enough to win two elections.

---

2   For a group-by-group breakdown of who pays income taxes, how that compares to total federal revenues, and what is paid by others, see latest figures in Tommy Newberry, *The War on Success: How the Obama Agenda Is Shattering the American Dream* (Washington, DC: Regnery, 2010), 59.

3   This is only one of the policies we will explore later.

Awaiting the City

The *second* galvanizing event was the terrorist attacks directed at the World Trade Center towers and the Pentagon on September 11, 2001. These attacks, forming in tandem (along with another failed attempt on an unknown target) an enemy's one-point protest against American interests, were so significant as to be truly "historic." "Never before" has never been so true for Americans. Their bloody and tragic nature alone gave, and still gives, thoughtful Americans pause for near-apocalyptic reflection. But it is not just the blood of thousands, the vast piles of rubble, and the heroic acts of so many that draws our attention here. What is even more compelling is the "cause" in which these attacks were launched. This was no mere military attack to carry out some narrow political purpose.

It can be fairly argued, based on what we know of the attackers' stated motivations, that the whole value system of American and Western civilization is the target of the extremist Islamic group(s) behind this onslaught. American (and to a lesser extent, Western) prosperity was symbolized in the World Trade Center towers. American and Western-style governance and the ability to project both political and economic power are symbolized in the US military's headquarters at the Pentagon. The fact that these events took place on live TV, projected globally by the finest modern technology, could not be ignored as merely coincidental. The whole scenario appeared to have been originated and planned as a master statement pitting one worldview against another, and subsequent events and communications have not put the quietus on this conviction.

Christians could not dismiss lightly the debate this ignited from many quarters as questions arose about the "justness" of American and Western ways of life, business, and politics. Many said that the United States got what it deserved because of its *opulent* lifestyle, which ignores not only the "poor" in the United States but the far more destitute "poor" of third and fourth world nations—especially those in the Muslim world. These accusations continued and intensified as the "war on terror" escalated.[4] Such charges require a biblical and theological Christian response. Moreover, the fact that terror is an instrument used primarily against civilian targets requires a personal response since all alike are threatened. There simply is no place to hide.

---

4   For concise discussion of these charges and response to them, see Jean Bethke Elshtain, *Just War against Terror: The Burden of American Power in a Violent World* (New York: Basic Books, 2003).

Awaiting the City

A *third* event that focused attention on the economic life of the United States and the West is actually a series of events played out in one sector of American society—the world of "big business" (specifically the world of publicly traded companies) and the financial markets. Beginning with the bankruptcy filing of the Enron corporation in December 2001, a veritable avalanche of business failures and scandals rocked the American and global economy. Firm after firm was found to be at or near dissolution, while apparently unethically and illegally covering up financial facts rightfully required by investors to make proper decisions. Accountants and auditors were found to be making false reports to boards of directors and the public.[5] High-ranking executives were found to be cashing in on stock sales while employee retirement plans became relatively worthless. Stock brokerage firms were found to be advising stock purchasers to buy company stocks that they knew were not sound or involved illegal "kickback" schemes.

These developments in the business of America were not just isolated incidents occurring in obscure, little-traded corporations. Rather, the list of companies caught in some way in this web included the titan Enron Corporation (largest bankruptcy in American history to that point, followed by the even larger collapse of WorldCom, Inc.), Arthur Andersen LLP (largest accounting firm in America and auditor/accountant for an untold number of publicly traded American corporations), Merrill Lynch (which paid a $100 million fine to settle charges of illegal touting of client company shares), Sotheby's Auction House (whose chairman was sentenced to prison and fined $7.5 million for price fixing), Adelphia Communications (filed for bankruptcy amid SEC investigation), Rite Aid (illegal accounting scheme resulting in the greatest corporate earnings restatement in US history to that time), Qwest Communications (SEC investigation for illegal accounting practices), and Tyco International (making $8 billion in acquisitions not made public). Ultimately over

---

5   For an account of what one Christian did to seek to stem the tide of fraud at Enron, see *Time* magazine's person of the year for 2002, Sherron Watkins, http://www.time.com/time/specials/packages/0,28757,2022164,00.html. Richard Lacayo and Amanda Ripley, "Persons of The Year 2002: The Whistleblowers," Time, December 30, 2002, http://www.time.com/time/magazine/article/0,9171,1003998,00.html. There is also a brief account in Darrow L. Miller, with Marit Newton, *LifeWork: A Biblical Theology for What You Do Every Day* (Seattle: YWAM Publishing, 2009), 214.

Awaiting the City

two thousand publicly traded companies switched accounting firms to create at least the public *impression* of a clean slate, and in 2002 a record number of firms restated their financial reports to set the record straight.[6]

The result of these and many other similar revelations in the mass media on an almost daily basis in 2002 led to a never-before-seen phenomenon in American economic life. For the first time in its history the American economy seemed to be recovering from a recession without a *corresponding* recovery in the financial markets. Fear gripped many investors like no time since the Great Depression of the 1930s. The markets plunged and rose erratically as the downward spiral of the indices seemed to continue without abatement. Some observed that only trading mechanisms that had been put in place after the crash of 1987 prevented the kind of implosion that destroyed the markets in 1929. With the additional pressure of the waiting game surrounding attempts to get United Nations backing for a preemptive strike on Iraq's weaponry of mass destruction and mayhem, US financial markets experienced ever-increasing downward motion.

The lesson supposedly learned through hard experience during this time, however, was not that man-made barriers to uncontrolled sell-offs can save a market gone wild. Only restoration of the "trust factor," a return to some certainty about future developments in the world, would be the answer to investors' natural fears. Financial markets react most strongly to the *uncertainty* factor. Nothing produces uncertainty like the absence of truth-telling in the corporate world and disequilibrium in world politics. Millions of working-class individual investors learned for the first time how important *ethics* and *political stability* are in the world of high finance.

Of course, this period was finally marked by the eventual operation of laws and regulations that had been intended to prevent just such a situation from developing. Ultimately the front pages of newspapers and the TV news cameras bore witness to the sight of once high-flying executives being carted off to jail, some even in handcuffs (doing the now infamous "perp walk"). But the damage had already been done to millions who lost their savings and investment portfolios in the disastrous fall that came after human depravity wreaked its havoc.

---

6   Many online and print news sources corroborate these facts.

Awaiting the City

Then, after seemingly having resumed the barely interrupted rush to permanent prosperity, the American economy and public were subjected to an even
worse economic shock as the recession of 2008 bit in hard and led to the largest
stock market retreat since the Great Depression. This time the culprit was a housing "bubble" brought on by financing schemes fueled by Washington politics and
a lending industry acting irresponsibly and sometimes in a *predatory* manner toward those with marginal abilities to pay for mortgages. The accumulation of un-
collectible loans and falling real estate prices led to the failure of banks in numbers
not seen for twenty years (a pattern that continues right up to publication of this
volume) and ultimately the complete restructuring of the American auto industry
through government "bailouts" ultimately to be financed by deficit accumulation
for future taxpayers and inflation of the currency through monetary policy.[7]

Riding the wave of the bad news came the first African American candidate for the presidency with a clear and legitimate opportunity to win the
White House, a feat he proceeded to pull off with great promises of "hope"
and "change" that would "remake America." Those of us who lived through
the '60s as young adults and college students recalled quickly how little hope
such an event (election of a black president) seemed to have for accomplishment any time soon. Now, the election of a man who might not have even had
the right to vote in the South of forty years before was a reality, but at what
price? The early days of 2009 proved to be a *socialist's* dream come true as big
government collectivist program after program began its journey through a
willing and united Congress threatening to change the political and economic
landscape for generations to come. Among the cheerleaders for the new agenda were not just those who longed to see the day of color-blind elections,[8] but
those whose hopes to *reinvent* American economics and politics along utopian
socialistic lines have their best opportunity for fruition since the 1930s.

How then should Christians respond to such events?

---

7 For a full and accurate treatment of the facts in this historic meltdown, see Thomas Sowell,
   The Housing Boom and Bust (New York: Basic Books, 2009), and Peter Schweizer, *Architects
   of Ruin: How Big Government Liberals Wrecked the Global Economy—and How They Will
   Do It Again If No One Stops Them* (New York: HarperCollins, 2009).
8 Many of these advocates of such change who nevertheless deplore the direction of the
   Obama presidency, and saw it coming in advance, could not vote for him on the simple
   ground that skin color was representative of a long struggle for equality and opportunity.

Awaiting the City

CHRISTIANS IN ECONOMIC LIMBO

The Enron debacle, mentioned above, illustrates the dilemma of how to *think and act as a Christian* in times such as these. Many a pundit opined about the "rich corporate executives" who appeared to have used their inside information to manipulate their corporate stock prices and cash in on sales of personally owned stock to enrich themselves (and later the pundits opined about those who were subject to government "bailouts" pocketing big bonuses). Enron was not the only place this happened, but its story serves our purpose well. Enron was like many publicly traded corporations whose boards turned the operation over to a highly sought-after CEO. The bidding for such talent produced outrageous salary packages and large blocks of stock options. Believing they should give executives a clear stake in the company's stock pricing, boards of directors thought this the best way to insure diligence on the part of its leadership. However, the law of unintended consequences was set in motion when corporate executives became tempted to manipulate stock prices in the short term by illegal and/or unethical practices.

Enron Corporation was like hundreds of corporations in the 1990s—riding a huge wave of stock investing by a new generation of investors flush with disposable income and driven by tax policies (for 401[k]s, IRAs, SEPs, etc.) to stash money in attractive stocks. Not to be lost in this is also the undeniable fact that Enron was a prime mover in the attempt to *convert* the American economy to an engine for the massive *transfer* of wealth to companies engaged in "environmental" technologies that depend on large government involvement to succeed in the marketplace.[9] The further irony in all this is that at Enron and many other businesses, executives and ordinary employees alike had incentives to buy their own company stock and watch it rise on the stock exchanges. However, sometimes rules about the timing of purchase and resale of their own company stock created periods when 401(k) stock could not be sold. At Enron, such a moment occurred after executives had begun and/or

---

9 Recall Thomas DiLorenzo's distinction between *market* entrepreneurs and political entrepreneurs, Enron thus representing the latter (see chap. 19). The best treatment on Enron is Bethany McLean and Peter Elkind, *The Smartest Guys in the Room: The Amazing Rise and Scandalous Fall of Enron* (New York: Portfolio, 2004).

finished liquidation of *their own* declining stock. Enron stock fell from values in the $60s per share to the single digits per share over about nine months. Late in this decline, 401(k) shares were frozen by previously enacted rules and could not be sold.

Here is where the ethics of the situation becomes much more complicated. Stocks are sold by investors for many reasons, but the primary ones are these: (1) the investor believes the stock has gone up enough for her to solidify a profit by selling, (2) the investor believes a stock has gone up as far as it will and decides if he waits to sell he might not make as much as he can now, or (3) the investor sees a stock declining, believes it will continue to do so, and decides to sell now to cut future losses.

All stocks experience ups and downs based on investor perception of their values and the decisions made by buyers and sellers at any given time. Enron stock had a phenomenal run-up and at one point made all kinds of people (executives and employees) "paper millionaires"—i.e., their millions were in paper stock certificates and could only be turned into "real money" by selling those pieces of paper. Whatever the motives for selling stock, if enough shares of any stock go on the market at any given time, the price can fall, simply from the *volume* of availability and the mentality that this can foster.

Enron's stock began to fall as executives sold—probably for a number of reasons. Any time "insiders" in a company sell, it is time for Wall Street professionals and savvy investors to pay attention. This is an alert that all may not be well with a company. Usually this information can be found by research into the finances of all publicly traded companies—*unless* someone is covering up the data, which is exactly what was going on at Enron.

Many people (executives and others) got out of the stock as it was falling. The primary motivation became to curtail losses and cash out as much of the "paper profits" as possible. Those at the top made out very well, and those at the bottom got hurt relative to what had once been huge potential cash gains. Be sure to note, however, that every seller of a stock must find a buyer. And, what a seller is selling is confidence that a stock will go up and the buyer is buying that same value—even if he realizes a stock may decline further before going up.

As Enron's stock hit bottom, the company entered bankruptcy proceedings and the facts began to be known. One of the most distressing revelations

Awaiting the City

was that, because of the rules in force at the time (made so by government mandates), lower-level employees of the corporation had been locked out of selling their Enron 401(k) stock for a period of time while executives were still able to sell theirs. Now there was added to the charge of *unethical* and *illegal* insider manipulations, along with accounting and disclosure cover-ups, a charge of sheer "unfairness" or "injustice." After all, the "rich" executives profited while the "common people" were unable to do the same. This aspect of the situation was seized upon as a "rich vs. poor" issue by many commentators, some of them specifically Christian.[10]

What is a fully Christian response to this story? Of course, it begins with the obvious—"You shall not steal, bear false witness against your neighbor, etc." means don't manipulate the market to your gain and another's loss. Be particularly careful not to take advantage of a situation where you are able to exert overwhelming power at the expense of an "innocent" person. This bare minimum is incorporated in SEC regulations and has become the cause for widespread prosecutions, convictions, and punishments.

But is this *all* a Christian has to say to this peculiarly modern morality tale? We think not—and this will illustrate our methodology. Christians should be contemplating ethical issues well beyond the mere fact that the "rich and powerful" sometimes manipulate and do harm to the "poor and weak" because of greed, lust, covetousness, and sheer murderous intent. What about the "ordinary investor" type in this situation? Is there no ethical question for him in selling a stock he has reason to believe will keep going down? All along the way of Enron's decline, "ordinary investors" directly selling shares and indirectly selling them through mutual funds saved losses for themselves by passing them along to their buyers. At the end, the woeful 401(k) investors who were unable to sell lamented that they had not been allowed to do the same as those above them—thus showing their own *envy* and *covetousness*. Were these "poor and weak" only less guilty of sin because of the absence of means to do as others did?

---

10 See weekly e-mail newsletter from *Sojourners* founding editor-in-chief Jim Wallis, "The Moral Failures of Enron Execs," *Sojomail*, January 16, 2002, http://sojo.net/sojo-mail/2002/01/16. Wallis regularly goes about the country touting the "morality" or lack thereof of government budgets—Tom has heard him repeatedly in Denver.

Awaiting the City

Surely the Ten Commandments encompass the full range of human depravity that sometimes only *awaits* a moment of opportunity. Accordingly, Jesus in his "fulfilling" ethic of the Law warns that "lust in the heart" and inappropriate "anger" toward another as well as the language of disrespect for persons (see in Matt. 5:22 *rhaka*, "fool," a term that impugns a person's moral capacity) are offenses that, without the work of grace, will exclude one from the kingdom and bring on damnation. A fully biblical Christian ethics says that all persons—poor and rich, weak and mighty, young and old, male and female, brother and alien—stand before the bar of God's just demands in need of *equal* amounts of grace.

The Complexity of Ethical Judgments

The foregoing discussion elucidates the motivation we have had in writing this book. We believe that Christians in this new marketplace—a truly "political economy"[11]—have increasingly been placed in ethical dilemmas where they tend to do one of three things: (1) make *snap decisions* based on incomplete information or emotional manipulation by outside forces (religious, political, and/or social), (2) *go along* with whatever requires the least rational and spiritual consideration because the times are presenting such complex situations (a new situational ethics), or (3) *do the homework* necessary to embody a *thoroughly Christian* moral perspective in any present or future marketplace.

The simple choices that Christians have made at times in the past are now made thornier by the forces inherent in the events with which we began this chapter. First is the dynamic of American politics—and ever more pervasively global politics. Americans generally (if polling data can be trusted), and their politicians in particular, have (for the time being, at least) decided, or perhaps just acquiesced, in favor of what is euphemistically called "big government"

---

11 See Michael Burleigh, *Earthly Powers: The Clash of Religion and Politics in Europe, from the French Revolution to the Great War* (New York: HarperCollins, 2005), for a full discussion of this terminology and its implications. The term "political economy" does appear to have derived originally from the discussion of Smith's *Wealth of Nations* in the academic community of the time and over the next forty years. See Stewart Davenport, *Friends of the Unrighteous Mammon: Northern Christians and Market Capitalism, 1815–1860* (Chicago: University of Chicago Press, 2008).

and its increasing intervention in the daily lives of its citizens. By 2009 they had apparently enthusiastically embraced an activist agenda to reshape completely the American economic experience along *collectivist* lines. How it finally washes out is the stuff of elective politics.[12] Christians, unless they are ready simply to opt out of the process, will need more and more to think and act out their economic ethic through their political involvement. This process is now heavily influenced by events that seem to be out of control and beyond the ability of even the strongest political entities to direct.

With the "baby boomer" generation now moving toward retirement and a looming Social Security system crisis on the horizon, the ethico-political struggle will be a truly *personalized* battle. And, "battle" may not be an overly strong term to describe the clash between generations over tax policy, the payment for what will be considered "entitled" benefits, and the future of the next generation's retirement funding. Who are the "rich" and the "poor" when politicians use those terms to *promote* their *projects* and their *election campaigns*? Who's really "mean-spirited," and who's "compassionate"? What price should one part of the electorate be required to pay for the benefits thought due to another?[13]

The crux of the debate in modern American politics on the domestic front is, "How can each group seated at the table of federal largesse get its 'fair share' of the pie, and what is the obligation of the nation to global justice?" More importantly, ordinary Americans who have never individually thought to "scam the system" are now doing so.[14] Increasingly, it is considered sheer stupidity, at least, and political

---

12 This is by no means a settled future prospect. See Arthur C. Brooks, *The Battle: How the Fight between Free Enterprise and Big Government Will Shape America's Future* (New York: Basic Books, 2010).

13 Witness Jesse Jackson in a CNN interview, July 1, 2009, referring to the Supreme Court reversal of an affirmative action decision in New Haven, Connecticut, that he said opted not to "inconvenience" white candidates for a firefighter position who scored higher on testing than did black applicants.

14 Ordinary people in the street are now getting wise to the political chicanery that is a part of the manipulation of economic factors. See the recent scandals on this level where large numbers of people are attempting to refinance their home mortgages by falsifying their credit worthiness *downward* (by understating their incomes, overstating their debts and deliberately running up credit card bills), and falsifying applications for food stamps (EBT), welfare, and Medicaid benefits by using correcting fluid on utility bills and lease agreements. See Allison Sherry, "Fraud Claims Climb Steeply," *Denver Post*, August 3, 2009, 1, and Miles Moffeit, "Banks Here Nixing Aid to Small Businesses," *Denver Post*, August 1, 2009, 1. Articles online at http://www.denverpost.com/. Additionally, many are

suicide for sure, not to be part of a constituency seeking, yea, *demanding* to receive federal and state goodies—either monetary or in the form of in-kind services or intangibles. Thus, virtually no politician can be elected to national office without promising to "bring home the bacon." Additionally, some evangelicals suggest that global justice demands deeper and deeper sacrifices by the American public for the sake of foreign aid projects. Is there a biblical Christian perspective on these things, and is it clear enough to command a consensus of biblically informed Christians? We believe we have begun to lay out the answer to both questions. The exegesis of Scripture and the consideration of theology in its historical context has led us to the consideration now of the facts before us in daily economic and political life.

The second dynamic from which American Christians (and arguably the worldwide Christian community) cannot isolate themselves is a foreign enemy that for the first time in our history has made its goal the destruction of the American way of life—more specifically, its economic success, its politico-military might, and its Judeo-Christian orientation.[15] We will *concede* that its stated antipathy is for the sins and perversions of an America gone soft and materialistic because of its wealth and becoming ever more perverted by various influences because it has forsaken its core values. This justification can appear to have the ring of *truth* at its surface, and many Christian Americans rightly bemoan the apparent accuracy of such criticisms.

However, the view that this is all there is to Islamic extremism is terribly shallow. The primary stimulus to the September 11, 2001, attacks is an understanding of the Muslim holy book that demands that all the world be converted to Islam or be destroyed. This conviction is further fueled by the belief that Western civilization with American economic, political, and military might at the forefront threatens the culture and stability of the Islamic world. Therefore, what we view as an act of cowardice and terrorism sells in the mind of Islamic extremists as an act of war and self-defense. In the world of these "warriors" it is only right and moral for them to attack our entire way of life as a threat to theirs. Consequently, *any* target is legitimate.[16]

---

now simply walking away from homes with payable mortgages because real estate values do not match the mortgages.

15 This is increasingly an agenda pointed at the entirety of Western European civilization.

16 See Elshtain, *Just War against Terror*, on this paragraph.

Awaiting the City

This means that for the first time since the American Civil War, American soil is a true battleground. There can be no discharge even to the civilian population, for the enemy considers *all* its designated opponents[17] to be combatants. This is true even if all one does is go to work in the New York financial district. Thus do plain working people, Christian and non-Christian, become enemies of Allah and Muhammad.

As we have noted, some would have us to believe that the terrorist cause is at least "more just" than that of America and the West because the "poor" Islamic societies suffer under American exploitation. Further, they say, our Middle Eastern politics, based on supporting Israel as a stabilizing influence to protect the flow of Arabian oil for our profligate use, is worthy of attack. Others would add that the sheer in-your-face affluence of American society is an affront to God and should bring down his righteous wrath upon it in any form available. Tony Campolo opined that the Crusades of previous centuries were justification enough for the atrocity of 9/11: "We don't know much about the Crusades, but there isn't a Muslim in the world that doesn't know about the Crusades. Where, in the name of Jesus, we slaughtered how many hundreds and thousands of innocent people, many of them women and children."[18] Even more troubling to some is the charge by large groups of activist demonstrators at world economic summits that the United States is the primary culprit in the "rape" of the planet and should be the object of violent protest and opposition.

How should Christians respond to such external threats and internal critiques and the questions they raise? Is our "way of life" an affront to God? Do we support un-Christian foreign policies that exploit the weak and poor? Do we immorally invest in companies that pillage other societies? Many on the evangelical left would have us believe that these charges have great merit and that Christians in the pew do indeed have a serious responsibility to address them in radical ways, such as redistribution of wealth and reparations to aggrieved peoples and support for the

---

17 That means all who have not converted to Islam, known as "infidels."
18 Tony Campolo, "It's Friday, but Sunday's Comin'," (chapel address at North Park University, Chicago, Illinois, October 9, 2001), quoted in Elshtain, *Just War against Terror*, 117. This sentiment was echoed by former president Bill Clinton at the time and many others then and now. For a thorough treatment of the actual nature of the Crusades vis-à-vis Muslim attitudes and actions then and now, see Rodney Stark, *God's Battalions: The Case for the Crusades* (New York: HarperOne, 2009).

Awaiting the City

usual litany of monetary and service transfers such as progressive taxation, minimum wage legislation, debt cancellation for undeveloped countries, and all the usual welfare state programs.[19] Craig Blomberg is perhaps the most vehement (vitriolic?) in denouncing American economic dominance when he says that previous candidates (the former Soviet Union, Iraq, the European Union) for identification with the "evil empire" of Revelation 17 and 18 "have never wielded the commercial clout of North America, with its multi-national corporations and its politics of national interest that lead to the impoverishment of countless millions around the world with scarcely a tear shed."[20] He finds this to be "frightening," not because of the rise of socialist cultural engineering and political coercion but because of "the downfall of communism and the resurgence of worldwide capitalism."[21]

---

19 See Sider, Wallis, and Blomberg previously cited in introduction. See further Ronald J. Sider, *The Scandal of the Evangelical Conscience: Why Are Christians Living Just Like the Rest of the World?* (Grand Rapids, MI: Baker, 2005); Jim Wallis, *God's Politics: Why the Right Gets It Wrong and the Left Doesn't Get It* (San Francisco: HarperCollins, 2005); Obery M. Hendricks, *The Politics of Jesus: Rediscovering the True Revolutionary Nature of the Teachings of Jesus and How They Have Been Corrupted* (New York: Doubleday, 2006); David P. Gushee, ed., *Toward a Just and Caring Society: Christian Responses to Poverty in America* (Grand Rapids, MI: Baker, 1999); and John Howard Yoder, *The Politics of Jesus*, 2nd ed. (Grand Rapids, MI: Eerdmans, 1994). In a work hard to classify, but which has major assumptions economically and theologically with which we cannot agree, John E. Stapleford, *Bulls Bears, and Golden Calves: Applying Christian Ethics in Economics* (Downers Grove, IL: InterVarsity Press, 2002), appears to be attempting some middle-of-the-road thinking.

20 Craig L. Blomberg, *Neither Poverty nor Riches* (Downers Grove, IL: InterVarsity Press, 1999), 238. The economic and political myopia of such posturing is unfortunately not confined to just a few radicals at the extreme left, but is becoming prevalent within evangelicalism, as Blomberg demonstrates. That Blomberg intends that his warnings be taken seriously by ordinary working American Christians is demonstrated later, when he opines, that "certain extremes of wealth and poverty are inherently intolerable," that those of us who have what he calls "excess income (*i.e.*, most readers of this book!)" are obligated to go beyond what we are apparently now doing in paying nearly forty percent of our incomes in taxes and levees in addition to our tithes and offerings to "help at least a few of the desperately needy in our world" (247). Lest we misunderstand his meaning, at this point in a footnote (2) he quotes David Murchie: "From the NT perspective, Christians may serve only as conduits by which God's gracious material provision is equitably distributed to the world." "The New Testament View of Wealth Accumulation," *Journal of the Evangelical Theological Society* 21 (1978): 343. The key phrase there is "equitably distributed." We would like to see a little more definition. Finally, Blomberg advocates that we support the minimum wage, boycott Nike because it hires people in other countries for much less than they would pay here, that we "divest ourselves of our unused or unnecessary possessions," believe a thoroughly uninformed "study" that purports to demonstrate that Christian tithing could eliminate worldwide poverty, and in a note suggests that it is difficult to label "any as truly 'worthy poor.'" *Neither Poverty nor Riches*, 252, 252n6. More on this "study" in chap. 28, the final chapter of this book.

21 Blomberg, *Neither Poverty nor Riches*, 238.

Awaiting the City

The dynamics of domestic politics and external challenges are further brought home to working people (as opposed to the idle "rich") by the ebb and flow of the financial markets. Never before in American history have so many individual working families been so affected by events on Wall Street. The "new investor class" has had its appetite whetted for making profits from disposable income and is not likely to simply go away, especially in light of the failure of government to "fix" such promised entitlement programs as Social Security and the constant drumbeat of warning that all must learn to be responsible for their own future in old age. Further, political realities are apt to make this new class of investor a *target* for manipulation and exploitation. How can "soccer moms," single parents, baby boomers, senior citizens, GenXers, blue and white collar workers, bankers, lawyers—in short, every conceivable constituency—respond to the need for ethical processes to assure that the playing field is level for all?

In 1929 bankers and financial officers and Wall Street professionals were the primary victims of the October Crash, though we have noted the beginning involvement of working-class Americans. The great American masses were not affected until the banks began to fail, factories were closed and workers were laid off, and farms and businesses were repossessed. Today's stock market swoon immediately impacts Main Street America. Dishonesty and greed along with lust and covetousness have immediate impacts that force more people than ever before to contemplate what's right and wrong. Even more, the constant onslaught of condemnations of Western civilization in the media and through the public school system demand an answer.

The following chapters are designed to facilitate that contemplation by addressing specific issues in the marketplace of political economics in the twenty-first century.

Awaiting the City

Chapter 24

The Morality of Market Economics

"The free society is an experiment, not a guarantee."[1]
Michael Novak

THE SHEER SUCCESS AND POWER of free-market economics, popularly labeled "capitalism," is no longer seriously debated. At no time in human history on this planet have so *many* benefited so much from so *little* labor and toil than in the past 250 to 300 years. However, utilitarian success cannot in itself settle the moral questions raised by its motives, goals, methods, and unintended consequences. Those are the issues we will now address.

FREE MARKET ECONOMICS

As we have previously noted, the conceptual origin of free-market thinking is largely the original work of one man, Adam Smith, whose *Wealth of Nations* appeared in 1776.[2] Prior to that time (from about the fifteenth to the eigh-

---

1   Michael Novak, *The Catholic Ethic and the Spirit of Capitalism* (New York: Free Press, 1993), 86. For further Catholic perspectives, see Thomas E. Woods Jr., *The Church and the Market: A Catholic Defense of the Free Economy*, Studies in Ethics and Economics (Lanham, MD: Lexington Books, 2005).
2   Novak has noted on Smith that he wrote his treatise with the motivation that for the first time in history there was available a means of alleviating massive poverty in the world. See Michael Novak, *Business as a Calling: Work and the Examined Life* (New York: Free Press, 1996), 66. He also attributes this motivation to Hume's work of the same time period. Although the ideas Smith put together were anticipated by other thinkers (particularly by

teenth century) the predominant economic system, if such it can be called, was a nationalistic and imperialistic hodgepodge of mostly state-dominated processes that Smith labeled "mercantilism."[3] That "system," as we have documented, was based on the idea that there was a finite amount of wealth in the world and the more one acquired, the less others must have. The primary locus of wealth was believed to consist in commodities, scarce metals, and mineral stores, to be found in the ground or in the possession of others. Thus, the wealth of a nation or people group was built up by making sure the income was greater than the outflow of these goods, an idea that naturally took a dim view of free and unrestricted trade. The management of this situation was commandeered by governments, mostly monarchical on the European Continent and parliamentarian after 1688 in England, whose job was thought to be, in the economic sphere, to make sure the balance of trade went the right direction. This meant government management by monopoly licensing to individuals and groups charged with the acquiring of goods, especially precious metals, called bullion or specie. The accumulation of *specie* was the goal of successful economics and those engaged in this business were handsomely rewarded and came from lordly and aristocratic classes.

As we have noted under such a system there was very little if any mobility socially, politically, or economically unless one came upon the opportunity to engage in such business through acquiring influence in the halls of government. In fact, this economic philosophy led to controlling power being brokered throughout the society, as it permitted little if any movement between stations in life, villages or cities, or occupations, crafts, common labors, or agrarian pursuits. Systems of *licensing* and *guilds* made sure no disruptions occurred in the relative number of participants in any of the various endeavors of economic life, and it was quite often necessary to have approval from government to move about the land or country or from village to village. This system was mostly static in terms of development, and encouraged little, if any, individual effort or innovation. There

---

Catholic Scholastics; see chap. 10, note 3, and chap. 11), his originality was in articulating these ideas in the way he did and when he did, the result of which was remarkable (see discussion of Smith in chap. 15).

3   But see Rondo Cameron and Larry Neal, *A Concise Economic History of the World: From Paleolithic Times to the Present*, 4th ed. (New York: Oxford University Press, 2003), for corrective analysis.

was change and progress to be sure, but the process was so slow that one might not typically notice it through a single lifetime. Such a situation is understandable when it is noted that about eighty percent of the population was required to be at work in food-production pursuits for the societies to feed themselves.[4]

This modified stasis was the condition of humankind economically from the time of civilization's rise in Mesopotamia till near the close of the eighteenth century. "Feudalism," a term used to describe medieval societies, though now disputed in its usefulness, had reigned in the West since the demise of Roman culture and civilization from ca. A.D. 600 till about the fifteenth century as the military means of societal control and domination. "Manorialism," the underlying economic arrangement of the period had dominated since the late Roman Empire—a system whereby lands were ruled by lords,[5] with peasantry bound to the land for life as servant/slaves (our terminology) with no prospects for the future. Secular government, the Roman Church, and aristocratic elites who had land holdings dominated politically, culturally, and economically throughout the states of Europe. Interestingly, the church was the *largest single* landholder during this period, with its own manors, and was consequently perhaps the strongest player in the economics of the period. At the least it was the strongest counter and/or ally to government in the accumulation and distribution of wealth and economic development and power.

Forms of modified "capitalistic" enterprise had appeared already (as we document elsewhere) in the work of the monasteries and the banking and trading activities centered in northern Italy, primarily traveling merchant activity providing trade goods from the Orient to European destinations. Rodney Stark and Michael Novak have made a strong case for the preindustrial development among Catholic clergy-related enterprise, and numerous studies have now made the case that the Middle Ages and the Scholastic period was not the "Dark Ages" (a calumny fostered by the writings of "Enlightenment"

---

4   See discussion of these phenomena in Joyce Appleby, *The Relentless Revolution: A History of Capitalism* (New York: W. W. Norton, 2010), esp. Kindle loc. 109–17.

5   "No land without a lord, no lord without a land." Cameron and Neal, *Concise Economic History of the World*, 45. See also now Deirdre N. McCloskey, *Bourgeois Dignity: Why Economics Can't Explain the Modern World* (Chicago: University of Chicago Press, 2010), for volume 2 of several in her ongoing update to Adam Smith.

Awaiting the City

philosophers, politicians, and "scientists").[6] This same period saw the rise of capitalistic thought and activity in the Islamic world as well.[7]

However, at no time during the millennia from the time of Sumerian civilization till the time of the American and French revolutions did the average economic state of the human race change substantially. The very rich have always been there, and the destitute have always been there, each at their respective end of the spectrum. In between has almost always been a vast percentage of the population that lived at or near subsistence levels or at risk almost daily of returning to that level. At no time did the general population look forward to a secure future or one in which the family/clan might actually rise above its station in life economically, culturally, or politically.[8] The possibility that one might work hard, get an education, save, invest, and postpone spending so as to become "successful" in such a way as to pass to the next generation a substantial advantage or to move from one class of society to the next was virtually nil. This way of life would be considered normal to about ninety percent of the people who have lived on this earth between the cave and the Europe of the eighteenth century. People's lives were controlled more by war, pestilence, and famine than by any other factors when they were not being manipulated by local and area "government." Without access to modern

---

6   See Novak, *Catholic Ethic and the Spirit of Capitalism*, and Rodney Stark, *The Victory of Reason: How Christianity Led to Freedom, Capitalism, and Western Success* (New York: Random House, 2005). Thomas E. Woods Jr. has also produced a credible defense of Roman Catholic contributions to the development of capitalism in *How the Catholic Church Built Western Civilization* (Washington, DC: Regnery, 2005). Rodney Stark has also contributed toward identifying the false impressions created by the purveyors of "Dark Ages" accusations in *For the Glory of God: How Monotheism Led to Reformations, Science, Witch-Hunts and the End of Slavery* (Princeton, NJ: Princeton University Press, 2003).

7   See economist Arthur Laffer's crediting of Islamic economic thinker Ibn Khaldun with the original idea that fuels "supply-side" economics, as cited in Abdul Azim Islahi, "Ibn Khaldun's Theory of Taxation and Its Relevance Today" (paper, Conference on Ibn Khaldun, Madrid, Spain, November 3–5, 2006), 17, 22n4, http://www.uned.es/congreso-ibn-khaldun/ponencia.htm.

8   See esp. Gregory Clark, *A Farewell to Alms: A Brief Economic History of the World* (Princeton, NJ: Princeton University Press, 2008), on this subject, and see Appleby, *Relentless Revolution*, and McCloskey, *Bourgeois Dignity* and Deirdre N. McCloskey, *Bourgeois Virtues* (Chicago: University of Chicago Press, 2006), on the huge development of worldwide wealth in the past three hundred years. McCloskey documents at length that Switzerland has the highest comparative wealth, calculated at more than thirty times the per capita accumulation and use of goods compared to the millennia that led up to the massive change. The average in the world is on the order of sixteen times the previous value.

Awaiting the City

sanitation, medical care, adequate food, and clean housing, average life spans
hovered around twenty-five to thirty years, a figure heavily distorted by the
widespread instance of infant and youth mortality and the ravages of war and
plague. This has changed *suddenly*, by comparison to the millennia that led up
to it, and *outrageously*, to use a term loaded with secondary meaning, as our
sources document.

The sudden nature of the change that ensued at the end of the eighteenth
century can be seen in the graph found in the appendix.[9] In the short span of
less than two and a half centuries, man's lot on average has ascended from little
above the cave to walking on the moon and returning safely while broadcast-
ing the achievement to hundreds of millions on planet earth even at the moment it is happening. More dramatically, it is only sixty-six years from Kitty
Hawk to the moon. With such massive disruption of the seemingly "natural"
course of events by "unnatural" forces, it is not so surprising that *criticism*,
both secular and religious, should arise. Previous chapters have documented
the give-and-take, both secular and religious, on this subject. Are human beings themselves or their environment to blame for the inequality and apparent
unfairness of economic life in a world that changes so fast? Is the "problem"
moral or political or economic or all of the above?

As we have seen, much of the criticism of the rapid changes that began to
overtake the Western world arose out of the romantic age conception of chivalry
and duty and the divine right of kings and the lordship of the Roman Catholic
Church. Suddenly the pace of change overtook the generations in such a way
that one could see significant movement and displacement in a *single* lifetime,
with attendant breakdowns in cultural norms and expectations. Displacement
of families and individuals from their expected roles and obligations by economic events (what Schumpeter has labeled "creative destruction")[10] seemed
somehow immoral. Intellectuals, as they have since the time of Aristotle, saw
in themselves and their thinking, wisdom above that of the masses that could

---

9 Clark, *Farewell to Alms*, 2. See appendix for Clark's graph and our explanation.
10 Joseph A. Schumpeter, *History of Economic Analysis*, rev. ed. (1954; New York: Oxford
   University Press, 1994). See also our discussion of Schumpeter in chap. 19.

Awaiting the City

interpret and accurately critique these events.[11] The culture of merchant and shopkeeping life that developed, labeled *bourgeois* by its intellectual despisers, was seen as the enslaver of the working masses, the proletariat. Marx despised these *proles* he sought to lead in revolution and simply advised manipulating them for their own good and governmental power, a mark of Marxist thought into the twentieth century.[12] Some like Dickens could actually see the nature of true evil and the personal nature of true charity, while *deploring* the conditions in the cities of England and looking expectantly for a hoped-for *conversion* in humanity to bring order and good out of apparent chaos.[13] Dostoyevsky seems to have *despaired* in his conception of evil as predominating over a hopeless landscape, or so it seemed to him. Others had a vision of Christian *charity* as the way to ameliorate the condition of the poor through immediate relief efforts, education, and moral reform. Marvin Olasky has brilliantly told the story of the course of these kinds of efforts in the United States.[14] Fogel has traced it through its attachment to religious awakening periods as he sees them having developed over almost three hundred years.[15] Both note that what was once a private, primarily religious, movement(s), has become a *societal* commitment to some form of egalitarian justice with mixed results in its actual effects.

Social Justice and Economic Decision-Making

According to some, the term *social justice* was invented by critics of capitalism to circumvent the normal discussion of justice. Political commentator and

---

11 For a fully accessible study of this subject, see Thomas Sowell, *Intellectuals and Society* (New York: Basic Books, 2009). Paul Johnson has also written well on this subject in his *Intellectuals: From Marx and Tolstoy to Sartre and Chomsky* (New York: HarperCollins, 2007).

12 See Mark Skousen, *The Making of Modern Economics*, 2nd ed. (Armonk, NY: M. E. Sharpe, 2009), 133–68, for biographical summary of Marx and his thought. This was the ideal for both Fidel Castro and Che Guevara. One must use whatever means to gather the unthinking masses into a controllable movement.

13 See Charles Dickens, *A Christmas Carol* (London: Chapman & Hall, 1843).

14 Marvin Olasky, *The Tragedy of American Compassion* (Wheaton, IL: Crossway, 1992). Also, see his call for a renewal of private effort in Marvin Olasky, *Renewing American Compassion: How Compassion for the Needy Can Turn Citizens into Heroes* (Washington, DC: Regnery, 1997).

15 Robert W. Fogel, *The Fourth Great Awakening and the Future of Egalitarianism* (Chicago: University of Chicago, 2000).

leading architect of neoconservatism Irving Kristol argued that if the question is whether capitalism is compatible with social justice, the answer must be "no." This is because the term can only and has only been defined in such a way as to *exclude* the particular type of justice implied in free-market exchanges labeled as "capitalism" by its critics, the first of which was Karl Marx. As the term is used today, Kristol said, it can only be defined with an overwhelmingly *egalitarian* and *authoritarian* thrust.[16] Kristol is probably referring to Friedrich Hayek's contention that the term cannot refer in any way to personal justice, and society cannot be held accountable for such an ideal.[17]

The term *social justice*, though possibly as old as the mid-nineteenth century[18] appears to have been introduced in a formal sense (thus, "canonized," as Hayek noted) in 1931 by Pope Pius XI in an encyclical, addressing conditions as he saw them in Europe between the two great wars. Prior to this time, Rousseau had spoken for the French revolutionists, insisting that human beings in their natural and pure state did not produce societal injustice, rather society imposed this upon them such that society's reform must *precede* the reform of humanity itself.[19] The Methodist statement of its "Social Creed" in 1908 called for "equal rights and complete justice for all men" and may be the first usage of "justice" in this context.[20]

Typically, the public conception of social justice is that it is something imposed by the *state* that produces something like a "common good." In this form it resembles what Novak has called a "rock skipping across the pond" of history.[21] Wherever it settles, it emboldens and empowers the state to impose its own vision. The *state* is that entity or those entities within the confines of a geographical location that makes and enforces laws upon the people of the

---

16 Cited in Ronald H. Nash, *Social Justice and the Christian Church* (Milford, MI: Mott Media, 1983), 111–13.

17 See our discussion of justice as a theological and biblical idea in part 1, esp. chaps. 3 and 5; and for his general argument, see F. A. Hayek, *The Fatal Conceit: The Errors of Socialism*, Collected Works of F. A. Hayek 1, ed. W. W. Bartley III (Chicago: University of Chicago Press, 1991..

18 See Novak, *Catholic Ethic and the Spirit of Capitalism*, 62–69, for background. See Friedrich Hayek, *The Road to Serfdom*, 50th anniversary ed. (1944; Chicago: University of Chicago Press, 1994), esp. chap. 8, "Who, Whom?";

19 This is the general contention of the "social gospel" of the early twentieth century.

20 Fogel, *Fourth Great Awakening*, 124.

21 Novak, *Catholic Ethic and the Spirit of Capitalism*, 69.

Awaiting the City

society with coercive force. It may have merely received such power from the machinations of society, but it is not the same as the society. The *society* may have certain coercive pressures and measures in its own operations, but it is not the same thing as the state. Societies are *voluntary* in their essential makeup, but they do become coercive under certain conditions of cultural domination by received opinions and ideas. The state under these conditions must of course "allow" or condone such situations. Societies are the entities that in the West have formed "states" to do their bidding through elective politics and have increasingly become the instruments of what is widely called "social justice." Michael Novak has contended for a three-pronged approach forging a balance among economic, governmental, and cultural institutions.[22] This is essentially the model used by economists Victor Claar and Robin Klay as well.[23]

Pope Pius specifically denied that the state through socialistic methods could be trusted to produce what he was calling social justice. *Statism* is the term that describes the condition or mind-set of a society increasingly looking to the state's coercive force to accomplish the perceived "good" (now being denominated "social justice") of all society. This is the distinction to be drawn between Babylon and the Beast in the book of Revelation. The adulterated society gives its power and consent to the Beast, who proceeds to subject all things and people to his will by coercion and deception. *All* statist thinking tends to such *totalitarianism*. The dedicated statist tends to see the state as an end in itself. Hegel *deified* the state. Marx looked for a time when this would not be necessary, but his vision depended upon the development (evolution) of a new man. Prior to that, in Marx's view, is the dictatorship of the proletariat through the *imposition* of totalitarian elite rule with the explicit disrespect for the ability of the nonelite intellectual classes (businessmen and workers) to make their own decisions. This is the heart and soul of "Progressivism" as we have outlined it in this book.

Many gravitate politically to this model because of the desire to exercise power over others, and this is the quickest way to that end. Some are merely

---

22 Michael Novak, *The Spirit of Democratic Capitalism*, 2nd ed. (Lanham, MD: Madison, 1991).

23 Victor V. Claar and Robin J. Klay, *Economics in Christian Perspective* (Downers Grove, IL: InterVarsity Press, 2007).

meddlesome in the affairs of their fellows out of an exaggerated sense of their own ability to see what is best for everyone.[24] Others believe that humanitarian considerations demand that the state be involved in coercive activities to accomplish goals for "the common good" or some other notion tied to the social justice terminology. Their defense of such activities is that one cannot truly be free without "power" to possess desired ends, economic and social (the definition of "democracy" in the progressivist lexicon). Therefore, so long as any are unable to accomplish their preferred life desires and goals (often loosely defined as "need"), there is no real freedom. In the early days of the twentieth century the conviction that societal evils causing poverty led to the moral degradation of the cities, especially in the slums, forced many social gospelers to seek state action as a corrective to produce egalitarian outcomes. We delineated this development in previous chapters (see chaps. 17–21).

Nonstatist thinkers counter that the evil that people do to one another is *more than* economic and cultural and tends to *intensify* wherever coercive power is concentrated.[25] Thus, human beings are most free when they are *not coerced* by such power. The use of coercive power is not perfectible because human nature and society are not perfectible. In fact, Lord John Acton's axiom that "[p]ower tends to corrupt, and absolute power corrupts absolutely" is nearer the truth. In such a circumstance, rewards and distributions will no longer be based on economic merit or even moral merit[26] but political merit, that is, service to the state (bring on 666). We contend that statist "solutions" invariably lead to loss of "power" for the masses of the people and accumulation in the hands of *coercive elites* that exploit group disparities to their own advantage. Furthermore, the failure of the state actually to do what only it can do well, which is to prevent the violence men and women do to one another, results in the injustice that the Bible condemns.

---

24 Think here of your own neighborhood or local church "busybody," only now with the money and power to do real damage.

25 Refer to our previous interaction with Thomas Sowell, *A Conflict of Visions: Ideological Origins of Political Struggles*, rev. ed. (New York: Basic Books, 2007), The statist position reflects the unconstrained vision, the attempt to coerce an outcome no matter the cost because the outcome is preferable to those in the ruling elite. The position we are espousing is the constrained vision.

26 This is a favorite category of the Left denoting the superiority of one way of making a living over another, as in such assertions as "It's immoral for football players to make millions more than university professors."

Awaiting the City

The Market for Power

Power itself, whether seen as authority to act or the force with which action is carried out, is a *commodity*, of course, that has trade value in any kind of market, be it strictly monetary or otherwise denominated. Human relationships, whether individual or societal, being what they are, as concentrations of power tend to have the highest "value" to those most enslaved by the human situation of depravity. Commodities such as *ideas*, or ideals, require *power* to execute their ends. It is no accident that Hegelian ideals such as the Superman awaited a concentration of power capable of putting them into practice. Only a political entity such as the German Reich was capable of translating an *idea* into rolling boxcars of human cargo and crematoria capable of exterminating six million human beings. Those who glibly call for governmental answers to human societal problems seem unaware of this kind of market where the exchange medium is power. There are no records of monopoly *businesses* intentionally exterminating whole *ethnic groups*, but the record of monstrous slaughter of millions waited till the twentieth century allowed the accumulation of totalitarian power in a few hands that willingly sent upwards of 100 million people to early and horrible deaths, not to mention gruesome torture and starvation. All this was done in the name of *social reform*, the greater good of the many over the few, and the righting of economic wrongs (among others). In such a scenario, what are the lives of a few tens of millions? After all, you can't make an omelet without cracking some eggs. Historian Niall Ferguson[27] has documented the terrible toll in terms of human life and destruction of civilizations that attended both the rise of the welfare state and the increased economic volatility that came from governmental interference in markets that had been globalized by the British Empire prior to the year 1914 and warns of such a scenario as a possibility for the twenty-first century.

Still, some would point to an evil such as chattel *slavery* as the product of systemic economic violence that did not depend on political power to survive.

---

27 Niall Ferguson, *War of the World: Twentieth-Century Conflict and the Descent of the West* (New York: Penguin Books, 2006).

We counter that it is *only* political power that allows or stops such activity.[28] Chattel slavery is a violence between human beings that is unjust by definition and is one of the most legitimate places for governmental action. This most egregious of all economic evils originated in state imperialism and conquest and has been mankind's sorrow for millennia and across the whole world.[29] The failure of the American founders to *eliminate* this scourge from the continent at the outset simply proves the case. Slavery could not have existed as it did if *political power swaps* had not been the order of the day, rather than simple economic transactions.[30] It should never have existed in this country!

A number of studies have shown the economic disadvantage incurred by the South in protecting its "peculiar institution."[31] Strangely, strictly economic considerations probably would have eventually demanded the cessation of a system unable to compete efficiently with the industrialized North. It is possible to imagine a scenario arising that would have had the southern route for railroad building bring a new economy to the South, ending the dependency on slavery.[32] Stephen Douglas, however, was bound to seek the supremacy of economic interests in Illinois through governmental action and *curried favor* with the South to extend slavery into Kansas-Nebraska territory.[33] Consequently, moral and cultural failures in southern society were *ratified* by governmental action and extended the misery until political solutions

---

28 See Matthew Mason, *Slavery and Politics in the Early American Republic* (Chapel Hill: The University of North Carolina Press, 2006).

29 See esp. Thomas Sowell, *Race and Culture: A World View* (New York: Basic Books, 1994), 186–223. Also, Dinesh D'Souza, *The End of Racism* (New York: Free Press, 1995), 67–115.

30 See Robert P. Murphy, *The Politically Incorrect Guide to Capitalism* (Washington, DC: Regnery, 2007), 41–47, for argument and documentation that slavery required government to prop it up or it would have died on its own.

31 See Robert William Fogel and Stanley L. Engerman, *Time on the Cross: The Economics of American Negro Slavery* (1974; repr., New York: Norton, 1995), and Herbert G. Gutman, *Slavery and the Numbers Game: A Critique of Time on the Cross*, Blacks in the New World (1975; repr., Chicago: University of Illinois Press, 2003), for pros and cons on this subject.

32 This would have happened in the absence of the Kansas-Nebraska Act of 1854 that extended slavery into the new territories so that Stephen Douglas could argue persuasively for the northern route to connect the east-west portions of the United States. This was to Douglas' political benefit and the economic benefit of his constituents.

33 See Lewis E. Lehrman, *Lincoln at Peoria: The Turning Point; Getting Right with the Declaration of Independence* (Mechanicsburg, PA: Stackpole Books, 2008), Kindle loc. 984–1015, for a full discussion of this situation and its attendant political implications during this period.

Awaiting the City

failed and the catastrophic war ensued. The English, by contrast, found an economic solution that avoided war. This is perhaps the *one place* where a conjunction of societal activism and political action combined to produce actual justice without the fallout of destroying one person or group's rights for the sake of another's.[34]

The *myth* of the state as an *instrument* of social justice dies hard. The literature proving the massive failures of governmental economic maneuvering and the welfare state in the United States go back thirty to forty years.[35] The fact that governmental scandal is almost always found to be about currying favor with economic interests goes back almost to the founding of the country.[36] The Civil War was more about the economic implications of North-South competition than it was about slavery itself, and that is sad.[37] The fact that government itself through its bureaucracies is the *primary recipient* of welfare dollars through taxation is *undeniable*. The fact that minimum wage legislation *never* helps those it is touted to help while making them less employable at the higher wage, helping instead those receiving union wages based on the federally mandated wage minimum, is indisputable. The fact that "affordable housing" legislation leads to *ghettoization* in the short run followed by *gentrification* of blighted areas and skyrocketing land values is everywhere evident. The fact that governmental licensing procedures, such as that for taxicabs

---

34 See our earlier discussion in chap. 18 of Wilberforce and his efforts to abolish the slave trade in Britain and its colonies.

35 The most famous early critique comes from the Daniel Moynihan–led cabinet department report in 1965, which was widely panned as "racist." See *The Negro Family: The Case for National Action* (Washington, DC: US Government Printing Office, 1965), http://www.dol.gov/oasam/programs/history/webid-meynihan.htm. See also chap. 25, note 54.

36 For a discussion and documentation of the actual development formally of the "transfer society" idea (the presumption that some have the right to the wealth of others and may take it through governmental action), see Terry L. Anderson and Peter J. Hill, *The Birth of a Transfer Society* (1979; repr., Lanham, MD: University Press of America, 1989).

37 Even for the Northern soldiers, at the beginning of the war the cause célèbre for fighting was preserving the Union, but "The sentiment toward slavery among the Union soldiers began to change once they ventured south." David Goldfield, *America Aflame: How the Civil War Created a Nation* (New York: Bloomsbury, 2011), 246. They came to see that preserving the Union meant that they had "to first 'wipe [out] the institution' of slavery." "Enlisted soldier," Third Wisconsin, to *Wisconsin State Journal*, October 1861, near Harpers Ferry, Virginia, Quiner Papers, Reel 1, vol. 1, 179, quoted in Chandra Manning, *What This Cruel War Was Over: Soldiers, Slavery, and the Civil War* (New York: Alfred A. Knopf, 2007), 45, cited in Goldfield, *America Aflame*, 559n4.

Awaiting the City

in New York City, create markets that cannot be entered by anyone but the wealthy (e.g., "medallions" to run a cab in the City of New York are sold for over $600,000, and hot-dog vendorships for as much as $350,000) is common knowledge.[38] The fact that all this is widely known and documented, without resulting in changes of policy or advocacy of more workable and less oppressive actions, tends to make the case that *another agenda* is at work—an agenda motivated by lust for power and control over people's lives, and perhaps the long-standing *disdain* of intellectuals for businessmen in general. If the welfare state is the answer, exactly what was the question?[39]

Robert Fogel has concluded that "[d]espite the enormous gains in life expectancy, health, education and real income and the nineteen-fold increase in real income for the poor, the social gospelers' effort to reform human nature, to crush evil, and to create God's kingdom on earth through income redistribution has failed." He then quotes the famous remark of H. Richard Niebuhr that in this scheme, "A God without wrath brought men without sin into a kingdom without judgment through the ministrations of a Christ without a Cross."[40] Wayne Grudem may be onto something when he says, "[I]f the devil himself wanted to keep people created by God in the wretched bondage of lifelong poverty, it is hard to think of a better way he could do it

---

38 See on this the latest documentation from the Hoover Institution, Walter E. Williams, *Race and Economics: How Much Can Be Blamed on Discrimination?* (Stanford, CA: Hoover Institution Press, 2011), 62. Williams gives the history of this growth in the price from $60,000 to an individual price of $603,000 and a corporate price of $781,000.

39 A partial listing of sources on this paragraph includes Mona Charen, *Do-Gooders: How Liberals Hurt Those They Claim to Help (and the Rest of Us)* (New York: Penguin, 2004); Fogel, *Fourth Great Awakening*; Olasky, *Tragedy of American Compassion*; D'Souza, *End of Racism*; Walter E. Williams, *The State against Blacks*, Manhattan Institute for Policy Research (New York: McGraw Hill, 1982); Walter E. Williams, *Race and Economics*; Thomas Sowell, with Lynn D. Collins, *American Ethnic Groups* (Washington, DC: Urban Institute, 1978); Thomas Sowell, *Affirmative Action Around the World* (New Haven, CT: Yale University Press, 2004); Charles Murray, *Losing Ground: American Social Policy 1950–1980* (New York: Basic Books, 1984); George Gilder, *Wealth and Poverty*, new ed. (1981; Washington, DC: Regnery, 2012); Martin Fridson, *Unwarranted Intrusions: The Case against Government Intervention in the Marketplace* (Hoboken, NJ: John Wiley & Sons, 2006); David W. Hall, ed., *Welfare Reformed: A Compassionate Approach* (Phillipsburg, NJ: P&R, 1994); Charles M. North and Bob Smietana, *Good Intentions: Nine Hot-Button Issues Viewed through the Eyes of Faith* (Chicago: Moody, 2008); Charles Murray, *In Our Hands: A Plan to Replace the Welfare State* (Washington, DC: AEI Press, 2006).

40 Fogel, *Fourth Great Awakening*, 171.

Awaiting the City

than to make people think that business is fundamentally evil, so they would avoid entering into it or would oppose it at every turn. And so I suspect that a profoundly negative attitude toward business in itself—not toward distortions and abuses, but toward business activity in itself—is ultimately a lie of the Enemy who wants to keep God's people from fulfilling his purposes."[41] The market that sells and buys the right to exercise political and military power is the most *seductive* of all, for on it the greatest *fortunes* in the history of mankind have been and are built. From such lofty heights come the delusions of godlike wisdom and beastly superiority to the hoi polloi of the streets and countryside.[42]

A clear corollary to this statist preference is that personal and nongovernmental charity becomes superfluous in the minds of many and noxious to others. After all, "charity" is demeaning and implies lack of just desert on the part of the recipient. This means that the biblical idea of communal and individual care and charity must be subsumed into political activism. Righteous or "good" deeds now become *political* deeds. Hence Jim Wallis and others can argue that governmental budgets are *moral documents* in state capitals around the country and in Washington, DC.[43] Given his premise, not a biblical one, it is not hard to see how he could come to such a conclusion. We need a corrective.

The System as We Know It

As noted earlier, the term *capitalism* was used pejoratively first by Karl Marx to describe what he saw in the industrialization of Europe and the opening of markets to disburse mass goods through *specialization* of labor skills and the *accumulation* of monetary and other "capital" for investment in enterprises

---

41 Wayne Grudem, *Business for the Glory of God: The Bible's Teaching on the Moral Goodness of Business* (Wheaton, IL: Crossway, 2003), 82–83.

42 For a view and documentation on the manner in which big government colludes with big business, see Timothy P. Carney, *The Big Ripoff: How Big Business and Big Government Steal Your Money* (Hoboken, NJ: John Wiley & Sons, 2006).

43 Restating this option as a "right" does not make it so. The Bill of Rights in our Constitution enumerates nothing that will cost another to provide. A "right" to food, shelter, health care or any other commodity implies someone else will pay for it. This is not a "right," it is charity.

for profit. Marx himself was not drawing his conclusions from observations formed in the Gilded Age of the great American industrialists but rather from what he called the bourgeoisie, the middle-class businessmen, "shopkeepers."[44] His alleged concern was for the proletariat, the workers, whom he supposed were being exploited by the other classes, since it was the workers in his theory of labor that actually produced "surplus wealth."

Since that time, the word *capitalism* has been used to describe any market system that is deemed to be "free" from outside interference. The term serves very little purpose in current discussions except when describing theoretical models. The reason is that *no* known system is truly free from outside interference. The issue is the *degree* and *kind* of such interference. In fact, the term *market system*, which is supposed to distinguish capitalistic from socialistic systems is a misnomer. Socialism is a market system. It just has a different unit of exchange and different rules for making exchanges, but it is a market system nonetheless. It is a political market system that trades in *influence peddling* for the profit of power and position and from these positions of power controls to its own advantage the goods that economic markets trade through the medium of money or its equivalents. This kind of market system justifies itself as having altruistic interest only in the "common good."

Such a system, however, we submit is as "capitalistic" as any supposed free-market economic system, because it relies on the accumulation of capital for the purpose of investment to the profit of the investor. The capital need not be monetary or concrete, but it is capital to be spent in the right place and at the right time to the maximum advantage of the dispenser. The old Soviet Union is just the most fully developed of such a system where the aristocrats of the party *never* stood in bread lines or huddled around a single stove in a freezing apartment or starved in the countryside while famine swept the Siberian wastes. The black market in necessities and the finest luxury goods never ceased to function for the Communist Party elite. But the common people were subjected to the most *demeaning* lives imaginable and the most outra-

---

44 It was Napoleon who seems to have coined the phrase "nation of shopkeepers" to refer to the British disdainfully.

Awaiting the City

geous atrocities, all in the name of the "common good."[45] At the end of *this type* of capitalistic market system there is always in human history some form of gulag for those who long for freedom from its enslavement.[46]

Equally as perverse is the *supposed* opposition to the Soviet model, which was known in the last century as Fascism. We have previously noted its development as a political "alternative" to communist ascendancy in Europe. Unfortunately, the language of our time has been *corrupted* to the point that "fascist" has become a designation for any defense of the free-market system that seeks to maintain freedom for individual and corporate economic action from governmental interference. Far from a correct rendering of history and political philosophy, this designation and use of the language is one of *gross distortion*, as we have already discussed. Rather the *collusion* of government and business for direction of the economy at the expense of free markets *is* the common denominator of fascist philosophy. The gradual descent of the American system into fascist experimentation[47] has led in our day to multiplied thousands of well-paid lobbyists at the seat of national government vying for a place at the table, lest they be "on the menu."

---

45 This is clearly not unlike the refusal of American political elites to subject themselves to the vagaries of social security, the failure of the DC public school system, the onerous future likely to occur under Obamacare, and many other federally mandated intrusions into the lives of ordinary citizens.

46 Alexander I. Solzhenitsyn, *The Gulag Archipelago, 1918–1956: An Experiment in Literary Investigation*, 3 vols., trans. Thomas P. Whitney (vols. 1–2) and Harry Willetts (vol. 3), Harper Perennial Modern Classics (1973–78; repr., New York: HarperCollins, 2007).

47 From Teddy Roosevelt's tinkering with the economy and the courts, to Wilson's attempts to bring in a modified Hegelian understanding of the state, to FDR's entitlement reforms and attempts to overrun the Supreme Court, to LBJ's massive buildup of the welfare system, to Obamacare, all of these are clearly *fascist* undertakings in the *classical* meaning of that word (though not in the sense that it has come down to us in the late twentieth century). In Goldberg's words, "Conservatives are the more authentic classical liberals [in terms of political economy], while many so-called liberals are 'friendly' fascists." Jonah Goldberg, *Liberal Fascism: The Secret History of the American Left from Mussolini to the Politics of Meaning* (New York: Doubleday, 2006), 8. A heavy-handed federal government, at the behest of the executive branch, took to itself previously unprecedented powers in order to accomplish its objective, over the protests, usually, of the majority of Americans. That some aspects of these legislative maneuvers are justifiable is likely the case. It is often the *manner* in which they was adopted and enforced that is problematic, Obamacare being the clearest example. "Fascism is a religion of the state.... It takes responsibility for all aspects of life, including our health and well-being, and seeks to impose uniformity of thought and action, whether by force or through regulation and social pressure." Ibid., 23.

Awaiting the City

Some will now argue that these aberrations (Soviet Communism and German Nazism) are but extreme examples of what promises to be adaptable to more benign uses in the hands of "Social Democrats." Some form of this designation is attached to most attempts to concentrate capital in political power for the purpose of manipulating people and their business lives in such a way as to achieve the "common good." The idea here is to create competing factions that engage in partisan politics to gain the biggest piece of the capital accumulation of the society in which they live. Today there are roughly 35,000 registered lobbyists in the United States (working primarily in Washington, DC, offices) representing competing factions to cut up the economic, political, tax, and regulative pie.[48] This is how any society with democratic institutions in the place of dictatorships and totalitarianism is presumed to work. "The people" now are allowed to decide their fate through elective politics and petitioning their representatives. In functioning models outside the United States this results in coalition governments based on the trade-offs of otherwise oppositional factions who form "governments" headed by leaders chosen from among the factions or elected by the people at large. The *trades* in these cases are the political market. The *capital* hoarded is the ability to influence other factions to support one's own partisan interests, which translate to the private interests of the constituency represented.

In the United States two-party system there is simply one party of winners and one party of losers. In the legislative branch the party that has the most seats in each house controls all the committees that manage and bring to a vote any part of its agenda. Without power the losing party must content itself with only modifying or slowing the process unless it has strength for a filibuster in the Senate. If the two houses are led by different parties, bills must be reconciled in a bipartisan conference in which trade-offs are made. If the houses of the legislature do not align with the president's party, he is forced to negotiate any agenda he wishes to advance through multiple layers of partisan interest groups that engage in trades for support on their own constituent issues. This is *also* a market that trades in power, position, and influence peddling, with requisite financial advantage and disadvantage. Only when the Congress and

---

48 Ibid., Kindle loc. 5525–41.

Awaiting the City

the president's party are fully aligned do we get what amounts to a green light for full implementation of a program. However, the whole process, regardless of its elective outcome is a market where political capital is spent to gain the right to dispense benefits in monetary or in-kind services (goods doled out that do not necessarily come in the form of a check or its equivalent) and burdens in the form of rules and regulation and especially taxation.

In the democratic West this form of market has come to dominate the scene even *more* than the strictly economic market. This system is rightly designated a political economy by Michael Burleigh and others in greater numbers recently.[49] Economists normally will ask you what you want most, knowing that trade-offs are always involved in a world where no one can have absolutely everything he or she wants in unlimited quantities. Rather, we must trade one "good" for another.

The politician will typically ask you what you want, period, implying an ability to deliver it without trade-offs. However, constituencies abound for every conceivable "interest" and group, and it is the politician's job to balance these *through trade-offs* so as to get elected again and again.[50] The term *special interest* is now used primarily and to designate the constituency of one's opponents pejoratively. "My opponent is guided by special interest groups, but of course, I am not." It is not that monetary considerations do not play a part in the corruption of the process. It is just that money is not the *primary* means of exchange.[51] It is one of the elements that form the capital of a politician. But influence, position, seniority, access, public perception, and a host of other factors come into play along with and even before the money. Trade-offs in

---

49 Michael Burleigh, *Earthly Powers: The Clash of Religion and Politics in Europe from the French Revolution to the Great War* (New York: HarperCollins, 2005).

50 The practice of this kind of economic politics is now increasingly labeled "crony capitalism." It usually stands in for another term, "corporate welfare." The language is dominated by the liberal media and left-leaning politicos who would never refer to "union welfare" or "movie-star welfare" or "big-media welfare," etc. We believe all constituencies are "cronies" and deserve to be treated with equal caution.

51 With the exception of a recent criminal debacle in Illinois. See Pete Williams, The Associated Press, and Reuters, "Feds: Governor Tried to 'Auction' Obama's Seat," NBC News.com, December 9, 2008, http://www.nbcnews.com/id/28139155/ns/politics/t/feds-governor-tried-auction-obamas-seat/#.UYp0bMoU1BB. Blagojevich was convicted and sentenced. See Michael Winter, "Blagojevich Guilty of Trying to Sell Obama's Old Senate Seat," USATODAY.com, June 27, 2011, http://content.usatoday.com/communities/on-deadline/post/2011/06/blagojevich-guilty/1#.UYp-w8oU1BB.

Awaiting the City

the "old boy system," as some call it, make this one of the most dynamic and influential markets on earth. In the United States, no life and especially no business is unaffected by it. As Goldberg opines, "This is one of the underappreciated consequences of the explosion of the size of government. So long as some firms are willing to prostitute themselves to Uncle Sam, every business feels the pressure to become a whore."[52] Blunt, but accurate!

Some Definitions

This discussion leads us to some definitions that fit the kind of system we deal with most often today. A *market* is formed anywhere among human beings where scarce commodities (that is, those that may not be held in unlimited amounts, no matter how large that amount may be) are voluntarily traded between partners to the trade process. This presupposes *no* violent coercive force is used—"violent" meaning fraudulent, confiscatory (theft), or acquisitive without the voluntary consent of both parties. *Governments* rightly exist to set the terms for such transactions in law and provide penalties for violation. In such situations it is presumed that parties make choices between what is being acquired and all other possible goods that might be made with the same exchange medium.

Capital is that accumulation of goods that include money and concrete items that might be traded or bartered for other goods, but it is not limited to such goods. Human capital is whatever one might bring to a market that might be traded for any good existing in the material realm. Such goods might be moral character traits that enhance trust and reputation, abilities or skills learned that enable productivity, sheer physical or mental strength that allow intensive labor and/or athletic achievement, educational achievement and knowledge accumulation, raw talent endowed through birth and environment, family history and connections, influence within certain circles of power and position, cultural dispositions that favor certain usages over others, etc. The list is almost endless.

Profit is the term that describes the *added value* any party to a market exchange attaches to the transaction subjectively. A valuation can be in the

---

52 Goldberg, *Liberal Fascism*, Kindle loc. 5510–25.

Awaiting the City

form of additions to the bottom line financially (this is the limited traditional definition of profit) or whatever form each party is using to find satisfaction in the exchange. This is the terminology Jesus is using when he asks what "profit" a man has if he "gains the whole world and loses his soul" (Matt. 16:26). In each situation the parties to voluntary exchange evaluate it in terms of their own values and desires at the time to determine if it has been profitable. In this sense the term "profit" is a *value judgment* attached to every transaction entered into voluntarily. If I am simply selling products to make a living, money is the bottom line in some ways, but it does not exclude my satisfaction in producing goods that enhance the lives of others, while allowing me to continue in business. At any time, I may decide that my *personal satisfaction* or my *moral standard* is a greater profit than a monetary bottom line, and I may decide to change my occupation. If I am buying a good, I have decided that there is more profit for me in acquiring whatever it is I buy, rather than holding on to the money, which I might have invested or saved for some other purpose. In each case the parties decide on the nature of the profit they seek and obtain. If each did not think they were *better off* from the exchange, they would not engage in it. This is true regardless of what any other nonparticipant in the transaction may think.

INTERVENTIONISM, COMPETITION, MONOPOLIES, AND THE BUSINESS CYCLE

Interventionism is the term that describes attempts to coerce behaviors in a market that are believed to produce some other good that might not otherwise be expected of a completely voluntary exchange. This is an activity of government generally, but in some parts of the world it might be exercised by gangs or other criminal types or by outside forces aligned one way or another with the different parties. Interventionism is the system under which virtually all supposedly capitalistic and free-market transactions take place today. *Laissez-faire* (noninterference) is *not* and *never* really has been a property of capitalistic free-market practice in the Western world. It is now used as a pejorative term to justify further interference in transactions that were already heavily regulated, protected, favored, penalized and/or taxed, or not taxed for a myriad of reasons settled by political means.

Awaiting the City

Because of the predominance of such interventionist policies by governing authorities, the *market of politics* has become the guiding marketplace. The recognition of this factor has caused the coining of the term *political economy* to describe what now dominates the economic thinking of the West. This is what we contend actually makes market economics or capitalism a "system." Laissez-faire economics is simply capitalistic markets working without *systematic interference*. Typically only pure Libertarianism now contends for the actual practice of laissez-faire economics either theoretically or practically. Consequently, the most invasive and powerful forces in the lives of ordinary people are governmental in *origin* and economic in *effect*. The real danger in this approach is that the government becomes the source and end of everything— the next thing to God. Increasingly it becomes the only agency that effectively assigns benefits and burdens across a society. It alone determines who wins and loses in transactions. And since governments never suffer business failure (go out of business) and since they hold the gun (the power to coerce compliance), the bottom line (profit) becomes *power* as opposed to money, although power inevitably leads to monetary gain, in this case the ability to tax and dispense it and take some "from the bag." Even so, most in the political and administrative process find far more capital gain and pleasure in the exercise of power and the attainment of position than in the acquisition of money.[53] This is hardly a choice that offers moral alternatives.

Economic systems do not differ from one another by the inclusion or exclusion of markets. Markets exist as a consequence of the necessity implied in human choices. The difference is in the nature of the *marketplace*. Does the market offer virtually unlimited choices, or does it seek to narrow the range of choices to certain continuums based on predetermined desired outcomes decided by *someone other* than those making exchanges through their choices? Seen another way, are the choices made by one elite group controlling the choices offered to nonelite groups? From another perspective, will the goods

---

53 But for the latest documentation of political insider-dealing for profit of serious monetary value, see Peter Schweizer, *Throw Then All Out: How Politicians and Their Friends Get Rich off Inside Stock Tips, Land Deals, and Cronyism That Would Send the Rest of Us to Prison* (New York: Houghton Mifflin Harcourt, 2011). This book prompted a segment on CBS's *60 Minutes* program and was followed by a typical congressional "quick fix" that promises no real solution to both parties' use of political power for heavyweight monetary gain.

Awaiting the City

exchanged be predominantly material, monetary, or political? The clear advantage of strictly economic choice-making is that it is not coercive and happens in a marketplace where someone else enforces predetermined rules and where parties that fail to obey the rules can be jailed and/or put out of business, or be otherwise forced to comply with the rules. When the government predominates, the rules do not apply and/or may be changed at any time for the convenience of whatever constituency has the ear of political power through whatever means has the greatest effect—public sentiment, direct lobbying, political contributions, *quid-pro-quo* wheeling and dealing, etc.[54] This is where the moral issue is to be settled. Why should it be thought more just or moral to deliver choice making to *interventionist* entities who are beset by the same moral failings as those whose fate they hold hostage to political considerations and pressure tactics?

Another criticism from the Christian moral perspective concerns this very process called "competition." The market system is flawed, they say, because it induces people to compete against their fellows rather than cooperate for communal good, thus further exacerbating the breakdown of true community. Once again the perception is wide of the mark in reality. Fundamental to the operation of efficient markets is the necessity of accurately and efficiently meeting the needs of others in a timely fashion. There will be no market absent these underlying principles. Consequently, the very nature of the competitive enterprise is to see how well one can follow these principles in order to meet the needs of others. This is a competitive situation to be sure, absent any coercive action, legal or illegal. However, it is not like two prizefighters in the ring seeking to knock one another out to win the jackpot. This is a place where the person who meets the *needs of others* best "wins" and in the process raises the level of effort of others to do the same.

Yes, some will be shown that they are not suited to the particular area of "competition" they have chosen, but this only gives them the information they need to seek out other ways to serve their fellows more efficiently. In this way the market encourages hard work, intelligence, attention to others' needs,

---

54 The only defense against such arbitrary rule is a written constitution interpreted according to original intent and not plasticized by calling it a "living" document—meaning we can interpret it as we see fit now in the middle of the game.

Awaiting the City

cooperation with those involved in the making and distribution of products, and combats human tendencies to self-satisfaction and a false sense of security. Even if the avaricious and greedy turn limited parts of the market into an opportunity to outcompete in such a way as to put some disliked competitor out of business and into another line of work, the only way they can do it is by *meeting the needs of others*, if they are held to the standard of noncoercive intervention. Furthermore, this competition, if left unsullied by governmental protectionist mechanisms, is a marvelous alternative to war, when cultures clash and understanding is weak. Surely it is far better to "compete" economically and learn about one another's needs and wants, and how to meet them, than to "compete" militarily. Arguably, this is what ended the Cold War of the last century and is marking the latest competition between Western democracies and Oriental empire builders (think China).

It is from the conjunction of politics, used primarily to eliminate unwanted and feared competition, and the human tendency to seek the easy way to prosperity and economic dominance that monopolies are built in the marketplace. While it is common to suppose that monopolies are one of the *primary reasons* for governmental intervention in the economic marketplace, it is a more accurate representation of the facts that the *opposite* is the case.[55] No business, however large, can monopolize a segment of the market, except narrowly and on a short-lived leash, without governmental assistance, either through protectionist or exclusionary regulation or taxation. The late nineteenth- and early twentieth-century industrialists charged with monopoly tactics were actually the products of misbegotten governmental interference, not the other way around. Protective trade tariffs, licensing regulations, price fixing, and preferential tax policy originate in "business" people who do not want to be subject to the open market but who wish rather to make government the means of protecting their favored status.[56] However, so long as

---

55 For a discussion of the entire subject of antitrust legal action and enforcement, see Robert H. Bork, *The Antitrust Paradox: A Policy at War with Itself*, 2nd ed. (New York: Free Press, 1993).

56 See Carney, *Big Ripoff*; Paul A. London, *The Competition Solution: The Bipartisan Secret behind American Prosperity* (Washington, DC: AEI Press, 2005); Burton W. Folsom Jr., *The Myth of the Robber Barons*, 6th ed. (1987; Herndon, VA: Young America's Foundation, 2010); H. W. Brands, *The Money Men: Capitalism, Democracy, and the Hundred Years' War Over the American Dollar*, Enterprise (New York: W. W. Norton, 2006); Charles R. Morris, *The Tycoons: How Andrew Carnegie, John D. Rockefeller, Jay Gould, and J. P. Morgan Invented the American Supereconomy*, Enterprise (New York: Henry Holt, 2005). A careful

government maintains a stance that truly leaves the market "open" to *all partici-pants*, no matter their origins, and uses its police power to punish *genuine* fraud and violence in the marketplace, monopolies cannot be maintained. The market has its own way of punishing the desire for relative stasis instead of innovation and change—it puts businesses out of business.

This factor is what leads to the collusion between labor and management in the protection of industries from competition. Since neither management nor labor prefers the "creative destruction" that comes from true competition, they tend to become partners in the use of government to exclude new businesses and new workers from entering their chosen fields of production. Consequently, the issue of whether government should be on the side of employer or employee is largely irrelevant in many industries. The more relevant issue is whether government should be on the side of those *seeking employment* and entry into business or of those *already established* and wishing to be *protected* from outside competition. This becomes particularly important morally when the losers may be destitute people in the underdeveloped world working in sugar, textiles, steel, agriculture, and other highly labor intensive areas of production. This very issue has been at the heart of repeated and heated debates over tariffs and free trade and regulation and deregulation and "tax incentives" (either in the form of rebates or deductions or direct subsidies) for various industries and segments of the economy in all Western democracies. Seldom is the real issue addressed: How can certain groups be *protected* from or *advantaged* over other individuals and groups who wish to have an open opportunity to compete for sales and innovative services? Such activity by interventionist government in Western democracies is rightly called "corporate welfare."

Misbegotten attempts to control the business cycle also play a large role in the justification of governmental interventionism. Market-based economies depend on *supply and demand* and pricing to determine the most efficient, and ultimately the most "just," distribution of goods and services to the widest number of people. They are subject to time lags between demand build up and supply availability and to the monetary system, which provides financing to

---

reading of current biographical materials of this period in American history will show that it was the attempts to curry governmental favor that led to monopolist evils.

Awaiting the City

suppliers and manufacturers and over the years increasingly to buyers as well. Not only is timing a factor, but a number of other elements determine whether buyers and sellers arrive in the market felicitously so as to promote prosperity widely and meet the needs and desires of the most the most efficiently. New products can overturn prior expectations about what is needed. Weather phenomena can disrupt expected supplies catastrophically or seasonally. War in one part of the world can affect events in other parts of the world. Epidemics can force allocation of resources to unforeseen emergencies. The mood of consumers can affect willingness to buy one thing over another based on events in the world or faddish whims. All these calculations, and more, enter economic situations and change them from season to season and year to year as producers and sellers attempt to exercise prescience. This will cause fluctuations in the cycle of the *realization* of need (demand) and the *provision* for the need (supply). In its simplest form, this is called the *business cycle*, and it is recognized and regulated by the *pricing mechanism*. The catchall term for the calculation of these factors is *risk assessment* on which we will comment elsewhere.

What we have not mentioned, of course, is the "boom-and-bust" nature of the cycle, which began in the West as market-based economies began to experience the incredible growth of economic prosperity brought on by industrialization and the creation of a consumer-oriented society. Prior to that time, the primary societal economic upheavals had been demographic swings caused by epidemics and wars and famines, which were the result of failure to grow food or drought and the actions of governments manipulating the allocation of food supplies.[57] Ferguson is the latest to document the unprecedented economic power that is inherent in modern banking systems.[58] When capitalistic enterprises began to replace mercantilistic systems, banking and monetary policy became the lifeline of industrialization. Many studies con-

---

57 See Robert William Fogel, *The Escape from Hunger and Premature Death, 1700–2100* (Cambridge: Cambridge University Press, 2004); Clark, *Farewell to Alms*; Cameron and Neal, *Concise Economic History of the World*, et al. for discussion on this and analysis of which factors held sway at what times.

58 Niall Ferguson, *The Ascent of Money: A Financial History of the World* (New York: Penguin Books, 2008). He notes significantly that it is understanding how money works that accentuates the differences between people and businesses in their relative economic success. There is a disproportionate advantage to those who are able to take advantage of their knowledge of money. Ibid., Kindle loc. 209.

Awaiting the City

firm that boom-and-bust cycles are primarily created when monetary policy is allowed to distort and disrupt the market on a societal scale, creating misery and havoc up and down the scale of wealth and poverty and usually harming the poor the most in relative terms (that is, they have the least to lose without suffering starvation, homelessness, nakedness).[59]

Localized mistakes in the process of allocating supplies to meet demands efficiently (profitably) happen all the time in markets, but they are short lived and do not affect entire nations, or increasingly, the global community. It requires governmental manipulation of the cycle through monetary and banking policy set by central banking systems to bring about such rapid and painful shifts across nations and the world. They may also, when fairly and wisely administered, stabilize and minimize economic catastrophes. Arguably, all the great depressions (known also at times as "panics") and serious recessions of American history (1837, 1873, 1892, 1929, 1972, 1987, 2009) have been preceded by such periods of central interference that distorted credit markets and created artificial pressures on the pricing mechanism.[60] Quite often this has been exacerbated by political manipulation of industries and employment and pricing through tariff policy designed to protect an entrenched group at the expense of those wishing to enter the market. Indeed, the current ten-

---

59 See Thomas Sowell, *Housing Boom and Bust* (New York: Basic Books, 2009); Amity Shlaes, *The Forgotten Man: A New History of the Great Depression* (New York: HarperCollins, 2007); Burton Folsom Jr., *New Deal or Raw Deal: How FDR's Economic Legacy Has Damaged America* (New York: Simon & Schuster, 2008); Ronald H. Nash, *Poverty and Wealth: The Christian Debate Over Capitalism* (Westchester, IL: Crossway, 1986), 126–45. Also see our previous discussion of the Great Depression in chap. 20.

60 Note that sources vary in the years given for these recessions. For documentation in historical contexts, see Milton Friedman and Anna Jacobson Schwartz, *A Monetary History of the United States, 1867–1960*, Studies in Business Cycles 12 (Princeton, NJ: Princeton University Press, 1963). This is an academic work written for trained economists, making it less readable to a general audience. More readable summaries include Milton and Rose Friedman, "The Anatomy of Crisis," in *Free to Choose: A Personal Statement* (New York: Harcourt, 1990), 70–90; Milton Friedman, "A Summing Up," in *The Essence of Friedman*, ed. Kurt R. Leube (Stanford, CA: Hoover Institution Press, 1987), 676–700. Comparisons of United States and worldwide monetary issues are in Milton Friedman, *Money Mischief: Episodes in Monetary Policy* (New York: Harcourt Brace Jovanovich, 1992). Finally, for a convenient summary in short form, see Milton Friedman, *Why Government Is the Problem*, Essays in Public Policy 39 (Stanford, CA: Hoover Institution Press, 1993), which explains how various concentrated and dispersed interests combine and compete to produce a broken system.

dency of every presidential election in the United States to come down to "it's-the-economy-stupid" rhetoric fuels attempts to manipulate the cycle to one or the other party's advantage. The net effect is to make government both the problem and the "answer." No conception of justice or morality includes the idea that the entity that *causes* the problem in the first place gets to label *itself* dispenser of justice and morality when it repents and starts the same cycle again, while blaming the victims (businesses, investors, bankers, consumers) for the original problem.

MORALITY AND THE PRODUCTION OF WEALTH: ANSWERING SOME CHARGES

Does the Free Market Create Economic Suffering?

It is widely believed and disseminated among Statist advocates for social justice that the adverse conditions arising in the cities of Europe and the United States in the last two hundred years or so are the product of capitalistic market freedom.[61] Eighteenth-century diatribes and historical reviews of the past blaming the Industrial Revolution[62] for the appalling conditions in cities in England and Europe ignore the fact that such poverty had existed for millennia.[63] Ironically, it was Marx and Engels who noted that industrialization made it possible for millions to flee "the idiocy of rural life."[64] So it was not until the time of industrialization that such poverty became *concentrated* in cities instead of dispersed in the countryside. Only now was the problem more visible to large numbers of people and publicized accordingly. This transition period simply moved the problem, first across Europe and then into the cities of the United States, but it did not *cause* it.

---

61 For a book-length discussion of some of these charges and others from a Christian perspective, see Jay W. Richards, *Money, Greed, and God: Why Capitalism Is the Solution and Not the Problem* (New York: HarperOne, 2009). Richards has included lengthy analyses of a number of issues we must give only passing consideration here.

62 As we have noted before, even the term "Industrial Revolution" is problematic. Cameron and Neal, *Concise Economic History of the World*, 163–64.

63 See, for instance, Peter Ackroyd, *London: The Biography* (New York: Nan A. Talese, Doubleday, 2001), 55–58, 96, 100–103, 128–30.

64 Cited in Ferguson, *War of the World*, xxxvi.

Awaiting the City

In fact, government policies in England had as much to do with the living conditions of the poor as anything—tariffs on foreign lumber, taxes on windowed buildings and bricks, along with restrictions on interest rates, making it difficult to obtain financing for construction. Child labor was an answer to starvation, which had gone on in the countryside for ages. It was not until the industrialization of societies advanced that men were able to earn enough to support an entire family on their own.[65] The same situation applies in the underdeveloped world today, where "sweat shops" and "child labor" are a way out of poverty, not a consequence of globalization. Were it not for these opportunities, the "victims" would simply die of starvation and/or disease or be selling themselves on the streets for sexual favors and risking death from AIDS or other such dangers of life on the street.

The argument over the "exploitation" of labor ignores the fact that the worker, who produces products for sale from the invested capital of an employer, is likely willing to accept such an arrangement because of the mutual advantage it affords him. But it is the *employer* who assumes the risks of failure—inability to market and sell effectively the products manufactured, competitors' price strategies and product improvements, product defects, worker damages and injuries, economic disruptions caused by catastrophes, war, or sabotage, to name just a few. Likewise, the employer provides the tools for production, buys and transports the raw materials, packages and ships to market, and manages anything else that keeps the worker doing what he does best—producing the product—while paying the worker a wage based on his value-added contribution in advance of the sale and delivery of products. Even if workers were to provide their own tools for production, thus increasing their productivity at their own expense, they would not be accounting for the myriad other factors that turn raw materials into money, or whatever unit of exchange is being used. A worker is only justified in complaining of "excess profits" made by the employer on the workers' labor if the worker is also willing to suffer loss and failure (that is, accept risk) with the employer when these events happen, as they frequently do. It is no accident of history that wealthy

---

65 See Clark, and Cameron and Neal, cited in note 57, for discussions and documentation on this time period of industrial development.

Awaiting the City

labor unions with huge stores of capital and workers do not regularly (never) develop employee-owned businesses. It is also the reason that politicians do not rush to have "bailout" hearings when oil is twenty dollars per barrel, and drillers and oil companies take huge losses from their investments in exploration and research, and some just go out of business. It is only when those who take risks begin to cash in on their efforts that complaints and hearings take place over so-called price-gouging or "windfall profits." Some people will always be willing to assume the risks involved in developing a new product or enterprise or geographical location, and others will trade risk-taking for the security of fixed income and other values. There is nothing unjust in a system that allows such choices.[66]

Likewise, it is not just the capitalistic countries in the global economy that can be found "exploiting" the poorer countries and their workers. Socialistic countries have the same kinds of relationships in the global economy. Sometimes this criticism (of capitalism and the global market system) is equated with the old colonial system that began as mercantilistic (characterized by a concept of "money" as precious metals in coinage with the state as the primary possessor of wealth) enterprises that sought to exploit raw materials from regions that had very little else to offer. However, this argument ignores the fact that these regions were not made poor by capitalism. They were already poor in the first place, and those regions of the world that were the most associated with colonial empire building and "exploitation" are the most developed and well off in the current situation vis-à-vis the rest of the underdeveloped world. There is a net advantage in history to being "exploited" in such a way, whether that exploitation is justifiable or not.[67]

---

66 The primary reason Christians seem to be led astray on these matters is a failure to understand basic economics. See our prior citations for helpful guides to the nature of economic choices. Additionally, see Nash, *Poverty and Wealth*, and Samuel Gregg, *Economic Thinking for the Theologically Minded* (Lanham, MD: University Press of America, 2001).

67 The literature supporting our position on globalization is large and includes at least the following: Jeffry A. Frieden, *Global Capitalism: Its Fall and Rise in the Twentieth Century* (New York: W. W. Norton, 2006); Johan Norberg, *In Defense of Global Capitalism*, rev. ed., trans. Roger Tanner, with Julian Sanchez (Washington, DC: Cato Institute, 2005); Joseph E. Stiglitz, *Globalization and Its Discontents* (New York: W. W. Norton, 2002); Martin Wolf, *Why Globalization Works* (New Haven, CT: Yale University Press, 2004); and William Easterly, *The White Man's Burden: Why the West's Efforts to Aid the Rest Have Done So Much Ill and So Little Good* (New York: Penguin Books, 2006).

Awaiting the City

Does the Free Market Create Winners and Losers?

Those who charge that capitalism is based on pandering to selfishness, greed, ambition, and competitiveness fail to see the illogic of the charge. Such character traits are inherent in the human condition and will be there in any situation, economic or otherwise. It is the free market that tames rather than causes these vices. No one engaging in free exchange without fraud, theft, extortion, or some other form of violence can satisfy their greed or selfishness except by providing for the needs of someone else at an acceptable price that the other is willing to offer.[68] Criminal behavior is endemic to all human societies and is a matter for retributive justice and the law. Criminality is not, however, an inherent part of a free-market exchange of values. Absent the free market, the greed, selfishness, ambition, and competitiveness of fallen human nature will simply resort to other means to achieve its ends, and the only other avenues will be coercive—political and/or military. Free markets tame human desires and channel them to constructive purposes and raise the issue of choices—i.e., what things of value to me (including my soul and my relationship to God) am I willing to trade to satisfy my desires/lusts, ambition, and greediness?

The charge that capitalism always has winners and losers in market exchanges ignores the simple fact that each person is allowed to choose something he or she values more than what that person already possesses and to offer without coercion to swap one commodity for the other. In such a situation, no one loses; both win. It is not for some outside judge of the situation to declare that one or the other is the loser because somehow one or the other made a "bad choice." If no fraud or violence was involved, the choice was personal and satisfying to both parties or no one would have bothered. I or someone else might not have made either choice for whatever reasons, moral or otherwise, but it is not the market or the system that is at fault. It is the inherent nature of human decision making that some will make foolish, immoral, shortsighted,

---

68 This is even true in the supposedly exploitative situation of catastrophic emergencies. In those cases people make hard decisions about what they actually need the most and deploy whatever resources they have to satisfy their true needs accordingly—they define for themselves what is an "acceptable" price by buying or declining to do so in favor of some other value.

Awaiting the City

and/or hasty decisions. The market simply allows experimentation and learning to proceed without coercion. It does not guarantee the absence of human foibles or outright corruption, nor can any other system.[69]

Does the Free Market Cause Consumers to Make Bad Choices?

Akin to the winner/loser charge is the argument that Ronald Nash has labeled the "puritanical argument."[70] In other contexts it might be labeled the "nanny" argument, so-called because it presupposes that someone besides the ordinary consumer knows what's best for all and should be allowed to make choices for all as to the nature and provenance of products on offer in the market. Since the days of Aristotle, the discussion about the general intelligence and decision-making ability of the masses has fascinated the intellectually and politically elite communities. In our time it is especially intense because the mass market is filled to overflowing with items on offer that are shoddy, trivial, immoral, habit-forming, fattening (and otherwise bad for health), glitzy, faddish, and qualifying for a dozen other pejorative descriptions. The argument goes that it is unfair and unjust to have a system that exploits the ignorant and impulsive masses, who are incapable of controlling their impulses and making good decisions. Of course, the gullibility and naïveté of human beings has no apparent end, but that is not the fault of capitalism. Consequently, the inner logic of the argument fails, because it does not account for the gullibility and naïveté of elites (also human), who achieve high political office or sit ensconced in chairs of intellectual superiority. If someone is to be given such power to choose products for all, who might it be? And how might he or she or they be chosen? Surely not democratically, for the masses could not possibly be trusted to make such delicate choices! The only resort in such a situation is the coercive totalitarian one. John Stuart Mill was not the first or the last to come to this conclusion and opt for the coercive totalitarian "solution." We prefer William F. Buckley Jr., who often

---

69 See Thomas Sowell, *Knowledge and Decisions* (New York: Basic Books, 1980), for a clear discussion of the implications of real-life decision making.
70 Nash, *Social Justice and the Christian Church.*

opined that he would rather be governed by the first hundred names in the Boston phone directory than the faculty at Harvard.

Many charge that the role of advertising in market economics is a systemic evil that conjures up the sense of need and want in individuals and groups where none existed before. In truth, this is the concept taught in some forms of advertising theoretical models. In essence one must create the market for one's product where one did not exist before. It is then said to follow that this is a form of evil and unjust manipulation. Once again the attempt to connect human evil to the system in which it operates is illogical. Advertising in itself is nothing more than the announcement of the presence of a product to meet certain needs. In its primitive form it is just a hot dog or burrito vendor on the street corner setting up a sign and/or calling out to passersby and perhaps positioning himself downwind of the traffic for olfactory advantage. The newspaper boys of days gone by used to do the same thing in the streets of major cities as they cried, "Extra, extra, read all about it!"

Technological advances and sophisticated communication methodologies only enhance the basic practice, which is as old as Yahweh warning Adam about a certain tree or piquing Moses' curiosity with a bush aflame that would not burn up or out. It makes known that which was not generally known and causes the curious to investigate and see for themselves what is on offer. The charge that desire or acquisitiveness is incited where none was before is not a valid condemnation of the practice itself, nor is it an accurate theological analysis in general. In fact, without such "advertising" there could be no gospel preaching, for preaching is itself the attempt to create desire and investigative curiosity where none was before in order to convert the disinterested and distracted by announcing a new thing. The fact that false prophets exist and are successful does not delegitimize the true prophet or turn his convert into some gullible dupe who has been exploited by a dubious scheme. False advertising, just like false prophets, are the product of human depravity, and market economics is no more accountable for that than Yahweh is for the falsifiers of his chosen methodology. Government exists to police the most obvious cases of this as fraud, and buyers of any good on offer in any market are personally responsible for their choices. There is no injustice in such a system.

Awaiting the City

Does the Free Market Cause Alienation?

Finally, the market system is often condemned for its alienation of human beings from their work, their fellows, their community and themselves individually because the system emphasizes mass production of goods for an impersonal market through the process of specialization in labor activity. Thus, the worker is reduced to a cog in the massive machine of industrialization and market dynamics. As in each of the other cases, however, this argument falls upon the original situation of the very first humans coming out of Eden. They are clearly shown to be alienated first from their God by sin and condemned to a life of "toil" such that the man will "eat bread in the sweat of his brow" (Gen. 3:19). This is a universal condition that cannot be eliminated in this present age, only ameliorated through grace, both common and redemptive. The biblical and Christian answer to this is personal salvation and calling into service through all areas of life, especially daily work. No system can promise to eliminate "toil," for that is endemic, not systemic.

Furthermore, the market system has proved to provide the widest opportunity for the most people that has ever been devised on earth. No one is forced to remain in monotonous and uninspiring work unless he or she makes the choice directly or indirectly (by failing to get educated and equipped to do something else). In fact, the origins of this argument go back to the early days of the industrialization of the West when mass production began to be the salvation of the masses through the distribution of vast new wealth throughout the population. During that early transition people moved to centers of production to take advantage of new opportunities to earn their way in life so rapidly that populations grew faster than any society could ever have been expected to anticipate and provide their needs for shelter, clothing, and food efficiently or to deliver up educational opportunity in a timely fashion. No free-market, capitalistic society fails to provide these things at the present time. The issue now seems to be a matter of degree and supposed inequities.

Sometimes the idea of the "dead-end job" substitutes in for this argument. By that it is meant that all one is able to do for a living is flip burgers or work

Awaiting the City

at the car wash or some other apparently boring and/or "demeaning" task.[71] What is not emphasized is that these are overwhelmingly front-end jobs, not dead ends. They are where basic work skills and habits are learned for those who will go on to educate themselves and prepare for better opportunities in the future. This is where first jobs are supposed to lead, not end. This is "injustice" only in the eyes of a jaundiced beholder. On the contrary, this is precisely the kind of situation that allows the Christian to discover spiritual and other "gifts" that may be exercised for both profit and fulfillment. The injustice would be if some other entity were allowed to allocate human resources to whatever area some planning agency might arbitrarily see fit.

Conclusion

We have attempted here to address some of the moral implications of capitalistic market economics as we encounter it in the twenty-first century and as it has been encountered over the past three hundred years. This part of the discussion deals only with certain charges made against the process by which wealth is produced. How wealth is produced and accumulated and invested is the subject that must precede any distributive consideration. No books are written on the subject of how to become poverty stricken. Wealth must be accumulated to be distributed, and in this world as we know it, no approach to its production begins to compete with capitalistic free markets. And no other approach leaves humankind freer to profit by serving the needs of one's fellows and advancing the overall good of all people. No coercive system has the ability to tame humanity's innate tendency to lord it over one's brother or sister or neighbor like the free market. In another chapter we will deal more extensively with the implications of how that wealth is distributed, and in another we will address the issue of humanity in their destiny as ruler of this planet and its implications for technological advance and competitive destruction.

---

71 Quite often the ones who use this argument do not consider it "demeaning" to accept a welfare check or food stamps or housing assistance at public expense.

Awaiting the City

Chapter 25

Social Justice and Distribution: Wealth, Poverty, and Human Need

"JACQUES ELLUL IS ONE CULTURAL ANALYST who gives expression to modern thinking about the dehumanizing function of money. He observes that in both socialism and capitalism money has the function of measuring value, and that it therefore leads people to pursue the goal of having something instead of *being* something."[1] In other words, both rich and poor had best be wary of the corrosive power of fixation on money.

GOD, THE STATE, AND THE POOR

The concern for distributional justice, a dubious phraseology if ever there was one, is at the heart of the debate over Socialism (or, now Progressivism, the new self-designation), Fascism, and capitalism. "Having something," however it is received, drives humanity to a greater or lesser degree wherever we find economic activity. Whether one believes in a Socialist/Fascist means to that end or a free-market capitalistic means, if the end of having money (that is, hoarding for the sense of the security it brings) becomes the justification for economic and/or political activity, one has made a god of money and turned it

---

[1] George M. Stulac, "Appendix: The Identity of the Rich in James," in *Commentary on James*, IVPNTC 16, ed. Grant R. Osborne (Downers Grove, IL: InterVarsity Press, 1993), Laridian digital ed., 200, citing this observation from Jacques Ellul, *Money and Power*, trans. LaVonne Neff (Downers Grove, IL: InterVarsity Press, 1984), 22.

into mammon. The claim by either system for a more moral or ethical or just system of distribution generally raises this question: What is the end you seek? More of what others have? More of what is simply available? Or just more? The subject of this chapter is the consideration that it is men and women who make these choices, regardless of what system they choose to support in order to receive what they consider to be "just distribution" of "societal wealth" (another dubious use of language).

A more or less universal statement of the will of God and the true force of social justice for many on the Left is "God is on the side of the poor." We have sought to determine the precise origin of this terminology, and though it comes from discussions surrounding what has been known as liberation theology, we cannot find its origins outside the work of Ron Sider.[2] Craig Blomberg cites this origin in his work, which we have repeatedly cited, and traces the concept to Latin American bishops of the Roman Catholic Church in 1979 who stated that God has a "preferential option for the poor."[3] Peter Beyerhaus has also traced this conception (though not the precise terminology) to a conference in Melbourne, Australia, in 1980.[4] It is clearly an ambiguous turn of phraseology,

---

2   James 2:5 is sometimes asserted to have in it a "preference" for the poor, but this is by no means universally accepted. See also our discussion of this passage previously in chap. 8. While the phrase "God is on the side of the poor" appears to come from Sider, we recognize that the historical roots of as well as the term *liberation theology* (or *theologies*) clearly comes from outside of and predates Sider. See, e.g., John Yu, comp., "A Chronology of Liberation Theology 1512–1986," Liberation Theologies, http://liberationtheology.org/articles/john-yu-document-collection/chronology/. According to Peruvian Catholic theologian Gustavo Gutiérrez, in a new introduction to his work titled *Teología de la Liberación*: "The name and reality of 'liberation theology' came into existence in Chimbote, Peru, in July 1968, only a few months before Medillín," referring to the Medillín Conference of Latin American Bishops in Columbia (CELAM II). Prior to the conference he presented a paper titled "Hacia una teología de la liberatión" ("Towards a Theology of Liberation") at the Encuentro National del Movimiento Sacertdotal ONIS. Gustavo Gutiérrez, *A Theology of Liberation: History, Politics, and Salvation*, trans. Caridad Inda and John Eagleson (1971; Maryknoll, NY: Orbis Books, 1973), "Introduction to the Revised Edition: Expanding the View." Thus the term entered the English language with the 1973 translation of Gutiérrez's seminal work. Sergio Silva cites this Medillín conference as the second of four aspects of the origins of liberation theology. Cited in J. David Turner, *An Introduction to Liberation Theology* (Lanham, MD: University Press of America, 1994), chap. 1. We are indebted to our editor, Paul J. Brinkerhoff, for his sleuthing and contribution to this note.

3   Craig L. Blomberg, *Neither Poverty nor Riches*, 22.

4   Peter Beyerhaus, "Blessed Are the Poor in Spirit: 'The Theology of the Poor in Biblical Perspective,'" in *God Who Is Rich in Mercy*, ed. Peter T. O'Brien and David G. Peterson (Homebush West, NSW, Australia: Lancer Books; Grand Rapids, MI: Distributed in North

made more so by Dr. Sider's attempts to explain what it does and does not mean. Ron Nash has done a fine job of critiquing its use and abuse in *Social Justice and the Christian Church*.[5] In his latest contribution Sider sees this supposed preference for the poor as indicating God's going out of his way to correct inequities economically just as a parent would in helping a D-grade student more than an A-grade student. The problem is and remains (other than the specifically designated biblical poor) how to answer the question: How do the politically designated poor of our time relate to the biblical mandates to "help the poor"? Sider continues to threaten hellfire upon those who fail to take his assertions at face value, those who "neglect to share."[6] Our take on it is that the terminology is marginally useful to some for generating vague concern (guilt?) on the part of sincere Christian people who take the Bible seriously and do not wish to be "against" the poor and needy.[7]

America by Baker, 1986), 153–63. Beyerhaus in his treatment shows the Marxist background and untenable foundations of the attempt to read redistributional economics into the theological statement of Jesus.

5   Ronald H. Nash, *Social Justice and the Christian Church* (Milford, MI: Mott Media, 1983), 161–67. Sider has updated his position in his essay "Justice, Rights, and Human Government," in *Toward an Evangelical Public Policy* (Grand Rapids, MI: Baker, 2005), 163–93. His updated position is somewhat less polemical than others of his we cite, but he does not offer correctives to his previous work, and he still favors coercive government redistributive policies (183), minimum wage legislation (191), "finding mechanisms that offer everyone the opportunity to share in the ownership of" information services (seen as education) and factories (seen as equivalent to land in the Bible; 181). Blomberg takes the position that Nash's work is "unsophisticated and one-sided," citing, e.g., Humberto Belli and Ronald H. Nash, *Beyond Liberation Theology* (Grand Rapids, MI: Baker, 1992) a critique with which we could not be more in disagreement. Blomberg, *Neither Poverty nor Riches, 22.*

6   Sider, "Justice, Rights, and Human Government," 173. He asserts here that God's attitude toward those who do not give to the poor is the same as it is to those who actually oppress the poor. He uses the rich man and Lazarus passage and Sodom as examples.

7   Sider has previously made clear his Marxist take on the Bible in Stephen Mott and Ronald J. Sider, "Economic Justice: A Biblical Paradigm," in *Toward a Just and Caring Society*, ed. David P. Gushee (Grand Rapids, MI: Baker, 1999), 15–45. Mott and Sider conclude that "[t]he traditional criterion of distributive justice which comes closest to the biblical paradigm is distribution according to needs." Ibid., 45. That resonates the old Socialist line "From each according to his ability, to each according to his need!" This is also the position taken by Stephen Charles Mott in his essay "The Partiality of Biblical Justice: A Response to Calvin Beisner," in *Christianity and Economics in the Post–Cold War Era*, ed. Herbert Schlossberg, Vinay Samuel, Ronald J. Sider (Grand Rapids, MI: Eerdmans, 1994), 81–99. Mott and Sider allow a role for "[a]chievement," but state that "it must be subordinate." They understate when they say finally that a successful effort to implement their program would take "dramatic change, both in the U.S. and in every nation on earth." Mott and Sider, "Economic Justice," 45. Where have we heard that kind of talk before? William

Awaiting the City

In fact, except for the genetic engineers, planned-parenting abortion advocates, Darwinists, and various Hegelian fascist types at the close of the nineteenth and beginning of the twentieth century who advocated (by selective breeding and passive euthanasia) eliminating the chronic bearers of the various syndromes that kept the poor in abject poverty,[8] the mass murders of the Socialist/Communist twentieth century,[9] the African dictators and thugs who pile up relief supplies in depots for sale to the highest bidder while hundreds of thousands starve to death,[10] the bureaucratic types who soak up large percentages of the budget allocations in the United States reserved

---

Voegeli argues brilliantly that it is patently impossible to have a stopping point in welfare-state spending because there will always be those at the margins of whatever criteria is set for eligibility who will cry out to be included until their political muscle prevails. *Never Enough: America's Limitless Welfare State* (New York: Encounter Books, 2010). E. Calvin Beisner has also answered these arguments in his essay "Justice and Poverty: Two Views Contrasted," in *Christianity and Economics in the Post–Cold War Era*, 57–80. See also our related comments on Sider's thoughts on distributive justice in chap. 3, note 59.

8   See Benjamin J. Wiker, *10 Books That Screwed Up the World* (Washington DC: Regnery, 2008), 126–43. Further, see John G. West, "Darwin's Public Policy: Nineteenth Century Science and the Rise of the American Welfare State," in *The Progressive Revolution in Politics and Political Science: Transforming the American Regime*, ed. John Marini and Ken Masugi (New York: Rowman & Littlefield, 2005), 253–86. Also, see the recent controversy over Obama Administration science czar John Holdren's advocacy of coercive measures (compulsory abortion and sterilization substances added to public water supplies) to control certain populations, cited in Emily Belz, "Political Science," *World Magazine*, August 15, 2009, 6, http://www.worldmag.com/2009/07/political_science (posted July 31, 2009), and Terence P. Jeffrey, "The Global Redistributionist at Obama's Left Hand," *Human Events*, August 3, 2009, 18, http://www.humanevents.com/2009/08/05/the-global-redistributionist-at-obamas-left-hand/ (posted August 5, 2009). For extensive documentation on the origins of eugenic population control, see Connie Hair, "The Facts about the Freedom of Choice Act (FOCA)," *Human Events*, suppl., July 27, 2009, http://www.humanevents.com/2009/08/05/the-facts-about-the-freedom-of-choice-act-foca/ (posted August 5, 2009). This is just the latest in governmental societal engineering from the Obama administration.

9   See William Willimon's comments about Nazi "benevolence" to the "less fortunate" in David W. Hall, "Toward a Post-Statist Theological Analysis of Poverty," in *Welfare Reformed: A Compassionate Approach*, ed. David W. Hall (Phillipsburg, NJ: P&R, 1994), 25.

10 See Robert Calderisi, *The Trouble with Africa: Why Foreign Aid Isn't Working* (New York: Palgrave MacMillan, 2006), for full treatment, and Keith B. Richburg, *Out of America: A Black Man Confronts Africa* (1997; repr., New York: Basic Books, 2009), for anecdotal evidence. Additional documentation is in R. Glenn Hubbard and William Duggan, *Aid Trap: Hard Truths about Ending Poverty* (New York: Columbia University Press, 2009). One of the latest catastrophes was in Haiti where the government was last seen holding thousands of "Buckets of Hope" given by American Southern Baptists, while people went hungry and food rotted in the rain and mud.

Awaiting the City

as transfer payments to the poor,[11] it is hard to think of anyone not "on the side of the poor."[12] Of course there are the environmentalists who stopped the use of DDT in the last century after the developed world had used it to effectively eliminate the scourge of malaria, the leading cause of 1.5 to 2.7 million deaths per year.[13]

---

11 See numerous studies based on governmental statistics and accounting documents. Hall, "Toward a Post-Statist Theological Analysis of Poverty," 7–28, reflects at length on the brokenness of the system of welfare in our time. Thomas Sowell is cited by Walter Block, noting that a simple transfer of money from the federal allocations for social welfare programs to the "poor" would amount to about $70,000 per year. Our latest calculation based on government publications is $83,000. See Walter Block, "Private Property, Ethics, and Wealth Creation," in *The Capitalist Spirit: Toward a Religious Ethic of Wealth Creation*, ed. Peter L. Berger (San Francisco: ICS Press , 1990), 116. This number coincides with about the same figure from all state, local, and federal outlays for transfers from government to the "poor" and near-poor. It amounts to about twenty percent of the US GDP per year (totalling on the order of $17 trillion in needs-based outlays since the advent of Great Society legislation, according to Heritage Foundation expert Robert Rector, "The Facts about Poverty in America," *Human Events*, February 7, 2012, http://www.humanevents.com/2012/02/07/the-facts-about-poverty-in-america/). Large portions of this largesse are absorbed by the governmental entities (workers, consultants, providers, etc.) that do the distributing. Average federal wages as of 2009 total $71,206, not counting bonuses, overtime, fringe benefits, pension accruals, etc. Civil service salaries average more than $100,000. All this is at a time when private sector salaries average $40,331. Figures supplied in Michael Knox Beran, "The Descent of Liberalism," *National Review*, April 5, 2010, 24, http://www.nationalreview.com/articles/229520/descent-liberalism/michael-knox-beran (posted April 12, 2010).
12 Our intent in this reversal of the concept is to highlight the elasticity of this pejorative use of terminology to elicit guilt from audiences to whom the terminology is addressed.
13 See Richard Stearns, *The Hole in Our Gospel* (Nashville: Thomas Nelson, 2009), 142, and his graphic account of the manner in which people die from and suffer with malaria. Tim Zeimer, senior director of World Relief, says approximately a million of these are children under the age of five. Emily Belz, "Survivor," *World Magazine*, March 13, 2010, http://www.worldmag.com/2010/02/survivor (posted February 26, 2010). Much of the world's mania about DDT is based on a book published in the early sixties by marine biologist Rachel Carson, *Silent Spring* (Boston: Houghton Mifflin, 1962), which has been shown by subsequent research to be filled with bad science and worse journalism. The book was dedicated to Albert Schweitzer, a man she claimed was opposed to DDT, while his own writings called the chemical "a ray of hope." See Jack Cashill, *Hoodwinked: How Intellectual Hucksters Have Hijacked American Culture* (Nashville: Thomas Nelson, 2005), 199–206. In addition Rael Jean Isaac and Erich Isaac, *The Coercive Utopians: Social Deception by America's Power Players* (Chicago: Regnery Gateway, 1983), 69–71, detail the unscientific political process that banned DDT. For the most thorough debunking of the "science" behind the ban, see George Claus and Karen Bolander, *Ecologocal Sanity: A Critical Examination of Bad Science, Good Intentions and Premature Doomsday Announcements of the Ecology Lobby* (New York: David McKay, 1977), and for the most recent definitive work since the '70s, see Roger E. Meiners, Pierre Desrochers, and Andrew P. Morriss, eds. *Silent Spring at 50: The False Crises of Rachel Carson* (Washington, DC: Cato Institute, 2012).

Awaiting the City

The question is how to do what the terminology implies vaguely in a concrete and just manner. That is, since consideration of some kind for the needs of the poor shows up in almost every area of the Bible, how does one go about being obedient to its teaching?[14] The political and cultural divide over this issue may be broadly stated as the difference between private/voluntary action and statist/coercive action, for virtually no one actually suggests that nothing at all should be done in behalf of "the poor," despite some of the rhetoric used in political and theological discourse. The first position (private action) regards as inevitable the existence of economic disparities in society because of a myriad of reasons, not all or even many "unjust."[15] Further, so long as the stratification is not permanent and intractable and solidified into caste-like separations that preclude relatively equal opportunity for improvement,[16] no coercive action is justified except where specific misappropriation of wealth has taken place. Private action may be urged for many reasons and can include but not be limited to immediate relief, education, lifestyle counseling, job training, personal moral training, or regular care for the permanently disabled, widowed, and orphaned, with special attention also paid to those not native to the society. This conception of economics views production of wealth as a vast interconnected process that inevitably results in variable and unequal outcomes, over time and in the short run, that are not unjust in the aggregate (as opposed to the individualistic) and expects rational compassion to be exercised as a virtue cultivated by all voluntarily and at the persuasion of others.

The second position proceeds along the set of ideas flowing from a presup-

---

14 However, the Bible's teaching about the poor is not nearly as ubiquitous or specific in its denotation to the modern world or fraught with as much eternal significance as many are claiming.

15 See esp. Edgar K. Browning, *Stealing from Each Other: How the Welfare State Robs Americans of Money and Spirit* (Westport, CT: Praeger, 2008), 4–18, and other parts of the book for thorough discussion of the various forms of "just inequalities" in the market system. See p. 11 for discussion of the work disparities between the top 20 percent of wage earners and the bottom twenty percent in American society. The difference in time spent working between these households is on the order of seven hundred percent. Latest government agency and Census Bureau surveys of the "poor" as designated by government standards show that fully sixty-seven percent of these say they did not work one full week in the previous year. Another twenty-five percent worked only part-time.

16 This is in fact a description of the actual situation that has prevailed in the ancient world of biblical times, especially in the Roman world of the New Testament and the period up to about three hundred years ago in the West.

Awaiting the City

position that wealth (especially anything considered "excessive") is really "societal wealth," that is, not the possession justly and rightly of those who may now be said to "own" it in some narrow sense, but rather the possession of all within a given state, and for some, ultimately, the world of states. That means that it is a "right" to have some kind of equalizing redistribution of wealth done coercively because it is a matter of social "justice." The assumption is that for anyone to have what some consider "excess," they must have acquired it at the expense of someone(s) else. Those in government who take this view will often contend that failure to tax individuals and corporations at higher rates amounts to a "subsidy." In other words, all wealth actually belongs to government as the representative of the society charged with the responsibility of seeing that everybody "gets their fair share." This is the famous zero-sum view of economics that says there is only so much wealth in the world, and what I have or get came out of someone else's rightful share or from exploitation of something that belongs to them.[17] This idea is what turns economic and cultural equalization of outcomes into a dispute over "rights."[18] To look to some form of compassion and personal virtue to do the job is to fail to grasp that those who have less are aggrieved parties to society's misallocation of its wealth. Thus, the very idea of "charity" (a derivative of the King James Bible's use of "love" language) is offensive, for equality of distribution is a matter of pure "justice" and/or "rights."

The defense of coercive intervention by government requires a justification for action that the private and personal does not, because the former has no resources to satisfy the aggrieved without taking them from someone else either through taxation or regulation or both. Private works of charity and redress, on the other hand, proceed from "donors" who give and/or establish

---

17 This zero-sum conception of wealth appears to have originated in the writings of Rousseau.
18 See Thomas Sowell, *Civil Rights: Rhetoric or Reality?* (New York: William Morrow, 1984), for a discussion of the issues that have faced Americans since 1954 on this subject of "rights." William Willimon's insight is illuminating in this vein: "The notion of 'rights' is not a biblical idea. It is a legacy of the European Enlightenment. The notion of rights has been helpful in forming liberal societies, that is, societies formed without reference to God. No one needs to feel grateful or to say 'thank you' in a society of rights." William H. Willimon, "The Effusiveness of Christian Charity," *Theology Today* (April 1992): 79–80, quoted in David W. Hall, "A Response to Johan D. van der Vyver's 'The Jurisprudential Legacy of Abraham Kuyper and Leo XIII," *Journal of Markets & Morality* 5, no. 1 (Spring 2002): 258, http://www.marketsandmorality.com/index.php/mandm/article/viewFile/732/pdf.

Awaiting the City

their own vehicles for distribution of goods and services. Consequently, to justify coercive measures charges against the supposed inherent inadequacies and/or outright evils of capitalistic market-driven distribution of wealth must be made and sustained in the public arena. There is no want of such charges, as we will now demonstrate.[19]

"Robber Barons" vs. the Politburo—Where Is the Capital Concentrated?

Discussions about the unequal and supposedly unjust accumulation (also called "distribution") of capital usually begin with recitation of facts and figures to prove that, particularly in the United States, there is a vast inequality from top to bottom of the spectrum, and more recently, that the middle class is "disappearing" or at least under heavy siege.[20] These "facts" are highly misreported and misapplied in the literature of those lobbying for governmental coercive measures to secure "equality."[21] We will not go into the massive data available online and in the print media. We refer you to this material in our notes and the discussion in our previous chapters. For our purposes here, we assume that the United States is the most "equal" of all societies in world history in its economic distribution of benefits and opportunities and that any supposed unacceptable inequalities or "injustices" are not the result of market-driven capitalistic forces.[22] Rather, they

---

19 For an early look at the groups (and their offspring) that now command attention in the media on the subject of limiting economic growth and development, see Isaac and Isaac, *Coercive Utopias*. This book demonstrates the long-standing agenda of utopian groups that will use whatever captures the public's imagination to create "crisis" mentalities and hysteria.

20 See to the contrary Ron Haskins, "The Myth of the Disappearing Middle Class," *Washington Post*, Opinions, March 29, 2012, http://articles.washingtonpost.com/2012-03-29/opinions/35450048_1_income-distribution-income-inequality-income-growth.

21 See paper by professor of economics J. Bradford DeLong, "Robber Barons," (paper, University of California at Berkeley, and NBER, 2nd draft, January 1, 1998), http://www.uni-muenster.de/PeaCon/eliten/Robber%20Barons.htm (see also his Web site http://delong.typepad.com/sdj/) for a discussion of the nature of the accumulation of vast wealth by individuals in the present and the bygone era.

22 See Browning, *Stealing from Each Other*, and Alan Reynolds, *Income and Wealth* (Westport, CT: Greenwood Press, 2006). The other kind of "equalization" involves societal poverty—that is, instead of vast wealth being shared, poverty is shared by all. This is what Socialist and Communist systems produce—not to mention the thuggish regimes of Africa. See Ron Haskins and Isabel Sawhill, *Creating an Opportunity Society* (Washington, DC: Brookings Institution Press, 2009), and Claudia Goldin and Lawrence F. Katz, *The Race*

come from interventionist government policies and/or cultural remnants of sinful attitudes such as racism or ethnocentrism that prevent cultural assimilation. Immense wealth does concentrate in the hands of a few at some times and in a relatively few industries, and some complain that this concentration is growing rather than stabilizing or decreasing.[23] Brad DeLong, cited in an earlier footnote, has noted the threefold causes[24] of such vast accumulations in the hands of a very few, noting also that such accumulations are rare indeed, are presently higher than they were fifty or so years ago, and are not particularly harmful to economies as a whole,[25] and we might add, not to individuals at all. Furthermore, the only way to "rectify" (a word we consider to be envious) that situation is to confiscate wealth outright by coercion, and that places the wealth in the hands of a different elite. It does not remedy the problem of concentration. It simply changes distribution into a political market where bidders and sellers exchange political capital for material capital.[26]

The choice between coercive and relatively free-market solutions to economic problems depends on none of the conclusions about the equality of distribution suggested above. The choice is to be made from an entirely different

---

between Technology and Education (Cambridge: Harvard University Press, 2008), for the causes of any inequalities of economic outcomes.

23 See Sider's update of Just Generosity: A New Vision for Overcoming Poverty in America, 2nd ed. (Grand Rapids, MI: Baker, 2007), for the ongoing recitation of "gaps" between those denominated "rich" and those called "poor" for the purposes of statistical categorization. The Bible is nowhere concerned about "gaps" between rich and poor but about direct oppression or hardhearted failure to give and help those who are clearly designated helpless.

24 DeLong says immense wealth is caused by (1) inheriting wealth accentuated by a stock market boom (think the inheritors of the 1980s and beyond), (2) persuading the government to do your industry a "truly massive favor" (think the railroad magnates of the nineteenth century), and/or (3) being in the right place at the right time to create an enterprise of truly enormous social utility—think Henry Ford or Bill Gates in the latter case.

25 The annual publication of "The Forbes 400" (http://www.forbes.com/forbes-400/) listing the richest individuals in America shows from year to year how volatile wealth accumulation at the highest levels is. There is a constant churn among the American wealthy and no evidence of stratifying. See also the constant movement in the "Fortune 500," noted by Carl J. Schramm, The Entrepreneurial Imperative: How America's Economic Miracle Will Reshape the World (and Change Your Life) (New York: HarperCollins, 2006), 90–91.

26 We have previously cited the latest work by James Davison Hunter, To Change the World: The Irony, Tragedy, and Possibility of Christianity in the Late Modern World (New York: Oxford University Press, 2010), as having come out late in the process of our finishing this book. His insights into the relationship between power and capital are compatible with what we lay out here. However, we note that the discussion here was written without reference to his work.

Awaiting the City

perspective that we have introduced in the previous chapter (chap. 24). We have already noted that the understanding of "capital" has been undergoing change and should now include all kinds of "goods" that go beyond monetary and material denominations. In fact, economic success is now invested more heavily in human capital than it is in the traditional understanding of monetary capital.[27] On the free-market side is the whole range of choices that present themselves to men and women that lead to economic prosperity—lifestyle, education, work habits, native talent, cultural inclinations, prudence, resourcefulness, delayed gratification, marital fidelity, sexual control, and others that could be named. To this must be added the value added by accidents of birth, the clear advantages gained by superior intellectual ability that is rewarded by entry to the world of elite educational institutions, and especially the value of political influence.

The near-miracle of what has happened in the West during the past two hundred to three hundred years is that for the first time in human history these choices have been allowed to work themselves out more or less freely in an atmosphere of at least nominal Judeo-Christian moral conviction. True wealth, the kind that produces choice and mobility and the ability to resist the state, has changed the world. The power of the state and caste-like aristocratic domination as well as that of state-church hierarchies has been eliminated, even as racist and ethnocentric prejudices have been waning. The result has been the unleashing of the human creative genius in ways never before dreamed. Suddenly (considering the long ages passed in near-stasis), like the Cambrian fossil explosion, what Weber and Novak (and now McCloskey) have denominated the "spirit" of democratic capitalism has changed the world and made the accumulation of human capital the most important of all "distributions." We will pursue this particular idea later in this chapter and in

---

27 A more troubling assessment has come of late from the ever-perceptive Charles Murray, *Coming Apart: The State of White America, 1960–2010* (New York: Crown Forum, 2012). His frightening analysis of the decline of human capital values in the population he has studied for his book confirms much of our ongoing analysis here. The growing "gaps" some are decrying can be traced to declines in the very values that once produced such great strength and diversity throughout the various social and economic classes of the United States. Murray is not optimistic about the future under these circumstances.

Awaiting the City

the next (chap. 26), but for now we must define some terms and clarify the underlying choices to be made.

Concentrations of Power

Plainly stated, the choice is between free-market concentrations on the one hand and coercive governmental choices on the other hand.[28] Where shall we concentrate the power and wealth accumulated by the aggregate effort of millions of working, thinking, inventing, and investing people? Will that aggregate effort be allowed to seek its own level through millions and billions of private choices (what Smith called the "invisible hand"),[29] or will it be concentrated in the hands of a political elite?[30]

That is the choice, because the very concentration of political power, as we have already noted, is a capital good to be spent by those who have it. That good is coercive power, and it stands on the foundation of government's ability to take something from one person and give it to another in the form of direct cash settlements (payments or credits) or benefits in kind that go to various constituencies whose interests come before others'. Government does not generate wealth; it can only take it and pass it out. Increasingly this is done not only by tax confiscations and distributions, but through regulation of the use of private goods justified by environmental, health, safety, and other concerns. Whether and how one may do business, what the price of raw materials and labor will be, what one must do to avoid taxes and regulations—all these concerns increasingly determine the business landscape and the distri-

---

28 For the most succinct discussion of this subject, see Thomas Sowell, *Intellectuals and Society* (New York: Basic Books, 2009), 65–70, with his documentation of counterarguments.

29 See Jim Wallis, *Rediscovering Values: On Wall Street, Main Street, and Your Street: A Moral Compass for the New Economy* (New York: Simon & Schuster, 2010), for the latest diatribe against Smith's turn of phrase. He says that "we were sold a lie" about the invisible hand, 21, Kindle loc. 385–400, without specifying who did the lying or what the lie exactly was.

30 See Charles E. Lindblom, *The Market System: What It Is, How It Works, and What to Make of It*, Yale ISPS (New Haven, CT: Yale University Press, 2001), for a thorough discussion of how this apparently uncoordinated "system" coordinates itself in this apparently invisible manner. Additional views on this subject include Peter L. Berger, ed., *The Capitalist Spirit: Toward a Religious Ethic of Wealth Creation* (San Francisco: ICS Press, 1990); Fred Catherwood, *The Creation of Wealth: Recovering a Christian Understanding of Money, Work, and Ethics* (Wheaton, IL: Crossway, 2002); and Brian Griffiths, *The Creation of Wealth: A Christian's Case for Capitalism* (Downers Grove, IL: InterVarsity Press, 1984).

Awaiting the City

bution of wealth through a society when the government takes an ever greater
role. These are denominated "costs" in any study of economics and are passed
along to consumers in the form of higher prices and taxes upon all to establish
the regulatory bureaucracies that enforce them. Furthermore, the custom of
"lobbying" the government through its representatives is the only wise choice
when others are doing the same for the purpose of being sure they do not end
up paying a higher price for their inactivity. Those who learn to cultivate this
form of capital are actually political entrepreneurs, in distinction from the
economic and technological entrepreneurs of bygone eras, though it is undoubtedly true that these political kind of fellows have always been among us.

In such an atmosphere the term "distribution" is extremely problematic,
for it treats wealth as something that appears on the ground each morning, like
manna, and awaits the gathering in. Some Christian commentators seem to
think this is what the analogy should be and use it to advocate egalitarian outcomes so that "he who gathered much had no leftover and he who gathered little
had no lack" (Exod. 16:18).[31] Further, since those who gathered too much found
spoilage the next morning, it should serve as a warning to the "rich." Apart from
the dubious derivation of such a message from the manna in the wilderness story, the fact is that wealth in any form small or great does not simply appear on
the ground for the taking. It is generated by the efforts of people in their practice
of the creative activity of God in everyday work and inventiveness. Wealth, if it
is not gained by fraud, violence, or theft, must be produced and earned. The law
against thievery makes personal possession of any wealth legal and just in itself,
if it has not been obtained by fraud or violence. To pass a law to take such wealth
from anyone and give it to another is nowhere counted as "just" in Scripture.[32]
Such "distribution" is first a legalized theft, before it becomes a gift to the receiv-
er.[33] Frédéric Bastiat stated it like this long ago:

---

31 See esp. Blomberg, *Neither Poverty nor Riches,* chap. 6, in his comments on Paul's exhor-
    tation to giving in 2 Cor. 8–9. See also our discussion of Paul's offering for "the poor" at
    Jerusalem in this same biblical passage (see chap. 8).
32 See our discussion of Calvin's view of "theft" in the previous historical treatment (see chap.
    12).
33 Lest some should think this language too harsh, it must be remembered that the ped-
    igree of the idea that such action is not theft is Rousseau's dictum that to have more
    than someone else is to have engaged in theft, thus justifying the excesses of the French
    Revolution. Marxists regularly espouse the idea that private property is theft.

Awaiting the City

When [the law] has exceeded its proper functions, it has not done so merely in some inconsequential and debatable matters. The law has gone further than this; it has acted in direct opposition to its own proper purpose. The law has been used to destroy its own objective: It has been applied to annihilating the justice that it was supposed to maintain; to limiting and destroying rights which its real appeal was to respect. The law has placed the collective force at the disposal of the unscrupulous who wish, without risk, to exploit the person, liberty, and property of others. It has converted plunder into a right, in order to protect plunder. And it has converted lawful defense into a crime, in order to punish lawful defense.[34]

This is the "taking" Samuel warned Israel about when the people demanded a king. Such taking from others is different from the rule of God himself, and it should not be confused with some conception of biblical justice.

Some will charge that this choice is to be preferred to others on offer. For instance, the so-called Gilded Age of the robber barons—when conspicuous consumption by the extremely wealthy rubbed the faces of the poor in the disparity between the so-called exploiters and the exploited—surely demanded that something be done to make things right. Or, more recently, do not cases where workers in the underdeveloped world work at extremely low wages for American and other companies, whose owners and managers fly around the world in private jets and live in mansions, so they can sell fast food and trivial consumer goods to overweight and bored Americans demand that "justice" be done?[35] Is this not a legitimate sphere for governmental action that Christians should support for reasons of theological conviction and conscience? Are the issues not obvious?

They are only if one is unaware of history as it relates to governmental practice and economics, and business as it literally spreads the wealth globally.

---

34 Frédéric Bastiat, *The Law*, 2nd ed., trans. Dean Russell (1850; Eng. trans., 1950; Irvington-on-Hudson, NY: Foundation for Economic Education, 1998), 32–33.

35 See arguments by D. Stephen Long, "Catholic Social Teaching and the Global Market," in *Wealth, Poverty, and Human Destiny*, ed. Doug Bandow and David L. Schindler (Wilmington, DE: ISI Books, 2003), 77–102. We argue that it is more likely that governmental looters of international aid programs will be the majority riding jets and yachts.

Awaiting the City

The early concentrations of wealth in private hands in the age of rapid and massive industrial change in the United States were unprecedented. It does seem like hitting the lottery in modern parlance until one reads the stories of the great entrepreneurs and their struggles from relative poverty to great riches.[36] Furthermore, some of the newly rich celebrated their new status and power in outrageous ways that were offensive to more than just the hardworking poor. They were often and loudly condemned, at times, by the media, religious institutions, and preachers.[37] Nevertheless, they did not make their wealth by illegitimate means, except as they were in league with governmental authorities to deny entry into their respective fields of activity by others, nor did most of them spend inordinate amounts of money on themselves compared to the size of their fortunes and their philanthropic pursuits. Novak says of these supposed villains of what someone has called a "fierce capitalism," that they (the robber barons, so-called) "were not always robbers and seldom barons; most were poor boys, badly educated, barely (if at all) gentlemen and aesthetically quite insecure."[38] The fact that some put themselves in league with the political entrepreneurs we mentioned above is deplorable. But it was only after they had pioneered in innovative processes and perfected them to their great advantage that they then sought monopoly control through governmental means of various kinds.[39] And, as we noted above, it appears they went

---

36 For studies of the attitudes of those wishing to see "redistribution" of such wealth, see Peter Schweizer, *Makers and Takers: Why Conservatives Work Harder, Feel Happier, Have Closer Families, Take Fewer Drugs, Give More Generously, Value Honesty More, Are Less Materialistic and Envious, Whine Less—and Even Hug Their Children More Than Liberals* (New York: Doubleday, 2008), where the persuasion that wealth is a matter of hitting the "lottery of life" rather than being produced by hard work, thrift, education, and entrepreneurial skill leads such political factions to prefer envy and destructiveness over engaging in the "Protestant work ethic."

37 Mark Twain and coauthor Charles Dudley Warner appear to have invented the term "Gilded Age" as a pejorative, in their thus-titled book, *The Gilded Age: A Tale of Today* (Hartford, CT: American Publishing Company, 1873).

38 Michael Novak, *The Spirit of Democratic Capitalism*, 2nd ed. (Lanham, MD: Madison Books, 1991), 213.

39 See Thomas J. DiLorenzo, *How Capitalism Saved America* (New York: Crown Forum, 2004), 110–33, for discussion and sources. See also Robert P. Murphy, *The Politically Incorrect Guide to Capitalism* (Washington, DC: Regnery, 2007), and Burton W. Folsom Jr., *The Myth of the Robber Barons*, 6th ed. (Herndon, VA: Young America's Foundation, 2010). For a strikingly fresh analysis of the origins of this phenomenon in American history, see Thomas J. DiLorenzo, *Hamilton's Curse* (New York: Crown Forum, 2008).

to school on the Standard Oil case and "learned" from it that it was better to get to the political table ahead of trustbusters like Theodore Roosevelt and muckrakers like Ida Tarbell.

Even the book that has made famous the term "robber barons," written by Matthew Josephson,[40] was a transparent attempt to arrive at a predetermined conclusion for political (Marxist) purposes and did so by distorting massively the facts and personalities involved.[41] We conclude that no amount of coercive governmental seizure of wealth will change the corruptibility of governments and businesspeople (or bohemian hagiographers) that always hovers around the accumulation of money.[42]

The net effect of the early industrial entrepreneurs and developers, in spite of the politically entrepreneurial activities that made some of them monopolists of a kind, was to open up whole new areas of employment, give access to goods for ordinary people that not even aristocrats and kings and queens had known, usher in the modern world of health and longer life, set the stage for a century of technological progress, and this at ever cheaper prices for all. Contrary to the criticisms of some, there has never been a case where an industry has been successfully monopolized to the detriment of consumers. It is would-be competitors who have marshaled government action against those

---

40 Matthew Josephson, *The Robber Barons* (1934; repr., New York: Harcourt, Brace & World, 1962).

41 For a full treatment of the origin of the book itself and the life of its author, see David Shi, *Matthew Josephson: Bourgeois Bohemian* (New Haven, CT: Yale University Press, 1981), 155–88. Allan Nevins (biographer of the Rockefeller family) characterized the book at the time as "a pamphlet or polemic as well as a vivid picture... by a man not expert in either history or economics. Its consistently critical and hostile tone makes little pretense to balance or impartiality." Quoted in ibid., 163. Shi is clear that this opinion squares with the facts of the case and that Josephson was writing to confirm the tone of political discourse of the times. Shi would not necessarily be in sympathy with our approach in this book, however.

42 More accurate representations of the period of the so-called Gilded Age are Allan Nevins, *John D. Rockefeller: The Heroic Age of American Enterprise*, 2 vols. (New York: Charles Scribner's Sons, 1940); Charles R. Morris, *The Tycoons: How Andrew Carnegie, John D. Rockefeller, Jay Gould and J. P. Morgan Invented the American Supereconomy* (New York: Henry Holt, 2005); Les Standiford, *Meet You in Hell: Andrew Carnegie, Henry Clay Frick and the Bitter Partnership That Transformed America* (New York: Crown, 2005); Edward J. Renehan Jr., *Dark Genius of Wall Street: The Misunderstood Life of Jay Gould, King of the Robber Barons* (New York: Basic Books, 2005); Ron Chernow, *Titan: The Life of John D. Rockefeller, Sr.* (New York: Random House, 1998); and Ron Chernow, *The House of Morgan: An American Banking Dynasty and the Rise of Modern Finance* (1990; repr., New York: Grove, 2001).

Awaiting the City

they wish to bring down to their level so prices could be higher, reflecting their own inefficiencies in bringing goods to consumers. Prices for all goods, necessities as well as luxuries, have steadily declined decade after decade as a relative percentage of the labor needed to purchase them.[43] For Christians, it would be well to consider how far afield the gospel would have proceeded without the burst of industrialization that brought rapid transportation and communication and educational opportunity to millions through just the entrepreneurial genius and philanthropy of Rockefeller and Carnegie[44] alone, much less the burgeoning of modern technology at affordable prices.

As for the "plight" of the workers in these industries, it is well to consider what their condition was before industrialization and the supposed exploitation of their efforts. The most lamented of them were new immigrants who were escaping abject poverty in their homelands to seek new opportunity in America. They suffered as all wanderers on this earth have as they took up the quest for new beginnings and looked in hope to the place they had never been before. They were like those who arrive in the United States today legally and illegally. They chose it as a better course than staying put in the home country. Supposedly they did so because it was a better place to be and live and work. Arguably, employers could have decided arbitrarily to pay them more than they did, but the competition among those needing work would quickly have driven the price for wages down again as more of those without work arrived and would agree to work for less just to have a job. The same situation obtains today when a global business relocates production in a developing part of the world and generally is forced to match local wages, lest it destroy the fledgling local pricing structures.

Then, as now, some of the loudest protesters of this situation were those displaced from jobs by the new arrivals. Such is the price of mobility and free-

---

43 For a telling analysis of both the history and legal proceedings of the accumulation of the great industrial fortunes and attempts to break them up, see Dominick T. Armentano, *Antitrust and Monopoly: Anatomy of a Policy Failure* (1972; New York: John Wiley & Sons, 1982). The government has yet to prove that any of the famous "robber barons" or anyone else has ever harmed the public by controlling prices and markets. So-called trust-busting is about other matters altogether.

44 Rockefeller was a lifelong tither, beginning with his first period of adult-level work in support of his family at the age of fourteen. See also Michael Novak's remarkably balanced assessment of Andrew Carnegie's life and his effort to give away his entire fortune in *Business as a Calling: Work and the Examined Life* (New York: Free Press, 1996).

Awaiting the City

dom and change. This is an unavoidable economic reality. Such displacement is not "unjust" except in the cosmic sense we discuss elsewhere.[45] It is the first step on the ladder of opportunity. And this is exactly the situation of workers in the undeveloped world today who take jobs offered at lower wages than those paid in the United States. It is a chimera of outrageous proportions to think that someone on the ground in that bygone era (or the present) could have wisely legislated who got to keep what job at the expense of someone else willing to work for less. Or, to decide what industry must survive at the expense of invention and innovation.[46] Whether private jets and mansions in our time are equivalent to the near-orgies of the Gilded Age is a judgment call that would require personal knowledge to condemn or justify. In any case, is it the job of government to take away mansions and jets to create "equality"? In most cases of that type it is not the displaced workers who are served by confiscations but the politicians and bureaucracies. Peter Schweizer has shown, amazingly, that a large percentage of redistributionists are so filled with envy that some politicians and bureaucrats care not whether they benefit from the process so long as the wealthy are damaged.[47]

Our concern here is to relate the issue of coercive power and choices to private alternatives. Just how would the government decide justly the proper dividing up of benefits and burdens for those involved in new enterprises and entrepreneurial efforts? Who has the wisdom to discern the market forces involved and do more good than harm at the outset and anticipate all the dips and turns inherent in new human endeavors as development proceeds?[48] The choice is between a politburo-like cadre of autocrats and a supposed bunch of robber barons. The difference is that one group has a gun (and cannot be put out of business without a revolution),

---

45   See our discussion of justice in the cosmic sense in conjunction with Sowell's constrained versus unconstrained vision of political means and goals for society at the end of the section under the heading "Equality and Justice" in chap. 27 as well as the section under the heading "A Conflict of Vision" in chap. 21. See also Thomas Sowell, *The Quest for Cosmic Justice* (New York: Free Press, 1999).

46   Yet this picking of winners and losers is, of course, what licensing, regulation, and tariffs are all about. Industry leaders join legislators to see to it that start-up companies can't compete and in order to monopolize the market.

47   See Schweizer, *Makers and Takers*, Kindle loc. 1249–65.

48   This is exactly the point of Friedrich Hayek's, *The Road to Serfdom*, 50th anniversary ed. (Chicago: University of Chicago Press, 1994). No one person or group of persons can do this—no mortal is sufficient to the task.

Awaiting the City

and the other does not.[49] Is God on the side of the gun? Or, is he on the side of uncoerced choices that may or may not lead to his blessing or judgment? On the one side is a "taking" to "give" to the highest political bidder. On the other is production to be sold at a market-clearing price in an open market where businesses go out of business every day for failure to keep up with consumer demand and desire and where their workers can move to new jobs or start their own businesses. Where will God be in such a situation? The Beast and Babylon beckon.

The Good Samaritan with a Gun

But surely it is the job of government to insure the "safety net" of services to the poor and needy so no one in a wealthy society need go hungry, stay outside in the cold, or want for decent clothing. We have no desire to see anyone without basic necessities of life, and we know of no one who advocates such a scenario. The issue has never been that simple, and we believe most people know that. The problem is twofold. The first question to be settled is whether this is a "right" of all people regardless of behavior and choices. Some insist it is unequivocally. From the Christian perspective, this is generally seen as the compassionate thing to do, without reference to other issues of justice. In this scenario strict justice becomes, as Carl Henry long ago warned, "a subset of compassion."[50] Others insist that there is no justice in taking from

---

49   The Homestead Steel Strike in 1892 is a case in point that is improperly used to blame capitalism for violent "taking" of labor. The strike escalated into a protracted conflict between the Amalgamated Association of Iron and Steel Workers (the AA) and the Carnegie Steel Company in Homestead, Pennsylvania, climaxing in armed clashes to coerce action on both sides. The government managed to turn its head and not enforce the law for various reasons. This dispute was central in the breakdown of the relationship between Andrew Carnegie and Henry Clay Frick, who served as chairman of the company and whose partnership with Carnegie ensured that Carnegie's steel mills had adequate supplies of coke. Politically, the result was a huge defeat for AA and set back efforts to unionize steelworkers. As one of the most serious disputes in US labor history, the Homestead strike has served those who want to make a whipping boy out of capitalism for its violent "taking" of labor. In point of fact, the exact opposite is the case. This aberration would not have been possible without the collusion and acquiescence of government. Government failed at this point, not capitalism. For further discussion, see Les Standiford, *Meet You in Hell: Andrew Carnegie, Henry Clay Frick and the Bitter Partnership That Transformed America* (New York: Crown, 2005).

50   Carl F. H. Henry, "Evangelicals in the Social Struggle," *Christianity Today*, October 8, 1965, 3–11, cited in Marvin Olasky, *The Tragedy of American Compassion* (Wheaton, IL: Crossway,

the hardworking and responsible to give to the indigent, lazy, and irresponsible, who have made and continue to make life choices that leave them in the condition they are in. The key concern here is the fact that government has to take something to give something, and it is penalizing good behavior and rewarding bad behavior and calling it *just* when it awards to one group a right to the earnings of another regardless of behavior patterns. No such definition should entice the biblical Christian, for it is nowhere taught in Scripture as a mark of justice. We have elsewhere noted Paul's first-century dictum to let the lazy learn from a growing appetite—a word of wisdom from other places in Scripture as well (Eph. 4:28; 2 Thess. 3:6–14; cf. Prov. 16:26; 19:15).

More near the mark of biblical teaching is the idea that compassion may cause the Christian to provide basic needs in the hope of converting the sinner from the error of his ways—the sin here involves lifestyle and choices contrary to God's will for all men and women. If such compassion is not received well so that training in good choices can proceed, the Christian is justified in abandoning the compassionate relief in hopes that at another time and under better or at least different circumstances the assistance will be more effective. There are enough "poor" to go around so that one does not need to waste time on those who should be taking care of themselves. After all, even Jesus made it plain he was not going to be the welfare king in Israel when the crowds searched him out for a second feeding after the one all four Gospels record.[51] He rather straightforwardly let the crowds and his disciples know that the bread they were seeking was secondary and his words were primary (John 6). He fed them the previous day in compassion, but it did not deter him from prioritizing his mission. Surely we will not accuse Jesus of injustice.

Part of that prioritizing is to see the "poor" as the Bible sees them. They are basically two groups: (1) the ones specifically oppressed by others (with emphasis on the remnant of the Old Testament and Jesus' disciples in the New Testament), whose oppression usually comes through the help of governmental

---

1992), 172. Henry proposed that making justice a subset of compassion "not only destroys the biblical view of God on the one hand, but also produces the welfare state on the other." Ibid.

51 See Matt. 14:13–21; Mark 6:30–44; Luke 9:10–17; and John 6:1–14. The feeding of the four thousand (Matt. 15:32–39 and Mark 8:1–10) appears to be clearly a matching miracle for a Gentile group. This gives the same message to all people, Jew and Gentile alike.

Awaiting the City

agents (kings and judges), and (2) those to whom life itself has dealt a bad hand: the widowed, the orphaned, the disabled (not through choices to abuse liquor and drugs or live in defiance of sexual prohibitions, however), the persecuted/ imprisoned for Christ's sake, and the cultural alien who needs help assimilating.[52] Together these two groups are a considerable crowd all by themselves, and truly caring for them would require some choices to forgo assistance to those who can take care of themselves in favor of those clearly mandated for assistance as delineated in Scripture. This is what we call "rational compassion"—taking time to discern what needs to be done, how best to do it cost-effectively, and allocating resources, human and material, accordingly. This we should do!

But the question is, who should and can do the best job caring for (emphasis on "caring") these needy folk, the "poor" of Scripture? Government cannot give compassion, nurture, or personal consideration—the things the Bible associates with love. It can give money and "services." The government does not make a good mother or father, and it does not build a home. It "houses" people. It "fosters" them. It pays them. And it can do none of those things without taking from someone else coercively as a matter of rights. This is the most important issue to recognize in turning the job over to government. No government can love my neighbor for me. It can only force my neighbor and me to go through the motions and activities that cannot possibly substitute for loving the truly oppressed and unfortunate. In fact, it is clear now that many, if not most, of those who normally expect government to take care of their responsibility to others, do actually refrain generally from hands-on approaches to caring and giving. Those who object to the governmental approach are also the ones who continue to do the most on a voluntary basis.[53]

---

52 It has now become clear over the past decades that the crusade on the evangelical and religious left is not even about this second group of the "poor" any more but about a general call to egalitarian redistribution based on arbitrary analysis of income and/or wealth "gaps" in the statistical tables.

53 See Arthur C. Brooks, *Who Really Cares: The Surprising Truth about Compassionate Conservatism; America's Charity Divide—Who Gives, Who Doesn't, and Why It Matters* (New York: Basic Books, 2006), and Schweizer, *Makers and Takers*, for extensive documentation on this phenomenon. For another interesting sidelight to this phenomenon pits the political parties in the same kind of comparison, see Joseph Fried, *Democrats and Republicans—Rhetoric and Reality: Comparing the Voters in Statistics and Anecdotes* (New York: Algora, 2008). We are not attempting to be apologists for the Republican Party, as we have said elsewhere in this volume.

Awaiting the City

The approach of coercive neighbor-love would have had the Good Samaritan standing by the road, or better yet, chasing down the priest and the Levite and sticking a gun in their ribs, saying "Gimme yer dough!" "What for?" they reply. "For your brother in the ditch! Don't you know God said to love your neighbor?" Then, if those two didn't have enough to meet the need themselves, the Samaritan would proceed at the inn to use the gun to secure a contribution from the innkeeper. Try reading it that way next Sunday in your church.

The government cannot and does not love its supposed beneficiaries. On the contrary, since the mid-twentieth century for certain and going back probably into the Depression-era attempt by the Roosevelt administration to nationalize and cartelize whole industries and establish government as the employer of last resort, government has proved itself to be the vehicle of dependency and cultural destruction. Nothing could have been calculated purposefully to destroy inner-city family life more effectively than government welfare policy from the 1960s onward.[54] Nor could any outright conspiracy have led to the burgeoning of crime and drug use and the destruction of whole neighborhoods that government programs have fostered. Attempts at housing projects and rent control have simply destroyed the very infrastructure that people need to have a sense of control and dignity in their lives.[55] Government can put a stop to violent and criminal behavior, and in so doing rescue the oppressed. It cannot restore hope and dignity to the human heart. That is a work of love.

---

54 This was first sensationally noted in the media with the famous quote from Daniel Patrick Moynihan, who himself was no "conservative" by today's standards and no fan of elimination of the social safety net: "The steady expansion of this welfare program, as of public assistance programs in general, can be taken as a measure of the steady disintegration of the Negro family structure over the past generation in the United States." "The Negro American Family," in *The Negro Family: The Case for National Action* (Washington, DC: US Government Printing Office, 1965), chap. 2, http://www.dol.gov/oasam/programs/history/moynchapter2.htm. For commentary on this statement, see Walter E. Williams, "'Black Progress' through Politics?" *Capitalism Magazine*, November 18, 2006, http://capitalismmagazine.com/2006/11/black-progress-through-politics/. Moynihan was widely labeled "racist" at the time his report appeared. For the latest compilation of statistical documentation on the continuing devastation of illegitimacy and its connection to poverty, see Duncan Currie, "Five Decades of Crisis," *National Review*, August 24, 2009, 35–36.

55 See our sources below in this chapter for extensive documentation.

Awaiting the City

Paying for Good Health

An area of human need that has now become a surefire object of political power-grabbing is health care. Certain to inspire heated debate and indignant denunciation is the suggestion that equality in the distribution of medical attention is not a right but should be considered a commodity to be purchased and dispensed on the market like any other good. In the United States no one goes without basic medical care.[56] This is often obscured in the rhetoric that loudly announces numbers of uninsured or "underinsured" persons and families. It is often implied that these uninsured, or more dubiously "underinsured," Americans are somehow being denied basic medical care. This is simply not so.[57]

No one may be turned away from an emergency room in the United States for want of insurance or ability to pay, if his or her condition demands immediate attention.[58] The process of recovering costs is different for these people than for the insured or self-paying patient, but care is not denied for

---

56 See Olaf Gerstemann, *Cowboy Capitalism: European Myths, American Reality* (Washington, DC: Cato Institute, 2004), 133–35, for analysis on providing basic medical care.

57 The widely reported figure (47 million) said to represent the "uninsured" in America is nothing but a momentary snapshot, akin to noting that at some time each year fifty million Americans might have a head cold. The Census Bureau in 2007 reported that 250 million Americans have health insurance (85 percent of the population) or are covered by Medicare, Medicaid, or SCHIP (State Children's Health Insurance Program). Those not covered at any given time temporarily number about thirty million who include students just out of school, millions of foreign-born (many here illegally), those between jobs, etc. The average family that goes without health insurance temporarily is reinsured within six months. Many of the uninsured are younger people who can afford it but choose to go without it as a gamble on their youth and good health. About 10.6 million people (less than five percent) go uninsured because they cannot afford it or are uninsurable due, e.g., to preexisting conditions. This is a manageable group through some form of charitable provision like food stamps (health-care stamps?). Thee is some role for government here, but it ought to be circumscribed. Latest figures accounting for the cost of the Patient Protection and Affordable Care Act (PPACA, commonly called Obamacare) show that the average annual cost for insurance in the market is $5,429 per person. This calculates to an annual cost of $58 billion if taxpayers simply bought insurance for the 10.6 million. By contrast the Obama administration says the annual cost will be $93 billion (the cost of central planning), whereas the Congressional Budget Office calculates $893 billion per year (the real cost). See Kevin D. Williamson, "The Central Plan," *National Review*, March 5, 2012, 22–23, https://www.nationalreview.com/nrd/articles/293360/central-plan.

58 Tom's wife works nights in just such an emergency room and has constant hands-on experience with this phenomenon involving not just the indigent poor but young urban professionals and their families and all other classes of people who simply choose not to purchase insurance. And now nothing in the recently passed health-care "reform package" in the US

---

these reasons. All payers pay more for their services because health-care providers must consider the non-payers as a part of the cost of doing business. Triage may determine that no procedure that would consume time and resources is necessary, or elaborate and expensive operations may not be used, but no one is turned away without what is needed to maintain life and relieve pain. The argument once again is not over basic needs provision but over the inequality of care given to those who are insured or can afford to self-pay. After all should not something as basic as health care be outside the market process? Why should the "rich" be able to get procedures that the "poor" cannot due to price considerations?

This can be answered from two perspectives. Every day people make decisions like this without considering justice issues. For instance, shouldn't everyone be able to afford steak instead of macaroni and cheese? Shouldn't everyone be allowed to drive a new BMW instead of a fifteen-year-old Ford Escort? Shouldn't everyone be able to wear a Broncos NFL jacket instead of a Walmart off-brand? The question can be asked a hundred ways. It is not unjust to require that one be able to actually pay for a $1,000 MRI through self-pay or insurance, if it is not a life-threatening case. The only way to make that MRI available to all regardless of ability to pay is to ration it on some other basis, because it is not possible to make it available to all regardless of cost. The machines and technicians must be paid for by some means to be available at all.

The American system allocates resources in a manner that all who truly need the procedure can get it. Some pay for it themselves or use their insurance (with prior approval), and others receive it according to immediate need. The only other choice is to have a health czar deciding who gets what and when and have everyone line up and wait—in places like Canada, for months on end, with sometimes tragic results. In fact, you can get an MRI for your *dog* faster than you can for your *child* in Canada.[59] Furthermore, such pressures inevitably cause choices to be made on the basis of cost-effective considerations that mean the handicapped and unborn and aging are and will be marginalized on the basis of "quality-of-life"

Congress will stop this phenomenon, for the "penalties" for failure to buy insurance will not outweigh the prices necessary to insure those now foregoing insurance for their own reasons.

59   For current wait times, simply Google "MRIs for dogs in Canada." Currently it is one day for pets and a month for humans.

Awaiting the City

considerations. There is nothing more "just" in a system like this.

The other perspective on this issue is that it is the wealthy who lead the way in experimental procedures that eventually become commonplace. Anywhere technology is in an experimental stage, whether it be computers or TVs or satellite radios or air conditioners or new drugs or MRIs, someone must pay the start-up costs and the research and development expenses through higher prices on the front end of public consumption. This is what drives the excellent health-care environment in the United States. Companies know they can profit from innovations that will at first not be affordable to the general public but will make enormous differences for all down the road. The wealthy pay for the initial experimental stages. Everyone benefits as prices go down. Even so, many somehow cannot see through what they consider to be a transparent argument to grasp the reality of health-care economics. Perhaps there is more to it. Clearly the actual outcome will be a new day of almost universal dependence for the population of the United States.[60] Could it be that the *political* desire for *control* of people's lives and choices is the *capital* being accumulated here?

The Politics of Envy

Olasky and Fogel have shown clearly that there was once a way of determining the true state of the indigent and poor and isolating the "deserving poor" as they were once called from the ones who chose to game the system and live off their neighbors. "Paupers" were those who have supposedly "given up" on ever rising out of this condition. Others needed a brief lift and could be soon sent on their way. Others needed a push and shove sometimes, but could be expected to move up the ladder with encouragement. This work was once almost universally done by private, mostly conservative religious groups.

Instead of this, government offers more and more of the same to more and more people as the definitions of "poverty" and "need" are stretched beyond any sense of normal meaning. The so-called *poverty line* is raised constantly to reflect not a basic market basket of essentials in goods and services below which no one should be expected to survive, but an ever-ascending spiral

---

60 See Mark Steyn, "Dependence Day," *National Review*, July 20, 2009, 31–33, http://www.nationalreview.com/corner/196681/happy-dependence-day/mark-steyn. Steyn is Canadian and has lived with such a system as a citizen of that country.

of goods that reflect a keeping-up-with-the-proverbial-Joneses approach and simplistic use of "gap" statistics on income and wealth to establish allegedly "unfair" or "unjust" conditions.[61] According the 2011 Census Bureau, people in the "poverty" group own their own homes (about forty-six percent), multiple TVs, air conditioning, multiple automobiles, use smart phones, and live in spaces most European middle-class people would be envious of.[62] Many smoke, drink, do drugs, have indiscriminate sex with multiple partners, refuse to take precautions to prevent AIDS and other STDs, and do not work nearly as long or hard as the ones whose money is taken to pay for their lifestyles.[63] A "need" now extends in 2009 to digital TV receivers. If you cannot afford one, the government will pay for it. We have served pastorally in places for many years where it is common to see a mother in a check-out line with a couple of grade-school-age children in tow (wearing the latest Nike sneakers and NFL team logo jackets) offering food stamps to pay for numerous items of junk food, while paying cash for more than one carton of cigarettes.[64] Sug-

---

61 Sider has constantly revised his definition of the poverty line until it now resembles something like poor people being able to take "full advantage" of all the benefits found in a society and could include access to ownership of "factories" that they did not build and the right not to work full time if they so choose. See esp. *Just Generosity*, chap. 2, for his "biblical" justification. He appears to have reached a number of 120 to 130 percent of the poverty line number used today by most welfare agencies. His position on work seems to vary between saying that those who do not work must repent and then justifying their failure to seek full-time work as part of the system's failure to pay enough and offer something that is fulfilling in the best biblical sense.

62 See interaction with the Census Bureau's 2011 annual poverty report in Robert Rector and Rachel Sheffield, "Understanding Poverty in the United States: Surprising Facts about America's Poor" (paper, Backgrounder No. 2607, Heritage Foundation, Washington, DC, September 13, 2011), http://www.heritage.org/research/reports/2011/09/understanding-poverty-in-the-united-states-surprising-facts-about-americas-poor.

63 Sider admits that only twenty-sven percent of the so-called poor have a full-time worker in the household and that those who work even part-time don't want or look for full-time work. *Just Generosity*, n. 10, Kindle loc. 3283–87. We have previously cited this disparity on work between the "poor" and the so-called "rich." See, e.g., section under heading "The American Success Story" in chap. 22.

64 Memorably, Tom experienced this repeatedly in years when, pastoring a small church, he and his family were eligible for the EITC (Earned Income Tax Credit) and refused it as not compatible with Christian views of provision for one's own. The only pair of name-brand sneakers his children ever wore was one pair of red "Air Jordans" bought for his oldest son during high school. They were on a bargain rack because they were two years out of date and style. No NFL logo jackets or paraphernalia were ever thought commensurate with good stewardship of money and possessions at our level.

Awaiting the City

gestions that it would be more appropriate to require lifestyle changes before true "need" can be assessed raise the cry that such judgments are "blaming the victim." None of this is in the biblical conception of "just" distribution of anything. Instead it only contributes to envy, because the rhetoric no longer is really about absolute poverty in real terms but of "income gaps" and "tax breaks for the rich," with the "rich" now defined in 2009 by President Obama as anyone with an income over $250,000 for couples.[65]

Furthermore, the politics of envy is now entrenched in tax systems in the West (and most importantly for our purposes, the United States) that take more and more people off the income tax rolls altogether, so that they have no incentive to elect politicians whose agenda is to stop the confiscations of other people's money or demand lifestyle changes.[66] We have arrived at that point where incitement to envy of others makes the best elective politics, for it is always about what group(s) are going to get who to do the paying for benefits to whomever else. Not everyone is going to pay, even on a supposedly "progressive" basis. Some will not pay at all; many others will become net tax receivers. No system of economics that relies on voluntary exchanges could ever be as insidious in encouraging envy as a coercive system that buys votes with someone else's money. To call this "just" is to twist the concept beyond any recognition.[67]

It has been noted before that every good idea that assumes the role of personal conviction becomes the cause that evolves through the movement

65 For complete analysis of the issue of supposed growing income gaps, see Robert W. Fogel, *The Fourth Great Awakening and the Future of Egalitarianism* (Chicago: University of Chicago, 2000), 218–22. Several of our other sources also have analyses. Sowell, *Intellectuals and Society*, explains how the statistics measure and do not measure pertinent facts related to our contentions here. See also David Murray, Joel Schwartz and S. Robert Lichter, *It Ain't Necessarily So: How the Media Remake Our Picture of Reality* (New York: Penguin Books, 2002), 71–81, 165–68, for analysis of these same phenomena and their usage as the reporting agencies have changed methodologies over the years.

66 This number is approaching fifty percent in the United States. See U.S. GAO (Government Accountability Office) statistics and other studies for this information. According to the American Enterprise Institute we are now approaching the level of forty-nine percent of the American population who pay no income taxes. See interview with AEI president Arthur Brooks by Marvin Olasky, "The Next 100 Years," *World Magazine*, January 16, 2010, 22, http://www.worldmag.com/2009/12/the_next_100_years.

67 See Schweizer, *Makers and Takers*, for documentation that this encouragement to envy is purposeful and actually part of the agenda of the Left, who observes that "the only way to determine what is equal is the absence of envy," citing what liberal thinker Ronald Dworkin called "the envy test." Kindle loc. 1256–64.

Awaiting the City

phase to become itself little more than a *racket*. Most movements for good are co-opted by those who have figured out how to profit from them—either monetarily or politically or socially or all of the above. This is what Gonzalo Fernández de la Mora calls the "demagogic promotion of envy," and it succeeds because all people are subject to its allure and the majority of any population at any given time will feel inferior to some minority.[68] Envy is mostly *pain* at the *happiness of others* and can be satisfied only when the other is made *less happy*, though it may not immediately seem evident that the other's diminishment has definitely benefited oneself. That is what makes this sin so evil—I need not directly benefit except by enjoying the diminishment of another. The politics of envy is driven by this human failing and not the direct distribution of benefits to the most needy.[69] This is what accounts for its success. It does not need to succeed at what it promises to do for *me*, only in what it does to the *other* that makes me feel better. In fact, at certain levels the economics of taxation and regulation that promises benefits to the less fortunate actually *harms* them. Minimum wage legislation, tariff barriers, licensing regulations, corporate tax rates, high personal tax rates on high income people, and many other popular soak-the-rich schemes actually *harm poorer people* through increased consumer prices, elimination of entry-level jobs, disincentives to businesses to expand and others to invest, and the decisions of wealthier people to work less and pay less in taxes.[70] But the politicians who enact such legislation are given the opportunity to exercise their *will to power* (Nietzsche) in so doing.

---

68 See Gonzalo Fernández de la Mora, *Egalitarian Envy: The Political Foundations of Social Justice*, trans. Antonio T. de Nicolás (1984; Eng. trans., 1987; repr., Lincoln, NE: iUniverse, 2000), 93. This is also Sowell's argument, without reference to envy, in *Civil Rights*. Nieztsche would call this "*ressentiment*," as does Hunter, *To Change the World*.
69 See Barack Obama's comment in an exchange with Charles Gibson that even if raising tax rates on the "rich" (in this case all investors who have capital gains) does not result in actual additional revenues to the government, it is still the "fair" thing to do. Arthur B. Laffer, Stephen Moore, and Peter J. Tanous, *The End of Prosperity: How Higher Taxes Will Doom the Economy—If We Let It Happen* (New York: Simon & Schuster, 2008), Kindle loc. 284. This is the very definition of envy.
70 See Mona Charen, *Do-Gooders: How Liberals Hurt Those They Claim to Help (and the Rest of Us)* (New York: Penguin, 2004). For a wide-ranging discussion of the politics associated with these issues from a Christian perspective, see Doug Bandow, *Beyond Good Intentions: A Biblical View of Politics*, Turning Point Christian Worldview (Westchester, IL: Crossway, 1988).

Awaiting the City

The Elephant in the Room

Many by now are wondering when the real issue of wealth and poverty in America will be addressed.[71] Is it not true that the United States owes a massive debt to one segment of its society that demands government intervention on whatever scale necessary to correct the evil? That is, the evil of *racism*. Is it not true that capitalistic free markets cannot redress such a monstrous wrong without direct government intervention in the marketplace to provide a level playing field on which the competitive dynamics of the market play out? What can two white guys (Chad and Tom) have to say about that? At the risk of also being labeled "racist" ourselves, we will attempt an answer, but not without the help of some of our African American brothers and sisters, several of whom would simply prefer to be called "black," or better "Mr." or "Mrs." or "Dr.,"[72] without any reference to skin color. It is part of the peculiar nature of the American situation that white and black people of our generation looked forward with Dr. Martin Luther King Jr. to a time when we could be color-blind. It seems we are no closer today to that ideal than we were more than forty years ago, and we mourn the apparent death (or at least coma) of a great dream. In today's American politics, there is an unfortunate and cynical, almost sinister use of the label "racist," and its concomitant "Uncle Tom," to dismiss anyone who argues as we will, while documenting as we will.[73] Nevertheless, with Dr. Walter E. Williams' certificate of exoneration

---

71 See introductory remarks from James M. Lawson in the *Poverty and Justice Bible: Contemporary English Version*, ed. Sandie Butler, David Spriggs, Nick Page, and Claire Page (New York: American Bible Society, 2009): "Oppression is the primary trait of poverty in its varied forms in this country." He goes on to cite injustice practiced against the Native American population from the seventeenth century onward and 350 years of slavery and its aftermath.

72 The range of acceptable terminology to designate "people of color" (a relatively recent addition to the vocabulary) is confusing to many and fraught with the possibility of multiple offenses given and taken. We will stick to the "black" designation and hope for the best.

73 See esp. Randall Kennedy, *Sellout: The Politics of Racial Betrayal* (New York: Pantheon Books, 2008), for a highly nuanced discussion of the issues related to black group solidarity and the concomitant tendency in that group to label pejoratively and derisively those who oppose racial set-asides, known popularly as "affirmative action" and/or redistributional tax and regulation policies, from a black perspective.

in hand[74] and Dr. Shelby Steele's warning against "white guilt"[75] in our ears, we will proceed.

Frankly, this is where the problem of envy makes itself most savagely known with consequences of such far-reaching import that it is hard to take it all in. The monstrous crime against enslaved Africans on this continent perpetrated by a hypocritical elite claiming "all men are created equal" fairly begs to be punished in some way beyond some of its obvious consequences.[76] Abraham Lincoln suggested that the Civil War was in some sense an expiation in blood for crimes against the enslaved.[77] But no amount of blood spilled could right the wrong or redress the inequities and injustices that would follow. For another hundred years racism would enslave with chains unseen and consequences just as insidious.

If ever a crime justified envy as we have defined it above, surely this would be it, but in this case it would not be exactly envy but the desire for retribution and restitution that drives the sense of grievance. However, the facts of economic life once again trump such desires with a concreteness that defies the ideal one might wish to achieve. One is then left with envy only, the desire to diminish someone else regardless of its true consequences for me. The other person's happiness, truly undeserved to my own thinking, cannot be allowed to stand while I cannot achieve what that person has, at least at the pace I would like to achieve it.

Here are the facts that cannot be dismissed without further detriment to those previously wronged through slavery and racism. The greatest harm done has been the theft of human capital. Beginning with human dignity and progressing through familial destruction, social and cultural disruption, and educational

---

74 See printable certificate available from Walter E. Williams, "Proclamation of Amnesty and Pardon Granted to All Persons of European Descent," http://econfaculty.gmu.edu/wew/WalterWilliamsAmnestyProclamation.pdf. Written about twenty years ago, this proclamation is rementioned in Walter E. Williams, "Senate Slavery Apology," Townhall, July 8, 2009, http://townhall.com/columnists/walterewilliams/2009/07/08/senate_slavery_apology.

75 Shelby Steele, *White Guilt: How Blacks and Whites Together Destroyed the Promise of the Civil Rights Era* (New York: HarperCollins, 2006).

76 For samplings of the true feelings of many of the founders on the issue of slavery, see Thomas G. West, *Vindicating the Founders* (1997; repr., New York: Rowman & Littlefield, 2000), 1–36, and Walter E. Williams' selection of quotations, "What the Founders Said about Slavery," http://econfaculty.gmu.edu/wew/quotes/slavery.html.

77 See his second inaugural address. Abraham Lincoln, "Inaugural Address," March 4, 1865, online by Gerhard Peters and John T. Woolley, American Presidency Project, http://www.presidency.ucsb.edu/ws/?pid=25819.

Awaiting the City

deprivation, the slave culture of the South and the racist culture of the North and South before and after the Civil War created a class of people from whom was taken the basic building blocks of competitive opportunity in the industrialized world.[78] No amount of money, property or means of production can replace these fundamentals. Furthermore, they cannot be instantaneously restored, for they are the heritage of generations and cannot be acquired except over time and with constant sacrificial effort. In short, they cannot be given; they must be produced.[79] The response of government early on was to promise forty acres and a mule. This is the way government works through complex problems. It deals in quantifiable units and monetary/material "solutions." It cannot provide what family, social and cultural contacts, and habits of life do.[80] All these human factors play into the education of each generation to its accountability to those gone before and to itself. Government is capable of giving a *handout* but not a true *hand-up*. Without a prior reservoir of individual and communal capital, each generation must supply its own resolve to do the preparatory work of getting equipped to compete

---

78 A sampling of the literature includes Thomas J. Sugrue, *Sweet Land of Liberty: The Forgotten Struggle for Civil Rights in the North* (New York: Random House, 2008); Robert Higgs, *Competition and Coercion: Blacks in the American Economy, 1865–1914*, Hoover Institution Publication 163 (New York: Cambridge University Press, 1977); Robert William Fogel, *Without Consent or Contract: The Rise and Fall of American Slavery* (New York: W. W. Norton, 1989); Anthony S. Chen, *The Fifth Freedom: Jobs, Politics, and Civil Rights in the United States, 1941–1972*, Princeton Studies in American Politics (Princeton, NJ: Princeton University Press, 2009); Robert J. Norrell, *Up From History: The Life of Booker T. Washington* (Cambridge: Harvard University Press, 2009), to name only a few. The latest assessment of the impact of slavery and its aftermath up to the time of the great migration northward to the cities outside the South is Russell K. Nieli, *Wounds That Will Not Heal: Affirmative Action and Our Continuing Racial Divide* (New York: Encounter Books, 2012). Nieli's work is not uncontroversial, but it is a fair reading and goes to heart of our concerns here.
79 Several of the sources here cited note the remarkable fashion in which such a deprived people recovered in less than a hundred years and demonstrated the group integrity and grit to rise above huge injustice and disadvantage. Higgs, *Competition and Coercion*, shows statistically that competitive action is better than governmental coercion of redistribution. Additional studies show how business and business-friendly courts tend to undermine racism, such as Robert E. Weems Jr., *Desegregating the Dollar: African American Consumerism in the Twentieth Century* (New York: New York University Press, 1998); Stephanie Capparell, *The Real Pepsi Challenge: The Inspirational Story of Breaking the Color Barrier in American Business*, Wall Street Journal Book (New York: Free Press, 2007); and on the mixed bag in the relationship of labor to racism, see Paul D. Moreno, *Black Americans and Organized Labor: A New History* (Baton Rouge: Louisiana State University Press, 2006), and Sugrue, *Sweet Land of Liberty*.
80 We are not begrudging the "forty acres and a mule," merely pointing out that this did not really meet the real need, as witness the evils of "Redemption" and Jim Crow laws.

Awaiting the City

in the market. Lyndon Johnson's "Great Society" purported to address this very problem. He sold it to the American public as a program to bring all Americans to the starting line with the same equipment to run the race.[81] Unfortunately, it is at this time that one can begin to trace the decline in the reservoir of human capital in the black family and culture. The name attached to this governmental attempt to redress ancient wrongs came to be known as "affirmative action," the ideal of not simply ceasing to oppress but making every effort to make up for lost time and resources in the black community, and eventually an ever-widening circle of aggrieved minorities seeking to piggyback on the achievements of blacks politically. Today this term, and its companion "set-asides," is primarily attached to the positive attempt to insure actual entry into the job market and educational institutions for minority group Americans and special classes of citizens.

Most of the current generations of living Americans would probably trace the term's origins to the agitation and politics of the 1960s and '70s out of which LBJ's proposals were aroused. However, recent studies have shown that the actual beginnings of the search for equal protection of the law in employment practice can be traced to the 1940s, especially the time after World War II when returning veterans flooded the job market expecting a grateful nation to hire indiscriminately and generously. When black Americans were confronted in all regions of the country with evident racial discrimination in hiring, the modern political movement demanding fair employment practices (FEP) was born.[82]

The struggle for FEP legislative relief in the 1940s, where the term "affirmative action" first appeared, was a reference to "administrative orders requiring employers or unions to hire, reinstate, or promote individual workers who were the proven victims of discriminatory behavior." Eventually it would refer to "written plans for racial integration that all federal contractors were mandated to file as part of their bid for federal contracts, irrespective of what lawyers would later call a 'factual predicate' of discrimination."[83] These plans did not simply describe proactive steps employers or unions might take to insure equal treatment for prospective and current employees, but went on to set

---

81 See Nick Kotz, *Judgment Days: Lyndon Baines Johnson, Martin Luther King, Jr., and the Laws That Changed America* (New York: Houghton Mifflin, 2005), for the history of LBJ's agenda.
82 See Chen, *Fifth Freedom*, and Sugrue, *Sweet Land of Liberty*, above.
83 This was the language of the government mandate.

Awaiting the City

"goals and timetables" for equalizing representation of "selected racial groups over time.... By the early months of 1972, job discrimination had come to be regulated by a set of policies that would have appeared unrecognizable to anyone with clear memories of the original struggle for FEP."[84] Now public policy was a "bewildering labyrinth of federal and state statutes, administrative regulations and executive orders."[85] Anthony Chen documents throughout his work that the failure of coalitions opposed to the *original intent* of FEP legislation to join in *just* attempts to redress the wrongs of that era inadvertently laid the foundation for the more onerous actions of the later years, a development that undoubtedly fueled the increasing sense of *frustration and deprivation on one side and the sense of unfair compensatory action on the other side*. Add to this mix professional politicians, agitators, "consultants," and various pressure groups (read PACs) standing to gain from the ongoing strife, and the volatile cocktail of racial confrontation must inevitably explode, as it did in the '60s and '70s, and/or feed ever-increasing envy and discontent as it does today.

Perhaps of even greater import is the broad coalition in American politics that is determined to *bring down* the whole capitalistic system because they believe that it is in some way *inherently racist* and *discriminatory* and not reconcilable with corrective actions needed to redress these ancient wrongs.[86] Tom Sowell has eloquently reminded us that the facts are contrary to this agenda, illustrating it graphically in a tribute to Rosa Parks at the time of her death.[87] He reminds us that Jim Crow laws in the South were the product of *government* and *not capitalistic businesses*. Especially in the case of public transit systems, it was a small minority of racists (in a sea of racism) who persuaded governments to pass laws segregating the races in their seating. The bus companies (who were intent on profits both white and black) resisted the passage of the laws, went to court to strike the laws down, and resisted enforcement of the laws in some places for years until government began

---

84   Chen, *Fifth Freedom*, 6–7.
85   Ibid.
86   For a collection of thought on the subject of racism and capitalism, see Jonathan J. Bean, ed. *Race and Liberty in America: The Essential Reader*, Independent Studies in Political Economy (Lexington: University Press of Kentucky, 2009). The most obvious example in 2011–12 was the various protests of the Occupy Whatever "movement" around the country, fueled and fed by Washington bureaucrats and the left-wing media.
87   See Thomas Sowell, "Rosa Parks: Pursuit of Profit vs. Racism," *Capitalism Magazine*, October 27, 2005, http://capitalismmagazine.com/2005/10/rosa-parks-pursuit-of-profit-vs-racism/.

to punish employees for failure to enforce the segregation laws.[88] Racism is not inherent in any system of economics, but it is *endemic to the human race*. Markets do not cure racism, but they do tend to ameliorate the effects of it. Sowell describes the struggle for egalitarian solutions to this and other supposed failings of the market system as the conflict between "unlimited" and "limited" visions.[89] We have already spoken of this juxtaposition and will address this more specifically in a later chapter, but here we must note the counterproductive results of affirmative action and redistributional tax and regulation policy as we know it in twenty-first-century American political economy.[90]

---

88 See also Bean, *Race and Liberty in America*, 113–17, for primary source documentation on this incident.

89 See again, as we have frequently cited elsewhere, Thomas Sowell, *A Conflict of Visions: Ideological Origins of Political Struggles*, rev. ed. (New York: Basic Books, 2007).

90 Some of the foregoing and most of the following discussion is taken from numerous sources in the black community that include the following: Thomas Sowell, *Race and Culture: A World View* (New York: Basic Books, 1994); Thomas Sowell, *Affirmative Action Around the World: An Empirical Study* (New Haven, CT: Yale University Press, 2004); Sowell, *Civil Rights;* Thomas Sowell, *Black Rednecks and White Liberals: And Other Cultural and Ethnic Issues* (San Francisco: Encounter Books, 2005); Shelby Steele, *A Dream Deferred: The Second Betrayal of Black Freedom in America* (New York: HarperCollins, 1998); Shelby Steele, *The Content of Our Character: A New Vision of Race in America* (New York: St. Martin's Press, 1990); Juan Williams, *Enough: The Phony Leaders, Dead-End Movements, and Culture of Failure That Are Undermining Black America—and What We Can Do About It* (New York: Crown, 2006); Walter E. Williams, *The State against Blacks* (New York: McGraw Hill, 1982); John H. McWhorter, *Losing the Race: Self-Sabotage in Black America* (New York: Free Press, 2001); John McWhorter, *Winning the Race: Beyond the Crisis in Black America* (New York: Gotham Books, 2005); Larry Elder, *Ten Things You Can't Say in America* (New York: St. Martin's Press, 2000); Stan Faryna, Brad Stetson, and Joseph G. Conti eds., *Black and Right: The Bold New Voice of Black Conservatism in America* (Westport, CT: Praeger, 1997); Rev. Jesse Lee Peterson, *Scam: How the Black Leadership Exploits Black America* (Nashville: WND Books, 2003); C. Mason Weaver, *It's OK to Leave the Plantation*, 3rd ed., edited by Julie Reeder (Fallbrook, CA: Reeder, 2000); Kenneth R. Timmerman, *Shakedown: Exposing the Real Jesse Jackson* (Washington, DC: Regnery, 2002); Star Parker, with Lorenzo Benet, *Pimps, Whores and Welfare Brats: From Welfare Cheat to Conservative Messenger; The Autobiography of Star Parker* (New York: Pocket Books, 1997); Star Parker, *Uncle Sam's Plantation: How Big Government Enslaves America's Poor and What We Can Do about It* (Nashville: WND Books, 2003); Clarence Thomas, *My Grandfather's Son: A Memoir* (New York: HarperCollins, 2007); Ward Connerly, *Creating Equal: My Fight against Race Preferences*, rev. ed. (San Francisco: Encounter Books, 2007); Stephen L. Carter, *Reflections of an Affirmative Action Baby* (New York: Basic Books, 1991); Glenn C. Loury, *One By One from the Inside Out: Essays and Reviews on Race and Responsibility in America* (New York: Simon & Schuster, 1995).

Awaiting the City

Counterproductive and Destructive Political Action

Tom Sowell noted twenty-five years ago that it is demonstrable that political action designed nominally to lift whole communities economically is not just unproven as a strategy but actually counterproductive in its long-term effects, for it tends to exacerbate problems by polarizing groups.[91] Its primary effect is to elevate individual political leadership at the expense of group alienation in the larger culture. No biblical Christian can take solace in the idea that this is somehow more "just" and likely to promote some form of actual racial harmony.[92] "In short, despite the unpromising record of politics as a means of raising a group from poverty to affluence and despite the dangers of politicizing race, there are built-in incentives for individual political leaders to do just that."[93] This is becoming a common refrain.

Several of our sources also decry the reverse effects of affirmative action in the academic world and the job market. All groups subject to such preferential treatment, but especially blacks, are now *subjected to the suspicion* that they are actually inferior in ability but have arrived at the point of their present achievement through special treatment *whether this is the case or not*. On the other hand, many are actually placed in situations where they are likely to fail because they are not yet qualified to compete and prosper at the level to which they have been advanced through preferential treatment. This is especially insidious in the educational world because many of those thus trapped would succeed at a lower level of academic expectation and progress at their own rate, perhaps in the end to actual arrival at the higher level prematurely received. Instead, they are more likely to simply drop out and despair of future advancement. The apparent net effect is that the goal of community advancement through preferential treatment(s) is lost as the intellectual and economic elites[94] in the aggrieved community receive the most benefits, while the actual objects of the political exercise, the majority of the disadvantaged,

---

91   Sowell, *Civil Rights*, 29–35.
92   A number of our other sources confirm this diagnosis. We do not have the space here to cite sources again and again, but we do hope those who are sincerely interested in the facts will consult our listings in notes.
93   Sowell, *Civil Rights*, 35.
94   The intellectual elites will achieve without preferential treatment academically and the economic elites are the only ones capable of bidding on jobs and contracts set aside for minority applicants.

remain in the trap of despair. This double whammy—denigration through suspicion and setup for failure through misplaced zeal for "justice"—is a burden that no group should be required to bear, especially in light of prior deprivation and the evident proven group ability to achieve given proper opportunities.[95]

The phenomenon of "white guilt" is a condition foisted upon white and black alike to the detriment of any true ideal of justice. From the black perspective it taints racial relationships with condescension (from the white position) and inferiority feelings and complexes (from the black position) that are undeserved and perpetuate the myth of actual racial differences. From the white perspective it prevents the kind of actual personal dialogue that would lead to understanding and true brotherhood because the fear of being labeled "racist" through inadvertent conversational mistakes.[96] The ideal of color-blindness cannot flourish in such an atmosphere, and all kinds of pathologies flow from this well of suspicion and misinformation.

We have previously mentioned in passing the reverse effects of ongoing redistributional policies and preferential treatment on the actual group culture of those affected by these policies. Jason DeParle has movingly presented this story in *American Dream*[97] and has presented as well the telling effects for good and ill of the famous "welfare reform" legislation of the 1990s. There is no question that the most egregious effects of such political "solutions" have fallen upon the black community. This has made an evil that was once being overcome by the incredible resilience of the people upon whom it was perpetrated into an ongoing blight of even greater proportions. For it distorts the perceptions of both black and white of themselves and each other.[98]

The discouragement and disillusionment of the formerly legally oppressed mi-

---

95 Sowell discusses concisely the manipulation of statistics in the media and documents his remarks on affirmative action in *Intellectuals and Society*, 122–24.

96 Obama administration official Eric Holder recently called America a "nation of cowards on race."

97 Jason DeParle, *American Dream: Three Women, Ten Kids, and a Nation's Drive to End Welfare* (New York: Viking, 2004).

98 For the most recent treatment of the actual state of racial differences and perceptions in the United States (esp. in the light of affirmative action) see, Richard Sander and Stuart Taylor Jr., *Mismatch: How Affirmative Action Hurts Students It's Intended to Help and Why Universities Won't Admit It* (New York: Basic Books, 2012). Prior to this time the best treatment was Stephan Thernstrom and Abigail Thernstrom, *America in Black and White: One Nation, Indivisible* (New York: Simon & Schuster, 1997).

Awaiting the City

nority is being institutionalized in the form of generational poverty being passed along to a perpetual underclass that then overcompensates with behaviors that worsen the condition.[99] The former legal oppressors continue to operate in a condescending and guilty conspiracy with political coalitions that actually exacerbate the situation.[100] Black leadership is thus bound (some in the community feel) to support destructive policies for their own communities in order to stay at the political table. This is the source of much intraracial frustration in the black community between those who see these conditions differently and accuse one another of racial betrayal.

The need for group "solidarity" is an ongoing struggle for both survival in it and a challenge to individual accomplishment apart from it. In the process the hope of racial harmony through dialogue and personal interaction is lost in the politics of group identity. It is to be hoped that, despite the usual expected deference to this solidarity displayed by President Obama at a recent[101] NAACP meeting, the words he spoke additionally to black and white alike will have a positive effect. He warned that black kids, just like other poor children may face long odds, "[b]ut that's not a reason to get bad grades, that's not a reason to cut class, that's not a reason to give up on your education and drop out of school. No one has written your destiny for you. Your destiny is in your hands—you cannot forget that. That's what we have to teach all our children. No excuses. No excuses."[102]

These words highlight what is perhaps the most egregious result of this process, the failure of educational opportunity to materialize from the political morass we have outlined above. Abigail and Stephan Thernstrom have clearly

99 This is especially true in the educational community where getting properly prepared for life in society through schooling can be derided as "acting white," the entertainment industry where lawlessness and debauchery are glorified, and the jobless community where selling drugs and other criminal activity pay more monetarily in the short run than entry-level jobs, which traditionally have taught life skills.
100 Witness the coalition of unions (who perpetuate the myth of the minimum wage, a clear detriment to the black community), teachers' associations and unions (who refuse to bargain over vouchers and charters to remedy the deficiencies of inner-city schools that year by year do not educate poor black children for competitive success in society), and the abortion industry (which disproportionately assists in the killing of black children by a wide margin).
101 Recent to this writing.
102 Barack Obama, "Remarks by the President to the NAACP Centennial Convention," (speech, New York Hilton, New York, New York, July 17, 2009), http://blogs.suntimes.com/sweet/2009/07/obamas_naacp_speech.html, quoted in *National Review*, August 10, 2009, 8.

Awaiting the City

delineated the problem of the "racial gap in learning."[103] Their final chapter outlines the continuing roadblocks to significant change. The informed reader will see that this is a political swamp full of alligators. Perhaps nowhere else in American life is it more evident that what drives the political process and its economic results is not the need of the poor but the agenda of the politically connected and the recipients of governmental largesse in the bureaucratic establishments of government and education. This may be the greatest betrayal of a minority group in the history of the American experiment.

In 1993, then-president Bill Clinton spoke in the church in Memphis that was the last place Martin Luther King Jr., preached before he was killed. Jason Deparle notes that "Clinton chided the congregation to imagine what King would say to them now. 'I fought for freedom, he would say, but not for freedom of people to kill each other,' Clinton said. 'Not for freedom of children to have children and the fathers of those children to walk away from them as if they don't amount to anything.... I did not fight for the right of black people to murder other black people with reckless abandon.' A black audience in a poor black city interrupted with applause eleven times."[104] Our sentiments exactly.

---

103 Abigail Thernstrom and Stephan Thernstrom, *No Excuses: Closing the Racial Gap in Learning* (New York: Simon & Schuster, 2003).
104 DeParle, *American Dream*, 151.

Awaiting the City

Chapter 26

The Spirit of Competitive Destruction: Creation, Ecology, and the Destiny of Man

MICHAEL NOVAK HAS SPENT A GOOD PORTION of his public career seeking to ferret out and delineate the true "spirit" of democratic capitalism as a political economic system. Inspired by the original "spirit" analysis of Max Weber, he has especially sought to prove that it is not just a Protestant ethic that led to the ascendancy of the West economically, but that also the Catholic ethic has played its part. In addition, he has sought to tie the overwhelming success of the American experiment to a spirit of entrepreneurial bravado and innovative experimentation that characterizes so much of American life. It is not just capitalistic markets or banking enterprises or corporate structures or a work ethic derived from whatever Christian sources or even a combination of all these factors. There is something about the whole outlook of a culture and society that is willing to accept and foster change everywhere all the time and ongoing over time that constitutes a "spirit" that produces immense wealth from inventive genius and spreads it up and down the spectrum of economic distribution and literally changed and is changing the world. That this change is on balance good cannot be denied, if it is a "good" to improve humanity's material condition as opposed to leaving the vast majority of mankind in poverty, ill health and with a short horizon for human life. This is what constitutes the true "spirit of democratic capitalism."[1] This is also the theme of Dierdre McCloskey (*Bourgeois Dignity*) in her multivolume (planned) work.[2]

CREATIVE DESTRUCTION

A less optimistic view of the process of industrialization and modernization of the West and particularly the United States is the assessment of Joseph Schumpeter, who coined the term "creative destruction" to describe the ongoing rise and fall of businesses and whole industries as human inventiveness and competitiveness seeks ever more progress in the technological development of society and the planet.[3] This process can be seen as ruthless and materialistic from the standpoint of its effects on those caught in its seemingly inexorable march and is often criticized for its apparent exploitation of the planet, a charge that implies lack of care and proper stewardship. This last charge can be made by anyone from Christians who take the Bible seriously to earth-worshipers.[4] From this perspective the development of a growing economy fueled by the production and pursuit of "consumer goods" is a degrading materialistic spiral that feeds people's basest instincts and disregards the human costs of competitive market destruction and creation as well as destroys indigenous cultural values globally.

Bethany Moreton is one who (it seems to us) alternately appears to commend and then excoriate Walmart for having done just this by moving into a niche of consumer service in an untapped human market and developed it into the premier company of its kind in the world.[5] Along the way Sam Walton and his company have made consumer goods available to huge numbers of people at prices never before seen in the areas where his stores first appeared and now continue to appear globally. They hired local people and local managers and

---

1   Michael Novak, *The Spirit of Democratic Capitalism*, 2nd ed. (Lanham, MD: Madison Books, 1991).

2   McCloskey's first two volumes are *The Bourgeois Virtues* (Chicago: University of Chicago Press, 2006), and *Bourgeois Dignity* (Chicago: University of Chicago Press, 2010).

3   Joseph A. Schumpeter, *Capitalism, Socialism, and Democracy*, 3rd ed. (New York: Harper & Row, 1950), 82–83, inter alia. See also our discussion of Schumpeter in chap. 19.

4   Strangely, Jim Wallis even refers to the earth as our "mother" in his latest release, *Rediscovering Values* (New York: Simon & Schuster, 2010), Kindle loc. 1088–133.

5   Bethany Moreton, *To Serve God and Wal-Mart: The Making of Christian Free Enterprise* (Cambridge, MA: Harvard University Press, 2009).

found local money for finance and provided incentive investment plans that have made numbers of their lowest level employees millionaires. They have made flexible hourly employment available to people with other priorities besides full-time careers. They have forced the retailing industry as a whole to become more efficient and lower prices across the board. They have encouraged and supported educational institutions to train a new cadre of service-oriented employees and entrepreneurs. They have encouraged Christian behavior inside and outside the company itself. They have supported evangelical causes with money and personnel. And yet, and yet...[6]

Furthermore, the process is not "sustainable" because it depends on the continuing destructive exploitation of the planet, which is neither right nor limitless in its possibilities. Depending on such "growth" to eventually include all societies on earth in prosperity is wrong and shortsighted. Consequently national and international "solutions" must be sought to stop societal and global destructive economic growth, while simultaneously remedying the abject poverty and misery of the underdeveloped world.[7]

Both the paragraphs above assume an understanding of man, individually and communally, and mankind's role in the overall ecology of the planet and ultimately their destiny as human. Mankind as "human" will finally get to assume the proper role of dominion and rule and thus reflect or image God in the world the way they were meant to—now in part, but in the age to come in full. Yet human beings will not become a god or gods. Rather, as God's image-bearing creatures they will fulfill their God-given destiny. We have noted elsewhere that the idea of progress as a

---

6   Ibid., esp. 264–74
7   For discussion of the issues in this chapter, see Joseph A. Schumpeter, *History of Economic Analysis*, rev. ed. (New York: Oxford University Press, 1994); Larry Schweikart, *The Entrepreneurial Adventure: A History of Business in the United States* (New York: Harcourt College Publishers, 2000); William J. Baumol, Robert E. Litan, and Carl J. Schramm, *Good Capitalism, Bad Capitalism, and the Economics of Growth and Prosperity* (New Haven, CT: Yale University Press, 2007); Brian C. Anderson, *Democratic Capitalism and Its Discontents* (Wilmington, DE: ISI Books, 2007); John R. Lott Jr., *Freedomnomics: Why the Free Market Works and Other Half-Baked Theories Don't* (Washington, DC: Regnery, 2007); Gene Epstein, *Econospinning: How to Read Between the Lines when the Media Manipulate the Numbers* (Hoboken, NJ: John Wiley & Sons, 2006); Paul Collier, *The Bottom Billion: Why the Poorest Countries Are Failing and What Can Be Done about It* (New York: Oxford University Press, 2007); Tyler Cowen, *Creative Destruction: How Globalization Is Changing the World's Cultures* (Princeton, NJ: Princeton University Press, 2002); and Tyler Cowen, *In Praise of Commercial Culture* (Cambridge, MA: Harvard University Press, 1998).

Awaiting the City

Christian ideal has a long history. Western civilization and particularly the United States, culturally, politically and economically, are the product of this bias. This assumes that man in his private and societal self would not remain in stasis but would grow and change as the gradual accumulation of human knowledge and technology produced domination of his environment and freedom from debilitating disease and early aging through harsh labor and survival struggles. This conception of man says that it is better to struggle with the results of rapid change than it is to continue to live in perpetual fear of famine and disease at the mercy of one's environment. Better to *control it than be controlled by it*, even if the process is disruptive to a modern sense of security. Let the market and man's entrepreneurial inventiveness work.

It can be argued that the whole *critique* of capitalistic free markets and the civilization they spawn is an *antiprogress, antimodern* longing for a time gone by when life was supposedly simpler and less hectic, more fulfilling in terms of human contentment and more conducive to artistic and cultural pursuits. Life on Walden Pond or Lake Wobegon continues to have its allure, so long as someone can haul in the groceries and the satellite dish doesn't go on the fritz. This is what makes it strange that those once called "liberals" or "socialists" now wish to be called "progressive." In fact, they wish to roll back the tide of progress to another time, or at least hold back the current tide as it seems inexorably bound to change the world even further. Arguing that people were, in effect, meant to "stop and smell the roses" or at least plant some or paint some, the progressive agenda seeks the leveling that comes from penalizing the work of one person (through taxation or regulation or both) to benefit another, who may lack skill or talent or education or motivation or ambition or any of a dozen human characteristics that make this other person uncomfortable in a competitive atmosphere, where keeping up with the work load means choosing against the quieter, more reflective life he or she might have otherwise chosen. After all, are not the "values" of such a life more to be cherished and nourished than the apparently more "materialistic" life of the seemingly "driven" capitalistic entrepreneur? This criticism might be dubbed the European critique, because Europeans, who are far less productive and happy in their work, treasure their leisure time and government-provided sense of security.[8]

---

8   See Olaf Gerseman, *Cowboy Capitalism: European Myths, American Reality* (Washington, DC: Cato Institute, 2004).

Awaiting the City

More to the point, is not the destructiveness that results from the whole process of creative/competitive change *itself unjust*? The idea behind this charge is that a process that hurts someone at the bottom end of the distributional ladder must be inherently unjust. The example is often given that when change comes in some areas of the economy the distribution of incomes goes from 6/6/4/4/4 to 18/18/12/12/12 (these represent group distributions, not individuals, delineated by labor allocation in various trades), with each grouping apparently ascending the ladder proportionally. This would not be unjust, although to the strict egalitarian it is, since the lowest persons on the ladder move up proportionally, even though the relative distance between the groups widens. However, suppose the technological advance turns the distribution into 50/50/40/40/3.[9] Clearly this would appear to be an injustice, it seems. Except that this is exactly what happened when the automobile took over for the horse and carriage. The lowest rung was the buggy-whip industry, which eventually found its niche market virtually wiped out. Is this an injustice, or simply the price to be paid for civilizational progress?

This is the debate in unionized industries when innovation and automation takes over more and more tasks, and those whose skills are no longer needed are squeezed out of the industry. Is this not inherently unjust and a cause for Christian concern? We respond that it is not inherently unjust to expect people to change with the times and educate and reeducate themselves to improve their employable skills in the marketplace. It is of Christian concern to assist and encourage the displaced, but coercive disruption of the processes of modernization and progress is a sure way to introduce *political injustice* into the system.

GREED AND MOBILITY

It has been argued all during the Industrial and Technological Revolutions that the constant struggle to bring more and more efficiency to the work and productivity of humankind is really disguised greed. Christian and other critics of the great virtuosos of business in the West have seriously suggested among

---

9   See Ronald H. Nash, *Social Justice and the Christian Church* (Milford, MI: Mott Media, 1983), 43.

Awaiting the City

other things that it is greed to constantly strive to lower prices at the consumer level so more and more people will be able to take advantage of products that only the few were once able to afford, notably the very rich.[10] The lowering of prices to sell more at a lower profit margin is the economic mechanism at work in consolidation of industries and businesses to take advantage of efficiencies of scale. In this sense *larger* normally translates to *more actual profit made*, but the *consumer* is the one who benefits most, and in vast numbers, and workers whose jobs become more secure and productive through such consolidations also profit.[11] Nevertheless, men like John D. Rockefeller in oil, Andrew Carnegie in steel, James Hill and Cornelius Vanderbilt (and others) in commercial transportation, Henry Ford (and others) in personal transportation, and the Walton family and Bill Gates (and others) in retailing, along with many others in various other industry and business sectors, have had their names and reputations sullied and their businesses attacked despite all they have done and continue to do to make the lives of rich and poor alike on this earth easier.

The charge that industrialists and businesspeople of this type are simply "greedy" or that they are ruthless in their competition with others, since they exercise "control" in the marketplace and acquire "power," is *irrational*. The only "control" they have is offering goods at prices people will pay, that are lower than those at which someone else is willing or able to sell. Furthermore, the only alternative to fair competition in pricing is collusion and cartelization, through either government interference to pick winners and losers, or industry-wide conspiracies in pricing—a process that is patently illegal and always makes prices higher to consumers, rather than lower, and would be a true cause for ethical concern.[12] A situation such as this always hurts those at the lower scale of incomes (i.e., the relatively poorer) more than those at the upper end, because the former have less disposable income to pay the higher

---

10   We have documented this process elsewhere (e.g., see references to the Gilded Age in chap. 22 and allusions to the same phenomenon in the health-care issue in chap. 25).

11   See chap. 3, "Price Controls," in Thomas Sowell, *Basic Economics*, 3rd ed. (New York: Basic Books, 2007), for easily readable and thorough discussion of the pricing mechanism, and Thomas Sowell, *Intellectuals and Society* (New York: Basic Books, 2009), 62–70, for discussion of this era.

12   Such governmental interference was the very thing Herbert Hoover attempted to do at the outset of the Great Depression.

Awaiting the City

prices. Whenever governments have attempted to set prices arbitrarily, they have always caused shortages and higher prices than the market mechanism.[13]

It is sometimes argued additionally that businesses, which continue the search for profitability by moving about and disrupting local economics, both where they left from and where they go to, are unjust because they damage local workers and cause "mom and pop" businesses to lose customers and go out of business.[14] This is the age-old problem of humanity's disregard of the prime directive and the "go" implied in it all. To become dependent on anything, other than God as the "source" of our prosperity, even the company we work for or the industry we work in or the skill-set we have previously developed or the locale and culture in which we have always lived, is to make an idol out of it. The same people who would restrict businesses from making themselves more profitable by moving or buying automated equipment or "outsourcing" or building businesses in countries whose labor force can be hired at cheaper wages, would never think to restrict the movement of local workers, wherever in the world they wish to go—the very way industrialization was supplied with workers in this country and anywhere lots of jobs suddenly become available. These same people will be found arguing that anyone who needs work has a right to cross the US border and find sanctuary and work, legally or illegally. Are these people seeking profit from their labors "greedy" because they come to this country (or any other) and offer themselves for hire at lower wages than local workers are accustomed to receive? Are the folk who clamor for work in American factories that are being moved to the undeveloped world "greedy" because they see a way out of their destitution? If the answer is "No," then there is no basis morally or rationally to deny such a right to any other grouping, corporate or otherwise. The fundamental moral principle at work here is that the driving down of prices through business efficiency so that consumers can receive more for their dollar is neither unethical nor immoral.

---

13 See Robert L. Schuettinger and Eamonn F. Butler, *Forty Centuries of Wage and Price Controls: How Not to Fight Inflation* (Ottawa, IL: Green Hill, 1979), for a history of attempts to control pricing outside the market.

14 This premise is usually stated as if "mom and pop" have some moral right that someone else does not have to do business anywhere they wish. Nothing in the Bible confirms such a judgment. On the contrary, the mandate to "fill" the earth implies large businesses that employ thousands and more in the feeding, clothing, housing, medicating, and transporting of the huge population. This is clearly beyond "mom and pop."

Awaiting the City

Finally, greed is charged against the entrepreneurial and inventive people who profit "inordinately" (critics' terminology) from discoveries and innovations they have brought to the marketplace. That is, Henry Ford's conception of the assembly line and its economies of scale placed him in the position at the top of the "food chain" to profit in a way he should not have because it supposedly made him the recipient of the skill and labor of those below him—i.e., his employees, and secondarily his customers. Ford is only one of hundreds and thousands of examples that are marshaled to sustain this argument. But it is upside down when given only a cursory consideration. The fact is that Ford and others in this position are the only ones not benefiting from someone else's "gift." The inventive person is the one who adds value to everyone else's labor, not the other way around. The fact that a worker on the assembly line can simply push a button or throw a lever all day long and make a living wage and far beyond that is the result of Ford's inventiveness. It is Ford's gift to everyone down the line that the productivity of all has increased many times and makes everyone's work more valuable. To begrudge Ford his profits is envy and covetousness of the worst sort. Ford has made a gift to all who benefit from his inventiveness. He owes God accountability for his own giftedness, but he is not *necessarily greedy* to want to distribute his own profits as he sees fit.[15]

Sustaining Materialistic Consumers

Nevertheless, the argument continues that such a "system" degrades society and persons and threatens the planetary environment to boot. Three terms dominate this part of the debate: *materialism, consumerism,* and *sustainability.* Materialism is another one of those *plastic* terms that everybody seems to think they understand but that no one can precisely define. What exactly constitutes *materialism* and who is *materialistic* or what system of economics or politics fits the terminology are all questions that produce multiple answers.

---

15 See the study by Michael Novak, *Business as a Calling: Work and the Examined Life* (New York: Free Press, 1996), on many of the factors in the paragraphs above. It remains true today as in the past that the greatest satisfaction to most successful businesspeople is the opportunity for the exercise of creativity and achievement of goals rather than the acquisition of money.

Awaiting the City

The terminology is clearly pejorative in its usual *connotative* usages but not always in the same *denotative* intention. *First,* some seem to use the terminology to denigrate any conception of life that treats the materials of existence as good in themselves and worthy of use and enjoyment. This historically is what is broadly defined as the *Gnostic* view.[16] It presumes that nothing truly good is material in essence, nor can anything worthy of knowing be known through material means. Furthermore, one cannot come to true understanding or the truly "good" except through ascetic denial of the material in life. Gnostic ideas and conceptions of life have a long history of entangling themselves with Christian faith and practice (as we have shown) to deceive seekers after inward and transcendent peace and satisfaction with a religion of asceticism and self-denial not directly associated with material necessity. A version of this would be to urge "living more simply" as a way to Christian virtue, regardless of its actual assistance to others in need or some other immediate goal in the service of Christ on earth. Not that living more simply is a bad idea, and many of us could trim our budgets. But the idea that spending more money than we literally have to for subsistence is itself inherently wrong is a Gnostic notion.

A *second* common usage of the materialistic terminology is that which came out of the Enlightenment philosophical period. It posited that nothing that is real in the phenomenological world is immaterial. All phenomena can be explained in material terms. Among other things, this means that the mind or soul of a human being can be reduced to brain functions and bodily processes. A person's life is limited to the world of phenomena that can be observed and quantified. Nothing else is "real" or good, and natural processes explain everything. At least one derivative conclusion from this position is that miracles do not happen. They are excluded by definition. Consequently, the claims of religion to transcendent knowledge are to be viewed skeptically or assigned some source in the material realm.

Furthermore, it can be extrapolated from this, as Marx did, that religion is *no more* than an "opiate" that anesthetizes the senses of the oppressed so they will not demand relief in this life, but will seek it in some unseen world to come.[17]

---

16 See our discussion in chap. 10.
17 The phrase "pie in the sky" is a populist invention based on this philosophical idea. It was coined by Swedish-American Industrial Workers of the World (IWW) organizer Joe Hill (Joel Hägglund) in his song "The Preacher and the Slave," 1911. See Rodney Stark, *Triumph*

Awaiting the City

By this means religion becomes the servant of the oppressor classes. In the absence of a direct indictment against "rich" Christians for fraudulent acquisition of wealth, the attempt to cast them as oppressors or exploiters is little better than Marxian dogma. In the end, it must also cast Jesus in this role when he pronounces "blessed" on those who are "poor" or "poor in spirit," however one chooses to take the text. Jesus now becomes something other than the one who warns rich and poor alike not to turn life into a materialistic quest.

This warning then leads us properly to a *third* perspective on materialism—the term defines a practice of life that may purport to accept the existence and importance of immaterial values and goods but lives as if there really is nothing else worth pursuing in this life. To be a "materialist" in this sense is to live for the acquisition of materialistic goods and to *define one's worth and value* by what one has rather than *what one is* in some immaterial sense. This appears to be what Jacques Ellul is referring to as the problem of both capitalist and socialist, cited at the very beginning of the previous chapter. Unfortunately, this usage of materialistic terminology is disproportionately aimed by many on the left at the "rich," to the detriment of the moral and spiritual condition of the "poor," because *both rich and poor and all in between* are subject to evaluating their lives and spiritual conditions in terms of the acquisition of material goods. The only difference is in the *amounts acquired*, not in the perspective on life. The poor man can be just as fixated on material goods as the rich man. We (Tom and Chad) have both lived and worked in economically depressed communities where you were "rich" if you had *two cars* up on blocks! Or, as Tom's grandfather noted in the early twentieth century, if you have more than one mule. We have found that *materialism* can be as prevalent there as in gated communities. There is no inherent freedom from this problem through being poor. This is the reason that the motto "God is on the side of the poor" is meaningless at the very least and dangerous in its use by political shills seeking to generate class envy. A poor man can be just as bound up in the pursuit of material ends, but his materialism may now be originating in envy and outright claims to the goods of his neighbor. In this case, the "rich" man may be elevated above the "poor" man morally.

---

of *Christianity* (New York: HarperOne, 2011), 105. Stark notes here that the contrary is true: Christianity more often "puts the pie on the table."

Awaiting the City

Ironically the attempt to separate the acquisition of material goods such as cash benefits, food, clothing, housing, medical and other services in kind, educational and other assets from reference to effort, talent, work, ambition, ingenuity, lifestyle choices, frugality, self-denial, and a host of other human and divine virtues results in *another kind* of materialism. If material goods have no referent in their acquisition to *virtuous behaviors*, having been attached to a debased idea of "justice," one cannot have moral satisfaction in their attainment. It is this very problem that degrades human existence in some of the worst economic circumstances. For now one is completely reduced to material life without the values that make it worthwhile. This is perhaps the *worst kind* of degrading materialism.

Closely connected to materialistic terminology is the new pejorative use of *consumer* with an *-ism* on the end to designate something of a disease that is marked by "consumption" (an extension on the idea of "use," in its baser sense) of goods by the masses of society. This malady is considered to be the bane of modern capitalistic societies that feed off of a constant supply of new gadgetry and throwaway products that become objects of some vague sense of need and/or faddish delight. The "goods" may be substantial or nonsubstantial, as the Internet and the virtual universe have provided a whole new realm of want and freedom to innovate and advertise. The "consumer society" is considered to be a cultural and spiritual disaster in some quarters because it *degrades sensibilities and shortens attention spans* and causes people everywhere to go constantly from one new, never-before-seen thing to the next without consideration of the debilitating effects being let loose in such an environment. "Needs" are now things and objects of desire that may not even have been *invented* six months or a year ago, much less a decade or generation ago. Instead of majoring on lasting satisfaction with what one already has, the drive to acquire more and more "stuff" seems to lead to the idea that has often been expressed as "he who has the most stuff wins," the so-called game of life.[18]

---

18 For a range of takes on this phenomenon, see Stephen Moore and Julian L. Simon, *It's Getting Better All the Time: 100 Greatest Trends of the 20th Century* (Washington, DC: Cato Institute, 2000); Thomas Hine, *I Want That: How We All Became Shoppers* (New York: HarperCollins, 2002); Gregg Easterbrook, *The Progress Paradox: How Life Gets Better While People Feel Worse* (New York: Random House, 2003); and Brink Lindsey, *The*

It is, of course, this very engine that drives modern economies to higher and higher levels of growth, many times fueled by consumer credit that leads to higher and higher levels of cumulative societal debt. This engine is the primary cause of the 2008 collapse of the financial markets. Debt instruments in the finance industry became bloated with uncollectable mortgages (primarily) based on debased lending standards at interest rates that were certain to be adjusted upward. This produced both a housing valuation "bubble" that could not be sustained and a rush to borrow on real-estate equities that were inflated beyond reasonable levels. Consumer purchases of housing and the use of mortgaged equities to purchase consumer goods and services left too many people with too much debt and not enough equity to survive when the financial and real-estate markets adjusted. The ensuing collapse is indeed a warning about the perils of unchecked consumerism driven by debt.[19]

Nevertheless, the collapse of the economic bubble was inevitable not primarily because of the inherent weakness or evil of "consumerism," but because of *lending policies* that were driven by political pressure from Washington, DC. The lowering of lending standards to encourage "subprime" mortgages was a deliberately orchestrated process driven by *political posturing* and *threats* aimed at the banking and finance industry. The primary target was the political constituency in neighborhoods and among groups that were previously considered high risk for standard mortgage products. On the other hand, the constituency of banking industry types formed a line to get political favors through exemptions and set-asides. The pressure to make loans and avoid the charge of "redlining" (considered prejudice against certain neighborhoods) and outright racial or ethnic discrimination led to policies that

---

Age of Abundance: How Prosperity Transformed America's Politics and Culture (New York: HarperCollins, 2007).

19 For more on this, see esp. Thomas Sowell, *Housing Boom and Bust* (New York: Basic Books, 2009). Also, Peter Schweizer, *Architects of Ruin* (New York: HarperCollins, 2009). A very succinct description of the process leading to the crash of 2008 is offered in Peter Ferrara, "What Barack Obama Is Thinking," *American Spectator*, May 26, 2010, http://spectator.org/archives/2010/05/26/what-barack-obama-is-thinking. Latest treatment is from Gretchen Morgenson and Joshua Rosner, *Reckless Endangerment: How Outsized Ambition, Greed, and Corruption Led to Economic Armageddon* (New York: Henry Holt, 2011). Morgenson and Rosner are no right-wingers out to get the Left, but they have clearly indicted the proper suspects.

Awaiting the City

put people in mortgages and/or made loans on equities that would not have been made in the past.[20] All the while, the oversight groups in Congress continually lauded the process and claimed that all was well. When foreclosures began to mount, the *same politicians* who had pressured the financiers to make bad loans turned and blamed the people they had originally threatened with federal prosecutions for discrimination, for supposedly defrauding their customers by making the loans and then foreclosing on them. Additionally, the politicians themselves were found to have taken advantage of the arrangement to feather their own nests with cheap loans. This is a *common process* in the economic *interventionist system*—the political economy. The laudable goal of home ownership for as many as possible becomes the political hammer to enhance the power of government without actually reaching its goal. This *cannot* be called "justice."

The consumerist society is indeed problematic for a lot of reasons. It is not essentially *unjust*, however. Its problems do not stem from its systemic evils but from the inevitable human infatuation with the acquisition of more and the fascination of all things new—a situation Paul encountered at Athens in the first century long before the "consumer society" had been "invented" (see Acts 17:21). That took (arguably) until the introduction of the Sears catalogue in the late nineteenth century when goods could be pictured and ordered on the basis of sight alone and delivered from a central location at affordable prices such that all homes, even on the frontier, could be equipped with "modern conveniences." That is a problem for *human decision making*, not the inventor of new devices and ways to distribute them. Even if advertising has become a device for creating a sense of "need" where wiser heads might counsel caution, it is still for the *individual* to decide how to allocate his or her own resources. The fact that many people fall into the hole they have dug for themselves (Prov. 26:27) does not call for coercive governmental intervention. In fact, the scenario above shows that government can be just as manipulative of the market as anyone, only for *political capital* accumulation.

---

20 Many of our sources document this phenomenon. See esp. the latest from Walter E. Williams, *Race and Economics: How Much Can Be Blamed on Discrimination?* (Stanford, CA: Hoover Institution Press, 2011), 128–31.

Awaiting the City

"Saving the Planet" or Using Resources Wisely?

The latest shibboleth of egalitarian distributional advocacy is "save-the-planet" talk. It is cloaked in the euphemism "sustainable growth." This has arisen as it becomes more and more apparent that the underdeveloped world is not going to arise out of its poverty until it joins the party of modern development through consumer-oriented growth.[21] Since this has begun to be more and more apparent to politicians of every stripe, a new emphasis on the scarcity of everything from oil to air has become the mantra for governmental interventions into the economy on a massive and unprecedented scale. Whoever *controls* access and permits consumption of the *resources* involved will become the *most powerful* groups and individuals on earth. The double whammy of nostalgia for a supposedly happy and primitive past coupled with the greed and avarice of political power brokers and their allied business associates who stand to make a profit in new, supposedly green, but unprofitable technologies, threatens to drive the standard of living of the whole world down and doom the lowest economic classes to perpetual misery. What is judged to be "sustainable" growth to the one group, the one with the power, is the lifeline of the other group, the miserable "bottom billion" whose eventual rise out of misery depends entirely on the ability to "develop" along the lines of the rest of the world. No amount of "aid" will accomplish this goal.[22]

"Sustainability" is the concept that growth, to be acceptable and moral, must be justified by its nonexploitative use of planetary resources,[23] be they

---

21 See Thomas L. Friedmann, *Hot, Flat, and Crowded: Why We Need a Green Revolution—and How It Can Renew America* (New York: Farrar, Straus and Giroux, 2008), and Fareed Zakaria, *The Post-American World* (New York: W. W. Norton, 2008).

22 See Dambisa Moyo, *Dead Aid: Why Aid Is Not Working and How There Is a Better Way for Africa* (New York: Farrar, Straus, and Giroux, 2009); Robert Calderisi, *The Trouble with Africa: Why Foreign Aid Isn't Working* (New York: Palgrave Macmillan, 2006); Collier, *Bottom Billion*; Julian L. Simon, *Hoodwinking the Nation* (New Brunswick, NJ: Transaction, 2006); and R. Glenn Hubbard and William Duggan, *Aid Trap: Hard Truths about Ending Poverty* (New York: Columbia University Press, 2009).

23 Increasingly this means being sure "future generations" will have plenty left of whatever resource is in question after this generation is gone. This mantra completely ignores the long history of human achievement in switching from one resource to another as technological and scientific advance replace previously "irreplaceable" resources—such as whale oil, wood, or (literal) horsepower.

Awaiting the City

energy or land or air or water or wilderness or animal life or whatever happens to become the cause of whatever fashionable interest group at any given time. Sometimes the argument relates to the actual supposed scarcity of a resource,[24] such as petroleum (food was another), which has a long history of being nearly "used up" since the 1970s and the Carter-era "malaise."[25] At other times it has been animal life, to be preserved supposedly indefinitely no matter how many men, women, and children die from malaria in tropical areas of the world or how many innocents, including family pets and livestock, are mangled, destroyed or carried off by bears, wolves, or mountain lions. Land in and around great cities is made to assume this role when "sprawl," the natural growth at the outer edges of the population, is regulated in such a way that land prices skyrocket to the point that "affordable housing" is scarce and must be subsidized by taxpayers through rent assistance and public housing. "Wilderness preservation" becomes the issue when an elite few wish to preserve their ability to enjoy nature at the expense of the vast majority, who do not have their physical strength and skills or youthfulness to access the forbidden zones, or when they wish to buy for themselves areas of immense value to serve as private enclaves in the midst of otherwise developed land.[26]

---

24 A number of our sources agree with us that the term "resource" does not fit the actual corresponding object or organism being described as such. Nothing is truly a "resource" until human ingenuity and creativeness makes it so. Until that time it is only raw material waiting the resourcefulness of mankind to put it to use.

25 See Julian Lincoln Simon, *The Ultimate Resource 2*, rev. ed. (Princeton, NJ: Princeton University Press, 1998), for the best answer to the myth of diminishing resources we have seen. His previous work addresses this issue as well: Julian Lincoln Simon, ed., *State of Humanity* (1995; repr., Oxford: Blackwell, 1998). The latest is from Indur M. Goklany, *Improving State of the World* (Washington, DC: Cato Institute, 2007). The ultimate resource is the depository of mental and technical abilities given to humanity itself for sustaining life on the planet while carrying out the creation directives. E. Calvin Beisner, *Garden Meets Wilderness: Evangelical Entry into the Environmental Debate* (Grand Rapids, MI: Acton Institute for the Study of Religion and Liberty / Eerdmans, 1997), 59–65, addresses the issue of misinformation on this subject among evangelicals. His previous work, E. Calvin Beisner, *Prospects for Growth: A Biblical View of Population, Resources, and the Future* (Westchester, IL: Crossway, 1990), is a complete and comprehensible guide for Christians on the subject. See also Robert Bryce, *Power Hungry: The Myths of "Green" Energy and the Real Fuels of the Future* (New York: PublicAffairs, 2010), chaps. 1–7.

26 See esp. Steven Milloy, *Green Hell: How Environmentalists Plan to Control Your Life and What You Can Do to Stop Them* (Washington, DC: Regnery, 2009). One of the leading advocates of such policies, willing and able to put his money where his mouth is, is Ted Turner. He also is the second-largest private landowner in the United States. See Julie Zeveloff and

The examples can be multiplied depending on the area of the world that is in question.[27]

The latest "crisis" is the supposed disaster in the offing resulting from "climate change."[28] This is only the latest term used to panic the public through unproven predictions of planetary disaster brought on by man's callous disregard for his environment. Not one given to understatement, Gary Cook, legislative director of the Greenpeace climate campaign and their senior IT anaylist, warns "We are running out of sky, not oil."[29] Thirty or so years ago it was "global cooling." Recently it was "global warming." It is now "climate

---

Gus Lubin, "The 25 Biggest Landowners in America," Business Insider, October 23, 2012, http://www.businessinsider.com/the-25-biggest-landowners-in-america-2012-10?op=1.

27 Alvin Toffler, in his 1970 blockbuster book *Future Shock*, made predictions that available land would be used up, oil would be used up, we would be facing an unsustainable population in terms of food supplies, and many other similar predictions, and that all of this would happen before the end of the millennium. Alvin Toffler, *Future Shock* (New York: Bantam, 1970), see esp. 91–94, 228–37, and so on. While some of Toffler's social predictions have come true ("homosexual daddies," "drag queen movies," "the overstimulated individual," et al.), his predictions of planetary doom and gloom look silly in retrospect.

28 We have previously cited some of the literature on environmental alarmism and will discuss the issue further in the final two chapters. The best documentation on the current discussion in this chapter includes Ian Plimer, *Heaven and Earth: Global Warming, the Missing Science* (Lanham, MD: Taylor Trade, 2009); Bjørn Lomborg, *Cool It: The Skeptical Environmentalist's Guide to Global Warming* (New York: Alfred A. Knopf, 2007); Roy W. Spencer, *Climate Confusion: How Global Warming Hysteria Leads to Bad Science, Pandering Politicians and Misguided Policies That Hurt the Poor* (New York: Encounter Books, 2008) and his latest, Roy W. Spencer, *The Great Global Warming Blunder: How Mother Nature Fooled the World's Top Climate Scientists* (New York: Encounter Books, 2010); Lawrence Solomon, *The Deniers: The World-Renowned Scientists Who Stood Up against Global Warming Hysteria, Political Persecution and Fraud and Those Who Are Too Fearful to Do So* (Minneapolis: Richard Vigilante Books, 2008); Iain Murray, *The Really Inconvenient Truths: Seven Environmental Catastrophes Liberals Don't Want You to Know About—Because They Helped Cause Them* (Washington, DC: Regnery, 2008); Patrick J. Michaels, ed., *Shattered Consensus: The True State of Global Warming* (Lanham, MD: Rowman & Littlefield, 2005); S. Fred Singer and Dennis T. Avery, *Unstoppable Global Warming: Every 1,500 Years* (Lanham, MD: Rowman & Littlefield, 2007); John A. Baden, ed., *Environmental Gore: A Constructive Response to Earth in the Balance* (San Francisco: Pacific Research Institute for Public Policy, 1994); and Roger Pielke Jr., *The Climate Fix: What Scientists and Politicians Won't Tell You about Global Warming* (New York: Basic Books, 2010). Beisner has addressed many of the alarmist statements by evangelicals in *Garden Meets Wilderness*. Unfortunately, Block and Toly et al. in Noah J. Toly and Daniel I. Block, eds., *Keeping God's Earth: The Global Environment in Biblical Perspective* (Downers Grove, IL: InterVarsity Press, 2010), have not apparently dealt with any of this material, as their "crisis" language is everywhere apparent: 78, 86–89, 121–23, 128, 136–40, 228, 246–7, and 263, just to cite a few references.

29 Quoted in "Environmental Groups Troubled by Recent Merger," *Global Warming Today*, December 4, 1998, 1, cited in Steven F. Hayward, "Sustainable Development in

change" because it could go either way, depending on which "experts" you consult. The widespread change in the terminology testifies to the agenda that is behind the "crisis." When the science is questioned seriously and found to be wanting, the mantra must always be maintained. What is clear is that the "science" is garbled at best and tendentious at least and politically and economically motivated at worst.[30] When "Climategate" struck in 2010, some of the more volatile rhetoric died down, but under the hand of politicians who have much to gain in terms of power and influence, the politicization has not quieted. No one wins except the *politicians*, the parts of the economy preparing to take *tax subsidies* to develop resources that are not cost-effective without such measures,[31] and the various groups whose financial lifeline is linked to the regular creation of a *crisis mentality*—lobbying groups, media, advertising agencies, consultants, and especially those adept at writing proposals for government grants meant to study the crisis du jour.[32] The losers are first and foremost the poorest and least equipped to find their basic energy costs soaring and their development plans and hopes dashed because the planet must be "saved" at all costs.

The twofold tragedy is that no foreseeable option that is on the table could affect in any significant way the amount of "change" human beings make in the

---

the Balance," *Environmental Policy Outlook*, August 1, 2002, http://www.aei.org/article/energy-and-the-environment/sustainable-development-in-the-balance/.

30 The old argument on the "limits of growth" made popular by the famous 1972 study by Donella H. Meadows, Dennis L. Meadows, Jørgen Randers, and William W. Behrens III, *Limits to Growth: A Report for the Club of Rome's Project on the Predicament of Mankind* (London: Earth Island, 1972), has been abandoned by serious environmentalists as being wrongheaded. See leading environmental scientist and Cambridge University senior research associate Michael Grubb, "Relying on Manna from Heaven?" *Science* 294 no. 5545 (November 9, 2001): 1285–87, doi: 10.1126/science.1066014.

31 See the Solyndra scandal in 2011 where the administration in Washington gave more than $500 million in guaranteed loans to a "green" company whose bottom line was suspect before the check was cashed. The company subsequently filed bankruptcy.

32 On the media and research establishment and its bias, see esp. Christopher C. Horner, *Red Hot Lies: How Global Warming Alarmists Use Threats, Fraud and Deception to Keep You Misinformed* (Washington, DC: Regnery, 2008). Most recently is Robert M. Carter, *Climate: The Counter Consensus; A Palaeoclimatologist Speaks*, Independent Minds (London: Stacey International, 2010). Additionally, the Science and Public Policy Institute has published a report by Joanne Nova, "Climate Money: The Climate Industry; $79 billion So Far—Trillions to Come" (SPPI Original Paper, Haymarket, Virginia, July 21, 2009), http://scienceandpublicpolicy.org/originals/climate_money.html, detailing some of the interconnected financial interests feeding the hysteria.

Awaiting the City

climate of earth—it is minuscule when compared to the ninety-eight percent of other factors involved in any changes to climate and the cost of affecting that two percent (it is actually much less than this) would wreck the world economy and plunge humankind into the darkest of depressions and the poorest on earth into massive starvation and disease.[33] The other part of the tragedy is that too many Christians are buying the idea that planetary "stewardship" demands support for the agenda being pushed by the various groups who stand to profit if a massive "rescue" of the planet is enacted into coercive policies.[34] No more destructive program has been conceived by world politicians since the *takeover of the Soviet Union* in 1917. It is this realization that has caused some pundits to

---

33 Bjørn Lomborg, *The Skeptical Environmentalist* (Cambridge: Cambridge University Press, 2001), has calculated that if there is a factual reason to blame human beings for significant global climate change, the economic thing to do is prepare for the change, not severely curtail carbon emissions. On this subject, see also Goklany *Improving State of the World*, and Bryce, *Power Hungry*, both cited above.

34 This agenda is set forth as a positive strategy in Ted Nordhaus and Michael Shellenberger, *Break Through: From the Death of Environmentalism to the Politics of Possibility* (New York: Houghton Mifflin, 2007), and shown to be in operation in Milloy, *Green Hell*, cited above. Googling something like "Al Gore carbon footprint" will bring up all kinds of information on the profitability of this hysteria for certain people and the hypocrisy of their usage of resources compared to ordinary people. E.g., see Deborah Corey Barnes, "The Money and Connections behind Al Gore's Carbon Crusade," Bay Ledger, September 30, 2007, http://www.blnz.com/news/2008/05/13/Money_Connections_Behind_Gores_Carbon_8700.html. See also Stephen Spruiell, "Climate Profiteers," *National Review*, March 22, 2010, 32–36, https://www.nationalreview.com/nrd/articles/339222/climate-profiteers, for a compilation of companies standing to profit from this hysteria. Bryce, *Power Hungry*, chaps. 8–20, details the ins and outs of governmental subsidies to companies standing to profit from unprofitable and impractical "answers" to the energy "crisis." Also, Brian Sussman, *Climategate: A Veteran Meteorologist Exposes the Global Warming Scam* (Washington, DC: WND Books, 2010), chaps. 5 and 10. Carter, *Climate*, also details "Climategate." As we were writing this book the scandal of the IPCC (Intergovernmental Panel on Climate Change) report "science" was summarized and documented in Steven Mosher and Thomas Fuller, *Climategate: The CRUtape Letters* (Lexington: CreateSpace Publishers, 2010). Additionally, on January 27, 2012, sixteen scientists of world-renowned credentials wrote an op-ed (opposite the editorial page) in the *Wall Street Journal (WSJ)*, "No Need to Panic about Global Warming," saying that they found nothing in the current science to justify the widespread alarm over global warming that is being fostered by the IPCC of the United Nations. The op-ed was argued in replies that appeared in later issues, one a letter signed by Kevin Trenberth and thirty-seven other climate scientists, "Check with Climate Scientists for Views on Climate," *WSJ*, February 1, 2012, and another by American Physical Society president Robert L. Byer, "American Physical Society Responds," *WSJ*, February 6, 2012. These replies were then answered by the original group of scientists in "Concerned Scientists Reply on Global Warming," *WSJ*, February 21, 2012, http://online.wsj.com/article/SB1000 1424052970203646004577213244084429540.html (includes links to prior citations).

Awaiting the City

label the advocates of this so-called "green revolution," "watermelons"—meaning they are green on the outside and red on the inside. This is where most of the real heat is coming from—rhetoric that bandies about panicky slogans arising from hidden agendas that invite snide repartee.[35]

Equally tragic, it seems to us, is the intrusion into this area of concern of the usual suspects when it comes to amelioration of actual ecological disaster. In 2010 the Gulf of Mexico became home to one of the worst human-caused disasters in history outside of war. The destruction of a drilling platform with much loss of life was followed by the release of untold billions of gallons of oil into the Gulf and its eventual washing ashore on the Gulf Coast, destroying ecosystems and possibly even ways of life for humans followed for generations. This is the rightful province of government agencies acting in situations where the "commons" are actually catastrophically affected by huge businesses. The ensuing blame game between government and business interests will take years to sort out, but we predict it will eventually be proved that government and business were in collusion to skirt the rules and feather each others' nests, and the losers were the environment and innocent people who were not invited to the table where the cards were passed out.[36]

---

35 Nevertheless, there is clearly an organized attempt on the part of some to remake the world in Marxist/Socialistic terms (to wit, "red on the inside") and the "globalness" of the climate change hysteria fits the bill as an activator of the masses. See Sussman, *Climategate*. Also see James Delingpole, *Watermelons: The Green Movement's True Colors* (New York: Publius Books, 2011). A more detailed and therefore tedious study is A. W. Montford, *The Hockey Stick Illusion: Climategate and the Corruption of Science*, Independent Minds (London: Stacey International, 2010). The economic and political futility of proposed "solutions" to the "problem" is summarized in a shorter work by Christian Gerondeau, *Climate: The Great Delusion, A Study of the Climatic, Economic and Political Unrealities* (London: Stacey International, 2010). More troubling is the connection between the "green revolution" and various cultic religious commitments. See on this issue James Wanliss, *Resisting the Green Dragon: Dominion, Not Death* (Burke, VA: Cornwall Alliance for the Stewardship of Creation, 2010).

36 Among charges made in various press sources at the time were that the drillers were well beyond the limits of their permits, government oversight of the rules for such drilling was nil, no standing plans were in place on the side of either business or government to counter such a catastrophe, the government entities thought first of political gains to be made from the event, business had been engaged in political payoffs, a fire alarm had been at least partially disabled, and on it goes. For an ironic follow-up to developments in this area, see Diana Chandler, "Deepwater Horizon Saga: A 'Backdoor Blessing' to Coastal Churches in LA," *Baptist Press*, July 8, 2011, http://www.bpnews.net/BPnews.asp?ID=35718. Chandler documents the manner in which capitalistic entrepreneurs among local people have shown

Awaiting the City

What cannot be denied is that the human condition on this earth vis-à-vis famine, pestilence, and war has never been better in the aggregate than it is today, and that it is steadily improving at rates previously unknown prior to the last three hundred years,[37] and those who are still left behind cannot be moved out of their condition without access to the same tools, goods, and services that the rest of the world enjoy because of unprecedented economic growth. There is no *justice* in advocating policies that would deny that portion of the world its due opportunities to work out of the dire circumstances that make its existence miserable and *unsustainable*—there's that term in its proper use. The truth is that the West could divest itself of its wealth tomorrow and no "sustainable" change would be wrought for the bottom billion (now 350 million) without industrialization and technological advance and the provision of a host of intangible human capital goods being made available to them through their own labor and initiative.[38] The so-called "save-the-planet" movement has the same agenda that anti-"sprawl" advocates do in and around the great cities. It says in its effects on others, "I have mine. You stay out. But if you want to buy my property, it just doubled in price because land that can be legally developed easily just got much more scarce." How is this "justice"?

The moral choice in matters economic is always a *trade-off*. In this case the issue is whether human life on earth is "sustainable" in the face of severe *deprivation* that causes the premature death of millions, not whether resources are "sustainable."[39] The groups involved in this campaign are not as concerned about the future of human beings as they are about the earth itself. They

---

resilience in the face of adversity, restored much prosperity to the region, and brought blessing to the churches apart from government relief.

37 The first half of the opening sentence from the executive summary of a United Nations Millennium Project publication acknowledges this overall betterment of human life: "People around the world are becoming healthier, wealthier, better educated, more peaceful, and increasingly connected and they are living longer...." Jerome C. Glenn and Theodore J. Gordon, ed., *2007: State of the Future* (Washington: World Federation of United Nations Associations, 2007), http://www.millennium-project.org/millennium/sof2007-exec-summ.pdf. See also *2011: State of the Future* executive summary, cited in the bibliography, which begins almost verbatim the 2007 annual report. See also Goklany, *Improving State of the World*, Simon, *State of Humanity*, and others among our sources.

38 See chap. 28 for this discussion in full.

39 See Jay W. Richards, *Money, Greed, and God* (New York: HarperOne, 2009), 186–96, for an easily accessible discussion of resource sustainability, and Simon's massive work of documentation, *Ultimate Resource 2.*

Awaiting the City

tend to regard the species of man as earth's biggest problem, not its ruler, and they actively support disobedience to the *prime command* to fill the earth and subdue it.[40] Along with plans to limit use of the planet are ongoing plans to limit allowable births by *coercion*, if necessary—a situation already playing itself out in China. Justice on God's earth demands that the desperate need of men and women in God's image to obey God's creation mandate cannot be made to take a backseat to concerns over the quality of life of animals and the enjoyment of elites in untouched wilderness environs or the gradual depletion of energy resources as technology gradually replaces them. It is a sure sign of a hidden agenda when the need for energy that could be easily and sustainably had through nuclear power—a source that does not pollute the atmosphere and is in widespread use all over Europe and elsewhere[41] without panic over waste or disaster—is not allowed to develop in the United States because of politics.[42] "Using" resources wisely to meet the needs of humanity, even in a consumer-oriented global community is no vice. *Coercing* choices through governmental mandates that benefit interest groups who make it their "business" to accumulate *political power* and turn it into money is *no virtue.* Individuals should have choices that reflect their own true needs and values guided by self-control, frugality, truth telling and truth seeking, and wisdom accumulated over generations, not those limited by political entrepreneurs.[43]

---

40 See previously cited advocacy of population control through coercive "breeding" policies. The *Green Bible* (San Francisco: HarperCollins, 2008), deliberately cites and emphasizes the right of animal species to multiply and fill the earth without emphasizing the same command to human beings and goes on at several points in commentary to pit the right of animals to space against that of humankind. In addition, the "Canticle of the Creatures" by Saint Francis of Assisi is quoted for his advocacy of the familial relationship between the earth and humans (and offered as the patron saint of environmentalism): "Sir Brother Sun... Sister Moon... Brother Wind... Sister Water... Brother Fire... Sister Mother Earth... Sister Bodily Death." We are convinced from our reading of Francis that he did not have the same thing in mind as the modern Green extremists. Even to cite him is a case of anachronism.

41 Up to seventy percent of all power produced in some areas of the Eurozone and only twenty percent of US power.

42 The fallout (figuratively and literally) from the 2012 earthquake and tsunami that hit Japan with the nuclear power-plant damage as a result will no doubt impact future considerations worldwide. However, at the time we completed this volume we have no reason to discount future use of nuclear power.

43 For a full discussion and documentation on the issue of "sustainability," see Hayward, "Sustainable Development in the Balance," a paper and published by the American

Individuality and Creative Destruction

We noted in our biblical discussion of the creation and fall era that it was God himself who introduced creative destruction to a sinful world. When he observed that Adam and Eve were poorly dressed to enter the world now "subject to decay" (Rom. 8:20–21), he personally undertook the task of clothing them appropriately. This was the first act of creative destruction on the planet, although Christian astrophysicist Hugh Ross and others detail how this process is actually part and parcel of the original creation. The universe itself is in the process of creative decay, a process that allows for life as we know it, but when God himself undertook to kill and skin an animal or animals to make clothing, he became a teacher in technology to the unwise and sinful pair. It should be no surprise that humankind, taking its cue from this primeval lesson, would see the usage of every resource as appropriate and necessary for human beings, who now had become consumers. It is difficult to speculate on the initial reaction of the humans to God's acts in provision for them, but hard reality must have set in quickly as the blood of animals was shed to clothe them. If it didn't there, it surely did when Cain rose up against Abel in envy and jealousy. Each man and woman are responsible to God for his or her actions and worship and are now held personally accountable for his or her choices. Paths and lives separate according to individual choices, and culture and society develop through the innovations brought on by those choices.

Furthermore, this individual accountability and encouragement to personal trust in a personal God is part of the central metanarrative of Scripture. Individuals apostatize from God and disobey his will continually, but it is only when they band together in societies and cultures that they pose threats to the global will of God. This is the sin of Babel and Babylon. Rather than proceeding apace to distribute throughout the planet and "fill" it and "subdue" it, the migrating group set about to produce security and a reputation by building a monument to humanity itself and a figurative pathway to heaven, or more properly from heaven to earth from God's perspective. Whatever the positive effects of city

---

Enterprise Institute, August 2002 (see citation in n. 29). This paper was produced in advance of the Johannesburg "summit" on the environment (Earth Summit 2002).

Awaiting the City

building may be in terms of pooled efforts and fraternal relationships, the tendency is continually to enhance human pride and make man the source of his own security.[44] This destructive tendency is constantly disrupted by God's direct and indirect actions—here in the confusion of language, and throughout history in the rise and fall of pestilence, war, and natural disaster, and according to the prophets, the rise and fall of empires. These are treated biblically as times and places of judgment, which are typically followed by eras of new creative activity.[45] Here is "creative destruction" on a societal and global scale. It is the way of the world governed by the hand of God in history. It is the destiny spelled out in the declaration "Behold, I make all things new" (Rev. 21:5). The desire to circumvent this process by whatever means is the source of mankind's enduring rebellion against the rule (kingdom) of God. The usual manner in which this is done is to anoint a messiah figure (king, emperor, pharaoh, caesar, czar, kaiser, etc.) to make the process go away.

A fundamental flaw in the attempt to posit organized coercive systems as saviors of a sort against a supposedly out-of-control capitalistic market economics is the failure to recognize the source of abuse in all "systems" and the inherent dangers in concentration of force in any human endeavor. The lone economically powerful individual is not a global threat unless he controls the prerogatives of governmental power, which may be military, regulative, confiscatory, or a combination of these and others. If government is corrupted by his and/or others' influence, it is government wielded by corrupt individuals that is at fault, not capitalistic markets. If British Petroleum (BP) is allowed to pollute and destroy large areas of the Gulf Coast of the United States without appropriate punishment and compensatory payments, it is a fault of corrupt government, not capitalistic market economies.

A single, crazed individual sitting in a Landesburg prison cell seething with jealousy and rage over supposed crimes of the Jewish people had no power to muster the economic strength of the Krupp family to rain death and destruction on a supine Europe until he seized the power of government. The Krupp family of arms builders had no power (and no apparent desire) to force

---

44   Jacques Ellul, *The Meaning of the City*, trans. Dennis Pardee (Grand Rapids, MI: Eerdmans, 1970), 1–84.

45   James M. Hamilton Jr., *God's Glory in Salvation through Judgment: A Biblical Theology* (Wheaton, IL: Crossway, 2010), throughout.

Awaiting the City

their will on Europe and the world through use of their fortune and arms factories until government in the hands of a crazed politician elected by a dissatisfied and envious populous purchased through taxation and confiscation the products that brought death to more than twenty million people during World War II.[46] This is not the fault of market economics any more than it is the fault of an automobile, driven by a drunk, that it hits a child in the street, destroying her life.[47] Both Alfried Krupp (and his family) and Adolf Hitler (and his henchmen) are responsible for their life choices before God and history. The German people were responsible for their votes, and the nations that forced the Treaty of Versailles on a beaten German nation at the end of World War I are responsible for their actions. But market economics, which made possible the wealth that bought the arms and paid the military to kill and destroy, is not morally responsible for anything. It is an "it," not a moral agent.

This realization was almost an epiphany to the great Russian dissident, Aleksandr Solzhenitsyn. In *The Gulag Archipelago,* Solzhenitsyn relates how he and others were recruited by the Soviet government in 1938 to become members of the NKVD, the Soviet secret police. He notes that such an assignment would have had political and material advantages making them among the most comfortable and powerful members of Russian society. Rather than being consigned to poverty and want and the meager future of the masses, they would have exercised power and controlled their own destiny and received "perks" of every sort. It was here that he began to realize the nature of human evil, especially that kind of evil that is thrust into power over others and acquires "shoulder boards" (the insignia of rank in the armed forces or secret police)—"What would I have become? What do shoulder boards do to a human being?" he asked. His contemplation of evil through this time led him to the famous conclusion cited in many places:

---

46 For the full story of the Krupp family of arms builders, including their dealings with Adolf Hitler and the Nazis, see William Manchester, *The Arms of Krupp, 1587–1968* (New York: Little, Brown, 1968).

47 But note any week in a major newspaper in this country the times a headline and lead story line will blame the ubiquitous "SUV" for running down some poor soul or smashing a more environmentally friendly "hybrid." Only later do we discover that the supposedly crazed SUV was driven by an unnamed or named human being in the throes of drug or alcohol-induced dementia or even a seizure or mere road rage.

Awaiting the City

If only it were all so simple [to eliminate evil through political means]! If only there were evil people somewhere insidiously committing evil deeds, and it were necessary only to separate them from the rest of us and destroy them. But the line dividing good and evil cuts through the heart of every human being. And who is willing to destroy a piece of his own heart?[48]

Individuality and Human Achievement

On the other hand, when men and women turn their attention to helping and benefiting others through the creativity and energy that comes from the image of God in them, it is market economics that most efficiently powers their abilities and various inclinations. The world of the Bible is a world of incentives (incentivism could easily stand in for capitalism) to good and warnings against evil and its consequences. In truth, it is the free moral agency of human individuality that fuels human progress or demise at every level. Mankind is led along the road of God's plan to fill and subdue the planet by the innovative and faithful servant genius of individuals. They are also led astray by the deviousness of those who would gain power over and through the masses of their fellows. Governments that are made up of elected groups of individuals employ in this manner a class of specialists in manipulation of what others produce and own. Committees and commissars do not invent things, they manage and control them, and as soon as they can they tax and regulate them and sell the political clout that comes from this ability.

And, when societies and cultures get completely off-track, as did Germany in the twentieth century (or Israel and others in the Bible), it is the lone prophet—a Dietrich Bonhoeffer or Martin Niemöller or Helmut Thielicke or other individuals like them—that calls to account the criminals and their criminality. Even "the church" as a corporate entity has a difficult time finding itself on the right side of such situations. The biblical narrative plays out

---

48 Aleksandr I. Solzhenitsyn, *The Gulag Archipelago, 1918–1956: An Experiment in Literary Investigation*, trans. Thomas P. Whitney (parts 1–4) and Harry Willetts (parts 5–7), abr. Edward E. Ericson Jr. (New York: Harper & Row, 1985), 73–75.

this theme to its ultimate climax as a single individual of God's own choosing hangs on a cross. The final words of this one to his church, recorded by John (Rev. 2–3), urge again and again that "he that conquers" in spite of opposition within and without the church will be rewarded in the age to come. Satan's counterfeit is the beastly savior-government of the last days, insisting on *mass conformity* to a certain order so as to practice a trade or make a living. It is a true "mystery" that in this stage of history so much of the Christian church cannot see through the fog of rhetoric and outright fabrication being used to bring it aboard the bandwagon of socialistic (progressive), coercive political economics. Nothing saps the sense of *dependence on God* more than a cradle-to-grave *social caretaker*, constantly promising to take something from someone else to give it to me as a matter of "rights" or "justice."

Conversely, nothing grows dependence on God and faith in his provision like learning how to make do on my own, using God-given resourcefulness, ingenuity, frugality, postponement of gratification, Scriptural wisdom and principles for living, prayer, and wise counsel from fellow believers. There is simply no substitute for this in any life lived to the glory of God. It is also clear that even those who do not make any pretense of trusting God are far better off in this life using these same principles. It is part of the "blessing" (common grace) of God on the "just and the unjust." Nothing prepares the individual better to be open to the gospel message than the clear knowledge of personal accountability for all of life's choices. True, many make the mistake of seeing this as mere self-sufficiency, but it is surely no worse than dealing with those who believe that life and taxpayers owe them something.

Astrophysicist Hugh Ross masterfully demonstrates that man was created and placed on this planet in precisely this place in the universe at precisely this epoch in its life to be in a position as a result of the development of just this high-tech society to observe the glory of the creation and wonder at all the majesty of God, so that the more we learn, the more glorious he becomes to our eyes and minds.[49] No such scenario was even envisioned three hundred years ago, except in the mind's eye of a few individuals. And they were thought weird, possessed, and/or dangerous. It took

---

49   Hugh Ross, *Why the Universe Is the Way It Is* (Grand Rapids, MI: Baker, 2008); also Hugh Ross, *The Creator and the Cosmos: How the Greatest Scientific Discoveries of the Century Reveal God*, 3rd ed. (Colorado Springs: NavPress, 2001).

Awaiting the City

centuries of industrialization and technocratic development and vast capitalization to realize the visions of a few, but the human race is now on the cusp of obeying the creation mandate to fill and subdue in a manner previously inconceivable.

From Kitty Hawk to the moon in sixty-six years is the kind of achievement that shows what government can do when it harnesses and enhances individual freedom and initiative to projects that only government is equipped to do.[50] It fits the general area of enhancement of the lives of all, through advancing technology and human achievement, and undertakings too large for private individuals or companies (though a very good case can be made for private projects of this sort)[51] because the risks and start-up costs are too great. But the temptations to corruption remain, in any great project, and the space program is like all others of its type—a bane and a blessing.[52] The blessing is that spin-offs from the space program benefit the lives of all people on earth every day, and the exploratory nature of it shows the handiwork of God regularly. While it can surely be argued that teamwork was and is indispensable in any world-changing endeavor, it is the teamwork of highly trained and rarely gifted individuals pooling immense effort and unstinting personal sacrifice that produces results of this kind. One does not produce or encourage that without incentives to achievement that are born out of market-oriented rewards.

The primary challenger in this area to American dominance was the Soviet Union, which did not expect its scientific elites to live at the level of the common folk whose lives were full of breadlines, cold apartments, overcrowded living spaces, and shortages of every kind of necessities. Just like her "amateur" athletes who competed regularly in the Olympics, Soviet aristocratic and technocratic elites did not share the daily deprivations of the Russian people. Nevertheless, the competition proved too much for a system not designed to access fully the innovative capacity of humanity made in the image of God. Market forces prevailed in more

---

50 Unfortunately, such government-enabled achievements and advances were more the product of war, both hot and cold, in that terrible century than of peaceful development.

51 See Burton W. Folsom Jr., *The Myth of the Robber Barons*, 6th ed. (Herndon, VA: Young America's Foundation, 2010), for a take on this very idea, which relates to our earlier discussion of James Hill, who built a railroad on his own (see chap. 19). Also recall our discussion concerning Henry Clay's notion of the "American System" (see chap. 18).

52 See a discussion of this issue in Jonathan Leaf, *The Politically Incorrect Guide to the Sixties* (Washington, DC: Regnery, 2009), ad loc.

Awaiting the City

ways than one. Even in the American effort, just like in all monopoly-induced escapes from the discipline of the market, the space program has become a questionable enterprise of dubious value to the taxpaying public except as it keeps people seeking to reach further into the frontiers of the creation, a mere symbol of its once heroic-seeming mission. Now, it is the kind of bureaucratic program that James DeLong has described as "captured, inch by inch, by its staffers, and its market power is then turned to their benefit, which may take the form of money, ease, ideological satisfaction, or all three."[53] Of course, NASA is now but a shell of what it once was. If it is to be resurrected, it must be on a different platform.

On the other hand, the work of men and women in garages and home studios that produced the information revolution (think Bill Gates, Paul Allen, Steve Jobs, Michael Dell, and many others) with minimal risk and small start-up costs shows how all peoples benefit from the initiative and genius of a few. It is no exaggeration to say that Bill Gates, and his enterprises, alone have done more through inventiveness and business expertise to remove poverty and hunger and want from this earth than all the modern benevolent enterprises of the West put together in his lifetime. Certainly Silicon Valley in California can make this claim. This is not to denigrate those benevolent efforts, but neither should anyone who engages in them denigrate the great businesspeople or technological genius for being involved in something apparently so mundane as building a world that is rich and accommodating to human material needs, so that poverty and want and disease can be pushed farther and farther to the periphery of earth's inhabited surface and so that the problem of scarcity is not nearly the daunting threat that it once was to nearly all the earth.[54]

Unless one believes that humans were created to spend their poor and miserable lives squatting around a campfire, picking lice and mud off themselves, and waiting for an even more miserable death, one must believe in the good of technological advance.[55] Even in the presence of sin, this is clearly the better alternative. If the planet was intended to be "filled" and "subdued," it is hard to imagine any goal much different from what has been achieved to this point, despite the inroads of sin and its destructiveness. Furthermore, the destruction

---

53   James V. DeLong, "Black and White and Dead All Over," *National Review*, April 6, 2009, 28.
54   The best defense of these lines is in Novak, *Business as a Calling*.
55   Recall Hobbes' words that in the state of nature the life of man is "solitary, poor, nasty, brutish, and short." *Leviathan*, 13.9.

that comes from the digging and plowing and wood chopping and steel making and water diverting and disease defeating and famine eliminating and countless other benefits of modern life is no worse than God's own act of killing and skinning animals for clothing for the first human pair. And just like any building project, it requires cleanup after all the apparent destruction and disruption of the *natural* processes. We highlight the word "natural," for it is by no means proven that somehow it is "unnatural" for humans to engage in similar so-called destruction and disruption in light of the command of God to fill and subdue.

Cleanup is the product of wealthy societies, not that of the destitute. It can and should be done, but it takes capital that can be produced only by first "destroying" to produce wealth. The gigantic hole in the ground that was filled with ugly steel and concrete and made to bear the load of a home or an apartment building or a skyscraper that will soon be colorfully and artistically decorated to show mankind's aesthetic sensibilities[56]—this hole-turned-habitat, surrounded by newly planted flora and landscaping that control drainage and erosion, will take the place of blank prairie that could not sustain a single person, much less a family or several families or numerous businesses. This, and the invention and building and launching of something like the Hubble Space Telescope that allows physicists and astronomers to map and transmit images of the stars that testify to the glories of God, is the destiny of human beings in God's image. Those who look nostalgically to the days when hunter-gathers roamed vast areas forget, either deliberately or naïvely, that such a society spends more time raiding[57] than building and subduing. One must fill and subdue before one can "tend" what has been created. To that subject we turn finally.

---

56 Witness the fact that craftsmen of the age of building European cathedrals spent hours and hours, day after day, creating artwork on the roofs that only they and God would see.

57 Niall Ferguson's terminology in *The Ascent of Money* (New York: Penguin Books, 2008).

Awaiting the City

Chapter 27

Tending the Garden: Changing the World or Rational Compassion

"We are beginning to wipe out the line that divides the practical
from the ideal; and in so doing we are fashioning an instrument of
unimagined power for the establishment of a morally better world."[1]
Franklin D. Roosevelt

"The central conservative truth is that it is culture, not politics,
that determines the success of a society. The central liberal truth
is that politics can change a culture and save it from itself."[2]
Daniel Patrick Moynihan

---

1   Franklin D. Roosevelt, "Inaugural Address," January 20, 1937, online by Gerhard Peters
    and John T. Woolley, American Presidency Project, http://www.presidency.ucsb.edu/ws/
    index.php?pid=15349, quoted in Amity Shlaes, *The Forgotten Man: A New History of the
    Great Depression* (New York: HarperCollins, 2007), 299. This was Roosevelt's second inau-
    gural address.
2   This is a widely disseminated quotation by Moynihan. For a discussion of how the "central
    liberal truth" works out or does not work out in the third and fourth world, see Lawrence E.
    Harrison, *The Central Liberal Truth* (New York: Oxford University Press, 2006). Harrison
    has done extensive work on the subject of culture and economic issues and is proposing
    ways that politics might engender cultural change leading to economic success where
    failure has prevailed.

Rousseau was famous for saying, "Nature has established equality among men and they have established inequality."[3] Such was the battle cry of the French Revolution that ultimately failed to carry the day and led to the kind of confusion that inexorably proceeded to the Napoleonic egomania—one more messianic "deliverance" from pestilence and disease and war. Across the pond in the same era a document was produced proclaiming the essential "equality" of all men as an endowment of creation's God. Along with this equality went "unalienable rights." Among those rights, the document continues, are "Life, Liberty and the pursuit of Happiness." It further opined, "That to secure these rights, Governments are instituted among Men, deriving their just powers from the consent of the governed." Upon these ideals stand much of the discussion of justice and injustice in American society today. Just what is the nature of the "equality" men and women share, and what is the role of the Creator and government in "securing" it?

The preceding chapters have made the case for market economics as the better choice for wealth production, accumulation, and distribution, and for fulfilling the biblical mandate to fill and subdue the creation. We are aware that "making the case" is in the eye of the beholder and that some will never be convinced because they have a completely different "vision"[4] of the nature and destiny of humanity. This vision of the way things ought to be, as opposed to the way things are, is a matter of ideological conviction and the search for a satisfying involvement in at least attempting to "change" the world as it is to something better.[5] Our premises involve especially an understanding of human nature as fallen and thus sinful in all endeavors and therefore dangerous to a person's fellow human beings when that person accumulates too much coercive

---

3   Jean-Jacques Rousseau, *Discourse on the Origin and Foundations of Inequality among Men* (1754; Eng. trans., 1761; repr., trans. and ed. Helena Rosenblatt, Bedford Series in History and Culture (New York: Bedford / St. Martin's Press, 2011), quoted in Gonzalo Fernández de la Mora, *Egalitarian* Envy, trans. Antonio T. de Nicolás (1984; Eng. trans., 1987; repr., Lincoln, NE: iUniverse, 2000), 177. De la Mora's citation of the title and original date of publication differ, however, from the edition cited above.

4   See Thomas Sowell, *A Conflict of Visions: Ideological Origins of Political Struggles*, rev. ed. (New York: Basic Books, 2007), and Thomas Sowell, *Vision of the Anointed: Self-Congratulation as a Basis for Social Policy* (New York: Basic Books, 1995).

5   See James Davison Hunter, *To Change the World* (New York: Oxford University Press, 2010), for the most balanced representation of this attempt by both Right and Left and outsiders to the political spectrum.

Awaiting the City

power and especially dangerous when such a person couches his or her coercive measures in moralistic formulations that imply that disagreement comes only from an evil to which his or her own heart is not subject.[6] From this condition proceed the societal and cultural structures that we call "the world" here, and we contend that no "system" on earth can escape them without divine intervention. John Kekes is surely right when he commends what was until the 1960s a consensus in American political life that ideologues must be avoided in favor of the kind of political accommodation that attempts to solve practical problems with practical solutions, cope with emergencies, and reconcile conflicting interests.[7] The ideologues are out to "change the world," and woe to any human being that gets in the way.[8] This observation applies equally to the Right and the Left politically and to Christian and non-Christian as well.

"THE PROBLEM WITH CAPITALISM . . ."

William F. Buckley famously reminded his readers annually in *National Review* that "[t]he problem with socialism is socialism; the problem with capitalism is capitalists."[9] Another way of putting it is that when capitalism runs to extremes, we get executives at Lehman Brothers, AIG, Countrywide Financial, and Fannie Mae and Freddie Mac carting off billions in bonuses as the housing bubble bursts. When Socialism runs to extremes, we get Lenin, Stalin, Mao, Pol Pot, and Castro, and when all of that is combined in one century with the

---

6   On the special propensity of the Left to take on this style politically, see Thomas Sowell, *Intellectuals and Society* (New York: Basic Books, 2009), esp. 83–88.

7   The previous deviations from this consensus essentially got in "through the back door." Few of those who voted for Woodrow Wilson in 1912 or 1916 knew that in his academic writings he had called for an *abandonment* of the Constitution, the very Constitution that he twice swore to uphold many years later! See our discussion of Wilson's Progressivism (fascism) in chap. 19.

8   John Kekes, *The Art of Politics: The New Betrayal of America and How to Resist It* (New York: Encounter, 2008). See also the discussion in Andy Crouch, "Why We Can't Change the World," in *Culture Making: Recovering Our Creative Calling* (Downers Grove, IL: InterVarsity Press, 2008), 187–201. Hunter, *To Change the World*, follows this same line with Hunter's discussion of *ressentiment* (a term also used earlier by Nietzsche for the attitude that animates the politics of envy), Kindle loc. 1441–60, 1918–30, and elsewhere.

9   The quote is attributed by Buckley to William Schlamm more than fifty years ago. Schlamm, an Austrian American and ex-Communist, encouraged Buckley to found the conservative magazine *National Review*.

Awaiting the City

nationalistic extreme that was called Fascism, we get Hitler and Mussolini and Hirohito to boot and more than 100 million lives lost in the devastations of war, deliberate starvation, and killings in the millions by governments bent on restructuring societies.

More than sixty years ago Reinhold Niebuhr, in the face of the century's greatest bloodletting crisis, lamented the possibility even of the survival of what was classical democratic liberalism,[10] reminding us of the underlying problem of human corruption: "Our modern civilization... was ushered in on a wave of boundless social optimism. Modern secularism is divided into many schools. But all the various schools agreed in rejecting the Christian doctrine of original sin." He went on to emphasize that failure to deal with this essential Christian doctrine leads to all kinds of folly, for it ignores "a fact which every page of human history attests." That is, that "there is no level of human moral or social achievement in which there is not some corruption of inordinate self-love.... That is why it conceived so many fatuous and futile plans for resolving the conflict between the self and the community; between the national and the world community." Problems are viewed in terms of "social organization" so that one school holds that people would be good if only political institutions would not corrupt them; another believes that they would be good if the prior evil of a faulty economic organization could be eliminated. Or another school thinks of this evil as no more than ignorance, and therefore waits for a more perfect educational process to redeem the human race from its partial and particular loyalties. But no school asks how it is that an essentially good human being could have produced corrupting and tyrannical political organizations or exploiting economic organizations or fanatical and superstitious religious organizations.[11]

More recently N. T. Wright has commented on the demise of democratic liberalism as follows:

---

10 The conception at the core of Adam Smith and the thought of others.
11 Reinhold Niebuhr, *The Children of Light and the Children of Darkness: A Vindication of Democracy and a Critique of Its Traditional Defence* (New York: Scribner's, 1944), 16–17. Niebuhr tellingly notes throughout his essay that according to his diagnosis this problem of failure to account for human depravity is the fault of the "children of light", based on Luke 16:8.

Awaiting the City

Politicians and the media used to pretend that a little more social progress, a little more Western-style democracy in the world, would solve the ills that were still visible. We now know that this was a lie; not only is the world not a significantly better place for having more democracy, but the Western powers themselves have been shown up as riddled with corruption, selfishness masked as public service, and sexual and financial scandals.…. There is such a thing as Sin, which is more than the sum total of human wrongdoing. It is powerful, and this power infects even those with the best intentions. If it could make even the holy Torah its base of operations, how much more the muddled intentions of well-meaning do-gooders.[12]

As many have said, government has nothing to give anybody except what it takes from somebody else, and a government big enough to give us everything we want is big enough to take away everything we have. Margaret Thatcher is famous for putting it like this: "The problem with Socialism is that you keep running out of other people's money." Thus, giving someone actual coercive power over yours or my economic life is a *far more daunting prospect* (to us) than having someone "compete" with me to sell products and services in such a way that might cause me inconvenience, disruption, displacement, reeducation, or any number of things that might not fulfill my most cherished desires at the present time, not to mention having to live without the vices that enslave human beings morally, socially, and economically. We (Tom and Chad) would rather *suffer these things* than have *government* take from someone else and give to us, because we know it can reverse the process and do *worse harm to us* than the competition can. As Pauline believers in the providence of God (Rom. 8:28), we prefer to be like David in the hands of an (even) angry God, rather than human militarists or famine (2 Sam. 24:14). With Jesus, we prefer to seek "blessing" as a daily exercise of faith, prayer, and effort, even if the greatest rewards are awaited in the *eschaton*. Furthermore, we believe this competitive atmosphere keeps us "on top of our game," more dependent on

---

12 N. T. Wright, "Romans," *The New Interpreter's Bible: Acts–1 Corinthians*, vol. 10 (Nashville: Abingdon, 2002), 588, commenting on the exposition of Rom. 7. We are aware that Wright would not necessarily agree with our solutions.

Awaiting the City

the Lord as our source and sustenance, and less likely to find ourselves floating comfortably along in some *delusive world* of false messianic security.[13]

We also regard it as our mandate to *assist* and *encourage* our fellows with the hand and heart of *compassion* and *justice* so they and we will enjoy the commendation of the God who made us, for these are gifts that government cannot give. More importantly, we regard it as biblically crucial that we pursue the *betterment of our fellows* at more than the expense of taxation and regulation, for the cross demands self-sacrifice to the *point of death*[14] and not merely writing the IRS a check or "simpler living."[15] Finally, we value *personal freedom* as the context of moral choices that most reflects the will of the God of the Bible. The destiny of mankind is the "freedom of the glory of the children of God" (Rom. 8:21 ESV), a prospect that is entirely incompatible with working toward some earthbound goal through *coercive* governmental mandates for supposedly Christian behavior.

Given these commitments, what is the nature of the "equality" among human beings that we advocate, and how can that best be secured? More importantly, how does this equality translate into some kind of economic justice? Finally, how does a biblical stewardship of the planet relate to these issues? We cannot avoid thinking here of the Creator's mandate to Adam to "work" and "tend" the garden,[16] a command that naturally follows from the prior

---

13 See Anthony Gill and Erik Lundsgaarde, "State Welfare Spending and Religiosity: A Cross-National Analysis," *Rationality and Society* 99–436, for how the growth of government saps religious faith. Elsewhere, Michael Barone has detailed how the "softness" of certain parts of American life has led to the same sense of false security. See Michael Barone, *Hard America, Soft America: Competition vs. Coddling and the Battle for the Nation's Future* (New York: Crown Forum, 2002).

14 Matt. 16:24; Luke 9:23; Mark 8:34; John 15:13.

15 For a very recent attempt to integrate these concerns into a holistic approach to Christian compassionate involvement with the poor everywhere in our world, see Steve Corbett and Brian Fikkert, *When Helping Hurts: Alleviating Poverty Without Hurting the Poor—and Yourself* (Chicago: Moody, 2009). Additionally, see the compendium of interactive studies on Christian activism and poverty fighting by Judith M. Dean, Julie Schaffner, and Stephen L. S. Smith, eds., *Attacking Poverty in the Developing World: Christian Practitioners and Academics in Collaboration* (Waynesboro, GA: Authentic Media / Federal Way, WA: World Vision, 2005).

16 We previously noted Beisner's division of the creation and garden commands as having great merit; cf. E. Calvin Beisner, *Garden Meets Wilderness* (Grand Rapids, MI: Acton Institute for the Study of Religion and Liberty / Eerdmans, 1997). It might be more appropriate to consider the two commands as secular and sacred. However, this is a false

construction of something from nothing, implying that the garden is to be extended and kept up to God's standards. What follows we would put under the heading of "working and tending." Humankind is currently living in a "garden," rather a city, of unprecedented wealth, health, and longevity that must be nourished and tended if it is to be extended and made available to the last portion of the planet still languishing in the misery of millennia gone by—Hobbes' famous "solitary, poor, nasty, brutish, and short" existence.

TRUTH AND JUSTICE

Near the end of his denunciation of Israel's inability to achieve the justice that God seeks, in the fifty-ninth chapter of the book named for him, Isaiah notes that

> Justice is turned back,
>   and righteousness stands far away;
> for truth has stumbled in the public squares,
>   and uprightness cannot enter.
> Truth is lacking,
>   and he who departs from evil makes himself a prey.
> (Isa. 59:14–15 ESV)

This juxtaposition of the language associated with biblical justice is not accidental or incidental. Where truth is lacking, there can be no justice/righteousness, and this truth is always a referential truth—it speaks from facts as they are in the eyes of God, who sees with impartiality and complete understanding. Consequently, "truth," biblically speaking, more nearly denotes our term "trustworthiness." God does not construct narratives that merely approximate what someone wishes were the facts or mistakenly understands the facts

---

dichotomy in the end, for ultimately the entire earth will be the sanctuary of God's dwelling with redeemed humanity (Rev. 21–22). Nevertheless, subduing and dominating in Gen. 1 is akin to what God himself does to the chaos, and his planting of a garden for fellowship with mankind is another act altogether requiring another activity from people that resembles worship in the tabernacle. Only *death* resembles the *pristine state* of the earth as a wilderness, for humans returns to the unorganized state of dust from which the first man came.

Awaiting the City

to be or maliciously intends to dupe the public by manufacturing. This is not my truth or your truth or the truth of the winners of the last war or the truth of the oppressors or the oppressed. It is the truth objectively seen and referenced to corresponding realities. Welcome to the pre-postmodern world. We cannot hope to achieve anything resembling equal justice for all in a society that gives itself to some other form of the truth or truth-telling, such as the indefinable "truthiness" of popular discourse, for justice must conform itself to the facts as they are. Nowhere is this more essential than in the discussion of economic issues.

Especially in market-oriented capitalism, trust is the number one product. Buyer and seller (including the buyers and sellers of political goods) must be able to trust that their exchanges of goods proceed without fraud or violence or some coercive intervention that subverts the process and that the information they are receiving about products and compensation can be trusted. The relative advantages achieved in the labor-management trade-off and the product-money trade-off must be measurable in some external manner that is understood and trusted by all to reflect reality. Otherwise, societal peace (*fraternité*) and freedom (*liberté*) break down, sometimes with disastrous results, such as the Reign of Terror after the onset of the French Revolution. Relative freedom and liberty in the context of some measure of equality (*égalité*) depend on truth-telling as a representation of facts, not a mere construct of imagination or assumption, or worse, propagandistic manipulation by demagogues.

Today's economic and political environment is coming dangerously close to tearing down this presumption of trust in capitalistic market economics and replacing it with coercive governmental mandates that cannot but issue in unprecedented societal disasters that would have global consequences. This condition proceeds partly from the conjunction of human greed and the development of monetary instruments that encourage individual CEOs (among others) at the top of the food chain to engage in behavior that amounts to speculative manipulation rather than investing in products and services for the long-run benefit of even their own businesses. On the other hand, a manipulative political climate that isolates regulatory and prosecutorial attention on such a small segment of the massive global economy can only serve to fuel envy and jealousy in the masses, who are being mined for

Awaiting the City

the votes necessary to political power. This has been part of the agenda of societal reconstructionists for generations and is characterized by the search for "enemies" at which to direct attention so that government will be given mandates to reshape societies globally. Stated succinctly by some of those given to this strategy:

> It would seem that humans need a common motivation, namely a common adversary, to organize and act together in the vacuum; such a motivation must be found to bring the divided nations together to face an outside enemy, either a real one or else one invented for the purpose. The common enemy of humanity is man. Democracy is no longer well suited for the tasks ahead and in searching for a new enemy to unite us, pollution, the threat of global warming, water shortages, famine, etc., would fit the bill.[17]

"There are ominous signs that the earth's weather patterns have begun to change dramatically and that these changes may portend a drastic decline in food production—with serious political implications for just about every nation on earth," states an article we recently read on climate change. It predicted "climate change" and went on to assert, "The evidence in support of these predictions has now begun to accumulate so massively that meteorologists are hard-pressed to keep up." You might conclude that this is just one of many stories on global warming in our time, but you would be wrong. It is from *Newsweek*, April 28, 1975, and it concerns "global cooling," the environmental myth of thirty-five years ago.[18] Global warming is only the latest in a series of hysterical scares to be perpetrated upon an unsuspecting public to justify governmental intervention on a massive scale to regulate and tax

---

17 Alexander King and Bertrand Schneider, *The First Global Revolution: A Report by the Council of the Club of Rome* (New York: Pantheon Books, 1991), 71, 75, et al. quoted in Bruce Schlink, *Americans Held Hostage by the Environmentalist Movement* (Pittsburgh: RoseDog Books, 2012), 458.

18 Peter Gwynne, "The Cooling World," *Newsweek*, April 28, 1975, http://denisdutton.com/cooling_world.htm.

Awaiting the City

life and economics for millions, even billions.[19] In such an atmosphere, it matters not to many that no global warming, as it has been defined and supposedly tracked in the current debate, has occurred since 2001 (at least) in the statistical studies comparing actual facts with computerized models. At the very least we ought to be asking, "What's the hurry?" Instead, politicians want to ram through *immediate* and *life-changing regulations*, reducing twelve parts per billion of contaminants to one part per billion, at the cost of thousands of dollars per year passed on to *each household*. If people question this, they are accused of wanting "dirtier water and dirtier air." We say, "Let us let all the voices be heard," even the ones who do not work for universities that get large grants from government agencies to do environmental studies. According to the voices calling for dramatic regulation, rather than slow down and rethink "solutions," one must declare the debate to be "over" and change the terminology. This may fit a postmodern sense of truth-telling, but it will not suit the facts and cannot be allowed to determine our understanding of *justice*.[20]

---

19 See Julian L. Simon, *Hoodwinking the Nation* (New Brunswick, NJ: Transaction, 1999). Simon documents numerous hysterical claims foisted upon the American public for political purposes. The latest documentation on the actual science behind the global warming hysteria is Ian Plimer, *Heaven and Earth* (Lanham, MD: Taylor Trade, 2009). See also E. Calvin Beisner, "The Meltdown of Global Warming Alarmism," *Baptist Press*, March 10, 2010, http://www.bpnews.net/BPFirstPerson.asp?ID=32470, documenting the implications of the discovery of attempts to manipulate "scientific" findings in reports from the University of East Anglia to the United Nations committee reporting on climate change (IPCC). Also, Brian Sussman, *Climategate* (Washington, DC: WND Books, 2010), and A. W. Montford, *Hockey Stick Illusion* (London: Stacey International, 2010).

20 See Angelo M. Codevilla, "Scientific Pretense vs. Democracy," *American Spectator*, April 2009, 32–38, http://spectator.org/archives/2009/04/14/scientific-pretense-vs-democra, for the manner in which political rulers determine which "scientific" authorities are to be believed and which are to be excoriated as "unscientific" or prejudiced beyond credibility. Once this classification has been accepted as factual, the media carries the water for the received wisdom of the chosen politicians. For listings of signatories (now about four thousand) of so-called "deniers" of global warming hysteria in the scientific community, see the Heidelberg Appeal, http://legacy.library.ucsf.edu/tid/jmc24e00, which originated as a protest to the United Nations Earth Summit 1992, held in Rio de Janeiro. Also, see the Petition Project, http://www.petitionproject.org/, for scientific community signatories (more than 31,000) protesting the science behind the 1997 Kyoto Protocol, an international treaty agreement linked to the United Nations Framework Convention on Climate Change (UNFCCC) that sets binding obligations on industrialized countries to reduce emissions of carbon dioxide and other so-called greenhouse gases.

Awaiting the City

EQUALITY AND JUSTICE

Defining equality in this context is the first task. Rousseau's opinion and that of the founding document of the American Revolution allege that it is God himself who made/created all men "equal" in some sense and that it is the duty of governments to "secure" this against societal inroads. Rousseau opined that it was societies that made men unequal, thus paving the way for a wholesale re-ordering of society for egalitarian goals aided in his day by Jacobin bishops in the church. The American experiment proceeded from a different perspective, one that assumed equality to be a matter of "rights" (seen as natural standing but not natural giftedness); of standing before the law, not attainment in life; of opportunity to *succeed* and progress through equality of *opportunity*, not equality of *outcomes*. Thus, egalitarian goals could not be pursued except at the price of loss of liberty, a prospect confirmed in the experience of the French Revolution and eschewed vigorously by the American observers who visited the Continent during the American revolutionary period. The program of American governments in the nineteenth century for the relief of poverty was liberty,[21] and it succeeded marvelously in making poverty the exception rather than the rule in a nation with nearly the highest per capita income in the world at the turn of the twentieth century.[22]

The irony in both cases is that it is manifest that the Creator's idea of "equality" is clearly *not* that of the political classes who view it as their mission to level and redistribute the totality of human and economic capital according to some preconceived notion of "fairness" or justice.[23] Human beings are born decidedly unequal in physiology, psychology, mental capacity, genetic predispositions, skill sets, cultural settings, and innumerable other ways that testify to the uniqueness of each individual and his or her ability to contribute

---

21 See Lawrence W. Reed, "Government, Poverty, and Self-Reliance," (speech, inaugural con-ference, The Center for Vision & Values, Grove City College, Grove City, Pennsylvania, April 8, 2005), http://www.mackinac.org/7050. This online essay is an edited version of the original speech.

22 Though England per capita income was very close.

23 For thorough discussions of this issue, see John Kekes, *Illusions of Egalitarianism* (Ithaca, NY: Cornell University Press, 2003), and Fernández de la Mora, *Egalitarian Envy*, as well as Thomas Sowell's previously cited works. For another sort of take on the subject, see Rousas John Rushdoony, *The Politics of Guilt and Pity* (1970; repr., Fairfax, VA: Thoburn, 1978).

Awaiting the City

to human betterment or detriment. It is no accident that DNA markers are absolutely without prior precedent in each new birth. Failure to recognize and celebrate this reality is the unmistakable philosophical bias of collectivist organizers of societal uniformity. It is not the *Creator* who has made us all alike but societies, governments, and cultures that attempt to *homogenize* individuals into pliable units and building blocks for some imagined world without differences in outlook, ambition, opinion, values, or even effort,[24] as when unions seek to control the actual output of labor given by individuals so there will be no reason for unequal compensation,[25] or when schools eliminate competitive activities or sports leagues play without keeping score.

The decidedly unequal distribution of human capital in the act of human procreation renders null each generation's attempt at egalitarian outcomes.[26] The only way any apparent equality of outcomes could be simulated would be if each generation were steamrolled into indistinguishable masses of pliant and uninteresting, not to mention ugly and unhappy, communes whose function would be to make certain not to engage in any endeavor that might distinguish any individual from his fellows. Somewhere Orwell and Huxley are smiling in derision. This is what Thomas Sowell has labeled the "unlimited vision," and it suffers from a complete lack of comprehension of the human condition or the plan of a benevolent Creator. This is not a dream; it is a nightmare.

Charles Murray has detailed at length the benefits to all mankind of the pursuit of individual excellence and its rarity in the course of human history.[27] Such a vision of human seeking after the true "glory" of the image of God

---

24 Think of some of the worst examples of this in fiction, as in Aldous Huxley, *Brave New World: A Novel* (London: Chatto & Windus, 1932), Ray Bradbury, *Fahrenheit 451* (New York: Ballantine Books, 1953), or George Orwell, *Nineteen Eighty-Four* (London: Secker & Warburg, 1949). Progressives claim to love these books, but many of their policies would move us into the direction of emulating those scenarios.

25 I, Tom, have personally experienced this phenomenon and have had repeated conversations with those who have had the same experience.

26 See esp. on this subject Richard J. Herrnstein and Charles Murray, *The Bell Curve: Intelligence and Class Structure in American Life* (New York: Free Press, 1994); Abigail Thernstrom and Stephan Thernstrom, *No Excuses: Closing the Racial Gap in Learning* (New York: Simon & Schuster, 2003); William Wright, *Born That Way: Genes, Behavior, Personality* (New York: Routledge, 1999). This last work particularly discusses the famous "nature vs. nurture" debate.

27 Charles Murray, *Human Accomplishment: The Pursuit of Excellence in the Arts and Sciences, 800 B.C. to 1950* (New York: HarperCollins, 2003). Malcolm Gladwell has produced a

Awaiting the City

through creativity and work is not some aberrant "health and wealth" gospel invented by half-baked theological pygmies proof-texting the three friends of Job. The God who "makes his rain to fall on the just and the unjust" is the same God who superintends the formation of human DNA into the kind of genius that eventually changes the direction of the world through science, technology, industry, art, government, and a host of other endeavors. He is also the God who hovers over the creation of the child with Down's syndrome, whose contribution (if he or she is not aborted by a society seeking to level all human differences through idolatrous self-aggrandizement for the sake of convenience) is far different but just as unique.[28] As Murray avers, "Excellence exists,[29] and it is time to acknowledge and celebrate the magnificent inequality that has enabled some of our fellow humans to have so enriched the lives of the rest of us." In the further context, Murray continues,

> It is also time to render unto equality that which is appropriate to equality, and unto excellence that which is appropriate to excellence. Equality is a fine ideal, and should have an honored place. To have understood that each person is unique, that each person must be treated as an end not a means, that each person should be free to live his life as he sees fit, so long as he accords others the same freedom, that each person should be equal before the law and is equal in God's sight, and to incorporate these principles

---

much easier reading piece on the same subject with his *Outliers: The Story of Success* (New York: Little, Brown, 2008).

28 Tom will never forget during his junior-high-school years a young man named Phil McEnroe, whose mother would never have countenanced destroying him in the womb, his simple childlike love expressed in hugs all around, his faithful work on a Texas dairy farm, his warm and constant smile and gentle disposition, and the wonderful day when he came down an aisle in a little country church to receive Christ when my own father gave an invitation. My dad told me it was the only time in seven years of ministry in that church that he could actually fully understand Phil's speech without his mother or daddy there to translate. Chad was moved Sunday by Sunday at Gambrell Street Baptist Church in Ft. Worth, Texas, in seminary days to see Dr. and Mrs. T. B. Maston, longtime professor of ethics at The Southwestern Baptist Theological Seminary, wheel their grown son, severely handicapped, to church and sit with him and hold his hymnal while he did his best to articulate the words of the hymns we sang.

29 And we would add that excellence takes on different garbs from Phil McEnroe to Bill Gates, though this is not what Murray is specifying here.

Awaiting the City

into the governance of nations—these are among the greatest of all human accomplishments. But equality has nothing to do with the abilities, persistence, zeal, and vision that produce excellence. Equality and excellence inhabit different domains, and allegiance to one need not compete with allegiance to the other.[30]

Only envy would deny those who benefit mankind in this manner economic rewards that outstrip that which is given to billions of others, even if it is in the billions of dollars.

Yet, still the attempt to control outcomes from cradle to grave goes on in an educational system that insists on constant invasion of *parental rights*, a tax system that *punishes* entrepreneurial talent and risk-taking and rewards foolish and immoral behavior, a political dance that pits groups of supposed "have-nots" against those who have "won the lottery in life," courts that regard their task as exercising the "heart" and "empathy" to walk in someone else's shoes rather than *upholding the law* and the Constitution,[31] and attempts to reconstruct whole segments of the economy through "health-care reform" and "cap-and-trade" schemes to "save the planet." The equality this will "provide" is the equality of a vast *leveling down*, not a pulling up of the downtrodden to full enjoyment of the liberties and wealth of American society as we have known it.[32]

The equality that is achievable, and biblical as well, is that which gives every human being the *same standing* before the law and guarantees that the rules will not be changed *arbitrarily* by the previous court or the next higher court. Rather, the law is standardized in advance by a written Constitution to which all parties concerned with law enforcement are bound to give allegiance and service. There can be *no justice* where this is not found and fiercely upheld. *Chaos* and *anarchy* can be the only end result of discarding this principle. The *failure* of this process is what the Bible labels as *injustice*, or unrighteousness. When government and

---

30 Murray, *Human Accomplishment*, 450.
31 This is the promise Barack Obama campaigned on relating to the appointment of judges and has already at this writing begun to implement in the nomination of Judge Sonia Sotomayor, who was later confirmed by the Senate, followed by the nomination and subsequent confirmation of Judge Elena Kagan.
32 See on this Arthur B. Laffer, Stephen Moore, and Peter J. Tanous, *The End of Prosperity* (New York: Simon & Schuster, 2008).

Awaiting the City

human individuals collude to take from their fellows to give to themselves or their cronies, whether business or political cronies, it is called *theft* and *unjust gain*.[33] This collusion at every level is what creates Babylonish culture, the parody of the New Jerusalem. Let us never forget that the Babylon we should fear most is the one in the human heart of which Luther warned: "For all evils and seductions are done under the guise of godliness. Every calamity begins in God's name." These words were further echoed by Helmut Thielicke out of the Nazi tragedy: "Our towns are copied fragments from our breast; and all man's Babylons strive but to impart the grandeurs of his Babylonian heart."[34]

Those who posit that it is just a matter of time and money that separate the world community from some form of universal justice have the burden of proof to show that man in the aggregate has ever been more just to all his fellows than has man the individual. This is the false hope of all Babylonian dreams. Man the *individual* may see his "brother" in need, and in the absence of a communal option, seek to be the Samaritan option. However, in the group setting he is more likely to devise with others an unjust option or simply assume that *someone else* will do the dirty work for him.[35] The justice being sought in the *unconstrained vision* is a cosmic justice that can only be achieved by One who is of infinite wisdom to correct and level that which is bent and out of shape from a near-infinite passage of time and genetic and cultural variation and the ravages of sin.[36] The *unconstrained vision* belongs to God alone; we must be content with pursuing the *constrained vision*.

RATIONAL COMPASSION—THE JUSTICE THAT IS POSSIBLE

Changing the world sounds grand until you consider how poorly we do even at changing our own little lives. On a daily basis we break our promises, indulge

---

33 See Isa. 57:15; cf. Gen. 37:26; Exod. 18:21; Judg. 5:19; 1 Sam. 8:3; Ps. 119:36; Prov. 28:16; Mic. 4:13.

34 Quotations from Mark Seifrid, "Story-Lines of Scripture and Footsteps in the Sea," *SBJT* 12, no. 4 (Winter 2008): 101–2.

35 See Peter Schweizer, *Makers and Takers* (New York: Doubleday, 2008), for full documentation on the tendency of egalitarian political groupings to do just this.

36 For a complete treatment of this subject, take a journey through N. T. Wright's commentary on Romans (cited in n. 12), where the "righteousness of God" promises through Christ the very thing sought out by all would-be social engineers.

our addictions, and rehearse old fantasies and grudges that even we know we'd be better off without. We have changed less about ourselves than we would like to admit. Who are we to charge off to change the world?

Indeed, I sometimes wonder if breathless rhetoric about changing the world is actually about changing the subject—from our own fitfully suppressed awareness that we did not ask to be brought into this world, have only vaguely succeeded in figuring it out, and will end our days in radical dependence on something or someone other than ourselves. If our excitement about changing the world leads us into the grand illusion that we stand somehow outside the world, knowing what's best for it, tools and goodwill and gusto at the ready, we have not yet come to terms with the reality that the world has changed us far more than we will ever change it. Beware of world changers—they have not yet learned the true meaning of sin.[37]

It should be clear at this point that egalitarian governmental "solutions" to near-intractable human problems is a chimerical vision that cannot be sustained in any imaginable real world. What, then, can be done to show compassionate attention to people in situations demanding some sort of "action" beyond pity? A number of proposals, from a governmental direction, are already on the table involving minimal governmental coercion and interference even as they maximize personal human involvement with fellow human beings.

The welfare reforms of the 1990s emphasizing work requirements and limitations on amounts and timing of benefits have forced many to consider whether it is better to get on with self-sufficient alternatives than to continue in dependency.[38] Other proposals, such as the use of educational vouchers (for private schools) for parents and their children in school districts that are doing

---

37 Crouch, *Culture Making*, 200. We would classify Richard Stearns's and Jim Wallis' latest contributions as this category of work. Ron Sider is a constant advocate of this mentality as is Tony Campolo in works we have previously cited. There are others, of course, as well.

38 Jason DeParle, *American Dream* (New York: Viking, 2004), and Marvin Olasky, *Renewing American Compassion* (Washington DC: Regnery, 1997), have documented this process and its effectiveness and/or lack thereof. For insight to the intractability of inner-city problems and the worldview that sustains them, see, Kathryn Edin and Maria Kefalas, *Promises I Can Keep: Why Poor Women Put Motherhood before Marriage* (Berkeley: University of California Press, 2005), and Theodore Dalrymple, *Life at the Bottom: The Worldview That Makes the Underclass* (Chicago: Ivan R. Dee, 2001). Sadly, recent data indicate that non-marital births, after leveling off for a period after "welfare reform" in the 1990s, have begun to increase again, indicating more than economic disincentives at work in underclass

Awaiting the City

a poor job of preparing children for life in "hard America" are anathema to the educational establishment and are not being tried extensively, but in some places they have been and are successful.[39] Charter schools have also been successful (though the track record is mixed) and not as widely resisted by public school educators as vouchers are. Tax credits in various forms to be used in private charity efforts have been proposed but not adopted. Additionally, during the George W. Bush administration, the idea of "faith-based initiatives" was welcomed by some, excoriated by others, and tried without much satisfaction by others, and thus appears to have been mostly abandoned. Finally, throwing caution to the winds, Charles Murray, whose work on the failure of the welfare system[40] in 1984 arguably led to the discussion and implementation of reform in the 1990s, has proposed a complete replacement of the system of all entitlement spending in the United States with a *simple payment* once a year that would *eliminate all* political posturing and coercive interference, but *for that very reason* (in our opinion) it has no chance of implementation.[41]

Domestically, Olasky and others have advocated several ways of profitable interaction with the "deserving," *biblical poor.*[42] Here we mean by "deserving," those who will accept assistance in developing a self-sufficient and productive lifestyle within the parameters of unavoidable human limitations—that is, even if poor life choices and/or prior choices by others have led to despair and despondency; even

---

communities. And we have cited earlier the same alarming trend among middle-class white families, Charles Murray, *Coming Apart* (New York: Crown Forum, 2012).

39 The National Education Association has recently heavily subsidized antivoucher campaigns in Utah and Colorado and discouraged any hopefulness about future attempts to successfully win approval for vouchers in education by ballot initiative. This is one area where Sider has broken free from the Democrat coalition politically. See Ronald J. Sider, "Quality Education for Everyone," in *Just Generosity*, 2nd ed. (Grand Rapids, MI: Baker, 2007), chap. 7.

40 Charles Murray, *Losing Ground: American Social Policy 1950–1980* (New York: Basic Books, 1984).

41 Charles Murray, *In Our Hands: A Plan to Replace the Welfare State* (Washington, DC: AEI Press, 2006). Murray's proposal has no chance because modern politicians see political maneuvering and posturing as *the way* to exert their clout.

42 See among others, Olasky, *Renewing American Compassion*; David W. Hall, ed. *Welfare Reformed: A Compassionate Approach* (Phillipsburg, NJ: P&R, 1994); Corbett and Fikkert, *When Helping Hurts*; Myron Magnet, ed., *What Makes Charity Work? A Century of Public and Private Philanthropy* (Chicago: Ivan R. Dee, 2000); Richard John Neuhaus, *Doing Well and Doing Good: The Challenge of the Christian Capitalist* (New York: Doubleday, 1992); and publications and training opportunities afforded through Voice of Calvary Ministries in Mendenhall, Mississippi, founded by John Perkins.

if handicaps, language barriers, parental abandonment, death or abandonment of a spouse, educational deficiencies, or lack of basic life skills have led to an apparent dead-end condition; if considerate, timely, and respectful help can be given and received, then it *ought* to be given. Furthermore, for the Christian such help must be given at *whatever* expense may be required in terms of human and financial resources and *within biblical boundaries* and the guidance of the Holy Spirit. This is clearly within the mandate of Christ to his church to shine the light of kingdom values and the world to come into the present darkness.

Richard John Neuhaus reminds us that there is a universal appeal in the "truths" upon which this nation was founded that comes from a Puritan-Lockean foundation—"a curious mix of Scottish Enlightenment and Calvinist Christianity, shaped by the emergence of democratic insight among English dissenters, and colored by their idealization of republican Rome and Periclean Athens." He goes on to comment that Dr. Martin Luther King Jr., as leader in the generation of the '60s for universal human and civil rights, most clearly articulated this synthesis and would regularly seek to define his "dream" in terms of Christian ideals centered in "human dignity, creation, redemption, forgiveness, and the promise of the Kingdom." Dr. King was fond of saying, "Whom you would change you must first love, and they must know that you love them." Neuhaus comments significantly that the cameras and microphones were always on when King spoke of the political topics of the day but were turned off when he sought to articulate the *true meaning* of the cause for which he fought and died.[43] The current secularized American culture is not likely to turn to such leadership again barring a genuine heaven-sent spiritual awakening.

Given such a turn of events in this last fifty years, it is likely that Christians interested in actually affecting the situation of the poor in America—recognizing that very few in our land begin to compare with the destitute of the world outside the United States—must involve themselves in community development and identification with those in need and work without resort to governmental "solutions." Corbett and Fikkert clearly delineate the principles of operation that others have seen before them—that is, one must determine if the need of the moment is for relief (immediate life-saving assistance), rehabilitation (modifica-

---

43 Neuhaus, *Doing Well and Doing Good*, 4–7.

Awaiting the City

tion of life habits and skills and choices), or development (promoting ongoing personal and communal stability for self-sufficiency). All of these, having been stated in various ways by numerous others before, must include the indispensable use of correct timing to produce hopeful results.[44] The key to success in any endeavor of this sort is personal and communal involvement that restores, preserves, and develops human dignity in the image of God, so that the full potential for "glory" in human achievement can be realized.

HELP FOR GLOBAL POVERTY

Corbett and Fikkert apply these same criteria to helping the poor outside the United States. We agree that the literature overwhelmingly supports this approach and denies that the numerous attempts at massive financial intervention through loans and outright gifts and grants has had anything like the impact hoped for or in some cases claimed.[45] The greatest problem facing American Christians concerned about the inequities that exist globally is that cultures outside the West do not revere the values that underlie our civiliza-

---

44 Corbett and Fikkert, *When Helping Hurts*, 103–60, for full discussion and applicational guidance.
45 A sampling of the supporting documentation includes Keith B. Richburg, *Out of America* (1997; repr., New York: Basic Books, 2009); Robert Calderisi, *The Trouble with Africa* (New York: Palgrave Macmillan, 2006); Dambisa Moyo, *Dead Aid* (New York: Farrar, Straus and Giroux, 2009); Herbert Schlossberg, Pierre Berthoud, Clark H. Pinnock, and Marvin Olasky, *Freedom, Justice, and Hope: Toward a Strategy for the Poor and the Oppressed*, ed. Marvin Olasky, Turning Point Christian Worldview Series (Westchester, IL: Crossway, 1988); Lawrence E. Harrison, *Who Prospers? How Cultural Values Shape Economic and Political Success* (New York: Basic Books, 1992); Jagdish Bhagwati, *In Defense of Globalization* (New York: Oxford University Press, 2004); Hernando de Soto, *The Mystery of Capital: Why Capitalism Triumphs in the West and Fails Everywhere Else* (New York: Basic Books, 2000); and Hernando de Soto, *The Other Path: The Economic Answer to Terrorism* (New York: Basic Books, 1989); William Easterly, *The Elusive Quest for Growth: Economists' Adventures and Misadventures in the Tropics* (Cambridge, MA: MIT Press, 2002). Typical of the debate about development, taking different positions on the same data, are R. Glenn Hubbard and William Duggan, *The Aid Trap* (New York: Columbia University Press, 2009); William Easterly, *White Man's Burden* (New York: Penguin, 2006); and Jeffrey D. Sachs, *The End of Poverty: Economic Possibilities for Our Time* (New York: Penguin, 2005). A balanced weighing of the claims can be found in Don Eberly, *Rise of Global Civil Society* (New York: Encounter Books, 2008), who sides ultimately with the business development model (Easterly) with supplemental infrastructural development, keyed to country by country incentivized aid based on the elimination of corruption.

tion, values derived from the Reformation and the Enlightenment—freedom, equality, limited government, constitutionalism, individual rights, the protection of private property,[46] and the rule of law. Further, superstition about the creation and the fatefulness of history and human existence and the value and rightness of work to overcome environmental barriers bars the way to progress in too many places.[47] To a very great extent, a speech by President Barak Obama before the Ghanaian parliament in Accra states the obvious, from which we quote briefly: "Africa's future is up to Africans.... [T]he West is not responsible for the destruction of the Zimbabwean economy over the last decade, or wars in which children are enlisted as combatants.... Development depends on good governance, [which] is a responsibility that can only be met by Africans.... No business wants to invest in a place where the government skims 20 percent off the top."[48]

Furthermore, these non-Western cultures resent our excesses and failures. However, they do now seem to want our investment, while seeking to arrive at the day when they pass us economically and can then impose their own values on the rest of the world. The fact is that most of the world is not going to reach our level of economic success without the excesses of the consumer society. Wherever Islam and Confucianism or ancestral reverence and the more primitive tribalisms prevail, we are not likely to be successful at imposing any kind of economic reform. Certainly we will not succeed merely by divestiture in the evangelical community, even if only for our brethren caught in these situations.[49]

Claar and Klay support this assessment in their own way and opine that

---

46 Protection of private property, or rather the lack thereof, is a particularly egregious problem in the third and fourth worlds. See esp. De Soto, *Mystery of Capital*, on this. For the best (in our opinion) work on the subject of the importance of private property, see Tom Bethell, *The Noblest Triumph: Property and Prosperity through the Ages* (New York: Palgrave Macmillan, 1998).

47 On this subject, see esp. Udo Middelmann, *Christianity versus Fatalistic Religions in the War against Poverty* (Colorado Springs: Paternoster, 2007); Darrow L. Miller, *Discipling Nations* (Seattle: YWAM Publishing, 1988); and Darrow L. Miller, with Marit Newton, *Life Work: A Biblical Theology for What You Do Every Day* (Seattle: YWAM Publishing, 2009).

48 Barak Obama, "Remarks by the President to the Ghanaian Parliament," (speech, Accra International Conference Center, Accra, Ghana, July 11, 2009), http://www.whitehouse.gov/the-press-office/remarks-president-ghanaian-parliament.

49 See Robert W. Fogel, *The Fourth Great Awakening and the Future of Egalitarianism* (Chicago: University of Chicago Press, 2000), 231–33, for confirmation on these thoughts.

Awaiting the City

only development along the line of the West will save the undeveloped world.[50] In offering hope they cite ways Christians might meaningfully involve themselves while cautioning, with Albert Schweitzer from the previous century, that "[o]f all the will toward the ideal in mankind only a small part can manifest itself in public action. All the rest of this force must be content with small and obscure deeds. The sum of these, however, is a thousand times stronger than the act of those who receive wide public recognition. The latter, compared to the former, are like the foam on the wave of a deep ocean."[51] They further indicate that it is not exploitation by the West that makes the third and fourth world poor, but the exact opposite, as both D'Souza and Sowell have documented as well. Moreover, the only way an equalization of some kind can come is through the exportation of our human capital and making sure our markets are open to them. This would require wide-ranging educational efforts here and abroad, dislocation of workers here in industries that are now protected from foreign competition, large-scale relocation by American teachers, trainers, businessmen, investors, etc. In fact, it would probably take an effort comparable to the West's great evangelical missionary movement, or the e-word, establishment of empire. Oddly enough, the fact is that perhaps the greatest loss to the poorest nations of the world was the collapse of colonial empires, especially the British Empire.[52]

In light of such an assessment, major efforts are now under way to challenge American Christian business and technological talent to see their calling in terms of the opportunity to help the undeveloped world develop. Past efforts at "tentmaking" missionary work have not concentrated on the actual task of developing businesses and economic power within the nations targeted for missional effort. The business engagement has been only a pretext for entry to countries, not a genuine attempt to build businesses and industries within the chosen areas of service. Making this business development part of the mission itself is one of the most

---

50 Victor V. Claar and Robin J. Klay, *Economics in Christian Perspective* (Downers Grove, IL: InterVarsity Press, 2007), 143–44. See also Hubbard and Duggan who call for a new business "Marshall Plan." *Aid Trap*, 90–93. Please note that the Marshall Plan was a business plan for European recovery, not a massive giveaway of resources and capital. It was heavily incentivized.

51 Fogel, *Fourth Great Awakening*, 162. This is surely what Hunter, *To Change the World*, means by "faithful presence."

52 Fogel, *Fourth Great Awakening*, 223–25. We say that in full recognition that colonialism was a very mixed bag.

Awaiting the City

promising strategies now being explored, and if there is one way to carry out the mandate of Jesus in a holistic way, it is this.[53] It is at least worth considering that the widespread dislike of business and business people in the intellectual community, not least that of the Christian left, has led to a large gap in the understanding of Christian mission to the world. If we do believe in the holistic message of Jesus, there is no better way to take prosperity to the world than through the work of talented and zealous Christian people who are willing to give up the comfort of American life for the pioneer business life of the third and fourth world. Of course, this would involve dropping the agenda of the world leftist community that demands a stop to development and the divestiture of the West, especially that of North America. Envy never ceases in the human heart.

In 1995, Gregg Easterbrook[54] undertook to change the debate by introducing the idea that the vast improvements in the human condition, especially with reference to the environment, in the Western world were and are reasons to be optimistic and less hysterical about future prospects. He called for a new "eco-realism" that would recognize when exaggeration and hyperbole substitute for rational thought processes and realistic assessments of relative risks and consequences. American and Western environmentalism is concerned about acid rain, pesticide residues on vegetables and fruits, PCBs, dioxin, lead in paint, biodiversity degradation, ozone depletion, carbon dioxide emissions, spotted owl preservation and the cutting of old growth forests, toxic waste leaks from disposal sites, the cutting of rain forests, oil spills in the Gulf of Mexico and Alaska,[55] and preeminently climate change, not to mention any other localized cause that can

---

53 See Tetsunao Yamamori and Kenneth A. Eldred, eds., *On Kingdom Business: Transforming Missions through Entrepreneurial Strategies* (Wheaton, IL: Crossway, 2003), and Steve Rundle and Tom Steffen, *Great Commission Companies: The Emerging Role of Business in Missions* (Downers Grove, IL: InterVarsity Press, 2003). The latest and most comprehensive of these studies is C. Neal Johnson, *Business as Mission: A Comprehensive Guide to Theory and Practice* (Downers Grove, IL: InterVarsity Press, 2009). This is exactly what it claims to be. Another approach that has great promise is in microfinance, detailed in Peter Greer and Phil Smith, *The Poor Will Be Glad: Joining the Revolution to Lift the World out of Poverty* (Grand Rapids, MI: Zondervan, 2009), and other sources in our notes.

54 Gregg Easterbrook, *A Moment on Earth: The Coming Age of Environmental Optimism* (New York: Penguin Books, 1995). We are aware that Easterbrook would not necessarily support all of our proposals, but that makes him all the more relevant to our case at this point.

55 None of these conditions or events has ever been proved to cause human death or sickness in any significant numbers, though wildlife death and harm, habitat disturbance and degradation, aesthetics, and job loss have at times resulted.

Awaiting the City

be used for raising money and activists. On the other hand, millions of children in the undeveloped world die from diarrhea caused by drinking polluted water (not industrial waste but human and animal waste)[56] and breathing polluted air caused by the burning of dung and other biomass materials for cooking and heating.[57] The greatest air pollution is particulates from unpaved roads and streets. The likely cause of forest depletion is more from penniless farmers clearing land and cutting wood to fuel cooking and heating.[58]

Easterbrook goes on to document the activities of "institutional environmentalism," which is in opposition to the full development of the undeveloped world,[59] and among other remarks that have made him less than a hero to many who would otherwise have embraced his studies, he opines,

> Institutional environmentalism focuses on the real but comparatively minor problems of developed nations in part to support the worldview that Western material production is the root of ecological malevolence. The trough of such thinking was reached at the Earth Summit in Rio in 1992. There, having gotten the attention of the world and of its heads of state, what message did institutional environmentalism choose to proclaim? That global warming is a horror. To make Rio a fashionably correct event about Western guilt-tripping, the hypothetical prospect of global warming—a troubling but speculative concern that so far has harmed no one and may never harm anyone—was put above palpable, urgent loss of lives from Third World water and smoke pollution.[60]

---

56 Easterbrook cites 3.8 million such deaths of children under five years of age in 1993, a number higher than all deaths from all causes in the United States and the European Union combined. *Moment on Earth*, 578.

57 Ibid. The number estimated here is an additional 4 million.

58 Easterbrook, *Moment on Earth*, 579–82.

59 Ibid., 580–600.

60 Ibid., 579–80. While this is an opinion from two decades ago, we have found nothing at the present time in the literature to change this assessment. We have elsewhere cited Easterbrook taking very much the same position of development in the undeveloped world (see chap. 26, note 18). Gregg Easterbrook, *The Progress Paradox: How Life Gets Better While People Feel Worse* (New York: Random House, 2003).

Awaiting the City

In commenting further on the green agenda of limiting production and consumption, Easterbrook goes on to state,

> There is a famous statistic that the United States has 4 percent of the world's population and consumes 40 percent of current resources. Environmental orthodoxy says this proves U.S. resource use must go way down. What the statistic really tells you is that Third World resource consumption must go way up. United States resource use is in fact too high. But it will be impossible to raise the standard of living of the world's impoverished to anything like a morally equitable level without a significant rise in net global consumption of resources.

Finally, from a secular perspective, but not without ramifications for Christian mission, Bjørn Lomborg has compiled a list of projects that are doable now, that would have the greatest impact in the short run and require the least expenditure (that is, the most affordable and likely to be attempted) of capital for the developed world in behalf of the undeveloped world.[61] They are ranked from best to worst in terms of impact, doability, and cost-effectiveness, and the supporting data are massively documented. An international panel was assembled to assess the data and recommend strategy and rank the projects. Global warming projects rank dead last, with HIV/AIDS projects first, followed by projects for malnutrition and hunger, other communicable diseases (notably malaria), and sanitation and water projects. It is a tragedy that the world is full of hysterical alarm over "climate change" at a time when its attention should be turned to those things that could actually impact the third and fourth worlds for good in this generation. No scenario proposed by any national or international political grouping(s) reckons on making a measurable impact on the climate for the next fifty to hundred years, but Lomborg and his associates show what could actually be done for the destitute poor of

---

61 Bjørn Lomborg, ed., *Global Crises, Global Solutions* (Cambridge: Cambridge University Press, 2004).

Awaiting the City

the world now.[62] No construal of the Christian conception of "justice" can possibly ignore this strange juxtaposition of misplaced zeal for the problem that is *not*, in place of the solutions for the problem that *is*.

EPILOGUE: CAUSE FOR HOPE?

"Six years ago Richard Cizik, former vice president for governmental affairs of the National Association of Evangelicals (NAE), called 'climate change denialism' a 'heresy committed against all of creation, nothing less than a monstrous wrong.'"[63] So said E. Calvin Beisner in a 2011 *Baptist Press* news article. He also noted that the intervening years appear to have Protestant pastors, especially evangelicals, "jumping on the heresy bandwagon in droves." Beisner cites in support of this conclusion a LifeWay Research poll from October 2010, reported just in time for Earth Day in the United States (April 22), that "a majority of evangelicals (68 percent) disagree strongly (44 percent) or somewhat (24 percent) that global warming is real and man-made, compared to 45 percent mainline pastors." The response was to the statement "I believe global warming is real and man-made." This represents a significant "jump of over 50 percent from the 27 percent who gave that answer in 2008."[64] It is not heresy to point out that such alarmism and hysteria are the sound and fury of political entrepreneurs and neo-mercantilists, signifying nothing while they and their governmental coterie make handsome profits using other people's money.

The present situation is indeed daunting, but there is hope. One example is how a significant group of natural scientists, theologians, and economists are making the case against policies elevating man-made global warming to a catastrophic cause for massive governmental interference in our lives and those of billions around the world. Read the Cornwall Alliance's official evangelical declaration on global warming to see how they are "bringing a proper and balanced biblical view of stewardship to the critical issues of environment and

---

62 For his honest efforts to aid the world in understanding and doing positive things about the poor and the environment, Lomborg has been widely and viciously attacked by the community that was once his home—radical environmentalists.

63 E. Calvin Beisner, "Revisiting 'Climate Change Denialism,'" *Baptist Press*, April 19, 2011, http://www.bpnews.net/BPFirstPerson.asp?ID=35090.

64 Cited in ibid.

Awaiting the City

development."[65] Such responses are helpful, instructive, and necessary, and they also inspire hope for developing a way forward with attention to the concerns addressed in our study of the biblical, historical, and theological aspects of Christian faith and political economy. We turn now in the last chapter to final considerations for engaging God's creation/cultural mandate in our current context and time in history in view of God's redemptive mandate to bring the whole gospel to the whole person to the whole world.

---

65 G. Cornelis van Kooten, E. Calvin Beisner, and Pete Geddes, "A Renewed Call to Truth, Prudence, and Protection of the Poor: An Evangelical Examination of the Theology, Science, and Economics of Global Warming," Cornwall Alliance for the Stewardship of Creation, http://www.cornwallalliance.org/docs/a-renewed-call-to-truth-prudence-and-protection-of-the-poor.pdf. Quotation from "What is the Cornwall Alliance?" Cornwall Alliance Frequently Asked Questions, http://www.cornwallalliance.org/about/faq/.

Awaiting the City

Chapter 28

Fickle Prophets, Biblical Realism, and Rational Compassion

"The strongest moral claim for democratic capitalism
is that it is the most practical hope of the world's
poor: no magic wand, but the best hope."[1]
Michael Novak

"Of all the tyrannies, tyranny sincerely expressed for the good of
its victims may be the most oppressive. It may be better to live
under robber barons than under omnipotent moral busybodies."[2]
C. S. Lewis

"Freedom of choice places the whole blame of failure on the
shoulders of the individual. And as freedom encourages a
multiplicity of attempts, it unavoidably multiplies failure and
frustration.... We join a mass movement to escape individual responsibility, or, in the words of a young Nazi, 'to be free from freedom.'"[3]
Eric Hoffer

1   Michael Novak, *The Spirit of Democratic Capitalism*, 2nd ed. (Lanham, MD: Madison Books, 1991), 421.
2   C. S. Lewis, "The Humanitarian Theory of Punishment," *God in the Dock*, ed. Walter Hooper (1970; repr., Grand Rapids: Eerdmans, 2008), 292.
3   Eric Hoffer, *The True Believer: Thoughts on the Nature of Mass Movements* (1951; repr., New York: Harper & Row, 2002), 31.

"The only means by which the rich can get richer at the expense
of the poor is by the exercise of extortionary powers. This is
done by the use of government authority, by the exercise of
monopoly power, and by controlling the single element of
economic production that can't be enlarged, namely, land."[4]
William F. Buckley Jr.

"[I]f there is no truth to guide and direct political activity, then
ideas and convictions can easily be manipulated for reasons of
power. As history demonstrates, a democracy without values
easily turns into open or thinly disguised totalitarianism."[5]
John Paul II (Karol Wojtyla)

"The lessons of history, confirmed by the evidence immediately
before me, show conclusively that continued dependence upon
relief induces a spiritual disintegration fundamentally destructive
to the national fiber. To dole out relief in this way is to administer a
narcotic, a subtle destroyer of the human spirit. It is inimical to the
dictates of a sound policy. It is in violation of the traditions of America.
Work must be found for able-bodied but destitute workers."[6]
Franklin D. Roosevelt

THOMAS WOODS JR. HAS ARGUED from a Catholic perspective for the necessity
of the use of reason and logic in the consideration of economic matters from a
Christian perspective. He avers, "Economics is a bona fide science, whose laws
are binding whether we like them or not." Woods continues, "[I]f economic

---

4   William F. Buckley Jr., "Ignoring the Rich," *National Review*, January 31, 2006, 55, http://
     old.nationalreview.com/buckley/wfb200601311229.asp.
5   John Paul II (Karol Wojtyla), *Centesimus Annus*, Encyclical letter on the 100th anniversary
     of *Rerum Novarum*, regarding capital and labour, and regarding Catholic social teaching,
     Vatican Web site, May 1, 1991, par. 46, http://www.vatican.va/holy_father/john_paul_ii/
     encyclicals/documents/hf_jp-ii_enc_01051991_centesimus-annus_en.html, quoted in
     Richard John Neuhaus, *Doing Well and Doing Good* (New York: Doubleday, 1992), 277.
6   Franklin D. Roosevelt, "Inaugural Address," March 4, 1933, online by Gerhard Peters and
     John T. Woolley, American Presidency Project, http://www.presidency.ucsb.edu/ws/index.
     php?pid=14473.

analysis should conclude that living-wage legislation would have consequences exactly contrary to the wishes of its proponents, and would in fact throw men out of work entirely, then *it should not be controversial to conclude that living-wage legislation cannot be a moral imperative.*[7] The Christian advocates of "moral" government budgets and laws continue to advocate just such legislative "remedies," while loading guilt on the general population and Christian audiences in particular. In Woods's case the condemnation involves the charge of "dissent" from papal teaching, which he characterizes as an undeserved calumny based on the failure to submit moral teaching to rational processes. If a Christian insists that two-plus-two is five and declares to his fellows that this is a moral conclusion, no one is to be righteously condemned for declaring such "teaching" to be hokum and heresy. Neither should Christians be intimidated when confronted with irrational claptrap masquerading as biblical or ethical certitudes, such as minimum-wage legislation or boycotts of companies hiring destitute people in the undeveloped world. As Walter Williams has written again and again and spoken in various forums, "Truly compassionate policy requires dispassionate analysis."[8] Pascal is reputed to have said that the first moral duty of man is to think straight. If we have succeeded in moving anyone

---

7   Thomas E. Woods Jr., *The Church and the Market* (Lanham, MD: Lexington Books, 2005), 213. This kind of legislation is a regular feature of the advocacy on the evangelical left. For the latest explanation of how minimum-wage legislation hurts those it purports to help, see Kevin D. Williamson, "Keeping Blacks Poor," *National Review*, February 8, 2010, 30–33, https://www.nationalreview.com/nrd/articles/339716/keeping-blacks-poor. We have previously noted economist and professor Walter E. Williams, *The State against Blacks* (New York: McGraw Hill, 1982), and Walter E. Williams, "Race and Wage Regulation," in *Race and Economics* (Stanford, CA: Hoover Institution Press, 2011), 31–58, on this subject. See esp. the charts on pp. 42–43 for years 1948–2009. Latest figures on the effects of recent rises in the minimum wage may be found in "The Young and Jobless," *Wall Street Journal*, July 24, 2010, http://online.wsj.com/article/SB10001424052748703467304575383413669781840.html.

8   Williams, *State against Blacks*, 49. In his latest contribution on this subject, Williams cites the report of William E. Even and David A. Macpherson, "Unequal Harm: Racial Disparities in the Employment Consequences of Minimum Wage Increases," Employment Policies Institute, May 5, 2011, http://www.epionline.org/study/r137/, showing blacks, esp. in the 16–24 male demographic, suffering more than twice the unemployment difficulties in 2008 and following the "Great Recession" as the minimum wage goes up. Cited in Walter Williams, "How Minimum Wage Devastates Young Blacks," *Human Events*, May 23, 2011, 19; also published as Walter Williams, "Minimum Wage's Discriminatory Effects," Townhall, May 11, 2011, http://townhall.com/columnists/walterewilliams/2011/05/11/minimum_wages_discriminatory_effects. See also Williams, *Race and Economics*.

Awaiting the City

toward this ideal in economic/political considerations, we will have reached at least one goal of this book. To paraphrase what Mark Twain said, it's not what people don't know that is so harmful; it's what they know for sure that just ain't so. The uninformed and passionate ("do-gooders") never see the "invisible victims" of their policy "solutions," those displaced from any self-respecting work at all when "child labor" and "sweat shop" labor are eliminated or minimum wage legislation prices unskilled workers out of the market. In the process, especially in the case of youth, all the things that are learned and added to one's skill- and tool-set by early low-pay jobs is destroyed.[9] We find ourselves at a loss to understand why we should go along with this kind of politics.

THE PROBLEM WITH SOCIALISM

Richard John Neuhaus, commenting in the same vein on Marxist Socialistic theory, wondered,

> Why should the philosophy of a man who died a century ago, whose prophecies have been confounded, and whose followers have caused some of the greatest catastrophes in history, remain the single most important intellectual influence in the world today, more important by far than that of men of more profound insight? Marxism answers several needs. It has its arcana, which persuade believers that they have penetrated to secrets veiled from others, who are possessed of false consciousness. It appeals to the strongest of all political passions, hatred, and justifies it. It provides a highly intellectualized rationalization of a discreditable but almost universal and ineradicable emotion: envy. It forever puts the blame elsewhere, making self-examination unnecessary and self-knowledge impossible. It explains everything. Finally, it persuades believers that they have a special destiny in the world. For disgruntled intellectuals, nothing could be more gratifying. The end of Marxism is definitely not nigh.[10]

---

9   We are here summarizing Professor Williams, *State against Blacks*, 50–51.
10 Neuhaus, *Doing Well and Doing Good*, 22–23.

Awaiting the City

Peter Berger has mused on the same subject:

> It is possible that the mythic superiority of socialism is the fact
> that, or so it appears, its realization never takes place. It is a fugitive
> vision, tantalizing those who adhere to it from one near-miss to the
> other. But Tantalus goes on trying—and believing. Thus there is
> the unending quest for the first case of "true socialism" always just
> out of reach, the quest taken up again after each disappointment.
> There is no capitalist equivalent of this (profoundly mythological,
> indeed religious) quest. The benefits of capitalism *are* attainable.[11]

He further opines that once these benefits are attained, they appear cheap
and ordinary, no matter the effort put into their attainment. Thus, they do not
inspire to poetic sacrifice and lack popular appeal. This is not unlike the attempt
by many Christians to equate the wealth of the industrialized West with just so
much "manna" to be distributed, having no real idea what it took to produce it.

Having survived the threat (for the time being) of totalitarian
Fascist/Marxist/Socialistic militarism in the last century, too many moderns
have failed to see the far more subtle threat coming from this vision of some
form of "true socialism,"[12] now being increasingly heralded as progressivism,
especially since liberalism has acquired such a bad name with the general body
politic. This "new" socialistic progressivism is that which comes from

> men of good intentions and good will who wish to reform us.
> Impatient with the slowness of persuasion and example to achieve
> the great social changes they envision, they are anxious to use the
> power of the state to achieve their ends and confident of their own
> ability to do so.... Yet if they gained the power, they would fail to
> achieve their immediate aims and, in addition, would produce a

---

11   Peter L. Berger, *The Capitalist Revolution: Fifty Propositions about Prosperity, Equality, and Liberty* (New York: Basic Books, 1986), 208–9.

12   Not named as such today generally, but nevertheless functioning as statist monopoly on huge segments of economic life for the purpose of redistributive egalitarian policies with a variety of agendas. This is truly the ultimate patronage system.

Awaiting the City

collective state…. Concentrated power is not rendered harmless
by the good intentions of those who create it.[13]

These words are just as true today as they were more than half a century ago.
The would-be utopia of the unconstrained vision is the dream of the administrative state so admired by progressives at the turn of the twentieth century.

In the same vein we cited earlier William Buckley's reiteration of William
Schlamm's saying, "The problem with socialism is socialism; the problem with
capitalism is capitalists." He was pointing out with great candor that, while human beings will always be in general what they have always been since the fall,
*the systematic enthronement of the supposedly wise and benevolent over our economic
fate is doomed to enslave us* in a way that *voluntary association and competitive
activities* designed to benefit our fellows in the marketplace *never can or will*. We
may need someone with police power (we do!)[14] to apply and enforce the rules
that have been agreed to, but we dare not entrust to others just like ourselves the
ability to determine the outcomes of our personal spiritual/moral development,
our economic activities, the *cars* we drive, the *temperature* on our thermostats,
the *treatments* we may or may not get for our illnesses, or our *food* consumption
(just to name a few of the apparent goals of the current "nanny state"), anymore
than we would our *worship*. That is putting humans in the place of God. We will
get what we have been foolish enough to enthrone—antichrist.

---

13   Milton Friedman, with Rose D. Friedman, 40th anniversary ed., *Capitalism and Freedom* (Chicago: University of Chicago Press, 2002), 201.
14   The founders saw it this way: "For the Founders, then, the individual's existence and freedom in this crucial respect are not a gift of government. They are a gift of God and nature. Government is therefore always and fundamentally in the service of the individual, not the other way around. The purpose of government, then, is to enforce the natural law for the members of the political community by securing the people's natural rights. It does so by preserving their lives and liberties against the violence of others. In the founding, the liberty to be secured by government is not freedom from necessity or poverty. It is freedom from the despotic and predatory domination of some human beings over others." Thomas G. West and William A. Schambra, "The Progressive Movement and the Transformation of American Politics" (First Principles Series Report #12, Heritage Foundation, Washington, DC, July 18, 2007), http://www.heritage.org/research/reports/2007/07/the-progressive-movement-and-the-transformation-of-american-politics. This essay clearly delineates the progressive agenda to makeover humanity itself through governmental fiat. See a more thoroughgoing treatment in John Marini and Ken Masugi, eds., *The Progressive Revolution in Politics and Political Science: Transforming the American Regime* (New York: Rowman & Littlefield, 2005), and our own discussion in chap. 19 and some in chap. 20.

Awaiting the City

The purpose of this book has been to warn of this possibility and show why this is no path Christians should lead the world to walk. We have examined these issues through three lenses—the Bible, historical theology, and historical political economy. The world of those who would lead us down a statist path to a chimerical nirvana, on this earth of fallen humans and a creation in bondage, is a world created by intellectuals who do not have the knowledge, ability, or wisdom to actually produce what they lovingly caress in their mental world.[15] Unfortunately, they do not seem to need the corroboration of actual historical practice to hold many in thrall to their ideas. It is their stock-in-trade not to put into successful practice the things of which they speak but to speak and opine demagogically without benefit of producing concrete realities. This is what Sowell repeatedly calls "verbal virtuosity." Christians require a good set of lenses and filters to strain out the spurious from their own pronouncements and political opinions in order to be truly prophetic to their contemporaries. We began this project with a view to opening some windows into such a worldview.

BIBLICAL REALISM

Biblically and theologically, we have sought to shed light in the befogged shadows of moral/political posturing by canvassing the Scripture and Christian theology for their message on several themes. First, who is God, and what is his desire and plan for mankind? It seems fairly clear to us that he, the God of the Bible, has in mind redeemed humanity's eventual full rule and enjoyment of the universe as his own vice-regents, with no other one to rule them than themselves through moral and spiritual embodiment of all that he is in us. Best seen in Christ, this *imago Dei* is the ultimate plan and goal for all who come to him in faith. He has promised to bring this plan to fruition in the grand blessing of the new heavens and new earth and the new Jerusalem, which is both a city and a society. God desires his created beings to *prosper* along with his creation, and he will have it so.

Second, what is man in the image of God, and how do human beings show forth the glory of God? We are just as certain of this as we are of the first answer

---

15 See Thomas Sowell, *Intellectuals and Society* (New York: Basic Books, 2009), and Paul Johnson, *Intellectuals* (New York: HarperCollins, 2007).

above. It is that we *mirror* his creative genius and wise rule by taking what he has given us as good stewards of it and *making it more than it was when it was given to us*, just as the Creator took that which was "without form and void" and made what we see and know of the physical universe. People are not made simply to idle away their days in apparent satisfaction with what is, but they are to differentiate and cause to function and "name" for future reference and incorporation into other functional units all those elements around them that have not yet reached their full potential. This is *creativity*, and it is the true nature of the "work" God has given to all human beings, and it is embodied in the best examples of the Bible. By this work mankind's dominion will prosper and come to include all that has ever been contemplated in the mind of God. But no one is *guaranteed* any dominion who does not take *responsibility* for his or her own portion of the garden/city/land.[16]

Third, what is the nature of the stewardship of humans over the creative works of their own hands? To be a steward one must "own" in some sense differentiated from one's fellow humans the works of his or her own hands and mental capacities and have the right to make choices about the disposition of all that proceeds from this work. If a person does not have this right, and his or her fellows do not have the same right over the works of their own hands, there is *no stewardship*. No one is accountable, for no one has ownership before God. This stewardship of the individual before God in all things moral, spiritual, and social is the foundation of biblical truth and order in the creation and society. Ultimately, we learn that the simplest statement of people's moral stewardship (private and public) is the Decalogue, and its embodiment is in Jesus of Nazareth. We will have more to say on stewardship and property rights later in this chapter.

So far so good, but why do we need the Ten Commandments and Jesus of Nazareth? That's the fourth element: The human race has *broken relationship* with the God who holds them individually accountable from the beginning, and all kinds of bloody mischief has followed. There is something dreadfully wrong beneath the surface of mankind's quest for blessing and order and peaceful pursuit of earthly dominion. It is *pervasive sinfulness* at every turn that has become a massive leviathan strangling the life out of the

---

16 The first responsibility of each Israelite tribe, clan, family unit, and so on, was to wrest "possession" of the "land" itself away from idolatrous holders of it and put it to good use in the service of God. Any failure to do this was regarded as disobedience and faithlessness.

Awaiting the City

human race. Fallen human beings cannot rule themselves, but they insist on ruling their fellows through subtle and blatant acts of violence, and by whatever means are available they take what is not theirs (steal), pervert the procreative expression of love (commit adultery), violently assault those who resist (commit murder), defend themselves with calumny against the innocent (bear false witness), all the while plotting how they can get more of what belongs *rightfully* to their neighbor (covet). Human violence has at one time reached such heights that God himself took it in hand to bring universal destructive judgment and institute new rules of governance (Gen. 6–9).

Which leads us to the fifth question: What is the role of government in the process of societal development and control? It is to see that humans do not do violence to one another, in accordance with God's revealed will in the Decalogue and its accompanying casuistic interpretations, while staying out of the place of God. Governments are not sanctioned to replace God as either provider or distributor and are condemned when they become themselves the oppressors through applying violence to ordinary transactions among people, especially by taking from one to give to another or by determining who the winner shall be in any given transaction. In the only state experiment in theocratic rule, the human element was found woefully wanting and was justly warned and judged by the Law of Sinai,[17] but was also given a promise that this way of governance would one day be renewed and transformed for all mankind's blessing and prosperity.[18] Meanwhile, the governance against which God's law had been juxtaposed to serve as guiding light continues without benefit of theocratic leadership. In this state they become and prove themselves to be "beasts." They do this by building empires that ravage other societies and plunder goods produced by hands and minds not their own. They enslave peoples to regimes of ongoing plunder through taxation and outright confiscation and military theft (quintessentially Rome in the reincarnation of Babylon, whom the Lord himself claimed to have thrown down).[19] They take prisoners and force them into labor without compensation and sell them as slaves in public

---

17 The clearest statement of this failure is the charge that rulers reverse the meaning of "good" and "evil" and make judgments on that basis (e.g., Isa. 5:20–23, Mic. 3:1–2; Mal. 2:17).
18 See esp. Ezek. 21:25–26 for the final word on the Davidic earthly king and the echo of Gen. 49:10 with the ultimate fulfillment to come.
19 Jer. 51, esp. v. 11.

Awaiting the City

markets. They terrorize the recalcitrant with torture and public executions and imprisonment and the enforced starvation of millions through disruption of the normal process of food production. They rob them of the right to worship a God who holds even government accountable, placing themselves and their leaders in the place of God. When they establish "peace," (the *Pax Romana*, with its motto "peace and safety"[20] was just one instance) it is upon the ruins they themselves have created and that rides the backs of masses in poverty at the subsistence level. And on and on we could go!

All this leads us to the overwhelming human dilemma, the problem of theodicy—where is the goodness/justice of God? If he is behind all of this from the creation, what is the plan? Where is the promised blessing? If he rules and reigns for his glory and our blessing, what on earth (literally) is going on, and where is justice to be found (Mal. 2:17)? It is to be found in the court of the just God of the Bible, who will not acquit the guilty nor pervert justice nor take a bribe, and who knows the thoughts and plans of every heart and possesses the wisdom that cast the universe into space. The indictment for wrongs committed is *inscripturated* in the Decalogue and is *incarnate* in Jesus of Nazareth. The answer to the theodicy is the *cross*, and the plan is the rule of the Resurrected One. The "government shall be upon his shoulder," and of his kingdom there shall be no end (Isa. 9:6–7) because he "makes all things new," including especially the one(s) intended for rule and prosperity in the first place (2 Cor. 5:17).[21] This is the vision of Daniel fulfilled when "everlasting righteousness" shall prevail (Dan. 9:24).

This leads finally to the urgent question, "When shall these things come to pass, and how shall we now live?"[22] The Bible is unclear, and deliberately so, on the timing of the end and urges readiness expressed in current lifestyle and deci-

---

20 1 Thess. 5:3.

21 This is the culmination of Russell Moore's kingdom theology when he concludes that the substitutionary atonement as God's justice displayed is the source for all hopes of a just world to come. See Russell D. Moore, *The Kingdom of Christ: The New Evangelical Perspective* (Wheaton, IL: Crossway, 2004), 127–28. Also, see N. T. Wright's discussion of what "righteousness" must entail in his "Romans" *The New Interpreter's Bible: Acts–1 Corinthians*, vol. 10 (Nashville: Abingdon, 2002).

22 This well-known latter question from Francis Schaeffer has recently been updated in the work of N. T. Wright to "What time is it?"—one of his worldview-orienting questions in his works on the New Testament, esp. throughout his Christian Origins and the Question of God series (see bibliography).

Awaiting the City

sion making. That lifestyle is clearly expressed in *dependency* on the God of the Bible through faith in his Son, Jesus Christ, and in following him with readiness to *renounce* all at a moment's notice to do his bidding. No other life is worthy of his life or his blessing. We steward what he has given and is giving by obeying his revealed will in the Bible and daily doing whatever we find to do with all our strength as an offering to him who saves us. With the largesse he provides from our daily efforts we are expected to *provide for our own needs* and those of the ones dependent on us, and we can expect to have leftovers for *giving and investment* in the future of coming generations and assistance especially for those of our own households in the generation that came before us.

Furthermore, as the opportunities present themselves to us, we are to *help* those whose state in life has been truncated by circumstances beyond their control—the widowed, the orphaned, the disabled, the stranger to our culture. We are especially to support the work of preaching and teaching the gospel to the world (thus passing along the lifestyle that we seek to practice) and to welcome into our homes those called into this service vocationally,[23] for they are truly the brethren of Christ himself. And we ourselves are to seek out opportunities to teach, witness, and minister the full liberating gospel of God's way to salvation and blessing through obedience to Christ's commands—understood as consistent with everything commanded in the Scriptures (Matt. 28:19–20) for life and well-being and summed up in the commands to love God supremely and love our neighbors as ourselves, including our *enemies. Anybody getting tired yet?* Come, Holy Spirit! Increase our faith!

If this is indeed the Christian mission and lifestyle, how should we pray for government and all those in authority (according to Jer. 29:7, so that the nation/city of our sojourning will have "*shalom*" that will also be "*shalom*" to us)? How should we work toward establishing or influencing societal patterns and norms that will aid us, or at least leave us alone to follow the Master as we see fit? What kind of legal and political framework and economic structure is most conducive to this mission? Paul put it like this: pray "for kings and all who are in high positions, that we may lead a peaceful and quiet life, godly and dignified in every way. This is good, and it is pleasing in the sight of God our Savior, who desires

---

23 Though this is to be done with discernment (2 John 11–12).

Awaiting the City

all people to be saved and to come to the knowledge of the truth" (1 Tim. 2:2–4 ESV). Pray that our lives will be left alone enough to be "peaceful... quiet... godly... dignified" and bent on seeing that "all people" will be "saved" and enhanced by "knowledge of the truth." There is no dependency on government for our sustenance or our mission. It is a vision of freedom to operate in a kingdom way. To fulfill the creation command and our redemptive mandate, the Great Commission, by following the advice of Qoheleth (Eccl. 9:10) and Paul (Col. 3:22–24) to work mightily as those who see this basic activity as God-pleasing. Both of the above are placed in the context of an imperfect world: Qoheleth is contemplating the shortness and vapory nature of life itself with death as the outcome. Paul is advising slaves how to work for their "masters" in the ancient Roman world. Paul will counsel his addressees to "imitate me," as we have noted previously, in this hard-working day and night lifestyle (1 Cor. 10:31–11:1; 2 Thess. 3:6–15; also see discussion in chap. 8).

Therefore, we want government that lets us profit from the physical and mental labor we expend and does not tax away our surpluses for *dubious projects* of egalitarian social tinkering (for not even the world to come will be egalitarian in its rewards)[24] or military adventures that *oppress* others. We want freedom to worship and speak and move about as God may lead us. We want a police power that enforces the law and protects our property and that of others so we can make godly decisions about its use. We do not want a government that encourages laziness, vice, idleness, envy, covetousness, resentment, or outright theft of goods of any kind. We want a court system that treats every person the same before the law, with no favoritism for any class of claimants, and a legislature that is open to moral persuasion, not bribery. We want a process that depends upon *moral suasion* and not coercion in areas that involve personal and private *virtues*. We want it to punish the guilty and exonerate the innocent. And we want to be able to *participate* in its processes as participants in the deliberative and governing activities, if that is God's will for our lives.

Likewise, we want an *economic* situation that *coincides* with this governmental situation. We want to be able to work with our hands and our minds in as creative

---

24 See our previous discussion in part 1 concerning both Jesus' and Paul's teaching as well as the clear results in the tribes of Israel who failed to "possess their possessions."

Awaiting the City

a way as pleases the Lord and have the fruit of that labor and mental exercise available to us before it is for anyone else. Paul, in counseling the slaves, would say to get free, if it is offered, and stay free once you are (1 Cor. 7:20–24). We want the opportunity to work as long and as hard and as smart as we can to produce whatever wealth God sees fit to bless us with, as we praise him for whatever abilities we might have received from him. We want the right to advance in education, excel in accomplishment at whatever endeavor, grow in development of native talent and ability, lift of our economic and social position, ascend to whatever level of governance or military position is fitting, or to do anything else that is in the will of God for our lives, without having that opportunity closed off by prior constraints of society or law.[25] We want the right to give away or reinvest or save or spend what is ours as God's stewards, not the slaves of other men or of government, knowing that we shall give account to him as the righteous judge. What we want for *ourselves*, we want as well for *others*, so they may prosper in the way God intended for them. We do not wish to see them enslaved in dependency and held for political ransom or traded about as *constituencies* in societal class struggles.

These are the basic biblical mandates as we see them. But there is more.

HISTORICAL THEOLOGY AND THE RISE OF FASCISM

Our survey of historical theology as it has engaged the culture and politics of the West shows us that it is *these truths* (above) that have led to the prosperity of Western civilization as we know it today. The Reformation, Puritan, and Free Church emphases on individual justification before God personally (individual accountability), vocational calling beyond clerical exclusivity (the priesthood of all believers), the mandate to work as unto the Lord, and the separation of institutional church from state, among other factors, led inexorably to the civilization whose bounty we enjoy.[26] Strangely, also, it was the independence fostered by such thinking and its fundamental change of worl-

---

25 In effect, we do not want a society or economic situation that is "stratified," meaning solidified into classes and social groupings that cannot be penetrated by hard work and achievement.
26 As our earlier historical survey shows, we recognize that the Reformation, Puritan, and Free Church traditions understood separation of institutional church from state in differing ways. But there is continuity between them on the other issues we list.

Awaiting the City

dview that led persecuted thousands to cast off fear and timidity and head to a place where they might try out their new convictions. Further, it is the increasing application of these principles that is leading to the elimination of poverty and its attendant woes all around the world, even when societies that benefit do not share our cultural or religious values as such.

The tragedy (to use Olasky's word) is that what was once a matter of theological conviction and ecclesiological practice, born out of a vision of a city on a hill, has become more the sphere of secular political activism than of the practice of loving concern for the neighbor in need. As charitable giving and acting (i.e., acts of loving concern) have been crowded out by governmental mandates and political organizing into rival constituencies, the *administrative state* has become the source and end for the supposed redress of "rights." What was once a subject of theological reflection and an object of societal "revival" and *spiritual renewal* has now become the justification for all kinds of societal restructuring through the coercive power of completely secularized governmental mandate, exercised through taxing and regulating and distributing goods taken from one group and given to another group organized for the specific purpose of guaranteeing itself a proper (in its own eyes) piece of the pie. All of this has been done with an increasing transfer of power to the state and without ever actually alleviating the alleged wrongs of the capitalist market system, while fostering other even more detrimental consequences and behaviors.

Most distressing to us is the rise, in the evangelical community, of what we can only decry as misapplied biblical understanding and faulty theologizing in the service of wildly skewed econometric data and environmental "science," now under the heavy influence of governmental funding and mandates. The purveyors of this new cover for the political power to invade the lives and ministries of others are not only unafraid to call secular political budgets "moral" or "immoral," but also to call into question the eternal destiny and Christian character of those who oppose them. Couple this with the postmodern loss of confidence in objective truth claims and the widespread rise of therapeutic models (in evangelical theology and ecclesiology) for the amelioration of the human condition as a fallen race of sinful creatures. In the end you have a prescription for increasing *loss of freedom* and the rise of yet unimagined tyrannies, not to mention the loss of everlasting souls without salvation—namely, those who have been told (falsely) that their economic and social ills are the fault of other sinful creatures, not they themselves. It is naïve in the extreme to believe that this road can lead anywhere but to Hayek's "serfdom."

Fortunately there remains a residue of concern and *rational compassion* among all kinds and denominations of Christians that are aware of these issues. They continue to seek out ways to practice their compassion that do not yield the negative results or dispositions in the body politic that we have explored throughout our study. Nevertheless, the unrelenting challenge from the stance of those considering their politics to be morally superior to those engaged in personal works of mercy and love is disconcerting. It is surely a blunder for any Christian to stake out political positions that entail *faulty moralizing* supported by *irrational* assessments of economics and politics. It is worse still to actively denigrate and propagandize those who disagree with such assessments and to use dubious biblical and theological musings to lend weight to the politics of the hour. In the hope of balancing the scale in the ongoing in-house debates among those of us who hope for a biblical and theological take on political economy, we offer what follows.

POLITICAL ECONOMY AND THE AMERICAN DREAM

The purpose of the historical survey and discussion of (especially) the American political economy has been to show that there has actually never been before in the long history of human beings on this earth such a period as the last three hundred or so years of prosperity, upward mobility for large general populations, economic justice, concern for the poor and helpless, and opportunity for fulfilling the biblical mandates. It is fundamentally *untrue* to urge upon Christians, from whom money and commitment is expected, that poverty (of the kind envisioned in the Bible) and its attendant miseries is increasing, either domestically or globally. The three-hundred-year miracle of the West and now the rest of the world is the perspective that should guide our moral worldview in the face of millennia of poverty and oppression. What was once known as the "bottom billion" has now become the bottom 350 million over the last forty years, and this has primarily been the result of the adoption of capitalistic market economics, especially in places like India and China. Further, this has happened despite the fact that world population grew by 3 billion in the same time period.[27] This is, of course, against the overall backdrop of increase in population from 750 million to 6.5 billion since about 1750.

Our proposal has been juxtaposed against the ongoing criticisms of the market economies of the West and the increasing globalization of this economic process. It is a *commonplace* in political and philosophical discussions like this that presuppositions tend to remain and carry the day among those engaged in the debates. We are under no illusions in this matter. However, the only rational way to proceed is to ask and answer the two-headed question: Are the assertions we make about the success of market economics *valid*, and is widespread *justice* being done and increasing globally? Secondarily, if justice is *not being done, who or what is at fault*, and what should be done about it? Those unconvinced by our argumentation up to this point will answer an emphatic "no" to the first question(s). Consequently the diagnosis of "what is wrong," one of N. T. Wright's worldview questions, will lead to decidedly different remedies. Nevertheless we proceed with some concluding propositions.

THE ALMOST TRAGIC VISION[28]

Foremost of these propositions is that in a sinful world, the market system is the best attainable this side of the new heavens and new earth. As Michael Novak puts it,

> Democratic capitalism has as its ideal the upward push of the poor, the bright, the talented. It keeps alive the knowledge that, with skill or luck (or both), one may yet have a future different from one's

---

27 Maxim Pinkovsky and Xavier Sala-i-Martin, "Parametric Estimations of the World Distribution of Income" (NBER Working Paper, no. 15433, National Bureau of Economic Research, Cambridge, Massachusetts, issued October 2009), http://www.nber.org/papers/w15433. See also Indur M. Goklany, *Improving State of the World* (Washington, DC: Cato Institute, 2007); and Julian L. Simon, ed., *The State of Humanity* (1995; repr., Oxford: Blackwell, 1998), for full documentation of the progress of the past 250 years. Further, notice Richard Stearns, *Hole in Our Gospel* (Nashville: Thomas Nelson, 2009), 163, listing numerous measures of progress around the world. Somehow, however, he needs to say "the hole" is "getting bigger," 105. It can't be both ways.
28 The "tragic vision" is the terminology Sowell juxtaposes with the "unlimited vision" ("unconstrained vision") or the "vision of the anointed" in his many works.

Awaiting the City

present. In most societies, especially in administrative societies,[29] and in societies bearing the name socialism, one knows from the start just how high one can go. The only path upward is political favor. Democratic capitalism has its faults. The alternatives are worse.[30]

We further maintain that the flaws of democratic capitalism are attributable to human nature and governmental interference and not to some endemic evil in the "system." This is primarily because, as we have sought to show, it is interference by fallen creatures through governmental fiat that distorts outcomes the most and causes systemic displacements that might otherwise correct themselves or be punished as actual fraud and theft or environmental crimes in the marketplace. Since this is the case, we argue that many Christian critiques of "capitalism," wealth accumulation, free movement and establishment of businesses by ownership with a view to being maximally profitable and providing the best value economically to their customers (their partners in transactions), disparities between the most wealthy and the most poor, and a number of other criticisms do not pass the test of *rational thought* or moral claims to *ultimate truth*. More to the point, it is not possible to make a moral claim on anyone until rational thought has established *actual* guilt or innocence.[31]

As an example, we have cited above (see n. 27), Stearns, in his apparent ambivalence on whether things are getting better or worse in the fight against global poverty. It is, therefore, particularly egregious for him to juxtapose a quotation from John Berger next to Scripture, first saying, "The poverty of this century is unlike that of any other," because it "comes from a set of priorities imposed upon the rest of the world by the rich." Berger further notes that, "The twentieth-century economy has produced the first culture for which a beggar is a reminder of nothing," where the poor can be "written off as trash." This quotation is followed by Romans 8:22, which we presume is to be taken as interpretive of the Berger opinion, and offering a supposed biblical condemnation.[32] If, in fact,

---

29 We have elsewhere discussed the rise of such governing and its attendant evils.
30 Novak, *Spirit*, 214.
31 Jim Wallis wants to indict "the invisible hand" and "the market" with "sin" in his latest release, *Rediscovering Values* (New York: Simon & Schuster, 2010), Kindle loc. 2525–600. This is undoubtedly the strangest use of moral language we have seen or heard.
32 Quoted in Stearns, *Hole in Our Gospel*, 95.

Awaiting the City

the situation is getting better all the time around the world, how is it possible to sustain such a charge as that given by Berger biblically? Stearns engages in hyperbole all through his book for the purpose of challenging American churchgoers to give to poverty relief, perhaps especially to AIDS treatment and orphan relief. Such exaggeration for effect is common in the literature and polemical speech of advocacy and activism, which we have copiously cited as we have gone along. Such rhetoric does not make its position or approach to relief efforts ethically and morally acceptable, despite its claim to help the poor.

It follows from this that to charge moral evil to anyone unjustly (for that is what this kind of moralizing does) and propose the remedy of *confiscation* through the law is *also* unjust and immoral.[33] We will now proceed with the kinds of cases we have been discussing in the body of this third section of the book, without in any way pretending that we can here exhaust the subject. Hopefully we will give guidance that will be applicable to many other situations.

WORK AND CAPITAL FORMATION

Beginning literally at the beginning, it is clear that the natural state of mankind since the garden episode is poverty. It is not wealth. The "nakedness" that was originally one without "shame" became a "nakedness" of judgment that must be ameliorated with "toil… by the sweat of the brow."[34] It was and is the will of God that individuals and compatible groups and eventually nations begin at ground level and work up.[35] No understanding of wealth can be rational that does not begin with production and understand what it is. Production is the application of mind and effort to raw materials to make something arise out of something as yet formless. This is exactly what God himself has done in creation, except that he made the raw materials also. Accumulating wealth by nonviolent means and voluntary exchange cannot be immoral, no matter how profitable it becomes, otherwise he who made it all is himself immoral,

---

33 See calling "good evil and evil good" in note 17 above.
34 See our exposition of Gen. 2:25; 3:7; and Deut. 28:48 in chap. 2, which indicate that the latter "nakedness" is a judgment of God first on the original couple and then the nation of Israel.
35 Note that the last sad verse of Gen. 3 states plainly that God "drove" Adam and Eve out of the wealth of the garden into the poverty of the world of sin.

since he is by definition the owner of it all. God looks on the poverty that was once universal (and which he decreed by banishing Adam and Eve from the garden with just skins on their backs) and is now fading from the earth, and he has waited millennia for mankind to work out of it. What he condemned and destroyed in the flood was a world turned to unlimited violence as a way to achieve the creation mandate with its blessing. With the receding of the floodwaters he renewed the work mandate and removed the "curse" from the ground, in some measure, assuring that the blessing can be experienced through *hard work* without resort to violence.

In the light of this narrative God's remedy for poverty is work, seen as both an intellectual and physical pursuit, not merely the application of physical toil to material substances willy-nilly. It is presumed that this labor will be connected to profitable enterprises and will be rewarded with varying degrees of gain, that is, *wealth creation*.[36] Therefore, we conclude that *no job*, no matter how menial, is a *dead-end job*; it is a *front-end job*, for some, where one learns basic skills and establishes work habits and makes connections that will lead to further training/ education and a movement up the ladder of achievement. Or, it may be a job taken because it is simply what is *available* at the time. God himself blesses these efforts by providing a *stable environment*, which is what government either abets or deters, and the steady passage of "seasons," understood not just in the agrarian sense, so we may plan and reap "harvests" (once again not just agrarian). Jesus made this universal when he said that the Father makes his rain fall "on the just and the unjust." In this way the creation mandate and promise of blessing that mankind might fill and subdue the creation is to be fulfilled. Expecting everyone to begin somewhere is not unjust or immoral.

On the other hand, since the Decalogue anticipates familial and national ac- cumulations of moral and social capital through obedience to God, it is not im- moral or unjust that those who have such a "leg up" are not starting at the same point as others who have not had such an advantage. One person's productivity does make another person poor in an environment where governments do not interfere and where *biblical justice* is in place. To think otherwise is a false and

---

36 It is never assumed in Scripture that mankind's labors will be altruistic or unconnected to some degree of "profit" (seen as personal benefits related to the things one values most at the time).

Awaiting the City

envious view of the world and life.[37] Further, any accumulated capital beyond the moral and cultural is never condemned and is seen as a blessing for those who can pass it on to their children with godly character and a hope that they will be wise in its use, knowing they are accountable to God. It is not immoral to be the recipient of a father's wise use of his time and effort and skills. Nor is it immoral to receive additional compensation from the exercise of mental and physical inventiveness that makes the work of others more productive and less toilsome.

The fact that persons so engaged in the production and accumulation of goods have a right to those goods vis-à-vis their neighbors is embedded in the Decalogue with the words, "Thou shalt not steal." It would be irrational to think otherwise. A person with no clear right to his or her own production is *by definition* a slave. God did not create man in his image to be a slave. The fact that human beings have enslaved one another irrationally and violently for millennia without moral qualms is indisputable. It took till the time of Wilberforce in the West and abolitionism and civil war in the United States for mankind to begin to grasp the sheer *iniquitous perversity* of slavery.[38] In our day the extreme poverty that remains in the world is largely the result of *societal breakdowns* that disconnect work from *profit* and lead to the *same despair* that outright slavery induced in the past. This may be caused by ubiquitous corruption in ruling structures, lawlessness as a cultural pattern, cultural norms that deny opportunity because of race or religion or other factors not related to commercial activity, cultural/religious taboos, or the absence of any structural process that might be denominated a *business climate*.

What seems so hard to grasp for many still is that it is not rational to believe that people will work as hard or as efficiently when their labor and mental capacities are being stolen or diverted as they will when they partake of their own production for the free exercise of the rights of *property*, conceived as

---

37 The Old Testament Sabbath and charity mandates for the poor do not propose that the poor were made so by oppression of those required to forgive debts and return land in the Jubilee. This is considered a merciful thing, not a matter of "justice."

38 For the discussion of the phenomenon of slavery around the world and the legacy of the West, which bequeaths freedom from it and abhorrence to it, see Thomas Sowell, *Race and Culture: A World View* (New York: Basic Books, 1994), and Dinesh D'Souza, *The End of Racism* (New York: Free Press, 1995), cited in our notes in chap. 24. It is a libelous canard to charge the West and esp. the United States with some singular benefit achieved by a unique usage of slavery.

Awaiting the City

anything that makes physical existence possible. Slavery is *irrational* as well as immoral. Consequently, to charge with immorality or more commonly *greed or covetousness*, someone who wishes to keep and distribute what he or she has earned on his or her own or received as a legacy from obedient and industrious parentage is a gross distortion of moral terminology.

The Immorality of Redistribution

It follows from these propositions that "redistributive" schemes to *acquire* wealth among people (notice the word here is *acquire* not produce) are immoral. The earliest forms of this process were personal theft and dishonest business dealings for bartered goods. On a macroscale it involved groups getting together to raid and pillage. When coinage came to be a form of universal exchange, carving and chipping at the precious metals served the same purpose,[39] just as counterfeiting of coins and paper money did and do. The Bible condemns the dishonest scale or measure and other forms of marketplace deception. All kinds of cheating in the economic realm have been the common lot of mankind from time immemorial. The worst schemes, however, proceed under the guise of *legalized theft*. This was the sin of the kings of Israel and Judah who transgressed God's commands to benefit their "servants," so tellingly denounced by the prophets and punished in the exile. It is not the "beastly" theft of empire, but such thievish sin is condemned in the sight of God, though it be done by supposedly theocratic kings.[40] This is now the common practice of modern governments who, if democratic, organize constituencies to confiscate the wealth of other constituencies by *law*,[41] until those (and other) constituencies can seize

---

39 Hence the term "chiseler" to denote someone working around the edges of honesty to gain advantage. The Roman government was notorious for devaluing its money by reducing the content of precious metals in coinage.

40 See our exposition on the prophets in Jerusalem and the summary in Zeph. 3:1–5 in chap. 5.

41 If it is thought that the word "confiscate" is too pejorative, consider that almost fifty percent of all Americans now pay no income tax, and the top ten percent of all earners pay nearly seventy-one percent of all income taxes, and the top twenty-five percent of all pay more than eighty-six percent of all income taxes. Figures available as of 2007 with the IRS, quoted in Tommy Newberry, *The War on Success: How the Obama Agenda Is Shattering the American Dream* (Washington, DC: Regnery, 2010), 59. See also William Voegeli, *Never Enough: America's Limitless Welfare State* (New York: Encounter Books, 2010), for extensive

Awaiting the City

the power to do the same to others, and "redistribute" to chosen receivers, while taking some off the top for themselves (à la Judas and the bag).[42] It matters not whether the constituencies are denominated "rich" or "poor" or "corporate" or "private" or "Democrat" or "Republican."[43] Some might label it "gangster capitalism." No *rational* consideration of what is actually going on here can be called *moral*. This is immoral *by definition*, and to call it otherwise (often by degrading the language to obfuscate what is called in the jargon of the Left "unearned income")[44] and denounce from a Christian standpoint those who oppose it (as greedy or covetous or hateful or even "fascist") is a distortion of moral categories that leads to the unwinding of foundational concepts of human rights and ethical standards. This is precisely the kind of degradation of the language used by fascists to confuse the public and manipulate politics.

When such language claims to be "prophecy," sometimes called "speaking truth to power," and deliberately sets aside a transcendent definition of justice for a sentimental and cultural mythology of egalitarian "fairness," it has joined the ranks of the enemies of justice. The ethos involved is more a pre-Sinaitic Mesopotamian concept than it is Judeo-Christian, and is (even more frighteningly) associated with fascist philosophy and theology of the last century, now on the ascendancy

---

documentation and charts on this subject. This is widely disseminated information that is almost never brought into the discussion of "tax breaks for the rich."

42 Jouvenel noted long ago that the real redistribution here is not actually of money from the rich to the poor but "of power from the individual to the state." See Bertrand de Jouvenel, *The Ethics of Redistribution* (1951; repr., Indianapolis: Liberty Fund, 1990), 72.

43 For a concise study of the development of this process in American politics, see Terry L. Anderson and Peter J. Hill, *The Birth of a Transfer Society* (1979; repr., Lanham, MD: University Press of America, 1989). This kind of redistribution of wealth (aka legalized theft) began in the Jacksonian era (early to mid-1800s), long before the so-called robber barons became the excuse. Ibid., 53.

44 The latest to do this is the Obama administration calling for a high tax on "unearned income" to pay for "health-care reform." See "Mr. Obama's Plan," *Washington Post*, February 23, 2010, http://articles.washingtonpost.com/2010-02-23/business/36817164_1, and Alec MacGillis and Amy Goldstein, "Obama Offers a New Proposal on Health Care," *Washington Post*, February 23, 2010, http://articles.washingtonpost.com/2010-02-23/politics/36794799_1 (and others across the country), who carried the story of his "compromise" plan. This is money that has been previously "earned" by legitimate labor and intellectual enterprise and has been taxed accordingly and is now in various savings and investment vehicles for future use. It is in no sense moral to call earnings from this activity "unearned" as if it were illegitimately possessed.

Awaiting the City

again.[45] As Ezekiel said long ago, "[Y]ou have disheartened the righteous falsely, although I have not grieved him, and you have encouraged the wicked, that he should not turn from his evil way to save his life" (Ezek. 13:22 ESV).

Why does the conception persist among some Christians that it is somehow right for government to act as agent for confiscation and redistribution without reference to individual and corporate guilt or innocence? Nowhere in the long discourse on the separation of the sheep and the goats in Matthew 25 does Jesus condone *taking other people's money* to feed "the least of these my brethren." We know why the political establishment and governmental bureaucracies do it—they get their cut from the "bag," like Judas, no matter who is or is not helped. We know some Christian leaders and organizations will take salaries putting themselves in the top five percent (or higher) of wage earners and pile up wasteful administrative costs using money given to alleviate pain and suffering. That is also wrong.

But we know of no Christian who would learn of the need of a friend for transportation, who would then *steal* his neighbor's vehicle to give to the friend in the name of compassion or justice or "fairness." It appears that some, however, would agree to the idea that the person knowing of the need could petition government to allow him to take his neighbor's vehicle, since the neighbor has three vehicles and the friend has no vehicle. Thus, it is legal and not *technically* theft. After all, the friend in need is a widow, an orphan, an alien, a person with disability of some kind, or just out of work for the time being.[46] Of course, we don't do that, we just vote to have someone else do it for us, if we happen to be of this moral and political persuasion. Worse still, this same group that supports such redistribution will condemn in terms of moral indignation and supposed biblical authority those who oppose such political chicanery.[47]

---

45 See John H. Walton, *Ancient Near Eastern Thought* (Grand Rapids, MI: Baker, 2006), Kindle loc. 3192–402, for discussion of the Mesopotamian conceptions versus the Sinaitic revelation. See Gene Edward Veith Jr., *Modern Fascism: The Threat to the Judeo-Christian Worldview*, Concordia Scholarship Today (St. Louis: Concordia, 1993), for a thorough treatment of how moral categories are discarded and/or redefined in popular usage to make way for the brave new world of government-as-god. For a dystopian work of fiction that takes up similar notions with both natural and supernatural elements in play, see C. S. Lewis, *That Hideous Strength: A Modern Fairy-Tale for Grown-Ups* (London: Bodley Head, 1945).

46 If only these were the only recipients normally considered eligible for "relief" in our modern world!

47 Jason DeParle, *American Dream* (New York: Viking, 2004), 144, notes this phenomenon esp. during the fight over "welfare reform" during the Clinton presidency, when "Bishops

Awaiting the City

The tragedy is that not only has violence been done in the name of charity and fairness and goodwill, but the relief effort has the side effect of confirming in other constituencies a state of mind of envy and covetousness—if we will just organize, we can get some stuff for ourselves (Isa. 26:10). To obscure redistributive schemes with words like "compassion" or "fairness" does not make them pass muster as "just." It simply adds an emotional layer to otherwise rational discourse and moral thinking.[48] But the biblical Christian knows with Isaiah that when *God's kind of justice* is done, "the people of the world learn righteousness" (Isa. 26:9). Humans speak of "fairness" when they do not wish to engage in moral exactitude—in other words, when they wish to proceed with what seems right in their own eyes, rather than in God's eyes as he has revealed clearly in Scripture. Such fairness is what Veith has called a "vague ethical idealism" whose real and only purpose is "to serve the state by encouraging self-sacrifice and social solidarity."[49] Its actual effect is to turn the picture of hands holding hands in communal solidarity into a picture of the same people standing side by side, each with his hand in the other's hip pocket.

The same order of *emotional argumentation* (Sowell's verbal virtuosity) pits something called "human rights" against *property*[50] *rights.* It says something like this: but don't we have to value the human being above property when it comes to protecting rights? The answer depends upon what the understanding of property is. The term "property" has no meaning apart from its human context. Property is that which *allows* the human to exist in a *material world*. Without it the human person dies; he or she goes out of existence. *Property rights* are in fact *human rights*. It is a circular and fallacious *sophism* to form an argument contrasting the two "rights." To exist as human one *must* use property. If one does not have a claim on property, one has no claim on existence. For anyone to assert that this or that person has human rights that transcend the property rights of

---

wrote letters. Academics signed petitions. Marian Wright Edelman of the Children's Defense Fund published an 'open letter,' asking Clinton, 'Do you think the Old Testament prophets…or Jesus Christ would support such policies?'"

48 For a concise essay on this entire subject, see Jouvenel, *Ethics of Redistribution.*
49 Veith, *Modern Fascism*, Kindle loc. 926–31.
50 "Property" here means all that of a material or intellectual nature, which a human being may rightly call his or her own, by reason of one's own productivity or rightful possession, in distinction from that of another human being.

Awaiting the City

another is to assert that *one person* has the right to existence at the *expense* of another. This is not a biblical principle by any stretch of imagination. It is pure Marxist intellectual *sophistry*. It is like the theory of labor as value that would put the same value on digging a hole in the backyard and then filling it up as many in their "logic" would put on digging the Panama Canal.[51]

We could continue this discussion with the misappropriation of words like *greed* (seen as wanting to keep what one has earned rather than have it taxed away), *acquisitiveness* (as if to "acquire" something were evil, rather than the means or use or abuse of what is gained), *consume* (as in "consumerism," seen as immoral, when the fact is that our bodies and lives depend on consuming), *environmental degradation* (when mining, damming, developing, eating meat, using incandescent light bulbs, setting a thermostat at a personally comfortable level, or even expelling carbon dioxide from one's own lungs are seen as sin against the creation and Creator), and oh so many other pejoratives. Moralizing of this kind serves no rational or ethical purpose because the *categories* of discourse have been *confused*. But this is not the only place Christian discourse has been abused.

THE CHRISTIAN DUTY TO GIVE

The alternative to coercive redistribution is giving what is rightfully mine to another, whether motivated by philosophical philanthropism or biblical mandate. We have repeatedly honored this biblical principle. However, the undeniable truth is that no matter whether the largesse bestowed comes from taxation and confiscation or charitable giving, poverty cannot be permanently alleviated in this manner; it can only be temporarily relieved. The literature we cite throughout our study overwhelmingly proves that only work and productivity will alleviate poverty and produce the prosperity needed for all to enjoy the blessing provided by God in the creation. Some Christians persist in declaring otherwise, as it is widely thought and taught that "the amounts of money theoretically needed to *eradicate* world poverty could be amassed simply if all American Christians would tithe," a claim

---

51 This very activity was tried during the French Revolution as a way to make work for the unemployed and is what Roosevelt meant in the chapter-opening epigraph referring to putting people to work.

Awaiting the City

that is patently absurd on the surface of it and which cannot stand the light of actual economic and financial analysis.[52]

To the best of our knowledge the origin of this myth are John and Sylvia Ronsvalle whose book published in 1992 claims that raising $30 to $50 billion a year (an amount equivalent to the total estimated annual tithe of American Christians then) would be enough to eliminate poverty at home and abroad, and keep doing what churches are already doing locally and internationally in other ministries, and American Christians could do this if all of us would just tithe.[53] Anyone who has spent any time at all researching what is actually being done governmentally and philanthropically in our world to alleviate (eradicate?) poverty worldwide and at home knows that this figure was *meaningless* twenty years ago (as are Stearns' latest numbers) and is a teacup of water in an ocean of money that has flowed to the undeveloped world without coming close to eliminating poverty.[54] The latest iteration of

---

52 Craig L. Blomberg, *Neither Poverty nor Riches*, 252 (emphasis added). Blomberg, however, is not alone, and we have used italics to emphasize the broad statement that appears in many forms, literary and vocal. "Eradicate" is Blomberg's (and others') terminology. "Overcome/overcoming" is the latest code word for Ron Sider (note subtitle as well) in *Just Generosity: A New Vision for Overcoming Poverty in America.*

53 John Ronsvalle and Sylvia Ronsvalle, *The Poor Have Faces: Loving Your Neighbor in the 21st Century* (Grand Rapids, MI: Baker, 1992), 45, 80. Their claim is that $30 to $50 billion a year is what was needed then to eliminate poverty—it is "preventable" according to the back cover of the book. Stearns, *Hole in Our Gospel*, has revived this concept and raised the ante to $168 billion in tithes (if every church attender in America did so). He quotes Jeffrey D. Sachs, *The End of Poverty* (New York: Penguin, 2005), on the possibility of actually eliminating poverty with this money. We have previously dealt with the dubious nature of this claim. Sachs has refused interview requests with *World Magazine* (after having agreed to answer questions) and has answered the critique of William Easterly, "A Modest Proposal," review of *The End of Poverty: Economic Possibilities for Our Time* by Jeffrey D. Sachs, *Washington Post*, March 13, 2005, Economics, BW03, http://www.washington-post.com/wp-dyn/articles/A25562-2005Mar10.html, with an "ad hominem attack on his [Sachs'] 'crude... simplistic... vacuous... tendentious' critic." Jeffrey D. Sachs, "Up from Poverty," letter, *Washington Post*, March 27, 2005, Letters, BW12, http://www.washington-post.com/wp-dyn/articles/A64541-2005Mar24.html, quoted in Marvin Olasky, "Giving Wisely," *World Magazine*, September 1, 2007, 76, http://www.worldmag.com/2007/09/giving_wisely. Also see Easterly's response included after Sachs' above-cited letter. See also William Easterly, *The Elusive Quest for Growth* (Cambridge, MA: MIT Press, 2002), cited previously in chap. 27, note 45.

54 The amount is many trillions of dollars over the past forty to fifty years, and we have previously cited that private charity now amounts to approximately $500 billion per year for social services in the United States and beyond. See the body of literature we have cited in this book. The calls for forgiving debt in the undeveloped world are of the same nature

Awaiting the City

this argument is from Stearns, who compares what Americans spend on a lot of trivial things compared to a tithe of $168 billion from all American churchgoers. His number for comparison with the previous need ($30 to $50 billion) is $65 billion and just as unrealistic.

It is not giving away money and resources that produces wealth and alleviates poverty. It is *work* and *training/education* and *business acumen* and *risk-taking* and *entrepreneurship* and a host of other human character traits employed in the presence of *property rights protections*, the *rule of law*, and most of all, the *elimination of corruption* from the governments who rule where poverty exists. To load American Christians with guilt about the death of millions of children in the underdeveloped world[55] because of what they are not doing about tithing is *gross misuse* of supposed moral authority. We know of no pastor or Christian leader who would not urge Christians in America to be more faithful in giving. But it is time to question, in light of what we have cited of American generosity and the level of taxation for wealth transfers to the needy at home and around the world, whether "poverty-fighting" of the kind being practiced now is the best place to put more tithe dollars.[56] This is another case in our opinion of *irrational moralizing* of the worst sort.

Furthermore, it is debatable at the very least whether it is wise for American missionary strategy to pursue missions in the manner it has for so long—transferring Western methodologies and structures that require Western-style financing and maintenance—because of the dependencies they cause.[57] Would that American

---

as the claims here cited on tithing. No amount of debt forgiveness (which has been tried over and over again) will reach the actual victims suffering the conditions of poverty in the undeveloped world.

55 Ronsvalle and Ronsvalle used the figure thirty-eight thousand children dying per day on the back cover of their book at the time of their writing. Stearns, *Hole in Our Gospel*, puts it at twenty-six thousand children dying per day now.

56 By way of contrast, Southern Baptists in 2008 fell almost $30 million short of giving for their International Mission Board, an amount that, spread among the average eight million attenders at weekly services, amounts to less than $4 per person. The consequent contraction of missions efforts and sacrifices being made by those already on the field is tragic and unconscionable.

57 See Glenn J. Schwartz, *When Charity Destroys Dignity: Overcoming Unhealthy Dependency in the Christian Movement* (Bloomington, IN: AuthorHouse, 2007), for a full analysis of this issue. See esp. Schwartz's citation of David Barrett and others that giving on the order of two percent of incomes in the African church would fund all their ministries, training, pastoral support, facilities, and *development projects*. Ibid., 161.

Awaiting the City

Christians would give more generously, but good stewardship demands that we put that generosity to work where it actually does good and does not end up in Judas' pocket or create unhealthy dependencies. This is the lesson Paul teaches us in the administrative precautions he took with the Jerusalem offering(s) and his personal lifestyle and exhortations to work even by slaves for their masters in an unjust situation by our standards. Famed missiologist and professor Ralph Winter was not the first or last to note the following observation: "If all the world's wealth were redistributed there would still be two kinds of people: those who would use it and replace it because they could earn the replacement, and those who would use it and then be just as poor as ever."[58] We concur. The problem is deeper than many analysts, including evangelicals, want to make it out to be.

Fickle[59] Prophets of Doom and Gloom

The latest fad among many Christians is to baptize global warming hysteria into some form of argument for stewardship of the planet in support of massive statist economic and political schemes. These "solutions" would curtail development of the remaining poverty-stricken areas of the planet and charge the West (especially the United States) with the bill, no matter what the truth of the supposed "science" or the consequences for the poorest people on earth.[60] This is in line with previous alarmism about other aspects of environmental concern, including population control, which was a big concern before global cooling and now warming, and fears about the looming shortages first of coal and then natural gas and then petroleum and the general destruction of the planetary environment. Ron Sider opined years ago, in decrying the attempts of human beings to maintain and expand the mandate to subdue and have dominion on the planet (i.e., "material abundance"):

---

58 Quoted in Olasky, "Giving Wisely."
59 "Fickle" here is being used as in Zeph. 3:4 (ESV), meaning reckless and unreliable, unlike Yahweh who is as reliable as the rising and setting of the sun.
60 For a thorough debunking of this position from a Christian perspective, see G. Cornelis van Kooten, E. Calvin Beisner, and Pete Geddes, "A Renewed Call to Truth, Prudence, and Protection of the Poor: An Evangelical Examination of the Theology, Science, and Economics of Global Warming," Cornwall Alliance for the Stewardship of Creation, 2007, http://www.cornwallalliance.org/docs/a-renewed-call-to-truth-prudence-and-protection-of-the-poor.pdf. First published in 2000 and revised and updated in 2005 and 2007.

Economic life today, especially in industrialized societies, is producing such severe environmental pollution and degradation that
the future for everyone—rich and poor alike—is endangered.
We are destroying our air, forests, lands and water so rapidly that
we face disastrous problems in the next century unless we make
major changes.… We overfish our seas, pollute our atmosphere,
exhaust our supplies of fresh water, and destroy precious topsoil,
forests, and unique species lovingly shaped by the Creator.[61]

Further, in denouncing Christians for ecological crimes Lynn White cited
the dominion mandate as the culprit in our thinking.[62] He even chided Christians for destroying faith in "animism," a superstition that holds major portions
of the world in thrall to the worst kind of deprivation. Would-be prophets of
our time need to be held to the same standards given by Moses in Deuteronomy
18:22 about "presumptuous" speech. They have been preaching a *false alarmism*
for decades, and their sensationalism needs to be ignored—no, debunked![63]

Rather, the wisdom of Proverbs 14:4 must prevail as we develop the planet for
all to enjoy: "Where there are no oxen, the manger is clean, but abundant crops
come by the strength of the ox" (ESV). One gets the impression that many in our
time would indeed *welcome back* the day of the ox in agriculture, which would
mean the horse on city streets.[64] We wonder if they would volunteer for manure re-

---

61 Ronald J. Sider, *Rich Christians in an Age of Hunger* (Nashville: Thomas Nelson: 2005), 157,
    quoted from the 1997 revision. Cited in Jay W. Richards, *Money, Greed, and God* (New
    York: HarperOne, 2009), locs. 2966–81.
62 Lynn Townsend White Jr., "The Historical Roots of Our Ecologic Crisis," Science 155,
    no. 3767 (March 10, 1967): 1203–7, http://www.drexel.edu/~/media/Files/greatworks/
    pdf_fall09/HistoricalRoots_of_EcologicalCrisis.ashx, cited in Richards, *Money, Greed,
    and God*, locs. 2997–3014. Just before we completed our writing for this volume, Jonathan
    Merritt made many of the same arguments in *Green Like God: Unlocking the Divine Plan
    for Our Planet* (New York: Hachette Book Group, 2010). There is nothing new here.
63 For both sides of this ongoing blame game, see Beisner, *Garden Meets Wilderness* (Grand
    Rapids: Acton Institute for the Study of Religion and Liberty / Eerdmans, 1997), and Noah
    J. Toly and Daniel I. Block, eds., *Keeping God's Earth* (Downers Grove, IL: InterVarsity
    Press, 2010). This latest is mostly a reprise of crisis-touting language and very little, if any,
    interaction with the literature we have previously cited in our study.
64 Prior to the arrival of the automobile in sufficient numbers to replace animal transporta-
    tion, e.g., upwards of a hundred thousand horses trampled manure into fine particles for
    residents of the city of New York to breathe. Anyone who cannot laud the automobile and

Awaiting the City

moval in such a time as ours, or how they would handle the disease and pestilence that would come from the mountains of stinking offal that would ensue. Surely it is clear that the hope for sustaining a world in which God's blessing/command to the human race's progenitors pre-fall and post-flood was literally to "multiply" and be "fruitful" in order to "fill" the planet (Gen. 1:28; 9:1; cf. Isa. 45:18) presupposes the technology necessary to live without disease and pestilence and starvation from famines. The ox is now *industrial society*. Yes, without it everything would be *clean*. But, we would not be better off for it. And the wisdom writer and God know this. Therefore, the biblically sensible thing to do is what we always do: *dig* (or tear or plow or whatever) it up (or in some cases tear it down), *build* it up, *clean* it up. You cannot produce a crop or build an apartment complex without doing those things. It is a process we have documented heavily here, and no amount of posturing in indignation at the temporary disappointments and frustrations in the fallen obedience mankind gives to God's command will change the mandate. The alternative is raiding and pillaging, a choice too many prior "civilizations" have made and the politics of our time is reproducing with different weaponry.

The true biblical "doom and gloom" is not about ecology or economics and dwindling resources leading to a planetary catastrophe. It is about the coming judgment of all mankind on the basis of God's law and the incarnate Christ work of redemption in his cross and resurrection. When we cry to God for justice, we are really crying for his kingdom to "come" and his will to be done "on earth as it is in heaven." This means that to give "justice" to one (and the saints who cry out), he must root out the "tares" around him (Matt. 13:36–43), that is, all "causes of sin and all law-breakers" (v. 41 ESV). This is ever the prospect for true justice. Egypt was judged that Israel might be free. Canaan was judged that Israel might have a land. Israel was judged as a nation that the world might know and Israel's remnant might know that God is not to be trifled with, but he is still working on the blessing to come. Jesus, God's Son, was judged that the believing might go free. The world will be judged that the final persecuted remnant, the biblical "poor," might cease from suffering for all time. To fail to publicize in the widest possible venues that a real judgment is coming on the

---

its form of "pollution," now drastically limited, as a true improvement over times gone by is not thinking rationally or morally in our opinion.

Awaiting the City

world based on what each individual does about worship of the one living God through his Son, Jesus Christ, and that this judgment is at least being previewed in the fortunes of nations and individuals who do not acknowledge him, is to be "fickle" in the extreme. Leading the nations and individuals to believe that the situation of poverty and deprivation is nothing more than the imperialism of the West distorts the facts on the ground and God's Word as well, and is the very definition of reckless and undisciplined prophesying.

Doing Good and Random Acts of Piety

Many of us grew up in a culture where it was common at mealtime for a mom to tell her recalcitrant children, "Clean up your plate [meaning finish the last bit of food on it]; children in China don't get that much to eat all day long." The day I heard someone say, "I'll be glad to do that if you can show me how that will help children in China," was the day I first began to understand the difference between helping someone in their actual situation and doing something just to feel better about it. In this case, the issue to moms back then was wasting food that would be thrown out if not eaten. That is still a problem today. However, it is not what causes others to starve or go hungry. "Waste not; want not" is still a good and right slogan today. However, it is not the key to alleviating world hunger or poverty. It is simply a statement of personal accountability to our Creator and principles that will serve all humanity well if followed. We should not need to have guilt manipulation from world poverty statistics used on us to get compliance.

Jay Richards has coined the phrase "random acts of piety" to describe this phenomenon that would substitute feel-good, do-good acts and legislation with actually doing something tangible to alleviate the needs of others. This same terminology describes well the counsel to "live more simply," as if this would have planetary consequences. We would all likely benefit from consuming less and giving more as a general rule, but to clothe this with an alarmist slogan like "save the planet" or "feed the hungry" or "save the children" or any one of a dozen other popular slogans is to live in a world of unrealistic emotional piety. Actually to do the work that would push poverty and hunger to the far periphery of human existence is an entirely different matter.

Awaiting the City

We suspect that the whole attempt to manipulate economics for millions into the "live simpler" mode through governmental interference is to eliminate surplus and capital from the hands of millions in order to slow the process of markets and development so as to accommodate the vision of some intellectuals[65] of a world without competition and insecurity and "unfairness."[66] This vision presupposes that the problem of hunger and poverty is caused by the presence in the world of market capitalism and Western economic imperialism. We do not concur in this diagnosis, as we have attempted to show. To the contrary, we believe that for such intellectual notions to have time to root and grow and gain influence, *capitalistic markets* producing huge profits for philanthropic investment are *required*. Just consider university *endowments* and *eleemosynary* and investigative (think-tank) institutions of all kinds. They are all funded by capitalistic enterprises. Additionally, a huge tax base of capitalistic mass production and culture must be present to fund *governmental grants* and mandates to occupy the time and intellectual energy of those engaged in the process. Otherwise, these *intellectuals* would not eat or be clothed or housed or be carried worldwide by jet transportation to conferences and seminars and consultations and demonstrations. Nor could the *media*, through which the popular culture and political climate are influenced by the intellectuals we describe, be sustained without the same capitalistic structure. In other words we believe there is a *rational blindness* and *moral myopia* that feeds off the very "system" it condemns.[67] The Bible has a word for that—*hypocrisy*.

The rational, though tragic, and biblical vision sees no solution to humanity's eternal need in *economics itself*, but it offers the *best way out* of deprivation and hunger. No solution to abject and intractable poverty is likely anywhere in the world without changes of heart and thoroughgoing *reform of life* and practice toward *bib-*

---

65 We are using "intellectuals" here in the sense that Tom Sowell and Paul Johnson do to designate those whose expertise consists in exercises of the mind without the discipline of being held accountable for results in real-world terms.

66 Please note our earlier rejoinder that "trimming one's budget" is a salutary practice, and "living within one's means" is important, but we are dealing here with a different philosophical and theological issue.

67 This is the argument of Voegeli, *Never Enough*, with special reference to the need of liberal-left politics for capitalistic wealth to distribute ever more generously to growing constituencies.

Awaiting the City

lical values. This is and should be the primary Christian mission! The ultimate "prosperity promise" in the Bible is, "[y]our days may be long, and that it may go well with you in the land that the LORD your God is giving you" (Deut. 5:16 ESV; cf. Exod. 20:12; Eph. 6:2–3). It is attached to the generational obligation of "honor" to father and mother. Honor is a weight word; along with a promise children are enjoined in this command to add weight to the inheritance and legacy passed on to them from their parents, to develop what they receive beyond what their parents were able to achieve, with a view to the next generation and so forth. However, it is always the generational handoff that is muffed. But it is still a promise of inherited blessing to those who follow its mandate. This is a promise of a certain kind of cultural longevity that accumulates human capital with each passing generation.

Therefore, why should it be thought strange that even nominally Christian cultures, those who seek to pass from generation to generation the Judeo-Christian heritage and faith, should surpass in economic success those given over to *animistic* and *idolatrous* gods and philosophies? Even Israel today is an ongoing example of this.[68] Abraham appealed to God for Sodom and Gomorrah on the basis of a "justice" that would not destroy the righteous in small numbers with the majority of guilty ones. The presence of large numbers of actually Christian people praying that God will bless their work and their country (cf. Jer. 29:7) cannot be dismissed out of hand as jingoism and chauvinistic partisanship. It is what Psalm 33 invites the whole world to do.

The evils inherent in fallen human nature will show itself with a vengeance in a "free" (even libertine) society, and this we deplore, as do those cultures of the world that resent the export of our perverted values, most notably disseminated from Hollywood and other parts of the entertainment industries. But just as the breaking in of the kingdom for the individual Christian and the church means there really is an "already,"[69] so there is in the culture and

---

68 See George Gilder, *The Israel Test: Why the World's Most Besieged State Is a Beacon of Freedom and Hope for the World Economy*, 2nd ed. (New York: Encounter Books, 2012), for documentation of the Jewish and Israeli story of worldwide blessing and economic success. See also Thomas Cahill, *The Gifts of the Jews: How a Tribe of Desert Nomads Changed the Way Everyone Thinks and Feels* (New York: Nan A. Talese, Doubleday, 1998), which despite its evolutionary bias historically traces the same story from antiquity.

69 See George Eldon Ladd and other biblical theologians who make a distinction between the "already" and the "not-yet" of Christian eschatology.

Awaiting the City

society where it has "already" *broken in*. To condemn this and ignore it is to *refuse* to see what God is doing now and how that bodes well for the future glories to be revealed. We shall "inherit the cosmos" as Paul said of Abraham in Romans 4 (see esp. v. 13) and Jesus mirrored for the meek ("inherit the land") in the Sermon on the Mount. To fail to allow for an in-breaking *now* of this promise is to *truncate* the gospel and miss the point of the true blessing altogether. Furthermore, George Gilder shows very well in his latest work that the state of Israel is portraying the same thing economically, having scrapped a previously socialistic scheme for a *market economy* with minimal governmental interference. The Arab nations of the Middle East and the poverty-stricken of the underdeveloped world would profit immensely from following the Israeli model based on a biblical worldview.

Stearns notes, in his call for the North American church to take up the call for relief in the African AIDS crisis, that the orphaned multitudes of this troubled continent are losing the very people who might lead them (the orphans) out of this tragedy—losing them to AIDS. When asked what it will take to replace the loss of teachers and other professionals that are being lost, one leader candidly noted that they must *start over* with the children and raise up a new generation. It is ever so. It is *generational accumulation* of human capital that most determines the economic future of the world as well as its spiritual and cultural future.

A Biblical/Theological/Historical Mandate

Jesus advised his followers, rich and poor, to become a people who give without expecting reciprocity, as opposed to the patronal system taught and practiced so clearly by Rome and syncretized into the Jewish world of his time. He did not tell the poor to organize, get political representation, and petition Rome (or anyone else) for "just" distribution of "societal wealth." He advised "poor" people (the ones addressed in the Sermon on the Mount) to give to the person who filed suit for one's outer garment, one's inner garment as well. In many other ways and venues Jesus taught that suffering outright injustice by returning good for evil builds one's store of heavenly "treasure." This treasure includes the wealth of the age to come, but it is never confined *merely* to this, for the "rewards" of the present range from personal character building to material advantages as well.[70]

It is surely one of the exegetical and theological *blunders* of our time to misconstrue this manner in which our Lord promises his blessing to his faithful people as a mandate for *political* action to restructure society through political activism. The logical fallacy is that to attempt on the one hand to enhance the material lifestyle of one group, while morally denigrating the material lifestyle of another group and confiscating wealth from them to give to the other, creates a never-ending spiral of moral nitpicking that makes the Pharisees look like *libertarians*. If enhancing material lifestyle is good for one person, who is to determine where that one has enough and the other person has had enough taken away? Such a program can only lead to further disaster, as we have earlier warned. It needs to be called by the name it deserves—teaching *covetousness* as a form of *Christian politics*. But that is not all.

Roger Scruton has written in a vein that expresses our sentiments, and we believe he is worth citing extensively here.

> When gifts are replaced by rights, so is gratitude replaced by claims. And claims breed resentment. Since you are queuing on equal terms with the competition, you will begin to think of the special conditions that entitle you to a greater, a speedier, or a more effective care. You will be always one step from the official complaint, the court action, the press interview, and the snarling reproach against Them, the ones who *owed* you this right and also *withheld* it…. Agape, the contagious gentleness between people, survives only where there is a habit of giving. Take away gift, and agape gives way to the attitude that Nietzsche call *ressentiment*, the vigilant envy of others, and the desire to take from them what *I* but not *they* have a right to.[71]

---

70 See Jesus' words in Mark 10:29: "No one who has left [all] for my sake and for the gospel… will fail to receive a hundred times as much in this present age [homes, brothers, sisters, children and fields—and with them persecutions], and in the age to come, eternal life." Prosperity gospel preachers distort this teaching, but we must not ignore its real significance in terms of temporal blessings.

71 Roger Scruton, "Gratitude and Grace," *American Spectator*, April 2010, 54, http://spectator.org/archives/2010/04/02/gratitude-and-grace.

Awaiting the City

Scruton continues,

> Moreover, ingratitude grows in proportion to the benefits received. When those good things, like food, shelter, education, for which our ancestors had to struggle, are offered as right, and without cost or effort, then they are "taken for granted," as the saying is, which means quite the opposite from "taken as gifts." In such conditions there arises what we might call a culture of ingratitude—one that does not merely forget to give thanks, but regards thanks as somehow demeaning, a confession of weakness, a way of according to the other person an importance that he does not have. This thanklessness is growing round us today. It is written on the faces of pop idols and sports stars; it is announced in all kinds of ways by the media and by our political representatives. And it is one reason for the radical decline in public standards.[72]

Scruton concludes his analysis by reminding us that it is, in fact, most likely in human experience and certainly taught in the Scriptures and Christian theology that true gratitude is learned when *adversity* and *offense* to our persons are treated as *gifts of God* and we begin to see into ourselves and confront, overcome, and understand at the deepest level the truth about ourselves, so as to be able to give love to others. We contend that to substitute material success or prosperity (or even subsistence) for the wealth of this insight and practice is to elevate this world over the kingdom and to serve *mammon* rather than God. We call on our brothers and sisters in the church to confront this truth as the ultimate mark of the "saved" in the world to come, not the politics of envy and *ressentiment*. As William Law remarked in *A Serious Call to a Devout and Holy Life*, "[W]hatever seeming calamity befalls you, if you can thank and praise God for it, you turn it into a blessing."[73] No better commentary exists on the underlying theology of the Sermon on the Mount and the teachings of Christ on this subject.

---

72 Ibid., 54–55
73 William Law, *A Serious Call to a Devout and Holy Life Adapted to the State and Condition of All Orders of Christians* (London: Printed for William Innys, 1729), quoted in ibid., 56.

Awaiting the City

In all the history of mankind, since the ancient Babylonian city Babili claimed to be the "gate of God," only two political entities have laid claim from biblical precedent (as they supposed) to the title City of God—Jerusalem and the Puritan claim to be God's "City on a Hill." Jerusalem has received its judgment and awaits its redemption. Babylon stands as an unholy caricature and parody on earth of the heavenly Jerusalem to come. It is clearly not a stretch to see in American aspirations to be the ideal society, full of wealth and security and promise for the whole world, a candidate for the final manifestation of Babylonian arrogance and oppression. If it does in fact turn out to that end, it will not be the fault of capitalism. It will be the fault of pagan idolatries financed by the largesse of the treasuries of God sent as blessing. This is the greatest abomination of all, as the prophets of old inveighed against Israel—taking the riches of the heavenly King to fashion idols. Truly, they are idols for destruction.

Awaiting the City

Epilogue

Obama, Bull Moose, and the White Queen

As we approached final deadlines for finishing our work, the political season began to heat up with the presidential primaries of Republicans and the campaigning of the incumbent Democrat in anticipation of the crucial election of 2012. Several events and developments seem pertinent to our final thoughts. At times we have read and heard during the decade-long research and writing of this book that it is really quite alarmist to consider the politics of the American economy as somehow fraught with apparently apocalyptic overtones. In fact, we have warned of just such "hysteria" and "crisis" mentalities throughout the book's three sections. Is it really necessary to warn Christians and others of the impending possibilities of a government and political system gone viral on the heady promise of utopian visions fostered by governing elites? We think so.

Angelo Codevilla, a world-class scholar, distinguished professor, and prolific researcher at the Stanford-based Hoover Institution, wrote in 2010 in his book *The Ruling Class* that our system of governance has been co-opted by a class of politicians from the right and the left that is out of touch in the extreme with *ordinary* Americans.[1] He documents in telling fashion the attitudes and predilections of this special group of Americans (and other nationalities, of course) that goes into politics and government and rubs shoulders constantly with just one class of people, whose entire predisposition is to help the people understand

---

1   Angelo M. Codevilla, *The Ruling Class: How They Corrupted America and What We Can Do about It* (New York: Beaufort Books, 2010).

and do what's good for them—even, or especially, if they would just as soon remain in their apparent "*ignorance*" and backwardness. The hopes of voters that somehow, someday they might elect a group from one party or the other that would change all this and "clean up" Washington (especially) and/or state capitals are repeatedly dashed on the shores of this prevailing mind-set in the professional ruling class. Hence the promising young solons, the RINO and country-club Republicans, the yellow-dog Democrats, the Tea Partiers, the blue-dog Democrats, the mugwumps of old, the New Dealers, Fair Dealers, Square Dealers, Whigs, Libertarians, Bull Moosers, "occupiers" (maybe), and on and on go to Washington and other places and get caught up in the prevailing winds. Overwhelmingly, that wind blows more and more toward a "*soft*" totalitarianism that promises anything to keep the voters pacified while the ruling class rules—either already or planning to tell us what food and drink we and our children will be allowed to consume, what light bulb to buy, what toilet to flush, what car to drive, what fuel to use, what temperature to set in our homes, what medical insurance we *must* buy for whom and including what unconscionable products, what medical care we can have, what doctor to see, what school to attend and what textbooks will be used, whether we can go on living or must die, ad infinitum. This is no "future shock" scenario; it is everyday life!

This situation did not arrive overnight. In the late nineteenth century Otto von Bismarck, the Iron Chancellor of a newly unified German state, implemented one of the first truly modern forms of social insurance. He was a follower of Marx and/or Metternich, depending on the whim of the moment. He is not considered to be among the "liberal" or "progressive" elites of that time or any other. Nevertheless, his "reforms" served as the model for things still on the horizon of the next century in the West. He remarked, in defense of his policies in 1881, "Whoever has a pension for his old age is far more content and *far easier to handle* than one who has no such prospect" (emphasis added). His purpose in social "reform" (establishing the first *Socialstaat*) was not to empower the people but to make them more subservient and manageable and increase the power of the state. He secretly longed to be known as "the king of the poor," an eponym first sought by Frederick the Great before him.[2]

---

2   Otto von Bismark quoted in A. J. P. Taylor, *Bismarck: The Man and the Statesman* (New York: Vintage Books, 1967), 203. Also see Michael Knox Beran, *Pathology of the Elites: How the Arrogant Classes Plan to Run Your Life* (Chicago: Ivan R. Dee, 2010), 106–8.

Seeking the City

The American president Richard Nixon purposely and knowingly furthered these ideals. A politician once thought by his supporters to be a true "conservative," whose politics could be trusted to resist the encroachments of the "New Dealers" and social welfare establishment, Nixon was a secret admirer of Friedrich Nietzsche. He referred often to the German philosopher's *Beyond Good and Evil* as a guide in electoral politics.[3] Nixon believed (as he read Nietzsche) that America was in the time of its decadence, enervated by wealth and unable to strive for greater things. Consequently, he shaped policy and proposed "solutions" that paved the way for supposed "conservatives" to support policies and propose ideas the Iron Chancellor would applaud. Nixon is the author of "conservative" support for Great Society spending that reached forty percent of the budget in his term (twenty-eight percent in LBJ's day), high tariffs, wage and price controls, greater government regulation (he inaugurated the EPA), elimination of the gold standard supporting the currency, and a proposal as part of his Family Assistance Plan to guarantee a minimum income unconnected to work or achievement (though this was never enacted).[4] Famously, when his programs did not work to control prices and inflation, he declared, "Kick the chain stores."[5]

In light of the foregoing it should not be thought shocking that George W. Bush, in the name of "compassionate conservatism," pushed and got the greatest entitlement expansion since the Great Society legislation, the Medicare Prescription Drug Plan, and recruited the most reliably "liberal" Democrat senator of the past fifty years (arguably), "last lion" of the house of Kennedy, to help enact No Child Left Behind "education reform." Later he would orchestrate "bailouts" for huge businesses thought "too big to fail." Remember, this is "compassionate conservatism": Perhaps the City of God can be realized by the City of Man!

Now the Obama administration has put governance in the hands of thirty to thirty-five "czars" (depending on who's doing the counting) and encourages them at this writing to promulgate rules (at numerous agencies),

---

3   Beran, *Pathology of the Elites*, 106–8. Monica Crowley, who was assistant to Nixon in his later years, said that Nixon told her that Nietzsche's *Beyond Good and Evil* was the inspiration for his own book, *Beyond Peace*. Monica Crowley, *Nixon in Winter* (London: I. P. Tauris, 1998), 351.
4   Ibid., 108–10.
5   Quoted in Nigel Bowles, *Nixon's Business Authority and Power in Presidential Politics* (College Station: Texas A&M University Press, 2005), 100, 267n65.

Seeking the City

in defiance and without the consent or authorization of Congress (remember Locke's views on the legislative), all the while declaring on the campaign trail, "We can't wait [for Congress to act]." What happened to Locke's argument that the *legislative* is the true power in a commonwealth? Is it any wonder that the president's czar for medical care, Kathleen Sebelius, with great forethought and apparent political calculation ruled that the Patient Protection and Affordable Care Act (Obamacare or Affordable Care Act for short, depending on one's perspective) disallowed noncoverage of "preventive health" involving birth control of any kind? This means that no entity except actual churches, not their schools, agencies (charitable or otherwise), or affiliates of any kind not organized specifically as "churches," is exempt from providing such "care" regardless of the stated mission and/or faith/doctrinal position of the entity.[6] The rule applies to all forms of contraception and sterilization procedures including those considered abortifacient. The later interpretation that said the entities themselves do not have to pay for this insurance, but their insurance providers must make it available for no charge, only placed an accounting procedure between the entities and their provision of abortifacient "preventive health" for their employees.

At this writing millions of evangelicals and Catholics have joined in verbal protest and are now, for the first time since the 1960s, suggesting seriously that the time for "civil disobedience" has come. Many on the political right swell the chorus, regardless of their sense of conscience on contraceptive practice, in the name of liberty and particularly religious freedom.[7] On the left and in the predominant media many seem puzzled that this has caused such a stir, remarking in the vein of at least one observer, "Maybe the Founders were wrong to guarantee free exercise of religion in the First Amendment, but they did."[8] Nancy Pelosi had previously defended the provision in the Act for abortive ser-

---

6   The case of Hobby Lobby is still right in the news as of this writing and it is not clear that this company will survive.
7   More than forty lawsuits against Obamacare are pending at the time of this writing.
8   This from MSNBC reporter Melinda Henneberger of the *Washington Post* speaking to Chris Matthews. Quoted in Mark Steyn, "The Church of Big Government," *National Review*, March 5, 2012, 26. https://www.nationalreview.com/nrd/articles/293368/church-big-government. She was telling Matthews how she talks about this issue to her "liberal friends."

vices by questioning loudly "this conscience thing."[9] A number of pundits and polls have demonstrated semantic creep in their language by observing that the Constitution "allows" one to "worship" in freedom—implying in context that it does not "guarantee" this "right" nor does it hold out for "practice" of one's faith in the public square.[10]

The "ruling class" on the right, including the recent Republican presidential contenders, are in seeming disarray at this moment in time, though they certainly may make a recovery before the 2014 elections. Theodore Roosevelt made it plain that he understood and practiced the politics of the "ruling class" when he stated a century ago, "I believe in power…, I did greatly broaden the use of executive power…. The biggest matters I handled without consultation with anyone, for when a matter is of capital importance, it is well to have it handled by one man only…. I don't think that any harm comes from the concentration of power in one man's hands."[11] Again, whither Locke? And Roosevelt was a Republican! He, of course, intended this declaration as a statement of his moral purpose and intention to enact and propagate "social reform." President Obama kicked off his reelection campaign in 2011 with a speech in Osawatomie, Kansas (birthplace of Bull Moose-ism), channeling the Rooseveltian Bull Moose party's aspirations for the "new nationalism." He, like Roosevelt before him, is a man enamored with the power of his office and is apparently unimpressed with the founders' sense of the depravity of all human beings and their need for separation of "powers" to prevent just such concentrations.

C. S. Lewis years ago seemed to be warning of a terrible time and place where perpetual winter prevailed at the behest of the White Witch, Her Imperial Majesty Jadis, Queen of Narnia (or so she imagined herself), who deplored

---

9 Geoffrey Surtees and Jordan Sekulow, "Rep. Pelosi, Conscience Is More Than a 'Thing,'" *Washington Post*, December 6, 2011, http://www.washingtonpost.com/blogs/religious-right-now/post/rep-pelosi-conscience-is-more-than-a-thing/2011/12/06/gIQAUw7KZO_blog.html (accessed April 5, 2013).

10 See, for instance, this helpful essay by Wesley J. Smith, "Freedom of Worship's Assault on Freedom of Religion," *First Things*, July 13, 2012, http://www.firstthings.com/onthesquare/2012/07/freedom-of-worshiprsquos-assault-on-freedom-of-religion (accessed April 1, 2013).

11 Quoted by Jim Powell, "Obama and Teddy Roosevelt: Both Progressives, Both Clueless about the Economy," *Forbes*, December 8, 2011. http://www.forbes.com/sites/jimpowell/2011/12/08/obama-and-teddy-roosevelt-both-progressives-both-clueless-about-the-economy/ (accessed November 14, 2012).

Christmas and was defeated only when the sacrificial Aslan returned from among the dead to defeat her. His *Chronicles of Narnia*,[12] couched in the guise of childrens' stories, *teach* far more than fairy-tale lessons. In our opinion, if the real world of ruling-class, czarist fantasies continues to set the agenda, a long winter threatens the political economy and constitutional liberties of an enervated and supposedly secure populace with no Christmas in sight. Lewis was prescient: "Of all the tyrannies, tyranny sincerely expressed for the good of its victims may be the most oppressive. It may be better to live under robber barons than under omnipotent moral busybodies."[13] We must concur.

---

12 C. S. Lewis, *The Lion, The Witch, and the Wardrobe* (New York: HarperCollins, 1978). Originally published in 1950, first of the seven-volume Chronicles of Narnia series, shortly after the end of World War II.
13 C. S. Lewis, "The Humanitarian Theory of Punishment," *God in the Dock*, ed. Walter Hooper (1970; repr., Grand Rapids, MI: Eerdmans, 2008), 292.

Seeking the City

Appendix

THE FOLLOWING GRAPH ILLUSTRATES the divergence in wealth production and accumulation from the almost constant line of previous millennia. The upward line represents the phenomenal increase in wealth of the industrialized world.

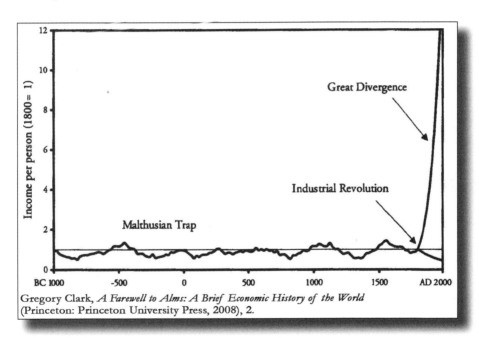

Gregory Clark, *A Farewell to Alms: A Brief Economic History of the World* (Princeton: Princeton University Press, 2008), 2.

The "Malthusian Trap" is the postulate of Thomas Malthus, whose calculations concluded that the human population on the earth was finite and based on the availability of food to sustain human numerical increase. His famous conclusion was that population grows in proportion to the ability of civilizations to feed themselves and naturally drops off when those numbers exceed productive ability. The divergence illustrated above coincides with the massive changes in productivity engendered by the Industrial Revolution in the West. The downward line shows the manner in which other cultures diverged as they received some of the benefits of Western productivity without developing their own economic capacities. The resulting increase in longevity for these groups produced more people with no increase in productivity, causing their overall economic condition per capita to deteriorate proportionally to the growth of population versus lack of productivity. This phenomenon, more than any other factor, explains the continuing problem of apparently intractable poverty in certain parts of the world.

Index

H